Structured COBOL

To Vivian

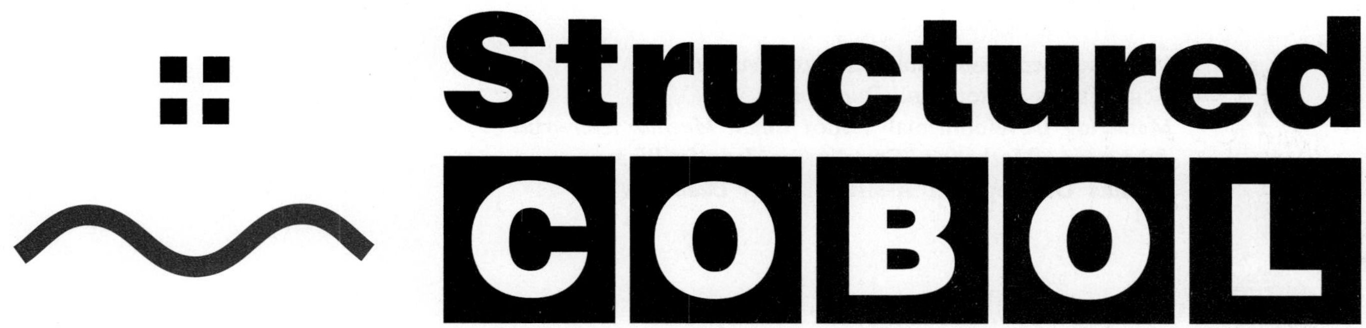

Structured COBOL

THIRD EDITION

Gerard A. Paquette

B&E TECH Business and Educational Technologies
A Division of Wm. C. Brown Communications, Inc.

Business and Educational Technologies
A Division of Wm. C. Brown Communications, Inc.

Vice President and Publisher *Susan A. Simon*
Acquisitions Editor *Paul Ducham*
Managing Developmental Editor *Linda Meehan Avenarius*
Advertising/Marketing Coordinator *Jennifer Wherry*
Product Development Assistant *Sandy Ludovissy*

Wm. C. Brown Communications, Inc.

Chief Executive Officer *G. Franklin Lewis*
Corporate Senior Vice President and Chief Financial Officer *Robert Chesterman*
Corporate Senior Vice President and President of Manufacturing *Roger Meyer*
Executive Vice President/General Manager, Brown & Benchmark Publishers *Tom Doran*
Executive Vice President/General Manager, Wm. C. Brown Publishers *Beverly Kolz*

The credits section for this book is on page 838, and is considered an extension of the copyright page.

Cover design by Sailer & Cook Creative Services

A Times Mirror Company

Library of Congress Catalog Card Number: 93-73870

ISBN 0-697-12394-4

Printed in the United States of America by Wm. C. Brown Communications, Inc.,
2460 Kerper Boulevard, Dubuque, IA 52001

10 9 8 7 6 5 4 3 2 1

Contents

Handy Reference to Rules for:

Preface

This text is written for the student who wants to develop effective problem-solving techniques while learning structured COBOL programming. It contains a number of features that make it stand out from other available texts.

Problem-Solving Procedure

A time-tested problem-solving procedure is presented and explained in the very first chapter, and then the "Turbo Manufacturing Company Employee Listing" program is used immediately to show the procedure in actual use. Every original program presented in the text is also systematically developed following the steps specified in the procedure.

Many textbooks do suggest a systematic approach to programming, but more often than not, the systematic approach is not used later in the text to develop sample programs, no further reference is made to it, and if students use it at all, it is on their own initiative. Since developing an effective approach to problem solving is so crucial to a novice programmer, repeated exposure to a specific method that is used in a consistent manner will go a long way toward achieving that goal. The net result is that the student retains the procedure as a productive "working" tool in later programming situations.

Problem-Oriented Approach

The text follows a problem-oriented approach. This approach allows the development of COBOL statements and features to be presented on a "need to know" basis, where they are applied immediately in the situation being discussed. The sample problems that have been selected as vehicles for the introduction of COBOL language features are presented at the very beginning of the chapter, thus setting the stage for what is to come in the rest of the chapter.

In Chapter 2, the program "Allied Stock Company Phone Sales Report" is presented and developed primarily to expose the students to the major functions of the four divisions of a COBOL program.

In Chapter 3, the same program is used as a vehicle to expand upon the features of the IDENTIFICATION DIVISION, the ENVIRONMENT DIVISION, and the DATA DIVISION. In Chapter 4, it is used to elaborate upon the features of the PROCEDURE DIVISION.

In Chapter 5, a new program, "Reliable Auto Parts Company Payroll Report," is presented and developed as a tool to introduce arithmetic statements, since the preparation of a payroll requires a number of arithmetic operations.

In Chapter 6, the program of Chapter 5 is expanded to prepare a summary payroll report that contains totals and averages for the company. The same program is then revised to include refinements in both the program and the printed report.

In Chapter 7, the program "Jocelyn Originals Company Annual District Sales Report" prepares a summary report by district. Because the records of the input file are in alphabetical order, the district code must be tested so that the sales figures can be added to the appropriate district accumulators. This leads into a discussion of conditional statements—simple, compound, and nested. Once the report has been produced, an alternative approach is developed to illustrate the use of CORRESPONDING statements and qualification of data names. Since the setting of the problem remains the same, students can more easily concentrate their attention on the new features.

In Chapter 8, two programs are presented to illustrate important applications of conditional statements. The "Sportsman Company Sales Analysis Report" program serves as an introduction to control breaks. One-level control breaks are examined first, and the program is then expanded to illustrate two-level control breaks. The "Sportsman Company Data Validation Report" program is then developed to examine various data validation procedures.

In Chapter 9, the "Monster Burger Stores Weekly Payroll Report" program has been designed to require the use of input-loaded and hard-coded tables. Its development leads into discussions of table organizations, levels in a table, table-loading procedures, and table-data retrieval procedures.

In Chapter 10, variations of the "Sportsman Company Sales Report" program are used to illustrate all the possible combinations of options of the SORT statement. PROCEDURE DIVISION sections are introduced in relation to the SORT statement. A final program is used to illustrate the MERGE statement.

In Chapter 11, the Jocelyn Originals Company provides a setting for the development of programs that create master files on tape or on disks. These files have sequential organization. Indexed files and relative files are also introduced, but complete programs are not included since the sequel to this book examines these two file organizations in detail.

Structured Programming Tools

Built into the design phase of the problem-solving procedure is the use of tools that result in structured programs. The system flowchart specifies the overall task of the program, in addition to identifying the required files. The structure chart begins with the overall task as its primary module, and then breaks it down into major subtasks, one per module. These major subtasks are further subdivided as needed, until the question "What has to be done?" is completely answered. The program pseudocode or the program flowchart then details the procedures that answer the question "How is the task to be done?"

In the structure chart, the first-level, or primary, module is numbered 100, the second-level modules are numbered consecutively from left to right in the 200s using increments of 10, the third-level modules are similarly numbered in the 300s, and so on for the remaining levels. If a particular module is needed at different levels in the structure chart, every occurrence of the module is assigned the number of the lowest level where it is needed, and the upper right-hand corner is darkened to clearly indicate its repetitive nature.

The paragraphs of the pseudocode and the modules in the flowchart retain the numeric prefixes and names first assigned in the structure chart. The paragraph names in the PROCEDURE DIVISION are then the same as those of the pseudocode or flowchart. Furthermore, by coding the paragraphs in ascending order of their numeric prefixes, program debugging is greatly facilitated, since the programmer can quickly scan margin A to locate a particular paragraph.

COBOL '85 Standards

The text implements the standards of COBOL '85. A student who learns the language as presented in this text will be well-prepared to write programs that include up-to-date syntax and structure. However, since most of COBOL '74 is still supported in the COBOL '85 standards, and since the new features are identified as such within the text, this text remains appropriate for use by students who are currently using a COBOL '74 compiler, and these students will have a handy reference when they first encounter a COBOL '85 compiler. Naturally, the new features cannot be incorporated in programs to be compiled by a '74 compiler, and features that are currently labeled as obsolete may be required entries. (Obsolete entries are not used in the sample programs of this text.)

Debugging Activities

Debugging exercises have been included at the end of every chapter. They are listed following the more traditional "review and practice" exercises and before the programming exercises. They include debugging data entry errors, misaligned entries on a printed report, data description errors that do not conform to prepared layouts, compiler-generated syntax errors, coding errors that do not represent the logic specified in either pseudocode or flowchart form, numeric and/or numeric-edited data description coding errors, errors in mathematical statements or expressions, errors related to missing data or incorrect values on a printed report, printed report errors related to incorrect handling of control breaks, coding errors related to table definitions, table loading, and data retrieval, sorting errors due to improperly sequenced keys, and control errors related to the use of sections within the PROCEDURE DIVISION.

These exercises are designed to draw attention to common errors and some less common ones. Students who successfully complete these exercises should be able to avoid making the same types of errors in their own programs.

Programming Assignments

There are four programming assignments at the end of each chapter, beginning with Chapter 3. In the spirit of "leading the student by the hand," the student is presented with the completed design phase of the problem-solving procedure in the first assignment; that is, the input record layout form and the printer spacing chart are prepared, and the system flowchart, the structure chart, and the program pseudocode and flowchart are completely developed. After studying these aids, the student can quickly move to the completion of the task—coding the program, debugging it as needed, and running it with a sample data file.

In the second assignment, the design phase of the problem-solving procedure is completed for the student except for the program pseudocode and the program flowchart. The student's task is to complete the design phase, and then implement the design.

The third and fourth assignments are full-scale assignments. The student must design the program "from scratch," and then carry out the implementation of the design.

Data sets for all programming assignments are provided in Appendix C, and are also available on magnetic disks for the convenience of instructors and students.

Program Documentation

All sample programs contain a number of documentation paragraphs in the IDENTIFICATION DIVISION. The student is aided in verbalizing the nature of the task that the program must accomplish by being expected to properly document the listing of the program. The better the task is defined, the easier it is to map out an appropriate strategy. Few textbooks provide this type of documentation or encourage students to do so.

Listing of Rules

Whenever COBOL language elements and statements are introduced, explained, and illustrated in a section of a chapter, all of the applicable rules are collected and summarized within that same section under a title beginning with "Rules Governing Use of. . . ." Students will find these sections convenient because everything they need to know about the feature or statement is there, assembled in one place. A list of these rules sections, complete with page references, is printed at the front of the book on page ix. The colored tabs that are visible on page edges mark the locations of these rules in the text.

Course Organization

There is ample material in this text for a quarter or a semester's work in a course that might be entitled "Structured COBOL Programming I." It is not intended as a complete treatment of the COBOL language, but rather as an effective teaching/learning tool for the developing programmer. The sequel to this text, *Advanced Structured COBOL,* takes the student into more advanced table handling, file organizations, master file updating procedures, subprograms and nested programs, and also introduces on-line interactive COBOL programs, even though a screen-handling facility is not yet included in ANSI COBOL Standards. A Report Writer supplement is also available upon request.

Ancillaries

The following ancillary materials have been prepared for the convenience of instructors using this text:

a. An Instructor's Manual that contains, for each chapter, an overview of the chapter, a discussion of the particularly significant topics of the chapter, some suggested coordinated activities for the student, answers to all the chapter exercises, solutions to all the debugging activities, and a complete set of solutions for all the programming exercises.

b. A complete set of transparency masters.

c. TestPak, a computerized testing program that an instructor can use in constructing class tests quickly and efficiently. TestPak is a computerized system that enables you to make up customized exams quickly and easily. For each exam, you can select up to 250 questions from the file and either print the test yourself or have Business and Educational Technologies print it.

d. A Data Disk that contains the data files used in the chapter sample programs and in the debugging activities programs, and data files that can be used as test data for all the programming exercises.

e. Source code disks that contain:
  i. The source code for all the chapter sample programs.
  ii. The source code for the programs used in the debugging activities at the end of each chapter. The source code for the completely debugged programs are also included.
  iii. The source code for the programs that must be developed in the programming exercises at the end of each chapter.

  These source code disks allow instructors to make changes to existing programs, thereby customizing the programs to their own needs without a major effort on their part.

Software

Structured COBOL can be purchased with the following excellent software packages:

a. The RM/COBOL-85 Educational Version Compiler, which offers complete language functionality, screen handling capabilities, and an application development environment. A Convenience Disk is included in the textbook for students who also purchase the RM/COBOL-85 Compiler for use on their personal computer. This disk contains the source code for the programs in the debugging exercises at the end of each chapter. It also contains all the data sets used in the chapter sample programs and the data sets needed for the programming exercises at the end of each chapter.

b. Micro Focus Personal COBOL, a full-featured, PC-based package that allows students to write, compile, debug, and test complete COBOL programs.

A Final Note

I wish to thank the staff of the Computer Center at the University of Massachusetts–Lowell for their cooperation whenever their technical assistance was needed.

I also wish to thank the members of my family for their patient understanding during the long development process, and in particular, my wife, Vivian, for her constant encouragement and support.

Notes on My Computer

1. Computer name: ____________________ Operating system: ____________________
2. Nonnumeric literals must be enclosed in ______________________________ (quotation marks or apostrophes).
3. Implementor-names to be used in the ASSIGN clause are:
   ____
   ____
   ____
4. ANSI COBOL compiler: __________ (1985 or 1974)
5. Procedures to log on to my system:
   ____
   ____
   ____
   ____
6. System commands to edit a file:
   ____
   ____
   ____
7. Commands to "run" a program:
   ____
   ____
   ____

Structured COBOL

■ Introduction

In this introduction, we take a brief look at the historical development of the modern computer and the COBOL programming language. We identify the major computer components and various languages that programmers use in giving instructions to computers.

If you are now undertaking your first course in computer programming, or if you feel a need to review the topics just listed, you are encouraged to spend an hour browsing through this introduction. ■

Historical Development of Computers

From time immemorial, people have had a need to gather and disseminate data. The caveman kept a record of his kill by carving notches in his spear; wise men preserved scientific observations for posterity by engraving in clay tablets; and the monks of old transcribed thousands of documents by hand. The development of the printing press greatly increased the speed by which accounts could be disseminated; and now, radio and television with the help of orbiting satellites make it possible to collect data and relay it immediately to any point on the globe.

In our need to collect and transmit data, we are constantly searching for better tools that enable us to accomplish our objectives. Historically, the collecting, processing, and dissemination of data have progressed through three stages: manual, mechanical, and now electronic. The earliest simple manual tool used for counting was the abacus, which is still in use today. In an effort to increase the capability of the abacus, the French mathematician Blaise Pascal developed the first mechanical calculator in about 1642. A few years later, the German mathematician Gottfried von Leibnitz also worked on a mechanical calculator that performed all the basic operations of arithmetic. By the mid-1800s, Charles Babbage partially constructed an automatic machine to perform calculations, but it was not until 1885 that William Burroughs developed the first useful and practical automatic calculator. These mechanical calculators had to be operated manually by a crank. They were improved and developed into electrical calculators.

By the mid to late 1930s, the threat of World War II provided additional impetus, and, very importantly, funding for research in the planning and development of electronic machines. Dr. Howard

An abacus

Pascal's mechanical calculator

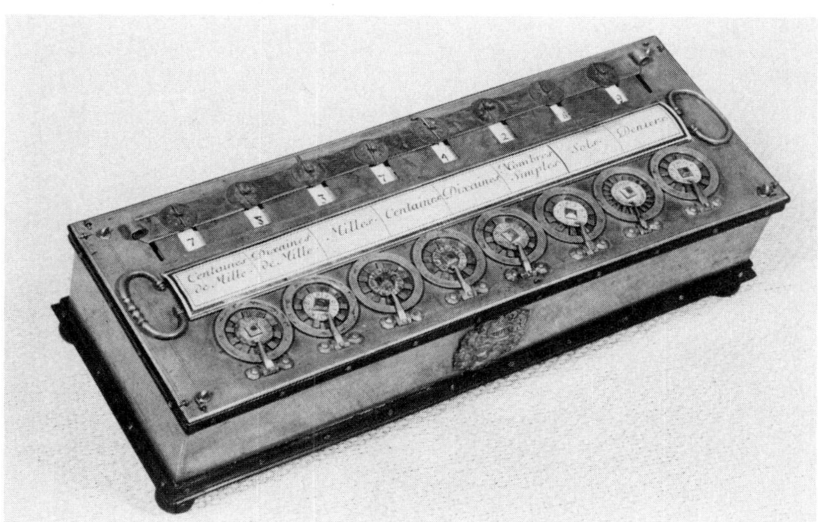

■ Burroughs automatic calculator

■ An IBM personal system/2

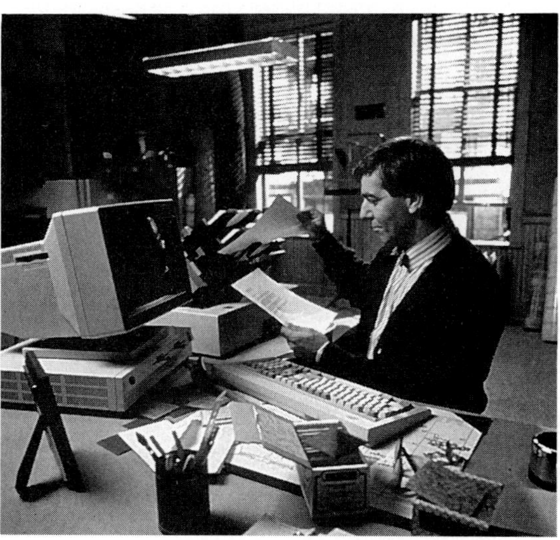

■ Transmission of data to and from the computer via satellite

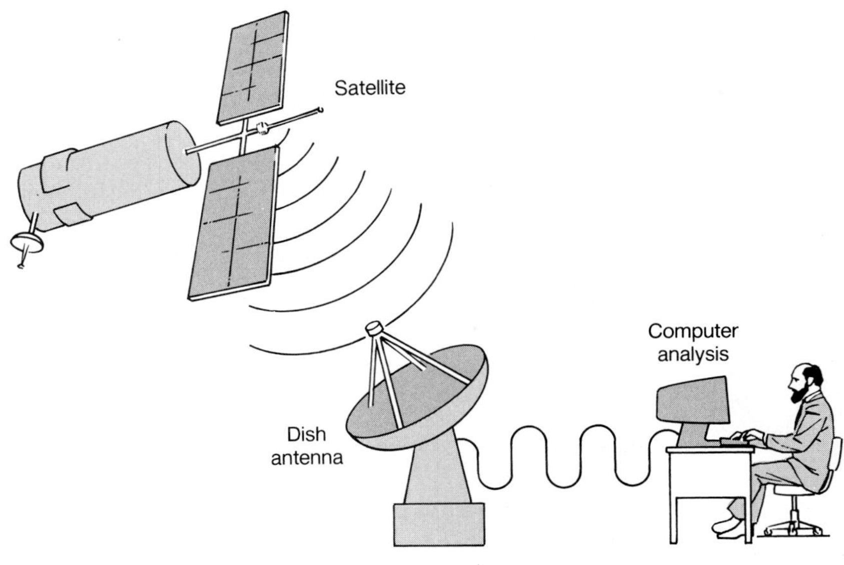

Aiken of Harvard University developed the Mark I in 1944. Dr. John Atanasoff of Iowa State University, with the help of his graduate student Clifford Berry, developed the ABC computer. But it was not until 1946 that the first electronic calculator, known as ENIAC, was produced by J. P. Echert and J. W. Mauchly at the University of Pennsylvania. (It became known much later that the key ideas developed by Mauchly had been obtained from Atanasoff.) From this time on, the development of computers has been so rapid and fantastic that it boggles the mind. John von Neumann developed the concept of *stored programs;* that is, how to keep programs (sets of instructions to the computer) in the computer's memory. Echert and Mauchly produced the first commercial computer, UNIVAC I, in 1950. (The head programmer of the UNIVAC was Dr. Grace Hopper, who later made very important contributions to the development of the COBOL language.)

As the technology improved, hundreds of vacuum tubes were replaced by tiny transistors, miles of wiring were replaced by printed circuits, and room-size computers were replaced by hand-held calculators. Today, the state of the art is still changing and leaping forward.

Historical Development of COBOL

The rapid technological advances of the 1950s made it necessary to increase the efficiency of programming languages. When computers were first brought on the market, all programming was written in *machine language*. This language is heavily dependent on the electronic makeup of a particular computer; hence, programs had to be written for specific computers. Programs prepared for one computer could not be used on another without substantial rewriting at substantial additional expense. Institutions could not share programs unless they had identical computers. If an industry updated its computer hardware, its applications programs had to be rewritten. Such a state of affairs was obviously unacceptable.

In 1959, a number of computer professionals representing the interests of the U.S. government, the world of finance, universities, the insurance industry, and a variety of commercial industries and computer manufacturers agreed to meet for the express purpose of developing a business-oriented programming language that would be machine-independent. This group was called the Conference on Data Systems Languages (CODASYL). Its efforts culminated in the publication in the latter part of 1960 of the first version of COBOL. The word *COBOL* is an acronym for COmmon Business-Oriented Language. Some of the important features CODASYL wanted to incorporate in this language were the following:

1. It was to be machine-independent, thus allowing the same program to be processed on more than one computer. This objective was achieved to a remarkable degree, as you will learn in subsequent chapters.

2. It was to be easily maintainable. It was to allow for expansion, and for the inclusion of additional features to take advantage of technological improvements anticipated in later-generation computers. The subsequent versions COBOL-61, COBOL-61 extended (1963), COBOL Edition 65 (1965), COBOL Edition 1974, and COBOL Edition 1985 attest to the success of this feature.

3. It was to be free of mathematical and scientific symbols. In fact, the syntax, as developed, looks very much like the English language. It has a sentence structure and uses verbs, names, phrases, and clauses. This structure, along with a great versatility in the selection of names, allows programs to be largely self-documenting.

Though CODASYL still assumes the responsibility to update and maintain the COBOL language, the American National Standards Institute (ANSI) entered the picture in 1968, when it established COBOL as a standard language. The versions of COBOL as specified by ANSI are referred to as ANS COBOL. Most computer manufacturers provide COBOL compilers for their computers that comply with the specifications established by ANSI, but they also include extended features that capitalize on the unique features of their hardware configurations.

In programming establishments throughout the country, the 1974 version of COBOL is gradually being replaced by the 1985 version. This text generally adheres to the newest version.

Computers

Today, there are computer systems of all sizes and capabilities. Microprocessors are used in cars to increase efficiency, minimize fuel consumption, display road maps, and control passenger area climate (see Figure i.1). Other microprocessors are used in home heating systems, controlling the amount of heat to be produced in relation to ambient outdoor temperatures according to a programmed time schedule.

■ Figure i.1 General Motors' Trav Tek system uses satellite communications and computer technology in the car (left) to provide the driver with precise on-board navigation information (right). (Illustration courtesy of General Motors.)

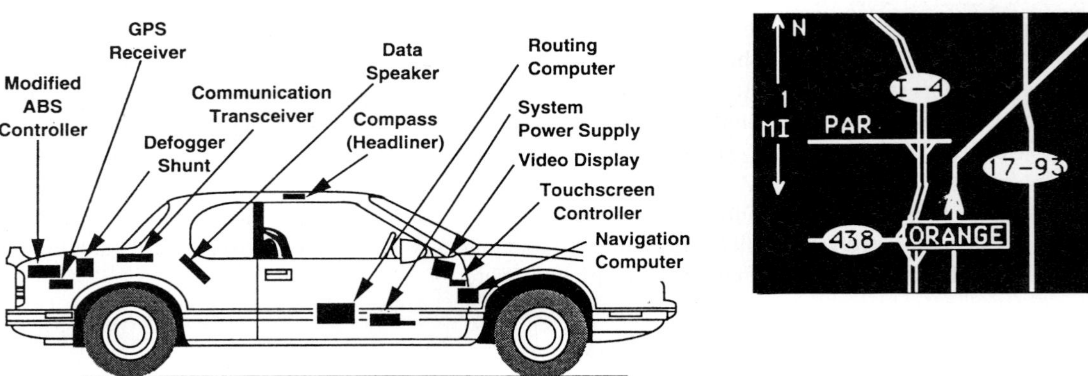

■ Figure i.2 An IBM personal system

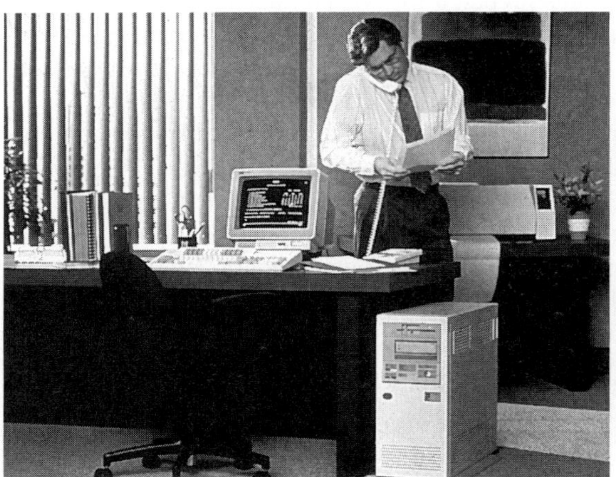

■ Figure i.3 Yesterday's mainframe

Microcomputers, also called personal computers, are found in many homes. They are used for educational purposes, for recreation, as word processors, as tools in managing home finances, even in the control of elaborate home security systems.

Personal computers are used extensively in schools, from elementary to university levels, for instructional purposes, for the management of student records, for the collection and analysis of data in scientific research, and so on.

Personal computers are also used in businesses of all sizes, from backyard operations to Fortune 500 companies (see Figure i.2). In small businesses, they can be used as simple bookkeeping tools or as sophisticated business analyzers, examining trends, making business projections, and the like. In a large business environment, the personal computer can be used as a stand-alone unit to help an individual manager, or it can be used as one of many units within a local area network (LAN) that allows sharing of data, interdepartmental communications, and so on.

Today's computers can have greater computing power than the large mainframes of the past (see Figure i.3). However, mainframe computers continue to be used by large businesses who process massive amounts of data.

■ Major Computer Components

Regardless of size, every computer consists of three major components: an *input unit,* a *processor unit,* and an *output unit,* as shown in Figure i.4.

Figure i.4 Major computer components

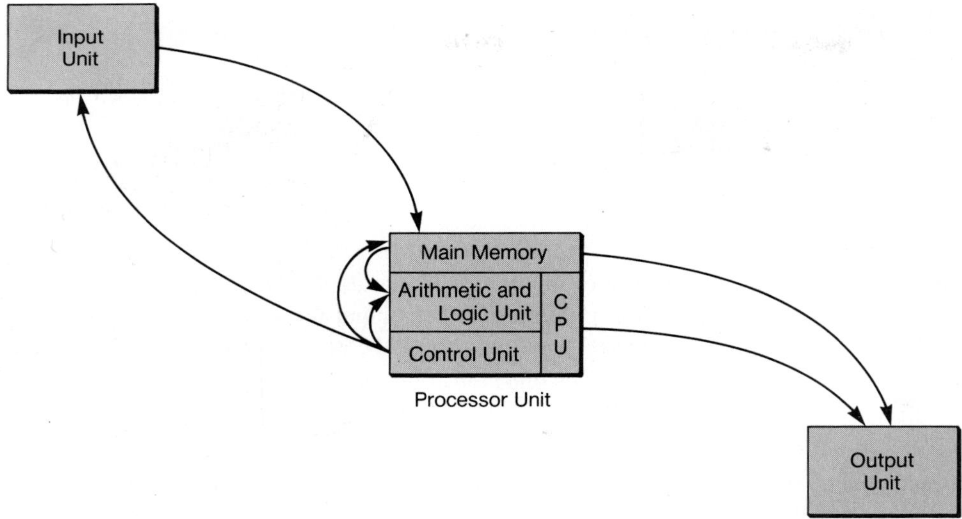

Input Unit

There are generally two kinds of input that must be supplied to the computer in the solution of a problem: *data* and *instructions.* The computer receives the instructions and the data through the use of some input device. Some of the most common types of input devices include a terminal keyboard, a magnetic disk drive, and a magnetic tape drive. Large computer installations may have a variety of such devices, whereas some very small microcomputers may have only one. In Figure i.2, the input device is the keyboard.

Processor Unit

The processor unit consists of two parts: the *central processing unit* (CPU) and the *main memory.*

The CPU is the component in which all required processing occurs. It is composed of two subcomponents: the *arithmetic and logic unit* (ALU) and the *control unit.*

The ALU is the component in which calculations and computations are performed. Most programs also contain conditional instructions; that is, instructions to be executed provided certain conditions are satisfied and not to be executed otherwise. The processing and evaluations necessary to make such decisions are carried out in this unit, specifically in the logic portion.

The control unit is the CPU component that controls the execution of the particular functions and processes required by the program. For instance, the control unit may command the input device to send data to main memory, or it may activate the ALU to perform some mathematical or logical operation, or it may direct the retrieval of stored information for further processing before outputting it on some output device such as a printer or magnetic tape drive. In short, the control unit is the control center of the entire computer system.

The main computer memory is used to store the program (set of instructions) as well as some or all of the data needed in the solution of a problem. The amount of main computer storage varies greatly from small to large computers. The memory capacity of a computer is expressed in terms of the number of characters (letters, digits, special symbols) that it can store. A computer with 640 KB (640 kilobytes) memory can store approximately 640,000 characters, or one character per byte. (K is actually equivalent to 2^{10}, or 1024, but it is usually read as "thousand.") A computer with 1 MB (1 megabyte = 1 million bytes) memory can store approximately 1,000,000 characters. Today, a typical personal computer has a main memory capacity in the range from 2 MB to 16 MB, expandable to 64 MB, whereas a large mainframe computer has a main memory capacity in the billions of characters, such as 1.2 GB (1.2 gigabytes = 1.2 billion bytes).

■ **Figure i.5** Components of main memory

Main Memory

Input Area	Working Storage	Output Area

In COBOL, the main storage area is treated as if it were physically separated into distinct compartments (see Figure i.5).

1. **Input memory** is reserved for the storage of input records as they are "read" into memory. (A buffer area is set aside in main memory for a file opened as an input file.)
2. **Output memory** is reserved for the storage of output records before they are "written" onto an output file. (A buffer area is set aside in main memory for a file opened as an output file.)
3. **Working storage** is reserved for data items that do not explicitly belong to an input or an output file.

This compartmentalizing of main memory is particularly important to the COBOL programmer because every program requires transferring data from one compartment to another. Detailed explanations will be provided in later chapters.

Output Unit

All the processing carried out by a computer is for the purpose of preparing and producing results, which are then recorded on some output device. A familiar device is the printer, which prints the output directly on paper. In certain applications programs, it may be preferable to record the output on some auxiliary storage device, such as a magnetic disk, where it will remain available for use or further processing later. Very often, the output is displayed on a TV-like screen, called a CRT (cathode ray tube), or a monitor, like the one in Figure i.2.

In general, a number of output devices are available for use in computer installations: the line printer, the laser printer, the magnetic tape or disk drive, the CRT or monitor, the plotter, and so on.

■ Computer Languages

The computer is a tool that people often use for help in the preparation and production of reports, in the processing and analysis of data, or in the solution of problems. Though a computer is a very powerful tool, it does nothing by itself to solve problems. It must receive specific instructions from the programmer; that is, the *programmer* (the person who writes the instructions) must communicate with the computer. This communication may occur at three different levels of languages: low, intermediate, and high.

Low-Level Languages

A low-level language can be characterized as the "native tongue" of the computer. The computer is a maze of electronic circuits, and each of these circuits may be in an "on" or "off" state. A language that specifies which of these circuits should be on and which should be off is called *machine language.* An instruction in machine language consists of a series of 0s and 1s, a 0 corresponding to off and a 1 corresponding to on. An example of such an instruction follows:

```
0100 1110 0101 1011
```

Since each kind of computer has its own peculiar circuitry, each one necessarily has its own machine language. Consequently, instructions written in machine language for a DEC VAX are not transferable to a CDC CYBER. Nontransferability of machine-language programs is a severe limitation of a low-level language, since much time, effort, and money must be spent duplicating programs if these same programs are to be processed on different makes of computers. Other negative aspects of low-level languages are also significant:

1. The machine-language programmer must be a specialist who is very knowledgeable about the electronic makeup of the computer. People who are to become machine-language programmers must spend a substantial amount of time just learning the intricacies and the specifications of the computer for which they will be writing instructions.

2. Since all the coding is done using 0s and 1s, it is very easy to make coding errors, but it is very difficult to locate and correct these errors.
3. Machine-language programmers must express all operations using specific numeric codes and must keep track of storage locations by using their addresses. This detailed and tedious work makes machine-language programming very difficult.

On the bright side, however, we must note the following:

1. Machine language is **indispensable** since it truly is the only language that a computer understands. It is its "native" tongue.
2. Machine language is a **most efficient** language because its instructions are directly implemented by the computer. Furthermore, instructions can be written so as to take advantage of the particular specifications of a computer.
3. Machine language is absolutely necessary in order to make the higher-level languages usable on a computer, as will be explained shortly.

Intermediate-Level Languages

When computers were first commercially produced, machine language was the only language available. However, the drawbacks mentioned above, coupled with the increasing need for programmers resulting from the general acceptance of computers in the business and scientific world, made it necessary to develop programming languages that could be learned more easily and that could also decrease coding errors.

The next step was the development of *symbolic assembly languages.* The major improvement consisted of replacing the *binary notations* (0s and 1s) with *mnemonics,* that is, groups of *alphanumeric characters* (letters of the alphabet and/or numeric digits). Thus, a machine-language instruction was replaced by an equivalent assembly-language instruction. While this change greatly facilitated the writing of instructions by eliminating much of the drudgery associated with machine language, an assembly language is still hampered by two major limitations:

1. An assembly language has to be written for a particular computer; therefore, an assembly-language program lacks transferability. An assembly language is machine-dependent, just like a machine language.
2. An assembly-language instruction falls far short of being clear in its meaning. When errors occur, it is a major task to find and correct them.

Since a computer understands only machine-language instructions, an assembly-language program must be translated into machine language before its instructions can be executed. This translation is effected by a *translator,* also called an *assembler.* A translator (or assembler) is not a piece of hardware, but rather a software package, specifically, a program usually stored permanently on some external storage medium, such as magnetic disk or tape. When a program written in assembly language is to be run on the computer, the translator or assembler must be loaded into the main memory of the processor unit. It then takes over the task of reading the assembly-language instructions and translating them into machine-language instructions. The set of machine-language instructions produced by the translator is called the *object program,* whereas the assembly-language program written by the programmer is called the *source program.* The control unit of the CPU will then control the execution of the object program.

High-Level Languages

Though the development of assembly-language programming was an important step in facilitating the coding of instructions, the fact that it remained so heavily machine-dependent caused computer specialists and users to examine the feasibility of developing machine-independent programming languages that would be process-oriented or problem-oriented instead of machine-oriented. From these efforts, two types of high-level languages evolved:

1. **Procedural languages** (process-oriented) such as Pascal, COBOL, FORTRAN, BASIC, APL, and PL/1
2. **Problem-oriented languages** such as RPG, APT, SNOBOL, and LISP

Procedural languages are general-purpose languages designed to facilitate the writing of instructions that specify **processes.** A sample instruction in BASIC might be

```
LET X = 3 * Y + 4
```

and a sample instruction in COBOL might be

```
ADD REGULAR-PAY OVERTIME-PAY GIVING GROSS-PAY.
```

The meaning of these instructions is very clear. They closely resemble statements in the English language, and anyone with a knowledge of elementary algebra has no difficulty understanding the mathematical statements.

Problem-oriented languages are special-purpose languages designed to facilitate computer solutions of particular types of problems. Instead of stressing procedures, these languages stress input data specifications and characteristics, output format specifications, and specifications of certain aspects or parameters of the problem to be solved. For instance, the sample RPG calculation specifications form shown in Figure i.6 shows the following: The multiplication calculation is to be performed when the indicator 10 is **on;** its factors are RATE and HOURS, and the result is to be stored in PAY; PAY has a field length of 6 with 2 decimal places, and its value must be rounded. The acronym RPG stands for Report Program Generator. It is used specifically to design business reports.

The acronym APT stands for Automatic Programmed Tools. It is used to generate instructions for numerical control machines.

The acronym SNOBOL stands for StriNg-Oriented SymBOlic Language. It is designed to manipulate large strings of characters and is used in creating text editors and compilers.

The acronym LISP stands for LISt Processing. It is used in nonnumeric programming, such as in artificial intelligence (AI), where symbolic objects are manipulated, rather than numbers.

Important advantages of high-level languages are as follows:

1. They are almost 100 percent machine-independent, so that a program written to be processed on one computer can be processed with very few changes, if any, on other computers.
2. Computer instructions written in these languages resemble English and/or scientific statements or specifications. This feature greatly facilitates the learning of these programming languages. Coding errors are decreased substantially, and, if any exist, they can be found and corrected more readily.

Just as an assembly-language program must be translated into a machine-language program, so must a high-level language program be converted into a machine-language program before its instructions can be executed. Two kinds of translators are used to carry out this code conversion: *interpreters* and *compilers.*

Most students who have studied BASIC, for instance, have used a BASIC interpreter. Since the role of the interpreter is transparent to the user, that is, the interpreter remains "out of view" and is never explicitly referenced by the user, its use may have gone unnoticed. The interpreter was brought into action whenever the RUN command was entered. It translated one line of BASIC code into machine-language code and immediately executed it, or, in the case of a syntax error, generated a diagnostic. Then it translated the next line of BASIC code and executed it, and so on, following the logic built into the program.

A compiler, on the other hand, is designed to translate all of a program's source-code instructions into machine-language code first. This code or object program is saved in a separate file. A RUN command will then execute the whole object program.

■ **Figure i.6** Sample RPG calculation specifications form

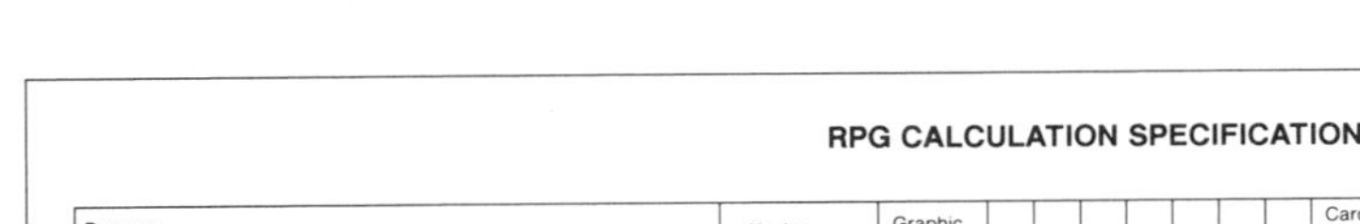
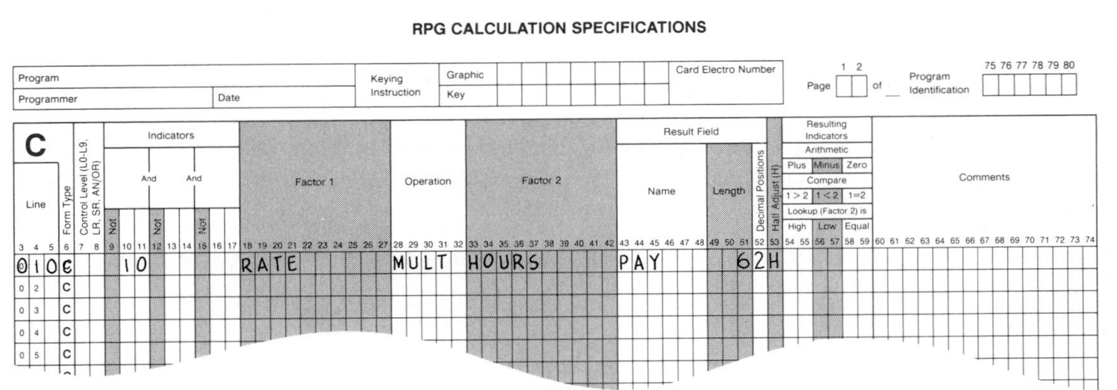

An interpreter is generally less efficient than a compiler, because the machine-language code it produces is not saved. Every time a program is executed, each source line is interpreted and then executed. So, if an instruction is contained in a loop, it must first be translated and then executed every time it is encountered. Furthermore, the interpreter must remain available in main memory during the execution of the program. With a compiler, however, the program is translated or compiled only once. Once compilation has occurred, the compiler can be returned to an on-line external storage medium, thus freeing main memory. The compiled program can then be executed repeatedly without any further need for the compiler.

Since each high-level language has its own set of specifications, its own rules of syntax, there must be distinct compilers and interpreters for each language that will be processed on a particular computer. For instance, if a computer is to be used to process Pascal programs, COBOL programs, and BASIC programs, it must have the corresponding translators readily available, such as a Pascal compiler, a COBOL compiler, a BASIC interpreter, and a BASIC compiler. (These translators are usually in on-line auxiliary storage.)

Moreover, since each brand of computer has its own machine-language specifications, a compiler or interpreter written to produce machine-language instructions for one computer cannot be used to produce machine-language instructions for another brand of computer. A COBOL compiler written for a CDC CYBER cannot be used to process a COBOL program on a DEC VAX. Compilers and interpreters are both machine-dependent and language-dependent programs.

Another very important role a translator plays is that of *diagnostician.* Before producing machine-language instructions, it checks each high-level language instruction to ascertain compliance with the rules of *syntax* (grammar and other language construction rules). If no error is found, then the *translation/compilation* process takes place—that is, machine-language code is generated—but if there are errors, the translator usually issues diagnostics. *Diagnostics* are error messages. The nature of diagnostics varies greatly from one translator to another. They may be just error codes, which must then be looked up in an error-code manual, or they may be detailed statements specifying the coding errors made. Compilers usually generate more extensive diagnostics than do interpreters. In any case, the translator is a powerful teacher, and the programmer soon learns to avoid the syntax errors it detects.

The preceding comments, applied to you as a COBOL student programmer, can be summarized as follows:

1. The programmer prepares the *source program,* that is, the high-level language instructions.
2. The source program is compiled by the compiler; that is, every properly coded instruction in the source program is translated into machine-language instructions. The resulting machine-language program is called the *object program.* It is usually stored in a separate file.

   If the source program contains serious syntax errors, the object program cannot be produced, and the compiler generates diagnostics related to the errors. (Note that **only syntax errors** are detected by the compiler. Logic errors are **your** responsibility.)
3. The computer processes the object program. The desired results are produced by the computer if no clerical errors and no logic errors exist in the program. The role of the compiler is illustrated in Figure i.7.

Computer Systems

Computer systems generally consist of one or more input devices, one or more output devices, and one or more processors. (Even a small personal computer has a keyboard, perhaps an optional mouse, one or more floppy-disk drives, and maybe a hard-disk drive as input devices and a monitor, a printer, and one or more disk drives as output devices.) Systems are usually classified according to the basic media used for input/output purposes (see Figure i.8). There are *disk systems, tape systems, card systems,* and combinations of these, though pure card systems today are almost nonexistent.

Typically, a disk system uses magnetic disks as input and output units (in addition to one or more keyboard video display terminals), and a processor unit. A small disk system has a minimum of two disk drives, each of these driving a disk pack consisting of several disks or platters. Each disk may contain from 200 to 800 magnetic tracks per surface.

A tape system uses a magnetic tape drive as an input unit (in addition to one or more keyboard video display terminals), another tape drive (and a printer) as an output unit, and a processor unit. A small tape system usually has a bank of at least four tape drives. The tape reels may contain from 250 to 3,600 feet of magnetic tape.

■ **Figure i.7** Major functions of the COBOL compiler

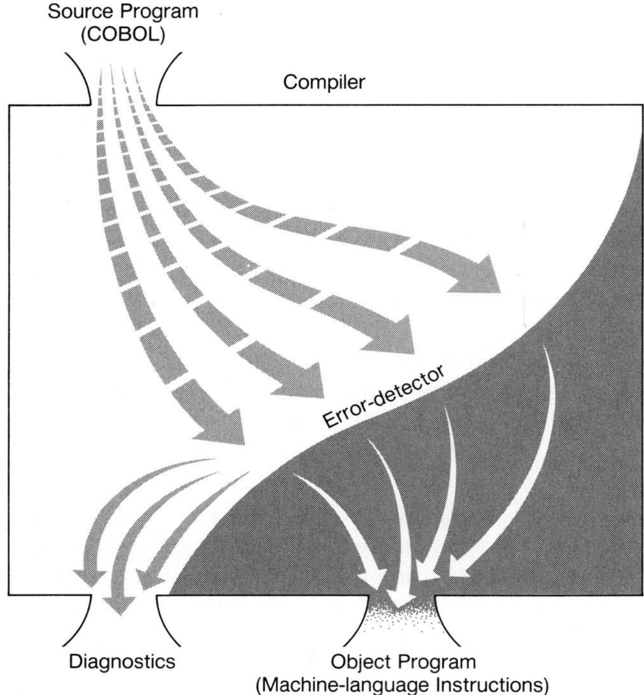

■ **Figure i.8** An IBM 370/138 information system

A combination system contains a variety of input/output devices and at least one processor unit. See Figure i.9.

Tape systems are characterized as *sequential access* systems. In these systems, records are processed in the physical sequence in which they reside on the file. If a record is stored at the 400-foot mark on a tape, the tape reel drive must pull the first 399 feet through the tape-reading head to reach the proper record.

On the other hand, disk systems are characterized as *direct-access* systems. Each disk or platter consists of as many as 800 concentric circles, called recording tracks, on each surface. The data recorded on any of these tracks can be accessed sequentially as well as directly by an access mechanism similar to the pick-up arm of a record player. The mechanism can place the read/write head at the appropriate spot on track 150, for instance, without scanning any of the 149 preceding tracks. In general, a record stored on a disk can be accessed directly in much less time than a record stored on tape.

■ **Figure i.9** A computer system with multiple facilities

Processing a Program

Processing a computer program requires the use of computer hardware and computer software. The hardware consists of an input unit, an output unit, and a processor unit. The required software consists essentially of three programs:

1. An executive program
2. A compiler program
3. An applications program

The *executive program* is an operating system program; it is the program that manages the operation of the computer system. It is generally loaded from disk storage into main computer storage at the beginning of the business's computer operations. From that time on, it controls the various functions and activities required to make the computer system operate efficiently. For instance, it activates the various input devices, sequences the various jobs or programs that must be run, selects and loads the appropriate compiler for each job, and activates I/O (input/output) devices, all with very little interference on the part of the computer operator. In short, it is the computer system manager.

The *compiler program* is the program whose prime task is to process the source program. In this text, the source program is always a COBOL program. As the compiler processes the program, it generates the corresponding object program, consisting of all the appropriate *machine-language* instructions specific to the computer that will execute the program. The object program may be stored on a disk for later use, or it may be stored directly in main memory for immediate use. This is the program that will be loaded by the *loader* or linked by the *linker* and subsequently "run" by the computer.

Another important task of the compiler is to provide diagnostics to the programmer regarding syntax errors that may exist in the program. Syntax errors may involve punctuation, spelling, spacing, or illegal statement formats. Not all errors have the same degree of severity. Some are disastrous and consequently will prevent execution of the program, whereas others generate only warnings. Warnings do not prevent program execution, but they may indicate possible unpredictable consequences when the program is run.

Diagnostic messages usually accompany the compiler-generated listing of the source program. The indicated errors must be corrected and the program recompiled before proper execution will occur. It is crucial for you to realize that the compiler detects syntax errors only; it does not detect logic errors. It is **your** responsibility to discover and correct logic errors.

Finally, the *applications program* is the COBOL program. In general, the applications program is written in a high-level language for the express purpose of solving a problem in a specific field of endeavor, such as business, science, engineering, or education. COBOL applications programs are written to solve business-oriented problems, such as the preparation of payroll, billing, and inventory reports. **The processing of applications programs is the ultimate purpose of a computer system.**

The relationships between the executive, compiler, and applications programs and the CPU are shown in Figure i.10.

Figure i.10 Essential software needed to run a program

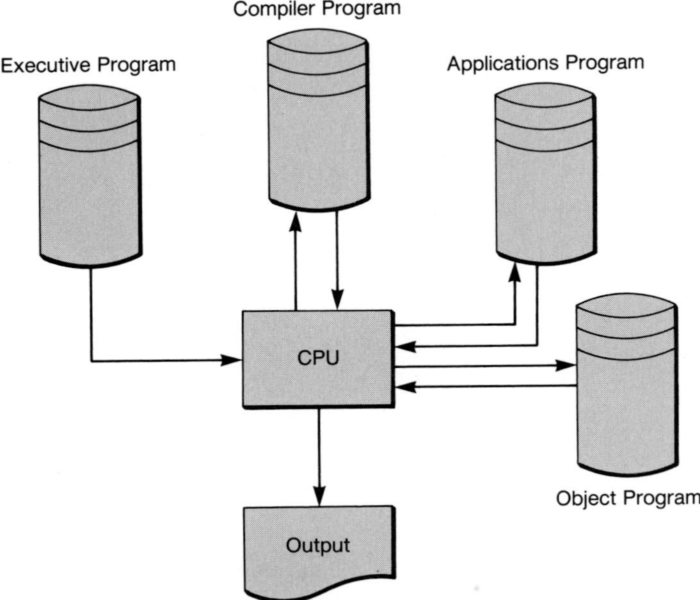

Conclusion

This completes the introduction. Before continuing to the next chapter, you should be able to identify the major components of a computer system and understand their main functions. You should know the subcomponents of the CPU and understand their relevance to COBOL programming. You should understand the essential function of translators: assemblers, interpreters, and compilers. And you should know the three kinds of software needed to process a computer program.

1 The Problem-Solving Procedure

The essential role of a computer **programmer** is that of a problem solver. A task is specified, and the programmer must plan just how it should be accomplished. In this chapter, you are presented with a **problem-solving procedure** that has proved to be a very effective tool toward that end. It will be applied systematically throughout the text in the development of the sample programs that are used to introduce you to **COBOL** concepts and syntax.

Additionally, in this chapter, a simple problem is presented to you for computer solution. You are then taken "by the hand" through the steps of the problem-solving procedure. Of course, at this very early stage, you are not expected to know any of the COBOL language requirements or understand any of the intricacies of a COBOL program. Consider this initial exposure as a bird's-eye view of the development of a COBOL program. In later chapters, you will learn everything you need to know to successfully design and code COBOL programs on your own. ■

Objectives You Should Achieve

After completing this chapter, you should:

1. Become aware of a standard problem-solving procedure that is most beneficial to COBOL programmers.

Problem-Solving Procedure

Typically, when a programmer is assigned the task of developing an applications program, the writing, or coding, of the program is one of the last activities to be performed. Experienced programmers are wont to say to beginners: "The sooner you begin to code, the longer it will take!" The point of the comment is to underscore the prerequisite need for analysis and good program design.

Initially, the programmer must obtain all the pertinent details regarding the nature of the problem, its specific objectives, the kind of output that is required, the data that will be provided as input, and so on. These details are obtained by the programmer during exploratory sessions with the person or persons requesting the program. This situation is analogous to your wanting a house built. Your request of the architect, contractor, and/or carpenter would not simply be "Build me a house." There would be lengthy meetings during which you would discuss in detail the features that you want included in your house. Then plans would be drawn up, and further discussions would take place before the first shovelful of dirt would be removed. After learning exactly what you want, the builder will then decide on a course of action: what must be done first, second, third, and so on.

Similarly, when the programmer has been made aware of all the program specifications, he or she spends a considerable amount of time designing and planning the program. This program *design phase* includes the preparation of output layout forms, if a printed report is needed, and input record layout forms. It includes a *system flowchart* that identifies the file(s) containing the data to be supplied as input to the program and the file(s) that receive the processed data from the program. It includes a *structure chart* that clearly specifies and illustrates the essential task to be accomplished, as well as the subtasks needed for a complete solution to the problem. It also includes a detailed listing of all the processing steps needed to complete the tasks specified in the structure chart. There are two different ways of providing these details. One way is to **write** them in English-like statements; the collection of all these statements is referred to as the *program pseudocode.* The other way is to **draw** a visual representation of the processing steps; this is referred to as the *program flowchart.* A programmer typically uses one or the other, but not both, since they accomplish the same objective. (In this text, the primary method we use is the program pseudocode. However, since some instructors have a strong preference for diagrams, we also include the corresponding program flowchart.)

This enumeration makes it very clear that the design phase is a most crucial task for the programmer. After preparing design materials, the programmer may request another meeting for the express purpose of explaining her or his plans and "walking through" the structure chart and the pseudocode or the program flowchart. Following the walk-through, further modifications may be required. If so, the programmer revises the plans. When all parties are sure that the plans meet all the problem requirements, the program design phase is complete.

The second phase is the *design implementation phase.* This is where the coding of the program finally begins.

Just as the contractor must take into account the local zoning laws, state and federal building codes, and the requirements of the buyer while executing the building plans, the programmer must also enter lines of coding into the program that abide by the rules of syntax for the language, all the while being guided by the program design. The successful completion of this task is greatly dependent on two factors:

1. The care, accuracy, and completeness of the design phase
2. The mastery of the rules of syntax and specifications of the programming language by the programmer

After completing the coding of the program, the programmer carefully reviews the entries on every line of the program to detect coding errors and any lack of compliance with the plans and design specified earlier. This is time and effort well invested, since it is much less costly to correct errors on paper than following a computer run. The programmer makes the necessary corrections and is then ready for the next step.

The next step in the implementation phase is *keying* or *entering* the program, that is, entering it line by line into a file. The file may reside on magnetic tape in a tape system, on a magnetic disk in a disk system, or on a floppy disk in a microcomputer. This is usually done by direct keyboarding on a microcomputer or keying at a remote-entry terminal on a large multiuser system. Each encoded line is a source record, and the complete set of encoded lines is called the *source program,* source file, or source code.

If the data to be processed by the program is not already in a file, then a data file has to be created as well. In keying data records, you must adhere exactly to the input record layout specifications noted in the design phase. Keying data in the wrong record positions may cause program execution to abort or at the least cause errors and/or garbage in the output. (In this text, sample data files that may be used in the programming exercises are available in the data sets in Appendix C. They are also available on a Data Disk that instructors who use this textbook may obtain from the publisher, and they are available on a Convenience Disk included in the textbook for students who purchase the RM/COBOL-85 compiler for use on their personal computer.)

After the source program has been stored in a file, it must be compiled; that is, it must be entered as input to the COBOL compiler. The compiler is normally directed to produce a listing of the lines of code in the program; as it does so, it numbers the lines sequentially. It then issues line-referenced diagnostics to notify you of the syntax errors that exist in the program. Syntax errors occur when coded entries do not conform to the requirements of the language. If diagnostics have been issued, it is your responsibility to make the necessary corrections by editing the corresponding records in the source program.

The process of calling the compiler must be repeated until all the serious errors have been removed from the program and a successful compilation has occurred. At this point, the compiler will have generated the *object* program. (We remind you again that the compiler does not detect logic errors.)

The next step in the implementation phase is to run the program. The procedure to follow in running the program always requires some system-related specific instructions to the executive program, and these vary with the computer system being used. The essential functions that must be completed by these instructions are (1) to resolve the meaning of symbolic references that exist in the program into representations meaningful to the operating system; and (2) to allocate the amount of memory required by the program. The result is an *executable image* of the program. On some systems, this is accomplished by the joint efforts of the translator and a program called a loader, as on a CDC CYBER; whereas on other systems, such as a DEC VAX, a linker program produces the final executable program image. (System commands generally indicate the process being used. LGO on a CYBER means "load and go." A LINK command followed by a RUN command on a VAX obviously means that a linker is called into the process. You must get additional system-specific information from your instructor or from your school's computer center.)

Assuming that all serious syntax errors were removed from the source program, and that the loader or linker successfully completed the executable image of the program, the computer executes the image, and the output is produced at this point. The programmer must then check the output for accuracy, completeness, readability, and even aesthetic form, and then discuss his or her findings with the person requesting the program to obtain a final approval. When this approval is obtained, the programmer provides final documentation for the program, and the program is then ready for use.

The explanation of the problem-solving procedure is visually presented in Figure 1.1.

The problem-solving procedure that we briefly explained in general terms above and illustrated in Figure 1.1 is formalized in Figure 1.2. (Note that step 3 in Figure 1.2 references specific COBOL program requirements.)

While developing the programs assigned in this text, the student is strongly advised to follow the problem-solving procedure systematically. The discussions and walk-through sessions that may be available to programmers in the "real world" are generally nonexistent while a student is writing programs as part of a course; consequently, the student may miss out on the important services that such meetings provide. It is therefore much more crucial for the student, working alone, to review her or his work often and very carefully. Of particular importance are the debugging steps of the problem-solving procedure.

Program Illustrating the Problem-Solving Procedure

We now present a simple programming assignment. In developing its solution, we will apply the steps of the problem-solving procedure systematically, just as we recommended earlier. As an additional aid at this point, we will label each step individually. You may want to refer to this sample later when you are faced with the task of developing a program on your own.

Note: It should be obvious that you are not expected to be able to do the work that follows all by yourself at this early stage. This sample program is being presented here so that you can have a complete picture of the problem-solving procedure "at work." The task of designing and writing a COBOL program is substantial. If you get lost in details later, you will always have this sample program development to refer to in order to reorient yourself.

■ **Figure 1.1** A visual presentation of the problem-solving procedure

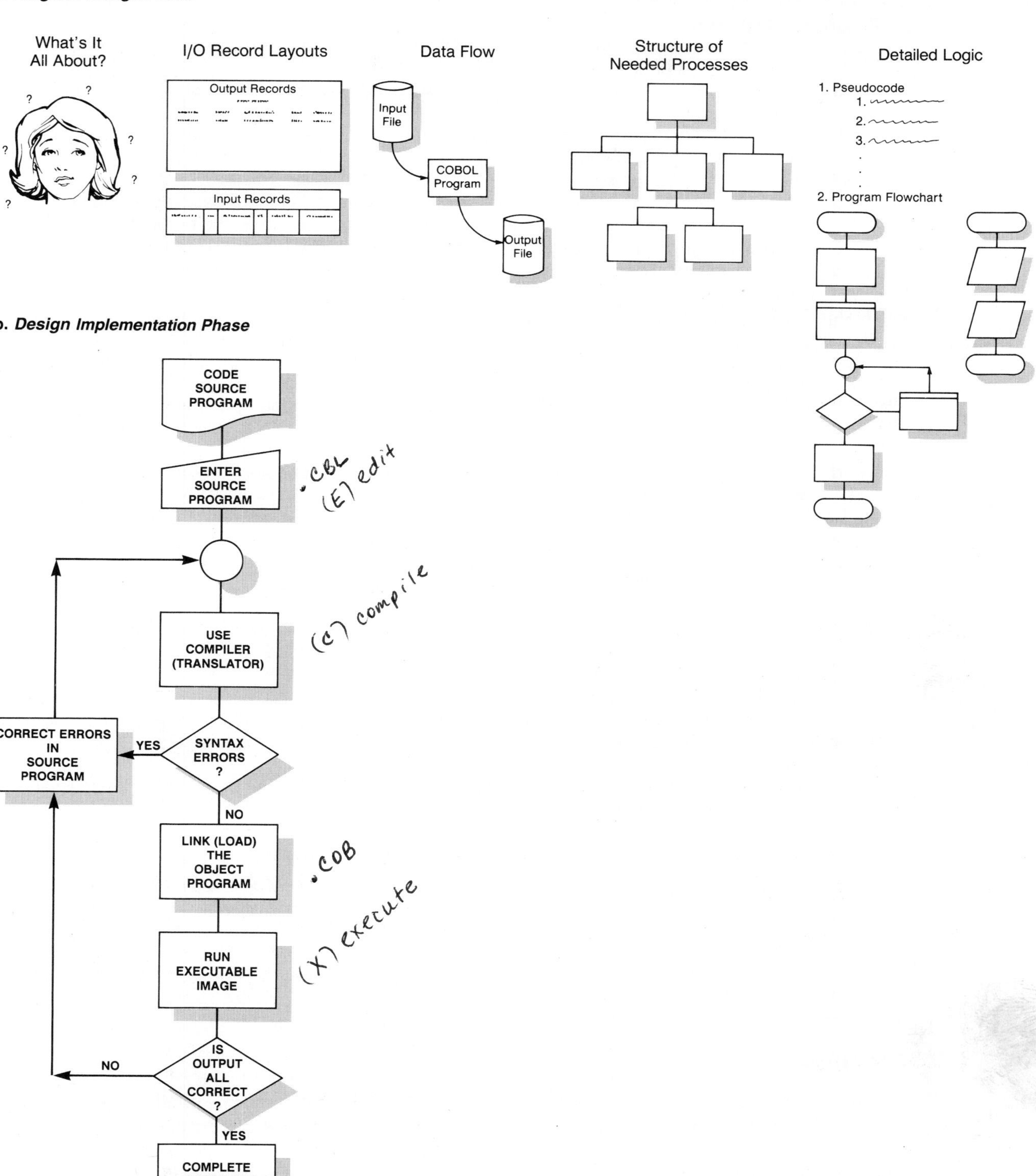

■ **Figure 1.2** The problem-solving procedure

The Problem-Solving Procedure

A. Program Design Phase

1. Develop a thorough understanding of the problem. Obtain all program specifications, and record these specifications on the appropriate forms.
   - **a.** Input record layout: identify and name data supplied; indicate position of data on record; name the record.
   - **b.** Output record layout(s): identify the types of records needed; plan the layout of each type; name the data fields; name the records.
2. Plan the solution to the problem.
   - **a.** Determine data flow (system flowchart): indicate the source of input data (name the input file), the function of the program, and the nature of the output file (name the output file).
   - **b.** Develop the structure chart: identify the overall task; specify functional subcomponents.
   - **c.** Convert each functional component into a specific set of processing steps; write the program pseudocode or design the program flowchart; walk through with sample data.

B. Design Implementation Phase

3. Code the COBOL program.
   - **a.** In the IDENTIFICATION DIVISION, name the program and include program documentation: author, date written, program description.
   - **b.** In the ENVIRONMENT DIVISION, specify the computers and the files needed by the program.
   - **c.** In the DATA DIVISION, define the files, and code all record data specifications. (Use layout forms as guides.)
   - **d.** In the PROCEDURE DIVISION, code all instructions corresponding to processing steps identified in the program pseudocode or flowchart.
4. Key (or enter) the program.
   - **a.** Create a new file.
   - **b.** Use a text editor to add the lines of coding to the file.
   - **c.** Get a listing of the file. (The file is the source program.)
   - **d.** Correct obvious errors.
5. Debug the program.
   - **a.** Use the compiler to identify all syntax errors in the source code.
   - **b.** Correct all syntax errors indicated by the compiler.
   - **c.** Repeat steps a and b until the program is free of syntax errors.
   - **d.** Compile the program, save the object program, and get a compiler listing of the source program.
   - **e.** If applicable, use the linker to produce an executable image of the program.
6. Test run the program.
   - **a.** Run the executable image with a sample input file; create the sample input file if necessary.
   - **b.** Check the output carefully to determine if all objectives are met.
   - **c.** Revise as necessary to meet all objectives.
7. Assemble the complete package for delivery to the person requesting it.
   - **a.** Input and output record layout forms
   - **b.** System flowchart
   - **c.** Structure chart
   - **d.** Program pseudocode or flowchart
   - **e.** Program listing produced by the compiler
   - **f.** Sample input file
   - **g.** Sample program output

Problem

The management of the Turbo Manufacturing Company wants a computer listing of all its employees. For each employee, the printed report must show the employee's Social Security number, name, job classification, and phone number.

An employee file contains a data record for each employee. The data in each record is stored as follows:

cc 1–9	Employee Social Security number
cc 10–29	Employee name
cc 30–49	Employee street address
cc 50–69	Employee city and state
cc 70–73	Employee job classification
cc 74–80	Employee phone number

(cc is used to mean character position; traditionally it meant card column)

Note: The employee file is shown in Figure 1.3 [DD/CD: V1C1SP.DAT].* (The column identifiers are inserted only to help you identify the data. They are not part of the data file itself.)

Solution

The steps of the problem-solving procedure are separated into two phases, the program design phase and the design implementation phase. Following is an explanation of how the problem will be explored in these phases.

The Program Design Phase

The first phase is the design phase. The programmer must plan the details and analyze the logical structure of the program.

Step 1. Developing of a Thorough Understanding of the Problem

In this example, the task is quite simple: The program must read an employee record and manipulate selected data on that record (Social Security number, name, job classification, and phone number) so it can print a corresponding line on the report. This procedure must be repeated for each employee record.

To reference data contained on an employee record, the programmer must tell the computer exactly where it is stored on the record. This calls for the following step.

Step 1a. Prepare Input Record Layout Forms

The layout of an input record shows the data fields that the record contains, where these fields are positioned on the record, and the names by which the fields can be referenced within the program. The record itself is also given a name.

Figure 1.4 has been developed by using information supplied in the statement of the problem. Note the data names assigned to the fields (subdivisions) of the record and the name assigned to the record itself.

For a program to be useful, it must produce some output. The programmer now attends to the following step.

Figure 1.3 Listing of the input file

Social Security number | Employee name | Street address | City and State | Job class | Phone number

```
714320025JOHN E. TURNER      436 ROCK ST.        FALL RIVER, MA      M-106832004
344024030JANET H. COLLINS    755 PLAIN AVE.      SWANSEA, MA         E-026841522
533254735EDWARD P. RILEY     1512 RIVERSIDE AVE. SOMERSET, MA        S-056833241
465114040BARBARA F. WOLSEY   515 GLOBE ST.       FALL RIVER, MA      M-056836432
547316545MICHELLE H. BOISE   843 TICKLE LANE     WESTPORT, MA        E-086851144
476561250GEORGE F. FAIRHURST 2450 OCEAN DRIVE    WESTPORT, MA        M-036853153
386471455SHAWN M. AINSWORTH  141 BUSH LANE       SWANSEA, MA         S-106846890
837684260CATHRYN E. CODY     844 FLINT ST.       FALL RIVER, MA      S-036837044
582784665ALEX B. GOULART     2415 PLAIN AVE.     SWANSEA, MA         S-026841139
664375170GLORIA J. NOWACK    1065 CENTER RD.     WESTPORT, MA        E-106857991
```

Figure 1.4 Sample input record layout

Record Layout Form

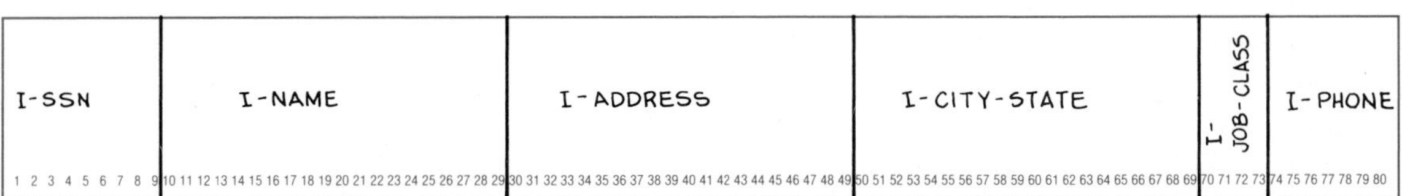

Record Name: EMPLOYEE-RECORD

*The employee file is file V1C1SP.DAT on the Data Disk (DD) and on the Convenience Disk (CD).

Step 1b. Prepare Output Record Layout Forms

If the output is a printed report, a printer spacing chart is used to plan the layout of each type of printed line needed on the report. If a line contains *constants,* that is, values that do not change during the execution of the program, such as column headers, the layout shows them properly positioned on the line. If a line will print *variables,* that is, field values that may change from one line to another or values that change from one run of the program to another run (such as a date field), the position and size of each of these fields are specified as strings of Xs, and names are assigned to the fields so that they can be referenced during the execution of the program.

If the output of the program is a file that will be stored on some magnetic medium, then the output record layouts will simply show the positions of the data fields that belong to the records of the file and the names by which these fields can be referenced.

In either case, the output records themselves are also assigned names.

In our sample program, we must now identify the kinds of records needed on the printed report. To keep the job simple we are skipping all headers, so that only one kind of line will be printed; specifically, the line that contains the information for an employee. There will be as many of these lines as there are employees, but all the lines will use the same format. We must prepare its layout. It should be obvious that the layout is related to the width of printer paper that is available. Let's suppose that wide (15-inch) continuous-form paper is used, and the printer can print 132 characters per line. You must decide which print positions will be used for the employee Social Security number, which print positions will be used for the employee name, and so on. For aesthetic considerations, programmers generally attempt to center a printed report across the width of the paper. The layout of the employee print line in our sample program is shown in Figure 1.5.

Step 2. Planning the Solution

The next part of the problem-solving procedure calls for planning the solution. The following step describes the first of those activities.

Step 2a. Prepare a System Flowchart

This flowchart shows the flow of data as required by the program. The data flow is generally from an input file, through the program, into an output file. (Data flow will be more involved later in the text.) Special symbols are used to illustrate the physical media on which the files reside, and file names are written within the symbols. A very brief description of the function of the program is also specified.

In the example, the data to be processed is obtained by the program from the input file. We have named this file EMPLOYEE-FILE, and the symbol shows that the file is stored on a magnetic disk. The printed output produced by the program has been named EMPLOYEE-LIST, and the symbol shows that the output file is a printed document. The system flowchart is shown in Figure 1.6.

The next planning activity is described in the following step.

Figure 1.5 Sample printer spacing chart

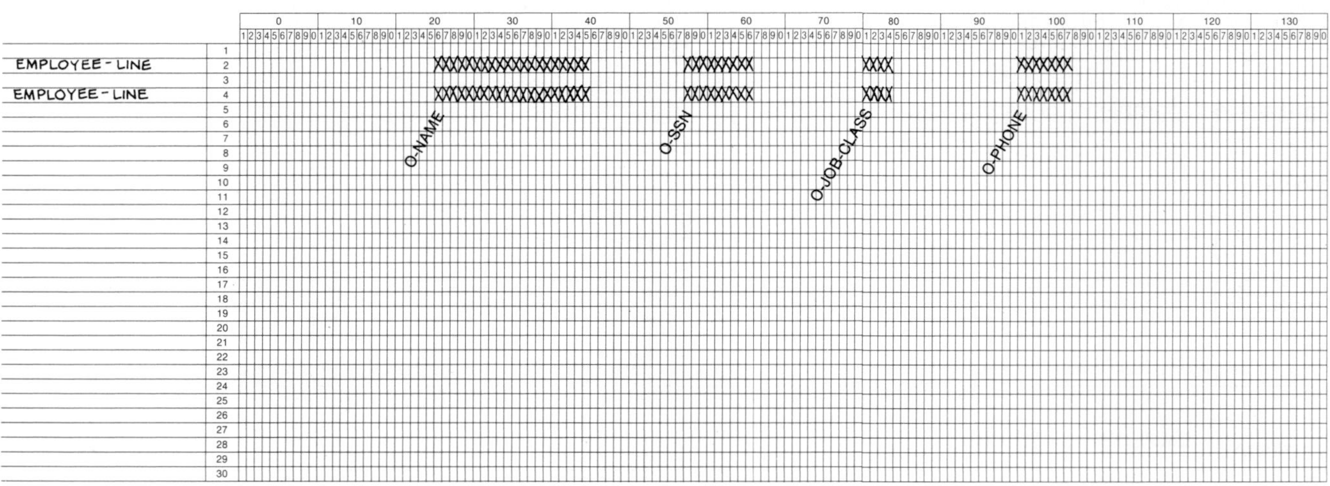

Figure 1.6 Sample system flowchart

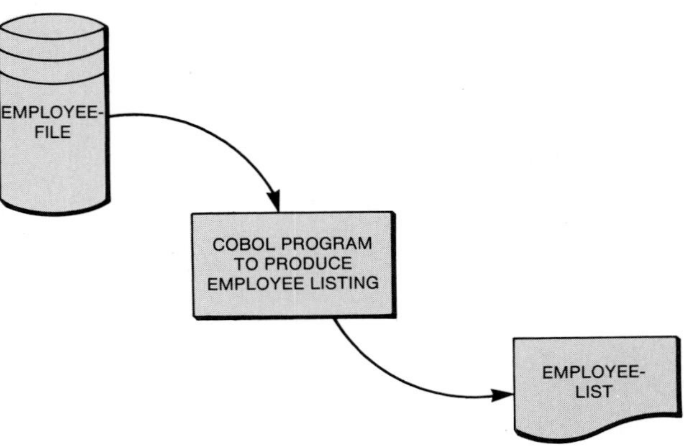

Figure 1.7 Sample structure chart

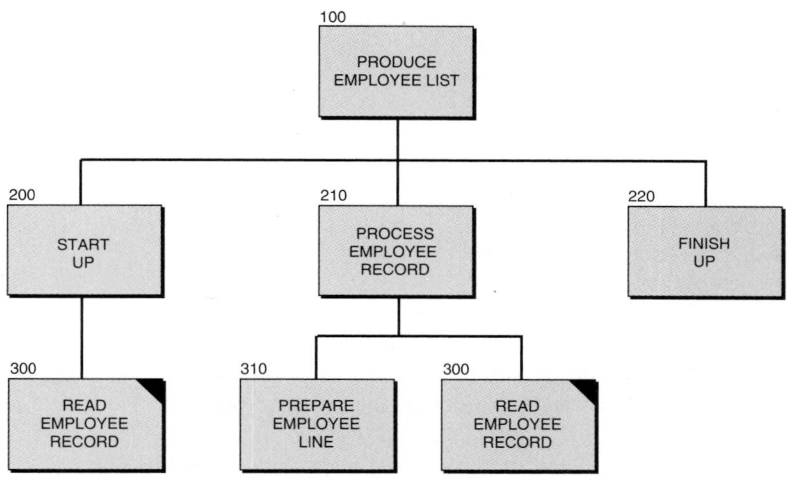

Step 2b. Prepare a Structure Chart

A *structure chart* is also called a *hierarchy chart.* A structure chart is a visual picture of the total task to be accomplished, broken down into its functional subcomponents. It is similar to an organization chart which is used to show the hierarchical relationships that exist between and among the various positions within the organization. The structure chart specifies the various functions that must be accomplished in order to complete the overall task. Any one of these major functions that in turn requires the completion of subtasks is further broken down into those subtasks.

The major function of the sample program is to produce the employee list. To accomplish this, a record must be read from the employee file, and then it must be processed. To process the employee record means to retrieve data from selected fields, move the data to the appropriate fields of the employee print line, and print the line. The process continues by reading the next record of the employee file. The structure chart for the sample program is shown in Figure 1.7. Note that the boxes in the chart are numbered. The numbering scheme, as well as the box labeled START UP and the box labeled FINISH UP, will be explained later.

The next task in planning the program is described in the next step.

Step 2c. Write the Program Pseudocode

The task specified in each box in the structure chart requires specific processing steps. They are itemized, within a paragraph, in the particular sequence in which they should occur, one paragraph per box in the structure chart. The term *pseudocode* (i.e., "fake" code) means that the statements written here closely resemble the actual COBOL statements that will be coded in the program itself.

For our sample program, the pseudocode that corresponds to the structure chart in Figure 1.7 is shown in Figure 1.8.

■ **Figure 1.8** Sample program pseudocode

100-Produce-Employee-List.

1. Perform 200-Start-Up.
2. Perform 210-Process-Employee-Record until no more records.
3. Perform 220-Finish-Up.
4. Stop the run.

200-Start-Up.

1. Open the files.
2. Set the end-of-file flag WS-MORE-RECORDS to "YES".
3. Perform 300-Read-Employee-Record.

210-Process-Employee-Record.

1. Perform 310-Prepare-Employee-Line.
2. Perform 300-Read-Employee-Record.

220-Finish-Up.

1. Close the files.

300-Read-Employee-Record.

1. Read an input employee record.
2. Test for the end-of-file record; if EOF record reached, move "NO " to the end-of-file flag.

310-Prepare-Employee-Line.

1. Move spaces to the Employee-Line area.
2. Move the input name to the Employee-Line name.
3. Move the input ssn to the Employee-Line ssn.
4. Move the input job-class to the Employee-Line job-class.
5. Move the input phone to the Employee-Line phone.
6. Move the Employee-Line to the output record area Printline.
7. After advancing 2 lines, write the output record Printline.

Note that the pseudocode consists of as many paragraphs as there are boxes in the structure chart. Each paragraph is assigned the functional name from within the box and uses the number next to the box as a prefix. The paragraphs are then written in ascending order of the numeric prefixes. More detailed explanations will be provided later.

The alternate suggested planning activity to detail the processing steps is described below.

Alternate Step 2c. Design the Program Flowchart

This alternate procedure is used for the purpose of producing a pictorial representation of the program logic. It is equivalent to the processing steps normally incorporated in the program pseudocode. The old adage, "a picture is worth a thousand words," is most appropriate here. For this reason, some programmers prefer using a flowchart to using pseudocode.

In the sample program, the program flowchart that corresponds to the pseudocode in Figure 1.8 is shown in Figure 1.9. Note that the flowchart is modular and that it contains as many modules as there are paragraphs in the pseudocode or boxes in the structure chart.

The five steps explained above constitute the program design phase. It should be emphasized that each of these steps should be examined and reexamined carefully before proceeding to the next step in line. Such activities are referred to as *debugging* activities. It is generally much easier to find and, in particular, to correct errors at **each** step of program development than it is much later when, supposedly, the job is complete.

We are now ready to proceed with the second phase of the problem-solving procedure.

The Design Implementation Phase

The second phase of program development is the design implementation phase. Put simply, now that the task has been planned, just do it. The design implementation phase includes the steps described below.

Step 3. Coding the COBOL Program

The efforts expended in the design phase begin to produce results here. Every COBOL program, regardless of how simple it is, contains four divisions. They are identified and explained briefly as follows.

a. **IDENTIFICATION DIVISION.** In this division the programmer must name the program, and she or he generally enters a brief explanation of the program.

■ **Figure 1.9** Sample program flowchart

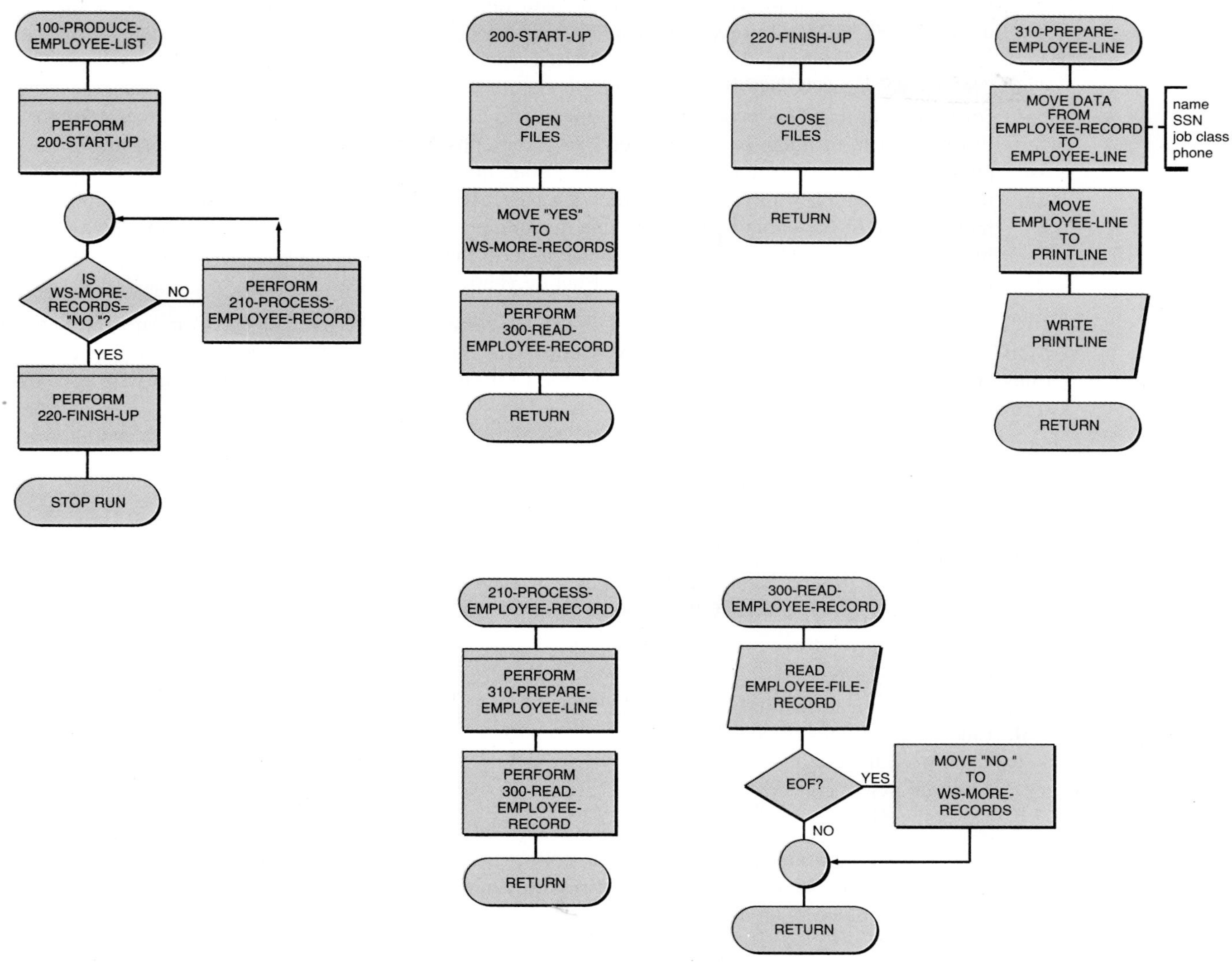

In the example, the program name is PRODUCE-EMPLOYEE-LISTING, and the documentation is enclosed within a box of asterisks.

b. ENVIRONMENT DIVISION. In this division the programmer identifies the computers that will run the program and names the files needed by the program. (The files have been identified previously in the system flowchart.)

In the example, the same computer (VAX-VMS-8650) plays the roles of both source computer and object computer. (The source computer processes the COBOL source program, and the object computer processes the machine-language object program.) The input file EMPLOYEE-FILE is assigned to COB$INPUT since it is the input file, and the output file EMPLOYEE-LIST is assigned to COB$OUTPUT.

Note: COB$INPUT and COB$OUTPUT are specific to the VAX. You must obtain entries for your computer from your instructor.)

c. DATA DIVISION. In this division the programmer provides complete specifications for all the data items needed within the program. Some of these items are the ones supplied on input records; other data items are those that will be prepared on output records; still other data items are needed internally to allow the program to do its job. A data item description must specify, among other things, the name of the storage area, its size (that is, the number of characters it can store), and the type of data that it will contain. The programmer uses the record layouts prepared during the design phase to direct much of the coding that is required here.

In our example, the input file is described in the paragraph that begins with FD EMPLOYEE-FILE, and the output file is described in the paragraph FD EMPLOYEE-LIST. Both of these are in the FILE SECTION. However, the output record whose layout was prepared on the printer spacing chart is described in the WORKING-STORAGE SECTION. This will be explained later.

d. PROCEDURE DIVISION. This division contains the actual COBOL instructions that correspond to the pseudocode written earlier, or to the processing steps contained in the program flowchart. The instructions are grouped into paragraphs, just as they are in the pseudocode. Or, equivalently, all instructions corresponding to one module in the program flowchart are grouped into one paragraph within the PROCEDURE DIVISION. To enhance program documentation, the names given to the paragraphs within this division are the same as those used to name the modules in the flowchart, the same as those used in the pseudocode, and also the same as the functions specified in the boxes of the structure chart.

In this example, the PROCEDURE DIVISION consists of six paragraphs. Compare the actual COBOL statements with those written in the pseudocode. Obviously, you must learn statement formats and rules of syntax before you can be expected to code COBOL statements on your own. You will learn the formats and rules in later chapters.

A tool used by programmers to facilitate the coding of COBOL programs is the COBOL coding form. Its use is illustrated in the sample program shown in Figure 1.10.

The next step calls for inputting your program.

Step 4. Keying or Entering the COBOL Program

With the coded program in hand, the programmer is ready to approach a terminal. The task is to create a file that ultimately contains the COBOL source program. In general, the programmer does the following:

- **a.** Logs on to the system
- **b.** Creates a new file name
- **c.** Calls an editor to facilitate entering the lines of coding into the file
- **d.** Enters all the lines of coding
- **e.** Exits from the editor
- **f.** Lists the newly created file
- **g.** Saves the file

The system commands and available editors required to create the file are specific to a computer installation. Your instructor will provide you with the necessary information. Nonetheless, Figure 1.11a is included as an illustration. In this case, the computer system is a DEC VAX, and the editor is the EDT editor.

In this illustration, the name given to the source file is C1SAMR.COB. The source program being entered into the file is the one coded in Figure 1.10. Figure 1.11b shows the contents of the file following the editing session.

Next, the programmer examines the listing of the program, looking for obvious errors. If some are found, the editor is called again, the corrections made, the editor is then released, and the corrected version of the file is listed and stored.

Now that the file (C1SAMR.COB) containing the COBOL source program is available on the system, the programmer calls the compiler to provide further assistance, as described in the next step.

Step 5. Debugging the Program

Recall that one function of the compiler is to be a tireless diagnostician. Figure 1.12a illustrates a call for the COBOL compiler (on a VAX) to check the program in file C1SAMR.COB for syntax errors.

Note: Ask your instructor for the corresponding system commands on your computer.

(On the VAX, the qualifier /ANSI specifies the ANSI version of the compiler; /LIS (or /LIST) specifies that the listing of the program produced by the compiler be stored in the file C1SAMR.LIS; the qualifier /NOOBJECT directs the compiler to check the program for syntax errors and generate diagnostics only—it does not generate the object program. Later, when the program is free of syntax errors, the /NOOBJECT qualifier will be removed. Ask your instructor if the compiler call system command for your computer allows this option. If it does, use it until all syntax errors have been corrected. It's a more efficient use of your computer facilities.) Figure 1.12b shows a copy of the file C1SAMR.LIS.

■ **Figure 1.10** Sample program on COBOL coding forms

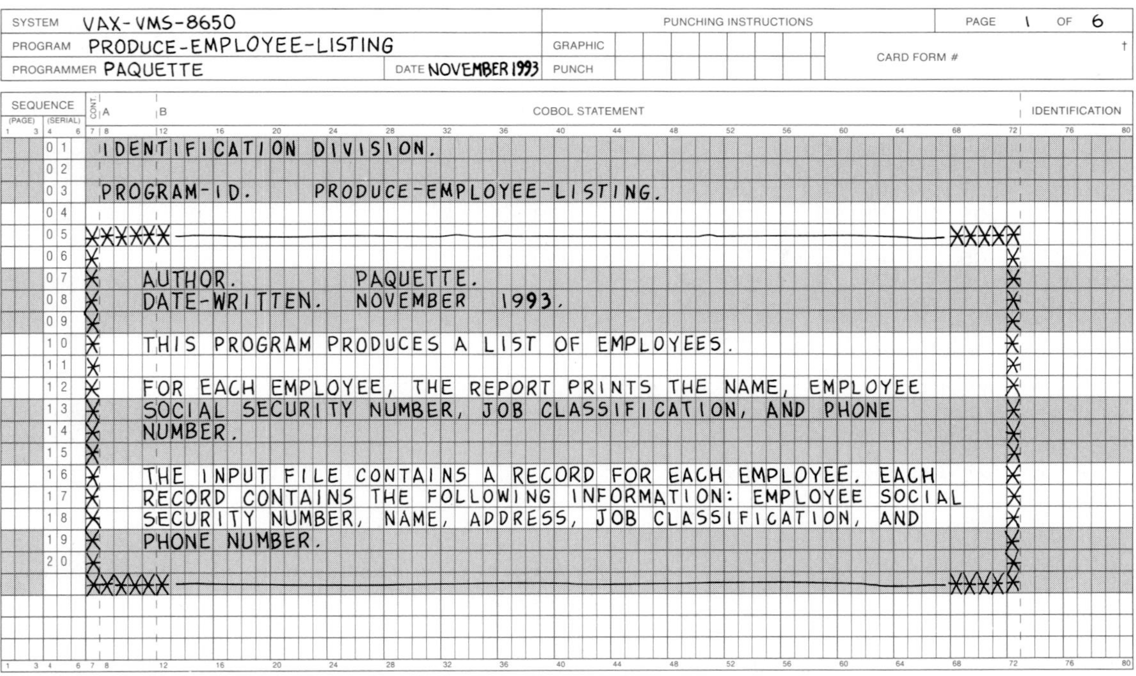

SYSTEM VAX-VMS-8650 | PUNCHING INSTRUCTIONS | PAGE 1 OF 6
PROGRAM PRODUCE-EMPLOYEE-LISTING | GRAPHIC | CARD FORM #
PROGRAMMER PAQUETTE | DATE NOVEMBER 1993 | PUNCH

```
01        IDENTIFICATION DIVISION.
02
03        PROGRAM-ID.      PRODUCE-EMPLOYEE-LISTING.
04
05       *****----------------------------------------------------------*****
06       *                                                                 *
07       *    AUTHOR.          PAQUETTE.                                   *
08       *    DATE-WRITTEN.    NOVEMBER  1993.                             *
09       *                                                                 *
10       *    THIS PROGRAM PRODUCES A LIST OF EMPLOYEES.                   *
11       *                                                                 *
12       *    FOR EACH EMPLOYEE, THE REPORT PRINTS THE NAME, EMPLOYEE      *
13       *    SOCIAL SECURITY NUMBER, JOB CLASSIFICATION, AND PHONE        *
14       *    NUMBER.                                                      *
15       *                                                                 *
16       *    THE INPUT FILE CONTAINS A RECORD FOR EACH EMPLOYEE. EACH     *
17       *    RECORD CONTAINS THE FOLLOWING INFORMATION: EMPLOYEE SOCIAL   *
18       *    SECURITY NUMBER, NAME, ADDRESS, JOB CLASSIFICATION, AND      *
19       *    PHONE NUMBER.                                                *
20       *                                                                 *
         *****----------------------------------------------------------*****
```

SYSTEM | PUNCHING INSTRUCTIONS | PAGE 2 OF 6
PROGRAM PRODUCE-EMPLOYEE-LISTING | GRAPHIC | CARD FORM #
PROGRAMMER | DATE | PUNCH

```
01        ENVIRONMENT DIVISION.
02
03        CONFIGURATION SECTION.
04
05        SOURCE-COMPUTER.      VAX-VMS-8650.
06        OBJECT-COMPUTER.      VAX-VMS-8650.
07
08        INPUT-OUTPUT SECTION.
09
10        FILE-CONTROL.
11            SELECT EMPLOYEE-FILE      ASSIGN TO COB$INPUT.
12            SELECT EMPLOYEE-LIST      ASSIGN TO COB$OUTPUT.
13
14        DATA DIVISION.
15
16        FILE SECTION.
17
18        FD  EMPLOYEE-FILE
19            RECORD CONTAINS 80 CHARACTERS.
20
```

The programmer examines the diagnostics to determine how the syntax errors should be corrected. Then, the editor is called again to make the corrections, and the corrected version of the source program is stored. The steps in Figure 1.12 are repeated again (and again if necessary) until all syntax errors have been removed from the program.

At this point, the programmer compiles the program (on the VAX, the /NOOBJECT qualifier must be removed from the COBOL compiler call statement). The compiler is directed to generate the object program,

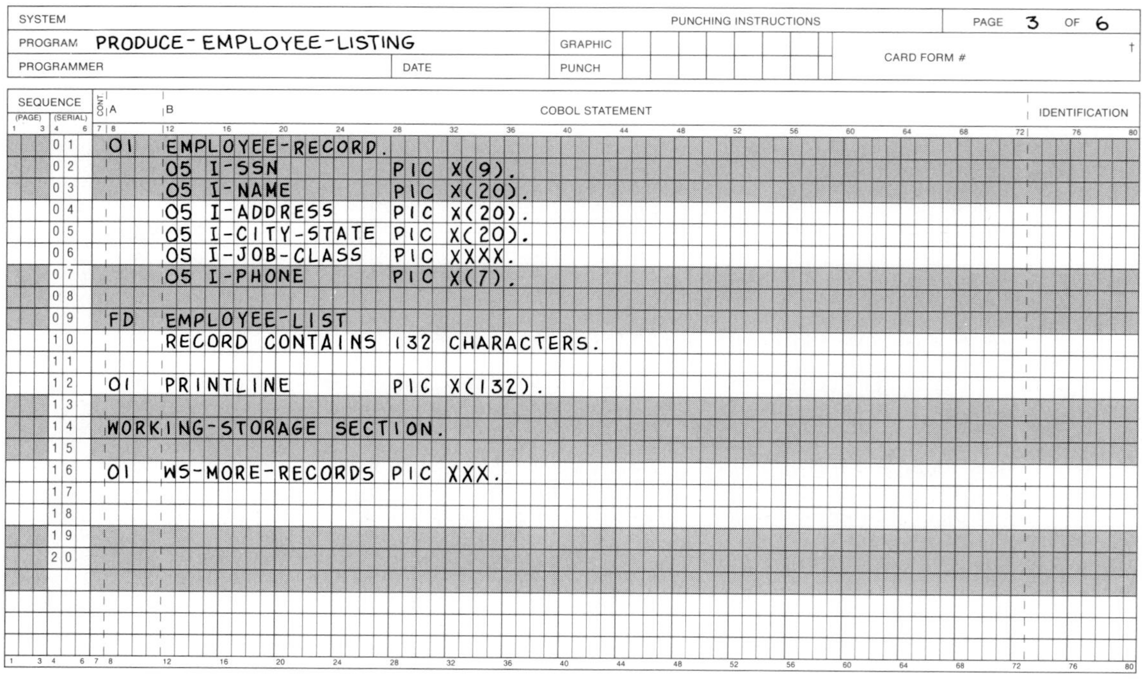

SYSTEM | PUNCHING INSTRUCTIONS | PAGE 3 OF 6
PROGRAM PRODUCE-EMPLOYEE-LISTING | GRAPHIC | CARD FORM #
PROGRAMMER | DATE | PUNCH

```
       01  EMPLOYEE-RECORD.
           05  I-SSN           PIC X(9).
           05  I-NAME          PIC X(20).
           05  I-ADDRESS       PIC X(20).
           05  I-CITY-STATE    PIC X(20).
           05  I-JOB-CLASS     PIC XXXX.
           05  I-PHONE         PIC X(7).

       FD  EMPLOYEE-LIST
           RECORD CONTAINS 132 CHARACTERS.

       01  PRINTLINE           PIC X(132).

       WORKING-STORAGE SECTION.

       01  WS-MORE-RECORDS PIC XXX.
```

SYSTEM | PUNCHING INSTRUCTIONS | PAGE 4 OF 6
PROGRAM PRODUCE-EMPLOYEE-LISTING | GRAPHIC | CARD FORM #
PROGRAMMER | DATE | PUNCH

```
       01  EMPLOYEE-LINE.
           05  FILLER          PIC X(25).
           05  O-NAME          PIC X(20).
           05  FILLER          PIC X(12).
           05  O-SSN           PIC X(9).
           05  FILLER          PIC X(14).
           05  O-JOB-CLASS     PIC XXXX.
           05  FILLER          PIC X(16).
           05  O-PHONE         PIC X(7).
           05  FILLER          PIC X(25).

       PROCEDURE DIVISION.

        100-PRODUCE-EMPLOYEE-LIST.
           PERFORM 200-START-UP.
           PERFORM 210-PROCESS-EMPLOYEE-RECORD
                  UNTIL WS-MORE-RECORDS = "NO ".
           PERFORM 220-FINISH-UP.
           STOP RUN.
```

the program consisting of the corresponding machine-language instructions. The object program is saved in a file (C1SAMR.OBJ on the VAX), and a compiler listing of the source program is also produced.

Now, we have reached the critical point of testing the program. If the operating system uses a loader, the programmer proceeds to step 6 for a sample run. If the operating system uses a linker, the object program must now be used as input to the linker. The purpose of the linker, as noted earlier, is to resolve the logical name references that may exist in the program, to attach other modules of machine code from system libraries if called by the program, and so on. The net result is the final executable version of the

■ **Figure 1.10** continued

SYSTEM | PUNCHING INSTRUCTIONS | PAGE 5 OF 6

PROGRAM PRODUCE-EMPLOYEE-LISTING | GRAPHIC | CARD FORM #

PROGRAMMER | DATE | PUNCH

```
200-START-UP.
    OPEN INPUT EMPLOYEE-FILE.
    OPEN OUTPUT EMPLOYEE-LIST.
    MOVE "YES" TO WS-MORE-RECORDS.
    PERFORM 300-READ-EMPLOYEE-RECORD.

210-PROCESS-EMPLOYEE-RECORD.
    PERFORM 310-PREPARE-EMPLOYEE-LINE.
    PERFORM 300-READ-EMPLOYEE-RECORD.

220-FINISH-UP.
    CLOSE EMPLOYEE-FILE.
    CLOSE EMPLOYEE-LIST.

300-READ-EMPLOYEE-RECORD.
    READ EMPLOYEE-FILE RECORD
        AT END
            MOVE "NO " TO WS-MORE-RECORDS.
```

SYSTEM | PUNCHING INSTRUCTIONS | PAGE 6 OF 6

PROGRAM PRODUCE-EMPLOYEE-LISTING | GRAPHIC | CARD FORM #

PROGRAMMER | DATE | PUNCH

```
310-PREPARE-EMPLOYEE-LINE.
    MOVE SPACES TO EMPLOYEE-LINE.
    MOVE I-NAME TO O-NAME.
    MOVE I-SSN TO O-SSN.
    MOVE I-JOB-CLASS TO O-JOB-CLASS.
    MOVE I-PHONE TO O-PHONE.
    MOVE EMPLOYEE-LINE TO PRINTLINE.
    WRITE PRINTLINE
        AFTER ADVANCING 2 LINES.
```

program. (On the VAX, the linker call is simple: LINK C1SAMR.OBJ; the output from the linker is the executable file C1SAMR.EXE.)

Step 6. Running a Test of the COBOL Program

A successful compilation of the program is not sufficient to assure that the program does what it was designed to do. The program must be put to the test. A sample data file, consisting of records selected to test every possible path within the program, is used as an input file, and the program is executed.

Figure 1.11a Using an editor to store the sample program in a file (partial)

```
EDIT C1SAMR.COB
*C
       IDENTIFICATION DIVISION.

       PROGRAM-ID.  PRODUCE-EMPLOYEE-LISTING.

      ***********************************************************
      *                                                         *
      *   AUTHOR.        PAQUETTE.                              *
      *   DATE WRITTEN.  NOVEMBER 1993.                         *
      *                                                         *
.
.
.
       PROCEDURE DIVISION.

       100-PRODUCE-EMPLOYEE-LIST.
           PERFORM 200-START-UP.
           .
           .
           .
       310-PREPARE-EMPLOYEE-LINE.
           MOVE SPACES TO EMPLOYEE-LINE.
           MOVE I-NAME TO O-NAME.
           MOVE I-SSN TO O-SSN.
           MOVE I-JOB-CLASS TO O-JOB-CLASS.
           MOVE I-PHONE TO O-PHONE.
           MOVE EMPLOYEE-LINE TO PRINTLINE.
           WRITE PRINTLINE
               AFTER ADVANCING 2 LINES.

[EOB]

*EXIT
```

Figure 1.11b Listing of the source program file

```
 IDENTIFICATION DIVISION.

 PROGRAM-ID.    PRODUCE-EMPLOYEE-LISTING.

*****************************************************************
*                                                               *
*   AUTHOR.        PAQUETTE.                                    *
*   DATE WRITTEN.  NOVEMBER 1993.                               *
*                                                               *
*   THIS PROGRAM PRODUCES A LIST OF EMPLOYEES.                  *
*                                                               *
*   FOR EACH EMPLOYEE, THE REPORT PRINTS THE NAME, EMPLOYEE     *
*   SOCIAL SECURITY NUMBER, JOB CLASSIFICATION, AND PHONE       *
*   NUMBER.                                                     *
*                                                               *
*   THE INPUT FILE CONTAINS A RECORD FOR EACH EMPLOYEE. EACH    *
*   RECORD CONTAINS THE FOLLOWING INFORMATION: EMPLOYEE SOCIAL  *
*   SECURITY NUMBER, NAME, ADDRESS, JOB CLASSIFICATION, AND     *
*   PHONE NUMBER.                                               *
*                                                               *
*****************************************************************

 ENVIRONMENT DIVISION.

 CONFIGURATION SECTION.

 SOURCE-COMPUTER.  VAX-VMS-8650.
 OBJECT-COMPUTER.  VAX-VMS-8650.

 INPUT-OUTPUT SECTION.

 FILE-CONTROL.
     SELECT EMPLOYEE-FILE    ASSIGN TO COB$INPUT.
     SELECT EMPLOYEE-LIST    ASSIGN TO COB$OUTPUT.

 DATA DIVISION.

 FILE SECTION.

 FD  EMPLOYEE-FILE
     RECORD CONTAINS 80 CHARACTERS.
```

■ **Figure 1.11b** continued

```
01   EMPLOYEE-RECORD.
     05 I-SSN         PIC X(9).
     05 I-NAME        PIC X(20).
     05 I-ADDRESS     PIC X(20).
     05 I-CITY-STATE  PIC X(20).
     05 I-JOB-CLASS   PIC XXXX.
     05 I-PHONE       PIC X(7).

FD   EMPLOYEE-LIST
     RECORD CONTAINS 132 CHARACTERS.

01   PRINTLINE        PIC X(132).

WORKING-STORAGE SECTION.

01   WS-MORE-RECORDS PIC XXX.

01   EMPLOYEE-LINE.
     05 FILLER        PIC X(25).
     05 O-NAME        PIC X(20).
     05 FILLER        PIC X(12).
     05 O-SSN         PIC X(9).
     05 FILLER        PIC X(14).
     05 O-JOB-CLASS   PIC XXXX.
     05 FILLER        PIC X(16).
     05 O-PHONE       PIC X(7).
     05 FILLER        PIC X(25).

PROCEDURE DIVISION.

100-PRODUCE-EMPLOYEE-LIST.
     PERFORM 200-START-UP.
     PERFORM 210-PROCESS-EMPLOYEE-RECORD
         UNTIL WS-MORE-RECORDS = "NO ".
     PERFORM 220-FINISH-UP.
     STOP RUN.

200-START-UP.
     OPEN INPUT EMPLOYEE-FILE.
     OPEN OUTPUT EMPLOYEE-LIST.
     MOVE "YES" TO WS-MORE-RECORDS.
     PERFORM 300-READ-EMPLOYEE-RECORD.

210-PROCESS-EMPLOYEE-RECORD.
     PERFORM 310-PREPARE-EMPLOYEE-LINE.
     PERFORM 300-READ-EMPLOYEE-RECORD.

220-FINISH-UP.
     CLOSE EMPLOYEE-FILE.
     CLOSE EMPLOYEE-LIST.

300-READ-EMPLOYEE-RECORD.
     READ EMPLOYEE-FILE RECORD
         AT END
             MOVE "NO " TO WS-MORE-RECORDS.

310-PREPARE-EMPLOYEE-LINE.
     MOVE SPACES TO EMPLOYEE-LINE.
     MOVE I-NAME TO O-NAME.
     MOVE I-SSN TO O-SSN.
     MOVE I-JOB-CLASS TO O-JOB-CLASS.
     MOVE I-PHONE TO O-PHONE.
     MOVE EMPLOYEE-LINE TO PRINTLINE.
     WRITE PRINTLINE
         AFTER ADVANCING 2 LINES.
```

■ **Figure 1.12a** Sample COBOL compiler call to check for syntax errors

```
COBOL/ANSI/NOOBJECT/LIST C1SAMR.COB
```

Figure 1.12b Listing generated by the compiler

```
PRODUCE-EMPLOYEE-LISTING        26-Nov-1993 09:47:21     VAX COBOL V3.2-42                    Page   1
Source Listing                  26-Nov-1993 09:47:05     SCIENCE$DISK:[MA6031.CHAPTER1]C1SAMR.COB;2

           IDENTIFICATION DIVISION.

           PROGRAM-ID.    PRODUCE-EMPLOYEE-LISTING.

          *****************************************************************
          *                                                               *
          *   AUTHOR.        PAQUETTE.                                    *
          *   DATE WRITTEN.  NOVEMBER 1993.                               *
          *                                                               *
          *   THIS PROGRAM PRODUCES A LIST OF EMPLOYEES.                  *
          *                                                               *
          *   FOR EACH EMPLOYEE, THE REPORT PRINTS THE NAME, EMPLOYEE     *
          *   SOCIAL SECURITY NUMBER, JOB CLASSIFICATION, AND PHONE       *
          *   NUMBER.                                                     *
          *                                                               *
          *   THE INPUT FILE CONTAINS A RECORD FOR EACH EMPLOYEE. EACH    *
          *   RECORD CONTAINS THE FOLLOWING INFORMATION: EMPLOYEE SOCIAL  *
          *   SECURITY NUMBER, NAME, ADDRESS, JOB CLASSIFICATION, AND     *
          *   PHONE NUMBER.                                               *
          *                                                               *
          *****************************************************************

           ENVIRONMENT DIVISION.

           CONFIGURATION SECTION.

           SOURCE-COMPUTER.  VAX-VMS-8650.
           OBJECT-COMPUTER.  VAX-VMS-8650.

           INPUT-OUTPUT SECTION.

           FILE-CONTROL.
               SELECT EMPLOYEE-FILE    ASSIGN TO COB$INPUT.
               SELECT EMPLOYEE-LIST    ASSIGN TO COB$OUTPUT.

           DATA DIVISION.

           FILE SECTION.

           FD  EMPLOYEE-FILE
               RECORD CONTAINS 80 CHARACTERS.

           01  EMPLOYEE-RECORD.
               05 I-SSN          PIC X(9).
               05 I-NAME         PIC X(20).
               05 I-ADDRESS      PIC X(20).
               05 I-CITY-STATE   PIC X(20).
               05 I-JOB-CLASS    PIC XXXX.
               05 I-PHONE        PIC X(7).

           FD  EMPLOYEE-LIST
               RECORD CONTAINS 132 CHARACTERS.

           01  PRINTLINE         PIC X(132).

           WORKING-STORAGE SECTION.

           01  WS-MORE-RECORDS PIC XXX.

           01  EMPLOYEE-LINE.
               05 FILLER         PIC X(25).
               05 O-NAME         PIC X(20).
               05 FILLER         PIC X(12).
               05 O-SSN          PIC X(9).
               05 FILLER         PIC X(14).
               05 O-JOB-CLASS    PIC XXXX.
               05 FILLER         PIC X(16).
               05 O-PHONE        PIC X(7).
               05 FILLER         PIC X(25).

           PROCEDURE DIVISION.

           100-PRODUCE-EMPLOYEE-LIST.
               PERFORM 200-START-UP.
               PERFORM 210-PROCESS-EMPLOYEE-RECORD
                   UNTIL WS-MORE-RECORDS = "NO ".
               PERFORM 220-FINISH-UP.
               STOP RUN.

```

Figure 1.12b continued

```
PRODUCE-EMPLOYEE-LISTING      26-Nov-1993 09:47:21      VAX COBOL V3.2-42                        Page   2
Source Listing                26-Nov-1993 09:47:05      SCIENCE$DISK:[MA6031.CHAPTER1]C1SAMR.COB;2

           200-START-UP.
               OPEN INPUT EMPLOYEE-FILE.
               OPEN OUTPUT EMPLOYEE-LIST.
               MOVE "YES" TO WS-MORE-RECORDS.
               PERFORM 300-READ-EMPLOYEE-RECORD.

           210-PROCESS-EMPLOYEE-RECORD.
               PERFORM 310-PREPARE-EMPLOYEE-LINE.
               PERFORM 300-READ-EMPLOYEE-RECORD.

           220-FINISH-UP.
               CLOSE EMPLOYEE-FILE.
               CLOSE EMPLOYEE-LIST.

           300-READ-EMPLOYEE-RECORD.
               READ EMPLOYEE-FILE RECORD
                   AT END
                       MOVE "NO " TO WS-MORE-RECORDS.

           310-PREPARE-EMPLOYEE-LINE.
               MOVE SPACES TO EMPLOYEE-LINE.
               MOVE I-NAME TO O-NAME.
               MOVE I-SSN TO O-SSN.
               MOVE I-JOB-CLASS TO O-JOB-CLASS.
               MOVE I-PHONE TO O-PHONE.
               MOVE EMPLOYEE-LINE TO PRINTLINE.
               WRITE PRINTLINE
                   AFTER ADVANCING 2 LINES.
```

In the example, there are only two possible paths: the one that processes the actual employee records and the path followed upon encountering the end-of-file marker.

If the sample file is not already available on the system, the programmer must create it. Let's assume that it must be created.

We must log on to the computer, create a new file name (we will call it C1SAMR.DAT), call an editor, enter the data in each record in the appropriate data fields as specified on the input record layout form, exit from the editor, and, finally, save the file.

The data file should then be listed and checked carefully to verify that all data has been entered in the correct positions on each record. Data entry errors are likely to produce garbage on the final computer output.

At this point in our example, all the employee data records are in data file C1SAMR.DAT, the COBOL source program is in file C1SAMR.COB, the object program is in file C1SAMR.OBJ, and the executable image is in file C1SAMR.EXE. We are ready for the test run. Figure 1.13a shows the RUN command for the VAX. Ask your instructor for the corresponding RUN command for your computer.

When the RUN command is executed, the data records of the input file shown in Figure 1.3 are processed, and the printed report shown in Figure 1.13b is produced as the output file.

By examining the output produced by the test run, the programmer can determine if the program has met all of its objectives. If it has not, then further debugging steps are required. Depending on the kinds of errors that are found in the program output, it may be necessary for the programmer to redo much of the work, even all the way back to step 1 of the design phase. It behooves the programmer to verify his or her work at **each** step of the problem-solving procedure. As noted above, errors detected early pay dividends later. Also realize that the compiler helps the programmer to detect *syntax errors,* but it does not help at all in detecting logic errors, errors in formulas, errors of omission (of needed instructions), and so on. This responsibility rests squarely on the shoulders of the programmer.

The test run of our sample program was successful, and consequently our job of illustrating the problem-solving procedure is complete.

Step 7. Assembling the Complete Package

If the program output indicates that all objectives have been met, then the programmer's job is done. All the following tools used in the job are assembled:

1. Input record layout forms
2. Output record layout forms

■ **Figure 1.13a** A sample run command

```
RUN C1SAMR.EXE
```

■ **Figure 1.13b** Output file produced by the program

```
JOHN E. TURNER            714320025     M-10     6832004
JANET H. COLLINS          344024030     E-02     6841522
EDWARD P. RILEY           533254735     S-05     6833241
BARBARA F. WOLSEY         465114040     M-05     6835432
MICHELLE H. BOISE         547316545     E-08     6851144
GEORGE F. FAIRHURST       476561250     M-03     6853153
SHAWN M. AINSWORTH        386471455     S-10     6846890
CATHRYN E. CODY           837684260     S-03     6837044
ALEX B. GOULART           582784665     S-02     6841139
GLORIA J. NOWACK          664375170     E-10     6857991
```

3. System flowchart
4. Structure chart
5. Program pseudocode or flowchart
6. Program listing (produced by the compiler)
7. Sample data file (used in the test run)
8. Program output (obtained in the test run)

The final package is submitted to the person requesting the program.

Debugging

Debugging programs is one task that beginning COBOL programmers find particularly annoying and, at times, even frustrating. Debugging activities are included at the end of each chapter for two main reasons: first, to draw your attention to common types of errors that students tend to make; and, second, to give you some practice at detecting and correcting them. If you work your way carefully through these exercises, it should help you avoid similar errors in your programs, and it should be easier for you to debug your programs.

Data Input to a COBOL Program

The sample program of this chapter has been designed to process data stored on records of a file. Generally, records are accumulated in a file over a period of time, such as days or weeks, and the whole *batch* of records is processed by the program at some designated moment, such as once a week or once a month. For obvious reasons, this is referred to as batch processing. There is very little, if any, communication between the program and the user of the program during program execution.

On the other hand, some COBOL programs are designed to process data that is supplied interactively by the user during the program execution. These programs are referred to as interactive COBOL programs, and the data processing is classified as *on-line processing.* Interactive programs make extensive use of the screen (or visual display terminal, VDT) in sending information to the user and in receiving data input from the user.

This text will teach you how to design and code batch programs only. There are two main reasons for this. COBOL was developed initially as a file-processing language, and consequently there are currently many more file-oriented COBOL applications in the business world. The second reason is that *ANSI* (American National Standards Institute) has not yet incorporated standards for a screen management facility into the COBOL language. Though various computer manufacturers and software development companies have developed their own extensions to the COBOL language, generally following the guidelines published by *CODASYL* (Conference on Data Systems Languages), the nonexistence of "standards" makes it particularly difficult to develop instructional materials that are universally applicable. (Nonetheless, the

Figure 1.14 Storing records in a sequential file

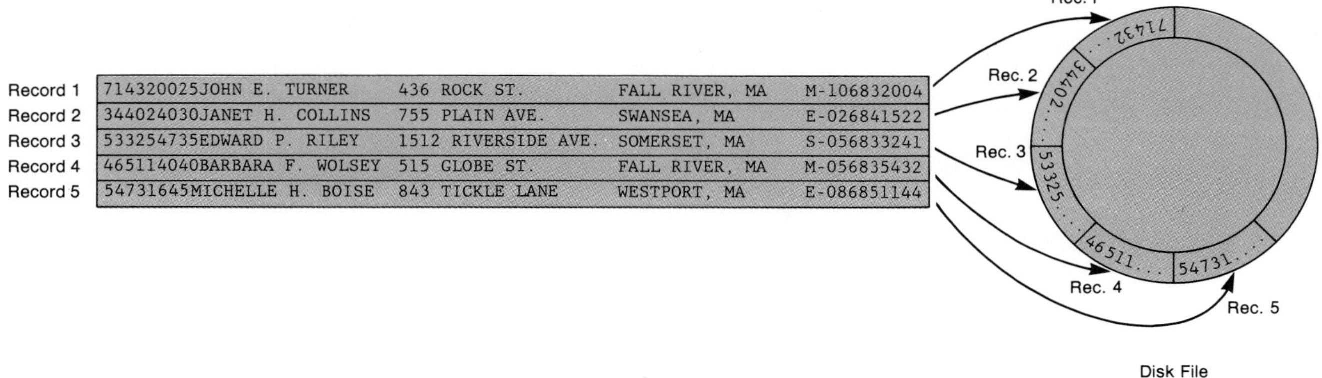

Figure 1.15 Reading a sequential file

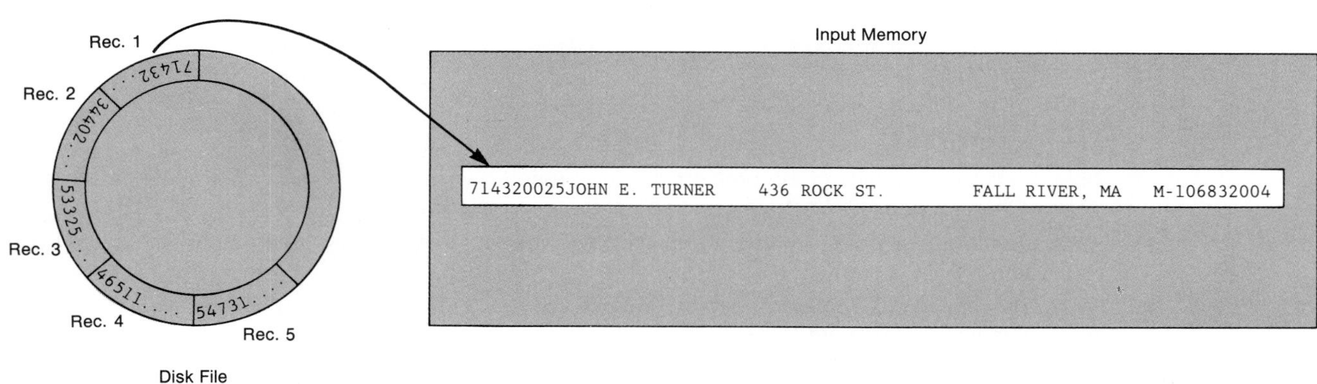

sequel to this text, *Volume II: Advanced Structured COBOL,* does address the topic "Interactive COBOL Programs," albeit with appropriate reminders of nonstandardized syntax.)

Files that are processed by batch COBOL programs are initially created with a specific organization. There are three standard file organizations: sequential, indexed, and relative. The last chapter of this text contains a detailed study of *sequential files* and an introduction to files with indexed and relative organizations. But it is important for you, the novice COBOL programmer, to understand that the programs of this text process only files with sequential organization. (The sequel to this text, *Advanced Structured COBOL,* examines indexed and relative files in detail.)

In a file with sequential organization, records are written onto the file in a certain sequence, one at a time, and they are stored in that same physical sequence. For instance, when an editor is used to create the data file for the sample program of the chapter, the resulting file is a sequential file. Figure 1.14 illustrates the first five records being stored on a disk.

When a program processes the records of a sequential file, the records are read from the file into the *input buffer,* one at a time, in the same sequence in which they were originally stored on the file. For instance, in the chapter program, when the input file is first read, record 1 (the first record written to the file) is copied into the input buffer. The program then goes on to process that record. When the record processing activities are complete and the input file is read again, record 2 is copied from the file into the input buffer, replacing record 1. (Only one record is kept in the input buffer at any one time.) Record 2 is then processed. The pattern repeats until the last record of the file has been read into the input buffer and subsequently processed. Figure 1.15 shows the employee file of the chapter program being read.

Students are often initially confused by the expression, "Read the file." Please note that when a file is read, **only one record is accessed** and copied into the input buffer, **not the whole file.** So, a file can be read as many times as the number of records it contains.

We state again that all the files, both input and output, referenced within the programs of this text have sequential organization. Files with other organizations will be studied later.

Important Terms in Chapter 1

ANSI
applications program
assembly language
batch
COBOL
CODASYL
compiler program
constants
CPU
debugging
diagnostic
executable image
executive program
hierarchy chart
input buffer
input unit
linker
loader
machine language
object program
on-line processing
output unit
problem-solving procedure
processor unit
program
programmer
sequential file
source program
structure chart
syntax error
translator
variables

Exercises

1. What does the acronym COBOL stand for?
2. What does ANSI mean? CODASYL?
3. What is the ultimate purpose of a computer system?
4. Briefly explain the functions of the compiler program.
5. What is an object program?
6. Is a COBOL program classified as a source program or an object program?
7. What are the three types of programs required to process a COBOL program?
8. What are the two phases of the problem-solving procedure presented in this chapter? What are the steps of the first phase? What are the steps of the second phase?
9. What are the critical points in the problem-solving procedure where debugging activities should be carried out?
10. Refer to the sample COBOL program in Figure 1.11b.
    a. How many divisions are there?
    b. What is the name of each division?
    c. What is the purpose of each division?

Debugging Activities

1. Examine the EMPLOYEE-RECORD layout shown in Figure 1.4. Suppose you are assigned the task of preparing five of these records. A listing of the records you have prepared is shown in Figure 1.16. Can you identify the errors in each record? (The top line has been inserted to help you position characters within the record.)
2. Suppose a COBOL program is stored in a file named PROG1.COB, and the data file to be processed by the program is stored in a file named PROG1.DAT. A student, told to compile the program, enters the following two statements. What's wrong?

```
COBOL PROG1.COB
COBOL PROG1.DAT
```

Figure 1.16

```
   1234567890123456789012345678901234567890123456789012345678901234567890
a. 311251670ROMANO, ROBIN  405 SNELL ST.  FALL RIVER, MA  E-056573214
b. 23214756CONDON, WILLIAM     271 HANCOCK ST.      SWANSEA, MA       S-056345611
c. 354123980RILEY, RUTH A.                          NEW BEDFORD, MA   M-097334578
d. 552374218HARDING, ELLEN     30 HUNTER ST.        SOMERSET, MA
e. COMSTOCK, BARRY             250 N. MAIN ST.      FALL RIVER, MA    M-066749578
```

Terminal Exercises

Given the employee data that follows, use the EMPLOYEE-RECORD layout of Figure 1.4 to create a record for each employee. Store the records in a file named C1EX1.DAT.

1. NAME: O'Brien, Michael
   ADDRESS: 166 Snell St.
   Swansea, MA
   PHONE #: 683-4132
   SSN: 447-13-2533
   JOB CLASS: M-04
2. NAME: Desautels, Carol
   ADDRESS: 204 High St.
   Fall River, MA
   PHONE #: 682-6765
   SSN: 385-75-4721
   JOB CLASS: S-08
3. NAME: Von Trapp, Arthur
   ADDRESS: 321 Millbury St.
   Somerset, MA
   PHONE #: 671-7746
   SSN: 414-56-2947
   JOB CLASS: P-05
4. NAME: Penn, Janice
   ADDRESS: 34 Oak Ave.
   Swansea, MA
   PHONE #: 686-6231
   SSN: 497-38-8413
   JOB CLASS: M-06
5. NAME: Boyer, George
   ADDRESS: 74 Palmer St.
   Fall River, MA
   PHONE #: 682-1152
   SSN: 331-53-2413
   JOB CLASS: S-10
6. NAME: Ridge, Paula
   ADDRESS: 381 Osborne St.
   New Bedford, MA
   PHONE #: 695-3325
   SSN: 302-33-6451
   JOB CLASS: M-05
7. NAME: Meehan, Sherry
   ADDRESS: 140 Essex St.
   Somerset, MA
   PHONE #: 684-7956
   SSN: 524-31-8978
   JOB CLASS: S-03
8. NAME: Foley, Patrick
   ADDRESS: 300 Ridge St.
   Fall River, MA
   PHONE #: 671-9215
   SSN: 332-21-3451
   JOB CLASS: P-08
9. NAME: Freeman, Joseph
   ADDRESS: 50 Laurel Dr.
   Swansea, MA
   PHONE #: 685-5334
   SSN: 514-25-5341
   JOB CLASS: M-05
10. NAME: Bigelow, Laura
    ADDRESS: 294 Hope St.
    Somerset, MA
    PHONE #: 684-9924
    SSN: 565-41-8156
    JOB CLASS: S-09

2 ■ A First Look at a COBOL Program

In this chapter, a problem is presented for computer solution. You are taken "by the hand," for a second time, through the steps of the problem-solving procedure introduced in Chapter 1. A main purpose is to illustrate the essential role of problem analysis in computer programming: determining the data flow, identifying the major functional components of the task, and detailing the processing steps needed to achieve each functional component. Another purpose is to illustrate how the analytical tools are related to the actual coding of the program.

A major objective of this text is the development of structured programs. The basic logic structures that are generally accepted as standard in structured programming are briefly introduced, illustrated, and explained.

In coding the sample chapter program, introductory information will be given on each of the four divisions of a COBOL program. ■

■ Objectives You Should Achieve

After studying this chapter, you should:

1. Know the phases of the problem-solving procedure.
2. Be able to identify the analytical tools used in the design phase of the problem-solving procedure.
3. Be able to apply the analytical tools used in the design phase of the problem-solving procedure, including the following:
   - **a.** Design a system flowchart
   - **b.** Prepare input and output record layout forms
   - **c.** Design a structure chart
   - **d.** Write the program pseudocode, or design the program flowchart
4. Know the steps of the design implementation phase.
5. Be able to enter a COBOL program into a file.
6. Be able to use a compiler to help identify syntax errors in a program.
7. Be able to create a data file.
8. Be able to "run" a COBOL program.
9. Know the basic logic structures used by programmers in structured programs.

■ The Problem

The Allied Stock Company is a business concern that sells its products using a variety of means: There are salespersons visiting customers out in the field, other customers come in and buy products over the counter, and other customers phone in their orders. For purposes of this example, the management wants the data processing department to prepare a sales report for all the telephone sales that were made to its regular customers during the business day.

As each phone sale occurred during the day, a salesperson entered a record of the sale at a terminal into a disk file reserved for phone sales, as illustrated in Figure 2.1. The records are stored in the file in the same sequence as the sales occurred during the day. (The file is classified as a *sequential* file.)

Each sale record contains the following data:

the customer number
the catalog number of the item sold
the unit cost of the item sold
the number of units purchased by the customer during the phone transaction

At the end of the day, the disk file contains records of all the phone sales. (The complete list of phone sale records for the sample program is shown in Figure 2.16b [DD/CD:VIC2SP.DAT].) The data processing department must execute a program that will access each of these records, compute the amount of the sale for each of the phone sales, and write the corresponding phone sale line on the sales report. For each phone sale, the sales report must show the following:

the customer number
the catalog number of the item sold
the unit cost of the item sold
the number of units sold to the customer
the net amount of the sale made to the customer

All of these items must be printed under descriptive column headers. When the sale amount is being computed, a 20 percent discount is applied to the gross sale amount if the customer purchased more than 100 units of a catalog item.

The task in this problem is to write a program that will process all the phone sales and produce the phone sales report, as illustrated in Figure 2.2. (You need not worry about the task, since it will be developed completely for you. The main objective here is to illustrate the application of the problem-solving procedure in a programming assignment.) (An argument could easily be made to have the report show the gross amount of the sale and the discount amount, in addition to the net amount of the sale. This would require additional COBOL language requirements that the author prefers not to introduce at this time. In the interest of greater simplicity in the sample program, only the net amount of the sale will be computed and printed on the report.)

■ **Figure 2.1** Phone sale terminal entry

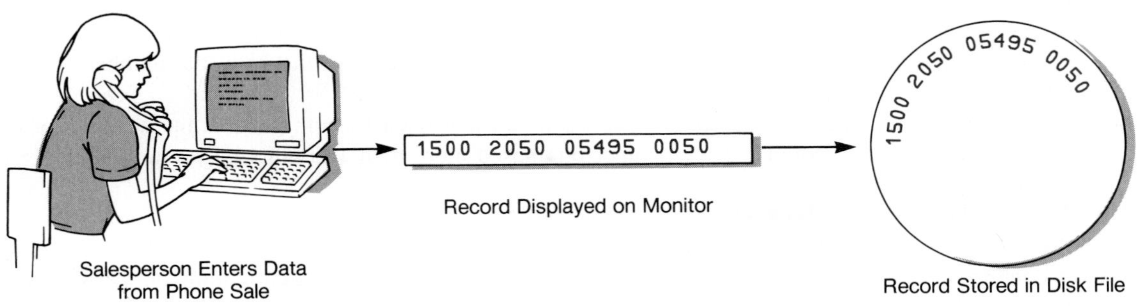

Figure 2.2 The main task of the sample program

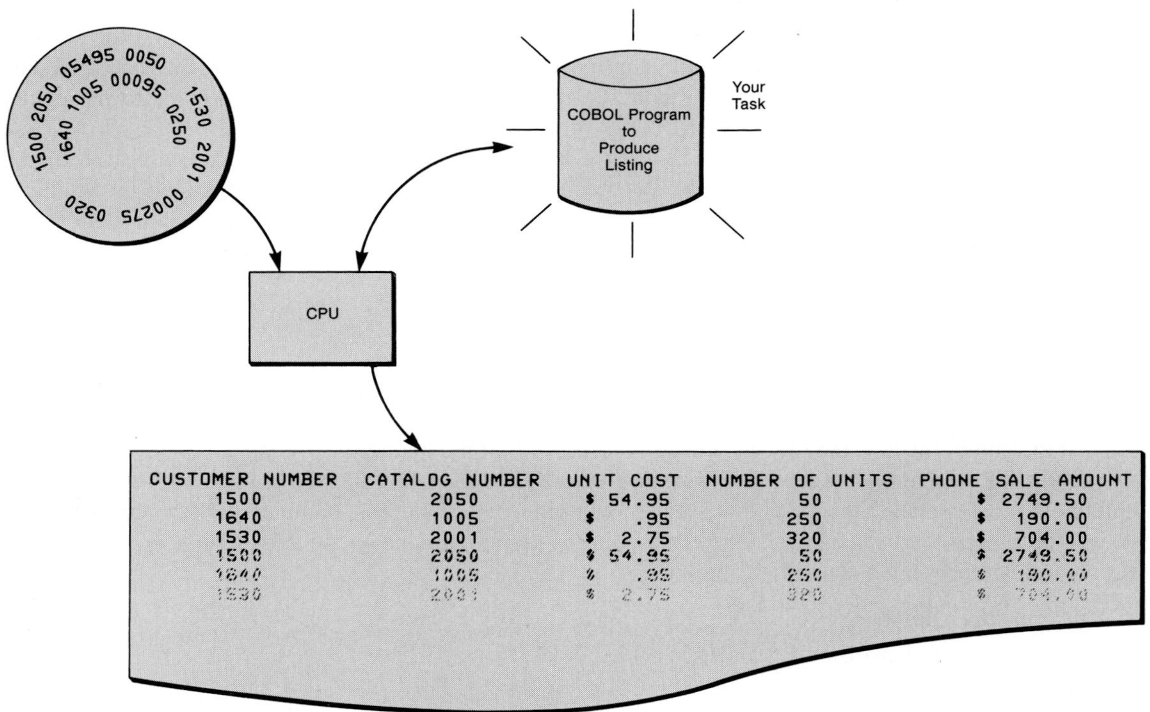

Program Design Phase

Step 1. Developing a Detailed Understanding of the Problem

The first task is to read the problem carefully and reread it as often as necessary to develop a clear understanding of the nature of the problem. Identify in detail the data that is to be provided as input to the program, the specifications of the report that the program must produce, and the relationship between the input and the output.

Some of the problem specifications are as follows:

1. For each phone sale, a record that exists in a file is supplied as input to the program. The data on the record consists of the customer number, the catalog number of the item that was sold, the unit cost of the item, and the number of units of that item sold to the customer.
2. The phone sales report to be produced by the program must have descriptive column headings to identify the data that will be printed under them.
3. For each phone sale record, the report must print a phone sale line that shows the customer number, the catalog number of the item that was sold, the unit cost of the item, the number of units sold to the customer, and the net amount of the sale.
4. As a phone sale record is being processed, the amount that must be computed as the net sale must include a 20 percent discount if the customer purchased more than 100 units of the item.

Step 1a. Prepare Layouts of Input Records

It is necessary to determine the exact layout of the data on each input record, specifically, which character positions contain the customer number, which character positions contain the catalog number, the unit cost of the item, and the number of units sold. A record layout form is used for this purpose.

It is determined that the customer number is stored in character positions 1–4, the catalog number in character positions 7–10, the unit cost in character positions 13–17, and the number of units sold in character positions 20–23. Vertical lines are drawn on the form to visually separate the record into the resulting fields, as shown in Figure 2.3.

■ **Figure 2.3** Layout of input record PHONE-SALE-RECORD

Record Layout Form

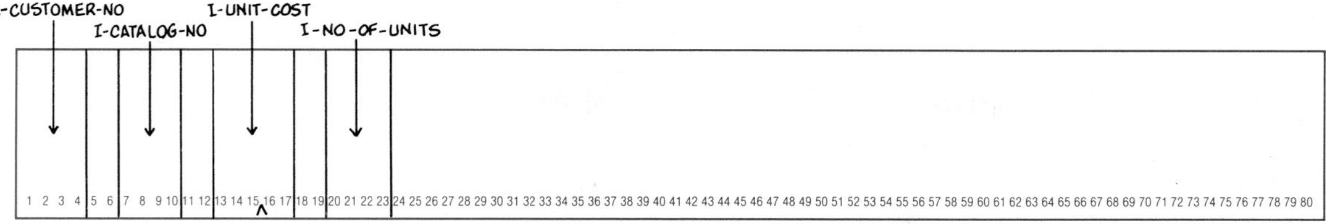

Record Name: PHONE-SALE-RECORD

Since the fields containing data have to be referenced within the program, they are assigned descriptive names: I-CUSTOMER-NO, I-CATALOG-NO, I-UNIT-COST, and I-NO-OF-UNITS. The prefix I- is a very convenient way of documenting the fact that these data names identify fields of an *input record.* Also note that a caret (^) is placed between character positions 15 and 16 in the data field I-UNIT-COST to indicate the location of an assumed decimal point. (If the value $25.95 is to be entered as the unit cost of the item, it is entered as the value 02595, and the caret is used to indicate where the decimal point belongs. More about this later.) The remaining groups of character positions are not assigned data names, since they are not referenced within the program.

Finally, the record itself is assigned a name: PHONE-SALE-RECORD. It is not necessary that the word RECORD be part of the name used to identify a record. For instance, the record could have been named PHONE-TRANSACTION. An important consideration in selecting names is the extent to which they will add clarity to the program. The more descriptive a name is, the more selfdocumentation it adds to the program.

Step 1b. Prepare Layouts of Output Records

The programmer next focuses on the requirements of the printed report. Each printed line is produced as an output from the program and thus is an output record. The programmer determines that two different kinds of lines are needed in this report: The first line prints the descriptive column headings, and the second line prints the phone sale line that corresponds to a phone sale that took place during the day. It should be obvious that all the phone sale lines will be printed using the same format. The programmer must now prepare the layout for each of these two types of output records.

An attempt is made to center the printed material across the width of the printer paper. The programmer decides that the column headers should be the following: CUSTOMER NUMBER, CATALOG NUMBER, UNIT COST, NUMBER OF UNITS, and PHONE SALE AMOUNT. Assuming that there are 132 print positions, and the column headers contain a total of 70 characters, that leaves 62 print positions to use as spacers. A decision is made to space the headers 8 print positions apart, thus leaving 30 unused print positions: 15 of them will be placed to the left of the first header and 15 to the right of the last header. The resulting layout is shown on line 2 in Figure 2.4, and it is given the name HEADINGS.

The second output record layout will be prepared so as to center the data fields under the headers. For instance, the customer number is a 4-character value. A 4-character field is centered under the header CUSTOMER NUMBER. To center it, subtract 4 from the header size (15), split the remainder (11) into 2 equal (or nearly equal) parts, count 6 spaces, and mark the 4-character field, as shown:

```
CUSTOMER NUMBER
------XXXX-----
   6        5
```

A string of Xs is used to denote the actual location of the data field. The same technique applies to the data fields that will contain the catalog number and the number of units purchased. The two remaining fields, however, will print dollar-and-cents values. In planning these two fields, the programmer takes into account the decimal point and the dollar sign and indicates exactly where these special editing characters should be placed. The resulting layout is shown on line 4 in Figure 2.4. The same layout is repeated again on line 6 to show that the phone sale lines are to be double-spaced. The programmer completes the preparation of this

■ **Figure 2.4** Layouts of output records HEADINGS and PHONE-SALE-LINE

Printer Spacing Chart

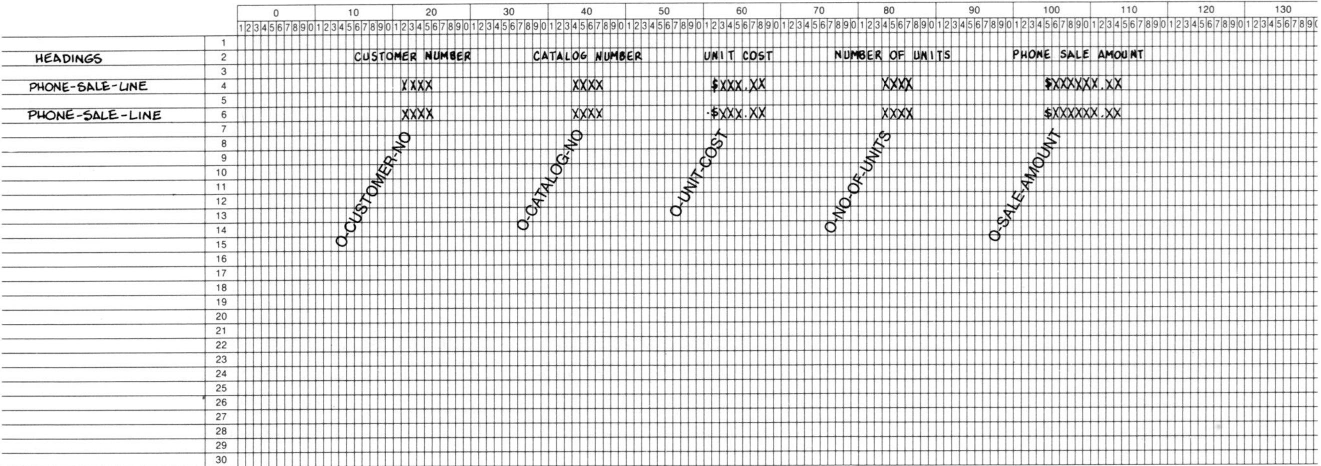

output record by giving a name to each data field and to the record itself. In this record, field names are given the prefix O- to help document the fact that they belong to an *output* record.

Note that the data fields of input records and output records that contain the same entities are given the same names, except of course for the prefixes I- and O-. This also helps to add clarity to the program.

Step 2. Planning the Solution to the Problem

Now that we have clearly identified the input data and determined exactly what data must be printed on the report, as well as the way the printed values should be displayed, we must plan the solution. The complete solution consists of a number of distinct steps.

Step 2a. Determine the Data Flow (System Flowchart)

In this situation, all the phone sales that occurred during the day have been entered sequentially as records in a disk file. This disk file, then, is the data file; that is, it contains all the data records that must be supplied as input to the program. In turn, the program must access the records of the data file sequentially, **one** at a time, in the same sequence as they are stored in the file. For each record, it must manipulate the values stored on that record in order to prepare and print a corresponding phone sale line on the report. The resulting data flow is shown in Figure 2.5. As shown, the program requires one input file; it has been named

■ **Figure 2.5** System flowchart for the chapter program

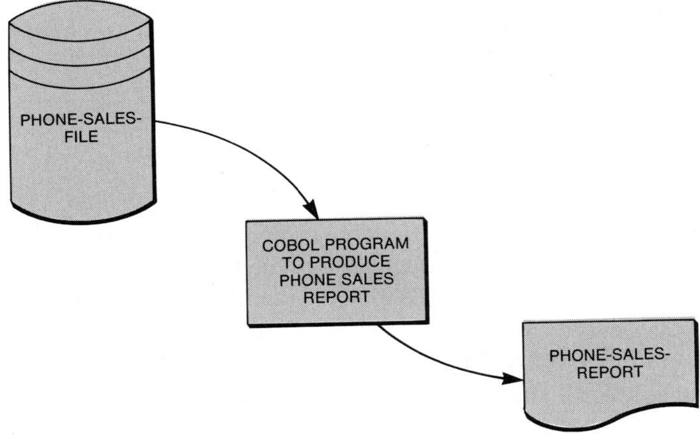

PHONE-SALES-FILE and it is stored on a disk, as denoted by the disk symbol. It needs one output file; it has been named PHONE-SALES-REPORT and the report will be a printed document. The essential function of the program is to produce the phone sales report.

Step 2b. Develop the Structure Chart

In developing the structure chart, the programmer's concern is to specify the functional tasks that must be performed by the program. This analysis is greatly facilitated by asking the question, "What must be accomplished?" that is, by concentrating on the **what** rather than the **how.**

The programmer generally begins by identifying "the whole job" as the primary or ultimate function that the program must accomplish. In this example, as noted on the system flowchart, the job is to "produce the phone sales report." The primary function is usually quite complex. In that case, the programmer separates the whole job into a number of separate "smaller jobs," or secondary jobs that, when all performed, complete the whole job. Again, if any of the secondary jobs can be reduced to groups of still smaller tasks, then these smaller tasks will be identified.

The result of decomposing a primary or "super" task into smaller "sub" tasks is a hierarchy of the functional components of the job. In other words, the whole job has been separated into modules, where each module is responsible for a specific task, function, or activity needed in the program. Thus, the program is being given a *modular structure*. (Conceptually, with a modular structure, a large programming assignment in the business world can be completed much more quickly because many programmers can be assigned to the project, each one responsible for a particular module or set of modules.) Many programmers initially begin this structure by separating the overall task into three subordinate modules: a start-up module, a processing module, and a finish-up module. This is the general procedure that we follow in this text.

The task of completing the development of the structure chart is not trivial. While the major function of the program may be fairly obvious, breaking it down into its **specific** subtasks generally requires a substantial amount of time and much concentrated analytical work. A productive starting point is the printer spacing chart prepared in step 1b of the problem-solving procedure. Typically, the programmer raises a series of questions like the following:

1. What's this report all about?
   (Answer: In the sample program, the report must list all the phone sales that occurred during the day.)
2. What must be printed first on the report?
   (Answer: In the sample program, the column headings must be printed at the top of the report. Since this requires writing a record to the output file, the file must have been opened earlier.)
3. What must be printed next on the report?
   (Answer: In the sample program, the phone sale line that corresponds to the first phone sale record in the data file.)
4. What must be done in order to be able to write this line on the report?
   (Answer: In the sample program, the first phone sale record must be read from the input file. To access an input file record, the programmer must have opened the file earlier. Once a record is read, it must be processed by the program. Specifically, this processing involves the computation of the sale amount. Then values must be assigned to the data fields of the phone sale line. Other than the sale amount, these values come from the input record. Finally, the phone sale line must be printed on the report.)
5. What must be done next?
   (Answer: In the sample program, writing the phone sale line on the report completes the processing of the current input record. Hence, the next step should be to read the next input record so that it can be processed.)
6. What must be done next?
   (Answer: In the sample program, all the records in the input file must be processed as described above. Then, when the job is complete, the files should be closed and the job terminated.)

Applying these notions of modularity to the chapter program, as briefly analyzed above, yields the structure (or hierarchy) chart shown in Figure 2.6. Each box corresponds to a module, and the entry in the box specifies the function to be accomplished within the module.

Note that the primary (or super) functional task is PRODUCE PHONE SALES REPORT. As noted earlier, this primary task is broken down into three subordinate tasks, yielding the module START UP, the

Figure 2.6 Structure (or hierarchy) chart for the chapter program

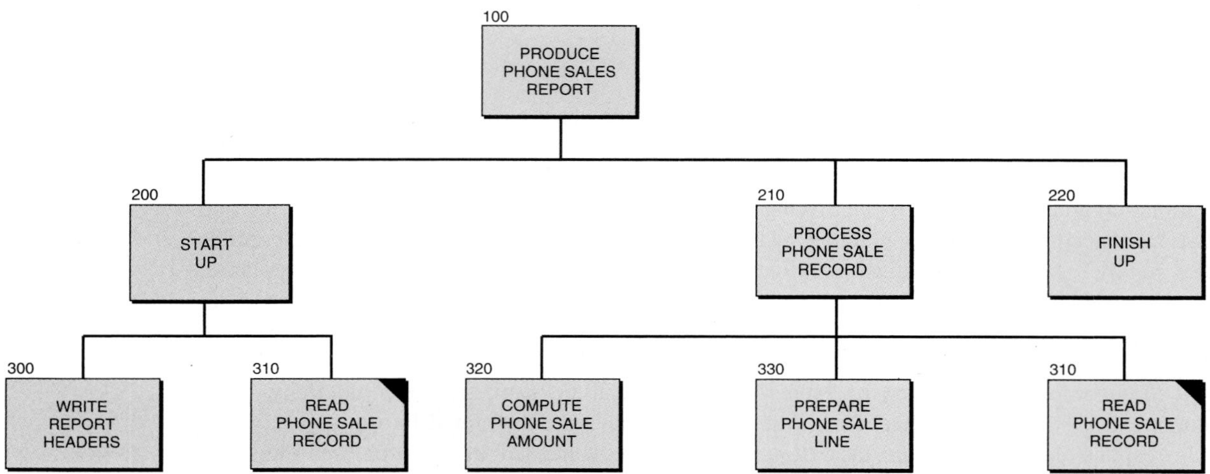

module PROCESS PHONE SALE RECORD, and the module FINISH UP. The brief analysis done earlier indicates that the report must begin with column headings. Hence, a subtask of module START UP is to print the headers on the report. And then, the next step is to start the processing of the records of the input file by accessing (reading) the first phone sale record. Thus, the two subtasks of module START UP have been identified as module WRITE REPORT HEADERS and module READ PHONE SALE RECORD.

The programmer then asks, "What does it mean to process the phone sale record?" It means that two essential subtasks must be accomplished: (1) compute the amount of the sale, and (2) prepare and print the phone sale line on the report. And then, when the current phone sale record has resulted in a phone sale line on the report, the next phone sale record must be accessed so that the job can continue until the processing reaches completion. Thus, the subtasks of module PROCESS PHONE SALE RECORD are the modules COMPUTE PHONE SALE AMOUNT, PREPARE PHONE SALE LINE, and READ PHONE SALE RECORD.

The FINISH UP module does not require any subtasks in this program. The complete structure chart is shown in Figure 2.6.

The numbers attached to the modules in the chart represent the relative positions of the specified functions within the hierarchy of functions. The most superior or super function is labeled 100. It is called the *primary module.* A function labeled in the 200s is immediately subordinate to the super function. Such a module is classified as a second-level module. A function labeled in the 300s is subordinate to a 200-level function and is a third-level module, and so on. It is possible for a function to be subordinate to more than one superior function, such as the function READ PHONE SALE RECORD in Figure 2.6. In that case, the number attached to the lowest-level occurrence of the function remains attached wherever the function is needed, and the upper right-hand corner is shaded to indicate its repetitive nature.

It will shortly become clear that the modular structure built into the structure chart carries through to the program itself. Specifically, each box or module in the chart corresponds to one paragraph of instructions in the PROCEDURE DIVISION of the COBOL program, and the paragraphs are coded in ascending order of the level numbers attached to the modules.

Step 2c. Write the Program Pseudocode

Developing the structure chart has identified **what** must be accomplished by the program. The purpose of the pseudocode is to specify the processing steps needed to accomplish the specified tasks. In other words, the pseudocode will show **how** to get the job done.

The programmer begins with the name of the primary module or the most superior function as a paragraph name. The paragraph will then consist of statements, each of which details a processing step related to the named function. Statements that must obviously be included are the ones directly responsible for performing the subordinate tasks. In fact, the key verb used in relation to each subordinate task is *perform.* The pseudocode begins with the following paragraph:

100-Produce-Phone-Sales-Report.

1. Perform 200-Start-Up.
2. Perform 210-Process-Phone-Sale-Record until no more records.
3. Perform 220-Finish-Up.
4. Stop the run.

Compare these entries with the connecting lines in the structure chart that exit from module 100. Do you see the correspondence? In other words, the second-level modules (those numbered in the 200s) are under direct control of the primary module. It should be clear that the second-level paragraphs in the pseudocode are under the control of the primary paragraph 100-Produce-Phone-Sales-Report. Consequently, the primary paragraph is the *main control paragraph.* That is, control begins in this paragraph; control passes to 200-level paragraphs only to return to the primary paragraph; and control leaves the program (to return to the operating system) from this paragraph when the step "Stop the run" is executed.

In general, the primary paragraph consists mainly of "perform" statements and the "Stop the run" instruction. When a perform statement is executed, control is transferred to the paragraph referenced in the statement, but it automatically returns to the "sending" paragraph after the last instruction in the performed paragraph has been carried out. The performs are executed in the order specified, and it is the programmer's responsibility to make sure that the specified sequence does in fact get the job done properly. When the "Stop the run" instruction is executed, control leaves the program to return to the operating system.

The programmer continues writing the pseudocode in this manner, generating all the processing steps needed to accomplish the function specified in each module. The paragraphs are written in ascending order of the level numbers attached to the modules of the structure chart.

The second paragraph is 200-Start-Up. Some start-up activities are needed in addition to the subtasks identified in the structure chart. Two very common activities in a start-up paragraph are opening the files that must be accessed by the program and initializing certain variable data items. In this program, as shown in the system flowchart of Figure 2.5, there is one input file, namely PHONE-SALES-FILE, and one output file, namely PHONE-SALES-REPORT. To read a record from the input file or to write a record to the output file, the file must be available to the program. This is the purpose of "opening" the files.

The start-up paragraph also initializes the variable (data item) WS-MORE-RECORDS. (In this text, the prefix WS- is used to identify data items defined in working storage.) Why is such an item needed? It should be clear that the steps needed to process a phone sale record have to be repeated for every record in the data file. In other words, these processing steps are contained within a loop. Some technique must be developed to provide an exit from the loop. To that end, the item WS-MORE-RECORDS is set up as a flag. It is initialized to "YES", but it is changed to "NO " when the end-of-file (EOF) record in the input file is encountered (during execution of the read function). The value of the flag is always either "YES" or "NO ". After reading the input file but before entering the procedure to process a phone sale record, the flag WS-MORE-RECORDS is checked. If it contains the value "YES", the data record processing steps are executed again, but if its value is "NO ", then control exits from the loop. The logic underlying the use of the flag is illustrated in Figure 2.7.

In the sample program, only one data item has to be initialized, so paragraph 200-Start-Up contains four steps:

200-Start-Up.

1. Open the files.
2. Set the end-of-file flag WS-MORE-RECORDS to "YES".
3. Perform 300-Write-Report-Headers.
4. Perform 310-Read-Phone-Sale-Record.

■ **Figure 2.7** Record-processing loop controlled by the flag WS-MORE-RECORDS

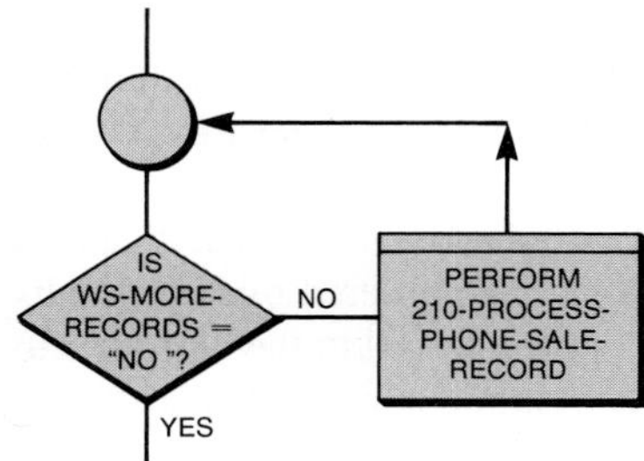

The next paragraph that must be attended to by the programmer is the one that corresponds to the structure chart module 210 PROCESS PHONE SALE RECORD. This module has three subordinate modules. Consequently, the corresponding paragraph in the pseudocode contains the three steps that control the execution of the subordinate modules. The paragraph is shown below:

210-Process-Phone-Sale-Record.

1. Perform 320-Compute-Phone-Sale-Amount.
2. Perform 330-Prepare-Phone-Sale-Line.
3. Perform 310-Read-Phone-Sale-Record.

Recall that step 3 in paragraph 210 is needed so that after the current phone sale record has been processed, the next one in the input file can be accessed and processed in turn.

The last module at the 200 level is 220 FINISH UP. The essential function of this module is to close the files that were made available to the program. The net effect of closing a file is to terminate access to the file from within the current program. The file then becomes available to other programs. It is the programmer's responsibility to properly close the files before exiting from the current run of the program. The corresponding paragraph in the pseudocode is shown below:

220-Finish-Up.

1. Close the files.

The first module in the structure chart at the 300 level is 300 WRITE REPORT HEADERS. The obvious task in this module is to write the headings for the report. The report is the output file PHONE-SALES-REPORT, so the task is really to write a record to the output file. COBOL requires that an output record be held physically in the buffer area reserved for the output file. We call the record in that area "Printline." However, most records ultimately written to an output file are generally prepared in another section of main memory known as *working storage.* The reasons for this will be explained later. So, the task of writing the headings requires, as a preliminary step, moving the headings from the working-storage area to the output record area Printline. Then, since the report should begin at the top of a new page, the paper is advanced in the printer, and finally the contents of Printline are written onto the report.

The next record that will be moved to the output area Printline is the phone sale line that must be prepared for the first phone sale record of the input file. A useful COBOL "housekeeping" step is to make sure that the preparation of this record area begins with a "clean slate." To do this, the programmer will move spaces to the record area Phone-sale-line.

Paragraph 300-Write-Report-Headers therefore contains three instructions, as shown below:

300-Write-Report-Headers.

1. Move Headings to the output area Printline.
2. After advancing to the top of a new page, write the output record Printline.
3. Clear the record area Phone-sale-line.

The next module in the structure chart at the 300 level is 310 READ PHONE SALE RECORD. The essential function of this module is to read a record from the data file PHONE-SALES-FILE. As a record is read, it is copied into the record area reserved in main memory for the input file. At some point, the read function will encounter the end-of-file record. It is at this moment that the end-of-file flag WS-MORE-RECORDS must be assigned the value "NO ". This logic is easily illustrated, as shown in Figure 2.8.

The processing steps specified in the pseudocode are shown below:

310-Read-Phone-Sale-Record.

1. Read an input Phone-sale-record.
2. Test for the end-of-file record; if EOF record reached, move "NO " to the end-of-file flag WS-MORE-RECORDS.

The next module in the structure chart at the 300 level is 320 COMPUTE PHONE SALE AMOUNT. The function of the module is stated very clearly. It is the programmer's responsibility to select the correct processing steps.

A key factor in determining the amount of the sale is the applicability of a discount. The specifications of the problem indicate that in order to earn the discount, the customer must have ordered over 100 units of the catalog item. Consequently, a test must be performed on the number of units sold to the customer to determine if it is greater than 100. If it is not, then the sale amount is computed without a discount. Specifically, the amount is simply the product of the number of units sold and the unit price of the catalog item. On the other hand, if the number of units sold is greater than 100, a 20 percent discount must be

Figure 2.8 Read-structure with test for end-of-file record

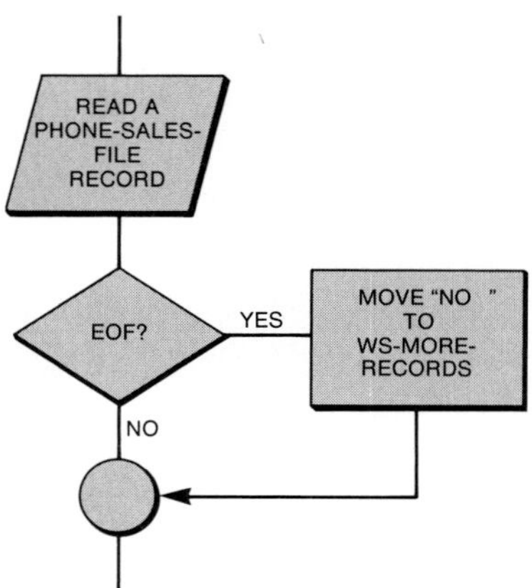

applied to the amount of the sale to yield the net sale amount. In other words, the customer will be charged only 80 percent of the total amount. Hence, the formula for the net amount of the sale is number of units sold "times" unit price of the item times 0.8.

This analysis yields the pseudocode paragraph that follows:

320-Compute-Phone-Sale-Amount.

1. If the input number-of-units > 100
    then
        compute the Phone-sale-line sale-amount = input number-of-units times
                                                  input unit-cost times .8
    else
        compute the Phone-sale-line sale-amount = input number-of-units times input unit-cost.

Finally, the last 300-level module in the structure chart is 330 PREPARE PHONE SALE LINE. In this paragraph, all the steps required to transfer data values from input record fields to the fields of the record PHONE-SALE-LINE must be specified. There are four such data transfers: the customer number, the catalog number, the unit cost of the item, and the number of units sold. The phone sale amount field has been assigned its value in the preceding paragraph, 320-Compute-Phone-Sale-Amount.

Once the record PHONE-SALE-LINE is completely prepared, that is, all its data fields have been assigned values, it must be moved to the output record area Printline. And finally, after advancing the printer paper the proper number of lines, the output record Printline is written on the report.

These detailed steps are shown below:

330-Prepare-Phone-Sale-Line.

1. Move input customer-number to Phone-sale-line customer-number.
2. Move input catalog-number to Phone-sale-line catalog-number.
3. Move input unit-cost to Phone-sale-line unit-cost.
4. Move input number-of-units to Phone-sale-line number-of-units.
5. Move the Phone-sale-line to the output record area Printline.
6. After advancing 2 lines, write the output record Printline.

This completes the program pseudocode. All the needed processing steps have been specified. They are assembled in Figure 2.9.

Alternate Step 2c. Design the Program Flowchart (Alternative to the Pseudocode)

For many years, the standard technique of mapping out the logic of a program consisted of developing a program flowchart. Today, the trend is to use the structure chart and the related program pseudocode instead of the program flowchart. However, many programmers (and instructors) still prefer the visual impact provided by the flowchart to the wordiness of the pseudocode. A picture is still worth a thousand words. To allow instructors to follow their preference, this text continues to present the program flowchart as an alternative to the program pseudocode. (It is unlikely that students will be expected to use both.)

The correspondence between the structure chart and the program flowchart is obvious. Just as the structure chart is based on modularity, so is the program flowchart of a modular design. For each functional

Figure 2.9 Pseudocode for the chapter program

100-Produce-Phone-Sales-Report.

1. Perform 200-Start-Up.
2. Perform 210-Process-Phone-Sale-Record until no more records.
3. Perform 220-Finish-Up.
4. Stop the run.

200-Start-Up.

1. Open the files.
2. Set the end-of-file flag WS-MORE-RECORDS to "YES".
3. Perform 300-Write-Report-Headers.
4. Perform 310-Read-Phone-Sale-Record.

210-Process-Phone-Sale-Record.

1. Perform 320-Compute-Phone-Sale-Amount.
2. Perform 330-Prepare-Phone-Sale-Line.
3. Perform 310-Read-Phone-Sale-Record.

220-Finish-Up.

1. Close the files.

300-Write-Report-Headers.

1. Move Headings to the output area Printline.
2. After advancing to the top of a new page, write the output record Printline.
3. Clear the record area Phone-sale-line.

310-Read-Phone-Sale-Record.

1. Read an input phone-sale-record.
2. Test for the end-of-file record; if EOF record reached, move "NO " to the end-of-file flag WS-MORE-RECORDS.

320-Compute-Phone-Sale-Amount.

```
1. If the input number-of-units > 100
      then
          compute the Phone-sale-line amount = input number-of-units times
                                               input unit-cost times .8
      else
          compute the Phone-sale-line amount = input number-of-units times input unit-cost.
```

330-Prepare-Phone-Sale-Line.

1. Move input customer-number to Phone-sale-line customer-number.
2. Move input catalog-number to Phone-sale-line catalog-number.
3. Move input unit-cost to Phone-sale-line unit-cost.
4. Move input number-of-units to Phone-sale-line number-of-units.
5. Move the Phone-sale-line to the output record area Printline.
6. After advancing 2 lines, write the output record Printline.

module (box) in the structure chart, there is a corresponding module in the program flowchart. The modules in the structure chart have functional names; the same names are attached to the modules in the program flowchart. Just as there are superior and subordinate modules in the structure chart, so are there "calling" and "called" modules in the program flowchart.

You should note, however, that the program flowchart, in addition to showing the relationship among modules, also specifies the exact sequence in which these modules are executed. This is readily accomplished by the presence of the *flow lines.* The assumption is that control flows through a flowchart module from top to bottom and from left to right, unless specified otherwise by the use of arrowheads on the flow lines. Furthermore, control is passed from one module to another by a *perform box* (a box with a double bar at the top). A *terminal symbol* with the key word RETURN returns control to the perform box it originally came from.

A program flowchart combines the hierarchical structure of the structure chart with the detailed processing activities specified in the program pseudocode. The program flowchart for the sample chapter program is shown in Figure 2.10. In this flowchart, module 100 and module 210 have been "stretched" to facilitate the insertion of dotted lines. These dotted lines show you how control flows between the modules of the flowchart. (These dotted lines are not usually included in a flowchart.)

■ **Figure 2.10** Program flowchart for the chapter program

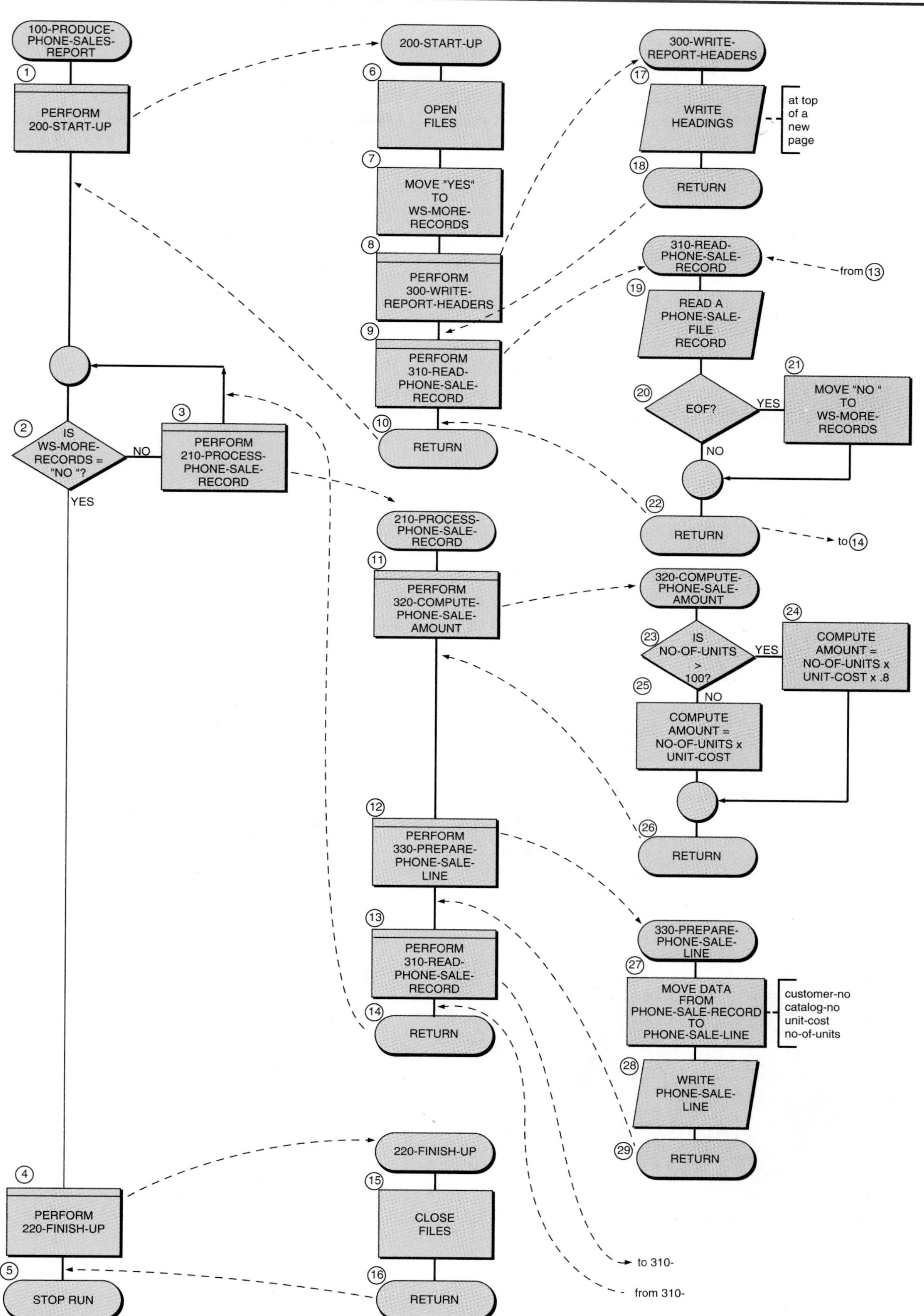

Again, note that the flowchart is modular in design. It consists of eight modules, one corresponding to each box in the structure chart.

Small numbered circles have been inserted in the flowchart to facilitate running a *trace* of the flowchart, that is, to show the sequence in which control passes from box to box. A cursory examination should make it clear that there are three possible paths in the overall logic: two are determined by the number of units sold to the customer, and the third is related to the end-of-file record.

The possible sequences are specified in Figure 2.11. Control begins in box 1, passes on to box 6 (as a result of the PERFORM), then to boxes 7 and 8, where control is sent to box 17, then 18. From box 18, control returns to box 9. In turn, box 9 sends control to box 19, and on to box 20, where an end-of-file test is executed. If the EOF condition is satisfied, control goes on to box 21, and then box 22 returns control to box 10. Box 10 returns control to box 2. In this case, the condition in box 2 is satisfied, and consequently, control goes on to boxes 4, 15, 16, and finally 5, which is obviously the end of this path, and the end of the program.

On the other hand, if the EOF condition back in box 20 is **not** satisfied, control goes on to box 22, which returns then to box 10. Box 10 returns control to box 2. In this case, the condition in box 2 is not true, and as a result, control goes on to box 3. Box 3 sends control to box 11. Box 11 sends control to box 23. If the condition in box 23 is true, then control flows to 24, then on to 26 and back to box 12. On the other hand, if the condition in box 23 is **not** true, control flows to 25, then 26, and then back to box 12. In either case, from box 12, control is sent to boxes 27, 28, and 29. Box 29 returns control to box 13. Box 13 sends control to box 19 again, and on to box 20, where the end-of-file test is executed. If the EOF condition is satisfied, control goes to box 21 and then to box 22. If the EOF condition is **not** satisfied, control goes to box 22 directly. Note that this time, control is returned from box 22 to box 14, and in turn, box 14 returns control to box 2, and the procedure continues as described above. The schematic in Figure 2.11 shows the trace of the flowchart.

It is important to note that the very first time module 310 is executed, control comes from box 9 and hence returns to box 10, whereas all the other times module 310 is executed, control comes from box 13, and hence control returns to box 14.

Use the records in the sample data file shown below, and carefully walk through the flowchart to see for yourself that the logic embedded in it does produce the required results. Record 1 follows the no-discount path; record 2 follows the 20 percent discount path; and record 3 triggers the exit from the processing loop.

Sample Data

Record Number	*Customer Number*	*Catalog Number*	*Unit Cost*	*Number of Units*
1	4000	1001	$2.00	50
2	5000	1002	$2.00	200
3	EOF record			

At this point, the program design phase is complete.

Figure 2.11 Trace of the program flowchart of Figure 2.10

```
                                    if EOF
1, 6, 7, 8, 17, 18, 9, 19, 20 ------> 21, 22, 10, 2, 4, 15, 16, 5 (End of program)
                              | if
                              | not
                              | EOF                 if>100
                              ------> 22, 10, 2, 3, 11, 23 ------> 24, 26
                                                   ___    | if
                                                          | not
                                                          |>100
                                                          |
                                                          ------> 25, 26
                                                          Then, from 26 in any case:

                                                                                if EOF
                                                          12, 27, 28, 29, 13, 19, 20 ------> 21, 22
                                                                                   | if
                                                                                   | not
                                                                                   | EOF
                                                                                   ------> 22
                                                          Then, from 22 in any case:

                                                                if true
                                                          14, 2 ------> 4, 15, 16, 5 (End of program)
                                                              | if
                                                              | not
                                                              | true
                                                              ------> 3, 11  and repeat as above at 11
                                                                         __                        __
```

Design Implementation Phase

In applying the steps of the problem-solving procedure diligently to the solution of the sample chapter program, we have reached the point where all the formal planning will now be implemented within the program itself.

Step 3. Coding the Program

The next task is writing, or coding, the program. The programmer assembles the materials she or he prepared during the program design phase, specifically, the system flowchart, the structure chart, and the pseudocode or the program flowchart. The programmer arranges these design tools and the original statement of the problem so that they can be referenced easily and reaches for a COBOL coding form. An IBM COBOL coding form is shown in Figure 2.12. A brief explanation of the form follows.

1. **Form Header.** The entries that the programmer makes in the header (top portion of the form) are obvious, with the possible exception of the PUNCHING INSTRUCTIONS area. To avoid misinterpreting the digit 0 for the letter O, the digit 1 for the letter I, the digit 2 for the letter Z, and so on, the programmer specifies to the data-entry operator the conventions being used. (Since you will do your own data entry, these entries are not needed.) Such a set of specifications is shown in Figure 2.13.
2. **Main Body.** The main body of the coding form is divided into 24 lines per page, 80 columns per line. The columns are grouped into areas as follows:
   a. **SEQUENCE area (columns 1 through 6).** This area is used to show a page number and a line number on that page. Lines are usually numbered in increments of 10. For instance, the sequence number 001030 corresponds to "line 3 on page 1."

      Gaps are left in line numbers so that if insertions are needed later, they can be made without affecting the rest of the sequence numbers. For instance, 001025 could be inserted between 001020 and 001030.

      Sequence numbers are optional but may be useful as points of reference when inserting new lines in a program, editing, and debugging a program. Your instructor will let you know if you should enter them or not.

Figure 2.12 IBM COBOL coding form

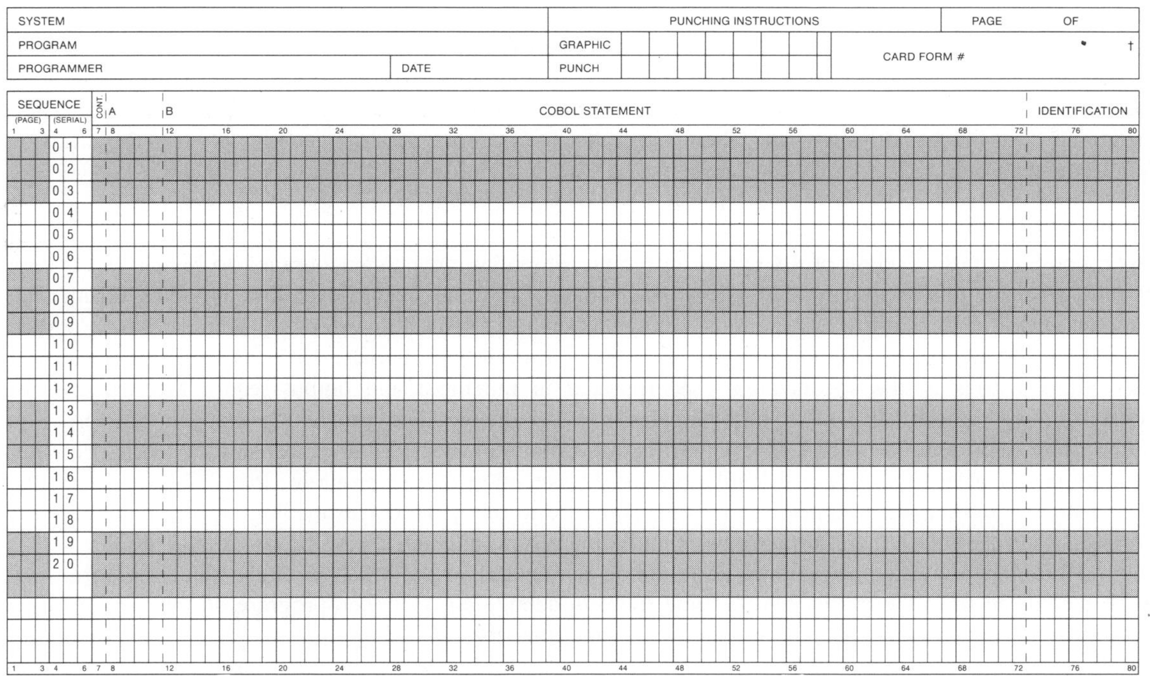

SYSTEM | PUNCHING INSTRUCTIONS | PAGE OF
PROGRAM | GRAPHIC | CARD FORM #
PROGRAMMER | DATE | PUNCH

SEQUENCE (PAGE) (SERIAL) | CONT. | A | B | COBOL STATEMENT | IDENTIFICATION

1 3 4 6 7 8 12 16 20 24 28 32 36 40 44 48 52 56 60 64 68 72 76 80

01
02
03
04
05
06
07
08
09
10
11
12
13
14
15
16
17
18
19
20

1 3 4 6 7 8 12 16 20 24 28 32 36 40 44 48 52 56 60 64 68 72 76 80

Figure 2.13 Data entry instructions related to coded characters

COBOL Coding Form

	PUNCHING INSTRUCTIONS							
	GRAPHIC	O	Ø	I	I	Ƶ	2	CARD FORM #
DATE	PUNCH	alpha	Zero	alpha	One	alpha	Two	

COBOL STATEMENT

b. CONTINUATION area (column 7). This column is reserved for a few special characters.

An asterisk (*) inserted in column 7 indicates that the entry on this line is to be treated as a comment. The asterisk must be entered on each comment line. This character is used extensively by programmers to provide documentation in programs. Typically, documentation is provided at the beginning of a program in the IDENTIFICATION DIVISION. However, it should be provided anywhere within a program where it is felt that additional explanations are useful.

A hyphen (-) can be inserted in column 7 to show that a literal or word begun on the preceding line is being continued on this line. A detailed explanation will be given in Chapter 3.

A slant or slash (/) inserted in column 7 will cause the printer to skip to the top of the next page while printing the listing of the program generated by the compiler. The slant is often used to begin the printing of each division at the top of a new page.

c. AREA A, columns 8 through 11. Some program entries must begin in this area, such as division and section headers, paragraph names, FD entries, and 01 level numbers. Naturally, an entry begun in area A may be continued into area B. When these entries are described later in this chapter and in later chapters, you will be reminded that their coding must begin in area A.

d. AREA B, columns 12 through 72. Source program entries other than the ones that must begin in Area A must be coded in Area B. Some of these are file names, all data names, level numbers 02–49, 66, 88, and all instructions in the PROCEDURE DIVISION. As we proceed in this chapter and into other chapters, these entries will be illustrated and explained in detail.

e. IDENTIFICATION area, columns 73 through 80. Traditionally, this area had been used to insert a program identification code, a useful feature in preventing source card decks for different programs from being mixed together. The use of this area is optional. Since card systems are almost extinct, some producers of COBOL coding forms no longer include this area on the form.

Program Coding

Writing the COBOL program on the coding forms is referred to as *coding* the program. The coding must be done very clearly and meticulously, since each line of coding is later entered on a keyboard exactly as it is coded, one line at a time.

Before a beginning programmer can reasonably be expected to write a COBOL program (regardless of how simple it is), he or she has much to learn. To facilitate this learning process, the complete program for the sample problem is presented in Figure 2.14. We will examine the general features of a COBOL program, division by division, and then return to the sample program to show how the division requirements were met.

Program Walk-through

Upon completing the coding of a COBOL program, the programmer is encouraged to review the coding carefully. During this important debugging process, the programmer checks each line of coding for missing punctuation, such as hyphens and periods, for syntax errors, for spelling errors of technical words (called COBOL reserved words), for inconsistent spelling of user-defined names, for conformity of the DATA DIVISION entries to the specifications incorporated in the input and output record layouts, and for conformity of the PROCEDURE DIVISION entries to the detailed processing steps in the program pseudocode or program flowchart. Coding errors that remain undetected will be transmitted to the computer and ultimately affect the proper compilation and/or execution of the program. When this happens, the programmer must recode the lines in error, use an editor to rekey the corresponding entries, recompile the program, and, assuming there are no new compilation errors, attempt to run the program again.

All of these repeated procedures are time-consuming and costly. It behooves the student programmer to be convinced from the outset that the time spent in debugging the coded program on the coding forms is time well spent. In general, the more productive the time spent in debugging, the greater the probability that the program will compile properly and have a successful first run.

■ Figure 2.14 Chapter program on coding forms

SYSTEM | PUNCHING INSTRUCTIONS | PAGE 1 OF 7
PROGRAM DAILY-PHONE-SALES-REPORT | GRAPHIC | CARD FORM #
PROGRAMMER PAQUETTE | DATE | PUNCH

SEQUENCE (PAGE) (SERIAL) | CONT. | A | B | COBOL STATEMENT | IDENTIFICATION

```
       IDENTIFICATION DIVISION.

       PROGRAM-ID.    DAILY-PHONE-SALES-REPORT.

      *****************************************************************
      *                                                               *
      *   AUTHOR.         PAQUETTE.                                   *
      *   DATE WRITTEN.   NOVEMBER   1993.                            *
      *                                                               *
      *   THIS PROGRAM PRODUCES A REPORT LISTING THE PHONE SALES THAT *
      *   OCCURRED DURING THE DAY.                                    *
      *                                                               *
      *   EACH INPUT RECORD IS A PHONE SALE RECORD THAT CONTAINS THE  *
      *   CUSTOMER NUMBER, THE CATALOG NUMBER, THE UNIT COST OF THE   *
      *   ITEM, AND THE NUMBER OF UNITS SOLD TO THE CUSTOMER.         *
      *                                                               *
      *   FOR EACH PHONE SALE, THE PHONE SALE LINE ON THE REPORT MUST *
      *   SHOW THE CUSTOMER NUMBER, THE CATALOG NUMBER, THE UNIT COST,*
      *   THE NUMBER OF UNITS SOLD, AND THE NET AMOUNT OF THE SALE.   *
      *   THE VALUES ON THE PHONE SALE LINES ARE LISTED UNDER APPRO-  *
      *   PRIATE COLUMN HEADINGS.                                     *
      *                                                               *
      *   THE AMOUNT OF THE SALE IS COMPUTED AS FOLLOWS: IF THE NUMBER*
      *   OF UNITS SOLD EXCEEDS 100, THE SALE AMOUNT IS DISCOUNTED 20%,*
```

SYSTEM | PUNCHING INSTRUCTIONS | PAGE 2 OF 7
PROGRAM DAILY-PHONE-SALES-REPORT | GRAPHIC | CARD FORM #
PROGRAMMER | DATE | PUNCH

SEQUENCE (PAGE) (SERIAL) | CONT. | A | B | COBOL STATEMENT | IDENTIFICATION

```
      *   THAT IS, SALE AMOUNT = NO. OF UNITS * UNIT COST * .8.  IF THE *
      *   NUMBER OF UNITS DOES NOT EXCEED 100, THE SALE AMOUNT = NO. OF *
      *   UNITS * UNIT COST.                                          *
      *                                                               *
      *****************************************************************

       ENVIRONMENT DIVISION.

       CONFIGURATION SECTION.

       SOURCE-COMPUTER.    VAX-VMS-8650.
       OBJECT-COMPUTER.    VAX-VMS-8650.

       INPUT-OUTPUT SECTION.

       FILE-CONTROL.
           SELECT PHONE-SALES-FILE       ASSIGN TO COB$INPUT.
           SELECT PHONE-SALES-REPORT     ASSIGN TO COB$OUTPUT.

       DATA DIVISION.

       FILE SECTION.

       FD  PHONE-SALES-FILE
```

■ Figure 2.14 continued

SYSTEM | PUNCHING INSTRUCTIONS | PAGE 3 OF 7

PROGRAM DAILY-PHONE-SALES-REPORT | GRAPHIC | CARD FORM #

PROGRAMMER | DATE | PUNCH

SEQUENCE (PAGE) (SERIAL) | CONT. | A | B | COBOL STATEMENT | IDENTIFICATION

```
           RECORD CONTAINS 23 CHARACTERS.

       01  PHONE-SALE-RECORD.
           05 I-CUSTOMER-NO      PIC X(4).
           05 FILLER             PIC XX.
           05 I-CATALOG-NO       PIC X(4).
           05 FILLER             PIC XX.
           05 I-UNIT-COST        PIC 999V99.
           05 FILLER             PIC XX.
           05 I-NO-OF-UNITS      PIC 9(4).

       FD  PHONE-SALES-REPORT
           RECORD CONTAINS 132 CHARACTERS.

       01  PRINTLINE             PIC X(132).

       WORKING-STORAGE SECTION.

       01  WS-MORE-RECORDS       PIC XXX.
```

SYSTEM | PUNCHING INSTRUCTIONS | PAGE 4 OF 7

PROGRAM DAILY-PHONE-SALES-REPORT | GRAPHIC | CARD FORM #

PROGRAMMER | DATE | PUNCH

SEQUENCE (PAGE) (SERIAL) | CONT. | A | B | COBOL STATEMENT | IDENTIFICATION

```
       01  HEADINGS.
           05 PIC X(15)     VALUE SPACES.
           05 PIC X(15)     VALUE "CUSTOMER NUMBER".
           05 PIC X(8)      VALUE SPACES.
           05 PIC X(14)     VALUE "CATALOG NUMBER".
           05 PIC X(8)      VALUE SPACES.
           05 PIC X(9)      VALUE "UNIT COST".
           05 PIC X(8)      VALUE SPACES.
           05 PIC X(15)     VALUE "NUMBER OF UNITS".
           05 PIC X(8)      VALUE SPACES.
           05 PIC X(17)     VALUE "PHONE SALE AMOUNT".
           05 PIC X(15)     VALUE SPACES.

       01  PHONE-SALE-LINE.
           05 FILLER             PIC X(21).
           05 O-CUSTOMER-NO      PIC X(4).
           05 FILLER             PIC X(18).
           05 O-CATALOG-NO       PIC X(4).
           05 FILLER             PIC X(14).
           05 O-UNIT-COST        PIC $ZZ9.99.
           05 FILLER             PIC X(15).
           05 O-NO-OF-UNITS      PIC ZZZ9.
           05 FILLER             PIC X(17).
           05 O-SALE-AMOUNT      PIC $Z(5)9.99.
```

Figure 2.14 continued

SYSTEM | PUNCHING INSTRUCTIONS | PAGE 5 OF 7
PROGRAM DAILY-PHONE-SALES-REPORT | GRAPHIC | CARD FORM #
PROGRAMMER | DATE | PUNCH

```
           05 FILLER                   PIC X(18).

       PROCEDURE DIVISION.

       100-PRODUCE-PHONE-SALES-REPORT.
           PERFORM 200-START-UP.
           PERFORM 210-PROCESS-PHONE-SALE-RECORD
                UNTIL WS-MORE-RECORDS = "NO ".
           PERFORM 220-FINISH-UP.
           STOP RUN.

       200-START-UP.
           OPEN INPUT PHONE-SALES-FILE.
           OPEN OUTPUT PHONE-SALES-REPORT.
           MOVE "YES" TO WS-MORE-RECORDS.
           PERFORM 300-WRITE-REPORT-HEADERS.
           PERFORM 310-READ-PHONE-SALE-RECORD.

       210-PROCESS-PHONE-SALE-RECORD.
           PERFORM 320-COMPUTE-PHONE-SALE-AMOUNT.
           PERFORM 330-PREPARE-PHONE-SALE-LINE.
           PERFORM 310-READ-PHONE-SALE-RECORD.
```

SYSTEM | PUNCHING INSTRUCTIONS | PAGE 6 OF 7
PROGRAM DAILY-PHONE-SALES-REPORT | GRAPHIC | CARD FORM #
PROGRAMMER | DATE | PUNCH

```
       220-FINISH-UP.
           CLOSE PHONE-SALES-FILE.
           CLOSE PHONE-SALES-REPORT.

       300-WRITE-REPORT-HEADERS.
           MOVE HEADINGS TO PRINTLINE.
           WRITE PRINTLINE
                AFTER ADVANCING PAGE.
           MOVE SPACES TO PHONE-SALE-LINE.

       310-READ-PHONE-SALE-RECORD.
           READ PHONE-SALES-FILE RECORD
                AT END
                    MOVE "NO " TO WS-MORE-RECORDS.

       320-COMPUTE-PHONE-SALE-AMOUNT.
           IF I-NO-OF-UNITS > 100
                THEN
                    COMPUTE O-SALE-AMOUNT = I-NO-OF-UNITS *
                                            I-UNIT-COST * .8
                ELSE
                    COMPUTE O-SALE-AMOUNT = I-NO-OF-UNITS *
                                            I-UNIT-COST.
```

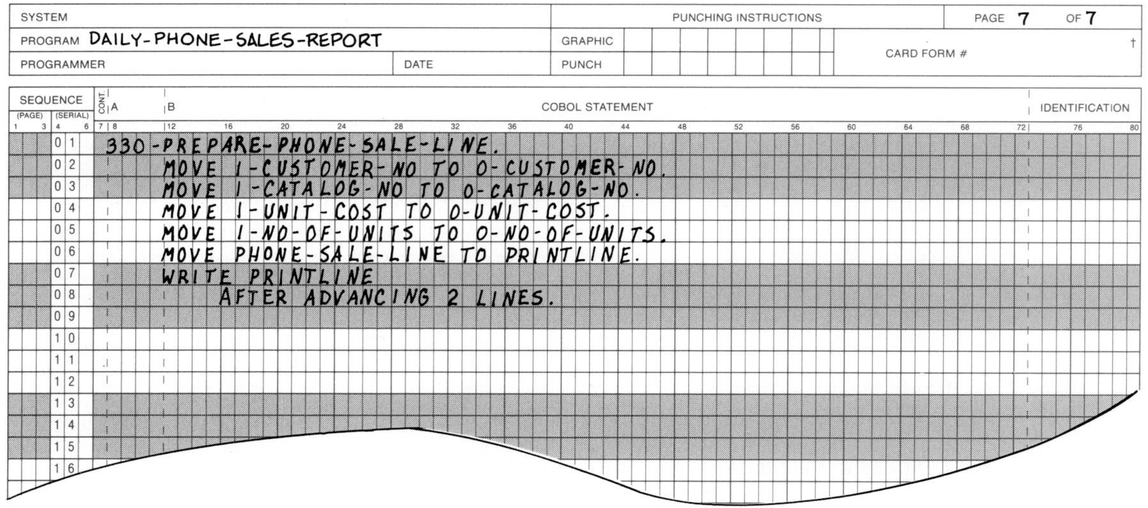

Step 4. Keying (or Entering) the Program

According to the problem-solving procedure, the next step in the design implementation phase is to create a file into which the program will be entered. Therefore, the time has come for the programmer to sit at a terminal, log on, create a new file, and use an editor to facilitate the job of entering the program into the file. Specific procedures to log on and specific information on available editors will be provided by your instructor.

Below are a few typical entries on a DEC VAX during which the EDT editor was used to load the chapter program into a file. In this example, the new file has been given the name C2SAMR.COB.

```
$ EDIT C2SAMR.COB
Input file does not exist
[EOB]
*CHANGE

        IDENTIFICATION DIVISION.

        PROGRAM-ID.  DAILY-PHONE-SALES-REPORT.

       ****************************************************************
       *                                                              *
       *  AUTHOR.        PAQUETTE.                                    *
       *  DATE WRITTEN: NOVEMBER 1993.                                *
       *                                                              *
       *  THIS PROGRAM PRODUCES A REPORT LISTING THE PHONE SALES THAT *
       *  OCCURRED DURING THE DAY.                                    *
       .
       .
       .
       .
        PROCEDURE DIVISION.

        100-PRODUCE-PHONE-SALES-REPORT.
            PERFORM 200-START-UP.
            .
            .
            .
        330-PREPARE-PHONE-SALE-LINE.
            MOVE I-CUSTOMER-NO TO O-CUSTOMER-NO.
            .
            .
            .
            WRITE PRINTLINE
                AFTER ADVANCING 2 LINES.

[EOB]

*EXIT
```

Step 5. Debugging the Program

The program must now be supplied as input to the COBOL compiler. The purpose is to use the compiler's role as diagnostician to "clean up" the program, that is, to identify the syntax errors that remain so that the programmer can correct them.

In producing error messages, the compiler generally does the following:

1. It classifies the error by its level of severity: fatal, nonfatal, or advisory. If an error is fatal, the program will not be compiled. The programmer must therefore correct all fatal errors.

   Nonfatal and advisory errors, though they may not prevent compilation, could very well interfere with the proper execution of the program and should therefore be examined carefully by the programmer.

   Except in rare circumstances, all errors, regardless of level of severity, should be corrected.
2. It attempts to isolate the error. The compiler generally assigns statement numbers to the entries in a program. Each diagnostic refers to one error and identifies the entry containing the error by referencing its statement number.
3. It identifies the type of error by providing an error code and/or a brief description of the error.

Figure 2.15 contains the diagnostics that were issued for the chapter program. (These errors are due to typing mistakes made when the program was entered from the coding forms into the file C1SAMR.COB.) Although the general appearance of the diagnostics and the particular wording of the messages will vary from one compiler to another, the functions of diagnostic messages will always be the same.

Step 5a. Correct All Syntax Errors

At this point, the programmer's task is to correct the syntax errors in the program. In Figure 2.15, eleven messages have been generated by the compiler. A closer examination will reveal that the program really

Figure 2.15 Use of the COBOL compiler to identify syntax errors in the chapter program

```
$ COBOL/ANSI/NOOBJECT/LIST C2SAMRX.COB
   38          INPUT OUTPUT SECTION.
               1
%COBOL-F-ERROR  117, (1) Invalid syntax
   40          FILE-CONTROL.
               1
%COBOL-W-ERROR  297, (1) Processing of source program resumes at this point
%COBOL-E-ERROR  453, (1) Missing INPUT-OUTPUT SECTION header assumed
   41              SELECT PHONE-SALES-FILE    ASSIGN TO COB$INPUT.
                          1
%COBOL-W-ERROR  239, (1) File is CLOSEd but is not OPENed
   42              SELECT PHONE-SALES-REPORT  ASSIGN TO COB$OUTPUT.
                          1
%COBOL-W-ERROR   16, (1) RECORD CONTAINS value is greater than length of longest record
   77              05 PIC X(15)    VALUE "NUMBER OF UNITS ".
                      1
%COBOL-E-ERROR   84, (1) Literal in VALUE clause conflicts with description - clause ignored
  107              OPEN INPUT PHONE-SALE-FILE.
                              1
%COBOL-F-ERROR  349, (1) Undefined name
  113              WRITE IPRINTLINE
                         1
%COBOL-F-ERROR  349, (1) Undefined name
  115              MOVE SPACES TO PHONE-SALE-LINE.
                   1
%COBOL-W-ERROR  297, (1) Processing of source program resumes at this point
  141              MOVE I-CUSTOMER-NO TO O-CUSTOMER-NO.
                                         1
%COBOL-F-ERROR  349, (1) Undefined name
  142              MOVE I-CATALOG-NO TO ON-CATALOG-NO.
                                        1
%COBOL-F-ERROR  349, (1) Undefined name
%COBOL-F-ENDDIAGS, SCIENCE$DISK:[MA6031]C2SAMRX.COB;3 completed with 11 diagnostics
```

contains only six errors. Quite often, a specific error triggers more than one message, as in the following examples:

1. The three messages at lines 38 and 40 are related to the missing hyphen (-) in the header INPUT-OUTPUT SECTION.
2. The message at line 41 and the one at line 107 are related. Correcting the spelling of the input file name at line 107 (it should be PHONE-SALES-FILE) will remove both error messages.
3. The message at line 42 is caused by specifying PIC X(130) for the output record PRINTLINE (at line 63), whereas the RECORD CONTAINS clause at line 61 specifies a size of 132 characters. Changing PIC X(130) to PIC X(132) will eliminate the error.
4. At line 77, the error is due to the size of the literal in the VALUE clause. There are 16 characters in the literal, but the PIC entry specifies a size of 15. To remove the conflict, delete the space at the end of the literal.
5. At line 113, the error is a misspelling of the record name PRINTLINE.
6. At line 141, the error is the prefix "zero" instead of the letter "O" in the data name O-CUSTOMER-NO.
7. At line 142, the error is the letter *N* in the prefix for the data name O-CATALOG-NO.

Once the errors have been identified, the programmer uses the editor to make the necessary corrections to the program. The compiler is called again (and again, if necessary) to finally produce a "clean" listing of the program. The listing is shown in Figure 2.16a. (As we proceed beyond this point, we assume that all the syntax errors have been corrected.)

Step 5b. Compile the Program

Now that the program is error-free, it is possible to compile it. Recall that to compile the program means to generate the object program (the machine-language instructions that correspond to the source program written by the programmer). In the business world, when a program is error-free and has been tested in several trial runs, a *production version* of the program will be saved in a file. In operating systems that use a loader, the production version is the object program. In operating systems that use a linker, the executable image produced by the linker is the production version. When the program is needed by the data processing department, it is executed directly and immediately, since it is already compiled. In a school environment, however, a student test runs a program with only a sample data file. A student does not usually make a production copy of a program, since assigned programs are only exercises designed to help students develop programming skills. Consequently, the program is usually compiled and run within the same job. This is the procedure we will follow with the chapter program. Now that we have assured ourselves that the program is free of syntax errors, we will compile and run the program in the next step.

Step 6. Performing a Test Run of the Program

In any computer system, the programs to be run are placed under the control of an operating system, a program that coordinates and sequences the various jobs to be performed by the computer system. The programmer must tell the operating system exactly what has to be done with the program, providing such specifics as the compiler that is needed to generate the object program, whether a listing of the program is wanted, any special input or output device requirements, and so on. The programmer communicates this information to the computer by means of operating system commands.

The particular set of operating system commands required for the proper execution of a COBOL program is a function of the computer system itself and consequently varies from one installation to another. Your instructor will provide you with a list of all the operating system commands required to run your program properly.

In general, the following activities will take place, assuming that output is produced at a printer:

1. The first set of operating system commands is entered.
2. The appropriate compiler is loaded into main memory.
3. The source program is entered and stored into main memory.
4. A listing of the source program is produced by the compiler. It contains the source code and the error messages, if there are any.

5. If there are no serious syntax errors, the object program is generated by the compiler.
6. The linker or loader is activated to produce the executable image of the program.
7. The "run" statement is processed, causing the computer to begin execution of the program.
8. Assuming no disastrous logic or programming error, the records of the input file are processed one at a time.
9. As the input records are processed, the program produces the corresponding output file records.
10. When the last COBOL program statement (STOP RUN) is processed, program execution stops.
11. A hard copy of the listing and of the output file is obtained from the printer, and the computer run is complete.

Step 6a. Run the Program with a Sample Input File

The following example shows the operating system commands that were used to compile, link, and run the chapter program and print the output on a remote high-speed printer.

Example:

```
$ COBOL/ANSI/LIS C2SAMR.COB
$ LINK C2SAMR.OBJ
$ ASSIGN C2SAMR.DAT COB$INPUT
$ ASSIGN C2SAMR.OUT COB$OUTPUT
$ RUN C2SAMR.EXE
$ PRINT/QUE = OS315 C2SAMR.LIS, C2SAMR.DAT, C2SAMR.OUT
```

In this example, the file that contains the COBOL source program is C2SAMR.COB, the file that contains the object program is C2SAMR.OBJ, and the file that contains the executable image of the program is C2SAMR.EXE. The sample data file is C2SAMR.DAT. The first ASSIGN statement equates the data file with the logical input file name COB$INPUT, coded, in the COBOL program, in the SELECT statement that specifies the input file (see line 41 in Figure 2.16a). The input file, known as PHONE-SALES-FILE within the program, is being equated to the user's file C2SAMR.DAT, which contains the phone sale records. The second ASSIGN statement equates the output file C2SAMR.OUT with the logical output file name COB$OUTPUT coded in the SELECT statement of the program that specifies the output file (see line 42 in Figure 2.16a). The report produced by the program, known as PHONE-SALES-REPORT within the program, will be stored in the user's file C2SAMR.OUT. Finally, the PRINT statement directs that the compiler-generated listing of the program, C2SAMR.LIS, the sample data file C2SAMR.DAT, and the file C2SAMR.OUT, which contains the report produced by the program, be printed on the high-speed printer identified by QUE=OS315.

Step 6b. Check the Output

The output produced by the commands in the last example is shown in Figure 2.16. Note that the printout contains three files: the compiler-generated listing of the source program (Figure 2.16a), the sample data file that contains the phone sale records (Figure 2.16b), and the output file that contains the phone sales report (Figure 2.16c). This report should be checked for accuracy and completeness. Its format should be checked against the line layouts prepared on the printer spacing chart. The programmer should use a calculator and verify that the results produced on the report are correct for selected entries representing the three possible paths in the program. Some typical questions are the following:

1. Is the report properly titled?
2. Are all column headings provided? Are they spaced properly?
3. Is the data output listed under the appropriate headings?
4. Is the data properly edited with, for example, dollar signs, decimal points, and commas?
5. Are the computed values accurate? In other words, do the mathematical instructions contain the proper arithmetic operations?
6. Does the output contain extraneous characters?

Faulty output requires the programmer to make the necessary corrections in the source program. The program must then be resubmitted for compilation and execution. This debugging cycle must continue until all specifications are met.

Only when all aspects of the program have been scrutinized and deemed to meet the requirements should the programmer conclude that the job is done.

Figure 2.16a Program listing produced by compiler

```
DAILY-PHONE-SALES-REPORT        26-Nov-1993 10:53:32    VAX COBOL V3.2-42                    Page   1
Source Listing                  26-Nov-1993 10:52:51    SCIENCE$DISK:[MA6031.CHAPTER2]C2SAMR.COB;3

           IDENTIFICATION DIVISION.

           PROGRAM-ID.  DAILY-PHONE-SALES-REPORT.

          *****************************************************************
          *                                                               *
          *  AUTHOR.         PAQUETTE.                                    *
          *  DATE WRITTEN:   NOVEMBER 1993.                               *
          *                                                               *
          *  THIS PROGRAM PRODUCES A REPORT LISTING THE PHONE SALES THAT  *
          *  OCCURRED DURING THE DAY.                                     *
          *                                                               *
          *  EACH INPUT RECORD IS A PHONE SALE RECORD THAT CONTAINS THE   *
          *  CUSTOMER NUMBER, THE CATALOG NUMBER, THE UNIT COST OF THE    *
          *  ITEM, AND THE NUMBER OF UNITS SOLD TO THE CUSTOMER.          *
          *                                                               *
          *  FOR EACH PHONE SALE, THE PHONE SALE LINE ON THE REPORT MUST  *
          *  SHOW THE CUSTOMER NUMBER, THE CATALOG NUMBER, THE UNIT COST, *
          *  THE NUMBER OF UNITS SOLD, AND THE NET AMOUNT OF THE SALE.    *
          *  THE VALUES ON THE PHONE SALE LINES ARE LISTED UNDER APPRO-   *
          *  PRIATE COLUMN HEADINGS.                                      *
          *                                                               *
          *  THE AMOUNT OF THE SALE IS COMPUTED AS FOLLOWS: IF THE NUMBER *
          *  OF UNITS SOLD EXCEEDS 100, THE SALE AMOUNT IS DISCOUNTED 20%, *
          *  THAT IS, SALE AMOUNT = NO. OF UNITS * UNIT COST * .8. IF THE *
          *  NUMBER OF UNITS DOES NOT EXCEED 100, THE SALE AMOUNT = NO. OF *
          *  UNITS * UNIT COST.                                           *
          *                                                               *
          *****************************************************************

           ENVIRONMENT DIVISION.

           CONFIGURATION SECTION.

           SOURCE-COMPUTER.  VAX-VMS-8650.
           OBJECT-COMPUTER.  VAX-VMS-8650.

           INPUT-OUTPUT SECTION.

           FILE-CONTROL.
               SELECT PHONE-SALES-FILE     ASSIGN TO COB$INPUT.
               SELECT PHONE-SALES-REPORT   ASSIGN TO COB$OUTPUT.

           DATA DIVISION.

           FILE SECTION.

           FD  PHONE-SALES-FILE
               RECORD CONTAINS 23 CHARACTERS.

           01  PHONE-SALE-RECORD.
               05 I-CUSTOMER-NO      PIC X(4).
               05 FILLER             PIC XX.
               05 I-CATALOG-NO       PIC X(4).
               05 FILLER             PIC XX.
               05 I-UNIT-COST        PIC 999V99.
               05 FILLER             PIC XX.
               05 I-NO-OF-UNITS      PIC 9(4).

           FD  PHONE-SALES-REPORT
               RECORD CONTAINS 132 CHARACTERS.

           01  PRINTLINE             PIC X(132).

           WORKING-STORAGE SECTION.

           01  WS-MORE-RECORDS       PIC XXX.

           01  HEADINGS.
               05 PIC X(15)     VALUE SPACES.
               05 PIC X(15)     VALUE "CUSTOMER NUMBER".
               05 PIC X(8)      VALUE SPACES.
               05 PIC X(14)     VALUE "CATALOG NUMBER".
               05 PIC X(8)      VALUE SPACES.
               05 PIC X(9)      VALUE "UNIT COST".
```

Figure 2.16a continued

```
DAILY-PHONE-SALES-REPORT          26-Nov-1993 10:53:32    VAX COBOL V3.2-42                        Page   2
Source Listing                    26-Nov-1993 10:52:51    SCIENCE$DISK:[MA6031.CHAPTER2]C2SAMR.COB;3

               05 PIC X(8)      VALUE SPACES.
               05 PIC X(15)     VALUE "NUMBER OF UNITS".
               05 PIC X(8)      VALUE SPACES.
               05 PIC X(17)     VALUE "PHONE SALE AMOUNT".
               05 PIC X(15)     VALUE SPACES.

           01  PHONE-SALE-LINE.
               05 FILLER            PIC X(21).
               05 O-CUSTOMER-NO     PIC X(4).
               05 FILLER            PIC X(18).
               05 O-CATALOG-NO      PIC X(4).
               05 FILLER            PIC X(14).
               05 O-UNIT-COST       PIC $ZZ9.99.
               05 FILLER            PIC X(15).
               05 O-NO-OF-UNITS     PIC ZZZ9.
               05 FILLER            PIC X(17).
               05 O-SALE-AMOUNT     PIC $Z(5)9.99.
               05 FILLER            PIC X(18).

           PROCEDURE DIVISION.

           100-PRODUCE-PHONE-SALES-REPORT.
               PERFORM 200-START-UP.
               PERFORM 210-PROCESS-PHONE-SALE-RECORD
                   UNTIL WS-MORE-RECORDS = "NO ".
               PERFORM 220-FINISH-UP.
               STOP RUN.

           200-START-UP.
               OPEN INPUT PHONE-SALES-FILE.
               OPEN OUTPUT PHONE-SALES-REPORT.
               MOVE "YES" TO WS-MORE-RECORDS.
               PERFORM 300-WRITE-REPORT-HEADERS.
               PERFORM 310-READ-PHONE-SALE-RECORD.

           210-PROCESS-PHONE-SALE-RECORD.
               PERFORM 320-COMPUTE-PHONE-SALE-AMOUNT.
               PERFORM 330-PREPARE-PHONE-SALE-LINE.
               PERFORM 310-READ-PHONE-SALE-RECORD.

           220-FINISH-UP.
               CLOSE PHONE-SALES-FILE.
               CLOSE PHONE-SALES-REPORT.

           300-WRITE-REPORT-HEADERS.
               MOVE HEADINGS TO PRINTLINE.
               WRITE PRINTLINE
                   AFTER ADVANCING PAGE.
               MOVE SPACES TO PHONE-SALE-LINE.

           310-READ-PHONE-SALE-RECORD.
               READ PHONE-SALES-FILE RECORD
                   AT END
                       MOVE "NO " TO WS-MORE-RECORDS.

           320-COMPUTE-PHONE-SALE-AMOUNT.
               IF I-NO-OF-UNITS > 100
                   THEN
                       COMPUTE O-SALE-AMOUNT = I-NO-OF-UNITS *
                                               I-UNIT-COST * .8
                   ELSE
                       COMPUTE O-SALE-AMOUNT = I-NO-OF-UNITS *
                                               I-UNIT-COST.

            330-PREPARE-PHONE-SALE-LINE.
                MOVE I-CUSTOMER-NO TO O-CUSTOMER-NO.
                MOVE I-CATALOG-NO TO O-CATALOG-NO.
                MOVE I-UNIT-COST TO O-UNIT-COST.
                MOVE I-NO-OF-UNITS TO O-NO-OF-UNITS.
                MOVE PHONE-SALE-LINE TO PRINTLINE.
                WRITE PRINTLINE
                    AFTER ADVANCING 2 LINES.
```

Figure 2.16b Sample input file

Customer number	Catalog number	Unit cost	Number sold
9999	0001	76750	0600
6001	0003	10500	0016
9009	0007	01000	0013
0046	0012	03800	0082
9551	0013	01250	0040
2150	0036	00999	0003
0008	0064	01510	0001
7752	0369	03999	3500
2200	0400	00100	1200
2201	0401	02199	0003
2203	0403	87500	0002
2205	0405	10000	0001
2207	0407	00300	0610
8611	0408	03650	0009
8612	0409	10130	0004
8614	0501	01299	0016
8617	0503	31000	0001
8618	0506	03100	0063
0105	0561	05915	0045
8619	0583	00250	0027
0061	0600	00900	0010
0700	0601	02800	0002
0701	0602	10001	0001
0702	0603	50000	0005
0703	0604	05112	0010
0704	0605	08999	0003
0705	0606	02500	1001
0706	0607	01289	0004
0707	0608	00500	0013
0708	0609	01389	0102
0709	0611	40000	0007
0711	0613	07189	0003
0713	0615	00125	0017
0715	0617	12589	0003
0717	0619	00360	0100
4121	0801	12009	5000
0037	1010	09999	0005
5213	1012	95000	0002
8515	1022	00399	0120
8633	1022	00399	0005
0530	1025	05500	3010
0003	1030	00099	0041
0210	1034	06760	0031
4203	1091	25099	0002
3200	1200	80050	0002
3201	1201	30000	0001
3203	1203	45000	0004
3205	1205	01199	0011
3207	1207	01500	0004
3209	1209	00500	0017

Note: The column identifiers are printed here only to help identify the data. They are not contained in the data file itself.

Figure 2.16c Phone sales report

CUSTOMER NUMBER	CATALOG NUMBER	UNIT COST	NUMBER OF UNITS	PHONE SALE AMOUNT
9999	0001	$767.50	600	$368400.00
6001	0003	$105.00	16	$ 1680.00
9009	0007	$ 10.00	13	$ 130.00
0046	0012	$ 38.00	82	$ 3116.00
9551	0013	$ 12.50	40	$ 500.00
2150	0036	$ 9.99	3	$ 29.97
0008	0064	$ 15.10	1	$ 15.10
7752	0369	$ 39.99	3500	$111972.00
2200	0400	$ 1.00	1200	$ 960.00

CUSTOMER NUMBER	CATALOG NUMBER	UNIT COST	NUMBER OF UNITS	PHONE SALE AMOUNT
2201	0401	$ 21.99	3	$ 65.97
2203	0403	$875.00	2	$ 1750.00
2205	0405	$100.00	1	$ 100.00
2207	0407	$ 3.00	610	$ 1464.00
8611	0408	$ 36.50	9	$ 328.50
8612	0409	$101.30	4	$ 405.20
8614	0501	$ 12.99	16	$ 207.84
8617	0503	$310.00	1	$ 310.00
8618	0506	$ 31.00	63	$ 1953.00
0105	0561	$ 59.15	45	$ 2661.75
8619	0583	$ 2.50	27	$ 67.50
0061	0600	$ 9.00	10	$ 90.00
0700	0601	$ 28.00	2	$ 56.00
0701	0602	$100.01	1	$ 100.01
0702	0603	$500.00	5	$ 2500.00
0703	0604	$ 51.12	10	$ 511.20
0704	0605	$ 89.99	3	$ 269.97
0705	0606	$ 25.00	1001	$ 20020.00
0706	0607	$ 12.89	4	$ 51.56
0707	0608	$ 5.00	13	$ 65.00
0708	0609	$ 13.89	102	$ 1133.42
0709	0611	$400.00	7	$ 2800.00
0711	0613	$ 71.89	3	$ 215.67
0713	0615	$ 1.25	17	$ 21.25
0715	0617	$125.89	3	$ 377.67
0717	0619	$ 3.60	100	$ 360.00
4121	0801	$120.09	5000	$480360.00
0037	1010	$ 99.99	5	$ 499.95
5213	1012	$950.00	2	$ 1900.00
8515	1022	$ 3.99	120	$ 383.04
8633	1022	$ 3.99	5	$ 19.95
0530	1025	$ 55.00	3010	$132440.00
0003	1030	$ 0.99	41	$ 40.59
0210	1034	$ 67.60	31	$ 2095.60
4203	1091	$250.99	2	$ 501.98
3200	1200	$800.50	2	$ 1601.00
3201	1201	$300.00	1	$ 300.00
3203	1203	$450.00	4	$ 1800.00
3205	1205	$ 11.99	11	$ 131.89
3207	1207	$ 15.00	4	$ 60.00
3209	1209	$ 5.00	17	$ 85.00

Step 7. Assembling the Complete Package

When the program has been completely debugged and the output for sample data has been determined as acceptable, the programmer then prepares a packet containing the following items:

1. Statement of the problem (as originally given)
2. Input and output record layout forms (Figures 2.3 and 2.4)
3. System flowchart (Figure 2.5)
4. Structure chart (Figure 2.6)
5. Program pseudocode (Figure 2.9) or program flowchart (Figure 2.10)
6. Program listing produced by the compiler (Figure 2.16a)
7. Sample input file (Figure 2.16b)
8. Sample program output (Figure 2.16c)

The packet is submitted to the one who requested the program, and this completes the programmer's task.

The Divisions of a COBOL Program

Every COBOL program consists of four divisions. They are always coded in the same order:

1. IDENTIFICATION DIVISION
2. ENVIRONMENT DIVISION
   a. CONFIGURATION SECTION
   b. INPUT-OUTPUT SECTION
3. DATA DIVISION
   a. FILE SECTION
   b. WORKING-STORAGE SECTION
4. PROCEDURE DIVISION

A general explanation of each division follows.

IDENTIFICATION DIVISION

As is obvious from the name, in the IDENTIFICATION DIVISION the program is identified. This is done by coding the name of the program in the PROGRAM-ID paragraph. The program name is user-defined. Though the COBOL standards allow up to 30 characters (letters, digits, and hyphens) for the name, some operating systems do not conform to the standards. Your instructor will let you know the particulars of your system.

Although the PROGRAM-ID paragraph is the only required entry in this division, programmers usually include additional program documentation, such as the name of the author of the program, the date written, and an explanation of the program.

ENVIRONMENT DIVISION

In the ENVIRONMENT DIVISION, the computer environment is clearly specified. In the CONFIGURATION SECTION, the computers are named. One is the SOURCE-COMPUTER. It processes the COBOL source program and, through its compiler, generates the object program (the corresponding machine-language instructions). The other computer is the OBJECT-COMPUTER. It executes the object program. In many cases, the same computer serves both functions.

In the FILE-CONTROL paragraph of the INPUT-OUTPUT SECTION, the hardware needed to handle the input and output files is identified by system-specific code names or by logical names. Each SELECT statement names a file and ASSIGNs it to its particular input or output device. In the sample program, the input file PHONE-SALES-FILE is assigned to the logical input device whose name is COB$INPUT, and the output file PHONE-SALES-REPORT is assigned to the logical output device whose name is COB$OUTPUT. (COB$INPUT and COB$OUTPUT are specific to the VAX operating system.) Note that the file names were first supplied by the programmer on the system flowchart. Within the program, the same file names are first coded in the SELECT statements.

Since the computer hardware varies from one installation to another, the programmer must obtain the specific names of the computers and the input and output devices for her or his own computer system. Your instructor will provide you with the required entries.

DATA DIVISION

In the DATA DIVISION, all the storage areas needed to store the data that must be supplied as input to the computer, all the storage areas needed to store the data that the computer must prepare for output, and all the work areas needed to store constants or intermediate results must be described in detail.

Of the first three divisions, this one is by far the most complex and the most difficult to learn. The DATA DIVISION is separated into sections. Of particular importance to us in this text are the FILE SECTION and the WORKING-STORAGE SECTION.

The task of coding the entries in these two sections is greatly facilitated if proper attention has been given to preparing the layouts of the input records and the output records as specified in steps 1a and 1b of the problem-solving procedure.

FILE SECTION

In the FILE SECTION, there must be a file description paragraph for each file that is accessed by the program. Recall that a file is a set of records; the set of all input records is an input file, and the set of all output records is an output file.

Since the sample program requires two files, there must be two file description (FD) paragraphs, one for the input file PHONE-SALES-FILE, the other for the output file PHONE-SALES-REPORT.

Each paragraph begins with the entry FD in area A, followed by the name of the file in area B and other entries that provide additional file information.

A 01 entry is then coded for each type of record that belongs to the file. The 01 is coded in area A, followed by the name of the record in area B. The 01 line is often followed by other coded lines that provide descriptions of the fields belonging to the record. It is here that the record layouts prepared earlier are particularly useful. They guide the programmer in entering the required coding. Generally, there are as many coded lines following the 01 entry as there are subdivisions of the record being described.

Each of these coded lines contains a level number (05 in this program), a field name, and a PICTURE clause (PIC) that specifies the field size and the type of value that will be stored in the field. The type is specified by code: **X** represents an alphanumeric character, **A** represents an alphabetic character, and **9** represents a numeric character. The number of times the code is repeated indicates the field size, that is, the maximum number of characters that can be stored in the field. For instance, PIC 9999 or PIC 9(4) indicates the field size as 4, and the type of character stored in the field as numeric. (A **V** in the PICTURE indicates the position of an assumed decimal point, as in PIC 999V99. Do you recall the use of the caret in Figure 2.3?)

The FD paragraph for the output file begins with the entry FD in area A and is followed by the name of the file, PHONE-SALES-REPORT, in area B. The 01 entry that follows describes the output record PRINTLINE as a one-field record whose size is 132. This may come as somewhat of a surprise, considering that the printer spacing chart contains the layouts of two types of lines to be printed on the report, HEADINGS and PHONE-SALE-LINE, and neither of these records is even mentioned here. Well, they could be, but we opted to describe them in the WORKING-STORAGE SECTION for reasons that will be explained below.

WORKING-STORAGE SECTION

In the WORKING-STORAGE SECTION, the programmer describes the following:

1. All the data items that are to be assigned constant or initial values
2. All the data items that are needed by the program as intermediate storage areas, but that are not part of either input or output records
3. All record descriptions whose data fields are to be assigned values by using the VALUE clause

The WORKING-STORAGE SECTION of the sample program contains three record descriptions: One is WS-MORE-RECORDS and its size is 3, another is HEADINGS and its size is 132, and the third is PHONE-SALE-LINE and its size is also 132.

In the WORKING-STORAGE SECTION, the VALUE clause can be used to assign initial or constant values to data fields. The availability of the VALUE clause is the main reason for describing the record HEADINGS in this section. All its fields can be assigned constant values. At the appropriate time during the execution of the program, the record as a whole is moved to the output record area PRINTLINE to be printed on the report. Detailed explanations will follow in Chapter 3.

When the COBOL program is compiled, the net effect of the coding in the DATA DIVISION is to set aside storage locations in main memory that can be referenced by specific names. In particular, storage is reserved in input memory for the input record PHONE-SALE-RECORD, in output memory for the

Figure 2.17 Main memory storage areas and data names for the chapter program

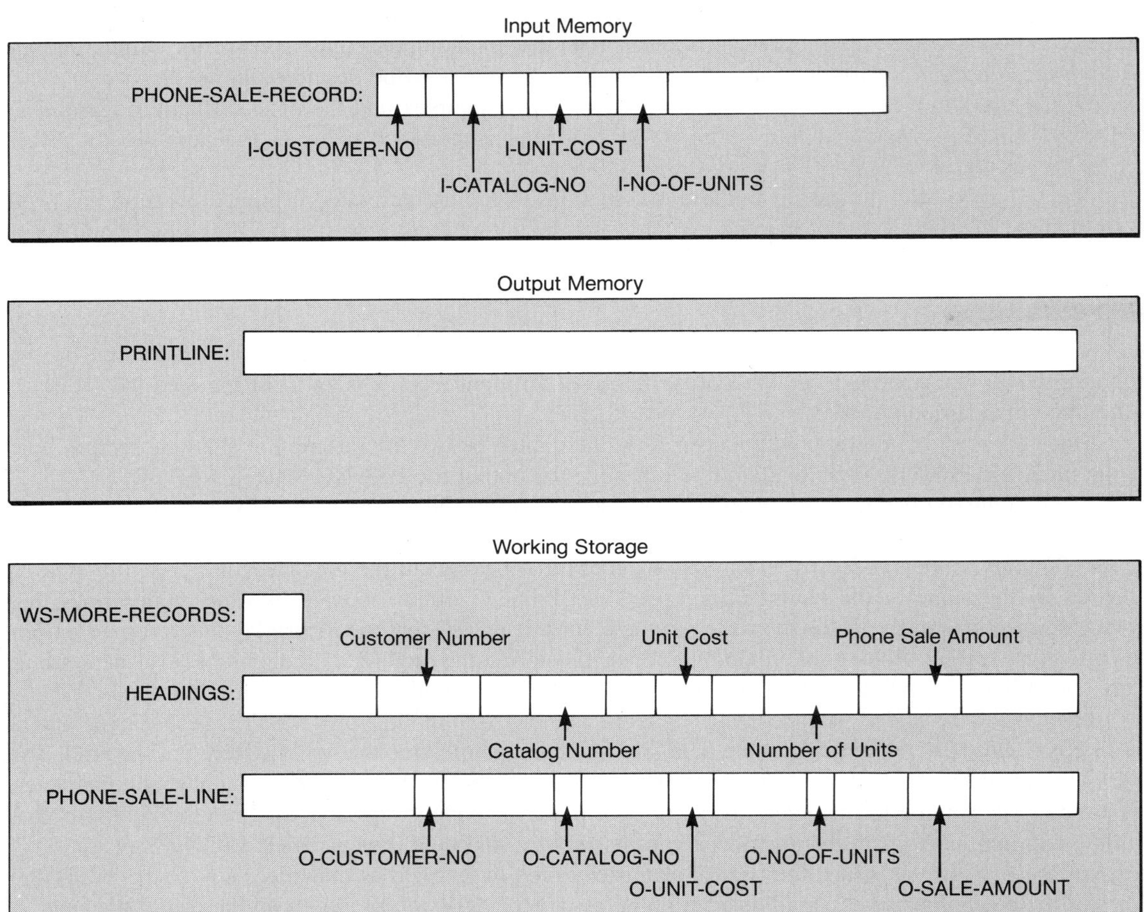

output record PRINTLINE, and in working storage for the flag item WS-MORE-RECORDS and for the records HEADINGS and PHONE-SALE-LINE, as shown in Figure 2.17.

PROCEDURE DIVISION

The PROCEDURE DIVISION must contain all the instructions corresponding to the processing steps specified in the program pseudocode or flowchart. Instructions are grouped into paragraphs. Each paragraph corresponds to a pseudocode paragraph or a flowchart module and is given the name of the paragraph or module. In the sample program, the paragraph names are 100-PRODUCE-PHONE-SALES-REPORT, 200-START-UP, 210-PROCESS-PHONE-SALE-RECORD, 220-FINISH-UP, 300-WRITE-REPORT-HEADERS, 310-READ-PHONE-SALE-RECORD, 320-COMPUTE-PHONE-SALE-AMOUNT, and 330-PREPARE-PHONE-SALE-LINE.

Paragraph names are coded in area A, but all instructions must be coded in area B. If an instruction begun on one line is continued on the next line, the continuation is normally indented for clarity.

The instructions in the PROCEDURE DIVISION are executed in the order in which they occur within a given paragraph. When a PERFORM instruction is encountered, control temporarily leaves the current paragraph, but it returns to execute the next instruction in line as soon as the last instruction in the paragraph specified in the PERFORM is executed. (You will find it very helpful to follow the dotted arrows in the program flowchart shown in Figure 2.10.) In the sample program, control leaves the primary paragraph 100-PRODUCE-PHONE-SALES-REPORT the first time when the instruction PERFORM 200-START-UP is executed. That is, control is transferred to the paragraph 200-START-UP. Here, the files are opened, the flag WS-MORE-RECORDS is set, and then control leaves the paragraph twice, once to execute the statement PERFORM 300-WRITE-REPORT-HEADERS, and then again to execute the statement PERFORM 310-READ-PHONE-SALE-RECORD. Following the execution of the last instruction in 200-START-UP, control returns to the primary paragraph to execute the next instruction: PERFORM 210-PROCESS-PHONE-SALE-RECORD UNTIL WS-MORE-RECORDS = "NO ". During the execution of this statement, control stays within a loop, that is, it is passed back and forth between the primary paragraph and the paragraph 210-PROCESS-PHONE-SALE-RECORD until the flag WS-MORE-RECORDS contains the value "NO ". At that time, control skips out of the loop to execute the next instruction: PERFORM 220-FINISH-UP. Again, control leaves the primary paragraph and, after closing the files, returns to execute the last instruction: STOP RUN. At this point, program execution stops, and control is returned to the operating system.

Within the loop established by the PERFORM-UNTIL statement in the primary paragraph, each time control enters the paragraph 210-PROCESS-PHONE-SALE-RECORD, it is passed to the paragraph 320-COMPUTE-PHONE-SALE-AMOUNT, then to the paragraph 330-PREPARE-PHONE-SALE-LINE, and then to the paragraph 310-READ-PHONE-SALE-RECORD.

After exiting from the program, control is returned to the operating system. At this point, all the records of the input file have been processed, and for each record a corresponding phone sale line has been printed on the report. The task is complete.

Note: You are encouraged to run through the instructions of the PROCEDURE DIVISION with the records of the input file shown in Figure 2.16a. This will help to deepen your understanding of the program.

Basic Logic Structures

It was established by Bohm and Jacopini during the mid-1960s, in their now-famous "Structure Theorem," that any programming logic, regardless of how complex, can be expressed by using only three basic logic structures or combinations of these structures:

1. Simple sequence
2. Selection
3. Iteration

They are presented here briefly, and they will be expanded upon in later chapters.

Note: Do not worry about the COBOL statements that are used as examples in this section. You will study them in detail later.

Simple Sequence

The simplest of the three basic structures is the *simple sequence structure.* It provides for control to pass unconditionally from one process to the next in line, as shown in Figure 2.18.

Each process in the simple sequence structure may consist of a single statement or a whole group of instructions, as might be required in complex computations. The key feature of this structure is the unconditional passing of control from one statement to the next in line.

For instance, the instructions

```
MULTIPLY REGULAR-HRS BY RATE GIVING REGULAR-PAY.
MULTIPLY OVERTIME-HRS BY DOUBLE-RATE GIVING OVERTIME-PAY.
```

illustrate the simple sequence structure. After the first instruction is executed, control automatically passes to the next instruction in line.

Figure 2.18 Basic logic structure: simple sequence

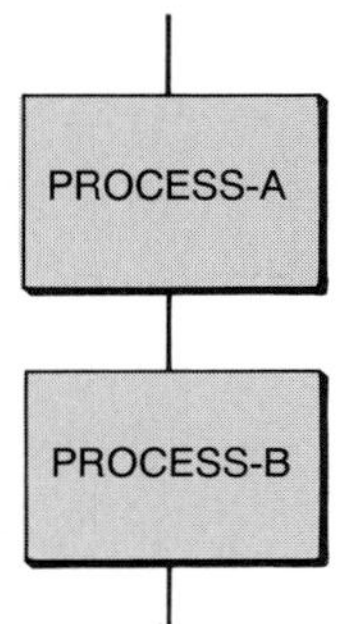

Selection

The *selection structure* begins with the testing of a condition and allows for alternate sets of instructions to be executed, depending on the condition being satisfied or not satisfied, as shown in Figure 2.19. The term IFTHENELSE is often used to refer to this structure, because it describes very clearly the basic logic of the structure: IF the tested condition is satisfied, THEN do what is specified in the THEN clause; otherwise, do what is specified in the ELSE clause.

The flowchart segment shows two branches exiting from the *decision box.* (The decision box is the diamond-shaped symbol.) These are labeled either YES or NO, TRUE or FALSE, ON or OFF, clearly indicating the alternate paths available. The two paths then merge at a connector, providing a single exit from the structure.

In Figure 2.19, the YES path leads to PROCESS-A and the NO path leads to PROCESS-B. Clearly, either PROCESS-A or PROCESS-B will be executed at any one time, never both at the same time; a selection must be made, hence the term selection structure.

The following COBOL statement illustrates the selection structure:

```
IF HOURS IS GREATER THAN 40
    THEN
        COMPUTE TOTAL-PAY = 40 * RATE + (HOURS - 40) * RATE * 2
    ELSE
        COMPUTE TOTAL-PAY = HOURS * RATE.
```

If in fact the number of hours is greater than 40, then the first COMPUTE instruction is executed, but if the number of hours is not greater than 40, then the second COMPUTE instruction is executed.

Two modifications of the selection structure are often encountered. These are shown in Figure 2.20. The logic illustrated by the figure on the left requires some specific instructions to be executed if the test holds true (PROCESS-A), but none if the test is false. The following COBOL statement illustrates this logic:

```
IF HOURS IS GREATER THAN 60
    THEN
        MOVE "HOURS ERROR" TO MESSAGE
    ELSE
        NEXT SENTENCE.
```

The condition being tested is HOURS IS GREATER THAN 60. If it is true, then the MOVE instruction is executed. If the tested condition is false, that is, HOURS is **not** greater than 60, the ELSE clause is executed, and control immediately passes to the sentence that follows the IF statement. (The clause ELSE NEXT SENTENCE is not required by the COBOL compiler; the IF statement can be terminated by placing a period immediately after the MOVE statement, as in the following example:

```
IF HOURS IS GREATER THAN 60
    THEN
        MOVE "HOURS ERROR" TO MESSAGE.
```

You will learn much more about the IF statement later.

■ **Figure 2.19** Basic logic structure: selection

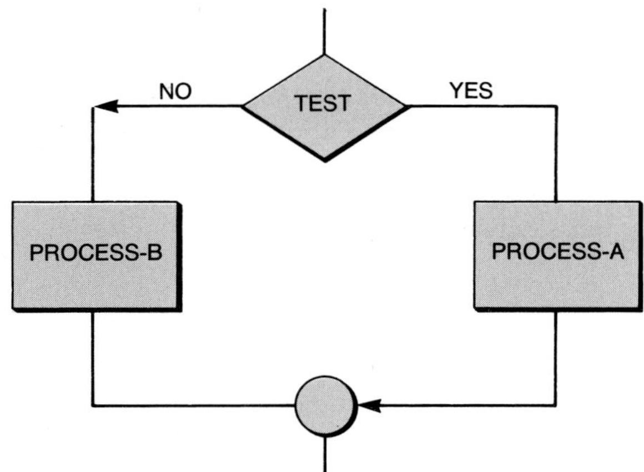

Figure 2.20 Variations of selection structure

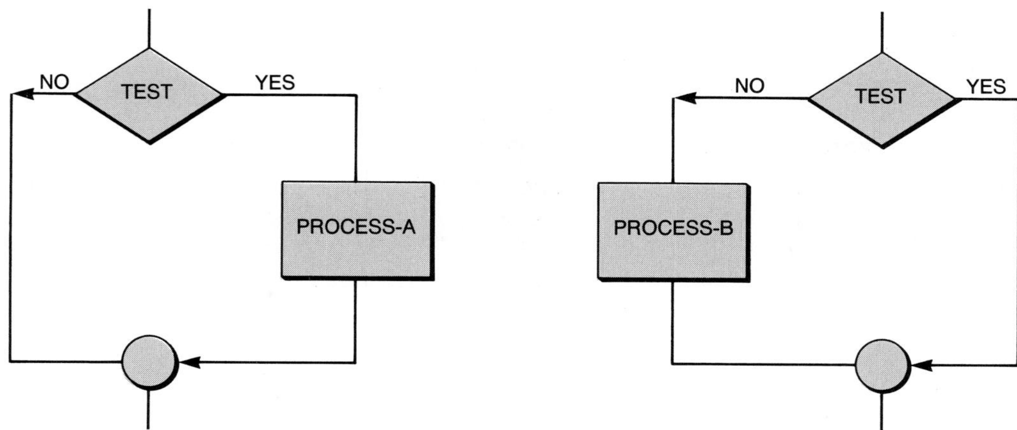

On the other hand, in the figure on the right, the logic requires that PROCESS-B be executed if the tested condition is false; otherwise, control must pass to the next sentence. A sample COBOL statement follows:

```
IF HOURS IS NOT GREATER THAN 60
    THEN
        NEXT SENTENCE
    ELSE
        MOVE "HOURS ERROR" TO MESSAGE.
```

Regardless of which form of the selection structure is used, a condition is tested, and one of two different courses of action is followed depending on the test being true or false.

Iteration

An *iteration structure* is a loop that is executed repeatedly until some exit condition occurs that transfers control out of the structure. There are two different kinds of iteration structures: the DOWHILE iteration and the DOUNTIL iteration. The basic forms are shown in Figure 2.21.

In the DOWHILE structure, it is obvious that the test indicated by the decision box must be performed **before** the instructions in PROCESS-A are executed. For this reason, this structure is also called *pretest iteration.* Depending on the outcome of the test, it is possible that PROCESS-A may not be executed even once. On the other hand, if control is passed to PROCESS-A, then, after the last instruction in PROCESS-A is executed, note that control returns just before the test, so that the test is performed again.

In the DOUNTIL structure, PROCESS-B is executed before the test is encountered; that is, the test is performed **after** PROCESS-B. For this reason, this structure is also called *posttest iteration.* In this structure, PROCESS-B must be executed at least once. Depending on the outcome of the test, PROCESS-B may be executed more than once.

The 1974 version of COBOL supports only the pretest iteration structure. The COBOL statement that implements this structure is PERFORM-UNTIL. As an example, the flowchart for the sample chapter program contains the segment shown in Figure 2.22.

Note that the flag WS-MORE-RECORDS must be tested **before** control is ever passed to the procedure 210-PROCESS-PHONE-SALE-RECORD. The COBOL statement corresponding to this iteration structure is as follows:

```
PERFORM 210-PROCESS-PHONE-SALE-RECORD
    UNTIL WS-MORE-RECORDS = "NO ".
```

Although it may not be perfectly clear from the format of the PERFORM-UNTIL statement that the condition in the UNTIL clause must be tested before sending control to the procedure specified in the PERFORM, that is in fact what occurs.

Figure 2.21 Basic logic structure: iteration

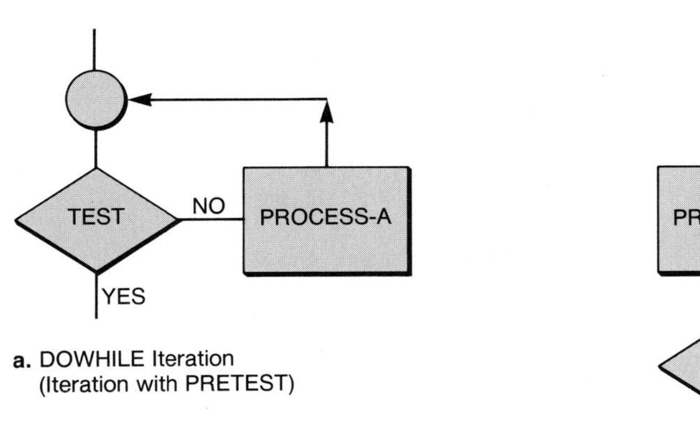

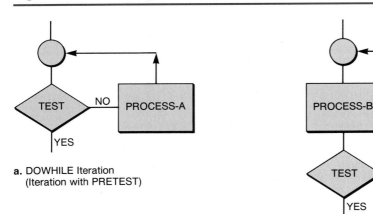

a. DOWHILE Iteration (Iteration with PRETEST)

b. DOUNTIL Iteration (Iteration with POSTTEST)

Figure 2.22 Example of PRETEST iteration

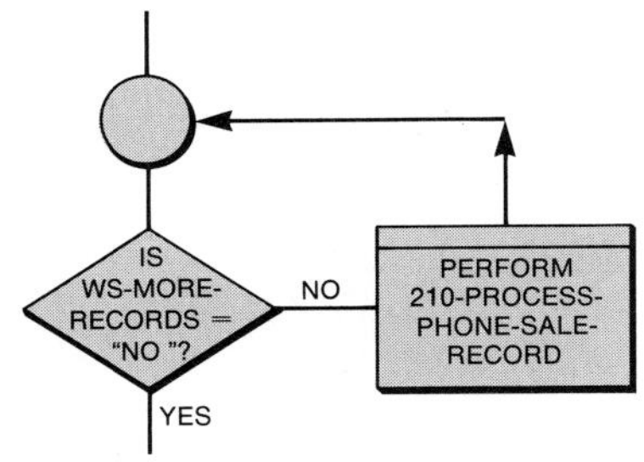

Figure 2.23 Example of POSTTEST iteration

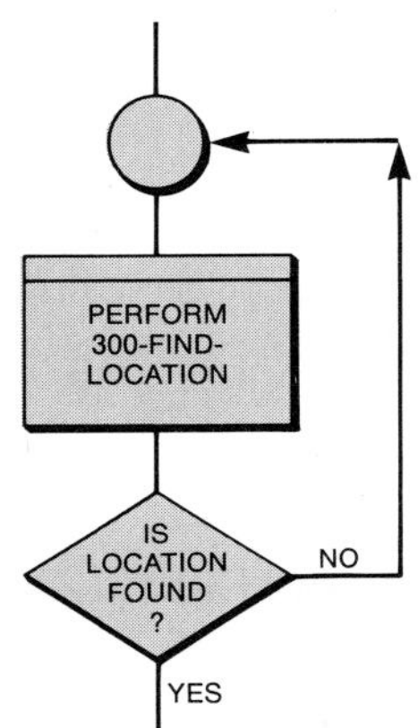

The latest version of COBOL (1985), which supports both forms of the iteration structure, removes any ambiguity. The format of the PERFORM statement has been enhanced to allow either of the following statements:

```
(DOWHILE or         1.  PERFORM procedure-name WITH TEST BEFORE
 pretest)                       UNTIL condition.

(DOUNTIL or         2.  PERFORM procedure-name WITH TEST AFTER
 posttest)                 UNTIL condition.
```

Note the explicit use of the phrases WITH TEST BEFORE and WITH TEST AFTER. In the chapter program, the statement

```
PERFORM 210-PROCESS-PHONE-SALE-RECORD WITH TEST BEFORE
    UNTIL WS-MORE-RECORDS = "NO "
```

could be used to code the logic represented by the flowchart segment in Figure 2.22. The placement of the test is made obvious.

Figure 2.23 illustrates the posttest iteration structure. The procedure 300-FIND-LOCATION is executed once. Upon returning from the procedure, the test is performed to determine if the location has been found. If it has, then an exit from the iteration process occurs. If it has not, control returns to the procedure 300-FIND-LOCATION again.

The example below shows the coding of this structure in the 1974 version of COBOL and in the 1985 version. Note that the use of the phrase WITH TEST AFTER now permits the programmer to code the structure directly and simply.

```
PERFORM 300-FIND-LOCATION.              PERFORM 300-FIND-LOCATION WITH TEST AFTER
PERFORM 300-FIND-LOCATION                         UNTIL LOCATION-IS-FOUND.
          UNTIL LOCATION-IS-FOUND.

          In 1974 COBOL                                In 1985 COBOL
```

Note: Whenever a programmer determines that an iteration structure is needed in a program, he or she must include within the procedure a mechanism that ultimately satisfies the condition being tested. Otherwise, an endless loop will result, and the program will either "hang" or "abort," depending on how the operating system is designed to handle such situations.

Combinations of the Three Simple Structures

In most programs, the simple structures explained above are usually used in combinations. A process box in any one of the structures may itself be replaced by one of the simple structures. For instance, in Figure 2.24, PROCESS-A of the simple sequence structure is replaced by a selection structure, and PROCESS-B is replaced by a pretest iteration structure.

Figure 2.25 shows PROCESS-D of Figure 2.24 replaced by a selection structure and PROCESS-E of Figure 2.24 replaced by a simple sequence structure. It can be seen quite readily that the three simple structures used in combinations can represent rather complex logic, and, conversely, complex logic can also be broken down into the three basic logic building blocks: simple sequence, selection, and iteration.

Note that each basic structure, whether it is used by itself, is nested within another, or contains other nested structures, has exactly one point of entry and one point of exit. No branching is allowed into the

Figure 2.24 Basic logic structures used in sequence in a flowchart segment

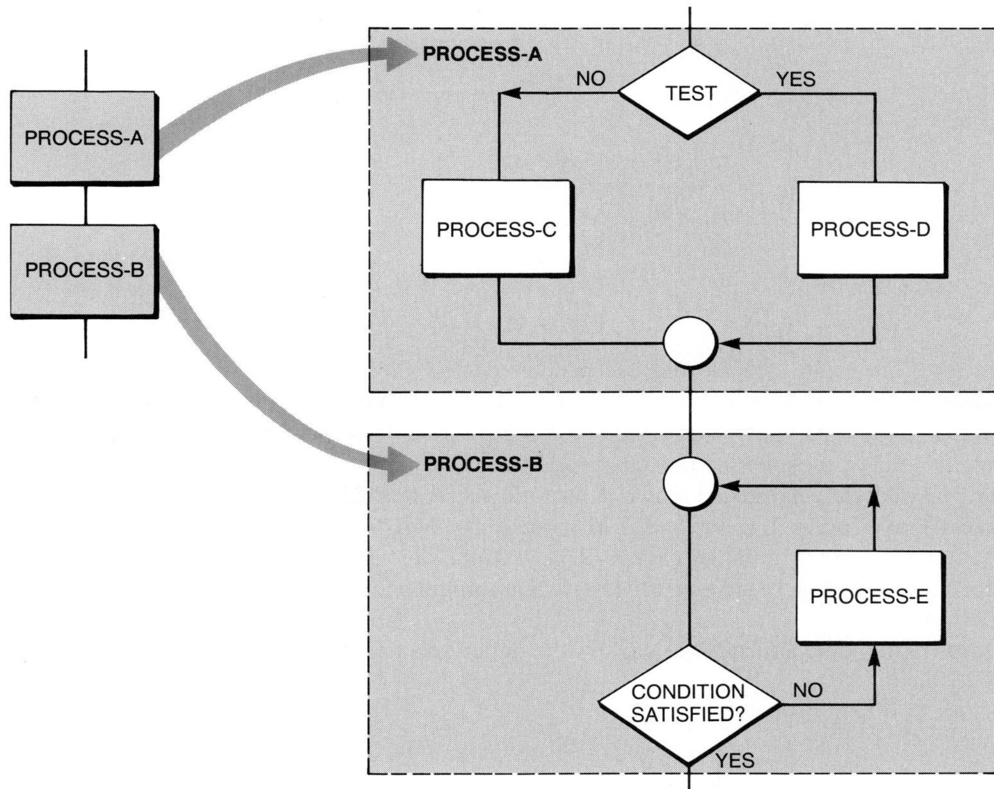

■ **Figure 2.25** Nested basic logic structures used in a flowchart segment

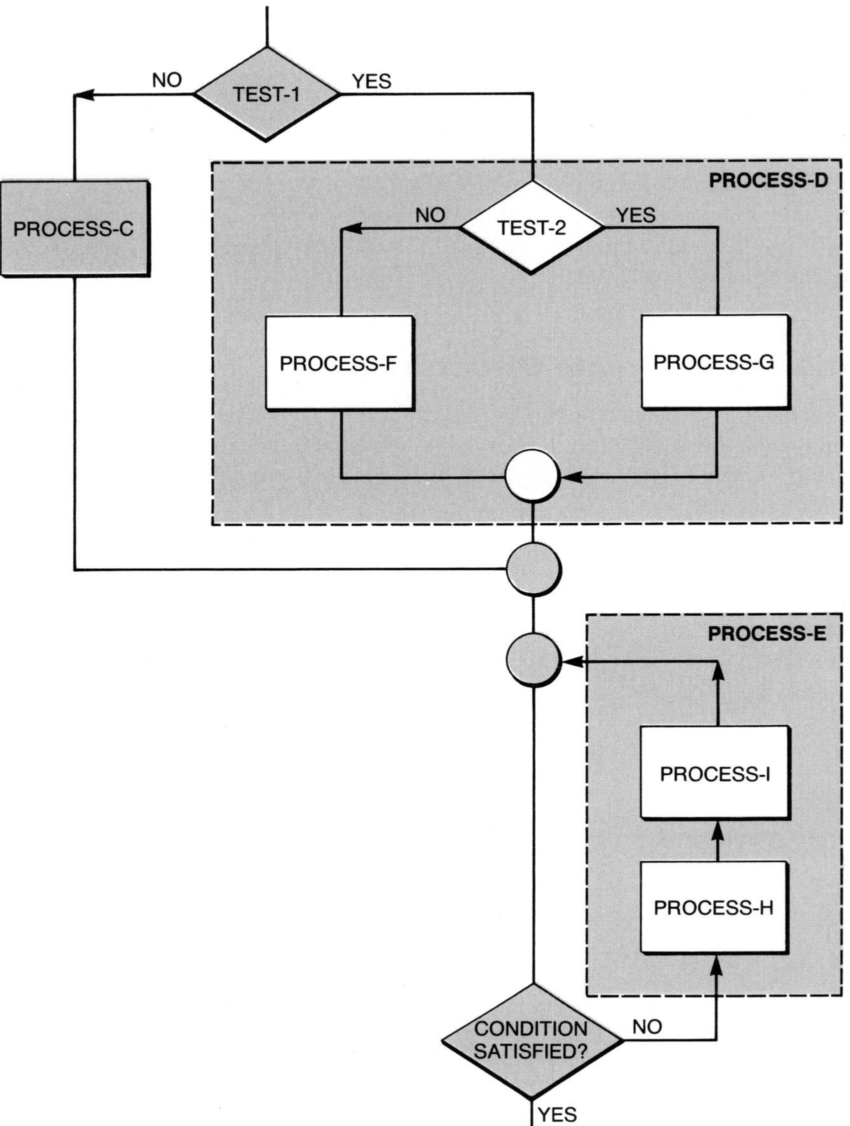

middle of a structure, nor is an exit allowed except after control flow has gone through the complete structure. A program in which control proceeds from the very first structure to the last structure through all intervening structures by entering and exiting each structure properly is called a *proper program.*

To illustrate this point, consider the flowchart in Figure 2.26.

Dotted-line *process boxes* have been drawn in each flowchart module. It should be clear that control flows from Process-1 to Process-2 to Process-3 in module 100-MAIN-ROUTINE. While control is in Process-2, it is sent to the second-level module 200-READ-WRITE in which it proceeds from Process-4 to Process-5 to Process-6 and then returns to Process-2. The program corresponding to this flowchart is therefore a proper program.

Can you identify the logic structures in each of the dotted process boxes in Figure 2.26?

■ **Figure 2.26** Combinations of the basic logic structures in a program flowchart

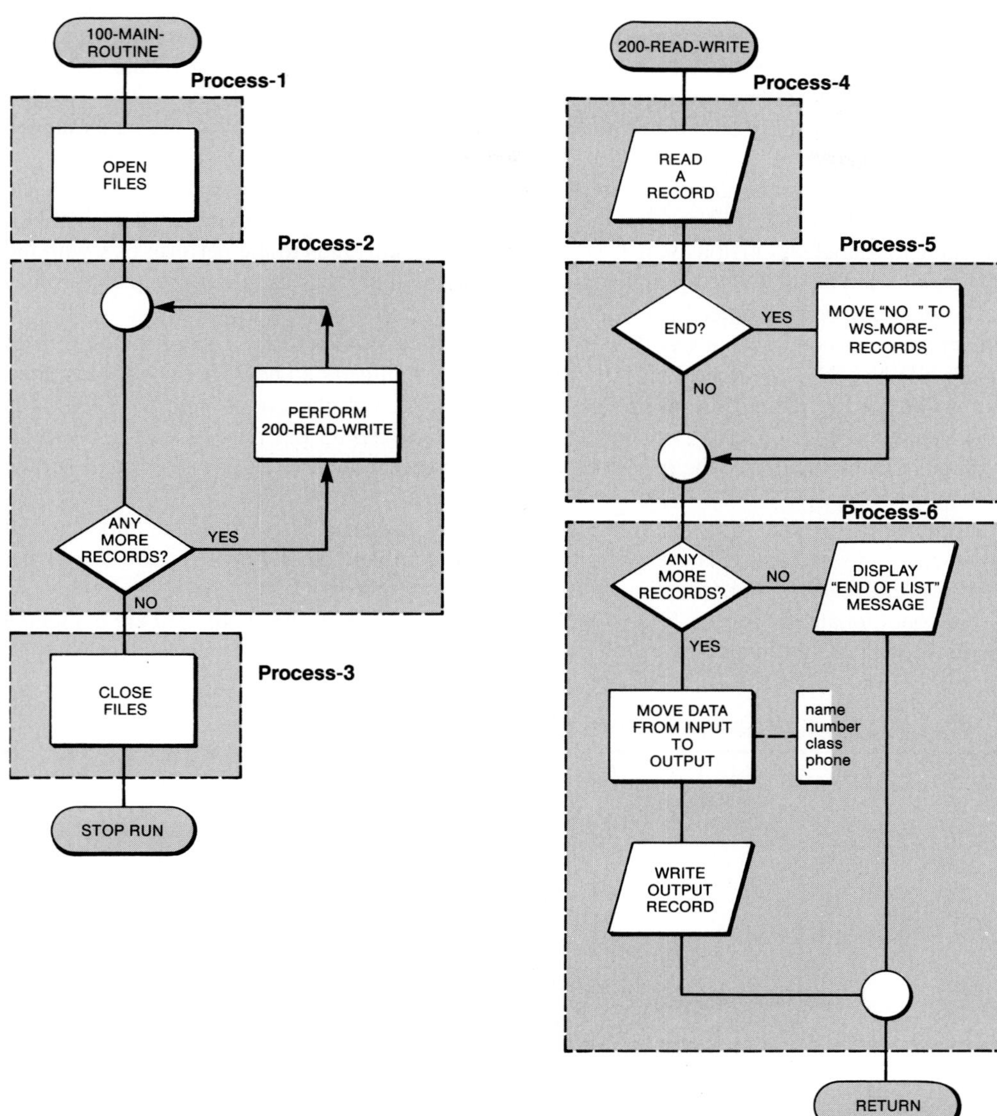

The Case Structure

The simple selection structure presented earlier is directly applicable only in those cases where there are only two possible outcomes. If, for instance, there are four possible outcomes, then the programmer must resort to "nested tests" to eventually test all possibilities. A simple example is shown in Figure 2.27.

The coding corresponding to the flowchart segment of Figure 2.27 is shown in Figure 2.28.

Note: You are not expected to fully understand the IF-ELSE statement at this point. It will be explained in detail in Chapter 7.

The logic of Figure 2.27 can be greatly simplified and clarified by using what is known as the *case structure*. It is illustrated in Figure 2.29. Note that there are five branches exiting from the decision symbol, and each branch is clearly labeled. Obviously, if I-REGION = 1, the path leads to the perform box with the entry PERFORM 300-UPDATE-REGION-1, and similar paths are available for the other acceptable values of I-REGION. The branch labeled "other" leads to an error-processing module.

To implement a case structure using COBOL-74, the programmer could use the coding in Figure 2.28 or the GOTO/DEPENDING ON statement. This last option will not be illustrated here for two reasons: first, it is too complex to be readily understood at this early stage, and second, the use of multiple GOTOs is frowned upon by structured COBOL programmers. Fortunately, COBOL-85 has introduced the EVALUATE statement specifically to streamline the implementation of the case structure. The new coding is shown in Figure 2.30.

The case structure is not one of the simple logic structures; rather, it is the result of the repeated application of the selection structure. It is presented here only to complete the set of logic constructs that programmers find useful in developing structured programs.

Note: The nested conditionals in Figure 2.28 and the EVALUATE statement in Figure 2.30 are explained in detail in Chapter 7. You are not expected to fully understand them at this early stage.

Figure 2.27 Example of nested selection structures

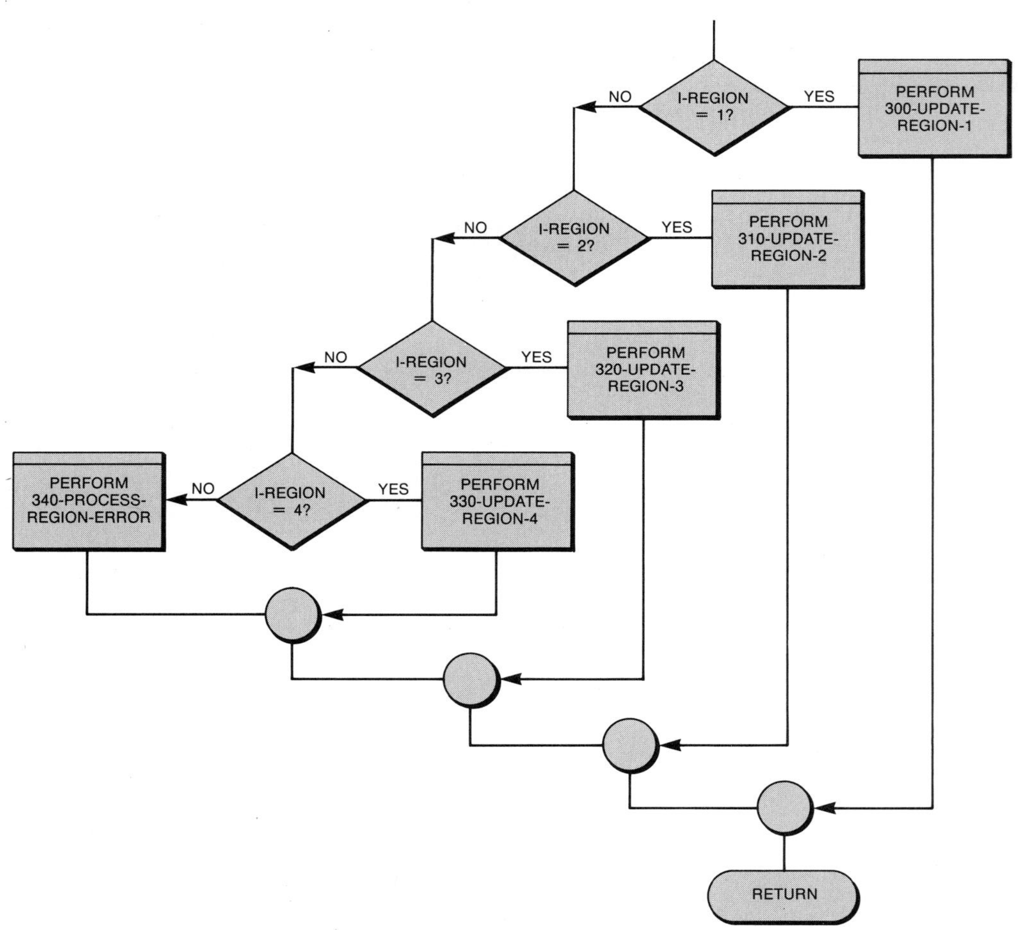

Figure 2.28 Coding of nested conditionals

```
IF I-REGION = 1
      THEN
            PERFORM 300-UPDATE-REGION-1
      ELSE
            IF I-REGION = 2
                  THEN
                        PERFORM 310-UPDATE-REGION-2
                  ELSE
                        IF I-REGION = 3
                              THEN
                                    PERFORM 320-UPDATE-REGION-3
                              ELSE
                                    IF I-REGION = 4
                                          THEN
                                                PERFORM 330-UPDATE-REGION-4
                                          ELSE
                                                PERFORM 340-PROCESS-REGION-ERROR.
```

Figure 2.29 Flowchart of the case structure

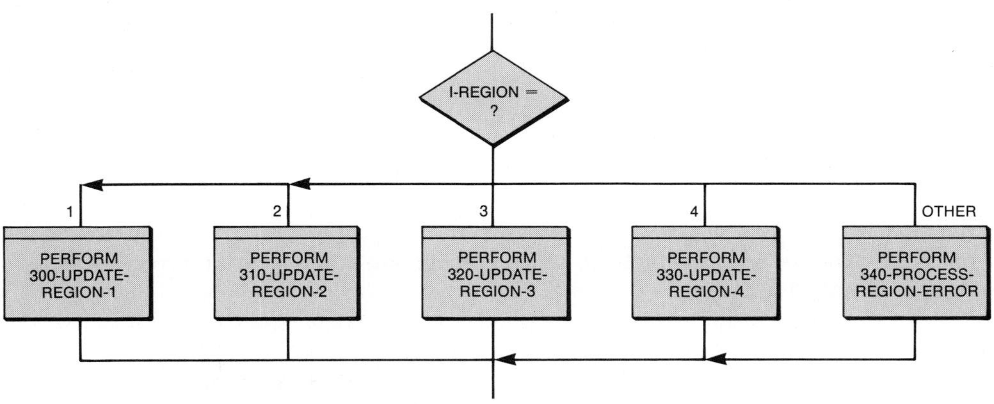

Figure 2.30 Sample use of the new EVALUATE statement

```
EVALUATE TRUE
    WHEN I-REGION = 1, PERFORM 300-UPDATE-REGION-1
    WHEN I-REGION = 2, PERFORM 310-UPDATE-REGION-2
    WHEN I-REGION = 3, PERFORM 320-UPDATE-REGION-3
    WHEN I-REGION = 4, PERFORM 330-UPDATE-REGION-4
    WHEN OTHER, PERFORM 340-PROCESS-REGION-ERROR.
```

Important Terms in Chapter 2

area A
area B
basic logic structure
case structure
COBOL coding form
COBOL reserved word
compiling a program
CONFIGURATION SECTION
continuation area
creating a data file
DATA DIVISION
data field
data field name
data file
debugging
decision box
descriptive name
design phase
design implementation phase
ENVIRONMENT DIVISION
EOF test
file
file name
FILE SECTION
flow lines
functional module
IDENTIFICATION DIVISION
input file
INPUT-OUTPUT SECTION
input record
input record layout
iteration structure
iteration test
keying a program into a file
main control paragraph
modular structure
output record
output record layout
perform box
posttest iteration
prefix I-
prefix O-
prefix WS-
pretest iteration
primary module
printer spacing chart
problem-solving procedure
PROCEDURE DIVISION
process box
production version
program flowchart
program pseudocode
program walk-through
proper program
record name
running a flowchart trace
running a program
second-level module
selection structure
sequence area
simple sequence structure
structure chart
structure chart module
system flowchart
terminal symbol
trace
user-defined name
WORKING-STORAGE SECTION

Exercises

1. Identify by name the two phases of the problem-solving procedure. What constitutes the first phase? What constitutes the second phase?

2. The manager of Nature Foods wants a payroll listing for the current week. The input file contains a record for each employee. Each record has been prepared as follows:

cc 1–9	Employee number
cc 11–30	Employee name
cc 31–32	Number of hours worked per day
cc 34	Number of days worked for the week
cc 40–43	Rate of pay per hour (dollars and cents)

The payroll listing must contain the employee number and name, the number of hours worked per day, the number of days worked during the week, the hourly rate of pay, and the wages earned during the week.

a. Name all the items that must be printed on the report.

b. Of the items on the printed report,

i. Which are obtained from the employee's input record?

ii. Which must be computed?

c. Show the layout of the data on the blank input record form shown in Figure 2.31. Draw full vertical lines to separate the record into data fields, and give an appropriate name to each field. Give an appropriate name to the input record.

Figure 2.31 Input record layout form

Record Layout Form

1 2 3 4 5 6 7 8 9 10 11 12 13 14 15 16 17 18 19 20 21 22 23 24 25 26 27 28 29 30 31 32 33 34 35 36 37 38 39 40 41 42 43 44 45 46 47 48 49 50 51 52 53 54 55 56 57 58 59 60 61 62 63 64 65 66 67 68 69 70 71 72 73 74 75 76 77 78 79 80

Record Name: ______________________

Figure 2.32 Printer spacing chart

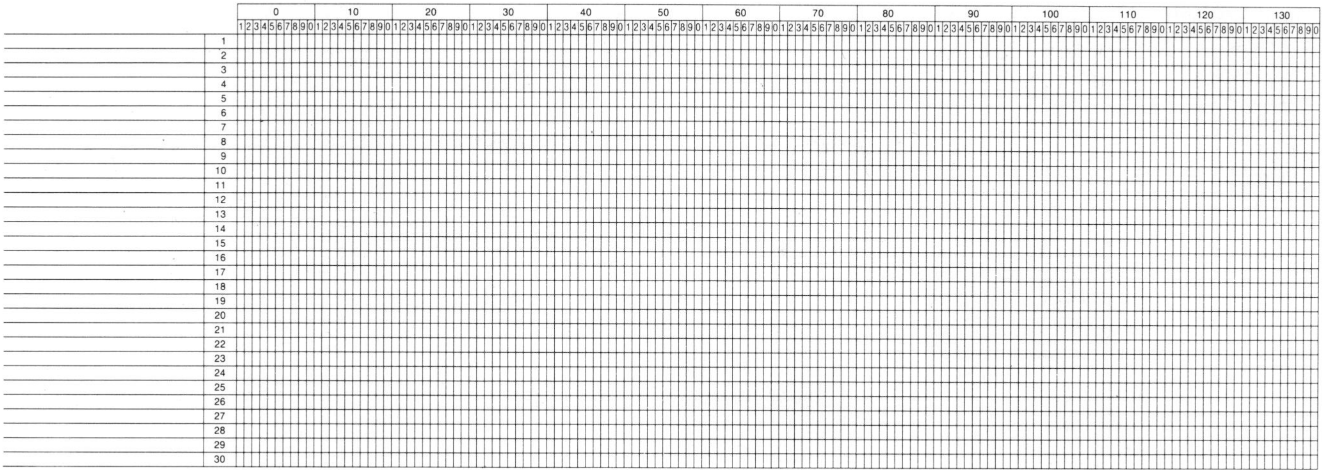

d. Assume that the payroll report is to be titled "Nature Foods Payroll Report." Prepare a title line, a headings line, and a pay line on a printer spacing chart like the one in Figure 2.32. Use the following headings: EMPLOYEE NUMBER, EMPLOYEE NAME, HOURS PER DAY, DAYS PER WEEK, PAY RATE, GROSS PAY. For the pay line, show each data field as a string of Xs, appropriately centered under the header. Give an appropriate name to each data field, then give a name to each record.

3. Refer to exercise 2 above. A COBOL program will have to be written to direct the computer to produce the payroll report.

a. Give a name to the input file.
b. Give a name to the output file.
c. Prepare a system flowchart for the job.
d. Identify the functional components of the program, and prepare a structure chart. (Use the chapter program as a guide.)

4. A professor in a programming course (18253—COBOL Programming) wants a program that will produce a grade report for the term. For each student, an input record is prepared as follows:

cc 1–7	Student ID number
cc 10–30	Student name
cc 32–34	Program-1 grade
cc 36–38	Program-2 grade
cc 40–42	Program-3 grade
cc 44–46	Program-4 grade
cc 48–50	Program-5 grade
cc 52–54	Midterm exam grade
cc 56–58	Final exam grade

The report must show the above information for each student, along with the course grade for the term. The course grade is determined as follows:

The five programs count for 50 percent of the course grade.
The two exams count for 50 percent of the course grade.

The system flowchart, input record layout, printer spacing chart, and structure chart appear in Figure 2.33. Answer the questions that follow.

a. What name is assigned to the input file? to the output file?
b. What name is assigned to the input record?
c. How many input records must be contained in the input file?
d. How many different types of output records are there on the printer spacing chart? Name them.
e. What is the name given to the output record that will contain a student's course grade?
f. How many printed lines should there be on the grade report?
g. What are the names assigned to the data fields of the input record?
h. What are the names assigned to the data fields of the output record GRADE-LINE?
i. What is the size of the input record data field I-STUDENT-ID?
j. What is the size of the output record data field O-STUDENT-ID?

■ Figure 2.33 Analytical information for exercise 4

System Flowchart

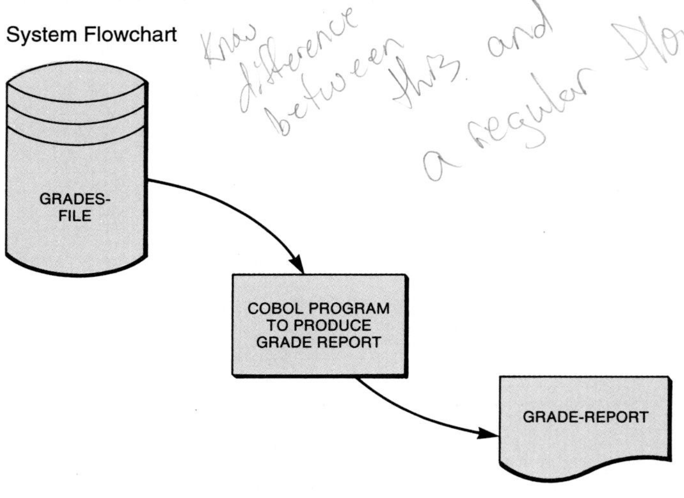

Record Layout Form

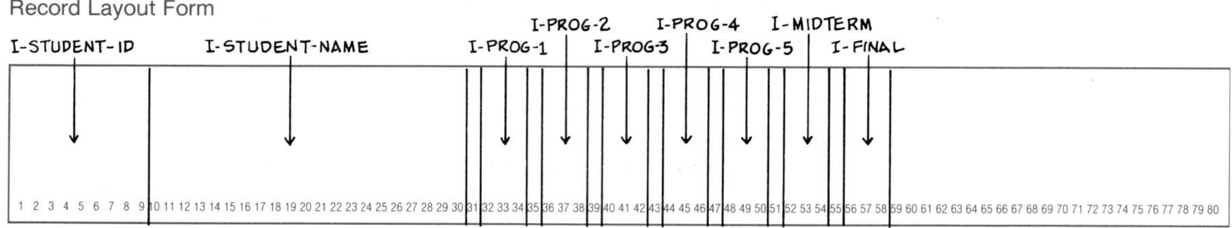

Record Name: STUDENT-RECORD

Printer Spacing Chart

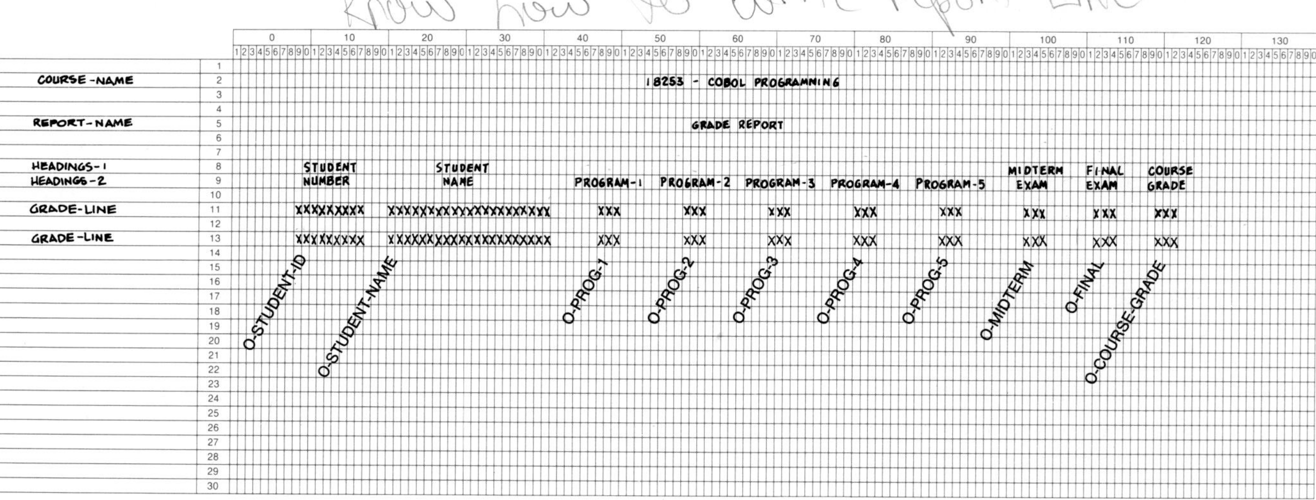

k. What is the size of the input record data field I-STUDENT-NAME?
l. What is the size of the output record data field O-STUDENT-NAME?
m. Which columns of the input record contain the midterm exam grade?
n. Which print positions of the output record GRADE-LINE contain the midterm exam grade?
o. Which of the output records must be printed first? second? third? fourth? fifth? sixth? tenth?
p. What functional subcomponents (modules) are required to produce the grade report?
q. In Figure 2.34, the program pseudocode that corresponds to the structure chart on page 79 has been partially written. Fill in the remaining blanks.
r. The program flowchart is shown in Figure 2.35. Fill in the blank flowchart symbols.
s. Generally, the PROCEDURE DIVISION contains as many paragraphs of instructions as there are modules in the structure chart, or the program pseudocode, or the program flowchart. So, the

Structure Chart

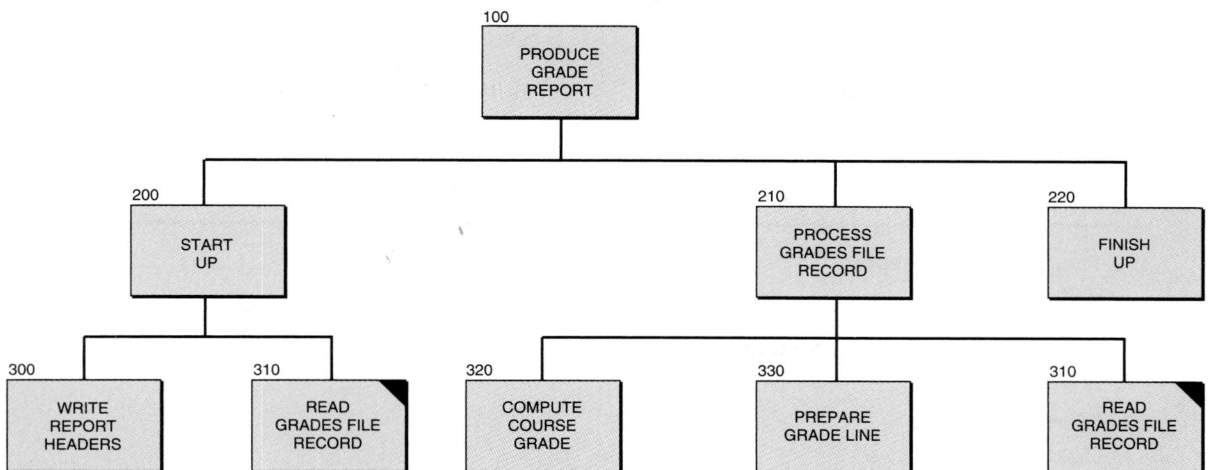

PROCEDURE DIVISION for this program will contain how many paragraphs? What names will be used as paragraph names?

t. In the following program segment, some key names have been omitted. In their place is a description within brackets ([ ]) of the kind of entry needed. Supply the appropriate entry by using information from above. (Names must be single words, so hyphenate as necessary.)

```
A   B
IDENTIFICATION DIVISION.
PROGRAM-ID.  PRODUCE-GRADE-REPORT.
ENVIRONMENT DIVISION.
CONFIGURATION SECTION.
SOURCE-COMPUTER.  VAX-VMS-8650.
OBJECT-COMPUTER.  VAX-VMS-8650.
INPUT-OUTPUT SECTION.
FILE-CONTROL.
    SELECT  [input-file name]   ASSIGN TO COB$INPUT.
    SELECT  [output-file name]  ASSIGN TO COB$OUTPUT.
DATA DIVISION.
FILE SECTION.
FD  [input-file name]
    RECORD CONTAINS 80 CHARACTERS.
01  [input-record name].
    05  I-STUDENT-ID            PIC X(9).
    05  [data-field name]       PIC X(21).
    05  FILLER                  PIC X.
    05  I-PROG-1                PIC 999.
    05  FILLER                  PIC X.
    05  [data-field name]       PIC 999.
    05  FILLER                  PIC X.
    05  I-PROG-3                PIC 999.
    05  FILLER                  PIC X.
    05  [data-field name]       PIC 999.
    05  FILLER                  PIC X.
    05  I-PROG-5                PIC 999.
    05  FILLER                  PIC X.
    05  [data-field name]       PIC 999.
    05  FILLER                  PIC X.
    05  [data-field name]       PIC 999.
    05  FILLER                  PIC X(22).
FD  [output-file name]
    RECORD CONTAINS 132 CHARACTERS.
01  PRINTLINE                   PIC X(132).
WORKING-STORAGE SECTION.
01  GRADE-LINE.
    05  FILLER                  PIC X(8).
    05  O-STUDENT-ID            PIC X(9).
    05  FILLER                  PIC XXX.
    05  [data-field name]       PIC X(21).
    05  FILLER                  PIC X(6).
    05  [data-field name]       PIC ZZ9.
    05  FILLER                  PIC X(8).
    05  O-PROG-2                PIC ZZ9.
    05  [COBOL reserved word]   PIC X(8).
    05  [data-field name]       PIC ZZ9.
    05  FILLER                  PIC X(8).
```

```
05  [data-field name]      PIC ZZ9.
05  FILLER                 PIC X(8).
05  [data-field name]      PIC ZZ9.
05  [COBOL reserved word]  PIC X(7).
05  [data-field name]      PIC ZZ9.
05  [COBOL reserved word]  PIC X(6).
05  [data-field name]      PIC ZZ9.
05  [COBOL reserved word]  PIC X(6).
05  [data-field name]      PIC ZZ9.
05  [COBOL reserved word]  PIC X(10).
```

Figure 2.34 Program pseudocode for exercise 4

100-Produce-Grade-Report.

1. Perform 200-Start-Up.
2. Perform 210-Process-Grades-File-Record until no more input records.
3. Perform 220- Finish-Up ________.
4. Stop the run.

200-Start-Up.

1. Open the Files ____.
2. Set the end-of-file flag WS-MORE-RECORDS to no ____.
3. Write the header ________.
4. Perform 310-Read-Grades-File-Record.

210-Process-Sales-File-Record.

1. Perform compute grade average ________.
2. Perform ________.
3. Perform read files ________.

220-Finish-Up.

1. Close the files ____.

300-Write-Report-Headers.

1. Move the Course Name record to the output area Printline.
2. After advancing to the top of a new page, write the output record Printline.
3. Move the Report Name record to the output area Printline.
4. ________.
5. Move the Headings-1 record to the output area Printline.
6. ________.
7. ________.
8. ________.
9. Clear the record area Grade-line.

310-Read-Grades-File-Record.

1. Read an input student-record.
2. Test for end-of-file record; if EOF record reached, ________.

320-Compute-Grade-Average.

1. Compute program-average = (input program-1 grade + input program-2 grade + input program-3 grade + input program-4 grade + input program-5 grade) divided by 5.
2. Compute exam-average = (input midterm-exam grade + input final-exam grade) divided by 2.
3. Compute the Grade-line course grade = (program-average + exam-average) divided by 2.

330-Prepare-Grade-Line.

1. Move input student-number to Grade-line student-number.
2. Move input student-name to ________.
3. Move ________ to Grade-line program-1 grade.
4. Move ________.
5. Move ________.
6. Move ________.
7. Move input program-5 grade to Grade-line program-5 grade.
8. Move input ________.
9. Move input ________.
10. Move the Grade-line to the output area Printline.
11. After advancing 2 lines, write the output record ________.

■ **Figure 2.35** Program flowchart for exercise 4

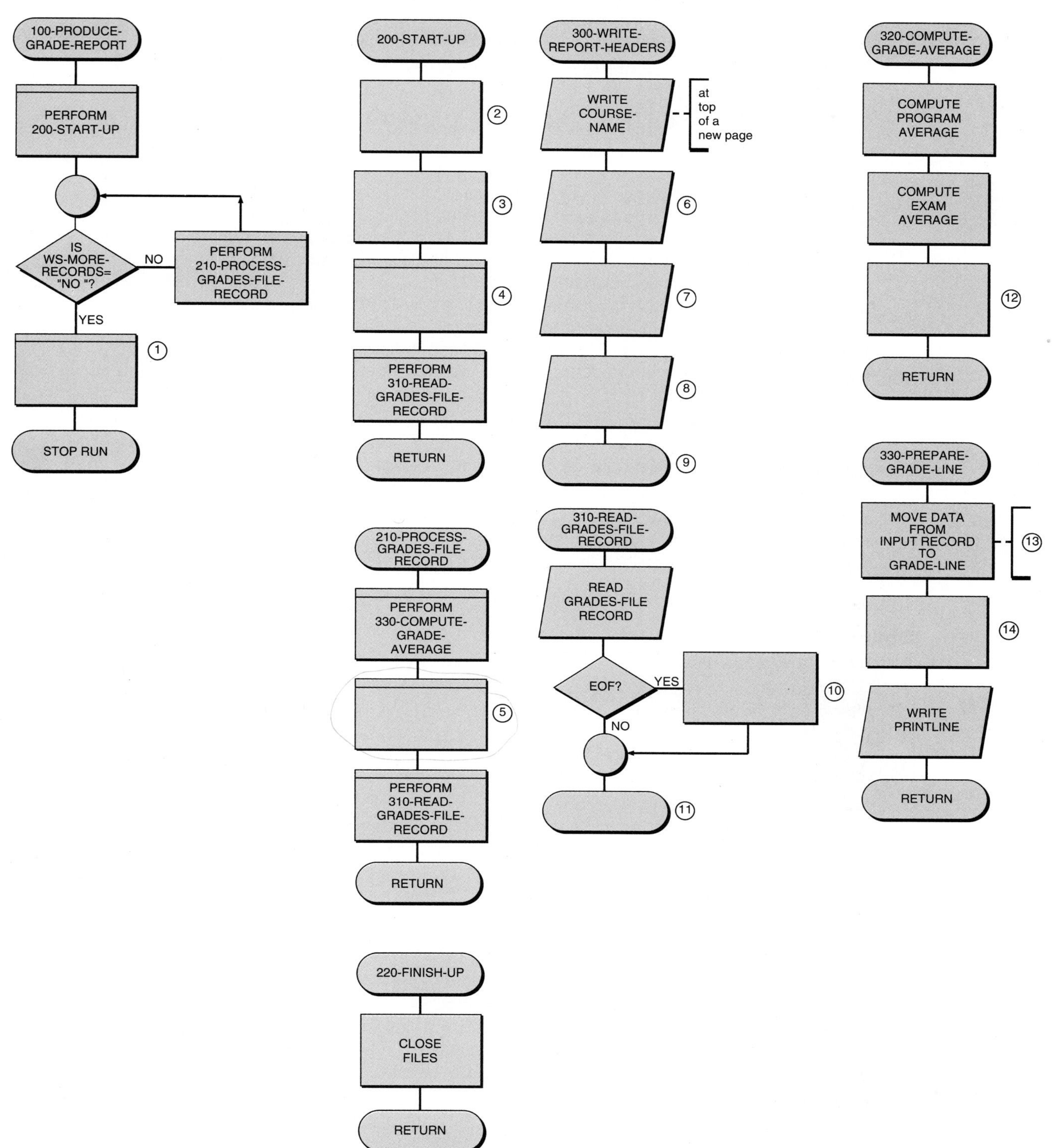

5. The Acme Supply Company wants the data processing department to produce a daily report listing the over-the-counter (OTC) cash sales and the total of the cash sales for the day. The record for each OTC cash sale contains the item number, the number of units sold, the unit retail price, and the amount of the sale. The computer report must list the above information for each sale and end with a last entry showing the total of the cash sales for the day. The system flowchart is shown in Figure 2.36.
   a. Give a name to the input file.
   b. Give a name to the output file.
   The input record layout form is shown in Figure 2.37.
   c. Give a name to the input record.
   d. Give a name to the data field that contains the amount of the sale.
   The printer spacing chart is shown in Figure 2.38.
   e. Give an appropriate name to each type of printed line needed on the report.
   f. Give a name to each data field shown on line 12 of the printer spacing chart.
   g. Give a name to the field that will print the total of the OTC cash sales.
   The structure chart is shown in Figure 2.39.
   h. Assign a number to each module in the second row of the structure chart.
   i. Assign a number to each module in the third row of the structure chart.
   j. Insert descriptive entries in each blank module in the structure chart.
   k. Write the program pseudocode to produce the OTC sales report, or design the program flowchart.

6. The management of ABC Hardware Company wants its data processing department to prepare an inventory report. The input record layout and the printer spacing chart are shown in Figure 2.40. For each inventory item, the new balance is computed as follows:

   new balance = old balance + receipts + returns − issues

   a. Design the system flowchart.
   b. Design the structure chart.
   c. Write the program pseudocode, or design the program flowchart.

Figure 2.36 System flowchart for exercise 5

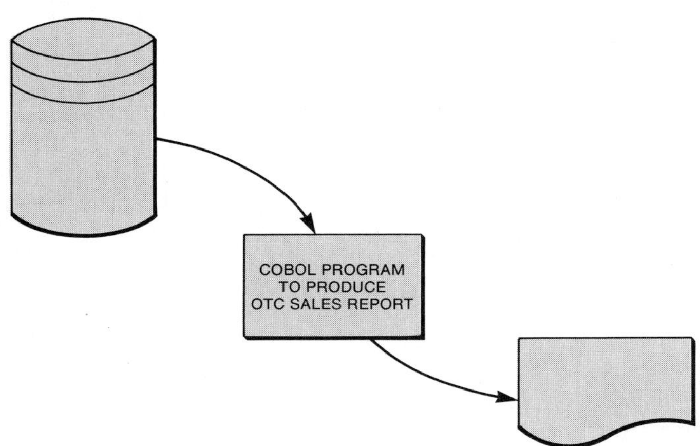

Figure 2.37 Input record layout form for exercise 5

Record Layout Form

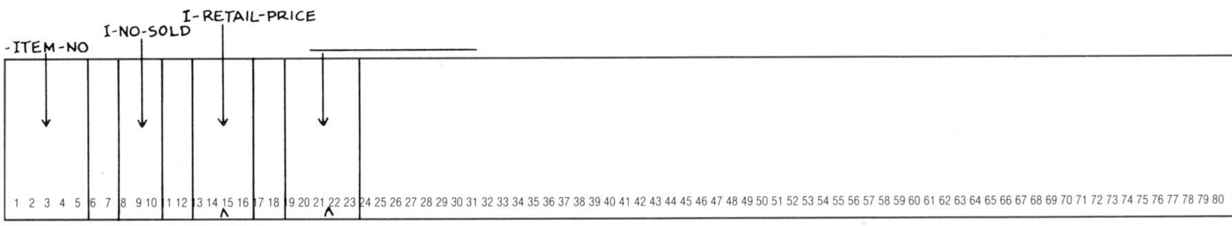

Record Name: ______________________

■ **Figure 2.38** Printer spacing chart for exercise 5

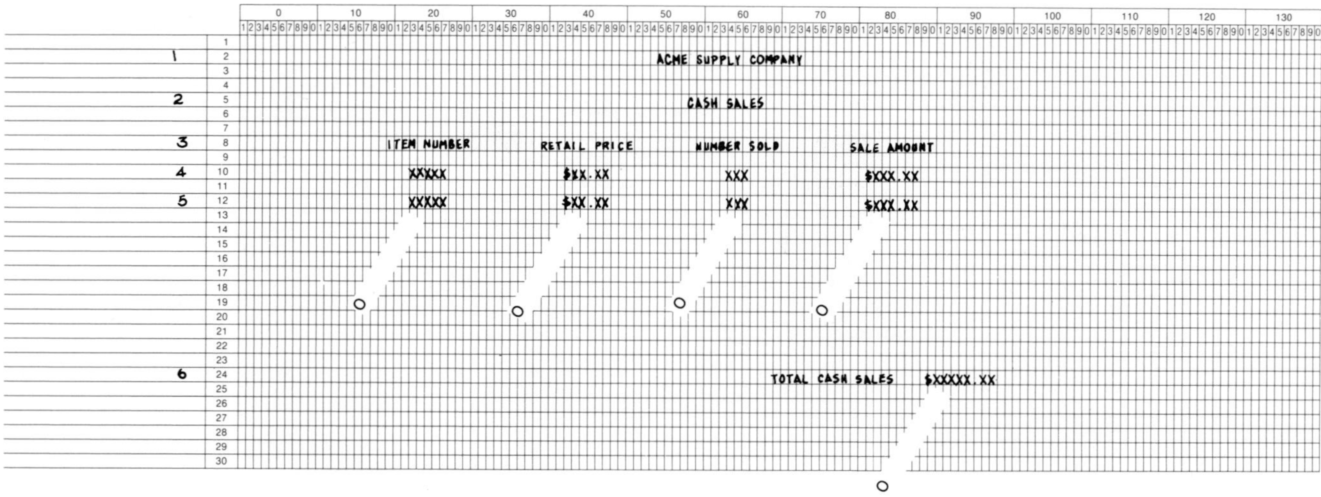

■ **Figure 2.39** Structure chart for exercise 5

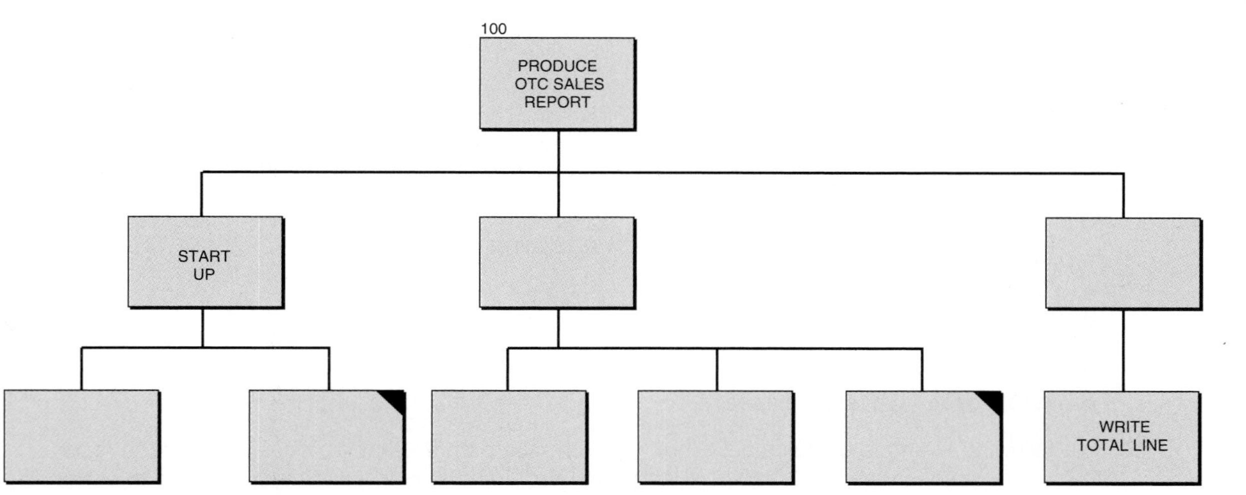

■ **Figure 2.40** Layout forms for exercise 6

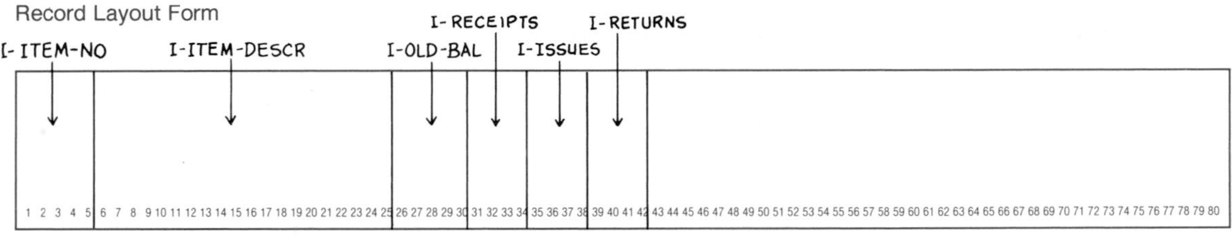

■ **Figure 2.40** continued

Printer Spacing Chart

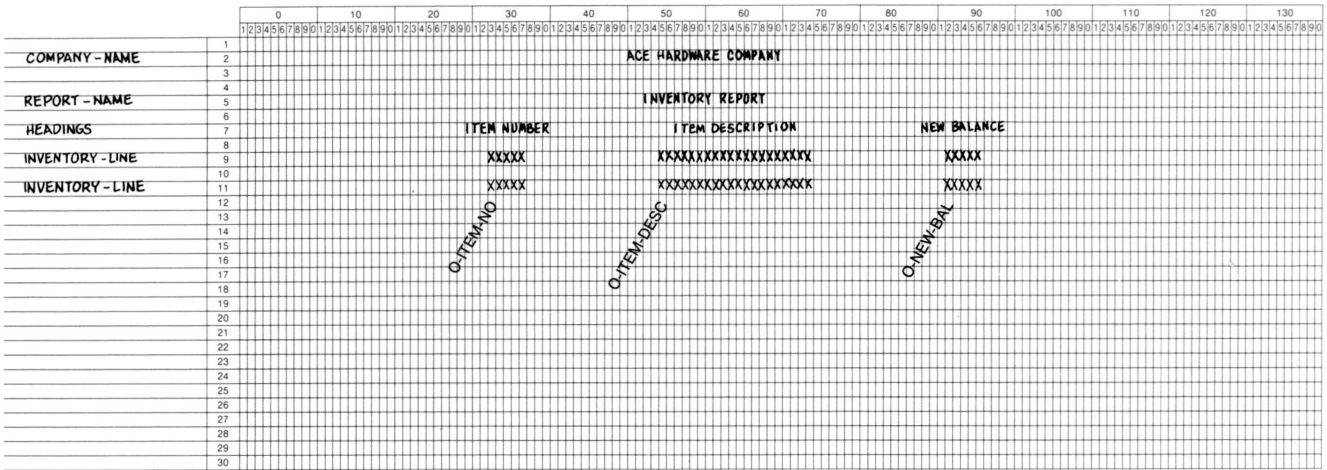

Debugging Activities

1. Given the PHONE-SALE-RECORD layout of Figure 2.3, suppose you are assigned the task of preparing five of these records. A listing of the records you have prepared is shown below. Can you identify the errors in each record? (The top line has been inserted to help you position characters within the record.)

```
   123456789012345678901234567890123456789012345678 90

a.  1980  345A  00285  0150
b. 2050  798B    475  0200
c. 1800  511X  00890  0050
d. 2435  634Y  05.40   790
e. 2815  395D  $025.50  0600
```

2. The following example contains a COBOL program, the data file that it processed, and the report that it produced. Examine the report. Identify the errors and specify what must be done to correct them.

Program:

```
 IDENTIFICATION DIVISION.

 PROGRAM-ID.    PRODUCE-EMPLOYEE-LISTING.

*****************************************************************
*                                                               *
*   AUTHOR.        PAQUETTE.                                    *
*   DATE WRITTEN.  NOVEMBER 1993.                               *
*                                                               *
*   THIS PROGRAM PRODUCES A LIST OF EMPLOYEES.                  *
*                                                               *
*   FOR EACH EMPLOYEE, THE REPORT PRINTS THE NAME, EMPLOYEE     *
*   SOCIAL SECURITY NUMBER, JOB CLASSIFICATION, AND PHONE       *
*   NUMBER.                                                     *
*                                                               *
*   THE INPUT FILE CONTAINS A RECORD FOR EACH EMPLOYEE. EACH    *
*   RECORD CONTAINS THE FOLLOWING INFORMATION: EMPLOYEE SOCIAL  *
*   SECURITY NUMBER, NAME, ADDRESS, JOB CLASSIFICATION, AND     *
*   PHONE NUMBER.                                               *
*                                                               *
*****************************************************************

 ENVIRONMENT DIVISION.

 CONFIGURATION SECTION.
```

```
SOURCE-COMPUTER.  VAX-VMS-8650.
OBJECT-COMPUTER.  VAX-VMS-8650.

INPUT-OUTPUT SECTION.

FILE-CONTROL.
    SELECT EMPLOYEE-FILE     ASSIGN TO COB$INPUT.
    SELECT EMPLOYEE-LIST     ASSIGN TO COB$OUTPUT.

DATA DIVISION.

FILE SECTION.

FD  EMPLOYEE-FILE
    RECORD CONTAINS 80 CHARACTERS.

01  EMPLOYEE-RECORD.
    05 I-SSN          PIC X(9).
    05 I-NAME         PIC X(20).
    05 I-ADDRESS      PIC X(20).
    05 I-CITY-STATE PIC X(20).
    05 I-JOB-CLASS  PIC XXXX.
    05 I-PHONE        PIC X(7).

FD  EMPLOYEE-LIST
    RECORD CONTAINS 132 CHARACTERS.

01  PRINTLINE         PIC X(132).

WORKING-STORAGE SECTION.

01  WS-MORE-RECORDS PIC XXX.

01  HEADINGS.
    05 PIC X(8)    VALUE SPACES.
    05 PIC X(13)   VALUE "EMPLOYEE NAME".
    05 PIC X(39)   VALUE SPACES.
    05 PIC XXX     VALUE "SSN".
    05 PIC X(5)    VALUE SPACES.
    05 PIC X(9)    VALUE "JOB CLASS".
    05 PIC X(14)   VALUE SPACES.
    05 PIC X(5)    VALUE "PHONE".
    05 PIC X(26)   VALUE SPACES.

01  EMPLOYEE-LINE.
    05 FILLER         PIC X(25).
    05 O-NAME         PIC X(20).
    05 FILLER         PIC X(12).
    05 O-SSN          PIC X(9).
    05 FILLER         PIC X(14).
    05 O-JOB-CLASS    PIC XXXX.
    05 FILLER         PIC X(16).
    05 O-PHONE        PIC X(7).
    05 FILLER         PIC X(25).

PROCEDURE DIVISION.

100-PRODUCE-EMPLOYEE-LIST.
    PERFORM 200-START-UP.
    PERFORM 210-PROCESS-EMPLOYEE-RECORD
        UNTIL WS-MORE-RECORDS = "NO ".
    PERFORM 220-FINISH-UP.
    STOP RUN.

200-START-UP.
    OPEN INPUT EMPLOYEE-FILE.
    OPEN OUTPUT EMPLOYEE-LIST.
    MOVE "YES" TO WS-MORE-RECORDS.
    PERFORM 300-WRITE-REPORT-HEADERS.
    PERFORM 310-READ-EMPLOYEE-RECORD.

210-PROCESS-EMPLOYEE-RECORD.
    PERFORM 320-PREPARE-EMPLOYEE-LINE.
    PERFORM 310-READ-EMPLOYEE-RECORD.

220-FINISH-UP.
    CLOSE EMPLOYEE-FILE.
    CLOSE EMPLOYEE-LIST.

300-WRITE-REPORT-HEADERS.
    MOVE HEADINGS TO PRINTLINE.
    WRITE PRINTLINE
        AFTER ADVANCING PAGE.

310-READ-EMPLOYEE-RECORD.
    READ EMPLOYEE-FILE RECORD
```

```
           AT END
               MOVE "NO " TO WS-MORE-RECORDS.

       320-PREPARE-EMPLOYEE-LINE.
           MOVE SPACES TO EMPLOYEE-LINE.
           MOVE I-NAME TO O-NAME.
           MOVE I-SSN TO O-SSN.
           MOVE I-JOB-CLASS TO O-JOB-CLASS.
           MOVE I-PHONE TO O-PHONE.
           MOVE EMPLOYEE-LINE TO PRINTLINE.
           WRITE PRINTLINE
               AFTER ADVANCING 2 LINES.
```

Data File [DD/CD:VIC2DBG2.DAT]:

```
714320025JOHN E. TURNER      436 ROCK ST.          FALL RIVER, MA      M-106832004
344024030JANET H. COLLINS    755 PLAIN AVE.        SWANSEA, MA         E-026841522
533254735EDWARD P. RILEY     1512 RIVERSIDE AVE.   SOMERSET, MA        S-056833241
465114040BARBARA F. WOLSEY   515 GLOBE ST.         FALL RIVER, MA      M-056835432
547316545MICHELLE H. BOISE   843 TICKLE LANE       WESTPORT, MA        E-086851144
476561250GEORGE F. FAIRHURST 2450 OCEAN DRIVE      WESTPORT, MA        M-036853153
386471455SHAWN M. AINSWORTH  141 BUSH LANE         SWANSEA, MA         S-106846890
837684260CATHRYN E. CODY     844 FLINT ST.         FALL RIVER, MA      S-036837044
582784665ALEX B. GOULART     2415 PLAIN AVE.       SWANSEA, MA         S-026841139
664375170GLORIA J. NOWACK    1065 CENTER RD.       WESTPORT, MA        E-106857991
```

Report:

```
EMPLOYEE NAME                                 SSN    JOB CLASS      PHONE

             JOHN E. TURNER               714320025         M-10           6832004

             JANET H. COLLINS             344024030         E-02           6841522

             EDWARD P. RILEY              533254735         S-05           6833241

             BARBARA F. WOLSEY            465114040         M-05           6835432

             MICHELLE H. BOISE            547316545         E-08           6851144

             GEORGE F. FAIRHURST          476561250         M-03           6853153

             SHAWN M. AINSWORTH           386471455         S-10           6846890

             CATHRYN E. CODY              837684260         S-03           6837044

             ALEX B. GOULART              582784665         S-02           6841139

             GLORIA J. NOWACK             664375170         E-10           6857991
```

Terminal Exercises

1. Create a file, and then copy into this file the COBOL program on the coding forms of Figure 2.14. Be very careful to begin each line in the correct column as coded on the forms. (Area A begins in column 8, and Area B begins in column 12.)
2. Compile the COBOL program of exercise 1. (Ask your instructor for the correct system commands.) Debug the program if necessary.
3. Create a file that contains the phone sale records listed on page 87. (Do not include the column identifiers.)

Customer number	Catalog number	Unit cost	Number sold
9999	0001	76750	0600
6001	0003	10500	0016
9009	0007	01000	0013
0046	0012	03800	0082
9551	0013	01250	0040
2150	0036	00999	0003
0008	0064	01510	0001
7752	0369	03999	3500
2200	0400	00100	1200
2201	0401	02199	0003
2203	0403	87500	0002
2205	0405	10000	0001
2207	0407	00300	0610
8611	0408	03650	0009
8612	0409	10130	0004
8614	0501	01299	0016
8617	0503	31000	0001
8618	0506	03100	0063
0105	0561	05915	0045
8619	0583	00250	0027
0061	0600	00900	0010
0700	0601	02800	0002
0701	0602	10001	0001
0702	0603	50000	0005
0703	0604	05112	0010
0704	0605	08999	0003
0705	0606	02500	1001
0706	0607	01289	0004
0707	0608	00500	0013
0708	0609	01389	0102
0709	0611	40000	0007
0711	0613	07189	0003
0713	0615	00125	0017
0715	0617	12589	0003
0717	0619	00360	0100
4121	0801	12009	5000
0037	1010	09999	0005
5213	1012	95000	0002
8515	1022	00399	0120
8633	1022	00399	0005
0530	1025	05500	3010
0003	1030	00099	0041
0210	1034	06760	0031
4203	1091	25099	0002
3200	1200	80050	0002
3201	1201	30000	0001
3203	1203	45000	0004
3205	1205	01199	0011
3207	1207	01500	0004
3209	1209	00500	0017

4. Ask your instructor for the system commands that you need to run the COBOL program of exercise 2, using the data file you created in exercise 3 as the input file. Run the program, and check the output carefully. If errors exist in the output, identify the causes, make the necessary corrections, and run the program again. Repeat these steps until the report is free of errors.

3 The Divisions of a COBOL Program: IDENTIFICATION, ENVIRONMENT, DATA

In this chapter, the first three divisions of a COBOL program are studied in some detail. The Chapter 2 sample program that you are already familiar with is used again to illustrate entries in these three divisions. Additional examples are included as needed to elaborate on some division features.

As a division is being coded, your attention is directed to the program design tools (system flowchart and input/output record layout forms) that contain the related information: the program name needed in the IDENTIFICATION DIVISION, the file names needed in the ENVIRONMENT DIVISION, the record names and their layouts that must be described in the DATA DIVISION.

In each division, the required entries and some of the optional entries are identified and explained. The DATA DIVISION is particularly crucial. Records, group items, and elementary items are carefully examined. The data item specifications (class and size) are presented in detail. You are also introduced to editing characters.

In the WORKING-STORAGE SECTION, the uses of the VALUE clause in assigning initial values to data items and in assigning constants to fields of a record are explained and illustrated. You will learn how to handle titles and headings and see why most programmers code such records in the WORKING-STORAGE SECTION.

Lists of rules are included for the construction of user-defined names and for the use of the VALUE clause.

The coding conventions used in this text are also noted, and you are made aware that coding requirements may be imposed on a programmer by "the business environment" in addition to those imposed by the COBOL language itself.

For your convenience, the design tools as well as the program developed in Chapter 2 are reproduced in Figure 3.1. As the divisions of a COBOL program are examined in greater detail, numerous references will be made to entries in this figure. ■

Objectives You Should Achieve

After studying this chapter, you should:

1. Be able to construct valid user-defined names.
2. Be able to specify the required and the optional entries in the IDENTIFICATION DIVISION.
3. Given the statement of a problem, be able to write a descriptive paragraph in the IDENTIFICATION DIVISION that explains the nature of the program.
4. Given a COBOL statement format specification, be able to identify the required components, the optional components, the COBOL reserved words, and the user-defined names that it contains.
5. Given a division name, be able to specify the area A entries and the area B entries in the division.
6. Given a system flowchart, be able to identify the files needed by the program.
7. Given a system flowchart, be able to code the FILE-CONTROL paragraph entries.
8. Given the entries of the ENVIRONMENT DIVISION, be able to identify the source computer, the object computer, and the names of the files.
9. Given a file description (FD) paragraph, be able to identify the required entries and the optional entries.
10. Given a file name and the layout of a record belonging to the file, be able to code the FD paragraph and the record description.
11. Given a record layout, be able to name the group items and the elementary items of the record.
12. Given an elementary data item description, be able to specify the class and size of the item.
13. Given the class of a data item and an actual value to be stored in the associated field, be able to determine if each character is an acceptable character in that class.
14. Given a numeric data item and a numeric value to be stored in the associated field, be able to specify the numeric character stored in each byte of the field.

15. Given a numeric-edited data item and a numeric value to be stored in the associated field, be able to specify the character stored in each byte of the field.
16. Given a WORKING-STORAGE SECTION data item, be able to correctly use the VALUE clause to assign an initial value to the item.
17. Given a printer spacing chart showing the layout of a line containing column headers, be able to correctly code the record as a WORKING-STORAGE SECTION record using the VALUE clause to assign values to each field of the record.
18. Given a programming assignment for which the completed design tools (I/O record layout forms, system flowchart, structure chart, pseudocode, and/or program flowchart) are provided, be able to successfully complete the task of coding the first three divisions of the COBOL program.
19. Given a programming assignment for which the completed I/O record layout forms, system flowchart, and structure chart are provided, be able to successfully complete the task of writing the program pseudocode and coding the first three divisions of the COBOL program.
20. Given a programming assignment whose purpose is to prepare a printed report that contains only data to be retrieved from input records, be able to successfully complete the design phase of the problem-solving procedure and code the first three divisions of the COBOL program.

User-Defined Names

As a programming language, COBOL has been designed to provide much self-documentation by allowing instructions to consist almost completely of English words. The words that a programmer can use fall into two categories: (1) *COBOL reserved words* and (2) *user-defined names.*

COBOL reserved words are the technical terms of the language. They have special meanings to the compiler and must not be used for any other than their intended technical purposes. These purposes will be pointed out as we proceed through the text. (A complete list of the COBOL reserved words is provided in Appendix D.)

User-defined names are the ones that must be supplied by the programmer to name such items as the program, files, records, fields of records, paragraphs, and special names that will be explained later. There are 21 different types of user-defined names. Within a program, most of the names that will be needed are generated during the design phase of the problem-solving procedure. For instance, in Figure 3.1a, the name given to the input record, specifically PHONE-SALE-RECORD, is a user-defined name, as are the names given to the data fields of the record (I-CUSTOMER-NO, I-CATALOG-NO, I-UNIT-COST, and I-NO-OF-UNITS). Note that all the names are single words.

In Figure 3.1b, the names given to the line layouts on the printer spacing chart, specifically, HEADINGS and PHONE-SALE-LINE, are user-defined names. The names given to the data fields of the record PHONE-SALE-LINE (O-CUSTOMER-NO, O-CATALOG-NO, O-UNIT-COST, and O-SALE-AMOUNT) are all user-defined names. Note, however, that the fields of the record HEADINGS have not been assigned names. The column headers are **values** stored in the fields (they will be printed on the report); they are **not** user-defined names. (The fields containing the column headers are not assigned names because they will not be referenced individually within the program.)

In Figure 3.1c, the names given to the input file and to the output file (PHONE-SALES-FILE and PHONE-SALES-REPORT) are also user-defined names.

Figure 3.1a Input record layout

Record Layout Form

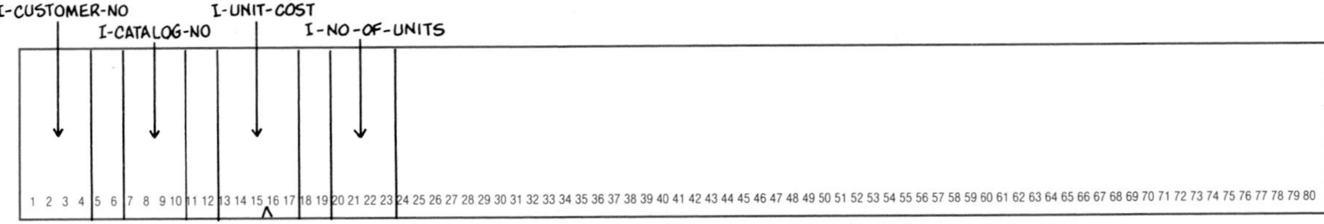

Record Name: PHONE-SALE-RECORD

Figure 3.1b Output record layout

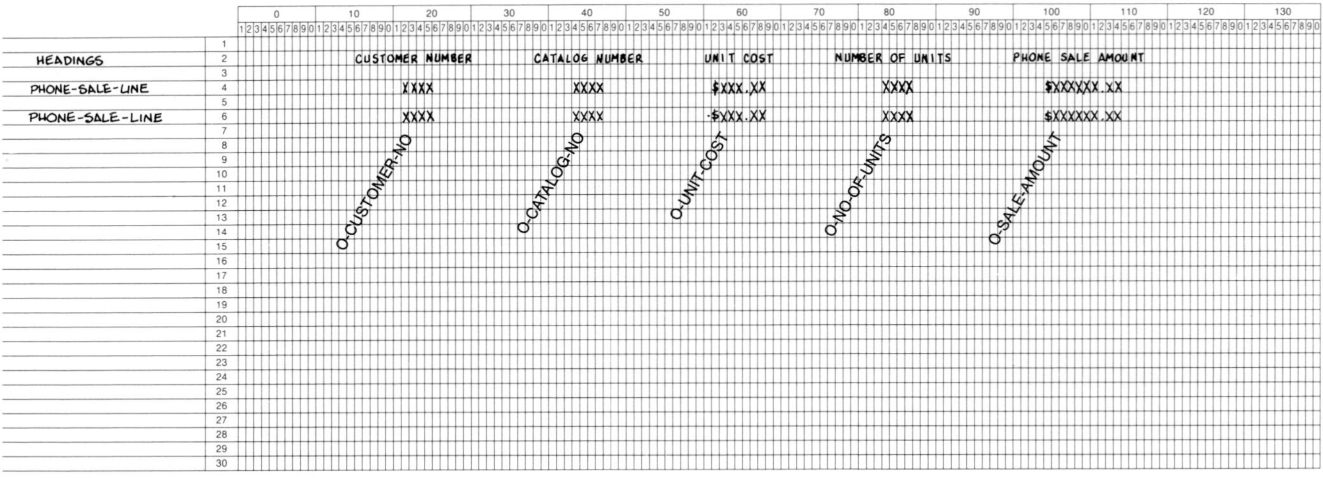

Figure 3.1c System flowchart

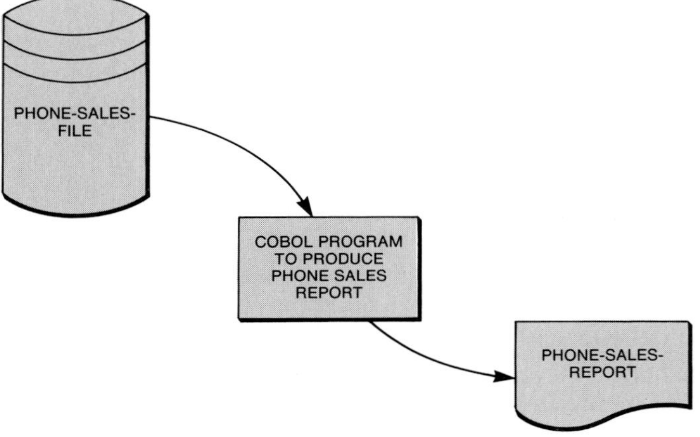

Figure 3.1d Structure chart

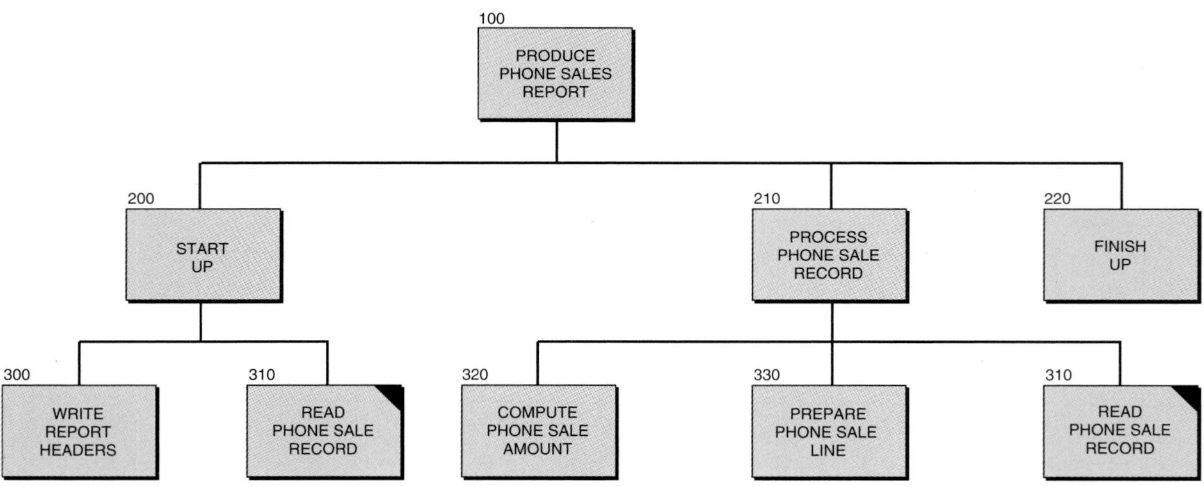

Figure 3.1e Program pseudocode

100-Produce-Phone-Sales-Report.

1. Perform 200-Start-Up.
2. Perform 210-Process-Phone-Sale-Record until no more records.
3. Perform 220-Finish-Up.
4. Stop the run.

200-Start-Up.

1. Open the files.
2. Set the end-of-file flag WS-MORE-RECORDS to "YES".
3. Perform 300-Write-Report-Headers.
4. Perform 310-Read-Phone-Sale-Record.

210-Process-Phone-Sale-Record.

1. Perform 320-Compute-Phone-Sale-Amount.
2. Perform 330-Prepare-Phone-Sale-Line.
3. Perform 310-Read-Phone-Sale-Record.

220-Finish-Up.

1. Close the files.

300-Write-Report-Headers.

1. Move Headings to the output area Printline.
2. After advancing to the top of a new page, write the output record Printline.
3. Clear the record area Phone-Sale-Line.

310-Read-Phone-Sale-Record.

1. Read an input phone-sale-record.
2. Test for the end-of-file record; if EOF record reached, move "NO " to the end-of-file flag WS-MORE-RECORDS.

320-Compute-Phone-Sale-Amount.

1. If the input number-of-units > 100
   then
   compute the Phone-sale-line amount = input number-of-units times input unit-cost times .8
   else
   compute the Phone-sale-line amount = input number-of-units times input unit-cost.

330-Prepare-Phone-Sale-Line.

1. Move input customer-number to Phone-sale-line customer-number.
2. Move input catalog-number to Phone-sale-line catalog-number.
3. Move input unit-cost to Phone-sale-line unit-cost.
4. Move input number-of-units to Phone-sale-line number-of-units.
5. Move the Phone-sale-line to the output record area Printline.
6. After advancing 2 lines, write the output record Printline.

■ **Figure 3.1f** Program flowchart

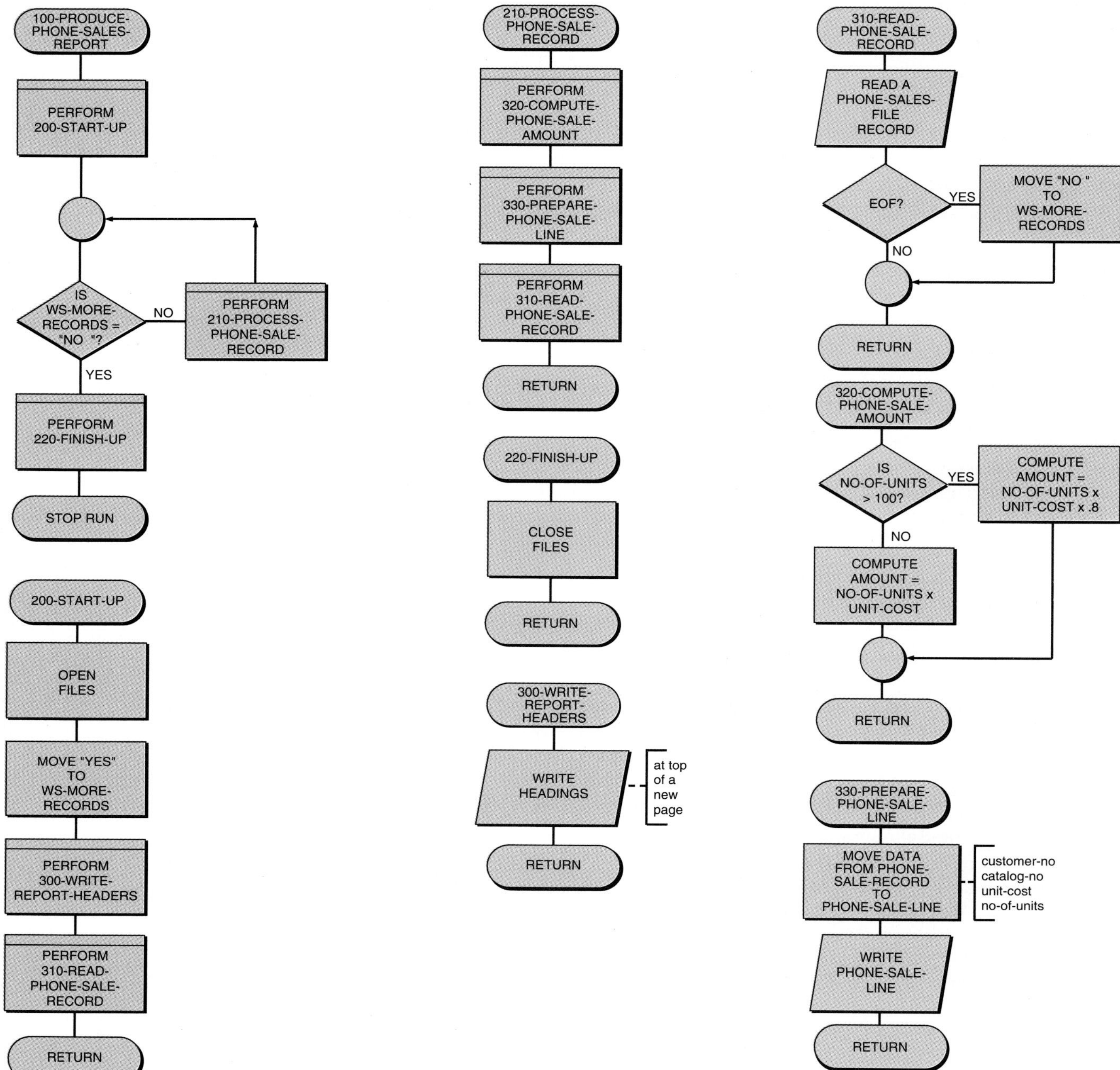

Figure 3.1g COBOL program

```
  IDENTIFICATION DIVISION.

  PROGRAM-ID.  DAILY-PHONE-SALES-REPORT.

******************************************************************
*                                                                *
*  AUTHOR.         PAQUETTE.                                     *
*  DATE WRITTEN:   NOVEMBER 1993.                                *
*                                                                *
*  THIS PROGRAM PRODUCES A REPORT LISTING THE PHONE SALES THAT   *
*  OCCURRED DURING THE DAY.                                      *
*                                                                *
*  EACH INPUT RECORD IS A PHONE SALE RECORD THAT CONTAINS THE    *
*  CUSTOMER NUMBER, THE CATALOG NUMBER, THE UNIT COST OF THE     *
*  ITEM, AND THE NUMBER OF UNITS SOLD TO THE CUSTOMER.           *
*                                                                *
*  FOR EACH PHONE SALE, THE PHONE SALE LINE ON THE REPORT MUST   *
*  SHOW THE CUSTOMER NUMBER, THE CATALOG NUMBER, THE UNIT COST,  *
*  THE NUMBER OF UNITS SOLD, AND THE NET AMOUNT OF THE SALE.     *
*  THE VALUES ON THE PHONE SALE LINES ARE LISTED UNDER APPRO-    *
*  PRIATE COLUMN HEADINGS.                                       *
*                                                                *
*  THE AMOUNT OF THE SALE IS COMPUTED AS FOLLOWS: IF THE NUMBER  *
*  OF UNITS SOLD EXCEEDS 100, THE SALE AMOUNT IS DISCOUNTED 20%, *
*  THAT IS, SALE AMOUNT = NO. OF UNITS * UNIT COST * .8.  IF THE *
*  NUMBER OF UNITS DOES NOT EXCEED 100, THE SALE AMOUNT = NO. OF *
*  UNITS * UNIT COST.                                            *
*                                                                *
******************************************************************

  ENVIRONMENT DIVISION.

  CONFIGURATION SECTION.

  SOURCE-COMPUTER.  VAX-VMS-8650.
  OBJECT-COMPUTER.  VAX-VMS-8650.

  INPUT-OUTPUT SECTION.

  FILE-CONTROL.
      SELECT PHONE-SALES-FILE     ASSIGN TO COB$INPUT.
      SELECT PHONE-SALES-REPORT   ASSIGN TO COB$OUTPUT.

  DATA DIVISION.

  FILE SECTION.

  FD  PHONE-SALES-FILE
      RECORD CONTAINS 23 CHARACTERS.

  01  PHONE-SALE-RECORD.
      05 I-CUSTOMER-NO      PIC X(4).
      05 FILLER             PIC XX.
      05 I-CATALOG-NO       PIC X(4).
      05 FILLER             PIC XX.
      05 I-UNIT-COST        PIC 999V99.
      05 FILLER             PIC XX.
      05 I-NO-OF-UNITS      PIC 9(4).

  FD  PHONE-SALES-REPORT
      RECORD CONTAINS 132 CHARACTERS.

  01  PRINTLINE             PIC X(132).

WORKING-STORAGE SECTION.

01  WS-MORE-RECORDS      PIC XXX.

01  HEADINGS.
    05 PIC X(15)      VALUE SPACES.
    05 PIC X(15)      VALUE "CUSTOMER NUMBER".
    05 PIC X(8)       VALUE SPACES.
    05 PIC X(14)      VALUE "CATALOG NUMBER".
    05 PIC X(8)       VALUE SPACES.
    05 PIC X(9)       VALUE "UNIT COST".
    05 PIC X(8)       VALUE SPACES.
    05 PIC X(15)      VALUE "NUMBER OF UNITS".
    05 PIC X(8)       VALUE SPACES.
    05 PIC X(17)      VALUE "PHONE SALE AMOUNT".
    05 PIC X(15)      VALUE SPACES.
```

```
01  PHONE-SALE-LINE.
    05 FILLER              PIC X(21).
    05 O-CUSTOMER-NO       PIC X(4).
    05 FILLER              PIC X(18).
    05 O-CATALOG-NO        PIC X(4).
    05 FILLER              PIC X(14).
    05 O-UNIT-COST         PIC $ZZ9.99.
    05 FILLER              PIC X(15).
    05 O-NO-OF-UNITS       PIC ZZZ9.
    05 FILLER              PIC X(17).
    05 O-SALE-AMOUNT       PIC $Z(5)9.99.
    05 FILLER              PIC X(18).

PROCEDURE DIVISION.

100-PRODUCE-PHONE-SALES-REPORT.
    PERFORM 200-START-UP.
    PERFORM 210-PROCESS-SALE-RECORD
        UNTIL WS-MORE-RECORDS = "NO ".
    PERFORM 220-FINISH-UP.
    STOP RUN.

200-START-UP.
    OPEN INPUT PHONE-SALES-FILE.
    OPEN OUTPUT PHONE-SALES-REPORT.
    MOVE "YES" TO WS-MORE-RECORDS.
    PERFORM 300-WRITE-REPORT-HEADERS.
    PERFORM 310-READ-PHONE-SALE-RECORD.

210-PROCESS-PHONE-SALE-RECORD.
    PERFORM 320-COMPUTE-PHONE-SALE-AMOUNT.
    PERFORM 330-PREPARE-PHONE-SALE-LINE.
    PERFORM 310-READ-PHONE-SALE-RECORD.

220-FINISH-UP.
    CLOSE PHONE-SALES-FILE.
    CLOSE PHONE-SALES-REPORT.

300-WRITE-REPORT-HEADERS.
    MOVE HEADINGS TO PRINTLINE.
    WRITE PRINTLINE
        AFTER ADVANCING PAGE.
    MOVE SPACES TO PHONE-SALE-LINE.

310-READ-PHONE-SALE-RECORD.
    READ PHONE-SALES-FILE RECORD
        AT END
            MOVE "NO " TO WS-MORE-RECORDS.

320-COMPUTE-PHONE-SALE-AMOUNT.
    IF I-NO-OF-UNITS > 100
        THEN
            COMPUTE O-SALE-AMOUNT = I-NO-OF-UNITS *
                                    UNIT-COST * .8
        ELSE
            COMPUTE O-SALE-AMOUNT = I-NO-OF-UNITS *
                                    I-UNIT-COST.

330-PREPARE-PHONE-SALE-LINE.
    MOVE I-CUSTOMER-NO TO O-CUSTOMER-NO.
    MOVE I-CATALOG-NO TO O-CATALOG-NO.
    MOVE I-UNIT-COST TO O-UNIT-COST.
    MOVE I-NO-OF-UNITS TO O-NO-OF-UNITS.
    MOVE PHONE-SALE-LINE TO PRINTLINE.
    WRITE PRINTLINE
        AFTER ADVANCING 2 LINES.
```

Rules for Constructing User-Defined Names

Any user-defined name must be constructed to conform to the following rules:

1. It can contain from 1 to 30 characters. (Some compilers that do not conform to the ANSI standards may allow a maximum of 8 characters only, while others may allow more than 30.)
2. The characters must be selected from the following:
   - **a.** the letters of the alphabet
   - **b.** the digits 0 through 9
   - **c.** the hyphen (-)
3. Any hyphen must be embedded within the name (it must not be the first or the last character).

Figure 3.2 Examples of nondescriptive and descriptive user-defined names

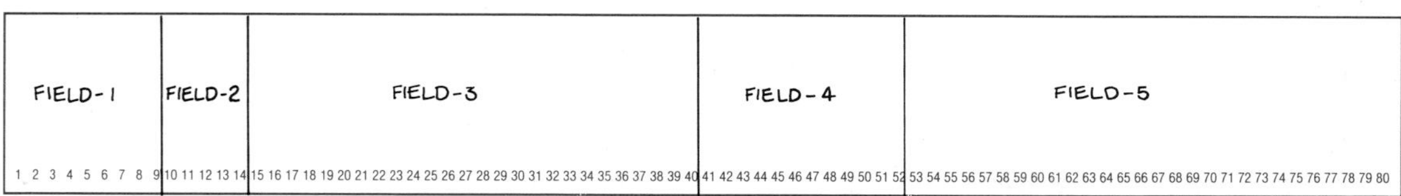

Record Name: RECORD-1

SOC-SEC-NO	CLASS	NAME	PHONE	OCCUPATION
1 2 3 4 5 6 7 8 9	10 11 12 13 14	15 16 17 18 19 20 21 22 23 24 25 26 27 28 29 30 31 32 33 34 35 36 37 38 39 40	41 42 43 44 45 46 47 48 49 50 51 52	53 54 55 56 57 58 59 60 61 62 63 64 65 66 67 68 69 70 71 72 73 74 75 76 77 78 79 80

Record Name: MEMBER-INFO-RECORD

4. There must not be any blanks within the name. The name must consist of a single word.
5. The name must contain at least one letter, except for paragraph names in the PROCEDURE DIVISION, which can be all numeric. (The author does not recommend all-numeric paragraph names.)

The programmer has the opportunity to make up names that are descriptive and, as such, contribute to the self-documentation of the program. For instance, if a program processes the payroll for the Modern Printing Company, a program name such as MODERN-PRINTING-CO-PAYROLL is much more descriptive than PROGRAM-1. Similarly, in the PROCEDURE DIVISION, if a paragraph contains instructions to read an input record, the paragraph name 310-READ-A-RECORD is more descriptive than the name 310.

Examine the records in Figure 3.2. Which record has field names that describe the contents of the fields? It is obvious that the names assigned to the fields of MEMBER-INFO-RECORD contribute to the documentation of the program, whereas the field names of RECORD-1 provide very little documentation. Similarly, the record name MEMBER-INFO-RECORD describes its contents, whereas the name RECORD-1 does not.

The names READ/WRITE and MODERN PRINTING CO. PAYROLL are not allowed as user-defined names because of the slash (/), blanks, and period. Nonhyphenated words can be used, but the programmer must check them against the list of COBOL reserved words to make sure they are legal user-defined names. Since few reserved words are hyphenated, the hyphen is used extensively in user-defined names.

Another note of caution regarding user-defined names: Some programmers have a tendency to construct abbreviated names. While they are acceptable to the compiler, names that are too greatly abbreviated tend to be nebulous, confusing, and irritating to other users. Examples are UNCST and UNORD. The author of such words has introduced elements of a guessing game: What do the names mean? With a little more effort, clarity and self-documentation are much better served. By constructing the names UNIT-COST and UNITS-ORDERED, the intent becomes perfectly clear.

Note: The programmer should make a conscious effort to use names that can be readily understood by anyone who uses the program.

The following examples further illustrate the comments in the two preceding paragraphs.

Valid Name	Invalid Name	Reason for Being Invalid
UNIT-COST	UNIT COST	Space not allowed
UNIT-COST	UNIT/COST	Slash (/) not allowed
UNIT-COST	UNIT-COST.	Period not allowed
MARK-UP-PERCENT	MARK-UP%	% symbol not allowed

Good Form	**Bad Form**
NEGATIVE-BALANCE	NBAL
PAY-RATE	PRATE
HIGH-LIMIT	HI-LIM
WS-TOTAL-COUNT	WS-TOT-CNT
WS-TOTAL-INCOME	WS-TOT-INC
WS-ACCOUNT-BALANCE	WS-ACT-BAL

As we proceed through the various divisions and examine the formats of entries, we will point out again the various names that must be supplied by the programmer. In each case, the programmer should carefully select names that are English-like and descriptive and that add to the documentation of the program. If this is done consistently, the program will be easier to read, understand, and maintain.

IDENTIFICATION DIVISION

The IDENTIFICATION DIVISION is always the first division of a COBOL program. Its purpose is to provide some means of identification for the program. Figure 3.3 shows the IDENTIFICATION DIVISION of the sample program.

PROGRAM-ID

The PROGRAM-ID paragraph is the only one that is required by the compiler. It must contain the external name of the program, that is, the name that identifies the program to its users. The name is constructed by the programmer at the time she or he is planning the program; it first appears on the system flowchart. When the coding of the program begins, the name is simply transferred to the COBOL coding form.

When constructing the program name, the programmer must abide by the requirements of the compiler. As noted earlier, many systems comply with the COBOL standards by allowing up to 30 characters, others allow more, and some may allow fewer. Your instructor will give you the appropriate information for your system.

Earlier versions of COBOL compilers also allowed additional optional identification information to be inserted in this division. The complete list of available paragraphs is shown in Figure 3.4. If these optional paragraphs are used, they must be entered in the sequence specified.

The 1985 ANSI standards for COBOL have labeled the AUTHOR, INSTALLATION, DATE-WRITTEN, DATE-COMPILED, and SECURITY paragraphs as **obsolete,** and they will be deleted in the next revision of the language. For this reason, this text will specify only the PROGRAM-ID paragraph in

Figure 3.3 IDENTIFICATION DIVISION for the chapter program: DAILY-PHONE-SALES-REPORT

```
  IDENTIFICATION DIVISION.

  PROGRAM-ID.   DAILY-PHONE-SALES-REPORT.

*****************************************************************
*                                                               *
*  AUTHOR.         PAQUETTE.                                    *
*  DATE WRITTEN:   NOVEMBER 1993.                               *
*                                                               *
*  THIS PROGRAM PRODUCES A REPORT LISTING THE PHONE SALES THAT  *
*  OCCURRED DURING THE DAY.                                     *
*                                                               *
*  EACH INPUT RECORD IS A PHONE SALE RECORD THAT CONTAINS THE   *
*  CUSTOMER NUMBER, THE CATALOG NUMBER, THE UNIT COST OF THE    *
*  ITEM, AND THE NUMBER OF UNITS SOLD TO THE CUSTOMER.          *
*                                                               *
*  FOR EACH PHONE SALE, THE PHONE SALE LINE ON THE REPORT MUST  *
*  SHOW THE CUSTOMER NUMBER, THE CATALOG NUMBER, THE UNIT COST, *
*  THE NUMBER OF UNITS SOLD, AND THE NET AMOUNT OF THE SALE.    *
*  THE VALUES ON THE PHONE SALE LINES ARE LISTED UNDER APPRO-   *
*  PRIATE COLUMN HEADINGS.                                      *
*                                                               *
*  THE AMOUNT OF THE SALE IS COMPUTED AS FOLLOWS: IF THE NUMBER *
*  OF UNITS SOLD EXCEEDS 100, THE SALE AMOUNT IS DISCOUNTED 20%,*
*  THAT IS, SALE AMOUNT = NO. OF UNITS * UNIT COST * .8.  IF THE*
*  NUMBER OF UNITS DOES NOT EXCEED 100, THE SALE AMOUNT = NO. OF*
*  UNITS * UNIT COST.                                           *
*                                                               *
*****************************************************************
```

■ **Figure 3.4** IDENTIFICATION DIVISION format

```
IDENTIFICATION DIVISION.
PROGRAM-ID. program-name.
*[AUTHOR. [comment-entry]...].
*[INSTALLATION. [comment-entry]...].
*[DATE-WRITTEN. [comment-entry]...].
*[DATE-COMPILED. [comment-entry]...].
*[SECURITY. [comment-entry]...].
```

*Marked for deletion in the next revision of ANSI COBOL standards.

the IDENTIFICATION DIVISION. The asterisk (in column 7) will be used freely to provide additional program documentation.

Since these optional paragraphs are still currently supported, a brief explanation is provided below.

AUTHOR

If the AUTHOR paragraph is used, the programmer simply enters his or her name. It can be entered in full, with ordinary punctuation, as in GERARD A. PAQUETTE.

INSTALLATION

If the INSTALLATION paragraph is used, the entry simply states the location of the computer center where the program will be run. More than one line can be used if needed.

DATE-WRITTEN

If the DATE-WRITTEN paragraph is used, the programmer enters the date on which the program was written.

DATE-COMPILED

If the DATE-COMPILED paragraph is used, most compilers supply the date of compilation automatically at the time the program is compiled. Often, the date of compilation is unknown to the programmer at the time the program is being coded. If an entry is made by the programmer, it is usually replaced by the actual date of compilation, and that date appears on the listing of the program.

SECURITY

The SECURITY paragraph specifies any restrictions placed on the availability and usage of the program. Some programs are highly classified and are to be used by personnel with required security clearance only. Other programs have no restrictions at all.

Use of Asterisk (*) in Program Documentation

As mentioned earlier, the asterisk can be used anywhere in a COBOL program to insert comments and provide documentation. It must be coded in column 7 of every line that contains comments. Throughout this text, initial program documentation will be inserted within a "box" of asterisks in the IDENTIFICATION DIVISION, as illustrated in Figure 3.3. This documentation will specify the author of the program and the date written and will contain a brief explanation of the program.

The programmer is encouraged to use the asterisk freely wherever it is felt that additional comments would improve the documentation of the program. To this end, the asterisk is generally used in the IDENTIFICATION DIVISION and in the PROCEDURE DIVISION.

Coding the IDENTIFICATION DIVISION

The division header, IDENTIFICATION DIVISION, and the paragraph names are coded in area A and are all followed by a period. The comment entries must all be coded in area B and end with a period.

The division header stands alone on a line, whereas the paragraph names are followed by the appropriate comment entries on one or more lines as needed. The comment entries can begin on the same line as the paragraph names, provided at least one space is left after the period. The comment entries can also begin on a separate line, as shown below. (In this text, the program name is on the same line as the paragraph name PROGRAM-ID.)

```
IDENTIFICATION DIVISION.

PROGRAM-ID.
    DAILY-PHONE-SALES-REPORT.

*****************************************************************
*                                                               *
*  AUTHOR.         PAQUETTE.                                    *
*  DATE WRITTEN:   NOVEMBER 1993.                               *
*                                                               *
*  THIS PROGRAM PRODUCES A REPORT LISTING THE PHONE SALES THAT  *
                              .
                              .
                              .
```

Many programmers insert blank lines in their programs for the purpose of making program listings easier to read. You are encouraged to do so, as illustrated in the sample program. In particular, note the blank lines before and after division and section headers, before a record description, and between paragraphs in the PROCEDURE DIVISION.

Technical Format Notation

As we proceed through the text, we will introduce the various entries available in each division of a COBOL program, some required and others optional. In presenting the formats of these entries, we will use the standard technical notation found in COBOL reference manuals. It is very important for the programmer to understand these specifications completely. In any COBOL format, the following conventions apply:

1. Capitalized words are COBOL reserved words. These have special meanings to the compiler. When they are used, they must be spelled exactly as shown.
2. Lowercase words denote entries that are to be supplied by the programmer. Some of these, like data names, are to be generated by the programmer. Others, like code names for the various pieces of hardware, must be obtained from the computer center or from your instructor.
3. Brackets ([ ]) indicate optional entries.
4. Any underlined reserved word is required if the entry containing it is used.
5. Any reserved word that is not underlined is optional. Such words are used to increase the clarity of statements.
6. The ellipsis (...) indicates that the entry preceding it can be repeated at the option of the programmer.
7. Braces ({ }) indicate alternatives, of which only one is to be used at a time.

As an example, examine the format of the ADD statement, shown in Figure 3.5. The following comments apply to the sample format:

Figure 3.5 Standard technical notation—example

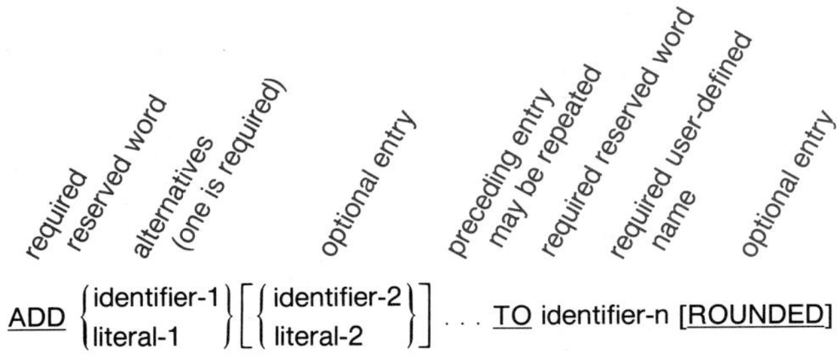

1. **ADD.** The verb ADD is a required COBOL reserved word.
2. $\left\{\begin{matrix}\text{identifier-1}\\ \text{literal-1}\end{matrix}\right\}$ The braces indicate that either an identifier or a literal is needed following the verb ADD. Identifier-1 is a user-defined name.
3. $\left[\left\{\begin{matrix}\textit{identifier-2}\\ \textit{literal-2}\end{matrix}\right\}\right]$. The brackets indicate that an optional second identifier or literal can be inserted after the first identifier or literal.
4. **... .** The ellipsis indicates that additional optional identifiers or literals can be inserted in the statement.
5. **TO.** This is a required COBOL reserved word.
6. **identifier-n** is a required user-defined name.
7. **[ROUNDED].** This is an optional entry. If it is used, the COBOL reserved word ROUNDED follows the user-defined name identifier-n.

For instance, in the statement

```
ADD COUNT-A COUNT-B 10 TO TOTAL-COUNT
```

the data items COUNT-A, COUNT-B, and TOTAL-COUNT are user-defined identifiers, the numeral 10 is a literal, and the words ADD and TO are COBOL reserved words.

Whenever a COBOL statement format is presented, the technical notation explained above will always be used.

ENVIRONMENT DIVISION

The second division of a COBOL program is the ENVIRONMENT DIVISION. Its key purpose is to provide information regarding the hardware that will be used to process the program. As a result, this division is truly machine-dependent. Of the four divisions, the ENVIRONMENT DIVISION is the only one whose entries are dictated by the computer components available at a given computer installation. (Recall that procedural languages were designed to be machine-independent. Obviously, that goal was not quite achieved in COBOL.) To complete the entries in this division, the programmer must obtain all hardware information from the computer center that will ultimately run the program. As a student, your instructor will provide you with the necessary entries.

The hardware is separated into two groups: the computers and the input and output devices. The computers are identified in the CONFIGURATION SECTION, and the input and output devices are identified in the INPUT-OUTPUT SECTION, as shown below.

```
ENVIRONMENT DIVISION.

CONFIGURATION SECTION.

SOURCE-COMPUTER.   VAX-VMS-8650.
OBJECT-COMPUTER.   VAX-VMS-8650.

INPUT-OUTPUT SECTION.

FILE-CONTROL.
    SELECT PHONE-SALES-FILE     ASSIGN TO COB$INPUT.
    SELECT PHONE-SALES-REPORT   ASSIGN TO COB$OUTPUT.
```

CONFIGURATION SECTION

The CONFIGURATION SECTION may contain three paragraphs: SOURCE-COMPUTER, OBJECT-COMPUTER, and SPECIAL-NAMES.

The SOURCE-COMPUTER paragraph is used to identify the computer that will process the source program. Recall that the source program is the one that consists of all the statements contained in your COBOL program. The source computer manages the compiler that will translate each source program statement into corresponding machine-language instructions. In the sample program, the VAX-VMS-8650 will process the source program.

The OBJECT-COMPUTER paragraph is used to identify the computer that will process the object program. The object program is produced by the compiler, and it consists of all the machine-language instructions corresponding to the COBOL statements of the source program. Usually, the object computer is the same as the source computer, but it does not have to be the same. In the sample program, the VAX-VMS-8650 will process the source program and also the object program.

Both the SOURCE-COMPUTER and OBJECT-COMPUTER paragraphs are optional and, when used, serve to provide documentation.

The third paragraph is SPECIAL-NAMES. Since very few programs in this text require the use of this section, specific details will be provided later whenever a program requires this section entry.

INPUT-OUTPUT SECTION

The INPUT-OUTPUT SECTION is used to identify the input and output devices that will be used to process the files needed in a given program. If a program does not process files, this section can be omitted in its entirety. In this text, however, this section is required, since all the programs will access files.

Files containing the data that must be processed by the program are input files, whereas files containing the processed data are output files. Realize that files produced as output by one program can be used as input to another. Printer files are exceptions, since they are exclusively output files. Typical files are shown in Figure 3.6.

In the first half of this text, there will generally be one input file and one output file. In later chapters, more than one input and/or output file may be needed. The entries that assign input files to input devices and output files to output devices are coded in the FILE-CONTROL paragraph.

FILE-CONTROL

The FILE-CONTROL paragraph must contain a SELECT statement for each file. The purpose of a SELECT statement is to ASSIGN a particular file by name to the particular external device that will process the file.

The format of the SELECT statement is:

```
SELECT file-name ASSIGN TO {implementor-name}
                           {literal          }
```

The verb SELECT is followed by the internal name of the file, that is, the name by which it will be referenced within the program. Recall that all file names are created by the programmer during the program design phase and first appear on the system flowchart.

Figure 3.6 Examples of files on various physical media

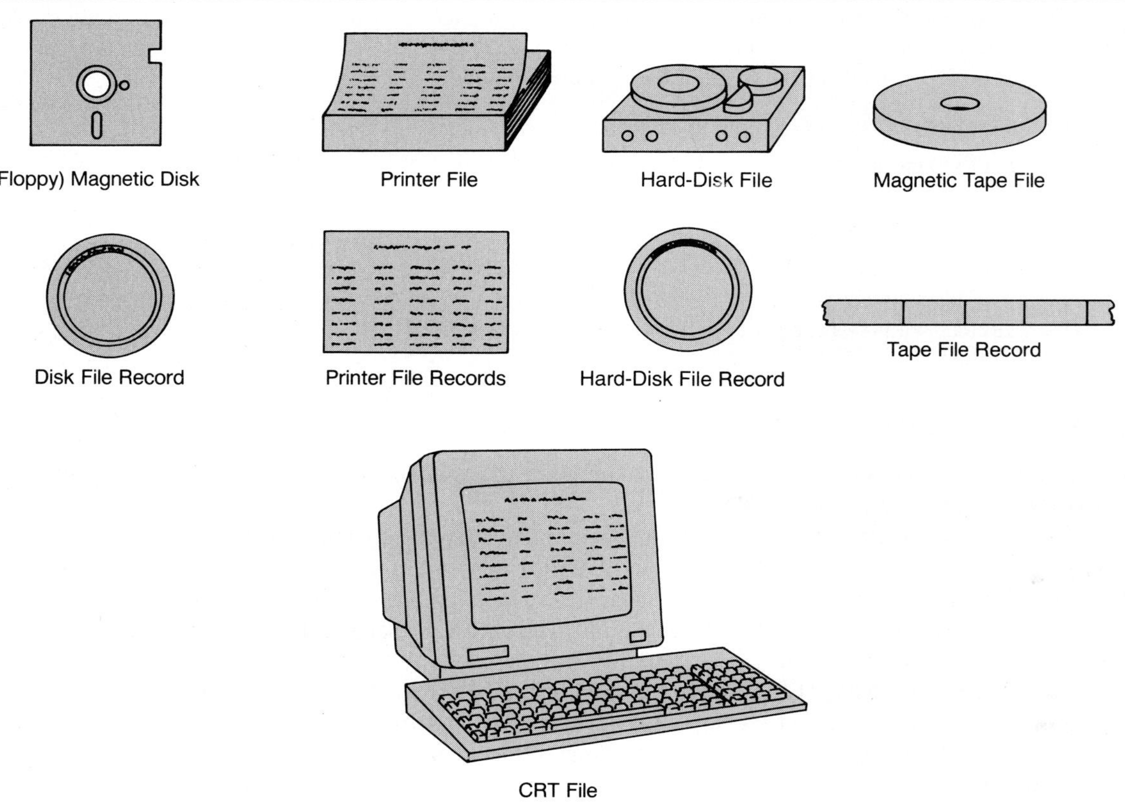

The ASSIGN clause then specifies one of the following:

1. **An implementor-name.** This is the name of the device that will process the file. This device is a physical link between the internal file name and the name of the file, external to the COBOL program, that actually contains the records. The external file can be stored on a disk, or tape, or printer paper, or some other medium. The implementor-names are system-specific.
2. **A literal.** This may be an actual file specification, such as a file name as it appears in a user's directory, or it may be a logical name. A logical name can be used to refer to a specific device, directory, or file within a directory. When a logical name is used, a system command must be used to establish the equivalence between the internal file name and an external file before the execution of the COBOL program. The literal must be nonnumeric.

Your instructor will give you the specific details for your computer system. The following examples illustrate the above statements.

Example 1:

```
SELECT PHONE-SALES-FILE ASSIGN TO "C2SAMR.DAT".
```

In this example, the internal file name is PHONE-SALES-FILE and the external file name is C2SAMR.DAT, that is, C2SAMR.DAT is the name of the data file as known within the user's **directory.** Within the **program,** the data file is referred to as PHONE-SALES-FILE. As a result of this SELECT statement, every time the program is executed, it has direct access to the records stored in file C2SAMR.DAT.

Example 2:

```
SELECT PHONE-SALES-FILE ASSIGN TO COB$INPUT.
```

In this example, COB$INPUT is a VAX logical name. To equate this logical name to the file name C2SAMR.DAT in the user's directory, a VAX command (not a COBOL program statement) such as $ ASSIGN C2SAMR.DAT COB$INPUT must be executed **before** running the program. COBOL programs can be made file-independent and device-independent by using logical names in the ASSIGN clause of the SELECT statement. Most programs in this text use this option.

Example 3:

```
SELECT PHONE-SALES-FILE ASSIGN TO SYS005-UR-2540R-S.
```

In this example, SYS005-UR-2540R-S is an implementor-name for an IBM-370. The records of the data file will be made available to the COBOL program through this particular device.

The sample program in this chapter contains SELECT statements of the form shown in example 2. They are:

```
SELECT PHONE-SALES-FILE   ASSIGN TO COB$INPUT.
SELECT PHONE-SALES-REPORT ASSIGN TO COB$OUTPUT.
```

The presence of the logical names COB$INPUT and COB$OUTPUT means that before the program is run, these names have to be associated with specific files in the user's directory. This is done by executing ASSIGN statements at the VAX command level. Here is the complete set of VAX commands that are needed to run the program:

```
$ COBOL/ANSI/LIS C2SAMR.COB
$ LINK C2SAMR.OBJ
$ ASSIGN C2SAMR.DAT COB$INPUT
$ ASSIGN C2SAMR.OUT COB$OUTPUT
$ RUN C2SAMR.EXE
```

The first ASSIGN statement associates the user's file C2SAMR.DAT with the logical name COB$INPUT, and the second ASSIGN statement associates the user's file C2SAMR.OUT with the logical name COB$OUTPUT. Then, when the program is executed, the SELECT statements in the FILE-CONTROL paragraph of the INPUT-OUTPUT SECTION complete the connection. That is, the user's file C2SAMR.DAT is connected through the logical name COB$INPUT to the internal input file name PHONE-SALES-FILE, and the user's file C2SAMR.OUT is connected through the logical name COB$OUTPUT to the internal output file name PHONE-SALES-REPORT.

■ **Figure 3.7** ENVIRONMENT DIVISION format (partial)

```
[ENVIRONMENT DIVISION.
[CONFIGURATION SECTION.
[SOURCE-COMPUTER. computer-name.]
[OBJECT-COMPUTER. computer-name.]
[SPECIAL-NAMES. implementor-name IS mnemonic-name.]]
[INPUT-OUTPUT SECTION.
[FILE-CONTROL.

    SELECT file-name    ASSIGN TO {implementor-name} . . .]]]
                                  {literal         }
```

On the other hand, if the SELECT statements in the chapter program had been of the form shown in example 1, specifically

```
SELECT PHONE-SALES-FILE   ASSIGN TO "C2SAMR.DAT".
SELECT PHONE-SALES-REPORT ASSIGN TO "C2SAMR.OUT".
```

then, at the VAX command level, the following commands would have been executed:

```
$ COBOL/ANSI/LIS C2SAMR.COB
$ LINK C2SAMR.OBJ
$ RUN C2SAMR.EXE
```

The sample programs in this text use the form shown in example 2 to maintain the file independence of the program.

Note: If you use the form of example 1, any change in the user's input and/or output file names requires the user to edit the COBOL program to change the names in the SELECT statements; whereas if you use the form of example 2, changes in the user's input and/or output file names leave the COBOL program intact since the new names need be specified only in the VAX ASSIGN statements when the program is executed.

The general format of the ENVIRONMENT DIVISION as specified in the 1985 version of ANSI COBOL and used in the sample program is shown in Figure 3.7. This format is incomplete. We will usually present only those portions of a format that are applicable to the current discussion. Complete formats are provided in the appendices.

Coding the ENVIRONMENT DIVISION

As noted earlier, all division and section headers must be coded in area A and end with a period. In this division, the headers are ENVIRONMENT DIVISION, CONFIGURATION SECTION, and INPUT-OUTPUT SECTION.

Paragraph names must also be coded in area A and end with a period. The CONFIGURATION SECTION contains three paragraphs: SOURCE-COMPUTER, OBJECT-COMPUTER, and SPECIAL-NAMES. In this text, the INPUT-OUTPUT section has only one paragraph: FILE-CONTROL.

The hyphens contained in the COBOL reserved words INPUT-OUTPUT, SOURCE-COMPUTER, OBJECT-COMPUTER, SPECIAL-NAMES, and FILE-CONTROL are all essential. Omission of hyphens, as well as the required periods, will cause the compiler to generate error messages.

The entries in a paragraph must be coded in area B. In particular, the computer names and the SELECT statements must be coded in area B and end with a period.

Some programmers prefer not to code on a line containing a paragraph name and to code the ASSIGN clauses indented on separate lines. Such coding is shown below.

Note: The programs in this text do not use the form illustrated below.

```
ENVIRONMENT DIVISION.

CONFIGURATION SECTION.

SOURCE-COMPUTER.
    VAX-VMS-8650.
OBJECT-COMPUTER.
    VAX-VMS-8650.
```

```
INPUT-OUTPUT SECTION.

FILE-CONTROL.
    SELECT PHONE-SALES-FILE
        ASSIGN TO COB$INPUT.
    SELECT PHONE-SALES-REPORT
        ASSIGN TO COB$OUTPUT.
```

DATA DIVISION

The third division of a COBOL program is the DATA DIVISION. The purpose of this division is to provide descriptions of all the data storage areas that will be needed by the program. A storage area known as an input buffer is reserved in input memory to store a data record as it is read from an input file. A storage area known as an output buffer is reserved in output memory to store an output record before its being written onto some external file, such as a printer file. In addition, a variety of storage areas are set aside in working storage for all other data items needed in the program.

In the sample program, the storage areas that are needed in input memory, output memory, and working storage are shown in Figure 3.8.

The storage area reserved in input memory and the storage area reserved in output memory must be described in the file section of the DATA DIVISION. The various storage areas reserved in working storage must be described in the WORKING-STORAGE SECTION of the DATA DIVISION. See the following:

```
DATA DIVISION.

FILE SECTION.

    (THIS SECTION MUST CONTAIN A DETAILED DESCRIPTION OF EACH FILE.
    A FILE DESCRIPTION INCLUDES A DETAILED DESCRIPTION OF THE RECORDS THAT
    BELONG TO THE FILE.)

WORKING-STORAGE SECTION.

    (THIS SECTION MUST CONTAIN A COMPLETE DESCRIPTION OF ALL THE DATA
    ITEMS THAT ARE NEEDED FOR THE PROPER PROCESSING OF THE PROGRAM BUT
    THAT DO NOT BELONG DIRECTLY TO INPUT OR OUTPUT RECORDS.)
```

FILE SECTION

Recall that in the ENVIRONMENT DIVISION, all the internal files needed in a program have been identified by name in the SELECT statements. Now, in the FILE SECTION of the DATA DIVISION, each file must be completely described.

The description of a file must contain two items:

1. An FD (file description) paragraph
2. A *01 entry* for each type of record belonging to the file

See the following.

```
FILE SECTION.

FD  PARAGRAPH
    (MUST SPECIFY THE NAME OF THE FILE. MAY PROVIDE OPTIONAL FILE DOCUMENTATION,
    SUCH AS THE SIZE OF ITS RECORDS.)

01  RECORD NAME.
    (DESCRIPTIONS OF DATA ITEMS BELONGING TO THIS TYPE OF RECORD.)

FD  PARAGRAPH
    (MUST SPECIFY THE NAME OF THE FILE. MAY PROVIDE OPTIONAL FILE DOCUMENTATION,
    SUCH AS THE SIZE OF ITS RECORDS.)

01  RECORD NAME.
    (DESCRIPTIONS OF DATA ITEMS BELONGING TO THIS TYPE OF RECORD.)

    ETC...
```

Figure 3.8 Storage areas needed in the main memory components for the chapter program

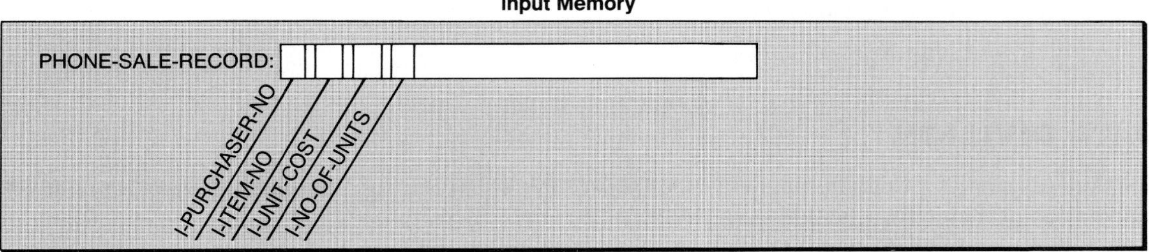

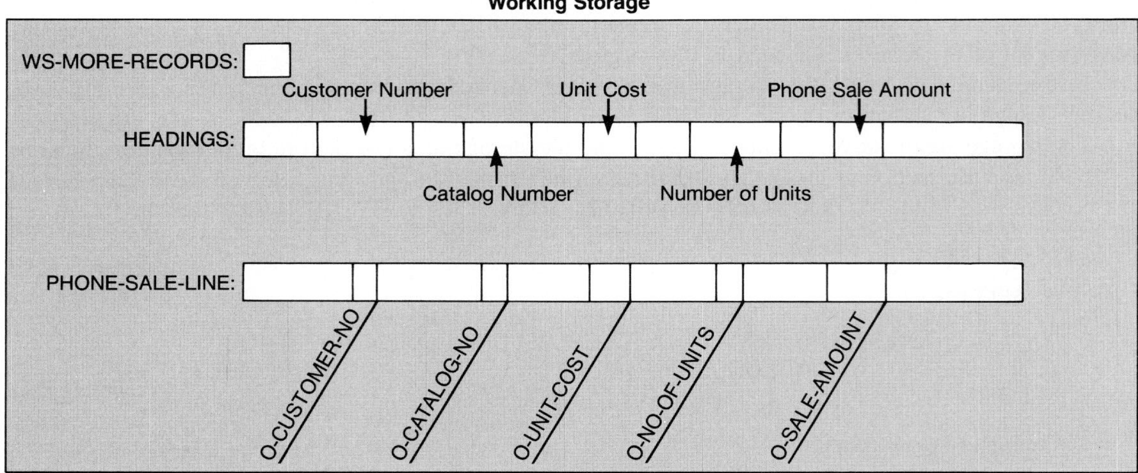

Output Memory

PRINTLINE:

The FD Paragraph

The FD or file description paragraph must name the file. Additionally, it can contain optional clauses that provide file documentation.

The format of the FD paragraph is shown in Figure 3.9.

Please note the following:

1. The paragraph name FD is coded in area A. This entry is required.
2. The name of the file is coded in area B, generally on the same line as the FD entry.
3. The clause RECORD CONTAINS or IS VARYING IN SIZE provides useful documentation. The compiler, however, determines the actual size from the record description that follows. Though the clause is optional, it is helpful in debugging situations, and the author recommends its use. (The VARYING IN SIZE option will be explained later when needed in relation to variable-length records.)
4. The optional clauses DATA RECORD IS (or DATA RECORDS ARE) and LABEL RECORDS ARE, though still supported in COBOL '85, are classified as obsolete and are scheduled for deletion when the standards are next revised. We will not use them in this text.
5. The format allows other clauses. They will be explained as needed in later chapters.
6. There must be only one period. It is inserted following the last clause, and it ends the FD paragraph.
7. The FD paragraph must be followed by one or more record description entries.

Figure 3.9 FD paragraph format

```
FD  file-name-1
           ⎧ CONTAINS integer-1 CHARACTERS                     ⎫
           ⎪ IS VARYING IN SIZE                                ⎪
  [RECORD  ⎨ [[FROM integer-2] [TO integer-3] CHARACTERS]       ⎬ ]
           ⎪  [DEPENDING ON data-name-1]                       ⎪
           ⎩ CONTAINS integer-4 TO integer-5 CHARACTERS        ⎭

  [DATA  { RECORD IS   } data-name-2...]
         { RECORDS ARE }

  [LABEL { RECORD IS   } { STANDARD }
         { RECORDS ARE } { OMITTED  }
```

Figure 3.10 Coding of a record containing subdivisions—example

```
01   PHONE-SALE-RECORD.
     05 I-CUSTOMER-NO      PIC X(4).
     05 FILLER             PIC XX.
     05 I-CATALOG-NO       PIC X(4).
     05 FILLER             PIC XX.
     05 I-UNIT-COST        PIC 999V99.
     05 FILLER             PIC XX.
     05 I-NO-OF-UNITS      PIC 9(4).
```

The 01 Record Description Entry

A 01 entry is needed for each type of record that belongs to the file. It is always coded in area A, and it tells the computer that a *record name* and a *record description* immediately follow.

The record name must be coded in area B. It is usually coded on the same line as the 01 entry. The record description then follows in either one of two ways:

1. If the record consists of a single field, that is, the record is **not** subdivided into fields, the description consists solely of a PICTURE clause following the record name, as in the following example:

```
01   PRINTLINE       PIC X(132).
```

2. If the record consists of more than one field, the record name is followed by a period. Then, on successive lines, higher-level entries (*entries with a level number between 02 and 49*) will be coded in area B for each field of the record. See Figure 3.10.

These entries specify the names of the fields, the characteristics of each field, the order in which the fields occur on the record, and the relationships that exist among the fields of the record.

FILE SECTION Examples

In the sample program, the FILE-CONTROL paragraph of the INPUT-OUTPUT SECTION of the ENVIRONMENT DIVISION contains two SELECT statements. This means that the FILE SECTION of the DATA DIVISION must contain two FD paragraphs, one for each file needed in the program. See Figure 3.11.

As another example, consider the FILE-CONTROL paragraph contained in Figure 3.12. In this case, there are three SELECT statements. The FILE SECTION of the DATA DIVISION must therefore contain three FD paragraphs, one for the file MASTER-FILE, one for the file DETAIL-FILE, and one for the file PRINT-FILE.

In Figure 3.11, the FD paragraph for the input file PHONE-SALES-FILE is followed by only one 01-level entry. This means that the file contains only **one type** of record. This is also the case for the output file PHONE-SALES-REPORT.

On the other hand, in Figure 3.12, the FD paragraph for the output file PRINT-FILE is followed by two 01-level entries, indicating that this file contains **two types** of records.

■ **Figure 3.11** Correspondence between the SELECT statements and FD paragraphs—example 1

```
INPUT-OUTPUT SECTION.

FILE-CONTROL.
    SELECT PHONE-SALES-FILE     ASSIGN TO COB$INPUT.
    SELECT PHONE-SALES-REPORT   ASSIGN TO COB$OUTPUT.

DATA DIVISION.

FILE SECTION.

FD  PHONE-SALES-FILE
    RECORD CONTAINS 23 CHARACTERS.

01  PHONE-SALE-RECORD.
    05 I-CUSTOMER-NO      PIC X(4).
    05 FILLER             PIC XX.
    05 I-CATALOG-NO       PIC X(4).
    05 FILLER             PIC XX.
    05 I-UNIT-COST        PIC 999V99.
    05 FILLER             PIC XX.
    05 I-NO-OF-UNITS      PIC 9(4).

FD  PHONE-SALES-REPORT
    RECORD CONTAINS 132 CHARACTERS.

01  PRINTLINE             PIC X(132).
```

■ **Figure 3.12** Correspondence between the SELECT statements and FD paragraphs—example 2

```
FILE-CONTROL.
    SELECT MASTER-FILE     ASSIGN TO "MASTER.DAT".
    SELECT DETAIL-FILE     ASSIGN TO COB$INPUT.
    SELECT PRINT-FILE      ASSIGN TO COB$OUTPUT.

DATA DIVISION.

FILE SECTION.

FD  MASTER-FILE
    RECORD CONTAINS 40 CHARACTERS.

01  DISK-RECORD.
    05 DELETE-CODE    PIC X.
    05 DK-SSN         PIC X(9).
    05 DK-NAME        PIC X(20).
    05 FILLER         PIC X(10).

FD  DETAIL-FILE
    RECORD CONTAINS 80 CHARACTERS.

01  DETAIL-RECORD.
    05 DETAIL-SSN     PIC X(9).
    05 FILLER         PIC X(71).

FD  PRINT-FILE
    RECORD CONTAINS 132 CHARACTERS.

01  PRINTLINE         PIC X(132).

01  PRINT-RECORD.
    05 FILLER         PIC X(10).
    05 PR-SSN         PIC X(9).
    05 FILLER         PIC X(5).
    05 PR-NAME        PIC X(20).
    05 FILLER         PIC X(88).
```

Record Field Descriptions

In Figure 3.11, the entry

```
05 I-NO-OF-UNITS    PIC 9(4).
```

is a record **field** description. The 05 is the **level number** of the field, I-NO-OF-UNITS is the **name** of the field, and PIC 9(4) specifies the *size* of the field and the *class* of character that will be stored in it.

The level number assigned to a field is a number in the range 02 through 49. It is used as follows:

1. All first-level subdivisions of a record are assigned the same level number. In the sample program, the input record PHONE-SALE-RECORD is separated into seven first-level subdivisions, as

Figure 3.13 First-level subdivisions of a record—example

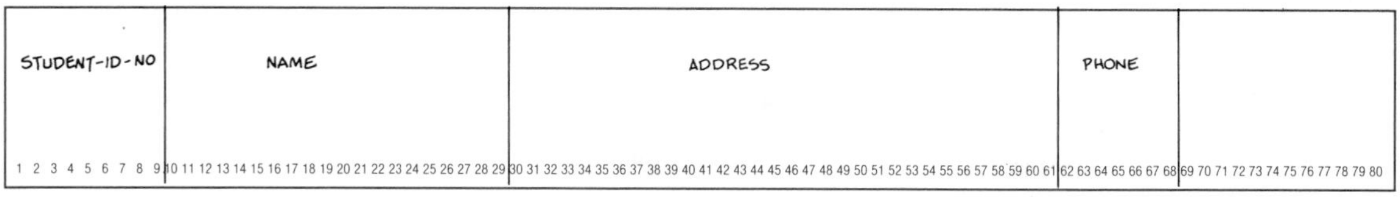

STUDENT-ID-NO	NAME	ADDRESS	PHONE	
1 2 3 4 5 6 7 8 9	10 11 12 13 14 15 16 17 18 19 20 21 22 23 24 25 26 27 28 29	30 31 32 33 34 35 36 37 38 39 40 41 42 43 44 45 46 47 48 49 50 51 52 53 54 55 56 57 58 59 60 61	62 63 64 65 66 67 68	69 70 71 72 73 74 75 76 77 78 79 80

Record Name: STUDENT-INFO

Figure 3.14 Multilevel subdivisions of a record—example

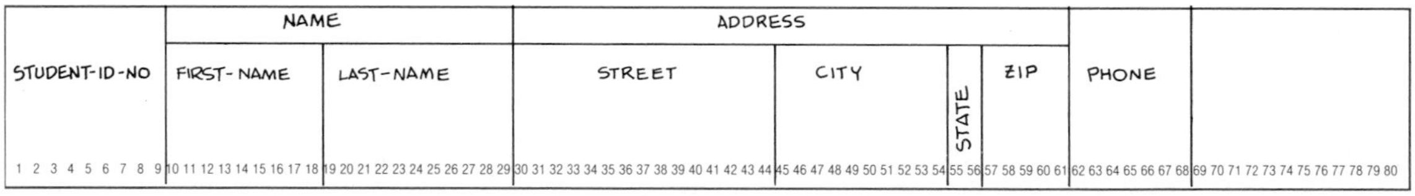

	NAME		ADDRESS					
STUDENT-ID-NO	FIRST-NAME	LAST-NAME	STREET	CITY	STATE	ZIP	PHONE	
1 2 3 4 5 6 7 8 9	10 11 12 13 14 15 16 17 18	19 20 21 22 23 24 25 26 27 28 29	30 31 32 33 34 35 36 37 38 39 40 41 42 43 44	45 46 47 48 49 50 51 52 53 54	55 56	57 58 59 60 61	62 63 64 65 66 67 68	69 70 71 72 73 74 75 76 77 78 79 80

Record Name: STUDENT-INFO

Figure 3.15 Use of level numbers in coding a record with multilevel subdivisions—example

```
01  STUDENT-INFO.
    05 STUDENT-ID-NO      PIC 9(9).
    05 NAME.
       10 FIRST-NAME      PIC A(9).
       10 LAST-NAME       PIC A(11).
    05 ADDRESS.
       10 STREET          PIC X(15).
       10 CITY            PIC A(10).
       10 STATE           PIC AA.
       10 ZIP             PIC 9(5).
    05 PHONE              PIC 9(7).
    05 FILLER             PIC X(12).
```

shown in Figure 3.1a. They have been assigned the level number 05. The level number 02, 04, 10, or any other could have been used. The important fact is that all the fields must be assigned the **same** level number, because they all are major subdivisions of the record.

The record shown in Figure 3.13 is separated into five major fields. Each of these must be given the same level number.

2. If a major subdivision of a record is itself subdivided, then the level number assigned to the subfields must be a higher number than the one assigned to the major field. In Figure 3.14, the major fields NAME and ADDRESS of Figure 3.13 have been subdivided. The subfields of NAME and the subfields of ADDRESS are assigned the higher-level number 10.

The coding of the record STUDENT-INFO (of Figure 3.14) is shown in Figure 3.15.

If any of the fields at the 10 level were further subdivided, the subdivisions would be third-level subdivisions and would be assigned level numbers higher than 10. The pattern continues in order to show the hierarchical relationships that exist among the data fields of the record.

In this text, first-level subdivisions are assigned level number 05; second-level subdivisions are assigned level number 10; third-level subdivisions are assigned level number 15, and so on, using increments of 5 at each level. Other programmers begin with level number 02 and use increments of 2.

3. All subdivisions of a record must be coded in area B. First-level subdivisions are usually coded beginning in column 12, second-level subdivisions in column 16, third-level subdivisions in column 20, and so on. The indentations in the coding of the record help to visually represent the hierarchy of data items within the record. They are not required by the compiler.

Elementary and Group Items

An *elementary item* is a data item that is not subdivided. Examples of elementary data items are PRINTLINE in the example on page 105, I-NO-OF-UNITS in Figure 3.10, and STUDENT-ID-NO and PHONE in Figure 3.15.

A *group item* is a data item that is subdivided. Examples of group data items are PHONE-SALE-RECORD in Figure 3.10 and NAME and ADDRESS in Figure 3.15. Group data items are also called *parent* items.

The PICTURE Clause

The purpose of the PICTURE clause is to specify data field characteristics as to size, class, and any special *editing* requirements. The format of the PICTURE clause is shown in Figure 3.16.

The PICTURE clause is required in the description of any elementary data item. It **must not** accompany a group item entry. For instance, in Figure 3.15, the group items NAME and ADDRESS are not followed by a PICTURE clause, but the elementary items belonging to the groups are each accompanied by a PICTURE clause.

Group data items are not given PICTURE specifications because specifying the PICTURE for each elementary item of a group details the specifications of the group item itself.

The character string contained in the PICTURE clause must identify the size of the data field, the class of the data field, and the editing characters that must be stored in the field. As noted earlier, the class means the kind of character that can be validly assigned to the field. It is specified by using one of three class codes: **9, A, X,** which are defined as follows:

1. The code **9** represents a *numeric* character.
2. The code **A** represents an *alphabetic* character or a *space.*
3. The code **X** represents an *alphanumeric* character, that is, any valid character, including the special characters on the keyboard.

If the character string consists solely of the code **9,** the data item (or field) is classified as a numeric item (or field). If the character string consists solely of the code **A,** the data item (or field) is classified as an alphabetic item (or field). If the character string contains at least one code **X,** the data item (or field) is classified as an alphanumeric item (or field). For instance, in Figure 3.15, the entry

```
10  STUDENT-ID-NO    PIC 9(9).
```

means that the field STUDENT-ID-NO is a numeric field; the entry

```
10  STREET           PIC X(15).
```

means that the field STREET is an alphanumeric field; and the entry

```
10  STATE            PIC AA.
```

means that the field STATE is an alphabetic field.

The **size** of the field is the maximum number of characters that can be stored in the field. These characters include the ones specified by the class code and certain editing characters. (Editing characters are examined briefly below.)

Examples (without editing characters):

PICTURE Clause	Class	Size
PIC 999	numeric	3
PIC XXXXXX	alphanumeric	6
PIC AA	alphabetic	2

Figure 3.16 Picture clause format

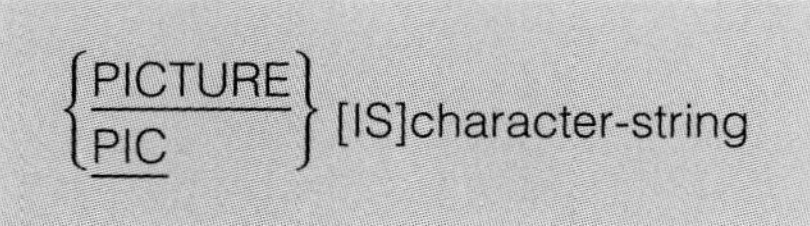

In the preceding examples, there are two ways of specifying the field size:

1. Repeat the class code the correct number of times, as shown.
2. Write a number within parentheses immediately following the class code, as in:

```
PIC 9(3)
PIC X(6)
PIC A(2)
```

The number within parentheses means that the class code is repeated this number of times. The PICTURE clauses PIC 999 and PIC 9(3) provide exactly the same information: The class is numeric, and the size is 3.

The use of parentheses is preferable if the same code is to be repeated more than four times, since less coding is required, as shown in the following:

X(6) is preferable to XXXXXX (4 keystrokes instead of 6)

Even though there are no official standards to follow, some programmers have developed a strong preference for the following scheme:

1. If the character string does not contain a V or editing characters, always denote the size by inserting it within parentheses. Examples: X(6), X(2), 9(1), and so on.
2. If the character string contains a V, use parentheses before the V, and use repetition after the V. Examples: 9(4)V99, 9(1)V999, and so on.
3. If the character string contains editing characters, use repetition only. Examples: $9,999.99, $ZZ,ZZ9.99–, and so on.

As a programmer, you will develop your own preference. In any case, the objective is to provide as much clarity as possible.

The special *editing* requirements of a field are those required to make printed (or displayed) values meaningful to the user. For instance, the date represented by 10/15/87 is easier to interpret than if it were represented by 101587. The slant or slash (/) is an editing character. More will be said about editing characters later.

Special Characters in the PICTURE of Numeric Items

We have just seen that if a character string consists exclusively of the code **9,** the item is a numeric item. There are, however, three special characters that may be present in the character string of a numeric item without affecting either its class or its size. These characters are the **V, S,** and **P.**

Note: These special characters must not be confused with editing characters. These three characters are used to make a **stored** value meaningful **to the computer,** not to the user.

The **V** in a numeric PICTURE indicates the position of an *assumed decimal* point.

Examples:

PICTURE	Field Characters	Value
99V99	1234	12.34
999V9	1234	123.4
9V999	1234	1.234
V9999	1234	.1234

It is important to note that the decimal point is **not** a character in the field. The **V** in the string of **9**s tells the computer to process the stored characters (1234 in the examples) as if there were a decimal point in that position.

Note 1: The decimal point must **never** be entered as a character in a numeric field when you are inputting data.

It should be obvious that the character strings **9999V** and **9999** are equivalent. That is, a **V** is never the rightmost character in a character string.

Note 2: The **V** in a character string does **not** count in determining the size of the field.

In the examples above, the field size is 4, not 5.

The special character **S** can be specified as the leftmost character in a numeric PICTURE. It tells the computer that the value in the field is to be processed as a *signed* number.

All arithmetic operations yield signed results. If the **S** is not specified for the field that will receive a signed result, then only the absolute value is stored. For instance, if the result of (2 – 5) is to be stored in an **unsigned** field, it is stored as the number 3; this is obviously an error. But if the result is to be stored in a **signed** field, it is stored as the number –3; this value is correct.

In a field properly defined as a signed numeric field, the sign is usually stored in the rightmost byte of the field, along with the rightmost digit.

Examine the description in the following example:

```
05  AMOUNT-A     PIC S999.
```

Note that this is a signed field whose size is 3. The storage area associated with this description may be represented as follows:

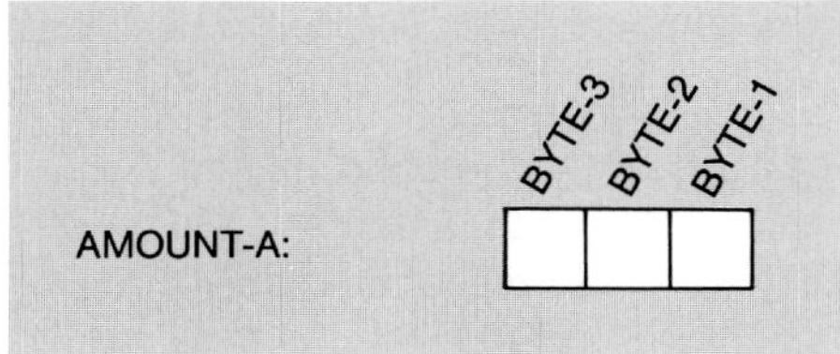

If the value +276 is to be stored in the field AMOUNT-A, the sign (+) **and** the digit 6 are stored in BYTE-1, the digit 7 in BYTE-2, and the digit 2 in BYTE-3, as follows:

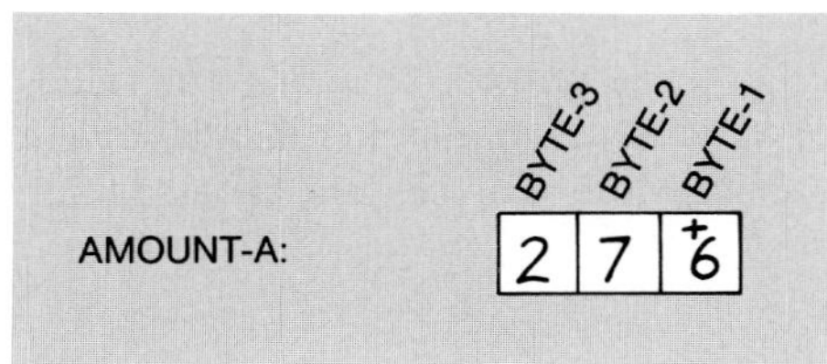

Since no two characters can physically occupy the same byte, the combination of the plus (+) sign and the digit **6** is represented internally as the letter **F,** as shown in the following:

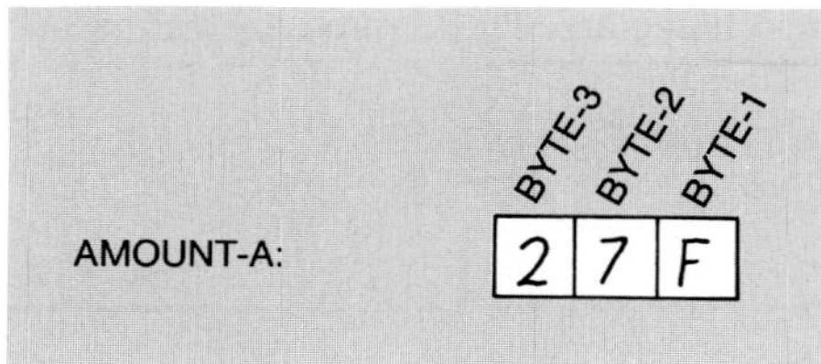

The **S** in the PICTURE that defines the field AMOUNT-A tells the computer that BYTE-1 contains a sign and a digit. When the sign is stripped from BYTE-1, what is left is the digit 6. That is, internally, **27F** means **+276.**

Similarly, if AMOUNT-B also has PIC S999, and if the number –348 is to be stored in the field, then each byte contains the characters shown below:

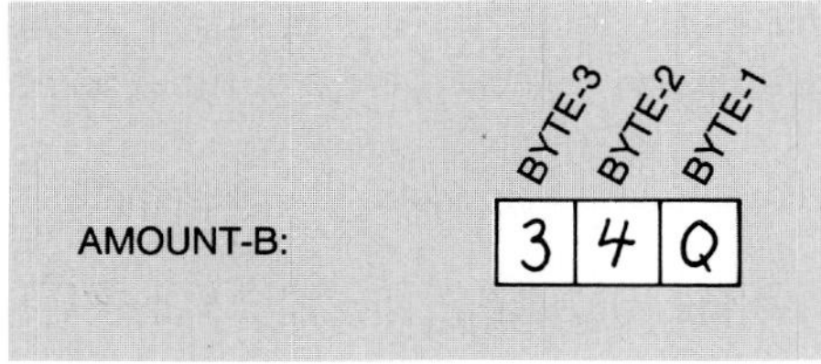

The **Q** in BYTE-1 is equivalent to the combination of the minus (–) sign and the digit 8.

Figure 3.17 Characters corresponding to signed digits

Digit	Sign	
	Positive	Negative
1	A	J
2	B	K
3	C	L
4	D	M
5	E	N
6	F	O
7	G	P
8	H	Q
9	I	R
0	{,[,?,0	},],:,!

The table in Figure 3.17 shows the characters that correspond to the signed digits.

Note 1: The **S** in a numeric PICTURE does not increase field size.

Note 2: The **S** should always be specified in the description of working storage numeric items that will be used in arithmetic operations. Signed items are processed more efficiently and are less likely to cause programming errors.

Note 3: If you (or any data entry operator) must enter signed numeric values into source fields, such as fields of input records, you must use extreme care to enter the sign along with the rightmost digit of the numeric value. For instance, enter +453 as 45C, and enter –945 as 94N.

Note 4: More sign-handling options are available to the programmer by using the SIGN clause in the description of the numeric data item. This clause is presented later, in Chapter 5.

The special character **P** can be entered in the character string of a numeric item. It represents an **assumed** zero and is used for scaling purposes, that is, to position the assumed decimal point.

Examples:

PICTURE	Field Characters	Value
99PPP	25	25000
VPPP99	25	.00025

Note 1: The **P** in a numeric PICTURE does not increase the size of the field. In the above two examples, the size of the numeric field is 2.

Note 2: The **P** can occur more than once, but only as consecutive contiguous characters, either at the left end or the right end of the character string.

Note 3: If the **P** is used as the leftmost character, then a **V** preceding it is redundant. Hence VPPP99 and PPP99 are interpreted the same way.

More on Numeric, Alphabetic, and Alphanumeric Classes

The programmer must be acutely aware of the way the COBOL compiler interprets each class of items, which can be any of the following:

1. **Numeric:** A data item (or field) is properly classified as numeric if the only characters it contains are the digits 0 through 9. It can also contain a + or – sign, provided the leftmost character in the character string of the PICTURE clause describing the item is an **S**.

   The PICTURE clause correctly defines an item as numeric if the character string in the clause consists only of the numeric class code **9,** the **V** to denote the position of an assumed decimal point, the **S** to allow the value stored in the field to be processed as a signed number, and the **P** as a scaling character representing an assumed zero.

   Note: A data item described by a numeric PICTURE can contain a maximum of eighteen digits. (Some systems may provide more or fewer digits than the COBOL standard.)

2. **Alphabetic:** A data item (or field) is properly classified as alphabetic if the only characters it contains are letters of the alphabet and/or spaces.

   The PICTURE clause correctly defines an item as alphabetic if the character string in the clause consists only of the alphabetic class code **A.**
3. **Alphanumeric:** A data item (or field) is properly classified as alphanumeric if it contains any combination of characters from the COBOL character set (digits, letters, spaces, special characters).

   The PICTURE clause correctly defines an item as alphanumeric if the character string in the clause contains the alphanumeric class code **X.** It can also contain some As and 9s, but it seldom does.

PICTURE-Related Issues

Since the COBOL compiler interprets the class of a data item as stated above, there are important issues the programmer must keep in mind. Consider the following PICTURE-related issues:

1. When data is being keyed into an input record, such as when creating a data file at a terminal, the characters assigned to a data field must be permissible characters for the class specified in the PICTURE clause describing the field. Storing the wrong type of character in a field is sufficient in many cases to cause the execution of the program to abort or, at the least, to cause unpredictable consequences.

   For instance, suppose we have the sales record description shown below.

```
01   SALES-RECORD.
     05 ITEM-NUMBER       PIC X(8).
     05 FILLER            PIC XX.
     05 SALE-DATE         PIC X(6).
     05 FILLER            PIC XX.
     05 NUMBER-SOLD       PIC 999.
     05 FILLER            PIC XX.
     05 PRICE-PER-ITEM    PIC 999V99.
     05 FILLER            PIC XX.
     05 SALESPERSON       PIC A(25).
     05 FILLER            PIC X(25).
```

   a. The data field ITEM-NUMBER is an alphanumeric field (code **X**). Values such as 155-CWF4, 84327611, AX-453, and 25001 are all valid. If the value does not consist of eight characters, the remaining positions are left blank, and blanks are also valid.

   b. The data field NUMBER-SOLD is a numeric field (code **9**). Values such as 150, 211, 060, and 001 are valid, but entries such as 25 and 7 are not valid. If 7 is the number sold, it must be entered as 007, since a blank is not permissible as a numeric character. The number 25 must be entered as 025. The entry 13F, for the value +136, is not valid since there is no **S** in the PIC clause.

   c. The data field PRICE-PER-ITEM is also a numeric field. Values such as 12550 and 00495 are valid, but 125.50 and 4.95 are not valid. The decimal point and spaces are not permissible in a numeric field. The **V** in the PICTURE clause specifies an assumed decimal point. The decimal point character itself must not be entered in the field. The numeric value will still be processed as a decimal numeric value, since the **V** specifies the position of the decimal point.

   d. The data field SALESPERSON is an alphabetic field (code **A**). A value such as LEE ROBERTS is valid, but the value LEE ROBERTS JR. is not. The period after JR is not permissible. To avoid problems with periods, hyphens, and apostrophes that appear in many names, simply change the class from alphabetic to alphanumeric by using code **X** rather than **A** in the PICTURE clause. In fact, the class code **A** is seldom used today.
2. On an input record, the following rules apply:

   a. When values are entered into an alphabetic or an alphanumeric field, the characters are normally keyed *left-justified* in the field, and excess positions are left blank.

   b. When values are entered into a numeric field, the characters are keyed *right-justified* in the field if there is no **V** in the PICTURE clause; otherwise, the characters are keyed in relation to the position of the decimal point. In either case, excess positions (to the left or to the right) are zero-filled. Examine the following examples.

Examples:

PICTURE	Value	Field Entry
9999	225	0225
99V99	2.25	0225
99V99	22.5	2250
999V99	22.5	02250
V9999	.25	2500
V9999	.025	0250

Figure 3.18 shows sample data correctly entered in a record following the specifications for the previous sales record example.

(Since an alphanumeric field allows for the storage of all the characters of the COBOL character set, the beginning programmer may ask why the class code **X** is not used exclusively. One most important reason is that numeric values stored in an alphanumeric field cannot be used for computational purposes; that is, arithmetic operations cannot be performed on such data. If a data item is to be used in arithmetic computations, it must be described as a numeric item; that is, the PICTURE clause that defines the item must contain the class code **9** [and the **V, P,** and **S** if needed]; otherwise, processing errors will occur, and the job is likely to abort.)

3. When data is transferred from one field of storage to another, such as from input storage to working storage, from input storage to output storage, or from working storage to output storage, and the PICTUREs specify different classes for these fields, the programmer must make sure that the characters being transferred into the receiving field are permissible in relation to the PICTURE clause defining that field.

Examples:

```
MOVE IN-NAME TO OUT-NAME.
```

	Sending Field		Receiving Field	
a.	IN-NAME	PIC A(20)	OUT-NAME	PIC X(20)
(Value:)	LEE ROBERTS JR		LEE ROBERTS JR	
b.	IN-NAME	PIC X(20)	OUT-NAME	PIC A(20)
(Value:)	LEE ROBERTS JR.		???????????????	

In the first example, the data transfer from IN-NAME to OUT-NAME is legal because the classes are compatible; that is, an alphabetic value can be moved into an alphanumeric field, since every alphabetic character is also an alphanumeric character.

In the second example, the data transferred from IN-NAME to OUT-NAME will generate a diagnostic, since not all the alphanumeric characters in the field are alphabetic characters. Specifically, the period after JR. is not an alphabetic character.

In general, the class of the field receiving the data must include all the characters currently in the sending field as permissible characters.

Note: Because class **A** accepts as valid characters only letters and spaces, many programmers omit its use in favor of class **X,** thereby avoiding problems that could occur with the presence of such characters as a

Figure 3.18 Correctly keyed input record—sample

```
155-CWF4  050381  072  00450  LEE ROBERTS
12345678901234567890123456789012345678901234567890123456789012345678901234567890
```

period, hyphen, apostrophe, and digit in fields intended essentially as name fields. However, as a student programmer, you still need to be aware of class **A**, as well as the constraints on its use.

First Look at Editing Characters in Output Record Fields

When the output of a program is a printed report, that is, the output file is a print file, the programmer is expected to prepare the formats of the output records so that the report is clear, easy to read, and meaningful to the user of the report. To that end, the COBOL language allows the programmer to insert certain editing characters in the PICTURE clause of numeric and alphanumeric data items.

Fields containing editing characters are known as edited fields. There are only two kinds of edited fields: numeric-edited fields and alphanumeric-edited *fields.*

A data item or field is properly classified as *numeric-edited* if the character string in the PICTURE clause contains any of the following editing characters in addition to the class code **9: B, Z, 0, ".", ",", *, +, –, CR, DB, $, /.**

Note: The use of these editing characters is explained in detail later.

A data item or field described by a numeric-edited PICTURE can contain a maximum of 18 digits. (Here also, some systems do not conform to the COBOL standard. They may allow more than or fewer than 18 digits.)

The output record PHONE-SALE-LINE of the sample program (see Figure 3.1) contains three edited fields:

```
05  O-UNIT-COST     PIC $ZZ9.99.
05  O-NO-OF-UNITS   PIC ZZZ9.
05  O-SALE-AMOUNT   PIC $Z(5)9.99.
```

In O-UNIT-COST, the editing characters are **$, Z,** and the decimal point (**.**); in O-NO-OF-UNITS, the editing character is **Z;** and in O-SALE-AMOUNT, the editing characters are **$, Z,** and the decimal point (**.**). The notation Z(5) means a string of five Zs, as in ZZZZZ, so PIC $Z(5)9.99 can be coded as $ZZZZZ9.99. In these PIC clauses, the dollar sign ($) and the decimal point (.) actually print in the specified positions, whereas the Zs cause leading zeros to be replaced by spaces.

Suppose the unit cost is two dollars and fifty cents. Without the editing characters shown in the description of the field O-UNIT-COST, the printed value would be 00250. With the editing characters as specified, the printed value is $ 2.50. Note the two spaces before the 2.

The editing characters in the example certainly make the printed value much clearer and much more meaningful.

A data item or field is properly classified as *alphanumeric-edited* if the character string in the PICTURE clause contains certain combinations of the following characters: **X, A, B, 0, 9, /.** These are explained in detail later.

Note: All editing characters inserted in the character string of an output record field are counted in determining the size of the item. For instance, the sizes of the edited fields O-UNIT-COST, O-NO-OF-UNITS, and O-SALE-AMOUNT are, respectively, 7, 4, and 10.

Coding the FILE SECTION of the DATA DIVISION

When you are ready to code the FILE SECTION of the DATA DIVISION, you should have the following design tools handy: input record layout forms, printer spacing chart, and system flowchart. These tools contain the file names, the record names, and the layouts of the input and output records. Figure 3.19 shows how these tools direct the coding of many entries in the DATA DIVISION. The coding conventions and requirements are summarized below.

Coding Conventions and Requirements

1. Division and section headers are coded in area A.
2. Blank lines are used to enhance listing readability, as follows:
   - **a.** A blank line precedes and follows a header.
   - **b.** A blank line precedes an FD paragraph.
   - **c.** A blank line precedes a record description (01 entry).

   Note: Blank lines are not required by the compiler. They are inserted to make it easier to read the listing of the program.
3. The FD paragraph coding requirements are as follows:
   - **a.** The FD paragraph name is coded in area A.
   - **b.** All other entries in the FD paragraph are coded in area B. The order in which the entries are coded is up to the programmer.

■ **Figure 3.19** Correspondence between design tools and DATA DIVISION entries

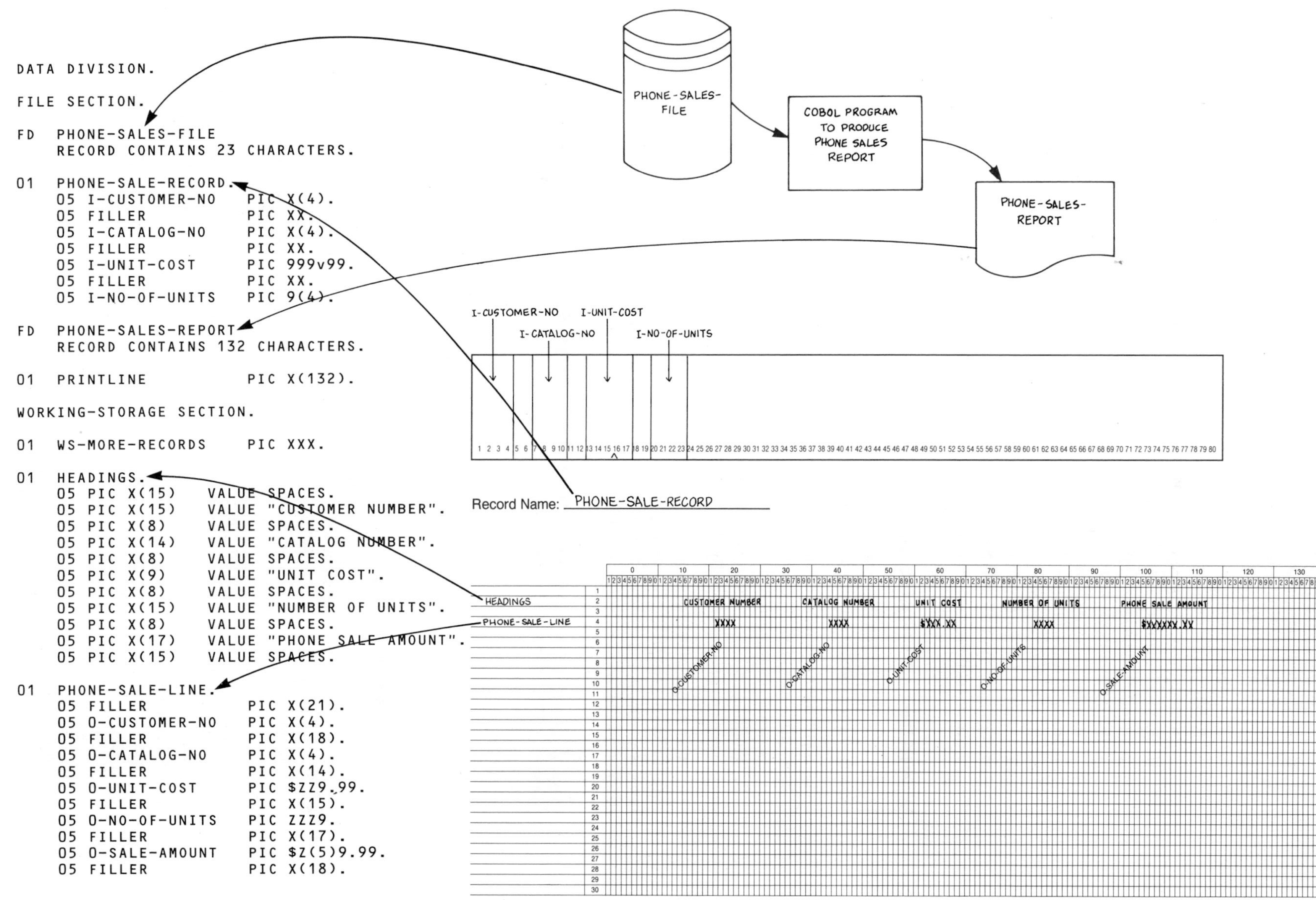


```
DATA DIVISION.

FILE SECTION.

FD  PHONE-SALES-FILE
    RECORD CONTAINS 23 CHARACTERS.

01  PHONE-SALE-RECORD.
    05 I-CUSTOMER-NO       PIC X(4).
    05 FILLER              PIC XX.
    05 I-CATALOG-NO        PIC X(4).
    05 FILLER              PIC XX.
    05 I-UNIT-COST         PIC 999v99.
    05 FILLER              PIC XX.
    05 I-NO-OF-UNITS       PIC 9(4).

FD  PHONE-SALES-REPORT
    RECORD CONTAINS 132 CHARACTERS.

01  PRINTLINE              PIC X(132).

WORKING-STORAGE SECTION.

01  WS-MORE-RECORDS        PIC XXX.

01  HEADINGS.
    05 PIC X(15)    VALUE SPACES.
    05 PIC X(15)    VALUE "CUSTOMER NUMBER".
    05 PIC X(8)     VALUE SPACES.
    05 PIC X(14)    VALUE "CATALOG NUMBER".
    05 PIC X(8)     VALUE SPACES.
    05 PIC X(9)     VALUE "UNIT COST".
    05 PIC X(8)     VALUE SPACES.
    05 PIC X(15)    VALUE "NUMBER OF UNITS".
    05 PIC X(8)     VALUE SPACES.
    05 PIC X(17)    VALUE "PHONE SALE AMOUNT".
    05 PIC X(15)    VALUE SPACES.

01  PHONE-SALE-LINE.
    05 FILLER              PIC X(21).
    05 O-CUSTOMER-NO       PIC X(4).
    05 FILLER              PIC X(18).
    05 O-CATALOG-NO        PIC X(4).
    05 FILLER              PIC X(14).
    05 O-UNIT-COST         PIC $ZZ9.99.
    05 FILLER              PIC X(15).
    05 O-NO-OF-UNITS       PIC ZZZ9.
    05 FILLER              PIC X(17).
    05 O-SALE-AMOUNT       PIC $Z(5)9.99.
    05 FILLER              PIC X(18).
```

   c. There must be a period following the last entry in the FD paragraph.
   d. No period can appear anywhere else in the paragraph.
4. A record is coded as follows:
   a. The 01 record indicator must be coded in area A.
   b. The record name must be coded in area B.
   c. Subdivisions of a record, as well as subdivisions of a field, must be coded in area B. Indentations are used to display the hierarchy of the data within a record.
   d. Only elementary items are followed by the PICTURE clause.
   e. All data item descriptions must be followed by a period.
   f. Level numbers assigned to subdivisions must be higher than the one assigned to the group item to which they belong. (In this text, level number 05 is assigned to first-level subdivisions of a record, level number 10 to second-level subdivisions, and so on.)
   g. The sum of the sizes of the elementary items must be the same as the size of the record itself.
5. The prefix **I-** is often attached to input record field names, the prefix **O-** to output record field names, and the prefix **WS-** to data items described in the WORKING-STORAGE SECTION. This practice facilitates debugging and increases the amount of program documentation.

WORKING-STORAGE SECTION

Recall that for COBOL programmers, it is useful to think of the main memory of a computer as being separated into three distinct parts (see Figure 3.8) as follows:

1. Input memory, used to store the contents of an input record as it is read from an input file
2. Output memory, used to store the contents of the various fields of an output record as that record is being prepared for printout or output to some other external output file
3. Working storage, used to store data that does not directly belong to either the input or output files, but data that is needed by the program

The layout of the storage areas (or buffers) in input memory and in output memory (for input and output records, respectively) are detailed in the FILE SECTION, as explained on the previous pages. The layouts of the storage areas in working storage for all the other data items needed by the program are detailed in the WORKING-STORAGE SECTION of the DATA DIVISION.

The data to be described in this section falls into two categories: elementary items and group items. The group items are classified as working storage **records** and are given level number 01. Noncontiguous elementary items are classified as *independent* data items and have traditionally been assigned level number 77. Level 77 data items are not subdivisions of other items and cannot themselves be subdivided. Essentially, they are identical to level 01 *elementary* items. For this reason, the level number 77 has fallen into disuse, and it is scheduled for deletion from the COBOL standards. Programmers today prefer describing noncontiguous elementary items as 01-level entries. In this text, we will not use level number 77.

01 Elementary Items

Elementary items described at the 01 level in working storage are used to store intermediate computed values, or to store constants needed in the program, or to set up control items such as an end-of-file flag. Such items are often called *work areas* to distinguish them from logical records.

In the sample program, the elementary item WS-MORE-RECORDS is the end-of-file flag. See Figure 3.19.

Suppose in the sample program we want to tally the number of records processed; that is, count the number of phone sales for the day, keep a running total of the number of units sold (regardless of the item numbers), and compute the total amount of the phone sales for the day. These are data items that will contain intermediate results, since their values change every time a new record is processed. The following example shows such items described as elementary items in the WORKING-STORAGE SECTION.

```
WORKING-STORAGE SECTION.

01  WS-RECORD-COUNT          PIC S999       VALUE 0000.
01  WS-TOTAL-UNITS-SOLD      PIC S9(8)      VALUE ZERO.
01  WS-TOTAL-SALES           PIC S9(8)V99   VALUE ZEROS.
```

Successful programmers generally prefer to group related elementary data items under a descriptive group name. For instance, the elementary items in the example above can be assigned as subordinate items of the group item WS-ACCUMULATORS, as shown below.

```
WORKING-STORAGE SECTION.

01  WS-ACCUMULATORS.
    05  WS-RECORD-COUNT        PIC S999      VALUE 0000.
    05  WS-TOTAL-UNITS-SOLD    PIC S9(8)     VALUE ZERO.
    05  WS-TOTAL-SALES         PIC S9(8)V99  VALUE ZEROS.
```

Grouping elementary items should be done judiciously, however: Assign to a group only those items that are somehow logically related. For instance, consider the following list of elementary items:

```
01  WS-MORE-RECORDS      PIC XXX        VALUE "YES".
01  WS-EMPLOYEE-CTR      PIC S9(4)      VALUE ZERO.
01  WS-REG-PAY           PIC S9(4)V99.
01  WS-OT-PAY            PIC S9(4)V99.
01  WS-LINE-CTR          PIC S99        VALUE ZERO.
01  WS-REG-PAY-ACCUM     PIC S9(8)V99   VALUE ZERO.
01  WS-TOTAL-PAY         PIC S9(4)V99.
01  WS-OT-PAY-ACCUM      PIC S9(8)V99   VALUE ZERO.
01  WS-TOTAL-PAY-ACCUM   PIC S9(8)V99   VALUE ZERO.
```

There is no advantage in the grouping shown in example a.

Example a:

```
01  INDEPENDENT-ITEMS.
    05  WS-MORE-RECORDS      PIC XXX        VALUE "YES".
    05  WS-EMPLOYEE-CTR      PIC S9(4)      VALUE ZERO.
    05  WS-REG-PAY           PIC S9(4)V99.
    05  WS-OT-PAY            PIC S9(4)V99.
    05  WS-LINE-CTR          PIC S99        VALUE ZERO.
    05  WS-REG-PAY-ACCUM     PIC S9(8)V99   VALUE ZERO.
    05  WS-TOTAL-PAY         PIC S9(4)V99.
    05  WS-OT-PAY-ACCUM      PIC S9(8)V99   VALUE ZERO.
    05  WS-TOTAL-PAY-ACCUM   PIC S9(8)V99   VALUE ZERO.
```

The groupings shown in example b, on the other hand, enhance self-documentation and also facilitate debugging. Searching a long list of elementary items is difficult. If they have been grouped carefully under descriptive names, it is much easier to locate the group that contains the elementary item you are searching for.

Example b:

```
01  PROGRAM-CONTROLS.
    05  WS-MORE-RECORDS      PIC XXX        VALUE "YES".
    05  WS-LINE-CTR          PIC S99        VALUE ZERO.
01  EMPLOYEE-WORK-AREAS.
    05  WS-REG-PAY           PIC S9(4)V99.
    05  WS-OT-PAY            PIC S9(4)V99.
    05  WS-TOTAL-PAY         PIC S9(4)V99.
01  COMPANY-ACCUMULATORS.
    05  WS-EMPLOYEE-CTR      PIC S9(4)      VALUE ZERO.
    05  WS-REG-PAY-ACCUM     PIC S9(8)V99   VALUE ZERO.
    05  WS-OT-PAY-ACCUM      PIC S9(8)V99   VALUE ZERO.
    05  WS-TOTAL-PAY-ACCUM   PIC S9(8)V99   VALUE ZERO.
```

The VALUE Clause

The description of any elementary (independent or subordinate) data item always includes the following:

1. A level number
2. The data item name (or the COBOL reserved word FILLER)
3. A PICTURE clause

The PICTURE clause indicates the class and the size of the storage area that must be reserved for the data item. It does not specify the actual value that the area will contain.

The COBOL language allows the use of the VALUE clause in the WORKING-STORAGE SECTION to assign an initial or constant value to the data item before the instructions in the PROCEDURE DIVISION are ever executed.

For instance, in the group item WS-ACCUMULATORS, coded on the preceding page, the data items WS-RECORD-COUNT, WS-TOTAL-UNITS-SOLD, and WS-TOTAL-SALES are all given an initial value of zero by using the VALUE clause as shown. (The three illustrated forms of the VALUE clause are equivalent.)

If the VALUE clause is **not** used in the description of the data item, no assumption should be made about its initial content. An instruction like

```
ADD 1 TO WS-RECORD-COUNT
```

will have unpredictable results, unless WS-RECORD-COUNT is initialized to zero.

Note: Some operating systems automatically assign **default** values to data items, if the VALUE clause is not specified. For instance, the VAX operating system assigns zero as the default value to numeric items and spaces to all other data items. Since these default values are not standard across all operating systems, it behooves the programmer not to make such assumptions.

VALUE Clause Format

The format for the VALUE clause is shown in Figure 3.20. In this format, the *literal* must conform to the PICTURE of the data item with regards to class and size. The following rules apply:

1. If the PICTURE clause specifies an alphabetic class, the literal must be completely alphabetic, and it must be enclosed within literal marks.
   Note: Some compilers require **single** literal marks (apostrophes) and others require **double** literal marks (quotation marks). You must obtain this information from your instructor or from the computer center where your program will be run. In this text, literal marks are represented by quotation marks.
2. If the PICTURE clause specifies an alphanumeric class, the literal can consist of any character from the system's character set, and it must be enclosed within literal marks.
3. If a numeric class is specified in the PICTURE clause, the literal must be numeric, and it must **not** be enclosed within literal marks. If the PICTURE clause contains a **V,** the numeric literal in the VALUE clause must contain a decimal point. If the PICTURE clause contains an **S,** the numeric literal must begin with a + or a – sign. The number of digits in the numeric literal must not exceed the size of the item.
4. If the PICTURE clause specifies an alphabetic or an alphanumeric class, the number of characters in the literal can be less than but not more than the size of the field.

In addition to the possibilities described above, the literal in the VALUE clause can be specified by a *figurative constant.* Figurative constants are COBOL reserved words. They are listed and explained on page 119.

The singular and plural forms of the figurative constants can be used interchangeably, either in the VALUE clause or in instructions in the PROCEDURE DIVISION.

The following examples illustrate the use of figurative constants:

1. In the record WS-ACCUMULATOR'S on page 117, the storage locations named WS-RECORD-COUNT, WS-TOTAL-UNITS-SOLD, and WS-TOTAL-SALES will all be filled with zeros when program execution begins.
2. **01 SEPARATION-LINE PIC X(132) VALUE IS ALL "*".** An asterisk (*) will be assigned to each of the 132 positions of the elementary item SEPARATION-LINE when program execution begins.

Figure 3.20 VALUE clause format

<u>VALUE</u> [IS] literal

■ Figurative Constants and Their Uses

Figurative Constants	Uses
ZERO, ZEROS, or ZEROES	Causes the numeric digit 0 to fill each space of the referenced *numeric* field.
SPACE or SPACES	Causes each position in the referenced *nonnumeric* field to be filled with a blank.
ALL "literal"	Causes the literal within the literal marks to be used as many times as needed to fill all the positions of the referenced *nonnumeric* field.
QUOTE or QUOTES	Represents a literal mark. Normally used to begin and end a literal when the literal itself begins and ends with a literal mark. Valid only in a *nonnumeric* field. Example: QUOTE "TOTAL UNITS" QUOTE.
HIGH-VALUE or HIGH-VALUES	Used to assign the highest value in the computer collating sequence. Valid only in an *alphanumeric* field.
LOW-VALUE or LOW-VALUES	Used to assign the lowest value in the computer collating sequence. Valid only in an *alphanumeric* field.

3. **MOVE SPACES TO PHONE-SALE-LINE.** A space will be assigned to each of the 132 positions of the record PHONE-SALE-LINE when the statement is executed.
4. **MOVE QUOTE "ACME SUPPLY CO." QUOTE TO NAME-FIELD.** Assuming that the size of NAME-FIELD is 17, the seventeen characters between the two QUOTE words will be assigned to the character positions of the data item NAME-FIELD when the statement is executed.

It should be emphasized that the VALUE clause can be used to assign initial or constant values to data items described in the WORKING-STORAGE SECTION only. Data items in the FILE SECTION are assigned values by executing instructions in the PROCEDURE DIVISION.

Rules Governing Use of the VALUE Clause

1. The VALUE clause can be used only in the WORKING-STORAGE SECTION to assign initial or constant values.
2. The VALUE clause can be used to assign initial values to elementary data items.
   a. If the PICTURE clause defines the item as numeric, then the literal must be numeric.
      i. The numeric literal must not be within literal marks.
      ii. The numeric literal must contain a decimal point if and only if the character string in the PICTURE clause contains a **V.**
      iii. The numeric literal must contain a sign (+ or –) if and only if the character string in the PICTURE clause begins with an **S.**
      iv. The numeric literal can contain a maximum of eighteen digits.
      v. The numeric value "zero" can be represented by the figurative constant ZERO, ZEROS, or ZEROES.
   b. If the PICTURE clause defines the item as alphabetic, alphanumeric, alphanumeric-edited, or numeric-edited, then the literal must be nonnumeric.
      i. The nonnumeric literal must be enclosed within literal marks, or it can be a figurative constant.
      ii. A nonnumeric literal can contain up to 160 characters. (This new maximum in COBOL '85 replaces the old maximum of 120. Some compilers allow up to 250 characters.)
      iii. Editing characters in the character string of the PICTURE clause have no effect on the literal specified in the VALUE clause. If the initial or constant value must contain editing characters, they must be included in the nonnumeric literal.
3. If the VALUE clause is used at the group level, then
   a. The literal must be a figurative constant or a nonnumeric literal.
   b. The group is initialized as if it were an elementary alphanumeric item.
   c. The VALUE clause cannot be used in the description of the group's subordinate items.

Examples:

The entries in group 1 illustrate correct uses of the VALUE clause.

Group 1.

```
01  WS-EOF-FLAG     PIC XXX     VALUE "YES".
01  WS-EOF-FLAG     PIC 9       VALUE 0.
01  WS-ITEM-CODE    PIC XXX     VALUE SPACE.
01  WS-UNIT-TOTAL   PIC 9(4)    VALUE ZEROS.
01  WS-TAX-FACTOR   PIC SV99    VALUE +.19.
01  WS-ITEM         PIC S999V9  VALUE +1.5.
```

The entries in group 2 illustrate incorrect uses of the VALUE clause. Identify the error in each case.

Group 2. (This group contains syntax errors.)

```
a. 01  WS-EOF-FLAG     PIC XXX     VALUE YES.
b. 01  WS-EOF-FLAG     PIC 9       VALUE "Y".
c. 01  WS-ITEM-CODE    PIC XXX     VALUE "ZEROS".
d. 01  WS-UNIT-TOTAL   PIC 9(4)    VALUE SPACES.
e. 01  WS-TAX-FACTOR   PIC V99     VALUE 19.
f. 01  WS-ITEM         PIC 999V9   VALUE 3425.5.
```

The errors in Group 2 are as follows:

1. In entry a, the literal YES must be enclosed within literal marks.
2. In entry b, the nonnumeric literal "Y" does not match the class specified in the PICTURE clause.
3. In entry c, the number of characters in the nonnumeric literal "ZEROS" exceeds the size specified in the PICTURE clause.
4. In entry d, the figurative constant SPACES denotes a character that is invalid for the class specified in the PICTURE clause.
5. In entry e, the numeric literal 19 must contain a decimal point in the position specified by the V in the PICTURE clause.
6. In entry f, the size of the numeric literal exceeds the size specified in the PICTURE clause.

An Alternative to the VALUE Clause

Examine the entries in the WORKING-STORAGE SECTION of the sample program. For convenience, they have been reproduced in Figure 3.21. Notice that the description of the elementary data item WS-MORE-RECORDS does not contain the VALUE clause. Recall that the function of this item is to serve as the end-of-file flag, which controls the loop that processes all the input records. To that end, it is assigned the initial value "YES". This value must remain unchanged until the EOF record is detected within the READ statement. At that time, WS-MORE-RECORDS is assigned the value "NO ", and, as a result, control will exit from the record-processing loop.

It should be clear from the discussion on the preceding pages that the flag WS-MORE-RECORDS could have been assigned the initial value "YES" as follows:

```
01  WS-MORE-RECORDS    PIC XXX   VALUE "YES".
```

Instead, the flag is assigned its initial value in the paragraph 200-START-UP by the execution of the instruction

```
MOVE "YES" TO WS-MORE-RECORDS.
```

As you work with more advanced programs, you will note that they usually contain a number of data items that must be initialized when a program starts up. Typical of these are accumulators and counters that must be set to zero and flags or switches that must be set to some initial state. Rather than use the VALUE clause in the data item descriptions, programmers often prefer to issue instructions in a start-up or initialize-variables paragraph to set all initial values. This approach increases the self-documentation of the PROCEDURE DIVISION, since it contains **all** the instructions that determine the values of these data items—the instructions that initialize the data items as well as the instructions that change the values.

Two kinds of instructions are used in a start-up paragraph to initialize data items. They are the MOVE instruction and the INITIALIZE instruction. Their formats will be examined in Chapter 4.

■ **Figure 3.21** Working storage section of the sample program

```
WORKING-STORAGE SECTION.

01  WS-MORE-RECORDS      PIC XXX.

01  HEADINGS.
    05 PIC X(15)     VALUE SPACES.
    05 PIC X(15)     VALUE "CUSTOMER NUMBER".
    05 PIC X(8)      VALUE SPACES.
    05 PIC X(14)     VALUE "CATALOG NUMBER".
    05 PIC X(8)      VALUE SPACES.
    05 PIC X(9)      VALUE "UNIT COST".
    05 PIC X(8)      VALUE SPACES.
    05 PIC X(15)     VALUE "NUMBER OF UNITS."
    05 PIC X(8)      VALUE SPACES.
    05 PIC X(17)     VALUE "PHONE SALE AMOUNT".
    05 PIC X(15)     VALUE SPACES.

01  PHONE-SALE-LINE.
    05 FILLER            PIC X(21).
    05 O-CUSTOMER-NO     PIC X(4).
    05 FILLER            PIC X(18).
    05 O-CATALOG-NO      PIC X(4).
    05 FILLER            PIC X(14).
    05 O-UNIT/COST       PIC $ZZ9.99.
    05 FILLER            PIC X(15).
    05 O-NO/OF/UNITS     PIC ZZZ9.
    05 FILLER            PIC X(17).
    05 O-SALE/AMOUNT     PIC $Z(5)9.99.
    05 FILLER            PIC X(18).
```

Records in the WORKING-STORAGE SECTION

When a COBOL program must produce a printed report, also called a print file, the layouts of the different kinds of lines that make up the report are prepared on the printer spacing chart. In the sample program of this chapter, there are only two different line layouts. They have been named HEADINGS and PHONE-SALE-LINE. Within a program, the layouts for the different kinds of lines that make up the print file are identified as records. Now, you could argue that since a print file is an output file, the records of the print file are therefore output records, and, consequently, they should be described within the file section, specifically within the file description of the output file. In the sample program, this implies the following coding in the FILE SECTION:

```
        FILE SECTION.

        FD  PHONE-SALE-FILE
            RECORD CONTAINS 23 CHARACTERS.

        01  PHONE-SALE-RECORD.
            .
            .
            .

        FD  PHONE-SALES-REPORT
            RECORD CONTAINS 132 CHARACTERS.

  ---->  01  HEADINGS.
            .
            .
            .

  ---->  01  PHONE-SALE-LINE.
            .
            .
            .
```

If you examine the listing of the sample program in Figure 3.1, you notice that the records HEADINGS and PHONE-SALE-LINE have been coded in the WORKING-STORAGE SECTION, not in the FILE SECTION.

It is very easy to justify this action for the record HEADINGS. All the fields of this record contain *constants.* The constants can be assigned to the fields very conveniently by using the VALUE clause. The VALUE clause is available for this purpose only in the WORKING-STORAGE SECTION.

A print file usually has a number of records whose fields contain constants, such as the record used to print the name of the company and the record used to print the name of the report, in addition to the one that prints the column headings. For the reasons just given, these records are also described in the WORKING-STORAGE SECTION.

By contrast, the fields of the record PHONE-SALE-LINE contain *variable* data; that is, the particular field values change for each recorded phone sale. Traditionally, this record would have been described in the file section, as an output record of the output file PHONE-SALES-REPORT, and the FD paragraph would have been coded as follows:

```
          FD   PHONE-SALES-REPORT
               RECORD CONTAINS 132 CHARACTERS.

          01   PRINTLINE          PIC X(132).

   ---->  01   PHONE-SALE-LINE.
               .
               .
               .
```

Obviously, this means that some of the print file line layouts prepared on the printer spacing chart (those that contain variable data fields) are coded in the FILE SECTION, whereas others (those that contain constants) are coded in the WORKING-STORAGE SECTION.

Today, most programmers use the approach illustrated in the sample program. One general-purpose output record area (PRINTLINE in the sample program) is described in the file description of the output file, but all the records that will eventually be written to the print file are prepared in sequence in the WORKING-STORAGE SECTION. By coding all of these records sequentially in one section, you are less likely to omit anything. This is the procedure that will be followed in this text.

Note that none of the fields of the record HEADINGS has been given a user-defined name. The reason is simply that the fields of this record do not need to be referenced individually in instructions within the PROCEDURE DIVISION. When the headings are to be printed on the report, the complete record HEADINGS is moved as a unit to the output record area PRINTLINE, and then the contents of PRINTLINE are copied on the report.

In the past, fields of a record that did not need user-defined names had to be assigned the COBOL reserved word FILLER. The latest revision of the ANSI COBOL standards has removed this requirement, so a blank field name is now acceptable. The coding of the record HEADINGS uses this option.

It should be clear from the coding of the record HEADINGS that bytes 1–15 are assigned spaces, bytes 16–30 are assigned the characters that make up the literal "CUSTOMER NUMBER," bytes 31–38 are assigned spaces, bytes 39–52 are assigned the characters that make up the literal "CATALOG NUMBER," and so on. The VALUE clauses have assigned 132 characters to the 132 bytes of the record. When the record HEADINGS is moved to PRINTLINE, the 132 characters are being copied in the same sequence into PRINTLINE. When PRINTLINE is written on the report, these characters require 132 print positions on a line of the report. Consequently, print positions 1–15 are left blank, print positions 16–30 contain the header CUSTOMER NUMBER, print positions 31–38 are left blank, print positions 39–52 contain the header CATALOG NUMBER, and so on.

By contrast, the fields of the record PHONE-SALE-LINE have been named FILLER or specific user-defined names, such as O-CUSTOMER-NO, O-CATALOG-NO, and so on. (As noted above, the word FILLER is not required.) The contents of the data fields will change from one phone sale to another. Instructions within the PROCEDURE DIVISION that process each phone sale must reference the data fields. All such references are in terms of the user-defined names assigned to the fields.

The VALUE SPACES clause could have been specified for each FILLER field, but the instruction MOVE SPACES TO PHONE-SALE-LINE in paragraph 300-WRITE-REPORT-HEADERS accomplishes the same result.

Adding a Title to the Report

Suppose that we also want the name of the company, The Allied Stock Company, to appear at the top of the report. This simple additional requirement forces us to make the appropriate changes in the design of the program. They are the following:

1. Prepare the layout of this new line on the printer spacing chart.
2. Revise the pseudocode paragraph 300-Write-Report-Headers (or revise the program flowchart module 300-WRITE-REPORT-HEADERS) to take this new function into account.

Corresponding changes must also be made in the design implementation phase, specifically the following:

3. Code this new record in the WORKING-STORAGE SECTION. Its coding should precede the coding of the record HEADINGS.
4. Recode the paragraph 300-WRITE-REPORT-HEADERS.
5. Recompile the program and check for syntax errors.
6. When compilation is successful, run the revised program.

Figure 3.22 shows the above tasks (1–4) and the revised headers on the report itself. (The report is not shown in its entirety since nothing else has changed.)

Figure 3.22 Revisions to the sample program:

Printer Spacing Chart

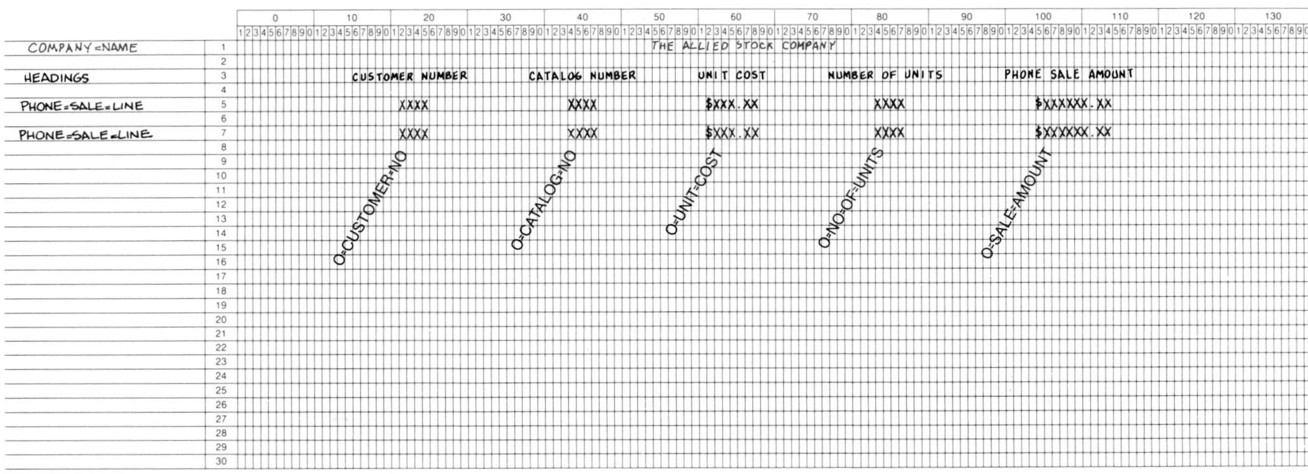

a. Task 1: Layout of new line COMPANY-NAME

300-Write-Report-Headers.

1. Move Company-Name to the output area Printline.
2. After advancing to the top of a new page, write the output record Printline.
3. Move Headings to the output area Printline.
4. After advancing 2 lines, write the output record Printline.
5. Clear the record area Phone-Sale-Line.

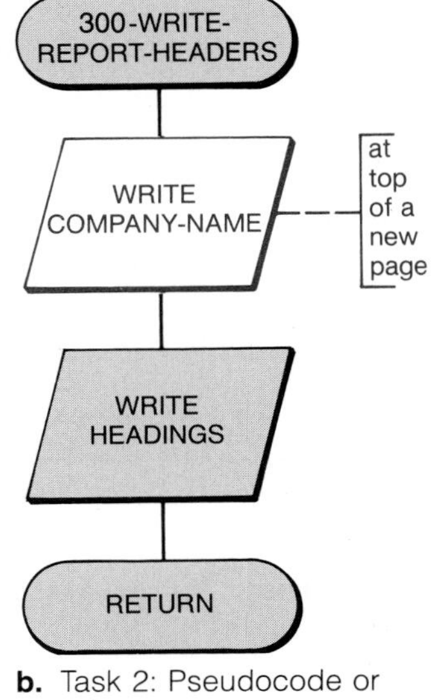

b. Task 2: Pseudocode or Program Flowchart

SYSTEM	PUNCHING INSTRUCTIONS	PAGE OF
PROGRAM	GRAPHIC	CARD FORM #
PROGRAMMER DATE	PUNCH	

```
       WORKING-STORAGE SECTION.

       01  WS-MORE-RECORDS          PIC XXX.

       01  COMPANY-NAME.
           05  PIC X(54)      VALUE SPACES.
           05  PIC X(24)      VALUE "THE ALLIED STOCK COMPANY".
           05  PIC X(54)      VALUE SPACES.

       01  HEADINGS.
           05  PIC X(15)      VALUE SPACES.
           05  PIC X(15)      VALUE "CUSTOMER NUMBER".
                 ⌇

       01  PHONE-SALE-LINE.
           05  FILLER               PIC X(21).
           05  O-CUSTOMER-NO        PIC X(4).
                 ⌇
```

c. Task 3: Coding of record COMPANY-NAME

SYSTEM	PUNCHING INSTRUCTIONS	PAGE OF
PROGRAM	GRAPHIC	CARD FORM #
PROGRAMMER DATE	PUNCH	

```
       300-WRITE-REPORT-HEADERS.
           MOVE COMPANY-NAME TO PRINTLINE.
           WRITE PRINTLINE
                 AFTER ADVANCING PAGE.
           MOVE HEADINGS TO PRINTLINE.
           WRITE PRINTLINE
                 AFTER ADVANCING 2 LINES.
           MOVE SPACES TO PHONE-SALE-LINE.
```

d. Task 4: Recoding of 300-WRITE-REPORT-HEADERS

```
                                  THE ALLIED STOCK COMPANY

CUSTOMER NUMBER       CATALOG NUMBER       UNIT COST       NUMBER OF UNITS       PHONE SALE AMOUNT

     9999                 0001              $767.50              600                $368400.00
     6001                 0003              $105.00               16                $   1680.00
     9009                 0007              $ 10.00               13                $    130.00
     0046                 0012              $ 38.00               82                $   3116.00
     9551                 0013              $ 12.50               40                $    500.00
     2150                 0036              $  9.99                3                $     29.97
     0008                 0064              $ 15.10                1                $     15.10
```

e. Revised headers on the report

Note: Step 3 at the top of page 123 requires the coding of the name of the company as the literal in the VALUE clause. Sometimes such a literal is too long to be coded on one line. Either of these two coding methods can be used to solve the problem:

1. The literal can be coded by itself on a separate line, as shown in the following example. Note that the VALUE clause does not end until the literal itself is coded. The period must be entered following the literal only.

```
01   COMPANY-NAME.
     05   PIC X(54)             VALUE SPACES.
     05   PIC X(24)             VALUE
          "THE ALLIED STOCK COMPANY".
     05   PIC X(54)             VALUE SPACES.
```

2. The literal can be started on the same line as the word VALUE, using all the possible positions on that line through column 72, and then it must be *continued* on the next line. In this case, a hyphen (-) must be coded in the continuation area (column 7), another literal mark must precede the continuation of the literal in area B, the rest of the literal is coded, a third literal mark is then coded to end the literal, and this is followed by the period, as shown below. Note that columns left blank, if any, at the end of the preceding line, through column 72, are included as part of the literal.

```
 01   COMPANY-NAME.
      05         PIC X(54)         VALUE SPACES.
      05         PIC X(24)         VALUE "THE ALLIED STOCK
-                                  "COMPANY".
      05         PIC X(54)         VALUE SPACES.
```

Coding the WORKING-STORAGE SECTION

When you are ready to code the WORKING-STORAGE SECTION, you should have the following design tools at your disposal:

1. The printer spacing chart, since it contains the layouts of all the different kinds of lines that must be printed on a report (if one is required by the program).
2. The program pseudocode (or the program flowchart), since it identifies all the program flags required, as well as the accumulators, counters, control items, work areas, and other intermediate storage areas needed by the program.

The coding conventions and requirements are summarized as follows:

Coding Conventions and Requirements

1. The first entry must be the section header, WORKING-STORAGE SECTION, coded in area A and followed by a period.
2. A blank line should precede and follow the header.
3. Elementary data items at the 01 level should be coded before group items and records at the 01 level. Knowing where to look for such items facilitates debugging.
4. It is preferable to group single elementary data items under descriptive group names rather than have a long list of elementary data items.
5. Records that will eventually be written onto a report should be coded in the sequence in which they will appear on the report.
6. The VALUE clause can be used to assign initial or constant values to data items described in this section.
7. The prefix **WS-** should be used in the data names of data items described in this section, except data names that belong to records that will be printed on a report, which should contain the prefix **O-**.
8. There is no restriction on the size of records defined in this section. The size restrictions imposed on input and output records are usually the result of the physical input and output devices available to the programmer. No such restriction applies to working-storage records.
9. The programmer should attempt to align PICTURE clauses and VALUE clauses within any one record. This facilitates debugging and produces clearer program listings.

■ **Figure 3.23** General format of a data item entry

level-number $\left\{\begin{matrix}\text{data-name}\\ \text{[FILLER]}\end{matrix}\right\}$ $\left[\left\{\begin{matrix}\underline{\text{PICTURE}}\\ \underline{\text{PIC}}\end{matrix}\right\} \text{IS character-string}\right]$ [$\underline{\text{VALUE}}$ IS literal].

The General Format of a Data Item Entry

We have seen that the most important function of the DATA DIVISION is to provide descriptions of all the storage areas needed in a program. The general format for a data item description is shown in Figure 3.23. (Other available options in this format will be presented later as needed. See Appendix A for the complete format).

In this format, the following rules apply:

1. The level number is as follows:
   a. 01 if the data item is a record described in the FILE SECTION or the WORKING-STORAGE SECTION, or a single elementary item in the WORKING-STORAGE SECTION.
   b. 02–49 if the data item is a subdivision of a record, or a subordinate of a group item.
   c. 77 if the data item is an independent item in the WORKING-STORAGE SECTION. (This level number has been classified as obsolete in the 1985 ANSI COBOL standards and is slated for deletion. It is not used in this text.)
2. The data name is defined by the programmer and must conform to applicable restrictions. (See "Rules for Constructing User-Defined Names" at the beginning of this chapter.)
   The COBOL reserved word FILLER can be used to name any storage area (field) that is not referenced individually during the execution of the program.
   The name entry can be left blank. In this case, it defaults to FILLER.
3. The PICTURE clause must be provided for all elementary data items. The character string must specify the class and size of the storage area, as well as editing requirements, if any.
4. The VALUE clause can be used to assign an initial value or a constant value to any data item in working storage. The literal can be numeric or nonnumeric, or it can be a figurative constant. It must conform to the class and size specified in the PICTURE clause.
5. The description of any data item must end with a period.

■ Important Terms in Chapter 3

alphabetic item
alphanumeric-edited item
alphanumeric item
ASSIGN clause
assumed decimal
asterisk (*)
blank field-name
character string
class codes: 9, A, X
class of a data item
CONFIGURATION SECTION
constant
DATA DIVISION
data item description entry
data item name
DATA RECORD IS clause
data transfer
editing characters
elementary item
ENVIRONMENT DIVISION
FD paragraph
figurative constant
  ALL "literal"
  HIGH-VALUE
  LOW-VALUE
  SPACE
  QUOTE
  ZERO
FILE-CONTROL
file name
FILE SECTION
FILLER
format notation
group (parent) item
IDENTIFICATION DIVISION
implementor-name
independent item
INPUT-OUTPUT SECTION
LABEL RECORDS ARE clause
left-justified
level number 77
literal continuation
nonnumeric literal
numeric-edited item
numeric item
numeric item characters: V, S, P
numeric literal
OBJECT-COMPUTER
PICTURE (PIC) clause
PROGRAM-ID
program name
RECORD CONTAINS clause
record description
record name
right-justified
SELECT statement
size of a data item
SOURCE-COMPUTER
SPECIAL-NAMES
user-defined name
VALUE clause
variable
work areas
WORKING-STORAGE SECTION
01 entry
02–49 level numbers

Exercises

1. Which of the following would be acceptable as user-defined names? If a name is unacceptable, explain why.

FIELD-1	NAME	DATE
IN-DATE	FIELD 1	END-OF-FILE
END-OF-PAGE	AREA	AREA-OF-TRIANGLE
ADRESS	LAST-FIELD	LINE-COUNTER
LINE-COUNT	-IN-FIELD	OUT-FIELD

2. Answer the following questions about the IDENTIFICATION DIVISION:
   a. Name the entry that is required in the IDENTIFICATION DIVISION, other than the header.
   b. What are the optional entries that can be used in the IDENTIFICATION DIVISION?
   c. How can a programmer provide a description of the program in the IDENTIFICATION DIVISION?
3. Answer the following questions about the ENVIRONMENT DIVISION:
   a. Are the entries in the ENVIRONMENT DIVISION mainly related to hardware or software?
   b. What are the section headers of the ENVIRONMENT DIVISION?
   c. Briefly explain the function of the entries SOURCE-COMPUTER and OBJECT-COMPUTER.
   d. Briefly explain the function of a SELECT statement in the FILE-CONTROL paragraph.
4. Write the IDENTIFICATION and ENVIRONMENT DIVISION entries, given the following information:
   a. The name of the program is CLASS-GRADES.
   b. The CPU to be used in processing the program is a VAX-VMS-8650.
   c. The input file name is GRADES-FILE, and the logical input device is COB$INPUT.
   d. The output file name is GRADES-REPORT, and the logical output device is COB$OUTPUT.
5. Refer to the system flowchart shown in Figure 3.24. Assume the name of the program is STUDENT-GRADE-PROGRAM, the CPU is a VAX-VMS-8650, the logical input device is COB$INPUT, and the logical output device is COB$OUTPUT. Code the entries of the IDENTIFICATION DIVISION and ENVIRONMENT DIVISION.
6. Examine each entry below. If the entry is correct, write OK on the corresponding line. If the entry contains errors, write in the correct coding.

```
A   B                                              A    B
IDENTIFICATION DIVISION.
PROGRAM ID.  TEST RUN.
*  THIS PROGRAM SEGMENT TESTS
*  YOUR KNOWLEDGE OF SOME COBOL
   LANGUAGE REQUIREMENTS.
ENVIRONMENT-DIVISION.
CONFIGURATION-SECTION.
    SOURCE COMPUTER.    VAX-VMS-8650.
    OBJECT COMPUTER.    VAX-VMS-8650.
```

7. Answer the following questions about the DATA DIVISION:
   a. What is the essential function of the DATA DIVISION?
   b. In the FILE SECTION of the DATA DIVISION, the first entry is FD. In which area is it coded? What does FD mean? What must be coded in area B immediately after FD? Which clause specifies the size of the records belonging to the file?

Figure 3.24

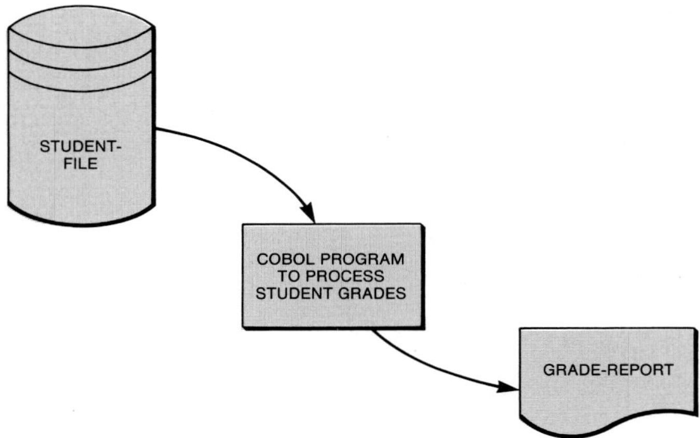

8. Given the following file description, answer the questions that follow it.

```
FD   OLD-CUSTOMER-MASTER
     RECORD CONTAINS 80 CHARACTERS.
01   OLD-CUSTOMER-RECORD.
     .
     .
     .
```

a. What is the name of the file?
b. What is the name of the record that belongs to the file?
c. What is the size of the record?

9. Consult the following record description when answering the questions that follow it:

```
01   EMPLOYEE-RECORD.
     05 SOC-SEC-NO              PIC X(9).
     05 NAME                    PIC X(15).
     05 DATE-OF-BIRTH.
         10 BIRTH-MONTH         PIC 99.
         10 BIRTH-YEAR          PIC 99.
     05 DATE-HIRED.
         10 MONTH-HIRED         PIC 99.
         10 YEAR-HIRED          PIC 99.
     05 LOCATION-CODE           PIC XX.
     05 EDUCATION-CODE          PIC X.
     05 CLASSIFICATION.
         10 CLASS-CODE          PIC XXX.
         10 DATE-OF-CLASS       PIC 9(4).
         10 RATING              PIC X.
     05 SALARY-INFO.
         10 SALARY              PIC S9(5)V99.
         10 DATE-OF-SALARY      PIC 9(4).
     05 FILLER                  PIC X(27).
```

a. What is the name of the record?
b. Identify all the group names in the record description.
c. Give the size and class of each of the following items:

```
DATE-OF-CLASS
SALARY
NAME
YEAR-HIRED
RATING
```

d. In which columns of the input record is the MONTH-HIRED value to be stored? the EDUCATION-CODE value? the DATE-OF-SALARY value?
e. What kinds of characters can properly be keyed into the field BIRTH-YEAR? LOCATION-CODE? SALARY? NAME? SOC-SEC-NO?
f. What is the effect of assigning the COBOL reserved word FILLER to the last field of the record?
g. Figure 3.25 shows the layout of the fields of the input record described above. Assign the corresponding name to each numbered field.

10. The input record layout in Figure 3.26 shows the name and class of each field. Assign a descriptive name to the record, and then write the appropriate record description entries as needed in the FILE SECTION of the DATA DIVISION.

11. Examine each entry below. If the entry is correct, write OK on the corresponding line. If the entry contains any error, write in the correct coding.

```
A    B                                                     A    B
DATA DIVISION
FILE-SECTION.
FD   INPUT-FILE.
     RECORD CONTAINS 50 CHARACTERS.
01   INPUT-RECORD
     05 I-SSN                      PIC X(9)
     05 I-NAME                     PIC X22.
     05 I ADRESS                   PIC X(15).
     05 I CITY-STATE               PICX (12.
     05 FILLER                     PIC 1X.
     05 I-PERSONAL-INFO            PIC X(15).
         10 I-SEX                  A1.
         10 I-MARITAL-STATUS       PIC X (1)
         10 I-DATE-OF-BIRTH        PIC 6X.
             15 I-MONTH BORN       PIC 99.
             15 I DAY BORN         PIC 9(2).
             15 I YEAR BORN        PIC 2 9s.
```

Figure 3.25

1	2	3 / 4	5	6 / 7	8	9	10	11 / 12	13	14	15 / 16	17	18
1 2 3 4 5 6 7 8 9	10 11 12 13 14 15 16 17 18 19 20 21 22 23 24	25 26	27 28	29 30	31 32	33 34	35	36 37 38	39 40 41 42	43	44 45 46 47 48 49	50 51 52 53	54 55 56 57 58 59 60 61 62 63 64 65 66 67 68 69 70 71 72 73 74 75 76 77 78 79 80

Figure 3.26

Record Layout Form

STUDENT-ID	STUDENT-NAME	COURSE		PROGRAM-GRADES				EXAMS		
		NUMBER	SECTION	PROG-1	PROG-2	PROG-3	PROG-4	MID-TERM	FINAL	
AN	A	AN	N	N	N	N	N	N	N	AN
1 2 3 4 5 6 7 8 9 10	11 12 13 14 15 16 17 18 19 20 21 22 23 24 25 26 27 28 29 30 31 32 33 34 35	36 37 38 39 40 41	42 43	44 45 46	47 48 49	50 51 52	53 54 55	56 57 58	59 60 61	62 63 64 65 66 67 68 69 70 71 72 73 74 75 76 77 78 79 80

AN: Alphanumeric
A: Alphabetic
N: Numeric

Record Name: ____________________

12. Refer to the layouts of output records shown in Figure 3.27. Write the record description entries for the record DETAIL-LINE.

13. Answer the following questions about the WORKING-STORAGE SECTION:

a. Describe some uses of the WORKING-STORAGE SECTION.

b. What level number is used to identify records in working storage?

c. In which area is level number 01 coded?

d. In which area is level number 05 coded?

e. What clause can be used to assign an initial value or a constant value to a data item described in the WORKING-STORAGE SECTION?

f. Compare the length of working-storage records with the length of unit records in input and output files.

14. Refer to the figure in exercise 12 (Figure 3.27). Code the records COMPANY-NAME, REPORT-NAME, and HEADINGS as would usually be done in the WORKING-STORAGE SECTION, and assign appropriate characters to each of the 132 character positions in each record.

Figure 3.27

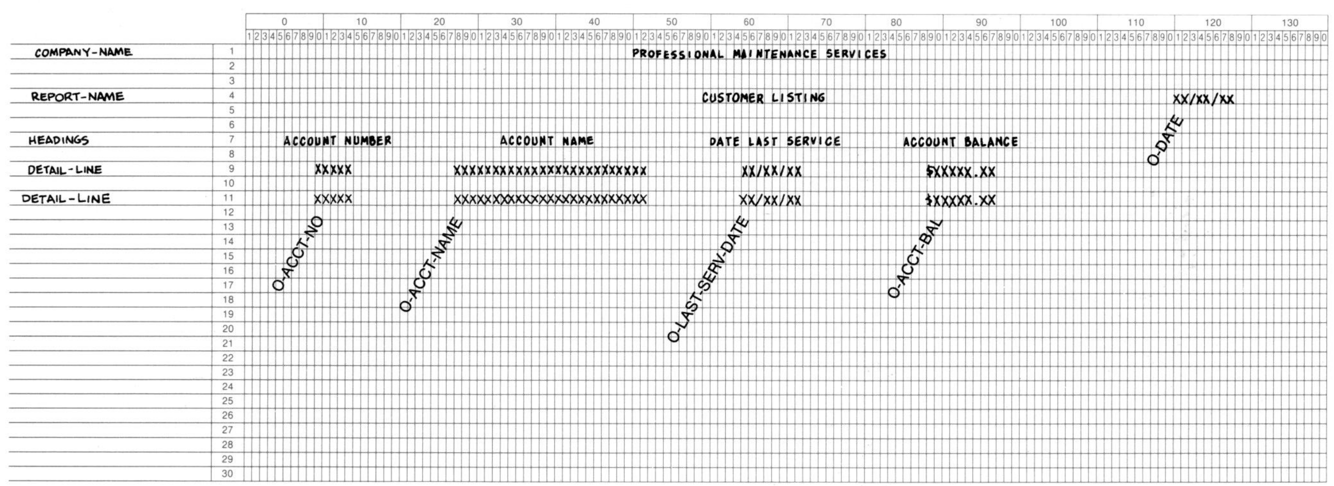

15. Show the characters that will be stored in each byte of the following data items:

```
a. FIELD-1     PIC 9(5)   VALUE 0.
b. FIELD-2     PIC 9(5)   VALUE 00000.
c. FIELD-3     PIC 9(5)   VALUE 25.
d. FIELD-4     PIC 9(5)   VALUE ZERO.
e. FIELD-5     PIC 9(5)   VALUE ZEROS.
f. FIELD-6     PIC X(5)   VALUE "ZERO".
g. FIELD-7     PIC X(5)   VALUE SPACE.
h. FIELD-8     PIC X(5)   VALUE "MARCH".
i. FIELD-9     PIC V99    VALUE .15.
j. FIELD-10    PIC S9V99  VALUE +2.25.
```

16. Examine each of the following uses of the VALUE clause. Explain why the clause is valid or why it is invalid.

```
a. PIC XXX     VALUE "YES".
b. PIC AAA     VALUE "YES".
c. PIC 999     VALUE "YES".
d. PIC XXX     VALUE "NO".
e. PIC AAA     VALUE "NO ".
f. PIC XX      VALUE "NO ".
g. PIC AA      VALUE NO.
h. PIC 999     VALUE "302".
i. PIC 99      VALUE 10.
j. PIC 99      VALUE +10.
k. PIC 999     VALUE +10.
l. PIC S99     VALUE +10.
m. PIC S99     VALUE -250.
n. PIC S99     VALUE 5.5.
o. PIC X(4)    VALUE "SANDY".
p. PIC XX9.9   VALUE 24.3.
q. PIC 99V999  VALUE 24.3.
r. PIC 9(4)    VALUE 24.3.
s. PIC S99V9   VALUE -24.
t. PIC X(6)    VALUE "2.8614".
```

17. Given the following input record description:

```
01  EMPLOYEE-RECORD.
    05 NAME          PIC X(20).
    05 FILLER        PIC X(4).
    05 SOC-SEC-NO    PIC 9(9).
    05 FILLER        PIC X(4).
    05 PAYRATE       PIC 99V99.
    05 FILLER        PIC XXX.
    05 LOCATION      PIC A(10).
    05 FILLER        PIC X(20).
```

Identify the records in Figure 3.28 that are properly prepared, and specify entry errors on the others.

Debugging Activities

1. Given the record layout shown in Figure 3.29a, a student generated the record description in part b. Find and correct the errors.
2. Given the record layout shown in Figure 3.30a, a student generated the coding in part b. Find and correct the errors.
3. Given the record layout in Figure 3.31a, a student generated the record description in part b. Find and correct the errors.
4. The sample program of Chapter 1 has been altered to produce the compiler listing shown in Figure 3.32. Correct the syntax errors that have been flagged by the compiler.

■ **Figure 3.28**

a.

```
LOUISE C. VONBURG       023456120     05.50     BURLINGTON
```

b.

```
SERAPHIM X. WHITEFIELD     142167392     10.25   MIDDLETON
```

c.

```
JOE DWYER         246-52-7314  4.75    LAKESIDE
```

d.

```
FRANK B. SKINNER        056-23-9120    0790    SALEM
```

e.

```
DEBORAH S. MCSHANE        042157421      1000    WEST BRIDGEWATER
```

■ **Figure 3.29**

a.

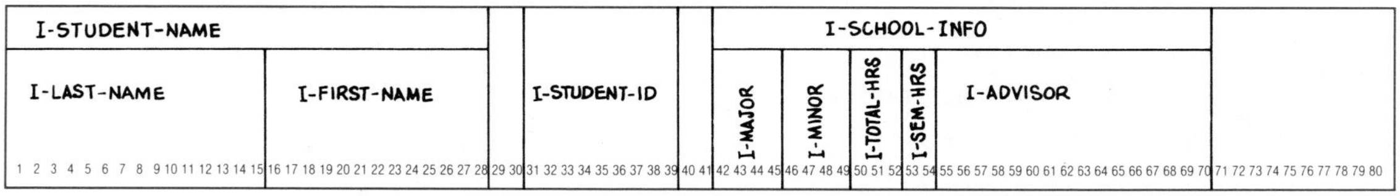

I-STUDENT-NAME					I-SCHOOL-INFO					
I-LAST-NAME (1–15)	I-FIRST-NAME (16–28)	(29–30)	I-STUDENT-ID (31–39)	(40–41)	I-MAJOR (42–45)	I-MINOR (46–49)	I-TOTAL-HRS (50–52)	I-SEM-HRS (53–54)	I-ADVISOR (55–70)	(71–80)

Record Name: STUDENT-RECORD

b.

```
A     B
01    STUDENT-RECORD.
      05 I-STUDENT-NAME    PIC X(28).
      05 I-STUDENT-ID      PIC X(9).
      05 I-SCHOOL-INFO     PIC X(29).
```

■ Figure 3.30

a.

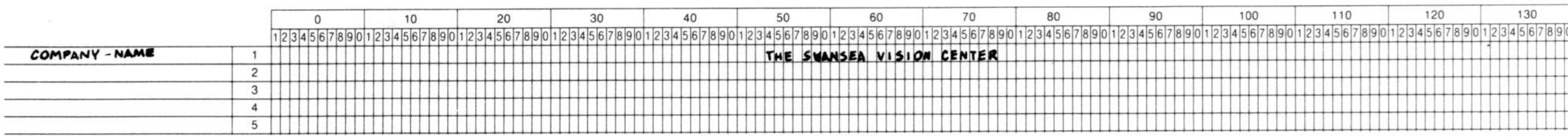

b.

```
A    B
01   COMPANY-NAME
     05 PIC X(53).
     05 PIC X(20)        VALUE "THE SWANSEA VISION CENTER".
     05 PIC X(54).
```

■ Figure 3.31

a.

I-SALESPERSON	I-SSN	I-AREA-CODE	I-MONTH-SALES	I-PREVIOUS-SALES	
1 2 3 4 5 6 7 8 9 10 11 12 13 14 15 16 17 18 19 20 21 22	23 24 25 26 27 28 29 30 31	32 33 34 35 36	37 38 39 40 41 42 43	44 45 46 47 48 49 50 51 52	53 54 55 56 57 58 59 60 61 62 63 64 65 66 67 68 69 70 71 72 73 74 75 76 77 78 79 80

Record Name: SALES - RECORD

b.

```
A    B
FD   SALES-FILE
     RECORD CONTAINS 80 CHARACTERS.

01   SALES-RECORD.
     05 I-SALESPERSON        PIC X(22).
     05 I-SSN                PIC X(9).
     05 I-AREA-CODE          PIC X(5).
     05 I-MONTH-SALES        PIC S9(5).99.
     05 I-PREVIOUS-TOTAL     PIC S9(7).99.
     05                      PIC X(28).
```

■ Figure 3.32

```
                                   17-Jul-1993 07:45:57    VAX COBOL V3.2-42                   Page   1
Source Listing                     17-Jul-1993 07:45:42    SCIENCE$DISK:[MA6031.CHAPTER3]C3FIG45.COB;3


             IDENTIFICATION DIVISION.

            PROGRAM-ID.    PRODUCE-EMPLOYEE-LISTING.

             ENVIRONMENT DIVISION
             1
%COBOL-F-ERROR  222, (1) "PROGRAM-ID" required at this point
%COBOL-E-ERROR   65, (1) Missing period is assumed
%COBOL-F-ERROR  226, (1) Missing required word

             CONFIGURATION SECTION.
             1
%COBOL-E-ERROR   65, (1) Missing period is assumed

             SOURCE-COMPUTER.  VAX-VMS-8650.
             OBJECT-COMPUTER.  VAX-VMS-8650.

             INPUT-OUTPUT SECTION.

             FILE-CONTROL.
                 SELECT EMPLOYEE-FILE     ASSIGN TO COB$INPUT.
                        1
%COBOL-W-ERROR   16, (1) RECORD CONTAINS value is greater than length of longest record
                 SELECT EMPLOYEE-LIST     ASSIGN TO COB$OUTPUT.
                        1
%COBOL-F-ERROR   52, (1) File has no definition in File Section - definition assumed
```

```
                              17-Jul-1993 07:45:57    VAX COBOL V3.2-42              Page   2
Source Listing                17-Jul-1993

        DATA DIVISION

        FILE SECTION.

        FD  EMPLOYEE-FILE
            RECORD CONTAINS 80 CHARACTERS.

        01  EMPLOYEE-RECORD.
            05 I-SSN          PIC X(9).
            02 I-NAME         PIC X(20).
               1
%COBOL-E-ERROR   36, (1) Items subordinate to same group item must have same level-number - error ignored
            05 I-ADDRESS      PIC X(20).
            05 I-CITY-STATE PIC X(20).
            05 I-JOB-CLASS   PIC XXXX.
            95 I-PHONE        PIC X(8).
            1
%COBOL-F-ERROR  117, (1) Invalid syntax

        FD  EMPLOYE-LIST
        1   2
%COBOL-W-ERROR  297, (1) Processing of source program resumes at this point
%COBOL-E-ERROR   51, (2) File has no definition in FILE-CONTROL paragraph - definition assumed
            RECORD CONTAINS 132 CHARACTERS.

        01  PRINTLINE               PIC X(132).

        WORKING STORAGE SECTION.
        1       2        3
%COBOL-E-ERROR   66, (1) Missing level-number - assumed same as previous
%COBOL-E-ERROR   81, (1) PICTURE clause required - PIC X or PIC 9 assumed, depending on usage
%COBOL-E-ERROR   65, (2) Missing period is assumed
%COBOL-E-ERROR   66, (2) Missing level-number - assumed same as previous
%COBOL-E-ERROR   81, (2) PICTURE clause required - PIC X or PIC 9 assumed, depending on usage
%COBOL-E-ERROR   65, (3) Missing period is assumed
%COBOL-F-ERROR  117, (3) Invalid syntax

        01  WS-MORE-RECORDS PIC XXX.
        1
%COBOL-W-ERROR  297, (1) Processing of source program resumes at this point

        01  EMPLOYEE-LINE.
            05                PIC X(25).
            05 O-NAME         PIC X(20).
            05                PIC X(12).
            05 O-SSN          PIC X(9).
            05                PIC X(14).
            05 O-JOB-CLASS    PIC XXXX.
            05                PIC X(16).
            05 O-PHONE        PIC X(7).
            05                PIC X(25).

        PROCEDURE DIVISION.

        100-PRODUCE-EMPLOYEE-LIST.
            PERFORM 200-START-UP.
            PERFORM 210-PROCESS-EMPLOYEE-RECORD
                UNTIL WS-MORE-RECORDS = "NO ".
            PERFORM 220-FINISH-UP.
            STOP RUN.

        200-START-UP.
            OPEN INPUT EMPLOYEE-FILE.
            OPEN OUTPUT EMPLOYEE-LIST.
            MOVE "YES" TO WS-MORE-RECORDS.
            PERFORM 300-READ-EMPLOYEE-RECORD.

        210-PROCESS-EMPLOYEE-RECORD.
            PERFORM 310-PREPARE-EMPLOYEE-LINE.
            PERFORM 300-READ-EMPLOYEE-RECORD.

        220-FINISH-UP.
            CLOSE EMPLOYEE-FILE.
            CLOSE EMPLOYEE-LIST.

        300-READ-EMPLOYEE-RECORD.
            READ EMPLOYEE-FILE RECORD
                AT END.
                    MOVE "NO " TO WS-MORE-RECORDS.

        310-PREPARE-EMPLOYEE-LINE.
            MOVE SPACES TO EMPLOYEE-LINE.
            MOVE I-NAME TO O-NAME.
            MOVE I-SSN TO O-SSN.
            MOVE I-JOB-CLASS TO O-JOB-CLASS.
            MOVE I-PHONE TO O-PHONE.
                 1
%COBOL-F-ERROR  349, (1) Undefined name
            MOVE EMPLOYEE-LINE TO PRINTLINE.
            1
%COBOL-W-ERROR  297, (1) Processing of source program resumes at this point
            WRITE PRINTLINE
                AFTER ADVANCING 2 LINES.
```

Programming Exercises

Programming Exercise I

The management of Express Auto Parts Warehouse wants its data processing department to prepare an inventory report for all its catalog items. For each item, there is a record in the inventory file containing the following data:

cc 1–5	Catalog number
cc 6–25	Item description
cc 26–30	Purchase price per unit (format: xxx.xx)
cc 31–35	Selling price per unit (format: xxx.xx)
cc 36–39	Quantity on hand
cc 40–43	Quantity on order
cc 44–47	Reorder point

This file is brought up-to-date weekly. The sample inventory file for this program is Data File Set 1 in Appendix C [DD/CD:VIC4EX1.DAT].

The inventory report must list all the catalog items. For each item, the report must specify the catalog number, description, quantity on hand, purchase price per unit, and selling price per unit. The report should begin at the top of a new page with appropriate descriptive information: company name, report name, and column headings.

The design phase has been completed for you. All the design tools are contained in Figure 3.33. Your assignment is as follows:

1. Study the program design, and then code the first three divisions of the program: IDENTIFICATION DIVISION, ENVIRONMENT DIVISION, and DATA DIVISION.
2. Use an editor to enter the partial program into a file.
3. Debug the partial program by calling the compiler to check for syntax errors.

Note a: Do not produce any object code, since the program is incomplete.

Note b: Do not be concerned about diagnostics that refer to a missing PROCEDURE DIVISION. This program will be completed at the end of Chapter 4.

Figure 3.33

Record Layout Form

I-CATALOG-NO	I-ITEM-DESCR	I-PURCHASE-PRICE	I-SELLING-PRICE	I-ON-HAND	I-ON-ORDER	I-REORDER-POINT	
1 2 3 4 5	6 7 8 9 10 11 12 13 14 15 16 17 18 19 20 21 22 23 24 25	26 27 28 ^ 29 30	31 32 33 ^ 34 35	36 37 38 39	40 41 42 43	44 45 46 47	48 49 50 51 52 53 54 55 56 57 58 59 60 61 62 63 64 65 66 67 68 69 70 71 72 73 74 75 76 77 78 79 80

Record Name: ITEM-RECORD

■ **Figure 3.33** continued

Printer Spacing Chart

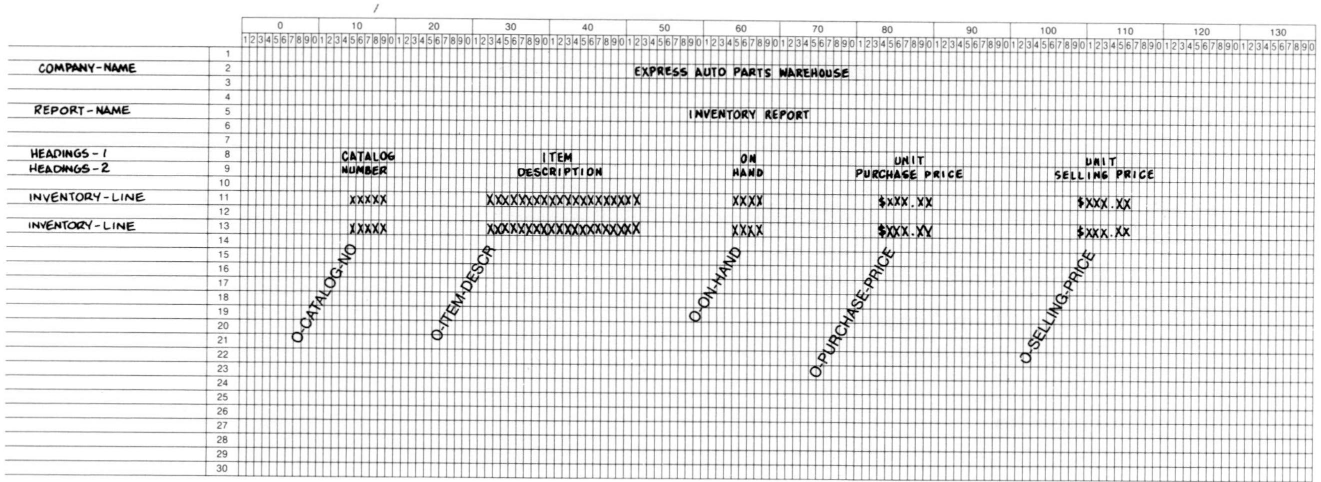

System Flowchart

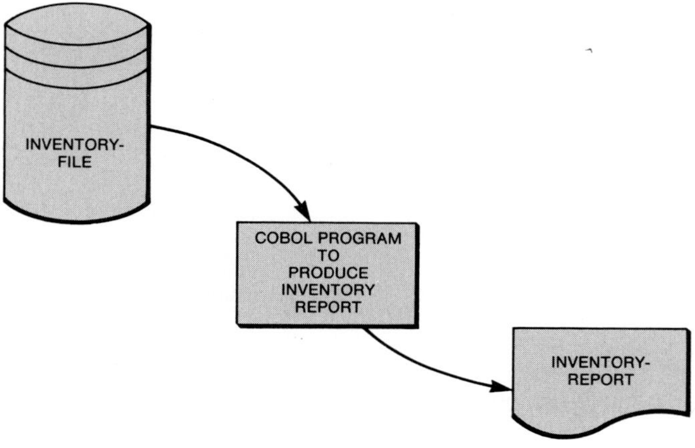

Structure Chart

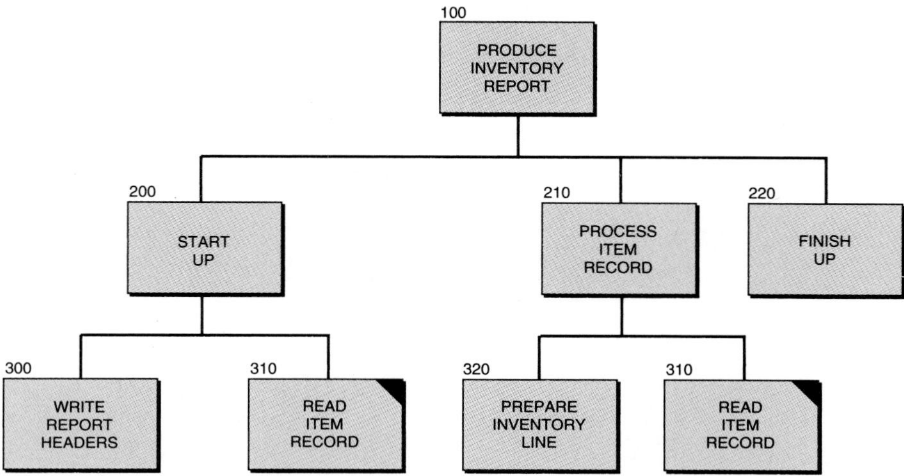

Program Pseudocode

100-Produce-Inventory-Report.

1. Perform 200-Start-Up.
2. Perform 210-Process-Item-Record until no more records.
3. Perform 220-Finish-Up.
4. Stop the run.

200-Start-Up.

1. Open the files.
2. Set the end-of-file flag WS-MORE-RECORDS to "YES".
3. Perform 300-Write-Report-Headers.
4. Perform 310-Read-Item-Record.

210-Process-Item-Record.

1. Perform 320-Prepare-Inventory-Line.
2. Perform 310-Read-Item-Record.

220-Finish-Up.

1. Close the files.

300-Write-Report-Headers.

1. Move the record Company-Name to the output area Printline.
2. After advancing to the top of a new page, write the output record Printline.
3. Move the record Report-Name to the output area Printline.
4. After advancing 3 lines, write the output record Printline.
5. Move the record Headings-1 to the output area Printline.
6. After advancing 3 lines, write the output record Printline.
7. Move the record Headings-2 to the output area Printline.
8. After advancing 1 line, write the output record Printline.
9. Clear the record area Inventory-Line.

310-Read-Item-Record.

1. Read an input item-record.
2. Test for the End-of-File record; if EOF record reached, move "NO " to the end-of-file flag WS-MORE-RECORDS.

320-Prepare-Inventory-Line.

1. Move input catalog-number to Inventory-line catalog-number.
2. Move input item-description to Inventory-line item-description.
3. Move input quantity-on-hand to Inventory-line quantity on hand.
4. Move input unit-purchase-price to Inventory-line unit-purchase-price.
5. Move input unit-selling-price to Inventory-line unit-selling-price.
6. Move the Inventory-line to the output record area Printline.
7. After advancing 2 lines, write the output record Printline.

Program Flowchart

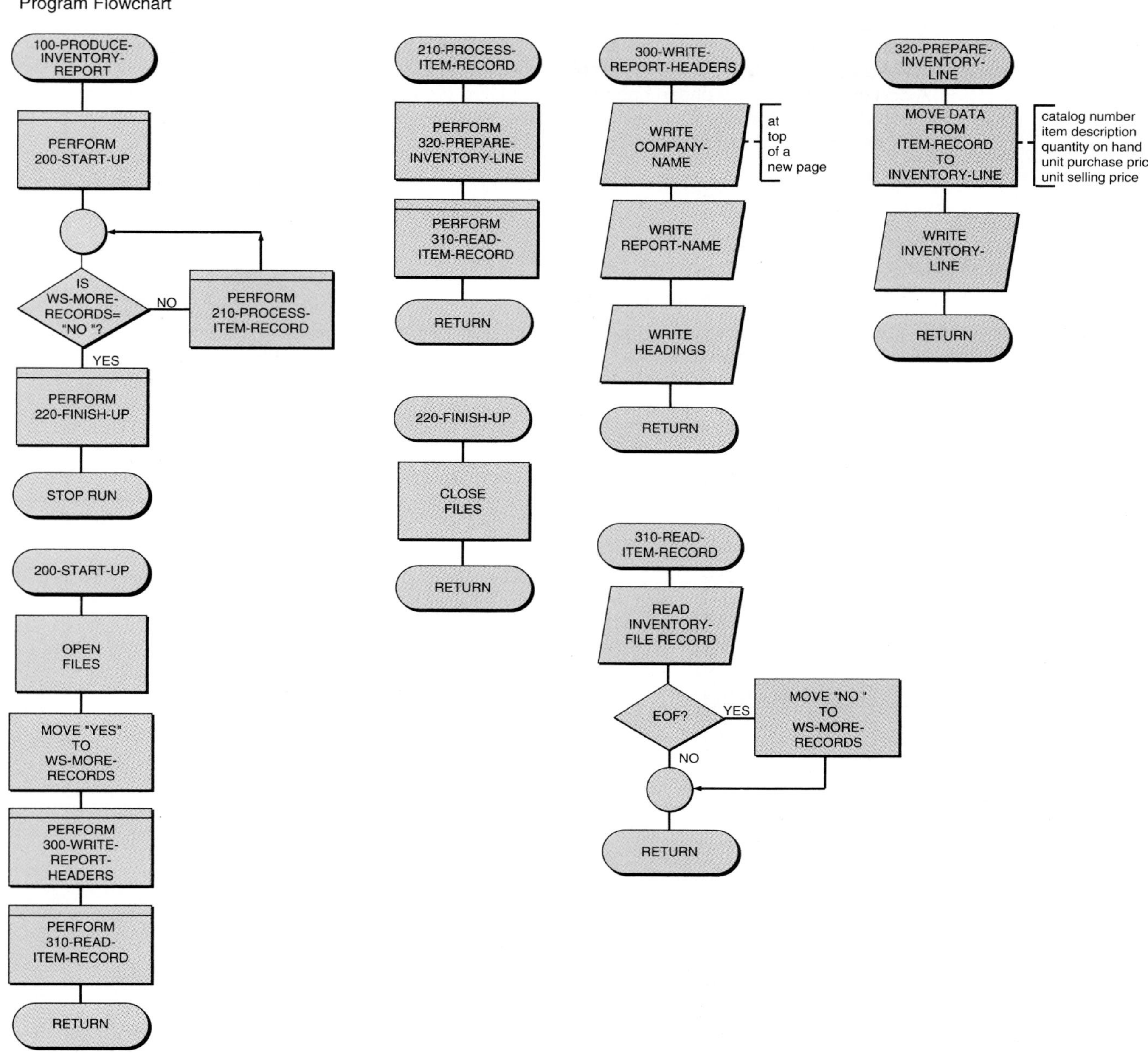

Programming Exercise II

The Ponagansett Electric Company wants a report that lists the previous and current meter readings for each of its customers for the current billing period.

Each customer record contains the following data:

cc 1–3	Area code
cc 4–9	Customer number
cc 10–29	Customer name
cc 30–34	Previous meter reading
cc 35–39	Current meter reading
cc 79–80	Month number

The records in the customer file are arranged sequentially by customer number within each area code. The meter readings are updated monthly. The sample customer file for this program is Data File Set 2 in Appendix C [DD/CD:VIC4EX2.DAT].

The report must begin at the top of a new page. It must contain the company name, the report name, and a detail line showing for each customer the area code, customer number and name, and previous and current meter readings, all listed under appropriate headings.

A portion of the design phase has been completed for you. Figure 3.34 contains the input and output record layouts, the system flowchart, and the structure chart.

Your assignment is as follows:

1. Complete the design phase; that is, write the program pseudocode or design the program flowchart.
2. Code the first three divisions of the program: IDENTIFICATION DIVISION, ENVIRONMENT DIVISION, and DATA DIVISION.
3. Use an editor to enter the partial program into a file.
4. Use the compiler to check for syntax errors.

Note a: Do not produce any object code, since the program is incomplete.
Note b: Do not be concerned about diagnostics that refer to a missing PROCEDURE DIVISION. This program will be completed at the end of Chapter 4.

Figure 3.34

Record Layout Form

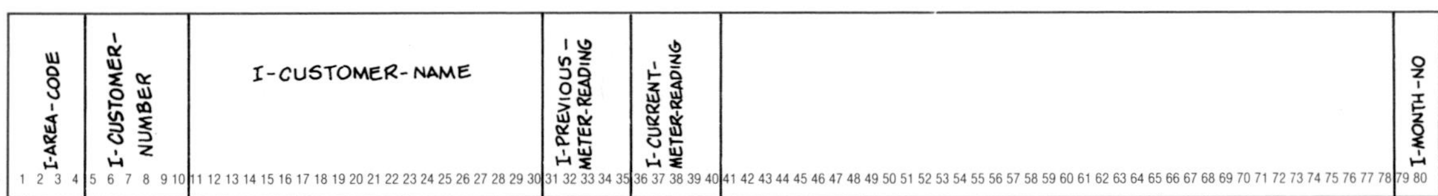

Record Name: CUSTOMER-RECORD

Printer Spacing Chart

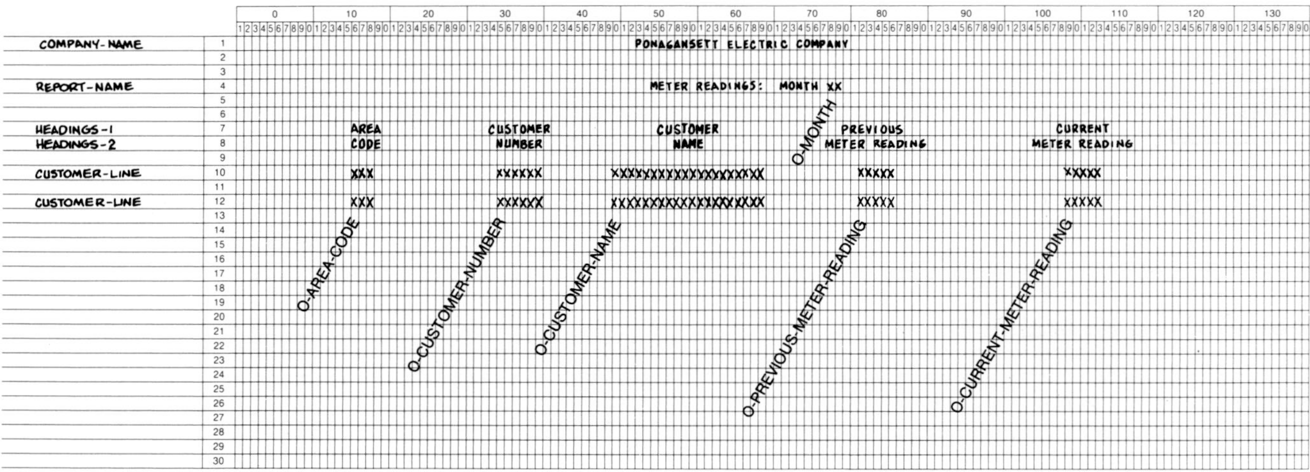

System Flowchart

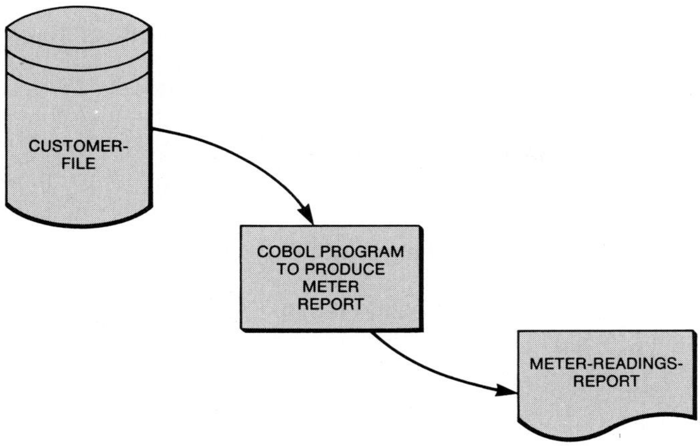

Structure Chart

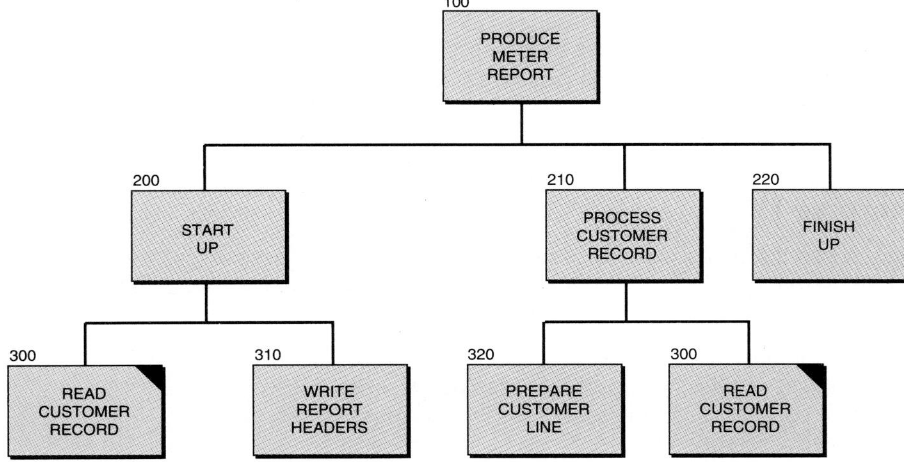

Programming Exercise III

The personnel director of the Modern Plastics Company wants the data processing department to prepare an employee register. The report must list all employees in seniority order within each department of each plant.

For each employee, there is a record in the personnel file containing the following data:

cc 3–4	Plant number
cc 5–6	Department number
cc 7–15	Social Security number
cc 16–35	Employee name
cc 36–38	Classification code
cc 39–42	Pay rate (format: xx.xx)
cc 77–80	Date hired

The sample personnel file for this program is contained in Data File Set 4 in Appendix C [DDKP:VIC4EX3.DAT].

The report must contain the following:

1. The company name, at the top of a new page
2. The name of the report
3. Descriptive column headings

4. For each employee, a detail line that shows
   plant number
   department number
   Social Security number
   employee name
   current pay rate
   date hired

Note: Before processing the employee records, the records must be arranged in seniority sequence within each department of each plant. (The data set that will be provided to you has been presorted in the proper sequence.)

Your assignment is as follows:

1. Design the program by completing the following steps:
   - **a.** Prepare the layout of the input record. (Be sure to indicate the position of the decimal point in the pay rate field.)
   - **b.** Prepare the layouts of all the different kinds of lines needed on the report. Use a printer spacing chart. (Edit the pay rate field.)
   - **c.** Draw the system flowchart.
   - **d.** Develop the structure chart.
   - **e.** Write the program pseudocode (or draw the program flowchart).
2. Code the first three divisions of the program: IDENTIFICATION DIVISION, ENVIRONMENT DIVISION, and DATA DIVISION.
3. Enter the partial program into a file.
4. Use the compiler to detect and correct all syntax errors.

Note a: Do not produce any object code, since the program is incomplete.
Note b: Do not be concerned about diagnostics that refer to a missing PROCEDURE DIVISION. This program will be completed at the end of Chapter 4.

Programming Exercise IV

The Allied Stock Company wants the data processing department to prepare a sales register for all the sales of the day. A sale can be made over-the-counter, by phone, or by mail order. For each sale, an input record is prepared in a sales file with the following data:

cc 7–12	Invoice number
cc 13	Sale code (1 = over-the-counter, 2 = phone, 3 = mail order)
cc 14	Payment code (1 = cash, 2 = charge, 3 = COD)
cc 15–17	Salesperson number
cc 18–22	Customer number
cc 23–26	Quantity sold
cc 27–46	Item description
cc 47–50	Item number
cc 51–55	Unit price (format: xxx.xx)

The sample sales file for this program is contained in Data File Set 3 in Appendix C [DD/CD:VIC4EX4.DAT].

The sales register should begin at the top of a page with the following:

1. The company name
2. The report name
3. Appropriate column headings

The report must then print a detail line for each sale made during the day. The detail line must show, in sequence, the following:

1. Invoice number
2. Customer number
3. Item number
4. Item description
5. Unit cost

6. Quantity sold
7. Salesperson number
8. Payment code
9. Sale code

Follow the steps of the problem-solving procedure to *design* the program. Next, code the first three divisions of the program, enter the partial program into a file, and use the compiler to debug it.

Note a: Do not produce any object code, since the program is incomplete.

Note b: Do not be concerned about diagnostics that refer to a missing PROCEDURE DIVISION. This program will be completed at the end of Chapter 4.

4 The Divisions of a COBOL Program: PROCEDURE DIVISION

In this chapter, we will examine the structure of the fourth and last division of a COBOL program, namely, the PROCEDURE DIVISION. We will continue working with the sample program from Chapter 2.

Just as selected design tools were used as guides in the coding of the first three divisions, the program pseudocode (or the program flowchart) that was generated from the structure chart is the essential guide in the coding of the PROCEDURE DIVISION. We will point out how the structure of this division reflects the structure incorporated first in the structure chart, which was then transmitted to the program pseudocode (or to the program flowchart).

As a paragraph is coded, we will explain the formats of the COBOL statements contained in the paragraph. Additional examples will be provided to illustrate the requirements as well as the options available for each of the COBOL statements. ■

Objectives You Should Achieve

After studying this chapter, you should:

1. Be able to correctly code a PERFORM statement to execute a procedure, either once or until a specified condition is satisfied.
2. Be able to correctly code an in-line PERFORM statement to execute a procedure that consists of a number of imperative statements.
3. Be able to correctly code a single PERFORM statement that executes a procedure once and then repeatedly until a certain condition is satisfied.
4. Be able to correctly code a statement to permanently stop the execution of a program.
5. Be able to correctly code a statement to make a file available to the program with a specified open mode.
6. Be able to correctly code a MOVE statement and then an INITIALIZE statement to assign a specified initial value to an elementary data item.
7. Be able to correctly code an INITIALIZE statement to assign specific values to subordinate items of a group data item.
8. Be able to correctly code a statement to read into memory the next record of a file with sequential organization and also make a copy of the record in another storage area.
9. Be able to correctly code a statement to write an output record at the top of a new page.
10. Be able to correctly code a PROCEDURE DIVISION paragraph that corresponds to a program pseudocode paragraph (or a program flowchart module), given the related DATA DIVISION entries.
11. Be able to correctly code the PROCEDURE DIVISION that corresponds to the program pseudocode (or the program flowchart), given the related DATA DIVISION entries.
12. Be able to correctly code a READ statement, given an input file name and input record name.
13. Be able to correctly code a WRITE statement, given an output file name and an output record name.
14. Be able to specify the contents of a receiving field following the execution of a MOVE statement, given appropriate field characteristics and a specific value in the sending field, or given a specific source value.
15. Be able to code two different sets of instructions to write a record to an output file if the record is described in the WORKING-STORAGE SECTION.
16. Be able to successfully complete the task of coding and running the program, if all the design tools are provided.
17. Be able to successfully complete the task of designing a program, coding, and running it, if the layouts of input and output records, the system flowchart, and the structure chart are provided.
18. Be able to successfully design, code, and run a program, given an adequate description of a programming assignment.

Planning the PROCEDURE DIVISION

The PROCEDURE DIVISION must contain all the COBOL instructions needed to access data, either from an external file or from internal storage; manipulate the data; transfer data from one storage area to another; perform computations and tests on data; prepare output records; and write them to a storage file or a print file: in short, all the instructions needed to carry out the procedures required to get the job done. Obviously, the specific instructions that must be issued and the sequence in which they must be executed are critical to the end result.

The design phase of the problem-solving procedure has addressed this issue in detail, beginning with step 1, which calls for developing a thorough understanding of the problem. Step 2 calls for the development of a structure chart. Recall that its purpose is to display the hierarchical structure of the functional subcomponents into which the whole job itself can be separated. Next, the program pseudocode converts each of these functional components into specific sets of instructions, or, equivalently, the program flowchart provides a visual representation of the detailed logic that corresponds to each module of the structure chart.

For your convenience, the structure chart, the program pseudocode, and the program flowchart for the current sample program are repeated in Figure 4.1.

Figure 4.1 Structure chart, pseudocode, and program flowchart for the sample program

Structure Chart

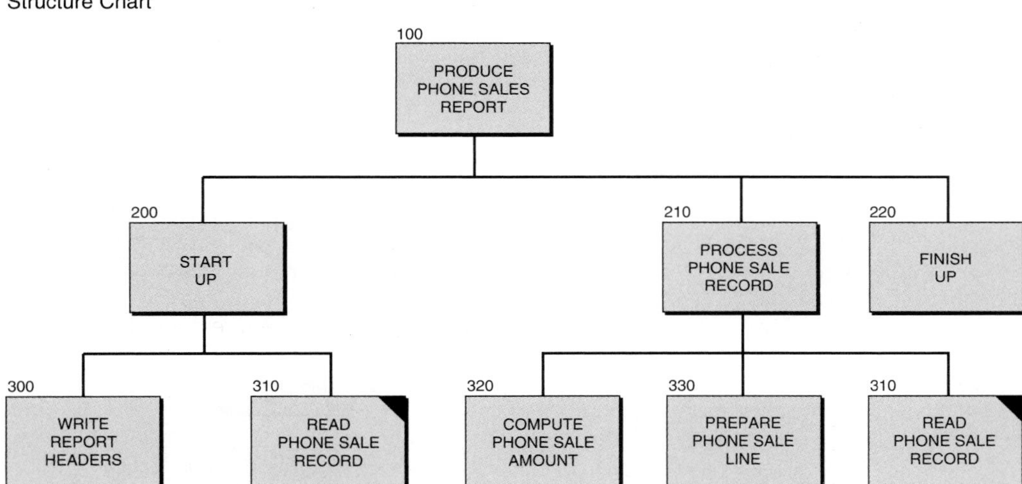

Program Pseudocode

100-Produce-Phone-Sales-Report.

1. Perform 200-Start-Up.
2. Perform 210-Process-Phone-Sale-Record until no more records.
3. Perform 220-Finish-Up.
4. Stop the run.

200-Start-Up.

1. Open the files.
2. Set the end-of-file flag WS-MORE-RECORDS to "YES".
3. Perform 300-Write-Report-Headers.
4. Perform 310-Read-Phone-Sale-Record.

210-Process-Phone-Sale-Record.

1. Perform 320-Compute-Phone-Sale-Amount.
2. Perform 330-Prepare-Phone-Sale-Line.
3. Perform 310-Read-Phone-Sale-Record.

220-Finish-Up.

1. Close the files.

300-Write-Report-Headers.

1. Move Headings to the output area Printline.
2. After advancing to the top of a new page, write the output record Printline.
3. Clear the record area Phone-sale-line.

310-Read-Phone-Sale-Record.

1. Read an input phone-sale-record.
2. Test for the end-of-file record; if EOF record reached, move "NO " to the end-of-file flag WS-MORE-RECORDS.

320-Compute-Phone-Sale-Amount.

1. If the input number-of-units > 100
   then
   compute the Phone-sale-line amount = input number-of-units times input unit-cost times .8
   else
   compute the Phone-sale-line amount = input number-of-units times input unit-cost.

330-Prepare-Phone-Sale-Line.

1. Move input customer-number to Phone-sale-line customer-number.
2. Move input catalog-number to Phone-sale-line catalog-number.
3. Move input unit-cost to Phone-sale-line unit-cost.
4. Move input number-of-units to Phone-sale-line number-of-units.
5. Move the Phone-sale-line to the output record area Printline.
6. After advancing 2 lines, write the output record Printline.

Program Flowchart

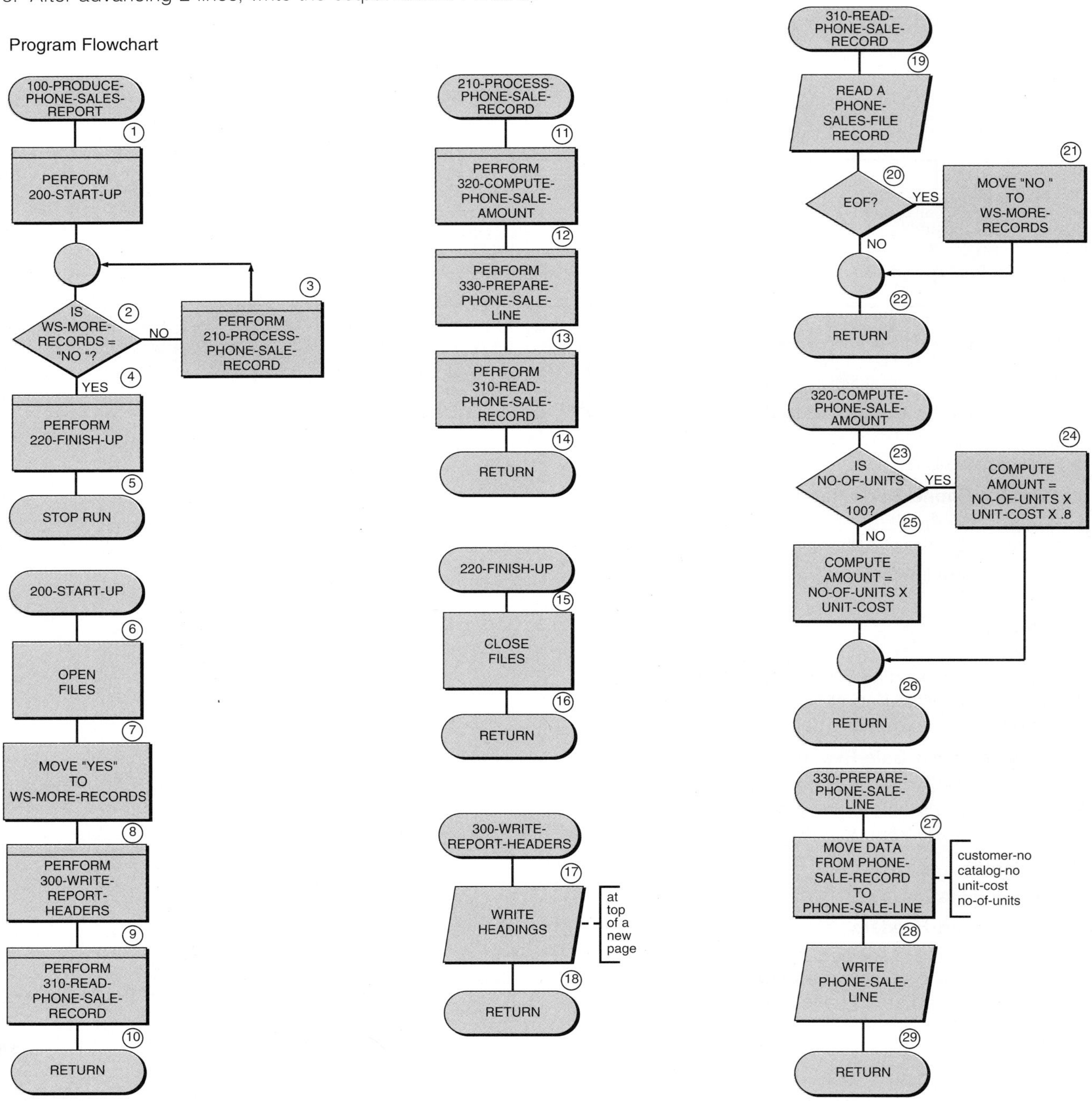

The program pseudocode (or the program flowchart) now guides the programmer in the coding of the PROCEDURE DIVISION. It was specifically developed to detail and to organize the processing steps required to accomplish the functions identified in each module of the structure chart. Note in Figure 4.1 that the pseudocode contains **one paragraph** of instructions for **each module** in the structure chart, and the program flowchart contains one flowchart module for each module in the structure chart.

Just as the pseudocode is composed of paragraphs, the PROCEDURE DIVISION is also composed of paragraphs. (Paragraphs are also called procedures.) Each paragraph in the PROCEDURE DIVISION contains the formal COBOL statements corresponding to the English statements in the corresponding pseudocode paragraph. There will be as many paragraphs or procedures in the PROCEDURE DIVISION as there are paragraphs in the pseudocode. The paragraph (or procedure) names are the same as the ones assigned to the corresponding paragraphs in the pseudocode.

The topmost module in the structure chart is called the *primary* or *main-control module.* In the PROCEDURE DIVISION, the paragraph that corresponds to this module is called the *primary* or *main-control paragraph.* Program control begins by executing the first instruction in this paragraph and always ends by executing the last instruction in this paragraph. All other instructions within the program are under the direct or indirect control of this paragraph.

Just as the modules in the second row of the structure chart are under the control of the primary module, so are all the second-level paragraphs (those with a numeric prefix in the 200s) under the direct control of the main-control paragraph. The modules in the third row of the structure chart are under the direct control of a second-level module, and the corresponding third-level paragraphs are under the direct control of a second-level paragraph. In the following example, black lines have been drawn from the statements in the main-control paragraph to the second-level paragraphs whose execution they control, and colored lines have been drawn from PERFORM statements in second-level paragraphs to the third-level paragraphs whose execution they control.

```
100-PRODUCE-PHONE-SALES-REPORT.
    PERFORM 200-START-UP.
    PERFORM 210-PROCESS-PHONE-SALE-RECORD
        UNTIL WS-MORE-RECORDS = "NO ".
    PERFORM 220-FINISH-UP.
    STOP RUN.

200-START-UP.
    OPEN INPUT PHONE-SALES-FILE.
    OPEN OUTPUT PHONE-SALES-REPORT.
    MOVE "YES" TO WS-MORE-RECORDS.
    PERFORM 300-WRITE-REPORT-HEADERS.
    PERFORM 310-READ-PHONE-SALE-RECORD.

210-PROCESS-PHONE-SALE-RECORD.
    PERFORM 320-COMPUTE-PHONE-SALE-AMOUNT.
    PERFORM 330-PREPARE-PHONE-SALE-LINE.
    PERFORM 310-READ-PHONE-SALE-RECORD.

220-FINISH-UP.
    CLOSE PHONE-SALES-FILE.
    CLOSE PHONE-SALES-REPORT.

300-WRITE-REPORT-HEADERS.
    MOVE HEADINGS TO PRINTLINE.
    WRITE PRINTLINE
        AFTER ADVANCING PAGE.
    MOVE SPACES TO PHONE-SALE-LINE.

310-READ-PHONE-SALE-RECORD.
    READ PHONE-SALES-FILE RECORD
        AT END
            MOVE "NO " TO WS-MORE-RECORDS.

320-COMPUTE-PHONE-SALE-AMOUNT.
    IF I-NO-OF-UNITS > 100
        THEN
            COMPUTE O-SALE-AMOUNT = I-NO-OF-UNITS *
                                    I-UNIT-COST * .8
        ELSE
            COMPUTE O-SALE-AMOUNT = I-NO-OF-UNITS *
                                    I-UNIT-COST.

330-PREPARE-PHONE-SALE-LINE.
    MOVE I-CUSTOMER-NO TO O-CUSTOMER-NO.
    MOVE I-CATALOG-NO TO O-CATALOG-NO.
    MOVE I-UNIT-COST TO O-UNIT-COST.
    MOVE I-NO-OF-UNITS TO O-NO-OF-UNITS.
    MOVE PHONE-SALE-LINE TO PRINTLINE.
    WRITE PRINTLINE
        AFTER ADVANCING 2 LINES.
```

You will note that all the paragraphs in the PROCEDURE DIVISION are coded in ascending order of their numeric prefixes. Except for the main-control paragraph, which must be coded first, the COBOL compiler does not require this ordering feature, but it greatly facilitates program documentation, debugging, and maintenance by enhancing the structure of the division.

Paragraph Names

All *paragraph* or *procedure names* are user-defined. Their construction must abide by the specifications listed in Chapter 3, pages 94–95.

We also highly recommend that a paragraph name be carefully selected so that it indicates the functions being carried out by the instructions contained in that procedure, thereby contributing to the self-documentation of the program. For instance, the names 1-GET-STARTED and 10-ENDIT are more descriptive than 1-A and 10-XYZ. In the sample program, 100-PRODUCE-PHONE-SALES-REPORT and 300-WRITE-REPORT-HEADERS provide more information than would the names 100-A and 300-B.

Notwithstanding the comments being made here, a programmer following the steps of the problem-solving procedure would normally create the paragraph names early in the design phase, namely, while constructing the structure chart.

Statements and Sentences

Other than paragraph names, the entries in the PROCEDURE DIVISION are classified as *statements* or as *sentences*. Technically, a statement is a valid combination of words (COBOL reserved, user-defined, and literals) and characters written according to specified rules of syntax.

Statements fall into four categories: imperative, conditional, delimited-scope, and compiler-directing. Each category is briefly explained in sections *a* through *d* below.

a. An *imperative* statement is one that must be executed unconditionally every time it is encountered. It always contains a verb and the verb's operands. The verb indicates the kind of processing the computer is being directed to do. For instance,

```
OPEN INPUT PHONE-SALES-FILE
```

is an imperative statement. The verb is OPEN, and the verb's operand is INPUT PHONE-SALES-FILE.

Some of the verbs used in the sample program to begin imperative statements are OPEN, PERFORM (without the UNTIL clause), COMPUTE, MOVE, WRITE, CLOSE, STOP.

b. A *conditional* statement always contains a condition that must be tested. The particular program action taken depends on the truth value of the tested condition. For instance,

```
IF I-NO-OF-UNITS > 100
    THEN
        COMPUTE O-SALE-AMOUNT = I-NO-OF-UNITS * I-UNIT-COST * .8
    ELSE
        COMPUTE O-SALE-AMOUNT = I-NO-OF-UNITS * I-UNIT-COST.
```

is a conditional statement. The condition being tested is I-NO-OF-UNITS > 100. If the condition is true, the first COMPUTE statement is executed, but if the condition is false, then the second COMPUTE statement is executed.

Another example of a conditional statement is the following:

```
READ PHONE-SALES-FILE RECORD
    AT END
        MOVE "NO " TO WS-MORE-RECORDS.
```

The MOVE statement is executed only if the condition AT END is true. (AT END means "if the record just read is the *end-of-file* record.")

The sample program contains a third example of a conditional statement:

```
PERFORM 210-PROCESS-PHONE-SALE-RECORD
    UNTIL WS-MORE-RECORDS = "NO ".
```

The condition is WS-MORE-RECORDS = "NO ". If the condition is false, then the PERFORM statement is executed; otherwise, it is not.

We will encounter many conditional statements in later chapters, and, when we do, we will draw your attention to them.

c. A *delimited-scope* statement is one that contains an explicit scope terminator. The sample program does not contain any of these. An example of a delimited-scope statement is the following:

```
READ PHONE-SALES-FILE RECORD
    AT END
        MOVE "NO " TO WS-MORE-RECORDS
        DISPLAY "NO MORE RECORDS IN THE DATA FILE"
END-READ.
```

The END-READ explicitly marks the scope of the READ statement. Note that the MOVE and DISPLAY statements are contained in the READ conditional statement, and they are executed only if the AT END condition is true. On the other hand, consider this statement:

```
READ PHONE-SALES-FILE RECORD
    AT END
        MOVE "NO " TO WS-MORE-RECORDS
END-READ
DISPLAY "NO MORE RECORDS IN THE DATA FILE".
```

Again, the READ statement ends at the scope terminator END-READ, but note where it is positioned. Consequently, the DISPLAY statement is independent of the READ statement, and it will be executed unconditionally, immediately following the execution of the READ statement.

Delimited-scope statements are a new feature of the 1985 ANSI COBOL standards. We will introduce them wherever they are appropriate throughout the text.

d. A *compiler-directing* statement is one that directs the compiler to take some specific action during the compilation phase of the program. There are only two of these, namely, COPY and USE. Suppose that in a business environment, a particularly lengthy record description (e.g., EMPLOYEE-RECORD) is needed in a number of distinct programs. Rather than recoding this record in each program that requires it, you can code it carefully once and then store it in a library of source code. Each program can then import the record description simply by coding

```
COPY EMPLOYEE-RECORD
```

at the point in the program where the record description is needed. These two statements (COPY and USE) will be used in advanced COBOL.

The above comments apply to statements. A *sentence* consists of one or more statements and ends with a period. The statements in a sentence can be separated by a blank, a comma, a semicolon, or the word THEN.

The following sentences are equivalent:

a. `CLOSE PHONE-SALES STOP RUN.`

b. `CLOSE PHONE-SALES, STOP RUN.`

c. `CLOSE PHONE-SALES; STOP RUN.`

d. `CLOSE PHONE-SALES THEN STOP RUN.`

In this text, however, we always code at most one statement per line. Using this convention, the preceding sentences are coded as follows:

a.
```
CLOSE PHONE-SALES
STOP RUN.
```

b.
```
CLOSE PHONE-SALES,
STOP RUN.
```

c.
```
CLOSE PHONE-SALES;
STOP RUN.
```

d.
```
CLOSE PHONE-SALES
    THEN
        STOP RUN.
```

Within the PROCEDURE DIVISION, a paragraph or procedure consists of a set of statements and/or sentences. Statements are always executed in the order in which they occur, except when branching instructions dictate otherwise.

Coding the PROCEDURE DIVISION

The coding of the PROCEDURE DIVISION begins with the division header in area A. Note again that a division header stands alone on a line, ends with a period, and is followed by a blank line.

All paragraph names are coded in area A and end with a period. In this text, no other entry is coded on the same line, though it is allowed by the compiler. A blank line precedes each paragraph name.

All statements and/or sentences must be coded in area B. Normally, at most one statement is coded per line. If a sentence or statement requires more than one line of coding, the coding on successive lines is indented four spaces to the right for clarity.

The coding in Figure 4.2 is allowed, but the author recommends the style shown in Figure 4.3.

As noted earlier, the paragraphs are coded in ascending order of their numeric prefixes. Within each paragraph, the COBOL statements are coded in the same sequence as their corresponding entries in the program pseudocode (or in the program flowchart module). For instance, the following example shows the correspondence between the pseudocode paragraph 300-Write-Report-Headers and the PROCEDURE DIVISION paragraph 300-WRITE-REPORT-HEADERS.

300-Write-Report-Headers.

1. Move Headings to the output area Printline.
2. After advancing to the top of a new page, write the output record Printline.
3. Clear the record area Phone-sale-line.

```
300-WRITE-REPORT-HEADERS.
    MOVE HEADINGS TO PRINTLINE.
    WRITE PRINTLINE
        AFTER ADVANCING PAGE.
    MOVE SPACES TO PHONE-SALE-LINE.
```

Now we will examine the formal COBOL language statements that can be used to carry out the functions specified in the program pseudocode.

The Main-Control Paragraph 100-PRODUCE-PHONE-SALES-REPORT

Figure 4.4 shows the related portions of the structure chart, the pseudocode, and the program flowchart that correspond to the paragraph 100-PRODUCE-PHONE-SALES-REPORT in the PROCEDURE DIVISION.

There are three kinds of statements in this paragraph: the PERFORM, the PERFORM-UNTIL, and the STOP RUN statements.

Figure 4.2 Example of unstructured style of coding

```
100-PRODUCE-PHONE-SALES-REPORT. PERFORM 200-START-UP.
        PERFORM 210-PROCESS-PHONE-SALE-RECORD UNTIL WS-MORE-RECORDS
        = "NO ". PERFORM 220-FINISH-UP. STOP RUN.
```

Figure 4.3 Example of structured style of coding

```
100-PRODUCE-PHONE-SALES-REPORT.
    PERFORM 200-START-UP.
    PERFORM 210-PROCESS-PHONE-SALE-RECORD
        UNTIL WS-MORE-RECORDS = "NO ".
    PERFORM 220-FINISH-UP.
    STOP RUN.
```

■ **Figure 4.4** The development of the procedure 100-PRODUCE-PHONE-SALES-REPORT

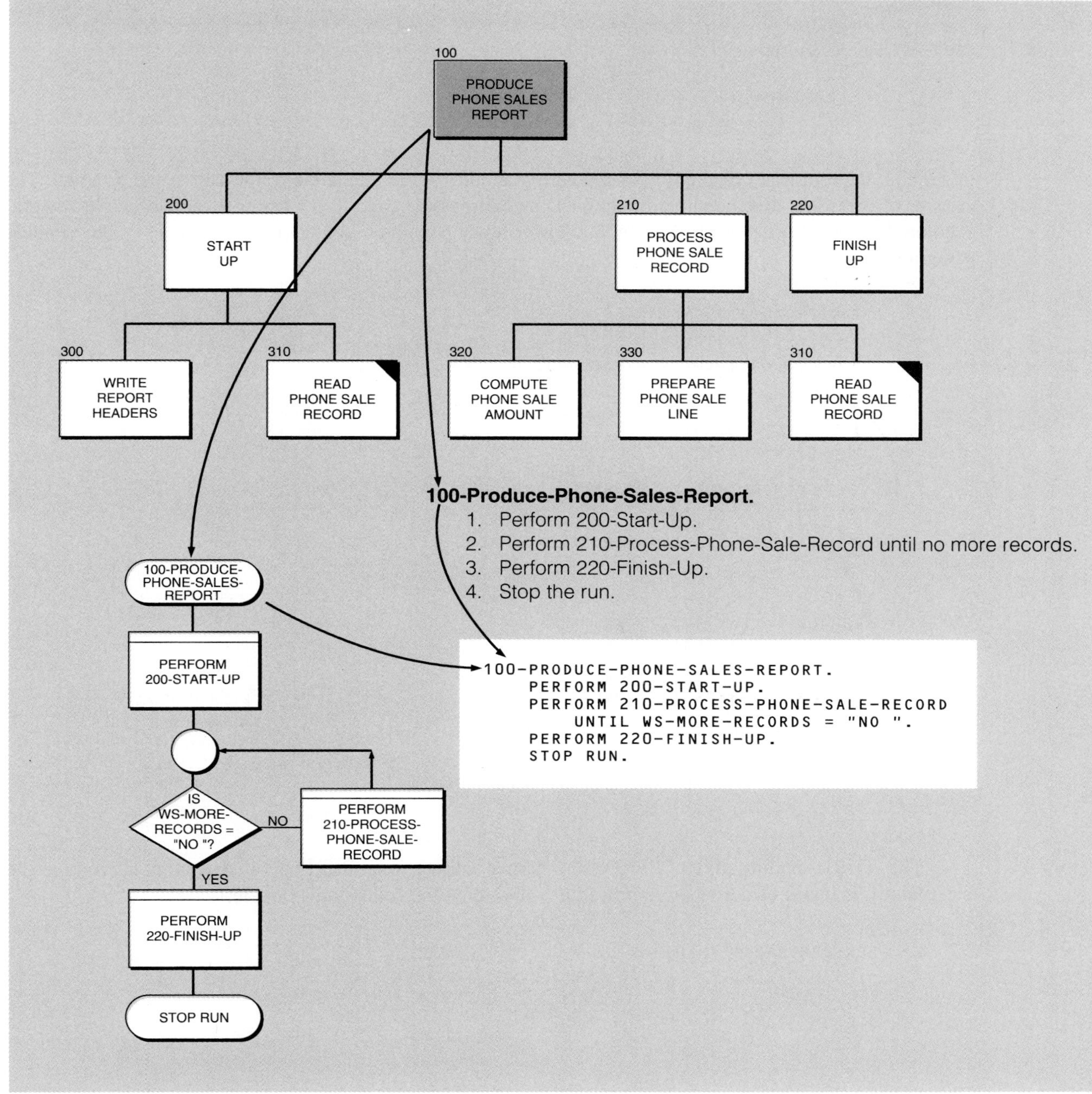

The PERFORM Statement

The format of the PERFORM statement is shown in Figure 4.5. The simplest option is "PERFORM procedure-name," and that is the one used in the sample program. The PERFORM is a control (or branching) statement. The verb PERFORM is followed by the name of the paragraph (procedure) to which control is being transferred. When the statement PERFORM 200-START-UP is executed, control leaves the current paragraph (100-PRODUCE-PHONE-SALES-REPORT), executes all the statements in the paragraph 200-START-UP, and then **automatically** returns to the statement following PERFORM 200-START-UP.

■ **Figure 4.5** PERFORM statement format

```
PERFORM [procedure-name-1 [{THRU   } procedure-name-2]]
                           {THROUGH}
        [imperative-statement . . . END-PERFORM]
```

In general, the return is triggered by encountering another paragraph name or the end of the program. The transfer of control is illustrated below. A black arrow transfers control to a lower-level paragraph, whereas a colored arrow returns control from the lower-level paragraph to the next sentence in the sending paragraph.

```
100-PRODUCE-PHONE-SALES-REPORT.
    PERFORM 200-START-UP.
    PERFORM 210-PROCESS-PHONE-SALES-RECORD
        UNTIL WS-MORE-RECORDS = "NO ".
    .
    .
200-START-UP.
    OPEN INPUT PHONE-SALES-FILE.
    OPEN OUTPUT PHONE-SALES-REPORT.
    MOVE "YES" TO WS-MORE-RECORDS.
    PERFORM 300-WRITE-REPORT-HEADERS.
    PERFORM 310-READ-PHONE-SALE-RECORD.
    .
    .
300-WRITE-REPORT-HEADERS.
    MOVE HEADINGS TO PRINTLINE.
    WRITE PRINTLINE
        AFTER ADVANCING PAGE.
    MOVE SPACES TO PHONE-SALE-LINE.

310-READ-PHONE-SALE-RECORD.
    READ PHONE-SALES-FILE RECORD
        AT END
            MOVE "NO " TO WS-MORE-RECORDS.
    .
    .
```

The THRU option of the PERFORM format allows **one** PERFORM statement to control the execution of a **series** of consecutive procedures. Examine the following example:

```
PAR-A.
    PERFORM PAR-C THRU PAR-E.
    .
    .
PAR-B.
    .
    .
PAR-C.
    .
    .
PAR-D.
    .
    .
PAR-E.
    .
    .
```

When the PERFORM statement is executed, control is passed to the first statement in PAR-C. From that point on, control will pass to every statement in PAR-C and **into every intervening paragraph** until it executes the last statement in PAR-E. Control then returns to PAR-A to execute the statement following the PERFORM.

The THRU option is seldom used in structured programs, mainly because it is unlikely that the set of procedures to be performed are actually coded in physical sequence within the program. The use of the

THRU option would then cause logic errors. For this reason, as well as other problems that can easily occur with the THRU option, it is not used in this text.

The last option of the PERFORM statement format allows the programmer to substitute imperative statements for a procedure name. The resulting statement is called an *in-line PERFORM.* The in-line PERFORM is a new feature introduced in COBOL '85. The example below is the in-line PERFORM version corresponding to the first PERFORM statement in the sample program. Note that the scope terminator END-PERFORM is a **required** entry in this option.

```
PERFORM OPEN INPUT PHONE-SALES-FILE
        OPEN OUTPUT PHONE-SALES-REPORT
        MOVE "YES" TO WS-MORE-RECORDS
        PERFORM 300-WRITE-REPORT-HEADERS
        PERFORM 310-READ-PHONE-SALE-RECORD
END-PERFORM.
```

Programmers may find an in-line PERFORM easier to code if the paragraph to be performed contains only a few instructions. Note that all the statements in an in-line PERFORM must be imperative statements. The example below is **invalid** because of the READ-AT END conditional statement.

```
PERFORM OPEN INPUT PHONE-SALES-FILE
        READ PHONE-SALES-FILE RECORD
            AT END
                MOVE "NO " TO WS-MORE-RECORDS
END-PERFORM.
```

A word of caution: An important goal of structured programmers is to enhance the clarity of the logic and the maintainability of their programs. It would be an inappropriate use of the in-line PERFORM if the achievement of these goals is impaired. For instance, the PROCEDURE DIVISION for the sample program has been recoded below with in-line PERFORMs. The output produced by the program remains unchanged, but the logic on which the structure of the PROCEDURE DIVISION rests has lost much of its clarity.

```
PROCEDURE DIVISION.

100-PRODUCE-PHONE-SALES-REPORT.
    PERFORM OPEN INPUT PHONE-SALES-FILE
            OPEN OUTPUT PHONE-SALES-REPORT
            MOVE "YES" TO WS-MORE-RECORDS
            PERFORM MOVE HEADINGS TO PRINTLINE
                    WRITE PRINTLINE
                        AFTER ADVANCING PAGE
                    MOVE SPACES TO PHONE-SALE-LINE
            END-PERFORM
            PERFORM 310-READ-PHONE-SALE-RECORD
    END-PERFORM.
    PERFORM WITH TEST BEFORE UNTIL WS-MORE-RECORDS = "NO "
        PERFORM 320-COMPUTE-PHONE-SALE-AMOUNT
        PERFORM 330-PREPARE-PHONE-SALE-LINE
        PERFORM 310-READ-PHONE-SALE-RECORD
    END-PERFORM.
    PERFORM CLOSE PHONE-SALES-FILE
            CLOSE PHONE-SALES-REPORT
    END-PERFORM.
    STOP RUN.

310-READ-PHONE-SALE-RECORD.
    READ PHONE-SALES-FILE RECORD
        AT END
            MOVE "NO " TO WS-MORE-RECORDS.

320-COMPUTE-PHONE-SALE-AMOUNT.
    IF I-NO-OF-UNITS > 100
        THEN
            COMPUTE O-SALE-AMOUNT = I-NO-OF-UNITS *
                                    I-UNIT-COST * .8
        ELSE
            COMPUTE O-SALE-AMOUNT = I-NO-OF-UNITS *
                                    I-UNIT-COST.

330-PREPARE-PHONE-SALE-LINE.
    MOVE I-CUSTOMER-NO TO O-CUSTOMER-NO.
    MOVE I-CATALOG-NO TO O-CATALOG-NO.
    MOVE I-UNIT-COST TO O-UNIT-COST.
    MOVE I-NO-OF-UNITS TO O-NO-OF-UNITS.
    MOVE PHONE-SALE-LINE TO PRINTLINE.
    WRITE PRINTLINE
        AFTER ADVANCING 2 LINES.
```

The PERFORM-UNTIL Statement

The format of the PERFORM-UNTIL statement is shown in Figure 4.6.

1. The simplest option available in the format is the one used in the sample program, specifically,

   ```
   PERFORM procedure-name UNTIL condition.
   ```

   It is most important to understand how this statement is executed. As control is passed to this statement, the condition in the UNTIL clause is tested first; then, if the condition is **true,** control is passed on immediately to the first statement beyond the scope of the PERFORM-UNTIL; if the condition is **false,** control is passed on to the procedure referenced by the PERFORM verb. The logic is perfectly illustrated by the repetition (or iterative, or loop) structure. See Figure 4.7.

   It is obvious that the condition is tested **before** the procedure is ever executed, and if the condition is true initially, the procedure is not executed at all.

   In the sample program, the function of this loop (or iteration) is to process all the records of the input file. The loop is under the control of the flag WS-MORE-RECORDS, as seen in the following statement:

   ```
   PERFORM 210-PROCESS-PHONE-SALE-RECORD
       UNTIL WS-MORE-RECORDS = "NO ".
   ```

   Recall that the flag is initialized to "YES" in the procedure 200-START-UP. The plan is to change the value of the flag to "NO " when the end-of-file record is detected within the procedure 310-READ-PHONE-SALE-RECORD. The change of the flag value must occur while control is within the procedure 210-PROCESS-PHONE-SALE-RECORD; otherwise, the record-processing loop would be an endless loop. Figure 4.8 highlights the essential aspects of the logic used to control the execution of the record-processing loop.

   Figure 4.9 shows the PROCEDURE DIVISION entries corresponding to the logic in Figure 4.8. Annotations provide additional explanations.
2. The format of the PERFORM-UNTIL statement also allows the use of the THRU option. The comments made earlier apply to this format as well, so no further explanations are provided here.

Figure 4.6 Format of the PERFORM-UNTIL statement

```
PERFORM [procedure-name-1 [{THRU   } procedure-name-2]]
                           {THROUGH}
        [WITH TEST {BEFORE}] UNTIL condition
                   {AFTER }
        [imperative-statement . . .END-PERFORM]
```

Figure 4.7 Logic of the PERFORM-UNTIL statement (pretest iteration)

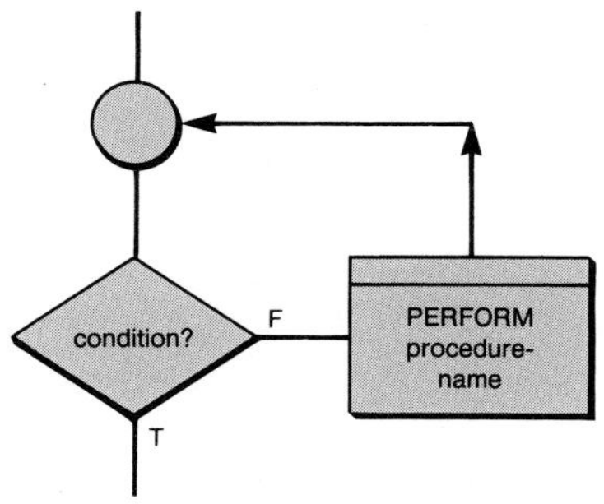

■ **Figure 4.8** Mechanisms that control execution of the record-processing loop

100-PRODUCE-PHONE-SALES-REPORT

PERFORM 200-START-UP

IS WS-MORE-RECORDS = "NO "?

NO

PERFORM 210-PROCESS-PHONE-SALE-RECORD

Record-processing loop. Exit occurs when flag contains the value "NO "

YES

200-START-UP

MOVE "YES" TO WS-MORE-RECORDS

The flag is initialized here

PERFORM 310-READ-PHONE-SALE-RECORD

This procedure will access the first record of the input file

RETURN

210-PROCESS-PHONE-SALE-RECORD

Record-processing activities

PERFORM 310-READ-PHONE-SALE-RECORD

Module contains mechanism to set flag to "NO "

RETURN

310-READ-PHONE-SALE-RECORD

READ A PHONE-SALE-RECORD

Test for end-of-file record

EOF?

YES

MOVE "NO " TO WS-MORE-RECORDS

Value of flag is changed to "NO " when end-of-file record is detected

NO

RETURN

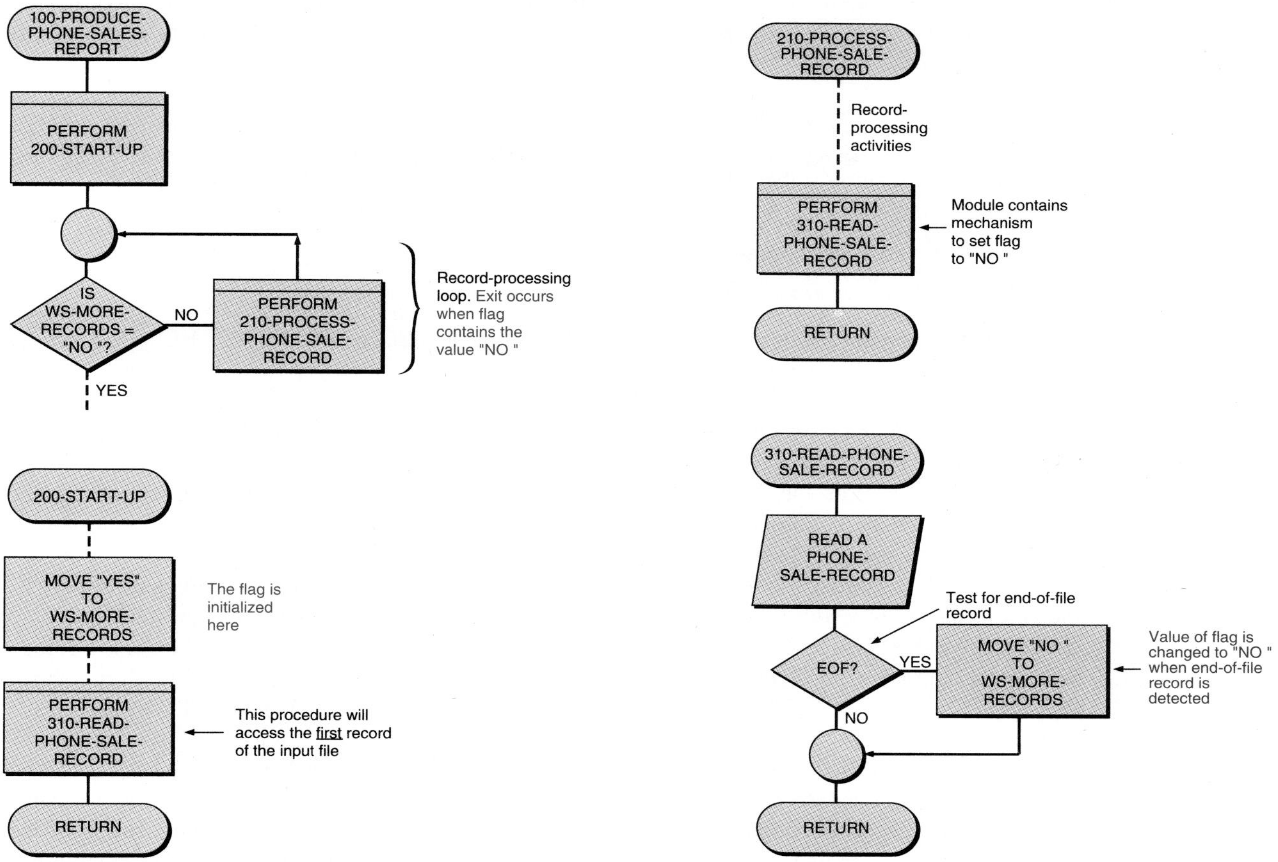

■ **Figure 4.9** PROCEDURE DIVISION entries that control execution of the record-processing loop

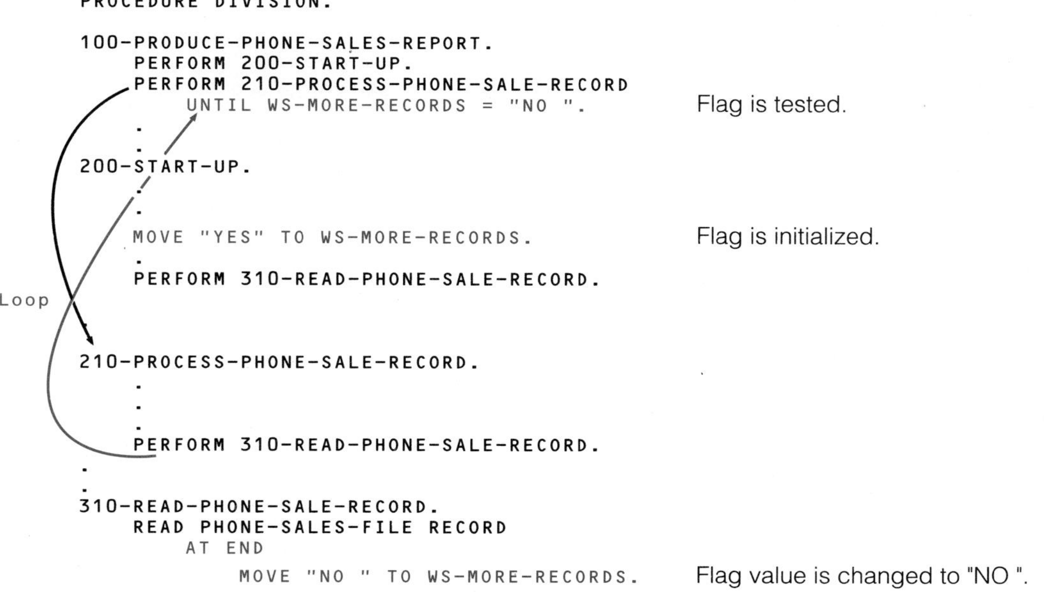

```
PROCEDURE DIVISION.

100-PRODUCE-PHONE-SALES-REPORT.
    PERFORM 200-START-UP.
    PERFORM 210-PROCESS-PHONE-SALE-RECORD
        UNTIL WS-MORE-RECORDS = "NO ".          Flag is tested.
    .
    .
200-START-UP.
    .
    .
    MOVE "YES" TO WS-MORE-RECORDS.              Flag is initialized.
    .
    PERFORM 310-READ-PHONE-SALE-RECORD.
Loop
210-PROCESS-PHONE-SALE-RECORD.
    .
    .
    .
    PERFORM 310-READ-PHONE-SALE-RECORD.
.
.
310-READ-PHONE-SALE-RECORD.
    READ PHONE-SALES-FILE RECORD
        AT END
            MOVE "NO " TO WS-MORE-RECORDS.      Flag value is changed to "NO ".
```

3. The phrases WITH TEST BEFORE and WITH TEST AFTER are new language features included in the 1985 ANSI standards. Their use **explicitly** indicates whether the condition specified in the UNTIL clause should be tested **before** or **after** execution of the procedure. From the explanations of the statement

```
PERFORM 210-PROCESS-PHONE-SALE-RECORD
    UNTIL WS-MORE-RECORDS = "NO "
```

given above, you can see that the option WITH TEST BEFORE is redundant. That is, the statement

```
PERFORM 210-PROCESS-PHONE-SALE-RECORD
     WITH TEST BEFORE
          UNTIL WS-MORE-RECORDS = "NO "
```

is logically equivalent to the above PERFORM without the phrase WITH TEST BEFORE, and as a result, the use of this phrase is optional.

On the other hand, situations occur when a procedure must be executed once, and then a decision has to be made whether it should be executed again. This logic is illustrated in Figure 4.10.

It is obvious from the flowchart segment that the condition is tested **after** the procedure has been executed. If the condition remains false, the procedure is executed again; when the tested condition is true, an exit from the loop or iteration occurs.

Figure 4.11 contains an example of a posttest PERFORM. The flowchart segment in part a indicates that the procedure 210-PROCESS-RECORD must be performed once, and then the condition WS-MORE-RECORDS = "NO " must be tested. Part b shows the cumbersome coding that a programmer would have to use if the TEST AFTER option were not available. Part c shows the simpler and more straightforward coding that results from the use of the TEST AFTER option.

4. The format of the PERFORM-UNTIL also allows the programmer to substitute imperative statements for a procedure name. Look at the example in Figure 4.12. It is clear from part a that the procedure 200-ADD contains only one statement. It seems to be particularly demanding of the language to require coding of a procedure to accomplish this little. In part b, the logic is simplified so that the loop contains only a process box rather than a perform box. The process box specifies the ADD function. An in-line PERFORM-UNTIL can be used to code the logic directly and more simply. In both cases, the phrase WITH TEST BEFORE is optional.

The coding of the PROCEDURE DIVISION on page 151 contains an in-line PERFORM-UNTIL that also includes the WITH TEST phrase. Note again that the scope of an in-line PERFORM must end with the explicit scope terminator END-PERFORM.

■ **Figure 4.10** Logic of the PERFORM-WITH TEST AFTER-UNTIL statement (posttest iteration)

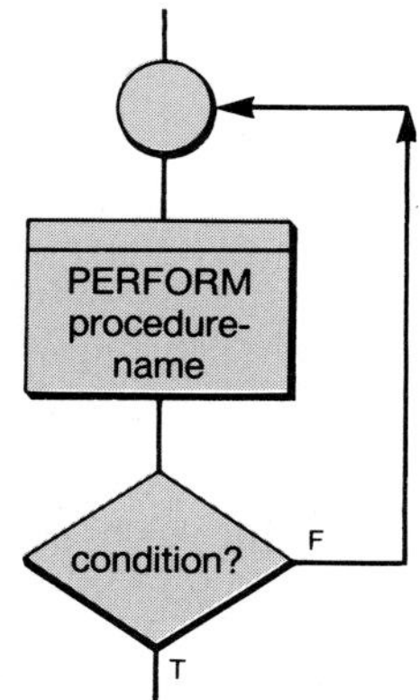

Figure 4.11 Iteration with test after—example

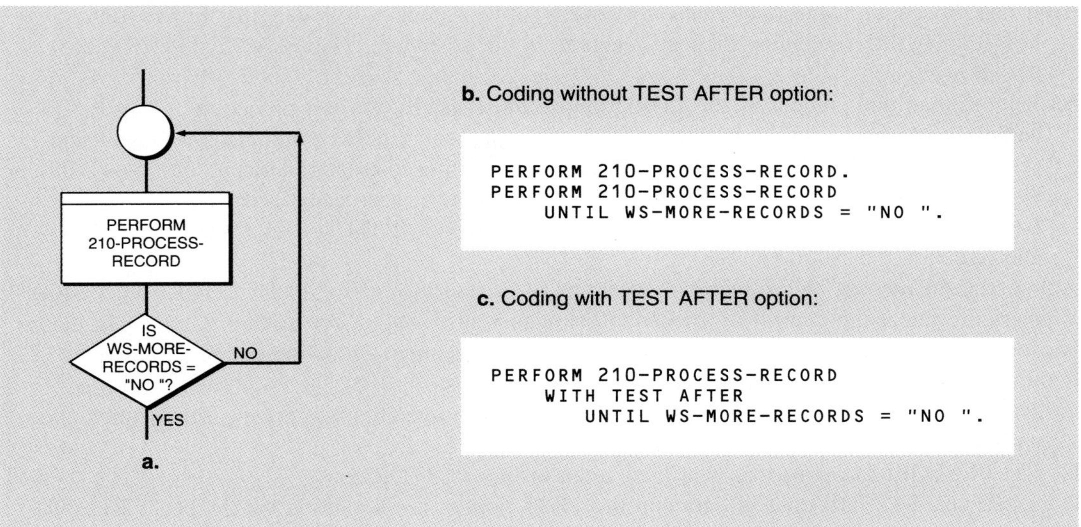
PERFORM
210-PROCESS-
RECORD
IS
WS-MORE-
RECORDS =
"NO "?
NO
YES
a.
b. Coding without TEST AFTER option:
PERFORM 210-PROCESS-RECORD.
PERFORM 210-PROCESS-RECORD
UNTIL WS-MORE-RECORDS = "NO ".
c. Coding with TEST AFTER option:
PERFORM 210-PROCESS-RECORD
WITH TEST AFTER
UNTIL WS-MORE-RECORDS = "NO ".

Figure 4.12 In-line PERFORM-UNTIL—example

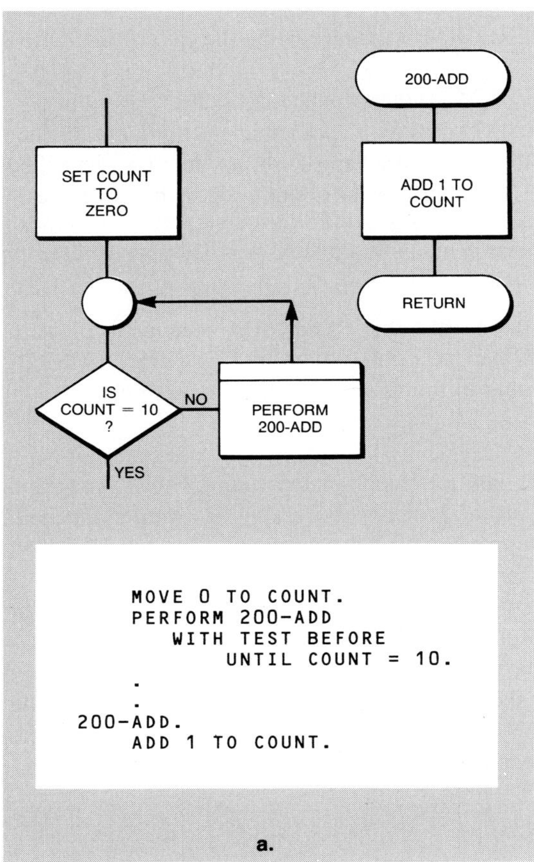
SET COUNT
TO
ZERO
IS
COUNT = 10
?
NO
YES
PERFORM
200-ADD
200-ADD
ADD 1 TO
COUNT
RETURN
MOVE 0 TO COUNT.
PERFORM 200-ADD
WITH TEST BEFORE
UNTIL COUNT = 10.
.
.
200-ADD.
ADD 1 TO COUNT.
a.

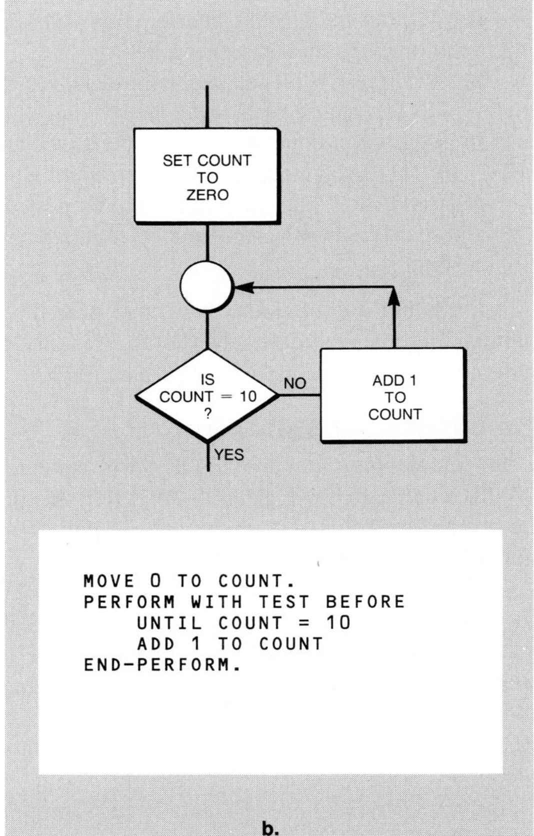
SET COUNT
TO
ZERO
IS
COUNT = 10
?
NO
YES
ADD 1
TO
COUNT
MOVE 0 TO COUNT.
PERFORM WITH TEST BEFORE
UNTIL COUNT = 10
ADD 1 TO COUNT
END-PERFORM.
b.

Rules Governing the Use of the PERFORM Statement

1. A PERFORM statement can execute one or more procedures.
   a. If one procedure, control automatically returns to the statement following the PERFORM immediately after executing the last statement in the procedure. The use of END-PERFORM is not allowed.
   b. If more than one procedure, the THRU option must specify the last procedure. Control automatically passes to every statement of every procedure between procedure-name-1 and procedure-name-2 (including these two) unless branching instructions dictate otherwise. In any event, all paths must lead ultimately to the last statement in procedure-name-2.
   Note: The use of the THRU option is not recommended. The use of END-PERFORM is not allowed.
2. A procedure name can be the name of a paragraph or a section of the PROCEDURE DIVISION.
3. A procedure under the control of a PERFORM statement that does not contain the UNTIL clause is executed only once. Control then passes to the first statement following the PERFORM.
4. If the PERFORM verb does not reference a procedure,
   a. The PERFORM statement must contain one or more imperative statements, and it must end with the scope terminator END-PERFORM.
   b. The PERFORM statement is classified as an in-line PERFORM.
5. If a PERFORM-UNTIL does not contain the TEST phrase, the default is WITH TEST BEFORE.
6. A procedure under the control of a PERFORM-UNTIL, without the TEST phrase or with the phrase WITH TEST BEFORE, need not be executed at all. This occurs if the condition in the UNTIL clause is satisfied initially.
7. A procedure under the control of a PERFORM-UNTIL with the phrase WITH TEST AFTER is executed at least once.
8. In an in-line PERFORM:
   a. Without the UNTIL clause, control leaves the PERFORM statement when the END-PERFORM scope terminator is encountered.
   b. With the UNTIL clause, control leaves the PERFORM statement when the condition in the UNTIL clause tests true.
   In either case, control passes to the first statement after the scope terminator END-PERFORM.
9. A PERFORM statement can be executed while under the control of another PERFORM statement. That is, PERFORM statements can be nested. They are not allowed to be recursive, however; that is, a nested PERFORM must not reference a procedure that contains it, directly or at an outer level of nesting.

It should be obvious from the preceding discussion that the PERFORM statement plays a commanding role in structured COBOL. It is used to control the execution of the PROCEDURE DIVISION paragraphs, except the main-control paragraph, corresponding to the modules of the structure chart.

The STOP RUN Statement

In the sample program, the STOP RUN statement is the last statement of the main-control paragraph 100-PRODUCE-PHONE-SALES-REPORT. At this point, all the required processing has been completed. The net result of this statement is to permanently stop the execution of the program, and control is then returned to the operating system. Its format is shown in Figure 4.13.

In COBOL '85, the execution of STOP RUN also implicitly closes all files that remain open. For program clarity, however, we recommend that files be closed explicitly using the CLOSE statement.

Note that the STOP RUN statement must be the last one executed in a program. It is generally explicitly coded as the last statement of the main-control paragraph. It should be clear, however, that it is not usually the last statement coded in the **program.** It is usually followed by the coding of all remaining paragraphs of the PROCEDURE DIVISION. (In this text, all paragraphs are coded in ascending order of their numeric prefixes.)

Figure 4.13 STOP statement format

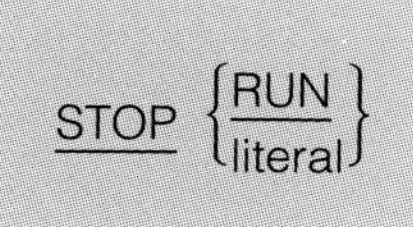

The format of the STOP statement also allows a literal to follow the verb STOP. This option temporarily interrupts execution of the program and displays the value of the literal at the terminal. Though the literal can be any literal or any figurative constant (other than ALL), it is usually a message that directs the operator to take some course of action. Program execution can then be resumed by entering a CONTINUE command. We will not need this option in this text. Furthermore, it has been made obsolete in COBOL '85 and is slated for removal from the standards.

The Second-Level Paragraph 200-START-UP

Figure 4.14 shows the related portions of the structure chart, the pseudocode, and the program flowchart that correspond to the paragraph 200-START-UP.

Figure 4.14 The development of the procedure 200-START-UP

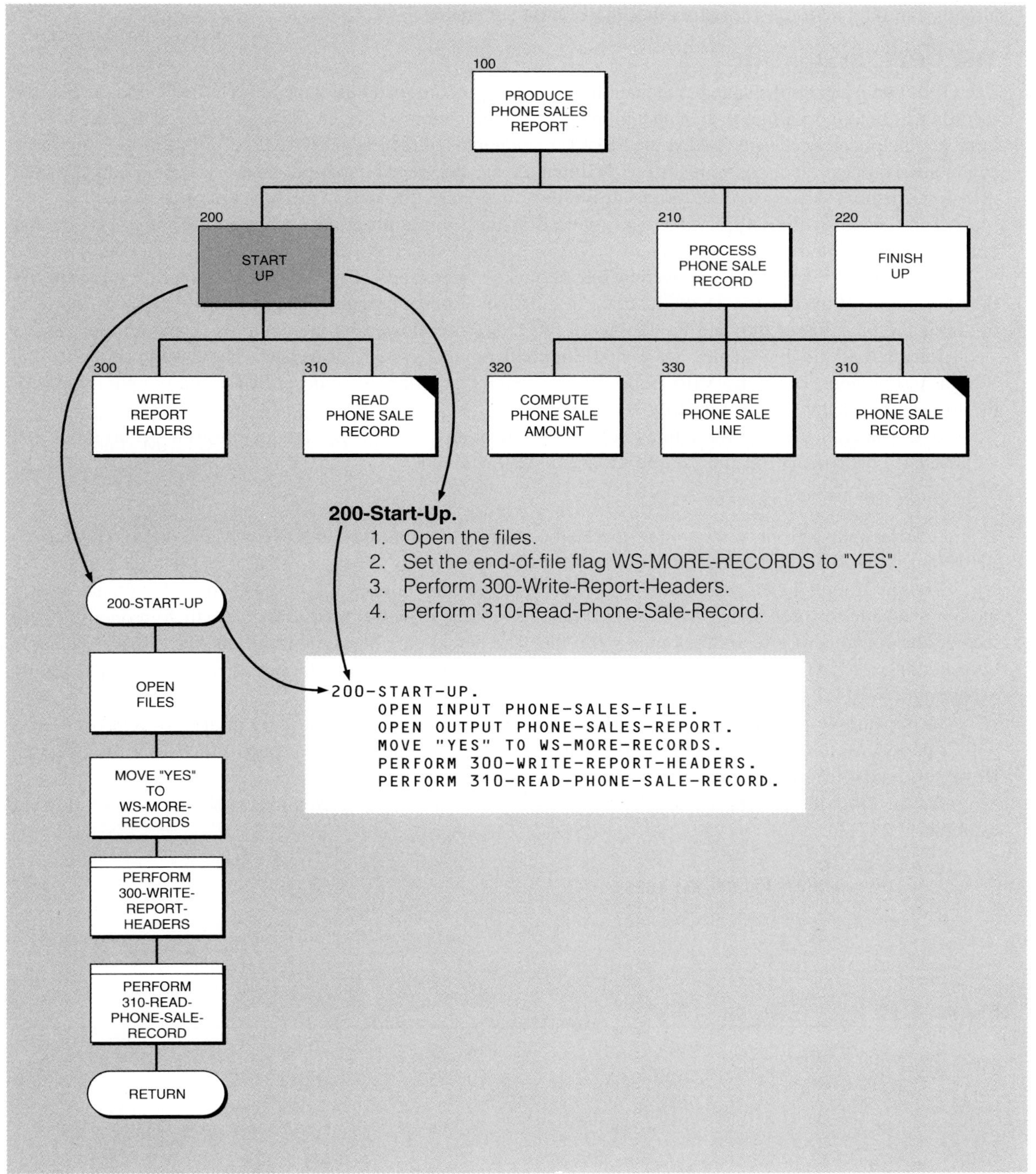

The general purpose of this type of procedure is to make the required files available to the program, to initialize variables (data items) such as accumulators and counters, to set flags to initial states, to begin the printing of a report if there is one, and to access the first record of the input file.

The specific purposes of the procedure 200-START-UP for the sample program are

1. To make the input file PHONE-SALES-FILE and the output file PHONE-SALES-REPORT available to the program. This is done by the execution of the OPEN statements.
2. To assign the initial value "YES" to the flag WS-MORE-RECORDS. This is done by a MOVE statement.
3. To control the execution of the procedure 300-WRITE-REPORT-HEADERS, whose function is to start the report by writing the required headings.
4. To control the execution of the procedure 310-READ-PHONE-SALE-RECORD, in order to access the first record of the input file.

We will examine the format of the OPEN statement and the format of the MOVE statement. (You are already familiar with the format of the PERFORM statement.)

The OPEN Statement

The OPEN verb begins the statements that direct the computer to ready the storage areas needed to process the records that belong to a file, to establish a line of communication with each file, and to check that the needed input and output devices (specified in the SELECT statements of the ENVIRONMENT DIVISION) are indeed available to process the files. No record of the input file can be "read" into input memory, and no output record in output memory can be written to a print file or to a storage file, unless the files are opened.

The format of the OPEN statement as used in the sample program is shown in Figure 4.15. (Other options are examined later.)

The verb OPEN must be followed by one of the key words INPUT or OUTPUT, as applicable, to specify the **open mode** of the file, that is, the function of the file within the program. The key word INPUT is followed by the name of an input file, and the key word OUTPUT is followed by the name of an output file.

Recall that the file names were first supplied on the system flowchart. They were coded in the SELECT statements of the ENVIRONMENT DIVISION, and they were described in the FD paragraphs of the file section of the DATA DIVISION.

It is essential that the file names not be altered in any way in any one of the four occurrences just mentioned. For instance, in the sample program, the statement

```
OPEN INPUT PHONE-SALE-FILE
```

would cause a disastrous error, since the name of the input file is PHONE-SALES-FILE. The name PHONE-SALE-FILE is not recognized as a valid file name.

The programmer must also realize that the OPEN statement does not by itself make the actual data in the file available for processing. All it does is make a storage or buffer area available which in due time will receive the contents of a record belonging to a file. The actual data on an input file record is made available by executing a READ statement, and the actual data on an output file record is written on the output file by executing a WRITE statement.

In the sample program, the two OPEN statements begin on separate lines in area B, and each ends with a period. Both could be coded on the same line, provided at least one space follows the first period. However, readability is enhanced by writing them on separate lines.

On the other hand, both files could be opened in the same OPEN statement, as shown in the following example:

```
200-START-UP.
    OPEN INPUT PHONE-SALES-FILE
         OUTPUT PHONE-SALES-REPORT.
    MOVE "YES" TO WS-MORE-RECORDS.
    .
    .
```

Figure 4.15 OPEN statement format

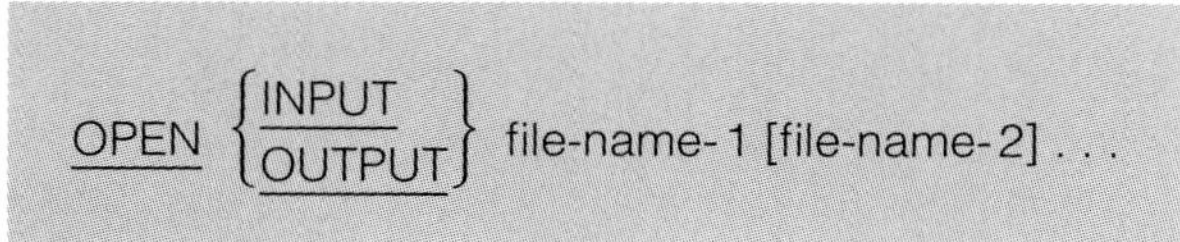

OPEN {INPUT / OUTPUT} file-name-1 [file-name-2] . . .

Note the following:

1. The verb OPEN is coded only once.
2. There is only one period; it follows the name of the output file.
3. The key word OUTPUT is aligned under INPUT, for readability.

It is important for the programmer to realize that no data belonging to a file can be processed unless the corresponding file has been opened by an OPEN statement.

Rules Governing the Use of the OPEN Statement

1. The OPEN statement makes a file available to the program.
2. The OPEN statement does not access a record of the file.
3. The file name must be that of a file described in the DATA DIVISION.
4. The open mode (function) of the file must be consistent with the SELECT statement in the FILE-CONTROL paragraph of the ENVIRONMENT DIVISION.
5. More than one file can be opened by a single OPEN statement.
6. A file can be opened more than once in the same program; however, it must have been closed before any subsequent OPEN.
7. A file must have been successfully opened before any INPUT or OUTPUT statement executes for that file.

The MOVE Statement

The next statement in the procedure 200-START-UP is a MOVE statement. Its purpose is to assign "YES" as the initial value of the flag WS-MORE-RECORDS. MOVE statements occur frequently in COBOL programs.

We have pointed out several times that the COBOL programmer must keep track of three distinct storage areas in the main memory: the input, the output, and the working-storage areas. The input storage area stores the contents of an input record as it is "read" into memory; the working-storage area usually stores intermediate computed values and contains storage areas for constants, flags, tables, and records that are ultimately written onto output files; and the output storage area stores the contents of an output record before it is written to an output file.

Data is generally transferred from input memory to output memory, from input memory to working storage, from one working-storage area to another, and from working storage to output memory. Such data transfers are accomplished by the MOVE statement.

Note: The verb MOVE and the expression "data transfer" may be misleading by suggesting a physical transfer of data. What actually happens is that the data is simply "copied" into the receiving field.

The format of the MOVE statement is shown in Figure 4.16. In this format, identifier-2, identifier-3, . . . name the receiving fields (the fields to which the data is being transferred); identifier-1 is the name of the source or sending field; and literal, if used, is the source value (the value being assigned to the receiving field).

In the statement

```
MOVE "YES" TO WS-MORE-RECORDS,
```

"YES" is the value being transferred to (or copied into) the receiving field WS-MORE-RECORDS. In the statement

```
MOVE HEADINGS TO PRINTLINE,
```

HEADINGS is the source field, and PRINTLINE is the receiving field.

Some problems may occur as data is moved from a source to a receiving field. Programmers must be aware of the valid and invalid moves. The table in Figure 4.17 summarizes the various data transfer options

■ **Figure 4.16** MOVE statement format

<u>MOVE</u> {identifier-1 / literal} <u>TO</u> identifier-2 [identifier-3] . . .

Figure 4.17 Summary of valid and invalid data transfers

Source Item Class	Receiving Item Class				
	Alphabetic	*Alphanumeric*	*Alphanumeric-edited*	*Numeric*	*Numeric-edited*
Alphabetic	V	V	V	I	I
Alphanumeric	V	V	V	V*	V*
Alphanumeric-edited	V	V	V	I	I
Numeric	I	V*	V*	V	V
Numeric-edited	I	V	V	V+	V+

* Integer only (sign is not stored)
\+ De-editing of source value occurs
V Valid move
I Invalid move

between sending and receiving fields and classifies the moves as valid or invalid. Restrictions on valid data transfers are also indicated.

Notes on Data Transfers

1. The recommended and most common data transfers are as follows:
   a. Alphabetic to alphabetic.
   b. Alphabetic to alphanumeric.
   c. Alphanumeric to alphanumeric.
   d. Alphanumeric to alphanumeric-edited.
   e. Numeric to numeric.
   f. Numeric to numeric-edited.
2. Whenever numeric data is transferred to a numeric field,
   a. It is stored right-justified in the receiving field if the receiving field does not contain a decimal point (assumed or explicit); the characters, if any, to the right of the decimal in the source value are lost; leading positions, if any, in the receiving field are zero-filled.
   b. It is positioned in the receiving field to align with the decimal point; leading and trailing positions, if any, are zero-filled.
   c. If the receiving field is signed, the sign of the source value is stored; if the source value is unsigned, a "plus" sign is stored.
   d. If the receiving field is unsigned, only the absolute value of the source value is stored.
   e. If the source value is edited, it will be de-edited before being moved to the receiving field. (De-editing is a new feature in COBOL '85.)
3. Whenever nonnumeric data is transferred, it is stored left-justified in the receiving field, unless the JUSTIFIED RIGHT clause is used in the field description entry.
4. If the source field is a group item, the data is handled as an alphanumeric data transfer.
5. If the receiving field is larger than the source field, then the extra spaces are
   a. Zero-filled if the transfer is numeric.
   b. Left blank if the transfer is nonnumeric.
6. If the receiving field is smaller than the source field, then:
   a. The leftmost digits (high-order characters) are truncated if the data is numeric and does not contain a decimal point.
   b. The extra digits to the left (high-order characters) and/or to the right (low-order characters) of the decimal point are truncated, if a decimal point exists.
   c. The rightmost (low-order) characters are truncated if the data is nonnumeric. If the JUSTIFIED RIGHT clause is used, the leftmost (high-order) characters are truncated.

These rules are illustrated in Figure 4.18. The sending field is SAMPLE-IN, and the receiving field is SAMPLE-OUT. In each case, a PICTURE is specified for the sending and the receiving fields. The contents of the fields are shown following the data transfer.

Note again that a MOVE statement does not physically remove the data from the source field; rather, it makes a copy of it in the receiving field. That is, it alters the contents of the receiving field but not the contents of the source field. To further illustrate this point, consider the next example:

```
MOVE ITEM-IN TO ITEM-OUT.
```

■ **Figure 4.18** Effect of PICTURE clause of receiving field on data transfer—examples

MOVE SAMPLE-IN TO SAMPLE-OUT

SAMPLE-IN		SAMPLE-OUT	
PIC	Contents	PIC	Contents
X(6)	NUMBER	X(6)	NUMBER
A(6)	NUMBER	X(4)	NUMB
X(6)	NUMBER	X(8)	NUMBER␣␣
X(6)	NUMBER	X(8) JUST	␣␣NUMBER
9(3)	356	9(3)	356
9(3)	356	9(5)	00356
9(3)	356	9(2)	56
999V999	273^258	99.9	73.2
999V99	273^25	9(5).999	00273.250
S9999V99	0023^0$\overset{+}{0}$	ZZZ9.99	␣␣23.00
S9999V99	1234^5$\overset{-}{6}$	$,$$9.99-	␣$234.56-
Z,ZZ9.99-	1,234.56-	999.999	234.560

Before Execution:

ITEM-IN	ITEM-OUT
PILLOWCASE	PANY-25␣GARDEN

After Execution:

ITEM-IN	ITEM-OUT
PILLOWCASE	PILLOWCASE␣␣␣␣

Transferring data into the field ITEM-OUT has erased the original data in the field and replaced it with the transferred data. Note that the extra spaces are left blank. After the MOVE, the value in ITEM-IN has not changed.

Data Classification

Before examining other uses of the MOVE statement, consider the various classifications of data shown in Figure 4.19.

Examples of constants include the following:

1. Numeric literal: 1, as in

```
ADD 1 TO LINE-CTR.
```

2. Nonnumeric literal: "PAYROLL REPORT", as in

```
MOVE "PAYROLL REPORT" TO REPORT-HEADER.
```

3. Figurative constant: SPACES, as in

```
MOVE SPACES TO PHONE-SALE-LINE.
```

Examples of types of variables (data names), as defined by the PICTURE clause, include the following:

1. Numeric, as in

```
05 I-ITEM-COST       PIC S999V99.
```

(Class code 9; no editing characters)

2. Alphabetic, as in

```
05 EOF-FLAG          PIC AAA.
```

(Class code A)

3. Alphanumeric, as in

```
05 I-CUSTOMER-NO     PIC X(4).
```

(Class code X; no editing characters)

■ **Figure 4.19** Data classification chart

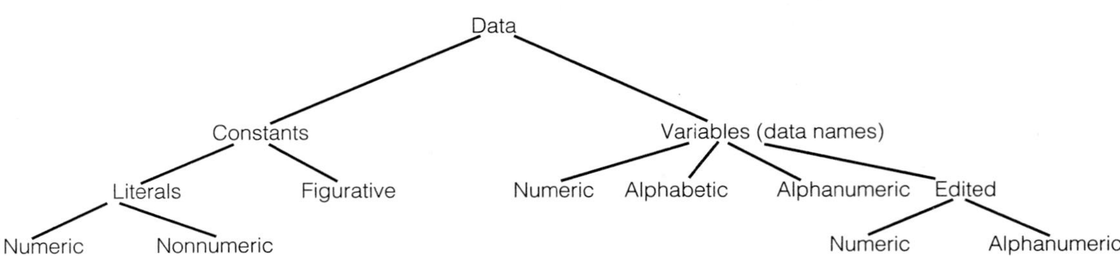

1. The value of a data name (variable) may
   a. vary
   b. be numeric, alphabetic, alphanumeric, numeric-edited, alphanumeric-edited.
2. The value of a constant does not vary. Its value is its face value.
3. A constant may be either a Literal or a Figurative Constant.
   a. Figurative Constants have been explained in Chapter 3.
   b. A Literal may be
      i. Numeric (any number consisting of up to 18 digits):
         It may have a plus or minus sign preceding it.
         It may have an embedded decimal point.
         It must not be enclosed within quotes.
      ii. Nonnumeric (any set of up to 160 characters):
         It must be enclosed within quotes.

4. Numeric-edited, as in

```
05 O-SALE-AMOUNT      PIC $Z(5)9.99-.
```

   (Class code 9, with editing characters $, Z, ., and -)

5. Alphanumeric-edited, as in

```
05 OUT-DATE           PIC XX/XX/XX.
```

   (Class code X, with editing character /)

Constants in a MOVE Statement

In the preceding discussion, we were concerned mainly with transferring data from one storage area to another by using the MOVE statement. This statement is often used to place constants into storage areas as well.

Note the effect of the MOVE statement in each example below. (Assume that the receiving fields are of the proper class and size.)

1. `MOVE SPACE TO PHONE-SALE-LINE.`

   The figurative constant SPACE is the source value. A blank is moved into each storage position (or byte) of the record PHONE-SALE-LINE. After execution, all the characters initially in the record area PHONE-SALE-LINE have been replaced by blank spaces.

2. `MOVE "THE ALLIED STOCK COMPANY" TO WS-COMPANY-NAME.`

   The source value is the nonnumeric literal THE ALLIED STOCK COMPANY. Note that the literal marks themselves are not part of the literal. After execution, the characters making up the literal are stored in the field WS-COMPANY-NAME. They are stored left-justified in the field. Excess positions to the right, if any, are left blank.

3. `MOVE 4.75 TO WS-PAY-RATE.`

   The source value is the numeric literal 4.75. A numeric literal is never enclosed in literal marks. After execution, the receiving field WS-PAY-RATE contains the value 4.75.

4. `MOVE ZEROS TO EMPLOYEE-COUNT, SALES-COUNT, TOTAL-SALES.`

   The figurative constant ZEROS is the source value. The numeric literal 0 could have been used instead, with the same result. After execution, the three receiving fields, EMPLOYEE-COUNT, SALES-COUNT, and TOTAL-SALES, are filled with zeros.

In summary, the MOVE statement can be used to **transfer** data from one storage area to another and to **place** constants into specific receiving fields.

Note: The rules for moving literals into receiving fields are the same as the ones that apply to data transfer from a source to a receiving field. (See the notes on data transfers, items 2, 3, 5, and 6, page 160.)

Literal Continuation

Nonnumeric literals can contain up to 160 characters in COBOL '85, replacing the prior maximum of 120. (Here also, some operating systems may have higher or lower maximums.) Consequently, sometimes they are too long to be coded on one line. This may occur when they are used in the VALUE clause in the WORKING-STORAGE SECTION of the DATA DIVISION, or when they are used as a source value in a MOVE statement in the PROCEDURE DIVISION. In either case, the problem can be resolved by using either of the two methods illustrated in Chapter 3.

JUSTIFIED RIGHT

When a nonnumeric value is moved into a receiving field, the characters are normally stored left-justified, with remaining low-order positions left blank. Sometimes, a report format may require that values assigned to a nonnumeric field be right-justified rather than left-justified, that is, that the characters be stored in the rightmost bytes of the storage area. This feature is implemented by coding the JUSTIFIED RIGHT clause in the DATA DIVISION entry used to describe the receiving field. (The entry JUSTIFIED RIGHT can be abbreviated simply JUST.)

Figure 4.20 shows the results of a MOVE statement in a field with the usual left justification (O-ITEM-NO) and in a field with right justification (O-ITEM-NO-X).

As another example, suppose the literal "THE ALLIED STOCK COMPANY" must be moved to the field WS-COMPANY-NAME of the record COMPANY-NAME in Figure 4.21a. The statement

```
MOVE "THE ALLIED STOCK COMPANY" TO WS-COMPANY-NAME
```

Figure 4.20 Effect of JUSTIFIED RIGHT on value in the receiving field—examples

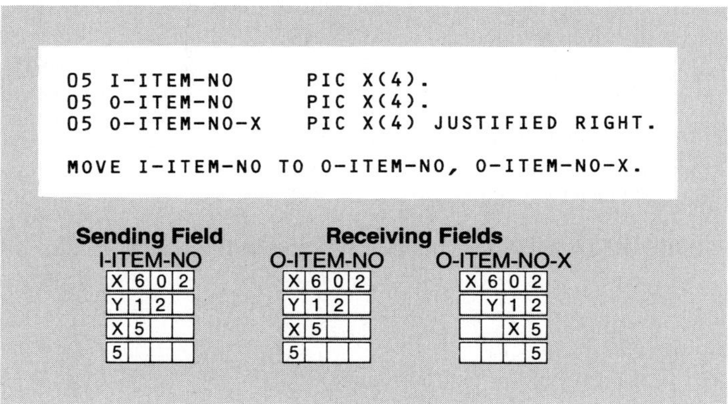

```
05 I-ITEM-NO       PIC X(4).
05 O-ITEM-NO       PIC X(4).
05 O-ITEM-NO-X     PIC X(4) JUSTIFIED RIGHT.

MOVE I-ITEM-NO TO O-ITEM-NO, O-ITEM-NO-X.
```


Figure 4.21 Example of JUSTIFIED RIGHT clause

```
       MOVE "THE ALLIED STOCK COMPANY" TO WS-COMPANY-NAME.

a.     01  COMPANY-NAME.
           05 WS-COMPANY-NAME       PIC X(78)  JUSTIFIED RIGHT.
           05 FILLER                PIC X(54)  VALUE IS SPACES.

     ** prints as shown below **
                                                        THE ALLIED STOCK COMPANY

b.     01  COMPANY-NAME.
           05 WS-COMPANY-NAME       PIC X(78).
           05 FILLER                PIC X(54)  VALUE IS SPACES.

     ** prints as shown below **
THE ALLIED STOCK COMPANY
```

stores the name in positions 53 through 78 of the record. When the record is printed, the company name is centered on the line, assuming the line has 132 print positions. On the other hand, in Figure 4.21b, the JUSTIFIED RIGHT clause is not used. The MOVE statement stores the company name in positions 1 through 24 of the record COMPANY-NAME. When the record is printed, the name is printed in print positions 1 through 24 of the printline.

Note: The clause JUSTIFIED RIGHT (or JUST) can be used in the description of nonnumeric fields only, at the elementary level, anywhere in the DATA DIVISION. It is operational only when it is applied to the *receiving field* specified in a MOVE statement.

The INITIALIZE Statement

The preceding pages contain information on data transfers brought about by the execution of MOVE statements. The reason that the MOVE statement was explained here in the chapter is that it was used in the procedure 200-START-UP to assign an initial value to the program flag WS-MORE-RECORDS. Most programs contain other data items that must also be initialized, such as accumulators and counters. All such items can also be initialized by using the appropriate MOVE statements. However, the 1985 COBOL ANSI standards now include the INITIALIZE statement for that purpose.

The format of the INITIALIZE statement is shown in Figure 4.22.

Rules Governing the Use of the INITIALIZE Statement

1. Identifier-1 is the name of the data item to receive an initial value.
2. The source value (that is, the value to be assigned to the receiving field) can be specified by a literal or by the name of the source field, identifier-2, referenced in the BY phrase.
3. If the REPLACING phrase is not used, the following default values are assigned to identifier-1:
   - **a.** SPACES, if the data item is alphabetic, alphanumeric, or alphanumeric-edited
   - **b.** ZEROS, if the data item is numeric or numeric-edited
4. Identifier-1 can be an elementary item or a group item.
   - **a.** If it is a group item, values are assigned to its elementary subitems as if they resulted from individual MOVE statements at the elementary level.
     - **i.** If the REPLACING phrase is not used, all elementary items will receive the default values.
     - **ii.** If the REPLACING phrase is used, only the elementary items whose class match the class specified in the phrase will receive the source value.
   - **b.** If it is an elementary item, its class must be the same as the one specified in the REPLACING phrase.
5. The source value must be compatible with the class specified in the REPLACING phrase. (Compatibility is determined by the rules for valid and invalid MOVE statements.)
6. A FILLER area is never affected by the INITIALIZE statement.

In the sample program, the flag WS-MORE-RECORDS can be assigned the initial value "YES" by the following statement:

```
INITIALIZE WS-MORE-RECORDS
    REPLACING ALPHANUMERIC DATA BY "YES".
```

In this statement:

1. The field being initialized is WS-MORE-RECORDS.
2. The source value is the literal "YES".
3. The class specified in the REPLACING phrase is ALPHANUMERIC; it is compatible with the class specified in the PIC clause that defines WS-MORE-RECORDS.

Figure 4.22 INITIALIZE statement format

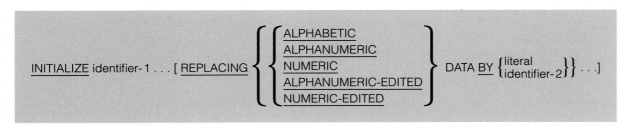

```
                                         { { ALPHABETIC          }                                  }
                                         { { ALPHANUMERIC        }                                  }
INITIALIZE identifier-1 . . . [ REPLACING { { NUMERIC             } DATA BY { literal      } } . . . ]
                                         { { ALPHANUMERIC-EDITED }         { identifier-2 } }
                                         { { NUMERIC-EDITED      }                                  }
```

Examine the following record descriptions and INITIALIZE statements.

Example 1:

```
01   COMPANY-WORK-AREAS.
     05 WS-TOTAL-FED-TAX        PIC S9(6)V99.
     05 WS-TOTAL-STATE-TAX      PIC S9(6)V99.
01   EMPLOYEE-WORK-AREAS.
     05 WS-FED-TAX              PIC S9(4)V99.
     05 WS-STATE-TAX            PIC S9(4)V99.
     05 WS-DEDUCTIONS           PIC S9(4)V99.
```

a. `INITIALIZE WS-TOTAL-STATE-TAX.`

The data item being initialized is the elementary item WS-TOTAL-STATE-TAX. It receives the default value of ZEROS, since the PIC that defines it classifies the field as numeric.

b. `INITIALIZE EMPLOYEE-WORK-AREAS.`

The data item being initialized is a group item. Since the REPLACING phrase is not part of the statement, default values are assigned to all of its elementary items. The default value is ZEROS, since each elementary item is defined as numeric.

Example 2:

```
01   ITEM-A.
     05 ITEM-B         PIC X(6).
     05 ITEM-C         PIC XX/XX.
     05 ITEM-D         PIC Z99.
     05 ITEM-E         PIC $Z9.99+.
     05 ITEM-F         PIC 9(4).
01   ITEM-P            PIC 9V9      VALUE 2.5.
01   ITEM-Q            PIC S99      VALUE -15.
01   ITEM-R            PIC XXX      VALUE "TAB".
```

a. `INITIALIZE ITEM-A.`

The elementary items of the group item ITEM-A are assigned default values as follows (*s* denotes a space):

```
ITEM-B:   ssssss
ITEM-C:   ss/ss
ITEM-D:   s00
ITEM-E:   $s0.00+
ITEM-F:   0000
```

b.
```
INITIALIZE ITEM-A
    REPLACING NUMERIC DATA BY ITEM-P.
```

The only elementary item of group ITEM-A that receives an initial value is ITEM-F, since it is the only numeric item. The value that is moved to ITEM-F is the value of ITEM-P, namely, 2.5. Since ITEM-F is an integer field, only the integer portion of 2.5 is actually stored, so the value of ITEM-F is 0002.

c.
```
INITIALIZE ITEM-A
    REPLACING ALPHANUMERIC DATA BY "YES"
              ALPHANUMERIC-EDITED DATA BY ITEM-R
              NUMERIC DATA BY ITEM-Q
              NUMERIC-EDITED DATA BY ITEM-Q.
```

After execution of the preceding statement, the elementary items of the group item ITEM-A contain the following values:

```
ITEM-B:   YESsss
ITEM-C:   TA/Bs
ITEM-D:   s15
ITEM-E:   $15.00-
ITEM-F:   0015
```

The above examples illustrate the flexibility of the INITIALIZE statement. It is a convenient alternative to the use of the VALUE clause in the WORKING-STORAGE SECTION and the use of explicit MOVE statements in the PROCEDURE DIVISION for those key data items that should be initialized.

The following example shows the coding of the procedure 200-START-UP of the sample program if the INITIALIZE statement is used instead of the MOVE statement to initialize the flag WS-MORE-RECORDS.

```
200-START-UP.
    OPEN INPUT PHONE-SALES-FILE
         OUTPUT PHONE-SALES-REPORT.
    INITIALIZE WS-MORE-RECORDS
        REPLACING ALPHANUMERIC DATA BY "YES".
      PERFORM 300-WRITE-REPORT-HEADERS.
      PERFORM 310-READ-PHONE-SALE-RECORD.
```

The Second-Level Paragraph 210-PROCESS-PHONE-SALE-RECORD

The next procedure to be executed in the sample program is 210-PROCESS-PHONE-SALE-RECORD. Figure 4.23 shows the related portions of the structure chart, the pseudocode, and the program flowchart that led to its development.

The only statements in this procedure are PERFORM statements. There is no new format to be examined here. Realize, however, that the PERFORMs reference third-level procedures. The execution of the procedures 320-COMPUTE-PHONE-SALE-AMOUNT, 330-PREPARE-PHONE-SALE-LINE, and 310-READ-PHONE-SALE-RECORD is nested within the execution of the current procedure 210-Process-Phone-Sale-Record. Equivalently, we can say that the PERFORMs in this procedure are nested within the PERFORM that controls the execution of the current procedure.

The essential function of this procedure is made very clear by its name. The processing of a phone sale record is separated into two parts: In the first part, the phone sale amount is computed; and in the second part, the remaining data fields of the record PHONE-SALE-LINE are assigned their values, so that

Figure 4.23 The development of the paragraph 210-PROCESS-PHONE-SALE-RECORD

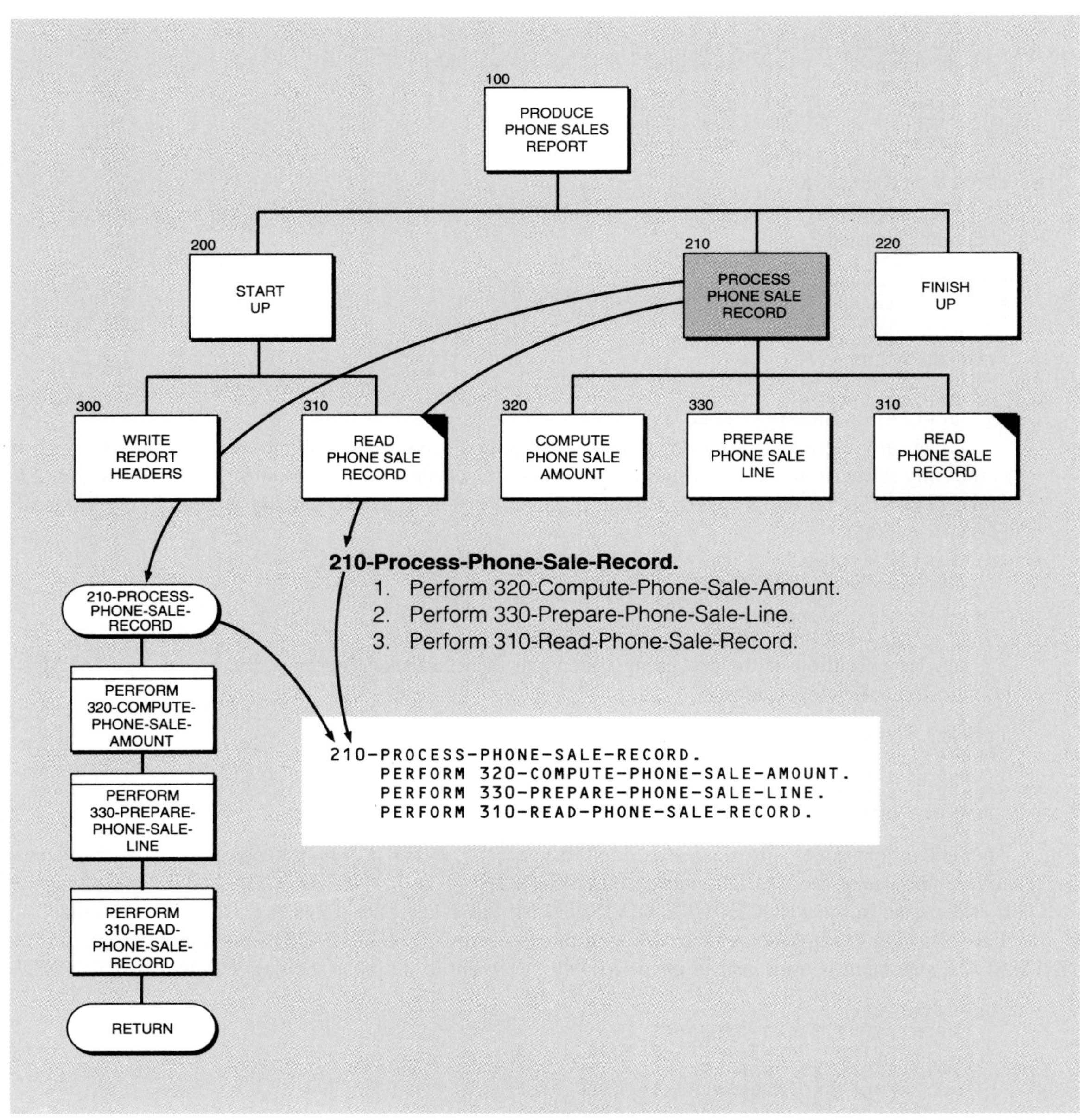

the output record can then be written to the output file. At this point, the processing of the input record (PHONE-SALE-RECORD) currently in input memory is complete. Therefore, the next phone sale record in the input file should be read so that it can be processed in turn.

The Second-Level Paragraph 220-FINISH-UP

The final procedure to be executed under the direct control of the main-control paragraph (100-PRODUCE-PHONE-SALES-REPORT) is 220-FINISH-UP. Figure 4.24 shows the related portions of the structure chart, the pseudocode, and the program flowchart that led to its development.

By the time control is sent to this procedure, the job of producing the report is complete. This paragraph takes care of "tidying up" system-related loose ends. In particular, the files that were made available to the program by the OPEN statements in the procedure 200-START-UP must now be closed. The COBOL statement that handles this function is the CLOSE statement. Its format is shown in Figure 4.25.

Figure 4.24 The development of the paragraph 220-FINISH-UP

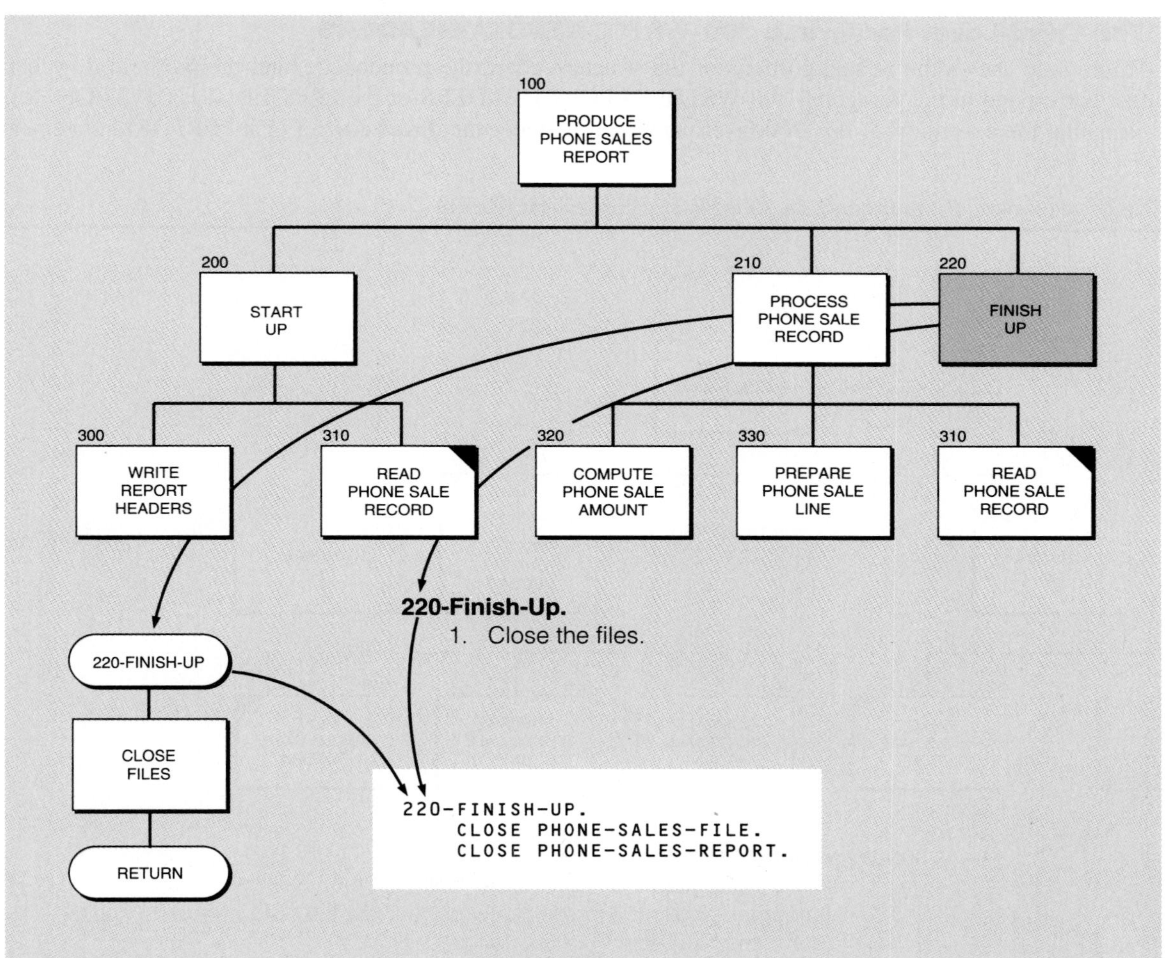

Figure 4.25 The CLOSE statement format

```
CLOSE file-name-1 [file-name-2] . . .
```

Rules Governing the Use of the CLOSE Statement

1. The CLOSE verb must be followed by the name of a file. The open mode for the file is not specified; that is, the words INPUT and OUTPUT are not entered in the statement. (Recall that the open mode **must** be specified in the OPEN statements.)
2. In order for the CLOSE statement to execute properly, the file must have been previously opened.
3. More than one file can be closed within one CLOSE statement. For instance,

```
CLOSE PHONE-SALES-FILE
      PHONE-SALES-REPORT
```

   is equivalent to the two statements in the paragraph 220-FINISH-UP.
4. A file that has been closed is no longer available to the program. It can be made available again only by the execution of another OPEN statement.

In the sample program, once the files have been closed within the procedure 220-FINISH-UP, control returns to the main-control paragraph. The next statement encountered is STOP RUN, and, following its execution, control returns to the operating system.

The procedure 220-FINISH-UP is the last of the second-level paragraphs. Now we will examine the third-level procedures.

The Third-Level Paragraph 300-WRITE-REPORT-HEADERS

Figure 4.26 shows the related portions of the structure chart, the pseudocode, and the program flowchart that correspond to the paragraph 300-WRITE-REPORT-HEADERS of the PROCEDURE DIVISION. It is clear that the execution of this 300-level paragraph is under the direct control of a PERFORM statement

Figure 4.26 The development of the procedure 300-WRITE-REPORT-HEADERS

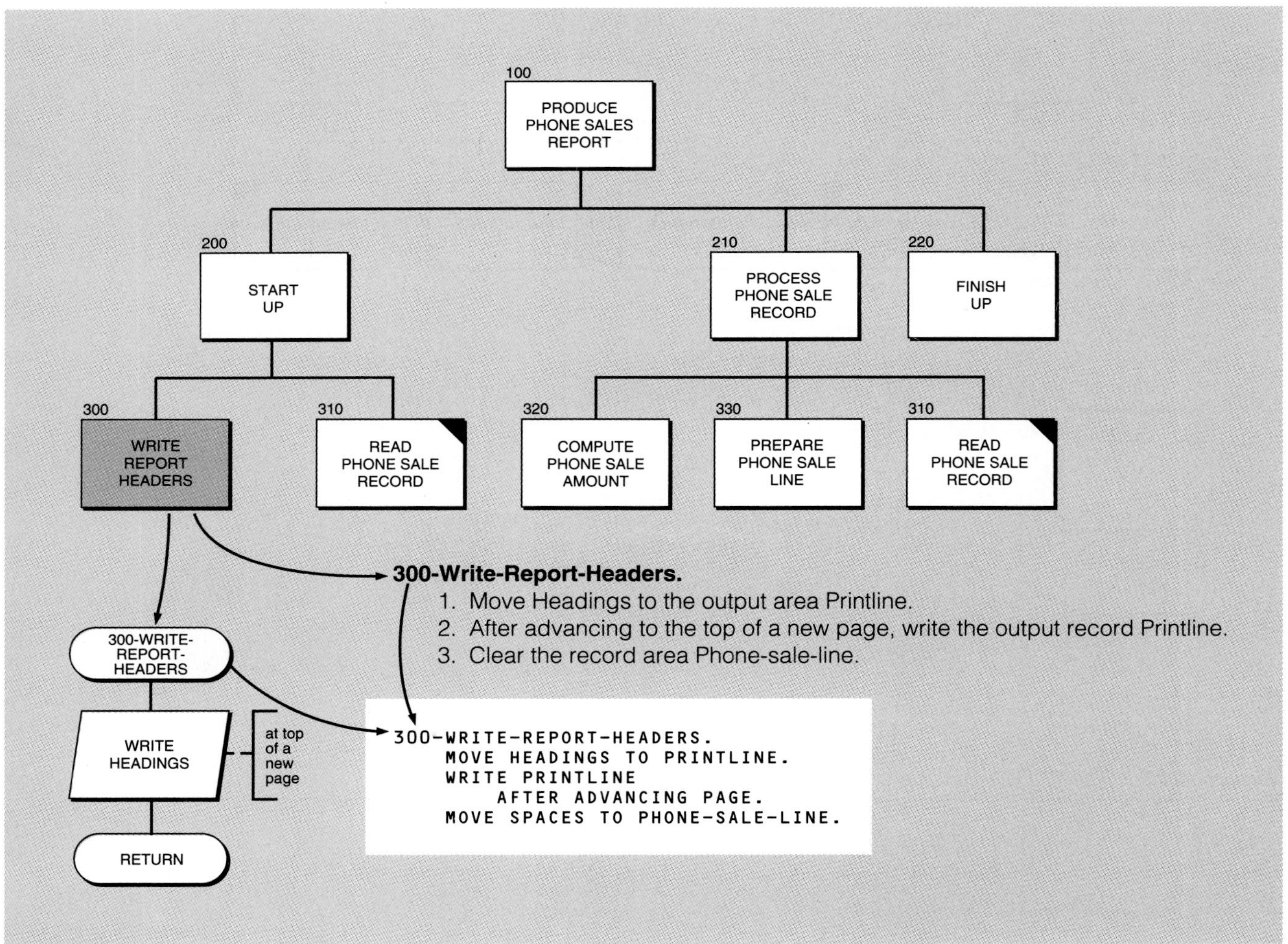

contained in paragraph 200-START-UP. Consequently, from within the primary paragraph 100-PRODUCE-PHONE-SALES-REPORT, the execution of the statement PERFORM 200-START-UP indirectly controls the execution of the paragraph 300-WRITE-REPORT-HEADERS.

This procedure contains two MOVE statements and one WRITE statement. The first statement, MOVE HEADINGS TO PRINTLINE, simply copies the contents of HEADINGS into PRINTLINE. Recall that the record HEADINGS was prepared in the WORKING-STORAGE SECTION because of the availability of the VALUE clause. However, in order to write it to the output file, it must be physically present in the output memory area so that it can be referenced by the WRITE statement. (We examine the WRITE statement below.)

The other MOVE is in the third statement: MOVE SPACES TO PHONE-SALE-LINE. The record PHONE-SALE-LINE is also defined in the WORKING-STORAGE SECTION. In general, there is no way of knowing which characters may be left in that storage area from its previous use. By moving spaces to it, the programmer is assured of beginning the preparation of the record with a "clean slate." The data fields of this record are assigned values later during execution of the record-processing loop.

The WRITE statement is the main function of the paragraph. When it is executed, it writes the contents of PRINTLINE, which contains a copy of the record HEADINGS, to the output file PHONE-SALES-REPORT.

We now examine the WRITE statement in some detail. More options are presented later.

The WRITE Statement

The format for the WRITE statement is shown in Figure 4.27.
In this format, the following rules apply:

1. The record name that follows the verb WRITE must be an output record that was defined in the output file description (FD) in the FILE SECTION of the DATA DIVISION. Note that the WRITE verb must be followed by the name of an output *record,* **not** the name of an output file.
2. The FROM option allows the programmer to write out the contents of identifier-1 as an output record. If this option were used in the sample program, the statement

   ```
   MOVE HEADINGS TO PRINTLINE
   ```

   would be eliminated, and the WRITE statement would be

   ```
   WRITE PRINTLINE FROM HEADINGS
       AFTER ADVANCING PAGE.
   ```

   In effect, the FROM option implicitly transfers identifier-1 to the output record area, and then the WRITE statement is executed. It is equivalent to a MOVE followed by a WRITE statement.

   Many programmers use the FROM option because it eliminates the explicit MOVE statements that transfer records from working storage to the output storage area.

   The revised paragraph of the sample program, shown below, uses the FROM phrase:

   ```
   300-WRITE-REPORT-HEADERS.
       WRITE PRINTLINE FROM HEADINGS
           AFTER ADVANCING PAGE.
       MOVE SPACES TO PHONE-SALE-LINE.
   ```

3. The ADVANCING clause in the WRITE statement is used in conjunction with print files to control line spacing during printing operations. This option is not used if the output file is a pure storage file.

Figure 4.27 WRITE statement format

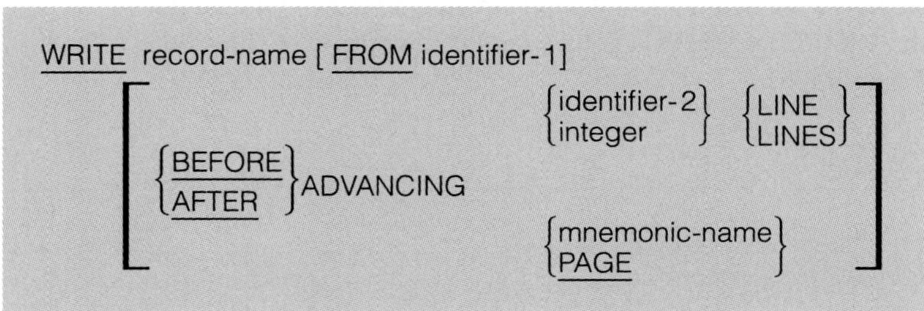

The AFTER ADVANCING option is used to advance the paper in the printer as specified before writing out the contents of the output record.

The BEFORE ADVANCING option causes the output record to be written to the file first, and then paper is advanced in the printer as specified.

In the sample program, the statement

```
WRITE PRINTLINE
    AFTER ADVANCING 2 LINES.
```

causes the printer carriage to first advance the paper two lines (skip one line), and then to write out the contents of the output record PRINTLINE.

If the ADVANCING clause is not used in conjunction with a print file, the default is AFTER ADVANCING 1 LINE.

4. In the ADVANCING clause, the particular entry that specifies the exact behavior of the printer can be any one of the following:

   a. Identifier-2 followed by the optional word LINE or LINES. In this case, identifier-2 must have a PICTURE that describes it as a nonnegative integer. The value of this data item must be in the range from 0 to 99, and it specifies the number of lines to be advanced on the printer paper.

   Example:

   ```
   WRITE PRINTLINE FROM PHONE-SALE-LINE
       AFTER ADVANCING WS-PROPER-SPACING.
   ```

   where the description of the data item WS-PROPER-SPACING might be

   ```
   05 WS-PROPER-SPACING   PIC 99.
   ```

   If the statement

   ```
   MOVE 2 TO WS-PROPER-SPACING.
   ```

   precedes the WRITE statement, then the contents of the record PHONE-SALE-LINE are printed after the paper is advanced **two** lines.

   On the other hand, if the statement

   ```
   MOVE 1 TO WS-PROPER-SPACING.
   ```

   precedes the WRITE statement, then the record PHONE-SALE-LINE is written on the **next** line.

   b. An integer followed by the optional word LINE or LINES. Its value must not be negative and must not exceed 99. It specifies the number of lines to be advanced on the printer paper. This is the option that is used in the sample program in the statement

   ```
   WRITE PRINTLINE
       AFTER ADVANCING 2 LINES.
   ```

   Obviously, the report produced in the sample program is double-spaced.

   c. The word PAGE. PAGE is a COBOL reserved word. Its use in the statement

   ```
   WRITE PRINTLINE FROM COMPANY-NAME
       AFTER ADVANCING PAGE.
   ```

   causes the printer to move the paper up so that the contents of the record COMPANY-NAME are printed on line 1 of the next page.

   d. A mnemonic name. This is a user-defined name set up to correspond to a print zone or channel on a printer page. A printer page is generally separated into 12 channels numbered 1 to 12 from top to bottom of a page. Correspondence between a channel and a mnemonic name is defined in the SPECIAL-NAMES paragraph. The SPECIAL-NAMES paragraph is an optional paragraph of the CONFIGURATION SECTION of the ENVIRONMENT DIVISION. It is coded on the line below the OBJECT-COMPUTER paragraph. Figure 4.28 shows the format of the SPECIAL-NAMES paragraph.

Figure 4.28 SPECIAL-NAMES paragraph format

<u>SPECIAL-NAMES.</u> implementor-name <u>IS</u> mnemonic-name . . .

In this format, the implementor names are supplied by the hardware manufacturer, and mnemonic names are supplied by the programmer. For instance, for an IBM-370, the implementor names C01, C02, . . . , C12 correspond to the 12 print channels. On a CDC-Cyber, "1" corresponds to the first print channel. On a VAX-8650, C01 corresponds to the first print channel. So, for different computers, the following two paragraphs are equivalent:

```
SPECIAL-NAMES.  C01 IS TO-NEW-PAGE.
SPECIAL-NAMES.  "1" IS TO-NEW-PAGE.
```

In each case, the mnemonic name TO-NEW-PAGE used in the statement

```
WRITE PRINTLINE FROM COMPANY-NAME
    AFTER ADVANCING TO-NEW-PAGE
```

causes the contents of COMPANY-NAME to be printed in channel 1 of the next printer page.

It should be clear that this result is the same as that obtained from using the much simpler PAGE option explained in item c above. (The SPECIAL-NAMES paragraph provides many other options. We do not mention them here because they do not pertain to the present discussion.)

Note: Some systems are set up to allow the programmer control over the 12 print channels. On other systems, channel control is more limited. You must obtain this specific information from your instructor or from the computer center.

Notes on the WRITE Statement

1. The verb WRITE is followed by the name of an output **record,** not the name of an output file. The record must belong to a file described in an FD paragraph of the FILE SECTION.
2. The WRITE statement writes a record to an output file.
3. The output file that contains the output record referenced in the WRITE statement must have been opened by an OPEN statement before the execution of the WRITE statement. For our current purposes, the open mode must be OUTPUT. In later applications, the mode can also be I-O or EXTEND.
4. The FROM option allows the writing of a record defined either in the WORKING-STORAGE SECTION or in another FD paragraph, but it has to be accessed through the name of an output record.
5. If the ADVANCING clause is not used when writing records on a print file, single spacing will necessarily occur between successive lines on the printout.
6. On some systems, if the ADVANCING option is used with one record of a print file, it must then be used in every WRITE statement that references a record of that file.
7. If the ADVANCING option is used, then the first byte of the output record is often reserved for the carriage-control character. Though this character does not print, the programmer must leave the first byte available for carriage control. Otherwise, the character assigned to the first byte is lost as it is replaced internally by the carriage-control character.

Some programmers explicitly reserve the first character position of any output record for carriage control. This is illustrated below. Note that the size of the record has been increased to 133 in order to still allow a total of 132 print positions on the printer paper.

```
FD   PHONE-SALES-REPORT
     RECORD CONTAINS 133 CHARACTERS.

01   PRINTLINE             PIC X(133).

WORKING-STORAGE SECTION.

01   WS-MORE-RECORDS       PIC XXX.

01   HEADINGS.
     05 CARRIAGE-CONTROL    PIC X.
     05 PIC X(15)     VALUE SPACES.
     05 PIC X(15)     VALUE "CUSTOMER NUMBER".
     05 PIC X(8)      VALUE SPACES.
     05 PIC X(14)     VALUE "CATALOG NUMBER".
     05 PIC X(8)      VALUE SPACES.
     05 PIC X(9)      VALUE "UNIT COST".
     05 PIC X(8)      VALUE SPACES.
     05 PIC X(15)     VALUE "NUMBER OF UNITS".
     05 PIC X(8)      VALUE SPACES.
     05 PIC X(17)     VALUE "PHONE SALE AMOUNT".
     05 PIC X(15)     VALUE SPACES.
```

```
01  PHONE-SALE-LINE.
    05 CARRIAGE-CONTROL PIC X.
    05 FILLER           PIC X(21).
    05 O-CUSTOMER-NO    PIC X(4).
    05 FILLER           PIC X(18).
    05 O-CATALOG-NO     PIC X(4).
    05 FILLER           PIC X(14).
    05 O-UNIT-COST      PIC $ZZ9.99.
    05 FILLER           PIC X(15).
    05 O-NO-OF-UNITS    PIC ZZZ9.
    05 FILLER           PIC X(17).
    05 O-SALE-AMOUNT    PIC $Z(5)9.99.
    05 FILLER           PIC X(18).
```

The Third-Level Paragraph 310-READ-PHONE-SALE-RECORD

Figure 4.29 shows the related portions of the structure chart, the pseudocode, and the program flowchart that correspond to the PROCEDURE DIVISION paragraph 300-READ-PHONE-SALE-RECORD.

The essential function of this paragraph is to access the next available record of the input file PHONE-SALES-FILE, so that it can be processed as needed by upcoming procedures. The key statement in this paragraph is obviously the READ statement.

Figure 4.29 The development of the paragraph 310-READ-PHONE-SALE-RECORD

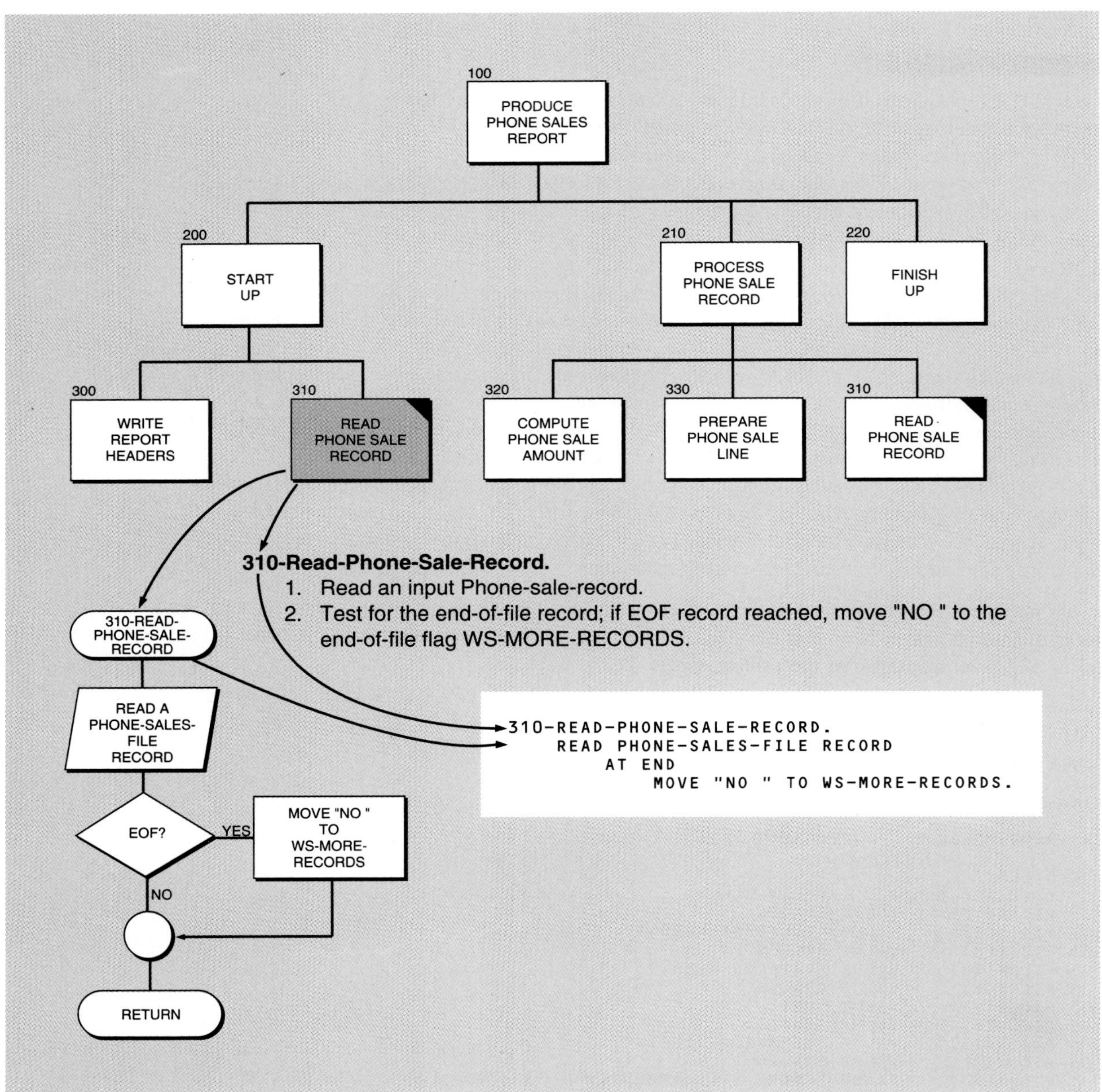

■ **Figure 4.30** The READ statement accesses data from an input record and stores it in input memory

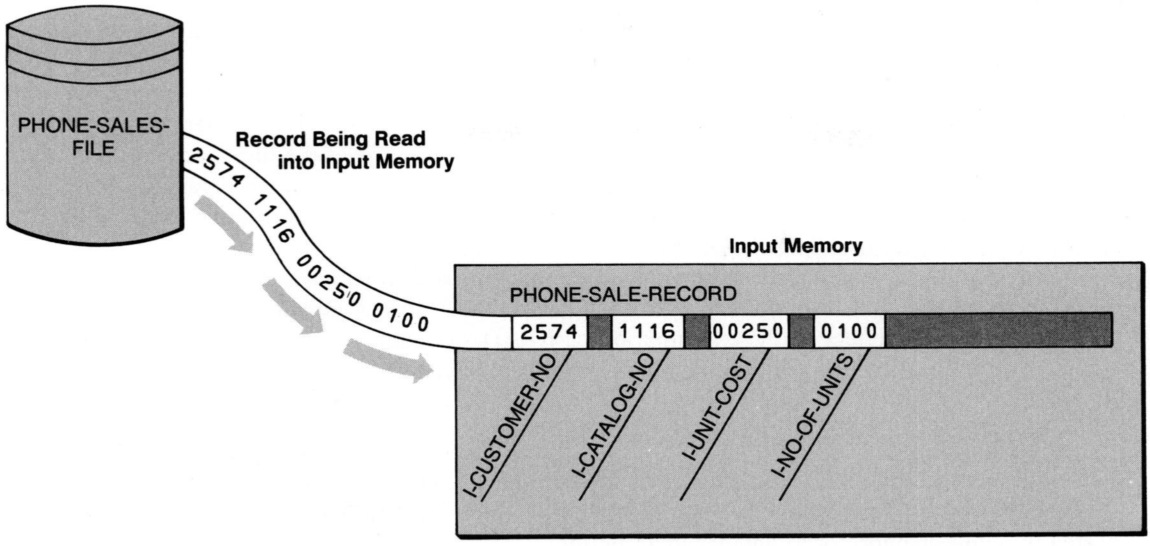

■ **Figure 4.31** Sequential access READ statement format

```
READ file-name [ NEXT ] RECORD [ INTO identifier]
    [AT END imperative-statement-1]
    [NOT AT END imperative-statement-2]
    [END-READ]
```

When the READ statement is first executed, the contents of the first record of the input file are copied into the input storage area. The data values that the record contains can then be referenced according to the format specified for that record in the FILE SECTION of the DATA DIVISION. Note that the entire input record is stored at one time, not just selected fields. See Figure 4.30.

The contents of this record are now available for further processing. The statements in the PROCEDURE DIVISION can access the data currently stored in input memory by using the data names that have been associated with the input record area fields in the FILE SECTION description of the record.

The record currently in input memory remains there until the execution of the next READ statement. At that time, the contents of the first record are lost, since they are replaced by the contents of the second record. In other words, the input records are accessed and processed **one at a time.**

In the case of sequential files, those files in which the records are accessed sequentially, the physical end of the file is an end-of-file (EOF) record or marker. The special characters it contains vary with the computer being used. When this record is read, the computer recognizes it as the end-of-file indicator and consequently executes the statements in the AT END clause of the READ statement.

In the sample program, when a record of the input file PHONE-SALES-FILE is read into input memory, the end-of-file test is performed. If the record just read is the EOF record, the computer is immediately directed to change the value of the flag WS-MORE-RECORDS to "NO "; otherwise, the flag retains its initial value of "YES".

The format of the READ statement used for sequential access files is shown in Figure 4.31.

Rules Governing the Use of the READ Statement

1. The READ verb must be followed by the name of the input **file,** not the name of the input record.

   Note: The READ verb references a **file** name, whereas the WRITE verb references a **record** name.
2. The file name must have been coded in a SELECT statement and assigned to an input device. (The input device specification is system-dependent.)

3. The file name must have been specified in an FD entry in the FILE SECTION of the DATA DIVISION.
4. The file named in the READ statement must have been opened in an OPEN statement before the READ statement can be executed. The OPEN mode must be specified as INPUT (or I-O, as we will see later).
5. The word RECORD is optional. Its use is encouraged for the following reason: The statement READ PHONE-SALES-FILE might give the impression to the novice programmer that the entire file PHONE-SALES-FILE is being read. Actually, **only one record** of the file is copied into input memory and is made available for processing when a READ statement is executed. By coding READ PHONE-SALES-FILE RECORD, it is clearer that the computer is directed to read **one record** of the input file PHONE-SALES-FILE.
6. The word NEXT is optional for sequential access files. If used, it simply emphasizes, in the coded statement, that the record to be read is the next one in the sequence in which they reside on the file. Its use has no effect on the execution of the READ statement.

   The READ statement in the sample program can be coded as

```
READ PHONE-SALES-FILE NEXT RECORD
    AT END ...
```

7. The identifier in the INTO option specifies a record described in the DATA DIVISION. It is generally a storage area defined in the WORKING-STORAGE SECTION, but it can be a storage area in output memory or in another input buffer.

   If this option is used, the contents of the input record are stored in the input storage area and then immediately transferred to (copied into) the identifier named in the INTO phrase. This phrase is equivalent to a READ followed by a MOVE. (See example 1 below.)
8. The AT END option must be used for sequential access files. Since the records of the file are being read sequentially, at some point the end of the file is reached. The AT END clause directs the computer to check each record as it is being read to determine if it is the end-of-file marker. The statements in the AT END clause are executed only when the AT END condition occurs.
9. The NOT AT END option allows the programmer to specify statements to be executed if the record just read is not the end-of-file marker. An example is given below. This option is a new feature of the '85 ANSI COBOL standards.
10. The END-READ option, also a new feature, is the explicit scope terminator for the READ statement. A READ statement can be terminated by either a period or an END-READ.

Example 1:

The statement

```
READ PHONE-SALES-FILE RECORD INTO WS-PHONE-SALE-RECORD
    AT END
        MOVE "NO " TO WS-MORE-RECORDS.
```

is equivalent to the two statements:

```
READ PHONE-SALES-FILE RECORD
    AT END
        MOVE "NO " TO WS-MORE-RECORDS.
MOVE PHONE-SALE-RECORD TO WS-PHONE-SALE-RECORD.
```

The INTO phrase in the first READ statement replaces the explicit MOVE statement above.

Example 2:

Consider the logic represented by the flowchart segment in Figure 4.32.

The coding corresponding to part a is the following:

```
READ EMPLOYEE-FILE RECORD
    AT END
        MOVE "NO " TO WS-MORE-RECORDS.
IF WS-MORE-RECORDS = "NO "
    NEXT SENTENCE
ELSE
    ADD 1 TO WS-RECORDS-READ-CTR.
```

■ **Figure 4.32** Logic of alternative paths with and without the NOT AT END option

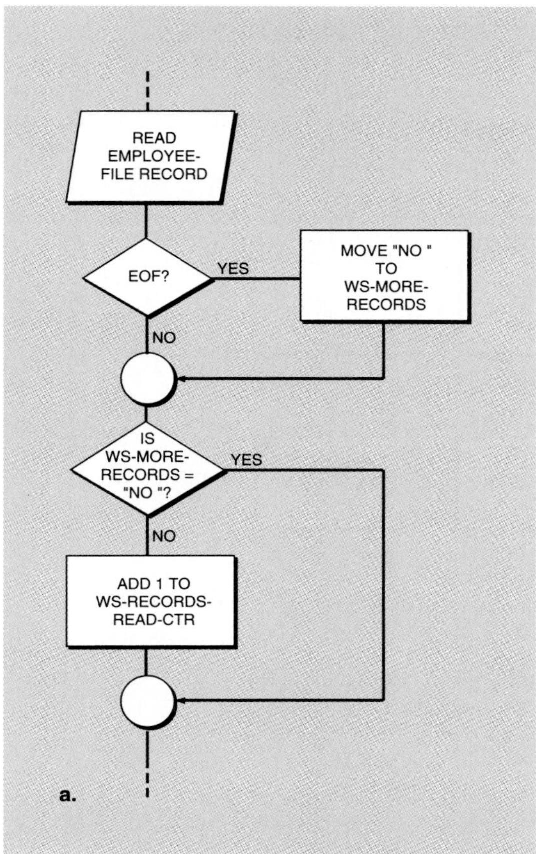

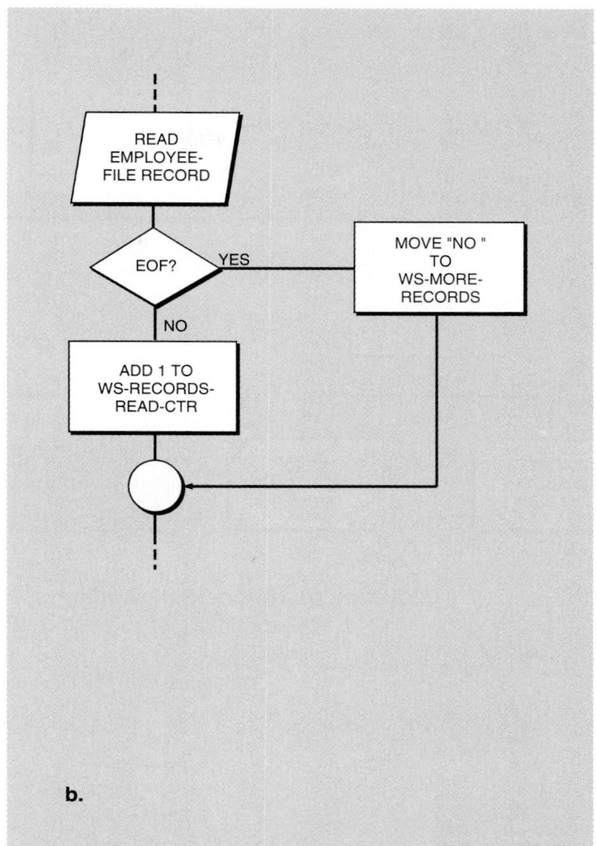

The coding corresponding to part b is the following:

```
READ EMPLOYEE-FILE RECORD
    AT END
        MOVE "NO " TO WS-MORE-RECORDS
    NOT AT END
        ADD 1 TO WS-RECORDS-READ-CTR
END-READ.
```

Note that the coding for part a requires two separate sentences: there are two periods. In part b, the availability of the alternative structure of the AT END/NOT AT END clauses allows all the coding to be included in **one** sentence, without any loss of clarity. The optional END-READ scope terminator terminates the READ statement. The END-READ entry could be eliminated by placing a period after the ADD statement with the same end result. That is, the period would also terminate the READ statement.

The Third-Level Paragraph 320-COMPUTE-PHONE-SALE-AMOUNT

Figure 4.33 shows the related portions of the structure chart, the pseudocode, and the program flowchart that correspond to the paragraph 320-COMPUTE-PHONE-SALE-AMOUNT.

To select the correct formula to compute the net amount of the phone sale, a test must be performed on the number of units purchased. The COBOL statement that lends itself readily to this situation is the IF-ELSE statement.

It is clear from the flowchart module in Figure 4.33 that the logic of the IF-ELSE statement parallels that of the selection structure first presented at the end of Chapter 2. Specifically, if a tested condition is true, then control passes to one set of instructions; but if the tested condition is false, then control passes to another set of instructions.

The format of the IF-ELSE statement is shown in Figure 4.34.

■ **Figure 4.33** The development of the paragraph 320-COMPUTE-PHONE-SALE-AMOUNT

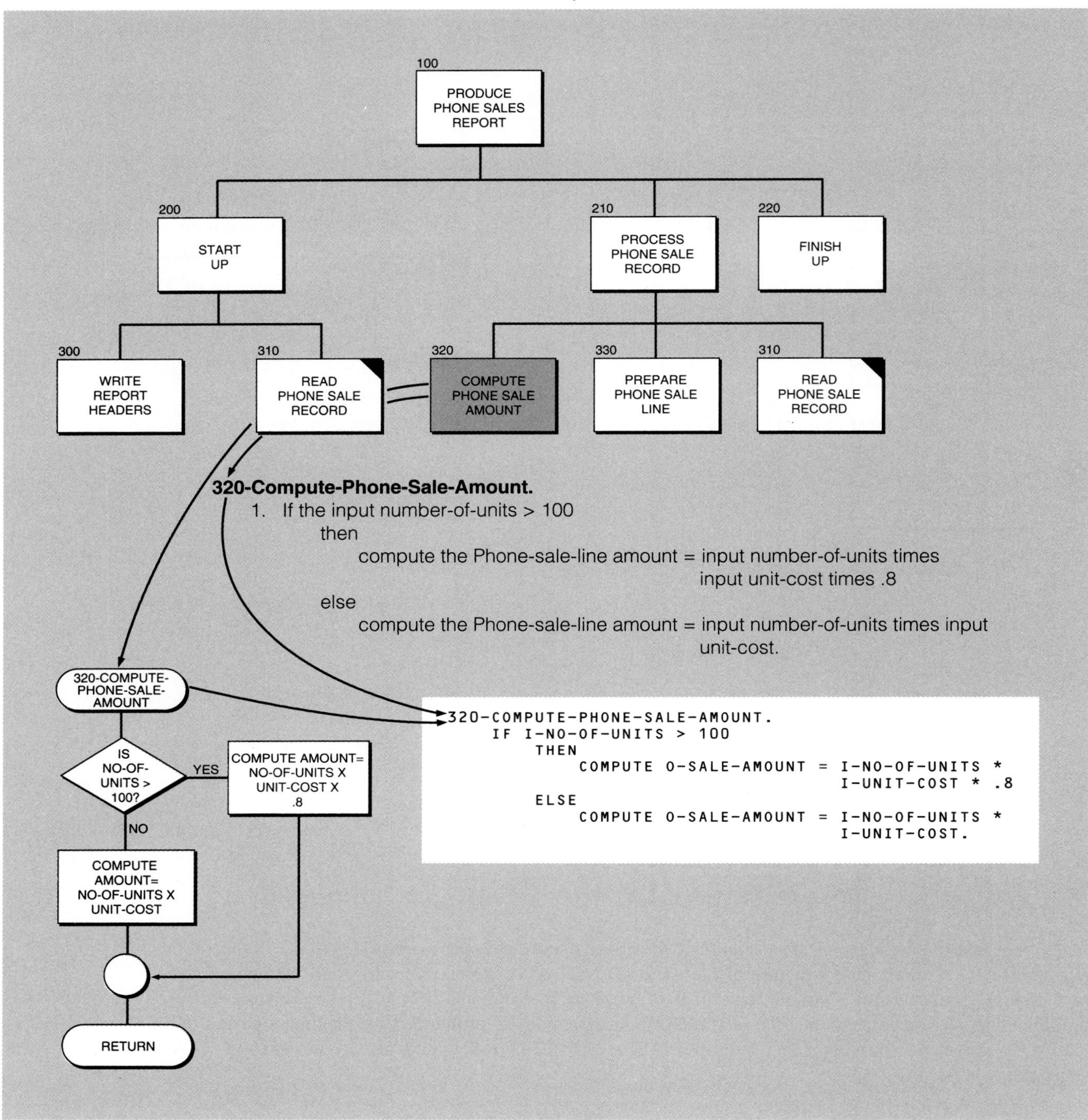

■ **Figure 4.34** IF-ELSE statement format

$$\underline{\text{IF}}\ \text{condition THEN} \left\{\begin{array}{l}\text{statement-1} \ldots \\ \underline{\text{NEXT SENTENCE}}\end{array}\right\}$$

$$\left[\left\{\begin{array}{l}\underline{\text{ELSE}}\{\text{statement-2}\} \ldots [\ \underline{\text{END-IF}}] \\ \underline{\text{ELSE NEXT SENTENCE}} \\ \underline{\text{END-IF}}\end{array}\right\}\right]$$

Since this statement will be studied in detail in a later chapter, we restrict our comments to the following selection of options:

```
IF condition
    THEN
        statement-1
    ELSE
        statement-2.
```

In Figure 4.33, the corresponding statement is

```
IF I-NO-OF-UNITS > 100
    THEN
        COMPUTE O-SALE-AMOUNT = I-NO-OF-UNITS *
                                I-UNIT-COST * .8

    ELSE
        COMPUTE O-SALE-AMOUNT = I-NO-OF-UNITS *
                                I-UNIT-COST.
```

The condition being tested is

```
I-NO-OF-UNITS > 100,
```

statement-1 is

```
COMPUTE O-SALE-AMOUNT = I-NO-OF-UNITS * I-UNIT-COST * .8,
```

and statement-2 is

```
COMPUTE O-SALE-AMOUNT = I-NO-OF-UNITS * I-UNIT-COST.
```

If the number of units is greater than 100, the first COMPUTE statement is executed; otherwise, the second COMPUTE statement is executed. In either case, the computed value is stored directly into the field O-SALE-AMOUNT of the output record PHONE-SALE-LINE.

It is important to understand how the IF-ELSE statement (in the sample program) works:

1. The IF-ELSE statement ends with a period. There must not be a period after statement-1 if the ELSE clause is used.
2. If the condition is satisfied, then the instructions making up statement-1 are executed, the ELSE clause is skipped, and control is sent to the first statement following the period.
3. If the condition is not satisfied, the instructions contained in the ELSE clause are executed, and then control is sent to the first statement following the period.

In general, there could be any number of processes along either or both branches of the selection structure. Similarly, the IF clause can contain any number of statements to be executed if the condition is satisfied, and the ELSE clause can contain any number of statements to be executed if the condition is **not** satisfied.

In the format of the IF-ELSE statement, the word THEN is a new option in COBOL '85. Consequently, we can code:

```
IF I-NO-OF-UNITS > 100
     COMPUTE O-SALE-AMOUNT = I-NO-OF-UNITS * I-UNIT-COST * .8
ELSE
     COMPUTE O-SALE-AMOUNT = I-NO-OF-UNITS * I-UNIT-COST.
```

The COMPUTE Statement

In the sample program, the instruction to be executed in each clause of the IF-ELSE statement is the COMPUTE arithmetic statement. Its format as used in this program is shown in Figure 4.35.

The identifier that follows the COMPUTE verb is the name of the field in which the computed value will be stored. The arithmetic expression contains the various operations that must be performed to produce the required computed value.

For instance, in the statement

```
COMPUTE O-SALE-AMOUNT = I-NO-OF-UNITS * I-UNIT-COST * .8,
```

■ **Figure 4.35** The COMPUTE statement format

<u>COMPUTE</u> identifier = arithmetic-expression

the name of the field in which the computed value is stored is O-SALE-AMOUNT, and the arithmetic expression that must be evaluated is I-NO-OF-UNITS * I-UNIT-COST * .8. The value stored in I-NO-OF-UNITS (a field of the input record PHONE-SALE-RECORD), the value stored in I-UNIT-COST (another field of the input record), and the numeric constant .8 are all multiplied together, and the resulting product is stored in the output record field named O-SALE-AMOUNT. (It is the programmer's responsibility to make sure that the receiving field is large enough to store the computed value.)

The COMPUTE statement is studied in greater detail in the next chapter. These comments are sufficient to explain the use of the COMPUTE statement in the sample program.

At this point in the sample program, control returns to the procedure 210-PROCESS-PHONE-SALE-RECORD, where the next PERFORM statement is executed. As a result, control is sent to the procedure 330-PREPARE-PHONE-SALE-LINE.

The Third-Level Paragraph 330-PREPARE-PHONE-SALE-LINE

Figure 4.36 shows the related portions of the structure chart, the pseudocode, and the program flowchart that correspond to the paragraph 330-PREPARE-PHONE-SALE-LINE.

Figure 4.36 The development of the paragraph 330-PREPARE-PHONE-SALE-LINE

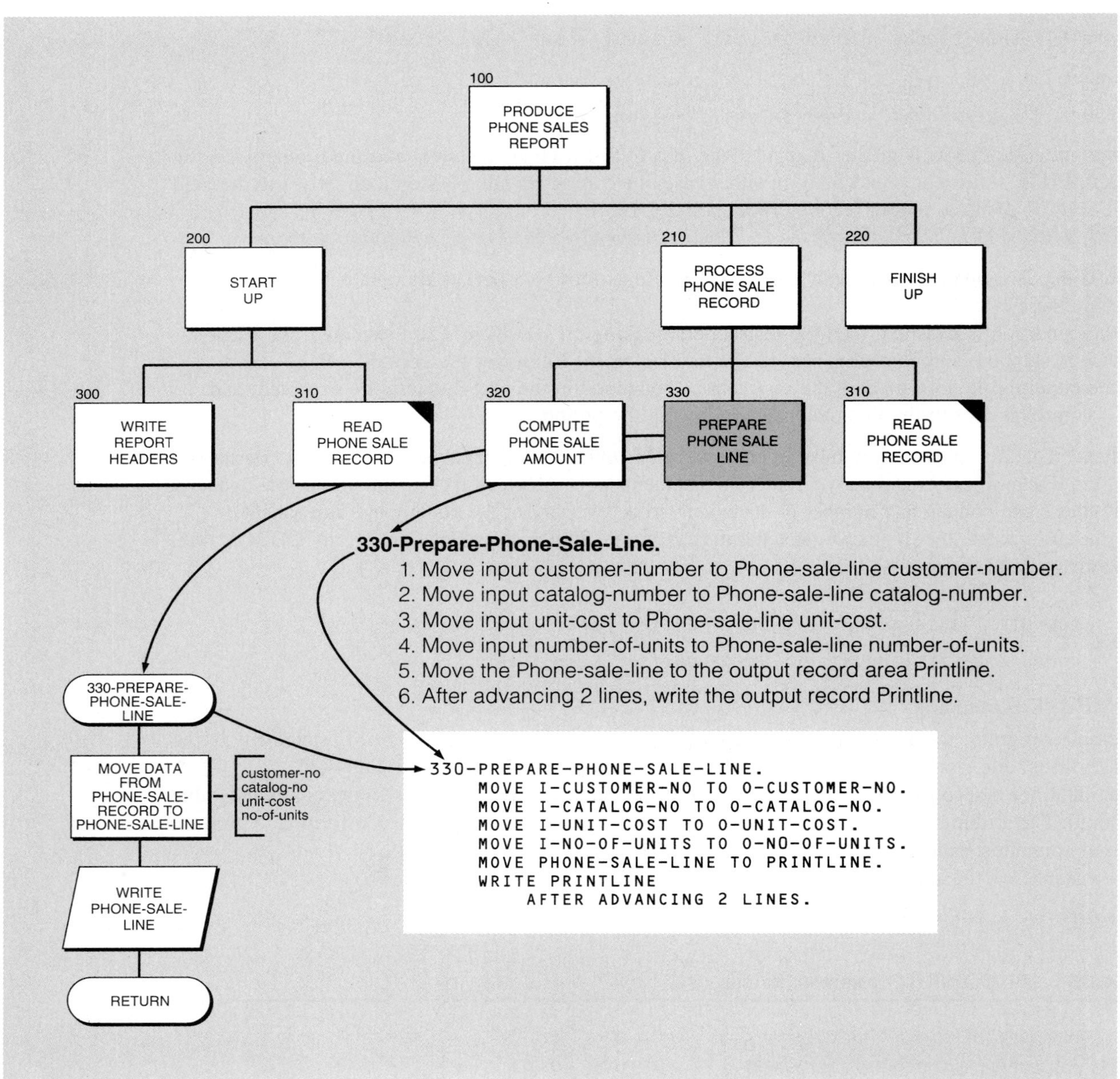


```
330-PREPARE-PHONE-SALE-LINE.
    MOVE I-CUSTOMER-NO TO O-CUSTOMER-NO.
    MOVE I-CATALOG-NO TO O-CATALOG-NO.
    MOVE I-UNIT-COST TO O-UNIT-COST.
    MOVE I-NO-OF-UNITS TO O-NO-OF-UNITS.
    MOVE PHONE-SALE-LINE TO PRINTLINE.
    WRITE PRINTLINE
        AFTER ADVANCING 2 LINES.
```

The essential function of this procedure is to complete the preparation of the output record PHONE-SALE-LINE and then to write it to the output file PHONE-SALES-REPORT. The field O-SALE-AMOUNT has already received its value from the COMPUTE statement in the preceding paragraph. The remaining fields, O-CUSTOMER-NO, O-CATALOG-NO, O-UNIT-COST, and O-NO-OF-UNITS, are now assigned copies of the values in the respective input record fields I-CUSTOMER-NO, I-CATALOG-NO, I-UNIT-COST, and I-NO-OF-UNITS. As noted earlier, the MOVE statement is used to effect these data transfers. The result of the MOVE statements is shown in Figure 4.37.

At this point, the output record is ready to be written to the output file. But since it resides in working storage, it must first be moved to the output memory area PRINTLINE (see Figure 4.37), and then the WRITE statement copies it to the output file. Since the WRITE statement is the last statement in this paragraph, control again returns to the sending paragraph 210-PROCESS-PHONE-SALE-RECORD. This completes the coding of the 300-level paragraphs.

As shown in the program flowchart of Figure 4.1, when control leaves module 330, it returns to module 210, only to be sent again to module 310, where the next record of the input file is read into input memory, replacing the previous one. As control returns from module 310, first to the end of module 210 and then back to the main-control module 100-PRODUCE-PHONE-SALES-REPORT, the flag WS-MORE-RECORDS is tested to determine if the last-executed READ statement accessed a valid record or detected the EOF record: if a valid record was accessed, control is returned to the module 210-PROCESS-PHONE-SALE-RECORD to run through all the processing steps again; if the EOF record was accessed, control exits from the PERFORM-UNTIL loop, where it is sent to module 220 to close the files, and upon returning from module 220, it stops the execution of the program.

The coding of the program is now complete.

Figure 4.37 Results of MOVE statements to transfer data between storage areas

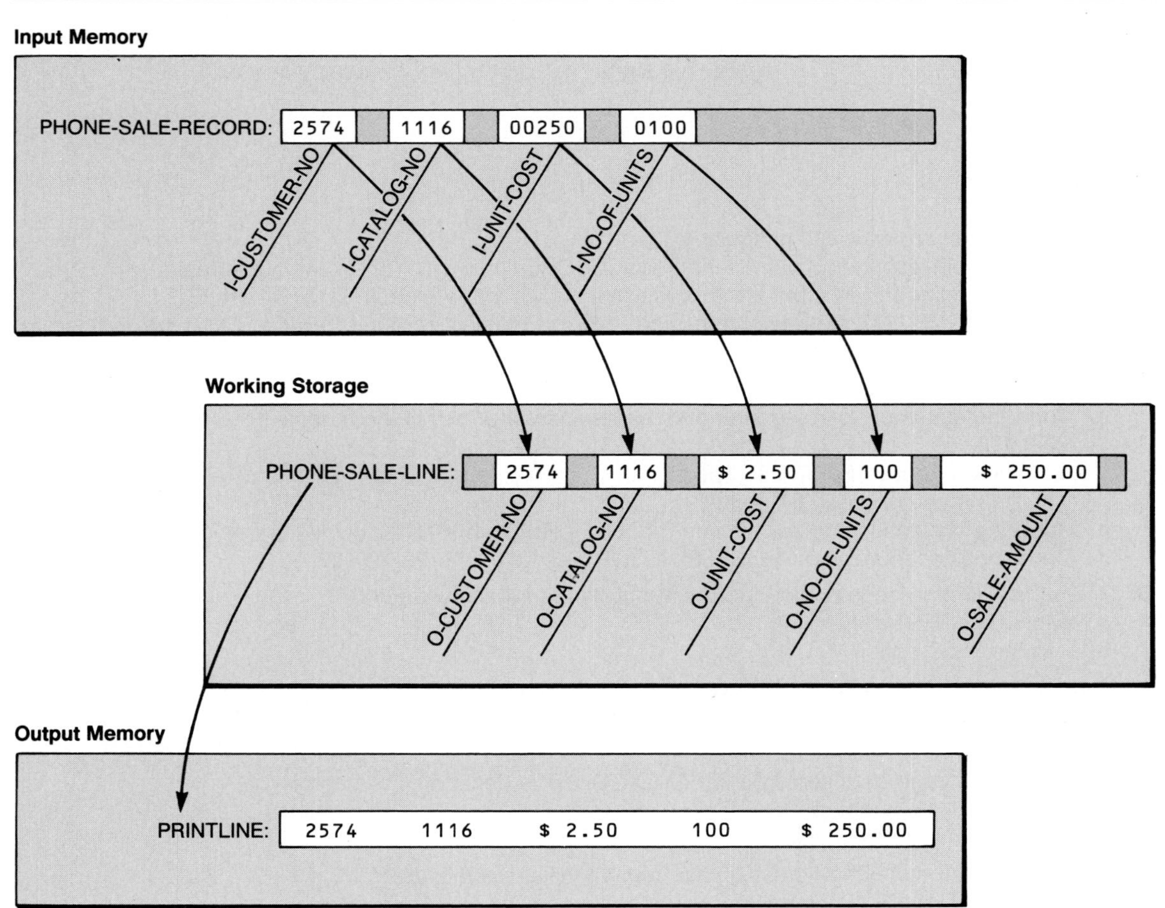

Conclusion

Recall from the problem-solving procedure that the remaining steps are the following:

1. Use an editor to enter the COBOL source program into a file.
2. Use the compiler to help you detect syntax errors in the program.
3. Once the program is free of syntax errors,
   a. Compile it.
   b. Link it, if your operating system uses a linker.
   c. Run it.
4. Check the output to make sure all the program specifications have been satisfied; select random values, and test their accuracy.
5. Complete the program documentation, if necessary.

Important Terms in Chapter 4

AFTER ADVANCING
AT END
carriage control
CLOSE
compiler directing statement
COMPUTE
conditional statement
data classification
delimited-scope statement
END-PERFORM
EOF record
high-order truncation
IF-ELSE
imperative statement
in-line PERFORM
invalid data transfer
JUSTIFIED RIGHT
literal continuation
low-order truncation
lower-level paragraph
main-control paragraph
mnemonic name
MOVE
NOT AT END
OPEN INPUT
OPEN OUTPUT
PAGE
paragraph name
PERFORM
PERFORM-UNTIL
PERFORM WITH TEST
print channel
PROCEDURE DIVISION
procedure name
READ
READ-INTO
receiving field
scope terminator
sending field
sentence
SPECIAL-NAMES paragraph
source field
source value
statement
STOP
valid data transfer
WRITE
WRITE-FROM

Exercises

1. Study the flowchart segment in Figure 4.38.
   a. Code the corresponding entries in a PROCEDURE DIVISION. (Show two paragraphs.)
   b. Code an in-line PERFORM for the procedure shown in the module 200-START-UP.
   c. Code an INITIALIZE statement to assign "YES" to the flag WS-MORE-RECORDS if it is defined as an alphanumeric item.
2. Study the flowchart segment in Figure 4.39.
   a. Code the statement corresponding to the iteration structure in the module 100-PRODUCE-REPORT:
      i. without the use of the TEST option.
      ii. with the use of the TEST option.
   b. Code the corresponding entries in a PROCEDURE DIVISION. (Show two paragraphs.)
   c. Code the procedure 210-PROCESS-RECORD as an in-line PERFORM.
3. Given the flowchart segment in Figure 4.40, code the iteration structure
   a. without the TEST option.
   b. with the TEST option.
4. Code a statement to make FILE-A available to a program
   a. as an input file.
   b. as an output file.
5. The working-storage data item WS-RECORD-COUNT is defined by the entry

```
05  WS-RECORD-COUNT     PIC 9(4).
```

   a. Use a MOVE statement to assign the item an initial value of zero.
   b. Use an INITIALIZE statement to assign the item an initial value of zero.

■ **Figure 4.38**

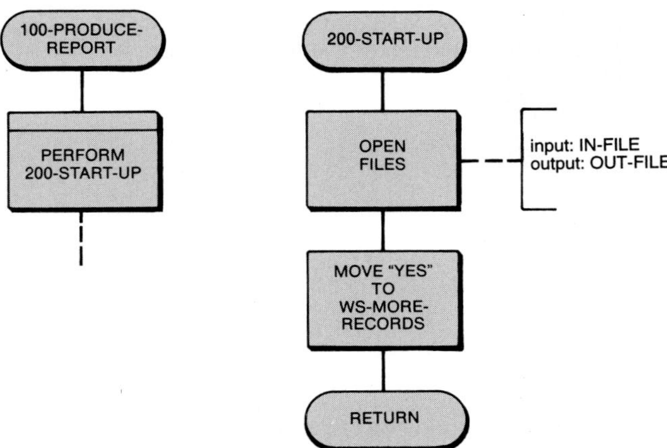

■ **Figure 4.39**

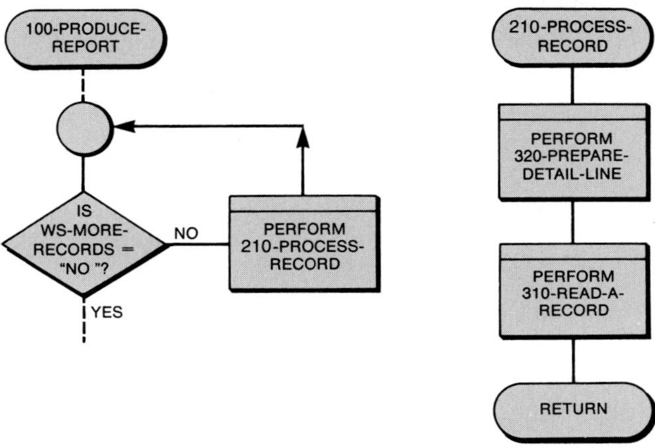

■ **Figure 4.40**

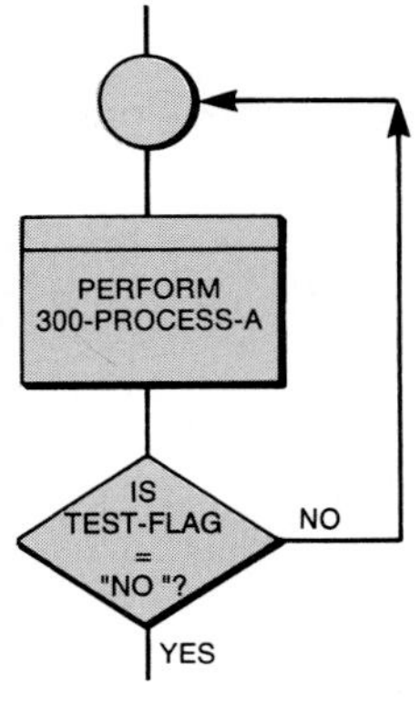

6. Given the following item description, answer the questions below.

```
01  GROUP-ITEM.
    05 ITEM-1               PIC XXX.
    05 ITEM-2               PIC A(4).
    05 SUB-GROUP.
       10 ITEM-3            PIC 999.
       10 ITEM-4            PIC 9V99.
       10 ITEM-5            PIC $ZZ9.99.
    05 ITEM-6               PIC X(10)  JUSTIFIED RIGHT.
    05 ITEM-7               PIC XX/XX/XX.
```

a. Describe the contents of each field following the statement

```
INITIALIZE GROUP-ITEM.
```

b. Identify and describe the contents of the fields affected by each of the following statements:

i.
```
INITIALIZE GROUP-ITEM
        REPLACING ALPHANUMERIC DATA BY "MARY".
```
ii.
```
INITIALIZE SUB-GROUP
        REPLACING NUMERIC DATA BY 18.5.
```
iii.
```
INITIALIZE SUB-GROUP
        REPLACING NUMERIC-EDITED BY 18.5.
```
iv.
```
INITIALIZE GROUP-ITEM
        REPLACING ALPHANUMERIC-EDITED DATA BY "101587".
```

7. Given an input file IN-FILE, with input record IN-RECORD,
- **a.** Code two statements to read a record of the input file and then to make a copy of it in the field WS-RECORD.
- **b.** Code a single statement to read a record of the input file and then to make a copy of it in the field WS-RECORD.

8. Given an output file PRINT-FILE with output record PRINTLINE and a working-storage record WS-RECORD,
- **a.** Code two statements to write the record WS-RECORD to the output file.
- **b.** Code a single statement to write the record WS-RECORD to the output file.

9. Code the PROCEDURE DIVISION paragraph that corresponds to the pseudocode paragraph shown below. Assume the input file is EMPLOYEE-FILE, and the output file is WORK-LOAD-REPORT.

200-Start-Up.
1. Open the files.
2. Set the end-of-file flag WS-MORE-RECORDS to "YES".
3. Set the accumulator WS-EMPLOYEE-CTR to zero.
4. Clear the record area EMPLOYEE-LINE.
5. Perform 300-Write-Report-Headers.
6. Perform 310-Read-Employee-Record.
7. If the flag WS-MORE-RECORDS is equal to "NO ",
   perform 320-Write-Error-Line.

10. Code the PROCEDURE DIVISION paragraph that corresponds to the pseudocode paragraph shown below. Assume the input file is CUSTOMER-FILE.

310-Read-Customer-Record.
1. Read an input Customer-record.
2. Test for end-of-file record;
   if EOF record reached, move "NO " to the end-of-file flag WS-MORE-RECORDS;
   if EOF record not reached, move input Customer-Record to storage area WS-CUSTOMER-RECORD.

11. Code the PROCEDURE DIVISION paragraphs that correspond to the modules shown in Figure 4.41. Assume the input file is EMPLOYEE-FILE, and the output file is WORK-LOAD-REPORT.

12. Write the complete sequence of statements for the flowchart segments in Figure 4.42.

13. In each case, show the value stored in the receiving field.

```
MOVE 1254 TO FIELD-Y.

FIELD-Y PICTURE
```
- **a.** 9(4)
- **b.** 9(6)
- **c.** 99
- **d.** 9(4)V99
- **e.** 99V99
- **f.** X(6)

```
MOVE -123 TO FIELD-X.

FIELD-X PICTURE
```
- **a.** 9(4)
- **b.** S9(6)
- **c.** S99
- **d.** S999V99
- **e.** 99V99
- **f.** X(6)

■ **Figure 4.41**

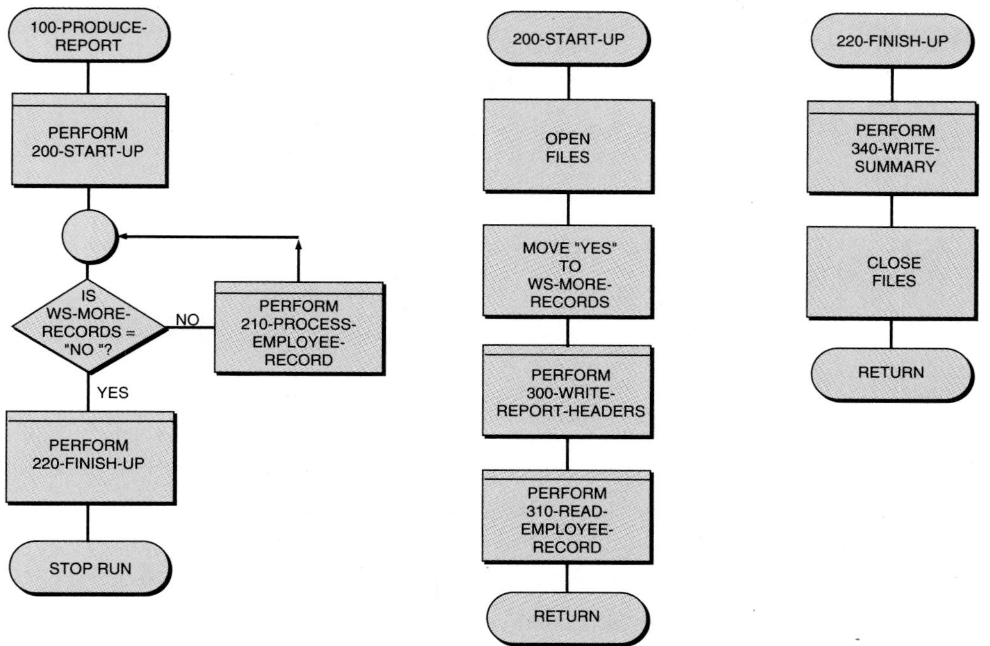

■ **Figure 4.42**

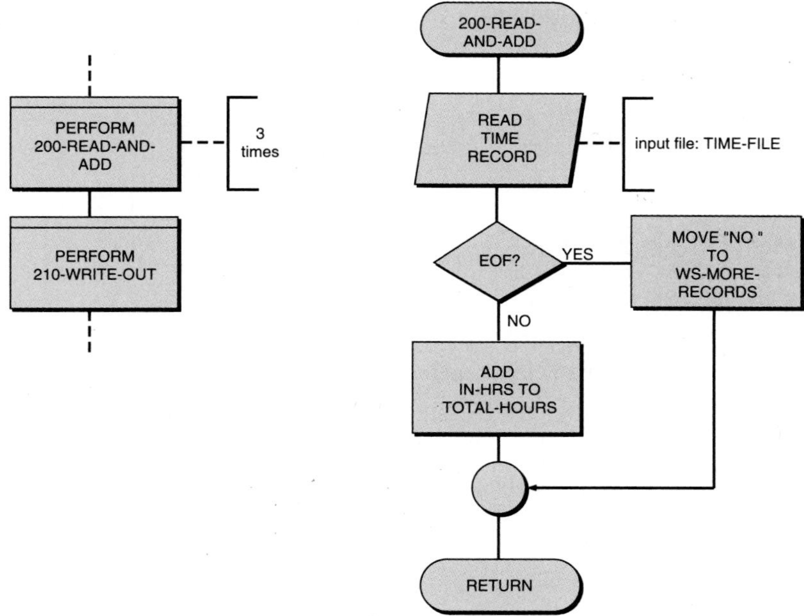

14. In each case, show the value stored in the source field and in the receiving field after the MOVE statement is executed. Indicate any invalid data transfer.

```
MOVE A TO B.
```

	Source Field A		Receiving Field B	
	PIC	Contents	PIC	Contents
a.	S99	+25	999	100
b.	99	25	99V99	42.50
c.	9V99	1.26	S999	-100
d.	S9V99	-1.26	99V9	42.5
e.	S9V99	-1.26	S9(4)V9999	+2345.6742
f.	99	25	X(4)	MARY
g.	999	325	XX	NO
h.	9V99	1.26	X(4)	MARY
i.	999	325	AAA	YES
j.	A(4)	MARY	AAA	YES
k.	A(4)	MARY	A(6)	FIDDLE
l.	A(4)	MARY	X(4)	JOHN
m.	X(4)	JOHN	A(4)	MARY
n.	X(4)	DC-3	X(6) JUST	MARYJO
o.	X(3)	123	S999	-345

15. Show two ways of coding the statement below. Assume that coding begins in column 16.

```
MOVE "THE PROPOSED BOSTON AND MAINE RAILROAD SECURITY SYSTEM" TO REPORT-TITLE.
```

16. Given the following file and record names, answer the questions below:

Input file: `EMPLOYEE-FILE`
Input records: `EMPLOYEE-RECORD, EMPL-TIME-RECORD`
Output file: `SALARY-FILE`
Output records: `SALARY-RECORD, PRINTLINE`

Which of the following statements are correct and which are wrong?

a. `READ EMPLOYEE-RECORD, AT END ...`
b. `READ EMPLOYEE-FILE, AT END ...`
c. `READ INPUT-FILE RECORD, AT END ...`
d. `READ EMPL-TIME-RECORD, AT END ...`
e. `READ EMPLOYEE-FILE RECORD, AT END ...`
f. `WRITE SALARY-FILE RECORD AFTER ADVANCING ...`
g. `WRITE SALARY-RECORD AFTER ADVANCING ...`
h. `WRITE PRINTLINE RECORD AFTER ADVANCING ...`
i. `WRITE OUTPUT-FILE RECORD AFTER ADVANCING ...`
j. `WRITE PRINTLINE AFTER ADVANCING ...`

17. Answer the following questions about READ and WRITE statements:

a. When a READ statement is executed, how many input records are stored in input memory?
b. When is the condition AT END satisfied?
c. When is the condition NOT AT END satisfied?
d. When a WRITE statement is executed, how many lines will be printed?
e. Explain the effect of the FROM entry in the statement

```
WRITE PRINTLINE FROM REPORT-NAME
    AFTER ADVANCING 2 LINES.
```

Debugging Activities

1. Given the flowchart segment in Figure 4.43a, a student generated the coding in part b. Identify and correct the errors.
2. Given the flowchart segments shown in Figure 4.44a (assume the input file is INPUT-FILE), a student generated the code in part b. Identify and correct the errors.
3. Given the following pseudocode paragraphs, a student generated the coding in part b. Find and correct the errors. Assume the input and output files are IN-FILE and OUT-FILE, respectively.

   a. **100-Produce-Inventory-Report.**
      1. Perform 200-Start-Up.
      2. Perform 210-Process-Item-Record until no more records.
      3. Perform 220-Finish-Up.
      4. Stop the run.

      200-Start-Up.
      1. Open the files.
      2. Set the end-of-file flag WS-MORE-RECORDS to "YES".
      3. Perform 300-Write-Report-Headers.
      4. Perform 310-Read-Item-Record.

   b.
```
100-PRODUCE-INVENTORY-REPORT
        PERFORM 200-START-UP
            OPEN IN-FILE
                OUT-FILE.
            MOVE YES TO WS-MORE-RECORDS.
            PERFORM 300-WRITE-REPORT-HEADERS.
        PERFORM 310-READ-ITEM-RECORD
            UNTIL WS-MORE-RECORDS = "NO ".
        PERFORM 210-PROCESS-ITEM-RECORD.
        PERFORM 220-FINISH-UP.
```

Figure 4.43

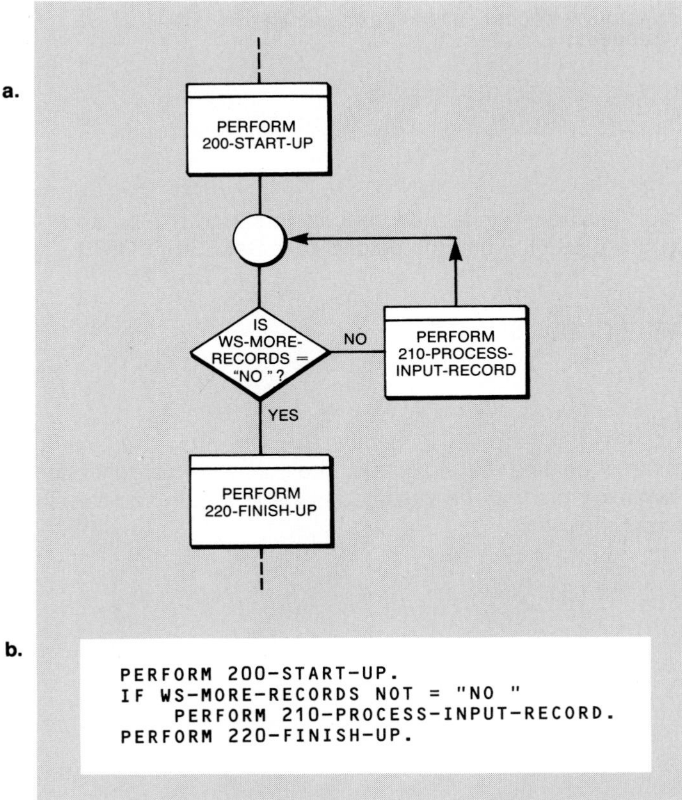


```
PERFORM 200-START-UP.
IF WS-MORE-RECORDS NOT = "NO "
    PERFORM 210-PROCESS-INPUT-RECORD.
PERFORM 220-FINISH-UP.
```

Figure 4.44

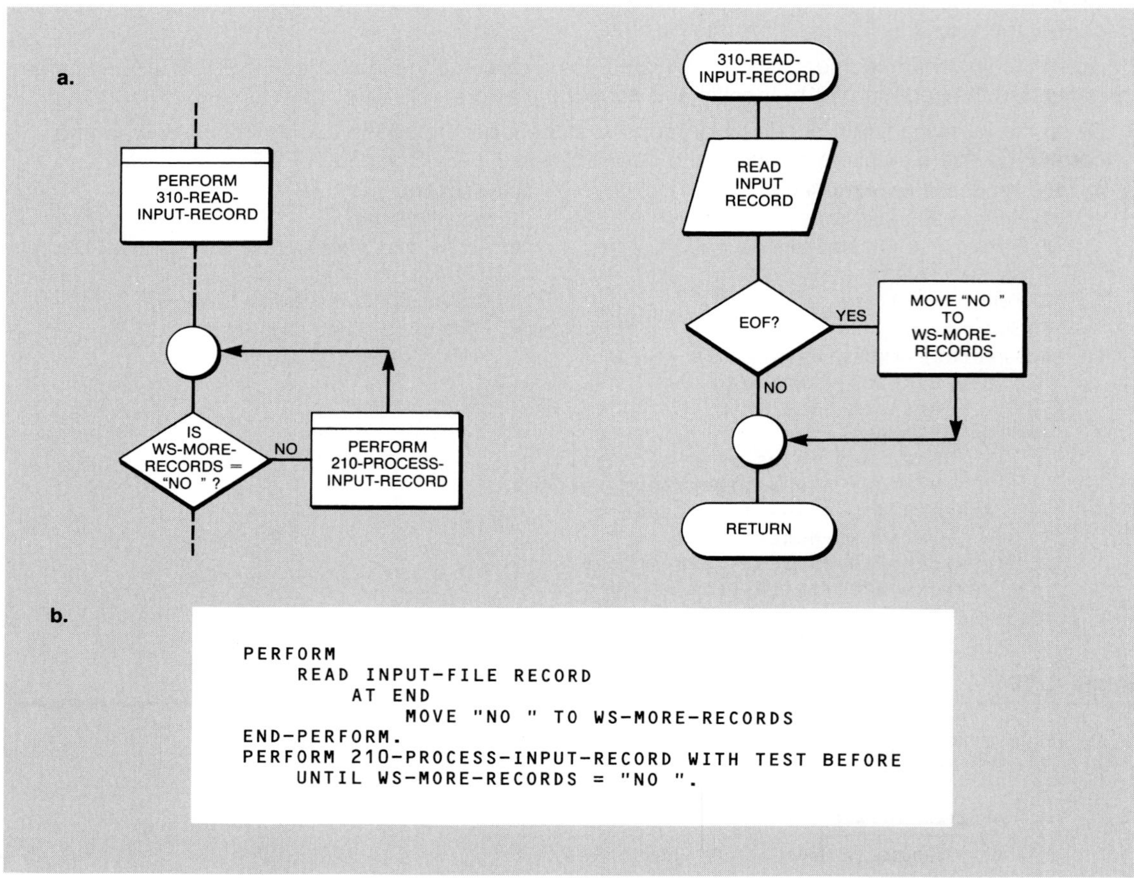

4. Given the following pseudocode paragraph, a student generated the coding in part b. Find and correct the errors. (Assume the input file is SALES-FILE and the output file is SALES-REPORT.)
   a. **200-Start-Up.**
      1. Open the files.
      2. Set the end-of-file flag WS-MORE-RECORDS to "YES".
   b.
```
200-START-UP.
        OPEN SALES-FILE.
        OPEN SALES-REPORT.
        SET WS-MORE-RECORDS = "YES".
```

5. A program has been written for the purpose of printing mailing labels. The compiler has generated the listing shown below. Correct all the syntax errors that are indicated in the listing. In addition, there is **one serious logic error.** Find and correct it.

```
        IDENTIFICATION DIVISION.

        PROGRAM-ID.  MAILING-LABELS-PROG.

        ENVIRONMENT DIVISION.

        CONFIGURATION SECTION.

        SOURCE-COMPUTER.   VAX-VMS-8650.
        OBJECT-COMPUTER.   VAX-VMS-8650.

        INPUT-OUTPUT SECTION.

        FILE-CONTROL.
            SELECT CLIENT-FILE     ASSIGN TO COB$INPUT.
                   1
%COBOL-W-ERROR  239, (1) File is CLOSEd but is not OPENed
            SELECT MAILING-LABELS  ASSIGN TO COB$OUTPUT.

        DATA DIVISION.

        FILE SECTION.

        FD  CLIENT-FILE
            RECORD CONTAINS 80 CHARACTERS.

        01  CLIENT-RECORD.
            05 I-CLIENT-NAME        PIC X(20).
            05 I-ADDRESS,
                10 I-STREET         PIC X(15).
                1
%COBOL-E-ERROR   65, (1) Missing period is assumed
                10 I-CITY-INFO.
                    15 I-CITY       PIC X(10).
                    15 I-STATE      PIC XX,
                    15 I-ZIP-CODE   PIC 9(5).
                    1
%COBOL-E-ERROR   65, (1) Missing period is assumed
            05                      PIC X(28).

        FD  MAILING-LABELS
            RECORD CONTAINS 32 CHARACTERS.

        01  PRINTLINE             PIC X(32).

        WORKING-STORAGE SECTION.

        01  WS-MORE-RECORDS       PIC XXX.

        01  SEPARATOR-LINE        PIC X(32)  VALUE ALL "*".
        1
%COBOL-E-ERROR   65, (1) Missing period is assumed

        01  LABEL-LINE            PIC X(32).

        PROCEDURE-DIVISION.

        100-PRODUCE-MAILING-LABELS.
            PERFORM 200-START-UP.
            PERFORM 210-PROCESS-CLIENT-RECORD.
            PERFORM 220-FINISH-UP.
            STOP.
                1
%COBOL-F-ERROR  321, (1) Invalid statement syntax

        200-START-UP.
            OPEN INPUT CLIENT-RECORD.
                          1
%COBOL-F-ERROR  259, (1) Operand must be a file-name defined by FD
            OPEN OUTPUT MAILING-LABELS.
            MOVE "YES" TO WS-MORE-RECORDS.
            PERFORM 300-READ-CLIENT-RECORD.
                    1
%COBOL-F-ERROR  349, (1) Undefined name

        210-PROCESS-CLIENT-RECORD.
        1
%COBOL-W-ERROR  297, (1) Processing of source program resumes at this point
            PERFORM 310-PREPARE-LABEL.
                    1
%COBOL-F-ERROR  349, (1) Undefined name
            PERFORM 300-READ-CLIENT-RECORD.
            1       2
%COBOL-W-ERROR  297, (1) Processing of source program resumes at this point
%COBOL-F-ERROR  349, (2) Undefined name

        220-FINISH-UP.
        1
%COBOL-W-ERROR  297, (1) Processing of source program resumes at this point
            CLOSE CLIENT-FILE
                  MAILING-LABELS.

        300-READ-CLEINT-RECORD.
            READ CLIENT-FILE RECORD
```

```
                  AT END
                      MOVE "NO " TO WS-MORE-RECORDS.

          310-PREPARE LABEL.
                      1
%COBOL-E-ERROR   65, (1) Missing period is assumed
%COBOL-F-ERROR  321, (1) Invalid statement syntax
              MOVE SPACES TO LABEL-LINE.
              1
%COBOL-W-ERROR  297, (1) Processing of source program resumes at this point
              WRITE PRINTLINE FROM SEPARATOR-LINE
                  AFTER ADVANCING 5 LINES.
              MOVE I-CLIENT-NAME TO LABEL-LINE.
              WRITE PRINTLINE FROM LABEL-LINE
                  AFTER ADVANCING 1 LINE.
              MOVE I-STREET TO LABLE-LINE.
                                  1
%COBOL-F-ERROR  349, (1) Undefined name
              WRITE PRINTLINE FROM LABEL-LINE
                  AFTER ADVANCING I LINE.
                                  1      2
%COBOL-F-ERROR  349, (1) Undefined name
%COBOL-W-ERROR  297, (2) Processing of source program resumes at this point
              MOVE I-CTY-INFOTO LABEL-LINE.
                  1
%COBOL-F-ERROR  349, (1) Undefined name
              WRITE PRINTLINE FROM LABEL-LINE
              1
%COBOL-W-ERROR  297, (1) Processing of source program resumes at this point
                  AFTER ADVANCING 1 LINE.
```

Programming Exercises

Programming Exercise I

The management of Express Auto Parts Warehouse wants its data processing department to prepare an inventory report for all its catalog items. For each item, there is a record in the inventory file containing the following data:

cc 1–5	Catalog number
cc 6–25	Item description
cc 26–30	Purchase price per unit (format: xxx.xx)
cc 31–35	Selling price per unit (format: xxx.xx)
cc 36–39	Quantity on hand
cc 40–43	Quantity on order
cc 44–47	Reorder point

This file is brought up-to-date weekly.

The inventory report must list all the catalog items. For each item, the report must specify the catalog number, description, quantity on hand, purchase price per unit, and selling price per unit. The report should begin at the top of a new page with appropriate descriptive information: company name, report name, and column headings.

The design tools (system flowchart, layout of input record, printer spacing chart, structure chart, program pseudocode, and program flowchart) have been developed for you and are shown in Figure 4.45.

Your assignment is to study the program design, and then complete the design implementation phase; that is, code, debug, and run the program. Use Data File Set 1 (see Appendix C) [DD/CD:VIC4EX1.DAT] as the inventory file.

Figure 4.45

Record Layout Form

I-CATALOG-NO	I-ITEM-DESCR	I-PURCHASE-PRICE	I-SELLING-PRICE	I-ON-HAND	I-ON-ORDER	I-REORDER-POINT	
1 2 3 4 5	6 7 8 9 10 11 12 13 14 15 16 17 18 19 20 21 22 23 24 25	26 27 28 29 30	31 32 33 34 35	36 37 38 39	40 41 42 43	44 45 46 47	48 49 50 51 52 53 54 55 56 57 58 59 60 61 62 63 64 65 66 67 68 69 70 71 72 73 74 75 76 77 78 79 80
		^	^				

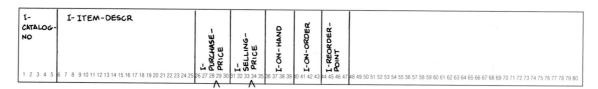

Record Name: ITEM-RECORD

■ Figure 4.45 continued

Printer Spacing Chart

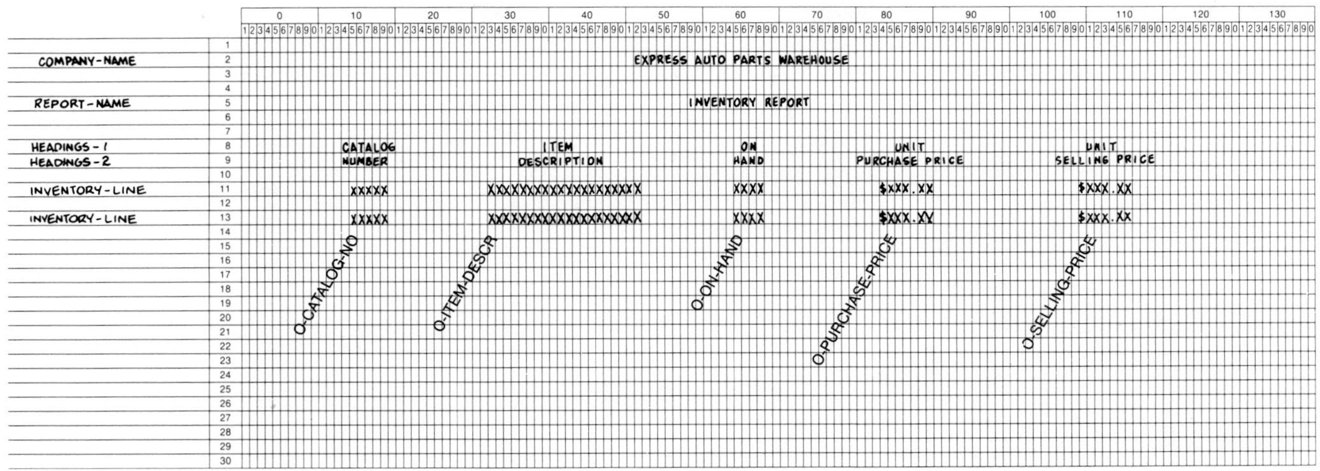

System Flowchart

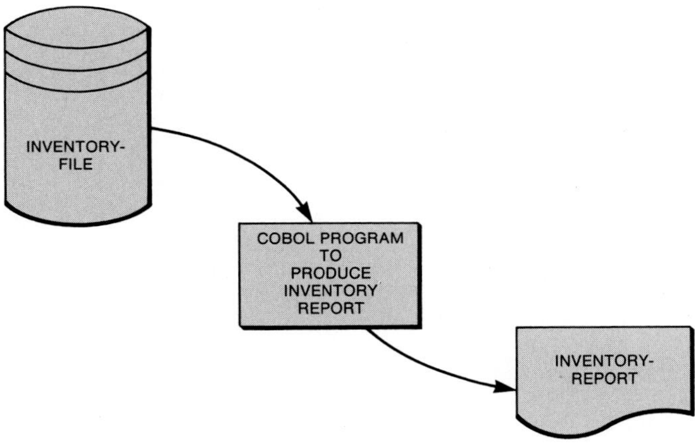

Structure Chart

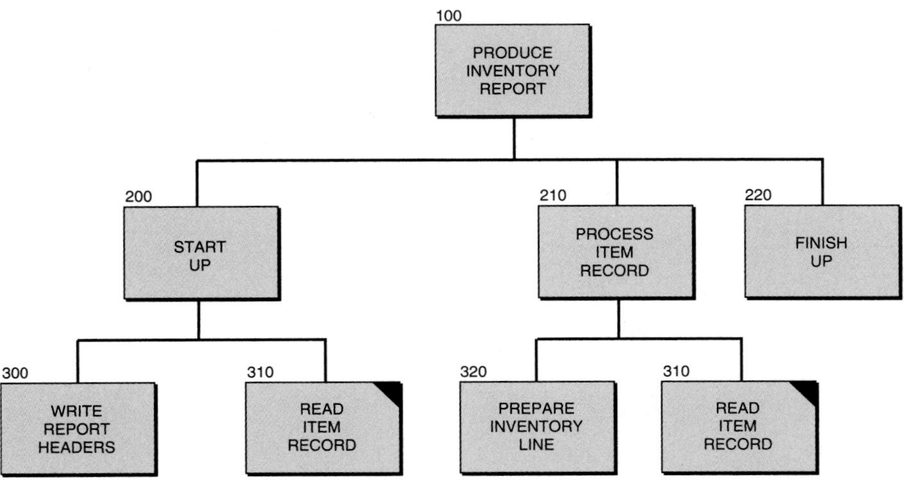

Program Pseudocode

100-Produce-Inventory-Report.

1. Perform 200-Start-Up.
2. Perform 210-Process-Item-Record until no more records.
3. Perform 220-Finish-Up.
4. Stop the run.

200-Start-Up.

1. Open the files.
2. Set the end-of-file flag WS-MORE-RECORDS to "YES".
3. Perform 300-Write-Report-Headers.
4. Perform 310-Read-Item-Record.

210-Process-Item-Record.

1. Perform 320-Prepare-Inventory-Line.
2. Perform 310-Read-Item-Record.

220-Finish-Up.

1. Close the files.

300-Write-Report-Headers.

1. Move the record Company-name to the output area Printline.
2. After advancing to the top of a new page, write the output record Printline.
3. Move the record Report-name to the output area Printline.
4. After advancing 3 lines, write the output record Printline.
5. Move the record Headings-1 to the output area Printline.
6. After advancing 3 lines, write the output record Printline.
7. Move the record Headings-2 to the output area Printline.
8. After advancing 1 line, write the output record Printline.
9. Clear the record area Inventory-line.

310-Read-Item-Record.

1. Read an input Item-record.
2. Test for the end-of-file record; if EOF record reached, move "NO " to the end-of-file flag WS-MORE-RECORDS.

320-Prepare-Inventory-Line.

1. Move input catalog-number to Inventory-line catalog-number.
2. Move input item-description to Inventory-line item-description.
3. Move input quantity-on-hand to Inventory-line quantity-on-hand.
4. Move input unit-purchase-price to Inventory-line unit-purchase-price.
5. Move input unit-selling-price to Inventory-line unit-selling-price.
6. Move the Inventory-line to the output record area Printline.
7. After advancing 2 lines, write the output record Printline.

Program Flowchart

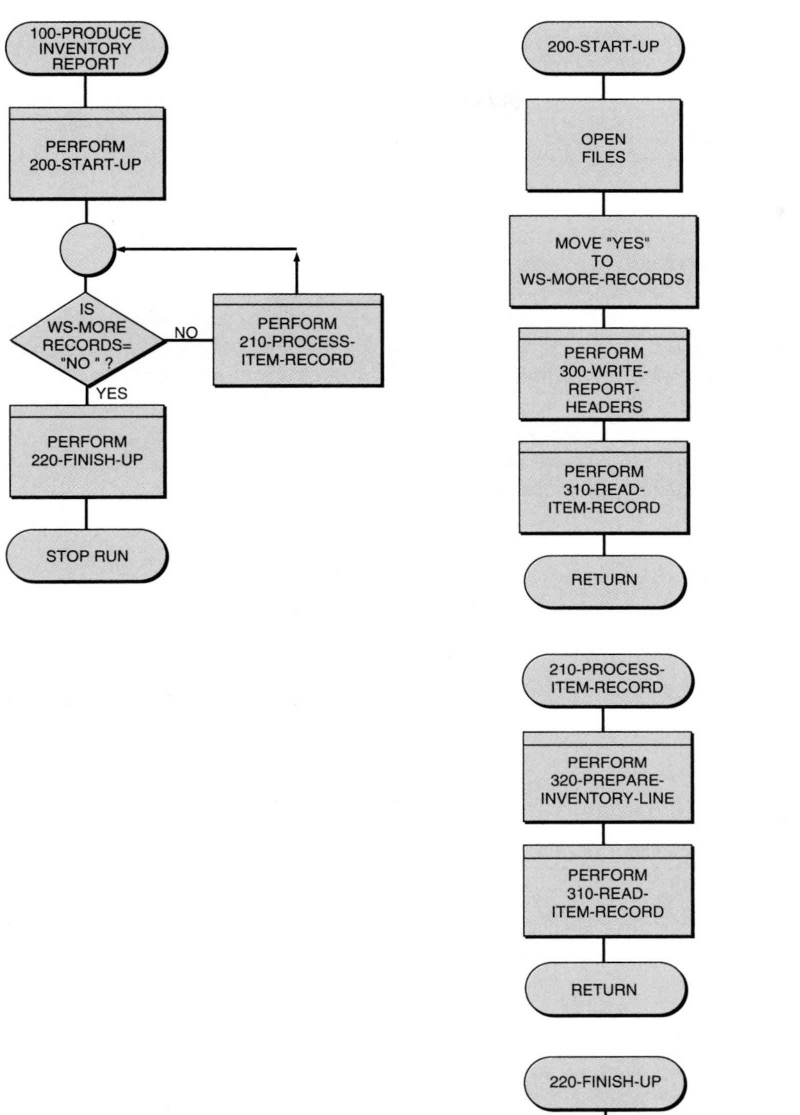

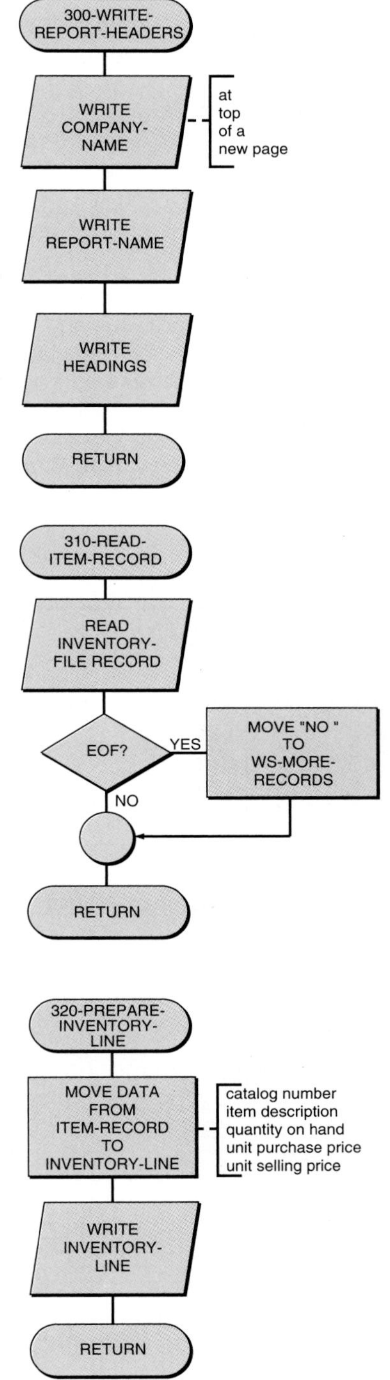

Programming Exercise II

The Ponagansett Electric Company wants a report that lists the previous and current meter readings for each of its customers for the current billing period.

Each customer record in the customer file contains the following data:

cc 1–3	Area code
cc 4–9	Customer number
cc 10–29	Customer name
cc 30–34	Previous meter reading
cc 35–39	Current meter reading
cc 79–80	Month number

The records in the customer file are arranged sequentially by customer number within each area code. The meter readings are updated monthly.

The report must begin at the top of a new page. It must contain the company name, the report name, and a detail line for each customer that specifies the area code, customer number and name, and previous and current meter readings, all listed under descriptive column headings.

The system flowchart, layout of input records, printer spacing chart, and structure chart have been completed for you and are shown in Figure 4.46.

Your assignment is to complete the design phase by writing the program pseudocode and by constructing the program flowchart. Then, you must code, debug, and run the program. Use Data File Set 2 (see Appendix C) [DD/CD:VIC4EX2.DAT] as the customer file.

Figure 4.46

Record Layout Form

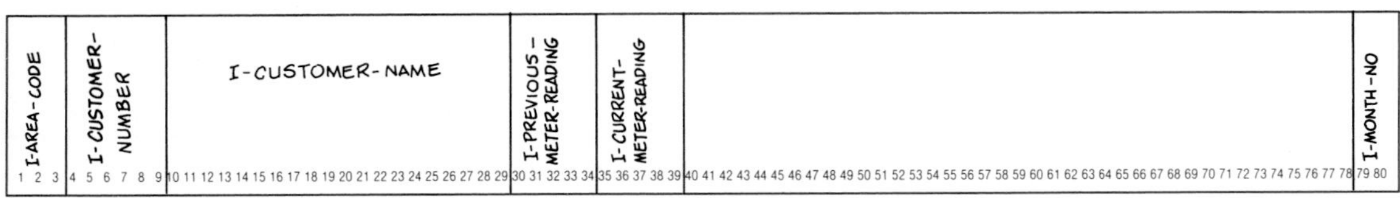

Record Name: CUSTOMER-RECORD

Printer Spacing Chart

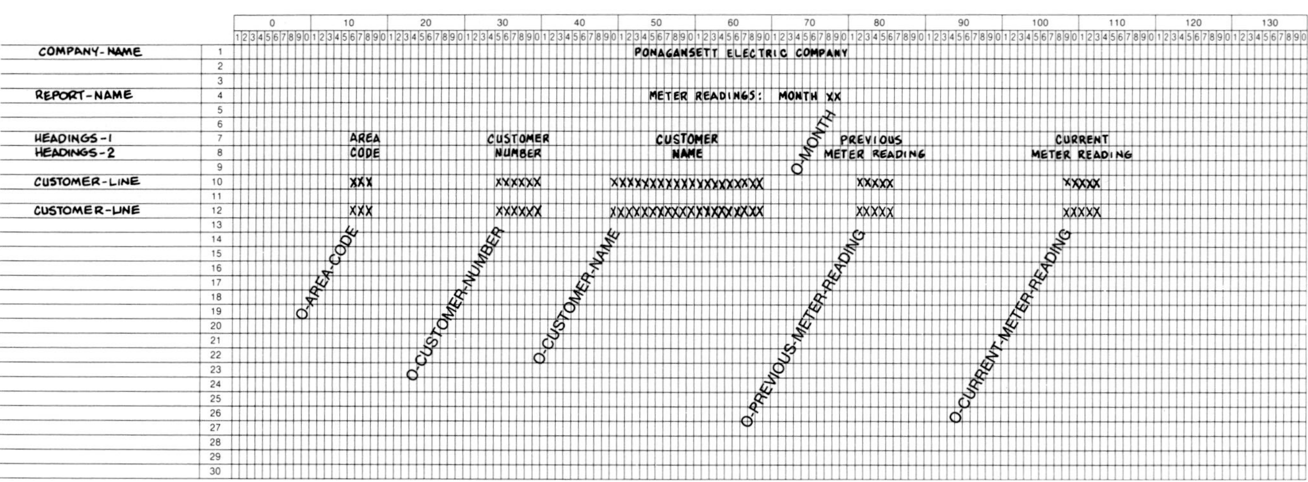

System Flowchart

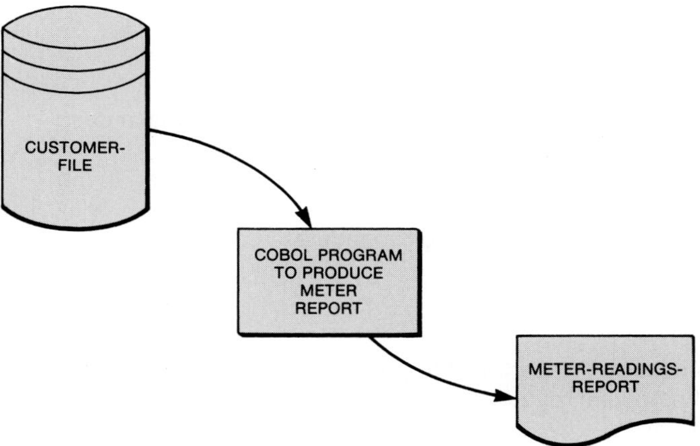

Structure Chart

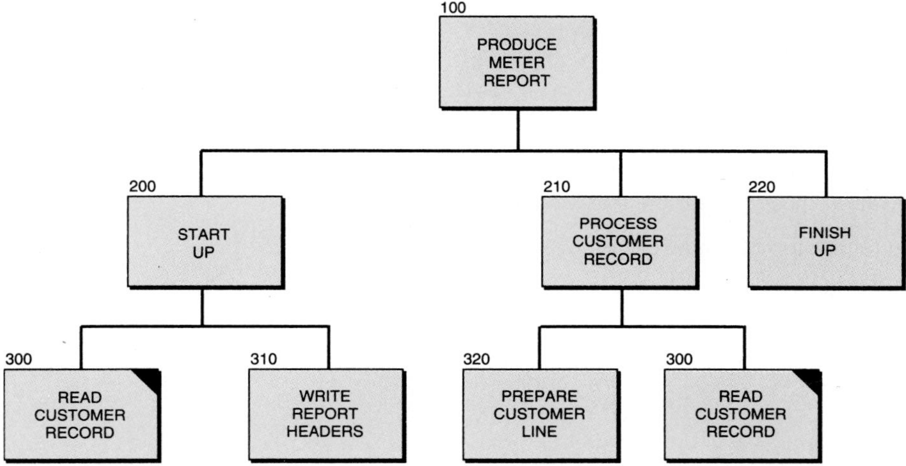

Programming Exercise III

The personnel director of the Modern Plastics Company wants the data processing department to prepare an employee register. The report must list all employees according to seniority by department within each plant.

For each employee, there is a record in the personnel file containing the following data:

cc 3–4	Plant number
cc 5–6	Department number
cc 7–15	Social Security number
cc 16–35	Employee name
cc 36–38	Classification code
cc 39–42	Pay rate (format: xx.xx)
cc 77–80	Date hired

The report must contain the following:

1. The company name, at the top of a new page.
2. The name of the report.
3. Descriptive column headings.

4. A detail line for each employee that shows:
   a. Plant number.
   b. Department number.
   c. Social Security number.
   d. Employee name.
   e. Current pay rate.
   f. Date hired.

Note that the records of the employee file must be arranged in seniority sequence within each department for each plant before processing them. Use Data File Set 4 (see Appendix C) [DD/CD:VIC4EX3.DAT] as the employee file. The records in this data set have been presorted in the required sequence.

You are encouraged to follow the steps of the problem-solving procedure.

Programming Exercise IV

The Allied Stock Company wants the data processing department to prepare a sales register for all the sales of the day. A sale can be made over the counter, by phone, or by mail order. For each sale, a record has been prepared with the following data:

cc 7–12	Invoice number
cc 13	Sale code (1 = over the counter, 2 = phone, 3 = mail order)
cc 14	Payment code (1 = cash, 2 = charge, 3 = COD)
cc 15–17	Salesperson number
cc 18–22	Customer number
cc 23–26	Quantity sold
cc 27–46	Item description
cc 47–50	Item number
cc 51–55	Unit price (format: xxx.xx)

These records have been assembled in a sales file.

The sales register report must contain the following information:

1. The company name (at the top of a new page)
2. The report name
3. Appropriate column headings
4. A detail line for each sale that specifies:
   a. Invoice number.
   b. Customer number.
   c. Item number.
   d. Item description.
   e. Unit cost.
   f. Quantity sold.
   g. Salesperson number.
   h. Payment code.
   i. Sale code.

You are encouraged to follow the steps of the problem-solving procedure. Use Data File Set 3 (see Appendix C) [DD/CD:VIC4EX4.DAT] as the sales file.

5 The Arithmetic Operations: Addition, Subtraction, Multiplication

Many data processing applications require that arithmetic calculations be performed. In this chapter, we will examine three of the arithmetic statements available in the COBOL language: ADD, SUBTRACT, and MULTIPLY.

To help us in this study, a sample program has been selected that includes all of the basic operations: addition, subtraction, multiplication, and division. The program produces a payroll report, and it is presented in two parts. In the first part, developed in this chapter, the program must compute payroll information for each employee, and in the second part, developed in Chapter 6, it must also calculate totals and averages for the company as a whole.

The various forms of the ADD, SUBTRACT, MULTIPLY, and DIVIDE statements and the COMPUTE statement are explained in detail within these two chapters, and they are applied as needed in the program.

In addition to examining the arithmetic operations, since the program must produce a printed report, we also explain how to use editing characters to make printed values more meaningful and useful to the end user. ■

Objectives You Should Achieve

After studying this chapter, you should:

1. Be able to identify the data items of an input record that will be needed within a program as arithmetic operands, given a statement of the programming problem and its input record specifications.
2. Be able to correctly identify and properly edit the data items of an output record that will be printed on a report.
3. Be able to group work areas needed in a program under appropriate group names that enhance the structure and self-documentation of a program.
4. Be able to correctly code a COBOL arithmetic statement that will store the sum of operands into a receiving field.
5. Be able to correctly code a COBOL arithmetic statement that will store the difference of two operands into a receiving field.
6. Be able to correctly code a COBOL arithmetic statement that will store the product of two operands into a receiving field.
7. Be able to correctly code a COBOL arithmetic statement that will store the product of more than two operands into a receiving field.
8. Given arithmetic operands, the PICTURE of the intended receiving field, and a specified arithmetic operation, be able to determine that *(a)* a low-order truncation will or will not occur; and *(b)* a high-order truncation will or will not occur.
9. Given arithmetic operands, the PICTURE of the intended receiving field, and a specified arithmetic operation, be able to code an appropriate COBOL arithmetic statement to minimize the effect of a low-order truncation.
10. Given arithmetic operands, the PICTURE of the intended receiving field, and a specified arithmetic operation, be able to code an appropriate COBOL arithmetic statement to prevent a high-order truncation.
11. Be able to successfully complete the task of coding and running a program that requires arithmetic operations, and for which the design tools (input and output record layouts, system flowchart, structure chart, and program pseudocode or program flowchart) are provided.
12. Be able to successfully develop the program pseudocode or the program flowchart and to code and successfully run a program that contains arithmetic operations, and for which some, but not all, of the design tools are provided.
13. Given a programming assignment whose purpose is to prepare a printed report that contains items whose values must be computed within the program, be able to successfully complete the design phase and the design implementation phase of the problem-solving procedure.

The Problem

The management of the Reliable Auto Parts Company wants its data processing department to prepare a weekly payroll report. The first part of the report must show the following information for each employee: the department in which the employee works, the employee's Social Security number, the employee's full name, the gross wages for the week, all the deductions (federal and state taxes, union dues, insurance premium), the total amount of deductions, and the net wages for the week. (The second part of the report will be developed later.)

A record has been prepared for each employee. Each record contains the following data:

cc 1–3	Department number
cc 4–12	Social Security number
cc 13–34	Employee's name
cc 35–36	Total hours worked during the week
cc 37–40	Employee's hourly pay rate (format: xx.xx)
cc 41–42	Federal tax rate (format: .xx)
cc 43–44	State tax rate (format: .xx)
cc 45–48	Union dues (format: xx.xx)
cc 49–52	Insurance premium (format: xx.xx)

The employee records are arranged first by department number (in ascending order) and then alphabetically within each department. This file is the input file for the program. (It is shown in Figure 5.27 [DD/CD:VIC5SP.DAT]).

Note: In developing this program, we will follow the steps of the problem-solving procedure first presented in Chapter 1. However, we will take detours wherever it is deemed useful to elaborate on a programming procedure or to introduce new COBOL statements.

Program Design Phase

Step 1

The first step specified in the problem-solving procedure is to develop a thorough understanding of the problem. This usually requires reading the statement of the problem a few times and then answering two questions very specifically:

1. What is given?
2. What is the required output?

In answering the first question, the programmer uses an input record layout form to prepare the layout of the data fields on the employee payroll record, as specified in the statement of the problem. The programmer must give a name to each data field and a name to the record itself. The result is shown in Figure 5.1.

Note: Recall that the decimal point is never entered in the field of an input record, but the programmer inserts a caret (^) to indicate where the decimal point belongs. The caret reminds the programmer to enter a V in the PICTURE clause of the data item description that must be coded later in the DATA DIVISION of the program. The caret is positioned as specified in the format (in parentheses) that follows the field entry. For instance, the format for the employee's pay rate field is xx.xx. Thus, a caret is placed between

Figure 5.1 Layout of input record for the chapter program

Record Layout Form

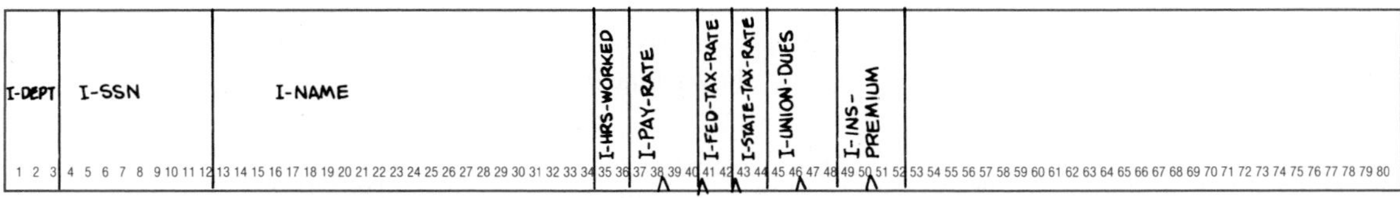

Record Name: EMPLOYEE-RECORD

Figure 5.2 Printer spacing chart for the chapter program

Printer Spacing Chart

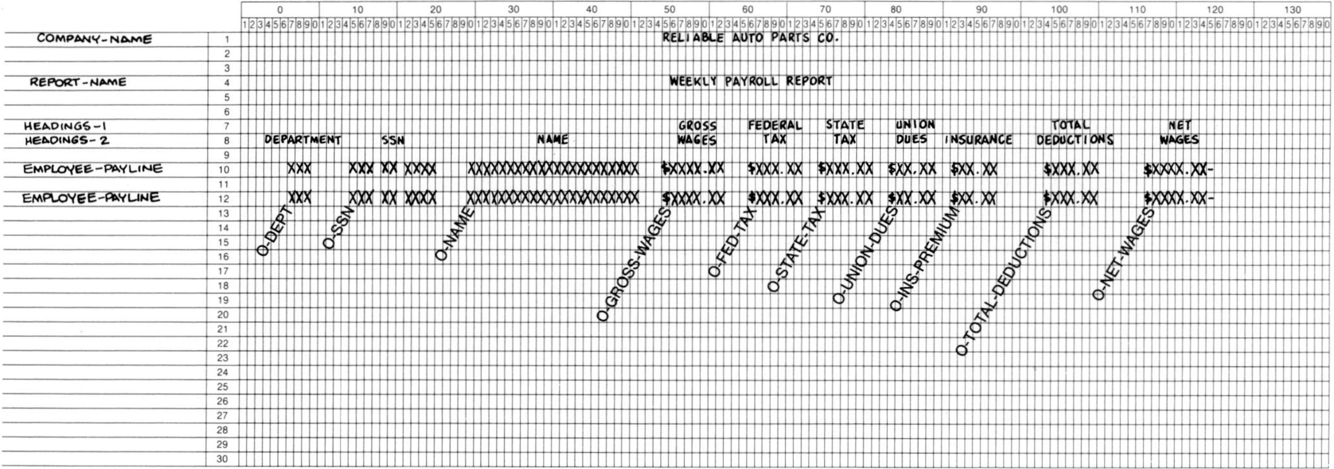

digit positions 2 and 3 in that field. The format for the state tax rate field is .xx, so a caret precedes the first digit position in the field.

In answering the second question, the programmer prepares the layouts of all the different kinds of lines that must be printed on the report. A printer spacing chart is used for this purpose.

In preparing printed reports, the programmer always attempts to make the printed data as meaningful as possible. This means that the report should be identified appropriately; columns of data should have descriptive headings; summary data, if any, should be identified as such; and so on.

The layouts of all the printed lines (or output records) needed for this report are shown in Figure 5.2. Note that there are five different kinds: one for the name of the company, one for the name of the report, two for appropriate column headings, and one for the employee's pay line. Descriptive names are given to each of the ten data fields of the employee's pay line and to each of the five different kinds of output records.

Note: The seven fields of the record EMPLOYEE-PAYLINE that contain "dollars and cents" values are edited so as to print the decimal point and the dollar sign. These editing characters will be inserted in the PICTURE clause of the data item descriptions when they are coded later in the DATA DIVISION of the program.

Step 2

The second step specified in the problem-solving procedure is to plan the solution. The essence of planning occurs at the thought-process level, since the programmer must analyze, organize, and synthesize. However, the programmer will use a selection of design tools to aid in this process. These design tools, along with the input and output record layout forms prepared above, will be retained to provide valuable documentation for the program that will be generated.

System Flowchart

The first of these design tools is the system flowchart. It is shown in Figure 5.3.

Recall that all the employee payroll records, prepared as shown in Figure 5.1, are contained in a file. The programmer must give a name to this data file. Figure 5.3 shows that it has been named EMPLOYEE-PAYROLL-FILE. This is the input file. The program must read an employee payroll record contained in this file, and it must process it as required to finally print a line on the payroll report. (The same procedure must be repeated for all the employee payroll records.) The report itself is the output file. This file must also be given a name. Figure 5.3 shows that the output file name is PAYROLL-REPORT-FILE.

The system flowchart shows very clearly that data flows from the input file (EMPLOYEE-PAYROLL-FILE) to the program and then from the program to the output file (PAYROLL-REPORT-FILE). Figure 5.4 shows a sample employee record being processed.

■ **Figure 5.3** System flowchart for the chapter program

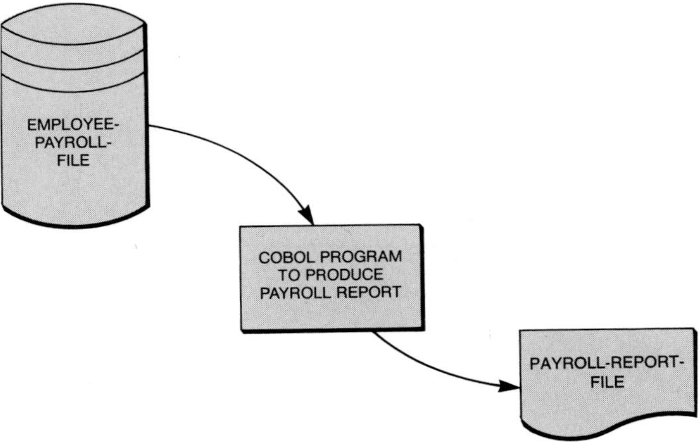

■ **Figure 5.4** A sample employee payroll record processed by the program

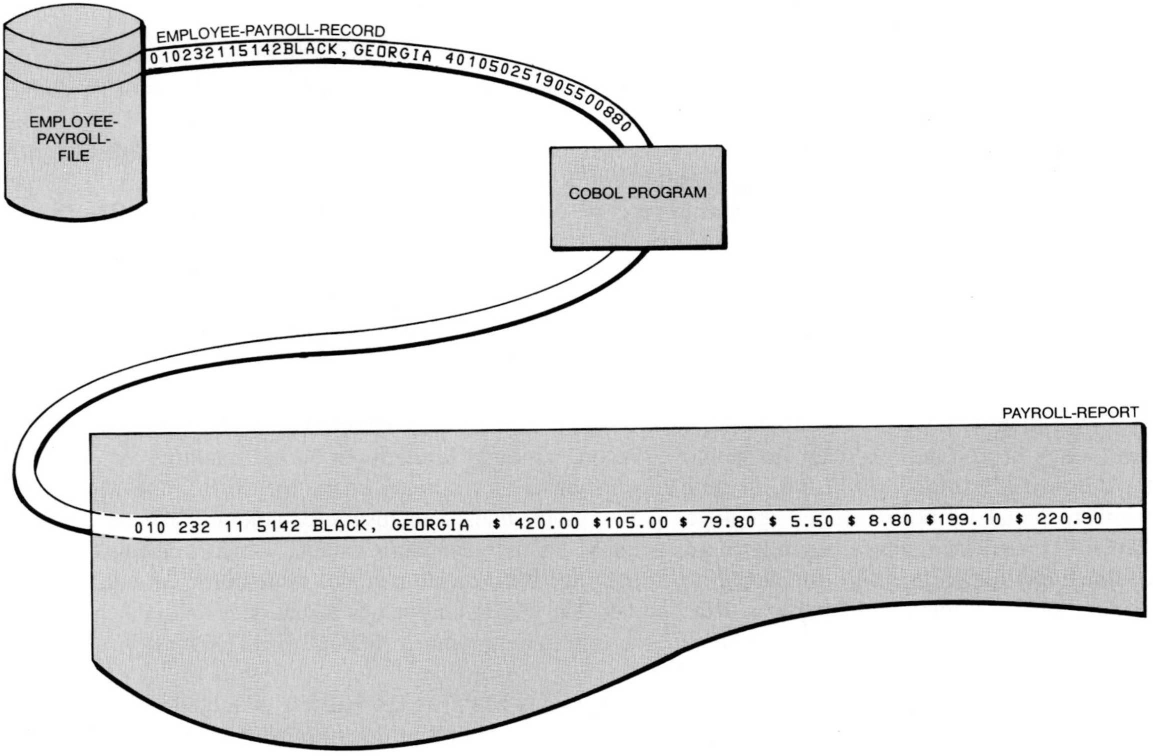

Structure Chart

The next design tool, the structure chart, helps us to focus on the role of the COBOL program itself, that is, **what** it must accomplish. Here, we begin by identifying the overall function of the program. We ask simply: What must the program do? The answer has already been stated in the system flowchart: COBOL PROGRAM TO PRODUCE PAYROLL REPORT. So, the top level of the structure chart consists of the module shown in Figure 5.5.

In a top-down development of the structure chart, we must identify the subtasks that must be performed in order to accomplish the ultimate task of producing the payroll report. In broad terms, we identify a need for start-up activities, for a record-processing module, and for some finish-up activities. These are shown in Figure 5.6.

Now, we know from having prepared the printer spacing chart that the report must begin with appropriate top-of-report documentation, specifically, the company name, the report name, and descriptive

Figure 5.5 Top level of the structure chart for the chapter program

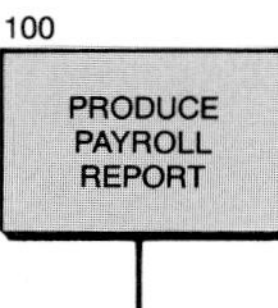

Figure 5.6 Developing the structure chart

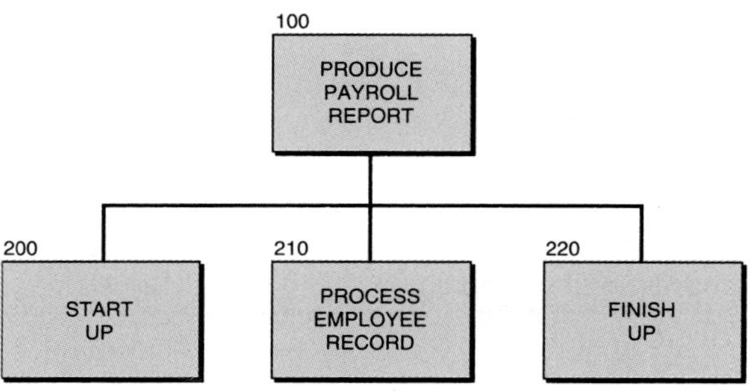

column headers. Printing these lines at the top of the report constitutes a subtask of module 200-START-UP, and the module designed to do this is 300-WRITE-REPORT-HEADERS.

Another important start-up activity is accessing the first record of the input file EMPLOYEE-PAYROLL-FILE so that upon entering module 210-PROCESS-EMPLOYEE-RECORD the very first time, there actually is in input memory a record to process. This subtask is accomplished in module 310-READ-EMPLOYEE-RECORD.

Recall, however, that before writing the top-of-report documentation to the output file (the printed report), and before accessing the first employee record from the input file, it is necessary to "open" the corresponding file. These activities, along with the initialization of certain variables such as the end-of-file flag, are start-up activities that are an integral part of module 200-START-UP.

The structure chart is now expanded as shown in Figure 5.7.

We then address the essential task of module 210-PROCESS-EMPLOYEE-RECORD, namely, to print a pay line on the report for the employee record currently in the input buffer. Examine the layout of the record EMPLOYEE-PAYLINE as prepared on the printer spacing chart. Notice that the department number, Social Security number, employee name, union dues, and insurance amounts can be obtained directly from the employee payroll record, whereas all the remaining values on that line must first be computed by the program. Consequently, we supply two subordinate modules to module 210: one that will contain all the required computations, and another that will assign values to the data fields of the record EMPLOYEE-PAYLINE and then write it out. We name these modules 320-COMPUTE-PAYROLL-ITEMS and 330-PREPARE-EMPLOYEE-PAYLINE.

At this point, the processing of an employee record is complete. To indicate that the next input record should now be accessed, the READ module is repeated as a subtask of module 210. The complete structure chart is then as shown in Figure 5.8. (Recall that the upper right-hand corner of a module is darkened if it occurs more than once in the structure chart.)

Program Pseudocode

The next task in the planning phase consists of writing pseudo instructions or drawing a detailed flowchart module for each module in the structure chart.

The main-control module 100-PRODUCE-PAYROLL-REPORT directly controls the execution of the second-level modules. The corresponding pseudocode paragraph is shown below.

100-Produce-Payroll-Report.

1. Perform 200-Start-Up.
2. Perform 210-Process-Employee-Record until no more records.
3. Perform 220-Finish-Up.
4. Stop the run.

Figure 5.7 Third-level modules subordinate to module 200-START-UP

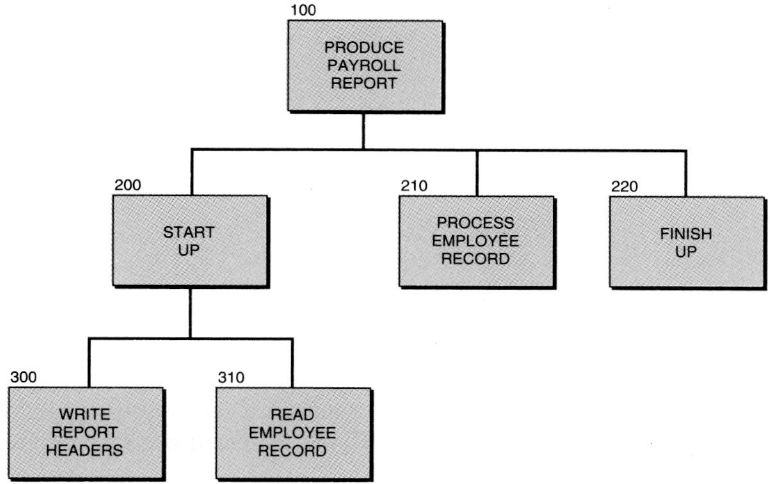

Figure 5.8 Structure chart for the chapter program

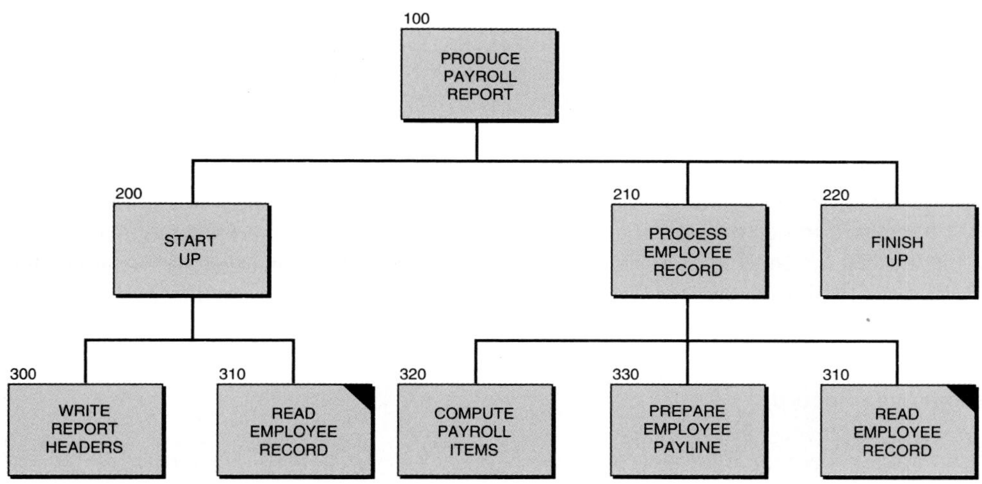

The functions of module 200-START-UP are to open the files in their proper mode for the program, to initialize variables, to control the execution of the module that begins the production of the report, and to control the execution of the Read module so as to access the first record of the input file. The system flowchart illustrates the open mode for each file: EMPLOYEE-PAYROLL-FILE is the **input** file, and EMPLOYEE-PAYROLL-REPORT is the **output** file for the program. Only one variable has to be initialized; it is the program flag. We call it WS-MORE-RECORDS, and we initialize it with the value "YES". The module that begins the production of the report is the third-level module 300-WRITE-REPORT-HEADERS, and the module that reads the input file is the third-level module 310-READ-EMPLOYEE-RECORD. The pseudocode for module 200-START-UP follows.

200-Start-Up.

1. Open the files.
2. Set the end-of-file flag WS-MORE-RECORDS to "YES".
3. Perform 300-Write-Report-Headers.
4. Perform 310-Read-Employee-Record.

Module 210-PROCESS-EMPLOYEE-RECORD directly controls the execution of three third-level modules: module 320-COMPUTE-PAYROLL-ITEMS that contains all the needed computations for the payroll record currently in input memory, module 330-PREPARE-EMPLOYEE-PAYLINE that ultimately writes the corresponding pay line on the report, and module 310-READ-EMPLOYEE-RECORD that will read the next record of the input file. The pseudocode for module 210 follows:

210-Process-Employee-Record.

1. Perform 320-Compute-Payroll-Items.
2. Perform 330-Prepare-Employee-Payline.
3. Perform 310-Read-Employee-Record.

In this program, module 220-FINISH-UP simply closes the files that were needed by the program. Its pseudocode is the following:

220-Finish-Up.

1. Close the files.

Now, we must generate the pseudocode for the 300-level modules. We do this in ascending order of the numeric prefixes, namely, 300, 310, 320, and 330.

The functions of module 300-WRITE-REPORT-HEADERS are to write the name of the company at the top of a new page, then the name of the report after advancing the number of lines specified on the printer spacing chart, and then the two lines containing the column headings, as specified on the printer spacing chart. The corresponding pseudocode follows:

300-Write-Report-Headers.

1. Move Company-Name to the output area Printline.
2. After advancing to the top of a new page, write the output record Printline.
3. Move Report-Name to the output area Printline.
4. After advancing 3 lines, write the output record Printline.
5. Move Headings-1 to the output area Printline.
6. After advancing 3 lines, write the output record Printline.
7. Move Headings-2 to the output area Printline.
8. After advancing 1 line, write the output record Printline.

The functions of module 310-READ-EMPLOYEE-RECORD are to read the next record of the input file and then to test the record to determine if it is a valid employee record or the end-of-file marker. If it is a valid record, no further action is needed here, but if it is the end-of-file marker, the program flag WS-MORE-RECORDS is assigned the value "NO ". Recall that this value will signal that the record-processing loop in step 2 of the main-control paragraph must come to an end. The pseudocode for this module follows:

310-Read-Employee-Record.

1. Read an input Employee-Payroll-Record.
2. Test for end-of-file record; if EOF record reached, move "NO " to the end-of-file flag WS-MORE-RECORDS.

The functions of module 320-COMPUTE-PAYROLL-ITEMS are as follows:

1. To compute the gross wages for the employee whose record is in input memory. This amount is the product of the hours worked and the pay rate. Both of these items are found in data fields of the employee record. The amount computed as the gross wages is stored in a data field in the working-storage area, since it will be needed in other computations shortly. See Figure 5.9, part 1.
2. To compute the amount of federal tax that must be withheld for the current pay period. This amount is the product of the gross wages and the federal tax rate. The applicable federal tax rate is currently available in a data field of the employee record in input memory, and the gross wages amount is in a data field in working storage. The amount computed as the federal tax is stored in another data field in working storage, since it will also be needed in another computation. See Figure 5.9, part 2.
3. To compute the amount of state tax to be withheld. The analysis for computing this tax is similar to that for computing the federal tax. The amount of state tax is stored in a data field in working storage. See Figure 5.9, part 3.
4. To compute the total deductions to be withheld for the pay period. This amount is the sum of the federal tax, the state tax, the union dues, and the insurance premium. The tax amounts are currently stored in working storage, and the other two amounts are contained in data fields of the employee record in input memory. The total deductions amount is also stored in a data field in working storage. See Figure 5.9, part 4.

Figure 5.9 The computed values in the chapter program

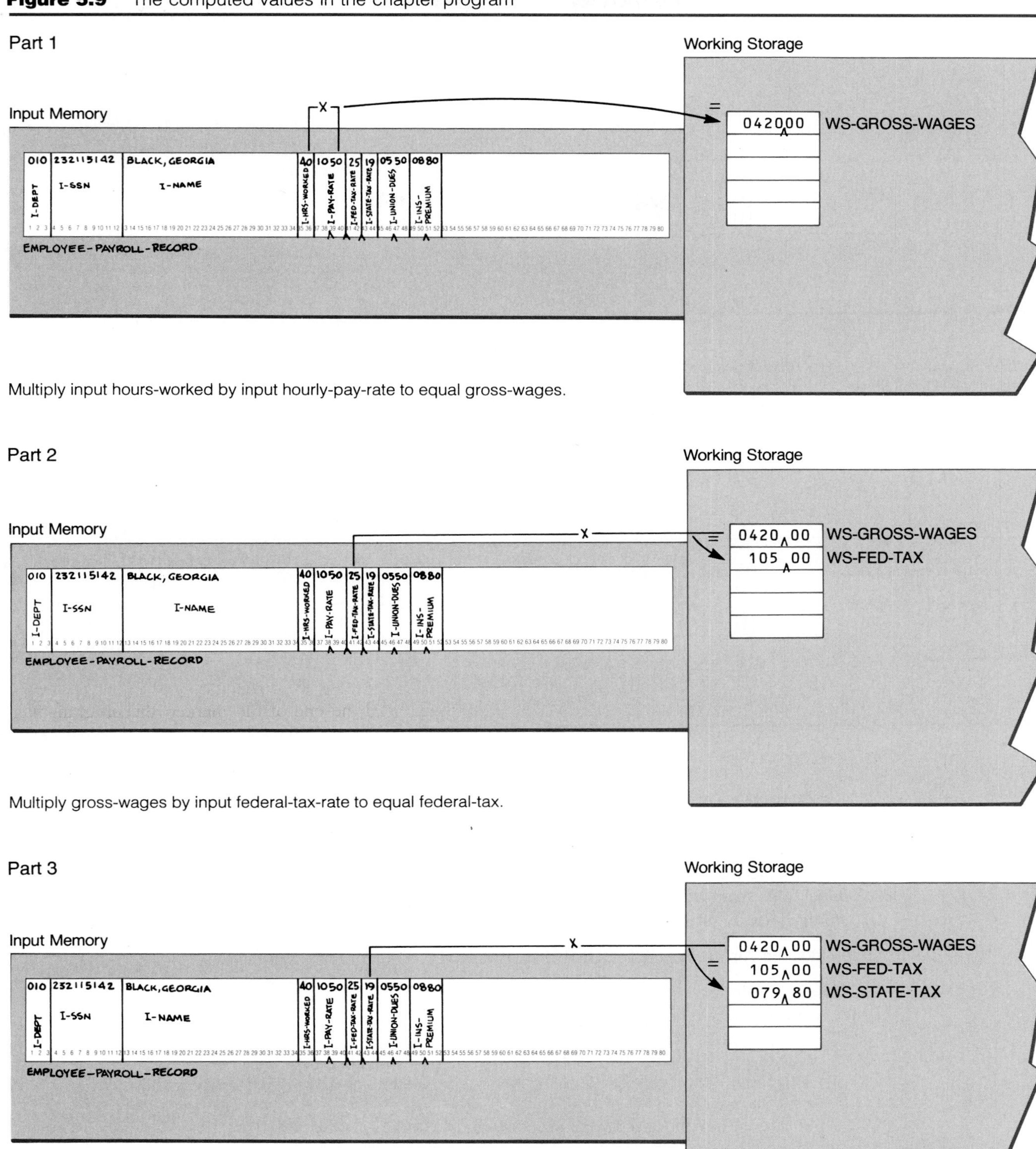

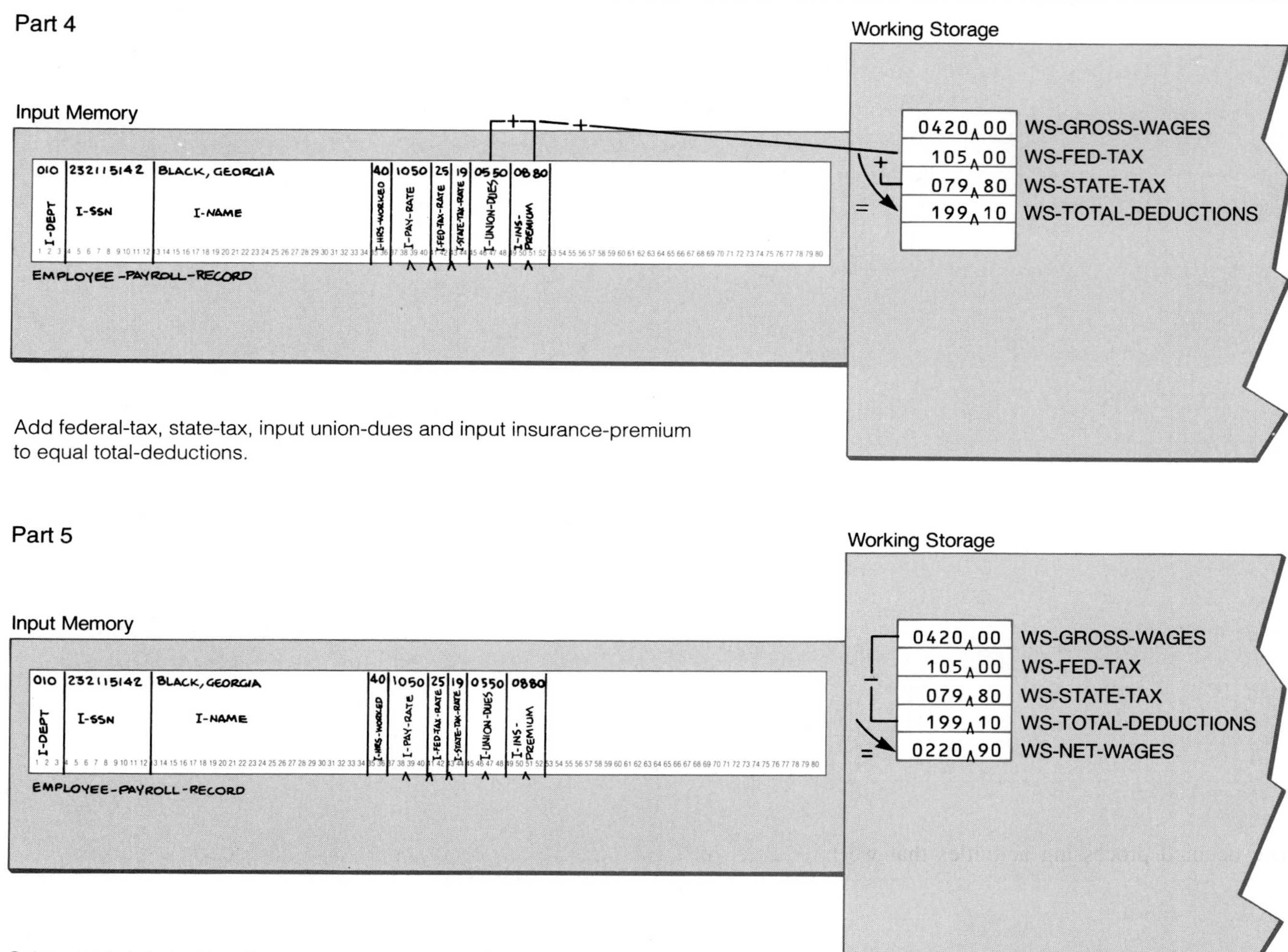

5. To compute the net wages for the pay period. This amount is obtained by subtracting the total deductions from the gross wages, and, for consistency, it is also stored in a data field in working storage. See Figure 5.9, part 5.

The pseudocode for module 320-COMPUTE-PAYROLL-ITEMS is shown below:

320-Compute-Payroll-Items.

1. Multiply input hours-worked by input-hourly-pay-rate to equal gross-wages.
2. Multiply gross-wages by input federal-tax-rate to equal federal-tax.
3. Multiply gross-wages by input state-tax-rate to equal state-tax.
4. Add federal-tax, state-tax, input union-dues, and input insurance-premium to equal total-deductions.
5. Subtract total-deductions from gross-wages to equal net-wages.

Finally, the essential functions of module 330-PREPARE-EMPLOYEE-PAYLINE are to prepare the output record EMPLOYEE-PAYLINE and then to write it to the output file EMPLOYEE-PAYROLL-REPORT. To prepare the record means to move all of the appropriate values to its data fields (see the printer spacing chart in Figure 5.2). Five of those values, specifically, the department number, the Social Security number, the employee's name, the amount to be withheld for union dues, and the amount to be withheld for the insurance premium, are currently stored in data fields of the input record EMPLOYEE-PAYROLL-RECORD (see Figure 5.9). The remaining five values are currently in working storage, specifically, the amount of gross wages, the federal and state tax amounts, the total deductions, and the net wages. After the values have been moved to the record EMPLOYEE-PAYLINE, the record is moved to the output buffer PRINTLINE and the line is finally written on the report.

The pseudocode for module 330-PREPARE-EMPLOYEE-PAYLINE is shown below, and the complete program pseudocode is contained in Figure 5.10.

330-Prepare-Employee-Payline.

1. Clear the record area Employee-Payline.
2. Move input department-number to Employee-Payline department-number.
3. Move input Social-Security-number to Employee-Payline Social-Security-number.
4. Move input name to Employee-Payline name.
5. Move input union-dues to Employee-Payline union-dues.
6. Move input insurance-premium to Employee-Payline insurance-premium.
7. Move gross-wages to Employee-Payline gross-wages.
8. Move federal-tax to Employee-Payline federal-tax.
9. Move state-tax to Employee-Payline state-tax.
10. Move total-deductions to Employee-Payline total-deductions.
11. Move net-wages to Employee-Payline net-wages.
12. Move Employee-Payline to the output area Printline.
13. After advancing 2 lines, write the output record Printline.

At this point, the programmer should "play computer" with the pseudocode. Begin by placing a blank sheet of paper on your desk to represent the output file or report. Then, select two records at random from the data file, as well as an end-of-file record. Follow the steps of the pseudocode "to the letter." Any write statement will produce a line on your paper (the output report). A read statement will access one of the sample records. Carry out the computations as specified. Use a calculator if you wish, and keep a record of the results. Once you have arrived at the "Stop the run" statement, check the report that was produced to determine if the program did what it was supposed to do. If you have written the pseudocode correctly, you will find that it did. If not, then you must locate the source of the errors, correct them, and "play computer" again until all the results are correct.

Program Flowchart

The detailed processing activities that we have listed in the program pseudocode could also have been visually represented by designing the program flowchart. Each module in the flowchart corresponds to the similarly named paragraph in the program pseudocode and/or module in the structure chart. The flowchart is contained in Figure 5.11.

At this stage of program development, the design phase is complete, but before going on to the design implementation phase, we need to emphasize again the importance of debugging the logic at this point. You must not lose sight of the fact that the compiler will help you to locate syntax errors in the program, but not logic errors. This remains **your** responsibility. By "playing computer" with the program pseudocode or the program flowchart, logic errors can be detected readily, and correcting them is easy, since the program has not yet been written.

■ **Figure 5.10** Program pseudocode

100-Produce-Payroll-Report.

1. Perform 200-Start-Up.
2. Perform 210-Process-Employee-Record until no more records.
3. Perform 220-Finish-Up.
4. Stop the run.

200-Start-Up.

1. Open the files.
2. Set the end-of-file flag WS-MORE-RECORDS to "YES".
3. Perform 300-Write-Report-Headers.
4. Perform 310-Read-Employee-Record.

210-Process-Employee-Record.

1. Perform 320-Compute-Payroll-Items.
2. Perform 330-Prepare-Employee-Payline.
3. Perform 310-Read-Employee-Record.

220-Finish-Up.

1. Close the files.

300-Write-Report-Headers.

1. Move Company-Name to the output area Printline.
2. After advancing to the top of a new page, write the output record Printline.
3. Move Report-Name to the output area Printline.
4. After advancing 3 lines, write the output record Printline.
5. Move Headings-1 to the output area Printline.
6. After advancing 3 lines, write the output record Printline.
7. Move Headings-2 to the output area Printline.
8. After advancing 1 line, write the output record Printline.

310-Read-Employee-Record.

1. Read an input Employee-Payroll-Record.
2. Test for end-of-file record; if EOF record reached, move "NO " to the end-of-file flag WS-MORE-RECORDS.

320-Compute-Payroll-Items.

1. Multiply input hours-worked by input hourly payrate to equal gross-wages.
2. Multiply gross-wages by input federal-tax-rate to equal federal-tax.
3. Multiply gross-wages by input state-tax-rate to equal state-tax.
4. Add federal-tax, state-tax, input union-dues, and input insurance-premium to equal total-deductions.
5. Subtract total-deductions from gross-wages to equal net-wages.

330-Prepare-Employee-Payline.

1. Clear the record area Employee-Payline.
2. Move input department-number to Employee-Payline department-number.
3. Move input Social-Security-number to Employee-Payline Social-Security-number.
4. Move input name to Employee-Payline name.
5. Move input union-dues to Employee-Payline union-dues.
6. Move input insurance-premium to Employee-Payline insurance-premium.
7. Move gross-wages to Employee-Payline gross-wages.
8. Move federal-tax to Employee-Payline federal-tax.
9. Move state-tax to Employee-Payline state-tax.
10. Move total-deductions to Employee-Payline total-deductions.
11. Move net-wages to Employee-Payline net-wages.
12. Move Employee-Payline to the output area Printline.
13. After advancing 2 lines, write the output record Printline.

Figure 5.11 Program flowchart

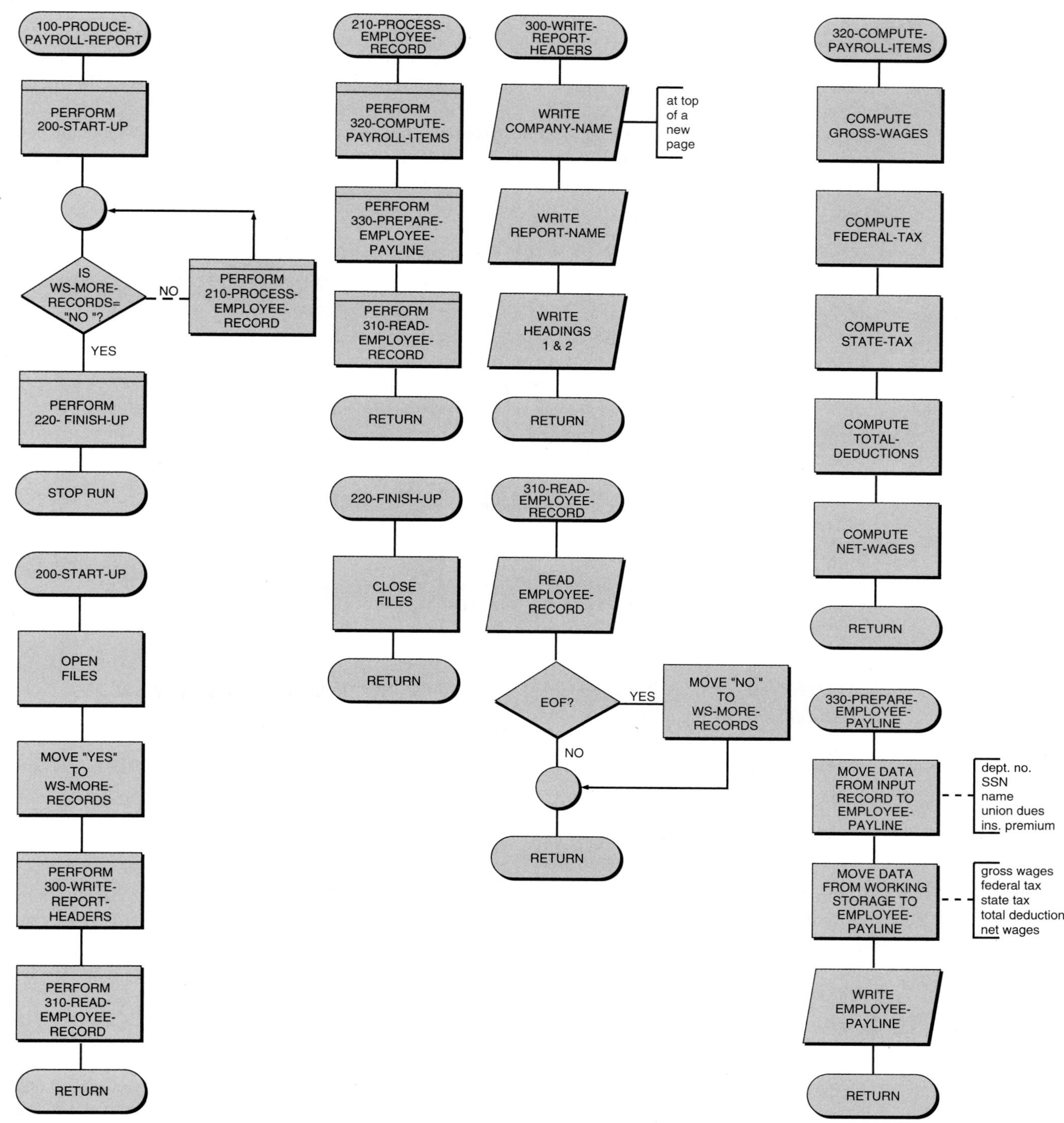

Design Implementation Phase

Step 3

The third step specified in the problem-solving procedure is to code the program. You may want to begin by reviewing the requirements of the IDENTIFICATION DIVISION and the ENVIRONMENT DIVISION as explained in Chapter 3.

The first two divisions for the sample program are shown below. Remember to obtain the system-related entries in the CONFIGURATION SECTION and in the SELECT statements of the FILE-CONTROL paragraph from your instructor. (The ones in this figure are for a VAX computer.)

```
 IDENTIFICATION DIVISION.

 PROGRAM-ID.     RELIABLE-AUTO-PAYROLL.

******************************************************************
*                                                                *
*  AUTHOR.          PAQUETTE.                                    *
*  DATE WRITTEN.    FEBRUARY 1993                                *
*                                                                *
*     THIS PROGRAM PREPARES A WEEKLY PAYROLL REPORT FOR THE       *
*  RELIABLE AUTO PARTS COMPANY.                                  *
*                                                                *
*     EACH RECORD OF THE INPUT FILE CONTAINS THE FOLLOWING        *
*  INFORMATION: AN EMPLOYEE'S DEPARTMENT, SOCIAL SECURITY NUMBER, *
*  NAME, HOURS WORKED DURING THE WEEK, PAY RATE, FEDERAL TAX RATE,*
*  STATE TAX RATE, UNION DUES, AND INSURANCE PREMIUM.            *
*                                                                *
*     FOR EACH EMPLOYEE, THE REPORT CONTAINS A PAY LINE WITH THE  *
*  FOLLOWING INFORMATION: THE DEPARTMENT NUMBER, SOCIAL SECURITY  *
*  NUMBER, NAME, GROSS WAGES, ALL DEDUCTIONS (FEDERAL TAX, STATE  *
*  TAX, UNION DUES, INSURANCE PREMIUM), TOTAL DEDUCTIONS, AND     *
*  NET WAGES. DATA IS PRINTED IN EDITED FORM.                    *
*                                                                *
*     THE REPORT BEGINS AT THE TOP OF A PAGE WITH THE COMPANY     *
*  NAME, FOLLOWED BY THE NAME OF THE REPORT, AND APPROPRIATE      *
*  COLUMN HEADINGS.                                              *
*                                                                *
******************************************************************

 ENVIRONMENT DIVISION.

 CONFIGURATION SECTION.

 SOURCE-COMPUTER.  VAX-VMS-8650.
 OBJECT-COMPUTER.  VAX-VMS-8650.

 INPUT-OUTPUT SECTION.

 FILE-CONTROL.
     SELECT EMPLOYEE-PAYROLL-FILE ASSIGN TO COB$INPUT.
     SELECT PAYROLL-REPORT-FILE   ASSIGN TO COB$OUTPUT.
```

Before beginning the coding of the DATA DIVISION, you should position three of the design tools, specifically the input record layout, the printer spacing chart, and the program pseudocode (or the program flowchart), so that they are immediately accessible. The reason is simply that the information they contain will direct most of the coding in this division.

While coding the DATA DIVISION, you must consider a number of important issues.

Issue 1

What class will be specified for the individual data fields of the input record? Some are alphanumeric, and others are numeric. If numeric, are there special features to be included, such as provisions for a sign (+ or –) and for a decimal point? If so, you must not forget to enter the special characters, S and V respectively, in the PICTURE clause.

Issue 2

When coding the data fields of output records, should editing characters be specified in order to make the printed values more readily understandable? If so, which ones? Some editing characters are appropriate for alphanumeric values and others for numeric values.

Issue 3

Other than the data fields of input records and output records, are other data items needed in this program? Typical of these are flags and work areas. Such items must be described in the WORKING-STORAGE

SECTION. What class and size should be specified in the PICTURE clause for these items? Are there any special concerns for numeric items, such as sign and assumed decimal points?

Comments on Issue 1: Class of Input Data Item

Any data item that will be used in arithmetic computations **must** have a **numeric** PICTURE. Only the class code 9 and the special characters V, S, and P are allowed in the character string of the PICTURE clause describing a numeric data item.

The presence of a V, an S, and/or a P in the character string of a PICTURE clause does not increase the size of the item being described.

The functions of each of these characters were explained in Chapter 3. For your convenience, a summary is shown in Figure 5.12.

The SIGN Clause

The most commonly used sign representation associated with the S in the PICTURE clause of a numeric item is the one that we discussed earlier, in Chapter 3; that is, the sign is stored in the rightmost byte along with the rightmost digit. Recall that the combination of a sign and digit is equivalent to the representation of a letter: the combinations +1 through +9 are equivalent respectively to the letters A through I; and the combinations –1 through –9 are equivalent respectively to the letters J through R. (The representation of +0 and –0 are system-dependent.) Thus, +453 is equivalent to 45C, and –453 is equivalent to 45L.

Other sign representations are also available, but they all require some additional entry following the PICTURE clause describing the numeric item to which they apply. The additional entries are the various options of the SIGN clause, whose format is shown in Figure 5.13.

The function of the SIGN clause is to specify the position and representation of the sign. The four possible positions are as follows:

1. SIGN IS TRAILING is the default position and representation if the SIGN clause is not used. This is the most common situation. Note that since the sign is stored in the rightmost (trailing) byte along with a digit, the special character S in the PICTURE clause does not increase the size of the item.
   The following two data description entries are equivalent:

```
ITEM-A   PIC S999.
ITEM-A   PIC S999   SIGN IS TRAILING.
```

2. SIGN IS LEADING indicates that the sign is stored in the leftmost (leading) byte along with the leftmost digit.

   Example:

```
ITEM-A   PIC S999   SIGN IS LEADING.
```

   The value +453 is stored as D53, and the value –453 is stored as M53. Note here also that the S in the PICTURE clause does not increase the size of the field.

■ **Figure 5.12** PICTURE clause characters for numeric items

Character	Explanation	Example		
		PICTURE	*Data in Field*	*Value*
9	Reserves storage for one numeric character.	999	023	23
V	Shows the position of an assumed decimal point.	9V99	134	1.34
S	Indicates the number is to be treated as a signed number (positive or negative).	S99	3$\overset{+}{4}$	+34
P	Indicates an assumed zero. It is used either to the right or the left of the decimal point to shift the numeric value.	99PPP	25	25000

■ **Figure 5.13** SIGN clause format

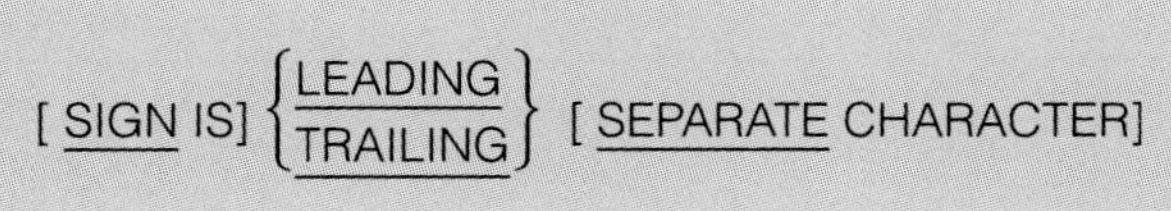

3. SIGN IS TRAILING SEPARATE CHARACTER indicates that the sign is stored in the trailing (rightmost) byte as a **separate** character. When this option is used, the size of the field is increased by 1.

   Example:

   ```
   ITEM-A    PIC S999   SIGN IS TRAILING SEPARATE CHARACTER.
   ```

   The value +453 is stored as 453+, and the value –453 is stored as 453–. It should be clear that the size of ITEM-A is *4,* not 3.
4. SIGN IS LEADING SEPARATE CHARACTER indicates that the sign is stored in the leading (leftmost) byte as a **separate** character. Here again, the SEPARATE CHARACTER entry clearly indicates that the S in the PICTURE clause increases the size of the field by 1.

   Example:

   ```
   ITEM-A    PIC S999   SIGN IS LEADING SEPARATE CHARACTER.
   ```

   The value +453 is stored as +453, and the value –453 is stored as –453.

In any case where you, or a data entry operator, must enter signed numbers into input records, it is essential to determine the appropriate sign position and representation.

Rules Governing the Use of the SIGN Clause

1. The SIGN clause specifies the sign's position and type of representation within a numeric field.
2. The SIGN clause can be used only in the description of a numeric item whose PICTURE contains an S.
3. The SIGN clause can be used at the group level or at the elementary level. If it is used at the group level, it applies to all the elementary numeric items that are subordinate to the group.
4. If the data description entry for a numeric item specifies the S in the PICTURE clause but does not include the SIGN clause, the position and representation of the sign are the same as specifying SIGN IS TRAILING, without the SEPARATE CHARACTER entry.
5. If the SEPARATE CHARACTER entry is specified, the sign (+ or –) is stored in a separate byte, and the S in the PICTURE clause increases the size of the field.
6. If the SEPARATE CHARACTER entry is not specified in the SIGN clause, then the sign is stored along with a digit, either in the rightmost (trailing) or leftmost (leading) byte, depending on the key word TRAILING or LEADING. The S in the PICTURE clause specifies the presence of a sign, but it does not increase the size of the field.

Input record data items that are not used in computations are generally assigned an alphanumeric PICTURE, described by using the class code X, regardless of the characters to be contained in the data field. See Figure 5.14. (Recall our comment that the alphabetic classification, class code A, is seldom used today. Though it is still supported in COBOL '85, it is slated for deletion from the standards at the next round of revisions.)

In the sample program of this chapter, the department, Social Security number, and name fields are given alphanumeric PICTUREs; the hours worked, the three rate fields, the union dues, and the insurance premium fields are given numeric PICTUREs, since these numeric values will all be used in arithmetic computations. In the character string of each numeric item (except hours worked), the V symbol is inserted to show the position of the assumed decimal point. The character string 99V99 for the hourly pay rate field allows values as high as ninety-nine dollars and ninety-nine cents. Sample rates are $4.50 per hour and $12.50 per hour. These values would be entered in the pay rate field as 0450 and 1250. The character string V99 for the federal tax rate field allows values such as 19 percent (.19) and 30 percent (.30). These values would be entered in the tax rate field as 19 and 30.

Figure 5.14 Class codes and related characters

Code	Characters Allowed in the Field	Example	
		PICTURE	*Data Value*
9	0,1,2,3,4,5,6,7,8,9 (+ or – if S in PICTURE)	S999	–024
A	Letters A through Z, spaces	AAA	NO
X	Any character in COBOL character set	X(5)	TR-31

The coding for the input record is shown below. Note that the PICTURE clauses of the numeric items do not contain the special character S. The numeric values in these fields are necessarily positive. If the S had been specified, then each field should also contain a + sign in the trailing byte in addition to a digit. Since no sign error is possible in this context, the character S is simply not specified.

```
01   EMPLOYEE-PAYROLL-RECORD.
     05 I-DEPT             PIC XXX.
     05 I-SSN              PIC X(9).
     05 I-NAME             PIC X(22).
     05 I-HRS-WORKED       PIC 99.
     05 I-PAY-RATE         PIC 99V99.
     05 I-FED-TAX-RATE     PIC V99.
     05 I-STATE-TAX-RATE   PIC V99.
     05 I-UNION-DUES       PIC 99V99.
     05 I-INS-PREMIUM      PIC 99V99.
     05 FILLER             PIC X(28).
```

Comments on Issue 2: Editing Fields of Output Records

Much of the processing carried out by COBOL programs is for the purpose of preparing printed reports. Since these reports are to be read and used by people, not by machines, their contents should be clear, readily understandable, and, to a reasonable extent, made aesthetically pleasing. To this end, editing of output records is a desirable and recommended feature.

There are numerous *editing characters.* They are generally classified into two groups: *insertion characters* and *replacement characters.*

Insertion editing characters are placed in the character string of a PICTURE clause of a data item so that they can be printed as part of the output. When used, they increase the size of the item. See the following example:

Data Item	PICTURE	Value	Printout
NUMBER-1	99	25	25
NUMBER-2	$99.00	25	$25.00

The PICTURE of NUMBER-1 contains no editing character. Its size is 2. The PICTURE of NUMBER-2 contains a dollar sign ($), a decimal point (.), and two zeros (0) as editing characters, increasing the size to 6. Note the difference in the printed value.

Replacement characters are included in the PICTURE of a data item to replace some output characters with more desirable output characters. Their use does not increase the size of the original item. Examine the following example:

Data Item	PICTURE	Value	Printout
NUMBER-3	9999	25	0025
NUMBER-4	ZZZ9	25	25

The PICTURE of NUMBER-3 specifies four numeric characters and contains no editing character; therefore, the printed value shows four digits, including two leading zeros. The PICTURE of NUMBER-4 makes provisions for four numeric characters also, but it contains the Z as an editing character. In the printed value, the leading zeros are replaced by blanks, since the Z editing character replaces leading zeros with spaces.

All the editing characters are listed, classified, explained, and illustrated in Figure 5.15.

Floating Characters

Some insertion characters are allowed to **float** so that they print in the rightmost position to the left of the first nonzero digit in the printout of a number. Look at the following example:

Data Item	PICTURE	Value	Printout
TOTAL-1	$9999.99	25.70	$0025.70

Suppose you want to have the dollar sign print just to the left of the 2, the first nonzero digit. In that case, the dollar sign must be used as a *floating character;* that is, a string of dollar signs must be specified in the PICTURE character string, as shown in the following example:

Data Item	PICTURE	Value	Printout
TOTAL-2	$$$$9.99	25.70	$25.70

In this way, a floating character deletes leading zeros, if there are any, and it will print in one of the positions occupied by the floating character in the character string of the PICTURE clause.

Figure 5.15 Editing characters: classification, explanation, and examples

Editing Character	Classification	Explanation	Examples: *Incoming Value*	Examples: *PICTURE*	Examples: *Printed (stored) as:*
Z	Replacement	It can appear more than once in a PICTURE character string as a replacement for the numeric code 9. It replaces leading zeros with spaces. It has no effect if the digit assigned to that position is not a leading zero. It cannot appear to the right of the numeric code 9. It is counted in determining the size of the item.	0250 0050 0000	ZZZ9 Z999 ZZZZ	250 050
*	Replacement	It can appear more than once in a PICTURE character string as a replacement for the numeric code 9. It replaces leading zeros with asterisks. It has no effect if the digit assigned to that position is not a leading zero or if it is aligned with an assumed decimal point. It cannot appear to the right of the numeric code 9. It can appear to the right of the decimal point only if all positions contain it. It is counted in determining the size of the item.	0250 0050 0000	***9 *999 ** **	*250 *050 ** **
$	Insertion	As an insertion character, it can appear only once in the PICTURE character string. It must occupy the leftmost position in the PICTURE character string. It assigns a dollar sign to that position. It is counted in determining the size of the item. The field size needed to store the data value should be increased by 1 to allow a position for the $ sign.	0250 4250	$99.99 $999	$02.50 $250
0	Insertion	It can appear more than once in a PICTURE character string. It assigns a 0 to each position it occupies in the PICTURE character string. If used to the right of the decimal point, it displaces digits to the right; if used to the left of the decimal point, it displaces digits to the left. It is counted in determining the size of the item.	0250 250.5 25 0250	990099 9999.09 99900 9900	020050 0250.05 02500 5000
.	Insertion	It can appear only once in a PICTURE character string. It assigns a decimal point to the position it occupies in the PICTURE character string. The actual or assumed decimal point in the numeric value is aligned with the decimal point in the PICTURE character string and the digits are then assigned to corresponding positions. It is counted in determining the size of the item.	02.50 250 2.245	99.99 999.99 99.99	02.50 250.00 02.24
,	Insertion	It can appear more than once in a PICTURE character string. It assigns a comma to each position it occupies in the PICTURE character string provided leading zeros to the left have not been eliminated. If they have, the comma can be replaced by a space, or some other zero suppression character such as $, *, +, or –.	1250 1250.50 25 240555	9,999 $999,999.99 Z,ZZ9 9,999,900	1,250 $001,250.50 25 4,055,500
+	Insertion	As an insertion character, it can appear only once in a PICTURE character string. It must be the leftmost or the rightmost character in the PICTURE character string. It assigns a + sign to the position it occupies if the value being stored in the field is positive or zero; it assigns a – sign if the value being stored in the field is negative. It cannot appear immediately to the right of the dollar sign. It is counted in determining the size of the item.	+250 +250 –250 –250	+999 999+ 999+ $999+	+250 250+ 250– $250–

■ **Figure 5.15** continued

Editing Character	Classification	Explanation	Examples		
			Incoming Value	*PICTURE*	*Printed (stored) as:*
–	Insertion	As an insertion character, it can appear only once in the PICTURE character string. It must be the leftmost or the rightmost character in the PICTURE character string. It assigns a – to the position it occupies if the value being stored in the field is negative. Otherwise, the position is left blank. It cannot appear immediately to the right of the dollar sign. It is counted in determining the size of the item.	+250 +250 –250 –250	–999 999– 999– $999.99–	250 250 250– $250.00–
B	Insertion	It can appear more than once in a PICTURE character string. It assigns a blank to each position that it occupies. It is counted in determining the size of the item.	250 032387 124578 250	9B99 XXBXXBXX 999B9B99 99BB9	2 50 03 23 87 124 5 78 25 0
/	Insertion	It can appear more than once in a PICTURE character string. It assigns a slash (/) to each position that it occupies. It is counted in determining the size of the item.	012582 BR102 080526	99/99/99 XX/XXX XX/XX/XX	01/25/82 BR/102 08/05/26
CR DB	Insertion	It can appear only once in a PICTURE character string. It must be the rightmost character in the PICTURE character string. It assigns the double character CR or DB if the value stored in the field is negative. Otherwise, the positions are left blank. CR is the credit symbol. DB is the debit symbol. It is counted in determining the size of the item (that is, add 2 to the size).	250 –250 –250	999CR 999CR 999DB	250 250CR 250DB

Notes:
1. The Z and * zero suppression characters cannot both be used in the same PICTURE character string.
2. The + and – cannot both be used in the same PICTURE character string.
3. The CR and DB cannot both be used in the same PICTURE character string.

The floating characters are listed and illustrated in Figure 5.16. When a floating character is used, the size of the data item must always be increased by 1. If there is no leading zero, the leftmost position specified for the floating character is the print position of the character.

Replacement and floating characters cannot be used in the same character string, but insertion and replacement or floating characters can. Some examples follow:

Data Item	PICTURE	Incoming Value A	Printed or Stored Value	Incoming Value B	Printed or Stored Value
NET-AMOUNT	$9999.99	25.50	$0025.50	1453.85	$1453.85
NET-AMOUNT	$9,999.99	25.50	$00025.50	1453.85	$1,453.85
NET-AMOUNT	$ZZZ9.99	25.50	$ 25.50	1453.85	$1453.85
NET-AMOUNT	$Z,ZZ9.99	25.50	$ 25.50	1453.85	$1,453.85
NET-AMOUNT	$$$$9.99	25.50	$25.50	1453.85	$1453.85
NET-AMOUNT	$***9.99	25.50	$**25.50	1453.85	$1453.85
NET-AMOUNT	$$999.99	25.50	$025.50	1453.85	$1453.85
NET-AMOUNT	$***9.00	25.50	$**25.00	1453.85	$1453.00
NET-AMOUNT	$*,**9.00	25.50	$***25.00	1453.85	$1,453.00

Note the effect of the comma as an editing character: If a nonzero digit is stored to its left, the comma is inserted as specified in the PICTURE; if there is no significant digit stored to its left, the comma is replaced by a zero, or a space, or an asterisk, depending on whether it is embedded in a string of 9s, Zs, or *'s, respectively.

■ **Figure 5.16** Floating characters: explanation and examples

Floating Characters	Explanations	Examples		
		Incoming Value	*PICTURE*	*Printed (Stored) as:*
$, +, –	The floating character aligned with the rightmost leading zero will be stored. Positions to the left will be left blank. Only one floating character can be used in a given PICTURE character string. The zero suppression characters Z and * cannot be used in a PICTURE character string that contains a floating character.	124.50 +124.50 –124.50 25425.10	$ $ $99.99 + + +99.99 – – – –9.99 $$$$9.99	$ 124.50 + 124.50 – 124.50 $5425.10

In the RELIABLE-AUTO-PAYROLL problem, the output record EMPLOYEE-PAYLINE contains eight fields that should be edited. The coding of the record is shown below. The layout prepared on the printer spacing chart was used to direct the coding.

```
01  EMPLOYEE-PAYLINE.
    05 CARRIAGE-CONTROL     PIC X.
    05 FILLER               PIC X(5).
    05 O-DEPT               PIC XXX.
    05 FILLER               PIC X(5).
    05 O-SSN                PIC XXXBXXBXXXX.
    05 FILLER               PIC X(4).
    05 O-NAME               PIC X(22).
    05 FILLER               PIC X(3).
    05 O-GROSS-WAGES        PIC $ZZZ9.99.
    05 FILLER               PIC XXX.
    05 O-FED-TAX            PIC $ZZ9.99.
    05 FILLER               PIC XX.
    05 O-STATE-TAX          PIC $ZZ9.99.
    05 FILLER               PIC XX.
    05 O-UNION-DUES         PIC $Z9.99.
    05 FILLER               PIC XX.
    05 O-INS-PREMIUM        PIC $Z9.99.
    05 FILLER               PIC X(6).
    05 O-TOTAL-DEDUCTIONS PIC $ZZ9.99.
    05 FILLER               PIC X(6).
    05 O-NET-WAGES          PIC $ZZZ9.99-.
    05 FILLER               PIC X(9).
```

Note the minus sign (–) editing character for the field O-NET-WAGES. Although the value assigned to this field is expected to be positive, if it ever prints as negative, then the sign will draw attention to the error. For this reason, many programmers automatically insert the minus sign editing character as the rightmost character in all numeric-edited fields. You are encouraged to do the same. (The sample program of this chapter illustrates the use of the minus sign editing character for only one field (O-NET-WAGES). Later programs will use it in all numeric-edited fields.)

Comments on Issue 3: Class of Working-Storage Data Items

Data fields, called work areas, that are needed to store intermediate values, such as computed values that will be used in later arithmetic computations and special data items that are used in the program for logic control purposes, can all be described as single elementary items at the 01 level in the WORKING-STORAGE SECTION.

In the payroll problem of this chapter, we want to set up five work areas and one field that is used as an end-of-file flag. The five work areas will store the computed gross wages, federal taxes, state taxes, total deductions, and net wages of an employee. The end-of-file flag is the same as the one used in Chapter 3, namely, WS-MORE-RECORDS. The coding of these items is shown below.

```
01  WS-MORE-RECORDS       PIC XXX.

01  WS-GROSS-WAGES        PIC S9999V99.

01  WS-FED-TAX            PIC S999V99.

01  WS-STATE-TAX          PIC S999V99.

01  WS-TOTAL-DEDUCTIONS PIC S999V99.

01  WS-NET-WAGES          PIC S9999V99.
```

In more advanced programs, the list of such items may become very long. Programmers generally prefer to group related items under a descriptive group name. In the following example, the work areas that pertain to an individual employee are grouped under the descriptive name WS-EMPLOYEE-PAYROLL-ITEMS, whereas the program flag WS-MORE-RECORDS is left to stand alone.

```
WORKING-STORAGE SECTION.

01   WS-MORE-RECORDS      PIC XXX.

01   WS-EMPLOYEE-PAYROLL-ITEMS.
     05 WS-GROSS-WAGES        PIC S9999V99.
     05 WS-FED-TAX            PIC S999V99.
     05 WS-STATE-TAX          PIC S999V99.
     05 WS-TOTAL-DEDUCTIONS   PIC S999V99.
     05 WS-NET-WAGES          PIC S9999V99.
```

Note: It is most important for you to understand that data items that are operands in arithmetic computations **must be numeric items**. That is, the character string in the PICTURE clause defining such an item must not contain characters other than 9, V, S, or P. Since most work areas are involved in arithmetic computations, their PICTURE clauses define them as numeric items.

Moreover, the results of computations carried out by the computer are always *signed numbers*. Such values are stored more efficiently if the receiving fields are also signed. Note the S as the first character in the character string of each PICTURE clause.

It should be obvious that if a computed value is negative and the receiving field is not signed, only the absolute value will be stored. This is a serious error. The error is compounded if the value is used in later computations. Consequently, it is always prudent to define receiving numeric fields as signed data items.

The complete coding of the DATA DIVISION for the RELIABLE-AUTO-PAYROLL problem is as follows:

```
DATA DIVISION.

FILE SECTION.

FD   EMPLOYEE-PAYROLL-FILE
     RECORD CONTAINS 80 CHARACTERS.

01   EMPLOYEE-PAYROLL-RECORD.
     05 I-DEPT            PIC XXX.
     05 I-SSN             PIC X(9).
     05 I-NAME            PIC X(22).
     05 I-HRS-WORKED      PIC 99.
     05 I-PAY-RATE        PIC 99V99.
     05 I-FED-TAX-RATE    PIC V99.
     05 I-STATE-TAX-RATE  PIC V99.
     05 I-UNION-DUES      PIC 99V99.
     05 I-INS-PREMIUM     PIC 99V99.
     05 FILLER            PIC X(28).

FD   PAYROLL-REPORT-FILE
     RECORD CONTAINS 133 CHARACTERS.

01   PRINTLINE            PIC X(133).

WORKING-STORAGE SECTION.

01   WS-MORE-RECORDS      PIC XXX.

01   WS-EMPLOYEE-PAYROLL-ITEMS.
     05 WS-GROSS-WAGES        PIC S9999V99.
     05 WS-FED-TAX            PIC S999V99.
     05 WS-STATE-TAX          PIC S999V99.
     05 WS-TOTAL-DEDUCTIONS   PIC S999V99.
     05 WS-NET-WAGES          PIC S9999V99.

01   COMPANY-NAME.
     05 PIC X(54)    VALUE SPACES.
     05 PIC X(24)    VALUE "RELIABLE AUTO PARTS CO.".
     05 PIC X(54)    VALUE SPACES.

01   REPORT-NAME.
     05 PIC X(55)    VALUE SPACES.
     05 PIC X(21)    VALUE "WEEKLY PAYROLL REPORT".
     05 PIC X(56)    VALUE SPACES.

01   HEADINGS-1.
     05 PIC X(56)    VALUE SPACES.
     05 PIC X(5)     VALUE "GROSS".
```

```
           05 PIC X(4)     VALUE SPACES.
           05 PIC X(7)     VALUE "FEDERAL".
           05 PIC XXX      VALUE SPACES.
           05 PIC X(5)     VALUE "STATE".
           05 PIC XXXX     VALUE SPACES.
           05 PIC X(5)     VALUE "UNION".
           05 PIC X(15)    VALUE SPACES.
           05 PIC X(5)     VALUE "TOTAL".
           05 PIC X(10)    VALUE SPACES.
           05 PIC XXX      VALUE "NET".
           05 PIC X(10)    VALUE SPACES.

       01  HEADINGS-2.
           05 PIC XXX      VALUE SPACES.
           05 PIC X(10)    VALUE "DEPARTMENT".
           05 PIC X(5)     VALUE SPACES.
           05 PIC XXX      VALUE "SSN".
           05 PIC X(17)    VALUE SPACES.
           05 PIC XXXX     VALUE "NAME".
           05 PIC X(14)    VALUE SPACES.
           05 PIC X(5)     VALUE "WAGES".
           05 PIC X(6)     VALUE SPACES.
           05 PIC XXX      VALUE "TAX".
           05 PIC X(6)     VALUE SPACES.
           05 PIC XXX      VALUE "TAX".
           05 PIC X(5)     VALUE SPACES.
           05 PIC XXXX     VALUE "DUES".
           05 PIC XX       VALUE SPACES.
           05 PIC X(9)     VALUE "INSURANCE".
           05 PIC XXX      VALUE SPACES.
           05 PIC X(10)    VALUE "DEDUCTIONS".
           05 PIC X(6)     VALUE SPACES.
           05 PIC X(5)     VALUE "WAGES".
           05 PIC X(9)     VALUE SPACES.

       01  EMPLOYEE-PAYLINE.
           05 CARRIAGE-CONTROL     PIC X.
           05 FILLER               PIC X(5).
           05 O-DEPT               PIC XXX.
           05 FILLER               PIC X(5).
           05 O-SSN                PIC XXXBXXBXXXX.
           05 FILLER               PIC X(4).
           05 O-NAME               PIC X(22).
           05 FILLER               PIC X(3).
           05 O-GROSS-WAGES        PIC $ZZZ9.99.
           05 FILLER               PIC XXX.
           05 O-FED-TAX            PIC $ZZ9.99.
           05 FILLER               PIC XX.
           05 O-STATE-TAX          PIC $ZZ9.99.
           05 FILLER               PIC XX.
           05 O-UNION-DUES         PIC $Z9.99.
           05 FILLER               PIC XX.
           05 O-INS-PREMIUM        PIC $Z9.99.
           05 FILLER               PIC X(6).
           05 O-TOTAL-DEDUCTIONS PIC $ZZ9.99.
           05 FILLER               PIC X(6).
           05 O-NET-WAGES          PIC $ZZZ9.99-.
           05 FILLER               PIC X(9).
```

Coding the PROCEDURE DIVISION

We are now ready to begin coding the PROCEDURE DIVISION. The design tool that the programmer uses as a guide for this task is the program pseudocode or the program flowchart. The transition from pseudocode to actual COBOL statements is very direct in most cases. (The transition from the program flowchart to the coding of the PROCEDURE DIVISION is illustrated in Figure 5.25.) The main-control paragraph 100-Produce-Payroll-Report of the pseudocode and the corresponding main-control paragraph 100-PRODUCE-PAYROLL-REPORT are shown on page 217.

Three procedures are under the direct control of the main-control paragraph. The first one, 200-START-UP, opens the files, thereby making them available to the program; it initializes the flag WS-MORE-RECORDS, and it controls the execution of two third-level procedures, one that begins the production of the report, and the other that accesses the first record of the input file and stores it in the input buffer.

The second procedure under direct control of the primary paragraph is 210-PROCESS-EMPLOYEE-RECORD. Note, however, that control is not sent **automatically** to 210-PROCESS-EMPLOYEE-RECORD. A test must first be performed on the end-of-file-flag WS-MORE-RECORDS to see if it contains the value "NO ". If it does not, then control is sent to the paragraph so that the record in input memory can be processed. To underscore the fact that the test is performed first, we have included the optional phrase

100-Produce-Payroll-Report.
1. Perform 200-Start-Up.
2. Perform 210-Process-Employee-Record until no more records.
3. Perform 220-Finish-Up.
4. Stop the run.

```
100-PRODUCE-PAYROLL-REPORT.
    PERFORM 200-START-UP.
    PERFORM 210-PROCESS-EMPLOYEE-RECORD WITH TEST BEFORE
        UNTIL WS-MORE-RECORDS = "NO ".
    PERFORM 220-FINISH-UP.
    STOP RUN.
```

WITH TEST BEFORE in the PERFORM-UNTIL statement. (Do you recall at what point the flag is assigned the value "NO "?)

The third procedure under direct control of the primary paragraph, namely, 220-FINISH-UP, is executed only after control passes out of the loop created by the PERFORM-UNTIL statement. This procedure simply closes the files and then it returns control to the main-control paragraph, where the final statement, STOP RUN, is executed, thereby returning control from the program back to the operating system.

The correspondences between the 200-level paragraphs of the pseudocode and those of the PROCEDURE DIVISION are shown below.

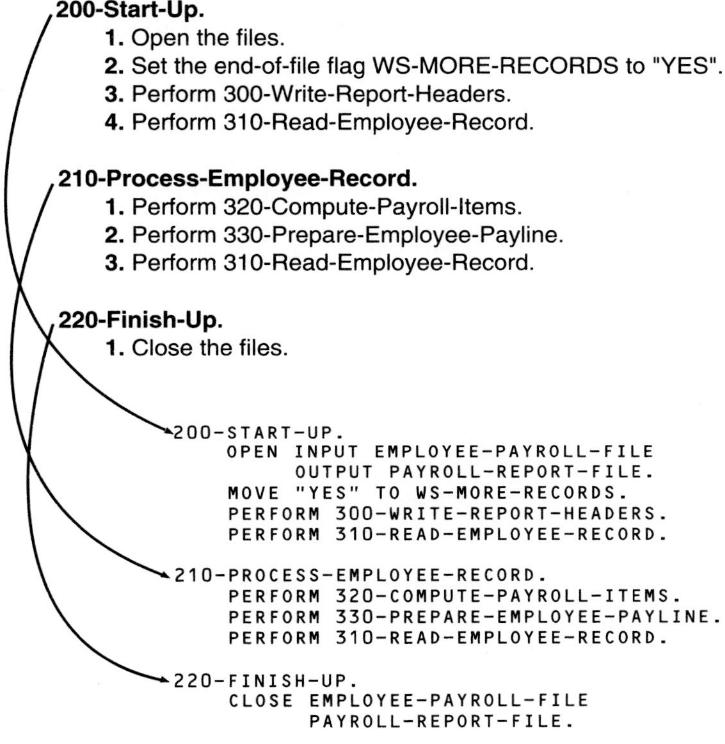

200-Start-Up.
1. Open the files.
2. Set the end-of-file flag WS-MORE-RECORDS to "YES".
3. Perform 300-Write-Report-Headers.
4. Perform 310-Read-Employee-Record.
210-Process-Employee-Record.
1. Perform 320-Compute-Payroll-Items.
2. Perform 330-Prepare-Employee-Payline.
3. Perform 310-Read-Employee-Record.
220-Finish-Up.
1. Close the files.
200-START-UP.
OPEN INPUT EMPLOYEE-PAYROLL-FILE
OUTPUT PAYROLL-REPORT-FILE.
MOVE "YES" TO WS-MORE-RECORDS.
PERFORM 300-WRITE-REPORT-HEADERS.
PERFORM 310-READ-EMPLOYEE-RECORD.
210-PROCESS-EMPLOYEE-RECORD.
PERFORM 320-COMPUTE-PAYROLL-ITEMS.
PERFORM 330-PREPARE-EMPLOYEE-PAYLINE.
PERFORM 310-READ-EMPLOYEE-RECORD.
220-FINISH-UP.
CLOSE EMPLOYEE-PAYROLL-FILE
PAYROLL-REPORT-FILE.

The Procedure 210-PROCESS-EMPLOYEE-RECORD

As noted earlier in the development of the structure chart, the details required to process an employee payroll record are contained in two third-level modules. The paragraph 210-PROCESS-EMPLOYEE-RECORD simply controls the execution of those procedures. Control is sent to the procedure 320-COMPUTE-PAYROLL-ITEMS to compute the gross wages, federal and state taxes, total deductions, and net wages, and then control is sent to the procedure 330-PREPARE-EMPLOYEE-PAYLINE to assign values to all the data fields of the record EMPLOYEE-PAYLINE and finally to write it out.

The writing of an employee's pay line on the printed report completes the processing of the employee record currently in memory. Control is then sent to the procedure 310-READ-EMPLOYEE-RECORD so that the next employee record can be accessed from the input file. (You know by now that at some point the EOF record is read here. When that happens, the flag WS-MORE-RECORDS is given the value "NO " just before control returns to the PERFORM-UNTIL statement in the main-control paragraph.)

Note again that the functions of the procedure 210-PROCESS-EMPLOYEE-RECORD are executed repeatedly until there are no more records in the input file.

Coding the Procedure 320-COMPUTE-PAYROLL-ITEMS

As the procedure name indicates, all the computations that must be performed for an individual employee are contained in the procedure 320-COMPUTE-PAYROLL-ITEMS. According to the pseudocode paragraph 320-Compute-Payroll-Items in Figure 5.10, the first item to be computed is the employee's gross wages. As noted in the pseudocode, the arithmetic is simple:

gross wages = number of hours × the hourly pay rate

The programmer must ask two questions:

1. Which COBOL statement(s) can be used to direct the computer to do a multiplication?
2. Where should the gross wages be stored?

In answer to the latter, the computed gross wages should be stored in the employee work area WS-GROSS-WAGES, since it will be needed as an operand when the taxes and the net wages are computed. If it were stored directly into the field O-GROSS-WAGES, then it could not be used as an operand, since this field contains editing characters. (Operands **must** be stored in **numeric** fields, not numeric-edited fields.)

In answer to the first question, COBOL provides two kinds of arithmetic statements in which multiplications can be performed: the MULTIPLY statement and the COMPUTE statement. We will explain the MULTIPLY statement here and the COMPUTE statement later.

The MULTIPLY Statement

Two standard formats are available for each of the simple arithmetic statements ADD, SUBTRACT, MULTIPLY, and DIVIDE. The formats of the MULTIPLY statement are shown in Figure 5.17. The formats for the others are shown later.

Since the computation of gross wages involves three data items (the operand hours worked, the operand pay rate, and the receiving field gross wages), the second format is the appropriate one to use, as follows:

```
MULTIPLY I-HRS-WORKED BY I-PAY-RATE GIVING WS-GROSS-WAGES.
```

The value stored in I-HRS-WORKED is multiplied by the value stored in I-PAY-RATE, and the result is stored in the work area WS-GROSS-WAGES. (See part 1 of Figure 5.9.)

The values stored in I-HRS-WORKED and I-PAY-RATE remain unchanged after the statement is executed. The only field whose value is changed by the instruction is the receiving field, that is, the field in which the product is stored, WS-GROSS-WAGES.

In general, in format 1, the receiving fields are the ones named after the word BY, and in format 2, the receiving fields are the ones named after the word GIVING. When a numeric value is assigned to a

Figure 5.17 MULTIPLY statement formats and options

```
1. MULTIPLY {identifier-1} BY {identifier-2 [ ROUNDED ]} . . .
            {literal-1   }
        [ON SIZE ERROR imperative-statement-1]
        [NOT ON SIZE ERROR imperative-statement-2]
        [END-MULTIPLY]

2. MULTIPLY {identifier-1} BY {identifier-2}
            {literal-1   }    {literal-2   }
        GIVING {identifier-3 [ ROUNDED ]} . . .
        [ON SIZE ERROR imperative-statement-1]
        [NOT ON SIZE ERROR imperative-statement-2]
        [END-MULTIPLY]
```

receiving field, the numeric characters are stored following the same rules that apply to numeric data transfers, as explained in Chapter 4, "Notes on Data Transfer." A brief summary follows:

1. If the receiving field is an integer field, only the integer portion of the computed value is stored, and it is stored right-justified.
2. If the receiving field is not an integer field, the value is aligned with the decimal point in the receiving field, and then the characters are assigned to the positions to the right and to the left of the decimal point, in each case starting at the decimal point.
3. If the receiving field is a signed field, then the sign is stored as specified by the data description entry for the field. If the receiving field is not a signed field, then only the absolute value is stored, and the sign is lost.

In the examples that follow, a PICTURE is specified for each data item. Sample data values contained in the fields are shown **before** the MULTIPLY statement is executed. The last column shows the values in the fields **after** the statement is executed. An asterisk (*) is used to identify the receiving field.

Example 1:

```
MULTIPLY I-HRS-WORKED BY I-PAY-RATE GIVING WS-GROSS-WAGES.
```

Item	PICTURE	Value Before	Value After
I-HRS-WORKED	99	40	40
I-PAY-RATE	99V99	08.50	08.50
*WS-GROSS-WAGES	S9999V99	+0100.00	+0340.00

The product, 40 × 08.50 = +340.00, is to be stored in WS-GROSS-WAGES. The decimal points in the product and in the receiving field are aligned. Two digits are stored to the right of the decimal point, four to the left, and the sign is stored in the trailing byte. Note that the initial value of +0100.00 in WS-GROSS-WAGES is simply replaced by the incoming value +0340.00.

Example 2:

```
MULTIPLY I-HRS-WORKED BY I-PAY-RATE GIVING WS-GROSS-WAGES.
```

Item	PICTURE	Value Before	Value After
I-HRS-WORKED	99	60	60
I-PAY-RATE	99V99	20.00	20.00
*WS-GROSS-WAGES	S999V99	+340.00	+200.00

The product, 60 × 20.00 = +1200.00, is to be stored in WS-GROSS-WAGES. By aligning the decimal point in the computed value with the one in the receiving field, the positions to the right of the decimal point are assigned zeros. The positions to the left of the decimal point are assigned characters starting at the decimal point; thus, a 0 is stored in the units position, a 0 in the tens position, and a 2 in the hundreds position. There is no remaining byte for the leftmost digit (1). It overflows the receiving field and is truncated. The stored value is +200.00, which is obviously a serious error.

In this example, the receiving field was not large enough to store the product, so a *high-order truncation* occurred. A high-order truncation occurs when the leftmost characters are lost due to an overflow. The programmer must be aware of such possibilities and must guard against them. A simple precaution is to figure out the largest product that could be produced by multiplying hours by pay rate (in this case), and then assign a PICTURE to the receiving field large enough to store the maximum value. For example: 99 (hours) × 99.99 (pay rate) = 9899.01. A PICTURE of S9999V99 for WS-GROSS-WAGES is adequate for all possible values.

Example 3:

```
MULTIPLY RATE BY HOURS.
```

Item	PICTURE	Value Before	Value After
RATE	99V99	05.40	05.40
*HOURS	99	17	91

This is an example of format 1. The receiving field is HOURS. The computed value is 05.40 × 17 = +91.80. Because the receiving field is an *integer* field, the characters to the right of the decimal point in the computed value are lost, the stored value is 91, and the plus (+) sign generated internally is lost, since the receiving field is not signed.

In this statement, the operands are RATE and HOURS, but HOURS is also the receiving field. Note that before the statement is executed, HOURS in fact contains an hours value, whereas after the statement is executed, HOURS contains a wage value. (Some self-documentation is lost by using this format of the MULTIPLY statement unless the first operand is a numeric literal.)

Example 4:

```
MULTIPLY HOURS BY RATE.
```

Item	PICTURE	Value Before	Value After
*RATE	99V99	05.40	91.80
HOURS	99	17	17

In this case, the receiving field is RATE. In storing the computed value, the decimal points in the computed value and in the receiving field are aligned, and all the characters are stored properly. Since the RATE field is not signed, the plus (+) sign is not stored.

Example 5:

```
MULTIPLY .0605 BY WS-GROSS-WAGES.
```

Item	PICTURE	Value Before	Value After
*WS-GROSS-WAGES	S999V99	+340.48	+020.59

In this case, the numeric literal .0605 and the initial value of WS-GROSS-WAGES are multiplied. The product, .0605 × (+340.48) = +20.59904, is to be stored in WS-GROSS-WAGES. By aligning the decimal point in the product with the decimal point in the receiving field, it is obvious that a *low-order truncation* must occur. The stored value is +20.59. The plus (+) sign is stored (in the trailing byte), since the receiving field is signed.

Arithmetic Statement Options

The preceding examples illustrated the following two kinds of errors that can occur when a numeric value is stored into a receiving field:

1. Low-order characters may be lost, as shown in examples 3 and 5.
2. High-order characters may be lost, as shown in example 2.

While it may be true that losing low-order characters is not generally as serious as losing high-order characters, neither should be allowed to happen due to careless programming.

COBOL provides optional entries that can be included in arithmetic statements to prevent high-order truncation and to minimize the effect of low-order truncation. They are the SIZE ERROR and the ROUNDED options, respectively.

ROUNDED

The word ROUNDED can be coded in an arithmetic statement immediately following the name of the receiving field. Its effect is to round off the computed value according to the PICTURE of the receiving field before it is stored in the field.

In the preceding example 3, by using the statement

```
MULTIPLY RATE BY HOURS ROUNDED,
```

the computed value (+91.80) is rounded to the nearest integer, since the PICTURE of HOURS (PIC 99) defines it as an integer. As a result, the value stored in HOURS will be 92, not 91.

The built-in rounding off procedure is the familiar one: If the digit to the right of the position to be rounded is 5, 6, 7, 8, or 9, the value in that position is increased by 1; otherwise, the value is left unchanged. In either case, all the digits to the right of that position are then truncated.

In example 5, the receiving field is WS-GROSS-WAGES. By using the ROUNDED option in the statement

```
MULTIPLY .0605 BY WS-GROSS-WAGES ROUNDED,
```

the product must be stored rounded to the nearest hundredth, since the PICTURE of WS-GROSS-WAGES is S999V99. The value +20.59904 rounded to the nearest hundredth is +20.60. With the ROUNDED option, the value stored in WS-GROSS-WAGES is therefore +020.60, not +020.59.

It is most important to understand that the ROUNDED entry directs the computer to round off the computed value **according to the PICTURE of the receiving field.** If the receiving field has a PICTURE as specified in the following examples, note the effect of the ROUNDED option.

Receiving Field PICTURE	Value Rounded to:
9999	nearest unit (integer)
999V9	nearest tenth (to 1 decimal place)
99V99	nearest hundredth (to 2 decimal places)
9V999	nearest thousandth (to 3 decimal places)

Note: As a general rule, the ROUNDED option should be used in a MULTIPLY statement if the number of decimal places in the receiving field is less than the sum of the decimal places in the factors.

ON SIZE ERROR

To avoid high-order truncation as shown in the preceding example 2, the entry "ON SIZE ERROR imperative-statement" can be coded in an arithmetic statement immediately following the name of the receiving field or after the word ROUNDED if it is used. For instance, the statement

```
MULTIPLY I-HRS-WORKED BY I-PAY-RATE GIVING WS-GROSS-WAGES
    ON SIZE ERROR
        PERFORM 400-PROCESS-SIZE-ERROR
```

directs the computer to proceed as follows:

1. Find the product of I-HRS-WORKED and I-PAY-RATE.
2. Compare the computed value with the size of the receiving field.
3. If the computed value can be stored in WS-GROSS-WAGES without causing an overflow or a high-order truncation, store it, and bypass the instructions in the ON SIZE ERROR clause.
4. If the computed value cannot be stored in WS-GROSS-WAGES without causing a high-order truncation, **do not store it;** simply execute the statements in the ON SIZE ERROR clause.

Example 2 is repeated below, to show the effect of the ON SIZE ERROR option if it is used in the MULTIPLY statement:

Item	PICTURE	Value Before	Value After
I-HRS-WORKED	99	60	60
I-PAY-RATE	99V99	20.00	20.00
*WS-GROSS-WAGES	S999V99	+340.00	+340.00

The product of I-HRS-WORKED and I-PAY-RATE is $60 \times 20.00 = +1200.00$. If +1200.00 were stored in WS-GROSS-WAGES, a high-order truncation would occur. The computed value +1200.00 is therefore **not** stored; WS-GROSS-WAGES retains its initial value of +340.00; and the PERFORM statement in the ON SIZE ERROR clause is executed.

Example 5 is repeated below with the ON SIZE ERROR entry:

```
MULTIPLY .0605 BY WS-GROSS-WAGES
    ON SIZE ERROR
        PERFORM 400-PROCESS-SIZE-ERROR.
```

Item	PICTURE	Value Before	Value After
*WS-GROSS-WAGES	S999V99	+340.48	+020.59

The product of .0605 and WS-GROSS-WAGES is $.0605 \times (+340.48) = +20.59904$. If +20.59904 is stored in WS-GROSS-WAGES, a low-order truncation occurs, but not a high-order truncation. The computed value is therefore stored as +20.59, and the statement in the ON SIZE ERROR clause is bypassed, because there is no size error.

Note: A size error occurs only when the computed value is (mathematically) greater than the largest value that can be stored in the receiving field. In the preceding example, the largest value that can be stored in WS-GROSS-WAGES is 999.99. It is clear that 20.59904 is not greater than 999.99, and consequently there is no size error.

Consider the next example:

```
MULTIPLY ITEM-A BY ITEM-B GIVING ITEM-C
    ON SIZE ERROR
        ADD 1 TO WS-ERROR-CTR
        MOVE MULT-ERROR-MESSAGE TO ERROR-LINE
        WRITE PRINTLINE FROM ERROR-LINE
END-MULTIPLY.
```

In this case, the following statements are true:

1. If the product of the values in ITEM-A and ITEM-B can be stored in ITEM-C without a high-order truncation, it is stored in ITEM-C, and control bypasses the ON SIZE ERROR clause to execute the first statement that follows the scope terminator END-MULTIPLY.
2. If the product of the values in ITEM-A and ITEM-B cannot be stored without causing a high-order truncation, it is not stored, and control passes into the ON SIZE ERROR clause to execute the three statements it contains. Following execution of the WRITE statement, control passes to the first statement following the END-MULTIPLY scope terminator.

Since the ON SIZE ERROR option may contain a number of statements, the END-MULTIPLY can be used to indicate the end of the MULTIPLY statement. In this example, it should be clear that the scope of the MULTIPLY statement could just as well be terminated by a period following the WRITE statement. There are situations, however, in which the period could cause a logic error. Consider the example in Figure 5.18.

In Figure 5.18, it should be clear from the flowchart segment that **two** statements must be executed if ITEM-A < ITEM-X, namely, the MULTIPLY statement (including the SIZE ERROR test) and the statement MOVE ITEM-A TO ITEM-X. If the END-MULTIPLY is removed from the coding, the statement MOVE ITEM-A TO ITEM-X becomes part of the ON SIZE ERROR clause, and it would be executed **only** if there is a size error. Of course, that is not the intent shown in the flowchart segment. Inserting a period

■ **Figure 5.18** Example of END-MULTIPLY scope terminator

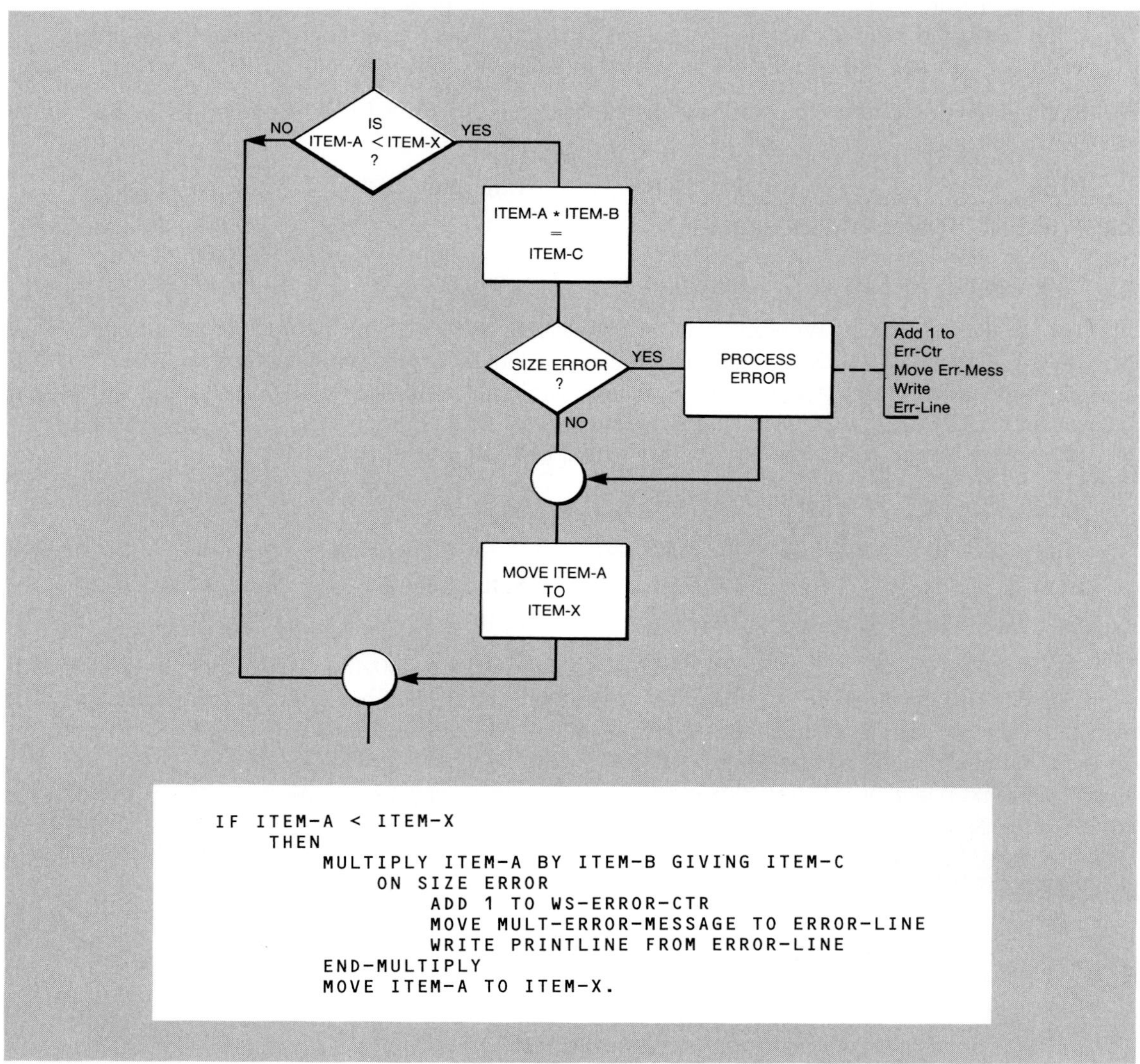


```
IF ITEM-A < ITEM-X
    THEN
        MULTIPLY ITEM-A BY ITEM-B GIVING ITEM-C
            ON SIZE ERROR
                ADD 1 TO WS-ERROR-CTR
                MOVE MULT-ERROR-MESSAGE TO ERROR-LINE
                WRITE PRINTLINE FROM ERROR-LINE
        END-MULTIPLY
        MOVE ITEM-A TO ITEM-X.
```

following the WRITE statement would prevent the statement MOVE ITEM-A TO ITEM-X from being included in the ON SIZE ERROR clause, but it would create another logic error of its own. The period would not only terminate the MULTIPLY statement, but it would terminate the IF statement as well, so that the statement MOVE ITEM-A TO ITEM-X would be executed regardless of the condition ITEM-A < ITEM-X.

You can see that the scope terminator END-MULTIPLY is a simple solution to the kinds of logic problems briefly discussed here.

Note: As a general rule, the ON SIZE ERROR option should be coded in a MULTIPLY statement if the number of positions to the left of the decimal point in the receiving field is less than the sum of the number of digits to the left of the decimal points in the fields containing the factors.

NOT ON SIZE ERROR

COBOL '85 allows the programmer to code an alternate path to the SIZE ERROR path by using the NOT ON SIZE ERROR option. The flowchart segment for the logic of the MULTIPLY statement with the SIZE ERROR test is illustrated by the example shown in Figure 5.19.

If there is a size error, the PERFORM statement in the ON SIZE ERROR clause is executed. When control returns from the procedure 400-PROCESS-SIZE-ERROR, it passes immediately to the first statement following END-MULTIPLY.

If there is no size error, the product is stored into the field WS-GROSS-WAGES, and then control is passed to the NOT ON SIZE ERROR clause. Here, it executes the MOVE statement and then passes on to the first statement following END-MULTIPLY.

Without the availability of the NOT ON SIZE ERROR clause, more cumbersome procedures would have to be used. Such a case is illustrated in Figure 5.20.

The end result obtained in Figure 5.20 is the same as that of Figure 5.19. However, the programmer must define a flag, such as WS-SIZE-ERROR-FLAG, set it to an initial value before the MULTIPLY statement is executed, and then test it to determine if its value has changed upon exiting from the MULTIPLY statement. If it has changed, a size error occurred, and the MOVE statement is not executed; otherwise, the MOVE statement is executed. The alternative paths provided by the two clauses ON SIZE ERROR and NOT ON SIZE ERROR greatly simplify the handling of the previously described situation.

Figure 5.19 SIZE ERROR test paths for the MULTIPLY statement

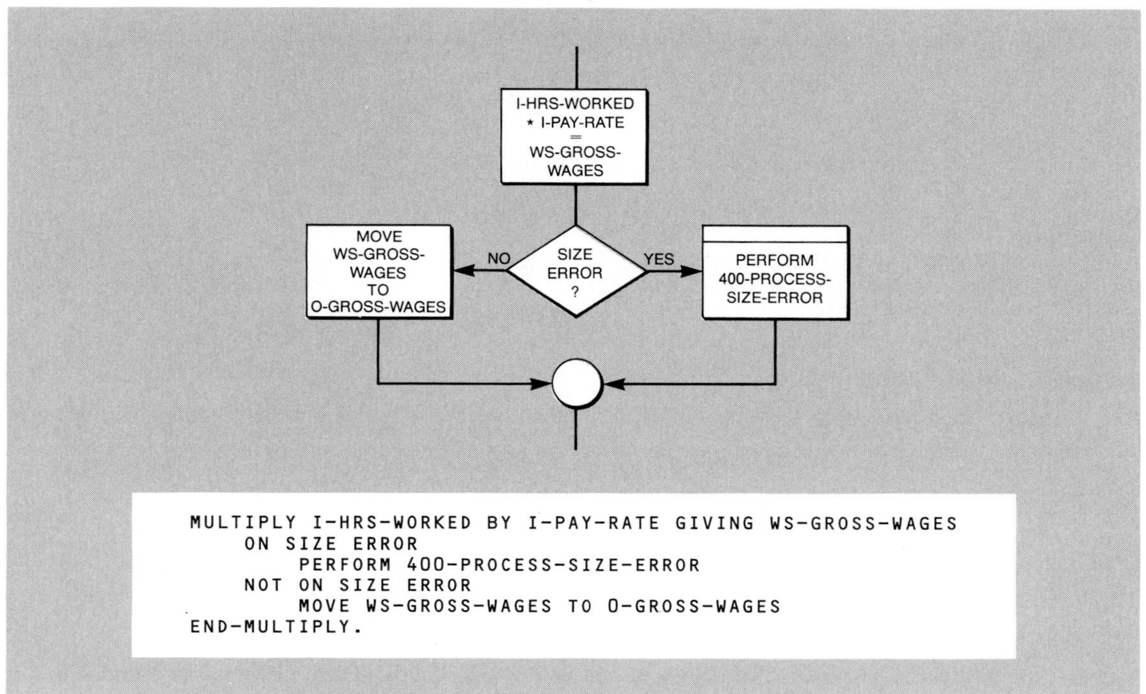


```
MULTIPLY I-HRS-WORKED BY I-PAY-RATE GIVING WS-GROSS-WAGES
     ON SIZE ERROR
          PERFORM 400-PROCESS-SIZE-ERROR
     NOT ON SIZE ERROR
          MOVE WS-GROSS-WAGES TO O-GROSS-WAGES
END-MULTIPLY.
```

■ **Figure 5.20** Logic of Figure 5.19 without the NOT ON SIZE ERROR clause

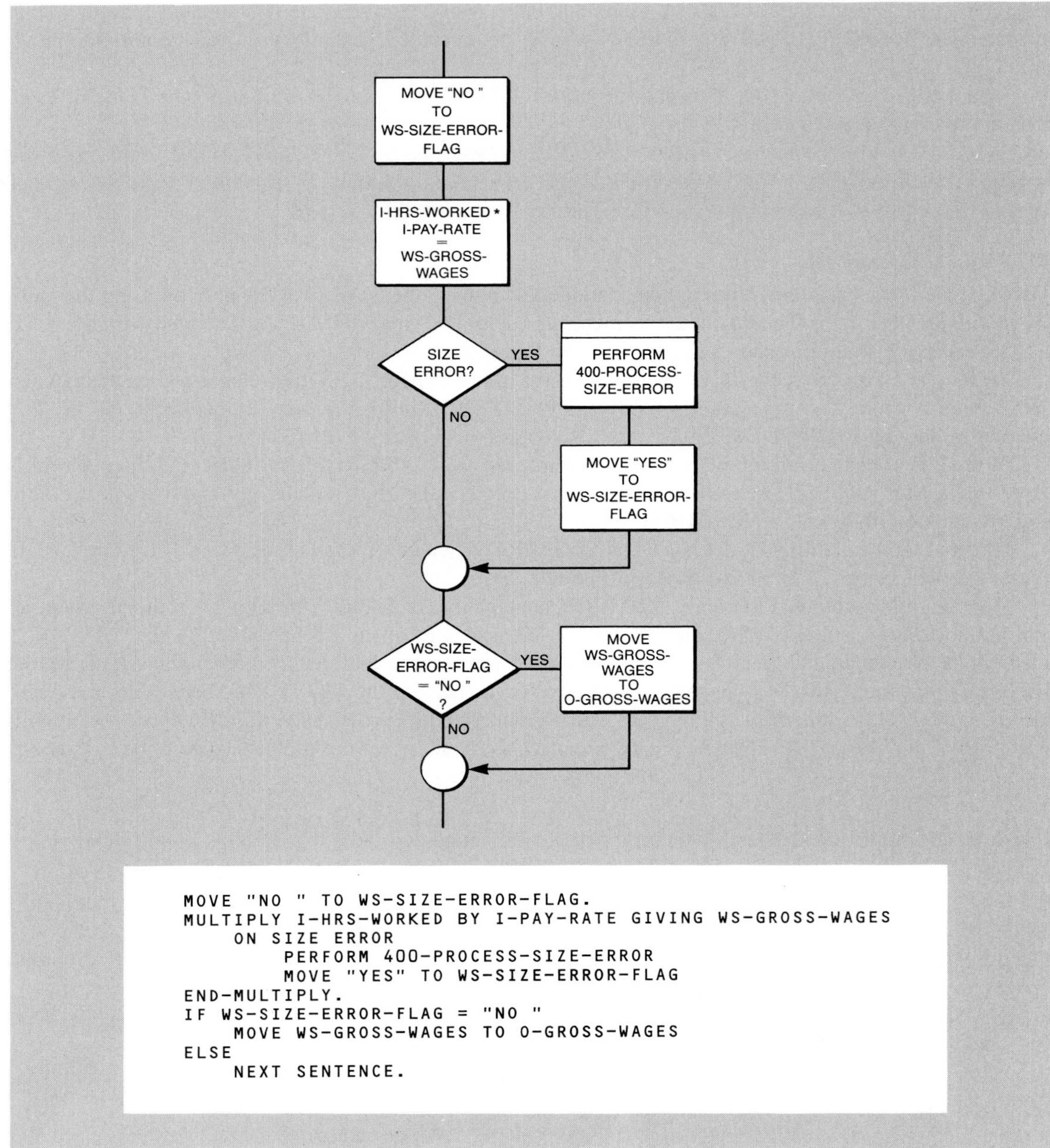

MOVE "NO " TO WS-SIZE-ERROR-FLAG
I-HRS-WORKED * I-PAY-RATE = WS-GROSS-WAGES
SIZE ERROR?
YES
PERFORM 400-PROCESS-SIZE-ERROR
NO
MOVE "YES" TO WS-SIZE-ERROR-FLAG
WS-SIZE-ERROR-FLAG = "NO " ?
YES
MOVE WS-GROSS-WAGES TO O-GROSS-WAGES
NO
MOVE "NO " TO WS-SIZE-ERROR-FLAG.
MULTIPLY I-HRS-WORKED BY I-PAY-RATE GIVING WS-GROSS-WAGES
    ON SIZE ERROR
        PERFORM 400-PROCESS-SIZE-ERROR
        MOVE "YES" TO WS-SIZE-ERROR-FLAG
END-MULTIPLY.
IF WS-SIZE-ERROR-FLAG = "NO "
    MOVE WS-GROSS-WAGES TO O-GROSS-WAGES
ELSE
    NEXT SENTENCE.

Multiple Receiving Fields

Both formats of the MULTIPLY statement allow more than one receiving field to be specified. For instance, the statement

```
MULTIPLY I-HRS-WORKED BY I-PAY-RATE GIVING WS-GROSS-WAGES ROUNDED
                                           O-GROSS-WAGES
```

is equivalent to the two statements

```
MULTIPLY I-HRS-WORKED BY I-PAY-RATE GIVING WS-GROSS-WAGES ROUNDED.
MULTIPLY I-HRS-WORKED BY I-PAY-RATE GIVING O-GROSS-WAGES.
```

Note that the product is rounded before being stored in WS-GROSS-WAGES, but it is not rounded before being stored in O-GROSS-WAGES. That is, the ROUNDED option must be specified for each receiving field for which rounding should occur.

Consider the following situation:

Data Item	PICTURE	Initial Value
ITEM-A	S99	+08
ITEM-B	S99	−35
ITEM-C	S99	+05
ITEM-D	S99	+10
ITEM-X	S99	+30

```
MULTIPLY ITEM-A BY ITEM-B ITEM-C ITEM-D
    ON SIZE ERROR
        MOVE -5 TO ITEM-X
END-MULTIPLY
MULTIPLY ITEM-X BY ITEM-A ITEM-B ITEM-C ITEM-D.
```

A size error condition occurs in the first MULTIPLY statement if **any** of the products to be stored in the receiving fields ITEM-B, ITEM-C, or ITEM-D causes an overflow. However, only the fields for which an overflow would occur retain their initial values; the other fields receive the computed values. The results are shown below:

Values In	After the First MULTIPLY	After the Second MULTIPLY
ITEM-A	+08	−40
ITEM-B	−35	+75
ITEM-C	+40	−25
ITEM-D	+80	−50
ITEM-X	−05	−05

The second MULTIPLY statement does not contain the SIZE ERROR clause. Note the high-order truncation that occurred in ITEM-B.

Rules Governing the Use of the MULTIPLY Statement and Its Options

1. In both formats, the MULTIPLY statement multiplies two operands and stores the result. Both operands must be **numeric** items.
2. In format 1, the value of identifier-1 (or literal-1) is multiplied by the value of identifier-2. The product is stored in identifier-2, thereby replacing its initial value. Identifier-2 is the receiving field.
3. In a MULTIPLY statement of format 1 with multiple receiving fields, each receiving field stores the product of identifier-1 or literal-1 and its initial value.
4. In format 2, the operands are the identifiers or literals preceding the word GIVING. The identifiers following the word GIVING are the receiving fields. The product of the operands is stored in each of the receiving fields, replacing initial values. The receiving fields can be defined as numeric-edited items.
5. Only the value in a receiving field is affected by a MULTIPLY statement. The data values in all other fields remain unchanged.
6. The product is stored in a receiving field following the rules for numeric MOVE statements:
   a. Integer values are stored right-justified in an integer receiving field or to the left of the decimal point (assumed or explicit) in a noninteger receiving field.
   b. Noninteger values are stored on the basis of decimal point (assumed or explicit) alignment.

   Note: Be aware of possible low-order and/or high-order truncation.
7. The sign of a product is stored only if the PICTURE clause that defines the receiving field contains an S in the character string. The sign is stored as specified by the rules for the SIGN clause.
8. If the ROUNDED option is used, the word ROUNDED immediately follows the name of the receiving field. The computed value is rounded according to the PICTURE specified for the receiving field. The effect of a low-order truncation is minimized. If there are multiple receiving fields, rounding occurs only for the receiving fields to which the word ROUNDED is attached.
9. If the ON SIZE ERROR option is used, the phrase ON SIZE ERROR immediately follows the name(s) of the receiving field(s), or the word ROUNDED if it is used. No high-order truncation occurs. Rounding or low-order truncation takes place before the size error check. If there is a size error in any receiving field, the product is **not** stored in that field, and the imperative statement following the phrase ON SIZE ERROR is executed. If there is no size error in any receiving field,

the product is stored in the receiving field(s), and the statement contained in the ON SIZE ERROR clause is not executed. If there are multiple receiving fields, only the fields for which a size error occurs retain their initial values. The other receiving fields store the product.

10. The NOT ON SIZE ERROR option is permissible only as an alternative path to the ON SIZE ERROR option. If there is no size error, the statement in the NOT ON SIZE ERROR clause is executed after the product is stored.
11. The statements in the [NOT] ON SIZE ERROR options must be imperative statements. No conditional statement is allowed.
12. END-MULTIPLY is the scope terminator. A MULTIPLY statement can be terminated either by a period or by the END-MULTIPLY.
13. The use of the ROUNDED and ON SIZE ERROR options is recommended as noted to minimize the effect of low-order truncations and to prevent high-order truncations of computed values, respectively.

Back to the Paragraph 320-COMPUTE-PAYROLL-ITEMS

In the sample program, the instruction to compute the gross wages

```
MULTIPLY I-HRS-WORKED BY I-PAY-RATE GIVING WS-GROSS-WAGES
```

does not require the use of the ROUNDED or the ON SIZE ERROR options for the following reasons:

1. There are as many decimal places in the receiving field WS-GROSS-WAGES as there are in the factors (only two are needed).
2. There are as many positions to the left of the decimal point in WS-GROSS-WAGES as the sum of the positions to the left of the decimal points in the factors (four are needed).

The next entry in the pseudocode paragraph 320-Compute-Payroll-Items indicates that the federal tax on the employee's gross wages must be computed. The applicable federal tax rate is supplied on the input record in the field I-FED-TAX-RATE. The amount of gross wages is stored in the employee's work area WS-GROSS-WAGES.

The programmer must ask the same two questions again:

1. Which arithmetic statements can be used?
2. Where should the federal tax amount be stored?

In answer to the first question, two COBOL statements can be used, the MULTIPLY and the COMPUTE. We will use the MULTIPLY statement again. In answer to the second question, we will store the federal tax in the work area WS-FED-TAX. (See part 2 of Figure 5.9.)

The MULTIPLY statement is as follows:

```
MULTIPLY WS-GROSS-WAGES BY I-FED-TAX-RATE
    GIVING WS-FED-TAX ROUNDED.
```

Note that the ROUNDED option is used because there are four decimal places in the factors WS-GROSS-WAGES and I-FED-TAX-RATE, but only two in the receiving field WS-FED-TAX. The computed tax will be rounded to the nearest penny (nearest hundredth), since the PICTURE of WS-FED-TAX is PIC S999V99. The sign is stored in the trailing byte.

The ON SIZE ERROR option could be used, but it is not reasonable to expect that the federal tax will exceed $999.99 on weekly wages.

The next entry in the pseudocode paragraph 320-Compute-Payroll-Items indicates that the state tax on the employee's gross wages must be computed. The state tax rate is supplied on the employee's input record in the field I-STATE-TAX-RATE, and the gross wages are stored in the employee's work area WS-GROSS-WAGES. We will store the result in the employee's work area WS-STATE-TAX. (See part 3 of Figure 5.9.) The required calculation is again a multiplication, and we decide to use the following MULTIPLY statement:

```
MULTIPLY WS-GROSS-WAGES BY I-STATE-TAX-RATE
    GIVING WS-STATE-TAX ROUNDED.
```

Note that the ROUNDED option is used, and the ON SIZE ERROR option is not used, for the reasons stated above.

The fourth entry in the pseudocode paragraph 320-Compute-Payroll-Items indicates that the employee's total payroll deductions should now be computed. Note that at this point in the processing of the employee payroll record, the amounts to be deducted for the union dues and insurance premium are still contained in input memory in the fields I-UNION-DUES and I-INS-PREMIUM, respectively, and the amounts to be deducted for the federal and state taxes are in the employee's work areas WS-FED-TAX and WS-STATE-TAX, respectively.

The programmer again asks the two questions:

1. Which arithmetic statement should be used to find the total deductions?
2. Where should the total of the deductions be stored?

COBOL allows additions to be performed in either ADD statements or COMPUTE statements. We will use the ADD statement here and explain the COMPUTE statement later. In answer to the second question, the total deductions should be stored in the employee's work area WS-TOTAL-DEDUCTIONS, since this amount will be needed as an operand to compute the net wages for the week. (See part 4 of Figure 5.9.)

The ADD Statement

Two formats of the ADD statement are shown in Figure 5.21.

In format 1, all the data items are *operands,* whereas in format 2, only the data items that precede the word GIVING are operands; in format 1, the data items following the word TO are *receiving fields* as well, whereas in format 2, the data items following the word GIVING are receiving fields only.

In our program, the operands are WS-FED-TAX, WS-STATE-TAX, I-UNION-DUES, and I-INS-PREMIUM, and their sum is to be stored in WS-TOTAL-DEDUCTIONS. In this case, format 2 is more appropriate, and the ADD statement is as follows:

```
ADD WS-FED-TAX WS-STATE-TAX I-UNION-DUES I-INS-PREMIUM
    GIVING WS-TOTAL-DEDUCTIONS.
```

In this statement, the values currently stored in WS-FED-TAX, WS-STATE-TAX, I-UNION-DUES, and I-INS-PREMIUM are added, and the result is stored in the receiving field WS-TOTAL-DEDUCTIONS.

Consider the following examples. (The asterisk [*] identifies the receiving field.)

Example 1:

```
ADD ON-HAND ON-ORDER TO TOTAL.
```

Item	PICTURE	Value Before	Value After
ON-HAND	999	235	235
ON-ORDER	999	500	500
*TOTAL	S999	+150	+885

In this case, there are three operands: ON-HAND, ON-ORDER, and TOTAL. The value in the field ON-HAND is added to the value in the field ON-ORDER, and this sum is added to the value in the field TOTAL. The result is then stored in the field TOTAL, with its sign in the trailing byte.

Figure 5.21 ADD statement formats and options

```
1. ADD {identifier-1} . . . TO {identifier-2 [ ROUNDED ]} . . .
       {literal-1   }
       [ON SIZE ERROR imperative-statement-1]
       [NOT ON SIZE ERROR imperative-statement-2]
       [END-ADD]

2. ADD {identifier-1} . . . TO {identifier-2}
       {literal-1   }          {literal-2   }
       GIVING {identifier-3 [ ROUNDED ]} . . .
       [ON SIZE ERROR imperative-statement-1]
       [NOT ON SIZE ERROR imperative-statement-2]
       [END-ADD]
```

Example 2:

```
ADD ON-HAND ON-ORDER GIVING TOTAL.
```

Item	PICTURE	Value Before	Value After
ON-HAND	999	235	235
ON-ORDER	999	500	500
*TOTAL	S999	+150	+735

In this case, there are only two operands: ON-HAND and ON-ORDER. The value in the field ON-HAND is added to the value in the field ON-ORDER, and this sum is then stored in the receiving field TOTAL, with its sign in the trailing byte. Note that the previous value in the field TOTAL is **not** an operand; it is simply replaced by the sum of the values in ON-HAND and ON-ORDER.

In both examples, the values of ON-HAND and ON-ORDER remain unchanged after the execution of the ADD statement, but the value of TOTAL has changed. Again, note that there are three operands in example 1, but only two in example 2.

Example 3:

```
ADD ON-HAND TO ON-ORDER GIVING TOTAL.
```

In format 2, the word **TO** is a new option supported in COBOL '85. It is not allowed in earlier standards. The net effect of this statement is identical to that of example 2. The receiving field is TOTAL, and the operands ON-HAND and ON-ORDER retain their initial values.

Example 4:

```
ADD ON-HAND ON-ORDER TO TOTAL.
```

Item	PICTURE	Value Before	Value After
ON-HAND	999	250	250
ON-ORDER	999	500	500
*TOTAL	S999	+250	+000

In this case, the ADD statement has produced the sum 1000. This sum must be stored in the field TOTAL. Since the receiving field is defined as a three-byte field, only the three rightmost digits can be stored, and an overflow condition occurs. The programmer must always guard against high-order truncations. A simple procedure is to make the receiving field of a computed value always large enough to store the largest possible value. In this ADD statement, simply defining TOTAL as a four-byte field would have been sufficient to avoid the overflow.

ADD Statement Options

The two options discussed in relation to the MULTIPLY statement, the ROUNDED and ON SIZE ERROR options, can also be used in any of the formats of the ADD statement. Examine the following examples:

Example 5:

```
ADD ON-HAND ON-ORDER TO TOTAL
    ON SIZE ERROR
        PERFORM 400-PROCESS-SIZE-ERROR.
```

Item	PICTURE	Value Before	Value After
ON-HAND	999	250	250
ON-ORDER	999	500	500
*TOTAL	S999	+250	+250

In this case, because of the ON SIZE ERROR option, the computed sum, +1000, is **not** stored, since a high-order truncation would occur. Rather, the imperative statement contained in the ON SIZE ERROR clause, namely, PERFORM 400-PROCESS-SIZE-ERROR, is executed, and the value initially in TOTAL remains unchanged.

Example 6:

```
ADD MED-EXP TAXES TO MISC-DEDUCTIONS
    GIVING TOTAL-DEDUCTIONS ROUNDED.
```

Item	PICTURE	Value Before	Value After
MED-EXP	9999V99	2342.35	2342.35
TAXES	9999V99	1974.76	1974.76
MISC-DEDUCTIONS	9999V99	8450.82	8450.82
*TOTAL-DEDUCTIONS	$ZZZZ9	$54320	$12788

In this case, the operands are MED-EXP, TAXES, and MISC-DEDUCTIONS. The receiving field is TOTAL-DEDUCTIONS. The computed sum, 2342.35 + 1974.76 + 8470.82 = +12787.93, must be rounded according to the PICTURE of the receiving field TOTAL-DEDUCTIONS. This is a numeric-edited field that stores only an integer value. The sum is therefore rounded to the nearest integer, and it is stored as $12788.

Example 7:

```
ADD ON-HAND ON-ORDER TO TOTAL
    ON SIZE ERROR
        PERFORM 400-PROCESS-SIZE-ERROR
    NOT ON SIZE ERROR
        MOVE TOTAL TO O-TOTAL
        WRITE PRINTLINE FROM TOTAL-LINE.
```

The three data items in the ADD statement are operands, and TOTAL is the receiving field. The ON SIZE ERROR and NOT ON SIZE ERROR options provide alternative paths based on the results of the size error test. For instance, with the data values and specifications in example 1, the sum of the operands is +885. The size error test indicates that there is no size error, so the sum, +885, is stored in the field TOTAL, and control bypasses the ON SIZE ERROR clause and executes the MOVE and WRITE statements in the NOT ON SIZE ERROR clause. With the data values and specifications in example 4, the sum of the operands is +1000. The size error test indicates that there is a size error. Therefore, the sum, +1000, is not stored in the receiving field TOTAL, and control executes the PERFORM statement in the ON SIZE ERROR clause and then bypasses the NOT ON SIZE ERROR clause to execute the first statement that follows the period.

The example in Figure 5.22 illustrates the ADD statement scope terminator END-ADD. You can see on the flowchart segment that if the value in the field WK-RECEIPTS is zero, then the ADD statement with the size error test is executed, and, regardless of the outcome of the size error test, a MOVE and a WRITE statement must be executed. That is, the alternative paths provided by the ON SIZE ERROR and NOT ON SIZE ERROR options must both ultimately lead to the MOVE statement. The END-ADD is properly positioned after the statement in the NOT ON SIZE ERROR clause. If there is a size error, the PERFORM in the ON SIZE ERROR clause is executed, and then control is sent to the first statement following END-ADD. If there is no size error, the PERFORM in the NOT ON SIZE ERROR clause is executed, and then control is sent to the first statement following END-ADD.

If the END-ADD scope terminator is removed from the coding, both the MOVE and WRITE statements necessarily become part of the NOT ON SIZE ERROR clause, and, consequently, are executed only if there is no size error. Of course, that is a logic error.

If a period is used to end the ADD statement, it also terminates the IF statement. As a result, the MOVE and WRITE statements are executed regardless of the value of WK-RECEIPTS. That is also a logic error.

The eight preceding examples have illustrated all the options of the ADD statement. Other than the nature of the arithmetic operations, these options are the same as the ones discussed earlier for the MULTIPLY statement, and they will also apply to the remaining arithmetic statements.

Rules Governing the Use of the ADD Statement and Its Options

1. In both formats, the ADD statement adds two or more operands and stores the sum. All operands must be **numeric** items.
2. In format 1, all the data items are operands. The values of the operands before the word TO are added. This sum is then added to the value of any identifier that follows the word TO, and the result is stored in that identifier. All identifiers that follow the word TO are receiving fields.

Figure 5.22 Example illustrating use of the END-ADD scope terminator

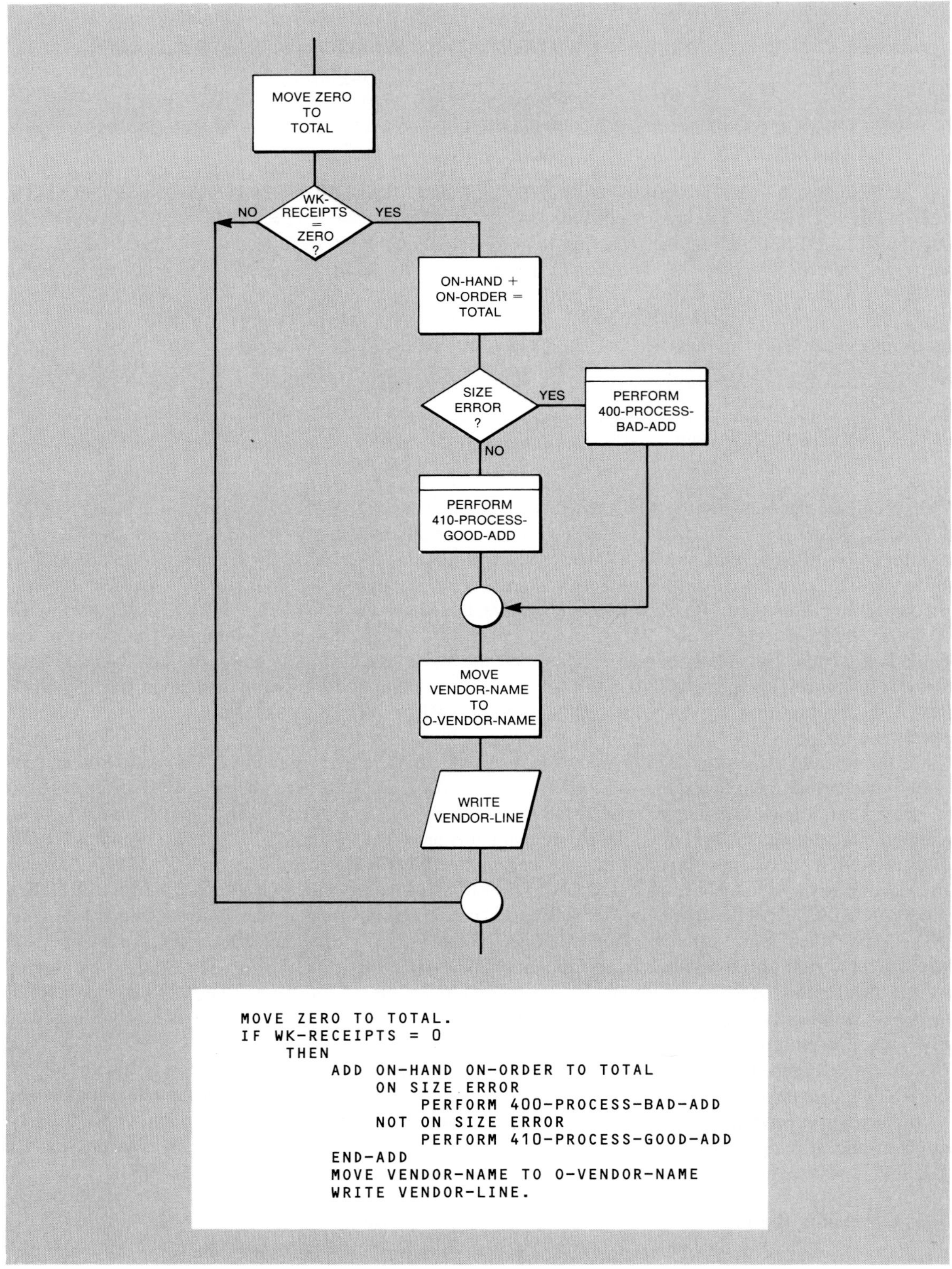


```
MOVE ZERO TO TOTAL.
IF WK-RECEIPTS = 0
    THEN
        ADD ON-HAND ON-ORDER TO TOTAL
            ON SIZE ERROR
                PERFORM 400-PROCESS-BAD-ADD
            NOT ON SIZE ERROR
                PERFORM 410-PROCESS-GOOD-ADD
        END-ADD
        MOVE VENDOR-NAME TO O-VENDOR-NAME
        WRITE VENDOR-LINE.
```

3. In format 2, the operands are the data items that precede the word GIVING. The values of the operands are added. This sum is then stored in each identifier that follows the word GIVING. All identifiers that follow the word GIVING are receiving fields. These receiving fields are allowed to be numeric-edited items.
4. Only the value in a receiving field is affected by an ADD statement. The values in all other fields remain unchanged.
5. The sum is stored in a receiving field following the rules for a numeric MOVE statement:
   a. Integer values are stored right-justified in an integer receiving field or to the left of the decimal point (assumed or explicit) in a noninteger receiving field.
   b. Noninteger values are stored on the basis of decimal point (assumed or explicit) alignment.

   Note: Be aware of possible low-order and/or high-order truncation.
6. The sign of a sum is stored only if the PICTURE clause that defines the receiving field contains an S in the character string. The sign is stored as specified by the rules for the SIGN clause.
7. If the ROUNDED option is used, the word ROUNDED immediately follows the name of the receiving field. The computed value is rounded according to the PICTURE specified for the receiving field. The effect of a low-order truncation is minimized. If there are multiple receiving fields, rounding occurs only for the receiving fields to which the word ROUNDED is attached.
8. If the ON SIZE ERROR option is used, the phrase ON SIZE ERROR immediately follows the name(s) of the receiving field(s), or the word ROUNDED if it is used. No high-order truncation occurs. Rounding or low-order truncation takes place before the size error check. If there is a size error in any receiving field, the sum is **not** stored in that field, and the imperative statement following the phrase ON SIZE ERROR is executed. If there is no size error in any receiving field, the sum is stored in the receiving field(s), and the statement contained in the ON SIZE ERROR clause is not executed. If there are multiple receiving fields, only the fields for which a size error occurs retain their initial values. The other receiving fields store the sum.
9. The NOT ON SIZE ERROR option is permissible only as an alternative path to the ON SIZE ERROR option. If there is no size error, the statement in the NOT ON SIZE ERROR clause is executed after the sum is stored.
10. The statements in the [NOT] ON SIZE ERROR options must be imperative statements. No conditional statement is allowed.
11. END-ADD is the scope terminator. An ADD statement can be terminated by either a period or END-ADD.
12. The use of the ROUNDED and ON SIZE ERROR options is recommended as noted to minimize the effect of low-order truncations and prevent high-order truncations of computed values.

Back to the Paragraph 320-COMPUTE-PAYROLL-ITEMS

In the sample program, the statement that computes the total deductions,

```
ADD WS-FED-TAX WS-STATE-TAX I-UNION-DUES I-INS-PREMIUM
    GIVING WS-TOTAL-DEDUCTIONS,
```

does not include the ROUNDED and the ON SIZE ERROR options. The data in the data file has been validated, and it is felt that weekly deductions from gross wages will never exceed $999.99. In other arithmetic computations where the values are not restricted by real-life situations like the ones that exist in a payroll problem, it is advisable to use the options. Furthermore, whenever a programmer is concerned about possible data-entry errors, then the options should be used.

The fifth and final entry in the pseudocode paragraph 320-Compute-Payroll-Items indicates that the employee's net wages for the week must now be computed. Again, the arithmetic is simple: The net wages are obtained by subtracting the total deductions for the week from the gross wages for the week.

Once more, the programmer asks the two questions:

1. Which arithmetic statement can be used to compute the net wages?
2. Where should the net wages be stored?

In answer to the first question, either the SUBTRACT statement or the COMPUTE statement can be used. Our decision is to use the SUBTRACT statement. In answer to the second question, the amount of net wages is not needed as an operand in any other arithmetic statement, so the amount **could** be stored directly into the edited field O-NET-WAGES of the output record EMPLOYEE-PAYLINE. However, we will store it in the employee's work area WS-NET-WAGES for two reasons: First, the internal data organization is clearer and more consistent with the treatment of the other computed values; and second, it will be useful in the sample program of the next chapter. (See part 5 of Figure 5.9.)

The SUBTRACT Statement

Two formats of the SUBTRACT statement are shown in Figure 5.23. Of the two formats, the second one is more appropriate to compute the net wages. Recall that the needed values are stored in the employee's work areas WS-GROSS-WAGES and WS-TOTAL-DEDUCTIONS. The statement is simply as follows:

```
SUBTRACT WS-TOTAL-DEDUCTIONS FROM WS-GROSS-WAGES
    GIVING WS-NET-WAGES.
```

In this statement, the value in the field WS-TOTAL-DEDUCTIONS is subtracted from the value in the field WS-GROSS-WAGES, and the result is stored in the field WS-NET-WAGES.

In format 1, all the data items are operands, and the identifiers following the word FROM store the results; whereas in format 2, all the data items before the word GIVING are operands, and the identifiers following the word GIVING are receiving fields only. Consider the following examples.

Example 1:

```
SUBTRACT SOLD FROM ON-HAND.
```

Item	PICTURE	Value Before	Value After
SOLD	999	075	075
*ON-HAND	999	500	425

In this case, there are two operands, SOLD and ON-HAND. The value in the field SOLD is subtracted from the value in the field ON-HAND, and the result is stored in the field ON-HAND. Note that the value in the field SOLD does not change.

Example 2:

```
SUBTRACT SOLD DAMAGED FROM ON-HAND.
```

Item	PICTURE	Value Before	Value After
SOLD	999	075	075
DAMAGED	999	020	020
*ON-HAND	999	500	405

In this case, there are three operands, SOLD, DAMAGED, and ON-HAND. The value in the field SOLD is added to the value in the field DAMAGED, their sum is subtracted from the value in the field ON-HAND, and the result is stored in the field ON-HAND. The values in the field SOLD and in the field DAMAGED remain unchanged.

Figure 5.23 SUBTRACT statement formats and options

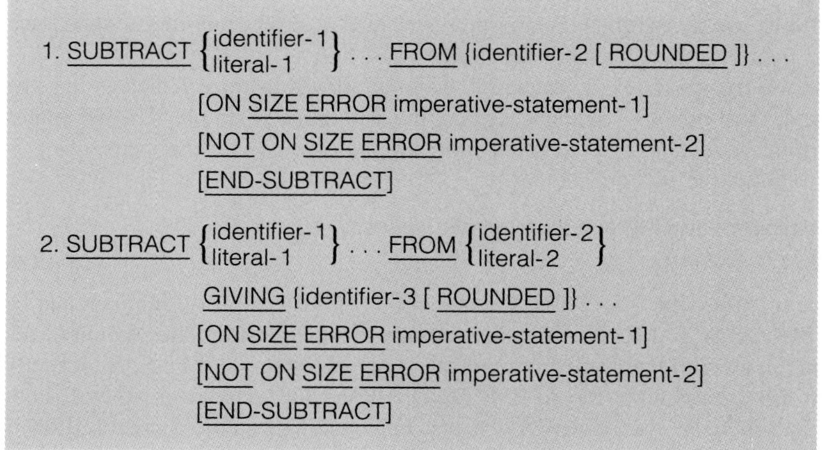

Example 3:

```
SUBTRACT SOLD DAMAGED FROM ON-HAND GIVING NET-AVAILABLE.
```

Item	PICTURE	Value Before	Value After
SOLD	999	075	075
DAMAGED	999	020	020
ON-HAND	999	500	500
*NET-AVAILABLE	999	595	405

In this case, the operands are again SOLD, DAMAGED, and ON-HAND. The sum of the values in the fields SOLD and DAMAGED is subtracted from the value in the field ON-HAND, and the result is stored in the field NET-AVAILABLE. The fields ON-HAND, SOLD, and DAMAGED retain their initial values, but the initial value in the field NET-AVAILABLE is replaced by the computed value.

Example 4:

```
SUBTRACT CHECK FROM ACCT-BALANCE.
```

Item	PICTURE	Value Before	Value After
CHECK	99999V99	00210.50	00210.50
*ACCT-BALANCE	S99999V99	+00050.00	–00160.50

In this case, the value in the field CHECK is subtracted from the value in the field ACCT-BALANCE, and the result is stored in ACCT-BALANCE.

It is important to realize that a subtraction can produce a negative remainder. An overdrawn checking account is unfortunately a too-common occurrence. The programmer must make provisions for storing negative values by inserting S in the character string of the PICTURE clause that defines such an item.

In example 4, if the S were removed from the PICTURE clause, only the absolute value of the result, namely 160.50, would be stored in the field ACCT-BALANCE. The operating system does not flag such errors. It is solely the programmer's responsibility to define any data item as *signed* data.

There are two precautions the programmer should exercise to make sure that signs (+ and –) attached to numeric values are not unintentionally dropped:

1. If the signed value is to be stored in a numeric field, the character string defining the numeric field should begin with an S.
2. If the signed value is to be stored in a numeric-edited field (for printout purposes), the editing character "+" or the editing character "–" should be inserted either as the leftmost or as the rightmost character in the character string that defines the edited field. (In some particular applications, the editing characters CR and DB are preferable to the plus and minus signs.)

Example 5:

```
SUBTRACT CHECK FROM ACCT-BALANCE GIVING OUT-BALANCE.
```

Item	PICTURE	Value Before	Value After
CHECK	99999V99	00210.50	00210.50
ACCT-BALANCE	S99999V99	+00050.00	+00050.00
*OUT-BALANCE	$ZZ,ZZ9.99–	$ 1,450.95	$ 160.50–

In this case, the value in the field CHECK is subtracted from the value in the field ACCT-BALANCE, and the result is stored in the field OUT-BALANCE. The values of the data items CHECK and ACCT-BALANCE remain unchanged. If there were no sign editing character, "–" in this case, the value –160.50 would simply be stored without the minus sign and would then be printed as the unsigned number $ 160.50. A serious error indeed!

The ROUNDED and ON SIZE ERROR options that were illustrated for the MULTIPLY and ADD statements are both available for use in the SUBTRACT statement as well, and their functions are the same. The ROUNDED option rounds off the computed value according to the PICTURE of the receiving field, and it minimizes the effect of a low-order truncation. The ON SIZE ERROR option tests the computed value against the receiving field, and if a high-order truncation is to occur, the value is not stored; rather, the imperative statement in the ON SIZE ERROR clause is executed, thus preventing a high-order truncation from taking place. The NOT ON SIZE ERROR clause provides an alternative path to the SIZE ERROR clause, and the entry END-SUBTRACT can be used as the scope terminator for the SUBTRACT statement.

Rules Governing the Use of the SUBTRACT Statement and Its Options

1. In both formats, the SUBTRACT statement subtracts one numeric item, or the sum of two or more numeric items, from one or more numeric items, and stores the result(s). All operands must be **numeric** items.
2. In format 1, all the data items are operands. The sum of the data items before the word FROM is subtracted from any identifier following the word FROM, and the result is stored in that identifier. All identifiers following the word FROM are receiving fields.
3. In format 2, the operands are the data items that precede the word GIVING. The sum of the data items that precede the word FROM is subtracted from the data item following the word FROM, and the result is stored in each identifier following the word GIVING. All identifiers following the word GIVING are receiving fields. These receiving fields are allowed to be numeric-edited items.
4. Only the value in a receiving field is affected by a SUBTRACT statement. The values in all other fields remain unchanged.
5. The result of a SUBTRACT statement is stored following the rules for a numeric MOVE statement:
   a. Integer values are stored right-justified in an integer receiving field or to the left of the decimal point (assumed or explicit) in a noninteger receiving field.
   b. Noninteger values are stored on the basis of decimal point (assumed or explicit) alignment.
   Note: Be aware of possible low-order and/or high-order truncation.
6. The sign of the result of a subtraction is stored only if the PICTURE clause that defines the receiving field contains an S in the character string. The sign is stored as specified by the rules for the SIGN clause.
7. If the ROUNDED option is used, the word ROUNDED immediately follows the name of the receiving field. The computed value is rounded according to the PICTURE specified for the receiving field. The effect of a low-order truncation is minimized. If there are multiple receiving fields, rounding occurs only for the receiving fields to which the word ROUNDED is attached.
8. If the ON SIZE ERROR option is used, the phrase ON SIZE ERROR immediately follows the name(s) of the receiving field(s), or the word ROUNDED if it is used. No high-order truncation occurs. Rounding or low-order truncation takes place before the size error check. If there is a size error in any receiving field, the result of the subtraction is **not** stored in that field, and the imperative statement following the phrase ON SIZE ERROR is executed. If there is no size error in any receiving field, the result of the subtraction is stored in the receiving field(s), and the statement contained in the ON SIZE ERROR clause is not executed. If there are multiple receiving fields, only the fields for which a size error occurs retain their initial values. The other receiving fields store the computed value.
9. The NOT ON SIZE ERROR option is permissible only as an alternative path to the ON SIZE ERROR option. If there is no size error, the statement in the NOT ON SIZE ERROR clause is executed after the result of the subtraction is stored.
10. The statements in the [NOT] ON SIZE ERROR options must be imperative statements. No conditional statement is allowed.
11. END-SUBTRACT is the scope terminator. A SUBTRACT statement can be terminated by either a period or END-SUBTRACT.
12. The use of the ROUNDED and ON SIZE ERROR options is recommended as noted to respectively minimize the effect of low-order truncations and prevent high-order truncations of computed values.

Back to the Paragraph 320-COMPUTE-PAYROLL-ITEMS

All the arithmetic operations specified in the pseudocode paragraph 320-Compute-Payroll-Items have now been coded as COBOL statements in the PROCEDURE DIVISION paragraph 320-COMPUTE-PAYROLL-ITEMS. The correspondence between these two paragraphs is shown on the next page. Note that the results of the arithmetic operations have been stored in the employee's work areas in working storage.

320-Compute-Payroll-Items.
1. Multiply input hours-worked by input hourly pay-rate to equal gross-wages.
2. Multiply gross-wages by input federal-tax-rate to equal federal-tax.
3. Multiply gross-wages by input state-tax-rate to equal state-tax.
4. Add federal-tax, state-tax, input union-dues, and input insurance-premium to equal total-deductions.
5. Subtract total-deductions from gross-wages to equal net-wages.

```
320-COMPUTE-PAYROLL-ITEMS.
    MULTIPLY I-HRS-WORKED BY I-PAY-RATE GIVING WS-GROSS-WAGES.
    MULTIPLY WS-GROSS-WAGES BY I-FED-TAX-RATE
        GIVING WS-FED-TAX ROUNDED.
    MULTIPLY WS-GROSS-WAGES BY I-STATE-TAX-RATE
        GIVING WS-STATE-TAX ROUNDED.
    ADD WS-FED-TAX WS-STATE-TAX I-UNION-DUES I-INS-PREMIUM
        GIVING WS-TOTAL-DEDUCTIONS.
    SUBTRACT WS-TOTAL-DEDUCTIONS FROM WS-GROSS-WAGES
        GIVING WS-NET-WAGES.
```

Coding the Procedure 330-PREPARE-EMPLOYEE-PAYLINE

The last pseudocode paragraph that must be converted to COBOL code is 330-Prepare-Employee-Payline. No new statements are needed in this paragraph, and the coding is direct. The first task is to transfer the appropriate data from the current source fields to the data fields of the record EMPLOYEE-PAYLINE. The employee's department number, Social Security number, name, union dues, and insurance premium are transferred from fields of the input record, whereas the gross wages, federal tax, state tax, total deductions, and net wages are transferred from the employee work areas. These data transfers are illustrated in Figure 5.24. They are coded as MOVE statements.

Figure 5.24 Data transferred to output record EMPLOYEE-PAYLINE from input memory and from working storage

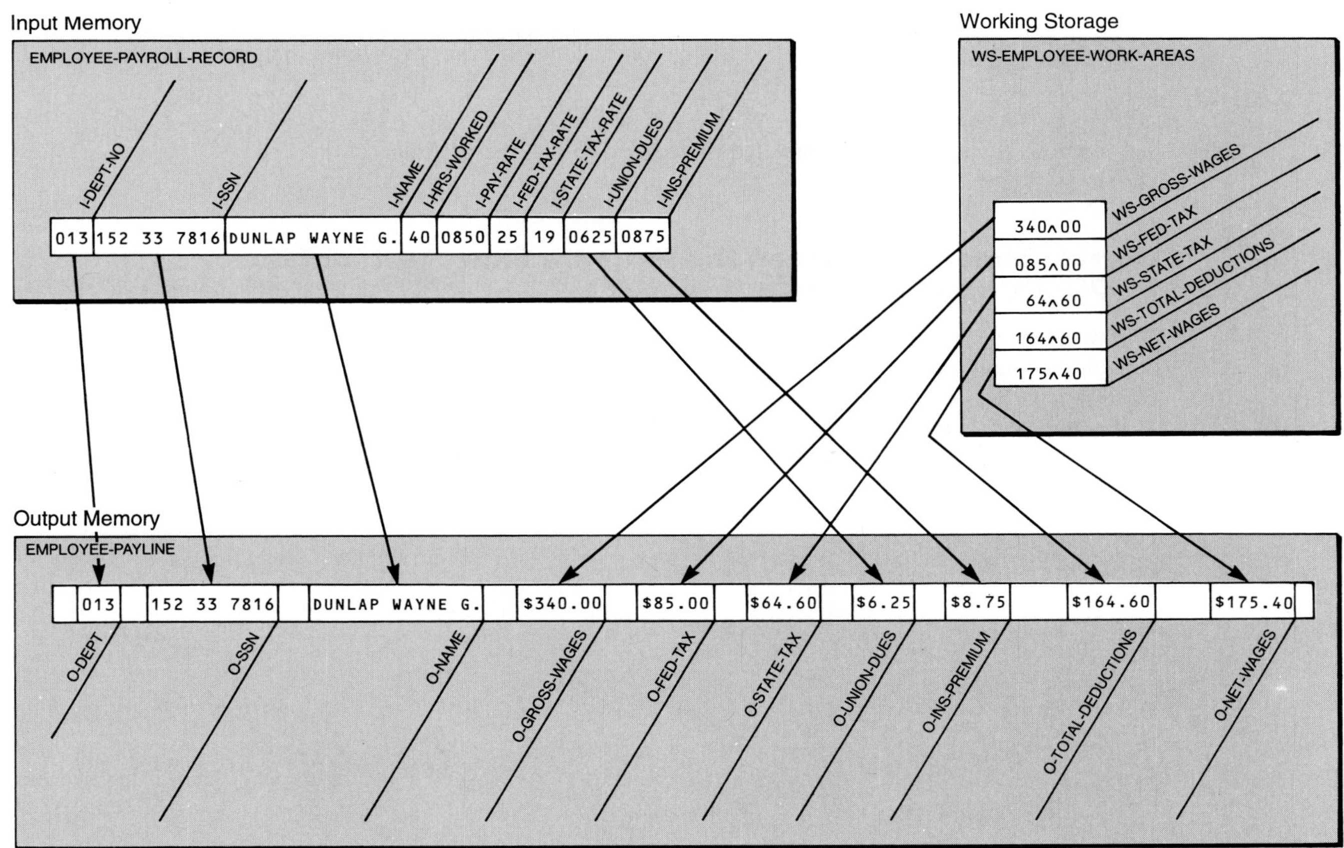

The final task consists of writing the output record EMPLOYEE-PAYLINE onto the print file PAYROLL-REPORT-FILE. The FROM phrase of the WRITE statement transfers the record from working storage to the output record area PRINTLINE, and the WRITE function then copies the record onto the output file.

The correspondence between the pseudocode paragraph 330-Prepare-Employee-Payline and the PROCEDURE DIVISION paragraph 330-PREPARE-EMPLOYEE-PAYLINE is shown below.

330-Prepare-Employee-Payline.

1. Clear the record area Employee-Payline.
2. Move input department-number to Employee-Payline department-number.
3. Move input Social-Security-number to Employee-Payline Social-Security-number.
4. Move input name to Employee-Payline name.
5. Move input union-dues to Employee-Payline union-dues.
6. Move input insurance-premium to Employee-Payline insurance-premium.
7. Move gross-wages to Employee-Payline gross-wages.
8. Move federal-tax to Employee-Payline federal-tax.
9. Move state-tax to Employee-Payline state-tax.
10. Move total-deductions to Employee-Payline total-deductions.
11. Move net-wages to Employee-Payline net-wages.
12. Move Employee-Payline to the output area Printline.
13. After advancing 2 lines, write the output record Printline.

```
330-PREPARE-EMPLOYEE-PAYLINE.
    MOVE SPACES TO EMPLOYEE-PAYLINE.
    MOVE I-DEPT TO O-DEPT.
    MOVE I-SSN TO O-SSN.
    MOVE I-NAME TO O-NAME.
    MOVE I-UNION-DUES TO O-UNION-DUES.
    MOVE I-INS-PREMIUM TO O-INS-PREMIUM.
    MOVE WS-GROSS-WAGES TO O-GROSS-WAGES.
    MOVE WS-FED-TAX TO O-FED-TAX.
    MOVE WS-STATE-TAX TO O-STATE-TAX.
    MOVE WS-TOTAL-DEDUCTIONS TO O-TOTAL-DEDUCTIONS.
    MOVE WS-NET-WAGES TO O-NET-WAGES.
    WRITE PRINTLINE FROM EMPLOYEE-PAYLINE
        AFTER ADVANCING 2 LINES.
```

At this point, we have completed the task of coding the program.

Correspondence between the Program Flowchart and the PROCEDURE DIVISION

If you opted to design the program flowchart rather than write the program pseudocode, then you must convert each module in the flowchart to a paragraph of instructions in the PROCEDURE DIVISION. The correspondence is direct, as illustrated in Figure 5.25. It should be obvious that the preceding discussions of the arithmetic statements apply here as well.

Figure 5.25 Correspondence between the flowchart and the PROCEDURE DIVISION

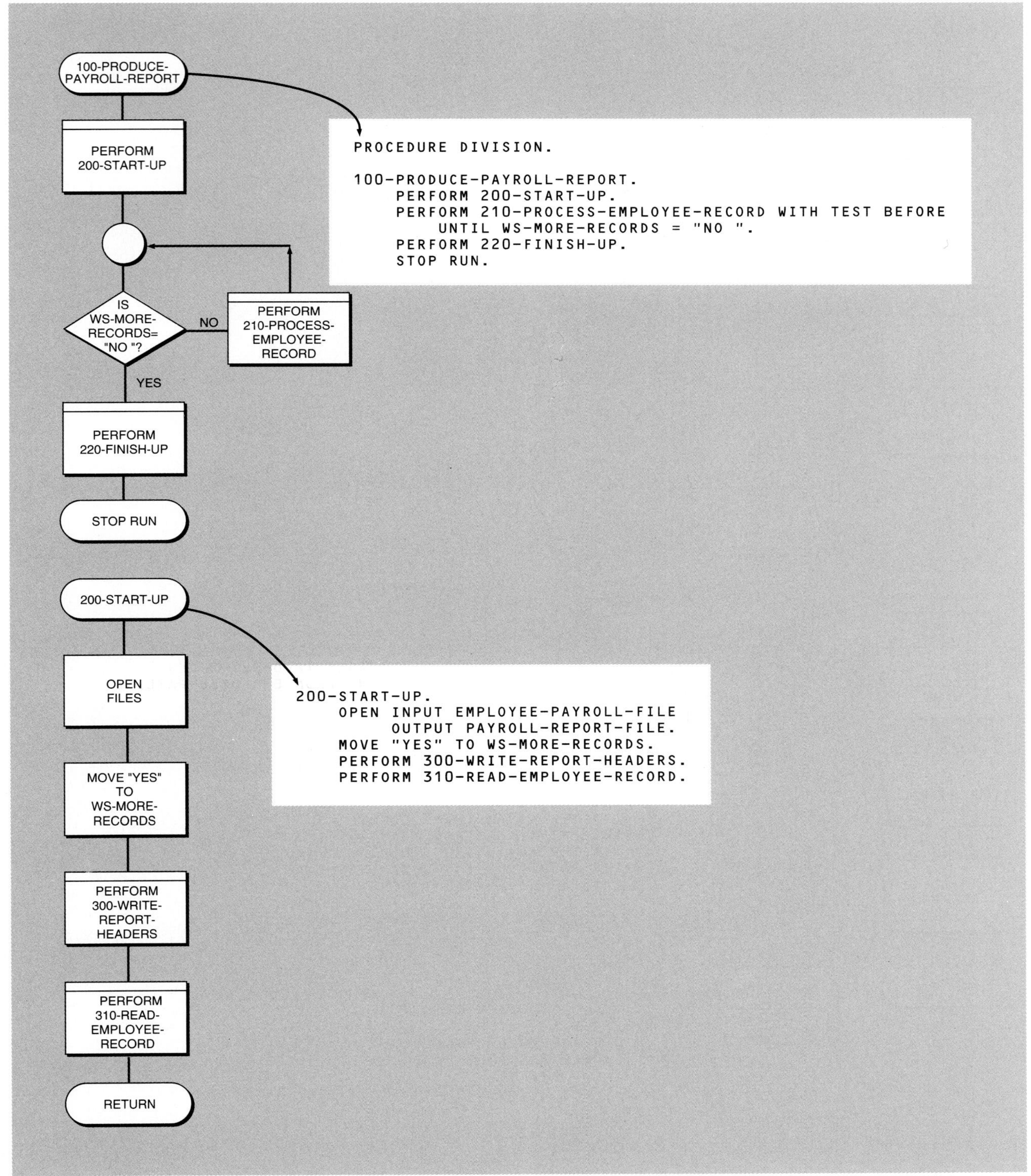


```
PROCEDURE DIVISION.

100-PRODUCE-PAYROLL-REPORT.
    PERFORM 200-START-UP.
    PERFORM 210-PROCESS-EMPLOYEE-RECORD WITH TEST BEFORE
        UNTIL WS-MORE-RECORDS = "NO ".
    PERFORM 220-FINISH-UP.
    STOP RUN.
```

```
200-START-UP.
    OPEN INPUT EMPLOYEE-PAYROLL-FILE
         OUTPUT PAYROLL-REPORT-FILE.
    MOVE "YES" TO WS-MORE-RECORDS.
    PERFORM 300-WRITE-REPORT-HEADERS.
    PERFORM 310-READ-EMPLOYEE-RECORD.
```

■ **Figure 5.25** continued

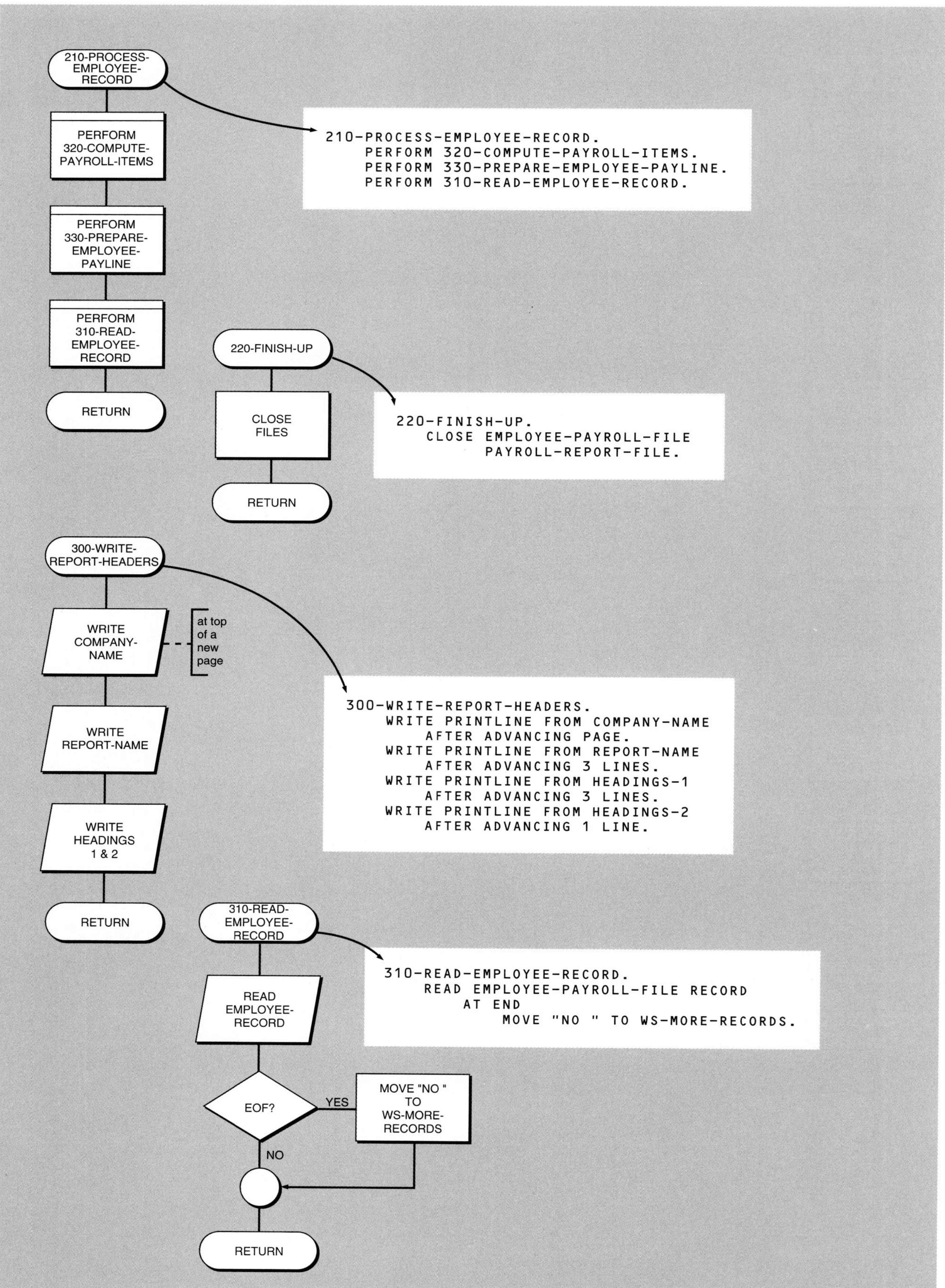

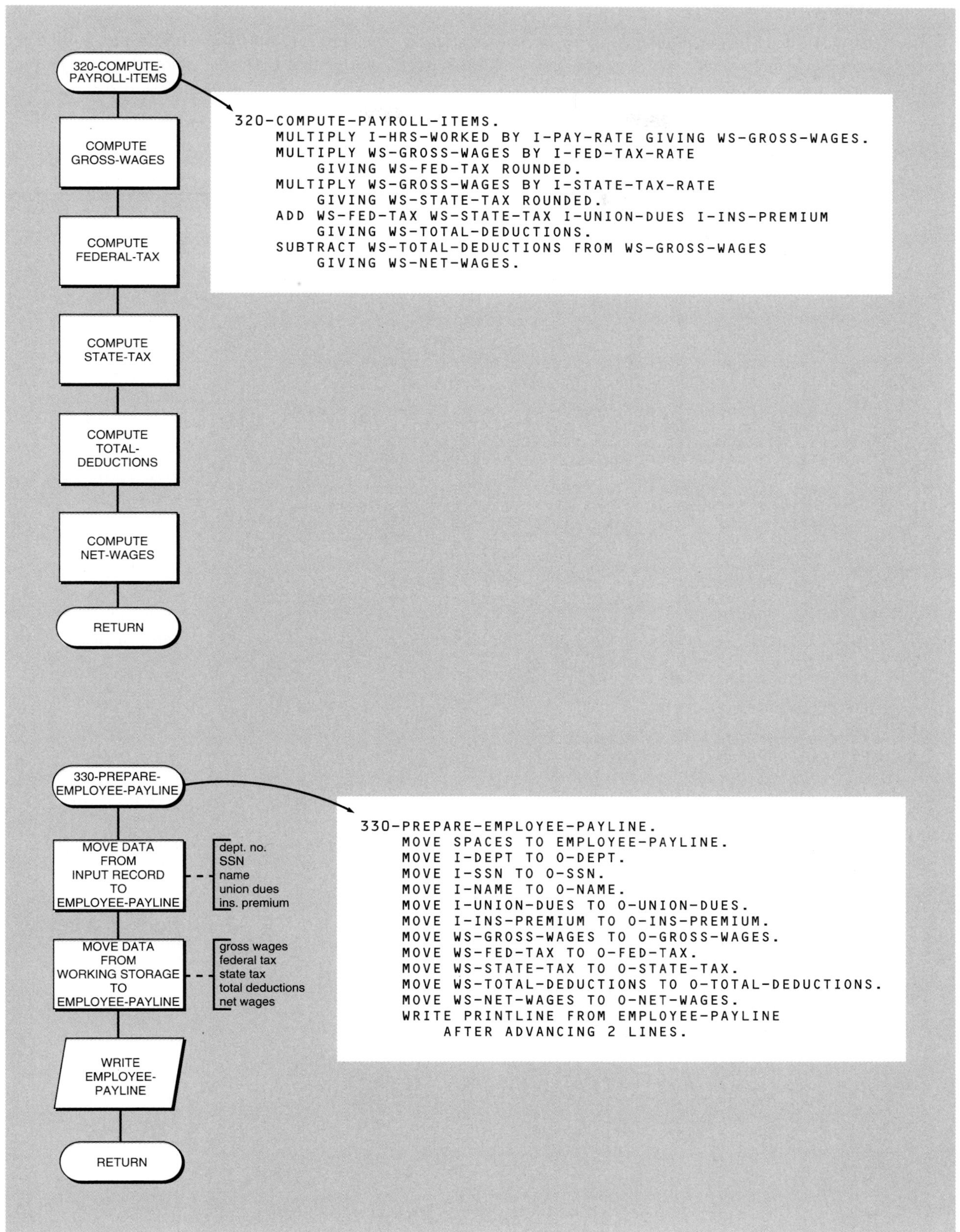


```
320-COMPUTE-PAYROLL-ITEMS.
    MULTIPLY I-HRS-WORKED BY I-PAY-RATE GIVING WS-GROSS-WAGES.
    MULTIPLY WS-GROSS-WAGES BY I-FED-TAX-RATE
        GIVING WS-FED-TAX ROUNDED.
    MULTIPLY WS-GROSS-WAGES BY I-STATE-TAX-RATE
        GIVING WS-STATE-TAX ROUNDED.
    ADD WS-FED-TAX WS-STATE-TAX I-UNION-DUES I-INS-PREMIUM
        GIVING WS-TOTAL-DEDUCTIONS.
    SUBTRACT WS-TOTAL-DEDUCTIONS FROM WS-GROSS-WAGES
        GIVING WS-NET-WAGES.
```

```
330-PREPARE-EMPLOYEE-PAYLINE.
    MOVE SPACES TO EMPLOYEE-PAYLINE.
    MOVE I-DEPT TO O-DEPT.
    MOVE I-SSN TO O-SSN.
    MOVE I-NAME TO O-NAME.
    MOVE I-UNION-DUES TO O-UNION-DUES.
    MOVE I-INS-PREMIUM TO O-INS-PREMIUM.
    MOVE WS-GROSS-WAGES TO O-GROSS-WAGES.
    MOVE WS-FED-TAX TO O-FED-TAX.
    MOVE WS-STATE-TAX TO O-STATE-TAX.
    MOVE WS-TOTAL-DEDUCTIONS TO O-TOTAL-DEDUCTIONS.
    MOVE WS-NET-WAGES TO O-NET-WAGES.
    WRITE PRINTLINE FROM EMPLOYEE-PAYLINE
        AFTER ADVANCING 2 LINES.
```

Design Implementation—Continued

Steps 4 and 5

The next steps in the problem-solving procedure consist of entering the program into a file, calling the compiler to help detect syntax errors, correcting the errors, and getting a "clean" listing of the program. The listing is shown in Figure 5.26.

Figure 5.26 The payroll program for the RELIABLE AUTO PARTS CO.

```
 IDENTIFICATION DIVISION.

 PROGRAM-ID.     RELIABLE-AUTO-PAYROLL.

*******************************************************************
*                                                                 *
*  AUTHOR.         PAQUETTE.                                      *
*  DATE WRITTEN.   FEBRUARY 1993                                  *
*                                                                 *
*     THIS PROGRAM PREPARES A WEEKLY PAYROLL REPORT FOR THE       *
*  RELIABLE AUTO PARTS COMPANY.                                   *
*                                                                 *
*     EACH RECORD OF THE INPUT FILE CONTAINS THE FOLLOWING        *
*  INFORMATION: AN EMPLOYEE'S DEPARTMENT, SOCIAL SECURITY NUMBER, *
*  NAME, HOURS WORKED DURING THE WEEK, PAY RATE, FEDERAL TAX RATE,*
*  STATE TAX RATE, UNION DUES, AND INSURANCE PREMIUM.             *
*                                                                 *
*     FOR EACH EMPLOYEE, THE REPORT CONTAINS A PAY LINE WITH THE  *
*  FOLLOWING INFORMATION: THE DEPARTMENT NUMBER, SOCIAL SECURITY  *
*  NUMBER, NAME, GROSS WAGES, ALL DEDUCTIONS (FEDERAL TAX, STATE  *
*  TAX, UNION DUES, INSURANCE PREMIUM), TOTAL DEDUCTIONS, AND     *
*  NET WAGES. DATA IS PRINTED IN EDITED FORM.                     *
*                                                                 *
*     THE REPORT BEGINS AT THE TOP OF A PAGE WITH THE COMPANY     *
*  NAME, FOLLOWED BY THE NAME OF THE REPORT, AND APPROPRIATE      *
*  COLUMN HEADINGS.                                               *
*                                                                 *
*******************************************************************

 ENVIRONMENT DIVISION.

 CONFIGURATION SECTION.

 SOURCE-COMPUTER.  VAX-VMS-8650.
 OBJECT-COMPUTER.  VAX-VMS-8650.

 INPUT-OUTPUT SECTION.

 FILE-CONTROL.
     SELECT EMPLOYEE-PAYROLL-FILE ASSIGN TO COB$INPUT.
     SELECT PAYROLL-REPORT-FILE   ASSIGN TO COB$OUTPUT.

 DATA DIVISION.

 FILE SECTION.

 FD  EMPLOYEE-PAYROLL-FILE
     RECORD CONTAINS 80 CHARACTERS.

 01  EMPLOYEE-PAYROLL-RECORD.
     05 I-DEPT            PIC XXX.
     05 I-SSN             PIC X(9).
     05 I-NAME            PIC X(22).
     05 I-HRS-WORKED      PIC 99.
     05 I-PAY-RATE        PIC 99V99.
     05 I-FED-TAX-RATE    PIC V99.
     05 I-STATE-TAX-RATE  PIC V99.
     05 I-UNION-DUES      PIC 99V99.
     05 I-INS-PREMIUM     PIC 99V99.
     05 FILLER            PIC X(28).

 FD  PAYROLL-REPORT-FILE
     RECORD CONTAINS 133 CHARACTERS.

 01  PRINTLINE            PIC X(133).

 WORKING-STORAGE SECTION.

 01  WS-MORE-RECORDS      PIC XXX.
```

Figure 5.26 continued

```
01  WS-EMPLOYEE-PAYROLL-ITEMS.
    05 WS-GROSS-WAGES          PIC S9999V99.
    05 WS-FED-TAX              PIC S999V99.
    05 WS-STATE-TAX            PIC S999V99.
    05 WS-TOTAL-DEDUCTIONS     PIC S999V99.
    05 WS-NET-WAGES            PIC S9999V99.

01  COMPANY-NAME.
    05 PIC X(54)    VALUE SPACES.
    05 PIC X(24)    VALUE "RELIABLE AUTO PARTS CO.".
    05 PIC X(54)    VALUE SPACES.

01  REPORT-NAME.
    05 PIC X(55)    VALUE SPACES.
    05 PIC X(21)    VALUE "WEEKLY PAYROLL REPORT".
    05 PIC X(56)    VALUE SPACES.

01  HEADINGS-1.
    05 PIC X(56)    VALUE SPACES.
    05 PIC X(5)     VALUE "GROSS".
    05 PIC X(4)     VALUE SPACES.
    05 PIC X(7)     VALUE "FEDERAL".
    05 PIC XXX      VALUE SPACES.
    05 PIC X(5)     VALUE "STATE".
    05 PIC XXXX     VALUE SPACES.
    05 PIC X(5)     VALUE "UNION".
    05 PIC X(15)    VALUE SPACES.
    05 PIC X(5)     VALUE "TOTAL".
    05 PIC X(10)    VALUE SPACES.
    05 PIC XXX      VALUE "NET".
    05 PIC X(10)    VALUE SPACES.

01  HEADINGS-2.
    05 PIC XXX      VALUE SPACES.
    05 PIC X(10)    VALUE "DEPARTMENT".
    05 PIC X(5)     VALUE SPACES.
    05 PIC XXX      VALUE "SSN".
    05 PIC X(17)    VALUE SPACES.
    05 PIC XXXX     VALUE "NAME".
    05 PIC X(14)    VALUE SPACES.
    05 PIC X(5)     VALUE "WAGES".
    05 PIC X(6)     VALUE SPACES.
    05 PIC XXX      VALUE "TAX".
    05 PIC X(6)     VALUE SPACES.
    05 PIC XXX      VALUE "TAX".
    05 PIC X(5)     VALUE SPACES.
    05 PIC XXXX     VALUE "DUES".
    05 PIC XX       VALUE SPACES.
    05 PIC X(9)     VALUE "INSURANCE".
    05 PIC XXX      VALUE SPACES.
    05 PIC X(10)    VALUE "DEDUCTIONS".
    05 PIC X(6)     VALUE SPACES.
    05 PIC X(5)     VALUE "WAGES".
    05 PIC X(9)     VALUE SPACES.

01  EMPLOYEE-PAYLINE.
    05 CARRIAGE-CONTROL     PIC X.
    05 FILLER               PIC X(5).
    05 O-DEPT               PIC XXX.
    05 FILLER               PIC X(5).
    05 O-SSN                PIC XXXBXXBXXXX.
    05 FILLER               PIC X(4).
    05 O-NAME               PIC X(22).
    05 FILLER               PIC X(3).
    05 O-GROSS-WAGES        PIC $ZZZ9.99.
    05 FILLER               PIC XXX.
    05 O-FED-TAX            PIC $ZZ9.99.
    05 FILLER               PIC XX.
    05 O-STATE-TAX          PIC $ZZ9.99.
    05 FILLER               PIC XX.
    05 O-UNION-DUES         PIC $Z9.99.
    05 FILLER               PIC XX.
    05 O-INS-PREMIUM        PIC $Z9.99.
    05 FILLER               PIC X(6).
    05 O-TOTAL-DEDUCTIONS PIC $ZZ9.99.
    05 FILLER               PIC X(6).
    05 O-NET-WAGES          PIC $ZZZ9.99-.
    05 FILLER               PIC X(9).
```

```
PROCEDURE DIVISION.

100-PRODUCE-PAYROLL-REPORT.
    PERFORM 200-START-UP.
    PERFORM 210-PROCESS-EMPLOYEE-RECORD WITH TEST BEFORE
        UNTIL WS-MORE-RECORDS = "NO ".
    PERFORM 220-FINISH-UP.
    STOP RUN.

200-START-UP.
    OPEN INPUT EMPLOYEE-PAYROLL-FILE
         OUTPUT PAYROLL-REPORT-FILE.
    MOVE "YES" TO WS-MORE-RECORDS.
    PERFORM 300-WRITE-REPORT-HEADERS.
    PERFORM 310-READ-EMPLOYEE-RECORD.

210-PROCESS-EMPLOYEE-RECORD.
    PERFORM 320-COMPUTE-PAYROLL-ITEMS.
    PERFORM 330-PREPARE-EMPLOYEE-PAYLINE.
    PERFORM 310-READ-EMPLOYEE-RECORD.

220-FINISH-UP.
    CLOSE EMPLOYEE-PAYROLL-FILE
          PAYROLL-REPORT-FILE.

300-WRITE-REPORT-HEADERS.
    WRITE PRINTLINE FROM COMPANY-NAME
        AFTER ADVANCING PAGE.
    WRITE PRINTLINE FROM REPORT-NAME
        AFTER ADVANCING 3 LINES.
    WRITE PRINTLINE FROM HEADINGS-1
        AFTER ADVANCING 3 LINES.
    WRITE PRINTLINE FROM HEADINGS-2
        AFTER ADVANCING 1 LINE.

310-READ-EMPLOYEE-RECORD.
    READ EMPLOYEE-PAYROLL-FILE RECORD
        AT END
            MOVE "NO " TO WS-MORE-RECORDS.

320-COMPUTE-PAYROLL-ITEMS.
    MULTIPLY I-HRS-WORKED BY I-PAYRATE GIVING WS-GROSS-WAGES.
    MULTIPLY WS-GROSS-WAGES BY I-FED-TAX-RATE
        GIVING WS-FED-TAX ROUNDED.
    MULTIPLY WS-GROSS-WAGES BY I-STATE-TAX-RATE
        GIVING WS-STATE-TAX ROUNDED.
    ADD WS-FED-TAX WS-STATE-TAX I-UNION-DUES I-INS-PREMIUM
        GIVING WS-TOTAL-DEDUCTIONS.
    SUBTRACT WS-TOTAL-DEDUCTIONS FROM WS-GROSS-WAGES
        GIVING WS-NET-WAGES.

330-PREPARE-EMPLOYEE-PAYLINE.
    MOVE SPACES TO EMPLOYEE-PAYLINE.
    MOVE I-DEPT TO O-DEPT.
    MOVE I-SSN TO O-SSN.
    MOVE I-NAME TO O-NAME.
    MOVE I-UNION-DUES TO O-UNION-DUES.
    MOVE I-INS-PREMIUM TO O-INS-PREMIUM.
    MOVE WS-GROSS-WAGES TO O-GROSS-WAGES.
    MOVE WS-FED-TAX TO O-FED-TAX.
    MOVE WS-STATE-TAX TO O-STATE-TAX.
    MOVE WS-TOTAL-DEDUCTIONS TO O-TOTAL-DEDUCTIONS.
    MOVE WS-NET-WAGES TO O-NET-WAGES.
    WRITE PRINTLINE FROM EMPLOYEE-PAYLINE
        AFTER ADVANCING 2 LINES.
```

Step 6

We are now ready to "test run" the program. The sample data file is shown in Figure 5.27 [DD/CD:VIC5SP.DAT], and the payroll report produced by the program is shown in Figure 5.28.

The programmer must check the payroll report carefully to make sure that it meets all of the original specifications for the program. Is the report properly documented? Are there obvious omissions? Do the column headers properly identify all the columns of data? Are the headers properly centered? Is every data item originally requested present on the report? Are the data fields properly edited? Are the computed values correct? Are there any "glaring" errors, such as total deductions greater than gross wages, or net wages greater than gross wages, or the like? Select a few records at random, and use a calculator to verify the accuracy of the entries.

If a close inspection of the report indicates that all the program objectives have been met, then the job is done. Assemble all the design tools, a listing of the program, the sample data file, and the results of the test run, and submit the package.

Figure 5.27 Sample input file to test run the program

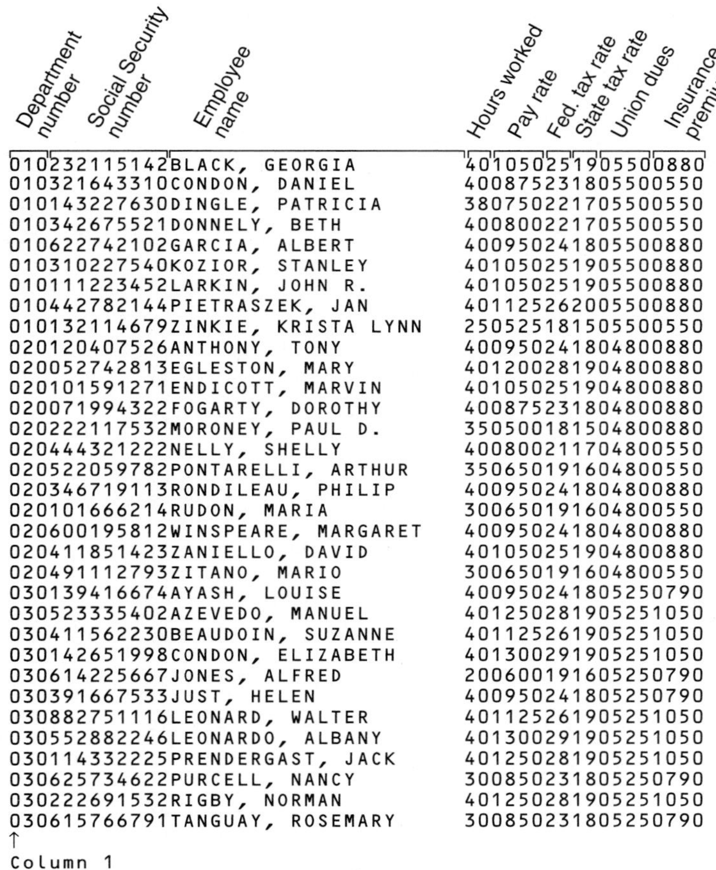


```
010232115142BLACK, GEORGIA           401050251905500880
010321643310CONDON, DANIEL           400875231805500550
010143227630DINGLE, PATRICIA         380750221705500550
010342675521DONNELY, BETH            400800221705500550
010622742102GARCIA, ALBERT           400950241805500880
010310227540KOZIOR, STANLEY          401050251905500880
010111223452LARKIN, JOHN R.          401050251905500880
010442782144PIETRASZEK, JAN          401125262005500880
010132114679ZINKIE, KRISTA LYNN      250525181505500550
020120407526ANTHONY, TONY            400950241804800880
020052742813EGLESTON, MARY           401200281904800880
020101591271ENDICOTT, MARVIN         401050251904800880
020071994322FOGARTY, DOROTHY         400875231804800880
020222117532MORONEY, PAUL D.         350500181504800880
020444321222NELLY, SHELLY            400800211704800550
020522059782PONTARELLI, ARTHUR       350650191604800550
020346719113RONDILEAU, PHILIP        400950241804800880
020101666214RUDON, MARIA             300650191604800550
020600195812WINSPEARE, MARGARET      400950241804800880
020411851423ZANIELLO, DAVID          401050251904800880
020491112793ZITANO, MARIO            300650191604800550
030139416674AYASH, LOUISE            400950241805250790
030523335402AZEVEDO, MANUEL          401250281905251050
030411562230BEAUDOIN, SUZANNE        401125261905251050
030142651998CONDON, ELIZABETH        401300291905251050
030614225667JONES, ALFRED            200600191605250790
030391667533JUST, HELEN              400950241805250790
030882751116LEONARD, WALTER          401125261905251050
030552882246LEONARDO, ALBANY         401300291905251050
030114332225PRENDERGAST, JACK        401250281905251050
030625734622PURCELL, NANCY           300850231805250790
030222691532RIGBY, NORMAN            401250281905251050
030615766791TANGUAY, ROSEMARY        300850231805250790
↑
Column 1
```

Figure 5.28 Payroll report produced by the test run of the program

RELIABLE AUTO PARTS CO.

WEEKLY PAYROLL REPORT

DEPARTMENT	SSN	NAME	GROSS WAGES	FEDERAL TAX	STATE TAX	UNION DUES	INSURANCE	TOTAL DEDUCTIONS	NET WAGES
010	232 11 5142	BLACK, GEORGIA	$ 420.00	$105.00	$ 79.80	$ 5.50	$ 8.80	$199.10	$ 220.90
010	321 64 3310	CONDON, DANIEL	$ 350.00	$ 80.50	$ 63.00	$ 5.50	$ 5.50	$154.50	$ 195.50
010	143 22 7630	DINGLE, PATRICIA	$ 285.00	$ 62.70	$ 48.45	$ 5.50	$ 5.50	$122.15	$ 162.85
010	342 67 5521	DONNELY, BETH	$ 320.00	$ 70.40	$ 54.40	$ 5.50	$ 5.50	$135.80	$ 184.20
010	622 74 2102	GARCIA, ALBERT	$ 380.00	$ 91.20	$ 68.40	$ 5.50	$ 8.80	$173.90	$ 206.10
010	310 22 7540	KOZIOR, STANLEY	$ 420.00	$105.00	$ 79.80	$ 5.50	$ 8.80	$199.10	$ 220.90
010	111 22 3452	LARKIN, JOHN R.	$ 420.00	$105.00	$ 79.80	$ 5.50	$ 8.80	$199.10	$ 220.90
010	442 78 2144	PIETRASZEK, JAN	$ 450.00	$117.00	$ 90.00	$ 5.50	$ 8.80	$221.30	$ 228.70
010	132 11 4679	ZINKIE, KRISTA LYNN	$ 131.25	$ 23.63	$ 19.69	$ 5.50	$ 5.50	$ 54.32	$ 76.93
020	120 40 7526	ANTHONY, TONY	$ 380.00	$ 91.20	$ 68.40	$ 4.80	$ 8.80	$173.20	$ 206.80
020	052 74 2813	EGLESTON, MARY	$ 480.00	$134.40	$ 91.20	$ 4.80	$ 8.80	$239.20	$ 240.80
020	101 59 1271	ENDICOTT, MARVIN	$ 420.00	$105.00	$ 79.80	$ 4.80	$ 8.80	$198.40	$ 221.60
020	071 99 4322	FOGARTY, DOROTHY	$ 350.00	$ 80.50	$ 63.00	$ 4.80	$ 8.80	$157.10	$ 192.90
020	222 11 7532	MORONEY, PAUL D.	$ 175.00	$ 31.50	$ 26.25	$ 4.80	$ 8.80	$ 71.35	$ 103.65
020	444 32 1222	NELLY, SHELLY	$ 320.00	$ 67.20	$ 54.40	$ 4.80	$ 5.50	$131.90	$ 188.10
020	522 05 9782	PONTARELLI, ARTHUR	$ 227.50	$ 43.23	$ 36.40	$ 4.80	$ 5.50	$ 89.93	$ 137.57
020	346 71 9113	RONDILEAU, PHILIP	$ 380.00	$ 91.20	$ 68.40	$ 4.80	$ 8.80	$173.20	$ 206.80
020	101 66 6214	RUDON, MARIA	$ 195.00	$ 37.05	$ 31.20	$ 4.80	$ 5.50	$ 78.55	$ 116.45
020	600 19 5812	WINSPEARE, MARGARET	$ 380.00	$ 91.20	$ 68.40	$ 4.80	$ 8.80	$173.20	$ 206.80
020	411 85 1423	ZANIELLO, DAVID	$ 420.00	$105.00	$ 79.80	$ 4.80	$ 8.80	$198.40	$ 221.60
020	491 11 2793	ZITANO, MARIO	$ 195.00	$ 37.05	$ 31.20	$ 4.80	$ 5.50	$ 78.55	$ 116.45
030	139 41 6674	AYASH, LOUISE	$ 380.00	$ 91.20	$ 68.40	$ 5.25	$ 7.90	$172.75	$ 207.25
030	523 33 5402	AZEVEDO, MANUEL	$ 500.00	$140.00	$ 95.00	$ 5.25	$10.50	$250.75	$ 249.25
030	411 56 2230	BEAUDOIN, SUZANNE	$ 450.00	$117.00	$ 85.50	$ 5.25	$10.50	$218.25	$ 231.75
030	142 65 1998	CONDON, ELIZABETH	$ 520.00	$150.80	$ 98.80	$ 5.25	$10.50	$265.35	$ 254.65
030	614 22 5667	JONES, ALFRED	$ 120.00	$ 22.80	$ 19.20	$ 5.25	$ 7.90	$ 55.15	$ 64.85
030	391 66 7533	JUST, HELEN	$ 380.00	$ 91.20	$ 68.40	$ 5.25	$ 7.90	$172.75	$ 207.25
030	882 75 1116	LEONARD, WALTER	$ 450.00	$117.00	$ 85.50	$ 5.25	$10.50	$218.25	$ 231.75
030	552 88 2246	LEONARDO, ALBANY	$ 520.00	$150.80	$ 98.80	$ 5.25	$10.50	$265.35	$ 254.65
030	114 33 2225	PRENDERGAST, JACK	$ 500.00	$140.00	$ 95.00	$ 5.25	$10.50	$250.75	$ 249.25
030	625 73 4622	PURCELL, NANCY	$ 255.00	$ 58.65	$ 45.90	$ 5.25	$ 7.90	$117.70	$ 137.30
030	222 69 1532	RIGBY, NORMAN	$ 500.00	$140.00	$ 95.00	$ 5.25	$10.50	$250.75	$ 249.25
030	615 76 6791	TANGUAY, ROSEMARY	$ 255.00	$ 58.65	$ 45.90	$ 5.25	$ 7.90	$117.70	$ 137.30

Important Terms in Chapter 5

ADD-GIVING
ADD-TO
ADD-TO-GIVING
edited field
editing character
END-ADD
END-MULTIPLY
END-SUBTRACT
floating character
high-order truncation
insertion character
integer numeric field
low-order truncation
multiple receiving fields
MULTIPLY-BY
MULTIPLY-BY-GIVING
noninteger numeric field
nonnumeric data item
NOT ON SIZE ERROR
numeric data item
ON SIZE ERROR
operand
receiving field
replacement character
ROUNDED
SEPARATE CHARACTER
SIGN IS LEADING
SIGN IS TRAILING
signed data field
signed number
SUBTRACT-FROM
SUBTRACT-FROM-GIVING
work area
zero suppressor

Exercises

1. Explain the effect of each of the following statements:
   a. `PERFORM 200-PROCESS-RECORD.`
   b. `PERFORM 200-PROCESS-RECORD 5 TIMES.`
   c. `PERFORM 200-PROCESS-RECORD UNTIL WS-MORE-RECORDS = "NO ".`
2. Which of the flowchart segments in Figure 5.29 properly illustrates the repetition structure corresponding to
   a. the PERFORM-UNTIL statement?
   b. the PERFORM-WITH-TEST-AFTER-UNTIL statement?
   c. the PERFORM-WITH-TEST-BEFORE-UNTIL statement?
3. Answer the following questions about data transfers:
   a. Which COBOL statement is used to transfer a data record from some external medium to the input memory area?
   b. Which COBOL statement is used to transfer data from the output memory area to some external medium?
   c. Which COBOL statement is used to transfer data from an internal source to another internal receiving field?
4. Given the system flowchart in Figure 5.30, complete the following:
   a. Identify the essential function of the program for which this is the system flowchart.
   b. Give the name of the file that contains the data records to be processed.
   c. Give the name of the output file.
5. Continue to refer to the system flowchart in Figure 5.30, and complete the following:
   a. Construct the first two levels of the structure chart corresponding to the system flowchart.
   b. Code the OPEN statements that correspond to the functions of the files specified in Figure 5.30.
6. Construct a system flowchart for a program that must process client records for the purpose of producing a list of all clients with a "past due" balance.

Figure 5.29

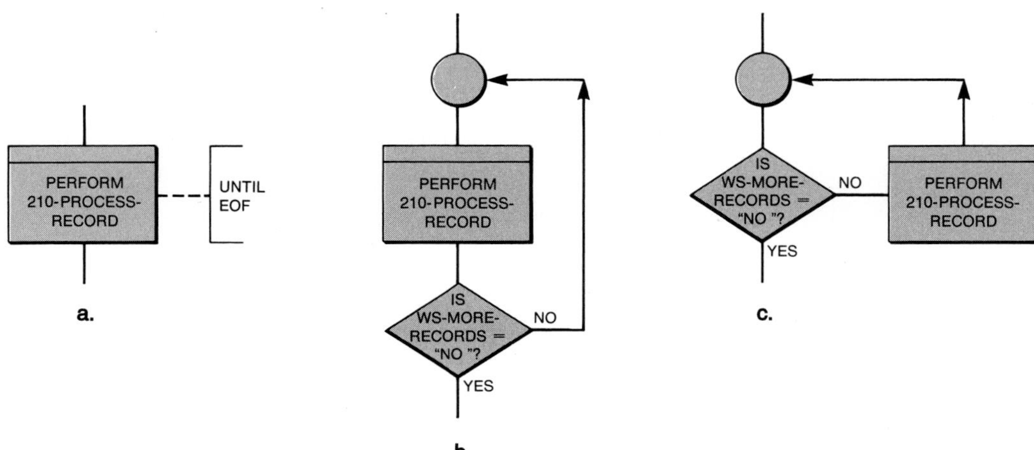

■ **Figure 5.30**

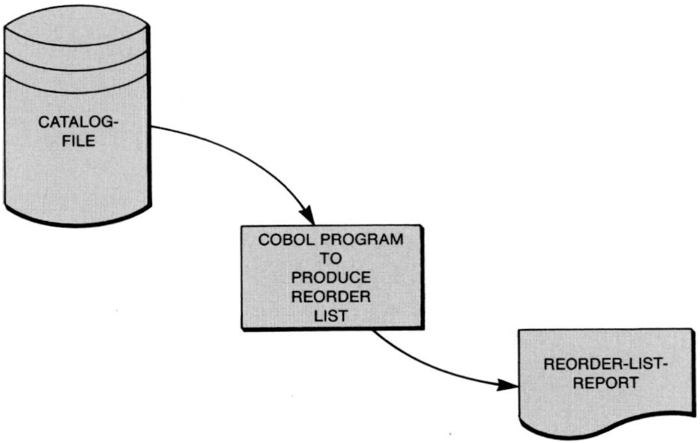

■ **Figure 5.31**

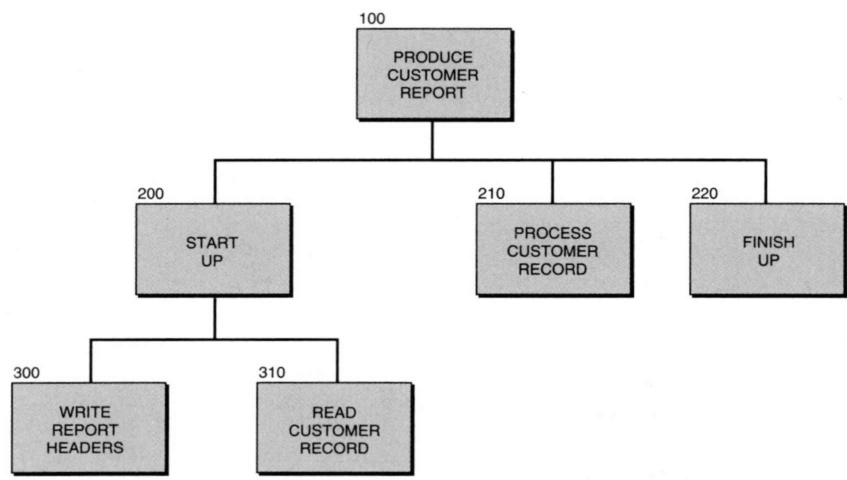

7. Given the partial structure chart in Figure 5.31, complete the following:
   a. Write the main-control paragraph of the program pseudocode, or draw the main-control module of the program flowchart. Assume that module 210 must be executed until there are no more records in the input file, and the end-of-file flag is WS-MORE-RECORDS.
   b. Code the main-control paragraph of the PROCEDURE DIVISION that corresponds to the pseudocode or flowchart module in part a.
8. Explain the procedure illustrated in the partial pseudocode of Figure 5.32a or in the partial flowchart of Figure 5.32b.
9. Code the PROCEDURE DIVISION entries that correspond to the pseudocode or flowchart of Figure 5.32a and b. Assume the input file is INVENTORY-FILE and the output file is INVENTORY-REPORT.

■ Figure 5.32a

100-Produce-Inventory-Report.

1. Perform 200-Start-Up.
2. Perform 210-Process-Inventory-Record until no more records.

.

.

200-Start-Up.

1. Open the files.
2. Set the end-of-file flag WS-MORE-RECORDS to "YES".
3. Perform 300-Read-Inventory-File-Record.

210-Process-Inventory-Record.

.

.

.

9. Move Inventory-Line record to the output area Printline.
10. After advancing 2 lines, write the output record Printline.
11. Perform 300-Read-Inventory-File-Record.

.

.

.

300-Read-Inventory-File-Record.

1. Read an input Inventory-File Record.
2. Test for end-of-file record; if EOF record reached, move "NO " to the flag WS-MORE-RECORDS.

■ Figure 5.32b

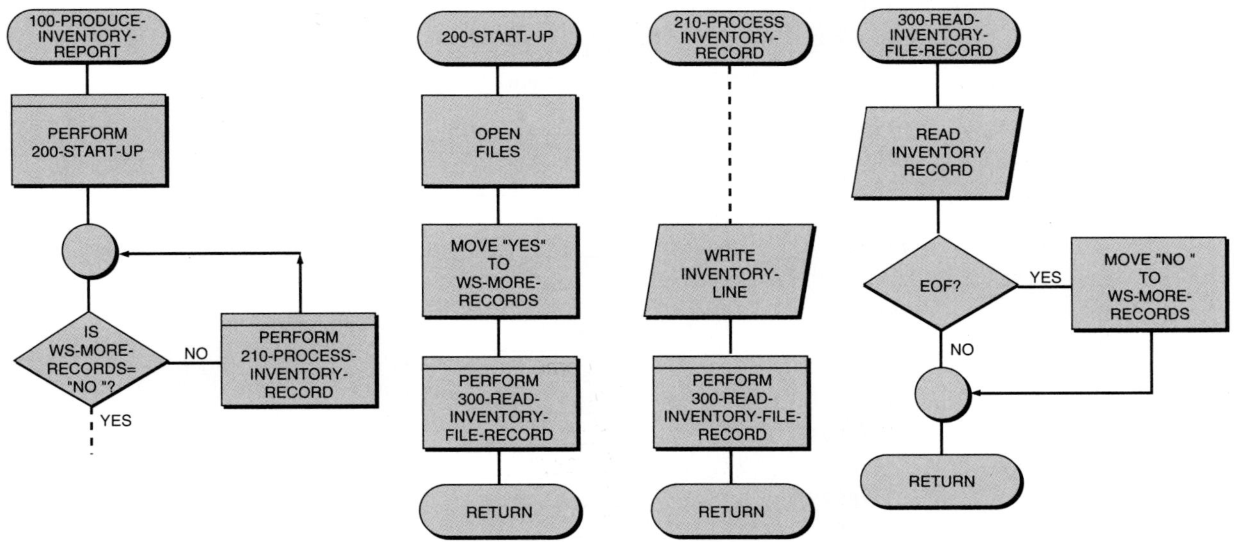

10. Use the numbers in the left column to show the order in which the statements below will be executed. Assume that the input file is not empty.

```
1          PERFORM 200-START-UP.
2          PERFORM 210-PROCESS-RECORD WITH TEST BEFORE
               UNTIL WS-MORE-RECORDS = "NO ".
3          PERFORM 220-FINISH-UP.
4          STOP RUN.

5      200-START-UP.
6          OPEN INPUT IN-FILE
                OUTPUT OUT-FILE.
7          MOVE "YES" TO WS-MORE-RECORDS.
8          PERFORM 300-WRITE-REPORT-HEADERS.
9          PERFORM 310-READ-A-RECORD.

10     210-PROCESS-RECORD.
11         MOVE IN-RECORD TO OUT-RECORD.
12         ADD 1 TO WS-RECORD-COUNT.
13         WRITE PRINTLINE FROM RECORD-LINE
               AFTER ADVANCING 1 LINE.
14         PERFORM 310-READ-A-RECORD.

15     220-FINISH-UP.
16         CLOSE IN-FILE
                 OUT-FILE.

17     300-WRITE-REPORT-HEADERS.
18         MOVE TITLE-LINE TO PRINTLINE.
19         WRITE PRINTLINE
               AFTER ADVANCING PAGE.

20     310-READ-A-RECORD.
21         READ IN-FILE RECORD
22             AT END
23                 MOVE "NO " TO WS-MORE-RECORDS.
```

11. In each case below, show the contents of the receiving field after the following MOVE statement is executed:

```
MOVE FIELD-A TO FIELD-B.
```

	FIELD-A		FIELD-B	
	Contents	**PICTURE**	**PICTURE**	**Contents**
a.	1453	9999	9999	1453
b.	453	999	9999	0453
c.	1453	9999	999	453
d.	1453	999V9	999V9	145^3
e.	1453	999V9	99V99	45^30
f.	1453	999V9	999.9	145.3
g.	453	999P	9999	4530
h.	453	999P	9V999	0^000
i.	453	999P	$99.99	$30.00
j.	4	9PPP	$99.99	$ 00.00
k.	453	VP999	$99.99	$ 00.04
l.	453	VP999	$ZZ.99	$.04
m.	453	VP999	$**.99	$**.04
n.	453	9V99	$*(4).99	$***.53
o.	453+	S999	999+	453+
p.	453+	S999	Z99-	453
q.	453-	S999	Z99+	453 -
r.	453-	S999	999-	453 -
s.	453-	S9V99	$ZZ9.99-	$ _ _ 4.53-
t.	453-	S9V99	$**9.99+	$** 4.53

12. For each entry of exercise 11, give the class and the size of FIELD-A and of FIELD-B.

13. Construct appropriate edited PICTUREs for the following items.

	Data Item	PICTURE	Edited PICTURE
a.	NO-OF-WORKERS	999	________
b.	UNIT-COST	9V99	________

c.	PROFIT	S999V99	________
d.	CHECK-AMOUNT	9(4)V99	________
e.	ACCOUNT-BALANCE	S9(5)V99	________
f.	REPORT-DATE	X(6)	________
g.	NEAREST-DOLLAR	999V99	________

14. Use the following data items with PICTUREs and initial values as specified to complete the exercises that follow.

	PICTURE	Value Before Execution
FIELD-A	S99999	00300+
FIELD-B	S9999	4533+
FIELD-C	S9999	5800+
FIELD-D	S999V9999	125.0554+
FIELD-E	S99	34-
FIELD-F	S99V99	80.25-
FIELD-G	S999V9	750.8+
FIELD-H	$9(4).0099	$0038.0055
FIELD-I	$Z9.99	$ 4.80

In each case below, specify the contents of each data item after the statement is executed.

a.
```
ADD FIELD-A TO FIELD-C.
```
b.
```
ADD FIELD-A FIELD-B TO FIELD-C.
```
c.
```
ADD FIELD-A FIELD-B GIVING FIELD-C.
```
d.
```
ADD FIELD-A FIELD-B TO FIELD-C
    ON SIZE ERROR
        SUBTRACT FIELD-A FROM FIELD-C.
```
e.
```
ADD FIELD-A FIELD-B TO FIELD-C
    ON SIZE ERROR
        SUBTRACT FIELD-C FROM FIELD-B GIVING FIELD-A.
```
f.
```
SUBTRACT FIELD-A FROM FIELD-G GIVING FIELD-C ROUNDED.
```
g.
```
SUBTRACT FIELD-F FROM FIELD-E ROUNDED
    ON SIZE ERROR
        ADD 1 TO FIELD-A
    NOT ON SIZE ERROR
        SUBTRACT 1 FROM FIELD-A.
```
h.
```
SUBTRACT FIELD-F FROM FIELD-D GIVING FIELD-I ROUNDED.
```
i.
```
SUBTRACT FIELD-E FROM FIELD-D GIVING FIELD-H ROUNDED
    ON SIZE ERROR
        MOVE ZERO TO FIELD-E
    NOT ON SIZE ERROR
        ADD 1 TO FIELD-E.
```
j.
```
MULTIPLY 5 BY FIELD-E.
```
k.
```
MULTIPLY 5 BY FIELD-E GIVING FIELD-A.
```
l.
```
MULTIPLY FIELD-E BY FIELD-F GIVING FIELD-H ROUNDED.
```
m.
```
MULTIPLY FIELD-F BY FIELD-D
    ON SIZE ERROR
        SUBTRACT FIELD-F FROM FIELD-D GIVING FIELD-E ROUNDED.
```

15. Suppose that each data item below has PICTURE S99V9. For each set of values (a through e), determine the value stored in ITEM-D and the value in ITEM-X after the ADD statement shown below is executed.

	ITEM-A	ITEM-B	ITEM-C	ITEM-D	ITEM-X
a.	+25.2	+10.8	+40.5	+60.4	+30.5
b.	+52.4	+10.8	+40.5	+60.4	+30.5
c.	+38.5	+25.5	-42.4	+50.8	+10.5
d.	-38.5	-25.5	-42.4	+50.8	+10.5
e.	+34.5	-14.5	+50.5	-40.5	-20.5

```
ADD ITEM-A ITEM-B ITEM-C GIVING ITEM-D
    ON SIZE ERROR
        SUBTRACT 15 FROM ITEM-X
    NOT ON SIZE ERROR
        MULTIPLY -3 BY ITEM-X.
```

16. In each part of this exercise, you must code an arithmetic statement.

a. Write a statement to sum REGION-1-SALES, REGION-2-SALES, and REGION-3-SALES, and store the total in COMPANY-SALES.

b. Write a statement to compute the tax on PURCHASE-AMOUNT and store it in PURCHASE-TAX if the applicable tax rate is TAX-RATE.

c. Write a statement to compute NEW-CHCK-ACCT-BAL if checks for amounts CHECK-1, CHECK-2, and CHECK-3 have been issued. Assume the beginning balance is OLD-CHCK-ACCT-BAL.

d. Write a statement to compute STOCK-VALUE for a stock item if its purchase price is PURCH-PRICE and the quantity in stock is IN-STOCK. If there is a size error, execute the procedure 400-ERROR-ROUTINE.

e. Write a statement to compute BONUS when the following rule is applied: if MONTH-SALES is greater than 10 percent above QUOTA, the bonus for the month is 2 percent of the sales for the month; otherwise, the bonus is .5 percent of the sales. The bonus value should be rounded.

Debugging Activities

1. Given the record layout shown in Figure 5.33a, a student generated the coding in part b. On the assumption that selected fields will be operands in arithmetic operations, find and correct the coding errors.
2. Given the output record layout shown in Figure 5.34a, a student generated the coding in part b. On the assumption that fields containing numeric values should be properly edited (leading zeros should be eliminated, and monetary values should contain a decimal point, commas, and a dollar sign), find and correct the coding errors.
3. Using the input record layout of activity 1, a program must compute the markup for each catalog item. A student generated the following relevant code. Identify and correct the errors.

```
FILE SECTION.
.
.
.
01   CATALOG-ITEM-RECORD.
     05 I-CATALOG-NO            PIC X(10).
     05 I-ITEM-DESCR            PIC X(20).
     05 I-UNIT-PURCHASE-PRICE   PIC X(5).
     05 I-UNIT-SELLING-PRICE    PIC X(5).
     05 I-QUANTITY-ON-HAND      PIC X(4).
     05                         PIC X.
     05 I-REORDER-POINT         PIC X(4).
.
.
.
WORKING-STORAGE SECTION.

01   ITEM-WORK-AREAS.
     05 WS-MARKUP     PIC S99V99.
.
.
.
PROCEDURE DIVISION.
.
.
.
     SUBTRACT I-UNIT-SELLING-PRICE FROM I-UNIT-PRUCHASE-PRICE
         GIVING WS-MARKUP.
.
.
.
```

4. A COBOL program was prepared for the purpose described in the IDENTIFICATION DIVISION. The compiler generated the listing shown in Figure 5.35. Correct all the syntax errors.
5. Assuming that all the syntax errors in Figure 5.35 have been corrected, the execution of the program has then produced the report shown in Figure 5.36. A cursory examination of the report shows a number of programming errors that were not flagged by the compiler. Find and correct the errors.

■ Figure 5.33

a.

I-CATALOG-NO	I-ITEM-DESCR	I-UNIT-PURCHASE-PRICE	I-UNIT-SELLING-PRICE	I-QUANTITY-ON-HAND		I-REORDER-POINT
1 2 3 4 5 6 7 8 9 10	11 12 13 14 15 16 17 18 19 20 21 22 23 24 25 26 27 28 29 30	31 32 33 34 ^ 35 36	37 38 39 40 ^ 41 42	43 44 45 46	47 48 49 50 51 52 53 54 55 56 57 58 59 60 61 62 63 64 65 66 67 68 69 70 71 72 73 74 75 76	77 78 79 80

Record Name: CATALOG-ITEM-RECORD

b.

```
01  CATALOG-ITEM-RECORD.
    05 I-CATALOG-NO              PIC X(10).
    05 I-ITEM-DESCR              PIC X(20).
    05 I-UNIT-PURCHASE-PRICE     PIC X(5).
    05 I-UNIT-SELLING-PRICE      PIC X(5).
    05 I-QUANTITY-ON-HAND        PIC X(4).
    05                           PIC X.
    05 I-REORDER-POINT           PIC X(4).
```

■ Figure 5.34

a.

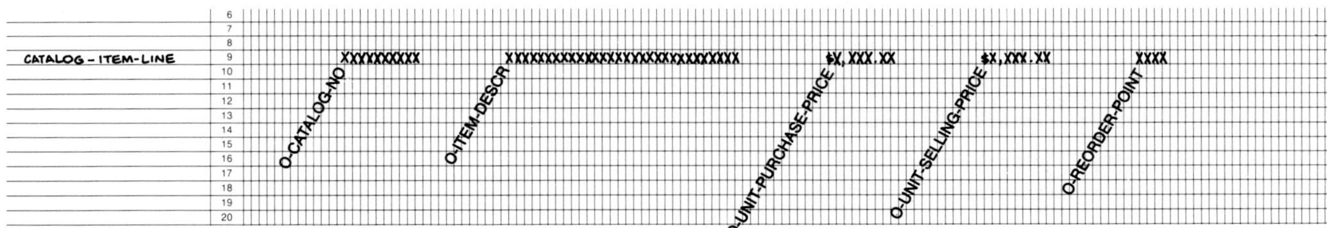

b.

```
01  CATALOG-ITEM-LINE.
    05                           PIC X(3).
    05 O-CATALOG-NO              PIC X(10).
    05                           PIC X(11).
    05 O-ITEM-DESCR              PIC X(300.
    05                           PIC X(11).
    05 O-UNIT-PURCHASE-PRICE     PIC X(5).XX.
    05                           PIC X(11).
    05 O-UNIT-SELLING-PRICE      PIC X(5).XX.
    05                           PIC X(11)
    05 O-REORDER-POINT           PIC X(4).
    05                           PIC X(13)
```

■ Figure 5.35

```
INT-HAB-PAY-REPORT                              18-Nov-1993 13:56:41    VAX COBOL V5.1-10                     Page   1
Source Listing                                  18-Nov-1993 13:02:12    FACULTY$DISK:[PAQUETTEG.WCBTXT]C5DBG4.CB1;1

            IDENTIFICATION DIVISION.

            PROGRAM-ID.   INT-HAB-PAY-REPORT.

           *****************************************************************
           *                                                               *
           *       THE PURPOSE OF THIS PROGRAM IS TO PRODUCE A PAY REPORT  *
           *  FOR THE INTERNATIONAL HABERDASHERY COMPANY.                  *
           *       EACH SALESPERSON RECEIVES A BASE SALARY AND A COMMISSION *
           *  BASED ON THE SALES FOR THE PAY PERIOD.  BOTH PAY COMPONENTS  *
           *  ARE SUPPLIED ON THE SALESPERSON'S INPUT RECORD.              *
           *       THE REPORT MUST BEGIN AT THE TOP OF A NEW PAGE WITH THE *
           *  COMPANY NAME, FOLLOWED BY THE NAME OF THE REPORT, AND THEN   *
           *  APPROPRIATE COLUMN HEADERS.  FOR EACH SALESPERSON, THE REPORT *
           *  MUST PRINT THE SOCIAL SECURITY NUMBER, THE PERSON'S NAME,    *
           *  THE BASE SALARY, THE COMMISSION, AND FINALLY, THE TOTAL PAY  *
           *  FOR THE CURRENT PAY PERIOD.                                  *
           *                                                               *
           *****************************************************************

            ENVIRONMENT DIVISION.

            CONFIGURATION SECTION.

            SOUCE-COMPUTER.  VAX-VMS-8650.
            1
%COBOL-F-ERROR  117, (1) Invalid syntax
            OBJECT-COMPUTER.  VAX-VMS-8650.
            1
%COBOL-W-ERROR  297, (1) Processing of source program resumes at this point

            INPUT-OUTPUT SECTION.

            FILE-CONTROL.
                SELECT EMPLOYEE-FILE   ASSIGN TO COB$INPUT.
                       1
%COBOL-E-ERROR   17, (1) Longest record is longer than RECORD CONTAINS value - Longest record size used
                SELECT PAY-REPORT      ASSIGN TO COB$OUTPUT.
                       1
%COBOL-E-ERROR   17, (1) Longest record is longer than RECORD CONTAINS value - Longest record size used

            DATA DIVISION.

            FILE SECTION.

            FD  EMPLOYEE-FILE
                RECORD CONTAINS 41 CHARACTERS.

            01  SALESPERSON-RECORD.
                05 I-SSN             PIC X(9).
                05 I-SALESPERSON     PIC X(20).
                05 I-SALARY          PIC 9999.99.
                05 I-COMMISSION      PIC 9999.99.

            FD  PAY-REPORT
                RECORD CONTAINS 133 CHARACTERS.

            01  PRINTLINE            PIC X(1332).

            WORKING-STORAGE SECTION.

            01  WS-MORE-RECORDS      PIC XXX.

            01  SALESPERSON-WORK-AREAS.
                05 WS-TOTAL-PAY      PIC XXX.XX-.
                                         1
%COBOL-F-ERROR  156, (1) Invalid PICTURE character-string

            01  COMPANY-NAME
                05 PIC X(54)  VALUE SPACES.
                1
%COBOL-E-ERROR   65, (1) Missing period is assumed
                05 PIC X(26)  VALUE "INTERNATIONAL HABERDASHERY".
                05 PIC X(53)  VALUE SAPCES.
                                    1
%COBOL-F-ERROR  119, (1) Invalid clause in record description

            01  REPORT-NAME.
                05 PIC X(62)  VALUE SPACES.
                05 PIC X(10)  VALUE "PAY REPORT".
                05 PIC X(61)  VALUE SPACES.

            01  HEADINGS.
                05 PIC XXX    VALUE "SSN.
                    1               2
%COBOL-E-ERROR   84, (1) Literal in VALUE clause conflicts with description - clause ignored
```

■ **Figure 5.35** continued

```
INT-HAB-PAY-REPORT                              18-Nov-1993  13:56:41    VAX COBOL V5.1-10                        Page   2
Source Listing                                  18-Nov-1993  13:02:12    FACULTY$DISK:[PAQUETTEG.WCBTXT]C5DBG4.CB1;1

%COBOL-F-ERROR  147, (2) Nonnumeric literal improperly continued
                  05 PIC X(15)  VALUE SPACES.
                  1
%COBOL-E-ERROR   65, (1) Missing period is assumed
                  05 PIC X(10)  VALUE "SALESPERSON".
                     1
%COBOL-E-ERROR   84, (1) Literal in VALUE clause conflicts with description - clause ignored
                  05 PIC X(15)  VALUE SPACES.
                  05 PIC X(6)   VALUE "SALARY".
                  05 PIC X(15)  VALUE SPACES.
                  05 PIC X(10)  VALUE "COMMISSION".
                  05 PIC X(15)  VALUE SAPCES
                                      1
%COBOL-F-ERROR  119, (1) Invalid clause in record description
                  05 PIC X(9(   VALUE "TOTAL PAY".
                  1  2   3
%COBOL-E-ERROR   65, (1) Missing period is assumed
%COBOL-E-ERROR   84, (2) Literal in VALUE clause conflicts with description - clause ignored
%COBOL-F-ERROR  178, (3) Invalid repetition factor
                  05 PIC X(17)  VALUE SPACES.

              01  PAY-LINE.
                  05                   PIC X(13).
                  05 O-SSN             PIC XXXBXXBXXXX.
                  05                   PIC X(7).
                  05 O-SALESPERSON     PIC X(20).
                  05                   PIC X(9).
                  05 O-SALARY          PIC $Z,ZZ9.99.
                  05                   PIC X(13).
                  05 O-COMMISSION      PIC $Z,ZZ9.99.
                  05                   PIC X(16).
                  05 O-TOTAL-PAY       PIC $ZZ9.99.
                  05                   PIC X(17).

              PROCEDURE DIVISION.

              100-PRODUCE-PAY-REPORT.
                  PERFORM 200-START-UP.
                  PERFORM 210-PROCESS-SALESPERSON-REC.
                      UNTIL WS-MORE-RECORDS = "NO ".
                      1
%COBOL-F-ERROR  321, (1) Invalid statement syntax
                  PERFORM 220-FINISH-UP.
                  1
%COBOL-W-ERROR  297, (1) Processing of source program resumes at this point
                  STOP RUN.

              200-START-UP.
                  OPEN INPUT EMPLOYEE-FILE
                       OUTPUT PAY-REPORT.
                  MOVE "YES" TO WS-MORE-RECORDS.
                  MOVE SPACES TO PAY-LINE.
                  PERFORM 300-WRITE-REPORT-HEADERS.
                  PERFORM 310-READ-SALESPERSON-REC.
                          1
%COBOL-F-ERROR  349, (1) Undefined name

              210-PROCESS-SALESPERSON-REC.
              1
%COBOL-W-ERROR  297, (1) Processing of source program resumes at this point
                  PERFORM 320-COMPUTE-TOTAL-PAY.
                  PERFORM 330-PREPARE-PAYLINE.
                          1
%COBOL-F-ERROR  349, (1) Undefined name
                  PERFORM 310-READ-SALESPERSON-REC.
                  1       2
%COBOL-W-ERROR  297, (1) Processing of source program resumes at this point
%COBOL-F-ERROR  349, (2) Undefined name

              220-FINISH-UP.
              1
%COBOL-W-ERROR  297, (1) Processing of source program resumes at this point
                  CLOSE FILES.
                        1
%COBOL-F-ERROR  349, (1) Undefined name

              300-WRITE-REPORT-HEADERS.
              1
%COBOL-W-ERROR  297, (1) Processing of source program resumes at this point
                  WRITE PRINTLINE FROM COMPANY-NAME
                      AFTER ADVANCING PAGE.
                  WRITE PRITLINE FROM REPORT-NAME
                        1
%COBOL-F-ERROR  349, (1) Undefined name
                      AFTER ADVANCING 3 LINES.
                  WRITE PRINTLINE FROM HEADINGS
                  1
```

■ Figure 5.35 continued

```
INT-HAB-PAY-REPORT                     18-Nov-1993  13:56:41   VAX COBOL V5.1-10                    Page   3
Source Listing                         18-Nov-1993  13:02:12   FACULTY$DISK:[PAQUETTEG.WCBTXT]C5DBG4.CB1;1

%COBOL-W-ERROR  297, (1) Processing of source program resumes at this point
                         AFTER ADVANCING 3 LINES.

                 310-READ-SALESPERSON-RECORD.
                     READ EMPLOYEE-FILE RECORD
                         AT END
                             MOVE "NO " TO WS-MORE-RECORDS.

                 320-COMPUTE-TOTAL-PAY.
                     ADD I-SALARY I-COMMISSION GIVING WS-TOTAL-PAY
                         1        2                  3
%COBOL-F-ERROR  276, (1) Operand must be a numeric data-name or a numeric literal
%COBOL-F-ERROR  276, (2) Operand must be a numeric data-name or a numeric literal
%COBOL-F-ERROR  275, (3) Operand must be a numeric or numeric edited data-name
                         ON SIZE ERROR
                             MOVE ZERO TO WS-TOTAL-PAY
                     END-ADD.

                 330-PREPARE-PAY-LINE.
                     MOVE I-SSN TO O-SSN.
                     MOVE I-SALESPERSON TO O-SALESPERSON.
                     MOVE I-SALARY TO O-SALARY.
                     MOVE WS-TOTAL-PAY TO O-TOTAL-PAY.
                     WRITE PRINTLINE FROM PAY-LINE
                         AFTER ADVANCING 2 LINES.
```

■ Figure 5.36

```
                                              INTERNATIONAL HABERDASHERY

                                                      PAY REPORT

SSN                  SALESPERSON                  SALARY            COMMISSION          TOTAL PAY

              623 45 5100      CAHILL, PAULA R.      $  985.50      $  125.00      $  0.00

              611 72 3510      CUSTER, GEORGE P.     $  735.40      $   95.00      $830.40

              315 78 1243      GAMELIN, JOSEPH       $1,230.00      $  810.00      $  0.00

              201 86 1752      JONES, EARLE B.       $  675.00      $   85.50      $760.50

              795 28 8916      BERARD, NORBERT V.    $1,005.00      $  225.00      $  0.00

              186 73 7565      PAQUIN, BRIDGET       $  960.50      $  375.50      $  0.00

              269 31 3905      RENAUD, ANNE          $1,125.00      $  340.00      $  0.00

              519 39 2407      LEMAIRE, HERVE        $  870.50      $  230.50      $  0.00

              056 41 9426      IWANSKI, JENNIE       $1,050.25      $  550.00      $  0.00

              353 22 8728      MALTAIS, VICTORIA     $  650.00      $  100.00      $750.00
```

Programming Exercises

Programming Exercise I

The management of Express Auto Parts Warehouse wants its data processing department to prepare an inventory report showing the activity during the past week for each of its catalog items. For each item, there is a record in the inventory file containing the following data:

cc 1–5	Catalog number
cc 6–25	Item description
cc 36–39	Quantity on hand at the beginning of the week
cc 40–43	Quantity on order at the beginning of the week
cc 44–47	The reorder point
cc 48–51	Quantity received during the week
cc 52–55	Quantity sold during the week
cc 56–59	Quantity returned by customers during the week

The inventory file is updated weekly.

The inventory report must list all the catalog items. For each item, the report must specify the catalog number, the item description, the quantity on hand at the beginning of the week, the quantity received during the week, the quantity returned by customers during the week, the quantity sold during the week, the new balance (quantity on hand) at the end of the week, the quantity that remains on order at the end of the week, and the reorder point.

The report must begin at the top of a new page with appropriate descriptive information: the company name, the report name, and column headings.

The design tools (layout of input record, printer spacing chart, system flowchart, structure chart, program pseudocode, and program flowchart) have been fully developed for you and are shown in Figure 5.37.

Your assignment is to study the program design and then to complete the design implementation phase; that is, code the program, enter it into a file, debug it with the help of the compiler, and then run it.

Use Data File Set 1 (see Appendix C) [DD/CD:VIC5EX1.DAT] as the inventory file.

Figure 5.37

Record Layout Form

I-CATALOG-NO	I-ITEM-DESCR		I-ON-HAND	I-ON-ORDER	I-REORDER-POINT	I-WK-RECEIPTS	I-WK-SALES	I-WK-RETURNS	
1 2 3 4 5	6 7 8 9 10 11 12 13 14 15 16 17 18 19 20 21 22 23 24 25	26 27 28 29 30 31 32 33 34 35	36 37 38 39	40 41 42 43	44 45 46 47	48 49 50 51	52 53 54 55	56 57 58 59	60 61 62 63 64 65 66 67 68 69 70 71 72 73 74 75 76 77 78 79 80

Record Name: INVENTORY-RECORD

Printer Spacing Chart

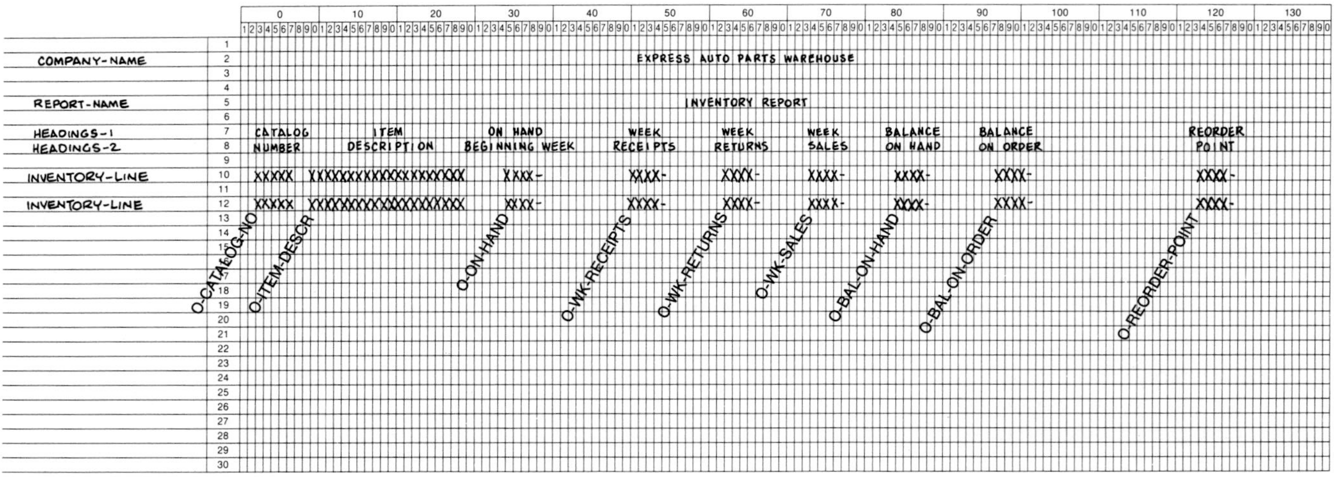

System Flowchart

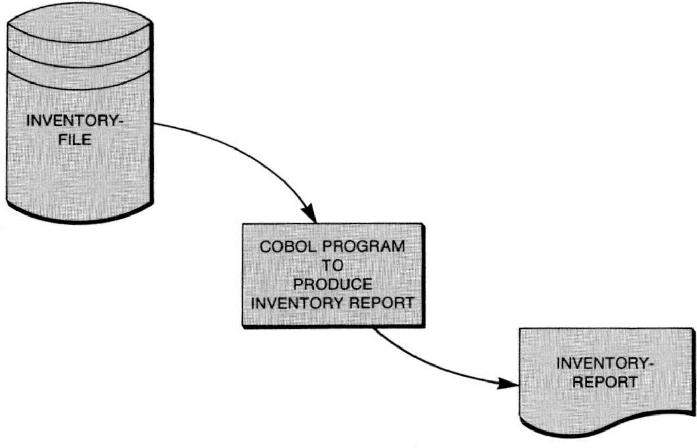

Structure Chart

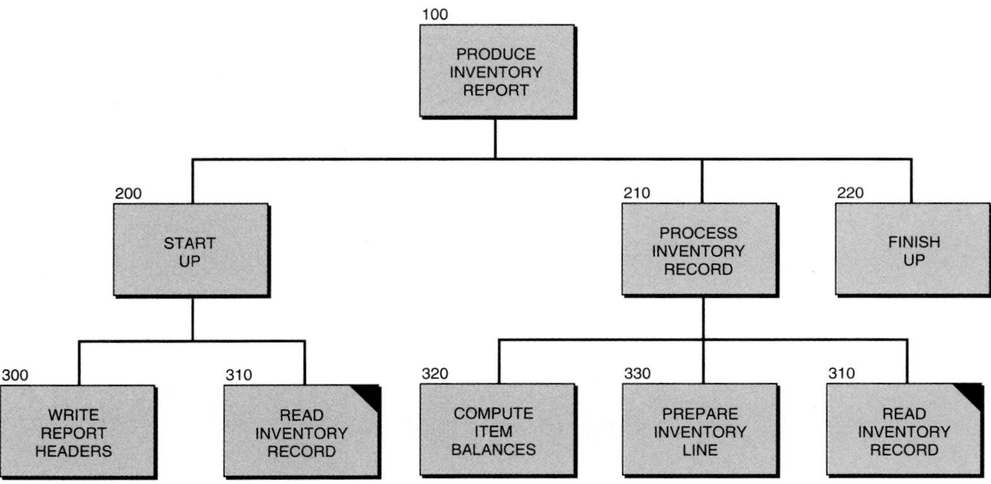

Program Pseudocode

100-Produce-Inventory-Report.

1. Perform 200-Start-Up.
2. Perform 210-Process-Inventory-Record until no more records.
3. Perform 220-Finish-Up.
4. Stop the run.

200-Start-Up.

1. Open the files.
2. Set the end-of-file flag WS-MORE-RECORDS to "YES".
3. Clear the record area Inventory-Line.
4. Perform 300-Write-Report-Headers.
5. Perform 310-Read-Inventory-Record.

210-Process-Inventory-Record.

1. Perform 320-Compute-Item-Amounts.
2. Perform 330-Prepare-Inventory-Line.
3. Perform 310-Read-Inventory-Record.

220-Finish-Up.

1. Close the files.

300-Write-Report-Headers.

1. Move the record Company-Name to the output area Printline.
2. After advancing to the top of a new page, write the output record Printline.
3. Move the record Report-Name to the output area Printline.
4. After advancing 3 lines, write the output record Printline.
5. Move the record Headings-1 to the output area Printline.
6. After advancing 2 lines, write the output record Printline.
7. Move the record Headings-2 to the output area Printline.
8. After advancing 1 line, write the output record Printline.

310-Read-Inventory-Record.

1. Read an input Inventory-record.
2. Test for the end-of-file record; if EOF record reached, move "NO " to the end-of-file flag WS-MORE-RECORDS.

320-Compute-Item-Amounts.

1. Compute new balance-on-hand by adding input quantity on-hand, input week-receipts, input week-returns, and then subtracting input week-sales.
2. Subtract input week-receipts from input balance on-order to equal new balance on-order.

330-Prepare-Inventory-Line.

1. Move input catalog-number to Inventory-Line catalog-number.
2. Move input item-description to Inventory-Line item-description.
3. Move input quantity-on-hand to Inventory-Line quantity-on-hand.
4. Move input week-receipts to Inventory-Line week-receipts.
5. Move input week-sales to Inventory-Line week-sales.
6. Move input week-returns to Inventory-Line week-returns.
7. Move input reorder-point to Inventory-Line reorder-point.
8. Move new balance on-hand to Inventory-Line balance on-hand.
9. Move new balance on-order to Inventory-Line balance on-order.
10. Move the Inventory-Line to the output record area Printline.
11. After advancing 2 lines, write the output record Printline.

■ **Figure 5.37** continued

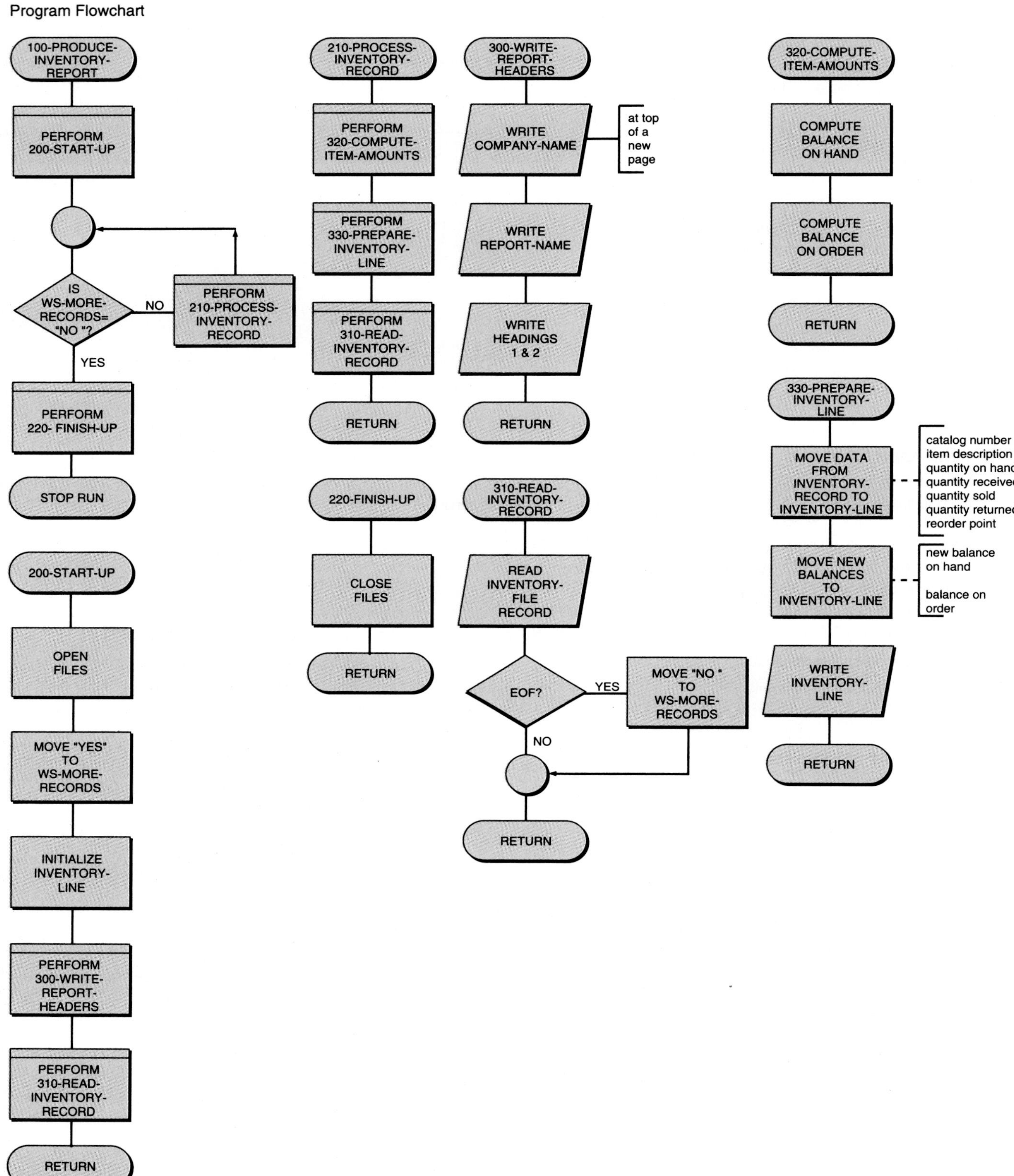

Programming Exercise II

The management of Express Auto Parts Warehouse wants its data processing department to prepare a sales report showing sales figures for the past week for each catalog item. For each item, there is a record in the sales file containing the following data:

cc 1–5	Catalog number
cc 6–25	Item description
cc 26–30	Purchase price per unit
cc 31–35	Selling price per unit
cc 52–55	Quantity sold during the week
cc 56–59	Quantity returned during the week

The sales file is updated weekly.

The sales report must list all the catalog items. For each catalog item, the report must identify the catalog number, the item description, the purchase price per unit, the selling price per unit, the quantity sold during the week, the quantity returned during the week, the gross income from sales during the week, the net income from sales during the week (quantity sold minus quantity returned times selling price), and the net profit or loss.

The report must begin at the top of a new page with appropriate descriptive information: company name, report name, and column headings.

Figure 5.38 contains the layout of the input record, the printer spacing chart, the system flowchart, and the structure chart.

Your assignment is as follows:

a. Complete the design phase by (1) assigning names to the data fields of the output record SALES-LINE, and (2) developing the program pseudocode or the program flowchart.

b. Code the program, enter it into a file, and debug it.

c. Run the program successfully.

Use Data File Set 1 (see Appendix C) [DD/CD:VIC5EX2.DAT] as the sales file.

■ Figure 5.38

Record Layout Form

I-CATALOG-NO	I-ITEM-DESCR	I-PURCHASE-PRICE-PER-UNIT	I-SELLING-PRICE-PER-UNIT		I-WK-SALES	I-WK-RETURNS	
1 2 3 4 5	6 7 8 9 10 11 12 13 14 15 16 17 18 19 20 21 22 23 24 25	26 27 28 ^ 29 30	31 32 33 ^ 34 35	36 37 38 39 40 41 42 43 44 45 46 47 48 49 50 51	52 53 54 55	56 57 58 59	60 61 62 63 64 65 66 67 68 69 70 71 72 73 74 75 76 77 78 79 80

Record Name: SALES-RECORD

■ Figure 5.38 continued

Printer Spacing Chart

Record	Line	Print positions 1–130
	1	
COMPANY-NAME	2	EXPRESS AUTO PARTS WAREHOUSE
	3	
	4	
REPORT-NAME	5	SALES REPORT
	6	
HEADINGS-1	7	CATALOG · ITEM · PURCHASE PRICE · SELLING PRICE · WEEK · WEEK · AMOUNT · AMOUNT · NET
HEADINGS-2	8	NUMBER · DESCRIPTION · PER UNIT · PER UNIT · SALES · RETURNS · GROSS INCOME · NET INCOME · PROFIT/LOSS
	9	
SALES-LINE	10	XXXXX · XXXXXXXXXXXXXXXXXXXX · $XXX.XX- · $XXX.XX- · XXXX- · XXXX- · $X,XXX,XXX.XX- · $X,XXX,XXX.XX- · $X,XXX,XXX.XX-
	11	
SALES-LINE	12	XXXXX · XXXXXXXXXXXXXXXXXXXX · $XXX.XX- · $XXX.XX- · XXXX- · XXXX- · $X,XXX,XXX.XX- · $X,XXX,XXX.XX- · $X,XXX,XXX.XX-

System Flowchart

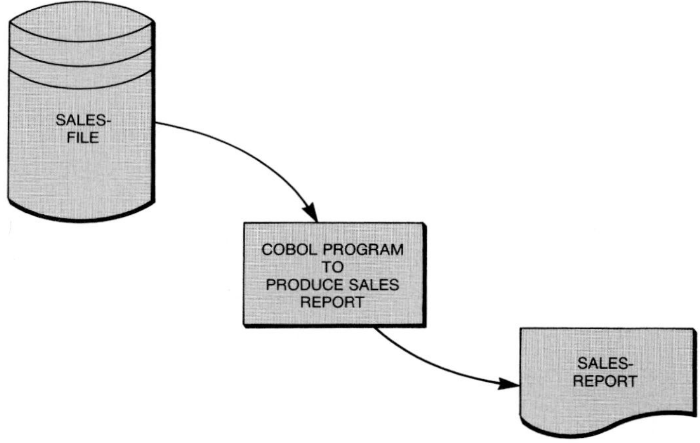

Structure Chart

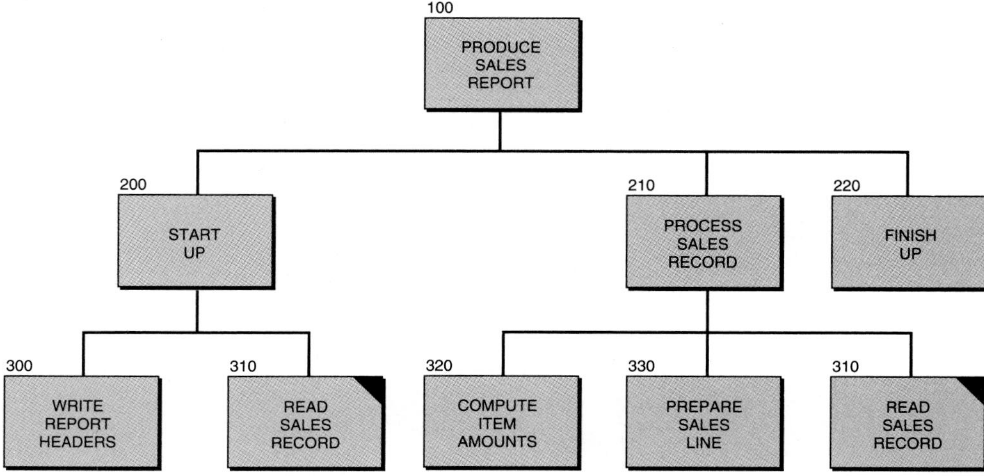

Programming Exercise III

The Ponagansett Electric Company wants a billing report that will list the bill amount for each of its customers for the current billing period. Each record in the customer file contains the following data:

cc 1–3	Area code
cc 4–9	Customer number
cc 10–29	Customer name
cc 30–34	Previous meter reading
cc 35–39	Current meter reading
cc 77–78	Flat rate in cents per KWH (format: x.x)
cc 79–80	Month number

The records in the customer file are arranged sequentially by customer number within area code. This file is updated monthly.

The billing report must contain the following information for each of its customers: the area code, the customer number, the customer name, the previous and current meter readings, the kilowatt-hours used, and the bill amount.

The report must begin at the top of a page with the company name, the report name, and appropriate column headings.

You are encouraged to follow the steps of the problem-solving procedure in developing the program.

Use Data File Set 2 (see Appendix C) [DD/CD:VIC5EX3.DAT] as the customer file.

Programming Exercise IV

The management of the Modern Plastics Company wants the data processing department to prepare a payroll report. For each employee, there is a record in the payroll file containing the following data:

cc 5–6	Department number
cc 7–15	Social Security number
cc 16–35	Employee name
cc 39–42	Pay rate (format: xx.xx)
cc 43–44	Hours worked at regular pay
cc 45–46	Hours worked at overtime pay (time and a half)
cc 77–80	Date hired

The records of the file are arranged in seniority sequence by department.

The payroll report must contain the following information for each employee: department number, Social Security number, name, regular pay, overtime pay, total pay, federal tax deduction (assume 20 percent of total pay), state tax deduction (assume 15 percent of the federal tax), union dues (assume 1 percent of total pay), retirement plan contribution (assume 5 percent of total pay), and net pay (total pay minus all deductions).

The report must begin at the top of a page and be properly documented with the company name, the report name, and descriptive column headings.

You are encouraged to follow the steps of the problem-solving procedure in developing the program.

Use Data File Set 4 (see Appendix C) [DD/CD:VIC5EX4.DAT] as the payroll file.

6 More Arithmetic: Totals and Averages

In this chapter, we will examine the remaining arithmetic statements—DIVIDE and COMPUTE—and the arithmetic concepts of accumulators and counters. To provide a setting for this study, we continue the development of the payroll program begun in Chapter 5. The extension of the program must provide summary information for the company as a whole.

In addition, once the development of the program has been completed, we will revise it for the purpose of introducing refinement features, some related to the program itself and others related to printed reports. Program refinements include the USAGE clause (so that arithmetic operations can be executed more efficiently), the grouping of report headers in working storage, the minus sign in numeric-edited items, initializing record areas, the use of a separate module to initialize program variables, verifying that the input file is not empty, and inserting program documentation within the PROCEDURE DIVISION. Report refinements include dating the report, controlling vertical spacing on a page, limiting the number of detail lines on each page, numbering the pages, and printing an "End of Report" message. ■

Objectives You Should Achieve

After studying this chapter, you should:

1. Be able to correctly code a COBOL arithmetic statement that will store the quotient of two operands in a receiving field.
2. Be able to correctly code a COBOL arithmetic statement that will store the remainder of a division in a receiving field.
3. Given a programming situation in which a value must be obtained as the result of a combination of operations, be able to correctly code a COMPUTE statement that will perform the required operations and properly store the result.
4. Given report specifications that impose a limit on the number of detail lines to be printed on each page, be able to properly define a counter, initialize it, increment it, test it, and reset it as needed in the program.
5. Given a programming situation that requires the use of accumulators, be able to properly define them, initialize them, and subtotal the correct values in them.
6. Given report specifications that require the report date to be printed in edited form at the top of each page, be able to obtain the date from the system and manipulate it so as to print it as specified.
7. Given report specifications that require the numbering of pages, be able to properly implement the requirement.
8. Given a programming situation that requires testing for an empty input file, be able to properly implement the requirement.
9. Be able to implement the printing of an end-of-report message at the end of a report.
10. Be able to control vertical spacing of detail lines on a report by using the "identifier" option of the ADVANCING clause.
11. Be able to code report headers as subordinates of a group item.
12. Be able to use a trailing minus sign to signal negative values on a report.
13. Be able to successfully complete the task of coding and running a program (for which the design tools are provided) that requires accumulators and counters.
14. Be able to successfully develop the program pseudocode and to code and successfully run a program (for which the design tools, through the structure chart, are provided) that
    a. contains arithmetic operations.
    b. must produce a dated report with a specified number of detail lines per page.
    c. must test for an empty input file and print an appropriate message if it is empty.
    d. must print an end-of-report message.

15. Be able to successfully complete the design phase and the design implementation phase of the problem-solving procedure, given a programming assignment whose purpose is to prepare a printed report that
    a. requires the use of accumulators and counters.
    b. contains items whose values must be computed within the program by using any or all of the arithmetic statements.
    c. requires testing for an empty input file.
    d. requires that the current date be printed on the report.
    e. requires a limit on the number of detail lines to be printed on each page.

The Problem

The management of the Reliable Auto Parts Company wants its data processing department to prepare a weekly payroll report. The first part of the report must show the following information for each employee: the department in which the employee works, the employee's Social Security number, full name, the gross wages for the week, all the deductions (federal and state taxes, union dues, insurance premium), the total amount of deductions, and the net wages for the week.

The second part of the report must provide summary information for the company. Specifically, it must show totals for gross wages, and net wages, total amounts withheld for federal taxes, state taxes, union dues, and insurance premiums, the total number of employees on the current payroll, and the company average for gross wages and for net wages.

A record has been prepared for each employee and placed in the employee payroll file. (This file is shown in Figure 6.10. [DD/CD:VIC6SP.DAT]) The records are arranged first by department number (in ascending order) and then alphabetically within each department. Each record contains the following data:

cc 1–3	Department number
cc 4–12	Social Security number
cc 13–34	Employee's name
cc 35–36	Total hours worked during the week
cc 37–40	Employee's hourly pay rate (format: xx.xx)
cc 41–42	Federal tax rate (format: .xx)
cc 43–44	State tax rate (format: .xx)
cc 45–48	Union dues (format: xx.xx)
cc 49–52	Insurance premium (format: xx.xx)

Each part of the report should start on a new page and must be properly documented with company name, report name, and descriptive column headers. In part 2, averages should be printed separate from the totals.

Program Design Phase

Step 1

Designing this program is greatly facilitated by incorporation of the design features for the first part of the report from Chapter 5. We can therefore concentrate on the additions to the design for the summary part of the report.

The layout of the input record is the one shown in Figure 5.1, and the printer spacing chart for part 1 of the report is the one shown in Figure 5.2.

The second part of the report must begin with the company name, then the report name and descriptive column headers for the company totals, and then a line containing the payroll totals. Separate lines are to be produced for the company averages. Note that the fields designed to contain totals and averages must have an adequate size. For instance, if there are fewer than 100 employees and the maximum wage for any payroll period is $2,000.00, then the total wages field should be large enough to contain the value $200,000.00. That is, the field size should be at least 11, counting the editing characters. Similarly, the average wage field should be large enough to contain the value $2,000.00, and its size should then be 9, including editing characters. The printer spacing chart for the summary report is shown in Figure 6.1.

Figure 6.1 Printer spacing chart for the summary report

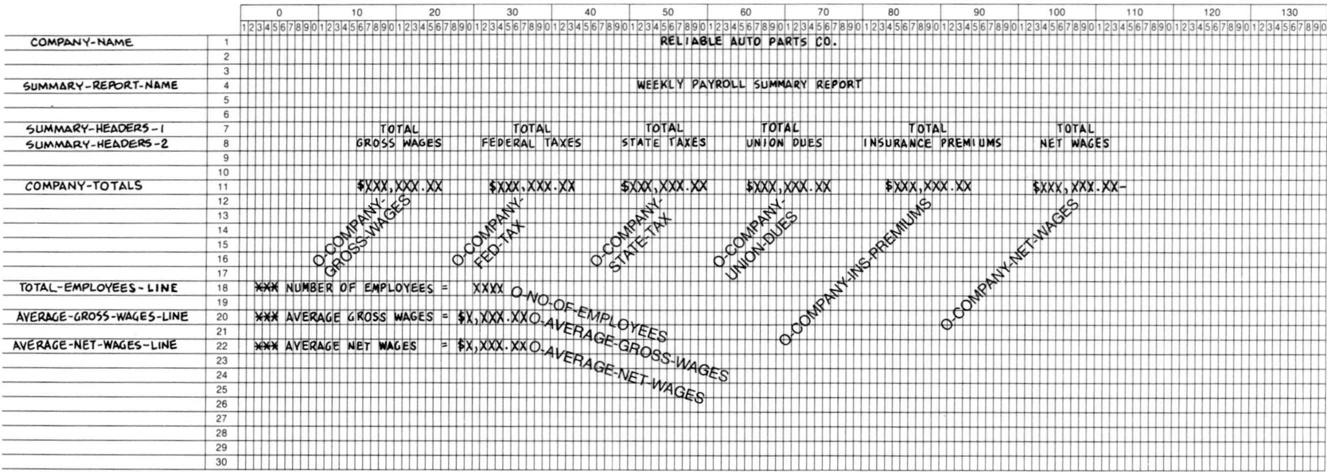

Step 2

In planning the solution to this programming problem, we will simply add to the design developed in Chapter 5.

A brief analysis of the task follows:

1. The first part of the report will be produced exactly as planned in Chapter 5.
2. To obtain totals for the company, "running" subtotals must be maintained while individual employee payroll records are being processed. Data items called *accumulators* are used for this purpose. They are set to zero initially, and once the gross wages, the payroll deductions (federal tax, state tax, union dues, and insurance premium), and the net wages have been computed for an employee, these values are added to the corresponding company accumulators, resulting in new subtotals. When the last employee payroll record has been processed, the subtotaling process will have yielded the final totals for the company.
3. To compute company averages (gross wages and net wages), it is necessary to count the number of employees on the current payroll. A counter must be defined for that purpose. It must be set to zero initially, and then it must be incremented by 1 each time an employee payroll record is processed.
4. The values that must be printed as part of the summary report are not known until all the employee payroll records have been processed. Consequently, the summary report must not be printed until control has passed out of the record-processing loop.

It should be clear that the system flowchart in Figure 5.3 remains unchanged: The records in the employee payroll file are supplied as input to the program, and the program processes the records to produce the payroll report.

On the other hand, the structure chart must take into account the additional task of producing the summary report. As noted in items 2 and 3 of the brief analysis above, the company accumulators must be updated every time an employee payroll record is processed subsequent to computing the payroll items for that employee. A module will be inserted in the structure chart for that purpose, and it will be placed under the control of module 210 PROCESS EMPLOYEE RECORD. Producing the summary report itself is the second of the two major tasks of the program. Since it cannot be done until all the employee records have been processed, it will be handled as a crucial final activity under the control of module 220 FINISH UP. The corresponding module is labeled 350 PRODUCE COMPANY SUMMARY. The production of the company summary is separated into three subordinate modules, one that prints the summary headers, another that prepares and writes the company totals, and a third that prepares and writes the company averages. The revised structure chart is shown in Figure 6.2.

The program pseudocode that details the processing steps corresponding to each module of the revised structure chart is shown in Figure 6.3. Asterisks and color have been used to draw your attention to the new entries.

In the primary paragraph 100-Produce-Payroll-Report, the overall tasks remain the same since there are no changes at the second level of the structure chart.

■ **Figure 6.2** Revised structure chart

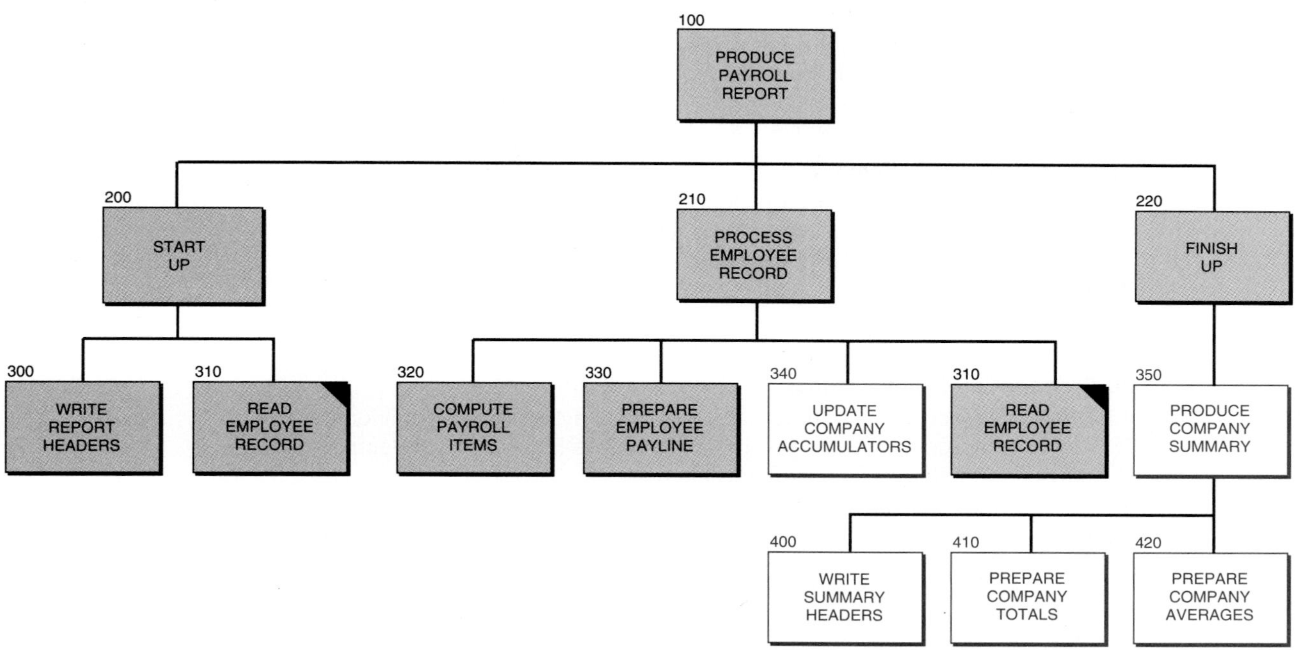

■ **Figure 6.3** Revised program pseudocode (* denotes new entries)

100-Produce-Payroll-Report.

1. Perform 200-Start-Up.
2. Perform 210-Process-Employee-Record until no more records.
3. Perform 220-Finish-Up.
4. Stop the run.

200-Start-Up.

1. Open the files.
2. Set the end-of-file flag WS-MORE-RECORDS to "YES".

*3. Set the company accumulators to zero.
*4. Clear the record area Employee-Payline and the record area Company-Summary.

5. Perform 300-Write-Report-Headers.
6. Perform 310-Read-Employee-Record.

210-Process-Employee-Record.

1. Perform 320-Compute-Payroll-Items.
2. Perform 330-Prepare-Employee-Payline.

*3. Perform 340-Update-Company-Accumulators.

4. Perform 310-Read-Employee-Record.

220-Finish-Up.

*1. Perform 350-Produce-Company-Summary.

2. Close the files.

300-Write-Report-Headers.

1. Move Company-Name to the output area Printline.
2. After advancing to the top of a new page, write the output record Printline.
3. Move Report-Name to the output area Printline.
4. After advancing 3 lines, write the output record Printline.
5. Move Headings-1 to the output area Printline.
6. After advancing 3 lines, write the output record Printline.
7. Move Headings-2 to the output area Printline.
8. After advancing 1 line, write the output record Printline.

310-Read-Employee-Record.

1. Read an input Employee-Payroll-Record.
2. Test for end-of-file record;
   if EOF record reached, move "NO " to the end-of-file flag WS-MORE-RECORDS.

320-Compute-Payroll-Items.

1. Multiply input hours-worked by input hourly payrate to equal gross-wages.
2. Multiply gross-wages by input federal-tax-rate to equal federal-tax.
3. Multiply gross-wages by input state-tax-rate to equal state-tax.
4. Add federal-tax, state-tax, input union-dues, and input insurance-premium to equal total-deductions.
5. Subtract total-deductions from gross-wages to equal net-wages.

330-Prepare-Employee-Payline.

1. Move input department-number to Employee-Payline department-number.
2. Move input Social-Security-number to Employee-Payline Social-Security-number.
3. Move input name to Employee-Payline name.
4. Move input union-dues to Employee-Payline union-dues.
5. Move input insurance-premium to Employee-Payline insurance-premium.
6. Move gross-wages to Employee-Payline gross-wages.
7. Move federal-tax to Employee-Payline federal-tax.
8. Move state-tax to Employee-Payline state-tax.
9. Move total-deductions to Employee-Payline total-deductions.
10. Move net-wages to Employee-Payline net-wages.
11. Move Employee-Payline to the output area Printline.
12. After advancing 2 lines, write the output record Printline.

***340-Update-Company-Accumulators.**

1. Add 1 to the employee-counter.
2. Add gross-wages to the gross-wages accumulator.
3. Add federal-tax to the federal-tax accumulator.
4. Add state-tax to the state-tax accumulator.
5. Add input union-dues to the union-dues accumulator.
6. Add input insurance-premium to the insurance-premium accumulator.
7. Add net-wages to the net-wages accumulator.

***350-Produce-Company-Summary.**

1. Perform 400-Write-Summary-Headers.
2. Perform 410-Prepare-Company-Totals.
3. Perform 420-Prepare-Company-Averages.

***400-Write-Summary-Headers.**

1. Move Company-Name to the output area Printline.
2. After advancing to the top of a new page, write the output record Printline.
3. Move Summary-Report-Name to the output area Printline.
4. After advancing 3 lines, write the output record Printline.
5. Move Summary-Headers-1 to the output area Printline.
6. After advancing 3 lines, write the output record Printline.
7. Move Summary-Headers-2 to the output area Printline.
8. After advancing 1 line, write the output record Printline.

***410-Prepare-Company-Totals.**

1. Move gross-wages accumulator to Company-Summary gross-wages.
2. Move federal-tax accumulator to Company-Summary federal-tax.
3. Move state-tax accumulator to Company-Summary state-tax.
4. Move union-dues accumulator to Company-Summary union-dues.
5. Move insurance-premiums accumulator to Company-Summary insurance-premiums.
6. Move net-wages accumulator to Company-Summary net-wages.
7. Move Company-Summary to the output area Printline.
8. After advancing 3 lines, write the output record Printline.

***420-Prepare-Company-Averages.**

1. Move employee-counter to Total-Employees-Line number-of-employees.
2. Move Total-Employees-Line to the output area Printline.
3. After advancing 5 lines, write the output record Printline.
4. Divide gross-wages accumulator by employee-counter to equal Average-Gross-Wages-Line average-gross-wages rounded.
5. Move Average-Gross-Wages-Line to the output area Printline.
6. After advancing 2 lines, write the output record Printline.
7. Divide net-wages accumulator by employee-counter to equal Average-Net-Wages-Line average-net-wages rounded.
8. Move Average-Net-Wages-Line to the output area Printline.
9. After advancing 2 lines, write the output record Printline.

In paragraph 200-Start-Up, the data items that will serve as the company accumulators are initialized to zero, and the two record areas Employee-Payline and Company-Summary are cleared. In the Chapter 5 program, you may recall that the record area Employee-Payline was cleared at the beginning of the paragraph 330-Prepare-Employee-Payline. Consequently, it was cleared every time a new employee record was processed. While such a procedure is fine, it is not necessary, since every data field of the record will receive new values for each employee record that is processed. The area is cleared initially to remove any extraneous characters that may be stored in bytes of the record that will not be referenced within the current program. Clearing the record area once at the beginning of the program is therefore sufficient and more efficient. Furthermore, it is a good practice to clear all record areas (except those that contain constants as specified by the VALUE clause in the record descriptions) within the Start-Up procedure.

In paragraph 210-Process-Employee-Record, the new entry Perform 340-Update-Company-Accumulators is specified as step 3. This position within the paragraph is not critical, but since it must add values that are computed in the execution of step 1, it must occur after step 1 and before the next record is read.

In paragraph 220-Finish-Up, the critical new task is to produce the summary report. The statement PERFORM 350-Produce-Company-Summary will send control to paragraph 350 where the job will get done. Once the summary report has been completed, the files are closed.

Since structure chart modules 300 through 330 specify the tasks needed to produce the detail report of Chapter 5, and no changes are needed in those modules for the revised program, additional comments are not needed here for the corresponding pseudocode.

In paragraph 340-Update-Company-Accumulators, all the accumulators are brought up-to-date by subtotaling the values that pertain to the employee record currently being processed. Specifically, the employee counter is incremented by 1, and the computed values (gross wages, federal tax, state tax, net wages) and the input record values for union dues and insurance premium are added to the corresponding company accumulators. Within the program, the data items that will serve as accumulators will have to be defined in working storage. They should be grouped under a descriptive group name.

In paragraph 350-Produce-Company-Summary, the three perform statements correspond to the three modules shown in the structure chart to be subordinate to module 350 PRODUCE COMPANY SUMMARY.

In paragraph 400-Write-Summary-Headers, the processing steps are a direct consequence of the statement of the problem and the printer spacing chart of Figure 6.1.

In paragraph 410-Prepare-Company-Totals, the final totals stored in the company accumulators are moved to the appropriate edited fields of the record Company-Summary. The prepared record is then printed on the report, via the output record area Printline.

In paragraph 420-Prepare-Company-Averages, the total accumulated in the employee counter is printed, and it is also used to divide into the accumulated gross wages and into the accumulated net wages to determine the averages for the company. These averages are printed along with appropriate messages.

The program flowchart in Figure 6.4 is the visual representation alternative of the program pseudocode. The parts of the flowchart that are related to the production of the summary report have been highlighted for your convenience.

Figure 6.4 Revised program flowchart

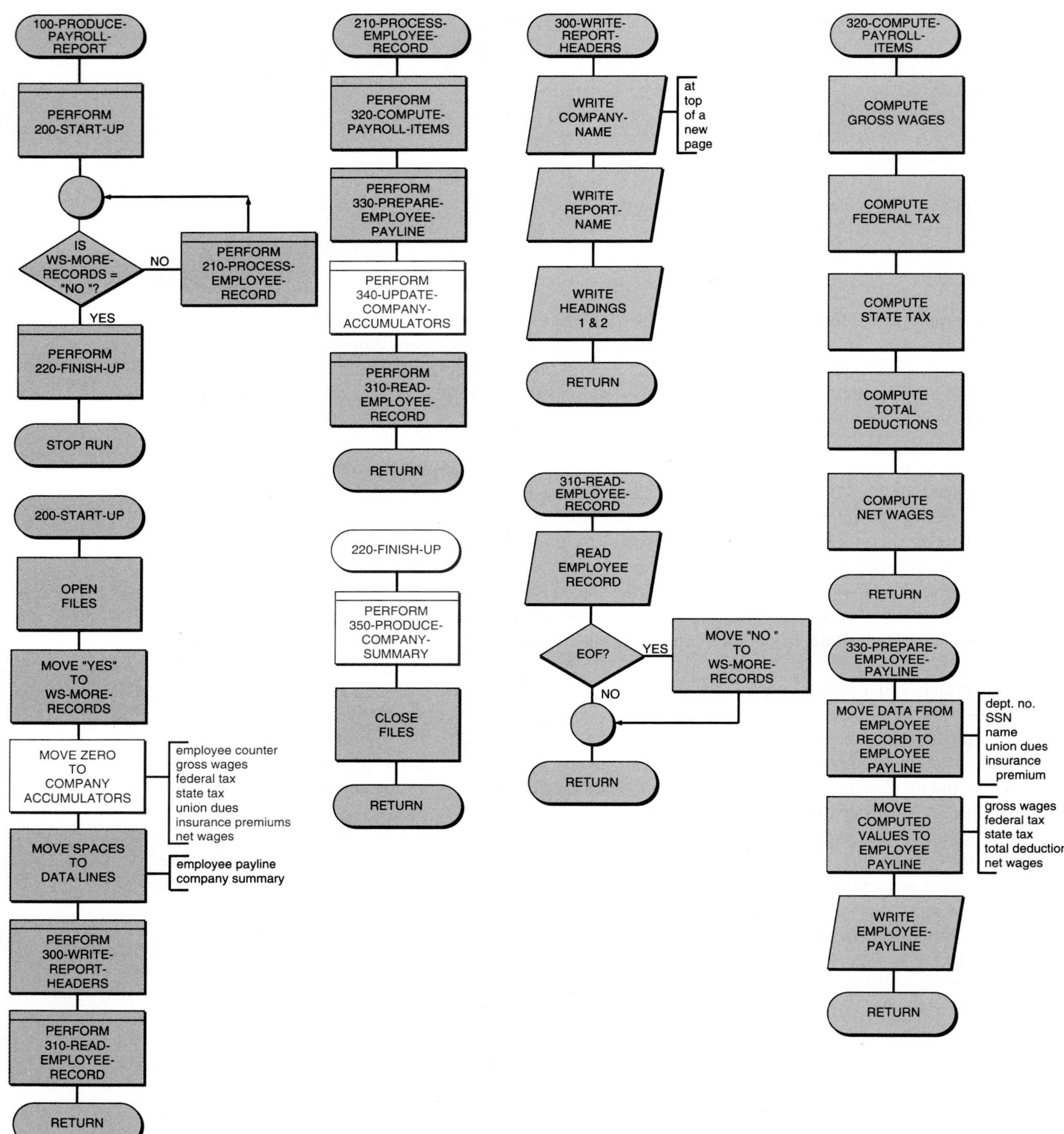

■ **Figure 6.4** continued

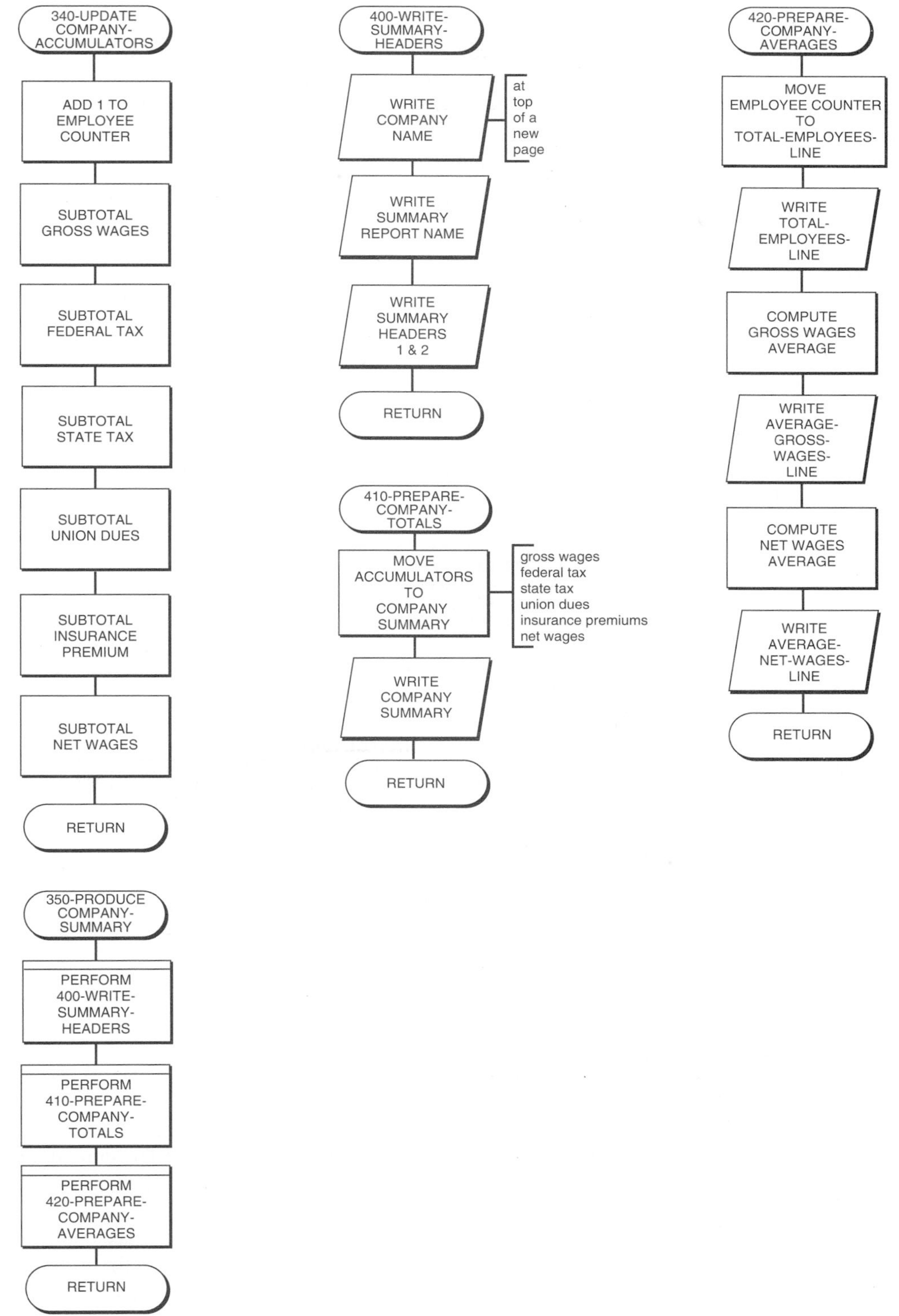

Design Implementation Phase

Step 3

We are now ready to begin coding the program. As you review the requirements of the first two divisions, it should be clear that the production of the summary report does not require any new entries. However, the program documentation within the IDENTIFICATION DIVISION should be updated to reflect the new program requirements.

The coding of the first two divisions of the program follows.

```
 IDENTIFICATION DIVISION.

 PROGRAM-ID.     RELIABLE-AUTO-PAYROLL.

*******************************************************************
*                                                                 *
*   AUTHOR.          PAQUETTE.                                    *
*   DATE WRITTEN.    APRIL 1993                                   *
*                                                                 *
*       THIS PROGRAM PREPARES A MULTILEVEL PAYROLL REPORT FOR THE  *
*   RELIABLE AUTO PARTS COMPANY.                                  *
*                                                                 *
*       THE FIRST PART OF THE REPORT CONTAINS A PAY LINE FOR EACH *
*   EMPLOYEE WITH THE FOLLOWING INFORMATION: THE DEPARTMENT       *
*   NUMBER, SOCIAL SECURITY NUMBER, NAME, GROSS WAGES, ALL        *
*   DEDUCTIONS (FEDERAL TAX, STATE TAX, UNION DUES, INSURANCE     *
*   PREMIUM), TOTAL DEDUCTIONS, AND NET WAGES.  DATA IS PRINTED   *
*   IN EDITED FORM.                                               *
*                                                                 *
*       THE SECOND PART OF THE REPORT IS A SUMMARY FOR THE COMPANY *
*   AS A WHOLE.  THE SUMMARY CONTAINS TOTALS FOR GROSS WAGES,     *
*   ALL DEDUCTIONS (FEDERAL TAX, STATE TAX, UNION DUES, INSURANCE *
*   PREMIUM), AND NET WAGES.  IT ALSO DISPLAYS THE TOTAL NUMBER   *
*   OF EMPLOYEES, AND THE AVERAGE FOR THE GROSS WAGES AND THE NET *
*   WAGES.                                                        *
*                                                                 *
*       EACH PART OF THE REPORT BEGINS AT THE TOP OF A PAGE WITH  *
*   THE COMPANY NAME, FOLLOWED BY THE NAME OF THE REPORT, AND     *
*   APPROPRIATE COLUMN HEADINGS.                                  *
*                                                                 *
*       EACH RECORD OF THE INPUT FILE CONTAINS THE FOLLOWING      *
*   INFORMATION: AN EMPLOYEE'S DEPARTMENT, SOCIAL SECURITY NUMBER, *
*   NAME, HOURS WORKED DURING THE WEEK, PAY RATE, FEDERAL TAX RATE,*
*   STATE TAX RATE, UNION DUES, AND INSURANCE PREMIUM.            *
*                                                                 *
*******************************************************************

 ENVIRONMENT DIVISION.

 CONFIGURATION SECTION.

 SOURCE-COMPUTER.  VAX-VMS-8650.
 OBJECT-COMPUTER.  VAX-VMS-8650.

 INPUT-OUTPUT SECTION.

 FILE-CONTROL.
     SELECT EMPLOYEE-PAYROLL-FILE ASSIGN TO COB$INPUT.
     SELECT PAYROLL-REPORT-FILE   ASSIGN TO COB$OUTPUT.
```

Coding the DATA DIVISION

Since the revised program uses the same input file (EMPLOYEE-PAYROLL-FILE) and the same output file (PAYROLL-REPORT-FILE) as in Chapter 5, no changes are required in the FILE SECTION. All the DATA DIVISION changes occur in the WORKING-STORAGE SECTION.

As noted earlier in the design phase, the program must define a total of seven company accumulators: one for gross wages, one for federal taxes, one for state taxes, one for union dues, one for insurance premiums, one for net wages, and, finally, an employee counter. The size of each of these must agree with the specifications contained on the printer spacing chart of Figure 6.1.

In Figure 6.5, the employee payroll record in input memory generates the values that will be stored in the data fields of the group WS-EMPLOYEE-PAYROLL-ITEMS. These values in turn, along with the values in the fields I-UNION-DUES and I-INS-PREMIUM in input memory, are then added to the corresponding accumulators in the group WS-COMPANY-ACCUMULATORS, and the employee counter is incremented by 1. (Figure 6.5 shows the **initial** values in the accumulators, since the input record for Georgia Black is the first one to be processed.) This occurs for each record in the EMPLOYEE-PAYROLL-

■ **Figure 6.5** Updating the company accumulators

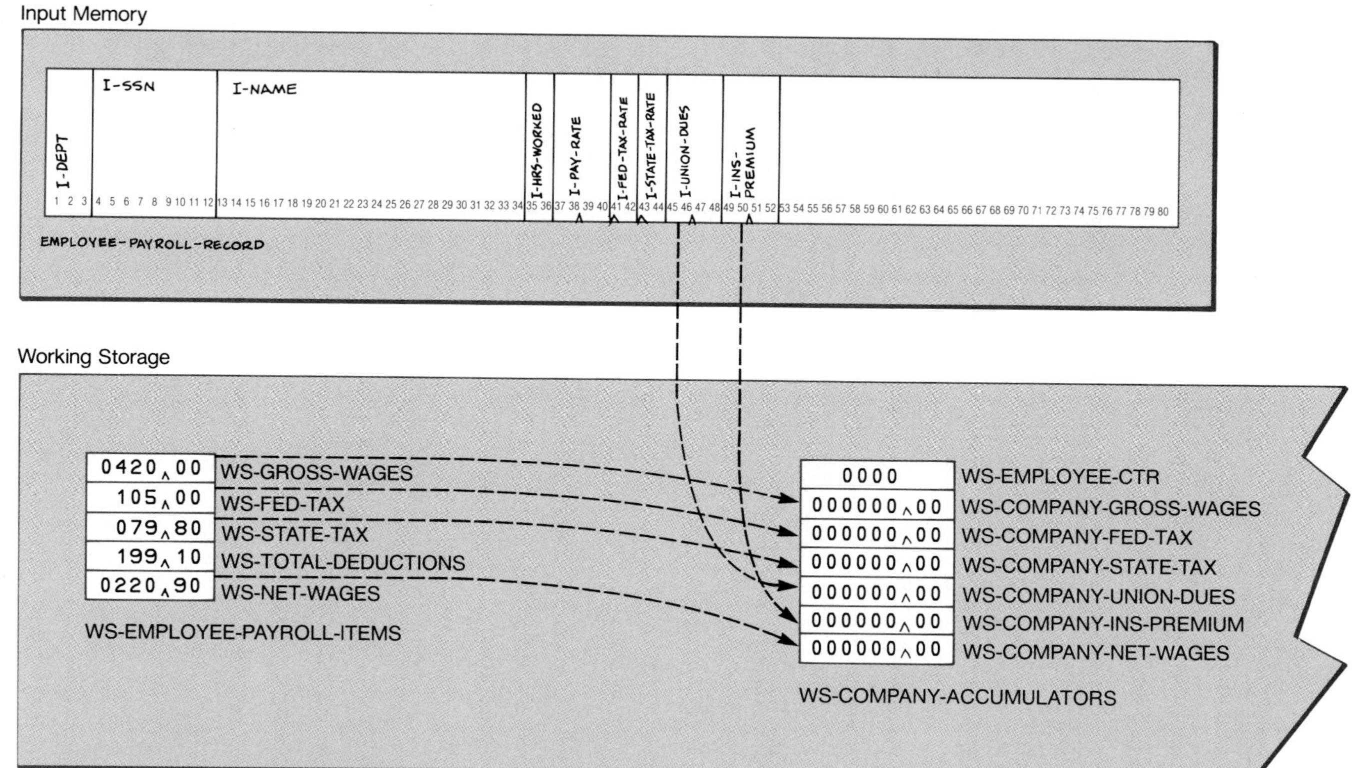

■ **Figure 6.6** Coding of program accumulators

```
*****************************************************************
*                                                               *
*  THE NEXT GROUP CONTAINS THE ACCUMULATORS THAT ARE NEEDED FOR *
*  THE SUMMARY REPORT.  THEY ARE INITIALIZED TO ZERO WITHIN THE *
*  MODULE 200-START-UP.                                         *
*                                                               *
*****************************************************************

 01  WS-COMPANY-ACCUMULATORS.
     05 WS-EMPLOYEE-CTR            PIC S9(4).
     05 WS-COMPANY-GROSS-WAGES     PIC S9(6)V99.
     05 WS-COMPANY-FED-TAX         PIC S9(6)V99.
     05 WS-COMPANY-STATE-TAX       PIC S9(6)V99.
     05 WS-COMPANY-UNION-DUES      PIC S9(6)V99.
     05 WS-COMPANY-INS-PREMIUMS    PIC S9(6)V99.
     05 WS-COMPANY-NET-WAGES       PIC S9(6)V99.
```

FILE. Consequently, after the last record has been processed, the accumulators will contain the final totals for the company.

The coding of the accumulators is shown in Figure 6.6. The programmer should always initialize accumulators to zero. This can be done in either of two ways: (1) use the VALUE IS ZERO clause in the description of the data item, or (2) use the statement MOVE ZERO TO accumulator-name or the alternate statement INITIALIZE accumulator-name within the start-up paragraph of the PROCEDURE DIVISION. This program will initialize the accumulators within the start-up paragraph because it provides a greater degree of self-documentation within the PROCEDURE DIVISION. (You may recall that in this text, the VALUE clause is used only to assign **constants** to data fields; in all other cases, fields that need to be initialized will receive their values as a result of MOVE or INITIALIZE statements.)

In addition to the accumulators, the revised WORKING-STORAGE SECTION must contain a record description for each of the eight lines that must be printed on the summary report. These lines have been prepared on the printer spacing chart of Figure 6.1. The corresponding coding is shown in Figure 6.7. Note that all data fields have been appropriately edited: Leading zeros will be eliminated, and the dollar sign ($), decimal point (.), and comma (,) will be inserted in dollar-amount fields.

Figure 6.7 Record descriptions corresponding to the printer spacing chart

```
******************************************************************
*                                                                *
*  THE NEXT 7 RECORDS ARE THE ONES THAT MUST BE PRINTED ON THE   *
*  SUMMARY REPORT.                                               *
*                                                                *
******************************************************************

 01   SUMMARY-REPORT-NAME.
      05 PIC X(51)    VALUE SPACES.
      05 PIC X(29)    VALUE "WEEKLY PAYROLL SUMMARY REPORT".
      05 PIC X(52)    VALUE SPACES.

 01   SUMMARY-HEADERS-1.
      05 PIC X(18)   VALUE SPACES.
      05 PIC X(5)    VALUE "TOTAL".
      05 PIC X(12)   VALUE SPACES.
      05 PIC X(5)    VALUE "TOTAL".
      05 PIC X(12)   VALUE SPACES.
      05 PIC X(5)    VALUE "TOTAL".
      05 PIC X(10)   VALUE SPACES.
      05 PIC X(5)    VALUE "TOTAL".
      05 PIC X(14)   VALUE SPACES.
      05 PIC X(5)    VALUE "TOTAL".
      05 PIC X(14)   VALUE SPACES.
      05 PIC X(5)    VALUE "TOTAL".
      05 PIC X(22)   VALUE SPACES.

 01   SUMMARY-HEADERS-2.
      05 PIC X(15)   VALUE SPACES.
      05 PIC X(11)   VALUE "GROSS WAGES".
      05 PIC X(5)    VALUE SPACES.
      05 PIC X(13)   VALUE "FEDERAL TAXES".
      05 PIC X(5)    VALUE SPACES.
      05 PIC X(11)   VALUE "STATE TAXES".
      05 PIC X(5)    VALUE SPACES.
      05 PIC X(10)   VALUE "UNION DUES".
      05 PIC X(5)    VALUE SPACES.
      05 PIC X(18)   VALUE "INSURANCE PREMIUMS".
      05 PIC X(5)    VALUE SPACES.
      05 PIC X(9)    VALUE "NET WAGES".
      05 PIC X(20)   VALUE SPACES.

 01 COMPANY-SUMMARY.
      05                             PIC X(15).
      05 O-COMPANY-GROSS-WAGES       PIC $ZZZ,ZZ9.99.
      05                             PIC X(6).
      05 O-COMPANY-FED-TAX           PIC $ZZZ,ZZ9.99.
      05                             PIC X(6).
      05 O-COMPANY-STATE-TAX         PIC $ZZZ,ZZ9.99.
      05                             PIC X(5).
      05 O-COMPANY-UNION-DUES        PIC $ZZZ,ZZ9.99.
      05                             PIC X(7).
      05 O-COMPANY-INS-PREMIUMS      PIC $ZZZ,ZZ9.99.
      05                             PIC X(8).
      05 O-COMPANY-NET-WAGES         PIC $ZZZ,ZZ9.99-.
      05                             PIC X(18).

 01   TOTAL-EMPLOYEES-LINE.
      05 PIC X(6)     VALUE "  *** ".
      05 PIC X(22)    VALUE "NUMBER OF EMPLOYEES = ".
      05 PIC X(2)     VALUE SPACES.
      05 O-NO-OF-EMPLOYEES        PIC ZZZ9.
      05 PIC X(99)    VALUE SPACES.

 01   AVERAGE-GROSS-WAGES-LINE.
      05 PIC X(6)     VALUE "  *** ".
      05 PIC X(22)    VALUE "AVERAGE GROSS WAGES = ".
      05 O-AVERAGE-GROSS-WAGES  PIC $Z,ZZ9.99.
      05 PIC X(96)    VALUE SPACES.

 01   AVERAGE-NET-WAGES-LINE.
      05 PIC X(6)     VALUE "  *** ".
      05 PIC X(22)    VALUE "AVERAGE NET WAGES   = ".
      05 O-AVERAGE-NET-WAGES    PIC $Z,ZZ9.99-.
      05 PIC X(94)    VALUE SPACES.
```

Coding the PROCEDURE DIVISION

The program pseudocode of Figure 6.3 or the program flowchart of Figure 6.4 is used to guide and direct the coding of the PROCEDURE DIVISION.

You have already learned the formats of all the statements that will be used to convert the pseudocode statements into COBOL code except for one, the DIVIDE statement, which is required in paragraph 420-PREPARE-COMPANY-AVERAGES. We will assume at this point that all the other paragraphs of the PROCEDURE DIVISION can be coded directly, and without any difficulty, from the program pseudocode or flowchart.

The DIVIDE statement is the last of the simple arithmetic statements. Although the COMPUTE statement is not used in this program, its format will be explained as well.

The DIVIDE Statement

The formats of the DIVIDE statement are shown in Figure 6.8. Of the three formats, the first two are used most often. Examine the following examples. (In these examples, the asterisk [*] denotes the receiving field.)

Example 1:

```
DIVIDE -5 INTO POINTS.
```

Item	PICTURE	Value Before	Value After
*POINTS	S99	+45	−09

In this statement, the operands are the numeric literal −5 and the data item POINTS. The *dividend* POINTS is divided by the *divisor* −5, and the *quotient* −9 is stored in the operand POINTS. Note that before execution of the instruction, POINTS contains the dividend (+45), but after execution, POINTS contains the quotient (−09). In other words, the function of the data item has changed. (Be aware that the clarity and self-documentation of the program are reduced whenever this happens. Such statements should be kept to a minimum.)

Example 2:

```
DIVIDE TOTAL-POINTS BY NO-OF-TESTS GIVING TEST-AVE ROUNDED.
```

Item	PICTURE	Value Before	Value After
TOTAL-POINTS	S999	+224	+224
NO-OF-TESTS	S99	+03	+03
*TEST-AVE	S99V9	+94.3	+74.7

Figure 6.8 DIVIDE statement formats

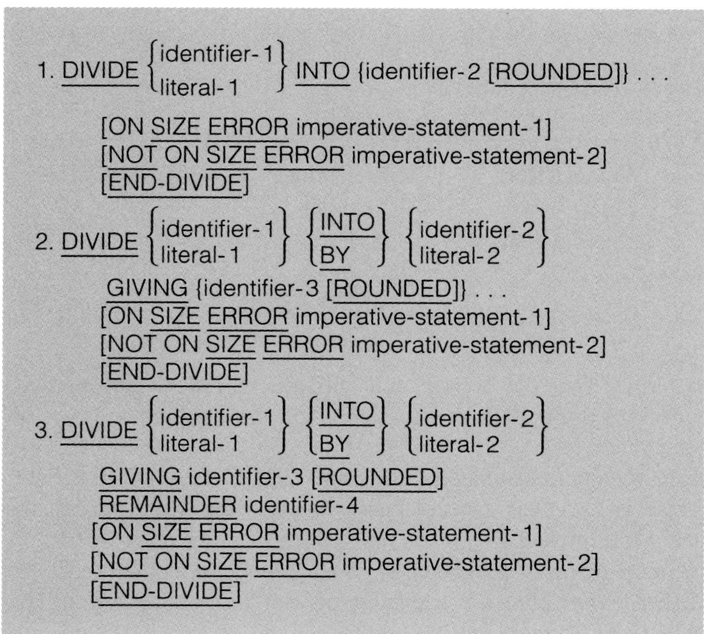

In this case, the dividend TOTAL-POINTS, with a value of +224, is divided by the divisor NO-OF-TESTS, with a value of +3, and the quotient +74.666... is stored rounded to the nearest tenth in TEST-AVE. The previous value in the receiving field TEST-AVE is simply replaced by the computed value +74.7, whereas the values in TOTAL-POINTS and in NO-OF-TESTS remain unchanged. (Note that the ROUNDED option applies to the PICTURE of the receiving field, TEST-AVE. The computed value +74.666... must be rounded to the nearest tenth. Hence, the stored value is +74.7.)

In the format used in this example, the initial function of each data item remains unchanged: TOTAL-POINTS is always the dividend, NO-OF-TESTS is always the divisor, and TEST-AVE is always the quotient.

The same results would be obtained by using the alternate form

```
DIVIDE NO-OF-TESTS INTO TOTAL-POINTS
     GIVING TEST-AVE ROUNDED.
```

Also note that in this alternate form, the functions of the data items remain unchanged: NO-OF-TESTS is the divisor, TOTAL-POINTS is the dividend, and TEST-AVE is the quotient.

Since a division very often yields a quotient that contains decimals, the ROUNDED option should always be used to round off the resulting value. For instance, in example 2, if the ROUNDED option is not used, the value stored in TEST-AVE is +74.6 rather than +74.7.

Example 3:

```
DIVIDE SSN BY FILE-SIZE GIVING QUOTIENT
     REMAINDER LOCATION-NO.
```

Item	PICTURE	Value Before	Value After
SSN	9(9)	334249502	334249502
FILE-SIZE	S9(4)	+0250	+0250
*QUOTIENT	S9(9)	+000031023	+001336998
*LOCATION-NO	S9(4)	+0152	+0002

In this case, the data item SSN is the dividend, FILE-SIZE is the divisor, QUOTIENT is the quotient, and LOCATION-NO stores the remainder. The remainder is the result of subtracting the product of the quotient and the divisor from the dividend. In this format, two data items receive a computed value: the item in the GIVING phrase and the item in the REMAINDER phrase.

Example 4:

```
DIVIDE ITEM-A BY ITEM-B GIVING ITEM-C ROUNDED
    ON SIZE ERROR
        MULTIPLY ITEM-A BY ITEM-B GIVING ITEM-D
    NOT ON SIZE ERROR
        ADD ITEM-A TO ITEM-B GIVING ITEM-D
END-DIVIDE
SUBTRACT ITEM-C FROM ITEM-A GIVING ITEM-E ROUNDED.
```

		Part 1		Part 2	
Item	**PICTURE**	**Value Before**	**Value After**	**Value Before**	**Value After**
ITEM-A	S99V99	+27.84	+27.84	+27.84	+27.84
ITEM-B	S9V99	−5.30	−5.30	+0.25	+0.25
ITEM-C	S99V99	+10.76	−05.25	−49.10	−49.10
ITEM-D	S999V99	−001.25	+022.54	+154.50	+006.96
ITEM-E	S99V9	+15.2	+33.1	−28.3	+76.9

In this case, ITEM-A is the dividend, ITEM-B is the divisor, and ITEM-C will store the quotient, rounded to two decimal places, if there is no size error. If there is a size error, the quotient will not be stored.

In part 1, there is no size error. Therefore, the quotient −5.25 is stored in ITEM-C, the ADD statement following the NOT ON SIZE ERROR phrase is executed, control passes beyond the scope terminator END-DIVIDE, and the SUBTRACT statement is executed.

In part 2, the quotient is +111.36. Since there is a size error, the quotient is not stored. The MULTIPLY statement following the ON SIZE ERROR phrase is executed, control then passes beyond the scope terminator END-DIVIDE, and the SUBTRACT statement is executed.

Rules Governing the Use of the DIVIDE Statement and Its Options

1. In all formats, the operands must be elementary items with numeric PICTUREs, and the literals must be numeric.
2. In format 1, identifier-1 and all identifiers following the word INTO are operands. Identifier-1 contains the divisor; each identifier following the word INTO contains a dividend before the division occurs, but each one contains its respective quotient after the division is performed.
3. In format 2, identifier-1 and identifier-2 are operands. Identifier-3, and any other identifier following the word GIVING, store the quotient; these identifiers are not operands and can have an edited PICTURE.
4. In format 3, identifier-1 and identifier-2 are operands. Identifier-3 stores the quotient. Identifier-4 stores the remainder; it is not an operand, and it can have an edited PICTURE. The remainder is obtained by subtracting the product of the quotient and the divisor from the dividend.
5. In any case, the computed value (quotient and/or remainder) is stored according to the PICTURE of the receiving field. If the receiving field contains a decimal point, assumed or edited, the positions are filled from the decimal point to the right and then to the left. If there is no decimal point, positions are filled from the rightmost. (Be careful: Low-order and high-order truncations may occur.)
6. If the ROUNDED option is used, the word ROUNDED immediately follows the name of the receiving field. The computed value is rounded according to the PICTURE of the receiving field. Its use minimizes the effect of a low-order truncation. If there are multiple receiving fields, rounding occurs only for the receiving fields to which the word ROUNDED is attached.
7. If the ON SIZE ERROR option is used, the phrase ON SIZE ERROR immediately follows the name(s) of the receiving field(s), or the word ROUNDED, if it is used. No high-order truncation will occur. Rounding or low-order truncation takes place before the size error check. If there is a size error in any receiving field, the quotient is not stored in that field, and the imperative statement following the ON SIZE ERROR phrase is executed. If there is no size error in any receiving field, the computed value is stored in the receiving field(s), and the statement following the ON SIZE ERROR phrase is not executed. If there are multiple receiving fields, only the fields for which a size error occurs retain their initial values. The other fields store the appropriate quotient.
8. The NOT ON SIZE ERROR option is permissible only as an alternate path to the ON SIZE ERROR option. If there is no size error, the statement following the NOT ON SIZE ERROR phrase is executed after the quotient(s) is (are) stored.
9. END-DIVIDE is the scope terminator. A DIVIDE statement can be terminated either by a period or by END-DIVIDE.
10. The sign of a quotient is stored only if the PICTURE clause that defines the receiving field contains an S.
11. The use of the ROUNDED and ON SIZE ERROR options is recommended as noted to minimize the effect of a low-order truncation and to prevent a high-order truncation, respectively.
12. Division by zero always causes a size error.

Coding the Paragraph 420-PREPARE-COMPANY-AVERAGES

Now that we have examined the formats of the DIVIDE statement, the coding corresponding to the pseudocode paragraph 420-Prepare-Company-Averages can be completed. Steps 4 and 7 are of particular concern, since they specify the need for the division operation.

In step 4, the value stored in the gross-wages accumulator WS-COMPANY-GROSS-WAGES must be divided by the value stored in the employee counter WS-EMPLOYEE-CTR. The resulting quotient is the "average" gross wages for the company, and it is stored directly into the edited field O-AVERAGE-GROSS-WAGES of the record AVERAGE-GROSS-WAGES-LINE.

It should be clear that format 2 of the DIVIDE statement is the most appropriate one to use. This format allows the following two choices:

Choice 1:

```
DIVIDE WS-COMPANY-GROSS-WAGES BY WS-EMPLOYEE-CTR
     GIVING O-AVERAGE-GROSS-WAGES ROUNDED.
```

Choice 2:

```
DIVIDE WS-EMPLOYEE-CTR INTO WS-COMPANY-GROSS-WAGES
     GIVING O-AVERAGE-GROSS-WAGES ROUNDED.
```

As an example, if WS-COMPANY-GROSS-WAGES contains the value 11928.75, and WS-EMPLOYEE-CTR contains the value 33, then the division

```
11928.75/33
```

yields the quotient 361.47727. This value must be rounded according to the PICTURE specified for the receiving field O-AVERAGE-GROSS-WAGES; that is, it must be rounded to the nearest hundredth. The stored value is therefore 361.48.

In step 7, the value stored in the net wages accumulator WS-COMPANY-NET-WAGES must be divided by the value stored in the employee counter WS-EMPLOYEE-CTR. The resulting quotient is the "average" net wages for the company, and it is stored directly into the edited field O-AVERAGE-NET-WAGES of the record AVERAGE-NET-WAGES-LINE.

Format 2 of the DIVIDE statement gives us the following two choices:

Choice 1:

```
DIVIDE WS-COMPANY-NET-WAGES BY WS-EMPLOYEE-CTR
    GIVING O-AVERAGE-NET-WAGES ROUNDED.
```

Choice 2:

```
DIVIDE WS-EMPLOYEE-CTR INTO WS-COMPANY-NET-WAGES
    GIVING O-AVERAGE-NET-WAGES ROUNDED.
```

If the value stored in WS-COMPANY-NET-WAGES is 6351.00, then the division

```
6351.00/33
```

yields the quotient 192.45455. This value must also be rounded to the nearest hundredth, and it is therefore stored in the receiving field O-AVERAGE-NET-WAGES as 192.45.

For both of these divisions, we have selected choice 1. The resulting coding is shown below.

```
420-PREPARE-COMPANY-AVERAGES.
    MOVE WS-EMPLOYEE-CTR TO O-NO-OF-EMPLOYEES.
    WRITE PRINTLINE FROM TOTAL-EMPLOYEES-LINE
        AFTER ADVANCING 5 LINES.
    DIVIDE WS-COMPANY-GROSS-WAGES BY WS-EMPLOYEE-CTR
        GIVING O-AVERAGE-GROSS-WAGES ROUNDED.
    WRITE PRINTLINE FROM AVERAGE-GROSS-WAGES-LINE
        AFTER ADVANCING 2 LINES.
    DIVIDE WS-COMPANY-NET-WAGES BY WS-EMPLOYEE-CTR
        GIVING O-AVERAGE-NET-WAGES ROUNDED.
    WRITE PRINTLINE FROM AVERAGE-NET-WAGES-LINE
        AFTER ADVANCING 2 LINES.
```

Since paragraph 420-PREPARE-COMPANY-AVERAGES is the last paragraph of the PROCEDURE DIVISION, the coding of the program is now complete.

Steps 4 and 5

The coded program must now be keyed into a file and debugged. A clean listing of the program is shown in Figure 6.9.

Step 6

Step 6 calls for a test run of the program. Figure 6.10 [DD/CD:VIC6SP.DAT] shows the data file that was used in the test run, and Figure 6.11 shows the report produced by the program.

This completes the initial development of the program.

Figure 6.9 Listing of chapter program

```
 IDENTIFICATION DIVISION.

 PROGRAM-ID.     RELIABLE-AUTO-PAYROLL.

*****************************************************************
*                                                               *
*  AUTHOR.         PAQUETTE.                                    *
*  DATE WRITTEN.   APRIL 1993                                   *
*                                                               *
*     THIS PROGRAM PREPARES A MULTILEVEL PAYROLL REPORT FOR THE *
*  RELIABLE AUTO PARTS COMPANY.                                 *
*                                                               *
*     THE FIRST PART OF THE REPORT CONTAINS A PAY LINE FOR EACH *
*  EMPLOYEE WITH THE FOLLOWING INFORMATION: THE DEPARTMENT      *
*  NUMBER, SOCIAL SECURITY NUMBER, NAME, GROSS WAGES, ALL       *
*  DEDUCTIONS (FEDERAL TAX, STATE TAX, UNION DUES, INSURANCE    *
*  PREMIUM), TOTAL DEDUCTIONS, AND NET WAGES.  DATA IS PRINTED  *
*  IN EDITED FORM.                                              *
*                                                               *
*     THE SECOND PART OF THE REPORT IS A SUMMARY FOR THE COMPANY *
*  AS A WHOLE.  THE SUMMARY CONTAINS TOTALS FOR GROSS WAGES,    *
*  ALL DEDUCTIONS (FEDERAL TAX, STATE TAX, UNION DUES, INSURANCE *
*  PREMIUM), AND NET WAGES.  IT ALSO DISPLAYS THE TOTAL NUMBER  *
*  OF EMPLOYEES, AND THE AVERAGE FOR THE GROSS WAGES AND THE NET *
*  WAGES.                                                       *
*                                                               *
*     EACH PART OF THE REPORT BEGINS AT THE TOP OF A PAGE WITH  *
*  THE COMPANY NAME, FOLLOWED BY THE NAME OF THE REPORT, AND    *
*  APPROPRIATE COLUMN HEADINGS.                                 *
*                                                               *
*     EACH RECORD OF THE INPUT FILE CONTAINS THE FOLLOWING      *
*  INFORMATION: AN EMPLOYEE'S DEPARTMENT, SOCIAL SECURITY NUMBER, *
*  NAME, HOURS WORKED DURING THE WEEK, PAY RATE, FEDERAL TAX RATE,*
*  STATE TAX RATE, UNION DUES, AND INSURANCE PREMIUM.           *
*                                                               *
*****************************************************************

 ENVIRONMENT DIVISION.

 CONFIGURATION SECTION.

 SOURCE-COMPUTER.  VAX-VMS-8650.
 OBJECT-COMPUTER.  VAX-VMS-8650.

 INPUT-OUTPUT SECTION.

 FILE-CONTROL.
     SELECT EMPLOYEE-PAYROLL-FILE ASSIGN TO COB$INPUT.
     SELECT PAYROLL-REPORT-FILE   ASSIGN TO COB$OUTPUT.

 DATA DIVISION.

 FILE SECTION.

 FD  EMPLOYEE-PAYROLL-FILE
     RECORD CONTAINS 80 CHARACTERS.

 01  EMPLOYEE-PAYROLL-RECORD.
     05 I-DEPT            PIC XXX.
     05 I-SSN             PIC X(9).
     05 I-NAME            PIC X(22).
     05 I-HRS-WORKED      PIC 99.
     05 I-PAY-RATE        PIC 99V99.
     05 I-FED-TAX-RATE    PIC V99.
     05 I-STATE-TAX-RATE  PIC V99.
     05 I-UNION-DUES      PIC 99V99.
     05 I-INS-PREMIUM     PIC 99V99.
     05                   PIC X(28).

 FD  PAYROLL-REPORT-FILE
     RECORD CONTAINS 133 CHARACTERS.

 01  PRINTLINE            PIC X(133).
```

```
 WORKING-STORAGE SECTION.

 01   WS-PROGRAM-CONTROLS.
      05 WS-MORE-RECORDS       PIC XXX.

 01   WS-EMPLOYEE-PAYROLL-ITEMS.
      05 WS-GROSS-WAGES        PIC S9999V99.
      05 WS-FED-TAX            PIC S999V99.
      05 WS-STATE-TAX          PIC S999V99.
      05 WS-TOTAL-DEDUCTIONS   PIC S999V99.
      05 WS-NET-WAGES          PIC S9999V99.

*****************************************************************
*                                                               *
*  THE NEXT GROUP CONTAINS THE ACCUMULATORS THAT ARE NEEDED FOR *
*  THE SUMMARY REPORT.  THEY ARE INITIALIZED TO ZERO WITHIN THE *
*  MODULE 200-START-UP.                                         *
*                                                               *
*****************************************************************

 01   WS-COMPANY-ACCUMULATORS.
      05 WS-EMPLOYEE-CTR            PIC S9(4).
      05 WS-COMPANY-GROSS-WAGES     PIC S9(6)V99.
      05 WS-COMPANY-FED-TAX         PIC S9(6)V99.
      05 WS-COMPANY-STATE-TAX       PIC S9(6)V99.
      05 WS-COMPANY-UNION-DUES      PIC S9(6)V99.
      05 WS-COMPANY-INS-PREMIUMS    PIC S9(6)V99.
      05 WS-COMPANY-NET-WAGES       PIC S9(6)V99.

 01   COMPANY-NAME.
      05 PIC X(54)    VALUE SPACES.
      05 PIC X(24)    VALUE "RELIABLE AUTO PARTS CO.".
      05 PIC X(54)    VALUE SPACES.

 01   REPORT-NAME.
      05 PIC X(55)    VALUE SPACES.
      05 PIC X(21)    VALUE "WEEKLY PAYROLL REPORT".
      05 PIC X(56)    VALUE SPACES.

 01   HEADINGS-1.
      05 PIC X(56)    VALUE SPACES.
      05 PIC X(5)     VALUE "GROSS".
      05 PIC X(4)     VALUE SPACES.
      05 PIC X(7)     VALUE "FEDERAL".
      05 PIC XXX      VALUE SPACES.
      05 PIC X(5)     VALUE "STATE".
      05 PIC XXXX     VALUE SPACES.
      05 PIC X(5)     VALUE "UNION".
      05 PIC X(15)    VALUE SPACES.
      05 PIC X(5)     VALUE "TOTAL".
      05 PIC X(10)    VALUE SPACES.
      05 PIC XXX      VALUE "NET".
      05 PIC X(10)    VALUE SPACES.

 01   HEADINGS-2.
      05 PIC XXX      VALUE SPACES.
      05 PIC X(10)    VALUE "DEPARTMENT".
      05 PIC X(5)     VALUE SPACES.
      05 PIC XXX      VALUE "SSN".
      05 PIC X(17)    VALUE SPACES.
      05 PIC XXXX     VALUE "NAME".
      05 PIC X(14)    VALUE SPACES.
      05 PIC X(5)     VALUE "WAGES".
      05 PIC X(6)     VALUE SPACES.
      05 PIC XXX      VALUE "TAX".
      05 PIC X(6)     VALUE SPACES.
      05 PIC XXX      VALUE "TAX".
      05 PIC X(5)     VALUE SPACES.
      05 PIC XXXX     VALUE "DUES".
      05 PIC XX       VALUE SPACES.
      05 PIC X(9)     VALUE "INSURANCE".
      05 PIC XXX      VALUE SPACES.
      05 PIC X(10)    VALUE "DEDUCTIONS".
      05 PIC X(6)     VALUE SPACES.
      05 PIC X(5)     VALUE "WAGES".
      05 PIC X(9)     VALUE SPACES.
```

```
 01  EMPLOYEE-PAYLINE.
     05 CARRIAGE-CONTROL     PIC X.
     05                      PIC X(5).
     05 O-DEPT               PIC XXX.
     05                      PIC X(5).
     05 O-SSN                PIC XXXBXXBXXXX.
     05                      PIC X(4).
     05 O-NAME               PIC X(22).
     05                      PIC X(3).
     05 O-GROSS-WAGES        PIC $ZZZ9.99.
     05                      PIC XXX.
     05 O-FED-TAX            PIC $ZZ9.99.
     05                      PIC XX.
     05 O-STATE-TAX          PIC $ZZ9.99.
     05                      PIC XX.
     05 O-UNION-DUES         PIC $Z9.99.
     05                      PIC XX.
     05 O-INS-PREMIUM        PIC $Z9.99.
     05                      PIC X(6).
     05 O-TOTAL-DEDUCTIONS   PIC $ZZ9.99.
     05                      PIC X(6).
     05 O-NET-WAGES          PIC $ZZZ9.99-.
     05                      PIC X(9).

*******************************************************************
*                                                                 *
*   THE NEXT 7 RECORDS ARE THE ONES THAT MUST BE PRINTED ON THE   *
*   SUMMARY REPORT.                                               *
*                                                                 *
*******************************************************************

 01  SUMMARY-REPORT-NAME.
     05 PIC X(51)    VALUE SPACES.
     05 PIC X(29)    VALUE "WEEKLY PAYROLL SUMMARY REPORT".
     05 PIC X(52)    VALUE SPACES.

 01  SUMMARY-HEADERS-1.
     05 PIC X(18)  VALUE SPACES.
     05 PIC X(5)   VALUE "TOTAL".
     05 PIC X(12)  VALUE SPACES.
     05 PIC X(5)   VALUE "TOTAL".
     05 PIC X(12)  VALUE SPACES.
     05 PIC X(5)   VALUE "TOTAL".
     05 PIC X(10)  VALUE SPACES.
     05 PIC X(5)   VALUE "TOTAL".
     05 PIC X(14)  VALUE SPACES.
     05 PIC X(5)   VALUE "TOTAL".
     05 PIC X(14)  VALUE SPACES.
     05 PIC X(5)   VALUE "TOTAL".
     05 PIC X(22)  VALUE SPACES.

 01  SUMMARY-HEADERS-2.
     05 PIC X(15)  VALUE SPACES.
     05 PIC X(11)  VALUE "GROSS WAGES".
     05 PIC X(5)   VALUE SPACES.
     05 PIC X(13)  VALUE "FEDERAL TAXES".
     05 PIC X(5)   VALUE SPACES.
     05 PIC X(11)  VALUE "STATE TAXES".
     05 PIC X(5)   VALUE SPACES.
     05 PIC X(10)  VALUE "UNION DUES".
     05 PIC X(5)   VALUE SPACES.
     05 PIC X(18)  VALUE "INSURANCE PREMIUMS".
     05 PIC X(5)   VALUE SPACES.
     05 PIC X(9)   VALUE "NET WAGES".
     05 PIC X(20)  VALUE SPACES.

 01 COMPANY-SUMMARY.
     05                            PIC X(15).
     05 O-COMPANY-GROSS-WAGES      PIC $ZZZ,ZZ9.99.
     05                            PIC X(6).
     05 O-COMPANY-FED-TAX          PIC $ZZZ,ZZ9.99.
     05                            PIC X(6).
     05 O-COMPANY-STATE-TAX        PIC $ZZZ,ZZ9.99.
     05                            PIC X(5).
     05 O-COMPANY-UNION-DUES       PIC $ZZZ,ZZ9.99.
     05                            PIC X(7).
     05 O-COMPANY-INS-PREMIUMS     PIC $ZZZ,ZZ9.99.
     05                            PIC X(8).
     05 O-COMPANY-NET-WAGES        PIC $ZZZ,ZZ9.99-.
     05                            PIC X(18).
```

```
 01  TOTAL-EMPLOYEES-LINE.
     05 PIC X(6)     VALUE "  *** ".
     05 PIC X(22)    VALUE "NUMBER OF EMPLOYEES = ".
     05 PIC X(2)     VALUE SPACES.
     05 O-NO-OF-EMPLOYEES       PIC ZZZ9.
     05 PIC X(99)    VALUE SPACES.

 01  AVERAGE-GROSS-WAGES-LINE.
     05 PIC X(6)     VALUE "  *** ".
     05 PIC X(22)    VALUE "AVERAGE GROSS WAGES = ".
     05 O-AVERAGE-GROSS-WAGES  PIC $Z,ZZ9.99.
     05 PIC X(96)    VALUE SPACES.

 01  AVERAGE-NET-WAGES-LINE.
     05 PIC X(6)     VALUE "  *** ".
     05 PIC X(22)    VALUE "AVERAGE NET WAGES   = ".
     05 O-AVERAGE-NET-WAGES    PIC $Z,ZZ9.99-.
     05 PIC X(94)    VALUE SPACES.

 PROCEDURE DIVISION.

*****************************************************************
*                                                               *
*  WITHIN THE PROCEDURE DIVISION, AN ASTERISK HAS BEEN INSERTED *
*  IN COLUMN 7 OF THE LINE PRECEDING AN ENTRY (OR ENTRIES) THAT *
*  IS (ARE) RELATED TO PRODUCING THE SUMMARY REPORT.  THE NEXT  *
*  ASTERISK INDICATES THE END OF THE ENTRY (ENTRIES).           *
*                                                               *
*****************************************************************

 100-PRODUCE-PAYROLL-REPORT.
     PERFORM 200-START-UP.
     PERFORM 210-PROCESS-EMPLOYEE-RECORD WITH TEST BEFORE
         UNTIL WS-MORE-RECORDS = "NO ".
     PERFORM 220-FINISH-UP.
     STOP RUN.

 200-START-UP.
     OPEN INPUT EMPLOYEE-PAYROLL-FILE
          OUTPUT PAYROLL-REPORT-FILE.
     MOVE "YES" TO WS-MORE-RECORDS.
*
     INITIALIZE WS-COMPANY-ACCUMULATORS.
     MOVE SPACES TO EMPLOYEE-PAYLINE
                    COMPANY-SUMMARY.
*
     PERFORM 300-WRITE-REPORT-HEADERS.
     PERFORM 310-READ-EMPLOYEE-RECORD.

 210-PROCESS-EMPLOYEE-RECORD.
     PERFORM 320-COMPUTE-PAYROLL-ITEMS.
     PERFORM 330-PREPARE-EMPLOYEE-PAYLINE.
*
     PERFORM 340-UPDATE-COMPANY-ACCUMULATORS.
*
     PERFORM 310-READ-EMPLOYEE-RECORD.

 220-FINISH-UP.
*
     PERFORM 350-PRODUCE-COMPANY-SUMMARY.
*
     CLOSE EMPLOYEE-PAYROLL-FILE
           PAYROLL-REPORT-FILE.

 300-WRITE-REPORT-HEADERS.
     WRITE PRINTLINE FROM COMPANY-NAME
         AFTER ADVANCING PAGE.
     WRITE PRINTLINE FROM REPORT-NAME
         AFTER ADVANCING 3 LINES.
     WRITE PRINTLINE FROM HEADINGS-1
         AFTER ADVANCING 3 LINES.
     WRITE PRINTLINE FROM HEADINGS-2
         AFTER ADVANCING 1 LINE.

 310-READ-EMPLOYEE-RECORD.
     READ EMPLOYEE-PAYROLL-FILE RECORD
         AT END
             MOVE "NO " TO WS-MORE-RECORDS.
```

```
 320-COMPUTE-PAYROLL-ITEMS.
     MULTIPLY I-HRS-WORKED BY I-PAY-RATE GIVING WS-GROSS-WAGES.
     MULTIPLY WS-GROSS-WAGES BY I-FED-TAX-RATE
         GIVING WS-FED-TAX ROUNDED.
     MULTIPLY WS-GROSS-WAGES BY I-STATE-TAX-RATE
         GIVING WS-STATE-TAX ROUNDED.
     ADD WS-FED-TAX WS-STATE-TAX I-UNION-DUES I-INS-PREMIUM
         GIVING WS-TOTAL-DEDUCTIONS.
     SUBTRACT WS-TOTAL-DEDUCTIONS FROM WS-GROSS-WAGES
         GIVING WS-NET-WAGES.

 330-PREPARE-EMPLOYEE-PAYLINE.
     MOVE I-DEPT TO O-DEPT.
     MOVE I-SSN TO O-SSN.
     MOVE I-NAME TO O-NAME.
     MOVE I-UNION-DUES TO O-UNION-DUES.
     MOVE I-INS-PREMIUM TO O-INS-PREMIUM.
     MOVE WS-GROSS-WAGES TO O-GROSS-WAGES.
     MOVE WS-FED-TAX TO O-FED-TAX.
     MOVE WS-STATE-TAX TO O-STATE-TAX.
     MOVE WS-TOTAL-DEDUCTIONS TO O-TOTAL-DEDUCTIONS.
     MOVE WS-NET-WAGES TO O-NET-WAGES.
     WRITE PRINTLINE FROM EMPLOYEE-PAYLINE
         AFTER ADVANCING 2 LINES.

*
 340-UPDATE-COMPANY-ACCUMULATORS.
     ADD 1 TO WS-EMPLOYEE-CTR.
     ADD WS-GROSS-WAGES TO WS-COMPANY-GROSS-WAGES.
     ADD WS-FED-TAX TO WS-COMPANY-FED-TAX.
     ADD WS-STATE-TAX TO WS-COMPANY-STATE-TAX.
     ADD I-UNION-DUES TO WS-COMPANY-UNION-DUES.
     ADD I-INS-PREMIUM TO WS-COMPANY-INS-PREMIUMS.
     ADD WS-NET-WAGES TO WS-COMPANY-NET-WAGES.

 350-PRODUCE-COMPANY-SUMMARY.
     PERFORM 400-WRITE-SUMMARY-HEADERS.
     PERFORM 410-PREPARE-COMPANY-TOTALS.
     PERFORM 420-PREPARE-COMPANY-AVERAGES.

 400-WRITE-SUMMARY-HEADERS.
     WRITE PRINTLINE FROM COMPANY-NAME
         AFTER ADVANCING PAGE.
     WRITE PRINTLINE FROM SUMMARY-REPORT-NAME
         AFTER ADVANCING 3 LINES.
     WRITE PRINTLINE FROM SUMMARY-HEADERS-1
         AFTER ADVANCING 3 LINES.
     WRITE PRINTLINE FROM SUMMARY-HEADERS-2
         AFTER ADVANCING 1 LINE.

 410-PREPARE-COMPANY-TOTALS.
     MOVE WS-COMPANY-GROSS-WAGES TO O-COMPANY-GROSS-WAGES.
     MOVE WS-COMPANY-FED-TAX TO O-COMPANY-FED-TAX.
     MOVE WS-COMPANY-STATE-TAX TO O-COMPANY-STATE-TAX.
     MOVE WS-COMPANY-UNION-DUES TO O-COMPANY-UNION-DUES.
     MOVE WS-COMPANY-INS-PREMIUMS TO O-COMPANY-INS-PREMIUMS.
     MOVE WS-COMPANY-NET-WAGES TO O-COMPANY-NET-WAGES.
     WRITE PRINTLINE FROM COMPANY-SUMMARY
         AFTER ADVANCING 3 LINES.

 420-PREPARE-COMPANY-AVERAGES.
     MOVE WS-EMPLOYEE-CTR TO O-NO-OF-EMPLOYEES.
     WRITE PRINTLINE FROM TOTAL-EMPLOYEES-LINE
         AFTER ADVANCING 5 LINES.
     DIVIDE WS-COMPANY-GROSS-WAGES BY WS-EMPLOYEE-CTR
         GIVING O-AVERAGE-GROSS-WAGES ROUNDED.
     WRITE PRINTLINE FROM AVERAGE-GROSS-WAGES-LINE
         AFTER ADVANCING 2 LINES.
     DIVIDE WS-COMPANY-NET-WAGES BY WS-EMPLOYEE-CTR
         GIVING O-AVERAGE-NET-WAGES ROUNDED.
     WRITE PRINTLINE FROM AVERAGE-NET-WAGES-LINE
         AFTER ADVANCING 2 LINES.
*
```

■ **Figure 6.10** Data file for the test run

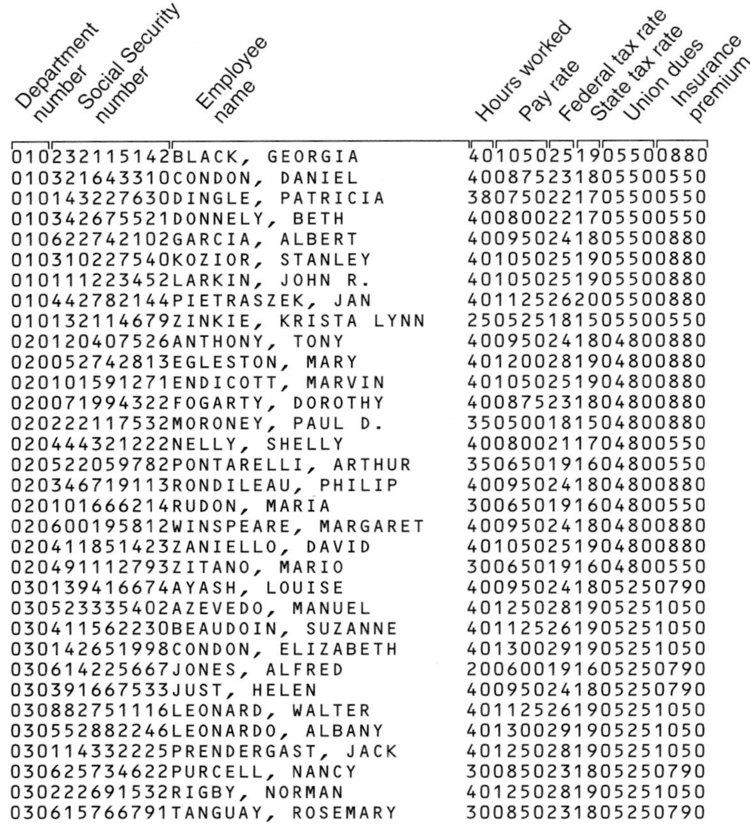


```
010232115142BLACK, GEORGIA            401050251905500880
010321643310CONDON, DANIEL            400875231805500550
010143227630DINGLE, PATRICIA          380750221705500550
010342675521DONNELY, BETH             400800221705500550
010622742102GARCIA, ALBERT            400950241805500880
010310227540KOZIOR, STANLEY           401050251905500880
010111223452LARKIN, JOHN R.           401050251905500880
010442782144PIETRASZEK, JAN           401125262005500880
010132114679ZINKIE, KRISTA LYNN       250525181505500550
020120407526ANTHONY, TONY             400950241804800880
020052742813EGLESTON, MARY            401200281904800880
020101591271ENDICOTT, MARVIN          401050251904800880
020071994322FOGARTY, DOROTHY          400875231804800880
020222117532MORONEY, PAUL D.          350500181504800880
020444321222NELLY, SHELLY             400800211704800550
020522059782PONTARELLI, ARTHUR        350650191604800550
020346719113RONDILEAU, PHILIP         400950241804800880
020101666214RUDON, MARIA              300650191604800550
020600195812WINSPEARE, MARGARET       400950241804800880
020411851423ZANIELLO, DAVID           401050251904800880
020491112793ZITANO, MARIO             300650191604800550
030139416674AYASH, LOUISE             400950241805250790
030523335402AZEVEDO, MANUEL           401250281905251050
030411562230BEAUDOIN, SUZANNE         401125261905251050
030142651998CONDON, ELIZABETH         401300291905251050
030614225667JONES, ALFRED             200600191605250790
030391667533JUST, HELEN               400950241805250790
030882751116LEONARD, WALTER           401125261905251050
030552882246LEONARDO, ALBANY          401300291905251050
030114332225PRENDERGAST, JACK         401250281905251050
030625734622PURCELL, NANCY            300850231805250790
030222691532RIGBY, NORMAN             401250281905251050
030615766791TANGUAY, ROSEMARY         300850231805250790
```

■ **Figure 6.11** Report produced during the test run

RELIABLE AUTO PARTS CO.

WEEKLY PAYROLL REPORT

DEPARTMENT	SSN	NAME	GROSS WAGES	FEDERAL TAX	STATE TAX	UNION DUES	INSURANCE	TOTAL DEDUCTIONS	NET WAGES
010	232 11 5142	BLACK, GEORGIA	$ 420.00	$105.00	$ 79.80	$ 5.50	$ 8.80	$199.10	$ 220.90
010	321 64 3310	CONDON, DANIEL	$ 350.00	$ 80.50	$ 63.00	$ 5.50	$ 5.50	$154.50	$ 195.50
010	143 22 7630	DINGLE, PATRICIA	$ 285.00	$ 62.70	$ 48.45	$ 5.50	$ 5.50	$122.15	$ 162.85
010	342 67 5521	DONNELY, BETH	$ 320.00	$ 70.40	$ 54.40	$ 5.50	$ 5.50	$135.80	$ 184.20
010	622 74 2102	GARCIA, ALBERT	$ 380.00	$ 91.20	$ 68.40	$ 5.50	$ 8.80	$173.90	$ 206.10
010	310 22 7540	KOZIOR, STANLEY	$ 420.00	$105.00	$ 79.80	$ 5.50	$ 8.80	$199.10	$ 220.90
010	111 22 3452	LARKIN, JOHN R.	$ 420.00	$105.00	$ 79.80	$ 5.50	$ 8.80	$199.10	$ 220.90
010	442 78 2144	PIETRASZEK, JAN	$ 450.00	$117.00	$ 90.00	$ 5.50	$ 8.80	$221.30	$ 228.70
010	132 11 4679	ZINKIE, KRISTA LYNN	$ 131.25	$ 23.63	$ 19.69	$ 5.50	$ 5.50	$ 54.32	$ 76.93
020	120 40 7526	ANTHONY, TONY	$ 380.00	$ 91.20	$ 68.40	$ 4.80	$ 8.80	$173.20	$ 206.80
020	052 74 2813	EGLESTON, MARY	$ 480.00	$134.40	$ 91.20	$ 4.80	$ 8.80	$239.20	$ 240.80
020	101 59 1271	ENDICOTT, MARVIN	$ 420.00	$105.00	$ 79.80	$ 4.80	$ 8.80	$198.40	$ 221.60
020	071 99 4322	FOGARTY, DOROTHY	$ 350.00	$ 80.50	$ 63.00	$ 4.80	$ 8.80	$157.10	$ 192.90
020	222 11 7532	MORONEY, PAUL D.	$ 175.00	$ 31.50	$ 26.25	$ 4.80	$ 8.80	$ 71.35	$ 103.65
020	444 32 1222	NELLY, SHELLY	$ 320.00	$ 67.20	$ 54.40	$ 4.80	$ 5.50	$131.90	$ 188.10
020	522 05 9782	PONTARELLI, ARTHUR	$ 227.50	$ 43.23	$ 36.40	$ 4.80	$ 5.50	$ 89.93	$ 137.57
020	346 71 9113	RONDILEAU, PHILIP	$ 380.00	$ 91.20	$ 68.40	$ 4.80	$ 8.80	$173.20	$ 206.80

■ **Figure 6.11** continued

020	101 66 6214	RUDON, MARIA	$ 195.00	$ 37.05	$ 31.20	$ 4.80	$ 5.50	$ 78.55	$ 116.45
020	600 19 5812	WINSPEARE, MARGARET	$ 380.00	$ 91.20	$ 68.40	$ 4.80	$ 8.80	$173.20	$ 206.80
020	411 85 1423	ZANIELLO, DAVID	$ 420.00	$105.00	$ 79.80	$ 4.80	$ 8.80	$198.40	$ 221.60
020	491 11 2793	ZITANO, MARIO	$ 195.00	$ 37.05	$ 31.20	$ 4.80	$ 5.50	$ 78.55	$ 116.45
030	139 41 6674	AYASH, LOUISE	$ 380.00	$ 91.20	$ 68.40	$ 5.25	$ 7.90	$172.75	$ 207.25
030	523 33 5402	AZEVEDO, MANUEL	$ 500.00	$140.00	$ 95.00	$ 5.25	$10.50	$250.75	$ 249.25
030	411 56 2230	BEAUDOIN, SUZANNE	$ 450.00	$117.00	$ 85.50	$ 5.25	$10.50	$218.25	$ 231.75
030	142 65 1998	CONDON, ELIZABETH	$ 520.00	$150.80	$ 98.80	$ 5.25	$10.50	$265.35	$ 254.65
030	614 22 5667	JONES, ALFRED	$ 120.00	$ 22.80	$ 19.20	$ 5.25	$ 7.90	$ 55.15	$ 64.85
030	391 66 7533	JUST, HELEN	$ 380.00	$ 91.20	$ 68.40	$ 5.25	$ 7.90	$172.75	$ 207.25
030	882 75 1116	LEONARD, WALTER	$ 450.00	$117.00	$ 85.50	$ 5.25	$10.50	$218.25	$ 231.75
030	552 88 2246	LEONARDO, ALBANY	$ 520.00	$150.80	$ 98.80	$ 5.25	$10.50	$265.35	$ 254.65
030	114 33 2225	PRENDERGAST, JACK	$ 500.00	$140.00	$ 95.00	$ 5.25	$10.50	$250.75	$ 249.25
030	625 73 4622	PURCELL, NANCY	$ 255.00	$ 58.65	$ 45.90	$ 5.25	$ 7.90	$117.70	$ 137.30
030	222 69 1532	RIGBY, NORMAN	$ 500.00	$140.00	$ 95.00	$ 5.25	$10.50	$250.75	$ 249.25
030	615 76 6791	TANGUAY, ROSEMARY	$ 255.00	$ 58.65	$ 45.90	$ 5.25	$ 7.90	$117.70	$ 137.30

RELIABLE AUTO PARTS CO.

WEEKLY PAYROLL SUMMARY REPORT

TOTAL GROSS WAGES	TOTAL FEDERAL TAXES	TOTAL STATE TAXES	TOTAL UNION DUES	TOTAL INSURANCE PREMIUMS	TOTAL NET WAGES
$ 11,928.75	$ 2,953.06	$ 2,183.19	$ 170.10	$ 271.40	$ 6,351.00

```
*** NUMBER OF EMPLOYEES =      33
*** AVERAGE GROSS WAGES = $   361.48
*** AVERAGE NET WAGES   = $   192.45
```

■ The COMPUTE Statement

Each of the simple arithmetic statements, ADD, SUBTRACT, MULTIPLY, and DIVIDE, contains only one kind of operation. A programmer encounters many computational situations in which more than one kind of operation is required. Consider the following example: Company X pays its employees weekly at a certain rate for the first forty hours and at twice the standard rate for overtime hours. Calculate an employee's gross pay.

Using the simple arithmetic statements MULTIPLY and ADD, the programmer could plan the following sequence of statements:

```
MULTIPLY REG-HOURS BY RATE GIVING REG-PAY.
MULTIPLY RATE BY 2 GIVING OVERTIME-RATE.
MULTIPLY OVERTIME-HOURS BY OVERTIME-RATE
     GIVING OVERTIME-PAY.
ADD REG-PAY OVERTIME-PAY GIVING GROSS-PAY.
```

If the COMPUTE statement is used, then the four statements above can be replaced by the following single statement:

```
COMPUTE GROSS-PAY = REG-HOURS * RATE + OVERTIME-HOURS * RATE * 2
```

In this statement, REG-HOURS * RATE is the regular pay, and OVERTIME-HOURS * RATE * 2 is the overtime pay. Their sum is the gross pay. It is readily seen that the COMPUTE statement greatly reduces the amount of coding that would be required otherwise.

The general format of the COMPUTE statement is shown in Figure 6.12.

■ **Figure 6.12** COMPUTE statement format and its options

```
COMPUTE {identifier-1 [ROUNDED]} . . . = arithmetic-expression
    [ON SIZE ERROR imperative-statement-1]
    [NOT ON SIZE ERROR imperative-statement-2]
    [END-COMPUTE]
```

■ **Figure 6.13** COBOL arithmetic operators

Arithmetic Operators	Meaning
+	Addition
–	Subtraction
*	Multiplication
/	Division
**	Exponentiation (Raising to a power)

■ **Figure 6.14** Hierarchy of arithmetic operations

Hierarchy of Operations	
1. **	Exponentiation
2. * and /	Multiplication and division in order of occurrence from left to right in the expression
3. + and –	Addition and subtraction in order of occurrence from left to right in the expression

In this format, identifier-1 is the receiving field. The arithmetic expression to the right of the equal sign (=) can be constructed of operands, arithmetic operators (see Figure 6.13), and parentheses for grouping purposes. The operands can be elementary numeric data items and/or numeric literals.

If an arithmetic expression contains more than one operator, it is important that the programmer understands very clearly the order in which the computer will execute them. The hierarchy of operations is shown in Figure 6.14.

Note that all exponentiations will be performed first, followed by all multiplications and divisions, followed by all additions and subtractions.

If the expression contains parentheses, then the following rules apply:

1. The operations within the parentheses are performed first, according to the hierarchy of operations as specified in Figure 6.14.
2. If parentheses are nested, the expressions within the parentheses are evaluated from the innermost to the outermost.
3. When all expressions within parentheses have been evaluated according to rules 1 and 2, then the normal hierarchy of operations applies to the remaining operations.

In Figure 6.15, sample arithmetic expressions are shown algebraically; they are then coded into COBOL; and, finally, the order in which the operations will be performed is shown by small numbers above each operator.

The arithmetic expression in a COMPUTE statement may be as simple as a numeric literal or a numeric data item, as illustrated in the first two examples that follow.

Example 1:

```
COMPUTE COUNT = 0.
```

In this case, the arithmetic expression consists of a single numeric literal. The net effect of this statement is the same as the simple MOVE statement: MOVE 0 TO COUNT.

Example 2:

```
COMPUTE NET-SAL = WS-NET-SAL.
```

In this case, the arithmetic expression consists of a single data name. The net effect of this statement is the same as the simple MOVE statement: MOVE WS-NET-SAL TO NET-SAL.

■ **Figure 6.15** Sequence of operations in arithmetic expressions—examples

In Algebra	In COBOL	Order of Operations
1. prt	P * R * T	1 2 P * R * T
2. 2l + 2w	2 * L + 2 * W	1 3 2 2 * L + 2 * W
3. $p(1 + r)^t$	P * (1 + R) ** T	3 1 2 P * (1 + R) ** T
4. $\frac{a + b}{2}$	(A + B) / 2	1 2 (A + B) / 2
5. $a + \frac{b}{2}$	A + B / 2	2 1 A + B / 2
6. $\frac{d}{(1 + i)^n}$	D / (1 + I) ** N	3 1 2 D / (1 + I) ** N

Since MOVE statements are internally simpler to execute than the COMPUTE statement, the author does not recommend the use of the COMPUTE statement wherever a simple MOVE statement is sufficient.

Examples 3 and 4 show situations in which the COMPUTE statement is particularly useful.

Example 3:

```
COMPUTE GROSS-PAY ROUNDED = BASE-PAY + .04 * (SALES - 1000).
```

In this case, the arithmetic expression will be evaluated by performing the operations in the following order: –, then *, and then +. The computed value will be stored in GROSS-PAY, rounded according to its PICTURE.

Example 4:

```
COMPUTE AMOUNT-ACC ROUNDED =
          PRINCIPAL * (1 + RATE) ** TIME-PERIODS
    ON SIZE ERROR
          PERFORM 400-PROCESS-ERROR-ROUTINE.
```

In this case, the arithmetic expression contains an exponentiation. The order in which these operations are performed is + first, then **, and finally *. If the receiving field AMOUNT-ACC is large enough to prevent high-order truncation, the computed value will be stored, rounded according to the PICTURE specified for AMOUNT-ACC. If the receiving field is not large enough to prevent high-order truncation, the computed value will not be stored, and the PERFORM statement following the ON SIZE ERROR phrase will be executed.

Though the COMPUTE statement is not used in the sample program of this chapter, it could have been used, for instance, to do the arithmetic specified in the paragraph 320-COMPUTE-PAYROLL-ITEMS, as shown in the following example.

```
320-COMPUTE-PAYROLL-ITEMS.
    COMPUTE WS-GROSS-WAGES = I-HRS-WORKED * I-PAY-RATE.
    COMPUTE WS-FED-TAX ROUNDED = WS-GROSS-WAGES * I-FED-TAX-RATE.
    COMPUTE WS-STATE-TAX ROUNDED =
        WS-GROSS-WAGES * I-STATE-TAX-RATE.
    COMPUTE WS-TOTAL-DEDUCTIONS =
        WS-FED-TAX + WS-STATE-TAX + I-UNION-DUES + I-INS-PREMIUM.
    COMPUTE WS-NET-WAGES = WS-GROSS-WAGES - WS-TOTAL-DEDUCTIONS.
```

We repeat that the COMPUTE statement is particularly useful in those situations where two or more arithmetic operations are required to compute the value of a data item.

Rules Governing the Use of COMPUTE and Its Options

1. Any identifier following the verb COMPUTE is a receiving field. The receiving fields are the only data items whose values are changed by the computation. A receiving field can have a numeric or a numeric-edited PICTURE.
2. In the arithmetic expression, all identifiers and literals are operands. That is, every identifier must be an elementary numeric item, and every literal must be numeric.
3. The arithmetic operations permissible in an arithmetic expression are exponentiation (**), multiplication (*), division (/), addition (+), and subtraction (–). Parentheses can be used as a grouping symbol.

4. The sequence in which operations are executed is exponentiation, multiplication and division in the order in which they occur from left to right in the expression, and, finally, addition and subtraction in the order in which they occur from left to right. Parentheses can be used to change the above sequence. If parentheses are used, the operations within the parentheses are performed first, from the innermost nested parentheses to the outermost.
5. The computed value is stored in the receiving field according to its PICTURE. If the receiving field contains a decimal point (assumed or edited), the positions are filled from the decimal point to the right first, and then to the left. If there is no decimal point, the positions are filled from the rightmost. Low-order and high-order truncations can occur.
6. Each identifier that must store the computed value rounded must be immediately followed by the word ROUNDED. The use of the ROUNDED option minimizes the effect of a low-order truncation.
7. If the ON SIZE ERROR option is used, the phrase ON SIZE ERROR immediately follows the arithmetic expression. No high-order truncation will occur. If there is a size error for a receiving field, the computed value is not stored in that receiving field, and the imperative statement that follows the ON SIZE ERROR phrase is executed. If there is no size error in any receiving field, the computed value is stored in each receiving field, and the statement following the ON SIZE ERROR phrase is not executed.
8. The NOT ON SIZE ERROR option is permissible only as an alternate path to the ON SIZE ERROR option. If there is no size error for any receiving field, the statement that follows the phrase NOT ON SIZE ERROR is executed after the computed value has been stored.
9. END-COMPUTE is the scope terminator. A COMPUTE statement can be terminated either by a period or by END-COMPUTE.
10. The sign of the computed value is stored only if the PICTURE of the receiving field contains an S.

Program Refinements

Up to this point in our work, we have been mainly concerned with writing programs that:

1. are developed systematically, by consistently following the steps of the problem-solving procedure.
2. are effective, that is, that produce the required results.
3. are clear and easy to understand. This was accomplished by selecting data names and procedure names that are descriptive and add to the self-documentation of the program.
4. are structured. This was accomplished by careful planning and by the development of structure charts.

While these concerns still hold, it is time to consider features that tend to make programs run more efficiently and that provide a greater degree of documentation.

The USAGE Clause

Characters are normally stored in memory in coded form. The coded form typically consists of strings of 0s and 1s. This is a direct consequence of the binary nature of a computer's circuitry: A circuit is either "on," represented by 1, or "off," represented by 0. The 0 and the 1 are *binary digits,* or *bits.*

There are different systems for representing characters as strings of 0s and 1s. Two of the most popular are the Extended Binary Coded Decimal Interchange Code, known as EBCDIC (pronounced "ebseedic"), and the American Standard Code for Information Interchange, known as ASCII (pronounced "askey"). Though both use an eight-bit configuration, that is, each character is represented by a string of eight binary digits, the schemes are different. For instance, in EBCDIC, the letter *A* is coded as 11000001, whereas in ASCII, the letter *A* is coded as 01000001. The internal storage required for each character is a *byte.* EBCDIC and ASCII use eight-bit bytes to store each character.

Of particular interest to the COBOL programmer, computer systems generally store data in character format. IBM mainframe computers, and IBM-compatible mainframe computers, use the EBCDIC format. DEC computers, such as the VAX, use the ASCII format. IBM microcomputers and IBM-compatible microcomputers use the ASCII format. However, when computers are directed to perform arithmetic operations on stored data, they must convert the data from character format to some appropriate computational form (such as binary form). Once the operation is complete, the result must be converted again, this time from the computational format back to character format so that it can be stored properly.

Figure 6.16 USAGE clause format

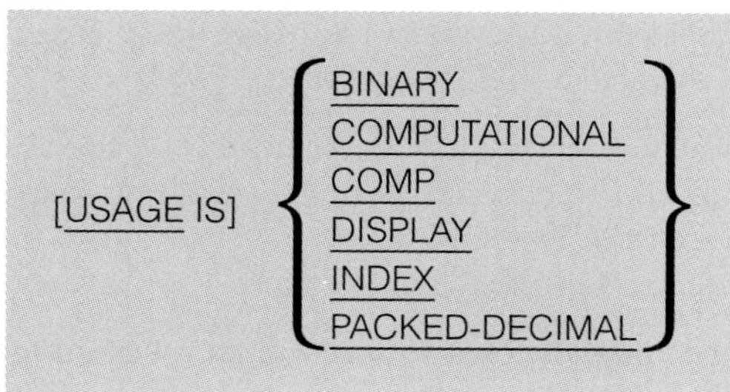

The COBOL language allows the programmer a limited degree of control over the format of stored data. To exercise this control, the programmer must specify the USAGE clause in data description entries. The format of the USAGE clause is shown in Figure 6.16.

It should be obvious from past programs that the USAGE clause is optional. If it is not used, then the default option is USAGE IS DISPLAY. This option is COBOL's way of specifying the computer system's standard data format, such as the EBCDIC and ASCII formats mentioned above.

While the DISPLAY option applies equally to numeric and to nonnumeric data items, the other options of the USAGE clause are appropriate only for numeric items.

When the programmer specifies USAGE IS COMPUTATIONAL, a numeric value is stored in a computational format appropriate for the computer system. This format is usually the binary form of the number, that is, the number written in base 2. For instance, the binary form of 312 is 100111000; the binary form of 1565.25 is 11000011111.01.

There are two advantages to the COMPUTATIONAL option. First, when the data item is needed as an operand, no data format conversion is required, since the value is already in a computational form, thus saving CPU time. Second, internal storage requirements are minimized; that is, fewer bytes are required to store a binary number than the corresponding decimal number. The decimal number 312 requires three bytes of storage, whereas its binary form (100111000) requires only two bytes (in an eight-bit byte configuration). The decimal number 1565.25 requires six bytes, whereas its binary form requires only four.

The BINARY option is a new feature of COBOL '85. Its use simply makes the computational form more explicit. For those systems where the COMPUTATIONAL option is binary, the two usages are equivalent. For those systems where the COMPUTATIONAL option does not mean binary, the BINARY usage provides an alternate computational form.

The PACKED-DECIMAL option is also a new feature of COBOL '85. This numeric format stores two digits per byte, thereby reducing data storage requirements. This format, first introduced by IBM and widely implemented by other computer manufacturers, has traditionally been available as an extension to the COBOL standards under the label COMPUTATIONAL-3. Because of its general availability, it has now been included in the new standards.

The USAGE IS INDEX option will be examined later in relation to the organization and processing of table data.

A complete technical explanation of the options of the USAGE clause is beyond the intended scope of this text. Furthermore, a reasonable argument can be made regarding omitting the USAGE clause altogether. In many COBOL programs, the quantity of mathematical computations is minimal. The overhead in CPU time that results from converting numeric data from DISPLAY format to a computational format is not noticeable. And, the cost per unit of storage has decreased so drastically over the past few years that reducing numeric data storage requirements has lost much of its importance. Nonetheless, since the USAGE clause is part of the language standards, you need to be aware of its availability so that it can be implemented in those few COBOL programs that demand a heavy use of arithmetic operations.

Rules Governing the USAGE Clause

1. The USAGE clause specifies the internal format of a data item.
2. The USAGE clause can be used in any data description entry with a level number other than 66 or 88.
3. If the USAGE clause is at a group level, it applies to every elementary item of the group.
4. The clause USAGE IS DISPLAY specifies that the data item is in the standard data format for the computer system.

5. If no USAGE clause applies to an elementary item, its usage is DISPLAY by default.
6. COMP is the abbreviation for COMPUTATIONAL.
7. If the usage is specified as BINARY, COMP, or PACKED-DECIMAL, then the PICTURE clause that defines the elementary item must contain only the characters 9, S, V, and P.

   Note: If a programmer decides to specify the USAGE clause, the author recommends that the two words USAGE and IS **not** be used, since they do not add to the clarity of the resulting entry. Similarly, the abbreviated form COMP is preferable to COMPUTATIONAL.
8. Elementary items belonging to a record of a print file must be in DISPLAY format.

In the current revision of the chapter sample program, the computational format will be specified for the working-storage data items that are used as operands in arithmetic statements. Note that, in the example below, COMP has been entered at the group level for the group item WS-COMPANY-ACCUMULATORS. When this item is referenced in the INITIALIZE statement of paragraph 200-START-UP, its elementary items will all receive the value zero in the appropriate binary form.

```
01   WS-PROGRAM-CONTROLS.
     .
     05 WS-LINE-CTR           PIC S99     COMP.
     .
     05 WS-PAGE-NO            PIC 99      COMP.

01   WS-EMPLOYEE-PAYROLL-ITEMS.
     05 WS-GROSS-WAGES        PIC S9999V99      COMP.
     05 WS-FED-TAX            PIC S999V99       COMP.
     05 WS-STATE-TAX          PIC S999V99       COMP.
     05 WS-TOTAL-DEDUCTIONS   PIC S999V99       COMP.
     05 WS-NET-WAGES          PIC S9999V99      COMP.

01   WS-COMPANY-ACCUMULATORS      COMP.
     05 WS-EMPLOYEE-CTR           PIC S999.
     05 WS-COMPANY-GROSS-WAGES    PIC S9(5)V99.
     05 WS-COMPANY-FED-TAX        PIC S9(5)V99.
     05 WS-COMPANY-STATE-TAX      PIC S9(5)V99.
     05 WS-COMPANY-UNION-DUES     PIC S9(5)V99.
     05 WS-COMPANY-INS-PREMIUMS   PIC S9(5)V99.
     05 WS-COMPANY-NET-WAGES      PIC S9(5)V99.
```

Note: If the COMP usage had been specified for each elementary item of the group WS-COMPANY-ACCUMULATORS, a problem could result if the INITIALIZE statement referenced the group item. The statement assigns the **character** zero to the numeric elementary items of the group, that is, zero in display mode. Zero in display mode is not the same as zero in binary form. Subsequent arithmetic operations could yield erroneous results. The problem can be avoided by referencing the elementary items in the INITIALIZE statement, or by specifying COMP at the group level, as was done in the last example.

Grouping Report Headers

Recall that the printer spacing chart is used to prepare the layout of each line that must be printed on a report. It was also recommended that the records corresponding to these lines be coded in the sequence in which these lines are to be printed. We now extend this notion one step further.

In the sample program of this chapter, there are four headers for the payroll report. These headers have been named COMPANY-NAME, REPORT-NAME, HEADINGS-1, and HEADINGS-2. Whenever the record COMPANY-NAME is printed, it is expected that the other three headers will also be printed. Internal data structure is improved by coding these records under **one** group name, such as REPORT-HEADERS. See the following illustration. (The records TOP-LINE and ERROR-LINE will be explained shortly.)

```
01   REPORT-HEADERS.

     05   TOP-LINE.
          10 PIC X(15)    VALUE    " REPORT-DATE:    ".
          .
          .
     05   COMPANY-NAME.
          10 PIC X(54)    VALUE SPACES.
          .
          .
     05   REPORT-NAME.
          10 PIC X(55)    VALUE SPACES.
          .
```

```
     .
05   HEADINGS-1.
     10 PIC X(56)    VALUE SPACES.
     .
     .
05   HEADINGS-2.
     10 PIC XXX      VALUE SPACES.
     .
     .
05   ERROR-LINE.
     10 PIC X(6)     VALUE   " *****  ".
     .
     .
```

Another benefit of this grouping occurs in "virtual storage" environments. (And there are many VMS [virtual memory storage] operating systems in use today.) When the record COMPANY-NAME is to be written on the report, it must be brought into "real memory." Data is usually copied into real memory one "logical page" at a time. It is very likely that the "page" will also contain the other three records. Hence, no additional paging is required in order to write **all** the headers, so the grouping procedure increases virtual storage efficiency.

The grouping method in the last example will be used for the headers of the summary report as well, shown below. In general, an effort should be made to code logically related data adjacent to each other in the program.

```
01   SUMMARY-REPORT-HEADERS.

     05   SUMMARY-REPORT-NAME.
          10 PIC X(51)    VALUE SPACES.
          10 PIC X(29)    VALUE "WEEKLY PAYROLL SUMMARY REPORT".
          10 PIC X(52)    VALUE SPACES.

     05   SUMMARY-HEADERS-1.
          10 PIC X(18)   VALUE SPACES.
          10 PIC X(5)    VALUE "TOTAL".
          10 PIC X(12)   VALUE SPACES.
          10 PIC X(5)    VALUE "TOTAL".
          10 PIC X(12)   VALUE SPACES.
          10 PIC X(5)    VALUE "TOTAL".
          10 PIC X(10)   VALUE SPACES.
          10 PIC X(5)    VALUE "TOTAL".
          10 PIC X(14)   VALUE SPACES.
          10 PIC X(5)    VALUE "TOTAL".
          10 PIC X(14)   VALUE SPACES.
          10 PIC X(5)    VALUE "TOTAL".
          10 PIC X(22)   VALUE SPACES.

     05   SUMMARY-HEADERS-2.
          10 PIC X(15)   VALUE SPACES.
          10 PIC X(11)   VALUE "GROSS WAGES".
          10 PIC X(5)    VALUE SPACES.
          10 PIC X(13)   VALUE "FEDERAL TAXES".
          10 PIC X(5)    VALUE SPACES.
          10 PIC X(11)   VALUE "STATE TAXES".
          10 PIC X(5)    VALUE SPACES.
          10 PIC X(10)   VALUE "UNION DUES".
          10 PIC X(5)    VALUE SPACES.
          10 PIC X(18)   VALUE "INSURANCE PREMIUMS".
          10 PIC X(5)    VALUE SPACES.
          10 PIC X(9)    VALUE "NET WAGES".
          10 PIC X(20)   VALUE SPACES.
```

The Trailing Minus Sign

It is a good practice to insert a trailing minus sign in every numeric-edited PICTURE. Even if a programmer never expects a particular field to receive a negative value, if it ever does, then the minus sign will flag the occurrence. The user can then determine if further actions are warranted.

Naturally, in order for the minus sign to be an effective safeguard, it is necessary that the **source** field be a signed field. Consider the next two examples.

Example 1:

Data Item	PICTURE
WS-NET-WAGES	9(4)V99
O-NET-WAGES	$ZZZ9.99–

```
MOVE WS-NET-WAGES TO O-NET-WAGES.
```

Even if the computed value of net wages is negative, when it is stored in the unsigned field WS-NET-WAGES, only the absolute value is stored, and the sign is lost. The MOVE statement then copies an **unsigned** value into O-NET-WAGES. Consequently, the minus sign is never printed.

Example 2:

Data Item	**PICTURE**
WS-NET-WAGES	S9(4)V99
O-NET-WAGES	$ZZZ9.99–

```
MOVE WS-NET-WAGES TO O-NET-WAGES.
```

In this case, the data item WS-NET-WAGES is always a signed number, due to the S in its PICTURE. The MOVE statement copies a signed number into O-NET-WAGES. If the number is positive, the minus sign is replaced by a space, but if the number is negative, then the minus sign is stored, and it will print in the trailing position.

Note that inserting a trailing minus sign in a numeric-edited PICTURE never "hurts" the output, but it may be very useful in signaling errors that would not be detected otherwise. This feature is included in the revision of the sample program. As an example, the record EMPLOYEE-PAYLINE is shown below.

```
01   EMPLOYEE-PAYLINE.
     05 CARRIAGE-CONTROL     PIC X.
     05                      PIC X(5).
     05 O-DEPT               PIC XXX.
     05                      PIC X(5).
     05 O-SSN                PIC XXXBXXBXXXX.
     05                      PIC X(4).
     05 O-NAME               PIC X(22).
     05                      PIC X(3).
     05 O-GROSS-WAGES        PIC $ZZZ9.99-.
     05                      PIC XX.
     05 O-FED-TAX            PIC $ZZ9.99-.
     05                      PIC X.
     05 O-STATE-TAX          PIC $ZZ9.99-.
     05                      PIC X.
     05 O-UNION-DUES         PIC $Z9.99-.
     05                      PIC X.
     05 O-INS-PREMIUM        PIC $Z9.99-.
     05                      PIC X(5).
     05 O-TOTAL-DEDUCTIONS PIC $ZZ9.99-.
     05                      PIC X(5).
     05 O-NET-WAGES          PIC $ZZZ9.99-.
     05                      PIC X(9).
```

Checking for an Empty Data File

In all the sample programs that have been developed until now, a tacit assumption was made that the input files were valid files; that is, that they contained the kinds of records that the programs were designed to process. As a result, no coding was generated within any program to detect invalid records or empty files.

As a first step toward correcting this shortcoming, the current program will be revised to verify that the input file is not empty. A brief initial analysis follows:

1. Begin by writing the report headers on the report.
2. Attempt to access (read) the first record of the input file.
3. If the attempt is not successful, then write an error message on the report that clearly explains the situation.
4. Follow through with the necessary steps to terminate execution of the program.

To formalize this brief analysis, we use the problem-solving procedure as a guide to performing the following steps:

1. A new record layout must be prepared on the printer spacing chart. It is shown in Figure 6.17.
2. The structure chart is revised to include the test for an empty input file in the start-up module. This segment of the structure chart is shown in Figure 6.18.

   Module 200-START-UP now contains a new subordinate module, specifically, the one that writes an error line on the report if the input file is empty.
3. The program pseudocode or the program flowchart is updated to detail the revised processing steps.

■ **Figure 6.17** Layout of the record ERROR-LINE

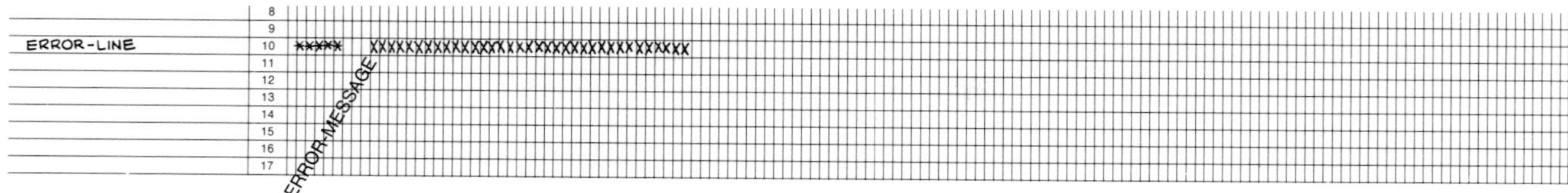

■ **Figure 6.18** Revised structure chart to check for an empty file

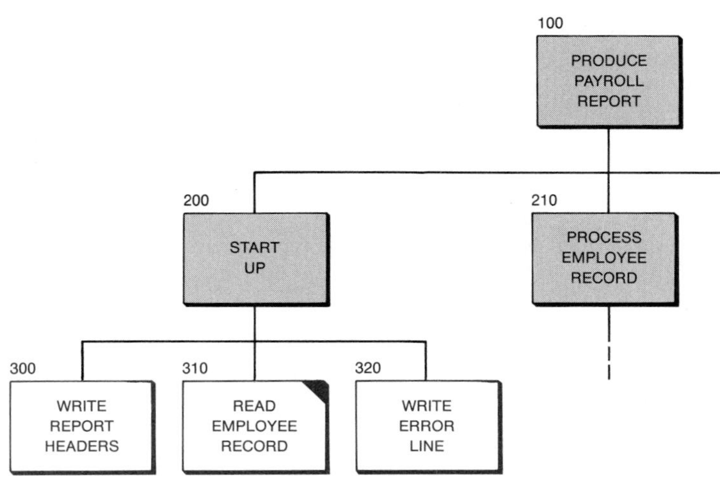

It should be obvious that if the input file is empty, the summary report should not be produced. Note the appropriate test in paragraph 220-Finish-Up.* The changes to paragraphs 200-Start-Up and 220-Finish-Up of the program pseudocode are shown in Figure 6.19a. Step 7 of the paragraph 200-Start-Up contains the test to determine if the input file is empty. If the file is empty, then the procedure 320-Write-Error-Line must be executed and the summary report under the control of paragraph 220-Finish-Up must not be produced. The corresponding changes in the flowchart are shown in Figure 6.19b.

4. Revisions to the COBOL program are made. The data description entries for the record ERROR-LINE must be coded in the WORKING-STORAGE SECTION. ERROR-LINE is added to the end of the group REPORT-HEADERS, since if it is needed, it will be the next record printed after HEADINGS-2.

The PROCEDURE DIVISION entries corresponding to the pseudocode or flowchart modules in Figure 6.19 must be coded. These revisions are contained in Figure 6.20. This completes the task of updating the program in order to test for an empty input file.

Inserting Documentation within the PROCEDURE DIVISION

Program documentation can be entered in a program anywhere the programmer feels that explanations are beneficial to the user. (For instance, see the documentation entered in the WORKING-STORAGE SECTION in Figure 6.9.) It is a common practice to insert documentation in the IDENTIFICATION DIVISION. Occasionally, documentation is inserted preceding paragraphs of the PROCEDURE DIVISION. These explanations usually cover the major functions of the paragraph and also specify where control comes from as it enters the paragraph and where it returns to upon exiting from the paragraph.

The documentation can be made obvious by using the format shown in Figure 6.21.

Note: The need for additional comments is greatly reduced if a program is well structured, and if the programmer made a serious effort to select data names and procedure names that are truly descriptive.)

The revised program at the end of the chapter contains documentation inserts within the PROCEDURE DIVISION.

*As an alternative procedure to the use of the employee counter, the programmer could define a data item to be used as a switch, initialize it to "off" in the paragraph 200-Start-Up, set the switch to "on" if the file is empty, and later, test the switch to determine if the summary report should be printed.

■ **Figure 6.19a** Revisions to the pseudocode to check for an empty file

100-Produce-Payroll-Report.

1. Perform 200-Start-Up.
2. Perform 210-Process-Employee-Record until no more records.
3. Perform 220-Finish-Up.
4. Stop the run.

200-Start-Up.

1. Open the files.
2. Set the end-of-file flag WS-MORE-RECORDS to "YES".
3. Set the company accumulators to zero.
4. Clear the record areas Employee-Payline and Company-Summary.
5. Perform 300-Write-Report-Headers.
6. Perform 310-Read-Employee-Record.
7. If the flag WS-MORE-RECORDS is not equal to "YES",
   perform 320-Write-Error-Line.

.
.
.

220-Finish-Up.

1. If employee-counter is not equal to zero,
   perform 360-Produce-Company-Summary.
2. Close ...

.
.
.

320-Write-Error-Line.

1. Move the message "No Records in Employee Payroll File" to
   error-message field of Error-Line.
2. Move Error-Line to the output area Printline.
3. After advancing 10 lines, write the output record Printline.

.
.
.

■ **Figure 6.19b** Revisions to the flowchart to check for an empty file

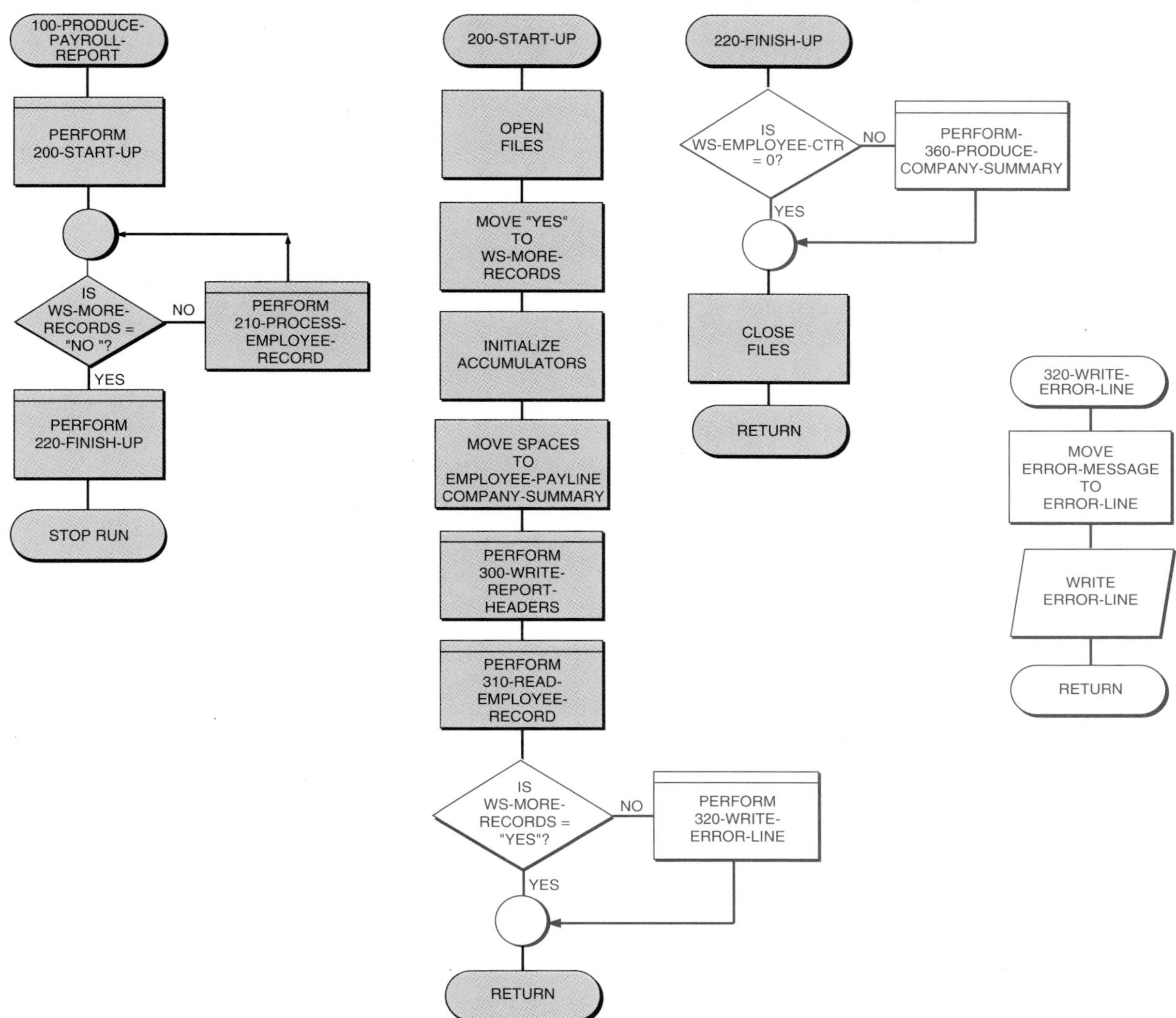

■ **Figure 6.20** Revisions to the COBOL program to check for an empty file

```
    .
    .
    .
    05  ERROR-LINE.
        10 PIC X(6)         VALUE " *****".
        10 PIC XXX          VALUE SPACES.
        10 ERROR-MESSAGE    PIC X(35).

    .
    .
PROCEDURE DIVISION.

100-PRODUCE-PAYROLL-REPORT.
    PERFORM 200-START-UP.
    PERFORM 210-PROCESS-EMPLOYEE-RECORD WITH TEST BEFORE
        UNTIL WS-MORE-RECORDS = "NO ".
    PERFORM 220-FINISH-UP.
    STOP RUN.

200-START-UP.
    OPEN INPUT EMPLOYEE-PAYROLL-FILE
         OUTPUT PAYROLL-REPORT-FILE.
    MOVE "YES" TO WS-MORE-RECORDS.
    INITIALIZE WS-COMPANY-ACCUMULATORS.
    MOVE SPACES TO EMPLOYEE-PAYLINE
                   COMPANY-SUMMARY.
    PERFORM 300-WRITE-REPORT-HEADERS.
    PERFORM 310-READ-EMPLOYEE-RECORD.
    IF WS-MORE-RECORDS = "YES"
        NEXT SENTENCE
    ELSE
        PERFORM 320-WRITE-ERROR-LINE.
.
.

220-FINISH-UP.
    IF WS-EMPLOYEE-CTR NOT = ZERO
        PERFORM 360-PRODUCE-COMPANY-SUMMARY
    ELSE
        NEXT SENTENCE.
    CLOSE EMPLOYEE-PAYROLL-FILE
          PAYROLL-REPORT-FILE.
.
.
320-WRITE-ERROR-LINE.
    MOVE "NO RECORDS IN EMPLOYEE PAYROLL FILE" TO ERROR-MESSAGE.
    WRITE PRINTLINE FROM ERROR-LINE
        AFTER ADVANCING 10 LINES.
```

■ **Figure 6.21** Use of asterisks (*) to highlight program documentation

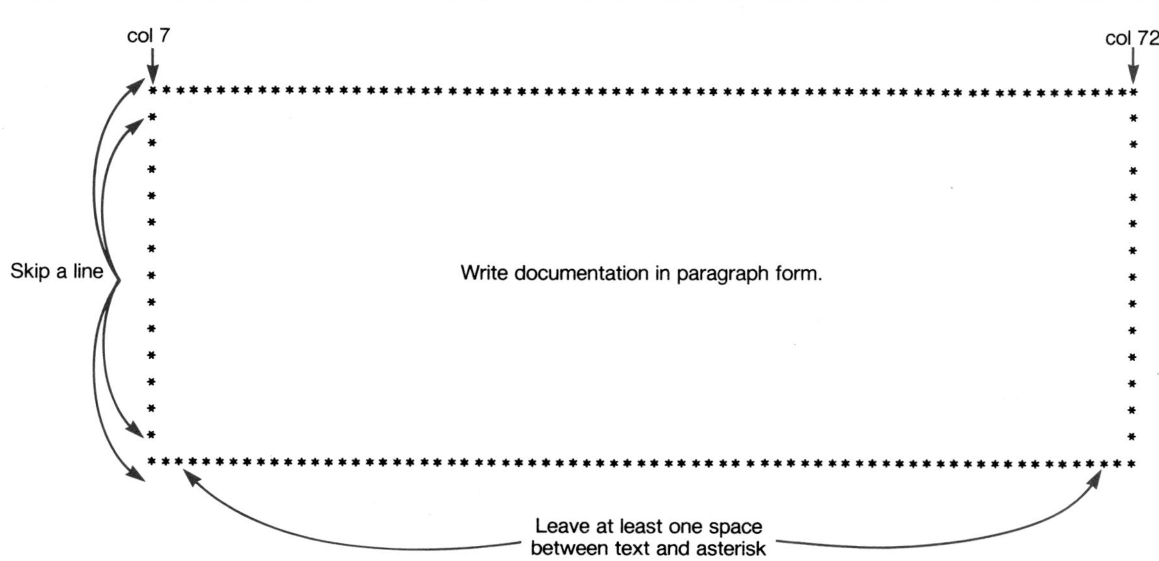

■ **Figure 6.22** WRITE statement format with identifier option for line spacing control

```
WRITE output-record-name FROM identifier-1
    AFTER ADVANCING identifier-2
```

Report Refinements

In this section, we consider some features that improve the quality of the reports produced by COBOL programs. In particular, we examine procedures to exercise greater control over vertical spacing of detail lines, to number the pages of the report, to date the report, to control the number of detail lines to be printed on each page, and to print an "End of Report" message at the end of the report.

Vertical Spacing

It is generally recommended to provide appropriate spacing between different types of lines on a report. One such scheme is as follows:

1. Skip two lines between a title and a subtitle, between a subtitle and column headings, or between a title and column headings.
2. If column headings require more than one line, write them on consecutive lines.
3. Skip one line between the column headers and the first detail line.
4. Print detail lines on consecutive lines.

The programs that have been developed until now satisfy steps 1–3 of this scheme; however, the detail lines have been double-spaced. This has been due to the format of the WRITE statement used in these programs:

```
WRITE PRINTLINE FROM DETAIL-LINE
    AFTER ADVANCING 2 LINES.
```

Note that the very first execution of this WRITE statement leaves one blank line between the column headers and the first detail line. However, since the same statement is used to print all the detail lines, the report is necessarily double-spaced.

To allow for greater control over vertical spacing of detail lines, the programmer can use the format of the WRITE statement shown in Figure 6.22.

By using the identifier option in the AFTER clause, the programmer can change its value as needed during program execution. For instance, the previous WRITE statement can be changed to

```
WRITE PRINTLINE FROM DETAIL-LINE
    AFTER ADVANCING WS-PROPER-SPACING.
```

The identifier WS-PROPER-SPACING is a data item described in the WORKING-STORAGE SECTION.

Since one blank line must be left between the headers and the first detail line, the item WS-PROPER-SPACING must have an initial value of 2 at the top of each page. But thereafter, it must have a value of 1 to prevent double-spacing on the rest of the page.

This control can be achieved by moving the numeric value 2 to WS-PROPER-SPACING immediately after writing the headings, assuring one blank line before writing the first detail line, and then by moving the numeric value 1 to WS-PROPER-SPACING after writing the first detail line. Note the coding that follows. (The data item WS-PROPER-SPACING is entered as an elementary item of the group item WS-PROGRAM-CONTROLS.)

```
01  PROGRAM-CONTROLS.
    05 WS-MORE-RECORDS      PIC XXX.
    05 WS-PROPER-SPACING    PIC 9.
.
.
PROCEDURE DIVISION.
.
.
300-WRITE-REPORT-HEADERS.
    .
    .
    WRITE PRINTLINE FROM HEADINGS-2
```

```
        AFTER ADVANCING 1 LINE.
    MOVE 2 TO WS-PROPER-SPACING.

.
.
340-PREPARE-EMPLOYEE-PAYLINE.
    MOVE I-DEPT TO O-DEPT.
    MOVE I-SSN TO O-SSN.
    MOVE I-NAME TO O-NAME.
    MOVE I-UNION-DUES TO O-UNION-DUES.
    MOVE I-INS-PREMIUM TO O-INS-PREMIUM.
    MOVE WS-GROSS-WAGES TO O-GROSS-WAGES.
    MOVE WS-FED-TAX TO O-FED-TAX.
    MOVE WS-STATE-TAX TO O-STATE-TAX.
    MOVE WS-TOTAL-DEDUCTIONS TO O-TOTAL-DEDUCTIONS.
    MOVE WS-NET-WAGES TO O-NET-WAGES.
    WRITE PRINTLINE FROM EMPLOYEE-PAYLINE
        AFTER ADVANCING WS-PROPER-SPACING.
    MOVE 1 TO WS-PROPER-SPACING.
.
.
```

This procedure is included in the revised program at the end of the chapter. Examine the report in Figure 6.39 to see the effect of vertical spacing control.

"End of Report" Message

Since most reports are printed on continuous-form paper, and the paper is torn off the printer at a perforated fold, the question could easily arise: "Do we have **all** the pages of the report?" One easy way of assuring that the report is complete is to print an "End of Report" message at the very end of the report.

The mechanics to accomplish this are very simple:

1. Plan the layout of an "End of Report" line on the printer spacing chart.
2. Define the corresponding record in the WORKING-STORAGE SECTION. It should be the last record in the section, since the line it generates is the very last line of the report.
3. Insert the statements needed to print this line within the finish-up paragraph.

Figure 6.23 shows the record layout in part a, the entries in pseudocode paragraph 220-Finish-Up in part b, and the corresponding coding in part c.

Limiting the Number of Detail Lines per Page

The reports that are printed as output from computer programs generally require many pages. Very often these pages are separated and collated in booklet form. To increase the clarity of printed material and to facilitate the retrieval of meaningful values from any page of the report, it is a common practice to properly document the report at the top of each page (by writing the company name, the report name, and column headings), and to number the pages consecutively. Consequently, a line counter is used to control the number of detail lines to be printed on each page of the report. The maximum number of lines that can be printed on a sheet is a function of the size of the continuous-form printer paper used, the size of the print characters available on the printer, and the kind of spacing required on the report.

When the required number of lines has been printed on a page, then the program must direct the computer to advance the paper in the printer to the top of a new page. There it should write the appropriate top-of-page documentation before continuing to print detail lines.

Within the program, these requirements can be accomplished as follows:

1. Determine the maximum number of lines to be printed on each page. This number can refer to detail lines only, or it can refer to all types of lines to be printed on a page. In the WORKING-STORAGE SECTION, define a data item such as WS-LINE-LIMIT and assign it the appropriate constant value by coding the VALUE clause. In the sample program, the maximum number of detail lines is set to 20, and it is decided that WS-LINE-LIMIT refers to detail lines only. Thus, the data item entry is

   ```
   05  WS-LINE-LIMIT     PIC S99     VALUE +20.
   ```

   (If the data item included all types of lines, then the constant in the VALUE clause would be 20 plus the number of lines needed for the top-of-page documentation, including all blank lines.)
2. Define another data item to be the line counter, such as WS-LINE-CTR. Since the line counter in this program counts only detail lines, it is initialized to zero at the top of each page, and it is incremented by 1 each time a detail line is printed. (If the counter counted **all** types of lines, it

■ **Figure 6.23** Preparations for an "end of report" message

a.

	28	
	29	
END-LINE	30	** END OF REPORT **

b.

100-Produce-Payroll-Report.

1. Perform 200-Start-Up.
2. Perform 210-Process-Employee-Record until no more records.
3. Perform 220-Finish-Up.
4. Stop the run.

.

.

.

220-Finish-Up.

1. If employee-counter is not equal to zero,
   perform 360-Produce-Company-Summary.
2. Move End-Line to the output area Printline.
3. After advancing 10 lines, write the output record Printline.
4. Close the files.

c.

```
.
.
01   END-LINE.
     05 PIC X(57)   VALUE SPACES.
     05 PIC X(19)   VALUE "** END OF REPORT **".
     05 PIC X(56)   VALUE SPACES.
.
.
.
100-PRODUCE-PAYROLL-REPORT.
     PERFORM 200-START-UP.
     PERFORM 210-PROCESS-EMPLOYEE-RECORD WITH TEST BEFORE
         UNTIL WS-MORE-RECORDS = "NO ".
     PERFORM 220-FINISH-UP.
     STOP RUN.

.
.
.
220-FINISH-UP.
     IF WS-EMPLOYEE-CTR NOT = ZERO
         PERFORM 360-PRODUCE-COMPANY-SUMMARY
     ELSE
         NEXT SENTENCE.
     WRITE PRINTLINE FROM END-LINE
         AFTER ADVANCING 10 LINES.
     CLOSE EMPLOYEE-PAYROLL-FILE
           PAYROLL-REPORT-FILE.
.
.
```

would be initialized to the number of lines needed for the top-of-page documentation after those lines have been printed on the page.)

3. For each record being processed, the line counter must be tested to determine if its detail line is to be printed on the current page or on the next page. The detail line must be printed on the current page if the line counter has not reached the value specified in the data item WS-LINE-LIMIT, specifically 20 in the sample program. If the line counter has reached the value of WS-LINE-LIMIT, then the detail line must be printed on the next page, but only after the top-of-page documentation lines have been printed. (Recall that every time a new page is started, the line counter must be reinitialized for that page, and this action is included in the module that writes the top-of-page documentation.)

The logic for the test on the line counter is shown in Figure 6.24. The test will be executed before the statement that writes the detail line in module 340-PREPARE-EMPLOYEE-PAYLINE, but since it is

Figure 6.24 Logic to produce 20 detail lines per report page

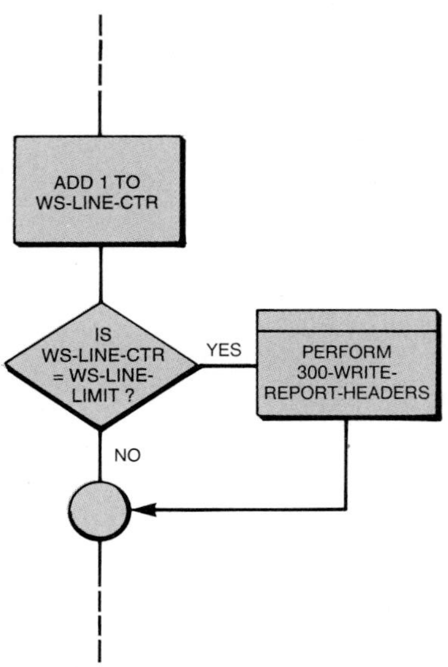

Figure 6.25 Change to the structure chart due to the use of the record counter

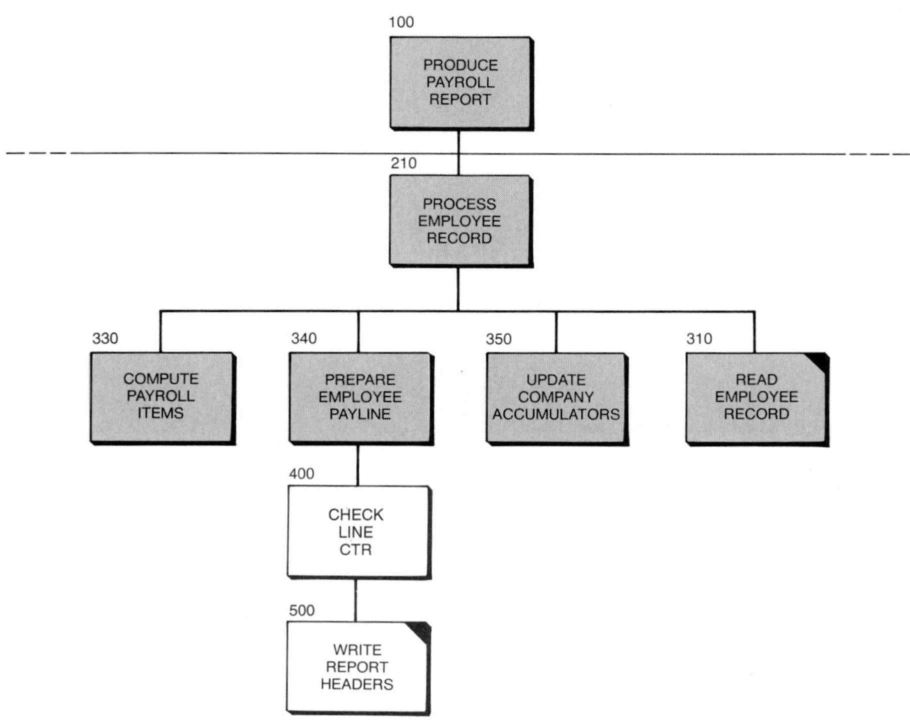

a separate function from that of module 340, it will be placed in a separate module, say 400-CHECK-LINE-CTR, and it will be executed by a PERFORM statement from within module 340. The revised portion of the structure chart is shown in Figure 6.25. (The test on the line counter is executed before the WRITE statement rather than after the WRITE statement to avoid the possibility of printing top-of-page documentation when there are no more detail lines to be printed. This would occur whenever the number of records in the input file is a multiple of the maximum number of detail lines to be printed on a page.)

Note that module 400-CHECK-LINE-CTR controls the execution of module 300-WRITE-REPORT-HEADERS (this occurs when the line counter has reached the line limit for the current page), and thus the WRITE module becomes subordinate to module 400. Consequently, the WRITE module is renumbered as

■ **Figure 6.26** Revisions to the pseudocode due to the record counter

.

.

.

340-Prepare-Employee-Payline.

1. Move input department-number to Employee-Payline department-number.
2. Move input Social-Security-number to Employee-Payline Social-Security-number.
3. Move input name to Employee-Payline name.
4. Move input union-dues to Employee-Payline union-dues.
5. Move input insurance-premium to Employee-Payline insurance-premium.
6. Move gross-wages to Employee-Payline gross-wages.
7. Move federal-tax to Employee-Payline federal-tax.
8. Move state-tax to Employee-Payline state-tax.
9. Move total-deductions to Employee-Payline total-deductions.
10. Move net-wages to Employee-Payline net-wages.
11. Perform 400-Check-Line-Ctr.
12. Move Employee-Payline to the output area Printline.
13. After advancing proper-spacing, write the output record Printline.
14. Add 1 to the line-counter.
15. Set proper-spacing to 1.

.

.

.

400-Check-Record-Ctr.

1. If line-counter is greater than or equal to line-limit, perform 500-Write-Report-Headers.

.

.

.

500-Write-Report-Headers.

1. Move Company-Name to the output area Printline.
2. After advancing to the top of a new page, write the output record Printline.
3. Move Report-Name to the output area Printline.
4. After advancing 3 lines, write the output record Printline.
5. Move Headings-1 to the output area Printline.
6. After advancing 3 lines, write the output record Printline.
7. Move Headings-2 to the output area Printline.
8. After advancing 1 line, write the output record Printline.
9. Set proper-spacing to 2.
10. Set the line-counter to zero.

■ **Figure 6.27** Revisions to the COBOL program due to the record counter

```
.
.
01  PROGRAM-CONTROLS.
    05 WS-MORE-RECORDS       PIC XXX.
    05 WS-PROPER-SPACING     PIC 9.
    05 WS-LINE-CTR           PIC S99     COMP.
    05 WS-LINE-LIMIT         PIC S99     COMP VALUE +20.
.
.
.
340-PREPARE-EMPLOYEE-PAYLINE.
    MOVE I-DEPT TO O-DEPT.
    MOVE I-SSN TO O-SSN.
    MOVE I-NAME TO O-NAME.
    MOVE I-UNION-DUES TO O-UNION-DUES.
    MOVE I-INS-PREMIUM TO O-INS-PREMIUM.
    MOVE WS-GROSS-WAGES TO O-GROSS-WAGES.
    MOVE WS-FED-TAX TO O-FED-TAX.
    MOVE WS-STATE-TAX TO O-STATE-TAX.
    MOVE WS-TOTAL-DEDUCTIONS TO O-TOTAL-DEDUCTIONS.
    MOVE WS-NET-WAGES TO O-NET-WAGES.
    PERFORM 400-CHECK-LINE-CTR.
    WRITE PRINTLINE FROM EMPLOYEE-PAYLINE
        AFTER ADVANCING WS-PROPER-SPACING.
    ADD 1 TO WS-LINE-CTR.
    MOVE 1 TO WS-PROPER-SPACING.
.
.
400-CHECK-LINE-CTR.
    IF WS-LINE-CTR >= WS-LINE-LIMIT
        PERFORM 500-WRITE-REPORT-HEADERS
    ELSE
        NEXT SENTENCE.

500-WRITE-REPORT-HEADERS.
    WRITE PRINTLINE FROM COMPANY-NAME
        AFTER ADVANCING PAGE.
    WRITE PRINTLINE FROM REPORT-NAME
        AFTER ADVANCING 3 LINES.
    WRITE PRINTLINE FROM HEADINGS-1
        AFTER ADVANCING 3 LINES.
    WRITE PRINTLINE FROM HEADINGS-2
        AFTER ADVANCING 1 LINE.
    MOVE 2 TO WS-PROPER-SPACING.
    MOVE ZERO TO WS-LINE-CTR.
```

the first module at the fifth level, namely, 500-WRITE-REPORT-HEADERS, and every occurrence of the WRITE module is so renumbered.

The considerations we have just discussed are incorporated in the partial pseudocode shown in Figure 6.26. (See the corresponding flowchart entries in Figure 6.37.)

Figure 6.27 shows the definitions of the data items WS-LINE-CTR and WS-LINE-LIMIT as elementary items of the group WS-PROGRAM-CONTROLS, and it also shows the PROCEDURE DIVISION entries corresponding to the pseudocode of Figure 6.26.

This development can be summarized as follows:

1. Every time a detail line is ready to be printed, a test is performed to determine if the line counter has reached the line limit set for each page (20 in our example), and if it has, then the page headers must be printed at the top of the next page, the line counter must be reset to the appropriate initial value (0 in our example), and finally the detail line is printed on the new page. Otherwise, the detail line is printed on the current page.
2. Every time a detail line is printed on the report, the line counter is incremented by 1.

Dating the Report and Numbering the Pages

Reports of all kinds accumulate over time. Printing the report date on each report is critical to keeping related reports in their proper chronological sequence. There are many different ways of printing a report date, but two common ones are printing it on the top line of each page and printing it on the line that contains the report name. An example of the latter is the following:

```
INVENTORY REPORT   AS OF   93/05/31
```

In the revision of the sample program, we will print the date in the upper left corner of the first line of each page. Since we also want to number the pages, the top line of the first page will be as follows:

```
REPORT DATE:   93/05/31                                                      PAGE 1
```

This situation requires the layout of another line on the printer spacing chart. It is shown in Figure 6.28. A brief analysis follows:

1. The first line of each page will be as illustrated above, except for the page number.
2. Since this line is the first line of each page, it is part of the report documentation. Consequently, the writing of this line should be included in module 500-WRITE-REPORT-HEADERS.
3. Since the date is the same on all pages, it should be assigned to the date field only once. This should occur in the start-up paragraph along with other data items that must be initialized.
4. Since the page number must be incremented by 1 for each page of the report, the page number field should be initialized to zero in the start-up paragraph, and then it should be incremented by 1 at the beginning of the module that controls the writing of the report headers.

As we examine the structure chart while thinking of this brief analysis, we see that this task does not require a new module. Some of the required functions will be included in module 200-START-UP, and the others will be included in module 500-WRITE-REPORT-HEADERS.

For simplicity, we separate the task into two components, one dealing with the page number and the other dealing with the date.

The Page Number

The page number is to be printed in edited form; that is, leading zeros must be suppressed. Consequently, it is not possible to add 1 directly to the value in the field O-PAGE-NO, since this field is numeric-edited. As a result, it is necessary to set up a related data item, such as WS-PAGE-NO, to handle the arithmetic. The numeric value is then moved to the edited field.

The pseudocode related to the page number is shown in Figure 6.29, and the corresponding coding is shown in Figure 6.30.

The Date

The date on which a report is printed can generally be obtained directly from the operating system. The statement used to retrieve the date from the system is the ACCEPT statement. Two of its formats are shown in Figure 6.31.

Figure 6.28 Layout of TOP-LINE on the printer spacing chart

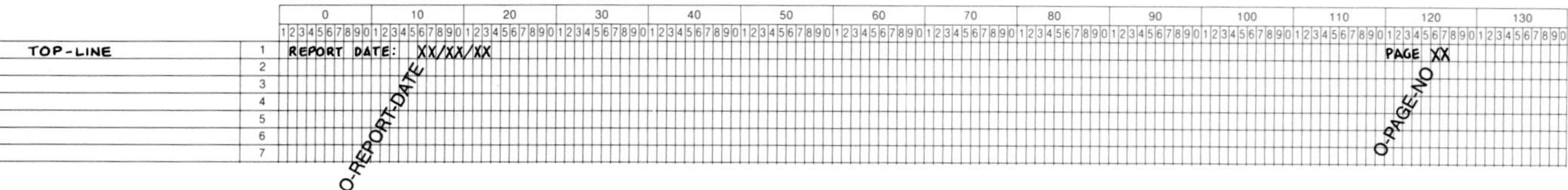

Figure 6.29 Pseudocode revisions related to the page number

.
.
.

200-Start-Up.

1. Open the files.
2. Set the end-of-file flag WS-MORE-RECORDS to "YES".
3. Set the company accumulators to zero.
4. Clear the record areas Employee-Payline and Company-Summary.
5. Set page-number to zero.
6. Perform 500-Write-Report-Headers.
7. Perform 300-Read-Employee-Record.
8. If the flag WS-MORE-RECORDS is not equal to "YES", perform 310-Write-Error-Line.

.
.
.

500-Write-Report-Headers.

1. Add 1 to page-number.
2. Move page-number to Top-Line page-number.
3. Move Top-Line to the output area Printline.
4. After advancing to the top of a new page, write the output record Printline.
5. Move Company-Name to the output area Printline.
6. After advancing 2 lines, write the output record Printline.
7. Move Report-Name to the output area Printline.
8. After advancing 3 lines, write the output record Printline.
9. Move Headings-1 to the output area Printline.
10. After advancing 3 lines, write the output record Printline.
11. Move Headings-2 to the output area Printline.
12. After advancing 1 line, write the output record Printline.
13. Set proper-spacing to 2.
14. Set line-counter to zero.

Figure 6.30 COBOL program entries related to the page number

```
.
.
01   PROGRAM-CONTROLS.
     05 WS-MORE-RECORDS        PIC XXX.
     05 WS-PROPER-SPACING      PIC 9.
     05 WS-LINE-CTR            PIC S99     COMP.
     05 WS-LINE-LIMIT          PIC S99     COMP VALUE +20.
     05 WS-PAGE-NO             PIC 99      COMP.
.
.
01   REPORT-HEADERS.

     05   TOP-LINE.
          10 PIC X(15)           VALUE " REPORT DATE:   ".
          10 O-REPORT-DATE       PIC XX/XX/XX.
          10 PIC X(97)           VALUE SPACES.
          10 PIC X(5)            VALUE "PAGE ".
          10 O-PAGE-NO           PIC Z9.
          10 PIC X(5)            VALUE SPACES.
.
.
200-START-UP.
     OPEN INPUT EMPLOYEE-PAYROLL-FILE
          OUTPUT PAYROLL-REPORT-FILE.
     MOVE "YES" TO WS-MORE-RECORDS.
     INITIALIZE WS-COMPANY-ACCUMULATORS
                WS-PAGE-NO.
     MOVE SPACES TO EMPLOYEE-PAYLINE
                    COMPANY-SUMMARY.
     PERFORM 500-WRITE-REPORT-HEADERS.
     PERFORM 300-READ-EMPLOYEE-RECORD.
     IF WS-MORE-RECORDS = "YES"
         NEXT SENTENCE
     ELSE
         PERFORM 310-WRITE-ERROR-LINE.
.
.
500-WRITE-REPORT-HEADERS.
     ADD 1 TO WS-PAGE-NO.
     MOVE WS-PAGE-NO TO O-PAGE-NO.
     WRITE PRINTLINE FROM TOP-LINE
         AFTER ADVANCING PAGE.
     WRITE PRINTLINE FROM COMPANY-NAME
         AFTER ADVANCING 2 LINES.
     WRITE PRINTLINE FROM REPORT-NAME
         AFTER ADVANCING 3 LINES.
     WRITE PRINTLINE FROM HEADINGS-1
         AFTER ADVANCING 3 LINES.
     WRITE PRINTLINE FROM HEADINGS-2
         AFTER ADVANCING 1 LINE.
     MOVE 2 TO WS-PROPER-SPACING.
     MOVE ZERO TO WS-LINE-CTR.
```

Figure 6.31 ACCEPT statement formats

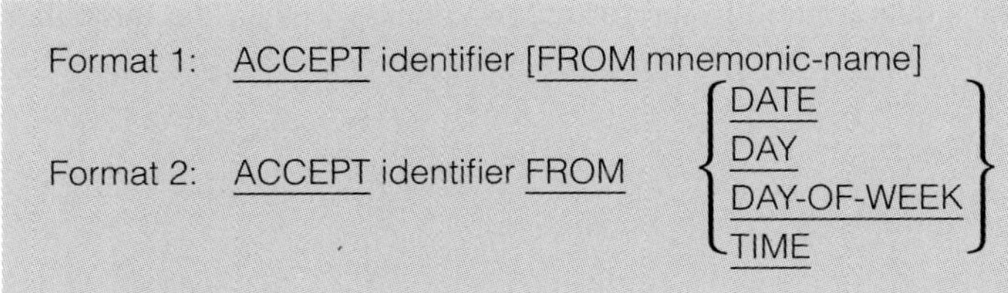

Format 1: ACCEPT identifier [FROM mnemonic-name]
Format 2: ACCEPT identifier FROM
DATE
DAY
DAY-OF-WEEK
TIME

Rules Governing the Use of the ACCEPT Statement

1. In both formats, the ACCEPT statement makes low-volume data available to the program.
2. In both formats, identifier is the receiving field.
3. In format 2:
   a. The option selected in the FROM phrase is the source value. These options are not data items. The programmer does not define them anywhere in the program.
   b. The DATE is received from the system as a six-digit value in the form YYMMDD, where YY is a two-digit year identifier, MM is a two-digit month identifier, and DD is a two-digit day identifier. Example: 930531 is May 31, 1993.
   c. The DAY is received from the system as a five-digit value in the form YYDDD, where YY is a two-digit year identifier, and DDD is a three-digit day identifier. Example: 93125 is the 125th day of the year 1993.
   d. The DAY-OF-WEEK is received from the system as a one-digit value, in the range from 1 to 7, where 1 corresponds to Monday, 2 to Tuesday, and so on, with 7 corresponding to Sunday.
   e. The TIME is received from the system as an eight-digit value in the form HHMMSSCC, where HH is a two-digit hour identifier on a 24-hour clock (in the range from 00 to 23), MM is a two-digit minute identifier in the range 00 through 59, SS is a two-digit second identifier in the range 00 to 59, and CC is a two-digit hundredths of a second identifier, in the range 00 through 99.
   f. The value supplied by the system is stored unedited and left-justified in the receiving field. Excess bytes in the receiving field are blank-filled. If the receiving field is too small, extra characters are truncated on the right.
4. In format 1:
   a. If the FROM phrase is not used, data is obtained from the system's default input device.
   b. The mnemonic-name in the FROM phrase must be defined in the SPECIAL-NAMES paragraph of the ENVIRONMENT DIVISION; that is, it must be associated with a system logical input device name.
   c. The source value is stored unedited and left-justified in the receiving field. Excess bytes in the receiving field are blank-filled. If the receiving field is too small, extra characters are truncated on the right.

You can see that format 2 is the appropriate one to use for our needs.

Since the date must be printed on the report in edited form, and since the ACCEPT statement does not edit the value as it is stored in the receiving field, it is necessary to use an intermediate storage area to receive the date from the system. Then the date is moved from the intermediate storage area to the edited field O-REPORT-DATE. We will define the data item WS-REPORT-DATE as the intermediate storage area. (See Figure 6.33.)

The entries in the pseudocode that are related to the date issue are shown in Figure 6.32, and the corresponding coding is shown in Figure 6.33.

This completes the report refinements that are to be included in the revision of the sample chapter program.

Handling Date Components

From the preceding discussion, you know that the date is obtained from the system in the format YYMMDD. If a report specification calls for a date printed in the format MM/DD/YY, then the three date components must be referenced individually.

Examine the following situation:

If WS-REPORT-DATE is defined as follows:

```
05 WS-REPORT-DATE.
    10 WS-YR      PIC XX.
    10 WS-MONTH   PIC XX.
    10 WS-DAY     PIC XX.
```

and O-REPORT-DATE is defined as follows:

```
05 O-REPORT-DATE.
    10 O-MONTH   PIC XX.
    10           PIC X VALUE "/".
    10 O-DAY     PIC XX.
    10           PIC X VALUE "/".
    10 O-YR      PIC XX.
```

then report specifications can be met with the following code:

■ **Figure 6.32** Pseudocode revisions related to the date

.
.
.

200-Start-Up.

1. Open the files.
2. Obtain the date from the system.
3. Move the date to Top-Line date.
4. Set the end-of-file flag WS-MORE-RECORDS to "YES".
5. Set the company accumulators to zero.
6. Clear the record areas Employee-Payline and Company-Summary.
7. Set page-number to zero.
8. Perform 500-Write-Report-Headers.
9. Perform 300-Read-Employee-Record.
10. If the flag WS-MORE-RECORDS is not equal to "YES", perform 310-Write-Error-Line.

.
.
.

■ **Figure 6.33** COBOL program entries related to the date

```
.
.
01  WS-PROGRAM-CONTROLS.
    05 WS-MORE-RECORDS       PIC XXX.
    05 WS-PROPER-SPACING     PIC 9.
    05 WS-LINE-CTR           PIC S99     COMP.
    05 WS-LINE-LIMIT         PIC S99     COMP VALUE +20.
    05 WS-REPORT-DATE        PIC X(6).
    05 WS-PAGE-NO            PIC 99.
.
.
    05  TOP-LINE.
        10 PIC X(15)         VALUE " REPORT DATE:   ".
        10 O-REPORT-DATE     PIC XX/XX/XX.
        10 PIC X(97)         VALUE SPACES.
        10 PIC X(5)          VALUE "PAGE ".
        10 O-PAGE-NO         PIC Z9.
        10 PIC X(5)          VALUE SPACES.
.
.
200-START-UP.
    OPEN INPUT EMPLOYEE-PAYROLL-FILE
         OUTPUT PAYROLL-REPORT-FILE.
    ACCEPT WS-REPORT-DATE FROM DATE.
    MOVE WS-REPORT-DATE TO O-REPORT-DATE.
    MOVE "YES" TO WS-MORE-RECORDS.
    INITIALIZE WS-COMPANY-ACCUMULATORS
               WS-PAGE-NO.
    MOVE SPACES TO EMPLOYEE-PAYLINE
                   COMPANY-SUMMARY.
    PERFORM 500-WRITE-REPORT-HEADERS.
    PERFORM 300-READ-EMPLOYEE-RECORD.
    IF WS-MORE-RECORDS = "YES"
        NEXT SENTENCE
    ELSE
        PERFORM 310-WRITE-ERROR-LINE.
```

```
ACCEPT WS-REPORT-DATE FROM DATE.
MOVE WS-MONTH TO O-MONTH.
MOVE WS-DAY TO O-DAY.
MOVE WS-YR TO O-YR.
```

Do you agree that the execution of the ACCEPT and the three MOVE statements will produce the correct results?

DISPLAY/ACCEPT

Another alternative is to supply the date as the source value in a format 1 ACCEPT statement, rather than the system-generated date. The following program entries implement this alternative:

```
ENVIRONMENT DIVISION.
.
.
.
OBJECT-COMPUTER.  ...
SPECIAL-NAMES.  CONSOLE IS TERMINAL.
.
.
.
DATA DIVISION.
.
.
.
        .
        .
        .
        05 O-REPORT-DATE    PIC X(8).
        .
        .
        .
PROCEDURE DIVISION.
.
.
.
        .
        .
        .
        ACCEPT O-REPORT-DATE FROM TERMINAL.
        .
        .
        .
```

The characters entered at the terminal will be stored left-justified in the receiving field. If the date is June 5, 1993, entering the string "06/05/93" will store the date in the correct format directly into the field O-REPORT-DATE.

Of course, it is important to know exactly when the program is requesting a terminal entry. Upon executing such an ACCEPT statement, systems generally display a terminal prompt, such as a question mark (?), or a brief message, such as "Awaiting Reply." This signals that the user should make the requested terminal entry.

As an aid to the user in determining the specifics of the required entry, such ACCEPT statements are generally preceded by one or more DISPLAY statements that provide the appropriate information to the user. An example follows:

```
DISPLAY "ENTER DATE IN FORMAT MM/DD/YY" UPON TERMINAL
```

where TERMINAL is a mnemonic name. In this example, it is the one that is also used in the ACCEPT statement.

Note: CONSOLE usually means the computer operator's console. You must use system-specific JCL (job control language) entries to assign CONSOLE or other logical input device names to your terminal. Ask your instructor for the specific commands that you need.

The message displayed at the terminal should be a clear statement of the value(s) to be entered by the user.

The format of the DISPLAY statement is shown in Figure 6.34.

Rules Governing the Use of the DISPLAY Statement

1. The DISPLAY statement transfers low-volume data from the program to the system's default output device or to the logical output device specified by the mnemonic-name.
2. Identifier is the name of a data item defined anywhere in the DATA DIVISION.
3. Literal can be any literal; it can also be any figurative constant except ALL.
4. No editing or data conversion occurs during the execution of DISPLAY.
5. If the UPON phrase is not specified, the data is transferred to the system's default output device.
6. If the UPON phrase is used, the mnemonic-name must be defined in the SPECIAL-NAMES paragraph of the ENVIRONMENT DIVISION.
7. The phrase WITH NO ADVANCING prevents normal positioning to the next line. If it is not specified, normal positioning occurs.

The DISPLAY/ACCEPT-FROM-CONSOLE statements will not be used in the revision of the sample program.

A New Module to Initialize Program Variables

In this chapter, we have introduced more data items that must be initialized at the start of the program, such as accumulators, a page number data item, and a date data item, in addition to the end-of-file flag WS-MORE-RECORDS. As the list of such items gets longer, it is more appropriate to initialize the items in a separate paragraph, thus enhancing the structure of the program. We now include this new feature in the revised program as module 300-INITIALIZE-ITEMS. The corresponding pseudocode and PROCEDURE DIVISION paragraph are shown below. (It is obvious that this new entry forces us to renumber all 300-level modules.)

300-Initialize-Items.

1. Obtain the date from the system.
2. Move the date to Top-Line date.
3. Set the end-of-file flag WS-MORE-RECORDS to "YES".

Figure 6.34 DISPLAY statement format

```
DISPLAY {identifier-1} . . . [UPON mnemonic-name]
        {literal-1   }
   [WITH NO ADVANCING]
```

4. Set the company accumulators to zero.
5. Set page-number to zero.
6. Clear the record areas Employee-Payline and Company-Summary.

```
300-INITIALIZE-ITEMS.
    ACCEPT WS-REPORT-DATE FROM DATE.
    MOVE WS-REPORT-DATE TO O-REPORT-DATE.
    MOVE "YES" TO WS-MORE-RECORDS.
    INITIALIZE WS-COMPANY-ACCUMULATORS
               WS-PAGE-NO.
    MOVE SPACES TO EMPLOYEE-PAYLINE
                   COMPANY-SUMMARY.
```

The Revised Program

All of the program refinements and all of the report refinements discussed on the preceding pages have been included in the revision of the chapter program.

The revised structure chart is shown in Figure 6.35. The revised program pseudocode is shown in Figure 6.36. The corresponding revised program flowchart is shown in Figure 6.37. The revised COBOL program is shown in Figure 6.38. And finally, the payroll report produced by the revised program is shown in Figure 6.39. In Figures 6.35-6.38, the revisions to the chapter program have been highlighted for your convenience.

Figure 6.35 Revised structure chart for the chapter program

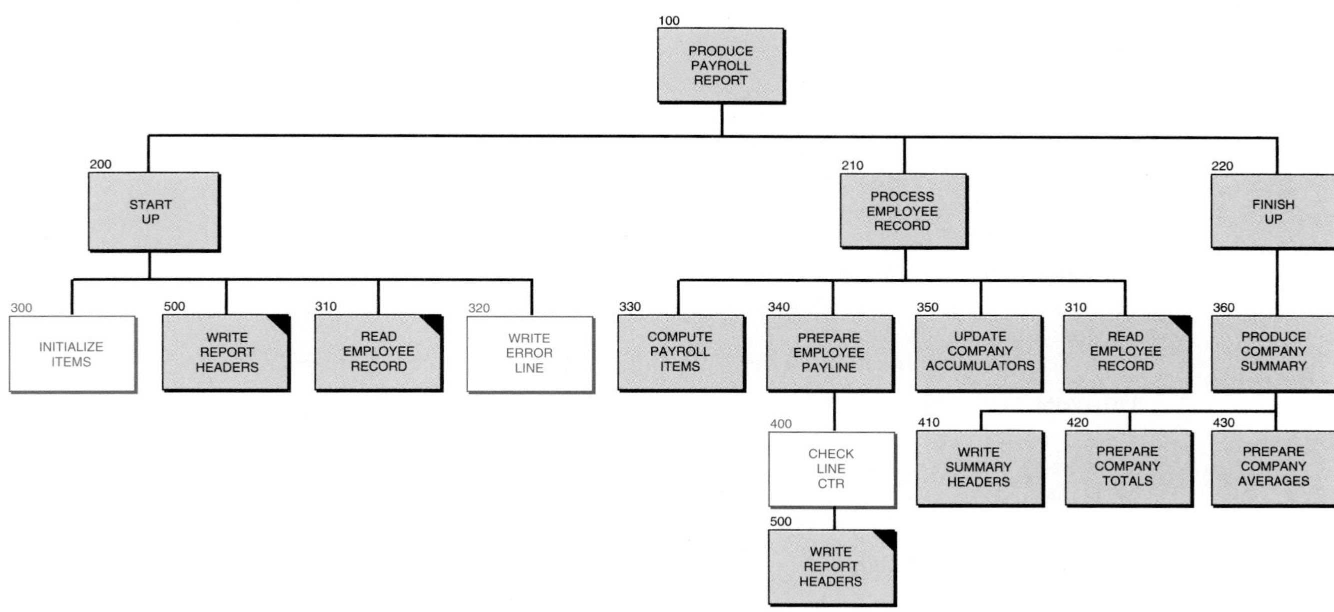

■ **Figure 6.36** Revised program pseudocode for the chapter program

100-Produce-Payroll-Report.

1. Perform 200-Start-Up.
2. Perform 210-Process-Employee-Record until no more records.
3. Perform 220-Finish-Up.
4. Stop the run.

200-Start-Up.

1. Open the files.
2. Perform 300-Initialize-Items.
3. Perform 500-Write-Report-Headers.
4. Perform 310-Read-Employee-Record.
5. If the flag WS-MORE-RECORDS is not equal to "YES",
   perform 320-Write-Error-Line.

210-Process-Employee-Record.

1. Perform 330-Compute-Payroll-Items.
2. Perform 340-Prepare-Employee-Payline.
3. Perform 350-Update-Company-Accumulators.
4. Perform 310-Read-Employee-Record.

220-Finish-Up.

1. If employee-counter is not equal to zero,
   perform 360-Produce-Company-Summary.
2. Move End-Line to the output area Printline.
3. After advancing 10 lines, write the output record Printline.
4. Close the files.

300-Initialize-Items.

1. Obtain the date from the system.
2. Move the date to Top-Line date.
3. Set the end-of-file flag WS-MORE-RECORDS to "YES".
4. Set the company accumulators to zero.
5. Set page-number to zero.
6. Clear the record areas Employee-Payline and Company-Summary.

310-Read-Employee-Record.

1. Read an input Employee-Payroll-Record.
2. Test for end-of-file record;
   if EOF record reached, move "NO " to the end-of-file flag WS-MORE-RECORDS.

320-Write-Error-Line.

1. Move the message "No Records in Employee Payroll File" to
   error-message field of Error-Line.
2. Move Error-Line to the output area Printline.
3. After advancing 10 lines, write the output record Printline.

330-Compute-Payroll-Items.

1. Multiply input hours-worked by input hourly payrate to equal gross-wages.
2. Multiply gross-wages by input federal-tax-rate to equal federal-tax.
3. Multiply gross-wages by input state-tax-rate to equal state-tax.
4. Add federal-tax, state-tax, input union-dues, and input insurance-premium to equal total-deductions.
5. Subtract total-deductions from gross-wages to equal net-wages.

340-Prepare-Employee-Payline.

1. Move input department-number to Employee-Payline department-number.
2. Move input Social-Security-number to Employee-Payline Social-Security-number.
3. Move input name to Employee-Payline name.
4. Move input union-dues to Employee-Payline union-dues.
5. Move input insurance-premium to Employee-Payline insurance-premium.
6. Move gross-wages to Employee-Payline gross-wages.
7. Move federal-tax to Employee-Payline federal-tax.
8. Move state-tax to Employee-Payline state-tax.
9. Move total-deductions to Employee-Payline total-deductions.
10. Move net-wages to Employee-Payline net-wages.
11. Perform 400-Check-Line-Ctr.
12. Move Employee-Payline to the output area Printline.
13. After advancing proper-spacing, write the output record Printline.
14. Add 1 to the line-counter.
15. Set proper-spacing to 1.

350-Update-Company-Accumulators.

1. Add 1 to the employee-counter.
2. Add gross-wages to the gross-wages accumulator.
3. Add federal-tax to the federal-tax accumulator.
4. Add state-tax to the state-tax accumulator.
5. Add input union-dues to the union-dues accumulator.
6. Add input insurance-premium to the insurance-premium accumulator.
7. Add net-wages to the net-wages accumulator.

360-Produce-Company-Summary.

1. Perform 410-Write-Summary-Headers.
2. Perform 420-Prepare-Company-Totals.
3. Perform 430-Prepare-Company-Averages.

400-Check-Line-Ctr.

1. If line-counter is greater than or equal to line-limit,
   perform 500-Write-Report-Headers.

410-Write-Summary-Headers.

1. Add 1 to page-number.
2. Move page-number to Top-Line page-number.
3. Move Top-Line to the output area Printline.
4. After advancing to the top of a new page,
   write the record Printline.
5. Move Company-Name to the output area Printline.
6. After advancing 2 lines, write the output record Printline.
7. Move Summary-Report-Name to the output area Printline.
8. After advancing 3 lines, write the output record Printline.
9. Move Summary-Headers-1 to the output area Printline.
10. After advancing 3 lines, write the output record Printline.
11. Move Summary-Headers-2 to the output area Printline.
12. After advancing 1 line, write the output record Printline.

420-Prepare-Company-Totals.

1. Move gross-wages accumulator to Company-Summary gross-wages.
2. Move federal-tax accumulator to Company-Summary federal-tax.
3. Move state-tax accumulator to Company-Summary state-tax.
4. Move union-dues accumulator to Company-Summary union-dues.
5. Move insurance-premiums accumulator to Company-Summary insurance-premiums.
6. Move net-wages accumulator to Company-Summary net-wages.
7. Move Company-Summary to the output area Printline.
8. After advancing 3 lines, write the output record Printline.

■ Figure 6.36 continued

430-Prepare-Company-Averages.

1. Move employee-counter to Total-Employees-Line number-of-employees.
2. Move Total-Employees-Line to the output area Printline.
3. After advancing 5 lines, write the output record Printline.
4. Divide gross-wages accumulator by employee-counter to equal Average-Gross-Wages-Line average-gross-wages rounded.
5. Move Average-Gross-Wages-Line to the output area Printline.
6. After advancing 2 lines, write the output record Printline.
7. Divide net-wages accumulator by employee-counter to equal Average-Net-Wages-Line average-net-wages rounded.
8. Move Average-Net-Wages-Line to the output area Printline.
9. After advancing 2 lines, write the output record Printline.

500-Write-Report-Headers.

1. Add 1 to page-number.
2. Move page-number to Top-Line page-number.
3. Move Top-Line to the output area Printline.
4. After advancing to the top of a new page, write the output record Printline.
5. Move Company-Name to the output area Printline.
6. After advancing 2 lines, write the output record Printline.
7. Move Report-Name to the output area Printline.
8. After advancing 3 lines, write the output record Printline.
9. Move Headings-1 to the output area Printline.
10. After advancing 3 lines, write the output record Printline.
11. Move Headings-2 to the output area Printline.
12. After advancing 1 line, write the output record Printline.
13. Set proper-spacing to 2.
14. Set line-counter to zero.

■ **Figure 6.37** Revised program flowchart for the chapter program

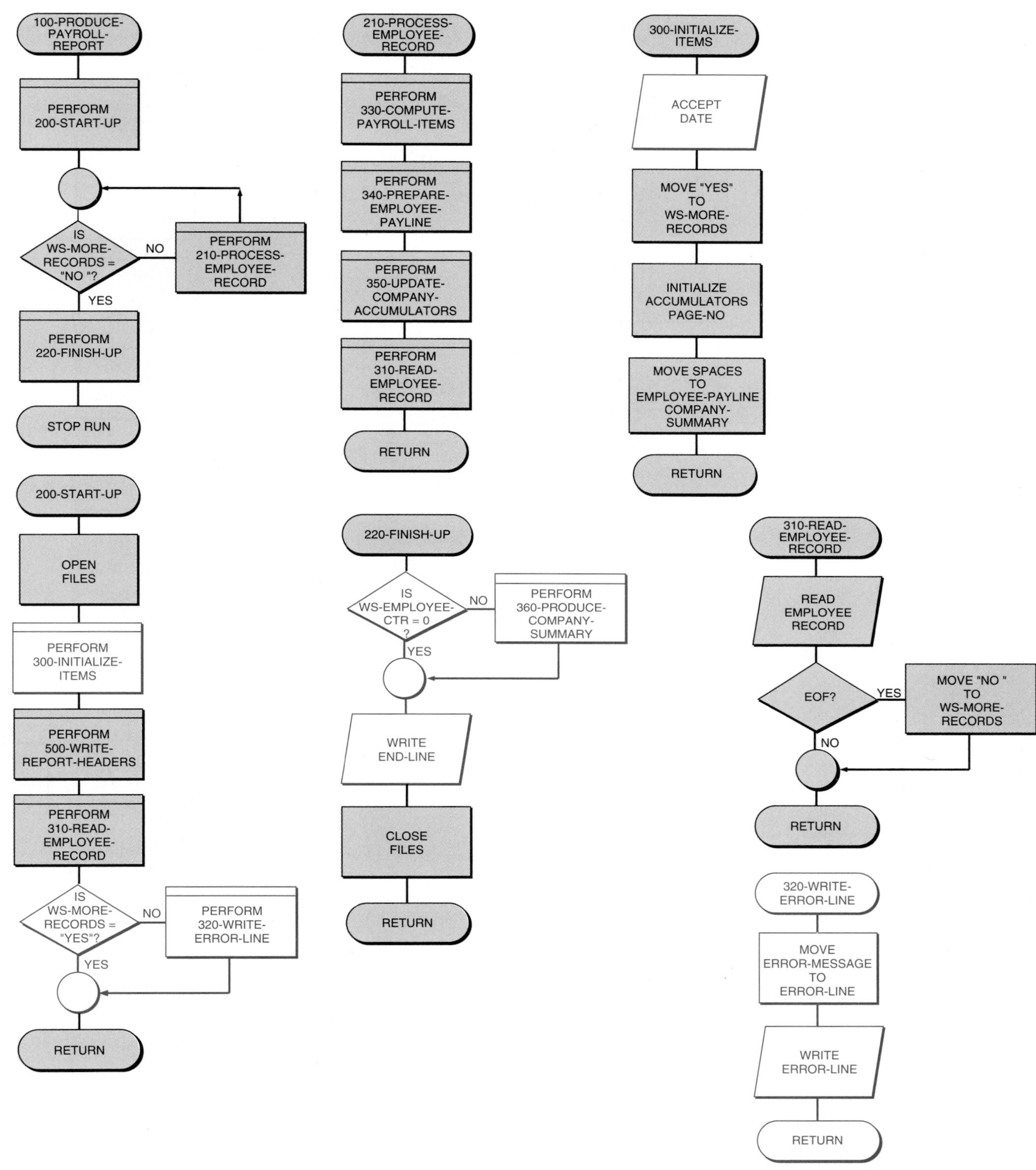

■ Figure 6.37 continued

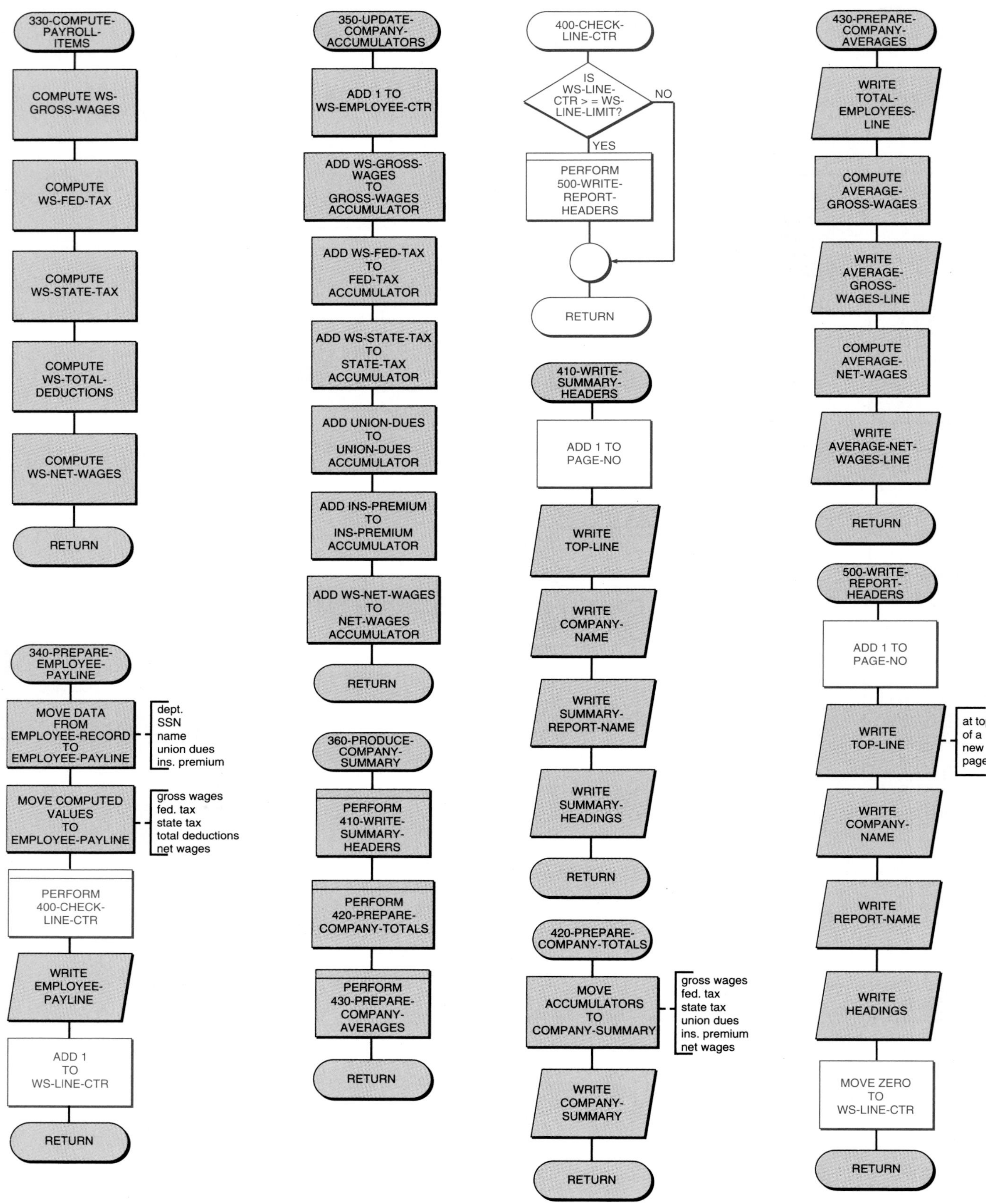

■ **Figure 6.38** Revised COBOL program

```
 IDENTIFICATION DIVISION.

 PROGRAM-ID.     RELIABLE-AUTO-PAYROLL.

*******************************************************************
*                                                                 *
*  AUTHOR.         PAQUETTE.                                      *
*  DATE WRITTEN.   APRIL, 1993                                    *
*                                                                 *
*     THIS PROGRAM PREPARES A MULTI-LEVEL PAYROLL REPORT FOR THE  *
*  RELIABLE AUTO PARTS COMPANY.                                   *
*                                                                 *
*     THE FIRST PART OF THE REPORT CONTAINS A PAY LINE FOR EACH   *
*  EMPLOYEE WITH THE FOLLOWING INFORMATION: THE DEPARTMENT        *
*  NUMBER, SOCIAL SECURITY NUMBER, NAME, GROSS WAGES, ALL         *
*  DEDUCTIONS (FEDERAL TAX, STATE TAX, UNION DUES, INSURANCE      *
*  PREMIUM), TOTAL DEDUCTIONS, AND NET WAGES.  DATA IS PRINTED    *
*  IN EDITED FORM.                                                *
*                                                                 *
*     A LINE COUNTER IS USED TO COUNT THE NUMBER OF PAY LINES     *
*  WRITTEN ON A PAGE.  WHEN THE LINE COUNTER EQUALS THE LINE      *
*  LIMIT, THE REPORT DOCUMENTATION IS PRINTED AT THE TOP OF THE   *
*  NEXT PAGE, AND MORE PAYLINES WILL BE PRINTED ON THAT PAGE.     *
*                                                                 *
*     THE SECOND PART OF THE REPORT IS A SUMMARY FOR THE COMPANY  *
*  AS A WHOLE.  THE SUMMARY CONTAINS TOTALS FOR GROSS WAGES,      *
*  ALL DEDUCTIONS (FEDERAL TAX, STATE TAX, UNION DUES, INSURANCE  *
*  PREMIUM), AND NET WAGES.  IT ALSO DISPLAYS THE TOTAL NUMBER    *
*  OF EMPLOYEES, AND THE AVERAGE FOR THE GROSS WAGES AND THE NET  *
*  WAGES.                                                         *
*                                                                 *
*     EACH PART OF THE REPORT BEGINS AT THE TOP OF A NEW PAGE.    *
*  THE FIRST LINE PRINTS THE REPORT DATE AND THE PAGE NUMBER,     *
*  FOLLOWED BY THE COMPANY NAME, THE NAME OF THE REPORT, AND      *
*  APPROPRIATE COLUMN HEADINGS.                                   *
*                                                                 *
*     THE REPORT ENDS WITH AN "END OF REPORT" MESSAGE.            *
*                                                                 *
*     EACH RECORD OF THE INPUT FILE CONTAINS THE FOLLOWING        *
*  INFORMATION: AN EMPLOYEE'S DEPARTMENT, SOCIAL SECURITY NUMBER, *
*  NAME, HOURS WORKED DURING THE WEEK, PAYRATE, FEDERAL TAX RATE, *
*  STATE TAX RATE, UNION DUES, AND INSURANCE PREMIUM.             *
*                                                                 *
*******************************************************************

 ENVIRONMENT DIVISION.

 CONFIGURATION SECTION.

 SOURCE-COMPUTER.  VAX-VMS-8650.
 OBJECT-COMPUTER.  VAX-VMS-8650.

 INPUT-OUTPUT SECTION.

 FILE-CONTROL.
     SELECT EMPLOYEE-PAYROLL-FILE ASSIGN TO COB$INPUT.
     SELECT PAYROLL-REPORT-FILE   ASSIGN TO COB$OUTPUT.

 DATA DIVISION.

 FILE SECTION.

 FD  EMPLOYEE-PAYROLL-FILE
     RECORD CONTAINS 80 CHARACTERS.

 01  EMPLOYEE-PAYROLL-RECORD.
     05 I-DEPT            PIC XXX.
     05 I-SSN             PIC X(9).
     05 I-NAME            PIC X(22).
     05 I-HRS-WORKED      PIC 99.
     05 I-PAYRATE         PIC 99V99.
     05 I-FED-TAX-RATE    PIC V99.
     05 I-STATE-TAX-RATE  PIC V99.
     05 I-UNION-DUES      PIC 99V99.
     05 I-INS-PREMIUM     PIC 99V99.
     05                   PIC X(28).

 FD  PAYROLL-REPORT-FILE
     RECORD CONTAINS 133 CHARACTERS.

 01  PRINTLINE            PIC X(133).
```

```
WORKING-STORAGE SECTION.

01  WS-PROGRAM-CONTROLS.
    05 WS-MORE-RECORDS        PIC XXX.
    05 WS-PROPER-SPACING      PIC 9.
    05 WS-LINE-CTR            PIC S99    COMP.
    05 WS-LINE-LIMIT          PIC S99    COMP  VALUE +20.
    05 WS-REPORT-DATE         PIC X(6).
    05 WS-PAGE-NO             PIC 99     COMP.

01  WS-EMPLOYEE-PAYROLL-ITEMS.
    05 WS-GROSS-WAGES         PIC S9999V99    COMP.
    05 WS-FED-TAX             PIC S999V99     COMP.
    05 WS-STATE-TAX           PIC S999V99     COMP.
    05 WS-TOTAL-DEDUCTIONS    PIC S999V99     COMP.
    05 WS-NET-WAGES           PIC S9999V99    COMP.

01  WS-COMPANY-ACCUMULATORS       COMP.
    05 WS-EMPLOYEE-CTR            PIC S999.
    05 WS-COMPANY-GROSS-WAGES     PIC S9(5)V99.
    05 WS-COMPANY-FED-TAX         PIC S9(5)V99.
    05 WS-COMPANY-STATE-TAX       PIC S9(5)V99.
    05 WS-COMPANY-UNION-DUES      PIC S9(5)V99.
    05 WS-COMPANY-INS-PREMIUMS    PIC S9(5)V99.
    05 WS-COMPANY-NET-WAGES       PIC S9(5)V99.

01  REPORT-HEADERS.

    05  TOP-LINE.
        10 PIC X(15)          VALUE " REPORT DATE: ".
        10 O-REPORT-DATE      PIC XX/XX/XX.
        10 PIC X(97)          VALUE SPACES.
        10 PIC X(5)           VALUE "PAGE ".
        10 O-PAGE-NO          PIC Z9.
        10 PIC X(5)           VALUE SPACES.

    05  COMPANY-NAME.
        10 PIC X(54)    VALUE SPACES.
        10 PIC X(24)    VALUE "RELIABLE AUTO PARTS CO.".
        10 PIC X(54)    VALUE SPACES.

    05  REPORT-NAME.
        10 PIC X(55)    VALUE SPACES.
        10 PIC X(21)    VALUE "WEEKLY PAYROLL REPORT".
        10 PIC X(56)    VALUE SPACES.

    05  HEADINGS-1.
        10 PIC X(56)    VALUE SPACES.
        10 PIC X(5)     VALUE "GROSS".
        10 PIC X(4)     VALUE SPACES.
        10 PIC X(7)     VALUE "FEDERAL".
        10 PIC XXX      VALUE SPACES.
        10 PIC X(5)     VALUE "STATE".
        10 PIC XXXX     VALUE SPACES.
        10 PIC X(5)     VALUE "UNION".
        10 PIC X(15)    VALUE SPACES.
        10 PIC X(5)     VALUE "TOTAL".
        10 PIC X(10)    VALUE SPACES.
        10 PIC XXX      VALUE "NET".
        10 PIC X(10)    VALUE SPACES.

    05  HEADINGS-2.
        10 PIC XXX      VALUE SPACES.
        10 PIC X(10)    VALUE "DEPARTMENT".
        10 PIC X(5)     VALUE SPACES.
        10 PIC XXX      VALUE "SSN".
        10 PIC X(17)    VALUE SPACES.
        10 PIC XXXX     VALUE "NAME".
        10 PIC X(14)    VALUE SPACES.
        10 PIC X(5)     VALUE "WAGES".
        10 PIC X(6)     VALUE SPACES.
        10 PIC XXX      VALUE "TAX".
        10 PIC X(6)     VALUE SPACES.
        10 PIC XXX      VALUE "TAX".
        10 PIC X(5)     VALUE SPACES.
        10 PIC XXXX     VALUE "DUES".
        10 PIC XX       VALUE SPACES.
        10 PIC X(9)     VALUE "INSURANCE".
        10 PIC XXX      VALUE SPACES.
        10 PIC X(10)    VALUE "DEDUCTIONS".
        10 PIC X(6)     VALUE SPACES.
        10 PIC X(5)     VALUE "WAGES".
        10 PIC X(9)     VALUE SPACES.
```

```
        05  ERROR-LINE.
            10 PIC X(6)         VALUE " *****".
            10 PIC XXX          VALUE SPACES.
            10 ERROR-MESSAGE    PIC X(35).

    01  EMPLOYEE-PAYLINE.
        05 CARRIAGE-CONTROL     PIC X.
        05                      PIC X(5).
        05 O-DEPT               PIC XXX.
        05                      PIC X(5).
        05 O-SSN                PIC XXXBXXBXXXX.
        05                      PIC X(4).
        05 O-NAME               PIC X(22).
        05                      PIC X(3).
        05 O-GROSS-WAGES        PIC $ZZZ9.99-.
        05                      PIC XX.
        05 O-FED-TAX            PIC $ZZ9.99-.
        05                      PIC X.
        05 O-STATE-TAX          PIC $ZZ9.99-.
        05                      PIC X.
        05 O-UNION-DUES         PIC $Z9.99-.
        05                      PIC X.
        05 O-INS-PREMIUM        PIC $Z9.99-.
        05                      PIC X(5).
        05 O-TOTAL-DEDUCTIONS PIC $ZZ9.99-.
        05                      PIC X(5).
        05 O-NET-WAGES          PIC $ZZZ9.99-.
        05                      PIC X(9).

    01  SUMMARY-REPORT-HEADERS.

        05  SUMMARY-REPORT-NAME.
            10 PIC X(51)   VALUE SPACES.
            10 PIC X(29)   VALUE "WEEKLY PAYROLL SUMMARY REPORT".
            10 PIC X(52)   VALUE SPACES.

        05  SUMMARY-HEADERS-1.
            10 PIC X(18)  VALUE SPACES.
            10 PIC X(5)   VALUE "TOTAL".
            10 PIC X(12)  VALUE SPACES.
            10 PIC X(5)   VALUE "TOTAL".
            10 PIC X(12)  VALUE SPACES.
            10 PIC X(5)   VALUE "TOTAL".
            10 PIC X(10)  VALUE SPACES.
            10 PIC X(5)   VALUE "TOTAL".
            10 PIC X(14)  VALUE SPACES.
            10 PIC X(5)   VALUE "TOTAL".
            10 PIC X(14)  VALUE SPACES.
            10 PIC X(5)   VALUE "TOTAL".
            10 PIC X(22)  VALUE SPACES.

        05  SUMMARY-HEADERS-2.
            10 PIC X(15)  VALUE SPACES.
            10 PIC X(11)  VALUE "GROSS WAGES".
            10 PIC X(5)   VALUE SPACES.
            10 PIC X(13)  VALUE "FEDERAL TAXES".
            10 PIC X(5)   VALUE SPACES.
            10 PIC X(11)  VALUE "STATE TAXES".
            10 PIC X(5)   VALUE SPACES.
            10 PIC X(10)  VALUE "UNION DUES".
            10 PIC X(5)   VALUE SPACES.
            10 PIC X(18)  VALUE "INSURANCE PREMIUMS".
            10 PIC X(5)   VALUE SPACES.
            10 PIC X(9)   VALUE "NET WAGES".
            10 PIC X(20)  VALUE SPACES.

    01  SUMMARY-REPORT-DATALINES.

        05 COMPANY-SUMMARY.
           10                          PIC X(15).
           10 O-COMPANY-GROSS-WAGES    PIC $ZZZ,ZZ9.99-.
           10                          PIC X(5).
           10 O-COMPANY-FED-TAX        PIC $ZZZ,ZZ9.99-.
           10                          PIC X(5).
           10 O-COMPANY-STATE-TAX      PIC $ZZZ,ZZ9.99-.
           10                          PIC X(4).
           10 O-COMPANY-UNION-DUES     PIC $ZZZ,ZZ9.99-.
           10                          PIC X(6).
           10 O-COMPANY-INS-PREMIUMS   PIC $ZZZ,ZZ9.99-.
           10                          PIC X(7).
           10 O-COMPANY-NET-WAGES      PIC $ZZZ,ZZ9.99-.
           10                          PIC X(18).
```

```
       05 TOTAL-EMPLOYEES-LINE.
          10 PIC X(6)           VALUE "  *** ".
          10 PIC X(22)          VALUE "NUMBER OF EMPLOYEES = ".
          10 PIC X(2)           VALUE SPACES.
          10 O-NO-OF-EMPLOYEES  PIC ZZZ9-.
          10 PIC X(98)          VALUE SPACES.

       05 AVERAGE-GROSS-WAGES-LINE.
          10 PIC X(6)               VALUE "  *** ".
          10 PIC X(22)              VALUE "AVERAGE GROSS WAGES = ".
          10 O-AVERAGE-GROSS-WAGES  PIC $Z,ZZ9.99-.
          10 PIC X(95)              VALUE SPACES.

       05 AVERAGE-NET-WAGES-LINE.
          10 PIC X(6)             VALUE "  *** ".
          10 PIC X(22)            VALUE "AVERAGE NET WAGES   = ".
          10 O-AVERAGE-NET-WAGES  PIC $Z,ZZ9.99-.
          10 PIC X(94)            VALUE SPACES.

    01  END-LINE.
        05 PIC X(57)  VALUE SPACES.
        05 PIC X(19)  VALUE "** END OF REPORT **".
        05 PIC X(56)  VALUE SPACES.

    PROCEDURE DIVISION.

   ******************************************************************
   *                                                                *
   *     THIS PARAGRAPH IS THE MAIN CONTROL PARAGRAPH.  IT CONTROLS *
   *  THE EXECUTION OF THE START-UP MODULE, THE EMPLOYEE-RECORD     *
   *  PROCESSING LOOP, AND THE PROGRAM TERMINATION FUNCTIONS.  IT   *
   *  IS ENTERED FROM AND EXITS TO THE OPERATING SYSTEM.            *
   *                                                                *
   ******************************************************************

    100-PRODUCE-PAYROLL-REPORT.
        PERFORM 200-START-UP.
        PERFORM 210-PROCESS-EMPLOYEE-RECORD WITH TEST BEFORE
            UNTIL WS-MORE-RECORDS = "NO ".
        PERFORM 220-FINISH-UP.
        STOP RUN.

   ******************************************************************
   *                                                                *
   *     THIS PARAGRAPH OPENS THE FILES, CONTROLS THE EXECUTION OF  *
   *  THE MODULE THAT INITIALIZES DATA ITEMS, CONTROLS THE PRINTING *
   *  OF THE REPORT HEADERS ON THE FIRST PAGE OF THE REPORT, READS  *
   *  THE INPUT FILE FOR THE FIRST RECORD, CHECKS TO MAKE SURE THE  *
   *  INPUT FILE IS NOT EMPTY, AND IF IT IS, CONTROLS THE EXECUTION *
   *  OF THE MODULE THAT WRITES AN ERROR MESSAGE ON THE REPORT.     *
   *  IT IS ENTERED FROM AND EXITS TO THE PARAGRAPH 100-PRODUCE-    *
   *  PAYROLL-REPORT.                                               *
   *                                                                *
   ******************************************************************

    200-START-UP.
        OPEN INPUT EMPLOYEE-PAYROLL-FILE
             OUTPUT PAYROLL-REPORT-FILE.
        PERFORM 300-INITIALIZE-ITEMS.
        PERFORM 500-WRITE-REPORT-HEADERS.
        PERFORM 310-READ-EMPLOYEE-RECORD.
        IF WS-MORE-RECORDS = "YES"
            NEXT SENTENCE
        ELSE
            PERFORM 320-WRITE-ERROR-LINE.

   ******************************************************************
   *                                                                *
   *     THIS PARAGRAPH CONTROLS THE EXECUTION OF THE MODULE THAT   *
   *  CONTAINS THE COMPUTATIONS, THE MODULE THAT PREPARES AND       *
   *  WRITES EMPLOYEE PAYLINES ON THE REPORT, THE MODULE THAT UP-   *
   *  DATES THE ACCUMULATORS, AND FINALLY THE MODULE THAT READS THE *
   *  NEXT RECORD OF THE INPUT FILE.  IT IS REPEATEDLY ENTERED FROM *
   *  AND EXITS TO THE PARAGRAPH 100-PRODUCE-PAYROLL-REPORT.        *
   *                                                                *
   ******************************************************************

    210-PROCESS-EMPLOYEE-RECORD.
        PERFORM 330-COMPUTE-PAYROLL-ITEMS.
        PERFORM 340-PREPARE-EMPLOYEE-PAYLINE.
        PERFORM 350-UPDATE-COMPANY-ACCUMULATORS.
        PERFORM 310-READ-EMPLOYEE-RECORD.
```

```
*****************************************************************
*                                                               *
*     THIS PARAGRAPH CONTROLS THE EXECUTION OF THE MODULE THAT  *
*  PRODUCES THE SUMMARY REPORT. IT ALSO WRITES THE "END OF      *
*  REPORT" MESSAGE AND THEN CLOSES THE FILES.  IT IS ENTERED    *
*  FROM AND EXITS TO THE PARAGRAPH 100-PRODUCE-PAYROLL-REPORT.  *
*                                                               *
*****************************************************************

 220-FINISH-UP.
     IF WS-EMPLOYEE-CTR NOT = ZERO
         PERFORM 360-PRODUCE-COMPANY-SUMMARY
     ELSE
         NEXT SENTENCE.
     WRITE PRINTLINE FROM END-LINE
         AFTER ADVANCING 10 LINES.
     CLOSE EMPLOYEE-PAYROLL-FILE
           PAYROLL-REPORT-FILE.

*****************************************************************
*                                                               *
*     THIS PARAGRAPH OBTAINS THE DATE FROM THE SYSTEM, SETS ALL *
*  ACCUMULATORS TO ZERO, SETS THE PAGE NUMBER TO ZERO, AND SETS *
*  THE END-OF-FILE FLAG WS-MORE-RECORDS TO "YES".  IT IS ENTERED *
*  FROM AND EXITS TO THE PARAGRAPH 200-START-UP.                *
*                                                               *
*****************************************************************

 300-INITIALIZE-ITEMS.
     ACCEPT WS-REPORT-DATE FROM DATE.
     MOVE WS-REPORT-DATE TO O-REPORT-DATE.
     MOVE "YES" TO WS-MORE-RECORDS.
     INITIALIZE WS-COMPANY-ACCUMULATORS
                WS-PAGE-NO.
     MOVE SPACES TO EMPLOYEE-PAYLINE
                    COMPANY-SUMMARY.

*****************************************************************
*                                                               *
*     THIS PARAGRAPH READS AN EMPLOYEE RECORD FROM THE INPUT    *
*  FILE AND SETS THE FLAG WS-MORE-RECORDS TO "NO " WHEN THE END *
*  OF THE FILE IS REACHED.  THE FIRST TIME, IT IS ENTERED FROM  *
*  AND EXITS TO THE PARAGRAPH 200-START-UP. THEREAFTER, IT IS   *
*  ENTERED FROM AND EXITS TO THE PARAGRAPH 210-PROCESS-EMPLOYEE- *
*  RECORD.                                                      *
*                                                               *
*****************************************************************

 310-READ-EMPLOYEE-RECORD.
     READ EMPLOYEE-PAYROLL-FILE RECORD
         AT END
             MOVE "NO " TO WS-MORE-RECORDS.

*****************************************************************
*                                                               *
*     THIS PARAGRAPH WRITES THE ERROR MESSAGE IF THE INPUT FILE *
*  IS INITIALLY EMPTY.  IT IS ENTERED FROM AND EXITS TO THE     *
*  PARAGRAPH 200-START-UP.                                      *
*                                                               *
*****************************************************************

 320-WRITE-ERROR-LINE.
     MOVE "NO RECORDS IN EMPLOYEE PAYROLL FILE" TO ERROR-MESSAGE.
     WRITE PRINTLINE FROM ERROR-LINE
         AFTER ADVANCING 10 LINES.

*****************************************************************
*                                                               *
*     THIS PARAGRAPH CARRIES OUT ALL THE PAYROLL COMPUTATIONS   *
*  FOR EACH EMPLOYEE.  IT IS ENTERED FROM AND EXITS TO THE PARA- *
*  GRAPH 210-PROCESS-EMPLOYEE-RECORD.                           *
*                                                               *
*****************************************************************

 330-COMPUTE-PAYROLL-ITEMS.
     MULTIPLY I-HRS-WORKED BY I-PAYRATE GIVING WS-GROSS-WAGES.
     MULTIPLY WS-GROSS-WAGES BY I-FED-TAX-RATE
         GIVING WS-FED-TAX ROUNDED.
     MULTIPLY WS-GROSS-WAGES BY I-STATE-TAX-RATE
         GIVING WS-STATE-TAX ROUNDED.
     ADD WS-FED-TAX WS-STATE-TAX I-UNION-DUES I-INS-PREMIUM
         GIVING WS-TOTAL-DEDUCTIONS.
     SUBTRACT WS-TOTAL-DEDUCTIONS FROM WS-GROSS-WAGES
         GIVING WS-NET-WAGES.
```

```
*****************************************************************
*                                                               *
*     THIS PARAGRAPH TRANSFERS ALL THE EMPLOYEE DATA TO THE     *
*  EMPLOYEE PAYLINE RECORD.  THEN BEFORE WRITING THE PAYLINE ON *
*  THE REPORT, IT CONTROLS THE EXECUTION OF MODULE 400-CHECK-   *
*  LINE-CTR TO DETERMINE IF A NEW PAGE IS NEEDED OR NOT.  IT    *
*  THEN WRITES THE PAYLINE RECORD ON THE REPORT AND ADDS 1 TO   *
*  THE LINE COUNTER.  IT IS ENTERED FROM AND EXITS TO THE PARA- *
*  GRAPH 210-PROCESS-EMPLOYEE-RECORD.                           *
*                                                               *
*****************************************************************

 340-PREPARE-EMPLOYEE-PAYLINE.
     MOVE I-DEPT TO O-DEPT.
     MOVE I-SSN TO O-SSN.
     MOVE I-NAME TO O-NAME.
     MOVE I-UNION-DUES TO O-UNION-DUES.
     MOVE I-INS-PREMIUM TO O-INS-PREMIUM.
     MOVE WS-GROSS-WAGES TO O-GROSS WAGES.
     MOVE WS-FED-TAX TO O-FED-TAX.
     MOVE WS-STATE-TAX TO O-STATE-TAX.
     MOVE WS-TOTAL-DEDUCTIONS TO O-TOTAL-DEDUCTIONS.
     MOVE WS-NET-WAGES TO O-NET-WAGES.
     PERFORM 400-CHECK-LINE-CTR.
     WRITE PRINTLINE FROM EMPLOYEE-PAYLINE
         AFTER ADVANCING WS-PROPER-SPACING.
     ADD 1 TO WS-LINE-CTR.
     MOVE 1 TO WS-PROPER-SPACING.

*****************************************************************
*                                                               *
*     THIS PARAGRAPH UPDATES ALL THE COMPANY ACCUMULATORS AS    *
*  EACH EMPLOYEE RECORD IS PROCESSED.  IT IS ENTERED FROM AND   *
*  EXITS TO THE PARAGRAPH 210-PROCESS-EMPLOYEE-RECORD.          *
*                                                               *
*****************************************************************

 350-UPDATE-COMPANY-ACCUMULATORS.
     ADD 1 TO WS-EMPLOYEE-CTR.
     ADD WS-GROSS-WAGES TO WS-COMPANY-GROSS-WAGES.
     ADD WS-FED-TAX TO WS-COMPANY-FED-TAX.
     ADD WS-STATE-TAX TO WS-COMPANY-STATE-TAX.
     ADD I-UNION-DUES TO WS-COMPANY-UNION-DUES.
     ADD I-INS-PREMIUM TO WS-COMPANY-INS-PREMIUMS.
     ADD WS-NET-WAGES TO WS-COMPANY-NET-WAGES.

*****************************************************************
*                                                               *
*     THIS PARAGRAPH CONTROLS THE EXECUTION OF THE MODULES THAT *
*  PRODUCE THE SUMMARY REPORT.  IT IS ENTERED FROM AND EXITS TO *
*  THE PARAGRAPH 220-FINISH-UP.                                 *
*                                                               *
*****************************************************************

 360-PRODUCE-COMPANY-SUMMARY.
     PERFORM 410-WRITE-SUMMARY-HEADERS.
     PERFORM 420-PREPARE-COMPANY-TOTALS.
     PERFORM 430-PREPARE-COMPANY-AVERAGES.

*****************************************************************
*                                                               *
*     THIS PARAGRAPH TESTS THE LINE COUNTER.  WHEN THE COUNTER  *
*  REACHES THE LINE LIMIT, THE MODULE THAT WRITES THE REPORT    *
*  HEADERS IS EXECUTED.  IT IS ENTERED FROM AND EXITS TO THE    *
*  PARAGRAPH 340-PREPARE-EMPLOYEE-PAYLINE.                      *
*                                                               *
*****************************************************************

 400-CHECK-LINE-CTR.
     IF WS-LINE-CTR >= WS-LINE-LIMIT
         PERFORM 500-WRITE-REPORT-HEADERS
     ELSE
         NEXT SENTENCE.

*****************************************************************
*                                                               *
*     THIS PARAGRAPH WRITES THE HEADERS FOR THE SUMMARY REPORT. *
*  IT IS ENTERED FROM AND EXITS TO THE PARAGRAPH 360-PRODUCE-   *
*  COMPANY-SUMMARY.                                             *
*                                                               *
*****************************************************************
```

Figure 6.38 continued

```
 410-WRITE-SUMMARY-HEADERS.
     ADD 1 TO WS-PAGE-NO.
     MOVE WS-PAGE-NO TO O-PAGE-NO.
     WRITE PRINTLINE FROM TOP-LINE
         AFTER ADVANCING PAGE.
     WRITE PRINTLINE FROM COMPANY-NAME
         AFTER ADVANCING 2 LINES.
     WRITE PRINTLINE FROM SUMMARY-REPORT-NAME
         AFTER ADVANCING 3 LINES.
     WRITE PRINTLINE FROM SUMMARY-HEADERS-1
         AFTER ADVANCING 3 LINES.
     WRITE PRINTLINE FROM SUMMARY-HEADERS-2
         AFTER ADVANCING 1 LINE.

******************************************************************
*                                                                *
*     THIS PARAGRAPH TRANSFERS THE ACCUMULATED AMOUNTS TO THE    *
*  COMPANY SUMMARY RECORD AND THEN WRITES IT OUT.  IT IS ENTERED *
*  FROM AND EXITS TO THE PARAGRAPH 360-PRODUCE-COMPANY-SUMMARY.  *
*                                                                *
******************************************************************

 420-PREPARE-COMPANY-TOTALS.
     MOVE WS-COMPANY-GROSS-WAGES TO O-COMPANY-GROSS-WAGES.
     MOVE WS-COMPANY-FED-TAX TO O-COMPANY-FED-TAX.
     MOVE WS-COMPANY-STATE-TAX TO O-COMPANY-STATE-TAX.
     MOVE WS-COMPANY-UNION-DUES TO O-COMPANY-UNION-DUES.
     MOVE WS-COMPANY-INS-PREMIUMS TO O-COMPANY-INS-PREMIUMS.
     MOVE WS-COMPANY-NET-WAGES TO O-COMPANY-NET-WAGES.
     WRITE PRINTLINE FROM COMPANY-SUMMARY
         AFTER ADVANCING 3 LINES.

******************************************************************
*                                                                *
*     THIS PARAGRAPH COMPUTES THE APPROPRIATE COMPANY AVERAGES   *
*  AND WRITES THEM OUT ON THE SUMMARY REPORT.  IT IS ENTERED     *
*  FROM AND EXITS TO THE PARAGRAPH 360-PRODUCE-COMPANY-SUMMARY.  *
*                                                                *
******************************************************************

 430-PREPARE-COMPANY-AVERAGES.
     MOVE WS-EMPLOYEE-CTR TO O-NO-OF-EMPLOYEES.
     WRITE PRINTLINE FROM TOTAL-EMPLOYEES-LINE
         AFTER ADVANCING 5 LINES.
     DIVIDE WS-COMPANY-GROSS-WAGES BY WS-EMPLOYEE-CTR
         GIVING O-AVERAGE-GROSS-WAGES ROUNDED.
     WRITE PRINTLINE FROM AVERAGE-GROSS-WAGES-LINE
         AFTER ADVANCING 2 LINES.
     DIVIDE WS-COMPANY-NET-WAGES BY WS-EMPLOYEE-CTR
         GIVING O-AVERAGE-NET-WAGES ROUNDED.
     WRITE PRINTLINE FROM AVERAGE-NET-WAGES-LINE
         AFTER ADVANCING 2 LINES.

******************************************************************
*                                                                *
*     THIS PARAGRAPH WRITES THE REPORT DOCUMENTATION AT THE TOP  *
*  OF EACH PAGE.  THE FIRST TIME, IT IS ENTERED FROM AND EXITS   *
*  TO THE PARAGRAPH 200-START-UP.  THEREAFTER, IT IS ENTERED     *
*  FROM AND EXITS TO THE PARAGRAPH 400-CHECK-LINE-CTR.           *
*                                                                *
******************************************************************

 500-WRITE-REPORT-HEADERS.
     ADD 1 TO WS-PAGE-NO.
     MOVE WS-PAGE-NO TO O-PAGE-NO.
     WRITE PRINTLINE FROM TOP-LINE
         AFTER ADVANCING PAGE.
     WRITE PRINTLINE FROM COMPANY-NAME
         AFTER ADVANCING 2 LINES.
     WRITE PRINTLINE FROM REPORT-NAME
         AFTER ADVANCING 3 LINES.
     WRITE PRINTLINE FROM HEADINGS-1
         AFTER ADVANCING 3 LINES.
     WRITE PRINTLINE FROM HEADINGS-2
         AFTER ADVANCING 1 LINE.
     MOVE 2 TO WS-PROPER-SPACING.
     MOVE ZERO TO WS-LINE-CTR.
```

■ **Figure 6.39** Payroll report produced by the revised program

```
REPORT DATE:  93/05/27                                                                          PAGE 1
                                                RELIABLE AUTO PARTS CO.

                                                 WEEKLY PAYROLL REPORT

                                                  GROSS     FEDERAL    STATE    UNION               TOTAL       NET
 DEPARTMENT      SSN              NAME             WAGES       TAX       TAX     DUES   INSURANCE  DEDUCTIONS   WAGES

    010     232 11 5142   BLACK, GEORGIA        $ 420.00   $105.00  $ 79.80  $ 5.50   $ 8.80    $199.10    $ 220.90
    010     321 64 3310   CONDON, DANIEL        $ 350.00   $ 80.50  $ 63.00  $ 5.50   $ 5.50    $154.50    $ 195.50
    010     143 22 7630   DINGLE, PATRICIA      $ 285.00   $ 62.70  $ 48.45  $ 5.50   $ 5.50    $122.15    $ 162.85
    010     342 67 5521   DONNELY, BETH         $ 320.00   $ 70.40  $ 54.40  $ 5.50   $ 5.50    $135.80    $ 184.20
    010     622 74 2102   GARCIA, ALBERT        $ 380.00   $ 91.20  $ 68.40  $ 5.50   $ 8.80    $173.90    $ 206.10
    010     310 22 7540   KOZIOR, STANLEY       $ 420.00   $105.00  $ 79.80  $ 5.50   $ 8.80    $199.10    $ 220.90
    010     111 22 3452   LARKIN, JOHN R.       $ 420.00   $105.00  $ 79.80  $ 5.50   $ 8.80    $199.10    $ 220.90
    010     442 78 2144   PIETRASZEK, JAN       $ 450.00   $117.00  $ 90.00  $ 5.50   $ 8.80    $221.30    $ 228.70
    010     132 11 4679   ZINKIE, KRISTA LYNN   $ 131.25   $ 23.63  $ 19.69  $ 5.50   $ 5.50    $ 54.32    $  76.93
    020     120 40 7526   ANTHONY, TONY         $ 380.00   $ 91.20  $ 68.40  $ 4.80   $ 8.80    $173.20    $ 206.80
    020     052 74 2813   EGLESTON, MARY        $ 480.00   $134.40  $ 91.20  $ 4.80   $ 8.80    $239.20    $ 240.80
    020     101 59 1271   ENDICOTT, MARVIN      $ 420.00   $105.00  $ 79.80  $ 4.80   $ 8.80    $198.40    $ 221.60
    020     071 99 4322   FOGARTY, DOROTHY      $ 350.00   $ 80.50  $ 63.00  $ 4.80   $ 8.80    $157.10    $ 192.90
    020     222 11 7532   MORONEY, PAUL D.      $ 175.00   $ 31.50  $ 26.25  $ 4.80   $ 8.80    $ 71.35    $ 103.65
    020     444 32 1222   NELLY, SHELLY         $ 320.00   $ 67.20  $ 54.40  $ 4.80   $ 5.50    $131.90    $ 188.10
    020     522 05 9782   PONTARELLI, ARTHUR    $ 227.50   $ 43.23  $ 36.40  $ 4.80   $ 5.50    $ 89.93    $ 137.57
    020     346 71 9113   RONDILEAU, PHILIP     $ 380.00   $ 91.20  $ 68.40  $ 4.80   $ 8.80    $173.20    $ 206.80
    020     101 66 6214   RUDON, MARIA          $ 195.00   $ 37.05  $ 31.20  $ 4.80   $ 5.50    $ 78.55    $ 116.45
    020     600 19 5812   WINSPEARE, MARGARET   $ 380.00   $ 91.20  $ 68.40  $ 4.80   $ 8.80    $173.20    $ 206.80
    020     411 85 1423   ZANIELLO, DAVID       $ 420.00   $105.00  $ 79.80  $ 4.80   $ 8.80    $198.40    $ 221.60
```

```
REPORT DATE:  93/05/27                                                                          PAGE 2

                                                RELIABLE AUTO PARTS CO.

                                                 WEEKLY PAYROLL REPORT

                                                  GROSS     FEDERAL    STATE    UNION               TOTAL       NET
 DEPARTMENT      SSN              NAME             WAGES       TAX       TAX     DUES   INSURANCE  DEDUCTIONS   WAGES

    020     491 11 2793   ZITANO, MARIO         $ 195.00   $ 37.05  $ 31.20  $ 4.80   $ 5.50    $ 78.55    $ 116.45
    030     139 41 6674   AYASH, LOUISE         $ 380.00   $ 91.20  $ 68.40  $ 5.25   $ 7.90    $172.75    $ 207.25
    030     523 33 5402   AZEVEDO, MANUEL       $ 500.00   $140.00  $ 95.00  $ 5.25   $10.50    $250.75    $ 249.25
    030     411 56 2230   BEAUDOIN, SUZANNE     $ 450.00   $117.00  $ 85.50  $ 5.25   $10.50    $218.25    $ 231.75
    030     142 65 1998   CONDON, ELIZABETH     $ 520.00   $150.80  $ 98.80  $ 5.25   $10.50    $265.35    $ 254.65
    030     614 22 5667   JONES, ALFRED         $ 120.00   $ 22.80  $ 19.20  $ 5.25   $ 7.90    $ 55.15    $  64.85
    030     391 66 7533   JUST, HELEN           $ 380.00   $ 91.20  $ 68.40  $ 5.25   $ 7.90    $172.75    $ 207.25
    030     882 75 1116   LEONARD, WALTER       $ 450.00   $117.00  $ 85.50  $ 5.25   $10.50    $218.25    $ 231.75
    030     552 88 2246   LEONARDO, ALBANY      $ 520.00   $150.80  $ 98.80  $ 5.25   $10.50    $265.35    $ 254.65
    030     114 33 2225   PRENDERGAST, JACK     $ 500.00   $140.00  $ 95.00  $ 5.25   $10.50    $250.75    $ 249.25
    030     625 73 4622   PURCELL, NANCY        $ 255.00   $ 58.65  $ 45.90  $ 5.25   $ 7.90    $117.70    $ 137.30
    030     222 69 1532   RIGBY, NORMAN         $ 500.00   $140.00  $ 95.00  $ 5.25   $10.50    $250.75    $ 249.25
    030     615 76 6791   TANGUAY, ROSEMARY     $ 255.00   $ 58.65  $ 45.90  $ 5.25   $ 7.90    $117.70    $ 137.30
```

```
REPORT DATE:  93/05/27                                                                          PAGE 3
                                         RELIABLE AUTO PARTS CO.

                                     WEEKLY PAYROLL SUMMARY REPORT

      TOTAL            TOTAL              TOTAL          TOTAL              TOTAL                 TOTAL
   GROSS WAGES     FEDERAL TAXES       STATE TAXES     UNION DUES     INSURANCE PREMIUMS        NET WAGES

   $ 11,928.75      $  2,953.06        $  2,183.19     $     170.10       $     271.40        $  6,351.00

*** NUMBER OF EMPLOYEES =      33

*** AVERAGE GROSS WAGES = $  361.48

*** AVERAGE NET WAGES   = $  192.45

                                          ** END OF REPORT **
```

Important Terms in Chapter 6

ACCEPT
accumulator
ADVANCING identifier
binary digit (bit)
bit (binary digit)
byte
COMPUTE
controlling vertical spacing
DISPLAY
DIVIDE
dividend
divisor
END-COMPUTE
END-DIVIDE
"End of Report" message
FROM DATE
FROM DAY
FROM DAY-OF-WEEK
FROM TIME
grouping report headers
initializing an accumulator
page number
program documentation
quotient
record counter
REMAINDER
report date
testing for an empty input file
trailing minus sign
USAGE IS BINARY
USAGE IS COMP
USAGE IS COMPUTATIONAL
USAGE IS DISPLAY
USAGE IS PACKED-DECIMAL

Exercises

1. Detail lines are written on a report by the following statement:

```
WRITE PRINTLINE FROM DETAIL-LINE
    AFTER ADVANCING 3 LINES
```

   a. How many blank lines are there between consecutive detail lines?
   b. Is the report double-spaced or triple-spaced?

2. Detail lines are written on a report by the following statement:

```
WRITE PRINTLINE FROM DETAIL-LINE
    AFTER ADVANCING 2 LINES
```

   a. How many blank lines are there between consecutive detail lines?
   b. Is the report double-spaced or single-spaced?

3. Detail lines are written on a report by the following statement:

```
WRITE PRINTLINE FROM DETAIL-LINE
    AFTER ADVANCING 1 LINE
```

   a. How many blank lines are there between consecutive detail lines?
   b. How many blank lines are left between the headers and the first detail line, assuming the preceding WRITE statement is the following:

```
WRITE PRINTLINE FROM HEADINGS
    AFTER ADVANCING 3 LINES.
```

4. If a given WRITE statement must provide flexibility in vertical spacing between lines on a report, which option of the ADVANCING clause should be used?
5. Answer the following questions about trailing minus signs:
   a. Explain the statement "It never hurts to insert a trailing minus sign in a numeric-edited field."
   b. What is the effect of a trailing minus sign in a receiving field when it receives an unsigned source value?
   c. What is the effect of a trailing minus sign in a receiving field when it receives a signed source value?
6. Answer the following questions about obtaining the date from the system:
   a. What is the COBOL statement that must be used to obtain the current date from the system?
   b. Code a statement to obtain the current date from the system and store it in the field WS-CURRENT-DATE.
   c. In part b above, given the following data item:

```
WS-CURRENT-DATE PIC XX/XX/XX.
```

   and the date June 30, 1993, list the characters that will be stored in the receiving field.
   d. Explain a procedure to print the current date in edited form.
7. Answer the following questions about the USAGE clause:
   a. What is the function of the USAGE clause?
   b. Which option of the USAGE clause corresponds to the standard data format of a computer system?
   c. List the options of the USAGE clause that cause arithmetic processes to be executed more efficiently.

8. If a data item is to be used as an accumulator,
   a. Explain the requirements of the PICTURE clause.
   b. Should it be initialized? If so, where and to what?
   c. Is it appropriate to specify the USAGE clause? Explain.

9. If one of the specifications of a printed report is to print a maximum of 30 detail lines on each page, explain what the programmer must include in the program to meet that requirement.

10. Use the following data items with PICTUREs and initial values as specified to complete the exercises below.

Data Item	PICTURE	Value Before Execution
FIELD-A	S99999	+00300
FIELD-B	S9999	+4533
FIELD-C	S9999	+5800
FIELD-D	S999V9999	+125.0554
FIELD-E	S99	−34
FIELD-F	S99V99	−80.25
FIELD-G	S999V9	+750.8
FIELD-H	$9999.0099	$ 0038.0055
FIELD-I	$Z9.99	$ 4.80

In each case below, specify the contents of each data item after the arithmetic statement is executed.

a.
```
DIVIDE FIELD-G BY FIELD-E GIVING FIELD-F ROUNDED.
```
b.
```
DIVIDE FIELD-F INTO FIELD-E ROUNDED.
```
c.
```
DIVIDE FIELD-B BY FIELD-A GIVING FIELD-F ROUNDED,
    ON SIZE ERROR
        DIVIDE FIELD-B BY FIELD-A GIVING FIELD-H.
```
d.
```
DIVIDE FIELD-C BY FIELD-E GIVING FIELD-I ROUNDED
    ON SIZE ERROR
        MULTIPLY FIELD-C BY FIELD-E GIVING FIELD-A ROUNDED
    NOT ON SIZE ERROR
        SUBTRACT FIELD-E FROM FIELD-B
END-DIVIDE.
```
e.
```
DIVIDE FIELD-B BY FIELD-A GIVING FIELD-G ROUNDED
    ON SIZE ERROR
        DIVIDE FIELD-B BY FIELD-A GIVING FIELD-H
    NOT ON SIZE ERROR
        ADD FIELD-E TO FIELD-F GIVING FIELD-D
END-DIVIDE.
```
f.
```
COMPUTE FIELD-A = (FIELD-B + FIELD-C) * 5.
```
g.
```
COMPUTE FIELD-G ROUNDED = FIELD-C / FIELD-E + FIELD-D * 5.
```
h.
```
COMPUTE FIELD-H = FIELD-A * FIELD-C * FIELD-E
    ON SIZE ERROR
        PERFORM 300-ERROR-ROUTINE.
```
i.
```
COMPUTE FIELD-H ROUNDED = (FIELD-F + FIELD-G) * FIELD-E
    ON SIZE ERROR
        ADD FIELD-A TO FIELD-C
    NOT ON SIZE ERROR
        ADD FIELD-A FIELD-B TO FIELD-C
END-COMPUTE.
```

11. Write a statement to compute COMPANY-SALES-AVE if the sales for each of its three regions are REGION-1-SALES, REGION-2-SALES, REGION-3-SALES. The average should be rounded.

12. Write a statement to compute the tax on the total of the purchases if the individual purchase amounts are ITEM-1, ITEM-2, and ITEM-3, and the applicable tax rate is TAX-RATE. The tax should be stored rounded in TAX-AMOUNT.

13. Write one or more statements to compute the total charge if individual item amounts are ITEM-1, ITEM-2, and ITEM-3, and the applicable tax rate is TAX-RATE. The total charge must be stored in TOTAL-CHARGE. (You can create other data names if needed.)

14. Write a statement to compute NEW-STOCK-BAL at the end of a period, given the beginning balance OLD-STOCK-BAL, period stock item sales of SALE-QTY-1, SALE-QTY-2, SALE-QTY-3, and period stock item receipts of RCVD-QTY-1 and RCVD-QTY-2. If a size error occurs, the procedure 400-ERROR-ROUTINE should be executed.

15. Write statements to compute an electric bill given the following:
   a. BASIC-CHARGE is assessed to all customers.
   b. USAGE-CHARGE is determined as follows: for KWHS-USED not exceeding 400 KWH, the cost per KWH is 9.722 cents; for the amount of KWHS-USED in excess of 400 KWH, the cost per KWH is 5.279 cents.
   c. The amount of the bill must be computed in dollars and cents and must be stored rounded in TOTAL-CHARGE.
16. Write a statement to compute the rounded value of *F1,* where

$$F1 = \frac{V}{N*(N+1)/2}$$

17. The amount of the monthly payment on a loan can be calculated by the following formula:

$$A = iP\frac{[(1 + i)^n]}{[(1 + n)^n - 1]}$$

where A = monthly payment
i = *monthly* interest rate expressed as a decimal
P = total amount of the loan
n = total number of monthly payments.
Write a statement to compute A as a rounded value.

Debugging Activities

1. Given the following coding, can you identify a potentially serious problem?

```
01   INPUT-RECORD.
     05 I-VALUE      PIC S999.
     .
     .
     .
01   WS-TOTAL-VALUE  PIC 9(6) COMP.
.
.
.
200-START-UP.
     .
     .
     .
     INITIALIZE WS-TOTAL-VALUE.
.
.
.
300-COMPUTE-SUB-TOTAL.
     ADD I-VALUE TO WS-TOTAL-VALUE.
```

2. Suppose a COBOL program is designed to print account balances as of a statement date. To compute the current balance, the total deposits and credits for the period must be added to the beginning balance, and then the total checks and debits must be subtracted. Relevant parts of the program are shown below. Find and correct all programming errors. In particular, note that a critical error (of omission) will prevent overdrawn accounts from being flagged on the report. It is crucial that this error be found.

```
FILE SECTION.

FD   ACCOUNTS-FILE
     RECORD CONTAINS 51 CHARACTERS.

01   ACCOUNT-RECORD.
     05 I-ACCOUNT-NO      PIC X(10).
     05 I-BEGIN-BALANCE   PIC S9(6)V99 SIGN LEADING
                                       SEPARATE CHARACTER.
     05 I-TOTAL-DEPOSITS  PIC 9(6)V99.
     05 I-TOTAL-CREDITS   PIC 9(6)V99.
     05 I-TOTAL-CHECKS    PIC 9(6)V99.
     05 I-TOTAL-DEBITS    PIC 9(6)V99.
.
.
.
WORKING-STORAGE SECTION.
```

```
01  PROGRAM-CONTROLS.
    05 WS-MORE-RECORDS    PIC XXX.
    05 WS-REPORT-DATE     PIC X(6).

01  ACCOUNT-WORK-AREAS.
    05 WS-TTL-DEP-CR       PIC 9(6)V99  COMP.
    05 WS-TTL-CHKS-DB      PIC 9(6)V99  COMP.
    05 WS-ACCOUNT-BALANCE  PIC 9(6)V99  COMP.

01  REPORT-HEADERS.
    05 TOP-LINE.
       10                  PIC X(5).
       10 O-REPORT-DATE    PIC XX/XX/XX.
       10                  PIC X(120).

    05 COMPANY-NAME.
       .
       .
       .
    05 REPORT-NAME.
       .
       .
       .
    05 HEADINGS.
       .
       .
       .
01  ACCOUNT-LINE.
    05                     PIC X(14).
    05 O-ACCOUNT-NO        PIC X(10).
    05                     PIC X(12).
    05 O-BEGIN-BALANCE     PIC $ZZZ,ZZ9.99-.
    05                     PIC X(12).
    05 O-TTL-DEP-CR        PIC $ZZZ,ZZ9.99-.
    05                     PIC X(12).
    05 O-TTL-CHCKS-DB      PIC $ZZZ,ZZ9.99-.
    05                     PIC X(12).
    05 O-ACCOUNT-BALANCE   PIC $ZZZ,ZZ9.99-.
    05                     PIC X(13).

PROCEDURE DIVISION.
.
.
.
200-START-UP.
    OPEN INPUT ACCOUNTS-FILE
         OUTPUT ACCOUNTS-REPORT.
    PERFORM 300-INITIALIZE-ITEMS.
    PERFORM 310-WRITE-REPORT-HEADERS.
    PERFORM 320-READ-ACCOUNT-RECORD.

210-PROCESS-ACCOUNT-RECORD.
    PERFORM 330-COMPUTE-ACCOUNT-AMOUNTS.
    PERFORM 340-PREPARE-ACCOUNT-LINE.
    PERFORM 320-READ-ACCOUNT-RECORD.

300-INITIALIZE-ITEMS.
    MOVE "YES" TO WS-MORE-RECORDS.
    MOVE WS-REPORT-DATE TO O-REPORT-DATE.
    MOVE SPACES TO ACCOUNT-LINE.
.
.
.
330-COMPUTE-ACCOUNT-AMOUNTS.
    ADD I-TOTAL-DEPOSITS + I-TOTAL-CREDITS GIVING WS-TTL-DEP-CR.
    ADD I-TOTAL-CHECKS + I-TOTAL-DEBITS GIVING WS-TTL-CHCKS-DB.
    COMPUTE WS-ACCOUNT-BALANCE = I-BEGIN-BALANCE +
                                 WS-TTL-DEP-CR - WS-TTL-CHKS-DB.

340-PREPARE-ACCOUNT-LINE.
    MOVE I-ACCOUNT-NO TO O-ACCOUNT-NO.
    MOVE I-BEGIN-BALANCE TO O-BEGIN-BALANCE.
    MOVE WS-TTL-DEP-CR TO O-TTL-DEP-CR.
    MOVE WS-TTL-CHCKS-DB TO O-TTL-CHCKS-DB.
    MOVE WS-ACCOUNT-BALANCE TO O-ACCOUNT-BALANCE.
    WRITE PRINTLINE FROM ACCOUNT-LINE
        AFTER ADVANCING 2 LINES.
```

3. A COBOL program was prepared for the purposes described in the IDENTIFICATION DIVISION. The compiler generated the following listing. Correct all the syntax errors.

```
INT-HAB-PAY-REPORTS                               18-Nov-1993 14:01:49    VAX COBOL V5.1-10                    Page   1
Source Listing                                    18-Nov-1993 13:02:49    FACULTY$DISK:[PAQUETTEG.WCBTXT]C6DBG3.CB1;1
            IDENTIFICATION DIVISION.

            PROGRAM-ID.    INT-HAB-PAY-REPORTS.

           ****************************************************************
           *                                                              *
           *       THE PURPOSE OF THIS PROGRAM IS TO PRODUCE A TWO-PART PAY *
           *  REPORT FOR THE INTERNATIONAL HABERDASHERY COMPANY.          *
           *       EACH SALESPERSON RECEIVES A BASE SALARY AND A COMMISSION *
           *  BASED ON THE SALES FOR THE PAY PERIOD.  BOTH PAY COMPONENTS   *
           *  ARE SUPPLIED ON THE SALESPERSON'S INPUT RECORD.             *
           *       THE FIRST PART OF THE REPORT MUST BEGIN AT THE TOP OF A  *
           *  NEW PAGE WITH THE COMPANY NAME, FOLLOWED BY THE NAME OF THE   *
           *  REPORT, AND THEN APPROPRIATE COLUMN HEADERS.  FOR EACH SALES- *
           *  PERSON, THE REPORT MUST PRINT THE SOCIAL SECURITY NUMBER, THE *
           *  PERSON'S NAME, THE BASE SALARY, THE COMMISSION, AND FINALLY,  *
           *  THE TOTAL PAY FOR THE CURRENT PAY PERIOD.                   *
           *       THE SECOND PART OF THE REPORT MUST BEGIN ON A SEPARATE   *
           *  PAGE WITH THE COMPANY NAME, FOLLOWED BY THE NAME OF THE RE-   *
           *  PORT, AND THEN SUMMARY INFORMATION FOR THE COMPANY:  TOTAL    *
           *  NUMBER OF EMPLOYEES ON THE CURRENT PAYROLL, THE TOTAL SAL-    *
           *  ARIES, THE TOTAL COMMISSIONS, THE AVERAGE SALARY, AND THE     *
           *  AVERAGE COMMISSION.                                         *
           *                                                              *
           ****************************************************************

            ENVIRONMENT DIVISION.

            CONFIGURATION SECTION.

            SOURCE-COMPUTER.  VAX-VMS-8650.
            OBJECT-COMPUTER.  VAX-VMS-8650.

            INPUT-OUTPUT SECTION.

            FILE-CONTROL.
                SELECT EMPLOYEE-FILE    ASSIGN TO COB$INPUT.
                       1
%COBOL-F-ERROR   52, (1) File has no definition in File Section - definition assumed
                SELECT PAY-REPORT       ASSIGN TO COB$OUTPUT.
                       1
%COBOL-W-ERROR  239, (1) File is CLOSEd but is not OPENed

            DATA DIVISION.

            FILE SECTION.

            FD  EMPLOYE-FILE
                1
%COBOL-E-ERROR   51, (1) File has no definition in FILE-CONTROL paragraph - definition assumed
%COBOL-E-ERROR   17, (1) Longest record is longer than RECORD CONTAINS value - Longest record size used
                RECORD CONTAINS 41 CHARACTERS.

            01  SALESPERSON-RECORD.
                05 I-SSN               PIC X(9).
                05 I-SALESPERSON       PIC X(20).
                05 I-SALARY            PIC $ZZZ9.99.
                05 I-COMMISSION        PIC $ZZZ9.99.

            FD  PAY-REPORT
                RECORD CONTAINS 133 CHARACTERS.

            01  PRINTLINE              PIC X(133).

            WORKING-STORAGE SECTION.

            01  PROGRAM-CONTROLS.
                05 WS-MORE-RECORDS        PIC X(3).
                05 WS-PAGE-NO             PIC S99.

            01  SALESPERSON-WORK-AREAS.
                05 WS-TOTAL-PAY           PIC $9999.99-  COMP.
                1
%COBOL-E-ERROR   42, (1) COMP and COMP-3 items must have numeric pictures - usage changed to DISPLAY

            01  COMPANY-ACCUMULATORS  COMP.
                05 WS-EMPLOYEE-CTR          PIC S999.
                05 WS-TOTAL-SALARIES        PIC S9(30V99.
%COBOL-F-ERROR  178, (1) Invalid repetition factor
                05 WS-TOTAL-COMMISSIONS  PIC S9(3)V99.

            01  COMPANY-WORK-AREAS  COMP.
                05 WS-AVERAGE-SALARY        PIC S99V99.
                05 WS-AVERAGE-COMMISSION PIC S99V99.

            01  COMPANY-NAME.
                05 PIC X(54)  VALUE SPACES.
                05 PIC X(26)  VALUE "INTERNATIONAL HABERDASHERY".
                05 PIC X(40)  VALUE SPACES.
                05 PIC X(5)   VALUE "PAGE ".
                05 O-PAGE-NO  PIC Z9.
                05 PIC X(6)   VALUE SPACES.

            01  REPORT-NAME.
                05 PIC X(62)  VALUE SPACES.
                05 PIC X(10)  VALUE "PAY REPORT".
                05 PIC X(61)  VALUE SPACES.
```

```
             01  HEADINGS.
                 05 PIC XXX    VALUE "SSN".
                 05 PIC X(15)  VALUE SPACES.
                 05 PIC X(11)  VALUE "SALESPERSON".
                 05 PIC X(15)  VALUE SPACES.
                 05 PIC X(6)   VALUE "SALARY".
                 05 PIC X(15)  VALUE SPACES.
                 05 PIC X(10)  VALUE "COMMISSION".
                 05 PIC X(15)  VALUE SPACES.
                 05 PIC X(9)   VALUE "TOTAL PAY".
                 05 PIC X(17)  VALUE SPACES.

             01  PAY-LINE.
                 05                  PIC X(13).
                 05 O-SSN            PIC XXXBXXBXXXX.
                 05                  PIC X(7).
                 05 O-SALESPERSON    PIC X(20).
                 05                  PIC X(9).
                 05 O-SALARY         PIC $Z,ZZ9.99-
                 05                  PIC X(13).
                 1
%COBOL-E-ERROR   65, (1) Missing period is assumed
                 05 O-COMMISSION     PIC $Z,ZZ9.99-
                 05                  PIC X(16).
                 1
%COBOL-E-ERROR   65, (1) Missing period is assumed
                 05 O-TOTAL          PIC $Z,ZZ9.99-
                 05                  PIC X(17).
                 1
%COBOL-E-ERROR   65, (1) Missing period is assumed

             01  SUMMARY-REPORT-LINES.

                 05  SUMMARY-REPORT-NAME.
                     10 PIC X(10)  VALUE SPACES.
                     10 PIC X(14)  VALUE "SUMMARY REPORT".
                     10 PIC X(10)  VALUE SPACES.

                 05  EMPLOYEE-COUNT-LINE.
                     10 PIC X(5)  VALUE "***  ".
                     10 PIC X(11) VALUE "EMPLOYEES ON PAYROLL:".
                          1
%COBOL-E-ERROR   84, (1) Literal in VALUE clause conflicts with description - clause ignored
                     10 O-TOTAL-EMPLOYEES PIC ZZZ9.

                 05  TOTAL-SALARIES-LINE.
                     10 PIC X(5)  VALUE "***  ".
                     10 PIC X(15) VALUE "TOTAL SALARIES:".
                     10 O-TOTL-SALARIES  PIC $ZZZ,ZZ9.99-.

                 05  TOTAL-COMMISSIONS-LINE.
                     10 PIC X(5)  VALUE "***  ".
                     10 PIC X(18) VALUE "TOTAL COMMISSIONS:".
                     10 O-TOTAL-COMMISSIONS  PIC $ZZZ,ZZ9.99-.

                 05  AVERAGE-SALARY-LINE.
                     10 PIC X(5)  VALUE "***  ".
                     10 PIC X(15) VALUE "AVERAGE SALARY:".
                     10 O-AVERAGE-SALARY  PIC $Z,ZZ9.99-.

                 05  AVERAGE-COMMISSION-LINE.
                     10 PIC X(5)  VALUE "***  ".
                     10 PIC X(10) VALUE "AVERAGE COMMISSION:".
                          1
%COBOL-E-ERROR   84, (1) Literal in VALUE clause conflicts with description - clause ignored
                     10 O-AVERAGE-COMMISSION PIC $Z,ZZ9.99-.

             PROCEDURE DIVISION.

             100-PRODUCE-PAY-REPORT.
                 PERFORM 200-START-UP.
                 PERFORM 210-PROCESS-SALESPERSON-REC
                     UNTIL WS-MORE-RECORDS = "NO ".
                 PERFORM 220-FINSH-UP.
                         1
%COBOL-F-ERROR  349, (1) Undefined name
                 STOP RUN.
                 1
%COBOL-W-ERROR  297, (1) Processing of source program resumes at this point

             200-START-UP.
                 OPEN INPUT EMPLOYEE-FILE.
                      OUTPUT PAY-REPORT.
                      1
%COBOL-F-ERROR  321, (1) Invalid statement syntax
                 PERFORM 300-INITIALIZE-ITEMS.
                 1
%COBOL-W-ERROR  297, (1) Processing of source program resumes at this point
                 PERFORM 310-WRITE-REPORT-HEADERS.
                 PERFORM 320-READ-SALESPERSON-REC.

             210-PROCESS-SALESPERSON-REC.
                 PERFORM 340-PREPARE-PAY-LINE.
                 PERFORM 330-COMPUTE-TOTAL-PAY.
```

```
           PERFORM 350-UPDATE-COMPANY-TOTALS.
           PERFORM 320-READ-SALESPERSON-REC.

       220-FINISH-UP.
           PERFORM 360-PRODUCE-COMPANY-SUMMARY.
           CLOSE EMPLOYEE-FILE
                 PAY-REPORT.

       300-INITIALIZE-ITEMS.
           INITIALIZE COMPANY-ACCUMULATORS
                      WS-PAGE-NO.
           MOVE "YES" TO WS-MORE-RECORDS.
           MOVE SPACES TO PAY-LINE.

       310-WRITE-REPORT-HEADERS.
           MOVE WS-PAGE-NO TO O-PAGE-NO.
           WRITE PRINTLINE FROM COMPANY-NAME
               AFTER ADVANCING PAGE.
           WRITE PRINTLINE FROM REPORT-NAME
               AFTER ADVANCING 3 LINES.
           WRITE PRINTLINE FROM HEADINGS
               AFTER ADVANCING 3 LINES.

       320-READ-SALESPERSON-REC.
           READ EMPLOYEE-FILE RECORD
               AT END
                   MOVE "NO " TO WS-MORE-RECORDS.

       330-COMPUTE-TOTAL-PAY.
           ADD I-SALARY TO I-COMMISSION GIVING WS-TOTAL-PAY
               1           2
%COBOL-F-ERROR  276, (1) Operand must be a numeric data-name or a numeric literal
%COBOL-F-ERROR  276, (2) Operand must be a numeric data-name or a numeric literal
               ON SIZE ERROR
                   MOVE ZERO TO WS-TOTAL-PAY
           END-ADD.

       340-PREPARE-PAY-LINE.
           MOVE I-SSN TO O-SSN.
           MOVE I-SALESPERSON TO O-SALESPERSON.
           MOVE I-SALARY TO O-SALARY.
           MOVE I-COMMISSION TO O-COMMISSION.
           MOVE WS-TOTAL-PAY TO O-TOTAL-PAY.
                                1
%COBOL-F-ERROR  349, (1) Undefined name
           WRITE PRINTLINE FROM PAY-LINE
               AFTER ADVANCING 2 LINES.

       350-UPDATE-COMPANY-TOTALS.
           ADD 1 TO WS-EMPLOYEE-CTR.
           ADD 1-SALARY TO WS-TOTAL-SALARIES
               1
%COBOL-F-ERROR  349, (1) Undefined name
               ON SIZE ERROR
                   MOVE ZERO TO WS-TOTAL-SALARIES.
                   1
%COBOL-W-ERROR  297, (1) Processing of source program resumes at this point
           ADD I-COMMISSION TO WS-TOTAL-COMMISSIONS
               1
%COBOL-F-ERROR  276, (1) Operand must be a numeric data-name or a numeric literal
               ON SIZE ERROR
                   MOVE ZERO TO WS-TOTAL-COMMISSIONS.

       360-PRODUCE-COMPANY-SUMMARY.
           PERFORM 400-WRITE-SUMMARY-HEADERS.
           PERFORM 410-COMPUTE-COMPANY-AVERAGES.
           PERFORM 420-PREPARE-SUMMARY-REPORT.

       400-WRITE-SUMMARY-HEADERS.
           ADD 1 TO WS-PAGE-NO.
           WRITE PRINTLINE FROM COMPANY-NAME
               AFTER ADVANCING PAGE.
           WRITE PRINTLINE FROM SUMMARY-REPORT-NAME
               AFTER ADVANCING 3 LINES.

       410-COMPUTE-COMPANY-AVERAGES.
           DIVIDE WS-TOTAL-SALARIES BY WS-EMPLOYEE-CTR
               GIVING WS-AVERAGE-SALARY ROUNDED
                   ON SIZE ERROR
                       MOVE ZERO TO WS-AVERAGE-SALARY.
           DIVIDE WS-TOTAL-COMMISSIONS BY WS-EMPLOYEE-CTR
               GIVING WS-AVERAGE-COMISSION ROUNDED
                      1
%COBOL-F-ERROR  349, (1) Undefined name
                   ON SIZE ERROR
                       MOVE ZERO TO WS-AVERAGE-COMMISSION.
                       1
%COBOL-W-ERROR  297, (1) Processing of source program resumes at this point

       420-PREPARE-SUMMARY-REPORT.
           MOVE WS-EMPLOYEE-CTR TO O-EMPLOYEE-CTR.
                                   1
%COBOL-F-ERROR  349, (1) Undefined name
           WRITE PRINTLINE FROM TOTAL-EMPLOYEES-LINE
                                1
```

```
INT-HAB-PAY-REPORTS                          18-Nov-1993 14:01:49      VAX COBOL V5.1-10                    Page   4
Source Listing                               18-Nov-1993 13:02:49      FACULTY$DISK:[PAQUETTEG.WCBTXT]C6DBG3.CB1;1

%COBOL-F-ERROR  349, (1) Undefined name
                    AFTER ADVANCING 3 LINES.
                                           1
%COBOL-W-ERROR  297, (1) Processing of source program resumes at this point
                MOVE WS-TOTAL-SALARIES TO O-TOTAL-SALARIES.
                                          1
%COBOL-F-ERROR  349, (1) Undefined name
                WRITE PRINTLINE FROM TOTAL-SALARIES-LINE
                    AFTER ADVANCING 2 LINES.
                MOVE WS-TOTAL-COMMISSIONS TO O-TOTAL-COMMISSIONS.
                WRITE PRINTLINE FROM TOTAL-COMMISSIONS-LINE
                    AFTER ADVANCING 2 LINES.
                MOVE WS-AVERAGE-SALARY TO O-AVERAGE-SALARY.
                WRITE PRINTLINE FROM AVERAGE-SALARY-LINE
                    AFTER ADVANCING 2 LINES.
                MOVE WS-AVERAGE-COMMISSION TO O-AVERAGE-COMMISSION.
                WRITE PRINTLINE FROM AVERAGE-COMMISSION-LINE
                    AFTER ADVANCING 2 LINES.
```

4. Suppose that all the syntax errors in exercise 3 have been corrected. The report produced by the program is shown below. It is obvious that there are programming errors that were not detected by the compiler. Find and correct them. (The data file that was used to produce this report is shown in Appendix C, Set 10 [DD:V1C6DBG4.DAT].)

```
                                                  INTERNATIONAL HABERDASHERY                                PAGE 0

                                                          PAY REPORT

SSN               SALESPERSON          SALARY               COMMISSION            TOTAL PAY

              623 45 5100                            $  985.50         $  125.00           $     0.00

              611 72 3510                            $  735.40         $   95.00           $1,110.50

              315 78 1243                            $1,230.00         $  810.00           $  830.40

              201 86 1752                            $  675.00         $   85.50           $2,040.00

              795 28 8916                            $1,005.00         $  225.00           $  760.50

              186 73 7565                            $  960.50         $  375.50           $1,230.00

              269 31 3905                            $1,125.00         $  340.00           $1,336.00

              519 39 2407                            $  875.50         $  230.50           $1,465.00

              056 41 9426                            $1,050.25         $  550.00           $1,106.00

              353 22 8728                            $  650.00         $  100.00           $1,600.25


                                                  INTERNATIONAL HABERDASHERY                                PAGE 0

          SUMMARY REPORT

***    EMPLOYEES ON PAYROLL:   10

***    TOTAL SALARIES:$      650.00

***    TOTAL COMMISSIONS:$      880.50

***    AVERAGE SALARY:$      65.00

***    AVERAGE COMMISSION:$      88.05
```

Programming Exercises

Programming Exercise I

The management of Express Auto Parts Warehouse wants its data processing department to prepare an item activity report showing the activity during the past week for each of its catalog items. The report is to consist of two parts: The first part will provide specific information on each catalog item, and the second part will provide summary information. For each item, there is a record in the item activity file containing the following data:

cc 1–5 Catalog number
cc 6–25 Item description
cc 36–39 Quantity on hand at the beginning of the week
cc 40–43 Quantity on order
cc 44–47 The reorder point
cc 48–51 Quantity received during the week
cc 52–55 Quantity sold during the week
cc 56–59 Quantity returned by customers during the week

The item activity file is updated weekly.

The first part of the item activity report must print the following information for each catalog item: the catalog number, the item description, the quantity on hand at the beginning of the week, the quantity received during the week, the quantity returned by customers during the week, the quantity sold during the week, the new balance (quantity on hand) at the end of the week, the quantity that remains on order at the end of the week, and the reorder point.

There should be no more than 30 items listed per page. The pages of the report should be numbered consecutively. Each page should be formatted as shown on the printer spacing chart. (Use the current date as the report date.)

The second part of the item activity report must print the following summary information: the total quantity received during the week, the total quantity returned by customers during the week, and the total quantity sold during the week. The summary report must be on a separate page, properly documented with company name, report name, and appropriate identifiers for the totals.

The program should write an error message on the report if the input file is empty. (Use an empty-file **switch** to determine if the summary report should be printed.)

The report should end with an "End of Report" message.

The design tools (layout of input record, printer spacing chart, system flowchart, structure chart, program pseudocode, and the program flowchart) have been fully developed for you and are shown in Figure 6.40.

■ Figure 6.40

Record Layout Form

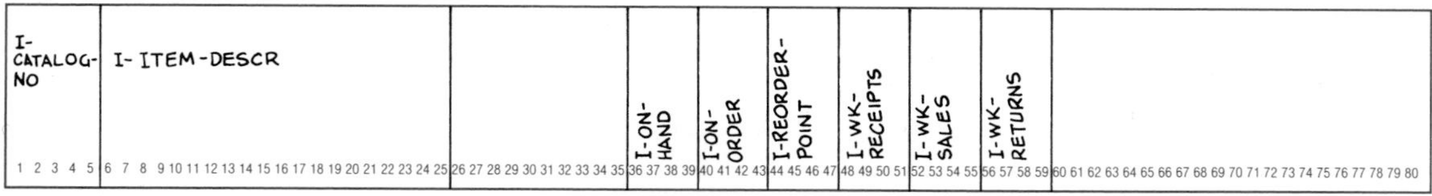

Record Name: ACTIVITY-RECORD

Printer Spacing Chart

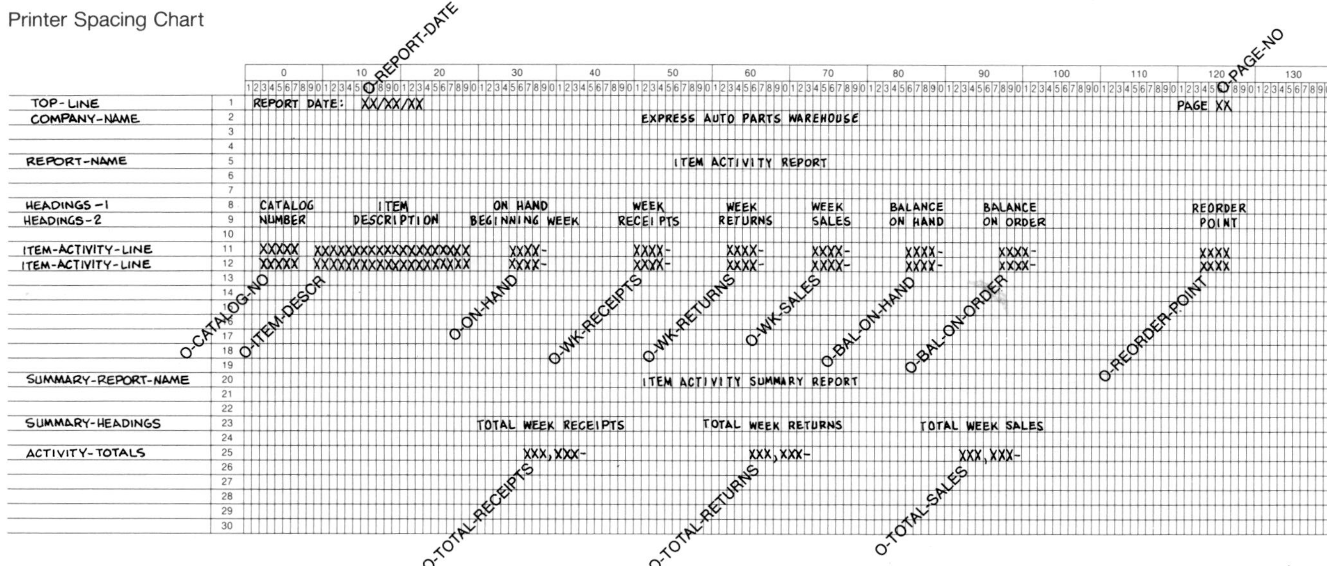

System Flowchart

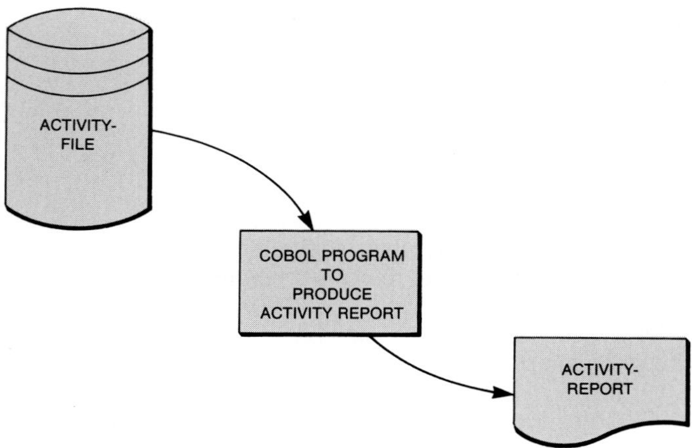

Structure Chart

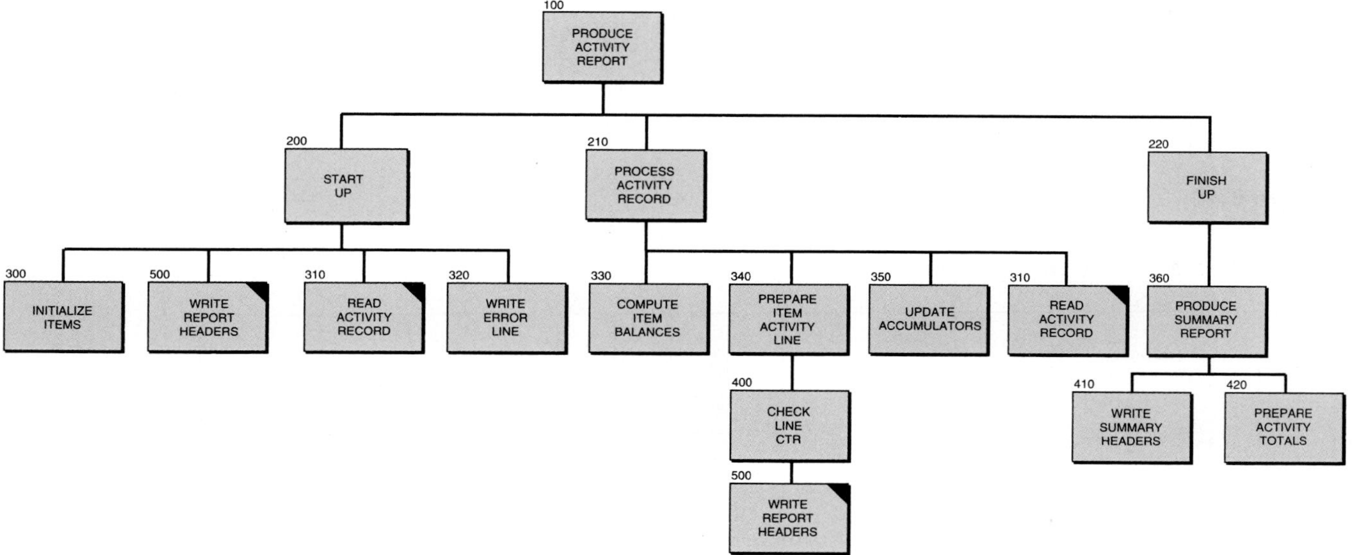

Program Pseudocode

100-Produce-Activity-Report.

1. Perform 200-Start-Up.
2. Perform 210-Process-Activity-Record until no more records.
3. Perform 220-Finish-Up.
4. Stop the run.

200-Start-Up.

1. Open the files.
2. Perform 300-Initialize-Items.
3. Perform 500-Write-Report-Headers.
4. Perform 310-Read-Activity-Record.
5. If the flag WS-MORE-RECORDS is not equal to "Yes",
   perform 320-Write-Error-Line.

210-Process-Activity-Record.

1. Perform 330-Compute-Item-Balances.
2. Perform 340-Prepare-Item-Activity-Line.
3. Perform 350-Update-Accumulators.
4. Perform 310-Read-Activity-Record.

220-Finish-Up.

1. If empty file switch is not "on",
   perform 360-Produce-Summary-Report.
2. Move End-Line to the output area Printline.
3. After advancing 10 lines, write the output record Printline.
4. Close the files.

300-Initialize-Items.

1. Obtain the date from the system.
2. Move the date to Top-Line date.
3. Set the end-of-file flag WS-MORE-RECORDS to "YES".
4. Set the accumulators to zero.
5. Clear the record areas Item-Activity-Line and Activity-Totals.
6. Set page-number to zero.
7. Set the empty-file switch to "off".

310-Read-Activity-Record.

1. Read an input Activity-Record.
2. Test for end-of-file record;
   if EOF-record reached, move "NO " to the end-of-file flag WS-MORE-RECORDS.

320-Write-Error-Line.

1. Move the message "No Records in the Activity File" to
   error-message field of Error-Line.
2. Move Error-Line to the output area Printline.
3. After advancing 10 lines, write the output record Printline.
4. Set the empty-file switch to "on".

330-Compute-Item-Balances.

1. Add input quantity on hand, input week-receipts, input week-returns,
   and then subtract input week-sales to equal balance on hand.
2. Subtract input week-receipts from input quantity on order to equal balance on order.

340-Prepare-Item-Activity-Line.

1. Move input catalog-number to Item-Activity-Line catalog-number.
2. Move input item-description to Item-Activity-Line item-description.
3. Move input on-hand to Item-Activity-Line on-hand.
4. Move input week-recepits to Item-Activity-Line week-receipts.
5. Move input week-returns to Item-Activity-Line week-returns.
6. Move input week-sales to Item-Activity-Line week-sales.
7. Move input reorder-point to Item-Activity-Line input reorder-point.
8. Move balance on hand to Item-Activity-Line balance on hand.
9. Move balance on order to Item-Activity-Line balance on order.
10. Perform 400-Check-Line-Ctr.
11. Move Item-Activity-Line to the output area Printline.
12. After advancing proper-spacing, write the output record Printline.
13. Set proper-spacing to 1.
14. Add 1 to line-counter.

350-Update-Accumulators.

1. Add input week-receipts to the week-receipts accumulator.
2. Add input week-returns to the week-returns accumulator.
3. Add input week-sales to the week-sales accumulator.

360-Produce-Summary-Report.

1. Perform 410-Write-Summary-Headers.
2. Perform 420-Prepare-Activity-Totals.

400-Check-Line-Ctr.

1. If line-counter is greater than or equal to line-limit, perform 500-Write-Report-Headers.

410-Write-Summary-Headers.

1. Add 1 to page-number.
2. Move page-number to Top-Line page-number.
3. Move Top-Line to the output area Printline.
4. After advancing to the top of a new page, write the record Printline.
5. Move Company-Name to the output area Printline.
6. After advancing 1 line, write the output record Printline.
7. Move Summary-Report-Name to the output area Printline.
8. After advancing 3 lines, write the output record Printline.
9. Move Summary-Heading to the output area Printline.
10. After advancing 3 lines, write the output record Printline.

420-Prepare-Activity-Totals.

1. Move week-receipts accumulator to Activity-Totals week-receipts.
2. Move week-returns accumulator to Activity-Totals week-returns.
3. Move week-sales accumulator to Activity-Totals week-sales.
4. Move Activity-Totals to the output area Printline.
5. After advancing 2 lines, write the output record Printline.

500-Write-Report-Headers.

1. Add 1 to page-number.
2. Move page-number to Top-Line page-number.
3. Move Top-Line to the output area Printline.
4. After advancing to the top of a new page, write the output record Printline.
5. Move Company-Name to the output area Printline.
6. After advancing 1 line, write the output record Printline.
7. Move Report-Name to the output area Printline.
8. After advancing 3 lines, write the output record Printline.
9. Move Headings-1 to the output area Printline.
10. After advancing 3 lines, write the output record Printline.
11. Move Headings-2 to the output area Printline.
12. After advancing 1 line, write the output record Printline.
13. Set proper-spacing to 2.
14. Set line-counter to zero.

■ **Figure 6.40** continued

Program Flowchart

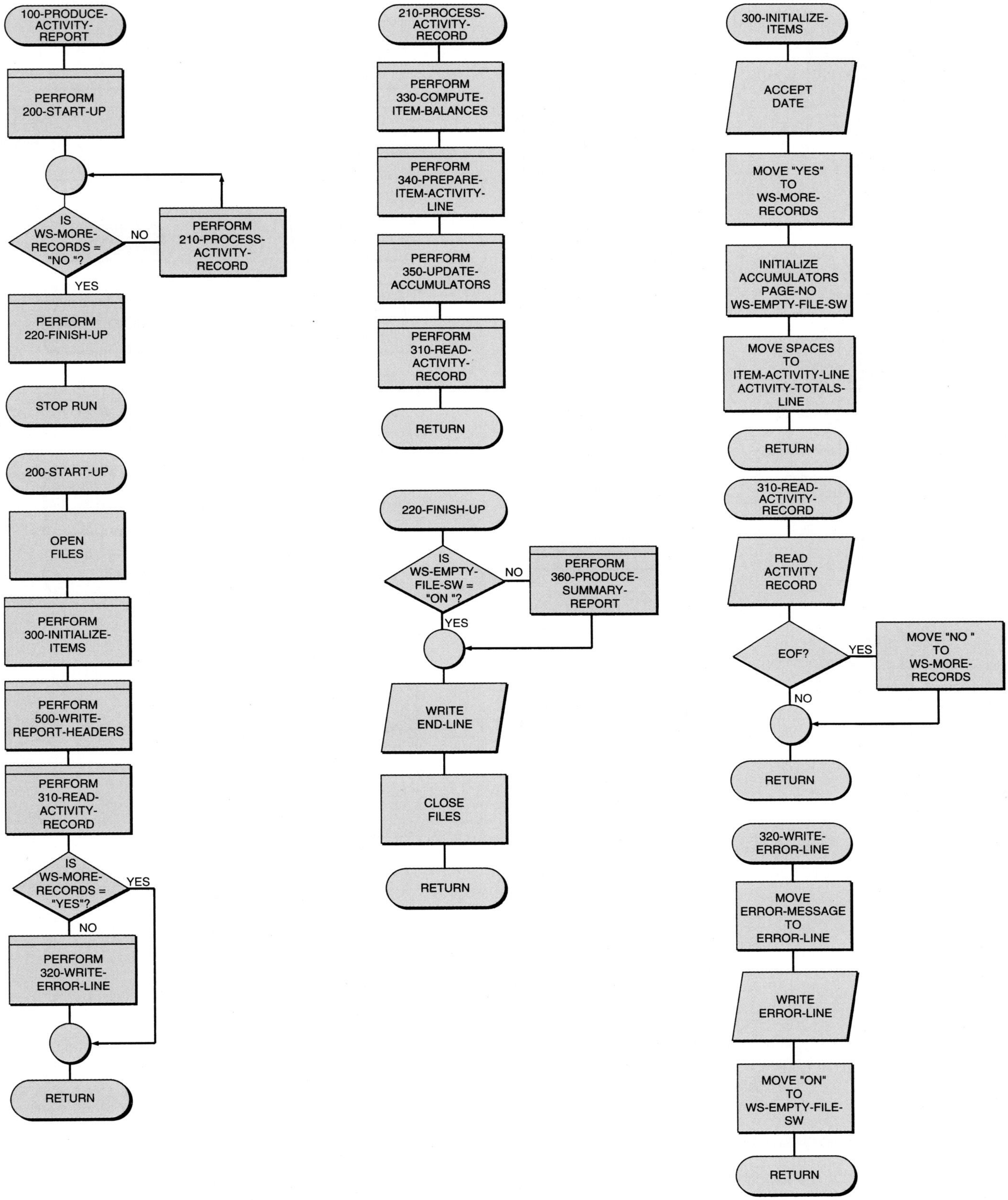

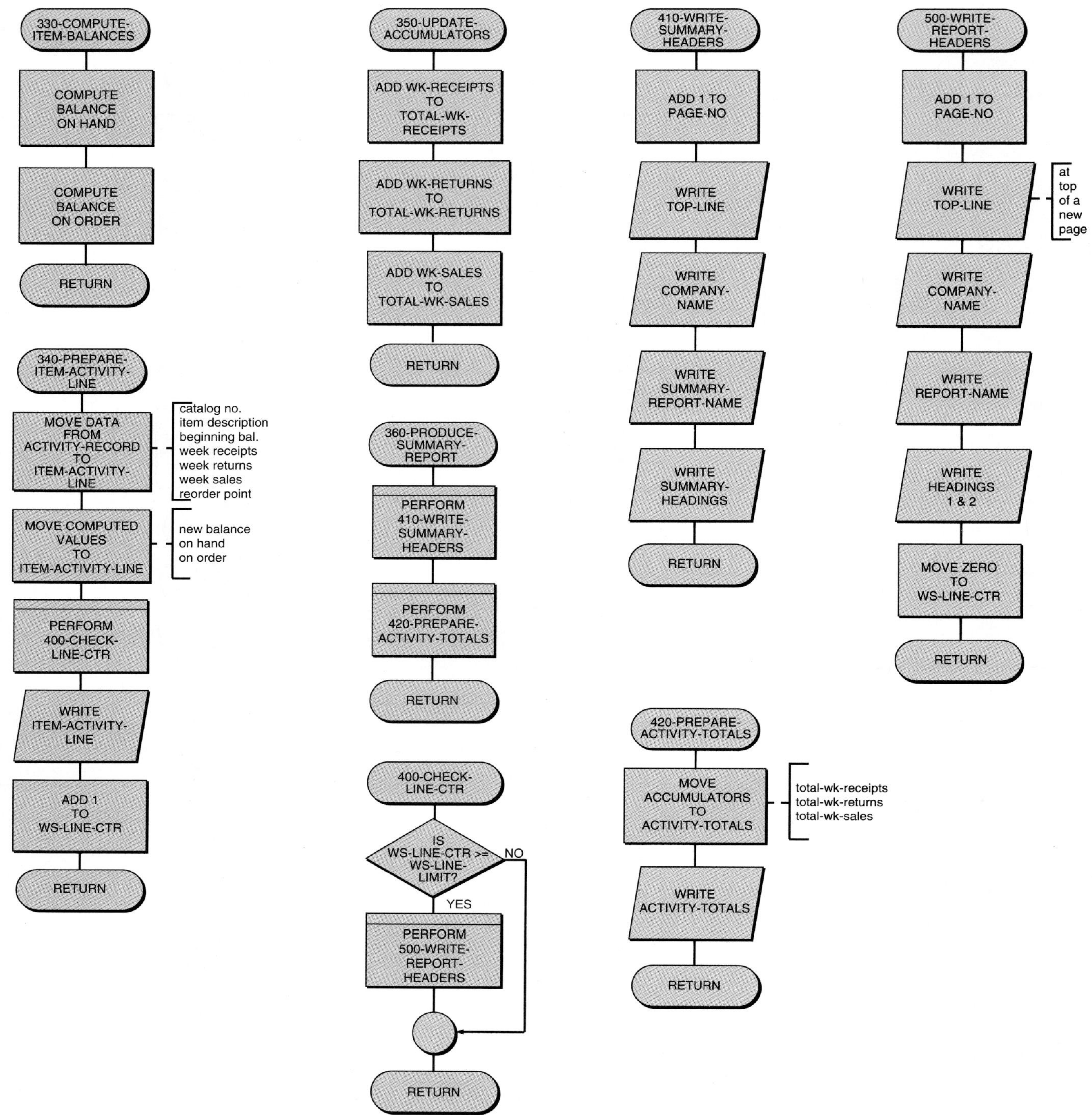

Your assignment is to study the program design and then to complete the design implementation phase; that is, code the program, enter it into a file, debug it with the help of the compiler, and then run it.

Use Data File Set 1 (see Appendix C) [DD/CD:VIC6EX1.DAT] as the item activity file.

Programming Exercise II

The management of Express Auto Parts Warehouse wants its data processing department to prepare a sales report showing sales figures for the past week for each catalog item and for the company as a whole. For each item, there is a record in the sales file containing the following data:

cc 1–5	Catalog number
cc 6–25	Item description
cc 26–30	Purchase price per unit
cc 31–35	Selling price per unit
cc 52–55	Quantity sold during the week
cc 56–59	Quantity returned during the week

The sales file is updated weekly.

The first part of the report must print the following information for each catalog item: the catalog number, the item description, the purchase price per unit, the selling price per unit, the quantity sold during the week, the quantity returned during the week, the gross income from sales during the week, the net income from sales during the week (quantity sold minus quantity returned times selling price), and the net profit or loss.

There should be no more than 30 items listed per page. The pages of the report should be formatted as shown on the printer spacing chart, and they should be numbered consecutively.

The second part of the report must print the following summary information: the total gross income from sales during the week, the total net income from sales during the week, and the total profit or loss. The summary report should be on a separate page and begin with appropriate top-of-page documentation.

The program should write an error message on the report if the input file is empty. (Use an empty-file switch to determine if the summary report should be printed.)

An end-of-report message should be printed at the end of the report.

Figure 6.41 contains the layout of the input record, the printer spacing chart, the system flowchart, and the structure chart.

Your assignment is as follows:

a. Complete the design phase by assigning appropriate names to all the data fields shown on the printer spacing chart, by developing the program pseudocode or drawing the program flowchart.

b. Code the program, enter it into a file, and debug it.

c. Run the program successfully.

Use Data File Set 1 (see Appendix C) [DD/CD:VIC6EX2.DAT] as the sales file.

■ Figure 6.41

Record Layout Form

I-CATALOG-NO	I-ITEM-DESCR	I-UNIT-PURCHASE-PRICE	I-UNIT-SELLING-PRICE		I-WK-SALES	I-WK-RETURNS	
1 2 3 4 5	6 7 8 9 10 11 12 13 14 15 16 17 18 19 20 21 22 23 24 25	26 27 28 29 30	31 32 33 34 35	36 37 38 39 40 41 42 43 44 45 46 47 48 49 50 51	52 53 54 55	56 57 58 59	60 61 62 63 64 65 66 67 68 69 70 71 72 73 74 75 76 77 78 79 80

Record Name: SALES-RECORD

■ Figure 6.41 continued

Printer Spacing Chart

Record	Line	Printed layout
TOP-LINE	1	REPORT DATE: XX/XX/XX PAGE XX
COMPANY-NAME	2	EXPRESS AUTO PARTS WAREHOUSE
	3	
	4	
REPORT-NAME	5	SALES REPORT
	6	
	7	
HEADINGS-1	8	CATALOG ITEM UNIT UNIT WEEK WEEK AMOUNT AMOUNT NET
HEADINGS-2	9	NUMBER DESCRIPTION PURCHASE PRICE SELLING PRICE SALES RETURNS GROSS INCOME NET INCOME PROFIT/LOSS
	10	
SALES-REPORT-LINE	11	XXXXX XXXXXXXXXXXXXXXXXXXX $XXX.XX $XXX.XX XXXX- XXXX- $X,XXX,XXX.XX- $X,XXX,XXX.XX- $X,XXX,XXX.XX-
	12	XXXXX XXXXXXXXXXXXXXXXXXXX $XXX.XX $XXX.XX XXXX- XXXX- $X,XXX,XXX.XX- $X,XXX,XXX.XX- $X,XXX,XXX.XX-
	13–19	
SUMMARY-REPORT-NAME	20	SALES REPORT SUMMARY
	21	
	22	
SUMMARY-HEADINGS	23	TOTAL GROSS INCOME TOTAL NET INCOME TOTAL PROFIT/LOSS
	24	
SUMMARY-TOTALS	25	$XXX,XXX,XXX.XX- $XXX,XXX,XXX.XX- $XXX,XXX,XXX.XX-
	26–29	
	30	** END OF REPORT **

System Flowchart

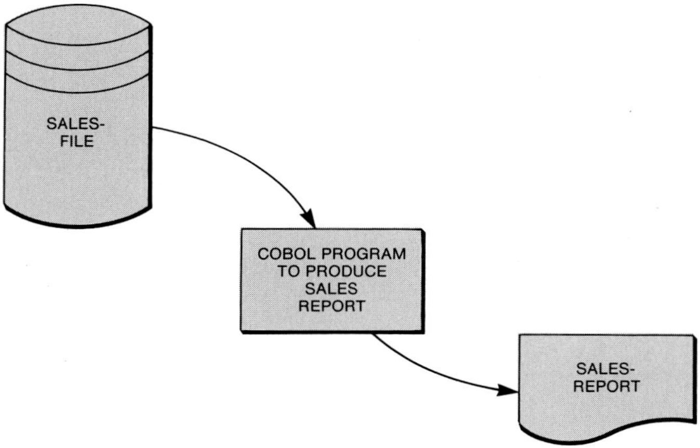

Structure Chart

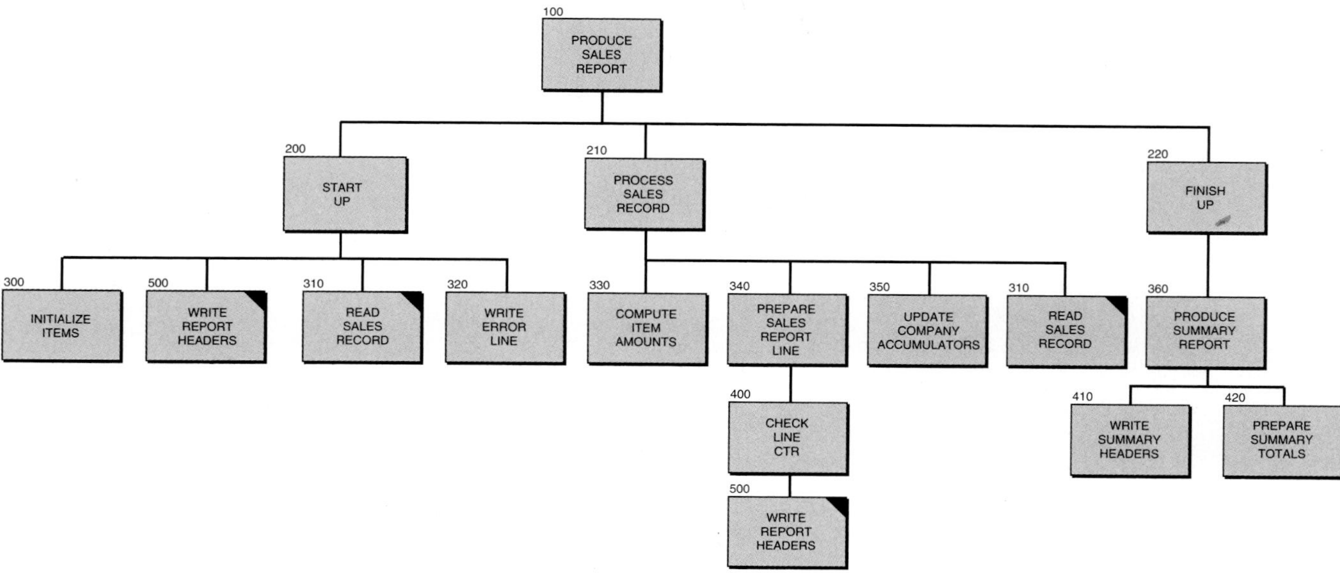

Programming Exercise III

The Ponagansett Electric Company wants a billing report that will list the bill amount for each of its customers for the current billing period and a summary report that will show the total KWHs sold and the total income to be derived from the sale of electricity to its customers.

Each record in the customer file contains the following data:

cc 1–3	Area code
cc 4–9	Customer number
cc 10–29	Customer name
cc 30–34	Previous meter reading
cc 35–39	Current meter reading
cc 77–78	Flat rate in cents per KWH (format: x.x)

The file is arranged sequentially by customer number within area code. It is updated monthly.

The billing report must contain the following information for each of its customers: the area code, the customer number, the customer name, the previous and current meter readings, the KWHs used, and the bill amount.

The summary report must show the total KWHs sold to its customers and the total income to be derived from the sale.

Each page of each report must begin with the report date line, the company name, the report name, and appropriate column headings. The pages must be numbered consecutively. There must be no more than 30 customers listed per page. The summary report must be printed on a separate, last page, and it must end with an "End of Report" message.

The program should test for an empty customer file and, if it is empty, print an appropriate error message on the report. (Use an empty-file switch to determine if the summary report should be printed.)

You are encouraged to follow the steps of the problem-solving procedure.

Use Data File Set 2 (see Appendix C) [DD/CD:VIC6EX3.DAT] as the customer file.

Programming Exercise IV

The management of the Modern Plastics Company wants the data processing department to prepare a payroll report and a payroll summary report. For each employee, there is a record in the payroll file containing the following data:

cc 5–6	Department number
cc 7–15	Social Security number
cc 16–35	Employee name
cc 39–42	Pay rate (format: xx.xx)
cc 43–44	Hours worked at regular pay
cc 45–56	Hours worked at overtime pay (time and a half)
cc 77–80	Year hired

The records of the file are arranged in seniority sequence by department.

The payroll report must contain the following information for each employee: department number, Social Security number, name, regular pay, overtime pay, total pay, federal tax deduction (assume 20 percent of total pay), state tax deduction (assume 15 percent of the federal tax), union dues (assume 1 percent of total pay), retirement plan contribution (assume 5 percent of total pay), and net pay (total pay minus all deductions).

The payroll summary report must contain the following information for the company as a whole: the total amount of money spent on regular salaries, on overtime salaries, and on total salaries; the total amount withheld for federal taxes, for state taxes, for the retirement plan, and for union dues; and the total net salaries paid to all employees.

Each page of the report must be properly documented: the first line must contain the report date and page number; line 2 must contain the company name; line 5 must contain the name of the report; lines 8 and 9 must contain the column headings. The employee pay lines must be single-spaced, but there must be a blank line between the column headers and the first pay line. There must be at most 30 pay lines per page.

The payroll summary report must be on a separate page, and an "End of Report" message must terminate the report.

All pages of the report must be numbered consecutively.

The program should test for an empty input file, and, if it is empty, print an appropriate error message on the report. (Use an empty-file switch to determine if the summary report should be printed!)

You are encouraged to follow the steps of the problem-solving procedure.

Use Data File Set 4 (see Appendix C) [DD/CD:VIC6EX4.DAT] as the payroll file.

7 Conditional Statements

In this chapter, we examine in greater detail the IF-ELSE and the EVALUATE conditional statements, and the various options that the COBOL language provides for them.

The sample program in this chapter produces a summary report. In this kind of report, data values are accumulated during the processing of the input records, and only the summary information is printed on the report. The program will provide opportunities to investigate sequential and nested IF statements, the EVALUATE statement, and some of the tests that can be coded in these statements. ■

Objectives You Should Achieve

After studying this chapter, you should:

1. Given a pseudocode paragraph or a flowchart module containing a group of tests, be able to correctly classify the group of tests as sequential or nested.
2. Given a pseudocode paragraph or a flowchart module containing sequential tests, be able to correctly code the corresponding PROCEDURE DIVISION paragraph.
3. Given a pseudocode paragraph or a flowchart module containing nested tests, be able to correctly code the corresponding PROCEDURE DIVISION paragraph.
4. Given a complete description of a programming situation in which distinct procedures must be executed depending on the value in a key field, be able to correctly write the appropriate pseudocode or flowchart the logic and correctly code the corresponding COBOL statements.
5. Given a flowchart segment containing a selection structure followed by a simple sequence, and sets of coded instructions, be able to select the sets of instructions that correctly correspond to the flowchart.
6. Given data item descriptions for which condition-names have been defined, and conditional statements using the data items in relational tests, be able to correctly rewrite the conditional statements using condition-names.
7. Given an input record description, be able to properly design a flowchart module or write pseudocode statements to test each data field for valid data.
8. Given pseudocode statements or a flowchart segment containing tests that can be treated as compound tests, be able to correctly code a conditional statement containing compound tests.
9. Given input record and output record descriptions that contain some identical data names, be able to
   a. correctly reference any data item using qualification.
   b. correctly code a MOVE statement to transfer one value from the input record to the identically named field of the output record.
   c. correctly code **one** MOVE statement to transfer simultaneously all values from the input record to the identically named fields of the output record.
10. Given a program, partial or complete, be able to correctly classify the test used in each conditional statement.
11. Given a data item for which a condition-name has been defined, be able to use a SET statement to move the condition-name value to the data item field.
12. Given a compound test in which the components consist of relation-condition tests, be able to code the compound test in its abbreviated form where applicable.
13. Given one or more data items which must be tested for different values in order to select specific procedures to be executed, be able to correctly code an EVALUATE statement to perform the tests.
14. Given a programming assignment in which the program must select some records of a file (and not others) for further processing, and for which the design tools are provided, be able to successfully complete the task of coding and running the program.
15. Given a programming assignment in which the program must produce a two-part report, the first part being a detail report and the second being a summary report, for which the input record layout, the

printer spacing chart, the system flowchart, and the structure chart are provided, be able to complete the design phase and develop the design implementation phase to a successful conclusion.

16. Given a programming assignment in which the program must produce a multipart report, and for which the printer spacing chart is provided, be able to successfully apply the steps of the problem-solving procedure in producing the required program.

The Problem

The Jocelyn Originals Company specializes in the creation of original designs. From a local "basement" operation, it has grown into a national business operating from coast to coast. The national sales manager wants an annual district sales report that will show the total quarterly sales of its sales force by district, the total sales for the year for each district, the previous year's total sales for each district, and the percent increase or decrease over the previous year's total sales. Similar information is to be provided for the company as a whole, that is, the total sales for each quarter and for the year, the previous year's total sales, and the percent increase or decrease over the previous year's total sales.

The input to the program will be a single record containing the company's total sales figures for the previous year, and a record for each salesperson, showing the salesperson's name, district code, total sales figures for each quarter of the year, and total sales for the year as a whole. The salesperson records are presorted in alphabetical order. (The sample input file is shown in Figure 7.45a [DD/CD:VIC7SPI.DAT].)

The layout of data on these two records is shown below.

Record 1 (Previous year's sales)

cc 1–4	Year of record
cc 5–14	District-1 total (format: xxxxxxxx.xx)
cc 15–24	District-2 total (format: xxxxxxxx.xx)
cc 25–34	District-3 total (format: xxxxxxxx.xx)
cc 35–44	District-4 total (format: xxxxxxxx.xx)
cc 45–54	Company total (format: xxxxxxxx.xx)

Record 2 (Salesperson data)

cc 1	Salesperson's district code
cc 2–26	Salesperson's name
cc 27–34	First quarter sales (format: xxxxxx.xx)
cc 35–42	Second quarter sales (format: xxxxxx.xx)
cc 43–50	Third quarter sales (format: xxxxxx.xx)
cc 51–58	Fourth quarter sales (format: xxxxxx.xx)
cc 59–66	Total sales for year (format: xxxxxx.xx)

Each of the districts is assigned a code as shown below:

District	Code
Eastern	1
Central	2
Mountain	3
Pacific	4

The output must show appropriate information identifying the report: the report date, company name, report name, fiscal year identifier, and column headings. All data output should be edited. The districts should be identified by name, not by code. If a district's total sales amount is less than the previous year's total, the percent increase amount should be negative. Similarly, if the company's total sales amount for the year is less than the previous year's total, a "–" sign should be printed next to the percent increase amount. The report must end with an "End of Report" message.

A Brief Analysis of the Problem

The annual district sales report that the program must produce is a summary report. As such, the program must process all the input records before the report can be printed. The report will begin with the top-of-report documentation as specified in the statement of the problem, followed by the summary information for each district, then the summary information for the company, and finally the End-of-Report message.

Since there are two kinds of input records, the record containing the previous year's sales figures by district (only one such record), and the salesperson record (one for each salesperson), the logic must be set up to process each kind properly. The record containing the previous year's sales figures will be read first, and the data will be transferred to storage areas in working storage for use later. As each salesperson record is read, the district must be identified so that the sales figures (quarterly and total) can be added to the correct district accumulators and then to the company accumulators. The four districts and the company must each be assigned a series of five accumulators in working storage, one for each quarter and one for the full year.

As noted previously, the sales figures needed for the report will not be known until all the salespersons' records have been processed. At that time, the percent increase or decrease for the first district must be determined, and all appropriate amounts for the first district must be printed. Then, the percent increase or decrease for the second district must be determined, and all appropriate amounts for that district must be printed. This pattern continues for the third district, the fourth district, and for the company as a whole.

When the End-of-Report message has been printed, the report is complete.

Program Design Phase

By now you are very familiar with the problem-solving procedure, so you know that during the design phase the programmer develops all the design tools. These tools are not only of immediate help to the programmer, but they also provide invaluable long-term documentation for the program.

Step 1

In this program, there are two kinds of input records: one that contains the company's sales totals for the previous year and one that contains a salesperson's data for the year being reported. Their layouts are shown in Figure 7.1.

Note that abbreviations have been used as data names. Although abbreviations are very acceptable to the compiler, they often impose an extra hardship on programmers who must maintain existing programs, since abbreviations often decrease the self-documentation that descriptive data names provide. Occasionally, full-length descriptive data names exceed the allowed maximum number of characters, and as a result there is no choice but to introduce abbreviations. Such is the case in this program. To assure that the self-documentation of data names does not suffer, a legend that equates an abbreviation with its full-length equivalent should be supplied by the programmer.

Figure 7.1 Layouts of input records for the chapter program

Record Layout Forms

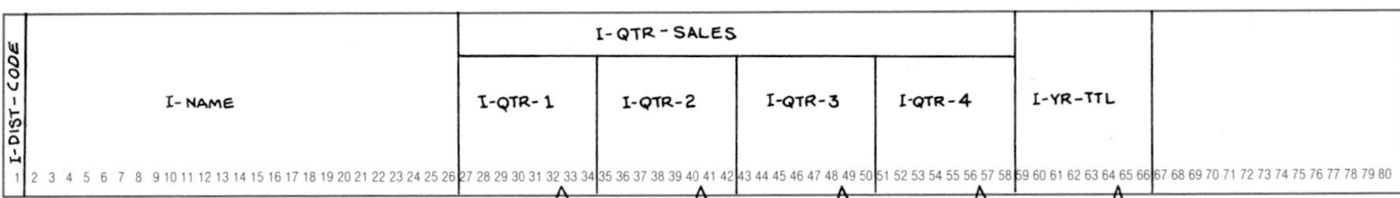

Record Name: SALESPERSON-RECORD

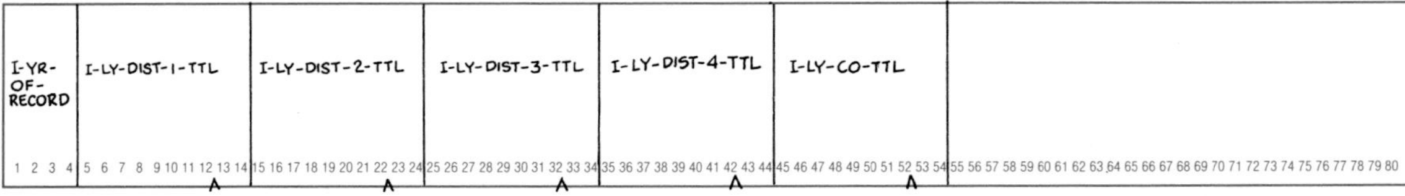

Record Name: LY-SALES-TOTALS-RECORD

■ **Figure 7.2** Printer spacing chart for the chapter program

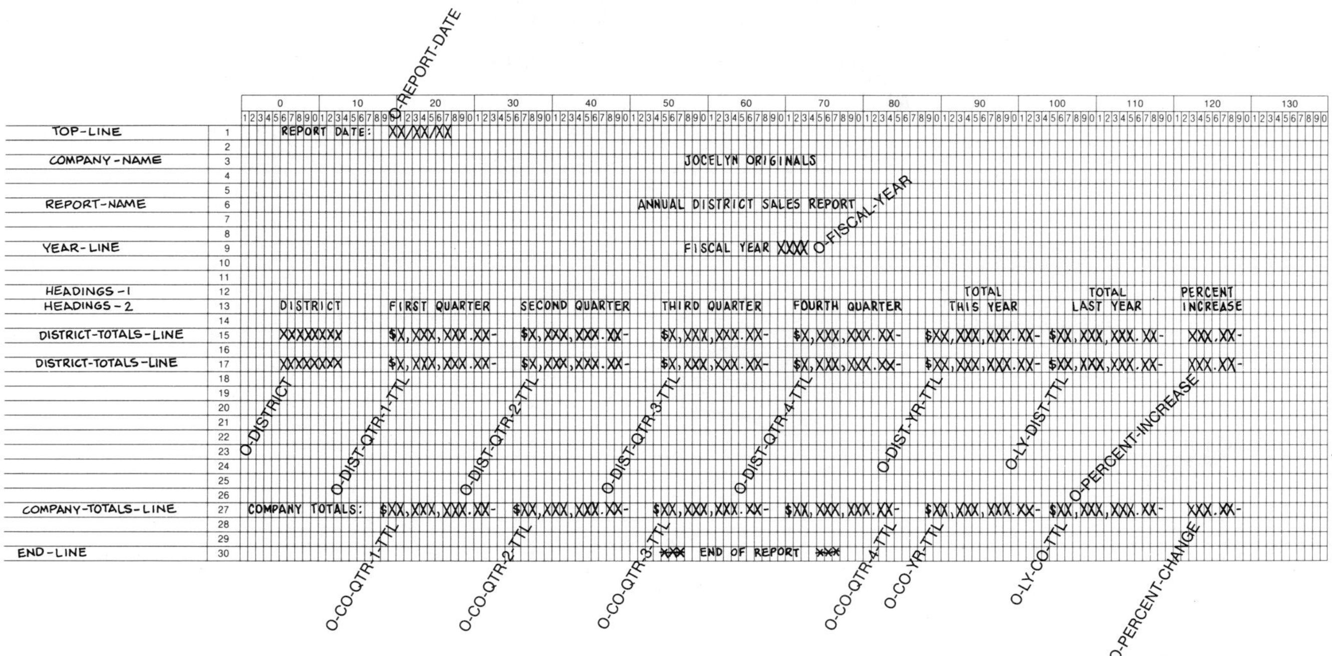

In this program, the following abbreviations have been used:

CO:	COMPANY
DIST:	DISTRICT
LY:	LAST YEAR
QTR:	QUARTER
TTL:	TOTAL
SUMRY:	SUMMARY

According to the requirements of the problem, the report must contain nine different kinds of lines. Their layouts are shown on the printer spacing chart of Figure 7.2.

Step 2

System Flowchart

In planning the solution to the problem, we must first determine the data flow requirements. It is clear from the brief analysis above that data will be obtained from a sales file, and it will be processed by the program in order to produce the summary report. The resulting system flowchart is shown in Figure 7.3.

Structure Chart

The system flowchart clearly indicates that the essential function of the program is to produce the sales summary report. Now we must break down this major task into manageable subtasks. We know, from previous programs, that certain start-up activities are generally needed. We also know, from the brief analysis above, that all the records of the sales file must be processed to accumulate the totals that must be printed on the summary report. And we know that the summary report must be printed, followed by the End-of-Report message. Now, unlike the previous "detail" reports that were printed in a piecemeal fashion (top-of-report documentation as a subtask of module 200 START UP, detail lines as a subtask of the main processing module 210 PROCESS RECORD, and End-of-Report message from within module 220 FINISH UP), the complete summary report will be printed as a subtask of module 220 FINISH UP. Thus, the first two levels of the structure chart are as shown in Figure 7.4.

■ **Figure 7.3** System flowchart for the chapter program

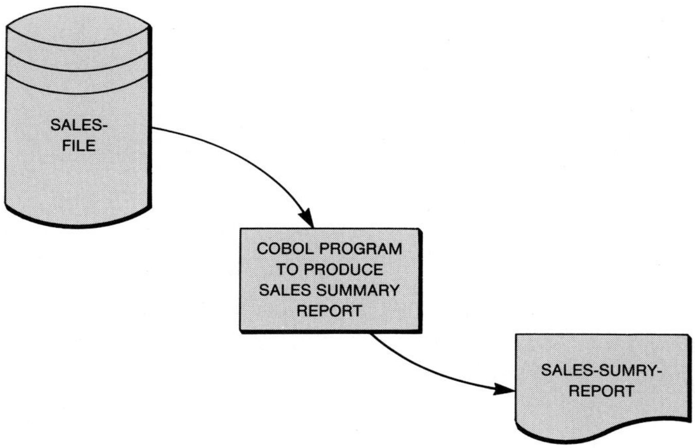

■ **Figure 7.4** First two levels of the structure chart

■ **Figure 7.5** Subtasks of module 200 START UP

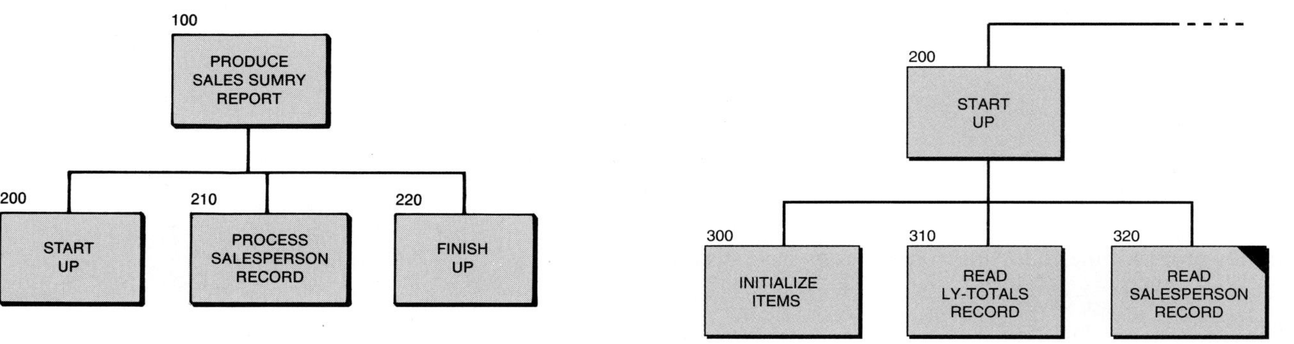

Module 200 START UP begins by opening the files, and then it will control the execution of three third-level modules. One module will obtain the date from the system, set the flag WS-MORE-RECORDS, and initialize all the program's accumulators. Another module will access the input record that contains the previous year's sales totals, and it will store them in working storage for use later. And the third module will access the first salesperson record. This structure is shown in Figure 7.5.

In module 210, the major task is to PROCESS a SALESPERSON RECORD. What's involved in processing a salesperson record? As noted in the brief analysis of the problem, once the district code on the record has been identified, the sales amounts for each quarter and for the year as a whole must be added to the appropriate district's accumulators, and they must also be added to the company accumulators. At this point the processing requirements for the current record are complete. Consequently, the next salesperson record should be accessed from the sales file so that it can be processed in turn. (Module 210 is executed repeatedly in a loop until all the salesperson records in the input file have been processed.) This breakdown is shown in Figure 7.6.

In module 220, the major task is to PREPARE the REPORT. This task, 350 PREPARE REPORT, can be readily broken down into six subtasks: The first subtask writes the top-of-report documentation, the next four subtasks produce a summary line for each of the four districts, and the final subtask produces the summary line for the company as a whole. Module 220 and its subtasks are shown in Figure 7.7.

When the components in Figures 7.4 through 7.7 are joined, the resulting structure chart is the one shown in Figure 7.8.

■ **Figure 7.6** Subtasks of module 210 PROCESS SALESPERSON RECORD

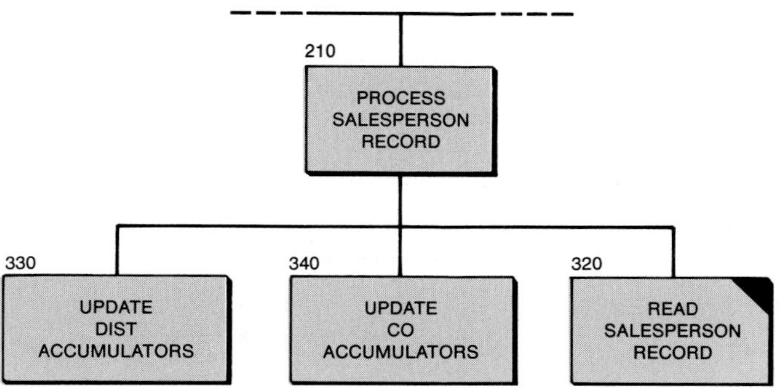

■ **Figure 7.7** Module 220 FINISH UP and its subtask module 350 PREPARE REPORT

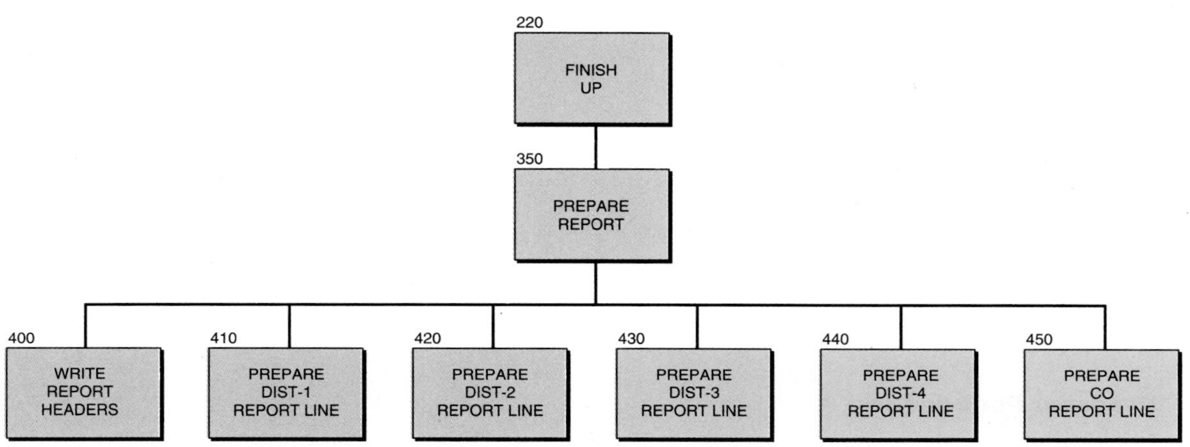

■ **Figure 7.8** Structure chart for the chapter program

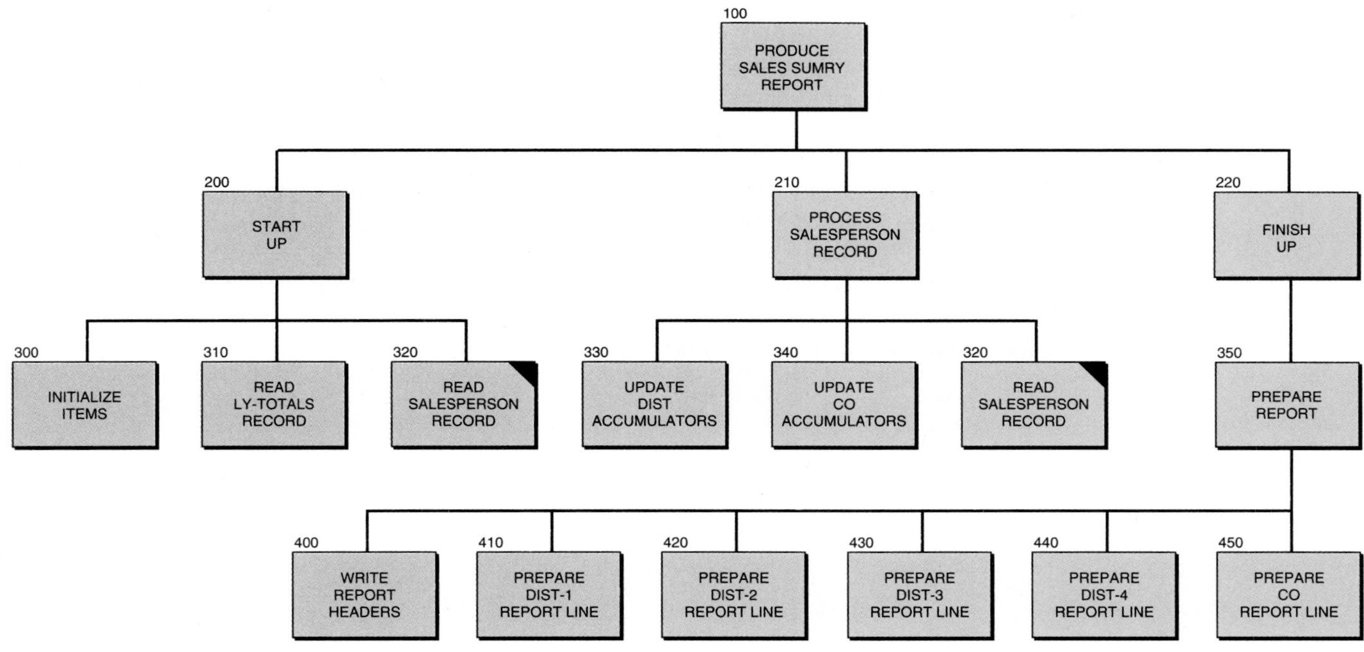

Figure 7.9 Primary pseudocode paragraph and flowchart module

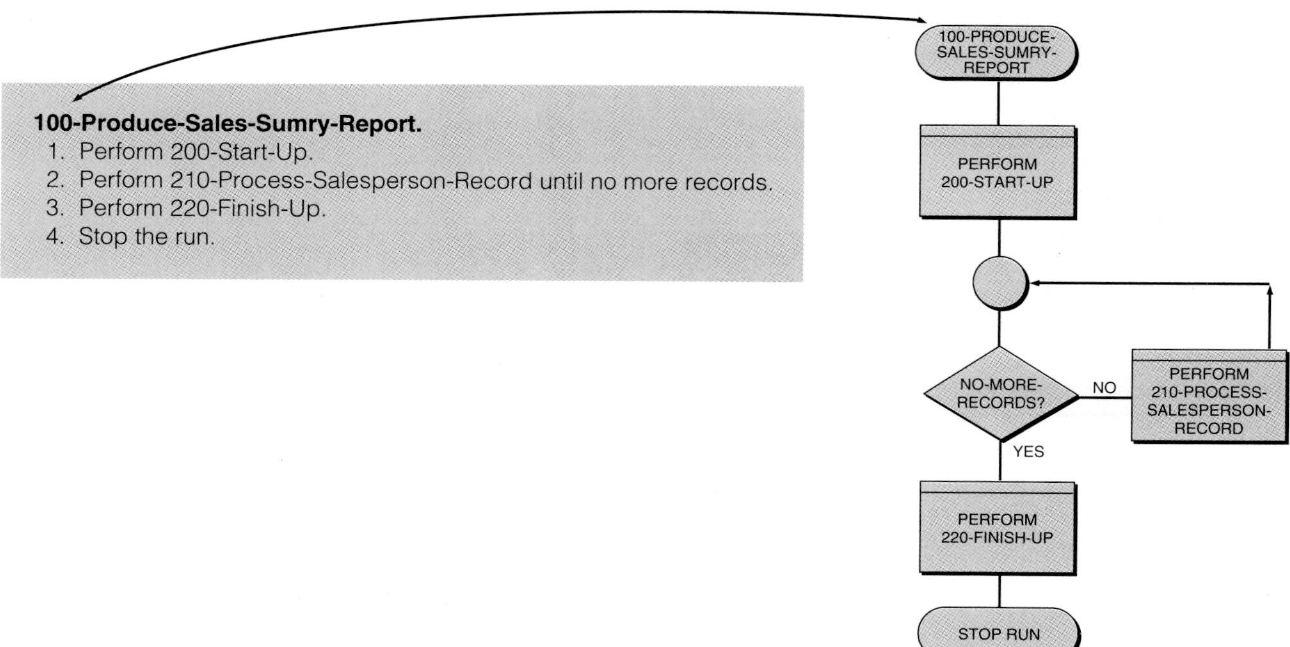

100-Produce-Sales-Sumry-Report.
1. Perform 200-Start-Up.
2. Perform 210-Process-Salesperson-Record until no more records.
3. Perform 220-Finish-Up.
4. Stop the run.
100-PRODUCE-SALES-SUMRY-REPORT
PERFORM 200-START-UP
NO-MORE-RECORDS?
NO
PERFORM 210-PROCESS-SALESPERSON-RECORD
YES
PERFORM 220-FINISH-UP
STOP RUN

Program Pseudocode

Now that the overall structure of the program has been established, we must detail the processing steps needed to accomplish the task specified in each module of the structure chart. The primary module 100 PRODUCE SALES SUMRY REPORT is the main control module. It controls the execution of the three 200-level modules: module 200 START UP that must be executed once, module 210 PROCESS SALESPERSON RECORD that must be executed as many times as there are salesperson records in the input file, and module 220 FINISH UP that must be executed only once. When those subtasks have been completed, the job is done and control must be returned to the operating system. The pseudocode paragraph for the primary module and the corresponding flowchart module are shown in Figure 7.9.

As noted earlier, structure chart module 200 START UP begins by opening the files, and then it controls the execution of three 300-level modules: module 300 INITIALIZE ITEMS, whose name specifies its function, module 310 READ LY TOTALS RECORD, whose task is to read the input record that contains the company's total sales figures for the previous year and then to store its contents in working storage for later use, and module 320 READ SALESPERSON RECORD, whose task is to access the first salesperson record and thus prime the loop that contains module 210 PROCESS SALESPERSON RECORD. The pseudocode paragraph and corresponding flowchart module for structure chart module 200 START UP and for each of its subordinate modules are shown in Figure 7.10.

■ **Figure 7.10** Pseudocode paragraphs and flowchart modules for 200-START-UP and its subordinate modules

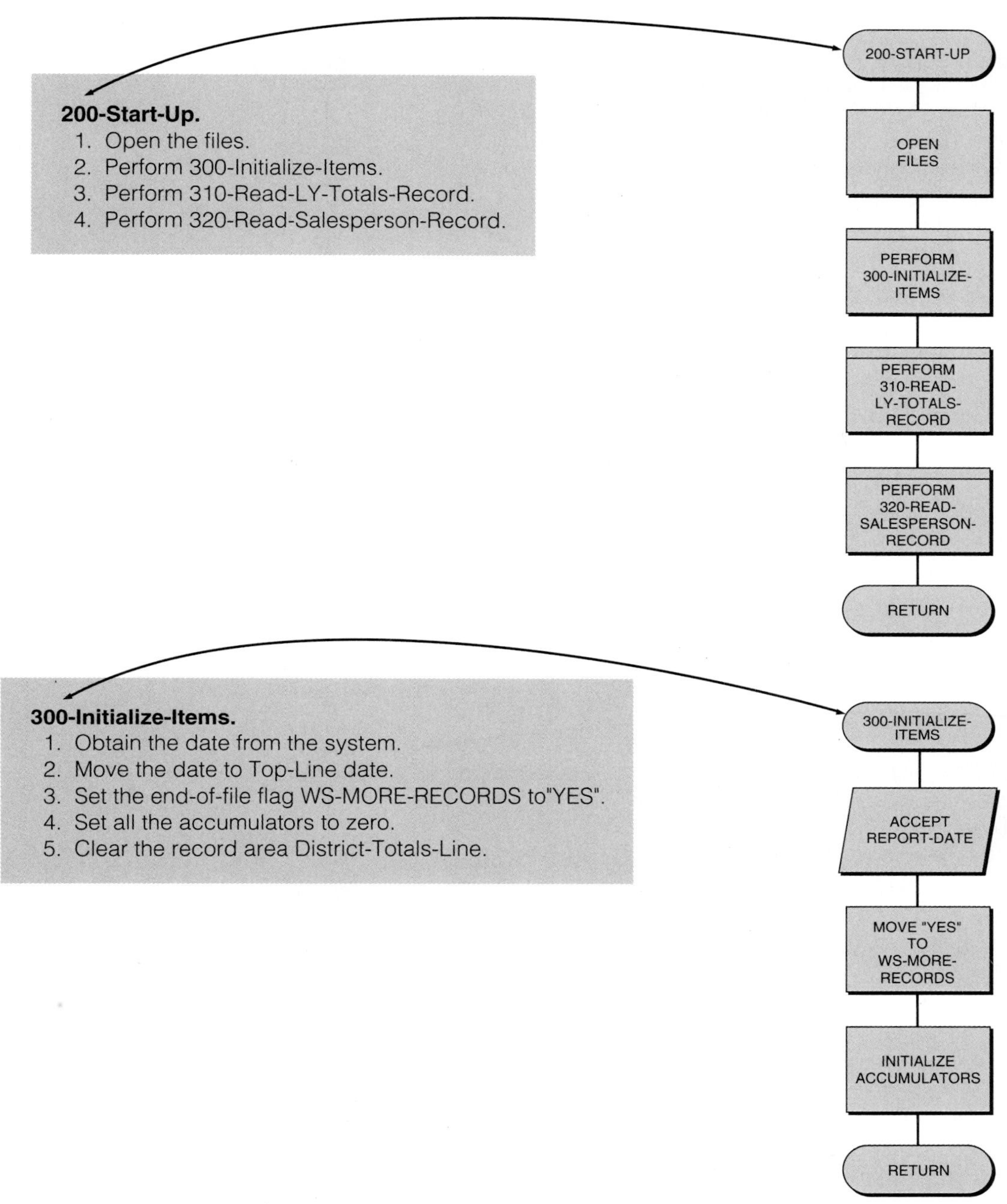
200-Start-Up.
1. Open the files.
2. Perform 300-Initialize-Items.
3. Perform 310-Read-LY-Totals-Record.
4. Perform 320-Read-Salesperson-Record.
200-START-UP
OPEN FILES
PERFORM 300-INITIALIZE-ITEMS
PERFORM 310-READ-LY-TOTALS-RECORD
PERFORM 320-READ-SALESPERSON-RECORD
RETURN
300-Initialize-Items.
1. Obtain the date from the system.
2. Move the date to Top-Line date.
3. Set the end-of-file flag WS-MORE-RECORDS to"YES".
4. Set all the accumulators to zero.
5. Clear the record area District-Totals-Line.
300-INITIALIZE-ITEMS
ACCEPT REPORT-DATE
MOVE "YES" TO WS-MORE-RECORDS
INITIALIZE ACCUMULATORS
RETURN

310-Read-LY-Totals-Record.

1. Read the input Last-Year-Sales-Totals-Record.
2. Test for end-of-file record;
   If EOF record reached, set the flag WS-MORE-RECORDS to "NO ".
   If not, move the record to LY-Sales-Totals area in
   working storage.

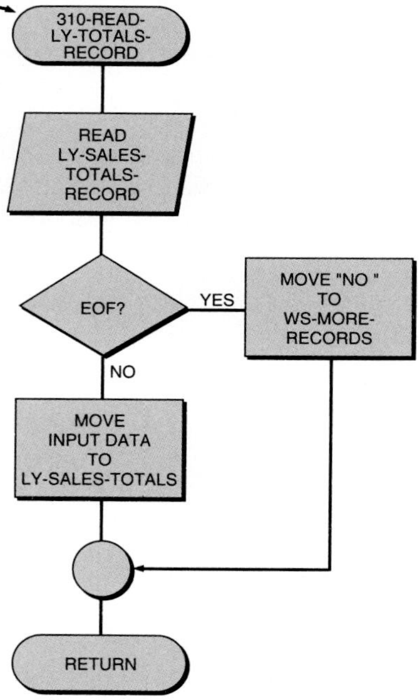

320-Read-Salesperson-Record.

1. Read an input Salesperson-Record.
2. Test for end-of-file record;
   If EOF record reached, set the flag WS-MORE-RECORDS to "NO ".

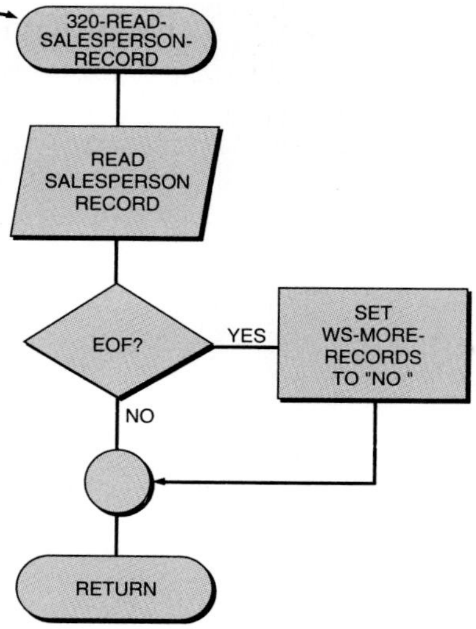

It is important to remember that one buffer (or record area) is reserved in memory for each file opened in a program. Since the two different kinds of records that exist in the input file SALES-FILE will be "read" into the same buffer, it is critical for us to make a copy of the record LY-SALES-TOTALS-RECORD in working storage to preserve the values it contains for later use. (This is done in module 310.) When the first salesperson record is read (module 320), its contents will replace last year's figures in the input buffer. This is illustrated in Figure 7.11.

As analyzed earlier, structure chart module 210 PROCESS SALESPERSON RECORD simply controls the execution of three 300-level modules: 330 UPDATE DIST ACCUMULATORS, 340 UPDATE CO ACCUMULATORS, and 320 READ SALESPERSON RECORD.

Module 330 UPDATE DIST ACCUMULATORS is crucial to the subtotaling process. The first task is to identify the district to which the salesperson, whose record is currently in input memory, belongs. On a salesperson's record, the district is specified by a code in column 1:

A **1** represents the Eastern district.

A **2** represents the Central district.

A **3** represents the Mountain district.

A **4** represents the Pacific district.

The logic is as follows:

1. If the district code is a 1, add the sales figures to the Eastern district accumulators.
2. If the district code is a 2, add the sales figures to the Central district accumulators.
3. If the district code is a 3, add the sales figures to the Mountain district accumulators.
4. If the district code is a 4, add the sales figures to the Pacific district accumulators.

The district code tests can be set up in sequence as shown in Figure 7.12. Part a shows the flowchart segment and part b shows the corresponding pseudocode. Note that the pseudocode is more detailed than the flowchart.

Although this logic would accomplish the module objective, it is important to realize that all the tests would have to be performed for each salesperson record. For instance, if the district code is a 1, the sales figures will be added to the Eastern district accumulators, but then the district code will be tested again to see if it is a 2, it will be tested again to see if it is a 3, and so on. Once the sales figures have been added to the appropriate accumulators, performing further tests on the district code is unnecessary and a waste of computer time.

Figure 7.11 Preserving last year's sales figures

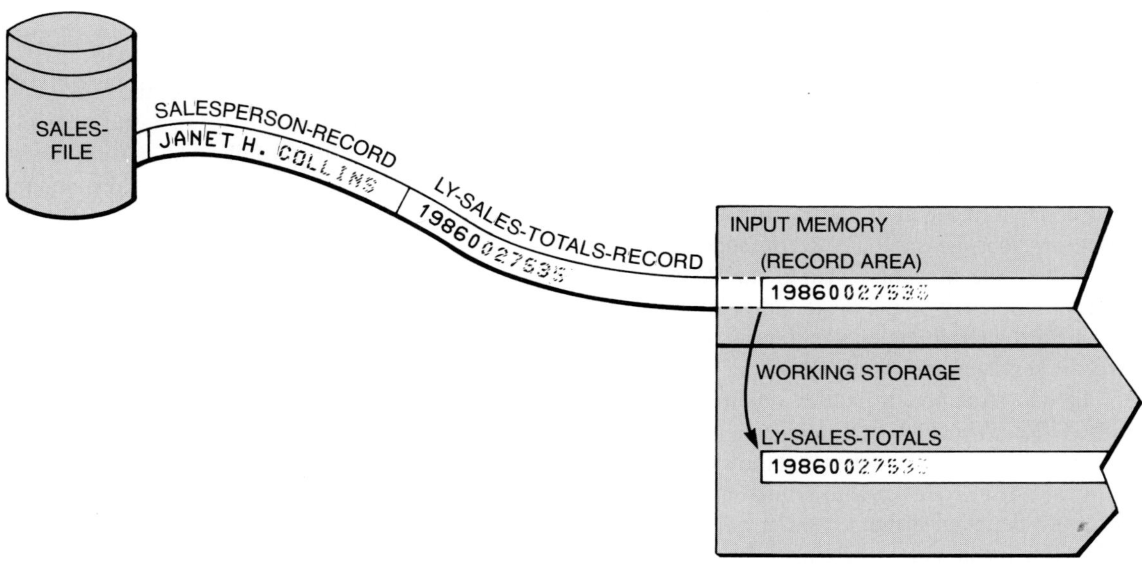

Figure 7.12 Using sequential tests to determine the district code

a. Flowchart Segment

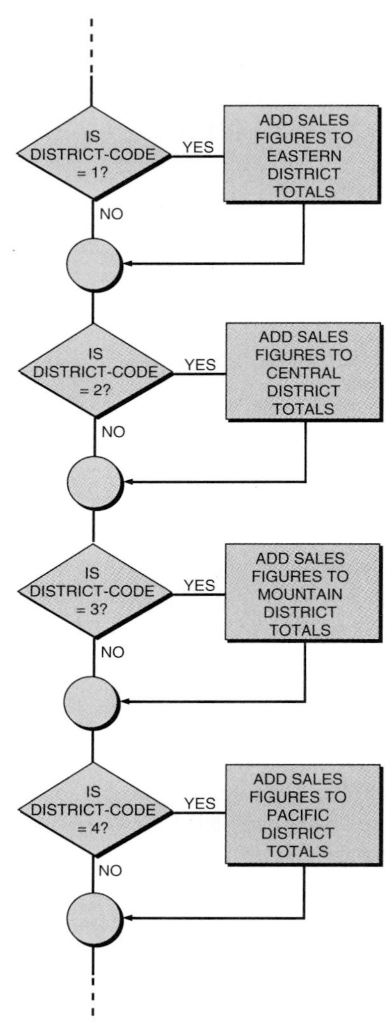

b. Pseudocode

1. **Test if input district-code = 1;**
   If it is, add input Quarter-1 to District-1-Quarter-1-Total,
   add input Quarter-2 to District-1-Quarter-2-Total,
   add input Quarter-3 to District-1-Quarter-3-Total,
   add input Quarter-4 to District-1-Quarter-4-Total,
   add input Year-Total to District-1-Year-Total;
   If it is not, continue.

2. **Test if input district-code = 2;**
   If it is, add input Quarter-1 to District-2-Quarter-1-Total,
   add input Quarter-2 to District-2-Quarter-2-Total,
   add input Quarter-3 to District-2-Quarter-3-Total,
   add input Quarter-4 to District-2-Quarter-4-Total,
   add input Year-Total to District-2-Year-Total;
   If it is not, continue.

3. **Test if input district-code = 3;**
   If it is, add input Quarter-1 to District-3-Quarter-1-Total,
   add input Quarter-2 to District-3-Quarter-2-Total,
   add input Quarter-3 to District-3-Quarter-3-Total,
   add input Quarter-4 to District-3-Quarter-4-Total,
   add input Year-Total to District-3-Year-Total;
   If it is not, continue.

4. **Test if input district-code = 4;**
   If it is, add input Quarter-1 to District-4-Quarter-1-Total,
   add input Quarter-2 to District-4-Quarter-2-Total,
   add input Quarter-3 to District-4-Quarter-3-Total,
   add input Quarter-4 to District-4-Quarter-4-Total,
   add input Year-Total to District-4-Year-Total;
   If it is not, continue.

5. . . .

It is more efficient to set up the logic so that when one of the tests is found to be true, the remaining ones are skipped. This can be accomplished by *nesting* the tests; that is, test-2 is performed only if test-1 fails, test-3 is performed only if test-2 fails, and test-4 is performed only if test-3 fails. The nesting of the tests is shown in Figure 7.13. Part a shows the flowchart segment and part b shows the corresponding pseudocode. (Note that if the district code does not specify the Eastern, Central, Mountain or Pacific district, an error message will be produced.)

Follow the flowchart path if the district code is a 1 in Figure 7.12 and then in Figure 7.13. The increased efficiency of the nested tests is obvious.

A third alternative available to us is to use the case structure shown in Figure 7.14. Part a shows the flowchart segment and part b shows the corresponding pseudocode.

In this structure, a path is set up for each case, that is, for each possible value of the key field DIST-CODE. When the key field contains a particular value, control goes directly to the corresponding path. This structure is sometimes referred to as a streamlined version of the nested tests. Although there are only four district codes, a fifth branch has been added to the case structure to specify the course of action that should be taken if there is an error in the specified code. (The only valid code values are 1, 2, 3, and 4.) This test for a code error makes the logical analysis more complete.

Each one of these three alternatives has specific coding requirements. They will be examined in detail shortly. In the current program, we will implement the case structure illustrated in Figure 7.14.

When the instructions along the selected path have been executed, the salesperson's sales figures will have been added to the appropriate district's accumulators, so the function of the module has been achieved.

Figure 7.13 Using nested tests to determine the district code

a. Flowchart Segment

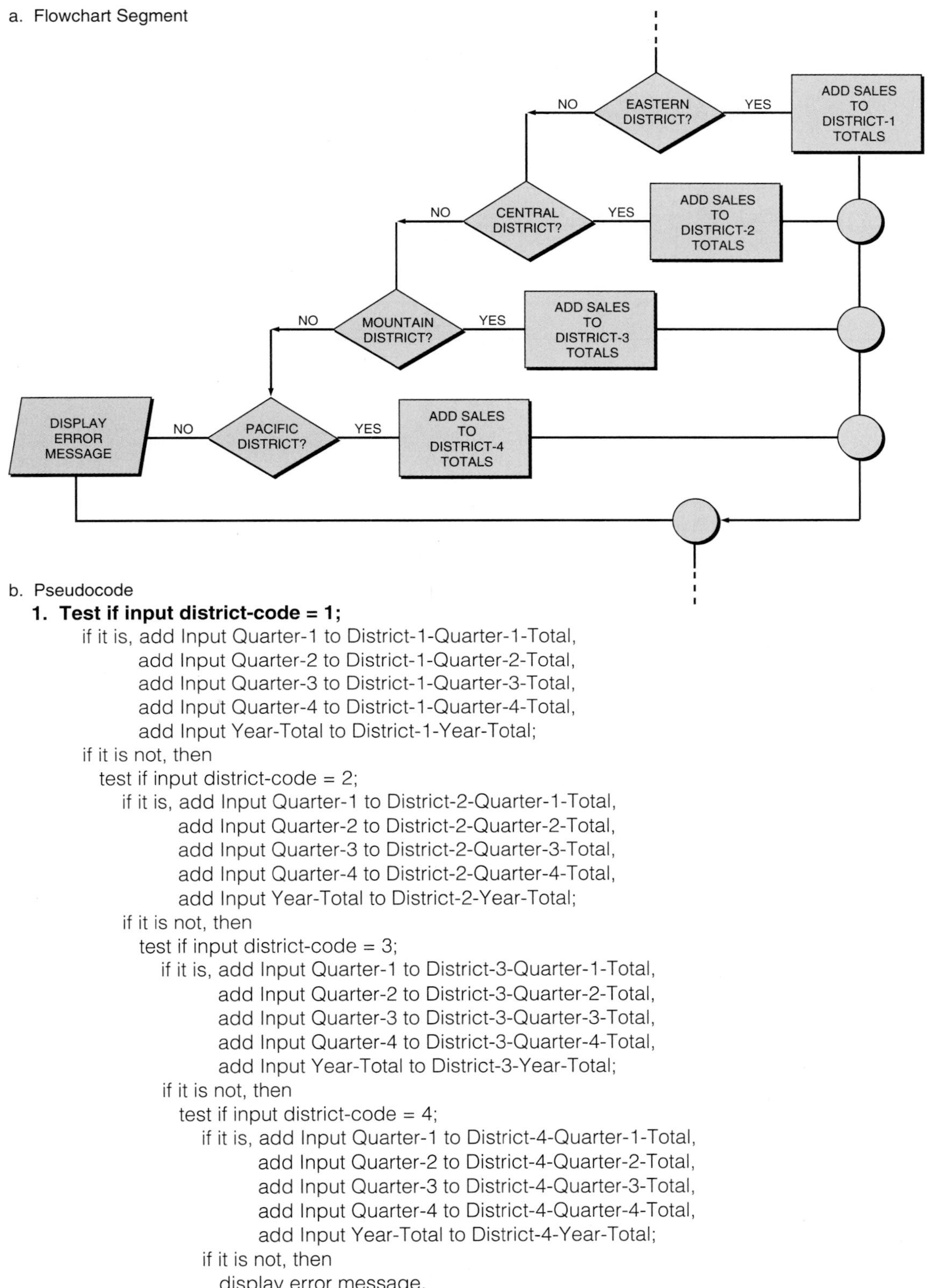

b. Pseudocode

1. Test if input district-code = 1;

```
if it is, add Input Quarter-1 to District-1-Quarter-1-Total,
          add Input Quarter-2 to District-1-Quarter-2-Total,
          add Input Quarter-3 to District-1-Quarter-3-Total,
          add Input Quarter-4 to District-1-Quarter-4-Total,
          add Input Year-Total to District-1-Year-Total;
if it is not, then
  test if input district-code = 2;
    if it is, add Input Quarter-1 to District-2-Quarter-1-Total,
              add Input Quarter-2 to District-2-Quarter-2-Total,
              add Input Quarter-3 to District-2-Quarter-3-Total,
              add Input Quarter-4 to District-2-Quarter-4-Total,
              add Input Year-Total to District-2-Year-Total;
    if it is not, then
      test if input district-code = 3;
        if it is, add Input Quarter-1 to District-3-Quarter-1-Total,
                  add Input Quarter-2 to District-3-Quarter-2-Total,
                  add Input Quarter-3 to District-3-Quarter-3-Total,
                  add Input Quarter-4 to District-3-Quarter-4-Total,
                  add Input Year-Total to District-3-Year-Total;
        if it is not, then
          test if input district-code = 4;
            if it is, add Input Quarter-1 to District-4-Quarter-1-Total,
                      add Input Quarter-2 to District-4-Quarter-2-Total,
                      add Input Quarter-3 to District-4-Quarter-3-Total,
                      add Input Quarter-4 to District-4-Quarter-4-Total,
                      add Input Year-Total to District-4-Year-Total;
            if it is not, then
              display error message.
```

The details to implement structure chart module 340 UPDATE CO ACCUMULATORS are much simpler, since each salesperson's sales figures, regardless of the district she or he works in, must be added to the company accumulators. The pseudocode paragraph and the corresponding flowchart for structure chart module 210 PROCESS SALESPERSON RECORD and for each of its subordinate modules are shown in Figure 7.15.

Figure 7.14 Using the case structure to determine the district code

a. Flowchart Segment

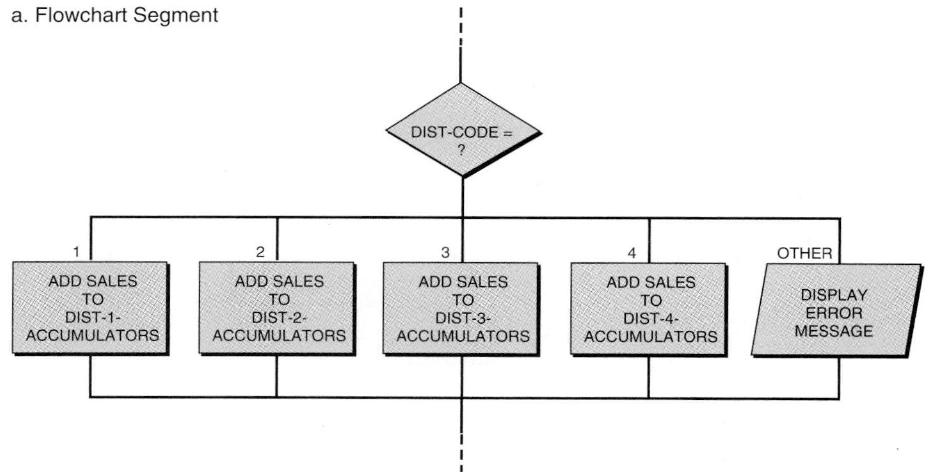

b. Pseudocode

1. Test input District-Code:

a. if "1": add input Quarter-1 to District-1-Quarter-1-Total,
add input Quarter-2 to District-1-Quarter-2-Total,
add input Quarter-3 to District-1-Quarter-3-Total,
add input Quarter-4 to District-1-Quarter-4-Total,
add input Year-Total to District-1-Year-Total.

b. if "2": add input Quarter-1 to District-2-Quarter-1-Total,
add input Quarter-2 to District-2-Quarter-2-Total,
add input Quarter-3 to District-2-Quarter-3-Total,
add input Quarter-4 to District-2-Quarter-4-Total,
add input Year-Total to District-2-Year-Total.

c. if "3": add input Quarter-1 to District-3-Quarter-1-Total,
add input Quarter-2 to District-3-Quarter-2-Total,
add input Quarter-3 to District-3-Quarter-3-Total,
add input Quarter-4 to District-3-Quarter-4-Total,
add input Year-Total to District-3-Year-Total.

d. if "4": add input Quarter-1 to District-4-Quarter-1-Total,
add input Quarter-2 to District-4-Quarter-2-Total,
add input Quarter-3 to District-4-Quarter-3-Total,
add input Quarter-4 to District-4-Quarter-4-Total,
add input Year-Total to District-4-Year-Total.

e. if other, display "District-Code error for " input Name.

When all the salesperson records in the input file have been processed, control exits from the loop that repeatedly executes structure chart module 210 PROCESS SALESPERSON RECORD, and it enters module 220 FINISH UP. Note that not even a single line has yet been printed on the report. This is because the required report in this program is a pure summary report. The major task of module 220 is to print the summary report. This is accomplished by module 350 PREPARE REPORT. Module 350 controls the execution of six structure chart modules: Module 400 WRITE REPORT HEADERS, module 410 PREPARE DIST 1 REPORT LINE, module 420 PREPARE DIST 2 REPORT LINE, module 430 PREPARE DIST 3 REPORT LINE, module 440 PREPARE DIST 4 REPORT LINE and module 450 PREPARE CO REPORT LINE. The pseudocode and corresponding flowchart for module 220 FINISH UP and for its subordinate module 350 PREPARE REPORT are shown in Figure 7.16.

Figure 7.15 Pseudocode paragraphs and flowchart modules for 210-PROCESS-SALESPERSON-RECORD and its subordinate modules

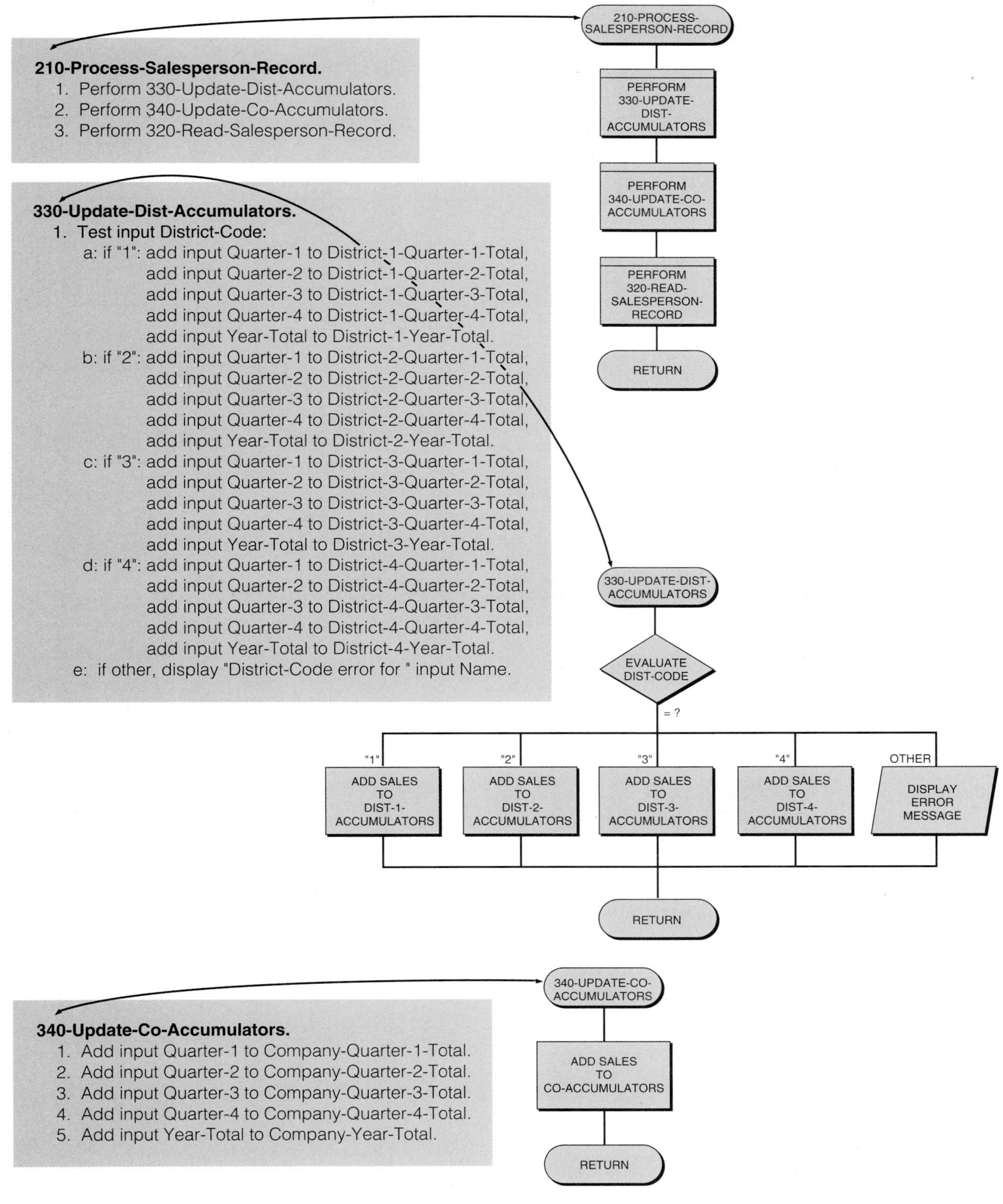

210-Process-Salesperson-Record.
1. Perform 330-Update-Dist-Accumulators.
2. Perform 340-Update-Co-Accumulators.
3. Perform 320-Read-Salesperson-Record.

330-Update-Dist-Accumulators.
1. Test input District-Code:
a: if "1": add input Quarter-1 to District-1-Quarter-1-Total,
add input Quarter-2 to District-1-Quarter-2-Total,
add input Quarter-3 to District-1-Quarter-3-Total,
add input Quarter-4 to District-1-Quarter-4-Total,
add input Year-Total to District-1-Year-Total.
b: if "2": add input Quarter-1 to District-2-Quarter-1-Total,
add input Quarter-2 to District-2-Quarter-2-Total,
add input Quarter-3 to District-2-Quarter-3-Total,
add input Quarter-4 to District-2-Quarter-4-Total,
add input Year-Total to District-2-Year-Total.
c: if "3": add input Quarter-1 to District-3-Quarter-1-Total,
add input Quarter-2 to District-3-Quarter-2-Total,
add input Quarter-3 to District-3-Quarter-3-Total,
add input Quarter-4 to District-3-Quarter-4-Total,
add input Year-Total to District-3-Year-Total.
d: if "4": add input Quarter-1 to District-4-Quarter-1-Total,
add input Quarter-2 to District-4-Quarter-2-Total,
add input Quarter-3 to District-4-Quarter-3-Total,
add input Quarter-4 to District-4-Quarter-4-Total,
add input Year-Total to District-4-Year-Total.
e: if other, display "District-Code error for " input Name.

340-Update-Co-Accumulators.
1. Add input Quarter-1 to Company-Quarter-1-Total.
2. Add input Quarter-2 to Company-Quarter-2-Total.
3. Add input Quarter-3 to Company-Quarter-3-Total.
4. Add input Quarter-4 to Company-Quarter-4-Total.
5. Add input Year-Total to Company-Year-Total.

210-PROCESS-SALESPERSON-RECORD
PERFORM 330-UPDATE-DIST-ACCUMULATORS
PERFORM 340-UPDATE-CO-ACCUMULATORS
PERFORM 320-READ-SALESPERSON-RECORD
RETURN
330-UPDATE-DIST-ACCUMULATORS
EVALUATE DIST-CODE
= ?
"1"
"2"
"3"
"4"
OTHER
ADD SALES TO DIST-1-ACCUMULATORS
ADD SALES TO DIST-2-ACCUMULATORS
ADD SALES TO DIST-3-ACCUMULATORS
ADD SALES TO DIST-4-ACCUMULATORS
DISPLAY ERROR MESSAGE
RETURN
340-UPDATE-CO-ACCUMULATORS
ADD SALES TO CO-ACCUMULATORS
RETURN

Figure 7.16 Pseudocode and flowchart modules for 220-FINISH-UP and its subordinate module

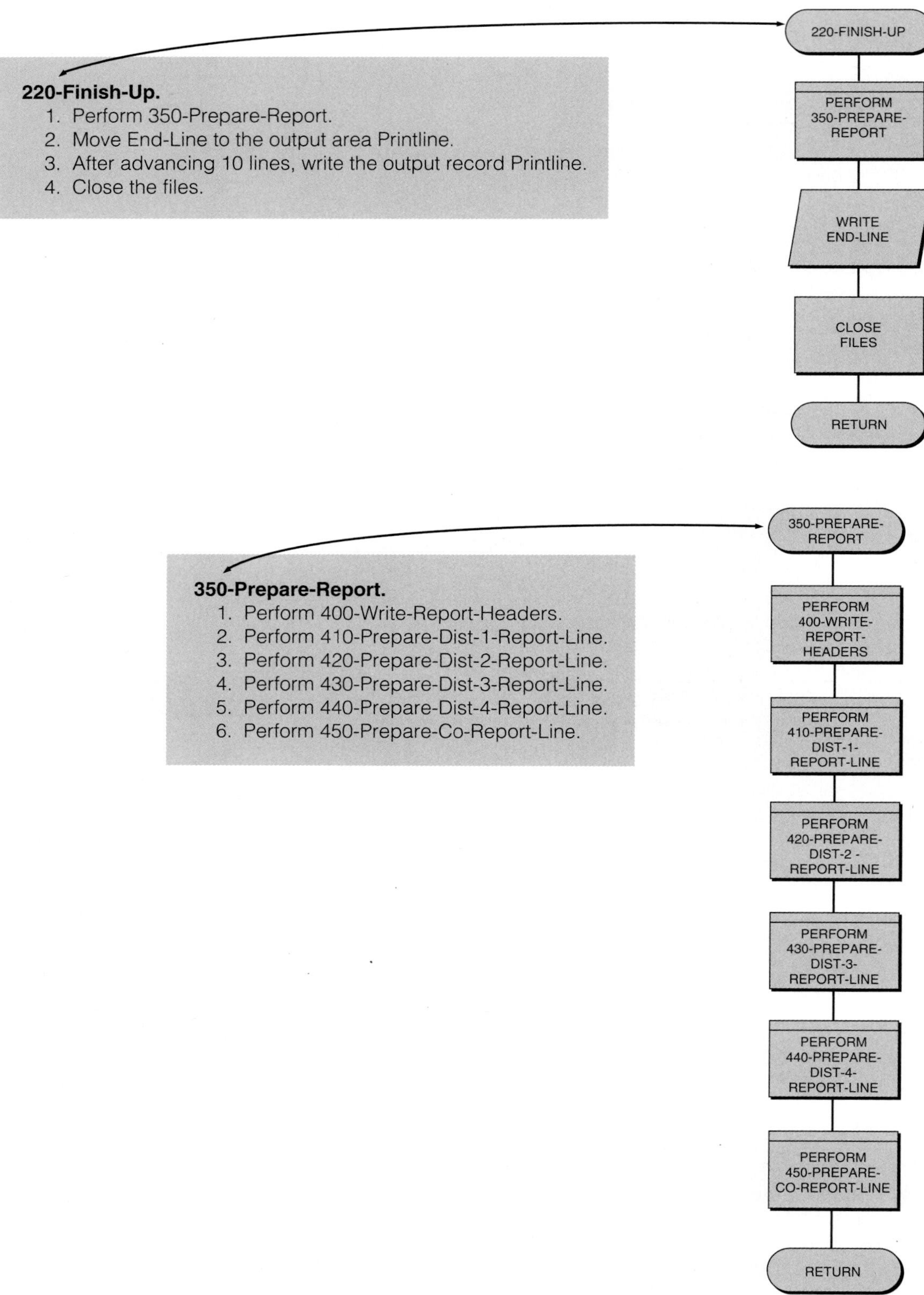

220-Finish-Up.
1. Perform 350-Prepare-Report.
2. Move End-Line to the output area Printline.
3. After advancing 10 lines, write the output record Printline.
4. Close the files.
220-FINISH-UP
PERFORM 350-PREPARE-REPORT
WRITE END-LINE
CLOSE FILES
RETURN
350-Prepare-Report.
1. Perform 400-Write-Report-Headers.
2. Perform 410-Prepare-Dist-1-Report-Line.
3. Perform 420-Prepare-Dist-2-Report-Line.
4. Perform 430-Prepare-Dist-3-Report-Line.
5. Perform 440-Prepare-Dist-4-Report-Line.
6. Perform 450-Prepare-Co-Report-Line.
350-PREPARE-REPORT
PERFORM 400-WRITE-REPORT-HEADERS
PERFORM 410-PREPARE-DIST-1-REPORT-LINE
PERFORM 420-PREPARE-DIST-2 -REPORT-LINE
PERFORM 430-PREPARE-DIST-3-REPORT-LINE
PERFORM 440-PREPARE-DIST-4-REPORT-LINE
PERFORM 450-PREPARE-CO-REPORT-LINE
RETURN

In structure chart module 400 WRITE REPORT HEADERS, the record YEAR LINE, the fourth line to be printed on the report, contains a field for the fiscal year identifier. There are different ways of obtaining this value, such as using the ACCEPT statement, but since it will always be one more than the previous year identifier, we decided to obtain it by a simple addition. The pseudocode paragraph for this module and its corresponding flowchart module are shown in Figure 7.17.

The function of module 410 is to prepare the report line for District 1. In preparing this line, the name of the district is moved to the first data field, the numeric values in the District 1 accumulators are moved to the appropriate edited fields, the total District 1 sales amount for the previous year is moved to its edited field, and finally the percent increase or decrease is computed and stored. This field is edited to print a minus sign if the percent change is a decrease. The report line is then printed on the report.

This procedure is repeated for each of the four districts and for the company as a whole. The corresponding pseudocode paragraphs and flowchart modules are shown in Figure 7.18.

This completes the design phase.

■ **Figure 7.17** Pseudocode paragraph and corresponding flowchart module for 400-WRITE-REPORT-HEADERS

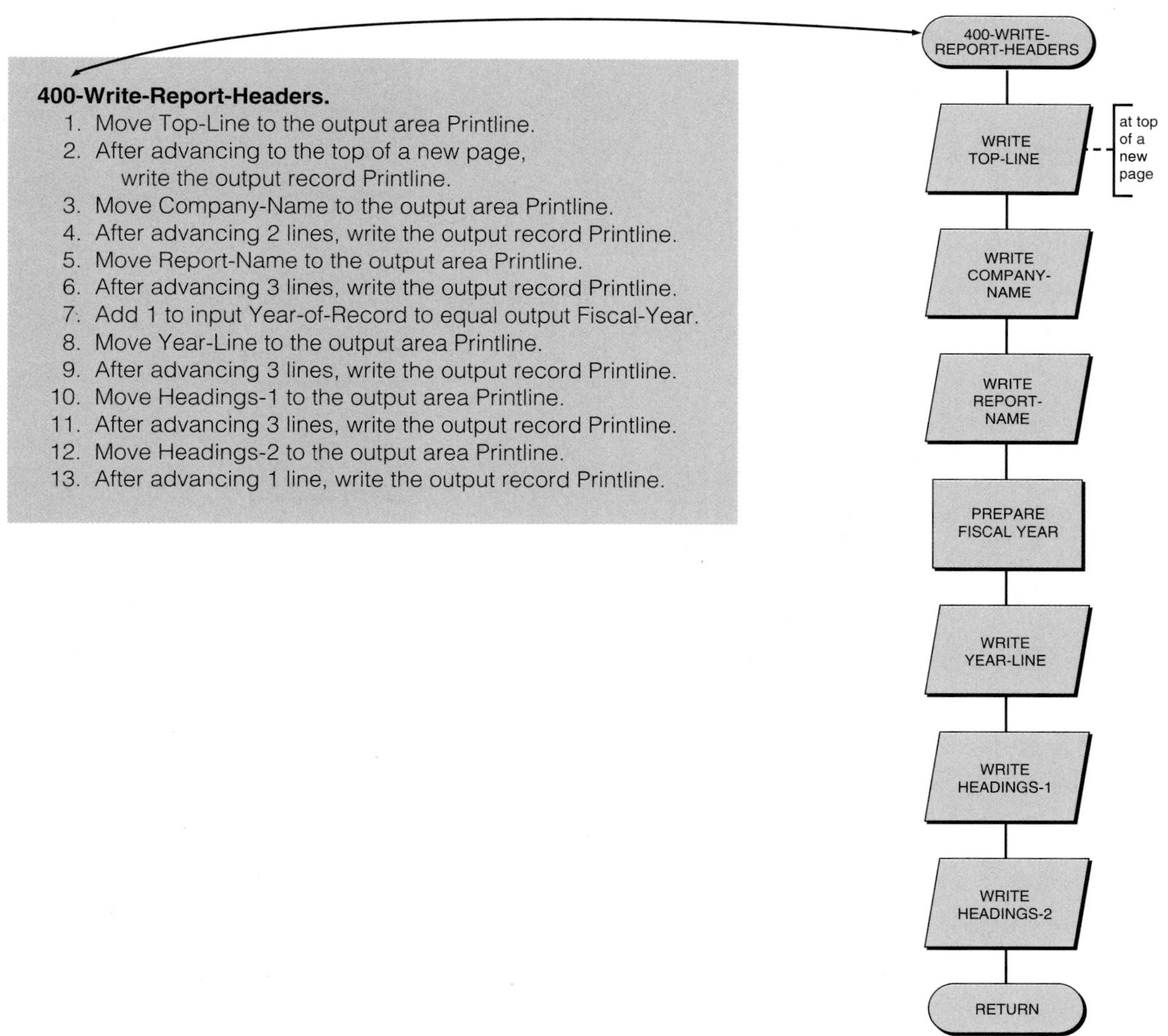

400-Write-Report-Headers.

1. Move Top-Line to the output area Printline.
2. After advancing to the top of a new page, write the output record Printline.
3. Move Company-Name to the output area Printline.
4. After advancing 2 lines, write the output record Printline.
5. Move Report-Name to the output area Printline.
6. After advancing 3 lines, write the output record Printline.
7. Add 1 to input Year-of-Record to equal output Fiscal-Year.
8. Move Year-Line to the output area Printline.
9. After advancing 3 lines, write the output record Printline.
10. Move Headings-1 to the output area Printline.
11. After advancing 3 lines, write the output record Printline.
12. Move Headings-2 to the output area Printline.
13. After advancing 1 line, write the output record Printline.

Figure 7.18 Pseudocode paragraphs and flowchart modules to prepare report lines

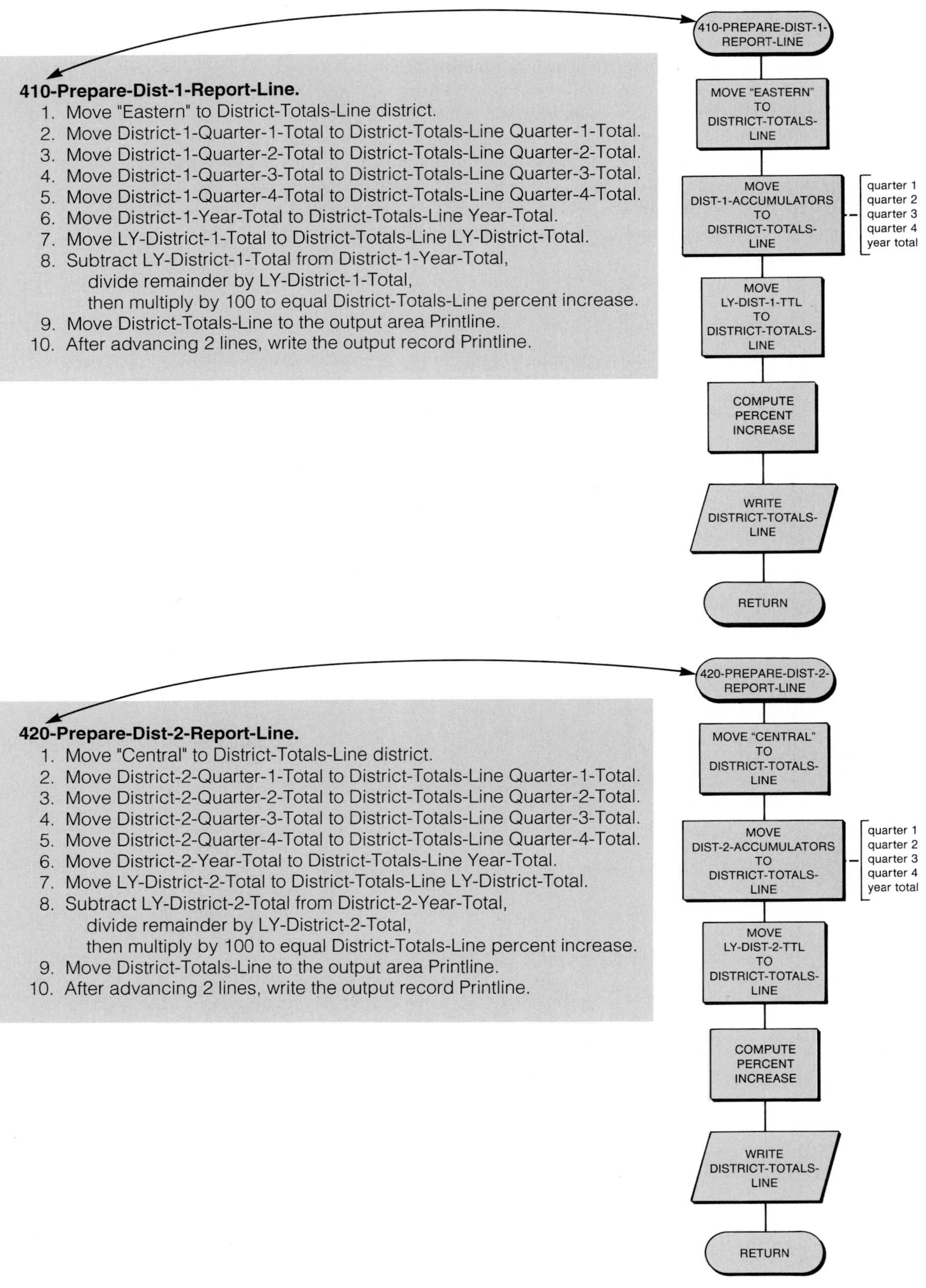

410-Prepare-Dist-1-Report-Line.
1. Move "Eastern" to District-Totals-Line district.
2. Move District-1-Quarter-1-Total to District-Totals-Line Quarter-1-Total.
3. Move District-1-Quarter-2-Total to District-Totals-Line Quarter-2-Total.
4. Move District-1-Quarter-3-Total to District-Totals-Line Quarter-3-Total.
5. Move District-1-Quarter-4-Total to District-Totals-Line Quarter-4-Total.
6. Move District-1-Year-Total to District-Totals-Line Year-Total.
7. Move LY-District-1-Total to District-Totals-Line LY-District-Total.
8. Subtract LY-District-1-Total from District-1-Year-Total,
divide remainder by LY-District-1-Total,
then multiply by 100 to equal District-Totals-Line percent increase.
9. Move District-Totals-Line to the output area Printline.
10. After advancing 2 lines, write the output record Printline.
410-PREPARE-DIST-1-REPORT-LINE
MOVE "EASTERN" TO DISTRICT-TOTALS-LINE
MOVE DIST-1-ACCUMULATORS TO DISTRICT-TOTALS-LINE
quarter 1
quarter 2
quarter 3
quarter 4
year total
MOVE LY-DIST-1-TTL TO DISTRICT-TOTALS-LINE
COMPUTE PERCENT INCREASE
WRITE DISTRICT-TOTALS-LINE
RETURN
420-Prepare-Dist-2-Report-Line.
1. Move "Central" to District-Totals-Line district.
2. Move District-2-Quarter-1-Total to District-Totals-Line Quarter-1-Total.
3. Move District-2-Quarter-2-Total to District-Totals-Line Quarter-2-Total.
4. Move District-2-Quarter-3-Total to District-Totals-Line Quarter-3-Total.
5. Move District-2-Quarter-4-Total to District-Totals-Line Quarter-4-Total.
6. Move District-2-Year-Total to District-Totals-Line Year-Total.
7. Move LY-District-2-Total to District-Totals-Line LY-District-Total.
8. Subtract LY-District-2-Total from District-2-Year-Total,
divide remainder by LY-District-2-Total,
then multiply by 100 to equal District-Totals-Line percent increase.
9. Move District-Totals-Line to the output area Printline.
10. After advancing 2 lines, write the output record Printline.
420-PREPARE-DIST-2-REPORT-LINE
MOVE "CENTRAL" TO DISTRICT-TOTALS-LINE
MOVE DIST-2-ACCUMULATORS TO DISTRICT-TOTALS-LINE
quarter 1
quarter 2
quarter 3
quarter 4
year total
MOVE LY-DIST-2-TTL TO DISTRICT-TOTALS-LINE
COMPUTE PERCENT INCREASE
WRITE DISTRICT-TOTALS-LINE
RETURN

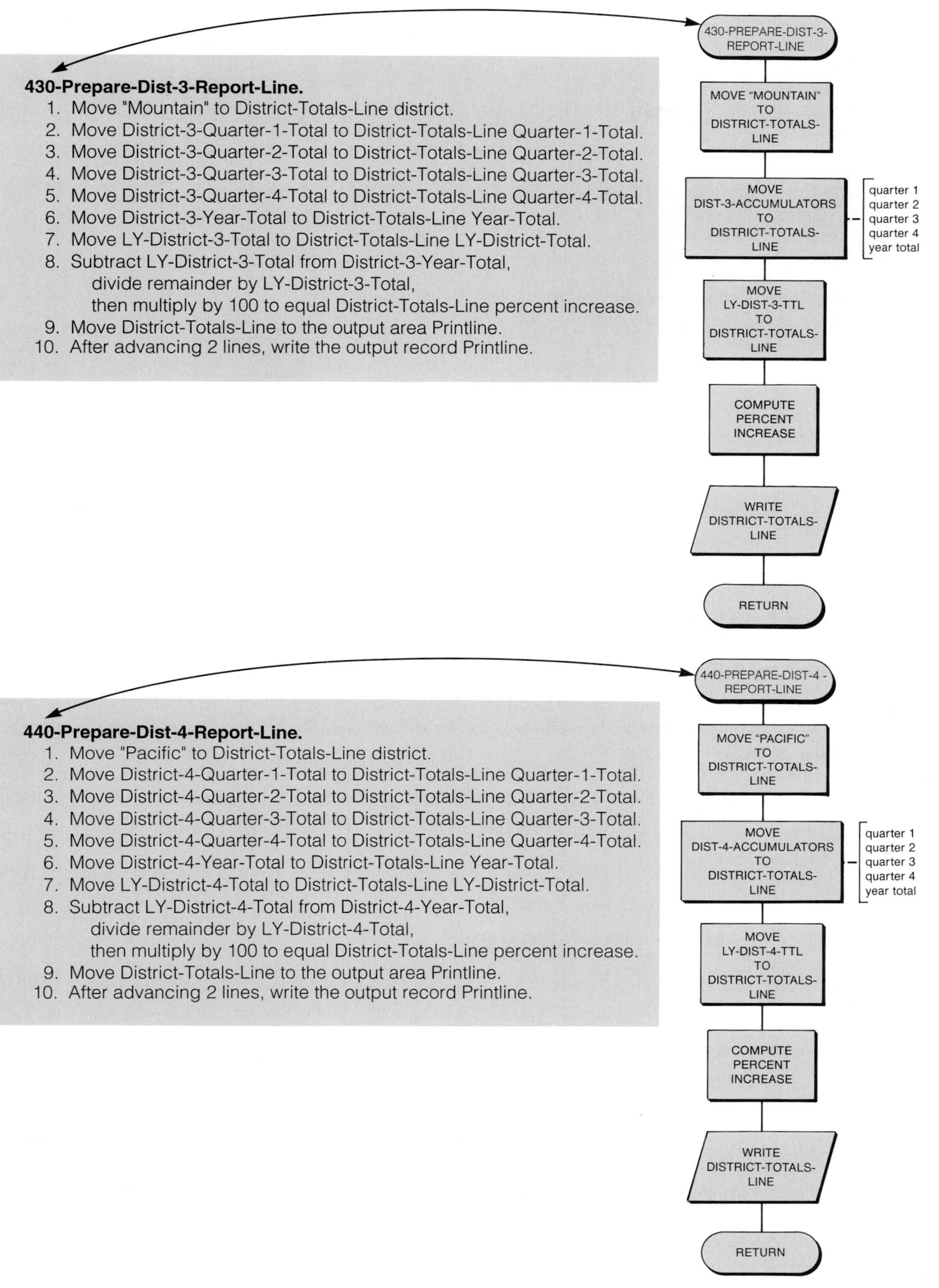

430-Prepare-Dist-3-Report-Line.

1. Move "Mountain" to District-Totals-Line district.
2. Move District-3-Quarter-1-Total to District-Totals-Line Quarter-1-Total.
3. Move District-3-Quarter-2-Total to District-Totals-Line Quarter-2-Total.
4. Move District-3-Quarter-3-Total to District-Totals-Line Quarter-3-Total.
5. Move District-3-Quarter-4-Total to District-Totals-Line Quarter-4-Total.
6. Move District-3-Year-Total to District-Totals-Line Year-Total.
7. Move LY-District-3-Total to District-Totals-Line LY-District-Total.
8. Subtract LY-District-3-Total from District-3-Year-Total,
   divide remainder by LY-District-3-Total,
   then multiply by 100 to equal District-Totals-Line percent increase.
9. Move District-Totals-Line to the output area Printline.
10. After advancing 2 lines, write the output record Printline.

440-Prepare-Dist-4-Report-Line.

1. Move "Pacific" to District-Totals-Line district.
2. Move District-4-Quarter-1-Total to District-Totals-Line Quarter-1-Total.
3. Move District-4-Quarter-2-Total to District-Totals-Line Quarter-2-Total.
4. Move District-4-Quarter-3-Total to District-Totals-Line Quarter-3-Total.
5. Move District-4-Quarter-4-Total to District-Totals-Line Quarter-4-Total.
6. Move District-4-Year-Total to District-Totals-Line Year-Total.
7. Move LY-District-4-Total to District-Totals-Line LY-District-Total.
8. Subtract LY-District-4-Total from District-4-Year-Total,
   divide remainder by LY-District-4-Total,
   then multiply by 100 to equal District-Totals-Line percent increase.
9. Move District-Totals-Line to the output area Printline.
10. After advancing 2 lines, write the output record Printline.

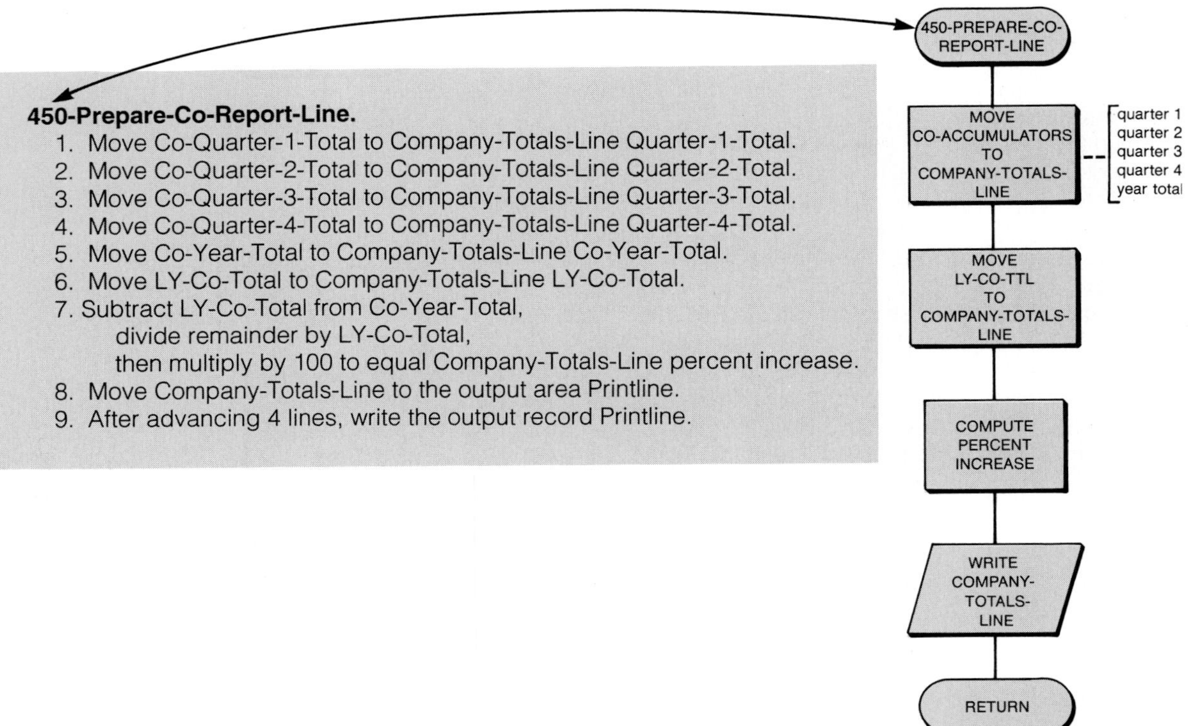

450-PREPARE-CO-REPORT-LINE
450-Prepare-Co-Report-Line.
1. Move Co-Quarter-1-Total to Company-Totals-Line Quarter-1-Total.
2. Move Co-Quarter-2-Total to Company-Totals-Line Quarter-2-Total.
3. Move Co-Quarter-3-Total to Company-Totals-Line Quarter-3-Total.
4. Move Co-Quarter-4-Total to Company-Totals-Line Quarter-4-Total.
5. Move Co-Year-Total to Company-Totals-Line Co-Year-Total.
6. Move LY-Co-Total to Company-Totals-Line LY-Co-Total.
7. Subtract LY-Co-Total from Co-Year-Total,
divide remainder by LY-Co-Total,
then multiply by 100 to equal Company-Totals-Line percent increase.
8. Move Company-Totals-Line to the output area Printline.
9. After advancing 4 lines, write the output record Printline.
MOVE CO-ACCUMULATORS TO COMPANY-TOTALS-LINE
quarter 1
quarter 2
quarter 3
quarter 4
year total
MOVE LY-CO-TTL TO COMPANY-TOTALS-LINE
COMPUTE PERCENT INCREASE
WRITE COMPANY-TOTALS-LINE
RETURN

■ Design Implementation Phase

Steps 3 and 4

In this program, no new entries are needed in the first two divisions. In the FILE SECTION of the DATA DIVISION, we must code record descriptions for the two different kinds of records that exist in the input file. That is, the FD paragraph for the input file is followed by two 01 paragraphs, one for the record LY-SALES-TOTALS-RECORD and one for the record SALESPERSON-RECORD, as shown in the following example. Since the two records do not contain the same number of characters, we decided to specify the minimum and maximum size of the records in the RECORD CONTAINS clause.

```
FD   SALES-FILE
     RECORD CONTAINS 54 TO 66 CHARACTERS.

01   LY-SALES-TOTALS-RECORD.
     05 I-YR-OF-RECORD     PIC 9999.
     05 I-LY-DIST-1-TTL    PIC 9(8)V99.
     05 I-LY-DIST-2-TTL    PIC 9(8)V99.
     05 I-LY-DIST-3-TTL    PIC 9(8)V99.
     05 I-LY-DIST-4-TTL    PIC 9(8)V99.
     05 I-LY-CO-TTL        PIC 9(8)V99.

01   SALESPERSON-RECORD.
     05 I-DIST-CODE.       PIC 9.
     05 I-NAME             PIC X(25).
     05 I-QTR-SALES.
        10 I-QTR-1         PIC 9(6)V99.
        10 I-QTR-2         PIC 9(6)V99.
        10 I-QTR-3         PIC 9(6)V99.
        10 I-QTR-4         PIC 9(6)V99.
     05 I-YR-TTL           PIC 9(6)V99.
```

In the WORKING-STORAGE SECTION, we must set aside a record area in which the contents of the input record LY-SALES-TOTALS-RECORD will be stored. We name that storage area LY-SALES-TOTALS. As noted earlier, we must also set up five accumulators for each of the four districts and for the company. We will group them all under the name SALES-ACCUMULATORS and specify the USAGE of the group as COMP. By doing this, we can initialize the 25 accumulators to zero simply by initializing the group.

The only other entries needed in this section are the descriptions of all the different report lines prepared on the printer spacing chart of Figure 7.2.

The coding of the WORKING-STORAGE SECTION is shown below. (The two 88-level entries attached to WS-MORE-RECORDS will be explained shortly.)

```
WORKING-STORAGE SECTION.

01  PROGRAM-CONTROLS.
    05 WS-MORE-RECORDS       PIC XXX.
        88 MORE-RECORDS      VALUE "YES".
        88 NO-MORE-RECORDS   VALUE "NO ".
    05 WS-REPORT-DATE        PIC X(6).

01  LY-SALES-TOTALS.
    05 WS-YR-OF-RECORD       PIC 9999.
    05 WS-LY-DIST-1-TTL      PIC S9(8)V99.
    05 WS-LY-DIST-2-TTL      PIC S9(8)V99.
    05 WS-LY-DIST-3-TTL      PIC S9(8)V99.
    05 WS-LY-DIST-4-TTL      PIC S9(8)V99.
    05 WS-LY-CO-TTL          PIC S9(8)V99.

01  SALES-ACCUMULATORS           COMP.
    05 WS-DIST-1-TTLS.
        10 WS-DIST-1-QTR-1-TTL   PIC S9(7)V99.
        10 WS-DIST-1-QTR-2-TTL   PIC S9(7)V99.
        10 WS-DIST-1-QTR-3-TTL   PIC S9(7)V99.
        10 WS-DIST-1-QTR-4-TTL   PIC S9(7)V99.
        10 WS-DIST-1-YR-TTL      PIC S9(8)V99.
    05 WS-DIST-2-TTLS.
        10 WS-DIST-2-QTR-1-TTL   PIC S9(7)V99.
        10 WS-DIST-2-QTR-2-TTL   PIC S9(7)V99.
        10 WS-DIST-2-QTR-3-TTL   PIC S9(7)V99.
        10 WS-DIST-2-QTR-4-TTL   PIC S9(7)V99.
        10 WS-DIST-2-YR-TTL      PIC S9(8)V99.
    05 WS-DIST-3-TTLS.
        10 WS-DIST-3-QTR-1-TTL   PIC S9(7)V99.
        10 WS-DIST-3-QTR-2-TTL   PIC S9(7)V99.
        10 WS-DIST-3-QTR-3-TTL   PIC S9(7)V99.
        10 WS-DIST-3-QTR-4-TTL   PIC S9(7)V99.
        10 WS-DIST-3-YR-TTL      PIC S9(8)V99.
    05 WS-DIST-4-TTLS.
        10 WS-DIST-4-QTR-1-TTL   PIC S9(7)V99.
        10 WS-DIST-4-QTR-2-TTL   PIC S9(7)V99.
        10 WS-DIST-4-QTR-3-TTL   PIC S9(7)V99.
        10 WS-DIST-4-QTR-4-TTL   PIC S9(7)V99.
        10 WS-DIST-4-YR-TTL      PIC S9(8)V99.
    05 WS-CO-TTLS.
        10 WS-CO-QTR-1-TTL       PIC S9(7)V99.
        10 WS-CO-QTR-2-TTL       PIC S9(7)V99.
        10 WS-CO-QTR-3-TTL       PIC S9(7)V99.
        10 WS-CO-QTR-4-TTL       PIC S9(7)V99.
        10 WS-CO-YR-TTL          PIC S9(8)V99.

01  REPORT-LINES.

    05 TOP-LINE.
        10 PIC X(6)          VALUE SPACES.
        10 PIC X(14)         VALUE "REPORT DATE:  ".
        10 O-REPORT-DATE     PIC XX/XX/XX.
        10 PIC X(105)        VALUE SPACES.

    05 COMPANY-NAME.
        10 PIC X(58)         VALUE SPACES.
        10 PIC X(17)         VALUE "JOCELYN ORIGINALS".
        10 PIC X(58)         VALUE SPACES.

    05 REPORT-NAME.
        10 PIC X(52)         VALUE SPACES.
        10 PIC X(28)         VALUE "ANNUAL DISTRICT SALES REPORT".
        10 PIC X(53)         VALUE SPACES.

    05 YEAR-LINE.
        10 PIC X(58)         VALUE SPACES.
        10 PIC X(12)         VALUE "FISCAL YEAR ".
        10 O-FISCAL-YEAR     PIC 9999.
        10 PIC X(59)         VALUE SPACES.

    05 HEADINGS-1.
        10 PIC X(94)         VALUE SPACES.
        10 PIC X(5)          VALUE "TOTAL".
        10 PIC X(11)         VALUE SPACES.
        10 PIC X(5)          VALUE "TOTAL".
        10 PIC X(7)          VALUE SPACES.
```

```
        10 PIC X(7)          VALUE "PERCENT".
        10 PIC XXXX          VALUE SPACES.

     05 HEADINGS-2.
        10 PIC X(6)          VALUE SPACES.
        10 PIC X(8)          VALUE "DISTRICT".
        10 PIC X(6)          VALUE SPACES.
        10 PIC X(13)         VALUE "FIRST QUARTER".
        10 PIC XXXX          VALUE SPACES.
        10 PIC X(14)         VALUE "SECOND QUARTER".
        10 PIC XXXX          VALUE SPACES.
        10 PIC X(13)         VALUE "THIRD QUARTER".
        10 PIC XXXX          VALUE SPACES.
        10 PIC X(14)         VALUE "FOURTH QUARTER".
        10 PIC X(6)          VALUE SPACES.
        10 PIC X(9)          VALUE "THIS YEAR".
        10 PIC X(7)          VALUE SPACES.
        10 PIC X(9)          VALUE "LAST YEAR".
        10 PIC X(5)          VALUE SPACES.
        10 PIC X(8)          VALUE "INCREASE".
        10 PIC XXX           VALUE SPACES.

     05 DISTRICT-TOTALS-LINE.
        10                       PIC X(6).
        10 O-DISTRICT            PIC X(8).
        10                       PIC X(6).
        10 O-DIST-QTR-1-TTL      PIC $Z,ZZZ,ZZ9.99-.
        10                       PIC XXX.
        10 O-DIST-QTR-2-TTL      PIC $Z,ZZZ,ZZ9.99-.
        10                       PIC XXXX.
        10 O-DIST-QTR-3-TTL      PIC $Z,ZZZ,ZZ9.99-.
        10                       PIC XXX.
        10 O-DIST-QTR-4-TTL      PIC $Z,ZZZ,ZZ9.99-.
        10                       PIC XXX.
        10 O-DIST-YR-TTL         PIC $ZZ,ZZZ,ZZ9.99-.
        10                       PIC X.
        10 O-LY-DIST-TTL         PIC $ZZ,ZZZ,ZZ9.99-.
        10                       PIC XXX.
        10 O-PERCENT-INCREASE PIC ZZ9.99-.
        10                       PIC XXX.

     05 COMPANY-TOTALS-LINE.
        10                     PIC XX     VALUE SPACES.
        10                     PIC X(17) VALUE "COMPANY TOTALS:  ".
        10 O-CO-QTR-1-TTL     PIC $ZZ,ZZZ,ZZ9.99-.
        10                     PIC XX     VALUE SPACES.
        10 O-CO-QTR-2-TTL     PIC $ZZ,ZZZ,ZZ9.99-.
        10                     PIC XXX    VALUE SPACES.
        10 O-CO-QTR-3-TTL     PIC $ZZ,ZZZ,ZZ9.99-.
        10                     PIC XX     VALUE SPACES.
        10 O-CO-QTR-4-TTL     PIC $ZZ,ZZZ,ZZ9.99-.
        10                     PIC XXX    VALUE SPACES.
        10 O-CO-YR-TTL        PIC $ZZ,ZZZ,ZZ9.99-.
        10                     PIC X      VALUE SPACES.
        10 O-LY-CO-TTL        PIC $ZZ,ZZZ,ZZ9.99-.
        10                     PIC XXX    VALUE SPACES.
        10 O-PERCENT-CHANGE   PIC ZZ9.99+.
        10                     PIC XXX    VALUE SPACES.

     05 END-LINE.
        10 PIC X(55)   VALUE SPACES.
        10 PIC X(23)   VALUE "***   END OF REPORT   ***".
        10 PIC X(55)   VALUE SPACES.
```

PROCEDURE DIVISION Considerations

Before doing any more coding, we will examine additional COBOL specifications that are relevant to some of the entries needed in the PROCEDURE DIVISION.

The Conditional Statement

The tests shown in Figure 7.12 and Figure 7.13 must be coded using the IF-ELSE conditional statement. Its general format, originally presented in Chapter 4, is shown again in Figure 7.19.

In this format, the word *condition* corresponds to the test indicated in the decision box (in Figure 7.12 or 7.13), the option *statement-1,* if used, corresponds to the processing specified along the YES (or TRUE) branch, and the option *statement-2,* if used, corresponds to the processing specified along the NO (or FALSE) branch of the selection structure. The word THEN, a new feature in COBOL '85, is always optional.

■ **Figure 7.19** IF-ELSE statement format

```
                  { [statement-1] . . . }    [ { ELSE [statement-2] . . . [END-IF] } ]
IF condition THEN {                     }    [ { ELSE NEXT SENTENCE              } ]
                  { NEXT SENTENCE       }    [ { END-IF                          } ]
```

■ **Figure 7.20** Logic of the simple IF-ELSE statement

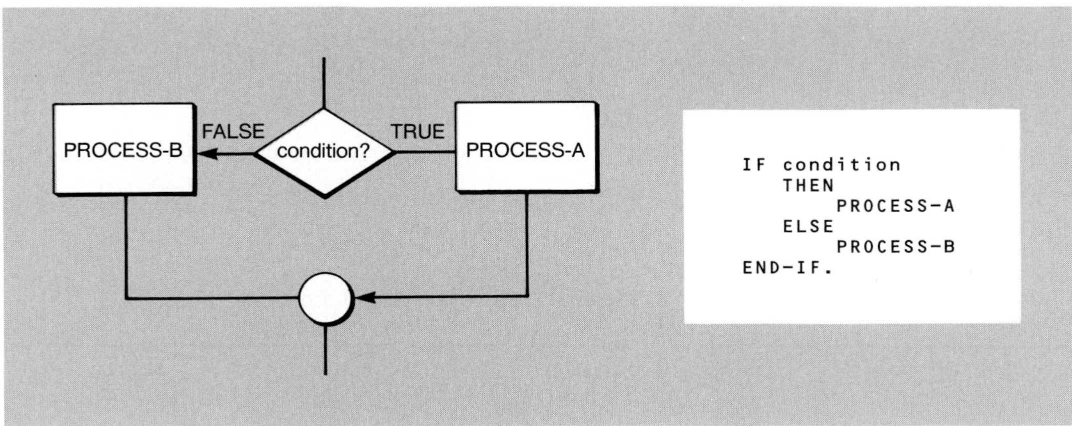

The IF-ELSE format allows for a number of variations, as illustrated in the following examples.

In Figure 7.20, PROCESS-A is executed if the condition is true; otherwise, PROCESS-B is executed. In either case, after PROCESS-A or PROCESS-B is executed, control passes to the next sentence. The next sentence is the one that follows the period or the scope terminator END-IF. Note that if a period is used to terminate the IF-ELSE sentence, it is placed after PROCESS-B.

In other words, if the condition is satisfied, PROCESS-A is executed, and then control skips around the ELSE clause and passes to the next sentence. If the condition is not satisfied, control skips PROCESS-A, passes to the ELSE clause, and executes PROCESS-B, so that when the period or the END-IF scope terminator is encountered, control is then passed on to the next sentence.

The tests in Figure 7.13 are of this form. However, in the first three tests, PROCESS-B is itself a test.

In Figure 7.21, PROCESS-A is executed if the condition is satisfied; otherwise, control passes to the next sentence. Note that the clause "ELSE NEXT SENTENCE" is optional. If it is not used, the statement may be terminated by placing a period immediately after PROCESS-A, or it may be terminated by placing the END-IF after PROCESS-A.

Note: A period must not follow PROCESS-A if the ELSE clause is coded.

The tests in Figure 7.12 are of the form shown in Figure 7.21. If the district code corresponds to the one being tested, then additions will be performed; otherwise, control passes immediately to the next test. For instance, the coding could be the following:

```
IF I-DIST-CODE = 1
    ADD I-QTR-1 TO WS-DIST-1-QTR-1-TTL
    ADD I-QTR-2 TO WS-DIST-1-QTR-2-TTL
    ADD ...
ELSE
    NEXT SENTENCE.
```

or it could be the following:

```
IF I-DIST-CODE = 1
    ADD I-QTR-1 TO WS-DIST-1-QTR-1-TTL
    ADD I-QTR-2 TO WS-DIST-1-QTR-2-TTL
    ADD ...
END-IF.
```

■ **Figure 7.21** Variation of the simple IF-ELSE statement—form 1

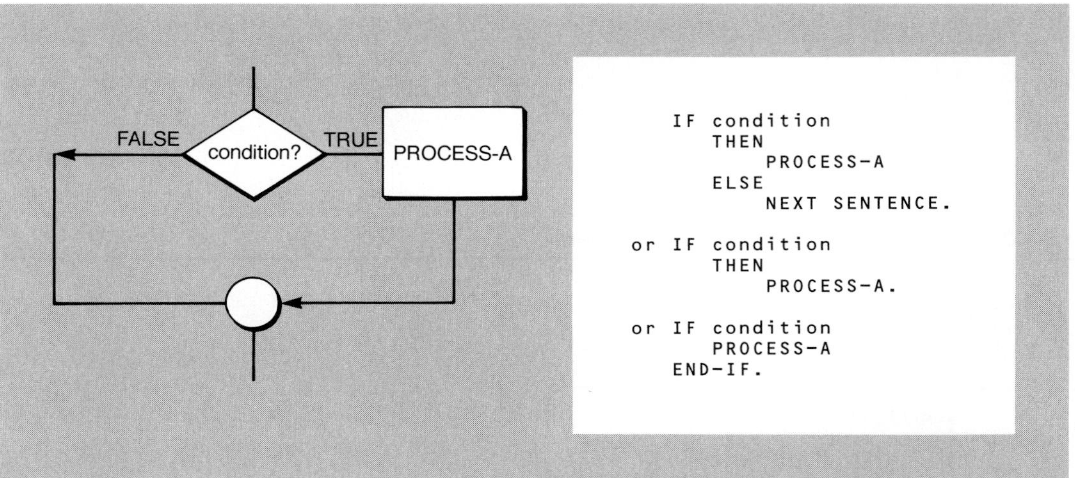

■ **Figure 7.22** Variation of the simple IF-ELSE statement—form 2

■ **Figure 7.23** Variation of the simple IF-ELSE statement—example 1

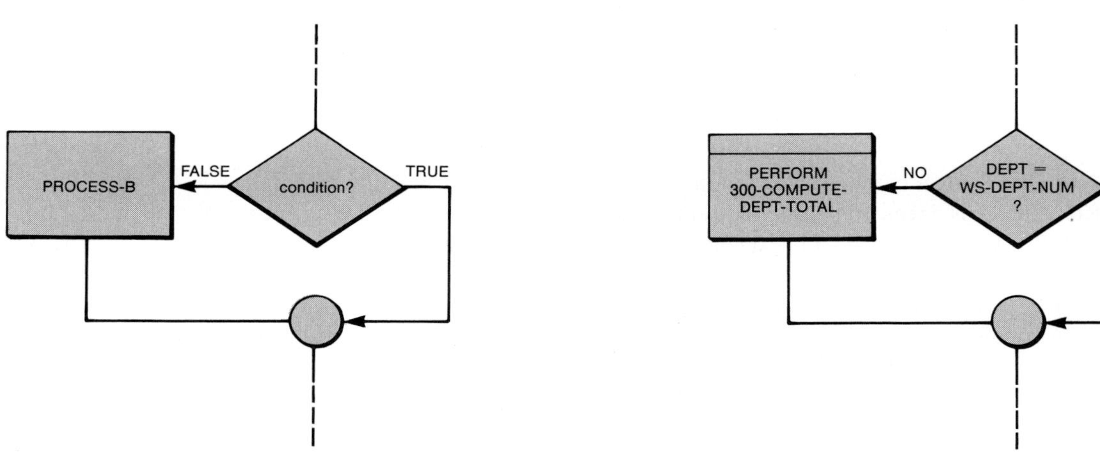

or it could simply be the following:

```
IF I-DIST-CODE = 1
    ADD I-QTR-1 TO WS-DIST-1-QTR-1-TTL
    ADD I-QTR-2 TO WS-DIST-1-QTR-2-TTL
    ADD ....
```

In Figure 7.22, if the condition is satisfied, no action is taken and control passes directly to the next sentence; otherwise, PROCESS-B is executed, after which control passes to the next sentence.

Consider Figure 7.23.

The coding for this flowchart segment is the following:

```
IF DEPT = WS-DEPT-NUM
    NEXT SENTENCE
ELSE
    PERFORM 300-COMPUTE-DEPT-TOTAL.
```

■ **Figure 7.24** Variation of the simple IF-ELSE statement—example 2

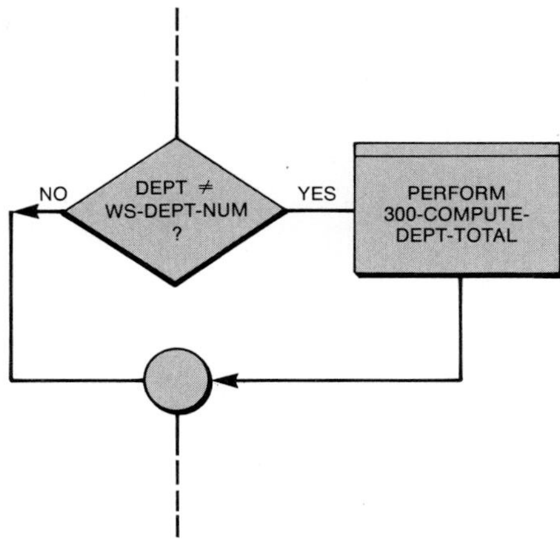

The logic shown in Figure 7.24 may be coded as follows:

```
IF DEPT NOT = WS-DEPT-NUM
    PERFORM 300-COMPUTE-DEPT-TOTAL
ELSE
    NEXT SENTENCE.
```

or, more simply, as follows:

```
IF DEPT NOT = WS-DEPT-NUM
    PERFORM 300-COMPUTE-DEPT-TOTAL
END-IF.
```

Do you see that the logic of Figure 7.23 and that of Figure 7.24 produce the same result? That is, regardless of the form being used, the statement

```
PERFORM 300-COMPUTE-DEPT-TOTAL
```

will be executed only if the value of DEPT is not the same as the value of WS-DEPT-NUM.

Rules Governing the Use of the Simple IF-ELSE Statement

1. The condition being tested may take the form of a relational test, a class test, a sign test, or a condition-name test.
2. If the tested condition is true, then statement-1 is executed, the ELSE clause is skipped, and control then passes to the next sentence.
3. If the tested condition is false and the ELSE clause is not used, control passes immediately to the next sentence.
4. If the tested condition is false and the ELSE clause is used, statement-2 is executed, and control then passes to the next sentence.
5. Statement-1 and statement-2 may each contain more than one instruction. An IF statement may be contained in either statement-1 or statement-2 or both.
6. The entry ELSE NEXT SENTENCE is optional if it is to be followed by a period.
7. The entries NEXT SENTENCE and END-IF cannot both be used in the same statement.
8. The IF-ELSE statement can be terminated either by a period or by the END-IF scope terminator. If an IF statement is nested within an IF statement, it can also be terminated by the ELSE associated with the preceding IF.
9. The word THEN is always optional. It is a new feature in COBOL '85.
10. For the sake of coding clarity, the word ELSE should be vertically aligned with the word THEN, if it is used, or, otherwise, with the word IF.

The CONTINUE Statement

The CONTINUE statement, whose format is simply CONTINUE, can be used to indicate that no executable statement is present. Whenever it is encountered, it implicitly transfers control to the next executable statement in line. The CONTINUE statement can be used whenever a conditional or imperative statement can be used.

The CONTINUE statement is introduced here because some programmers use it to replace NEXT SENTENCE in an IF-ELSE statement. For instance, the statement

```
IF DEPT = WS-DEPT-NUM
   NEXT SENTENCE
ELSE
   PERFORM 300-COMPUTE-DEPT-TOTAL.
```

can be replaced by

```
IF DEPT = WS-DEPT-NUM
   CONTINUE
ELSE
   PERFORM 300-COMPUTE-DEPT-TOTAL
END-IF.
```

When CONTINUE is encountered, it transfers control to the first executable statement beyond the scope terminator END-IF. Note that CONTINUE is **not** part of the IF-ELSE format. It is simply being used to replace the imperative statement NEXT SENTENCE.

As a second example, examine the following READ statement:

```
READ SALES-FILE RECORD
   AT END
       MOVE "NO " TO WS-MORE-RECORDS
   NOT AT END
       CONTINUE
END-READ.
```

The alternative paths are explicitly specified: If the AT END condition exists, the MOVE statement is executed, and if the AT END condition does not exist, the CONTINUE statement transfers control to the first executable statement beyond the scope terminator END-READ. Realize that except for clearer self-documentation, the above READ statement produces the same result as the familiar form:

```
READ SALES-FILE RECORD
   AT END
       MOVE "NO " TO WS-MORE-RECORDS.
```

The Relational Test

Up to this point, every time the IF-ELSE conditional statement has been used in a program, the condition being tested has been a relational condition. Specifically, the format of a relational condition test is that shown in Figure 7.25.

The relational operator can be any one of those listed in Figure 7.26, and the relational operands can be literals (numeric or nonnumeric), identifiers (data names), and/or arithmetic expressions.

Examples of conditional statements using a relational test are listed below:

1.
```
IF WS-LINE-CTR IS EQUAL TO 20
    PERFORM 400-WRITE-PAGE-SUMMARY
END-IF.
```

In the relational test WS-LINE-CTR IS EQUAL TO 20, the relational operator is IS EQUAL TO, the relational operands are WS-LINE-CTR and 20, WS-LINE-CTR is an identifier, and 20 is a numeric literal.

The test holds (or the condition is true) provided the value of WS-LINE-CTR is 20; otherwise, the test fails (or the tested condition is false).

■ **Figure 7.25** Relational condition format

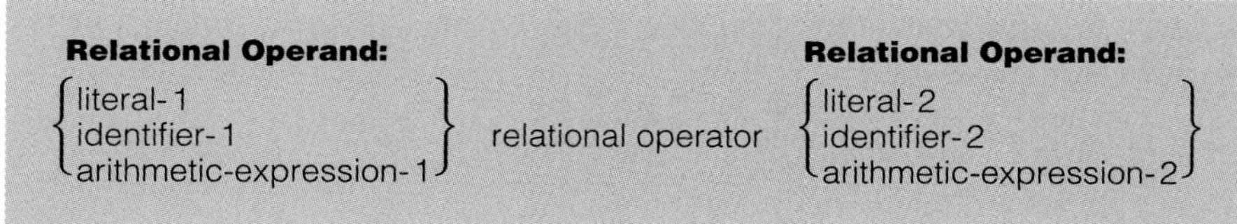

■ **Figure 7.26** COBOL relational operators

Relational Operators

IS [NOT] LESS THAN
IS [NOT] <
IS [NOT] EQUAL TO
IS [NOT =
IS [NOT] GREATER THAN
IS [NOT] >
*IS GREATER THAN OR EQUAL TO
*IS >=
*IS LESS THAN OR EQUAL TO
*IS <=
*New in COBOL '85

2.
```
IF NO-OF-UNITS > 100
     PERFORM 300-COMPUTE-DISCOUNT
ELSE
     CONTINUE.
```
In this case, the relational test is NO-OF-UNITS > 100. The relational operator is > (greater than), NO-OF-UNITS is an identifier, and 100 is a numeric constant (or literal).

The condition being tested is true provided the value of NO-OF-UNITS is greater than 100.

3.
```
IF TOTAL-HRS - REG-HRS >= .25 * DEPT-OVERTIME-HRS
     PERFORM 200-RESCHEDULE-OT-WORK.
```
In this case, the relational operator is >= (greater than or equal to), the operands are two arithmetic expressions, namely TOTAL-HRS – REG-HRS and .25 * DEPT-OVERTIME-HRS. The results of the computations will be compared to determine if the stated condition is satisfied or not satisfied.

4. In Figure 7.12, it should be clear that each decision box could be coded using a relational test, as follows:

```
IF I-DIST-CODE = 1
     ADD I-QTR-1 TO WS-DIST-1-QTR-1-TTL
     ADD I-QTR-2 TO WS-DIST-1-QTR-2-TTL
     ADD...
END-IF.
IF I-DIST-CODE = 2
     ADD I-QTR-1 TO WS-DIST-2-QTR-1-TTL
     ADD I-QTR-2 TO WS-DIST-2-QTR-2-TTL
     ADD ...
END-IF.
IF I-DIST-CODE = 3
     ADD I-QTR-1 TO WS-DIST-3-QTR-1-TTL
     ADD I-QTR-2 TO WS-DIST-3-QTR-2-TTL
     ADD ...
END-IF.
IF I-DIST-CODE = 4
     ADD I-QTR-1 TO WS-DIST-4-QTR-1-TTL
     ADD I-QTR-2 TO WS-DIST-4-QTR-2-TTL
     ADD ...
END-IF.
```

Nonnumeric Relational Operands

Whenever the relational operands have numeric values, it is quite simple even for the casual observer to determine if the condition being tested is true or false, since the relationship between two given numbers is common knowledge. However, if two relational operands do not have numeric values, their relationship is not at all clear.

To determine the relationship between two operands that are not both numeric, the programmer must be aware of the *collating sequence* (or ordering process) in use at the computer site. Collating sequences may vary from one computer installation to another, and, in fact, there may be more than one collating sequence available at any one time. If a particular collating sequence is not specified in a COBOL program, the operating system will, by default, use its "native" sequence. Procedures to define or select a collating sequence, other than the native sequence, are beyond the scope of this material.

Essentially, a collating sequence consists of numeric codes (in the range from 001 to 256) assigned to each character of the available character set. The two most common collating sequences are the EBCDIC and the ASCII sequences mentioned earlier. In the EBCDIC sequence, numeric codes are assigned in ascending order first to the special characters, then to the letters of the alphabet (from lowercase *a* to uppercase *Z*), and then to the digits 0 through 9. In the ASCII sequence, the numeric codes are assigned in ascending order to special characters, then to the digits 0 through 9, and finally to the letters of the alphabet (from uppercase *A* to lowercase *z*). These sequences can be summarized as shown below. (See the appendices for the listings of these collating sequences.)

COLLATING SEQUENCE

	ASCII	**EBCDIC**
Low	Blank space	Blank space
↓	Special characters	Special characters
	Digits (0–9)	Letters (a to Z)
High	Letters (A to z)	Digits (0–9)

Regardless of the particular collating sequence implemented on a computer, the comparison of operands that are not both numeric takes place on a character-by-character basis from the highest-order position (leftmost) to the lowest-order position (rightmost). Specifically, the first character of the first operand is compared with the first character of the second operand. If they have the same value (numeric code), then the second character of the first operand will be compared with the second character of the second operand. If these two corresponding characters have the same value, then the comparison process continues. When the first pair of unequal characters is encountered, the determination is made at that point that the operands are unequal, and the comparing process terminates.

For instance, in comparing THESE and THOSE, the determination will be made that THESE "is less than" THOSE when the third characters of each word are compared, since E occurs earlier in the alphabet than O. See below.

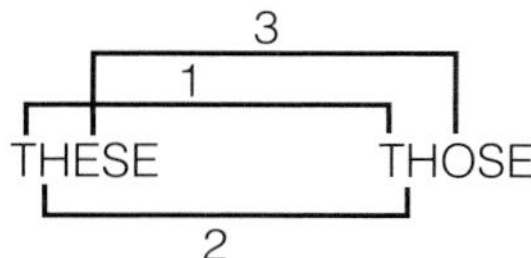

				Result
Step 1:	T	=	T	(Characters match; comparison continues with next pair)
Step 2:	H	=	H	(Characters match; comparison continues with next pair)
Step 3:	E	≠	0	(Characters do not match; comparison stops; 1st operand [THESE] has "smaller value" than 2nd operand [THOSE])

Similarly, if the names RICHARDS and RICHARDSON are compared, the first eight pairs of corresponding characters match. Since the second name has more characters than the first name, spaces are padded to the right of the shorter name to make the names equal in size. The name RICHARDSON is determined to have a larger value than the name RICHARDS, since the letter O has a higher numeric code than the corresponding "space" character.

Additional examples are shown below. Note that the data items A and B are alphanumeric.

A PIC X(8)	**B PIC X(10)**	**Result**
RICHARDS	BEDROSIAN	A > B
JOHN I	JOHN II	A < B
JUN5	JUNE 5	A< B in ASCII, A > B in EBCDIC
8	2542	A > B (Note PIC clause!)
8	EIGHT	A < B in ASCII, A > B in EBCDIC

Note the following:

1. If the relational operator is "=", the condition is satisfied provided all corresponding pairs of characters in the two operands are exactly the **same.** If one pair is mismatched, or if one operand is longer than the other, the condition fails.

2. If the relational operator is ">", the condition is satisfied provided that in the first pair of mismatched characters, the character from the first operand has a **greater value** than the character from the second operand; otherwise, the condition fails.
3. If the relational operator is "<", the condition is satisfied provided that in the first pair of mismatched characters, the character from the first operand has a **smaller value** than the character from the second operand; otherwise, the condition fails.

These few comments should be sufficient to indicate that it is possible to sort a list of names alphabetically by using the relational operator "IS LESS THAN."

Rules Governing the Use of the Relational Test

1. If the two operands are numeric (numeric literals, identifiers with numeric PICTUREs, arithmetic expressions), then their relationship is based strictly on their corresponding numeric values.
2. The two operands cannot both be literals.
3. If the operands are not both numeric, then their relationship is determined by a character-by-character comparison from highest- to lowest-order positions using the collating sequence implemented on the computer.
   a. They are equal if and only if they contain exactly the same characters in the same sequence.
   b. They are unequal if their sizes are different or if at least one pair of corresponding characters do not match.

The Condition-Name Test

In the preceding section, the relational tests used to code the logic of Figure 7.12 are meaningful to a person reading the program only if that person is aware of the numeric code assigned to each district. For instance, in the conditional statement

```
IF I-DIST-CODE = 3 ...
```

which district is assigned the numeric code 3?

Much clearer self-documentation can be provided in such instances by using condition-names. A *condition-name* is simply a user-defined name assigned to a particular value that a data name or identifier may have.

In the relational test I-DIST-CODE = 3, the data name is I-DIST-CODE. The various values it can have are 1, 2, 3, or 4. A condition-name can be assigned to each of the four values. Though any name could be constructed by the programmer, the obvious ones are the following:

EASTERN to correspond to the value 1

CENTRAL to correspond to the value 2

MOUNTAIN to correspond to the value 3

PACIFIC to correspond to the value 4

These codes provide the best documentation possible.

To assign these names as condition-names corresponding to the possible values of the identifier I-DIST-CODE, four *level-88* entries are made immediately following the description of the data name I-DIST-CODE, as shown in the following example. Recall that I-DIST-CODE is a field of the input record SALESPERSON-RECORD.

```
01   SALESPERSON-RECORD.
     05 I-DIST-CODE          PIC 9.
         88 EASTERN          VALUE 1.
         88 CENTRAL          VALUE 2.
         88 MOUNTAIN         VALUE 3.
         88 PACIFIC          VALUE 4.
     05 I-NAME               PIC X(25).
     .
     .
     .
```

Now, condition-name tests can be used instead of relational tests to code the decision boxes of Figure 7.12. Specifically, the statement

```
IF I-DIST-CODE = 1
    ADD I-QTR-1 TO WS-DIST-1-QTR-1-TTL ...
```

■ **Figure 7.27** 88-level entry format (definition of a condition-name)

$$\text{88 condition-name} \left\{ \begin{array}{l} \underline{\text{VALUE}}\ \text{IS} \\ \underline{\text{VALUES}}\ \text{ARE} \end{array} \right\} \text{literal-1} \left[\left\{ \begin{array}{l} \underline{\text{THROUGH}} \\ \underline{\text{THRU}} \end{array} \right\} \text{literal-2} \right]$$

$$\left[\text{literal-3} \left[\left\{ \begin{array}{l} \underline{\text{THROUGH}} \\ \underline{\text{THRU}} \end{array} \right\} \text{literal-4} \right]\right] \ldots$$

can be replaced by

```
IF EASTERN
    ADD I-QTR-1 TO WS-DIST-1-QTR-1-TTL ...
```

since the condition-name EASTERN is true whenever I-DIST-CODE contains the value 1; the statement

```
IF I-DIST-CODE = 2
    ADD I-QTR-1 TO WS-DIST-2-QTR-1-TTL ...
```

can be replaced by

```
IF CENTRAL
    ADD I-QTR-1 TO WS-DIST-2-QTR-1-TTL ...
```

since the condition-name CENTRAL is true whenever I-DIST-CODE contains the value 2, and so on.

In evaluating a condition-name condition, the computer checks to see if the value that corresponds to the condition-name is the one stored in the data item to which the condition-name is attached. For instance, in IF CENTRAL, the computer checks to see which value corresponds to the condition-name CENTRAL. It determines that CENTRAL means 2. Then, it checks to see if the data item to which CENTRAL is attached, namely I-DIST-CODE, contains a 2 or not. If it does, the condition-name condition is satisfied, and the ADD instructions are executed; otherwise, the condition-name condition is not satisfied, and the ADD instructions are not executed.

The use of condition-name tests in these cases provides two important advantages: they reduce the amount of coding, and they increase the self-documentation of the program.

The general format of the definition of a condition-name is shown in Figure 7.27.

Rules Governing the Use of Condition-Names

1. The level number 88 specifies a condition-name. It is coded in area B.
2. Each condition-name must be preceded by level number 88.
3. A condition-name should be descriptive to provide documentation for the program.
4. The literal(s) in the VALUE clause must agree in size and class with the PICTURE specified for the data item (or identifier) to which the condition-name is attached.
5. The VALUE clause can specify a single value, multiple distinct values, or a range of values.
6. A condition-name is a name assigned to correspond to a specific value, or any one of a set of values, that may be contained in the data item to which the name is attached.
7. Level-88 entries must immediately follow the description of the data items to which they apply.
8. Condition-names can be assigned only to elementary items.
9. In any case where a relational test can be used to test a value of a data item, the condition-name corresponding to that value can be used to replace the relational test.
10. The format of a condition-name test is simply:

```
[NOT] condition-name
```

More Condition-Name Examples

Here are additional examples to illustrate the use of the condition-name test.

Example 1:

```
01  WS-MORE-RECORDS     PIC XXX.
    88 MORE-RECORDS     VALUE "YES".
    88 NO-MORE-RECORDS  VALUE "NO ".
```

In the conditional statement

```
IF WS-MORE-RECORDS = "YES"
    PERFORM 200-PROCESS-LOOP
```

the relational test WS-MORE-RECORDS = "YES" can be replaced by the condition-name MORE-RECORDS, as in

```
IF MORE-RECORDS
    PERFORM 200-PROCESS-LOOP
```

since the condition MORE-RECORDS is true whenever the value of WS-MORE-RECORDS is "YES".

In the statement

```
PERFORM 210-PROCESS-SALESPERSON-RECORD
    UNTIL WS-MORE-RECORDS = "NO "
```

the relational test WS-MORE-RECORDS = "NO " can be replaced by the condition-name NO-MORE-RECORDS, as in

```
PERFORM 210-PROCESS-SALESPERSON-RECORD
    UNTIL NO-MORE-RECORDS
```

since the condition NO-MORE-RECORDS is true whenever the value of WS-MORE-RECORDS is "NO ".

Example 2:

```
01  EMPLOYEE-RECORD.
    05 SOC-SEC-NO       PIC X(9).
    05 SEX              PIC 9.
        88 MALE         VALUE 1.
        88 FEMALE       VALUE 2.
    05 NAME             PIC X(25).
    05 MARITAL-STATUS   PIC 9.
        88 MARRIED      VALUE 1.
        88 SINGLE       VALUE 2.
        88 WIDOWED      VALUE 3.
        88 DIVORCED     VALUE 4.
    05 PAY-CODE         PIC 9.
        88 PAID-HRLY    VALUE 1.
        88 SALARIED     VALUE 2.
```

In the conditional statement

```
IF SEX IS EQUAL TO 1
    ADD 1 TO MALE-COUNT
```

the relational test SEX IS EQUAL TO 1 can be replaced by the condition-name MALE, as in

```
IF MALE
    ADD 1 TO MALE-COUNT
```

since the condition MALE is true whenever the value stored in the data item SEX is a 1.

The statement

```
IF MARITAL-STATUS IS EQUAL TO 3 ...
```

can be replaced by the statement

```
IF WIDOWED ....
```

The compound relational test in the statement

```
IF SEX IS EQUAL TO 2 AND MARITAL-STATUS IS EQUAL TO 2 ...
```

can be replaced by the compound condition-name test, as in

```
IF FEMALE AND SINGLE ....
```

The statement

```
IF MARITAL-STATUS IS NOT EQUAL TO 4 ...
```

can be replaced by the statement

```
IF NOT DIVORCED ....
```

Figure 7.28a Line counter logic and coding without condition-names

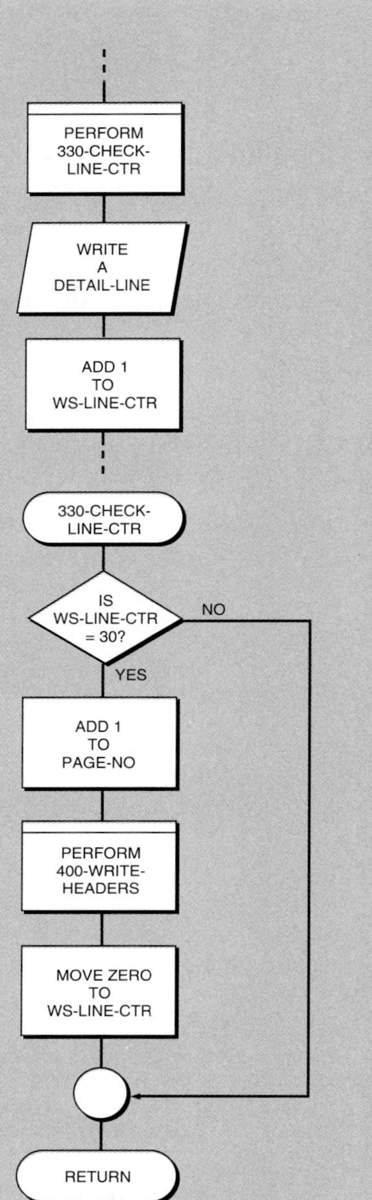


```
WORKING-STORAGE SECTION.
01 WS-LINE-CTR     PIC S99.

PROCEDURE DIVISION.
.
.
    PERFORM 330-CHECK-LINE-CTR.
    WRITE PRINTLINE FROM DETAIL-LINE
        AFTER ADVANCING 1 LINE.
    ADD 1 TO WS-LINE-CTR.
.
.
330-CHECK-LINE-CTR.
    IF WS-LINE-CTR = 30
        ADD 1 TO PAGE-NO
        PERFORM 400-WRITE-HEADERS
        MOVE 0 TO WS-LINE-CTR
    END-IF.
```

Figure 7.28b Line counter logic and coding with a condition-name

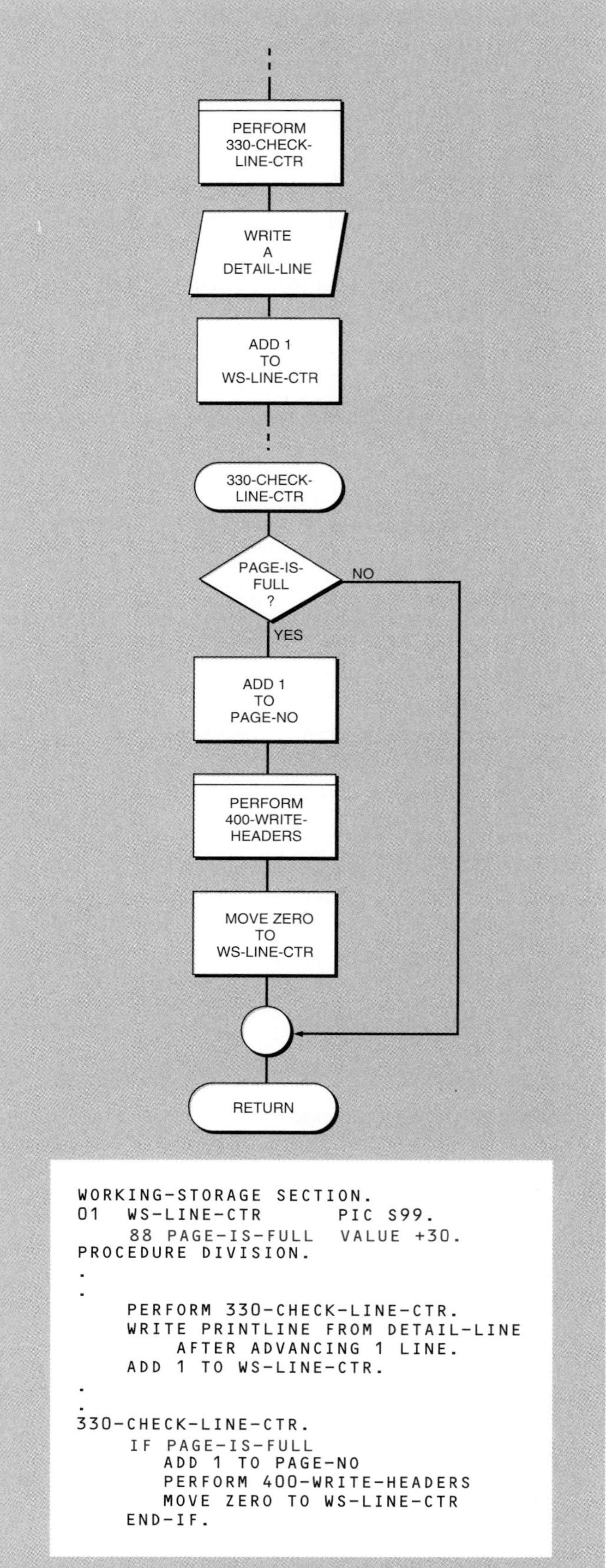


```
WORKING-STORAGE SECTION.
01  WS-LINE-CTR      PIC S99.
    88 PAGE-IS-FULL  VALUE +30.
PROCEDURE DIVISION.
.
.
    PERFORM 330-CHECK-LINE-CTR.
    WRITE PRINTLINE FROM DETAIL-LINE
        AFTER ADVANCING 1 LINE.
    ADD 1 TO WS-LINE-CTR.
.
.
330-CHECK-LINE-CTR.
    IF PAGE-IS-FULL
       ADD 1 TO PAGE-NO
       PERFORM 400-WRITE-HEADERS
       MOVE ZERO TO WS-LINE-CTR
    END-IF.
```

Note that in each case, the amount of coding is reduced and the item being tested is made much clearer by using descriptive condition-names.

Example 3:

Suppose the format of a printed report requires top-of-page information on each page and a maximum of 30 detail lines per page. A line counter should be set up in working storage, and its value should be increased by 1 every time a detail line is printed. When its value is 30, that is, after 30 detail lines are printed, appropriate top-of-page information should be printed at the top of the next page, the line counter should be reset to zero for this new page, and then normal record processing should continue. This logic and corresponding coding are shown in Figure 7.28a.

By attaching the condition-name PAGE-IS-FULL to WS-LINE-CTR, and defining it to represent the maximum number of lines allowed per page (30), the test WS-LINE-CTR = 30 can be expressed with the condition-name PAGE-IS-FULL as shown in Figue 7.28b.

Example 4:

Suppose the format of a printed report requires that the name of the company and the name of the report be printed only on the first page of the report, but that a page number line and the appropriate column headings be printed on each page. The flowchart module and coding in Figure 7.29 accomplish that objective.

Note that the condition-name FIRST-PAGE has been defined to correspond to the value 01 stored in the data item PAGE-NO. Therefore, the relational test PAGE-NO = 1 may be replaced by the condition-name FIRST-PAGE, as in

```
IF FIRST-PAGE
    WRITE PRINTLINE FROM COMPANY-NAME
        AFTER ADVANCING 2 LINES
    WRITE PRINTLINE FROM REPORT-NAME
        AFTER ADVANCING 3 LINES
ELSE
    CONTINUE.
```

■ **Figure 7.29** Logic testing value of PAGE-NO; allows use of condition-name

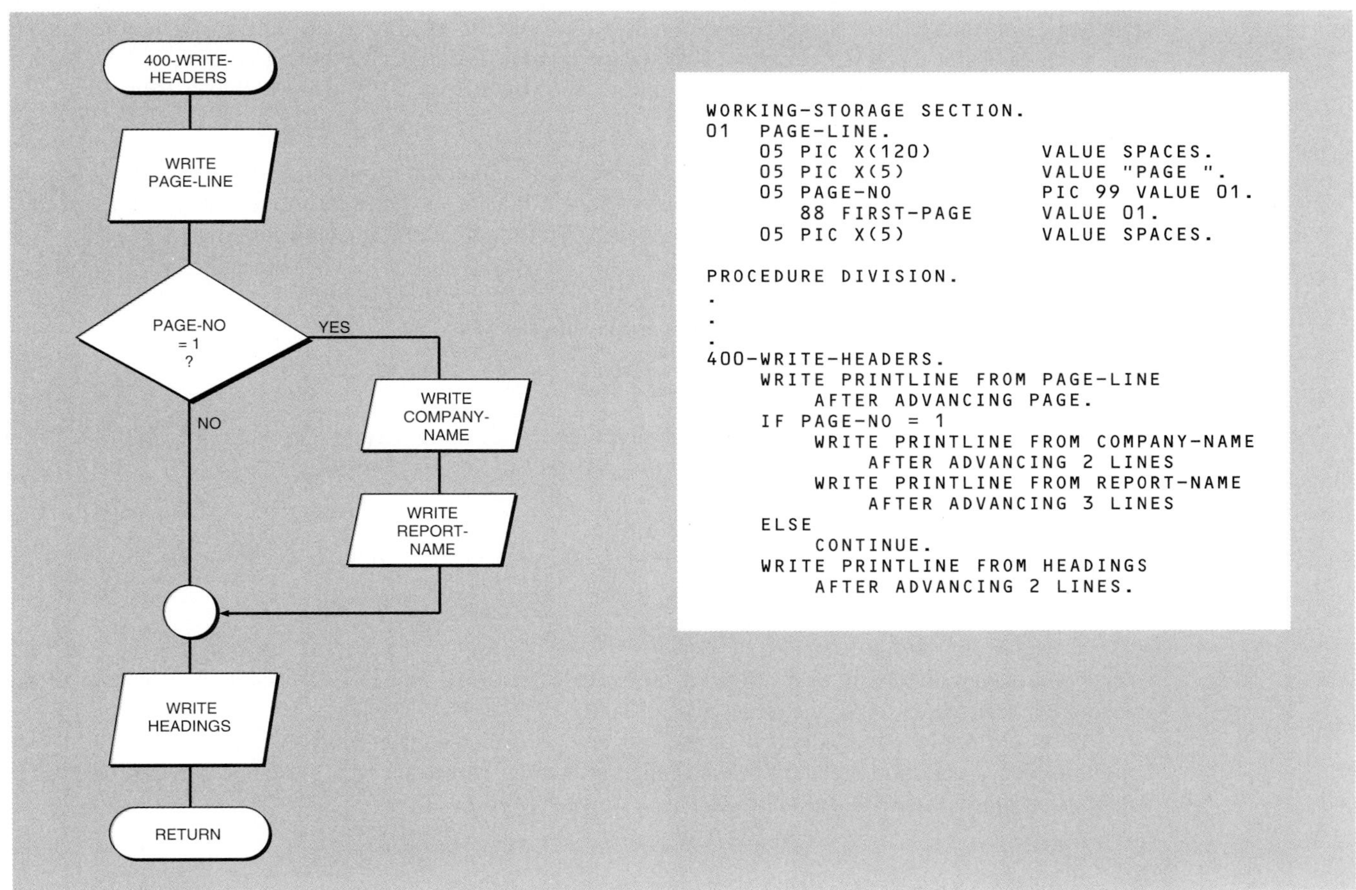


```
WORKING-STORAGE SECTION.
01  PAGE-LINE.
    05 PIC X(120)           VALUE SPACES.
    05 PIC X(5)             VALUE "PAGE ".
    05 PAGE-NO              PIC 99 VALUE 01.
       88 FIRST-PAGE        VALUE 01.
    05 PIC X(5)             VALUE SPACES.

PROCEDURE DIVISION.
.
.
.
400-WRITE-HEADERS.
    WRITE PRINTLINE FROM PAGE-LINE
        AFTER ADVANCING PAGE.
    IF PAGE-NO = 1
        WRITE PRINTLINE FROM COMPANY-NAME
            AFTER ADVANCING 2 LINES
        WRITE PRINTLINE FROM REPORT-NAME
            AFTER ADVANCING 3 LINES
    ELSE
        CONTINUE.
    WRITE PRINTLINE FROM HEADINGS
        AFTER ADVANCING 2 LINES.
```

Example 5:

The format in Figure 7.27 allows a condition-name to represent multiple values. As an example, consider the district codes in the chapter program. The only valid codes are 1, 2, 3, and 4. During the processing of a salesperson record, when the codes are being tested to determine which district accumulators should be updated, provisions should be made within the program to detect an invalid code. The pseudocode paragraph 330-Update-Dist-Accumulators in Figure 7.15 shows the following entry:

e. if other, display "District-Code error for " input Name.

The question is, What kind of COBOL statement can be coded for this entry?

One answer is to use a compound relational test (this type of test will be studied shortly), as follows:

```
IF I-DIST-CODE NOT = 1 AND
   I-DIST-CODE NOT = 2 AND
   I-DIST-CODE NOT = 3 AND
   I-DIST-CODE NOT = 4
   THEN
       DISPLAY "DISTRICT CODE ERROR FOR " I-NAME.
```

Another way is to define a condition-name such as VALID-CODE, to correspond to the values 1, 2, 3, and 4, as shown below:

```
05  I-DIST-CODE      PIC 9.
    88 EASTERN       VALUE 1.
    88 CENTRAL       VALUE 2.
    88 MOUNTAIN      VALUE 3.
    88 PACIFIC       VALUE 4.
    88 VALID-CODE    VALUES 1, 2, 3, 4.
```

With this condition-name, the above test becomes

```
IF NOT VALID-CODE
    DISPLAY "DISTRICT CODE ERROR FOR " I-NAME.
```

It should be obvious that the test is made much simpler, and, in addition, self-documentation of the statement is enhanced. Note that the condition VALID-CODE is true provided I-DIST-CODE contains any one of the values in the VALUE clause. If the value in I-DIST-CODE is anything other than 1, 2, 3, or 4, the condition VALID-CODE is false, and therefore, the condition NOT VALID-CODE is true.

Example 6:

The format in Figure 7.27 also allows a condition-name to represent any value within a specified range of values. For instance, consider assigning the letter-grade A if a student course average is 90 percent or better. Suppose the numeric average is stored in the field WS-GRADE-AVE, as defined below:

```
05  WS-GRADE-AVE   PIC S999.
```

One way of coding the test on the numeric average is

```
IF WS-GRADE-AVE >= 90 AND WS-GRADE-AVE <= 100
    MOVE "A" TO O-LETTER-GRADE.
```

This compound relational test can be greatly simplified by defining a condition-name, say A-GRADE, to correspond to any value in the range from 90 to 100, as in

```
05  WS-GRADE-AVE   PIC S999.
    88 A-GRADE     VALUES 90 THRU 100.
```

The test then becomes:

```
IF A-GRADE
    MOVE "A" TO O-LETTER-GRADE.
```

The condition A-GRADE is true provided the storage area WS-GRADE-AVE contains **any one** of the integers between 90 and 100, including 90 and 100.

If this example were extended to include tests for all the letter-grades A, B, C, D, and F, then condition-names could be defined for each range as follows (note that NOT VALID-AVE can be used to detect errors in the field WS-GRADE-AVE):

```
05  WS-GRADE-AVE    PIC S999.
    88 A-GRADE      VALUES 90 THRU 100.
    88 B-GRADE      VALUES 80 THRU 89.
    88 C-GRADE      VALUES 70 THRU 79.
    88 D-GRADE      VALUES 60 THRU 69.
    88 F-GRADE      VALUES 0 THRU 59.
    88 VALID-AVE    VALUES 0 THRU 100.
```

Note: In the sample program of this chapter, we will attach the condition-name NO-MORE-RECORDS to the data item WS-MORE-RECORDS as illustrated in example 1, and the condition-names EASTERN, CENTRAL, MOUNTAIN, PACIFIC, and VALID-CODE to the input record item I-DIST-CODE, as illustrated in example 5.

The SET Statement for Condition-Names

In every sample program developed thus far in this text, the end-of-file flag WS-MORE-RECORDS was used to control the loop that processes the records of the input file. The entries in the listing of the Chapter 2 program related to this flag are shown below.

```
             WORKING-STORAGE SECTION.

 67          01  WS-MORE-RECORDS      PIC XXX.
             .
             .
             .
 97          100-PRODUCE-PHONE-SALES-REPORT.
                 .
                 .
                 .
101              PERFORM 210-PROCESS-PHONE-SALE-RECORD
102                  UNTIL WS-MORE-RECORDS = "NO ".
                 .
                 .
                 .
             200-START-UP.
                 .
                 .
                 .
109              MOVE "YES" TO WS-MORE-RECORDS.
             .
             .
             .
117          310-READ-PHONE-SALE-RECORD.
118              READ PHONE-SALES-FILE RECORD
119                  AT END
120                      MOVE "NO " TO WS-MORE-RECORDS.
             .
             .
             .
```

On line 67, the data item WS-MORE-RECORDS is defined. On line 109, it is initialized to "YES". On line 102, it is tested to determine if control should remain in the loop or if control should exit from the loop. Control exits if the flag contains the value "NO ". On line 120, the MOVE statement assigns the value "NO " to the flag if the AT END condition is satisfied.

From the discussion on condition-names, and in particular in the preceding example 1, we know that the relational test on line 102 can be replaced nicely by a condition-name test, provided the definition of the item WS-MORE-RECORDS also includes the definition of an appropriate condition-name. Consequently, we can make the following revisions:

```
 67          01  WS-MORE-RECORDS      PIC XXX.
                 88 NO-MORE-RECORDS   VALUE "NO ".
             .
             .
             .
101          PERFORM 210-PROCESS-PHONE-SALE-RECORD
102              UNTIL NO-MORE-RECORDS.
             .
             .
             .
```

With these changes, when the statement on line 120, MOVE "NO " TO WS-MORE-RECORDS, is executed, the net effect is to make the condition-name NO-MORE-RECORDS true. That is, since the condition-name NO-MORE-RECORDS represents the condition that the data item WS-MORE-RECORDS contains the value "NO ", moving "NO " to the field WS-MORE-RECORDS makes the condition-name true.

■ **Figure 7.30** SET statement format

SET condition-name TO TRUE

COBOL '85 has introduced a new statement that allows the programmer an alternate way of moving the value "NO " to the flag WS-MORE-RECORDS. This procedure makes use of the availability of the condition-name. In this current example, the statement is simply:

```
SET NO-MORE-RECORDS TO TRUE.
```

The format for this new statement is shown in Figure 7.30.

Note the following about the SET statement:

1. If the condition-name corresponds to a single value, the SET statement moves that value to the associated data item. In example 1, page 364, the condition-name MORE-RECORDS corresponds to the single value "YES", and hence, the statement SET MORE-RECORDS TO TRUE is equivalent to the statement MOVE "YES" TO WS-MORE-RECORDS. Do you see that this is another way of initializing the end-of-file flag WS-MORE-RECORDS?
2. If the condition-name corresponds to multiple values, the SET statement moves the first value of the set to the associated data item. In example 5, page 368, the VALUE clause of the condition-name VALID-CODE specifies multiple values. The statement SET VALID-CODE TO TRUE is equivalent to the statement MOVE 1 TO I-DIST-CODE.
3. If the condition-name corresponds to a range of values, the SET statement moves the lowest value of the range to the associated data item. In example 6, page 368, the VALUE clause of the condition-name C-GRADE specifies the range of integers 70 thru 79. Hence, the statement SET C-GRADE TO TRUE is equivalent to the statement MOVE 70 TO WS-GRADE-AVE.

In the sample program of this chapter, we will make use of the SET statement in conjunction with condition-names whenever it is appropriate to do so.

The Sign Test

In the flowchart module 410-PREPARE-DIST-1-REPORT-LINE, a relational test could be used to determine if the total sales for the current year exceed the total sales of the preceding year. If the test holds true, then the percent change could be stored in a field such as O-SALES-UP; otherwise, the percent change could be stored in a field such as O-SALES-DOWN.

The test could take the form of a relational test, as in the following statement:

```
IF WS-DIST-1-YR-TTL > WS-LY-DIST-1-TTL
    COMPUTE O-SALES-UP = ...
ELSE
    COMPUTE O-SALES-DOWN = ....
```

An equivalent alternative test that could be used is the *sign test.* This test is used to determine if an arithmetic expression is positive (greater than zero), negative (less than zero), or zero; that is, it determines the **sign** of the value.

In the current example, if the quantity

```
(this year's sales - last year's sales)
```

is positive, then the sales are up for this year; otherwise, the sales are down. So, the relational test in the IF statement above can be replaced by the sign test as follows:

```
IF WS-DIST-1-YR-TTL - WS-LY-DIST-1-TTL IS POSITIVE
    COMPUTE O-SALES-UP = ...
ELSE
    COMPUTE O-SALES-DOWN = ....
```

The general format of the sign test is shown in Figure 7.31.

As noted above, the sign test is used to determine if the value stored in a numeric data field is or is not positive, negative, or zero, or if an arithmetic expression yields a value that is or is not positive, negative, or zero. In using this test, the programmer must understand under what conditions a particular form of the test is true (T), or false (F). The table to the right of Figure 7.31 summarizes these conditions.

■ **Figure 7.31** Sign test format

{identifier / arithmetic-expression} IS [NOT] {POSITIVE / NEGATIVE / ZERO}

Form of Test	Test Is	Provided Value of Identifier or Expression Is
IS POSITIVE	T	greater than zero
	F	equal to or less than zero
IS NOT POSITIVE	T	equal to or less than zero
	F	greater than zero
IS NEGATIVE	T	less than zero
	F	equal to or greater than zero
IS NOT NEGATIVE	T	equal to or greater than zero
	F	less than zero
IS ZERO	T	equal to zero
	F	less than or greater than zero
IS NOT ZERO	T	less than or greater than zero
	F	equal to zero

■ **Figure 7.32** Class test format

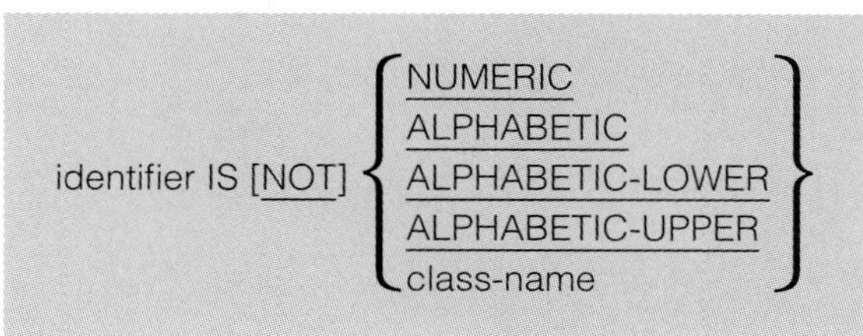

Some examples illustrating the use of the sign test follow:

1.
```
IF BALANCE - CHECK IS NEGATIVE
    PERFORM 400-PROCESS-OVERDRAWN-ACCT.
```
2.
```
IF NET-SALARY IS NOT POSITIVE
    PERFORM 300-CHECK-DEDUCTIONS-ROUTINE.
```
3.
```
PERFORM 200-ALLOCATE-FUNDS
    UNTIL FUNDS IS NEGATIVE.
```
4.
```
IF WS-ERROR-COUNTER IS POSITIVE
    PERFORM 300-PRINT-ERROR-ROUTINE.
```
5.
```
IF WS-LINE-CTR IS ZERO
    MOVE 2 TO WS-PROPER-SPACING.
```

It should be clear that any sign test can be written as a relational test. For instance, examples 1 and 2 above can be written as follows:

```
IF BALANCE - CHECK < 0
    PERFORM 400-PROCESS-OVERDRAWN-ACCT.
IF NET-SALARY NOT > 0
    PERFORM 300-CHECK-DEDUCTIONS-ROUTINE.
```

However, the sign test is preferable whenever the function of the test is to determine only the **sign** of the value, since the key words provide a greater degree of self-documentation.

The Class Test

A conditional statement can use a *class test* to determine if the characters stored in a data field are or are not alphabetic or numeric. This test is often used for data validation purposes. For instance, if a data field is specified by its PICTURE clause to be numeric, does it in fact contain only numeric characters? If a data field is specified by its PICTURE clause to be alphabetic, does it in fact contain only alphabetic characters and/or spaces? If a field is defined by its PICTURE as an alphanumeric field, it can be tested to determine if it contains only (or not only) alphabetic characters or only (or not only) numeric characters.

The general format for the class test is shown in Figure 7.32.

Rules Governing the Use of the Class Test

1. If the identifier has a numeric PICTURE, only the NUMERIC test can be used. The USAGE of the identifier must be DISPLAY.

2. If the identifier has an alphabetic PICTURE, only the alphabetic tests can be used, that is, ALPHABETIC, ALPHABETIC-LOWER, ALPHABETIC-UPPER.
3. If the identifier has an alphanumeric PICTURE, all forms of the test can be used.
4. The class of the identifier is numeric if the only characters contained in the field are the digits 0 through 9, including a sign, if so indicated by an S in the PICTURE string. The field must contain a sign if and only if the identifier is defined as a signed item.
5. The class of the identifier is ALPHABETIC if the only characters contained in the field are the letters of the alphabet A through Z, a through z, and/or spaces.
6. The class of the identifier is ALPHABETIC-LOWER if the only characters contained in the field are the lowercase letters of the alphabet, a through z, and/or spaces.
7. The class of the identifier is ALPHABETIC-UPPER if the only characters contained in the field are the uppercase letters of the alphabet, A through Z, and/or spaces.
8. Class-name is a user-defined set of characters to which a name is assigned in the SPECIAL-NAMES paragraph. The class of the identifier is class-name if the only characters contained in the field are characters belonging to the set specified in the definition of class-name.

Note: The last three options in the class test format (ALPHABETIC-LOWER, ALPHABETIC-UPPER, class-name) are new in COBOL '85. Furthermore, ALPHABETIC now includes lowercase letters. Earlier standards allowed only uppercase letters.

Consider the following examples.

Example 1:

Data Item	PICTURE	Contents
WAGE	99V99	450

```
IF WAGE IS NOT NUMERIC
    PERFORM 400-WAGE-ERROR-ROUTINE
ELSE
    COMPUTE SALARY = ....
```

In this case, the data field WAGE contains a space either in the leftmost byte or the rightmost byte. A space is not acceptable as a numeric character, and therefore the class is not numeric. Since the class test WAGE IS NOT NUMERIC is satisfied, the PERFORM statement will be executed. A leading or trailing zero should be inserted in the field WAGE to make all the characters numeric.

The test IF WAGE IS NOT ALPHABETIC is not a valid test, since WAGE has a numeric PICTURE. See rule 1.

Example 2:

Data Item	PICTURE	Contents
I-NAME	X(20)	RAYMOND C . BLOUNT

```
IF I-NAME IS ALPHABETIC-UPPER
    PERFORM 300-NORMAL-PROCESS
ELSE
    DISPLAY "NAME FIELD ERROR IN " I-NAME.
```

In this case, the data item I-NAME contains a nonalphabetic character, namely, the period after C, so the class test I-NAME IS ALPHABETIC-UPPER is false, and therefore the DISPLAY statement will be executed.

Note that I-NAME is defined as an alphanumeric data item. Its contents can be tested using any of the available class test options. See rule 3.

Example 3:

Data Item	PICTURE	Contents
PART-NUMBER	X(6)	1924-G

```
IF PART-NUMBER IS NOT NUMERIC
    PERFORM 400-NEW-LISTING.
```

In this case, the data item PART-NUMBER has an alphanumeric PICTURE, so any of the test options can be used. The class of the contents is in fact not numeric, since the hyphen and the letter G are not numeric characters. The class test PART-NUMBER IS NOT NUMERIC is therefore satisfied, and the PERFORM statement is executed.

Example 4:

Study the program entries below.

```
SPECIAL-NAMES.
    CLASS GREEK-ID IS "α, β, ψ, δ, ε".
.
.
.
01  TEST-RECORD.
    05 TEST-ID       PIC X.
    05 TEST-PHASE-1 PIC S999V9.
    05 TEST-PHASE-2 PIC S999V9.
    .
    .
    .
    IF TEST-ID IS NOT GREEK-ID
        PERFORM 300-WRONG-LABEL-ROUTINE
    ELSE
        PERFORM 310-COMPUTE-RESULTS.
```

In this example, the user defined a special class name, GREEK-ID, in the SPECIAL-NAMES paragraph. (See rule 8.) The objective is to check the field TEST-ID to see if it contains a character belonging to this class. If TEST-ID contains any one of the five special characters, then the class condition GREEK-ID is satisfied; otherwise, the class condition fails.

The format of the CLASS entry is shown in Figure 7.33. It allows more than one class name to be defined within a program.

The table following Figure 7.33 summarizes the pertinent class test information.

Negated Test

All the preceding types of tests can also be used in their negated form. This is accomplished simply by inserting the word *NOT* **before** the test. The format is shown in Figure 7.34.

In this format, if "test" is true, then "NOT test" is false, and if "test" is false, then "NOT test" is true. The only restriction is that the key word NOT must not be followed immediately by the word NOT, as in NOT NOT VALID. A bit of confusion initially arises here between the terms *negated test* and *negative test.* In a negative test, the word NOT is **part of the predicate;** in a negated test, the word NOT **precedes the test.** For instance,

```
IF WS-LINE-CTR IS NOT EQUAL TO 20 ...
```

is a negative test, and

```
IF NOT WS-LINE-CTR IS EQUAL TO 20 ...
```

is a negated test. Logically, the two forms are equivalent.

Consider the following examples.

Example 1:

Negative form:

```
IF YEAR-TOTAL IS NOT GREATER THAN LAST-YR-TOTAL ....
```

Negated form:

```
IF NOT YEAR-TOTAL IS GREATER THAN LAST-YR-TOTAL ....
```

Example 2:

Negative form:

```
IF BALANCE IS NOT NEGATIVE ....
```

Negated form:

```
IF NOT BALANCE IS NEGATIVE ....
```

Example 3:

Negative form:

```
IF RATE IS NOT NUMERIC ....
```

Figure 7.33 CLASS entry format

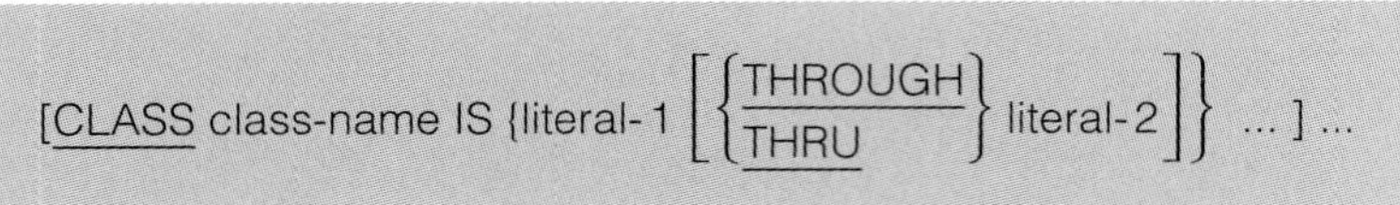

PICTURE of Identifier	Valid Tests	Test Is
Numeric (without S)	IS NUMERIC	T if the characters are only the digits 0–9 F if at least one character is not a digit
	IS NOT NUMERIC	T if at least one character is not a digit F if the characters are only the digits 0–9
Numeric (with S)	IS NUMERIC	T if the characters are only the digits 0–9, and a + or – F if at least one character is not a digit or the sign is not + or –
	IS NOT NUMERIC	T if at least one character is not a digit or the sign is not + or – F if the characters are only the digits 0–9, and a + or –
Alphabetic	IS ALPHABETIC	T if the characters are only the letters A–Z, a–z, or spaces F if at least one character is not a letter (upper- or lowercase) and not a space
	IS NOT ALPHABETIC	T if at least one character is not a letter (upper- or lowercase) and not a space F if the characters are only the letters A–Z, a–z, or spaces
	IS ALPHABETIC-LOWER	T if the characters are only the lowercase letters a–z, and spaces F if at least one character is not a lowercase letter or a space
	IS NOT ALPHABETIC-LOWER	T if at least one character is not a lowercase letter or a space F if the characters are only the lowercase letters a–z, and spaces
	IS ALPHABETIC-UPPER	T if the characters are only the uppercase letters A–Z, and spaces F if at least one character is not an uppercase letter or a space
	IS NOT ALPHABETIC-UPPER	T if at least one character is not an uppercase letter or a space F if the characters are only the uppercase letters A–Z, and spaces
Alphanumeric	All available	These tests are true or false under the same conditions as specified above
	IS class-name	T if the characters are only the ones specified in the definition of class-name F if at least one character is not among the ones specified in the definition of class-name
	IS NOT class-name	T if at least one character is not among the ones specified in the definition of class-name F if the characters are only the ones specified in the definition of class-name

Figure 7.34 Negated test format

NOT test

Negated form:

```
IF NOT RATE IS NUMERIC ....
```

It should be obvious from the preceding examples that the negated form of relational, sign, and class tests is more awkward than the more familiar negative form. Nevertheless, both forms are equally acceptable to the COBOL compiler.

The negated test is very useful in relation to condition-name tests, as shown in the next three examples.

Example 4:

```
IF NOT SALARIED ... (where SALARIED is a condition-name)
```

Example 5:

```
IF NOT FULL-PAGE ... (where FULL-PAGE is a condition-name)
```

Example 6:

```
IF NOT VALID-CODE ... (where VALID-CODE is a condition-name)
```

The negated test is also useful in relation to compound tests, which we now examine.

Compound Tests

There are many programming situations in which more than one condition must be tested. The logic of a program may require the conditions to be tested at different points in a program, or it may require them to be tested in a given sequence, or it may require them to be tested simultaneously. For instance, consider the flowchart segment in Figure 7.35.

It is obvious that in order to have NAME printed, it is necessary to satisfy **two** conditions at the same time; specifically, CATEGORY must have a value of "1A", and AGE must have a value less than 25. If either of these conditions fails, then NAME will not be printed.

Figure 7.35 Logic suggesting use of a conjunctive compound test—example

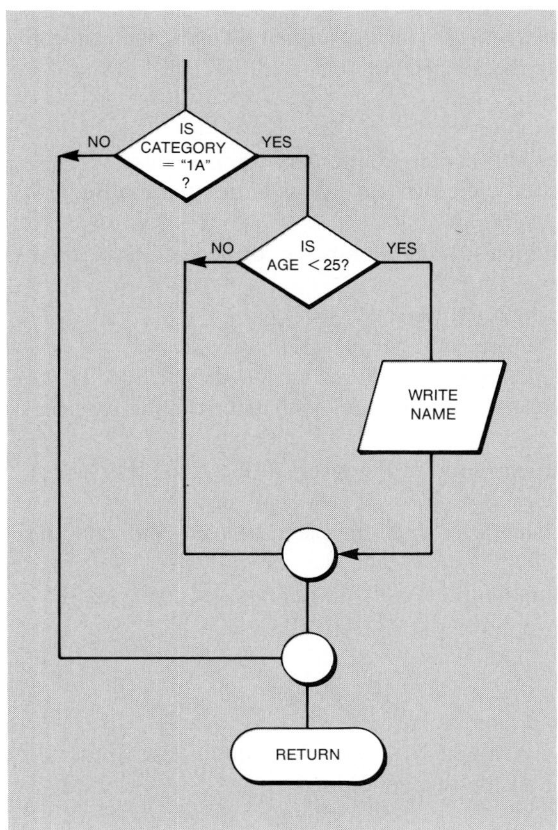

Figure 7.36 Compound test format

$$\text{condition-1} \left\{ \left\{ \begin{matrix} \underline{\text{AND}} \\ \underline{\text{OR}} \end{matrix} \right\} \text{condition-2} \right\} \ldots$$

If this flowchart segment were coded using simple conditional statements, the coding would be needlessly cumbersome, such as the following:

```
        IF CATEGORY = "1A"
            PERFORM TEST-2
        END-IF.
        .
        .
        .
    TEST-2.
        IF AGE IS LESS THAN 25
            MOVE NAME TO O-NAME
            WRITE PRINTLINE FROM NAME-LINE
                AFTER ADVANCING 1 LINE
        END-IF.
```

Fortunately, the COBOL language allows the programmer to form *compound tests.* They greatly simplify the coding, as well as the logic. Using the conjunction *AND* to join the two tests in Figure 7.35, the coding is simplified to the following:

```
    IF CATEGORY = "1A" AND AGE IS LESS THAN 25
        MOVE NAME TO O-NAME
        WRITE PRINTLINE FROM NAME-LINE
            AFTER ADVANCING 1 LINE
    END-IF.
```

The general format of compound tests is shown in Figure 7.36.

There are two kinds of compound tests: the *conjunctive test,* which is formed by using the connective *AND;* and the *disjunctive test,* which is formed by using the connective *OR.*

Rules Governing the Uses of Compound Tests

1. A conjunctive test (AND) is true provided both conditions are true; otherwise, it is false.
2. A disjunctive test (OR) is true provided at least one of the two conditions is true; otherwise, it is false.
3. Condition-1 and condition-2 can be relational, sign, class, condition-name, or negated tests, in any combination.
4. Condition-1 and condition-2 can themselves be compound tests.
5. In coding compound tests, there must be a space before and after each connective.
6. If the compound test contains more than two simple tests, parentheses can be used to specify the logical groupings of the tests. If parentheses are nested, the tests are evaluated from the innermost to the outermost.
7. If parentheses are not used to control the order of execution of the tests, all the AND tests are evaluated first, followed by all the OR tests.
8. To negate an AND or an OR test, the word NOT should precede the parenthesized compound test, as in NOT (test-1 AND test-2).
   (Be careful: in "NOT test-1 AND test-2", the compound test AND is **not** negated; only test-1 is negated.)

Examine the following examples.

Example 1:

In Figure 7.37, the MOVE box can be reached only by failing both specified conditions, whereas the COMPUTE box can be reached by satisfying either one of the two conditions.

Figure 7.37 Logic suggesting use of a compound test—example 1

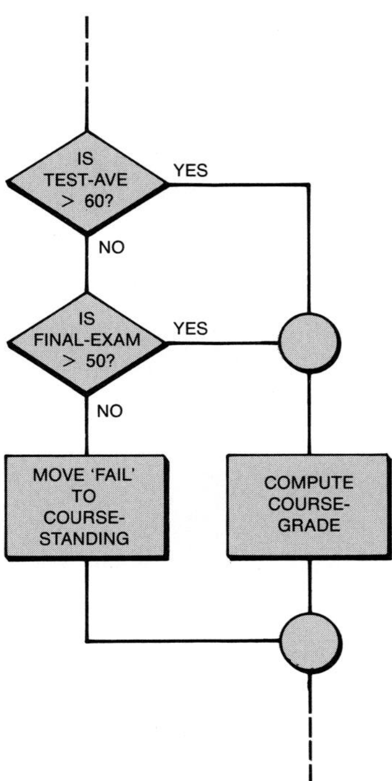

This flowchart segment can be coded in any one of three forms.

1. As a disjunction:

```
IF TEST-AVE > 60 OR FINAL-EXAM > 50
    COMPUTE COURSE-GRADE = ...
ELSE
    MOVE "FAIL" TO COURSE-STANDING.
```

2. As a conjunction:

```
IF TEST-AVE NOT > 60 AND FINAL-EXAM NOT > 50
    MOVE "FAIL" TO COURSE-STANDING
ELSE
    COMPUTE COURSE-GRADE = ....
```

3. As a negated disjunction:

```
IF NOT (TEST-AVE > 60 OR FINAL-EXAM > 50)
    MOVE "FAIL" TO COURSE-STANDING
ELSE
    COMPUTE COURSE-GRADE = ....
```

In Figure 7.38, two paths lead to the MOVE box: one is by simply satisfying the age requirement, the other is by being experienced (condition-name EXPERIENCED) **and** by being a high school graduate (condition-name HS-GRADUATE). Since the MOVE box can be reached either one way or the other, the coding calls for a disjunction:

```
IF AGE > 28 OR (EXPERIENCED AND HS-GRADUATE)
    MOVE NAME TO PRIORITY
END-IF.
```

Note that the parentheses around the conjunctive test are optional, since an AND test is evaluated before an OR test. Of course, you are encouraged to use parentheses for clarity. Also note that one test is relational, whereas the other two are condition-name tests.

Figure 7.38 Logic suggesting use of compound tests—example 2

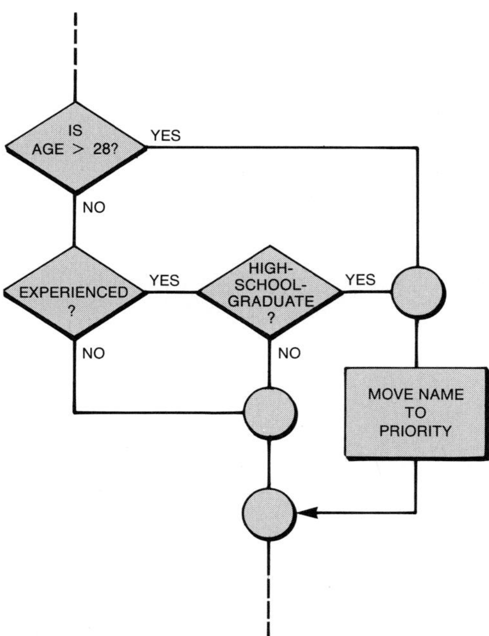

Abbreviated Compound Relational Tests

If a compound test contains a sequence of *relational tests,* it may be possible to write the relational test in an abbreviated form. Consider the following:

```
IF WS-INCOME > 40000 AND WS-INCOME NOT > 50000
    MOVE 4 TO WS-BRACKET-CODE
END-IF.
```

Since the subject of the relation is the same in both tests, it can be omitted in the second test, as in the following:

```
IF WS-INCOME > 40000 AND NOT > 50000
    MOVE 4 TO WS-BRACKET-CODE
END-IF.
```

As another example, consider the following:

```
IF ITEM-A > ITEM-X AND ITEM-A NOT < ITEM-B OR ITEM-A NOT < ITEM-C
    MOVE ITEM-A TO WS-SAVE-ITEM
END-IF.
```

In this case, ITEM-A is a common subject to all three tests, and, in addition, test-2 and test-3 also have the same predicate. The compound test can be abbreviated as follows:

```
IF ITEM-A > ITEM-X AND NOT < ITEM-B OR ITEM-C
    MOVE ITEM-A TO WS-SAVE-ITEM
END-IF.
```

Note that the first test in the sequence is always coded in full; only tests that occur later in the sequence can be abbreviated. If a subject is omitted in a test, the last preceding subject is substituted for the omission. If a relational operator is omitted, the last preceding relational operator is substituted for the omission.

The general format for abbreviated compound relational tests is shown in Figure 7.39. This is a new feature in COBOL '85.

In the format of Figure 7.39, the word NOT belongs to the relational operator if it is followed by one of the relational operators EQUAL, =, LESS, <, GREATER, or >. Otherwise, it is a logical operator that negates the omitted relational test.

Figure 7.39 Abbreviated compound relational test format

$$\text{relation-condition} \left\{ \left\{ \begin{array}{l} \underline{\text{AND}} \\ \underline{\text{OR}} \end{array} \right\} [\underline{\text{NOT}}]\ \text{[relational-operator] object} \right\} \ldots$$

Example 1:

```
ITEM-A = ITEM-B OR NOT > ITEM-C.
```

In this case, (1) the subject is omitted from the second test, and, therefore, the subject of the preceding test (ITEM-A) is implied; and (2) since the word NOT is followed by the relational operator >, it belongs to the predicate.

The explicit form of the test is as follows:

```
ITEM-A = ITEM-B OR ITEM-A NOT > ITEM-C.
```

Example 2:

```
ITEM-A = ITEM-B OR NOT ITEM-C.
```

In this case, (1) the subject and the predicate are omitted from the second test, and, hence, the subject and predicate of the preceding test are implied; and (2) since the word NOT is not followed by one of the relational operators, its role is to negate the relational test.

The explicit form of the test is the following:

```
ITEM-A = ITEM-B OR NOT (ITEM-A = ITEM-C).
```

Nested Conditional Statements

The general format of the IF-ELSE conditional statement is specified in Figure 7.19. In this general format, statement-1 and statement-2 are not restricted to being imperative statements. More specifically, they may be conditional statements themselves. If either one is a conditional statement, then this situation is referred to as *nested conditional statements.* Schematically, nested conditionals can be illustrated as shown in Figure 7.40.

In this figure, S1 is statement-1 for condition-1, and S2 is statement-2 for condition-1. Note that S1 and S2 themselves are *conditional statements.*

Consider the flowchart segment shown in Figure 7.41. Using nested conditionals, the coding becomes:

Line No.

```
1     IF NO-OF-UNITS IS GREATER THAN 100
2         IF NO-OF-UNITS IS GREATER THAN 300
3             COMPUTE BILL = NO-OF-UNITS * UNIT-COST * .7
4         ELSE
5             COMPUTE BILL = NO-OF-UNITS * UNIT-COST * .9
6         END-IF
7     ELSE
8         COMPUTE BILL = NO-OF-UNITS * UNIT-COST
9     END-IF.
10    WRITE PRINTLINE FROM BILL-LINE ...
```

Note how indentations are used to align the paired IF-ELSE statements, and how the scope terminator END-IF is used to explicitly mark the end of an IF-ELSE. Also note that control goes to line 2 only if the test on line 1 is satisfied; otherwise, control goes to line 7, the corresponding ELSE clause. If the test on line 2 is satisfied, control goes to line 3; otherwise, it goes to line 4, since line 4 contains the ELSE corresponding to the IF on line 2. Exit from the nested conditionals can occur at one of three points:

1. At the end of line 3 if NO-OF-UNITS is greater than 300
2. At the end of line 5 if NO-OF-UNITS is greater than 100 but not greater than 300
3. At the end of line 8 if NO-OF-UNITS is not greater than 100

■ **Figure 7.40** Schematic relating nested conditional statements to IF-ELSE format

```
┌ IF condition-1
│        ┌ IF condition-2
│     S1 │          statement-3
│        └ ELSE
│                   statement-4
└ ELSE
         ┌ IF condition-3
      S2 │          statement-5
         └ ELSE
                    statement-6
```

■ **Figure 7.41** Flowchart segment containing nested tests—example

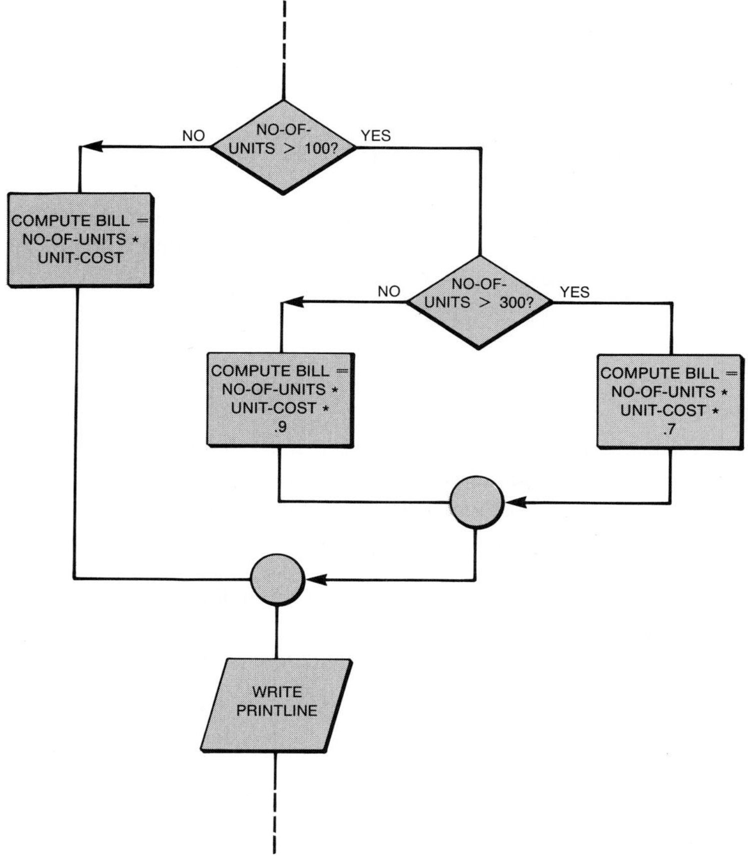

When any of these exits occurs, control is passed automatically to the next sentence; that is, the sentence that follows the END-IF on line 9. That sentence is the WRITE statement.

The flowchart segment of Figure 7.41 can also be coded as follows:

```
IF NO-OF-UNITS IS NOT GREATER THAN 100
    COMPUTE BILL = NO-OF-UNITS * UNIT-COST
ELSE
    IF NO-OF-UNITS IS NOT GREATER THAN 300
        COMPUTE BILL = NO-OF-UNITS * UNIT-COST * .9
    ELSE
        COMPUTE BILL = NO-OF-UNITS * UNIT-COST * .7
    END-IF
END-IF.
WRITE PRINTLINE FROM BILL-LINE ...
```

Here again, the IF-ELSE pairs are aligned and indented to enhance the clarity of the logic. In this coding, the nesting occurs within the ELSE clause of the outermost IF-ELSE statement, whereas in the previous coding, the nesting occurs within the IF clause of the outermost IF-ELSE statement.

Figure 7.42 Flowchart module consisting of nested tests—example

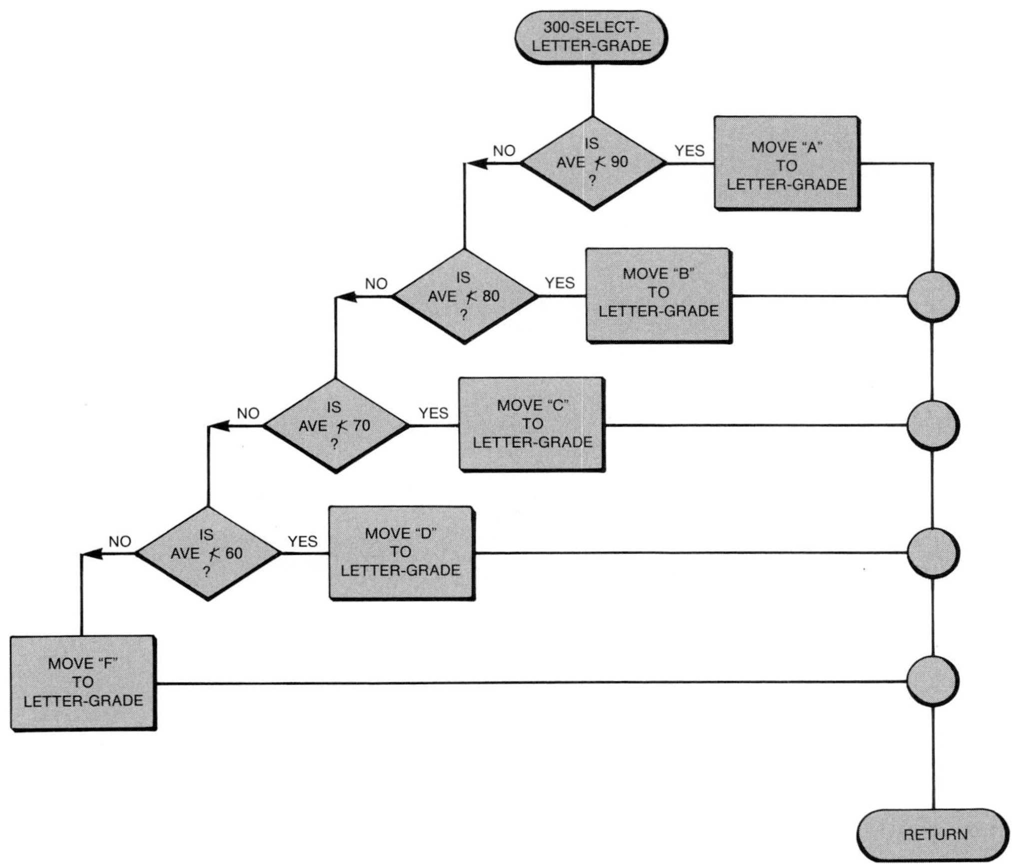

As a second example of nested conditionals, consider the flowchart module in Figure 7.42. The following nested IF-ELSE statements correspond to Figure 7.42:

```
IF AVE NOT < 90
    MOVE "A" TO LETTER-GRADE
ELSE
    IF AVE NOT < 80
        MOVE "B" TO LETTER-GRADE
    ELSE
        IF AVE NOT < 70
            MOVE "C" TO LETTER-GRADE
        ELSE
            IF AVE NOT < 60
                MOVE "D" TO LETTER-GRADE
            ELSE
                MOVE "F" TO LETTER-GRADE
            END-IF
        END-IF
    END-IF
END-IF.
```

(Recall that the END-IF scope terminators are optional. All of the IF-ELSE statements would be terminated by placing a period following the **last** MOVE statement. Nonetheless, for clarity, you are encouraged to use END-IFs.)

Suppose the value of AVE is 95. The relational test AVE NOT < 90 is true, and therefore the instruction MOVE "A" TO LETTER-GRADE is executed. Then control skips the ELSE clause to the matching END-IF. Note that this ELSE clause contains the rest of the nested conditionals, and therefore control has exited the structure altogether.

Suppose the value of AVE is 75. Trace the flow through the structure. Do you agree that the exit occurs just before the third ELSE?

As a third example of nested conditional statements, review the logic of Figure 7.13. Assume that the record description of SALESPERSON-RECORD is as follows:

```
01   SALESPERSON-RECORD.
     05 I-DIST-CODE       PIC 9.
     05 I-NAME            PIC X(22).
     05 I-QTR-SALES.
         10 I-QTR-1       PIC 9(6)V99.
         10 I-QTR-2       PIC 9(6)V99.
         10 I-QTR-3       PIC 9(6)V99.
         10 I-QTR-4       PIC 9(6)V99.
     05 I-YR-TTL          PIC 9(6)V99.
```

Following the logic of the flowchart segment, we can code nested conditionals as follows:

```
1     IF I-DIST-CODE = 1
2         ADD I-QTR-1 TO WS-DIST-1-QTR-1-TTL
3         ADD I-QTR-2 TO WS-DIST-1-QTR-2-TTL
4         ADD I-QTR-3 TO WS-DIST-1-QTR-3-TTL
5         ADD I-QTR-4 TO WS-DIST-1-QTR-4-TTL
6         ADD I-YR-TTL TO WS-DIST-1-YR-TTL
7     ELSE
8         IF I-DIST-CODE = 2
9             ADD I-QTR-1 TO WS-DIST-2-QTR-1-TTL
10            ADD I-QTR-2 TO WS-DIST-2-QTR-2-TTL
11            ADD I-QTR-3 TO WS-DIST-2-QTR-3-TTL
12            ADD I-QTR-4 TO WS-DIST-2-QTR-4-TTL
13            ADD I-YR-TTL TO WS-DIST-2-YR-TTL
14        ELSE
15            IF I-DIST-CODE = 3
16                ADD I-QTR-1 TO WS-DIST-3-QTR-1-TTL
17                ADD I-QTR-2 TO WS-DIST-3-QTR-2-TTL
18                ADD I-QTR-3 TO WS-DIST-3-QTR-3-TTL
19                ADD I-QTR-4 TO WS-DIST-3-QTR-4-TTL
20                ADD I-YR-TTL TO WS-DIST-3-YR-TTL
21            ELSE
22                IF I-DIST-CODE = 4
23                    ADD I-QTR-1 TO WS-DIST-4-QTR-1-TTL
24                    ADD I-QTR-2 TO WS-DIST-4-QTR-2-TTL
25                    ADD I-QTR-3 TO WS-DIST-4-QTR-3-TTL
26                    ADD I-QTR-4 TO WS-DIST-4-QTR-4-TTL
27                    ADD I-YR-TTL TO WS-DIST-4-YR-TTL
28                 ELSE
29                     DISPLAY "DISTRICT CODE ERROR FOR " I-NAME
30                END-IF
31            END-IF
32        END-IF
33    END-IF.
```

The END-IF on line 30 is the scope terminator for the innermost IF (line 22); the END-IF on line 31 is the scope terminator for the IF that begins on line 15, the END-IF on line 32 terminates the IF that begins on line 8, and the last END-IF terminates the first IF statement. An alternative to the use of the END-IFs is the placement of a period at the end of line 29, which would terminate the four IF statements. (You are encouraged to use the END-IF scope terminators.)

In this coding:

1. If the district code is 1, the statements on lines 2 through 6 are executed, and control then skips the ELSE clause that begins on line 7, branching to line 33, and then to the first statement that follows the period.
2. If the district code is 2, the test on line 1 fails, so control enters the ELSE clause on line 7; the condition on line 8 is satisfied, and therefore the statements on lines 9–13 are executed; control then skips the ELSE clause on line 14, branching to the END-IF scope terminator on line 32; and control then passes on to line 33 and exits the nested-IFs structure.
3. Can you determine the sequence for the other district code values?

As a final example, consider defining condition-names for the various values of I-DIST-CODE in the previous record description, as in the following:

```
05 I-DIST-CODE      PIC 9.
    88 EASTERN      VALUE 1.
    88 CENTRAL      VALUE 2.
    88 MOUNTAIN     VALUE 3.
    88 PACIFIC      VALUE 4.
```

Then, the relational tests in the above nested-IF statements can be replaced by the corresponding condition-name tests:

```
IF EASTERN
    ADD I-QTR-1 TO WS-DIST-1-QTR-1-TTL
    ADD I-QTR-2 TO WS-DIST-1-QTR-2-TTL
    ADD I-QTR-3 TO WS-DIST-1-QTR-3-TTL
    ADD I-QTR-4 TO WS-DIST-1-QTR-4-TTL
    ADD I-YR-TTL TO WS-DIST-1-YR-TTL
ELSE
    IF CENTRAL
        ADD I-QTR-1 TO WS-DIST-2-QTR-1-TTL
        ADD I-QTR-2 TO WS-DIST-2-QTR-2-TTL
        ADD I-QTR-3 TO WS-DIST-2-QTR-3-TTL
        ADD I-QTR-4 TO WS-DIST-2-QTR-4-TTL
        ADD I-YR-TTL TO WS-DIST-2-YR-TTL
    ELSE
        IF MOUNTAIN
            ADD I-QTR-1 TO WS-DIST-3-QTR-1-TTL
            ADD I-QTR-2 TO WS-DIST-3-QTR-2-TTL
            ADD I-QTR-3 TO WS-DIST-3-QTR-3-TTL
            ADD I-QTR-4 TO WS-DIST-3-QTR-4-TTL
            ADD I-YR-TTL TO WS-DIST-3-YR-TTL
        ELSE
            IF PACIFIC
                ADD I-QTR-1 TO WS-DIST-4-QTR-1-TTL
                ADD I-QTR-2 TO WS-DIST-4-QTR-2-TTL
                ADD I-QTR-3 TO WS-DIST-4-QTR-3-TTL
                ADD I-QTR-4 TO WS-DIST-4-QTR-4-TTL
                ADD I-YR-TTL TO WS-DIST-4-YR-TTL.
            END-IF
        END-IF
    END-IF
END-IF.
```

It is obvious from the examples in this section that nested conditionals are very useful in simplifying the coding of some otherwise complex and confusing programming. However, the programmer should be attentive to three items:

1. Avoid nesting so deeply in both branches of the initial IF-ELSE statement that the logic becomes too difficult to follow.
2. Be sure to properly align the matching IFs and ELSEs on the coding sheets to facilitate documentation as well as to guard yourself against omitting matching branches.
3. Use the END-IF scope terminator to enhance clarity in your own mind as well as in the coding itself.

The EVALUATE Statement

COBOL '85 has provided a new and very powerful tool for programmers to use in coding decision constructs that require multiple branches. It was first introduced at the end of Chapter 2 in relation to the case structure. This new statement is the EVALUATE statement. (See Figure 7.43.)

In its simplest form, the EVALUATE statement could be used as an alternative to a simple IF-ELSE statement, as in examples 1 and 2 below.

Example 1:

IF-ELSE statement:

```
IF WS-LINE-CTR = 30
    PERFORM 400-WRITE-REPORT-HEADERS
ELSE
    NEXT SENTENCE.
```

Corresponding EVALUATE statements:

a.
```
EVALUATE WS-LINE-CTR
    WHEN 30 PERFORM 400-WRITE-REPORT-HEADERS.
```

In this example, WS-LINE-CTR is the *subject* of the EVALUATE statement, and 30 is the *object*. When a match occurs between the subject and the object, that is, when WS-LINE-CTR is equal to 30, the PERFORM statement is executed. Note that the subject and the object belong to the same category; they are both numeric items.

■ **Figure 7.43** EVALUATE statement format

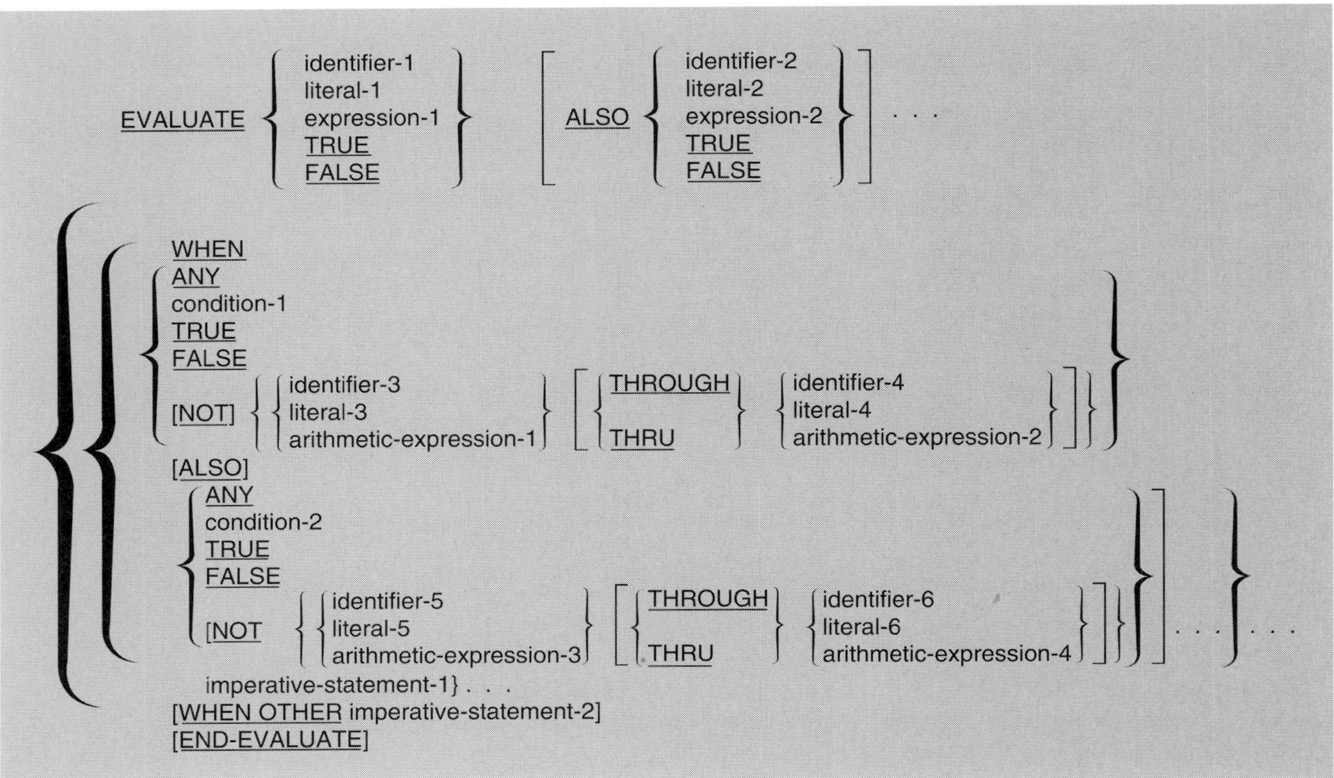

b. ```
EVALUATE WS-LINE-CTR = 30
    WHEN TRUE PERFORM 400-WRITE-REPORT-HEADERS.
```

In this case, the subject is the relational condition WS-LINE-CTR = 30, and the object is TRUE. In COBOL '85, TRUE and FALSE are two new conditional constants. Note again that the subject and object are of the same category: they are both conditionals. When the subject and object match, that is, in this application, when they are both "true," then the PERFORM statement is executed.

c. ```
EVALUATE TRUE
    WHEN WS-LINE-CTR = 30 PERFORM 400-WRITE-REPORT-HEADERS.
```

In this form, the subject and object of example b above have been interchanged. The same comments apply.

Example 2:

Assume that WS-LINE-CTR is defined as follows:

```
05 WS-LINE-CTR      PIC S99.
    88 PAGE-IS-FULL     VALUE +30.
```

The IF-ELSE of example 1 can be coded as follows:

```
IF PAGE-IS-FULL
    PERFORM 400-WRITE-REPORT-HEADERS
END-IF.
```

Corresponding EVALUATE statements can be coded as follows:

a. ```
EVALUATE TRUE
    WHEN PAGE-IS-FULL PERFORM 400-WRITE-REPORT-HEADERS
END-EVALUATE.
```

In this example, the subject is TRUE whereas the object is the condition-name PAGE-IS-FULL. Both are conditionals. When they match, that is, when both are "true," the PERFORM statement is executed.
```

b.
```
EVALUATE PAGE-IS-FULL
    WHEN TRUE PERFORM 400-WRITE-REPORT-HEADERS
END-EVALUATE.
```

In this example, the subject and object of the previous EVALUATE statement have been interchanged. The same comments again apply.

The strength of the EVALUATE statement is not as a substitute for a simple IF statement, but the two examples above begin to show you the versatility of the EVALUATE statement.

The format of the EVALUATE statement also allows for multiple conditions to be satisfied before a specified statement is executed. As a simple example, consider example 3, in which two conditions are required in each case.

Example 3:

Assume the following data item descriptions:

```
01   PROGRAM-CONTROLS.
     05 WS-MORE-RECORDS        PIC XXX.
         88 NO-MORE-RECORDS    VALUE "NO ".
     05 WS-LINE-CTR            PIC S99.
         88 PAGE-IS-FULL       VALUE +30.
```

a. Using nested IFs to code compound tests results in the following:

```
IF PAGE-IS-FULL AND NO-MORE-RECORDS
    PERFORM 410-END-OF-REPORT
ELSE
    IF PAGE-IS-FULL AND NOT NO-MORE-RECORDS
        PERFORM 400-WRITE-REPORT-HEADERS
        PERFORM 310-READ-A-RECORD
    ELSE
        IF NOT PAGE-IS-FULL AND NOT NO-MORE-RECORDS
            PERFORM 310-READ-A-RECORD
        ELSE
            IF NOT PAGE-IS-FULL AND NO-MORE-RECORDS
                SUBTRACT WS-LINE-CTR FROM 30
                    GIVING WS-PROPER-SPACING
                PERFORM 410-END-OF-REPORT
            END-IF
        END-IF
    END-IF
END-IF.
```

b. Using the EVALUATE statement to perform the same tests results in the following code:

```
EVALUATE PAGE-IS-FULL ALSO NO-MORE-RECORDS
  WHEN      TRUE      ALSO      TRUE          PERFORM 410-END-OF-REPORT
  WHEN      TRUE      ALSO      FALSE         PERFORM 400-WRITE-REPORT-HEADERS
                                              PERFORM 310-READ-A-RECORD
  WHEN      FALSE     ALSO      FALSE         PERFORM 310-READ-A-RECORD
  WHEN      FALSE     ALSO      TRUE          SUBTRACT WS-LINE-CTR FROM 30 GIVING WS-PROPER-SPACING
                                              PERFORM 410-END-OF-REPORT
END-EVALUATE.
```

In this example, combinations of truth values for the condition-names PAGE-IS-FULL and NO-MORE-RECORDS are being tested. Note the additional clarity of truth value pairings provided by the EVALUATE statement. Also note that there are two subjects, PAGE-IS-FULL and NO-MORE-RECORDS. Each WHEN clause must contain two objects. The paired subjects and objects must be of the same category. In this example, they are all conditionals. Also note that the new COBOL word ALSO separates the multiple subjects and the multiple objects. When the subjects have the same truth values as the paired objects in a particular WHEN clause, then the statements in that WHEN clause are executed, and control automatically passes beyond the scope of the EVALUATE statement.

Example 4:

In this example, we repeat the conditions tested in example 3 without using the condition-name NO-MORE-RECORDS. That is, we will test the data item WS-MORE-RECORDS itself for the two values that it may contain.

```
EVALUATE PAGE-IS-FULL ALSO WS-MORE-RECORDS
  WHEN      TRUE      ALSO      "NO "  PERFORM 410-END-OF-REPORT
  WHEN      TRUE      ALSO      "YES"  PERFORM 400-WRITE-REPORT-HEADERS
                                         PERFORM 310-READ-A-RECORD
  WHEN      FALSE     ALSO      "YES"  PERFORM 310-READ-A-RECORD
  WHEN      FALSE     ALSO      "NO "  SUBTRACT WS-LINE-CTR FROM 30 GIVING WS-PROPER-SPACING
                                         PERFORM 410-END-OF-REPORT
END-EVALUATE.
```

Note that the subject PAGE-IS-FULL is paired with either TRUE or FALSE as the object. They are both conditional items. The subject WS-MORE-RECORDS is an alphanumeric data item. Its matching objects are "YES" and "NO ", also alphanumeric values.

Example 5:

The chapter program provides us the opportunity for a simple application of the EVALUATE statement. The pseudocode paragraph 330-Update-Dist-Accumulators, or the corresponding flowchart module in Figure 7.15, tests the data item I-DIST-CODE for a value of 1, 2, 3, or 4. If I-DIST-CODE is defined as follows:

```
05  I-DIST-CODE    PIC 9.
    88 EASTERN     VALUE 1.
    88 CENTRAL     VALUE 2.
    88 MOUNTAIN    VALUE 3.
    88 PACIFIC     VALUE 4.
    88 VALID-CODE  VALUES 1, 2, 3, 4.
```

then the EVALUATE statement can be used to test the contents of the field I-DIST-CODE (see form 1 below) or to test the condition-names (see form 2).

Form 1:

```
EVALUATE I-DIST-CODE
    WHEN 1     ADD I-QTR-1 TO WS-DIST-1-QTR-1-TTL
               ADD I-QTR-2 TO WS-DIST-1-QTR-2-TTL
               ADD I-QTR-3 TO WS-DIST-1-QTR-3-TTL
               ADD I-QTR-4 TO WS-DIST-1-QTR-4-TTL
               ADD I-YR-TTL TO WS-DIST-1-YR-TTL
    WHEN 2     ADD I-QTR-1 TO WS-DIST-2-QTR-1-TTL
               ADD I-QTR-2 TO WS-DIST-2-QTR-2-TTL
               ADD I-QTR-3 TO WS-DIST-2-QTR-3-TTL
               ADD I-QTR-4 TO WS-DIST-2-QTR-4-TTL
               ADD I-YR-TTL TO WS-DIST-2-YR-TTL
    WHEN 3     ADD I-QTR-1 TO WS-DIST-3-QTR-1-TTL
               ADD I-QTR-2 TO WS-DIST-3-QTR-2-TTL
               ADD I-QTR-3 TO WS-DIST-3-QTR-3-TTL
               ADD I-QTR-4 TO WS-DIST-3-QTR-4-TTL
               ADD I-YR-TTL TO WS-DIST-3-YR-TTL
    WHEN 4     ADD I-QTR-1 TO WS-DIST-4-QTR-1-TTL
               ADD I-QTR-2 TO WS-DIST-4-QTR-2-TTL
               ADD I-QTR-3 TO WS-DIST-4-QTR-3-TTL
               ADD I-QTR-4 TO WS-DIST-4-QTR-4-TTL
               ADD I-YR-TTL TO WS-DIST-4-YR-TTL
    WHEN OTHER  DISPLAY "DISTRICT CODE ERROR FOR " I-NAME
END-EVALUATE.
```

Note the use of the COBOL '85 new reserved word OTHER. It is obviously a "catch-all" category that is satisfied if the value stored in the field I-DIST-CODE is other than a 1, a 2, a 3, or a 4. In this form, the subject and matching object are both numeric items (OTHER assumes the category specified for the subject). An alternative to coding WHEN OTHER is to code WHEN NOT 1 THRU 4. . . . The net result is the same.

Form 2:

```
EVALUATE TRUE
    WHEN EASTERN    ADD I-QTR-1 TO WS-DIST-1-QTR-1-TTL
                    ADD I-QTR-2 TO WS-DIST-1-QTR-2-TTL
                    ADD I-QTR-3 TO WS-DIST-1-QTR-3-TTL
                    ADD I-QTR-4 TO WS-DIST-1-QTR-4-TTL
                    ADD I-YR-TTL TO WS-DIST-1-YR-TTL
    WHEN CENTRAL    ADD I-QTR-1 TO WS-DIST-2-QTR-1-TTL
                    ADD I-QTR-2 TO WS-DIST-2-QTR-2-TTL
                    ADD I-QTR-3 TO WS-DIST-2-QTR-3-TTL
                    ADD I-QTR-4 TO WS-DIST-2-QTR-4-TTL
                    ADD I-YR-TTL TO WS-DIST-2-YR-TTL
    WHEN MOUNTAIN   ADD I-QTR-1 TO WS-DIST-3-QTR-1-TTL
                    ADD I-QTR-2 TO WS-DIST-3-QTR-2-TTL
                    ADD I-QTR-3 TO WS-DIST-3-QTR-3-TTL
                    ADD I-QTR-4 TO WS-DIST-3-QTR-4-TTL
                    ADD I-YR-TTL TO WS-DIST-3-YR-TTL
    WHEN PACIFIC    ADD I-QTR-1 TO WS-DIST-4-QTR-1-TTL
                    ADD I-QTR-2 TO WS-DIST-4-QTR-2-TTL
                    ADD I-QTR-3 TO WS-DIST-4-QTR-3-TTL
                    ADD I-QTR-4 TO WS-DIST-4-QTR-4-TTL
                    ADD I-YR-TTL TO WS-DIST-4-YR-TTL
    WHEN NOT VALID-CODE
        DISPLAY "DISTRICT CODE ERROR FOR " I-NAME
END-EVALUATE.
```

In this form, the subject and paired object are both conditional items. Each WHEN clause says: If this condition-name condition is true, perform the statements that follow. Form 2 is the one we will use in the chapter program.

The full format of the powerful and very versatile EVALUATE statement is shown in Figure 7.43.

Rules Governing the Use of the EVALUATE Statement

1. The entries following the verb EVALUATE and preceding the first WHEN are called the "subjects" of the EVALUATE statement. They form the "subject set."
2. In each WHEN clause, the entries that follow the word WHEN and precede the first statement are the "objects" of the EVALUATE statement. They form the "object set."
3. Multiple subjects and multiple objects are separated by the word ALSO.
4. There must be an object for each subject. An object in the object set is paired with the subject in the subject set on the basis of identical ordinal positions in the sets.
5. The subject and object belonging to a paired subject and object must be of the same category: numeric item with numeric item, alphanumeric item with alphanumeric item, conditional expression with conditional value.
6. TRUE and FALSE are conditional values that correspond to the truth values "true" and "false" respectively. The object ANY can correspond to any type of subject.
7. The words THRU and THROUGH are equivalent. The items connected by THRU must be of the same class and must be in ascending order. They specify the lowest and the highest values of the range.
8. Conditional expressions can be simple or compound.
9. In executing the EVALUATE statement,
   a. A value is assigned to each subject and to each object, following the familiar rules: An identifier is assigned the value it contains, a literal is assigned its explicit value, an arithmetic expression is evaluated, a conditional expression is assigned its truth value, and so on.
   b. The values of the subjects are compared with the values of the paired objects in a WHEN clause to see if the values match. If the paired values match, then the subject set is "satisfied" by the object set of the WHEN clause, and the WHEN clause is selected for execution. If the paired values do not all match, the subject set is "not satisfied," and the WHEN clause is not selected.
   c. If a WHEN clause is selected, statement-1 is executed, and control is then passed to the first statement beyond the scope of the EVALUATE statement.
   d. If no WHEN clause is selected, and there is no WHEN OTHER clause, control is passed to the first statement beyond the scope of the EVALUATE statement.
   e. If no WHEN clause is selected, and there is a WHEN OTHER clause, statement-2 is executed, and then control is passed to the first statement beyond the scope of the EVALUATE statement.

The next and final example is included to illustrate the kinds of complex decision-making situations that can be conveniently coded into a program by using the EVALUATE statement. Following the decision table (below) is the EVALUATE statement that codes it. Assume that WKLY-USAGE is a numeric data item for which HIGH and LOW are condition-names that correspond to ranges of values, QTY-ON-HAND and QTY-ON-ORDER are numeric data items, and LOCAL-VENDOR is a condition-name.

DECISION TABLE

WKLY-USAGE	QTY-ON-HAND	QTY-ON-ORDER	LOCAL-VENDOR	Action
HIGH	100–200	50–80	TRUE	Issue no order
HIGH	10–99	0	ANY	Issue rush order
LOW	0–9	0	TRUE	Issue normal order
ANY	20–50	0	FALSE	Issue normal order
LOW	ANY	10–20	ANY	Issue no order

Coding the decision table into an EVALUATE statement:

```
EVALUATE WKLY-USAGE ALSO QTY-ON-HAND  ALSO QTY-ON-ORDER ALSO LOCAL-VENDOR
   WHEN     HIGH    ALSO 100 THRU 200 ALSO  50 THRU 80  ALSO    TRUE       PERFORM 400-NO-ORDER
   WHEN     HIGH    ALSO  10 THRU 99  ALSO     ZERO     ALSO    ANY        PERFORM 420-RUSH-ORDER
   WHEN     LOW     ALSO   0 THRU 9   ALSO     ZERO     ALSO    TRUE       PERFORM 410-NORMAL-ORDER
   WHEN     ANY     ALSO  20 THRU 50  ALSO     ZERO     ALSO    FALSE      PERFORM 410-NORMAL-ORDER
   WHEN     LOW     ALSO      ANY     ALSO  10 THRU 20  ALSO    ANY        PERFORM 400-NO-ORDER
END-EVALUATE.
```

Back to the Program

We have left the chapter program many pages back. It should be useful at this time to review some of the specifications of the "Jocelyn Originals" program and to make some comments regarding their implementation.

1. The input file will contain two record descriptions: one designed to supply last year's total sales for the four districts and the company as a whole, the other supplying the report year's information for each salesperson. Since these records are not of the same size, we will use an optional form of the RECORD CONTAINS clause. Condition-names will be assigned to district codes.
2. The report date will be accessed from the system by using the ACCEPT statement. The fiscal year that is being reported will be determined from the record containing the previous year's totals. This record is the first one in the input file.
3. All the records needed for the report will be described in the WORKING-STORAGE SECTION as subgroups of the record REPORT-LINES.

   Other than the report documentation lines, the only type of line to be printed on the report is a summary line, containing summary figures for a district or for the company. For this reason, the report is classified as a pure summary report.
4. In working storage, a data item named WS-MORE-RECORDS will be assigned two condition-names: MORE-RECORDS to correspond to a "YES" value and NO-MORE-RECORDS to correspond to a "NO " value. The condition NO-MORE-RECORDS will cause an exit from the loop that processes the salespersons records. Wherever it is appropriate, the SET statement will be used in order to benefit from condition-name definitions.
5. When a salesperson record is read, the tests required to determine the district accumulators to which the sales amounts must be added will be implemented by using the EVALUATE statement. The WHEN clauses contain the condition-names assigned to the data item I-DIST-CODE.
6. When preparing the output record for a given district, we will use a minus sign editing character to signal a drop in the report year sales over the previous year's sales. The output record for the company will use a plus sign editing character to print a "+" if the percent change is positive and to print a "–" if the percent change is negative.

Coding the PROCEDURE DIVISION

We are finally ready to code the rest of the program. The tools that will guide us are the comments made above and the program pseudocode and/or the program flowchart developed earlier in Figures 7.9, 7.10, 7.15, 7.16, 7.17, and 7.18. The resulting coding is shown in Figure 7.44. We have inserted asterisks and color in the program to draw your attention to those entries that are related to the topics developed in this chapter. (For completeness, the first three divisions presented earlier are repeated again in Figure 7.44.)

Steps 5 and 6

The program shown in Figure 7.44 has been debugged. Figure 7.45a shows the sample input file [DD/CD:VIC7SP1.DAT], and Figure 7.45b shows the report produced by the program.

Figure 7.44 Complete COBOL program

```
 IDENTIFICATION DIVISION.

 PROGRAM-ID.  JOCELYN-ORIGINALS.

*****************************************************************
*                                                               *
*  AUTHOR.        PAQUETTE.                                     *
*  DATE WRITTEN.  JULY 1993.                                    *
*                                                               *
*       THIS PROGRAM PRODUCES AN ANNUAL SALES SUMMARY REPORT FOR *
*  THE JOCELYN ORIGINALS COMPANY.                               *
*                                                               *
*       FOR EACH DISTRICT AND FOR THE COMPANY AS A WHOLE, THE   *
*  REPORT SHOWS THE TOTAL SALES FOR EACH QUARTER AND FOR THE    *
*  YEAR, AND THE PERCENT INCREASE OR DECREASE OVER THE PREVIOUS *
*  YEAR'S SALES.                                                *
*                                                               *
*       AS INPUT, THERE ARE TWO KINDS OF RECORDS, ONE CONTAINING *
*  DISTRICT AND COMPANY SALES TOTALS FOR THE PRECEDING YEAR, THE *
*  OTHER CONTAINING A SALESPERSON'S DATA:  NAME, DISTRICT CODE, *
*  TOTAL SALES FOR EACH QUARTER AND FOR THE YEAR BEING REPORTED. *
*                                                               *
*       THIS PROGRAM CONTAINS THE FOLLOWING ABBREVIATIONS:      *
*                    CO:  COMPANY                               *
*                    DIST:  DISTRICT                            *
*                    LY:  LAST YEAR                             *
*                    QTR:  QUARTER                              *
*                    TTL:  TOTAL                                *
*                    SUMRY:  SUMMARY                            *
*                                                               *
*****************************************************************

 ENVIRONMENT DIVISION.

 CONFIGURATION SECTION.

 SOURCE-COMPUTER.  VAX-VMS-8650.
 OBJECT-COMPUTER.  VAX-VMS-8650.

 INPUT-OUTPUT SECTION.

 FILE-CONTROL.
     SELECT SALES-FILE           ASSIGN TO COB$INPUT.
     SELECT SALES-SUMRY-REPORT   ASSIGN TO COB$OUTPUT.

 DATA DIVISION.

 FILE SECTION.

 FD  SALES-FILE

*  THE NEXT ENTRY IS AN OPTIONAL FORM OF THE RECORD CONTAINS
*  CLAUSE.

     RECORD CONTAINS 54 TO 66 CHARACTERS.

 01  LY-SALES-TOTALS-RECORD.
     05 I-YR-OF-RECORD    PIC 9999.
     05 I-LY-DIST-1-TTL   PIC 9(8)V99.
     05 I-LY-DIST-2-TTL   PIC 9(8)V99.
     05 I-LY-DIST-3-TTL   PIC 9(8)V99.
     05 I-LY-DIST-4-TTL   PIC 9(8)V99.
     05 I-LY-CO-TTL       PIC 9(8)V99.

 01  SALESPERSON-RECORD.
     05 I-DIST-CODE       PIC 9.

*  THE NEXT 5 ENTRIES ARE CONDITION-NAME DEFINITIONS FOR THE
*  DATA ITEM I-DIST-CODE.

         88 EASTERN       VALUE 1.
         88 CENTRAL       VALUE 2.
         88 MOUNTAIN      VALUE 3.
         88 PACIFIC       VALUE 4.
         88 VALID-CODE    VALUES 1 THRU 4.
     05 I-NAME            PIC X(25).
```

```
          05 I-QTR-SALES.
              10 I-QTR-1        PIC 9(6)V99.
              10 I-QTR-2        PIC 9(6)V99.
              10 I-QTR-3        PIC 9(6)V99.
              10 I-QTR-4        PIC 9(6)V99.
          05 I-YR-TTL           PIC 9(6)V99.

      FD  SALES-SUMRY-REPORT
          RECORD CONTAINS 133 CHARACTERS.

      01  PRINTLINE             PIC X(133).

      WORKING-STORAGE SECTION.

      01  PROGRAM-CONTROLS.
          05 WS-MORE-RECORDS        PIC XXX.

     *   THE NEXT 2 ENTRIES ARE CONDITION-NAME DEFINITIONS FOR THE
     *   DATA ITEM WS-MORE-RECORDS.

              88 MORE-RECORDS       VALUE "YES".
              88 NO-MORE-RECORDS    VALUE "NO ".
          05 WS-REPORT-DATE         PIC X(6).

      01  LY-SALES-TOTALS.
          05 WS-YR-OF-RECORD        PIC 9999.
          05 WS-LY-DIST-1-TTL       PIC S9(8)V99.
          05 WS-LY-DIST-2-TTL       PIC S9(8)V99.
          05 WS-LY-DIST-3-TTL       PIC S9(8)V99.
          05 WS-LY-DIST-4-TTL       PIC S9(8)V99.
          05 WS-LY-CO-TTL           PIC S9(8)V99.

      01  SALES-ACCUMULATORS                COMP.
          05 WS-DIST-1-TTLS.
              10 WS-DIST-1-QTR-1-TTL    PIC S9(7)V99.
              10 WS-DIST-1-QTR-2-TTL    PIC S9(7)V99.
              10 WS-DIST-1-QTR-3-TTL    PIC S9(7)V99.
              10 WS-DIST-1-QTR-4-TTL    PIC S9(7)V99.
              10 WS-DIST-1-YR-TTL       PIC S9(8)V99.
          05 WS-DIST-2-TTLS.
              10 WS-DIST-2-QTR-1-TTL    PIC S9(7)V99.
              10 WS-DIST-2-QTR-2-TTL    PIC S9(7)V99.
              10 WS-DIST-2-QTR-3-TTL    PIC S9(7)V99.
              10 WS-DIST-2-QTR-4-TTL    PIC S9(7)V99.
              10 WS-DIST-2-YR-TTL       PIC S9(8)V99.
          05 WS-DIST-3-TTLS.
              10 WS-DIST-3-QTR-1-TTL    PIC S9(7)V99.
              10 WS-DIST-3-QTR-2-TTL    PIC S9(7)V99.
              10 WS-DIST-3-QTR-3-TTL    PIC S9(7)V99.
              10 WS-DIST-3-QTR-4-TTL    PIC S9(7)V99.
              10 WS-DIST-3-YR-TTL       PIC S9(8)V99.
          05 WS-DIST-4-TTLS.
              10 WS-DIST-4-QTR-1-TTL    PIC S9(7)V99.
              10 WS-DIST-4-QTR-2-TTL    PIC S9(7)V99.
              10 WS-DIST-4-QTR-3-TTL    PIC S9(7)V99.
              10 WS-DIST-4-QTR-4-TTL    PIC S9(7)V99.
              10 WS-DIST-4-YR-TTL       PIC S9(8)V99.
          05 WS-CO-TTLS.
              10 WS-CO-QTR-1-TTL        PIC S9(7)V99.
              10 WS-CO-QTR-2-TTL        PIC S9(7)V99.
              10 WS-CO-QTR-3-TTL        PIC S9(7)V99.
              10 WS-CO-QTR-4-TTL        PIC S9(7)V99.
              10 WS-CO-YR-TTL           PIC S9(8)V99.

      01  REPORT-LINES.

          05 TOP-LINE.
              10 PIC X(6)        VALUE SPACES.
              10 PIC X(14)       VALUE "REPORT DATE: ".
              10 O-REPORT-DATE   PIC XX/XX/XX.
              10 PIC X(105)      VALUE SPACES.

          05 COMPANY-NAME.
              10 PIC X(58)       VALUE SPACES.
              10 PIC X(17)       VALUE "JOCELYN ORIGINALS".
              10 PIC X(58)       VALUE SPACES.

          05 REPORT-NAME.
              10 PIC X(52)       VALUE SPACES.
              10 PIC X(28)       VALUE "ANNUAL DISTRICT SALES REPORT".
              10 PIC X(53)       VALUE SPACES.
```

```
       05 YEAR-LINE.
           10 PIC X(58)        VALUE SPACES.
           10 PIC X(12)        VALUE "FISCAL YEAR ".
           10 O-FISCAL-YEAR    PIC 9999.
           10 PIC X(59)        VALUE SPACES.

       05 HEADINGS-1.
           10 PIC X(94)        VALUE SPACES.
           10 PIC X(5)         VALUE "TOTAL".
           10 PIC X(11)        VALUE SPACES.
           10 PIC X(5)         VALUE "TOTAL".
           10 PIC X(7)         VALUE SPACES.
           10 PIC X(7)         VALUE "PERCENT".
           10 PIC XXXX         VALUE SPACES.

       05 HEADINGS-2.
           10 PIC X(6)         VALUE SPACES.
           10 PIC X(8)         VALUE "DISTRICT".
           10 PIC X(6)         VALUE SPACES.
           10 PIC X(13)        VALUE "FIRST QUARTER".
           10 PIC XXXX         VALUE SPACES.
           10 PIC X(14)        VALUE "SECOND QUARTER".
           10 PIC XXXX         VALUE SPACES.
           10 PIC X(13)        VALUE "THIRD QUARTER".
           10 PIC XXXX         VALUE SPACES.
           10 PIC X(14)        VALUE "FOURTH QUARTER".
           10 PIC X(6)         VALUE SPACES.
           10 PIC X(9)         VALUE "THIS YEAR".
           10 PIC X(7)         VALUE SPACES.
           10 PIC X(9)         VALUE "LAST YEAR".
           10 PIC X(5)         VALUE SPACES.
           10 PIC X(8)         VALUE "INCREASE".
           10 PIC XXX          VALUE SPACES.

       05 DISTRICT-TOTALS-LINE.
           10                      PIC X(6).
           10 O-DISTRICT           PIC X(8).
           10                      PIC X(6).
           10 O-DIST-QTR-1-TTL     PIC $Z,ZZZ,ZZ9.99-.
           10                      PIC XXX.
           10 O-DIST-QTR-2-TTL     PIC $Z,ZZZ,ZZ9.99-.
           10                      PIC XXXX.
           10 O-DIST-QTR-3-TTL     PIC $Z,ZZZ,ZZ9.99-.
           10                      PIC XXX.
           10 O-DIST-QTR-4-TTL     PIC $Z,ZZZ,ZZ9.99-.
           10                      PIC XXX.
           10 O-DIST-YR-TTL        PIC $ZZ,ZZZ,ZZ9.99-.
           10                      PIC X.
           10 O-LY-DIST-TTL        PIC $ZZ,ZZZ,ZZ9.99-.
           10                      PIC XXX.
           10 O-PERCENT-INCREASE PIC ZZ9.99-.
           10                      PIC XXX.

       05 COMPANY-TOTALS-LINE.
           10                  PIC XX     VALUE SPACES.
           10                  PIC X(17) VALUE "COMPANY TOTALS: ".
           10 O-CO-QTR-1-TTL   PIC $ZZ,ZZZ,ZZ9.99-.
           10                  PIC XX     VALUE SPACES.
           10 O-CO-QTR-2-TTL   PIC $ZZ,ZZZ,ZZ9.99-.
           10                  PIC XXX    VALUE SPACES.
           10 O-CO-QTR-3-TTL   PIC $ZZ,ZZZ,ZZ9.99-.
           10                  PIC XX     VALUE SPACES.
           10 O-CO-QTR-4-TTL   PIC $ZZ,ZZZ,ZZ9.99-.
           10                  PIC XXX    VALUE SPACES.
           10 O-CO-YR-TTL      PIC $ZZ,ZZZ,ZZ9.99-.
           10                  PIC XXX    VALUE SPACES.
           10 O-LY-CO-TTL      PIC $ZZ,ZZZ,ZZ9.99-.
           10                  PIC XXX    VALUE SPACES.
           10 O-PERCENT-CHANGE PIC ZZ9.99+.
           10                  PIC XXX    VALUE SPACES.

       05 END-LINE.
           10 PIC X(55)   VALUE SPACES.
           10 PIC X(23)   VALUE "***  END OF REPORT  ***".
           10 PIC X(55)   VALUE SPACES.

PROCEDURE DIVISION.

100-PRODUCE-SALES-SUMRY-REPORT.
    PERFORM 200-START-UP.
    PERFORM 210-PROCESS-SALESPERSON-RECORD
```

```
*  THE NEXT ENTRY CONTAINS A CONDITION-NAME TEST.

           UNTIL NO-MORE-RECORDS.
       PERFORM 220-FINISH-UP.
       STOP RUN.

   200-START-UP.
       OPEN INPUT SALES-FILE
            OUTPUT SALES-SUMRY-REPORT.
       PERFORM 300-INITIALIZE-ITEMS.
       PERFORM 310-READ-LY-TOTALS-RECORD.
       PERFORM 320-READ-SALESPERSON-RECORD.

   210-PROCESS-SALESPERSON-RECORD.
       PERFORM 330-UPDATE-DIST-ACCUMULATORS.
       PERFORM 340-UPDATE-CO-ACCUMULATORS.
       PERFORM 320-READ-SALESPERSON-RECORD.

   220-FINISH-UP.
       PERFORM 350-PREPARE-REPORT.
       WRITE PRINTLINE FROM END-LINE
           AFTER ADVANCING 10 LINES.
       CLOSE SALES-FILE
             SALES-SUMRY-REPORT.

   300-INITIALIZE-ITEMS.
       ACCEPT WS-REPORT-DATE FROM DATE.
       MOVE WS-REPORT-DATE TO O-REPORT-DATE.

*  THE NEXT ENTRY USES THE SET STATEMENT TO MOVE "YES" TO THE
*  FLAG WS-MORE-RECORDS.

       SET MORE-RECORDS TO TRUE.
       INITIALIZE SALES-ACCUMULATORS.
       MOVE SPACES TO DISTRICT-TOTALS-LINE.

   310-READ-LY-TOTALS-RECORD.
       READ SALES-FILE RECORD INTO LY-SALES-TOTALS
            AT END

*  THE NEXT ENTRY USES THE SET STATEMENT TO MOVE "NO " TO THE
*  FLAG WS-MORE-RECORDS IF THE AT-END CONDITION IS TRUE.

                SET NO-MORE-RECORDS TO TRUE.

   320-READ-SALESPERSON-RECORD.
       READ SALES-FILE RECORD
           AT END

*  THE NEXT ENTRY USES THE SET STATEMENT TO MOVE "NO " TO THE
*  FLAG WS-MORE-RECORDS.

                SET NO-MORE-RECORDS TO TRUE.

   330-UPDATE-DIST-ACCUMULATORS.

*  THIS PARAGRAPH USES THE EVALUATE STATEMENT TO IMPLEMENT THE
*  CASE STRUCTURE.

       EVALUATE TRUE
           WHEN EASTERN    ADD I-QTR-1 TO WS-DIST-1-QTR-1-TTL
                           ADD I-QTR-2 TO WS-DIST-1-QTR-2-TTL
                           ADD I-QTR-3 TO WS-DIST-1-QTR-3-TTL
                           ADD I-QTR-4 TO WS-DIST-1-QTR-4-TTL
                           ADD I-YR-TTL TO WS-DIST-1-YR-TTL

           WHEN CENTRAL    ADD I-QTR-1 TO WS-DIST-2-QTR-1-TTL
                           ADD I-QTR-2 TO WS-DIST-2-QTR-2-TTL
                           ADD I-QTR-3 TO WS-DIST-2-QTR-3-TTL
                           ADD I-QTR-4 TO WS-DIST-2-QTR-4-TTL
                           ADD I-YR-TTL TO WS-DIST-2-YR-TTL

           WHEN MOUNTAIN   ADD I-QTR-1 TO WS-DIST-3-QTR-1-TTL
                           ADD I-QTR-2 TO WS-DIST-3-QTR-2-TTL
                           ADD I-QTR-3 TO WS-DIST-3-QTR-3-TTL
                           ADD I-QTR-4 TO WS-DIST-3-QTR-4-TTL
                           ADD I-YR-TTL TO WS-DIST-3-YR-TTL
```

```
        WHEN PACIFIC        ADD I-QTR-1 TO WS-DIST-4-QTR-1-TTL
                            ADD I-QTR-2 TO WS-DIST-4-QTR-2-TTL
                            ADD I-QTR-3 TO WS-DIST-4-QTR-3-TTL
                            ADD I-QTR-4 TO WS-DIST-4-QTR-4-TTL
                            ADD I-YR-TTL TO WS-DIST-4-YR-TTL

        WHEN NOT VALID-CODE
            DISPLAY "DISTRICT CODE ERROR FOR " I-NAME
    END-EVALUATE.

340-UPDATE-CO-ACCUMULATORS.
    ADD I-QTR-1 TO WS-CO-QTR-1-TTL.
    ADD I-QTR-2 TO WS-CO-QTR-2-TTL.
    ADD I-QTR-3 TO WS-CO-QTR-3-TTL.
    ADD I-QTR-4 TO WS-CO-QTR-4-TTL.
    ADD I-YR-TTL TO WS-CO-YR-TTL.

350-PREPARE-REPORT.
    PERFORM 400-WRITE-REPORT-HEADERS.
    PERFORM 410-PREPARE-DIST-1-REPORT-LINE.
    PERFORM 420-PREPARE-DIST-2-REPORT-LINE.
    PERFORM 430-PREPARE-DIST-3-REPORT-LINE.
    PERFORM 440-PREPARE-DIST-4-REPORT-LINE.
    PERFORM 450-PREPARE-CO-REPORT-LINE.

400-WRITE-REPORT-HEADERS.
    WRITE PRINTLINE FROM TOP-LINE
        AFTER ADVANCING PAGE.
    WRITE PRINTLINE FROM COMPANY-NAME
        AFTER ADVANCING 2 LINES.
    WRITE PRINTLINE FROM REPORT-NAME
        AFTER ADVANCING 3 LINES.
    ADD 1 WS-YR-OF-RECORD GIVING O-FISCAL-YEAR.
    WRITE PRINTLINE FROM YEAR-LINE
        AFTER ADVANCING 3 LINES.
    WRITE PRINTLINE FROM HEADINGS-1
        AFTER ADVANCING 3 LINES.
    WRITE PRINTLINE FROM HEADINGS-2
        AFTER ADVANCING 1 LINE.

410-PREPARE-DIST-1-REPORT-LINE.
    MOVE "EASTERN" TO O-DISTRICT.
    MOVE WS-DIST-1-QTR-1-TTL TO O-DIST-QTR-1-TTL.
    MOVE WS-DIST-1-QTR-2-TTL TO O-DIST-QTR-2-TTL.
    MOVE WS-DIST-1-QTR-3-TTL TO O-DIST-QTR-3-TTL.
    MOVE WS-DIST-1-QTR-4-TTL TO O-DIST-QTR-4-TTL.
    MOVE WS-DIST-1-YR-TTL TO O-DIST-YR-TTL.
    MOVE WS-LY-DIST-1-TTL TO O-LY-DIST-TTL.
    COMPUTE O-PERCENT-INCREASE ROUNDED =
        (WS-DIST-1-YR-TTL - WS-LY-DIST-1-TTL)/ WS-LY-DIST-1-TTL
        * 100.
    WRITE PRINTLINE FROM DISTRICT-TOTALS-LINE
        AFTER ADVANCING 2 LINES.

420-PREPARE-DIST-2-REPORT-LINE.
    MOVE "CENTRAL" TO O-DISTRICT.
    MOVE WS-DIST-2-QTR-1-TTL TO O-DIST-QTR-1-TTL.
    MOVE WS-DIST-2-QTR-2-TTL TO O-DIST-QTR-2-TTL.
    MOVE WS-DIST-2-QTR-3-TTL TO O-DIST-QTR-3-TTL.
    MOVE WS-DIST-2-QTR-4-TTL TO O-DIST-QTR-4-TTL.
    MOVE WS-DIST-2-YR-TTL TO O-DIST-YR-TTL.
    MOVE WS-LY-DIST-2-TTL TO O-LY-DIST-TTL.
    COMPUTE O-PERCENT-INCREASE ROUNDED =
        (WS-DIST-2-YR-TTL - WS-LY-DIST-2-TTL)/ WS-LY-DIST-2-TTL
        * 100.
    WRITE PRINTLINE FROM DISTRICT-TOTALS-LINE
        AFTER ADVANCING 2 LINES.

430-PREPARE-DIST-3-REPORT-LINE.
    MOVE "MOUNTAIN" TO O-DISTRICT.
    MOVE WS-DIST-3-QTR-1-TTL TO O-DIST-QTR-1-TTL.
    MOVE WS-DIST-3-QTR-2-TTL TO O-DIST-QTR-2-TTL.
    MOVE WS-DIST-3-QTR-3-TTL TO O-DIST-QTR-3-TTL.
    MOVE WS-DIST-3-QTR-4-TTL TO O-DIST-QTR-4-TTL.
    MOVE WS-DIST-3-YR-TTL TO O-DIST-YR-TTL.
    MOVE WS-LY-DIST-3-TTL TO O-LY-DIST-TTL.
    COMPUTE O-PERCENT-INCREASE ROUNDED =
        (WS-DIST-3-YR-TTL - WS-LY-DIST-3-TTL)/ WS-LY-DIST-3-TTL
        * 100.
    WRITE PRINTLINE FROM DISTRICT-TOTALS-LINE
        AFTER ADVANCING 2 LINES.
```

■ **Figure 7.44** continued

```
440-PREPARE-DIST-4-REPORT-LINE.
    MOVE "PACIFIC" TO O-DISTRICT.
    MOVE WS-DIST-4-QTR-1-TTL TO O-DIST-QTR-1-TTL.
    MOVE WS-DIST-4-QTR-2-TTL TO O-DIST-QTR-2-TTL.
    MOVE WS-DIST-4-QTR-3-TTL TO O-DIST-QTR-3-TTL.
    MOVE WS-DIST-4-QTR-4-TTL TO O-DIST-QTR-4-TTL.
    MOVE WS-DIST-4-YR-TTL TO O-DIST-YR-TTL.
    MOVE WS-LY-DIST-4-TTL TO O-LY-DIST-TTL.
    COMPUTE O-PERCENT-INCREASE ROUNDED =
        (WS-DIST-4-YR-TTL - WS-LY-DIST-4-TTL)/ WS-LY-DIST-4-TTL
        * 100.
    WRITE PRINTLINE FROM DISTRICT-TOTALS-LINE
        AFTER ADVANCING 2 LINES.

450-PREPARE-CO-REPORT-LINE.
    MOVE WS-CO-QTR-1-TTL TO O-CO-QTR-1-TTL.
    MOVE WS-CO-QTR-2-TTL TO O-CO-QTR-2-TTL.
    MOVE WS-CO-QTR-3-TTL TO O-CO-QTR-3-TTL.
    MOVE WS-CO-QTR-4-TTL TO O-CO-QTR-4-TTL.
    MOVE WS-CO-YR-TTL TO O-CO-YR-TTL.
    MOVE WS-LY-CO-TTL TO O-LY-CO-TTL.
    COMPUTE O-PERCENT-INCREASE ROUNDED =
        (WS-CO-YR-TTL - WS-LY-CO-TTL)/ WS-LY-CO-TTL * 100.
    WRITE PRINTLINE FROM COMPANY-TOTALS-LINE
        AFTER ADVANCING 4 LINES.
```

■ **Figure 7.45a** Sample input file

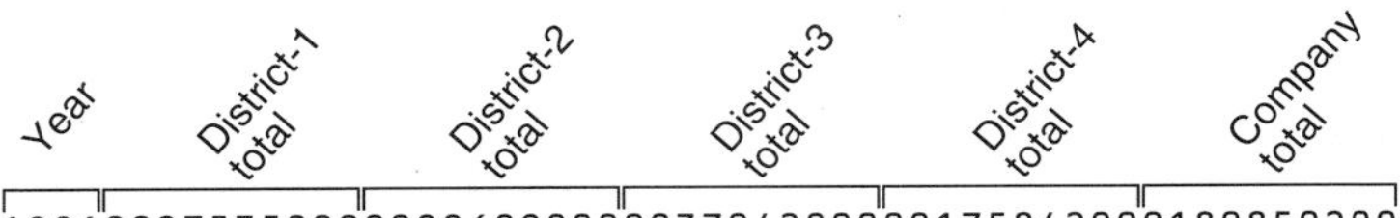

District | Name | Quarter-1 sales | Quarter-2 sales | Quarter-3 sales | Quarter-4 sales | Year total

```
1ABBRUZZI, KENNETH L.         0105755001296000015270500207808005958680
4AITKEN, THOMAS R.            0089800001125050012560000164505004924050
3ALTERMAN, MAUREEN E.         0143225001485070015380500203505006490420
1BAHR, LENA M.                0099505001276000013879000165425005313200
4BLAZUCK, JOSEPH A.           0125435001539550017190000223300006745900
2BUCCI, ELEANOR F.            0106655001239750015622500188855005757100
2BUXBAUM, JOAN M.             0082500001258050014350500217505005693150
1CARTER, AMELIA L.            0112900001359050009755500199555005459150
2COLETTI, SARAH T.            0106750001410050016685000234700006493050
3COUGHLIN, AILEEN M.          0115300000970000014790500183745005439500
1CYR, ROSARIO                 0125635001438400018260500259840007119200
3DURANT, MARIE L.             0109805001378840011325500207705005686490
3GAFFNEY, MARILYN             0123105001445050016828500217402506532975
2KACHADOURIAN, NATALIE A.     0143750001647050019850000243755007507100
1KRUGER, ALLEN                0101105001275050014278500167900005392950
2MARKARIAN, MARIAM            0113725000988500013700000193844005434190
3MCGEE, BERNARD W.            0124645001295050016684500203420006244150
1MOONEY, RONALD               0101905001282550015294500184845005679500
2OVERDEEP, CYNTHIA            0096255001433000016265500199700006019100
4PACCASASSI, DEBBIE           0119425001379250017225500234750006643550
4PRIMEAU, ISABEL              0124455001496000017369000217455006651600
2ROMA, GILDA                  0115800001336450016947500207755006266750
4SHERIDAN, RICHARD J.         0106507501428050018450000234855006686675
3STURDAHL, DEBRA              0129900001532550019470800226500007043630
3VELTRI, JOHN A.              0103350001228650017480500217400006184200
```

Figure 7.45b Report produced by the chapter program

```
REPORT DATE: 93/08/10
                                        JOCELYN ORIGINALS

                                    ANNUAL DISTRICT SALES REPORT

                                        FISCAL YEAR 1992


                                                                                      TOTAL            TOTAL        PERCENT
    DISTRICT        FIRST QUARTER    SECOND QUARTER    THIRD QUARTER    FOURTH QUARTER      THIS YEAR        LAST YEAR      INCREASE

    EASTERN         $   64,680.50    $   79,270.50    $   86,738.50    $  118,537.30    $  349,226.80    $  275,350.00     26.83

    CENTRAL         $   89,008.00    $  106,079.00    $  130,105.50    $  168,953.40    $  494,145.90    $  986,890.00     49.93-

    MOUNTAIN        $   72,468.50    $   80,401.60    $   95,276.30    $  125,625.75    $  373,772.15    $  370,420.00      0.90

    PACIFIC         $   56,562.25    $   69,679.00    $   82,794.50    $  107,486.50    $  316,517.75    $  175,842.00     80.00


COMPANY TOTALS    $   282,719.25   $   335,430.10   $   394,914.80   $   520,602.95   $ 1,533,662.60  $ 1,808,502.00



                                       ***  END OF REPORT  ***
```

An Alternate Program Development

The chapter program presents a unique opportunity to examine COBOL features that have not been used up to this point: qualification of data names and the CORRESPONDING option for the ADD and the MOVE statements. These features will be discussed briefly, and then the program will be rewritten to implement them.

Qualification

You have certainly learned by now, either through the text or from diagnostics generated by the compiler in response to errors in your programs, that data names or identifiers must be unique. Specifically, this means that the same identifier must not be used to name more than one storage area.

There are situations in which some benefits are obtained by using the same data name or identifier to name distinct storage areas. The benefits fall into two categories:

1. Enhancing the self-documentation of the program by using the same name for distinct fields that will contain the same data or the same type of data
2. Decreasing the number of distinct data names that must be constructed by the programmer and decreasing the amount of coding required in certain types of instructions

These benefits will be illustrated shortly.

The uniqueness property of data names must still be maintained, however. It is achieved by using *qualification,* that is, by specifying some unique group or record to which the nonunique item belongs. For instance, consider the input record EMPLOYEE-PAYROLL-RECORD and the output record DATA-LINE below.

```
01   EMPLOYEE-PAYROLL-RECORD.
     05 DEPT                  PIC X(5).
     05                       PIC X.
     05 SOC-SEC-NO            PIC X(9).
     05                       PIC X.
     05 NAME.
         10 FIRST-NAME        PIC A(10).
         10                   PIC X.
         10 I                 PIC A.
         10                   PIC X.
         10 LAST-NAME         PIC A(10).
     05                       PIC X.
     05 GROSS-SAL             PIC 999V99.
     05                       PIC X.
     05 FED-TAX               PIC 999V99.
     05                       PIC X.
     05 STATE-TAX             PIC 999V99.
     05                       PIC X.
     05 MISC-DED              PIC 99V99.
     05                       PIC X.
     05 TYPE-OF-INSURANCE     PIC A(6).
     05                       PIC X(11).

01   DATA-LINE.
     05                       PIC X(5).
     05 DEPT                  PIC X(5).
     05                       PIC X(4).
     05 SOC-SEC-NO            PIC XXXBXXBXXXX.
     05                       PIC XXX.
     05 NAME.
         10 FIRST-NAME        PIC A(10).
         10                   PIC X.
         10 I                 PIC A.
         10                   PIC X.
         10 LAST-NAME         PIC A(10).
     05                       PIC XXX.
     05 GROSS-SAL             PIC $ZZ9.99.
     05                       PIC XXX.
     05 FED-TAX               PIC $ZZ9.99.
     05                       PIC XX.
     05 STATE-TAX             PIC $ZZ9.99.
     05                       PIC XX.
     05 FICA                  PIC $Z9.99.
     05                       PIC XX.
     05 INSURANCE             PIC $Z9.99.
     05                       PIC X(6).
     05 MISC-DED              PIC $Z9.99.
     05                       PIC X(7).
     05 NET-SAL               PIC $ZZ9.99.
     05                       PIC X(11).
```

```
01  DEPT-SUM-TOTALS.
    05                      PIC X(86).
    05 NO-EMP               PIC ZZ9.
    05                      PIC X(8).
    05 DEPT-GROSS           PIC $ZZZZ9.99.
    05                      PIC XXX.
    05 DEPT-NET             PIC $ZZZZ9.99.
    05                      PIC XXX.
    05 NET-AVE              PIC $ZZZ9.99.
    05                      PIC XXXX.
```

The data names DEPT, SOC-SEC-NO, NAME, GROSS-SAL, FED-TAX, STATE-TAX, and MISC-DED name data fields that will contain the same data values in each of the first two records. Any one of these data items can be made unique by specifying the record to which it belongs, as in the following examples:

```
DEPT OF DATA-LINE,
GROSS-SAL OF EMPLOYEE-PAYROLL-RECORD.
```

The general format for qualification is shown in Figure 7.46.

Rules Governing Qualification

1. If two or more data fields are assigned the same name, or the same condition-name is applied to two or more data items, qualification must be used every time any one of these is referenced in a statement within the PROCEDURE DIVISION.
2. Qualification can be used even if a data name is assigned to only one field, or a condition-name is applied to only one data item.
3. The prepositions IN and OF are logically equivalent.
4. Data-name-1 or condition-name is the item being qualified; data-name-2 and file-name are qualifiers.
5. A qualifier must always have a higher-level number than the item being qualified. (01 is higher than 02, 05 is higher than 10, etc.)
6. More than one qualifier can be used if needed to make the data name or condition-name unique. In COBOL '85, up to 50 levels of qualification are permitted. (The previous limit was five.) Each qualifier must be of a successively higher level and within the same hierarchy as the name it qualifies.

Note the effect of rule 1 in the statements that follow:

1.
```
ADD FED-TAX OF EMPLOYEE-PAYROLL-RECORD
    STATE-TAX OF EMPLOYEE-PAYROLL-RECORD
    MISC-DED OF EMPLOYEE-PAYROLL-RECORD
        GIVING WS-TOTAL-DED.
```
2.
```
COMPUTE NET-SAL OF DATA-LINE =
    GROSS-SAL OF EMPLOYEE-PAYROLL-RECORD - WS-TOTAL-DED.
```

In the ADD statement, qualification is required for FED-TAX, STATE-TAX, and MISC-DED, since these data names identify fields of two distinct records, but qualification is not needed for WS-TOTAL-DED.

In the COMPUTE statement, NET-SAL is qualified. In this case, qualification is permissible but not required, since NET-SAL is the name of only one storage area. On the other hand, GROSS-SAL must be qualified. Why?

■ **Figure 7.46** Qualification format

```
{data-name-1   }  { {{IN}              } ... [{IN}           ] }
{condition-name}  { {{OF} data-name-2}       [{OF} file-name ] }
                  {  {IN}                                      }
                  {  {OF} file-name                            }
```

The MOVE CORRESPONDING Option

It is reasonable to expect that, at some time, the data stored in the fields of the input record EMPLOYEE-PAYROLL-RECORD will be moved to the corresponding fields of the output record DATA-LINE. The following set of instructions could be used to effect the data transfers:

```
MOVE DEPT OF EMPLOYEE-PAYROLL-RECORD TO DEPT OF DATA-LINE.
MOVE SOC-SEC-NO OF EMPLOYEE-PAYROLL-RECORD TO SOC-SEC-NO OF DATA-LINE.
MOVE NAME OF EMPLOYEE-PAYROLL-RECORD TO NAME OF DATA-LINE.
MOVE GROSS-SAL OF EMPLOYEE-PAYROLL-RECORD TO GROSS-SAL OF DATA-LINE.
MOVE FED-TAX OF EMPLOYEE-PAYROLL-RECORD TO FED-TAX OF DATA-LINE.
MOVE STATE-TAX OF EMPLOYEE-PAYROLL-RECORD TO STATE-TAX OF DATA-LINE.
MOVE MISC-DED OF EMPLOYEE-PAYROLL-RECORD TO MISC-DED OF DATA-LINE.
```

In situations like this one, where many data items are to be transferred from one record to another, the CORRESPONDING option of the MOVE statement is particularly valuable. The seven MOVE statements above can be replaced by the single MOVE CORRESPONDING statement below:

```
MOVE CORRESPONDING EMPLOYEE-PAYROLL-RECORD TO DATA-LINE.
```

Figure 7.47 shows sample contents of the data fields of the input record EMPLOYEE-PAYROLL-RECORD being moved to the corresponding fields of the output record DATA-LINE by the single MOVE CORRESPONDING statement.

Note that the data is transferred into each corresponding field of the output record according to the PICTURE specified for the receiving field. The PICTURE can be edited. That is, spaces are inserted in the Social Security number; the dollar sign and the decimal point are inserted in the dollar amounts for the gross salary, federal and state taxes, and miscellaneous deductions; and leading zeros are deleted. The type of insurance is not transferred, since there is no corresponding field in the output record. The field NET-SAL does not receive a value as a result of the MOVE CORRESPONDING, since there is no field by the name NET-SAL in the input record.

As readily seen in this example, the MOVE CORRESPONDING statement saves a considerable amount of coding. Its general format is shown in Figure 7.48.

Rules Governing the Use of MOVE CORRESPONDING

1. In this format, identifier-1 is called the source or sending group item, and identifier-2 is the receiving group item.
2. CORR is an abbreviation for CORRESPONDING.

Figure 7.47 Sample data transfers effected by a MOVE CORRESPONDING statement

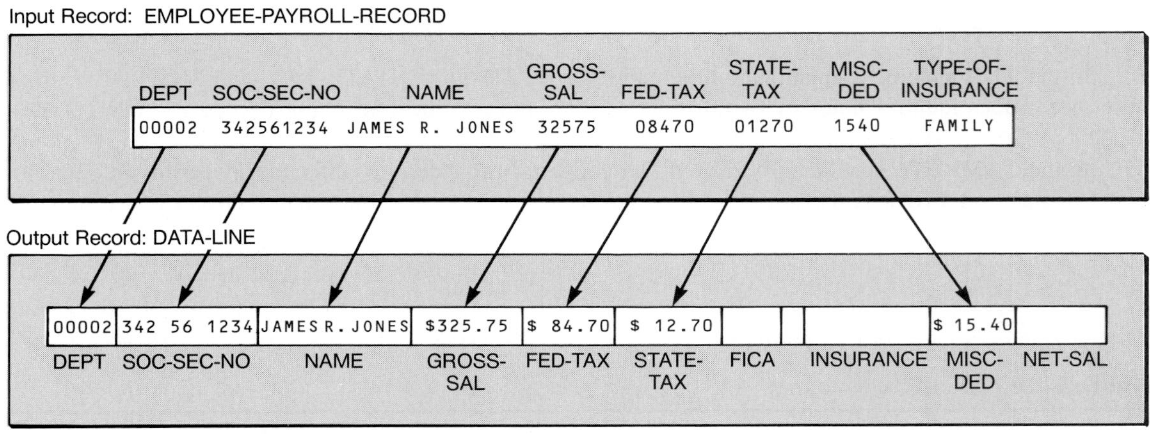

Figure 7.48 MOVE CORRESPONDING statement format

$$\underline{\text{MOVE}} \left\{ \begin{array}{l} \underline{\text{CORRESPONDING}} \\ \underline{\text{CORR}} \end{array} \right\} \text{identifier-1 } \underline{\text{TO}} \text{ identifer-2}$$

3. Transfer of data contained in fields of identifier-1 to fields of identifier-2 occurs only for those items that have the same name (and qualification if needed) in both source and receiving areas. **Note:** A data item in identifier-2 "corresponds" to a data item in identifier-1 only if *all* possible qualifiers of these data items are identical in both identifier-1 and identifier-2, except for the outermost qualifiers identifier-1 and identifier-2 themselves.
4. At least one of the data items in a matched pair must be an elementary item.
5. The data is transferred into the receiving field in conformity with the rules for simple MOVE statements.
6. Identifier-1 and identifier-2 must both be group items.
7. FILLER data items, explicit or by default, are ignored.

The ADD CORRESPONDING Option

A CORRESPONDING option is also available for the ADD and the SUBTRACT statements. The format for the ADD CORRESPONDING statement is shown in Figure 7.49.

Rules Governing the Use of the ADD CORRESPONDING Statement

1. In this format, CORR is an abbreviation for CORRESPONDING.
2. Identifier-1 and identifier-2 must be group data items.
3. All possible qualifiers for a data item contained in identifier-1 (excluding identifier-1 itself) must be identical to all possible qualifiers for the matching item in identifier-2 (excluding identifier-2 itself).
4. The values stored in numeric elementary items of identifier-1 are added to the values of the corresponding numeric elementary items (items of the same name and qualification) in identifier-2.
5. The numeric elementary items of identifier-2 are the receiving fields.
6. If the ON SIZE ERROR option is used, the test for a size error is made only after all additions have been performed; a receiving field for which there is a size error remains unchanged; if there is at least one size error, imperative-statement-1 is executed.
7. The NOT ON SIZE ERROR option provides an alternate path to the SIZE ERROR path. Imperative-statement-2 is executed only if there is no size error for any of the receiving fields.
8. The ADD CORR statement can be terminated either by a period or by the END-ADD scope terminator.

Suppose in a program that uses the input and output records of the example on pages 395 and 396, it is also necessary to print a summary line that will show the total of the gross salaries, as well as the total amounts withheld for federal and state taxes, and for miscellaneous deductions. First, it is necessary to set up accumulators in working storage, such as the following:

```
01   WS-COMPANY-ACCUMULATORS      COMP.
     05 GROSS-SAL     PIC S9(8)V99.
     05 FED-TAX       PIC S9(8)V99.
     05 STATE-TAX     PIC S9(8)V99.
     05 MISC-DED      PIC S9(8)V99.
```

When an employee record is processed, the pertinent amounts on that record must be added to the appropriate accumulators. This could be done as follows:

```
ADD GROSS-SAL OF EMPLOYEE-PAYROLL-RECORD TO GROSS-SAL OF WS-COMPANY-ACCUMULATORS.
ADD FED-TAX OF EMPLOYEE-PAYROLL-RECORD TO FED-TAX OF WS-COMPANY-ACCUMULATORS.
ADD STATE-TAX OF EMPLOYEE-PAYROLL-RECORD TO STATE-TAX OF WS-COMPANY-ACCUMULATORS.
ADD MISC-DED OF EMPLOYEE-PAYROLL-RECORD TO MISC-DED OF WS-COMPANY-ACCUMULATORS.
```

■ **Figure 7.49** ADD CORRESPONDING statement format

```
ADD {CORRESPONDING} identifier-1 TO identifier-2 [ROUNDED]
    {CORR         }
    [ON SIZE ERROR imperative-statement-1]
    [NOT ON SIZE ERROR imperative-statement-2]
    [END-ADD]
```

or, it could be done much more simply by using the ADD CORRESPONDING statement, as in the following:

```
ADD CORRESPONDING EMPLOYEE-PAYROLL-RECORD TO WS-COMPANY-ACCUMULATORS.
```

Note again that only the elementary numeric items that appear on both records are operands in the additions.

The SUBTRACT CORRESPONDING Option

The format for the SUBTRACT CORRESPONDING statement is shown in Figure 7.50. Other than the obvious substitution of the operation of subtraction for the operation of addition, the statements made about the ADD CORRESPONDING statement apply as well to the SUBTRACT CORRESPONDING statement.

The Alternate Program

In the chapter program, note the following:

1. The previous year's total sales for each district and for the company appear on an input record and are also stored in working storage. The same elementary field data names will be used for both of those records:

```
DIST-1-TTL
DIST-2-TTL
DIST-3-TTL
DIST-4-TTL
CO-TTL
```

2. Quarter-1, quarter-2, quarter-3, quarter-4, and year sales figures are needed for a salesperson (in input memory), for each of the four districts and for the company (in working storage accumulators), and for the four districts and the company on edited output records (although they are prepared in working storage). Rather than construct distinct names for each of these fields, it is more economical to assign the same standard names:

```
QTR-1
QTR-2
QTR-3
QTR-4
YR-TTL
```

3. The MOVE CORRESPONDING and the ADD CORRESPONDING statements will be used to replace multiple MOVE and ADD statements.
   Note: To implement the ADD CORRESPONDING statement, the description of the input record SALESPERSON-RECORD has been changed a little. The group name I-QTR-SALES has been removed and its elementary items renumbered at the 05 level to satisfy rule 3 of the ADD CORR format rules.
4. Qualification will be used whenever a particular one of these items is referenced in a statement.

Study the alternate program below. Comments and/or color have been inserted in the program to draw your attention to some of the entries related to the topics discussed in this chapter.

Figure 7.50 SUBTRACT CORRESPONDING statement format

```
SUBTRACT {CORRESPONDING} identifier-1 FROM identifier-2 [ROUNDED]
         {CORR         }
     [ON SIZE ERROR imperative-statement-1]
     [NOT ON SIZE ERROR imperative-statement-2]
     [END-SUBTRACT]
```

```
 IDENTIFICATION DIVISION.

 PROGRAM-ID.  JOCELYN-ORIGINALS-2.

******************************************************************
*                                                                *
*  AUTHOR.         PAQUETTE.                                     *
*  DATE WRITTEN.   JULY 1993.                                    *
*                                                                *
*       THIS PROGRAM PRODUCES AN ANNUAL SALES SUMMARY REPORT FOR *
*  THE JOCELYN ORIGINALS COMPANY.                                *
*                                                                *
*       FOR EACH DISTRICT AND FOR THE COMPANY AS A WHOLE, THE    *
*  REPORT SHOWS THE TOTAL SALES FOR EACH QUARTER AND FOR THE     *
*  YEAR, AND THE PERCENT INCREASE OR DECREASE OVER THE PREVIOUS  *
*  YEAR'S SALES.                                                 *
*                                                                *
*       AS INPUT, THERE ARE TWO KINDS OF RECORDS, ONE CONTAINING *
*  DISTRICT AND COMPANY SALES TOTALS FOR THE PRECEDING YEAR, THE *
*  OTHER CONTAINING A SALESPERSON'S DATA:  NAME, DISTRICT CODE,  *
*  TOTAL SALES FOR EACH QUARTER AND FOR THE YEAR BEING REPORTED. *
*                                                                *
*       THIS VERSION OF THE PROGRAM USES THE CORRESPONDING       *
*  OPTION OF THE ADD AND MOVE STATEMENTS, AND IT ALSO USES       *
*  QUALIFICATION WHERE NEEDED.                                   *
*                                                                *
*       THIS PROGRAM CONTAINS THE FOLLOWING ABBREVIATIONS:       *
*                    CO:   COMPANY                               *
*                    DIST:  DISTRICT                             *
*                    LY:  LAST YEAR                              *
*                    QTR:  QUARTER                               *
*                    TTL:  TOTAL                                 *
*                    SUMRY:  SUMMARY                             *
*                                                                *
******************************************************************

 ENVIRONMENT DIVISION.

 CONFIGURATION SECTION.

 SOURCE-COMPUTER.  VAX-VMS-8650.
 OBJECT-COMPUTER.  VAX-VMS-8650.

 INPUT-OUTPUT SECTION.

 FILE-CONTROL.
     SELECT SALES-FILE              ASSIGN TO COB$INPUT.
     SELECT SALES-SUMRY-REPORT      ASSIGN TO COB$OUTPUT.

 DATA DIVISION.

 FILE SECTION.

 FD  SALES-FILE

*  THE NEXT ENTRY IS AN OPTIONAL FORM OF THE RECORD CONTAINS
*  CLAUSE.

     RECORD CONTAINS 54 TO 66 CHARACTERS.

 01  LY-SALES-TOTALS-RECORD.
     05 I-YR-OF-RECORD    PIC 9999.
     05 DIST-1-TTL        PIC 9(8)V99.
     05 DIST-2-TTL        PIC 9(8)V99.
     05 DIST-3-TTL        PIC 9(8)V99.
     05 DIST-4-TTL        PIC 9(8)V99.
     05 CO-TTL            PIC 9(8)V99.

 01  SALESPERSON-RECORD.
     05 I-DIST-CODE       PIC 9.

*  THE NEXT 5 ENTRIES ARE CONDITION-NAME DEFINITIONS FOR THE
*  DATA ITEM I-DIST-CODE.

         88 EASTERN       VALUE 1.
         88 CENTRAL       VALUE 2.
         88 MOUNTAIN      VALUE 3.
         88 PACIFIC       VALUE 4.
         88 VALID-CODE    VALUES 1 THRU 4.
     05 I-NAME            PIC X(25).
     05 QTR-1             PIC 9(6)V99.
     05 QTR-2             PIC 9(6)V99.
     05 QTR-3             PIC 9(6)V99.
     05 QTR-4             PIC 9(6)V99.
     05 YR-TTL            PIC 9(6)V99.
```

```
FD  SALES-SUMRY-REPORT
    RECORD CONTAINS 133 CHARACTERS.

01  PRINTLINE              PIC X(133).

WORKING-STORAGE SECTION.

01  PROGRAM-CONTROLS.
    05 WS-MORE-RECORDS        PIC XXX.

*  THE NEXT 2 ENTRIES ARE CONDITION-NAME DEFINITIONS FOR THE
*  DATA ITEM WS-MORE-RECORDS.

        88 MORE-RECORDS       VALUE "YES".
        88 NO-MORE-RECORDS    VALUE "NO ".
    05 WS-REPORT-DATE         PIC X(6).

01  LY-SALES-TOTALS.
    05 WS-YR-OF-RECORD        PIC 9999.
    05 DIST-1-TTL             PIC S9(8)V99.
    05 DIST-2-TTL             PIC S9(8)V99.
    05 DIST-3-TTL             PIC S9(8)V99.
    05 DIST-4-TTL             PIC S9(8)V99.
    05 CO-TTL                 PIC S9(8)V99.

01  SALES-ACCUMULATORS        COMP.
    05 WS-DIST-1-TTLS.
        10 QTR-1     PIC S9(7)V99.
        10 QTR-2     PIC S9(7)V99.
        10 QTR-3     PIC S9(7)V99.
        10 QTR-4     PIC S9(7)V99.
        10 YR-TTL    PIC S9(8)V99.
    05 WS-DIST-2-TTLS.
        10 QTR-1     PIC S9(7)V99.
        10 QTR-2     PIC S9(7)V99.
        10 QTR-3     PIC S9(7)V99.
        10 QTR-4     PIC S9(7)V99.
        10 YR-TTL    PIC S9(8)V99.
    05 WS-DIST-3-TTLS.
        10 QTR-1     PIC S9(7)V99.
        10 QTR-2     PIC S9(7)V99.
        10 QTR-3     PIC S9(7)V99.
        10 QTR-4     PIC S9(7)V99.
        10 YR-TTL    PIC S9(8)V99.
    05 WS-DIST-4-TTLS.
        10 QTR-1     PIC S9(7)V99.
        10 QTR-2     PIC S9(7)V99.
        10 QTR-3     PIC S9(7)V99.
        10 QTR-4     PIC S9(7)V99.
        10 YR-TTL    PIC S9(8)V99.
    05 WS-CO-TTLS.
        10 QTR-1     PIC S9(7)V99.
        10 QTR-2     PIC S9(7)V99.
        10 QTR-3     PIC S9(7)V99.
        10 QTR-4     PIC S9(7)V99.
        10 YR-TTL    PIC S9(8)V99.

01  REPORT-LINES.

    05 TOP-LINE.
        10 PIC X(6)          VALUE SPACES.
        10 PIC X(14)         VALUE "REPORT DATE: ".
        10 O-REPORT-DATE     PIC XX/XX/XX.
        10 PIC X(105)        VALUE SPACES.

    05 COMPANY-NAME.
        10 PIC X(58)         VALUE SPACES.
        10 PIC X(17)         VALUE "JOCELYN ORIGINALS".
        10 PIC X(58)         VALUE SPACES.

    05 REPORT-NAME.
        10 PIC X(52)         VALUE SPACES.
        10 PIC X(28)         VALUE "ANNUAL DISTRICT SALES REPORT".
        10 PIC X(53)         VALUE SPACES.

    05 YEAR-LINE.
        10 PIC X(58)         VALUE SPACES.
        10 PIC X(12)         VALUE "FISCAL YEAR ".
        10 O-FISCAL-YEAR     PIC 9999.
        10 PIC X(59)         VALUE SPACES.

    05 HEADINGS-1.
        10 PIC X(94)         VALUE SPACES.
        10 PIC X(5)          VALUE "TOTAL".
        10 PIC X(11)         VALUE SPACES.
        10 PIC X(5)          VALUE "TOTAL".
```

```
        10 PIC X(7)        VALUE SPACES.
        10 PIC X(7)        VALUE "PERCENT".
        10 PIC XXXX        VALUE SPACES.

    05 HEADINGS-2.
        10 PIC X(6)        VALUE SPACES.
        10 PIC X(8)        VALUE "DISTRICT".
        10 PIC X(6)        VALUE SPACES.
        10 PIC X(13)       VALUE "FIRST QUARTER".
        10 PIC XXXX        VALUE SPACES.
        10 PIC X(14)       VALUE "SECOND QUARTER".
        10 PIC XXXX        VALUE SPACES.
        10 PIC X(13)       VALUE "THIRD QUARTER".
        10 PIC XXXX        VALUE SPACES.
        10 PIC X(14)       VALUE "FOURTH QUARTER".
        10 PIC X(6)        VALUE SPACES.
        10 PIC X(9)        VALUE "THIS YEAR".
        10 PIC X(7)        VALUE SPACES.
        10 PIC X(9)        VALUE "LAST YEAR".
        10 PIC X(5)        VALUE SPACES.
        10 PIC X(8)        VALUE "INCREASE".
        10 PIC XXX         VALUE SPACES.

PROCEDURE DIVISION.

100-PRODUCE-SALES-SUMRY-REPORT.
    PERFORM 200-START-UP.
    PERFORM 210-PROCESS-SALESPERSON-RECORD

*  THE NEXT ENTRY USES A CONDITION-NAME TEST.

        UNTIL NO-MORE-RECORDS.
    PERFORM 220-FINISH-UP.
    STOP RUN.

200-START-UP.
    OPEN INPUT SALES-FILE
         OUTPUT SALES-SUMRY-REPORT.
    PERFORM 300-INITIALIZE-ITEMS.
    PERFORM 310-READ-LY-TOTALS-RECORD.
    PERFORM 320-READ-SALESPERSON-RECORD.

210-PROCESS-SALESPERSON-RECORD.
    PERFORM 330-UPDATE-DIST-ACCUMULATORS.
    PERFORM 340-UPDATE-CO-ACCUMULATORS.
    PERFORM 320-READ-SALESPERSON-RECORD.

220-FINISH-UP.
    PERFORM 350-PREPARE-REPORT.
    WRITE PRINTLINE FROM END-LINE
        AFTER ADVANCING 10 LINES.
    CLOSE SALES-FILE
          SALES-SUMRY-REPORT.

300-INITIALIZE-ITEMS.
    ACCEPT WS-REPORT-DATE FROM DATE.
    MOVE WS-REPORT-DATE TO O-REPORT-DATE.

*  THE NEXT ENTRY USES THE SET STATEMENT TO MOVE "YES" TO THE
*  FLAG WS-MORE-RECORDS.

    SET MORE-RECORDS TO TRUE.
    INITIALIZE SALES-ACCUMULATORS.
    MOVE SPACES TO DISTRICT-TOTALS-LINE.

310-READ-LY-TOTALS-RECORD.
    READ SALES-FILE RECORD INTO LY-SALES-TOTALS
         AT END

*  THE NEXT ENTRY USES THE SET STATEMENT TO MOVE "NO " TO THE
*  FLAG WS-MORE-RECORDS IF THE AT END CONDITION IS TRUE.

              SET NO-MORE-RECORDS TO TRUE.

320-READ-SALESPERSON-RECORD.
    READ SALES-FILE RECORD
        AT END

*  THE NEXT ENTRY USES THE SET STATEMENT TO MOVE "NO " TO THE
*  FLAG WS-MORE-RECORDS.

            SET NO-MORE-RECORDS TO TRUE.

330-UPDATE-DIST-ACCUMULATORS.

*  THIS PARAGRAPH USES THE EVALUATE STATEMENT TO IMPLEMENT THE
*  CASE STRUCTURE.  IT ALSO USES THE ADD CORRESPONDING OPTION.
```

```
       EVALUATE TRUE
           WHEN EASTERN     ADD CORRESPONDING SALESPERSON-RECORD
                                TO WS-DIST-1-TTLS

           WHEN CENTRAL     ADD CORRESPONDING SALESPERSON-RECORD
                                TO WS-DIST-2-TTLS

           WHEN MOUNTAIN    ADD CORRESPONDING SALESPERSON-RECORD
                                TO WS-DIST-3-TTLS

           WHEN PACIFIC     ADD CORRESPONDING SALESPERSON-RECORD
                                TO WS-DIST-4-TTLS

           WHEN NOT VALID-CODE
               DISPLAY "DISTRICT CODE ERROR FOR " I-NAME
       END-EVALUATE.

   340-UPDATE-CO-ACCUMULATORS.
       ADD CORRESPONDING SALESPERSON-RECORD TO WS-CO-TTLS.

   350-PREPARE-REPORT.
       PERFORM 400-WRITE-REPORT-HEADERS.
       PERFORM 410-PREPARE-DIST-1-REPORT-LINE.
       PERFORM 420-PREPARE-DIST-2-REPORT-LINE.
       PERFORM 430-PREPARE-DIST-3-REPORT-LINE.
       PERFORM 440-PREPARE-DIST-4-REPORT-LINE.
       PERFORM 450-PREPARE-CO-REPORT-LINE.

   400-WRITE-REPORT-HEADERS.
       WRITE PRINTLINE FROM TOP-LINE
           AFTER ADVANCING PAGE.
       WRITE PRINTLINE FROM COMPANY-NAME
           AFTER ADVANCING 2 LINES.
       WRITE PRINTLINE FROM REPORT-NAME
           AFTER ADVANCING 3 LINES.
       ADD 1 WS-YR-OF-RECORD GIVING O-FISCAL-YEAR.
       WRITE PRINTLINE FROM YEAR-LINE
           AFTER ADVANCING 3 LINES.
       WRITE PRINTLINE FROM HEADINGS-1
           AFTER ADVANCING 3 LINES.
       WRITE PRINTLINE FROM HEADINGS-2
           AFTER ADVANCING 1 LINE.

   410-PREPARE-DIST-1-REPORT-LINE.
       MOVE "EASTERN" TO O-DISTRICT.
       MOVE CORRESPONDING WS-DIST-1-TTLS
            TO DISTRICT-TOTALS-LINE.
       MOVE DIST-1-TTL OF LY-SALES-TOTALS TO O-LY-DIST-TTL.
       COMPUTE O-PERCENT-INCREASE ROUNDED =
          (YR-TTL OF WS-DIST-1-TTLS - DIST-1-TTL OF LY-SALES-TOTALS)
           / DIST-1-TTL OF LY-SALES-TOTALS * 100.
       WRITE PRINTLINE FROM DISTRICT-TOTALS-LINE
           AFTER ADVANCING 2 LINES.

   420-PREPARE-DIST-2-REPORT-LINE.
       MOVE "CENTRAL" TO O-DISTRICT.
       MOVE CORRESPONDING WS-DIST-2-TTLS
            TO DISTRICT-TOTALS-LINE.
       MOVE DIST-2-TTL OF LY-SALES-TOTALS TO O-LY-DIST-TTL.
       COMPUTE O-PERCENT-INCREASE ROUNDED =
          (YR-TTL OF WS-DIST-2-TTLS - DIST-2-TTL OF LY-SALES-TOTALS)
           / DIST-2-TTL OF LY-SALES-TOTALS * 100.
       WRITE PRINTLINE FROM DISTRICT-TOTALS-LINE
           AFTER ADVANCING 2 LINES.

   430-PREPARE-DIST-3-REPORT-LINE.
       MOVE "MOUNTAIN" TO O-DISTRICT.
       MOVE CORRESPONDING WS-DIST-3-TTLS
            TO DISTRICT-TOTALS-LINE.
       MOVE DIST-3-TTL OF LY-SALES-TOTALS TO O-LY-DIST-TTL.
       COMPUTE O-PERCENT-INCREASE ROUNDED =
          (YR-TTL OF WS-DIST-3-TTLS - DIST-3-TTL OF LY-SALES-TOTALS)
           / DIST-3-TTL OF LY-SALES-TOTALS * 100.
       WRITE PRINTLINE FROM DISTRICT-TOTALS-LINE
           AFTER ADVANCING 2 LINES.

   440-PREPARE-DIST-4-REPORT-LINE.
       MOVE "PACIFIC" TO O-DISTRICT.
       MOVE CORRESPONDING WS-DIST-4-TTLS
            TO DISTRICT-TOTALS-LINE.
       MOVE DIST-4-TTL OF LY-SALES-TOTALS TO O-LY-DIST-TTL.
       COMPUTE O-PERCENT-INCREASE ROUNDED =
          (YR-TTL OF WS-DIST-4-TTLS - DIST-4-TTL OF LY-SALES-TOTALS)
           / DIST-4-TTL OF LY-SALES-TOTALS * 100.
```

```
    WRITE PRINTLINE FROM DISTRICT-TOTALS-LINE
        AFTER ADVANCING 2 LINES.

450-PREPARE-CO-REPORT-LINE.
    MOVE CORRESPONDING WS-CO-TTLS TO COMPANY-TOTALS-LINE.
    MOVE CO-TTL OF LY-SALES-TOTALS TO O-LY-CO-TTL.
    COMPUTE O-PERCENT-INCREASE ROUNDED=
        (YR-TTL OF WS-CO-TTLS - CO-TTL OF LY-SALES-TOTALS)
        / CO-TTL OF LY-SALES-TOTALS * 100.
    WRITE PRINTLINE FROM COMPANY-TOTALS-LINE
        AFTER ADVANCING 4 LINES.
```

Note: Many programmers feel that the advantages of the CORRESPONDING options are offset by the need to use qualification. As a result, they prefer using the scheme of assigning the same data name to fields containing the same data, but they use a prefix or a suffix to specify the fields as belonging to input memory, output memory, or working storage. The most common prefixes are I- or IN- for input memory items, O- or OUT- for output memory items, and WS- for working storage items. These prefixes generally provide adequate self-documentation and avoid the disadvantages of qualification.

As an individual programmer, you will develop your preferences, and as a member of a team of programmers, you will want to follow the directions you receive from the chief programmer.

Important Terms in Chapter 7

88-level entry
ADD CORRESPONDING
CLASS
class test
- ALPHABETIC
- ALPHABETIC-LOWER
- ALPHABETIC-UPPER
- CLASS-NAME
- NUMERIC

collating sequence
compound abbreviated conditionals
- implied subject
- implied predicate

compound test
- AND
- OR

condition-name
condition-name test
conditional statement
conjunction
CONTINUE
disjunction
EVALUATE
- ALSO
- ANY
- END-EVALUATE
- object
- subject
- WHEN OTHER

MOVE CORRESPONDING
negated compound test
negated test
negative test
- NOT

nested conditional statements
nested tests
nonnumeric relational operands
qualification
- IN
- OF

relational operands
relational test
- EQUAL TO
- GREATER THAN
- GREATER THAN OR EQUAL TO
- LESS THAN
- LESS THAN OR EQUAL TO

sequential tests
sign test
- NEGATIVE
- POSITIVE
- ZERO

SUBTRACT CORRESPONDING

Exercises

1. Which of the modules in Figure 7.51 illustrate sequential tests? nested tests?
2. Use IF statements to code the logic illustrated in Figure 7.51a.
3. Use IF statements to code the logic illustrated in Figure 7.51b.
4. Use IF statements to code the logic illustrated in Figure 7.51c.
5. a. Use IF statements to code the logic illustrated in Figure 7.51d.
   b. Use IF statements to code the logic illustrated in Figure 7.51e.
6. Assume that employees are either salaried or on commission. Salaried employees receive a fixed amount each week, whereas employees on commission receive a base pay and a commission. The commission is 10 percent of the individual's sales if the sales exceed the quota; otherwise, the commission is 8 percent. Design the flowchart segment that maps out the logic needed to compute the weekly pay.
7. Revise the flowchart of exercise 6 to add the computed amounts to a total pay accumulator.
8. Write the pseudocode paragraph corresponding to the flowchart segment in exercise 7.
9. Code the conditional statements corresponding to the flowchart segments in Figure 7.52. Consider each process name as a module or paragraph name.

■ **Figure 7.51**

a.

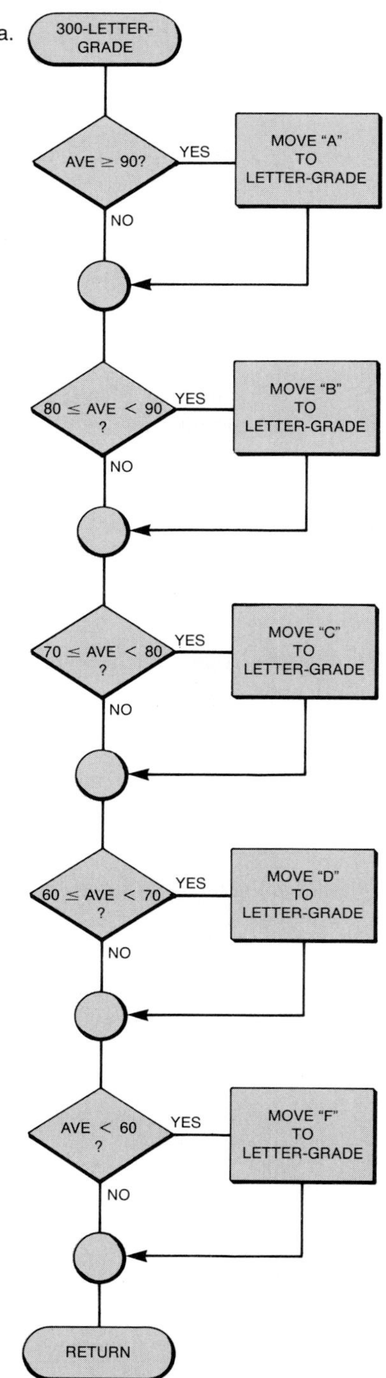

b.

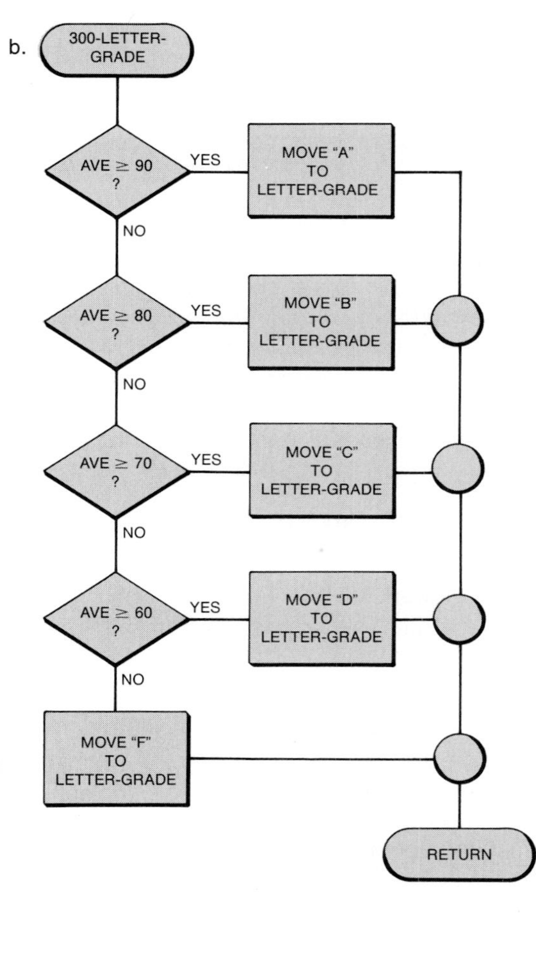

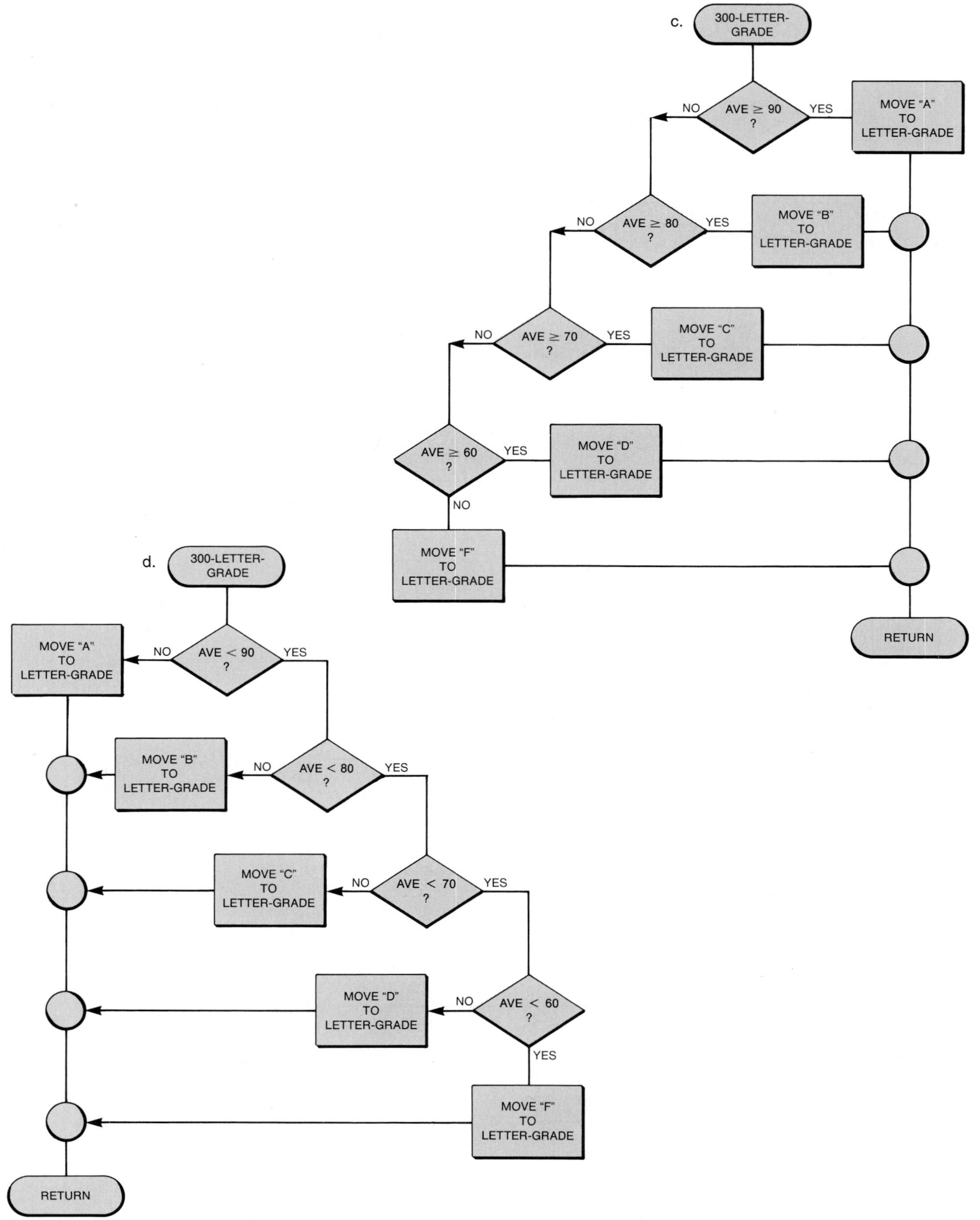
c.
300-LETTER-GRADE
AVE ≥ 90 ?
NO
YES
MOVE "A" TO LETTER-GRADE
AVE ≥ 80 ?
NO
YES
MOVE "B" TO LETTER-GRADE
AVE ≥ 70 ?
NO
YES
MOVE "C" TO LETTER-GRADE
AVE ≥ 60 ?
YES
MOVE "D" TO LETTER-GRADE
NO
MOVE "F" TO LETTER-GRADE
RETURN
d.
300-LETTER-GRADE
AVE < 90 ?
NO
YES
MOVE "A" TO LETTER-GRADE
AVE < 80 ?
NO
YES
MOVE "B" TO LETTER-GRADE
AVE < 70 ?
NO
YES
MOVE "C" TO LETTER-GRADE
AVE < 60 ?
NO
YES
MOVE "D" TO LETTER-GRADE
MOVE "F" TO LETTER-GRADE
RETURN

e.

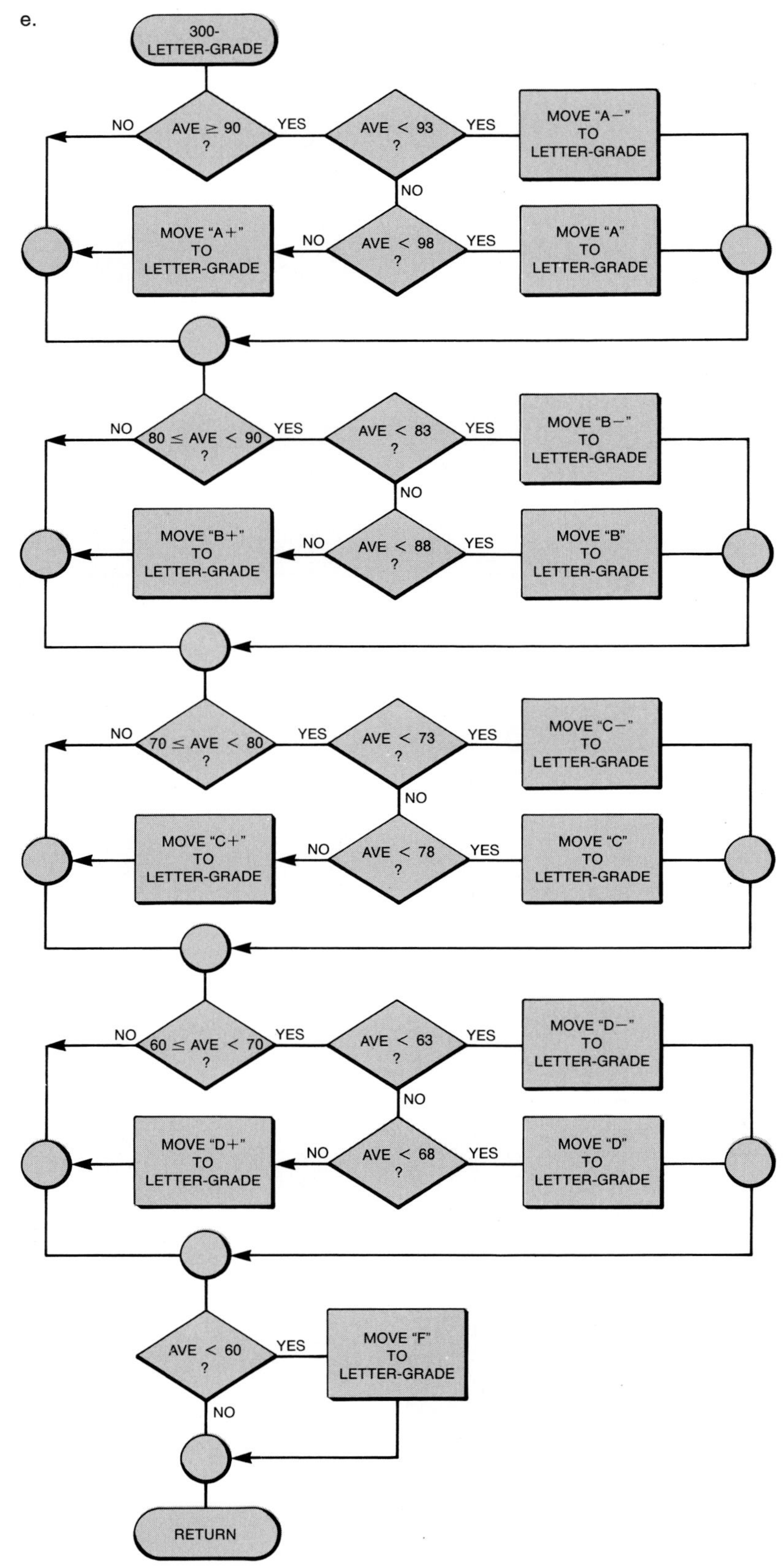
300-
LETTER-GRADE
AVE ≥ 90
?
NO
YES
AVE < 93
?
YES
MOVE "A−"
TO
LETTER-GRADE
NO
AVE < 98
?
NO
YES
MOVE "A+"
TO
LETTER-GRADE
MOVE "A"
TO
LETTER-GRADE
80 ≤ AVE < 90
?
NO
YES
AVE < 83
?
YES
MOVE "B−"
TO
LETTER-GRADE
NO
AVE < 88
?
NO
YES
MOVE "B+"
TO
LETTER-GRADE
MOVE "B"
TO
LETTER-GRADE
70 ≤ AVE < 80
?
NO
YES
AVE < 73
?
YES
MOVE "C−"
TO
LETTER-GRADE
NO
AVE < 78
?
NO
YES
MOVE "C+"
TO
LETTER-GRADE
MOVE "C"
TO
LETTER-GRADE
60 ≤ AVE < 70
?
NO
YES
AVE < 63
?
YES
MOVE "D−"
TO
LETTER-GRADE
NO
AVE < 68
?
NO
YES
MOVE "D+"
TO
LETTER-GRADE
MOVE "D"
TO
LETTER-GRADE
AVE < 60
?
YES
MOVE "F"
TO
LETTER-GRADE
NO
RETURN

■ **Figure 7.52**

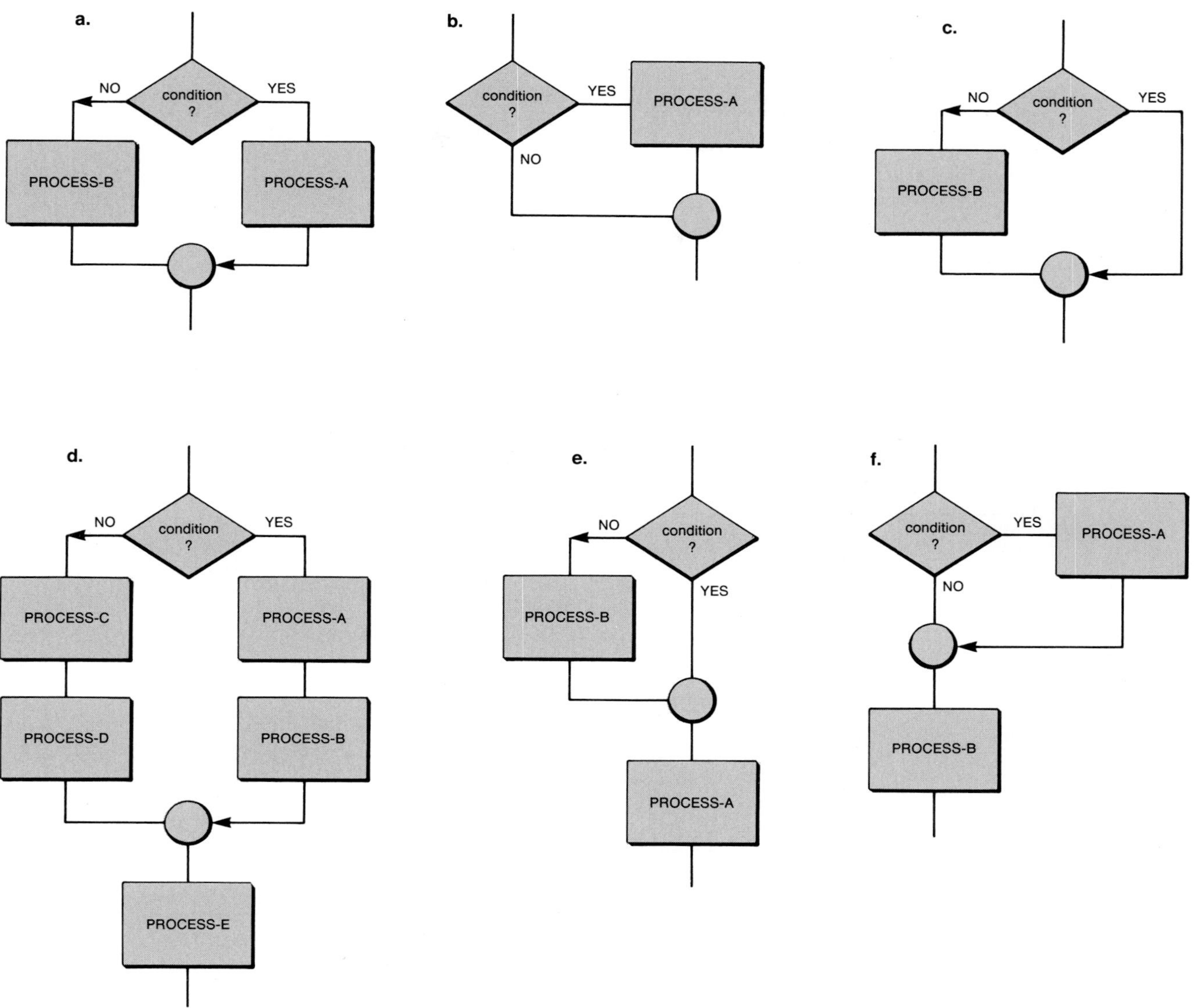

10. Refer to Figure 7.53. Which of the following coding groups corresponds to the flowchart?

a.
```
IF LINE-CTR = 20
    ADD 1 TO PAGE-NO.
        MOVE 0 TO LINE-CTR.
        PERFORM 300-WRITE-HEADERS.
    READ IN-FILE RECORD
        AT END
            MOVE "NO " TO WS-MORE-RECORDS.
```

b.
```
IF LINE-CTR IS NOT EQUAL TO 20
    READ IN-FILE RECORD
        AT END
            MOVE "NO " TO WS-MORE-RECORDS
    END-READ
ELSE
    ADD 1 TO PAGE-NO
    MOVE 0 TO LINE-CTR
    PERFORM 300-WRITE-HEADERS
END-IF.
```

c.
```
IF LINE-CTR = 20
    ADD 1 TO PAGE-NO
    MOVE 0 TO LINE-CTR
    PERFORM 300-WRITE-HEADERS
ELSE
    READ IN-FILE RECORD
        AT END
            MOVE "NO " TO WS-MORE-RECORDS
    END-READ
END-IF.
```

d.
```
IF LINE-CTR = 20
    ADD 1 TO PAGE-NO
    MOVE 0 TO LINE-CTR
    PERFORM 300-WRITE-HEADERS
ELSE
    CONTINUE.
READ IN-FILE RECORD
    AT END
        MOVE "NO " TO WS-MORE-RECORDS.
```

e.
```
IF LINE-CTR = 20
    ADD 1 TO PAGE-NO
    MOVE 0 TO LINE-CTR
    PERFORM 300-WRITE-HEADERS
END-IF.
READ IN-FILE RECORD
    AT END
        MOVE "NO " TO WS-MORE-RECORDS.
```

■ **Figure 7.53**

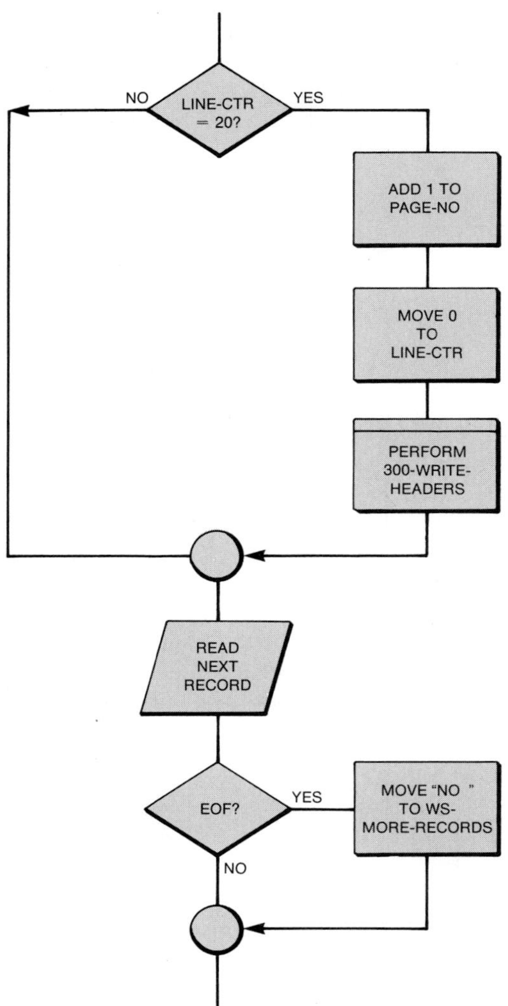

11. Use the following definitions to complete the exercises in parts 1 and 2 below:

```
01   PROGRAM-CONTROLS.
     05 WS-MORE-RECORDS            PIC XXX.
         88 THERE-IS-A-RECORD              VALUE "YES".
         88 NO-MORE-RECORDS                VALUE "NO ".
     05 LINE-CTR                   PIC 99.
         88 TOP-OF-PAGE                    VALUE 00.
         88 PAGE-IS-FULL                   VALUE 20.
     05 LINE-LIMIT                 PIC 99 VALUE 20.
```

Part 1. In each case, use a condition-name test to replace the relational test.

a. `IF LINE-CTR = LINE-LIMIT ...`

b. `IF WS-MORE-RECORDS IS EQUAL TO "YES" ...`

c. `IF LINE-CTR IS EQUAL TO 0 ...`

d. `IF LINE-CTR IS NOT = 0 ...`

e. `IF LINE-CTR IS NOT EQUAL TO 20 ...`

f.
```
IF WS-MORE-RECORDS = "YES"
    PERFORM 210-PROCESS-RECORD
        UNTIL WS-MORE-RECORDS = "NO ".
```

g.
```
IF WS-MORE-RECORDS = "YES" AND LINE-CTR = LINE-LIMIT
    PERFORM 300-WRITE-HEADERS.
```

Part 2. In each case, code a SET statement as an alternative to the MOVE statement.

a.
```
READ IN-FILE RECORD
    AT END
        MOVE "NO " TO WS-MORE-RECORDS.
```
b.
```
IF PAGE-IS-FULL
    PERFORM 300-WRITE-HEADERS
    MOVE ZERO TO LINE-CTR
END-IF.
```
c.
```
MOVE "YES" TO WS-MORE-RECORDS.
```
d.
```
IF NO-MORE-RECORDS
    MOVE 20 TO LINE-CTR
ELSE
    CONTINUE.
```

12. Use the following definitions to complete the exercises below:

```
05 AVE          PIC 999.
   88 A-GRADE   VALUES 90 THRU 100.
   88 B-GRADE   VALUES 80 THRU 89.
   88 C-GRADE   VALUES 70 THRU 79.
   88 D-GRADE   VALUES 60 THRU 69.
   88 F-GRADE   VALUES 0 THRU 59.
```

a. Use appropriate condition-names to code the statements corresponding to the flowchart module in Figure 7.51a.

b. Use appropriate condition-names to code the statements corresponding to the flowchart module in Figure 7.51c.

13. Given the input record and field specifications shown in Figure 7.54, write the pseudocode paragraph or design the flowchart module that will test each field for valid data. Set up an error counter to keep track of the number of errors. A blank field is also an error. If there is at least one error, display the record and the number of errors it contains.

14. Given the record layout shown in Figure 7.54, identify the fields of the records below that contain invalid characters.

```
                 1                   3 3 33   4 4
Col. 1           0                   0 2 45   0 2

     123456789FRANK BARBOZA      40 003   FAM
     432-77-8435JAMES HALLORAN   40 5 5   FAM.
     551 28 3240ANDREA POULITOS   40507   IND
     724662253   JILL SANMARTINO 400204   I
     154226684 DEAN ST. DENIS    40   08  F
```

15. Use appropriate compound tests to code the statements corresponding to the flowchart segments in Figure 7.55. Single-word entries in decision boxes are condition-names.

Figure 7.54

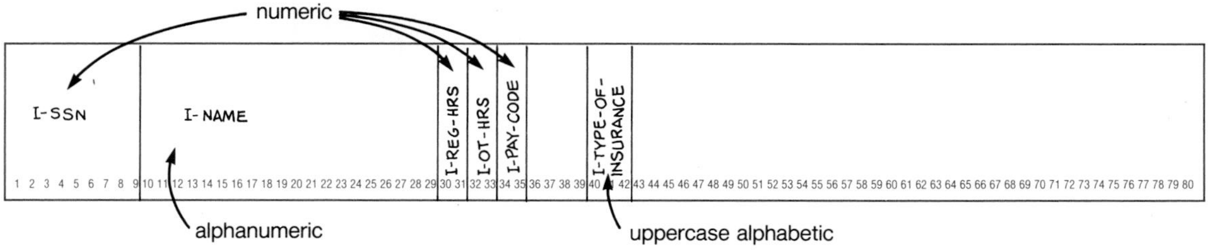

Field specifications:
I-REG-HRS <= 40
I-OT-HRS <= 20
I-PAY-CODE values 01–10
I-TYPE-OF-INSURANCE values FAM or IND

■ **Figure 7.55**

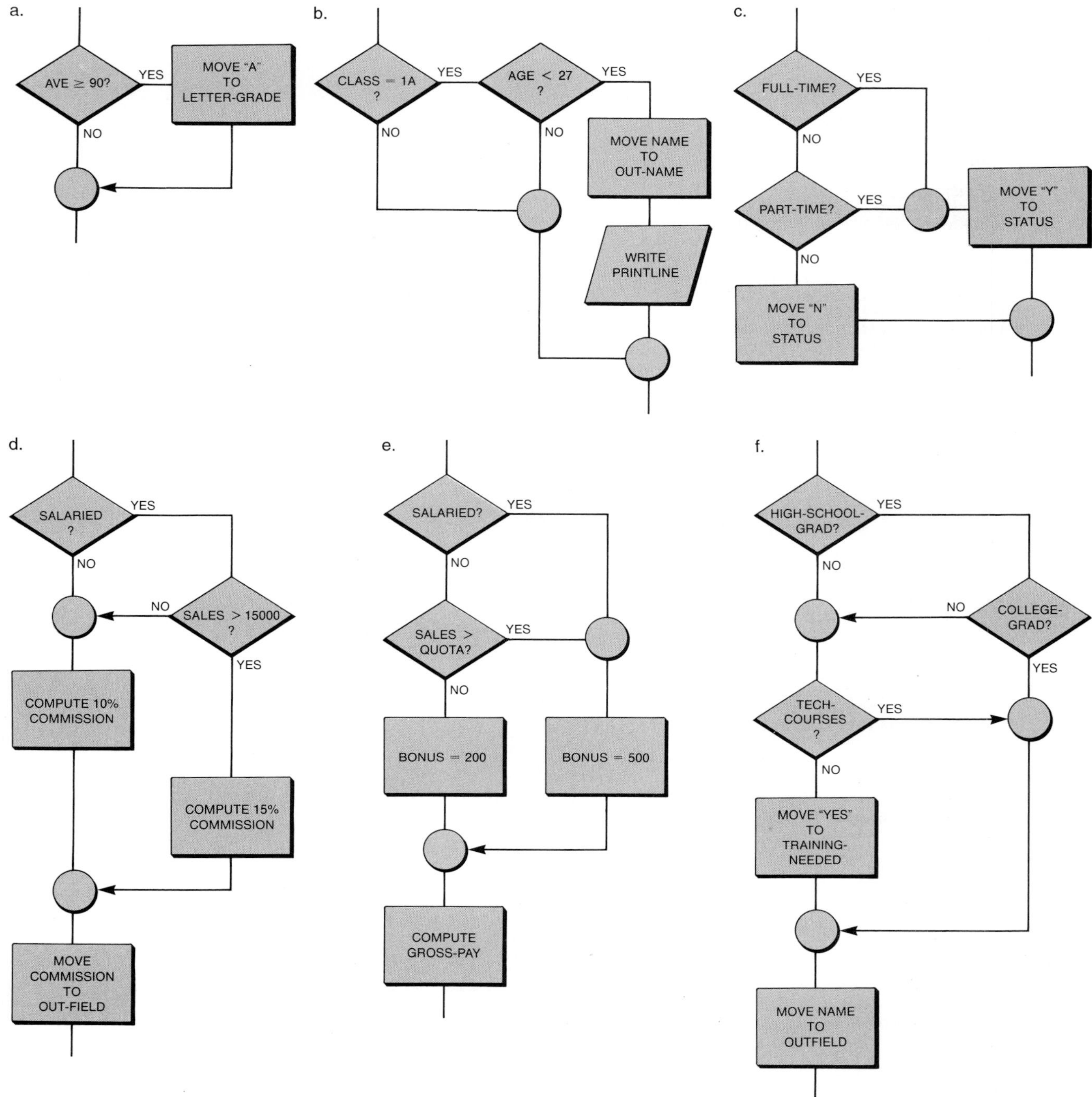
a.
AVE ≥ 90?
YES
NO
MOVE "A" TO LETTER-GRADE
b.
CLASS = 1A ?
YES
NO
AGE < 27 ?
YES
NO
MOVE NAME TO OUT-NAME
WRITE PRINTLINE
c.
FULL-TIME?
YES
NO
PART-TIME?
YES
NO
MOVE "Y" TO STATUS
MOVE "N" TO STATUS
d.
SALARIED ?
YES
NO
SALES > 15000 ?
NO
YES
COMPUTE 10% COMMISSION
COMPUTE 15% COMMISSION
MOVE COMMISSION TO OUT-FIELD
e.
SALARIED?
YES
NO
SALES > QUOTA?
YES
NO
BONUS = 200
BONUS = 500
COMPUTE GROSS-PAY
f.
HIGH-SCHOOL-GRAD?
YES
NO
COLLEGE-GRAD?
NO
YES
TECH-COURSES ?
YES
NO
MOVE "YES" TO TRAINING-NEEDED
MOVE NAME TO OUTFIELD

■ **Figure 7.56**

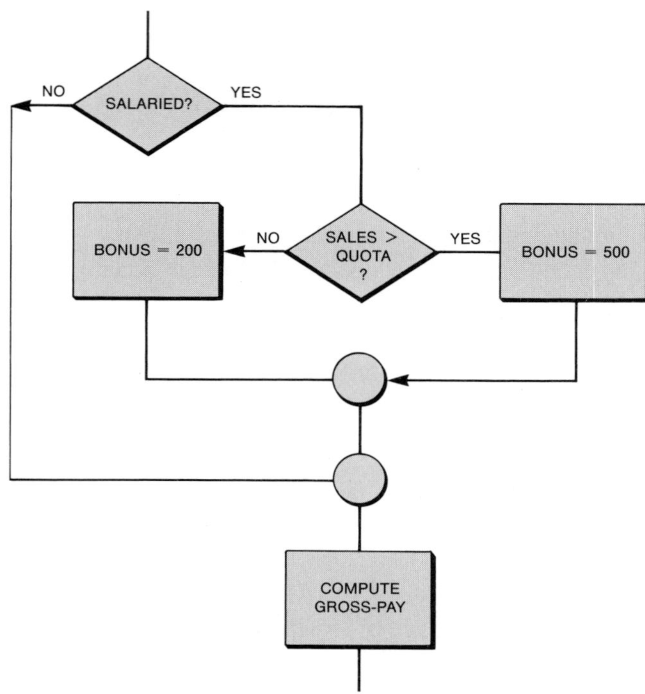

16. Given the flowchart segment in Figure 7.56, which of the following groups contain correct coding?

a.
```
IF SALARIED AND SALES > QUOTA
    MOVE 500 TO BONUS
ELSE
    MOVE 200 TO BONUS
END-IF.
COMPUTE GROSS-PAY = ...
```

b.
```
IF SALARIED
    IF SALES > QUOTA
        MOVE 500 TO BONUS
    ELSE
        MOVE 200 TO BONUS
ELSE
    COMPUTE GROSS-PAY = ...
```

c.
```
IF SALARIED
    THEN
        IF SALES > QUOTA
            MOVE 500 TO BONUS
        ELSE
            MOVE 200 TO BONUS
    ELSE
        NEXT SENTENCE.
COMPUTE GROSS-PAY = ...
```

d.
```
IF SALARIED
    IF SALES > QUOTA
        MOVE 500 TO BONUS
    ELSE
        MOVE 200 TO BONUS
END-IF.
COMPUTE GROSS-PAY = ...
```

e.
```
IF NOT SALARIED
    NEXT SENTENCE
ELSE
    IF SALES NOT > QUOTA
        MOVE 200 TO BONUS
    ELSE
        MOVE 500 TO BONUS
    END-IF
END-IF.
COMPUTE GROSS-PAY = ...
```

f.
```
EVALUATE SALARIED  ALSO  SALES > QUOTA
    WHEN   TRUE    ALSO      TRUE        MOVE 500 TO BONUS
    WHEN   TRUE    ALSO      FALSE       MOVE 200 TO BONUS
    WHEN   FALSE   ALSO      ANY         COMPUTE GROSS-PAY = ...
```

g.
```
EVALUATE SALARIED  ALSO  SALES > QUOTA
    WHEN   TRUE    ALSO      TRUE        MOVE 500 TO BONUS
    WHEN   TRUE    ALSO      FALSE       MOVE 200 TO BONUS.
COMPUTE GROSS-PAY = ...
```
h.
```
EVALUATE       TRUE      ALSO       TRUE
    WHEN     SALARIED    ALSO  SALES > QUOTA     MOVE 500 TO BONUS
    WHEN     SALARIED    ALSO  SALES NOT > QUOTA MOVE 200 TO BONUS
    WHEN   NOT SALARIED  ALSO        ANY         COMPUTE GROSS-PAY = ...
```
i.
```
EVALUATE       TRUE      ALSO       TRUE
    WHEN     SALARIED    ALSO  SALES > QUOTA     MOVE 500 TO BONUS
    WHEN     SALARIED    ALSO  SALES NOT > QUOTA MOVE 200 TO BONUS.
COMPUTE GROSS-PAY = ...
```

17. Use EVALUATE statements to code the flowchart segments shown in Figure 7.55.
18. Use IF statements to code the flowchart segments in Figure 7.57. Single-word entries in decision boxes are condition-names.
19. Use EVALUATE statements to code the flowchart segments in Figure 7.57.
20. Use the data item AVE in an EVALUATE statement to code the case structure in Figure 7.58.
21. Use the condition-names defined for the data item AVE in exercise 12 in an EVALUATE statement to code the case structure in Figure 7.58.
22. Given the following record descriptions, complete the exercises below:

```
01  IN-STUDENT-REC.
    05 NAME         PIC X(20).
    05 STUDENT-ID   PIC X(9).
    05 TEST-1       PIC 999.
    05 TEST-2       PIC 999.
    05 TEST-3       PIC 999.
```

```
01  OUT-STUDENT-REC.
    05              PIC X(5).
    05 NAME         PIC X(20).
    05              PIC X(4).
    05 TEST-1       PIC ZZ9.
    05              PIC XX.
    05 TEST-2       PIC ZZ9.
    05              PIC XX.
    05 TEST-3       PIC ZZ9.
    05              PIC XX.
    05 AVERAGE      PIC ZZ9.
    05              PIC X(10).
    05 STUDENT-ID PIC XXXBXXBXXXX.
```

Figure 7.57

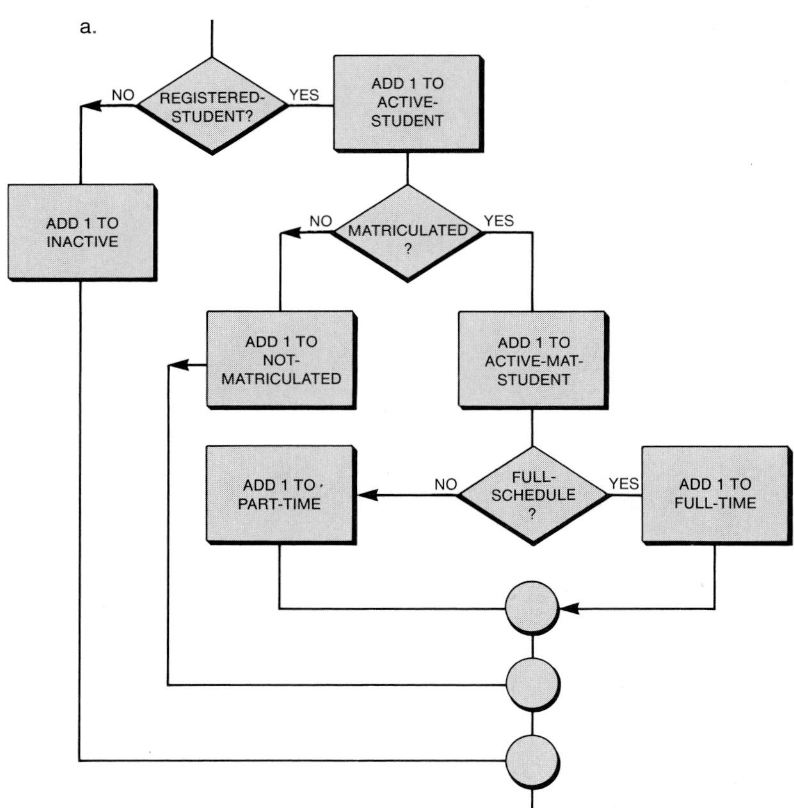

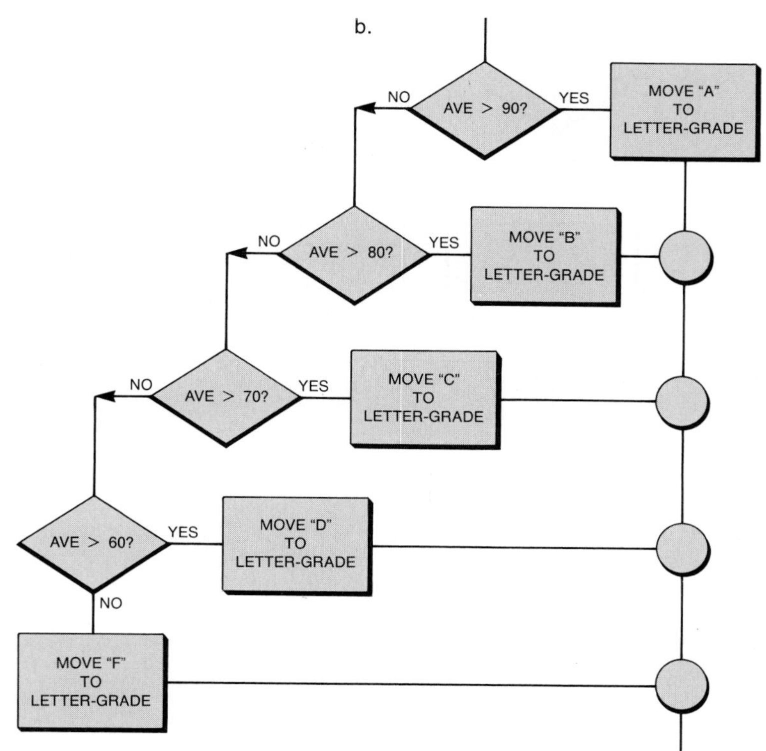
b.
AVE > 90?
NO
YES
MOVE "A" TO LETTER-GRADE
AVE > 80?
NO
YES
MOVE "B" TO LETTER-GRADE
AVE > 70?
NO
YES
MOVE "C" TO LETTER-GRADE
AVE > 60?
YES
MOVE "D" TO LETTER-GRADE
NO
MOVE "F" TO LETTER-GRADE

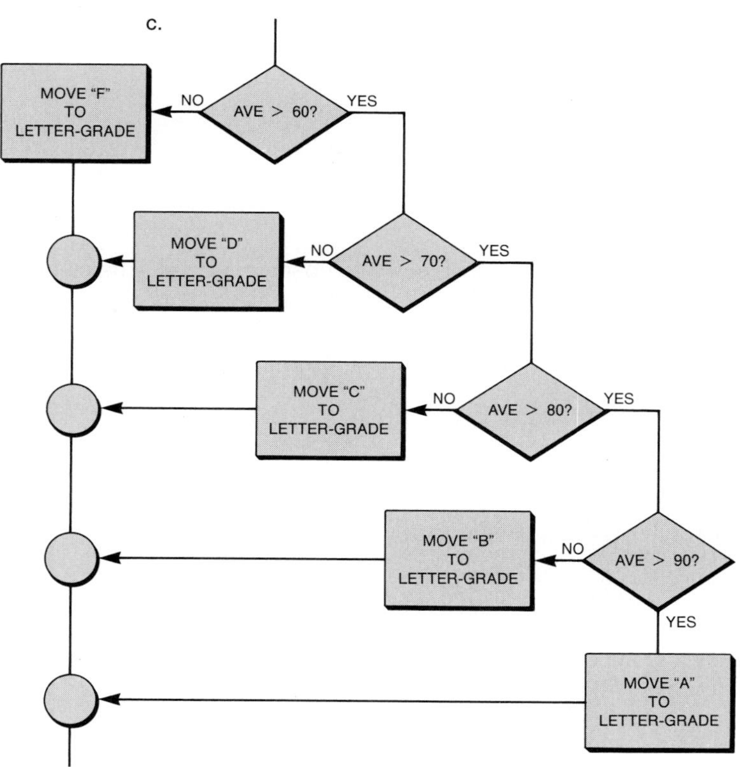
c.
AVE > 60?
NO
YES
MOVE "F" TO LETTER-GRADE
AVE > 70?
NO
YES
MOVE "D" TO LETTER-GRADE
AVE > 80?
NO
YES
MOVE "C" TO LETTER-GRADE
AVE > 90?
NO
MOVE "B" TO LETTER-GRADE
YES
MOVE "A" TO LETTER-GRADE

■ **Figure 7.58**

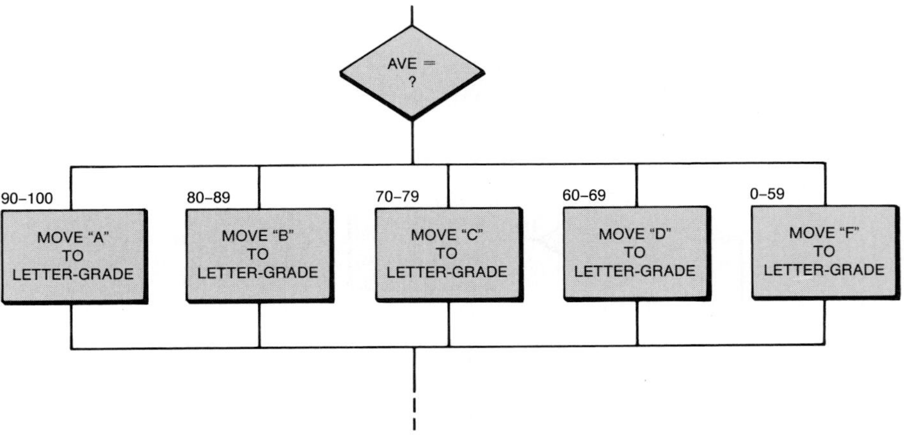

a. Use qualification to properly reference the elementary data items belonging to the records above.

b. Write the MOVE statements required to transfer the appropriate data from the record IN-STUDENT-REC to OUT-STUDENT-REC.

c. Write the MOVE CORRESPONDING statement required to transfer the data from the record IN-STUDENT-REC to OUT-STUDENT-REC.

d. Write the statement required to compute the average of the three tests and to store the resulting value in the field AVERAGE.

e. Rewrite the descriptions of the records above so that qualification will not be needed.

f. Use the data names you have assigned to the data fields in part e to:

  i. Move the values from IN-STUDENT-REC to OUT-STUDENT-REC.

  ii. Compute the average of the three tests and store the resulting value in the appropriate field of the output record.

■ Debugging Activities

1. A COBOL program must prepare a student report that lists the test grades, the numeric average, and a letter-grade for each student record in the input file. Unfortunately, the program contains a number of syntax errors. The listing produced by the compiler is shown in Figure 7.59. Your task is to correct all the syntax errors.

2. In this exercise, the syntax errors that are specified in Figure 7.59 have been corrected. The student file shown in part a (Debugging Activity Data File, Set 14 [DD/CD:VIC7DBG2.DAT]) was processed by the program, and the output that was produced is shown in part b.

   It should be obvious that the program is not producing the required report. Your task is to find and correct the remaining errors.

Part a:

```
FA8692-368-201232156742BORGES, JUDY        084091082
FA8692-368-201371421534CABANAUGH, JAMES R. 070064076
FA8692-368-201364153218ESPOSITO, PHIL      092085081
FA8692-368-201277821435MARSHALL, THERESA   068085091
FA8692-368-201537465322POTVIN, GARY        096091095
FA8692-368-201272117495RANGELY, DICK       087075083
FA8692-368-201436281726ROUSSEAU, MARY BETH 073087094
FA8692-368-201574392781SANTERRE, WILLIAM   100095098
FA8692-368-201513247132SILVIA, ROSEMARIE   081087079
FA8692-368-201431894142WORDEN, STEVE       064077085
```

■ Figure 7.59

```
COURSE-AVE-PROG                                        18-Nov-1993 15:46:43   VAX COBOL V5.1-10                    Page    1
Source Listing                                         18-Nov-1993 13:03:43   FACULTY$DISK:[PAQUETTEG.WCBTXT]C7DBG1.CB1;1

              IDENTIFICATION DIVISION.

              PROGRAM-ID.  COURSE-AVE-PROG.

             *************************************************************
             *                                                           *
             *  AUTHOR.         PAQUETTE.                                *
             *  DATE WRITTEN.   AUGUST  1993                             *
             *                                                           *
             *************************************************************

              ENVIRONMENT DIVISION.

              CONFIGURATION SECTION.

              SOURCE-COMPUTER.  VAX-VMS-8650.
              OBJECT-COMPUTER.  VAX-VMS-8650.

              INPUT-OUTPUT SECTION.

              FILE-CONTROL.
                  SELECT STUDENT-FILE     ASSIGN TO COB$INPUT.
                  SELECT STUDENT-REPORT   ASSIGN TO COB$OUTPUT.

              DATA DIVISION.

              FILE SECTION.

              FD  STUDENT-FILE
                  RECORD CONTAINS 52 CHARACTERS.

              01  STUDENT-RECORD.
                  05 SEMESTER        PIC X(4).
                  05 COURSE-ID       PIC X(10).
                  05 STUDENT-ID      PIC X(9).
                  05 STUDENT-NAME    PIC X(20).
                  05 TEST-GRADES.
                      10 TEST-1      PIC 999.
                      10 TEST-2      PIC 999.
                      10 TEST-3      PIC 999.

              FD  STUDENT-REPORT
                  RECORD CONTAINS 133 CHARACTERS.

              01  PRINTLINE          PIC X(133).

              WORKING-STORAGE SECTION.

              01  PROGRAM-CONTROLS.
                  05 WS-MORE-RECORDS          PIC XXX.
                     88 THERE-IS-A-RECORD     VALUE "YES".
                     88 NO-MORE-RECORDS       VALUE "NO ".
                  05 WS-REPORT-DATE           PIC X(6).
                  05 WS-PAGE-NO               PIC 99.
                  05 WS-LINE-CTR              PIC S99.
                  05 WS-LINE-LIMIT            PIC S99    VALUE +30.
                  05 WS-PROPER-SPACING        PIC 99.

              01  STUDENT-WORK-AREAS.
                  05 WS-GRADE-AVE       PIC S999   COMP.
                     88 A-GRADE         VALUES 90 THRU 100.
                     88 B-GRADE         VALUES 80 THRU 89.
                     88 C-GRADE         VALUES 70 THRU 79.
                     88 D-GRADE         VALUES 60 THRU 69.
                     88 F-GRADE         VALUES  0 THRU 59.
                                                1
%COBOL-F-ERROR  118, (1) Invalid record description
%COBOL-E-ERROR   65, (1) Missing period is assumed
                     88 VALID-AVE       VALUES  0 THRU 100.
                  05 WS-LETTER-GRADE    PIC X.
                  1

%COBOL-W-ERROR  297, (1) Processing of source program resumes at this point

              01  REPORT-HEADERS.
                  05 TOP-LINE.
                      10 PIC X(16)        VALUE "   REPORT DATE:   ".
                      10 O-REPORT-DATE    PIC XX/XX/XX.
                      10 PIC X(97)        VALUE SPACES.
                      10 PIC X(5)         VALUE "PAGE ".
                      10 O-PAGE-NO        PIC Z9.
                      10 PIC X(6)         VALUE SPACES.
                  05 REPORT-NAME.
                      10 PIC X(60)   VALUE SPACES.
                      10 PIC X(14)   VALUE "STUDENT REPORT".
                      10 PIC X(59)   VALUE SPACES.
```

Figure 7.59 continued

```
COURSE-AVE-PROG                          18-Nov-1993 15:46:43   VAX COBOL V5.1-10                            Page  2
Source Listing                           18-Nov-1993 13:03:43   FACULTY$DISK:[PAQUETTEG.WCBTXT]C7DBG1.CB1;1

               05 HEADINGS.
                   10 PIC X(5)    VALUE SPACES.
                   10 PIC X(8)    VALUE "SEMESTER".
                   10 PIC X(4)    VALUE SPACES.
                   10 PIC X(9)    VALUE "COURSE ID".
                   10 PIC X(5)    VALUE SPACES.
                   10 PIC X(10)   VALUE "STUDENT ID".
                   10 PIC X(8)    VALUE SPACES.
                   10 PIC X(12)   VALUE "STUDENT NAME".
                   10 PIC X(8)    VALUE SPACES.
                   10 PIC X(6)    VALUE "TEST 1".
                   10 PIC X(4)    VALUE SPACES.
                   10 PIC X(6)    VALUE "TEST 2".
                   10 PIC X(4)    VALUT SPACES.
                                  1    2
%COBOL-E-ERROR   65, (1) Missing period is assumed
%COBOL-E-ERROR   66, (1) Missing level-number - assumed same as previous
%COBOL-E-ERROR   81, (1) PICTURE clause required - PIC X or PIC 9 assumed, depending on usage
%COBOL-E-ERROR   65, (2) Missing period is assumed
%COBOL-F-ERROR  117, (2) Invalid syntax
                   10 PIC X(6)    VALUE "TEST 3".
                   1
%COBOL-W-ERROR  297, (1) Processing of source program resumes at this point
                   10 PIC X(4)    VALUE SPACES.
                   10 PIC X(14)   VALUE "COURSE AVERAGE".
                   10 PIC X(4)    VALUE SPACES.
                   10 PIC X(12)   VALUE "COURSE GRADE".
                   10 PIC X(4)    VALUE SPACES.

           01  STUDENT-LINE.
               05                PIC X(7).
               05 SEMESTER       PIC X(4).
               05                PIC X(6).
               05 COURSE-ID      PIC X(10).
               05                PIC X(4).
               05 STUDENT-ID     PIC X(9).
               05                PIC X(5).
               05 STUDENT-NAME   PIC X(20).
               05 SEMESTER-WORK.
                   10                PIC X(5).
                   10 TEST-1         PIC ZZ9.
                   10                PIC X(6).
                   10 TEST-2         PIC ZZ9.
                   10                PIC X(6).
                   10 TEST-3         PIC ZZ9.
                   10                PIC X(10).
                   10 COURSE-AVE     PIC ZZ9.
                   10                PIC X(15).
                   10 COURSE-GRADE   PIC X.
                   10                PIC X(10)

            01  END-LINE.
            1
%COBOL-E-ERROR   65, (1) Missing period is assumed
                05 PIC X(57)  VALUE SPACES.
                05 PIC X(19)  VALUE "** END OF REPORT **".
                05 PIC X(57)  VALUE SPACES.

            PROCEDURE DIVISION.

            100-PRODUCE-STUDENT-REPORT.
                PERFORM 200-START-UP.
                PERFORM 210-PROCESS-STUDENT-RECORD
                    UNTIL NO-MORE-RECORDS.
                PERFORM 220-FINISH-UP.
                STOP RUN.

            200-START-UP.
                OPEN INPUT STUDENT-FILE
                     OUTPUT STUDENT-REPORT.
                PERFORM 300-INITIALIZE-ITEMS.
                PERFORM 500-WRITE-REPORT-HEADERS.
                PERFORM 310-READ-STUDENT-RECORD.

            210-PROCESS-STUDENT-RECORD.
                PERFORM 320-COMPUTE-COURSE-GRADE.
                PERFORM 330-PREPARE-STUDENT-LINE.
                PERFORM 310-READ-STUDENT-RECORD.

              220-FINISH-UP.
                  WRITE PRINTLINE FROM END-LINE
                      AFTER ADVANCING 10 LINES.
                  CLOSE STUDENT-FILE
                        STUDENT-REPORT.
```

Figure 7.59 continued

```
COURSE-AVE-PROG                           18-Nov-1993 15:46:43   VAX COBOL V5.1-10                   Page   3
Source Listing                            18-Nov-1993 13:03:43   FACULTY$DISK:[PAQUETTEG.WCBTXT]C7DBG1.CB1;1

                300-INITIALIZE-ITEMS.
                    ACCEPT WS-REPORT-DATE FROM DATE.
                    MOVE WS-REPORT-DATE TO O-REPORT-DATE.
                    MOVE ZERO TO WS-PAGE-NO.
                    SET WS-MORE-RECORDS TO TRUE.
                        1
%COBOL-F-ERROR    348, (1) Operand must be a condition-name
                    INITIALIZE STUDENT-LINE.

                310-READ-STUDENT-RECORD.
                    READ STUDENT-FILE RECORD
                        AT END
                            SET NO-MORE-RECORDS TO TRUE.

                320-COMPUTE-COURSE-GRADE.
                    COMPUTE WS-COURSE-AVE ROUNDED =
                            1
%COBOL-F-ERROR    349, (1) Undefined name
                        TEST-1 + TEST-2 + TEST-3 / 3.
                        1        2        3
%COBOL-F-ERROR    337, (1) Ambiguous reference - check name qualification
%COBOL-F-ERROR    337, (2) Ambiguous reference - check name qualification
%COBOL-F-ERROR    337, (3) Ambiguous reference - check name qualification
                    EVALUATE WS-GRADE-AVE
                    1
%COBOL-W-ERROR    297, (1) Processing of source program resumes at this point
                        WHEN A-GRADE  MOVE "A" TO WS-LETTER-GRADE
                             1
%COBOL-F-ERROR    218, (1) Incompatible operands in relation condition
                        WHEN B-GRADE  MOVE "B" TO WS-LETTER-GRADE
                             1
%COBOL-F-ERROR    218, (1) Incompatible operands in relation condition
                        WHEN C-GRADE  MOVE "C" TO WS-LETTER-GRADE
                             1
%COBOL-F-ERROR    218, (1) Incompatible operands in relation condition
                        WHEN D-GRADE  MOVE "D" TO WS-LETTER-GRADE
                             1
%COBOL-F-ERROR    218, (1) Incompatible operands in relation condition
                        WHEN F-GRADE  MOVE "F" TO WS-LETTER-GRADE
                        WHEN NOT VALID-GRADE
                                     1
%COBOL-F-ERROR    349, (1) Undefined name
                            DISPLAY " ERROR IN GRADE AVERAGE FOR " STUDENT-NAME
                                                                   1
%COBOL-F-ERROR    337, (1) Ambiguous reference - check name qualification
                    END-EVALUATE.
                    1
%COBOL-F-ERROR    222, (1) "." required at this point

                330-PREPARE-STUDENT-LINE.
                1
%COBOL-W-ERROR    297, (1) Processing of source program resumes at this point
                    MOVE CORRESPONDING STUDENT-RECORD TO STUDENT-LINE.
                    MOVE WS-GRADE-AVE TO COURSE-AVE.
                    MOVE WS-LETTER-GRADE TO COURSE-GRADE.
                    PERFORM 400-CHECK-LINE-CTR.
                    WRITE PRINTLINE FROM STUDENT-LINE
                        AFTER ADVANCING WS-PROPER-SPACING.
                    MOVE 1 TO WS-PROPER-SPACING.
                    ADD 1 TO WS-LINE-CTR.

                400-CHECK-LINE-CTR.
                    IF PAGE-IS-FULL
                       1
%COBOL-F-ERROR    349, (1) Undefined name
                        PERFORM 500-WRITE-REPORT-HEADERS
                    ELSE
                    1
%COBOL-F-ERROR    222, (1) "." required at this point
                        CONTINUE.

                500-WRITE-REPORT-HEADERS.
                    ADD 1 TO WS-PAGE-NO.
                    MOVE WS-PAGE-NO TO O-PAGE-NO.
                    WRITE PRINTLINE FROM TOP-LINE
                        AFTER ADVANCING PAGE.
                    WRITE PRINTLINE FROM REPORT-NAME
                        AFTER ADVANCING 3 LINES.
                    WRITE PRINTLINE FROM HEADINGS
                        AFTER ADVANCING 3 LINES.
                    MOVE 2 TO WS-PROPER-SPACING.
                    INITIALIZE WS-LINE-CTR.
```

Part b:

```
REPORT DATE:   93/08/21                                                                                   PAGE   1
                                                      STUDENT REPORT

   SEMESTER   COURSE ID    STUDENT ID      STUDENT NAME      TEST 1   TEST 2   TEST 3   COURSE AVERAGE   COURSE GRADE

     FA86     92-368-201   232156742   BORGES, JUDY             0        0        0          202
     FA86     92-368-201   371421534   CABANAUGH, JAMES R.      0        0        0          159
     FA86     92-368-201   364153218   ESPOSITO, PHIL           0        0        0          204
     FA86     92-368-201   277821435   MARSHALL, THERESA        0        0        0          183
     FA86     92-368-201   537465322   POTVIN, GARY             0        0        0          219
     FA86     92-368-201   272117495   RANGELY, DICK            0        0        0          190
     FA86     92-368-201   436281726   ROUSSEAU, MARY BETH      0        0        0          191
     FA86     92-368-201   574392781   SANTERRE, WILLIAM        0        0        0          228
     FA86     92-368-201   513247132   SILVIA, ROSEMARIE        0        0        0          194
     FA86     92-368-201   431894142   WORDEN, STEVE            0        0        0          169


                                                  ** END OF REPORT **

ERROR IN GRADE AVERAGE FOR BORGES, JUDY
ERROR IN GRADE AVERAGE FOR CABANAUGH, JAMES R.
ERROR IN GRADE AVERAGE FOR ESPOSITO, PHIL
ERROR IN GRADE AVERAGE FOR MARSHALL, THERESA
ERROR IN GRADE AVERAGE FOR POTVIN, GARY
ERROR IN GRADE AVERAGE FOR RANGELY, DICK
ERROR IN GRADE AVERAGE FOR ROUSSEAU, MARY BETH
ERROR IN GRADE AVERAGE FOR SANTERRE, WILLIAM
ERROR IN GRADE AVERAGE FOR SILVIA, ROSEMARIE
ERROR IN GRADE AVERAGE FOR WORDEN, STEVE
```

Programming Exercises

Programming Exercise I

The management of Express Auto Parts Warehouse wants an analysis report for the week that will identify two kinds of items of questionable value to the company: (1) items that have not sold, and (2) items that have excessive returns (50 percent or more of sales). For each item, there is a record in the catalog file containing the following data:

cc 1–5	Catalog number
cc 6–25	Item description
cc 26–30	Unit purchase price
cc 36–39	Quantity on hand at the beginning of the week
cc 40–43	Quantity on order
cc 44–47	The reorder point
cc 48–51	Quantity received during the week
cc 52–55	Quantity sold during the week
cc 56–59	Quantity returned by customers during the week.

The report must be properly documented with a report-date line, company name, report name, and column headings. It must contain the following information for each item of questionable value: the catalog number, the item description, the purchase price, the quantity in stock (on hand + returns + received – sold), the total value of the stock (purchase price x quantity in stock), and the reason for current status (low sales or too many returns or both). At the end of the listing, an entry should specify the total value of the above items.

There should be no more than 30 items per page. The pages of the report should be numbered consecutively. An End-of-Report message should terminate the report.

The design tools have been provided for you in Figure 7.60. Your task is to complete the design implementation phase of the problem-solving procedure.

Use the current date as the report date, and use Data File Set 1 (see Appendix C) [DD/CD:VIC7EX1.DAT] as the input file.

■ Figure 7.60

Record Layout Form

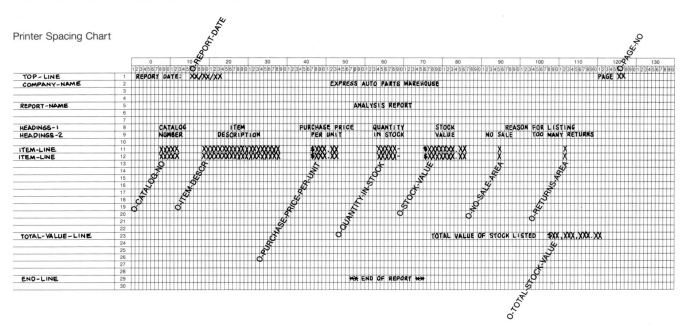

I-CATALOG-NO	I-ITEM-DESCR	I-PURCHASE-PRICE-PER-UNIT		I-ON-HAND	I-ON-ORDER	I-REORDER-POINT	I-WK-RECEIPTS	I-WK-SALES	I-WK-RETURNS	
1 2 3 4 5	6 7 8 9 10 11 12 13 14 15 16 17 18 19 20 21 22 23 24 25	26 27 28 ^ 29 30	31 32 33 34 35	36 37 38 39	40 41 42 43	44 45 46 47	48 49 50 51	52 53 54 55	56 57 58 59	60 61 62 63 64 65 66 67 68 69 70 71 72 73 74 75 76 77 78 79 80

Record Name: ITEM-RECORD

Printer Spacing Chart

Record	Line	Content
TOP-LINE	1	REPORT DATE: XX/XX/XX (O-REPORT-DATE) ... PAGE XX (O-PAGE-NO)
COMPANY-NAME	2	EXPRESS AUTO PARTS WAREHOUSE
	3	
	4	
REPORT-NAME	5	ANALYSIS REPORT
	6	
	7	
HEADINGS-1	8	CATALOG ITEM PURCHASE PRICE QUANTITY STOCK REASON FOR LISTING
HEADINGS-2	9	NUMBER DESCRIPTION PER UNIT IN STOCK VALUE NO SALE TOO MANY RETURNS
	10	
ITEM-LINE	11	XXXXX XXXXXXXXXXXXXXXXXXXX $XXX.XX XXXXX- $XXXXXXX.XX X X
ITEM-LINE	12	XXXXX XXXXXXXXXXXXXXXXXXXX $XXX.XX XXXXX- $XXXXXXX.XX X X
	13–22	
TOTAL-VALUE-LINE	23	TOTAL VALUE OF STOCK LISTED $XX,XXX,XXX.XX
	24–28	
END-LINE	29	** END OF REPORT **
	30	

Item-line field names: O-CATALOG-NO, O-ITEM-DESCR, O-PURCHASE-PRICE-PER-UNIT, O-QUANTITY-IN-STOCK, O-STOCK-VALUE, O-NO-SALE-AREA, O-RETURNS-AREA; total line: O-TOTAL-STOCK-VALUE

System Flowchart

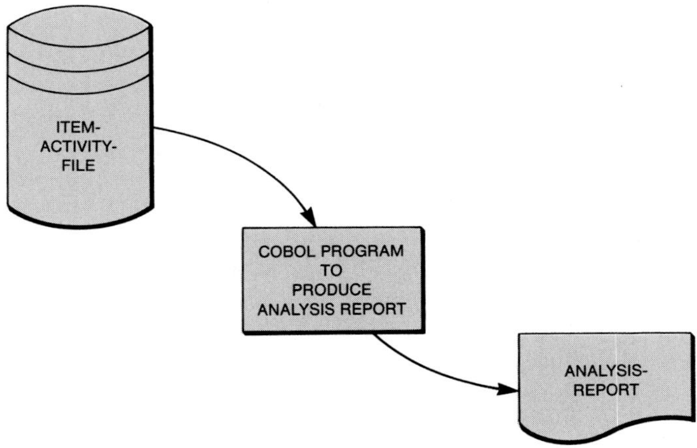

■ **Figure 7.60** continued

Structure Chart

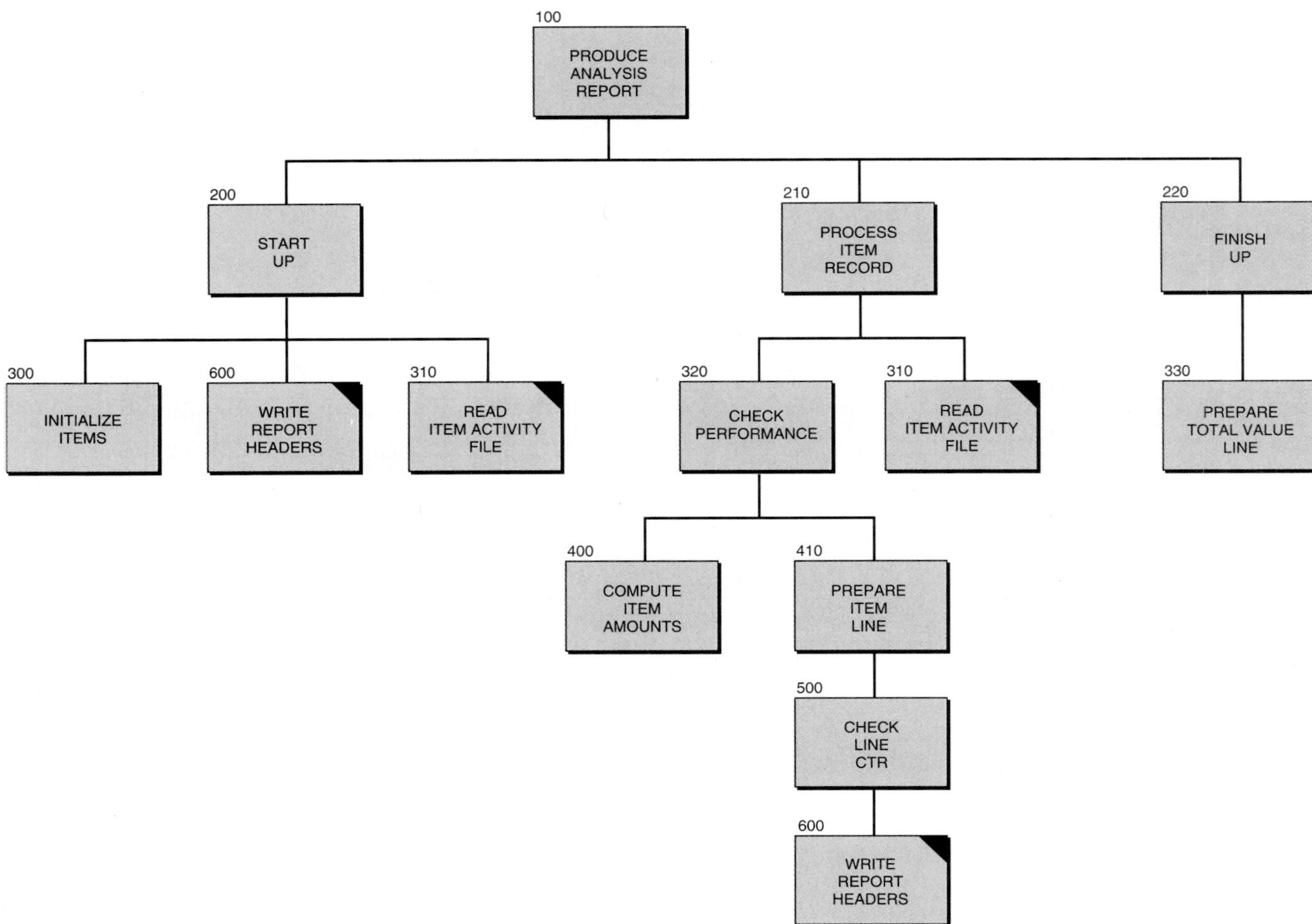

Pseudocode

100-Produce-Analysis-Report.

1. Perform 200-Start-Up.
2. Perform 210-Process-Item-Record until no more records.
3. Perform 220-Finish-Up.
4. Stop the run.

200-Start-Up.

1. Open the files.
2. Perform 300-Initialize-Items.
3. Perform 600-Write-Report-Headers.
4. Perform 310-Read-Item-Activity-File.

210-Process-Item-Record.

1. Perform 320-Check-Performance.
2. Perform 310-Read-Item-Activity-File.

220-Finish-Up.

1. Perform 330-Prepare-Total-Value-Line.
2. Move End-Line to the output area Printline.
3. After advancing 10 lines, write the output record Printline.
4. Close the files.

300-Initialize-Items.

1. Obtain the date from the system.
2. Move the date to Top-Line date.
3. Set page-number to zero.
4. Set the end-of-file flag WS-MORE-RECORDS to "YES".
5. Set the total-stock-value to zero.
6. Clear the record area Item-Line.

310-Read-Item-Activity-File.

1. Read an input Item-Record.
2. Test for end-of-file record;
   if it is, move "NO " to the end-of-file flag WS-MORE-RECORDS.

320-Check-Performance.

1. If input week-sales = zero or
   input week returns > half of input week-sales,
   perform 400-Compute-Item-Amounts and
   perform 410-Prepare-Item-Line.

330-Prepare-Total-Value-Line.

1. Move total-stock-value to Total-Value-Line total-stock-value.
2. Move Total-Value-Line to the output area Printline.
3. After advancing 5 lines, write the output record Printline.

400-Compute-Item-Amounts.

1. Add input on-hand, input week-returns, input week-receipts, and then subtract input week-sales to equal quantity-in-stock.
2. Multiply quantity-in-stock by input purchase-price-per-unit to equal stock-value.
3. Add stock-value to total-stock-value.

410-Prepare-Item-Line.

1. Move input catalog-number to Item-Line catalog-number.
2. Move input item-description to Item-Line item-description.
3. Move input purchase-price-per-unit to Item-Line purchase-price-per-unit.
4. Move quantity-in-stock to Item-Line quantity-in-stock.
5. Move stock-value to Item-Line stock-value.
6. If input week-sales = 0,
   move "X" to Item-Line no-sale-area.
7. If input week-returns > half of input week-sales,
   move "X" to Item-Line returns-area.
8. Perform 500-Check-Line-Ctr.
9. Move Item-Line to the output area Printline.
10. After advancing proper-spacing, write the output record Printline.
11. Set proper-spacing to 1.
12. Add 1 to the line-counter.

500-Check-Line-Ctr.

1. If line-counter is greater than or equal to line-limit,
   perform 600-Write-Report-Headers.

600-Write-Report-Headers.

1. Add 1 to page-number.
2. Move page-number to Top-Line page-number.
3. Move Top-Line to the output area Printline.
4. After advancing to the top of a new page,
   write the output record Printline.
5. Move Company-Name to the output area Printline.
6. After advancing 1 line, write the output record Printline.
7. Move Report-Name to the output area Printline.
8. After advancing 3 lines, write the output record Printline.
9. Move Headings-1 to the output area Printline.
10. After advancing 3 lines, write the output record Printline.
11. Move Headings-2 to the output area Printline.
12. After advancing 1 line, write the output record Printline.
13. Set proper-spacing to 2.
14. Set line-counter to zero.

Program Flowchart

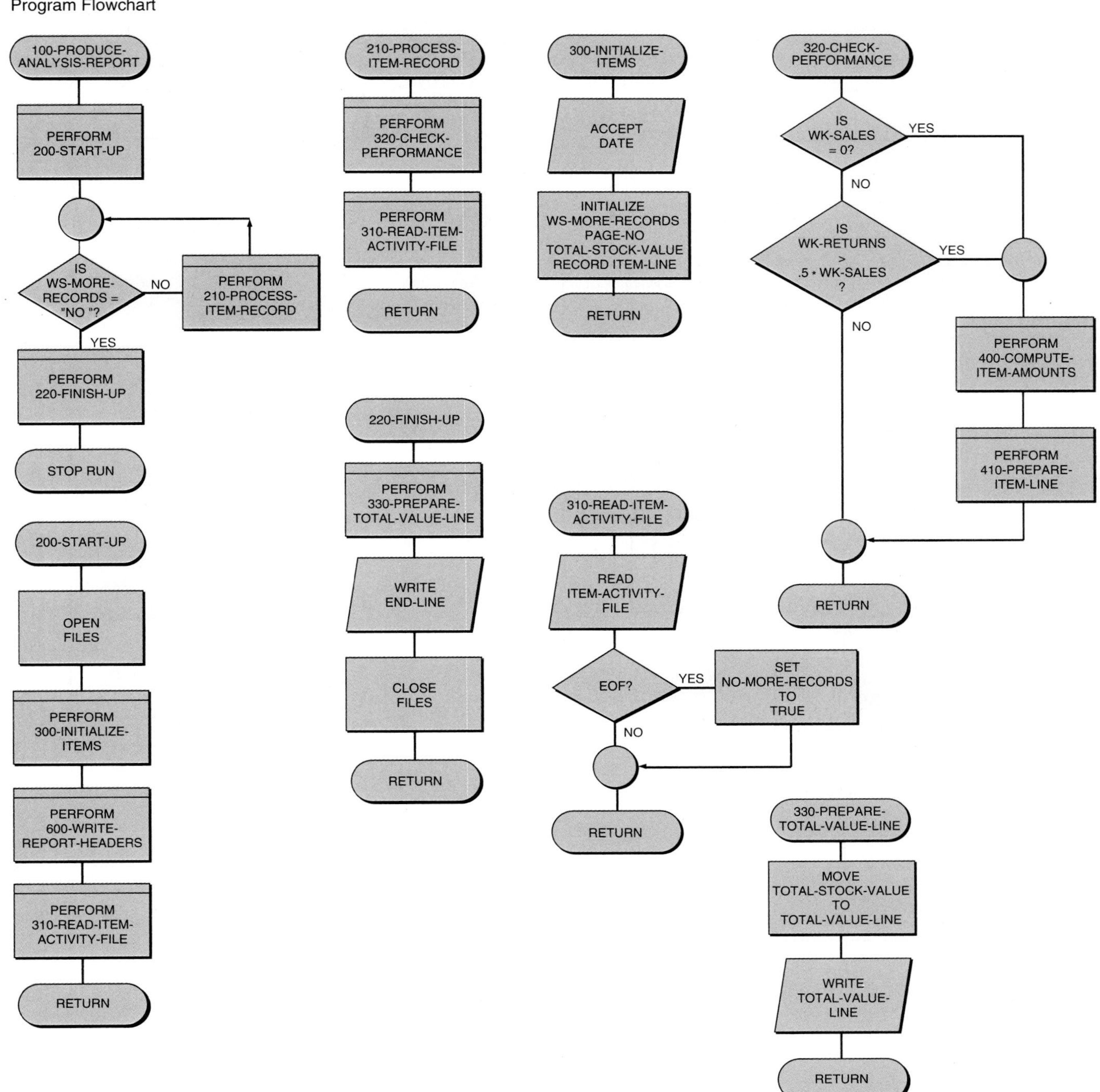

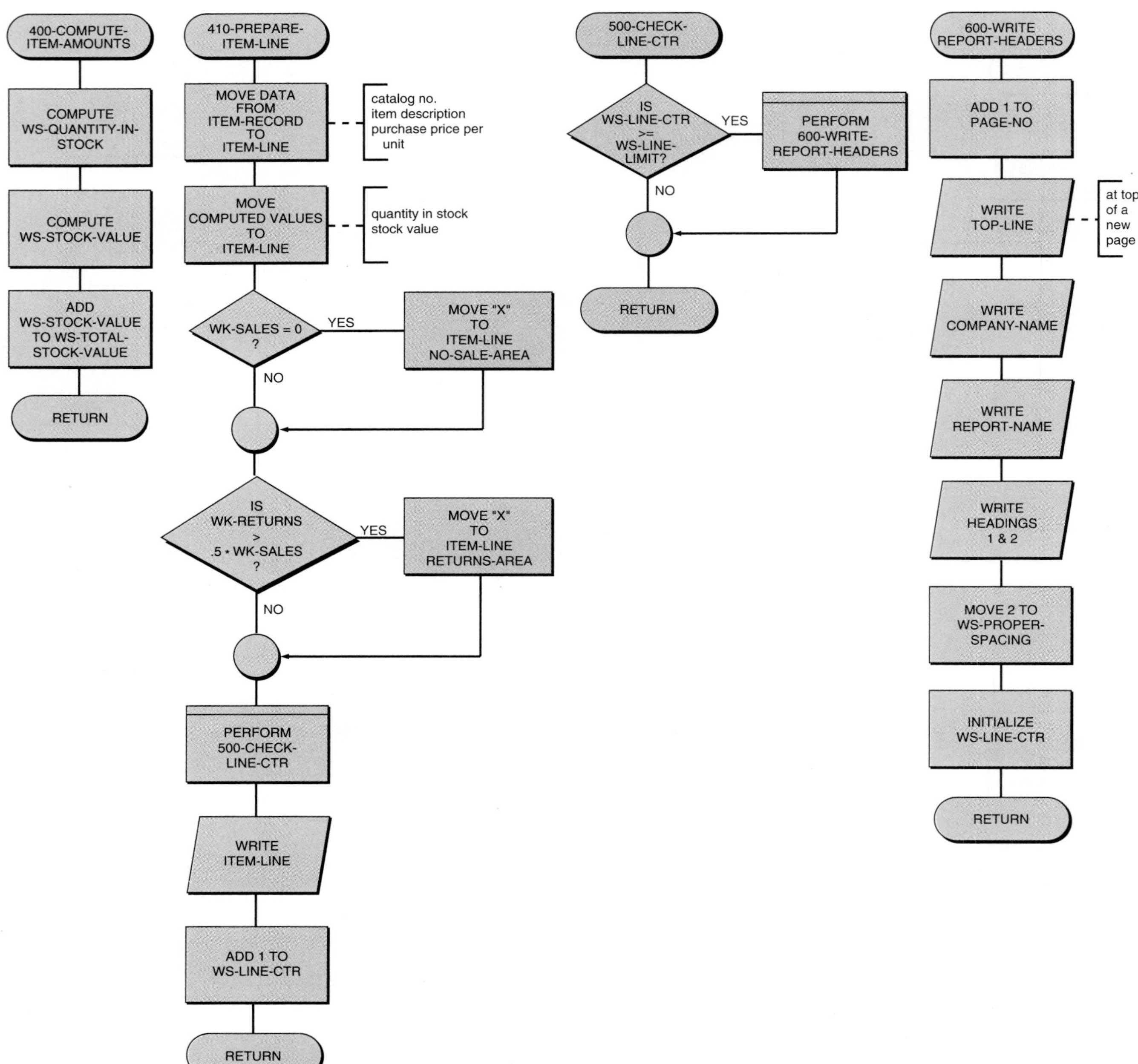

400-COMPUTE-ITEM-AMOUNTS
COMPUTE WS-QUANTITY-IN-STOCK
COMPUTE WS-STOCK-VALUE
ADD WS-STOCK-VALUE TO WS-TOTAL-STOCK-VALUE
RETURN
410-PREPARE-ITEM-LINE
MOVE DATA FROM ITEM-RECORD TO ITEM-LINE
catalog no.
item description
purchase price per unit
MOVE COMPUTED VALUES TO ITEM-LINE
quantity in stock
stock value
WK-SALES = 0 ?
YES
MOVE "X" TO ITEM-LINE NO-SALE-AREA
NO
IS WK-RETURNS > .5 * WK-SALES ?
YES
MOVE "X" TO ITEM-LINE RETURNS-AREA
NO
PERFORM 500-CHECK-LINE-CTR
WRITE ITEM-LINE
ADD 1 TO WS-LINE-CTR
RETURN
500-CHECK-LINE-CTR
IS WS-LINE-CTR >= WS-LINE-LIMIT?
YES
PERFORM 600-WRITE-REPORT-HEADERS
NO
RETURN
600-WRITE REPORT-HEADERS
ADD 1 TO PAGE-NO
WRITE TOP-LINE
at top of a new page
WRITE COMPANY-NAME
WRITE REPORT-NAME
WRITE HEADINGS 1 & 2
MOVE 2 TO WS-PROPER-SPACING
INITIALIZE WS-LINE-CTR
RETURN

Programming Exercise II

The management of International Haberdashery wants a sales analysis report that will list all of its salespersons. The report is a two-part report. In the first part, it must provide sales information for individual salespersons, and, in the second part, it must provide summary information for each store.

For each salesperson, the report must identify the store number, specify the current sales, interpret the current sales as a percent of the salesperson's quota, and provide a rating of the salesperson's performance: double star if sales are 20 percent or more above quota, and one star if sales are 10 percent or more (but less than 20 percent) above quota.

For each store, the second part of the report must identify the store's location, it must specify the total number of salespersons at that store, and it must specify the total sales, the average sales per salesperson, and the top store salesperson.

The input file consists of salespersons' records, arranged alphabetically by store, with store numbers in ascending order. Each record contains the following data:

cc 1–2	Store number
cc 3–22	Salesperson name
cc 48–55	Current sales (format: xxxxxx.xx)
cc 56–63	Sales quota (format: xxxxxx.xx)

The store codes and locations are as follows:

Store Code	**Location**
10	Providence
20	Hartford
30	Boston
40	Hyannis
50	Worcester

Each part of the report should begin on a new page and be properly documented with a report-date line, the company name, report name, and headings as needed. Pages are to be numbered consecutively, with no more than 30 detail lines per page.

The layout of the input record, the printer spacing chart, the system flowchart, and the structure chart are provided for you in Figure 7.61. Your task is to complete the design phase and then the design implementation phase of the problem-solving procedure.

Use the current date as the report date, and use Data File Set 5 (see Appendix C) [DD/CD:VIC7EX2.DAT] as the input file.

■ Figure 7.61

Record Layout Form

I-STORE-NO	I-SALESPERSON		I-CURRENT-SALES	I-SALES-QUOTA	
1 2	3 4 5 6 7 8 9 10 11 12 13 14 15 16 17 18 19 20 21 22	23 24 25 26 27 28 29 30 31 32 33 34 35 36 37 38 39 40 41 42 43 44 45 46 47	48 49 50 51 52 53 54 55	56 57 58 59 60 61 62 63	64 65 66 67 68 69 70 71 72 73 74 75 76 77 78 79 80

Record Name: SALES-RECORD

Printer Spacing Chart

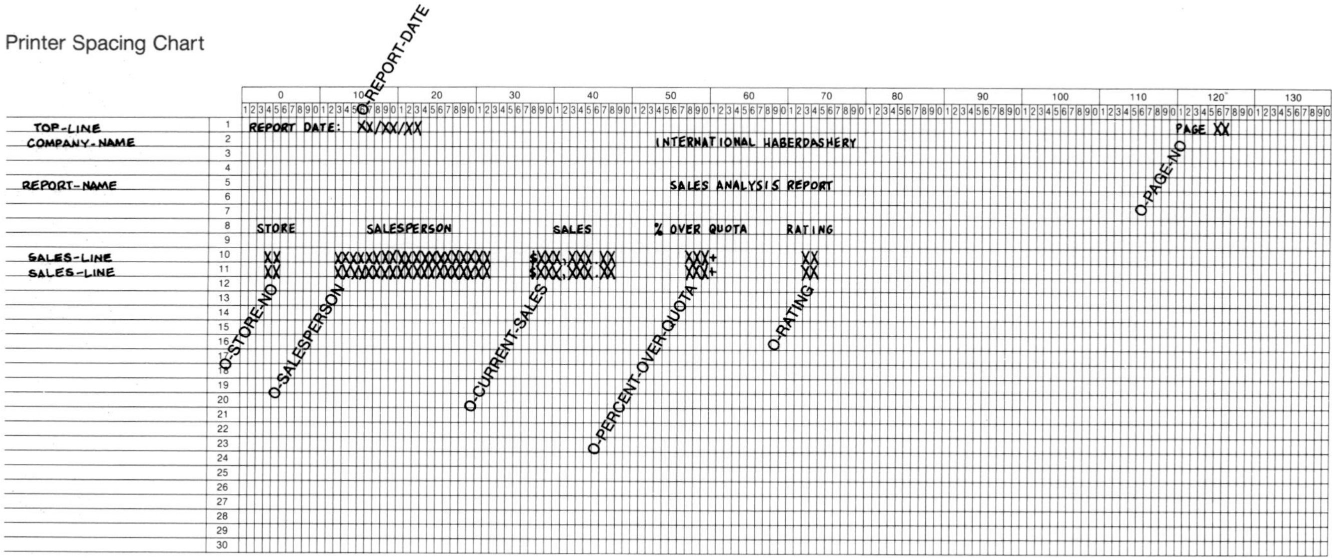

Printer Spacing Chart

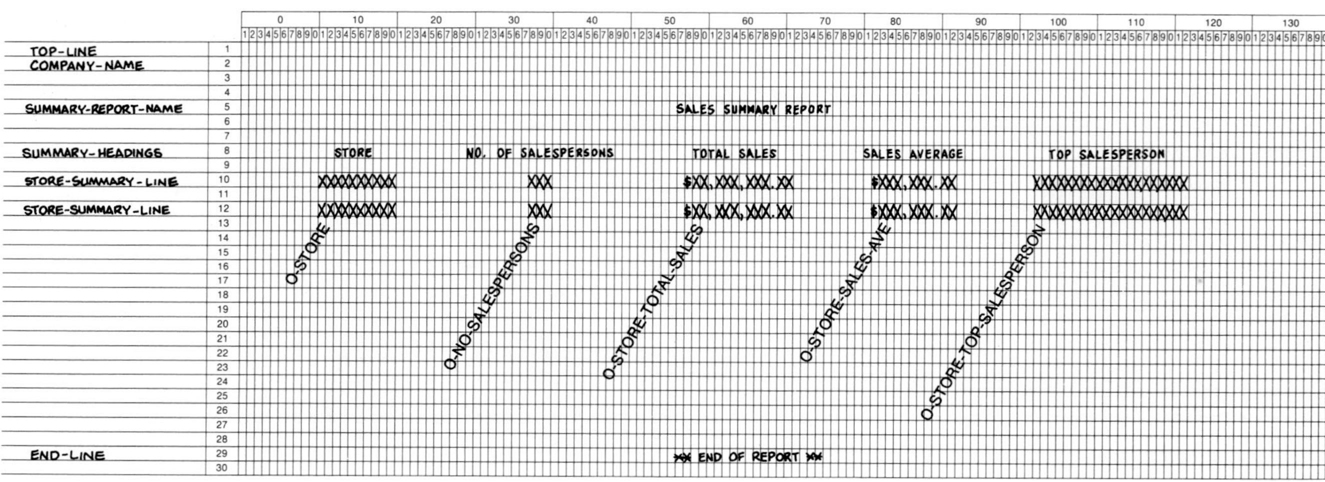

System Flowchart

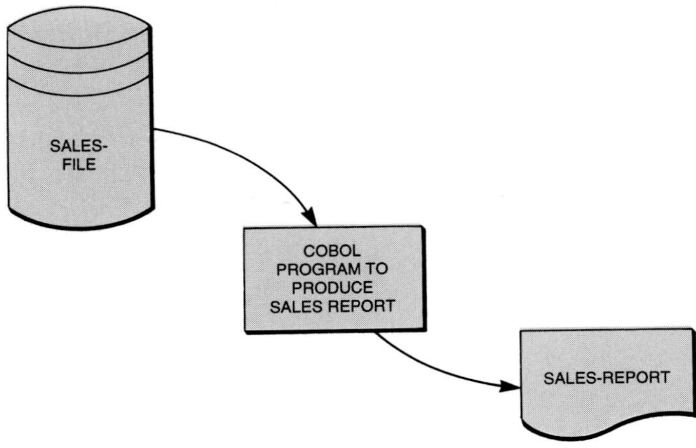

Figure 7.61 continued

Structure Chart

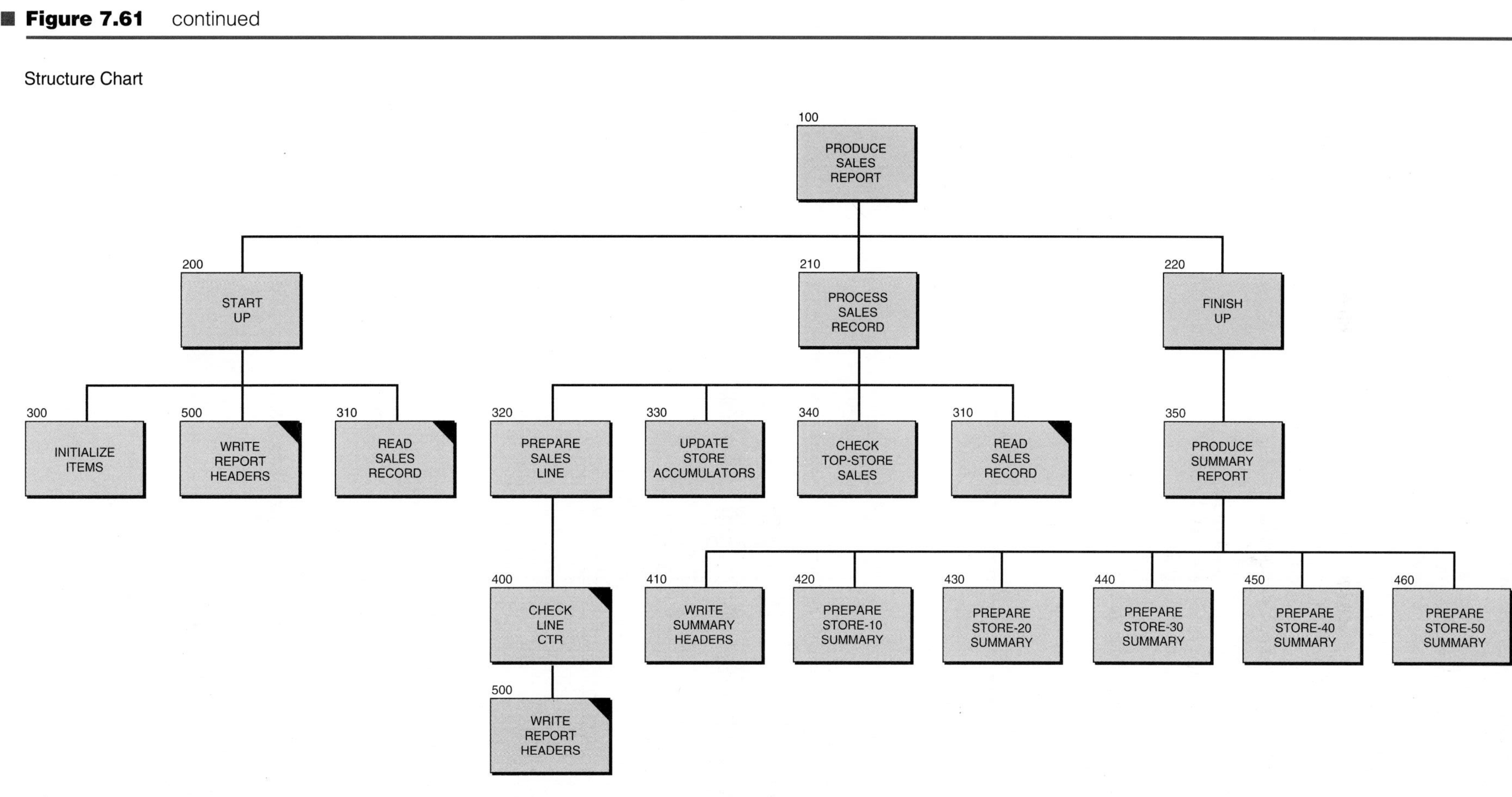

Programming Exercise III

The management of the Ponagansett Electric Company wants a usage report formatted as shown in Figure 7.62. It is a two-part report. The first part shows the usage and resulting charges for each of its customers. The second part provides summary information for each of its three service areas: Bristol (area code RI1), Essex (area code RI2), and South (area code RI3). For each area, the summary must specify the total usage by and the total charge assessed to all the residential customers, the total usage by and the total charge assessed to all the commercial customers, and the highest residential and commercial users.

The customer file contains a record for each customer. Each record contains the following data:

cc 1–3	Area code (RI1, RI2, RI3)
cc 4–9	Customer number
cc 10–29	Customer name
cc 30–34	Previous meter reading
cc 35–39	Current meter reading
cc 74–76	Rate schedule
cc 79–80	Month number

The file is arranged sequentially by customer number within each area code.

The rate schedules are as follows:

Figure 7.62

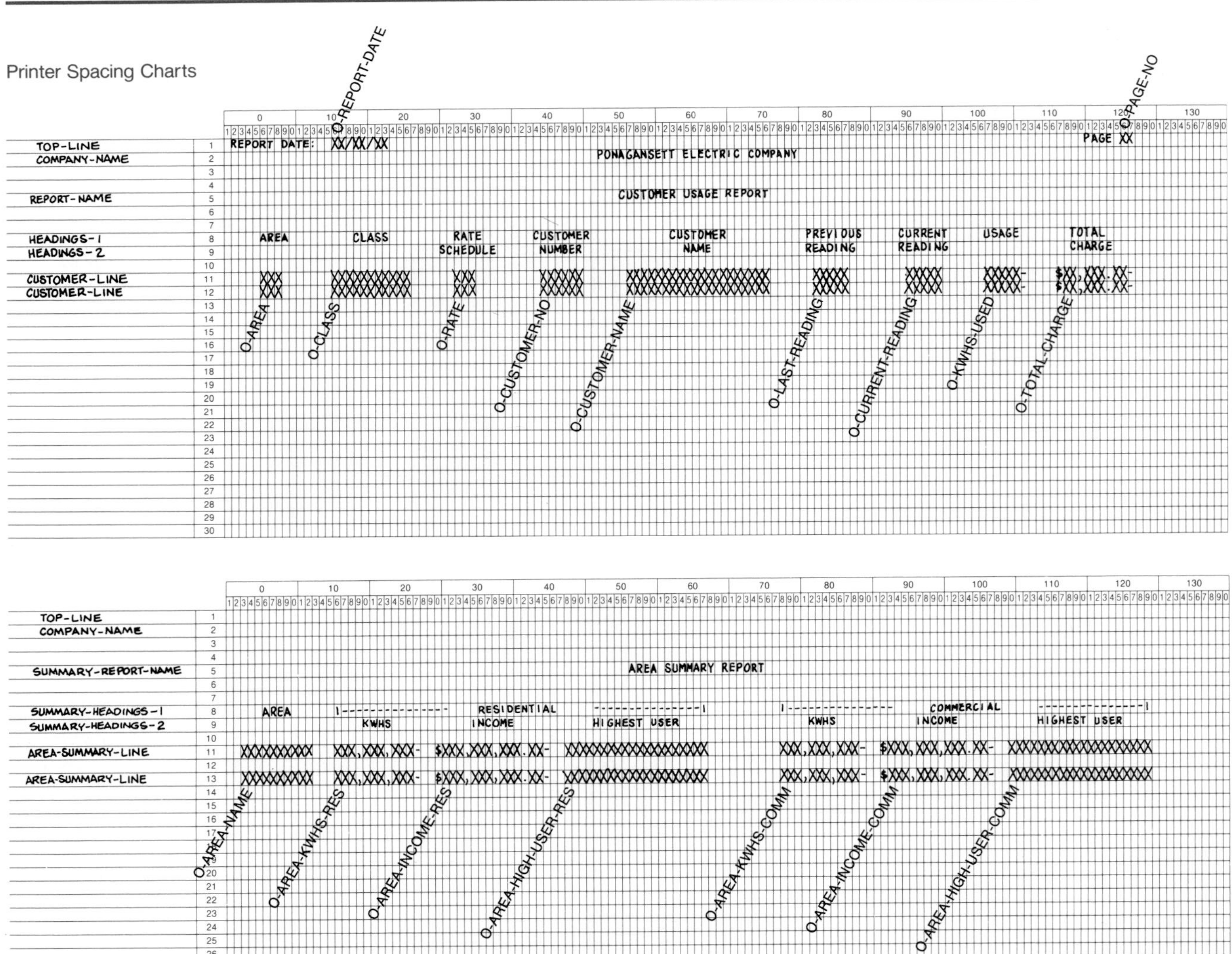

1. Residential: A10
   Customer Charge: $1.61 per month
   Energy Charge: 7.974 cents per KWH
2. Residential: A11 (Electric Water Heater)

$2.75	First	20 KWHS or less
10.435 cents per KWH	Next	30 KWHS
8.381 cents per KWH	Next	150 KWHS
5.529 cents per KWH	Next	350 KWHS
6.831 cents per KWH	Next	1450 KWHS
6.554 cents per KWH	Excess of 2000 KWHS	

3. Residential: A12 (All Electric)
   Same as A11
4. Commercial: C-2 (General Service, Small Business)
   Customer Charge: $4.75 per month
   Energy Charge:

8.913 cents per KWH	First	2000 KWHS
8.313 cents per KWH	Excess of 2000 KWHS	

In all classifications, the following additional charges apply: .006 cents per KWH for the Uniform Conservation Cost Adjustment, .042 cents per KWH for the Oil Conservation Adjustment, and .01413 cents per KWH Fuel Factor.

Each part of the report must begin on a new page. The first part must contain no more than 30 customers per page, and each page must be properly documented.

You are encouraged to follow the steps of the problem-solving procedure. Use the current date as the report date, and use Data File Set 2 (see Appendix C) [DD/CD:VIC7EX3.DAT] as the input file.

Programming Exercise IV

The management of the Modern Plastics Company wants its data processing department to prepare a three-part payroll report formatted as shown in Figure 7.63.

The first part prints information for each employee; the second part provides summary information for each store; and the third part provides summary information for the company as a whole.

Figure 7.63

Printer Spacing Charts

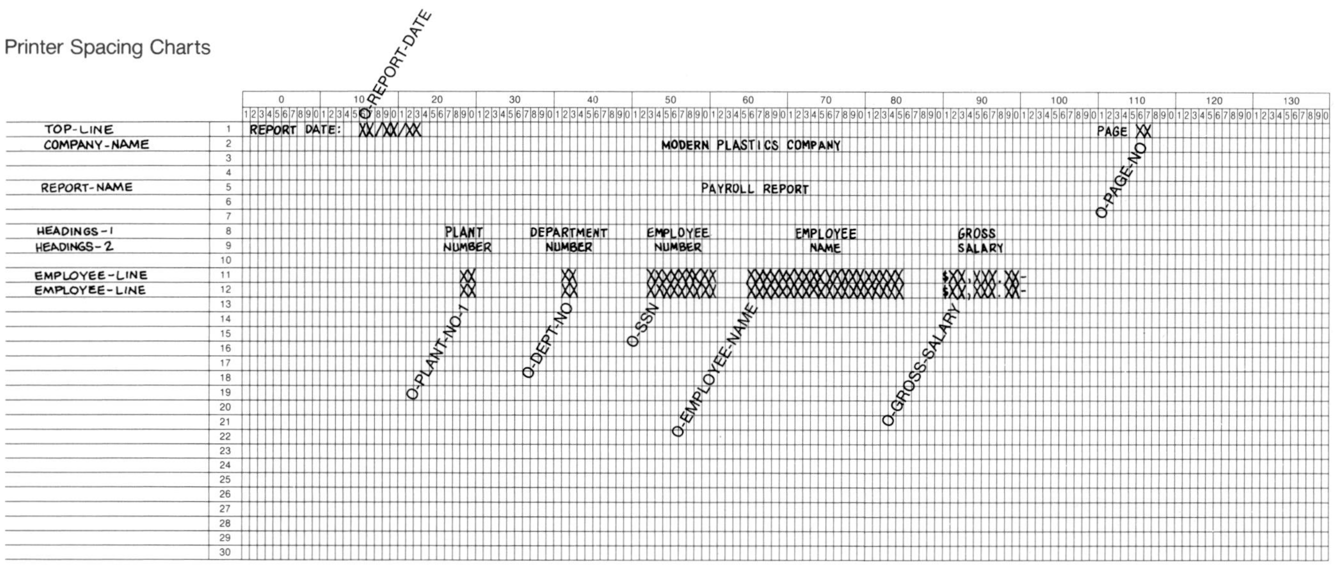

■ **Figure 7.63** continued

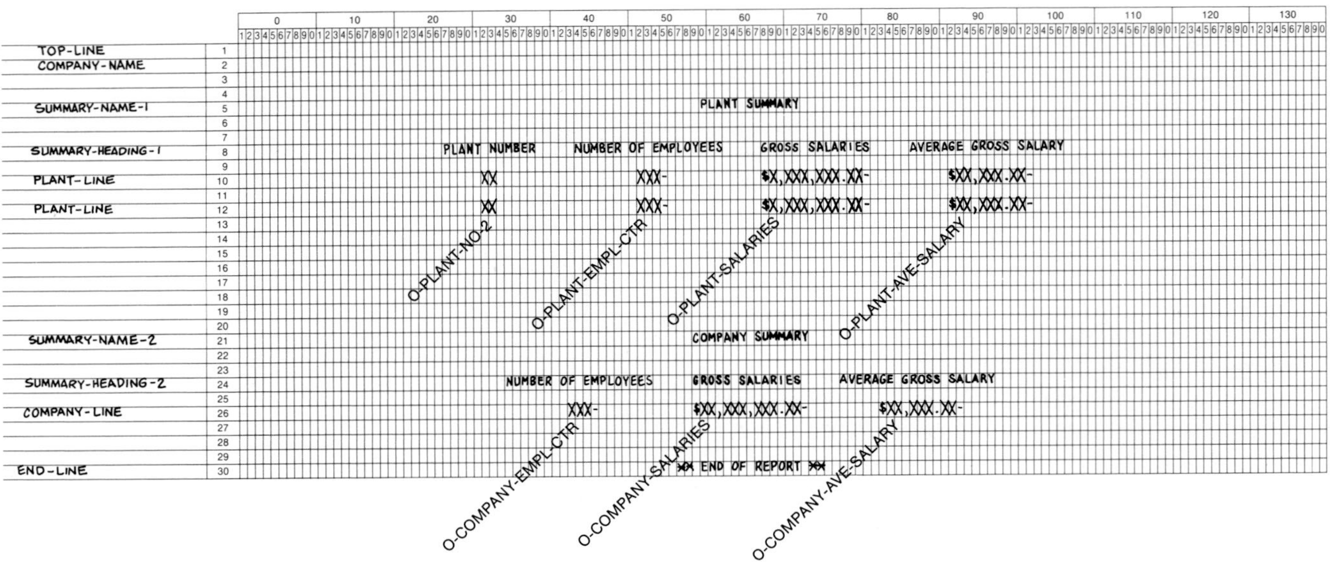

For each employee, there is a record in the payroll file containing the following data:

cc 3–4	Plant number
cc 5–6	Department number
cc 7–15	Social Security number
cc 16–35	Employee name
cc 39–42	Pay rate (format: xx.xx)
cc 43–44	Hours worked at regular pay
cc 45–46	Hours worked at overtime pay (time and a half)
cc 77–80	Date hired

The records of the input file are arranged in seniority sequence by department within each plant. The department numbers are in ascending order within each plant, and the plant numbers are in ascending order. There are five plants, and the plant numbers are 10, 20, 30, 40, and 50.

Each of the first two parts of the report must begin on a new page. The first part must list no more than 30 employees per page, and each page must be properly documented.

The company summary should be printed on the same page as the plant summaries.

You are encouraged to follow the steps of the problem-solving procedure. Use the current date as the report date, and use Data File Set 4 (see Appendix C) [DD/CD:VIC7EX4.DAT] as the input file.

8 Control Breaks and Data Validation

In this chapter, we will examine the use of conditional statements in two particular kinds of applications, namely, control breaks and data validation.

You have worked with programs that require printing a line on a report for each record accessed from the data file. Such reports are classified as **detail reports.** You have also worked with programs that process all the records of the data file, accumulating data in the process, and finally printing summary information on a report. These reports are classified as **summary reports.** Many situations require the printing of intermediate totals, in addition to the printing of detail lines and of final totals. These reports are classified as **multilevel reports.**

In a multilevel report, the decision to print intermediate summary information is usually based on new values being detected in one or more key data fields of an input record. For instance, if sales totals are to be printed at the department level (in a sales analysis program), the records of the sales file would contain a "department" field and they would have been presorted and grouped by department. During the processing of the sales file, when a new department value appears on an input record, it is clear that all the records with the preceding department value have been processed, and the sales totals for that department should be printed before processing of records for the next department begins. Situations such as this are known as **control breaks.** Control breaks may exist at more than one level within a program, such as at the department level, at the store level, at the city level, at the state level, and so on. In the first part of this chapter, we examine the use of control breaks within COBOL programs.

In the second part of the chapter, we present a data validation program in which data fields of an input record are tested for a variety of conditions. In addition to the use of conditional statements, we also present and use the INSPECT statement within various data validation procedures.

The chapter ends with a brief discussion of reference modification and of the REDEFINES clause. The REDEFINES clause allows the same storage area to be used to store different kinds of values; and reference modification allows access to the characters stored in particular bytes of a data item. ■

Objectives You Should Achieve

After studying this chapter, you should:

1. Given the layout of a multilevel report and program specifications, be able to correctly identify the lines that constitute a page heading, a control heading, a control footing, and a final footing.
2. Given a programming problem in which the program must contain a control break,
   - **a.** Be able to identify the key field of the input record that will trigger the control break.
   - **b.** Be able to identify the accumulators whose values must be printed during the control break.
3. Given a programming problem with multiple control breaks, be able to correctly use subtotaling and rolling forward at the appropriate levels to accumulate totals.
4. Given a programming assignment whose function is to prepare a multilevel report, and for which the design tools are provided, be able to complete the implementation phase and run the program successfully.
5. Given a programming assignment whose function is to prepare a multilevel report, and for which the input record layouts, the printer spacing chart, and the system flowchart are provided, be able to complete the design phase and successfully implement the design.
6. Given the statement of a programming assignment whose function is to prepare a multilevel report, be able to successfully accomplish the task.
7. Given an input record whose data fields must be validated for certain requirements, be able to correctly code the needed data validation procedures.
8. Given a programming assignment whose function is to prepare a data validation report, be able to successfully complete the task.
9. Given a data item that must be inspected for the presence of certain characters, be able to correctly code an INSPECT statement to do the inspection.
10. Given a data item in which certain characters must be replaced by other characters, be able to correctly code an INSPECT statement to carry out the task.

Control Breaks

As a first example, we develop a *one-level control break* program. The statement of the problem follows.

The Problem

The Sportsman Company owns a number of stores in different regions of the country. It caters to the real needs as well as the idiosyncracies of sportsmen everywhere. The vice president in charge of sales wants a weekly sales analysis report that lists the total sales of the salespersons of each store, the total sales for each store, and the total company sales.

The sales file contains a record for each salesperson. It is shown in Figure 8.18. The records in the file are sorted and grouped by store. Each record contains the following data:

cc 1–2	Store number
cc 3–4	Department number
cc 5–13	Social Security number
cc 14–33	Salesperson name
cc 34–39	Current sales (format: xxxx.xx)

The report must be formatted as shown in Figure 8.1.

Each page of the report must begin with a *page heading* consisting of the report-date line, followed by the company name and the report name lines. At most two stores must be reported per page. A store report begins with a *store control heading* consisting of a store identification line and the column headings line. A detail line (sales line) follows for each salesperson of that store. The store report ends with a *store control footing,* which consists of the store total line. This line is printed two lines below the last sales line for that store. On the last page of the report, the *company footing,* which consists of the company total line, must be printed three lines below the store control footing for the last store. The company total line shows the total sales for the company.

On the report, a store identification entry consists of two components: the store number and the city in which it is located. They are as follows:

10 – NEW YORK
20 – BOSTON
30 – CHICAGO
40 – SEATTLE

Figure 8.1 Report format for single-level control break program

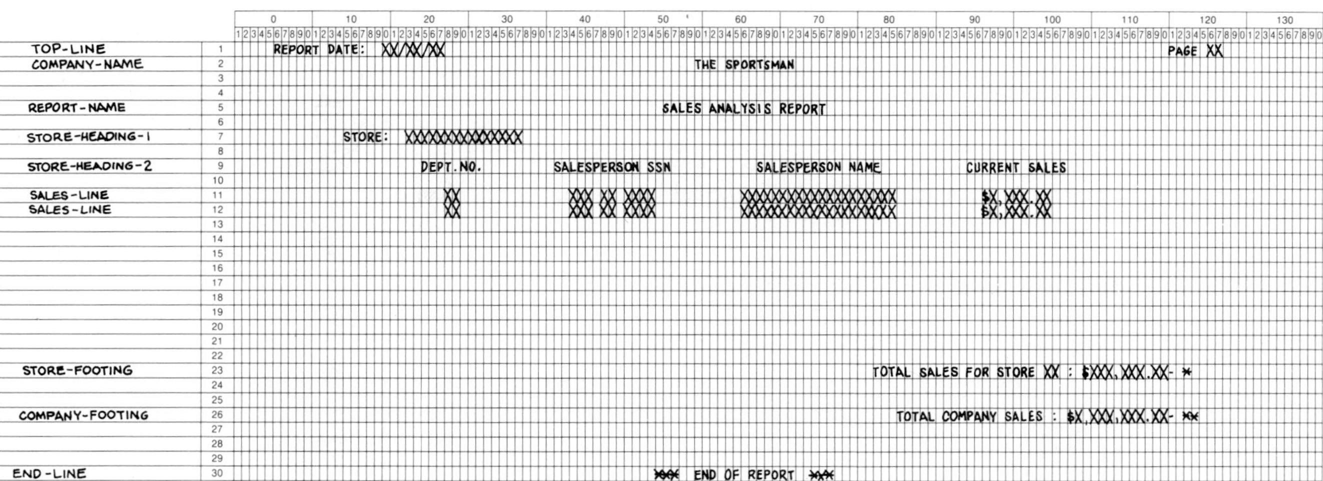

Brief Analysis of the Problem

After a careful examination of this problem, you will notice that no new COBOL statements are needed. What is new, however, is the requirement that *intermediate totals* be printed. In the preceding chapter, all the required totals were **final** totals printed at the end of the report; that is, totals were printed only subsequent to the processing of the last input record. In the current program, the pattern is as follows: a store control heading is printed for the store indicated on the first record of the sales file, then a detail line is printed for each salesperson of the store, and, following the last detail line for that store, a store control footing that contains the total sales for that store must be printed; then, a new store control heading is printed, a detail line is printed for each salesperson of this new store, and, following the last detail line for this store, the store control footing prints the total sales for this store; and the pattern continues for each store (with the limitation of two stores per page). Following the printing of the store footing for the last store, the total sales for the company must be printed.

The store control footing that must be produced for each store requires careful analysis. A number of important questions must be asked:

1. What does a store control footing consist of?
   Answer: It consists of a line that prints the store number and the total sales accumulated for the store.
2. When must a store control footing be printed?
   Answer: It must be printed after printing the sales lines for all the salespersons of that store.
3. What indicates that all the salespersons of a particular store have been processed?
   Answer: Each input record contains a field that specifies the salesperson's store number. Since the records of the input file are grouped by store, the appearance of a new store number on an input record indicates that the record is for the first salesperson of the next store. Hence, before the first record of a new store is processed, the store control footing for the previous store must be printed, and then the store control heading for the new store must be printed.
4. Does this mean that when a record is read, its store number must be compared with the store number of the previous record? If so, how can this be done, since upon reading in a new record, the contents of the previous one are lost?
   Answer: It is true that when a new record is read in, the contents of the previous one are lost. The procedure to use is the following:
   a. Set up a store control item in working storage.
   b. As the first record of the file is read, move its store number to the store control item. See Figure 8.2a.
   c. Before beginning the processing of a record, compare its store number with the one currently in the store control item in working storage. If they are the same, process the record, since it belongs to the same store as the previous one. If they are not the same, the record in input memory is the first record of a new store. Before the record is processed, the following steps must be performed (see Figure 8.2b):
      i. Print out the store control footing (store number and total sales) for the previous store.
      ii. Assign the new store number to the store control item in working storage so that store numbers of subsequent records can be compared to it.
      iii. Since no more than two stores must be reported on each page, decide if only the next store *control heading* is needed or if a new page is needed. If a new page is needed, then the page headings must be printed, followed by the store control heading for the new store.
      iv. Reset the store sales accumulator to zero for the next store whenever the store control heading is printed.

   Testing a control field to either temporarily interrupt normal processing to execute a specific procedure, or to continue with normal processing, is referred to as a *control break.* In this program, the control break is set up to print store summary information whenever a new store number is encountered.
5. How are the store sales totals accumulated?
   Answer: The programmer must define a store sales accumulator. It must be set to zero initially and reset to zero for each new store.

   Recall that in the Chapter 7 sample program, as many accumulators were needed as there were districts and quarters for which totals had to be accumulated, since the totals were printed as final totals only at the **end** of the report. In this program, only **one** store sales accumulator is needed, regardless of the number of stores, since once the total sales are printed for one store, the same accumulator can be reset to zero and then be used to accumulate the sales of the next store.

■ **Figure 8.2** Control break feature

a.

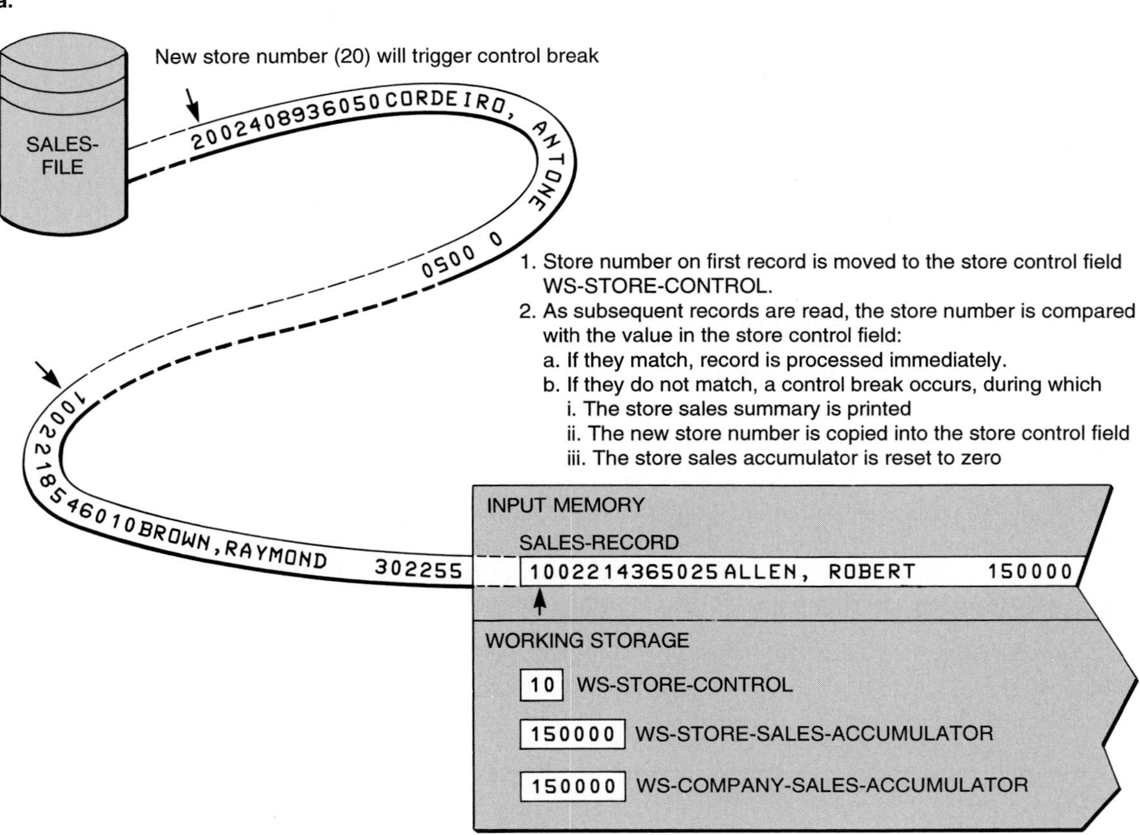
New store number (20) will trigger control break
SALES-FILE
2002408936050CORDEIRO, ANTONE
0500 0
1002218546010BROWN,RAYMOND
302255
1. Store number on first record is moved to the store control field WS-STORE-CONTROL.
2. As subsequent records are read, the store number is compared with the value in the store control field:
a. If they match, record is processed immediately.
b. If they do not match, a control break occurs, during which
i. The store sales summary is printed
ii. The new store number is copied into the store control field
iii. The store sales accumulator is reset to zero
INPUT MEMORY
SALES-RECORD
1002214365025ALLEN, ROBERT 150000
WORKING STORAGE
10 WS-STORE-CONTROL
150000 WS-STORE-SALES-ACCUMULATOR
150000 WS-COMPANY-SALES-ACCUMULATOR

b.

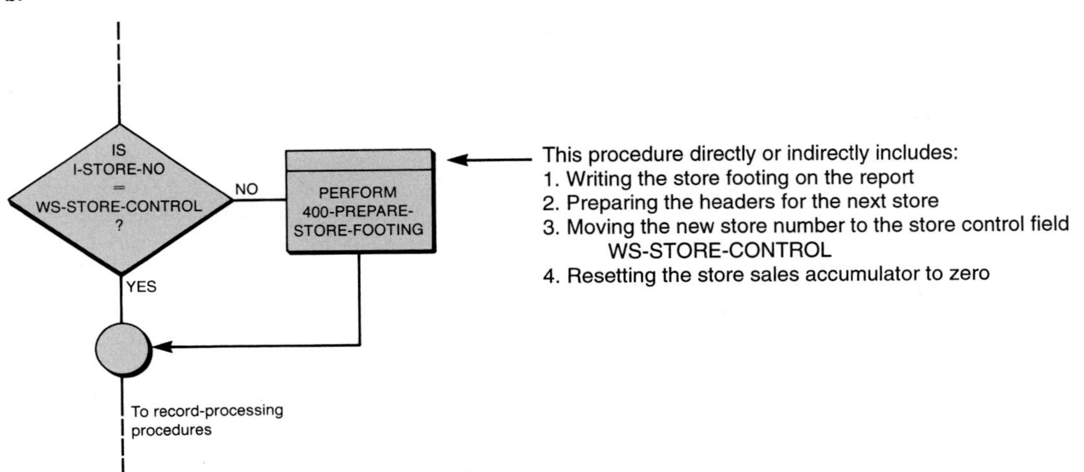
IS I-STORE-NO = WS-STORE-CONTROL ?
NO
YES
PERFORM 400-PREPARE-STORE-FOOTING
To record-processing procedures
This procedure directly or indirectly includes:
1. Writing the store footing on the report
2. Preparing the headers for the next store
3. Moving the new store number to the store control field WS-STORE-CONTROL
4. Resetting the store sales accumulator to zero

As a salesperson record is processed, the current sales on the record are added to the store sales accumulator. When the control break occurs, the accumulator will contain the total sales for that store. When the store footing has been printed on the report, the store sales accumulator will then be reset to zero before beginning to accumulate the sales for the next store.

6. If the printing of a store control footing is triggered by detecting a new store number, how does the summary for the very last store get printed, since there is no subsequent record with a new store number?

Answer: It is true that the control break cannot be used to signal the printing of the control footing for the last store. In fact, when the end-of-file flag is encountered, control will not even return to the processing module. One obvious way of solving the problem is to use the EOF record as a signal to print the last store footing. That is, when the EOF record is detected, set the program flag WS-MORE-RECORDS to "NO ", and also print the footing for the last store. However, the total sales for the company must also be printed as a final total. Since this is an important subtask of the report being prepared, a separate module can be set up to process the final totals. This is the procedure we will use.

The Design Phase

Step 1 of the problem-solving procedure can be completed easily by preparing the layout of the input record as specified in the statement of the problem and by attaching data names to the fields specified on the printer spacing chart of Figure 8.1. These are shown in Figure 8.3.

Flagging Summary Levels

When multilevel reports are prepared, it is useful to the users of the report (such as department managers, store managers, and the vice president in charge of sales) to include a feature that flags the level at which a summary is prepared. The feature is as follows:

1. A single asterisk (*) is printed to the right of a first-level summary, such as the store level in the Sportsman program. See the layout of STORE-FOOTING in Figure 8.3.
2. A double asterisk (**) is printed to the right of a second-level summary, such as the company summary in the Sportsman program. See the layout of COMPANY-FOOTING in Figure 8.3.
3. A triple asterisk (***) is printed to the right of a third-level summary, and so on.

Summary lines should be formatted in such a way that the asterisks stand out in the right margin.

Figure 8.3 Layouts of input and output records

Record Layout Form

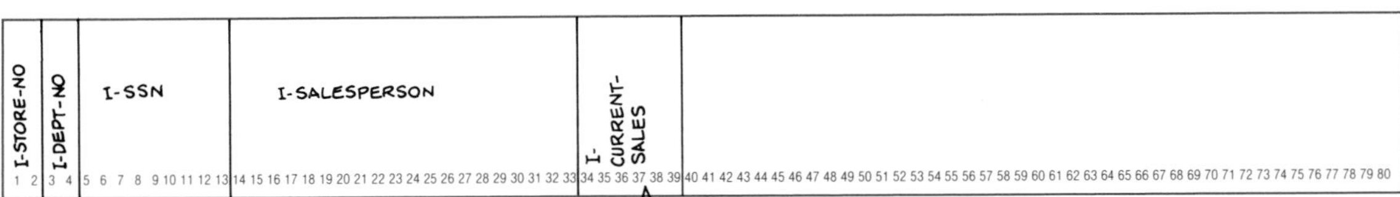

Record Name: SALES-RECORD

Printer Spacing Chart

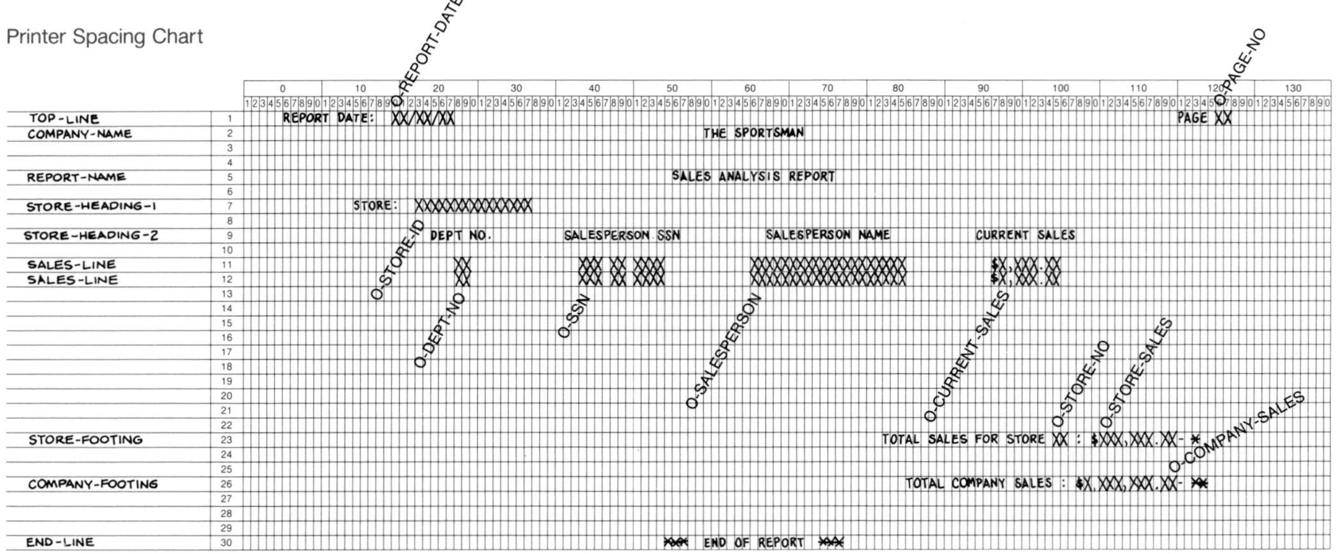

■ **Figure 8.4** System flowchart for the sample program

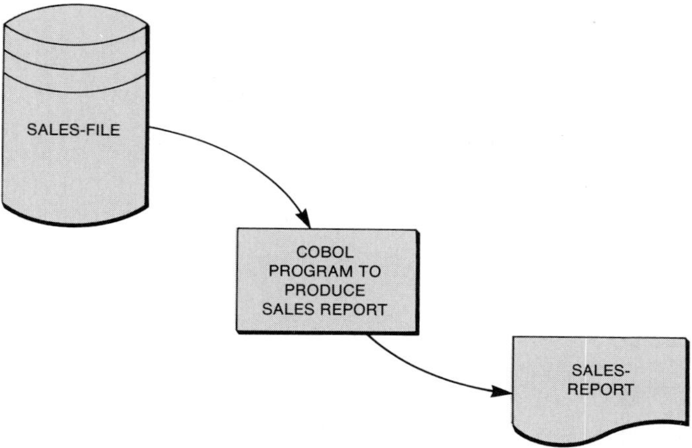

■ **Figure 8.5** First two levels of the structure chart

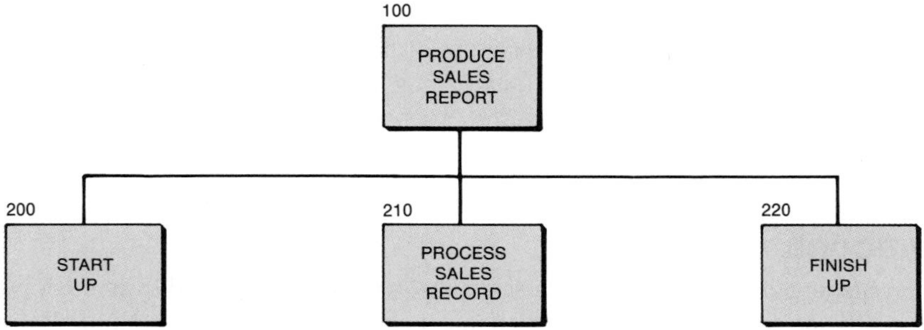

System Flowchart

Here again, the system flowchart is simple: The sales records must be read from the sales file and processed by the program to produce the multilevel sales report. The system flowchart is shown in Figure 8.4.

Structure Chart

It is clear that the primary task is to produce the sales report. This task is separated into the three standard modules: The first contains the start-up activities, the second is the record processing module, responsible for producing detail lines and intermediate store sales totals, and the third contains the finish-up activities, including printing final totals on the report.

The first two levels of the structure chart are shown in Figure 8.5.

200 START UP

The start-up activities usually include opening the files and controlling the execution of modules that initialize program variables (such as the date, flags, and accumulators) that write report headings, and that access the first record of the input file. Until now, all the headings were printed at the top of each page. That is, the report headings were also page headings. Now, as you examine the printer spacing chart in Figure 8.3, it should be clear that the page headings consist only of the three lines TOP-LINE, COMPANY-NAME, and REPORT-NAME. The two lines named STORE-HEADING-1 and STORE-HEADING-2 must be written for each store, and thus they make up what is called the store control heading.

Now, note that the field O-STORE-ID of the record STORE-HEADING-1 must contain an entry that identifies the store to which the first group of sales records belongs. Since the first store number must be obtained from the first salesperson's record, the input file must be read before the store control heading can be written for the first store. The store number on the first record is copied into the store control field in working storage to enable the control-break procedure to function properly. It is also used to determine the correct entry in the store-ID field O-STORE-ID. Though the structure chart is not designed to show the

■ **Figure 8.6** Modules subordinate to 200 START UP

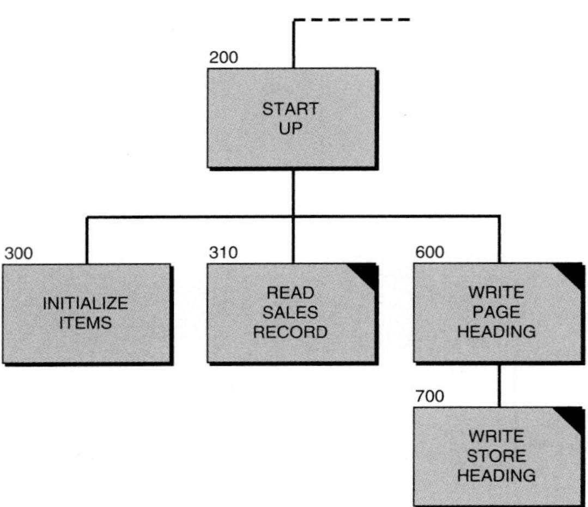

sequence of functions, an element of sequencing is introduced by positioning the modules from left to right. The resulting breakdown of module 200 START UP is shown in Figure 8.6.

Note that a separate module is required to indicate the printing of the store control heading, since it can be printed a second time on a page. For that reason, this function has to be separated from the one that writes the page heading at the top of each page. Also note that the numbers assigned to these modules are 600 and 700 respectively, because they are needed at the sixth and seventh levels of the structure chart, as you will see shortly.

210 PROCESS SALES RECORD

It was pointed out in the brief problem analysis above that as a salesperson record is accessed from the input file, the store number it contains must be compared with the one in the store control field to determine if this salesperson belongs to the same store as the previous salesperson record. If these two numbers are the same, then the record is processed; that is, the current sales are added to the store whose sales are currently being accumulated and are also added to the company accumulator, and the detail line Sales-Line is prepared and written on the report. If the store number on the input record is not the same as the one in the store control field, then a control break occurs to allow for the printing of the store control footing. Once the store summary has been printed on the report as part of the store control footing, a check must be made to determine if this is the second store footing on the current page. If it is, the next page of the report must be prepared. In either case, the store control heading must then be printed, after assigning the correct store ID to the field O-STORE-ID. In this same module, the new store number is copied into the store control field, and the store sales accumulator must be reset to zero. Then, the record that caused the control break is processed.

When the record in input memory has been processed, with or without the triggering of a control break, the next record in the input file is read, and the above functions are executed again.

The breakdown of module 210 PROCESS SALES RECORD is shown in Figure 8.7. Your attention is directed to module 320 CHECK FOR NEW STORE. This is the one that contains the control-break test. Note the subordinate modules that must be executed whenever a control-break occurs. (You also see the page heading module and the store heading module at the sixth and seventh levels of the structure chart.)

220 FINISH UP

As noted earlier, the control-break mechanism triggers the printing of a store control footing by detecting a new store number in input memory. However, since the last record of the last store does not have a successor record, the control-break mechanism does not apply. The program must **force** the printing of the store footing for the last store. An appropriate place to do this is in module 220 FINISH UP. But, since the company footing must also be printed before terminating the program, module 350 PRODUCE LAST FOOTINGS is assigned the task of producing the two last footings. Module 220 FINISH UP and its subordinate modules are shown in Figure 8.8.

The complete structure chart is shown in Figure 8.9.

■ **Figure 8.7** Modules subordinate to 210 PROCESS SALES RECORD

■ **Figure 8.8** Modules subordinate to 220 FINISH UP

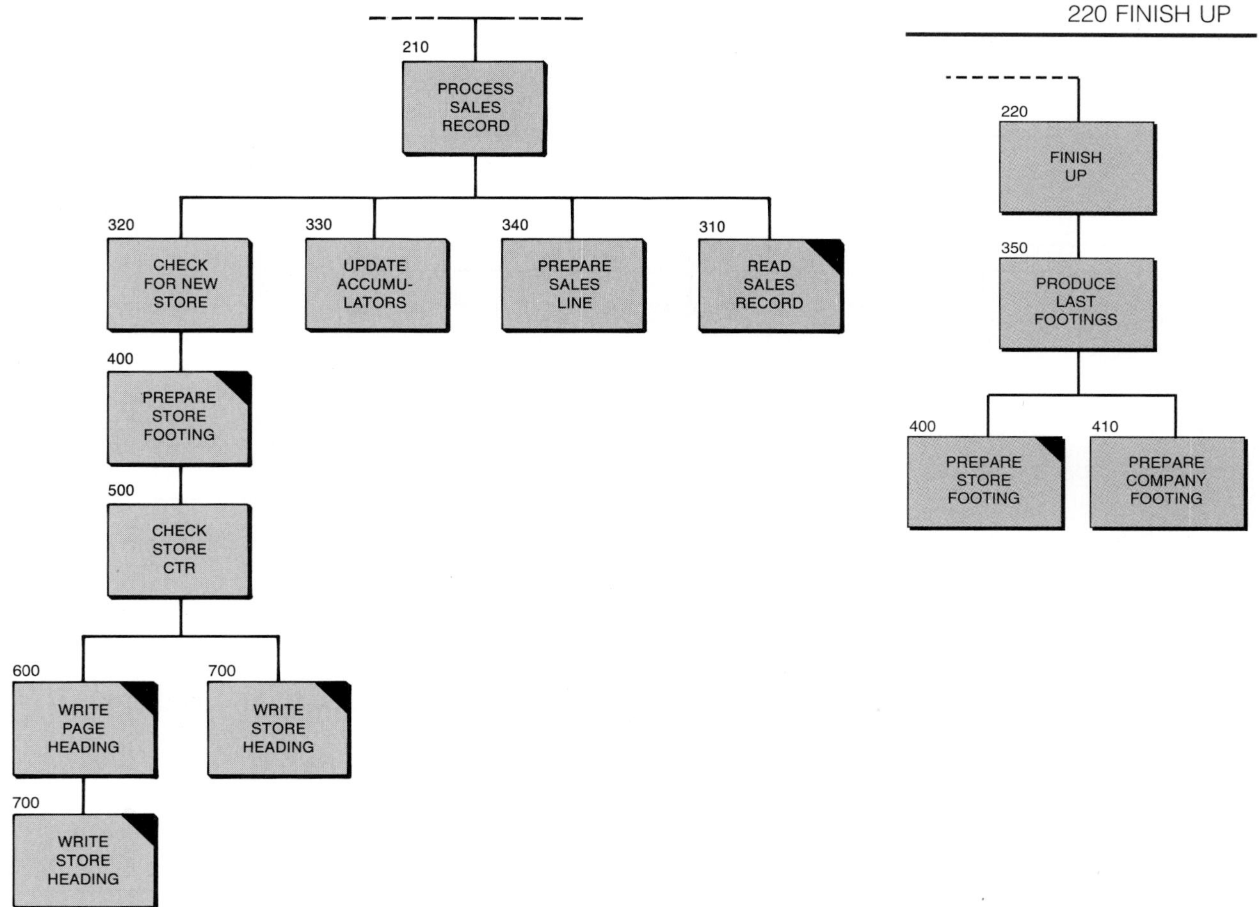

Program Pseudocode

The pseudocode specifies the details required to accomplish the functions identified in the modules of the structure chart. The paragraph corresponding to the primary module is simple and direct; no explanations are needed.

Figure 8.10 shows the pseudocode paragraph corresponding to structure chart module 200 START UP. Note that the files are opened before directing the execution of the three subordinate modules.

Subordinate module 300 INITIALIZE ITEMS obtains the date from the system and initializes the end-of-file flag, the page number data item, and the company sales accumulator.

Note: The store sales accumulator could be initialized in this module. However, it was decided to initialize it in module 700 WRITE STORE HEADING for two reasons: This accumulator has to be reset to zero for each new store, and the store heading must be printed for each store.

Subordinate module 310 READ SALES RECORD accesses the first record of the input file and stores it in input memory. Recall that the store number on this record must be moved to the store control field in working storage. That data transfer could be shown explicitly at this point. However, the same kind of data transfer will have to occur every time it is necessary to print the store control heading on the report. For this reason, the instruction to copy the new store number into the store control field will be contained in module 700 WRITE STORE HEADING.

Subordinate module 600 WRITE PAGE HEADING writes the top three lines on the report. Then it initializes the stores-per-page counter; that is, it sets the counter to zero at the top of each page. (Recall that no more than two stores must be reported per page.) The store control heading must then follow the page heading (see step 10 of pseudocode paragraph 600 in Figure 8.11).

■ **Figure 8.9** Structure chart for the sample program

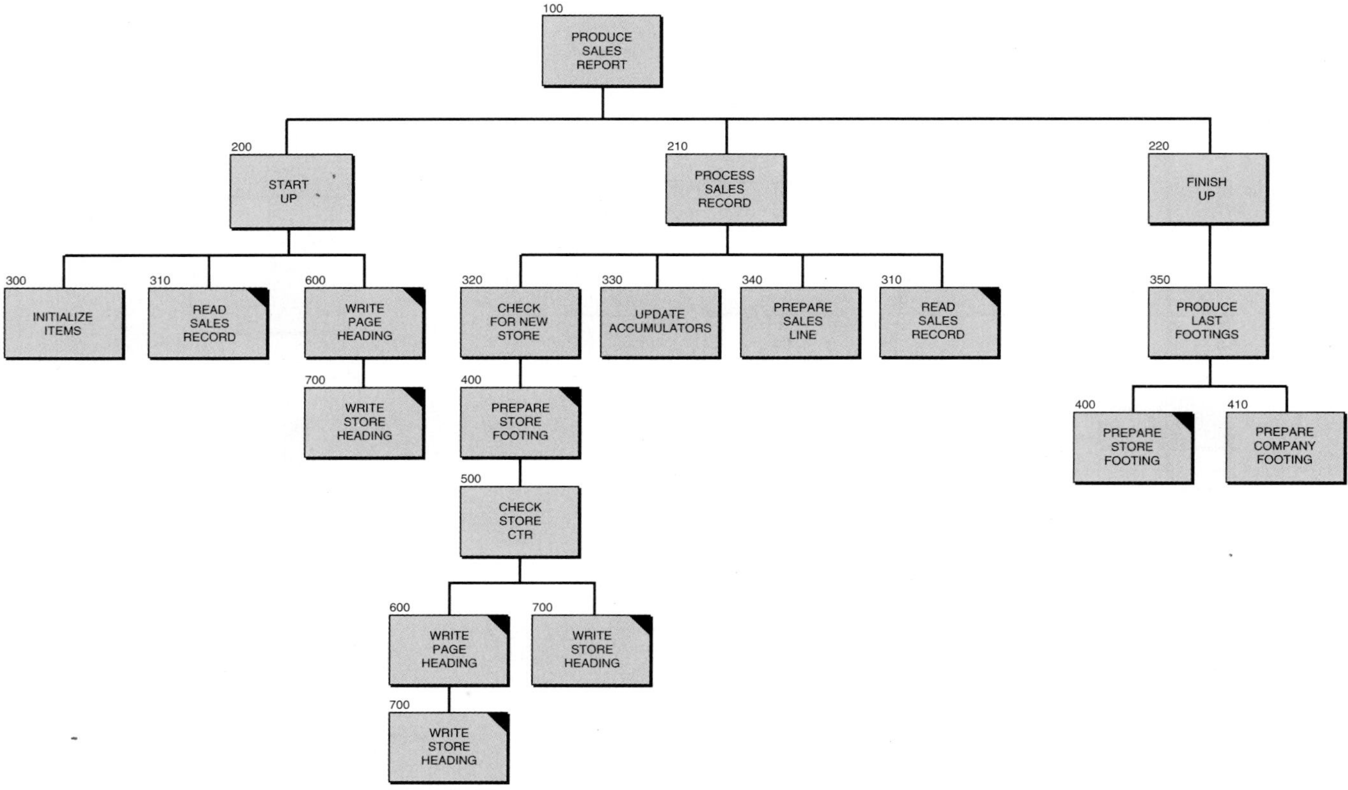

■ **Figure 8.10** Pseudocode paragraph corresponding to structure chart module 200 START UP

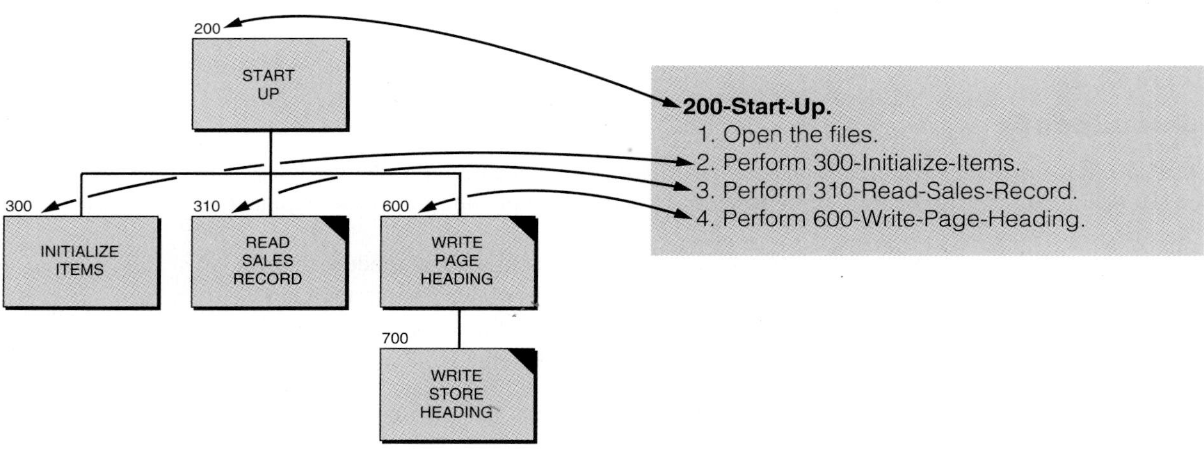

Structure chart module 700 WRITE STORE HEADING is subordinate to module 600. In this module, the new store number (currently in input memory) is moved into the store control field in working storage. Then, a test must be performed on the new store number to determine the correct store-ID entry needed on the first line of the store heading. The two lines that make up the store heading are then printed. And finally, the store sales accumulator is set to zero for this new store.

The pseudocode paragraphs corresponding to the modules subordinate to 200 START UP are shown in Figure 8.11.

Figure 8.12 contains the pseudocode paragraph 210-Process-Sales-Record that corresponds to module 210 PROCESS SALES RECORD of the structure chart. Recall that before processing the record in input memory, a test must be performed on the store number that it contains to determine if a control

■ **Figure 8.11** Modules subordinate to 200 START UP and their corresponding pseudocode paragraphs

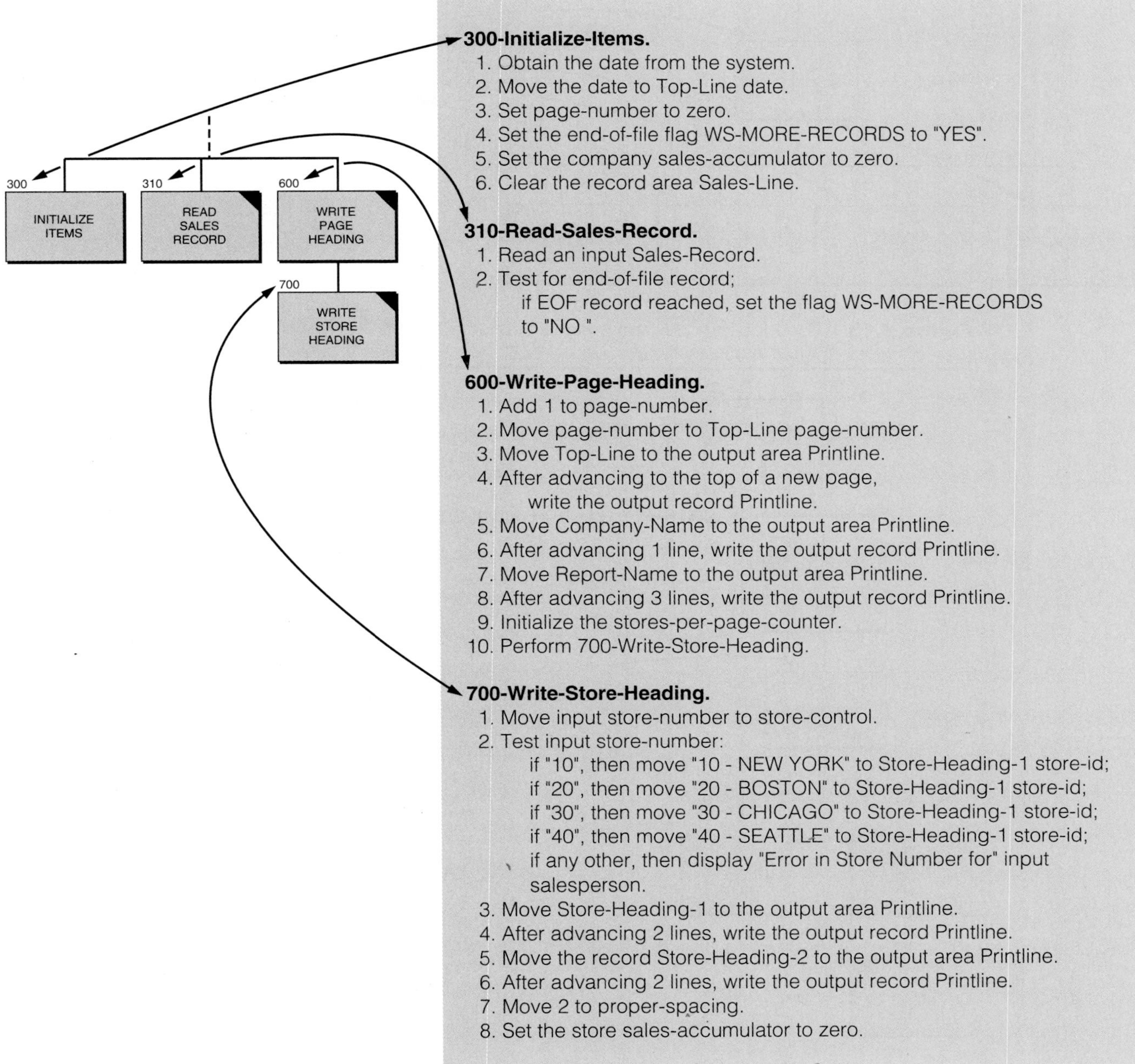

break should occur. Step 1 sends control to paragraph 320-Check-For-New-Store, where the test will be performed. Step 2 sends control to paragraph 330-Update-Accumulators. Step 3 sends control to paragraph 340-Prepare-Sales-Line and finally step 4 sends control to paragraph 310-Read-Sales-Record again, to access the next record of the input file.

300
INITIALIZE ITEMS
310
READ SALES RECORD
600
WRITE PAGE HEADING
700
WRITE STORE HEADING
300-Initialize-Items.
1. Obtain the date from the system.
2. Move the date to Top-Line date.
3. Set page-number to zero.
4. Set the end-of-file flag WS-MORE-RECORDS to "YES".
5. Set the company sales-accumulator to zero.
6. Clear the record area Sales-Line.
310-Read-Sales-Record.
1. Read an input Sales-Record.
2. Test for end-of-file record;
if EOF record reached, set the flag WS-MORE-RECORDS to "NO ".
600-Write-Page-Heading.
1. Add 1 to page-number.
2. Move page-number to Top-Line page-number.
3. Move Top-Line to the output area Printline.
4. After advancing to the top of a new page, write the output record Printline.
5. Move Company-Name to the output area Printline.
6. After advancing 1 line, write the output record Printline.
7. Move Report-Name to the output area Printline.
8. After advancing 3 lines, write the output record Printline.
9. Initialize the stores-per-page-counter.
10. Perform 700-Write-Store-Heading.
700-Write-Store-Heading.
1. Move input store-number to store-control.
2. Test input store-number:
if "10", then move "10 - NEW YORK" to Store-Heading-1 store-id;
if "20", then move "20 - BOSTON" to Store-Heading-1 store-id;
if "30", then move "30 - CHICAGO" to Store-Heading-1 store-id;
if "40", then move "40 - SEATTLE" to Store-Heading-1 store-id;
if any other, then display "Error in Store Number for" input salesperson.
3. Move Store-Heading-1 to the output area Printline.
4. After advancing 2 lines, write the output record Printline.
5. Move the record Store-Heading-2 to the output area Printline.
6. After advancing 2 lines, write the output record Printline.
7. Move 2 to proper-spacing.
8. Set the store sales-accumulator to zero.

Of the modules subordinate to module 210, only module 320 and its corresponding pseudocode need to be examined closely. Because this program contains a control break, paragraph 320-Check-For-New-Store is the most critical one. Without it, or some equivalent logic, no control break would occur, and no intermediate store totals could be printed on the report. Recall again that a control break must occur if the store number on the record currently in input memory is **not** the same as the store number in the store-control field in working storage. If that is the case, total sales for the previous store must be printed on the report before continuing to process the new record in input memory.

The pseudocode paragraphs corresponding to structure chart modules 320 CHECK FOR NEW STORE and 400 PREPARE STORE FOOTING are shown in Figure 8.13.

■ **Figure 8.12** Correspondence between pseudocode and module 210 PROCESS SALES RECORD

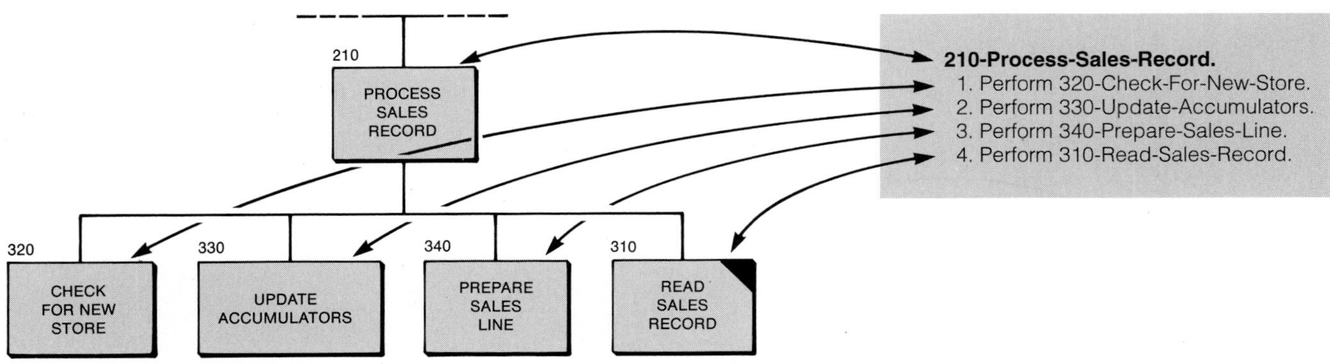

■ **Figure 8.13** Pseudocode corresponding to module 320 CHECK FOR NEW STORE and its subordinate modules

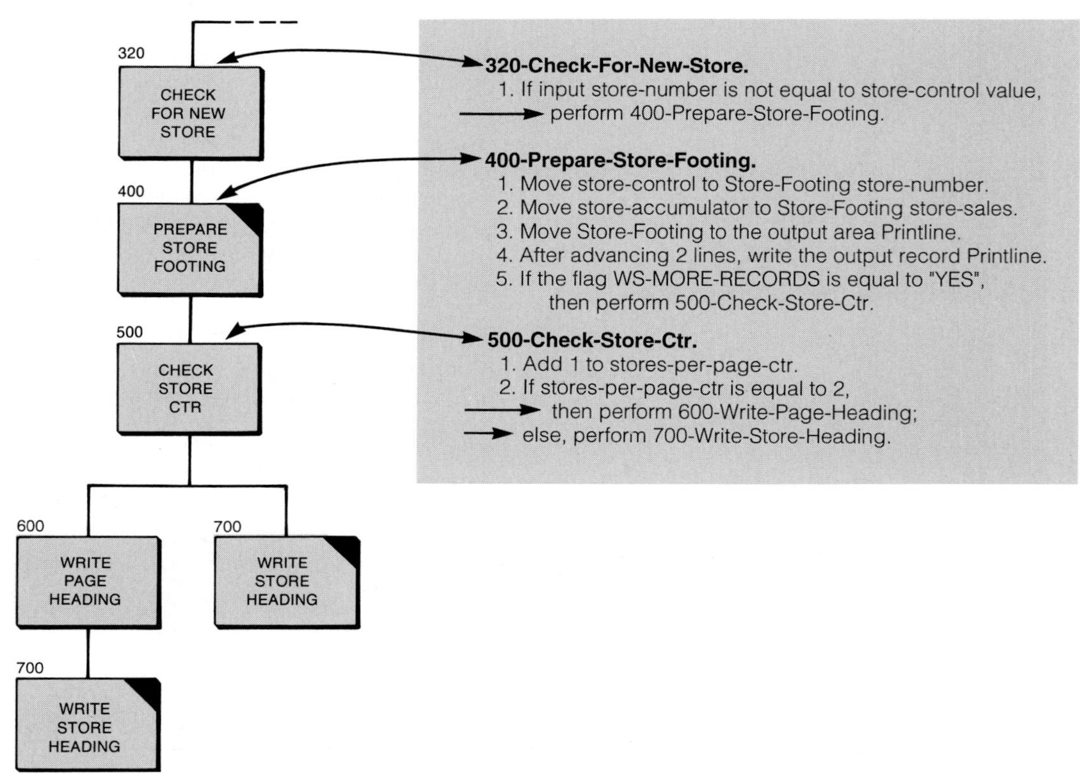

The printer spacing chart in Figure 8.3 shows that the store control footing line that prints the total sales for a store must also identify the store number. You must realize that control has been sent to this paragraph (400-Prepare-Store-Footing) as a result of a control break. This means that a new store number has appeared in input memory, but the store that must be identified on the store footing line is the previous store. That store number is still in the store control field in working storage. Step 1 of paragraph 400 moves the correct store number to the store footing line. Step 2 moves the total sales for the store to the store footing line and then the line is printed on the report.

Now, when is the new store number copied into the store control field? Do you recall that that occurs in paragraph 700-Write-Store-Heading? Realize also that after a store control footing is printed on the report, a test is performed to determine if the store control heading for the next store should be written on the current page or on the next page. If on the next page, the page heading must be printed first, followed by the store control heading. In either case, the new store number will have been copied into the store control field within paragraph 700. The pseudocode paragraph that corresponds to module 500 CHECK STORE CTR is also contained in Figure 8.13. (In step 5 of paragraph 400-Prepare-Store-Footing, note that paragraph 500-

Check-Store-Ctr is executed only if there are more records to process. That is, a page heading and/or a store heading should not be printed after the store footing for the very last store has been printed.)

The pseudocode paragraphs for modules 600 and 700 are not repeated in Figure 8.13, since they are already contained in Figure 8.11.

The conversion of structure chart modules 330 UPDATE ACCUMULATORS and 340 PREPARE SALES FILE into pseudocode is simple and direct, and no further explanations are needed.

Module 220 FINISH UP must handle the final tasks. There are two important ones: printing the total sales for the **last** store for which detail lines have been printed, and printing the total sales for the company as a whole. These two tasks are individually controlled from within structure chart module 350 PRODUCE LAST FOOTINGS. Recall that the program's control-break mechanism **does not trigger** the printing of the store footing for the last store. In fact, the printing of the total sales for the last store must be forced by the program, and this can logically occur only subsequent to encountering the EOF marker for the input file. It was decided to print the last store footing as a subtask of module 220, namely, in module 400 PREPARE STORE FOOTING.

After printing the store footing for the last store, the company footing is printed within module 410 PREPARE COMPANY FOOTING. Module 220 then prints the End-of-Report message and finally closes the files. Control then returns to the primary module, where program execution is terminated.

Figure 8.14 shows the pseudocode for module 220-FINISH-UP and its subordinate modules.

Figure 8.15 contains the complete program pseudocode.

■ **Figure 8.14** The pseudocode paragraphs corresponding to module 220 FINISH UP and its subordinate modules

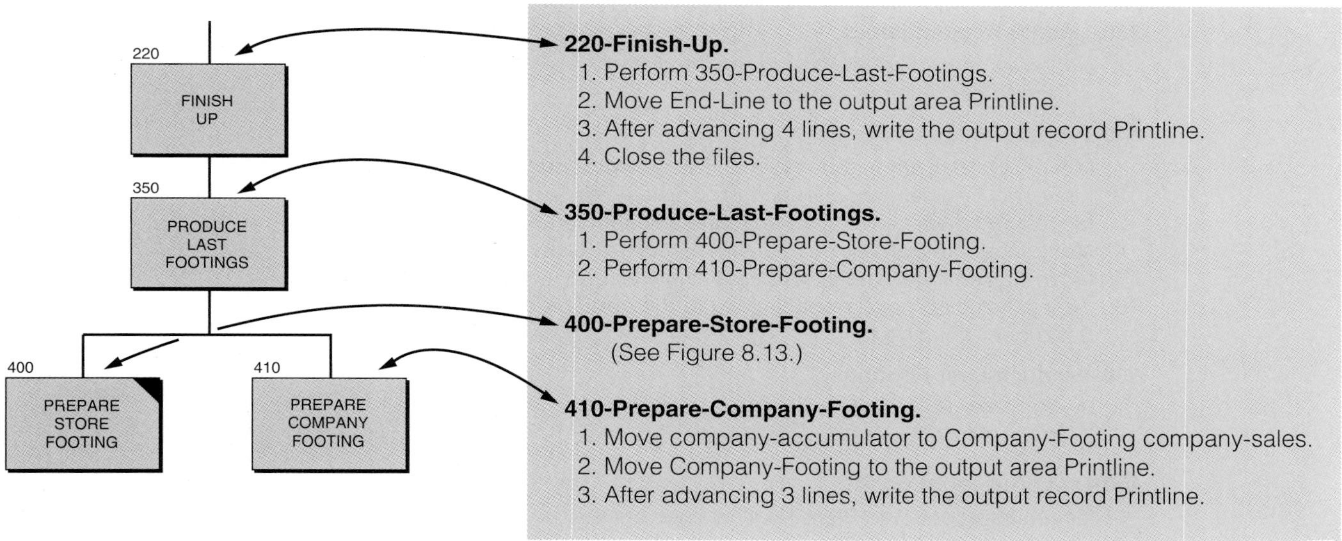
220
FINISH UP
350
PRODUCE LAST FOOTINGS
400
PREPARE STORE FOOTING
410
PREPARE COMPANY FOOTING
220-Finish-Up.
1. Perform 350-Produce-Last-Footings.
2. Move End-Line to the output area Printline.
3. After advancing 4 lines, write the output record Printline.
4. Close the files.
350-Produce-Last-Footings.
1. Perform 400-Prepare-Store-Footing.
2. Perform 410-Prepare-Company-Footing.
400-Prepare-Store-Footing.
(See Figure 8.13.)
410-Prepare-Company-Footing.
1. Move company-accumulator to Company-Footing company-sales.
2. Move Company-Footing to the output area Printline.
3. After advancing 3 lines, write the output record Printline.

■ **Figure 8.15** Program pseudocode for the sample program

100-Produce-Sales-Report.
1. Perform 200-Start-Up.
2. Perform 210-Process-Sales-Record until no more records.
3. Perform 220-Finish-Up.
4. Stop the run.

200-Start-Up.
1. Open the files.
2. Perform 300-Initialize-Items.
3. Perform 310-Read-Sales-Record.
4. Perform 600-Write-Page-Heading.

210-Process-Sales-Record.
1. Perform 320-Check-For-New-Store.
2. Perform 330-Update-Accumulators.
3. Perform 340-Prepare-Sales-Line.
4. Perform 310-Read-Sales-Record.

■ **Figure 8.15** continued

220-Finish-Up.

1. Perform 350-Produce-Last-Footings.
2. Move End-Line to the output area Printline.
3. After advancing 4 lines, write the output record Printline.
4. Close the files.

300-Initialize-Items.

1. Obtain the date from the system.
2. Move the date to Top-Line date.
3. Set page-number to zero.
4. Set the end-of-file flag WS-MORE-RECORDS to "YES".
5. Set the company sales-accumulator to zero.
6. Clear the record area Sales-Line.

310-Read-Sales-Record.

1. Read an input Sales-Record.
2. Test for end-of-file record;
   if EOF record reached, set the flag WS-MORE-RECORDS to "NO ".

320-Check-For-New-Store.

1. If input store-number is not equal to store-control value,
   perform 400-Prepare-Store-Footing.

330-Update-Accumulators.

1. Add input current-sales to store-accumulator
   and to company-accumulator.

340-Prepare-Sales-Line.

1. Move input department-number to Sales-Line department-number.
2. Move input social-security-number to Sales-Line social-security-number.
3. Move input salesperson to Sales-Line salesperson.
4. Move input current-sales to Sales-Line current-sales.
5. Move Sales-Line to the output area Printline.
6. After advancing proper-spacing, write the output record Printline.
7. Set proper-spacing to 1.

350-Produce-Last-Footings.

1. Perform 400-Prepare-Store-Footing.
2. Perform 410-Prepare-Company-Footing.

400-Prepare-Store-Footing.

1. Move store-control to Store-Footing store-number.
2. Move store-accumulator to Store-Footing store-sales.
3. Move Store-Footing to the output area Printline.
4. After advancing 2 lines, write the output record Printline.
5. If the flag WS-MORE-RECORDS is equal to "YES",
   then perform 500-Check-Store-Ctr.

410-Prepare-Company-Footing.

1. Move company-accumulator to Company-Footing company-sales.
2. Move Company-Footing to the output area Printline.
3. After advancing 3 lines, write the output record Printline.

500-Check-Store-Ctr.

1. Add 1 to stores-per-page-ctr.
2. If stores-per-page-ctr is equal to 2,
   then, perform 600-Write-Page-Heading;
   else perform 700-Write-Store-Heading.

600-Write-Page-Heading.

1. Add 1 to page-number.
2. Move page-number to Top-Line page-number.
3. Move Top-Line to the output area Printline.
4. After advancing to the top of a new page,
   write the output record Printline.
5. Move Company-Name to the output area Printline.
6. After advancing 1 line, write the output record Printline.
7. Move Report-Name to the output area Printline.
8. After advancing 3 lines, write the output record Printline.
9. Initialize the stores-per-page-counter.
10. Perform 700-Write-Store-Heading.

700-Write-Store-Heading.

1. Move input store-number to store-control.
2. Test input store-number:
   if "10", then move "10 - NEW YORK" to Store-Heading-1 store-id;
   if "20", then move "20 - BOSTON" to Store-Heading-1 store-id;
   if "30", then move "30 - CHICAGO" to Store-Heading-1 store-id;
   if "40", then move "40 - SEATTLE" to Store-Heading-1 store-id;
   if any other, then display "Error in Store Number for " input salesperson.
3. Move Store-Heading-1 to the output area Printline.
4. After advancing 2 lines, write the output record Printline.
5. Move the record Store-Heading-2 to the output area Printline.
6. After advancing 2 lines, write the output record Printline.
7. Move 2 to proper-spacing.
8. Set the store sales-accumulator to zero.

Program Flowchart

For those of you who prefer the development of a program flowchart to that of the program pseudocode, Figure 8.16 contains the flowchart. The comments made during the development of the pseudocode are appropriate here as well. All you need do is to substitute the flowchart module for the pseudocode paragraph of the same name, and make minor adjustments for those statements that refer to specific steps in the pseudocode.

This completes the design phase.

The Design Implementation Phase

Since this program does not include any new statement formats, the coding of the program does not present any new problems. However, we draw your attention to the following question: What statement will be used to code the tests in the pseudocode paragraph 400-Write-Store-Heading?

The two statements available to the programmer are the IF and EVALUATE statements. Both of these allow the tests to be coded with or without condition-names. The following examples illustrate the IF and EVALUATE statements with and without condition-names.

1. Coding the tests without condition-names.
   a. Using nested IF statements:

```
IF I-STORE-NO = "10"
    MOVE "10 - NEW YORK" TO O-STORE-ID
ELSE
    IF I-STORE-NO = "20"
        MOVE "20 - BOSTON" TO O-STORE-ID
    ELSE
        IF I-STORE-NO = "30"
            MOVE "30 - CHICAGO" TO O-STORE-ID
        ELSE
            IF I-STORE-NO = "40"
                MOVE "40 - SEATTLE" TO O-STORE-ID
            ELSE
                DISPLAY "ERROR IN STORE NUMBER FOR " I-SALESPERSON.
```

Figure 8.16 Program flowchart for the sample program

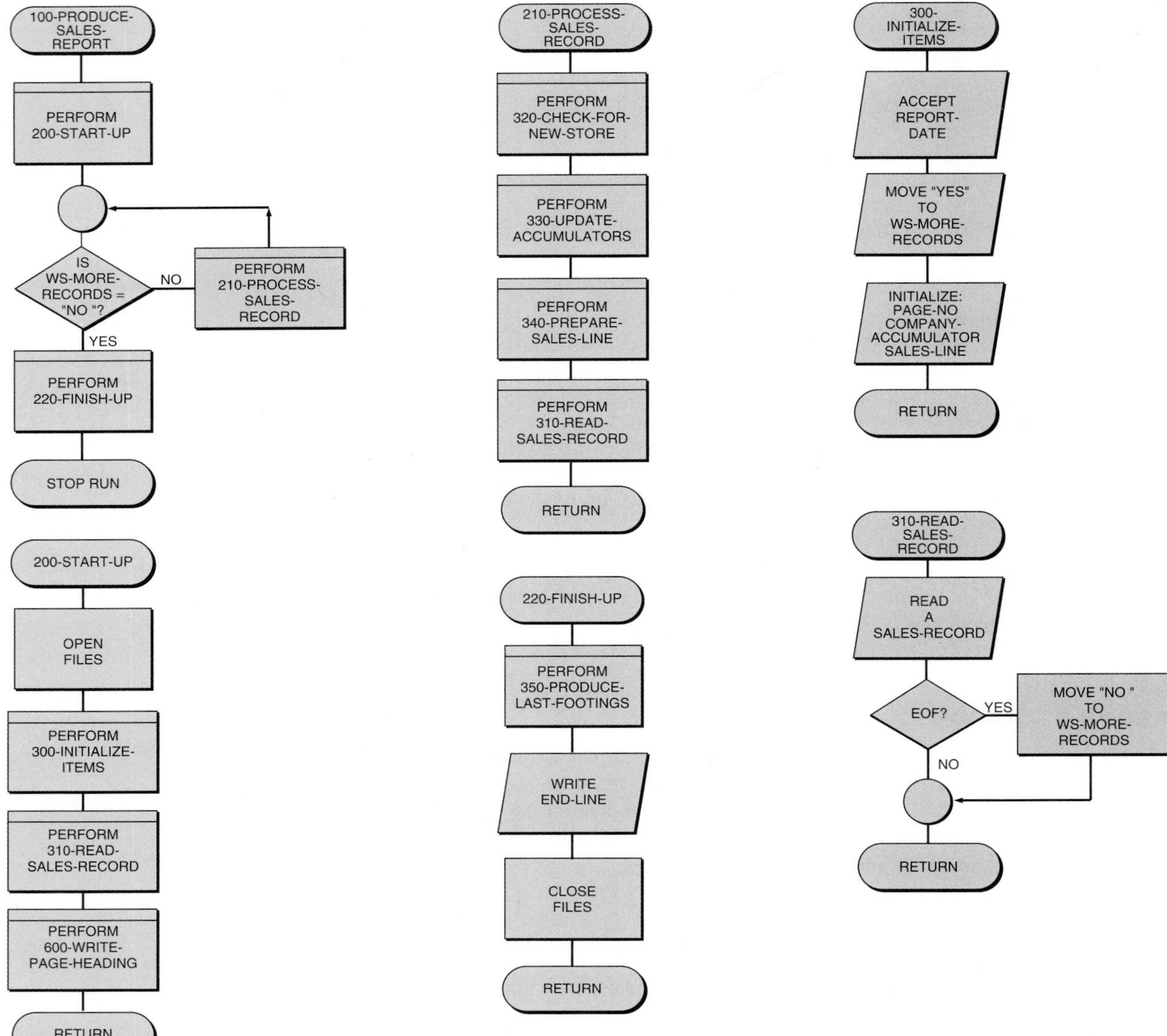

■ **Figure 8.16** continued

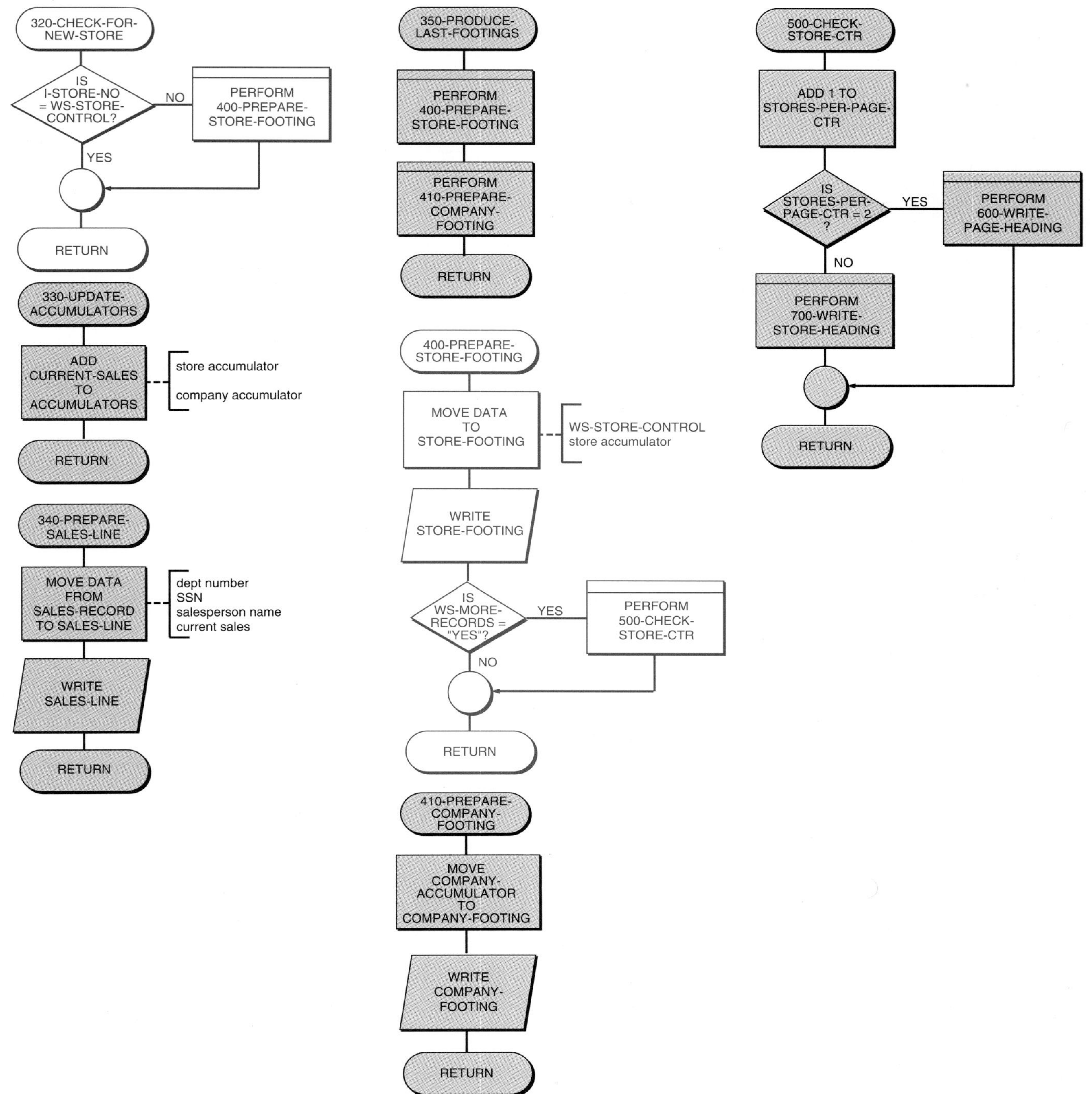

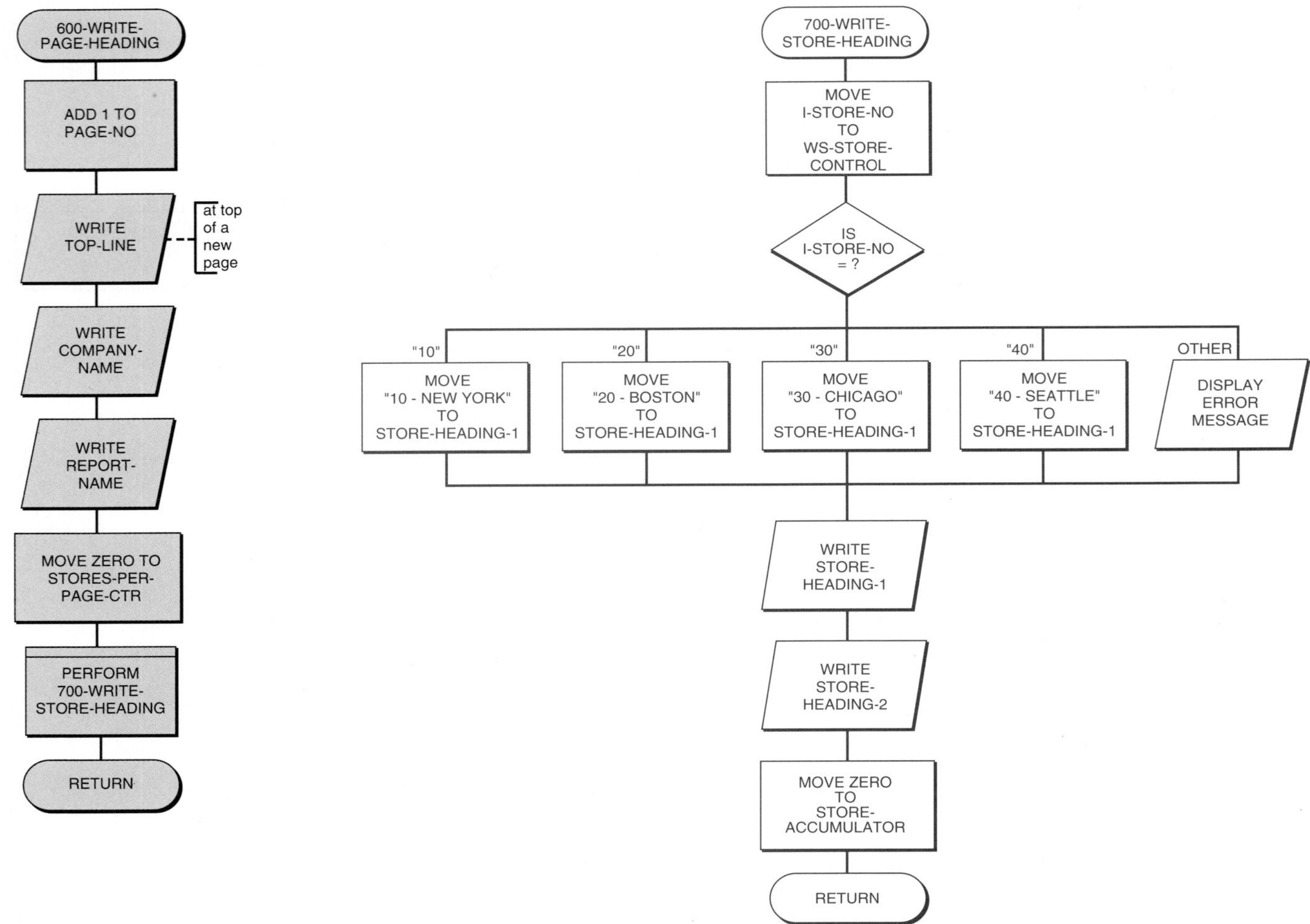

b. Using the EVALUATE statement:
Form 1.

```
EVALUATE I-STORE-NO
    WHEN "10" MOVE "10 - NEW YORK" TO O-STORE-ID
    WHEN "20" MOVE "20 - BOSTON" TO O-STORE-ID
    WHEN "30" MOVE "30 - CHICAGO" TO O-STORE-ID
    WHEN "40" MOVE "40 - SEATTLE" TO O-STORE-ID
    WHEN OTHER
        DISPLAY "ERROR IN STORE NUMBER FOR " I-SALESPERSON.
```

Form 2.

```
EVALUATE    TRUE
    WHEN I-STORE-NO = "10" MOVE "10 - NEW YORK" TO O-STORE-ID
    WHEN I-STORE-NO = "20" MOVE "20 - BOSTON" TO O-STORE-ID
    WHEN I-STORE-NO = "30" MOVE "30 - CHICAGO" TO O-STORE-ID
    WHEN I-STORE-NO = "40" MOVE "40 - SEATTLE" TO O-STORE-ID
    WHEN I-STORE-NO NOT = "10" OR "20" OR "30" OR "40"
        DISPLAY "ERROR IN STORE NUMBER FOR " I-SALESPERSON.
```

2. Coding the tests with condition-names.

In order to allow these options, condition-names must be defined for the data item I-STORE-NO, as follows:

```
05 I-STORE-NO           PIC XX.
   88 NEW-YORK          VALUE "10".
   88 BOSTON            VALUE "20".
   88 CHICAGO           VALUE "30".
   88 SEATTLE           VALUE "40".
   88 VALID-STORE-NO    VALUES "10", "20", "30", "40".
```

a. Using nested IF statements:

```
IF NEW-YORK
    MOVE "10 - NEW YORK" TO O-STORE-ID
ELSE
    IF BOSTON
        MOVE "20 - BOSTON" TO O-STORE-ID
    ELSE
        IF CHICAGO
            MOVE "30 - CHICAGO" TO O-STORE-ID
        ELSE
            IF SEATTLE
                MOVE "40 - SEATTLE" TO O-STORE-ID
            ELSE
                DISPLAY "ERROR IN STORE NUMBER FOR " I-SALESPERSON.
```

b. Using the EVALUATE statement:

```
EVALUATE   TRUE
    WHEN  NEW-YORK  MOVE "10 - NEW YORK" TO O-STORE-ID
    WHEN  BOSTON    MOVE "20 - BOSTON" TO O-STORE-ID
    WHEN  CHICAGO   MOVE "30 - CHICAGO" TO O-STORE-ID
    WHEN  SEATTLE   MOVE "40 - SEATTLE" TO O-STORE-ID
    WHEN NOT VALID-STORE-NO
        DISPLAY "ERROR IN STORE NUMBER FOR" I-SALESPERSON.
```

A listing of the coded program is shown in Figure 8.17. (The entries related to the control break have been highlighted.) The sample data file processed by the program is shown in Figure 8.18 [DD/CD:VIC8SP1.DAT], and the report produced by the program is shown in Figure 8.19.

Figure 8.17 The COBOL program

```
 IDENTIFICATION DIVISION.

 PROGRAM-ID.  SPORTSMAN-SALES-1.

*****************************************************************
*                                                               *
*  AUTHOR.        PAQUETTE.                                     *
*  DATE WRITTEN.  AUGUST 1993.                                  *
*                                                               *
*       THIS PROGRAM PRODUCES A MULTILEVEL SALES ANALYSIS RE-   *
*  PORT FOR THE SPORTSMAN COMPANY.                              *
*       THE REPORT CONTAINS A DETAIL LINE FOR EACH SALESPERSON, *
*  INTERMEDIATE SALES TOTALS FOR EACH STORE, AND A FINAL TOTAL  *
*  FOR THE COMPANY AS A WHOLE.                                  *
*       EACH SALESPERSON RECORD IN THE SALES FILE CONTAINS THE  *
*  FOLLOWING DATA:  THE SALESPERSON'S STORE NUMBER, DEPARTMENT  *
*  NUMBER, SOCIAL SECURITY NUMBER, NAME, AND CURRENT SALES FOR  *
*  THE PERIOD.                                                  *
*                                                               *
*****************************************************************

 ENVIRONMENT DIVISION.

 CONFIGURATION SECTION.

 SOURCE-COMPUTER.  VAX-VMS-8650.
 OBJECT-COMPUTER.  VAX-VMS-8650.

 INPUT-OUTPUT SECTION.

 FILE-CONTROL.
     SELECT SALES-FILE    ASSIGN TO COB$INPUT.
     SELECT SALES-REPORT  ASSIGN TO COB$OUTPUT.

 DATA DIVISION.

 FILE SECTION.

 FD  SALES-FILE
     RECORD CONTAINS 39 CHARACTERS.
```

```
01  SALES-RECORD.
    05 I-STORE-NO        PIC XX.
       88 NEW-YORK       VALUE "10".
       88 BOSTON         VALUE "20".
       88 CHICAGO        VALUE "30".
       88 SEATTLE        VALUE "40".
       88 VALID-STORE-NO VALUES "10", "20", "30", "40".
    05 I-DEPT-NO         PIC XX.
    05 I-SSN             PIC X(9).
    05 I-SALESPERSON     PIC X(20).
    05 I-CURRENT-SALES   PIC 9(4)V99.

FD  SALES-REPORT
    RECORD CONTAINS 133 CHARACTERS.

01  PRINTLINE    PIC X(133).

WORKING-STORAGE SECTION.

01  PROGRAM-CONTROLS.
    05 WS-MORE-RECORDS          PIC XXX.
       88 THERE-IS-A-RECORD     VALUE "YES".
       88 NO-MORE-RECORDS       VALUE "NO ".
    05 WS-STORE-CONTROL         PIC XX.
    05 WS-STORES-PER-PAGE-CTR   PIC 9.
    05 WS-PROPER-SPACING        PIC 99.
    05 WS-REPORT-DATE           PIC X(6).
    05 WS-PAGE-NO               PIC 99.

01  PROGRAM-ACCUMULATORS        COMP.
    05 WS-STORE-ACCUMULATOR     PIC S9(6)V99.
    05 WS-COMPANY-ACCUMULATOR   PIC S9(7)V99.

01  PAGE-HEADING.

    05 TOP-LINE.
       10                  PIC X(6)   VALUE SPACES.
       10                  PIC X(14)  VALUE "REPORT DATE:  ".
       10 O-REPORT-DATE    PIC XX/XX/XX.
       10                  PIC X(92)  VALUE SPACES.
       10                  PIC X(5)   VALUE "PAGE ".
       10 O-PAGE-NO        PIC Z9.
       10                  PIC X(6)   VALUE SPACES.

    05 COMPANY-NAME.
       10 PIC X(60)  VALUE SPACES.
       10 PIC X(13)  VALUE "THE SPORTSMAN".
       10 PIC X(60)  VALUE SPACES.

    05 REPORT-NAME.
       10 PIC X(56)  VALUE SPACES.
       10 PIC X(21)  VALUE "SALES ANALYSIS REPORT".
       10 PIC X(56)  VALUE SPACES.

01  STORE-HEADING.

    05 STORE-HEADING-1.
       10               PIC X(15)  VALUE SPACES.
       10               PIC X(8)   VALUE "STORE:  ".
       10 O-STORE-ID    PIC X(15).
       10               PIC X(95)  VALUE SPACES.

    05 STORE-HEADING-2.
       10 PIC X(25)   VALUE SPACES.
       10 PIC X(8)    VALUE "DEPT NO.".
       10 PIC X(9)    VALUE SPACES.
       10 PIC X(15)   VALUE "SALESPERSON SSN".
       10 PIC X(11)   VALUE SPACES.
       10 PIC X(16)   VALUE "SALESPERSON NAME".
       10 PIC X(11)   VALUE SPACES.
       10 PIC X(13)   VALUE "CURRENT SALES".
       10 PIC X(25)   VALUE SPACES.

01  SALES-LINE.
    05                    PIC X(28).
    05 O-DEPT-NO          PIC XX.
    05                    PIC X(14).
    05 O-SSN              PIC XXXBXXBXXXX.
    05                    PIC X(11).
    05 O-SALESPERSON      PIC X(20).
    05                    PIC X(11).
    05 O-CURRENT-SALES    PIC $Z,ZZ9.99.
    05                    PIC X(27).
```

```
01   STORE-FOOTING.
     05                  PIC X(83)   VALUE SPACES.
     05                  PIC X(22)   VALUE "TOTAL SALES FOR STORE ".
     05 O-STORE-NO       PIC XX.
     05                  PIC X(3)    VALUE " : ".
     05 O-STORE-SALES    PIC $ZZZ,ZZ9.99-.
     05                  PIC XX      VALUE " *".
     05                  PIC X(9)    VALUE SPACES.

01   COMPANY-FOOTING.
     05                    PIC X(86) VALUE SPACES.
     05                    PIC X(22) VALUE "TOTAL COMPANY SALES : ".
     05 O-COMPANY-SALES    PIC $Z,ZZZ,ZZ9.99-.
     05                    PIC X(3)  VALUE " **".
     05                    PIC X(8)  VALUE SPACES.

01   END-LINE.
     05 PIC X(55)  VALUE SPACES.
     05 PIC X(23)  VALUE "***  END OF REPORT  ***".
     05 PIC X(55)  VALUE SPACES.

PROCEDURE DIVISION.

100-PRODUCE-SALES-REPORT.
    PERFORM 200-START-UP.
    PERFORM 210-PROCESS-SALES-RECORD
        UNTIL NO-MORE-RECORDS.
    PERFORM 220-FINISH-UP
    STOP RUN.

200-START-UP.
    OPEN INPUT SALES-FILE
         OUTPUT SALES-REPORT.
    PERFORM 300-INITIALIZE-ITEMS.
    PERFORM 310-READ-SALES-RECORD.
    PERFORM 600-WRITE-PAGE-HEADING.

210-PROCESS-SALES-RECORD.
    PERFORM 320-CHECK-FOR-NEW-STORE.
    PERFORM 330-UPDATE-ACCUMULATORS.
    PERFORM 340-PREPARE-SALES-LINE.
    PERFORM 310-READ-SALES-RECORD.

220-FINISH-UP.
    PERFORM 350-PRODUCE-LAST-FOOTINGS.
    WRITE PRINTLINE FROM END-LINE
        AFTER ADVANCING 4 LINES.
    CLOSE SALES-FILE
          SALES-REPORT.

300-INITIALIZE-ITEMS.
    ACCEPT WS-REPORT-DATE FROM DATE.
    MOVE WS-REPORT-DATE TO O-REPORT-DATE.
    SET THERE-IS-A-RECORD TO TRUE.
    INITIALIZE WS-COMPANY-ACCUMULATOR
               WS-PAGE-NO.
    MOVE SPACES TO SALES-LINE.

310-READ-SALES-RECORD.
    READ SALES-FILE RECORD
        AT END
            SET NO-MORE-RECORDS TO TRUE.

320-CHECK-FOR-NEW-STORE.
    IF I-STORE-NO = WS-STORE-CONTROL
        NEXT SENTENCE
    ELSE
        PERFORM 400-PREPARE-STORE-FOOTING.

330-UPDATE-ACCUMULATORS.
    ADD I-CURRENT-SALES TO WS-STORE-ACCUMULATOR
                           WS-COMPANY-ACCUMULATOR.

340-PREPARE-SALES-LINE.
    MOVE I-DEPT-NO TO O-DEPT-NO.
    MOVE I-SSN TO O-SSN.
    MOVE I-SALESPERSON TO O-SALESPERSON.
    MOVE I-CURRENT-SALES TO O-CURRENT-SALES.
    WRITE PRINTLINE FROM SALES-LINE
        AFTER ADVANCING WS-PROPER-SPACING.
    MOVE 1 TO WS-PROPER-SPACING.

350-PRODUCE-LAST-FOOTINGS.
    PERFORM 400-PREPARE-STORE-FOOTING.
    PERFORM 410-PREPARE-COMPANY-FOOTING.
```

```
 400-PREPARE-STORE-FOOTING.
     MOVE WS-STORE-CONTROL TO O-STORE-NO.
     MOVE WS-STORE-ACCUMULATOR TO O-STORE-SALES.
     WRITE PRINTLINE FROM STORE-FOOTING
         AFTER ADVANCING 2 LINES.
     IF THERE-IS-A-RECORD
         PERFORM 500-CHECK-STORE-CTR
     ELSE
         CONTINUE.

 410-PREPARE-COMPANY-FOOTING.
     MOVE WS-COMPANY-ACCUMULATOR TO O-COMPANY-SALES.
     WRITE PRINTLINE FROM COMPANY-FOOTING
         AFTER ADVANCING 3 LINES.

 500-CHECK-STORE-CTR.
     ADD 1 TO WS-STORES-PER-PAGE-CTR.
     IF WS-STORES-PER-PAGE-CTR = 2
         PERFORM 600-WRITE-PAGE-HEADING
     ELSE
         PERFORM 700-WRITE-STORE-HEADING
     END-IF.

 600-WRITE-PAGE-HEADING.
     ADD 1 TO WS-PAGE-NO.
     MOVE WS-PAGE-NO TO O-PAGE-NO.
     WRITE PRINTLINE FROM TOP-LINE
         AFTER ADVANCING PAGE.
     WRITE PRINTLINE FROM COMPANY-NAME
         AFTER ADVANCING 1 LINE.
     WRITE PRINTLINE FROM REPORT-NAME
         AFTER ADVANCING 3 LINES.
     INITIALIZE WS-STORES-PER-PAGE-CTR.
     PERFORM 700-WRITE-STORE-HEADING.

 700-WRITE-STORE-HEADING.
     MOVE I-STORE-NO TO WS-STORE-CONTROL.
     EVALUATE I-STORE-NO
         WHEN "10"  MOVE "10 - NEW YORK" TO O-STORE-ID
         WHEN "20"  MOVE "20 - BOSTON" TO O-STORE-ID
         WHEN "30"  MOVE "30 - CHICAGO" TO O-STORE-ID
         WHEN "40"  MOVE "40 - SEATTLE" TO O-STORE-ID
         WHEN OTHER
             DISPLAY " ERROR IN STORE NO. FOR " I-SALESPERSON.

*  NESTED-IF STATEMENTS USING CONDITION-NAME TESTS COULD BE USED
*  AS AN ALTERNATE TO THE EVALUATE STATEMENT, AS FOLLOWS:

*    IF NEW-YORK
*        MOVE "10 - NEW YORK" TO O-STORE-ID
*    ELSE
*        IF BOSTON
*            MOVE "20 - BOSTON" TO O-STORE-ID
*        ELSE
*            IF CHICAGO
*                MOVE "30 - CHICAGO" TO O-STORE-ID
*            ELSE
*                IF SEATTLE
*                    MOVE "40 - SEATTLE" TO O-STORE-ID
*                ELSE
*                    DISPLAY " ERROR IN STORE NO. FOR "
*                              I-SALESPERSON
*                END-IF
*            END-IF
*        END-IF
*    END-IF.

     WRITE PRINTLINE FROM STORE-HEADING-1
         AFTER ADVANCING 2 LINES.
     WRITE PRINTLINE FROM STORE-HEADING-2
         AFTER ADVANCING 2 LINES.
     MOVE 2 TO WS-PROPER-SPACING.
     INITIALIZE WS-STORE-ACCUMULATOR.
```

■ Figure 8.18 Sample input file

Store number | Dept. number | Social Security number | Salesperson name | Current sales

```
1002214365025ALLEN, ROBERT        150000
1002218546010BROWN, RAYMOND       302255
1002641275050BRANNIGAN, NICOLE    087525
1002315463030FOGARTY, JANICE      105050
1002642754040MAIN, CHARLES        128000
1004685264065CARLSON, HOPE        090000
1004556234035CRANE, JOHN          105050
1004696996055DANIELS, JULIA       287050
1004251342020FARMER, SUSAN        162000
1004263452070FEINGOLD, HAROLD     125050
1004667451060HARRISON, LILY       142580
1006521244005DWYER, TERRENCE      142580
1006564451045EDWARDS, PETER       108050
1006644353075MANNING, ELIZABETH   135000
1008377568080HOWARD, RALPH        056050
1008482131015JANKOWSKI, STANLEY   135000
1008551164090KELLY, PATRICK       162500
1008599231085LANGFORD, SARAH      115050
1008521166100PRINGLY, ANNE        109805
2002408936050CORDEIRO, ANTONE     010050
2002509862005CORTON, ALEXANDRA    100000
2002509185045PINEAULT, NORMAN     098050
2002480755030TALBOT, JILLIAN      127580
2004479210065BARRESI, JOHN        065000
2004427560010COCHRANE, RUSSELL    146050
2004360902035PENTA, ROBERT        165025
2004472847080PROULX, PAULINE      115000
2004375701060QUINN, SUZANNE       132050
2006683309020COSTELLO, JAMES      167050
2006418090015CRAWFORD, SHIRLEY    139050
2006566127070FELDMAN, WALTER      147080
2006433406075FERNANDEZ, LOUISE    200000
2006571904025LEMERISE, DONALD     185050
2006572495090WORTHEN, MICHAEL     157000
2008762355100GOYETTE, FRANCES     095000
2008812133085KOSINSKI, KATHERINE  112500
2008804233040VERMETTE, GLORIA     156050
3002576400892KING, CHRISTOPHER    189070
3002416892014BERNARD, ISIDORE     203569
3002823144098MAHFUZ, IRENE        185025
3004566731251ROBINSON, GILBERT    210590
3004788230154DONOHUE, PHIL        087500
3004607044132CORRIGAN, ALENE      187550
3004745645270FURTADO, MAUREEN     201540
3006820788914ABALLO, NORMA        235075
3006785023157DOLLARHIDE, CHRIS    201570
3006745635164LINCOURT, LORETTA    149500
3008466587165BRAZ, JOAN           231560
3008557318974PRATT, ROBIN         215500
3008487251099MELANSON, GARY       190550
4002452677143BEAUDOIN, ROCKY      221500
4002787855623MARKLAND, MARY       198750
4002674451231BISBANO, HENRY       219055
4004720954670VELOZO, MARIO        242390
4004624166876PARISEAU, WILLIAM    178500
4004712133463PERRY, MARTA         194550
4006452892153CARDIN, FRANCIS      204590
4006551502546FORTIN, EMIL         225450
4006574930461GALLAGHER, MICHAEL   197675
4006683215467NOTTE, LORENZO       200500
4008721435472JOBIN, ANTONIO       214050
4008490234571MILLER, RENEE        190570
4008351566178TRAMONTE, ESTELLE    213500
```

Figure 8.19 Sales report produced by the program

```
REPORT DATE: 93/08/25                                                                    PAGE 1
                                    THE SPORTSMAN

                                 SALES ANALYSIS REPORT
        STORE: 10 - NEW YORK

                 DEPT NO.          SALESPERSON SSN            SALESPERSON NAME             CURRENT SALES

                    02              214 36 5025             ALLEN, ROBERT                  $1,500.00
                    02              218 54 6010             BROWN, RAYMOND                 $3,022.55
                    02              641 27 5050             BRANNIGAN, NICOLE              $  875.25
                    02              315 46 3030             FOGARTY, JANICE                $1,050.50
                    02              642 75 4040             MAIN, CHARLES                  $1,280.00
                    04              685 26 4065             CARLSON, HOPE                  $  900.00
                    04              556 23 4035             CRANE, JOHN                    $1,050.50
                    04              696 99 6055             DANIELS, JULIA                 $2,870.50
                    04              251 34 2020             FARMER, SUSAN                  $1,620.00
                    04              263 45 2070             FEINGOLD, HAROLD               $1,250.50
                    04              667 45 1060             HARRISON, LILY                 $1,425.80
                    06              521 24 4005             DWYER, TERRENCE                $1,425.80
                    06              564 45 1045             EDWARDS, PETER                 $1,080.50
                    06              644 35 3075             MANNING, ELIZABETH             $1,350.00
                    08              377 56 8080             HOWARD, RALPH                  $  560.50
                    08              482 13 1015             JANKOWSKI, STANLEY             $1,350.00
                    08              551 16 4090             KELLY, PATRICK                 $1,625.00
                    08              599 23 1085             LANGFORD, SARAH                $1,150.50
                    08              521 16 6100             PRINGLY, ANNE                  $1,098.05

                                                    TOTAL SALES FOR STORE 10 : $ 26,485.95 *
        STORE: 20 - BOSTON

                 DEPT NO.          SALESPERSON SSN            SALESPERSON NAME             CURRENT SALES

                    02              408 93 6050             CORDEIRO, ANTONE               $  100.50
                    02              509 86 2005             CORTON, ALEXANDRA              $1,000.00
                    02              509 18 5045             PINEAULT, NORMAN               $  980.50
                    02              480 75 5030             TALBOT, JILLIAN                $1,275.80
                    04              479 21 0065             BARRESI, JOHN                  $  650.00
                    04              427 56 0010             COCHRANE, RUSSELL              $1,460.50
                    04              360 90 2035             PENTA, ROBERT                  $1,650.25
                    04              472 84 7080             PROULX, PAULINE                $1,150.00
                    04              375 70 1060             QUINN, SUZANNE                 $1,320.50
                    06              683 30 9020             COSTELLO, JAMES                $1,670.50
                    06              418 09 0015             CRAWFORD, SHIRLEY              $1,390.50
                    06              566 12 7070             FELDMAN, WALTER                $1,470.80
                    06              433 40 6075             FERNANDEZ, LOUISE              $2,000.00
                    06              571 90 4025             LEMERISE, DONALD               $1,850.50
                    06              572 49 5090             WORTHEN, MICHAEL               $1,570.00
                    08              762 35 5100             GOYETTE, FRANCES               $  950.00
                    08              812 13 3085             KOSINSKI, KATHERINE            $1,125.00
                    08              804 23 3040             VERMETTE, GLORIA               $1,560.50

                                                    TOTAL SALES FOR STORE 20: $23,175.85*
```

Subtotaling Versus Rolling Forward

In the sample program of Figure 8.17, the current sales for a salesperson are added to the store sales accumulator as well as to the company sales accumulator. This procedure is called *subtotaling,* since adding the current sales to an accumulator produces a new subtotal in the accumulator.

An alternative procedure could easily be designed as follows: As a salesperson record is being processed, subtotal the current sales into the store sales accumulator only. When a control break occurs, and a store control footing is to be printed on the report, add the store total to the company sales accumulator. This procedure is called *rolling forward,* since the store total sales are "rolled forward" into the company sales accumulator.

It should be obvious that the results will be the same, although fewer additions involving the company sales accumulator are needed. Thus, the benefit to the program is a greater degree of efficiency.

If the rolling-forward procedure is used in the sample program, minor changes would be made to the program design. We list below, for instance, the changes that would be made to the program pseudocode:

1. In paragraph 210-Process-Sales-Record, the PERFORM statement in step 2 is replaced by

   Add input current-sales to store-accumulator.

   and paragraph 330-Update-Accumulators is eliminated.
2. In paragraph 400-Prepare-Store-Footing, we include the rolling-forward step. This step must **precede** the IF statement that sends control to paragraph 500, since within the subtasks of this

■ **Figure 8.19** continued

```
REPORT DATE: 93/08/25                                                                                  PAGE 2
                                          THE SPORTSMAN

                                        SALES ANALYSIS REPORT
          STORE:  30 - CHICAGO

                  DEPT NO.           SALESPERSON SSN             SALESPERSON NAME           CURRENT SALES

                     02               576 40 0892             KING, CHRISTOPHER               $1,890.70
                     02               416 89 2014             BERNARD, ISIDORE                $2,035.69
                     02               823 14 4098             MAHFUZ, IRENE                   $1,850.25
                     04               566 73 1251             ROBINSON, GILBERT               $2,105.90
                     04               788 23 0154             DONOHUE, PHIL                   $  875.00
                     04               607 04 4132             CORRIGAN, ALENE                 $1,875.50
                     04               745 64 5270             FURTADO, MAUREEN                $2,015.40
                     06               820 78 8914             ABALLO, NORMA                   $2,350.75
                     06               785 02 3157             DOLLARHIDE, CHRIS               $2,015.70
                     06               745 63 5164             LINCOURT, LORETTA               $1,495.00
                     08               466 58 7165             BRAZ, JOHN                      $2,315.60
                     08               557 31 8974             PRATT, ROBIN                    $2,155.00
                     08               487 25 1099             MELANSON, GARY                  $1,905.50

                                                           TOTAL SALES FOR STORE 30 : $ 24,885.99 *
          STORE: 40 - SEATTLE

                  DEPT NO.           SALESPERSON SSN             SALESPERSON NAME           CURRENT SALES

                     02               452 67 7143             BEAUDOIN, ROCKY                 $2,215.00
                     02               787 85 5623             MARKLAND, MARY                  $1,987.50
                     02               674 45 1231             BISBANO, HENRY                  $2,190.55
                     04               720 95 4670             VELOZO, MARIO                   $2,423.90
                     04               624 16 6876             PARISEAU, WILLIAM               $1,785.00
                     04               712 13 3463             PERRY, MARTA                    $1,945.50
                     06               452 89 2153             CARDIN, FRANCIS                 $2,045.90
                     06               551 50 2546             FORTIN, EMIL                    $2,254.50
                     06               574 93 0461             GALLAGHER, MICHAEL              $1,976.75
                     06               683 21 5467             NOTTE, LORENZO                  $2,005.00
                     08               721 43 5472             JOBIN, ANTONIO                  $2,140.50
                     08               490 23 4571             MILLER, RENEE                   $1,905.70
                     08               351 56 6178             TRAMONTE, ESTELLE               $2,135.00

                                                           TOTAL SALES FOR STORE 40 : $ 27,010.80 *

                                                              TOTAL COMPANY SALES : $ 101,558.59 **


                                       *** END OF REPORT ***
```

paragraph, the store accumulator will be reset to zero. So, for instance, we insert a new step 5, as follows:

Add store-accumulator to company-accumulator.

The original step 5 is then renumbered 6.

Note, however, that some self-documentation is lost, since updating the company accumulator is now "hidden" within the paragraph 400-Prepare-Store-Footing rather than being "obvious" in the original paragraph 330-Update-Accumulators. Similarly, updating the store accumulator is hidden within the paragraph 210-Process-Sales-Record. The programmer should strive for a proper balance between efficiency and clarity of the code. Obviously, if documentation lines precede each paragraph in the program (as illustrated in Chapter 6), these hidden functions are clearly stated.

Forcing the Last Store Footing

We have indicated earlier that the control break does not trigger the printing of the store control footing for the last store. The programming must force this printing to occur after processing the last input record. The program design has set up structure chart module 350 PRODUCE LAST FOOTINGS to document the fact that more than one footing line must be produced in that module, specifically, the one for the last store and the one for the company. This situation usually occurs in control-break programs, and the explicit documentation is therefore not necessary. The program can be redesigned to name the module 350 PREPARE COMPANY FOOTING, and the fact that the control footing for the last store is

■ **Figure 8.20** Design revision related to printing last footings

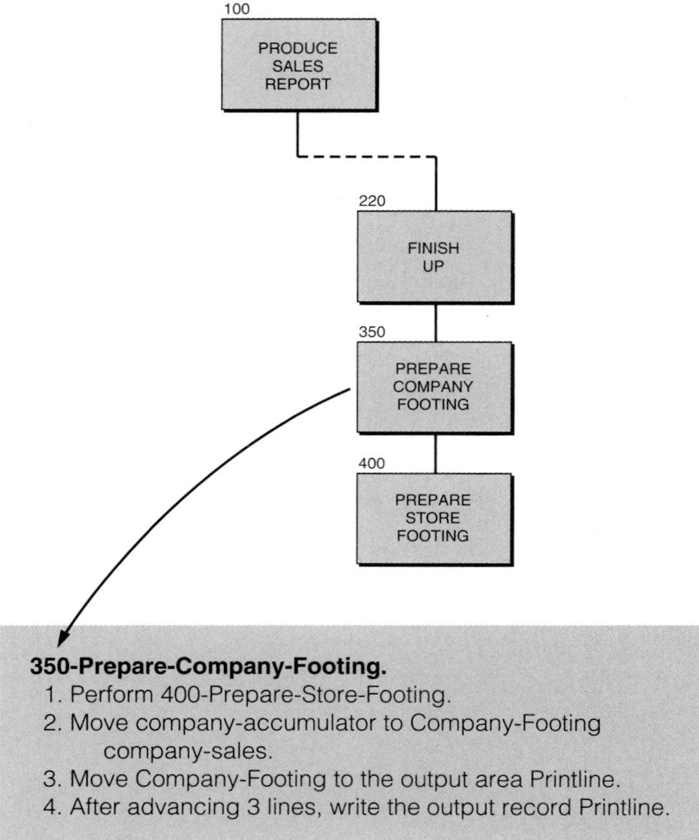

350-Prepare-Company-Footing.
1. Perform 400-Prepare-Store-Footing.
2. Move company-accumulator to Company-Footing company-sales.
3. Move Company-Footing to the output area Printline.
4. After advancing 3 lines, write the output record Printline.

also required can be documented in the structure chart by making module 400 PREPARE STORE FOOTING subordinate to module 350.

If this approach is used, then the revisions to the structure chart and to the program pseudocode are the ones shown in Figure 8.20. Note that original module 350 and the corresponding pseudocode paragraph are eliminated.

Multiple Control Breaks

Control breaks can occur at different levels. The chapter sample program is now revised to illustrate a *two-level control break.* Specifically, the revision requires the program to produce totals for each department within each store, in addition to intermediate totals for each store and a final total for the company.

When you examine the input file in Figure 8.18 or the report in Figure 8.19, you will notice that the records in the file have already been presorted by department number within each store. It should be clear that the two key fields of the input record are I-STORE-NO and I-DEPT-NO. Corresponding to these input record key fields, there must be two control items defined in working storage: the store control item WS-STORE-CONTROL, as in the previous program, and a department control item that we name WS-DEPT-CONTROL.

Notice in Figure 8.19 that each store consists of four departments. (Each store need not have the same departments or the same number of departments, though it is the case in our example.) Clearly, control breaks will occur at the department level before they occur at the store level, simply because a department has a smaller group of sales records than a store group. The collection of sales records for a department is referred to as a department control group and the collection of sales records for a store is referred to as a store control group. There are as many department control groups within a given store control group as there are departments in the given store, and there are as many store control groups as there are stores in the company. A department control group in this example is a minor control group, whereas a store control group is a major control group. Similarly, a control break at the department level is classified as a *minor control break,* and a control break at the store level is classified as a *major control break.* In working

Figure 8.21 Printer spacing chart for a sample two-level control-break program

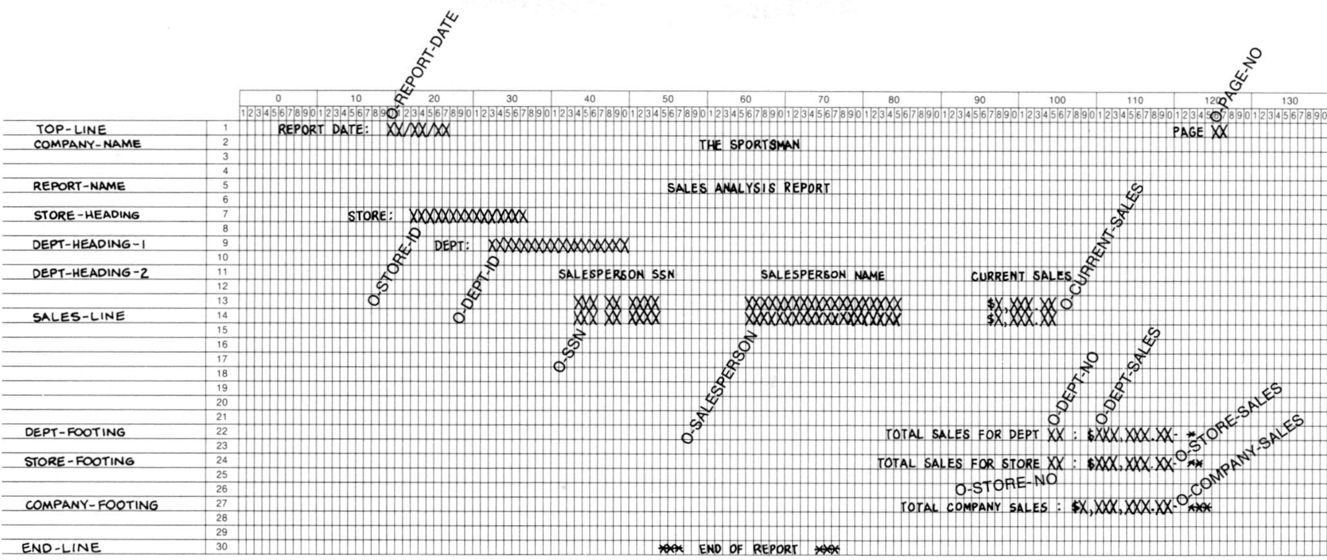

storage, WS-DEPT-CONTROL is the minor control item and WS-STORE-CONTROL is the major control item. Do you see that a minor control break can occur without a major control break occuring at the same time, but a major control break is necessarily accompanied by a minor control break? In other words, as you examine two consecutive records in the input file, the second record may have a different department number than the first without the store numbers necessarily being different. On the other hand, whenever you find two consecutive records with different store numbers, the departments will necessarily be different since they belong to different stores.

Now, in the two-level control break revision of the sample program, the layout of the input record remains unchanged, but the printer spacing chart must be revised to allow for a department heading and a department footing to accommodate the minor control break requirements. The revision is shown in Figure 8.21. Do you see that there are three new lines? They are DEPT-HEADING-1, DEPT-HEADING-2, and DEPT-FOOTING.

The data field in DEPT-HEADING-1 must contain one of the following entries:

02 – FOOTWEAR

04 – APPAREL

06 – EQUIPMENT

08 – LETTERING

In each of these entries, the first component is the department number, and the second component identifies the department by name.

In this revision, each store report must begin at the top of a new page. Note that the page heading consists of three lines, TOP-LINE, COMPANY-NAME, and REPORT-NAME. The store heading consists of only one line, STORE-HEADING. The department heading consists of two lines, DEPT-HEADING-1 and DEPT-HEADING-2. The detail line is SALES-LINE. There must be one of these detail lines for each salesperson in a department. The department footing DEPT-FOOTING is printed two lines below the last detail line for that department. Then, after advancing two more lines, the department heading (DEPT-HEADING-1 and DEPT-HEADING-2) for the next department must be printed. It is then followed by all the detail lines for that department, and these are followed by the department footing for that department. Following the department footing for the last department of a store, the store footing for that store must be printed. Then, before printing the first detail line of the first department of the next store, a new page must be prepared. The sequence described above is repeated for each store. The store footing for the last store must be followed by the company footing line.

Recall, from the previous program, that control breaks trigger the printing of the footing lines, except for the last department of the last store. The program must force the printing of the last department footing, the last store footing, and the company footing after the end of file (EOF) record for the input file has been encountered.

As we continue this brief analysis, note that three sales accumulators are needed: a department sales accumulator to accumulate the sales of a department control group, a store sales accumulator to accumulate the sales of a store control group, and a company sales accumulator. Subtotaling is used to accumulate the sales at the department level, rolling forward of department totals is used to accumulate the total sales for a store, and rolling forward of store totals is used to accumulate the total sales for the company. While it is obvious that the three accumulators must be set to zero initially, you must not forget to reset the department sales accumulator after a minor control break occurs, nor to reset the store sales accumulator after a major control break occurs. The simplest way to accomplish this is to set the department sales accumulator to zero within the procedure that prints the department header for a new department, and to set the store sales accumulator to zero within the procedure that prints the store header for a new store. These steps will be incorporated in the revision of the program.

Structure Chart

The structure chart for the revised program is shown in Figure 8.22. Note that the test for a major control break at the store level occurs in module 320, and the test for a minor control break at the department level occurs in module 400.

For a given input record, a store control break may or may not occur. If it does occur, it should be obvious that a department footing **must** precede the store footing, so no explicit test for a department control break is needed in this case. (Recall that a major control break is always accompanied by a control break at a lower level.) Following the store footing, a new page must be prepared. On the other hand, if the store control break does not occur, then a specific test for a department control break is required. If a department control break occurs, then a department footing must be printed, as well as the department heading for the next department.

The flowchart segment of Figure 8.23 illustrates the nested control breaks referred to in the preceding paragraph.

Program Pseudocode and Program Flowchart

The program pseudocode is contained in Figure 8.24. (The entries related to the control breaks are highlighted.)

Note the following:

1. The company sales accumulator is set to zero in step 5 of paragraph 300-Initialize-Items. The store sales accumulator is set to zero in step 5 of paragraph 600-Write-Store-Heading. The department sales accumulator is set to zero in step 8 of paragraph 700-Write-Dept-Heading.
2. The current sales for the record being processed are added to the department accumulator in step 2 of paragraph 210-Process-Sales-Record. This is the subtotaling process.
3. The amount in the department accumulator is added to the store accumulator during the department control-break procedure, as seen in step 3 of paragraph 500-Prepare-Dept-Footing. This is the rolling-forward process.
4. The amount in the store accumulator is added to the company accumulator during the store control-break procedure, as seen in step 4 of paragraph 410-Prepare-Store-Footing. This is again the rolling-forward process.
5. The test for a store control break (the major control break) occurs in paragraph 320-Check-For-New-Store.
6. The test for a department control break (the minor control break) occurs in paragraph 400-Check-For-New-Dept.

The flowchart corresponding to the pseudocode of Figure 8.24 is contained in Figure 8.25.

Figure 8.22 Structure chart for the sample two-level control-break program

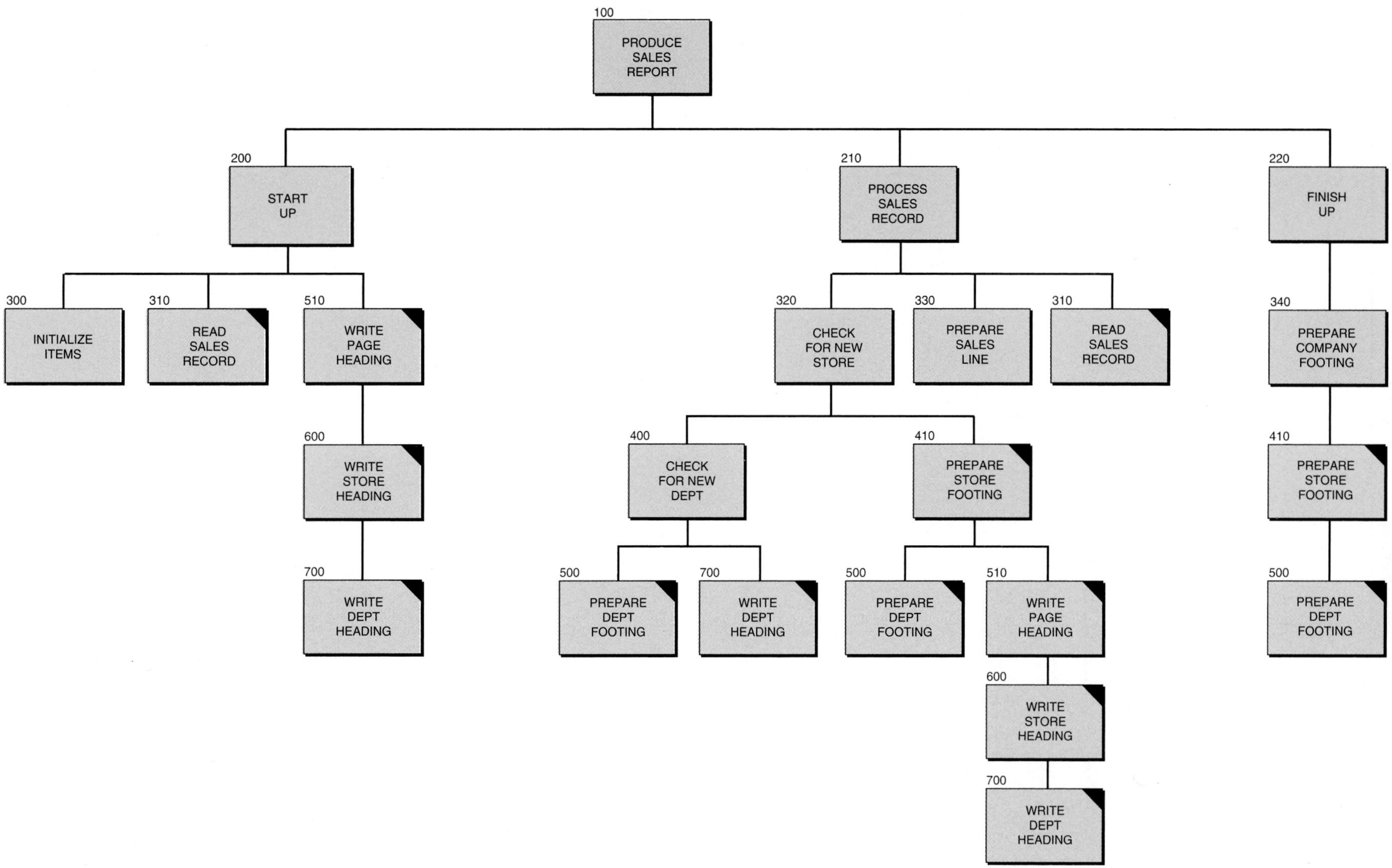

- 100 PRODUCE SALES REPORT
  - 200 START UP
    - 300 INITIALIZE ITEMS
    - 310 READ SALES RECORD
    - 510 WRITE PAGE HEADING
      - 600 WRITE STORE HEADING
        - 700 WRITE DEPT HEADING
  - 210 PROCESS SALES RECORD
    - 320 CHECK FOR NEW STORE
      - 400 CHECK FOR NEW DEPT
        - 500 PREPARE DEPT FOOTING
        - 700 WRITE DEPT HEADING
      - 410 PREPARE STORE FOOTING
        - 500 PREPARE DEPT FOOTING
        - 510 WRITE PAGE HEADING
          - 600 WRITE STORE HEADING
            - 700 WRITE DEPT HEADING
    - 330 PREPARE SALES LINE
    - 310 READ SALES RECORD
  - 220 FINISH UP
    - 340 PREPARE COMPANY FOOTING
      - 410 PREPARE STORE FOOTING
        - 500 PREPARE DEPT FOOTING

■ **Figure 8.23** Logic of nested control breaks

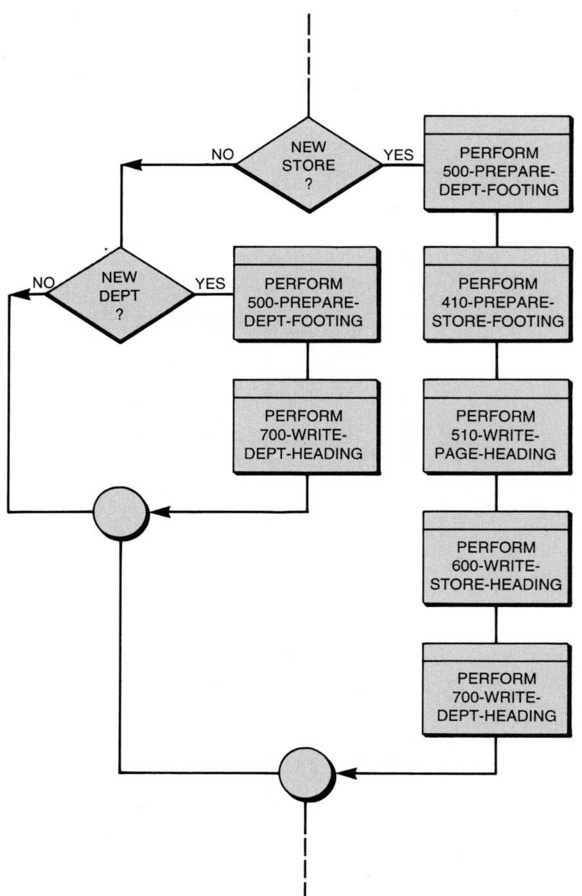

■ **Figure 8.24** Pseudocode for the revised program

100-Produce-Sales-Report.

1. Perform 200-Start-Up.
2. Perform 210-Process-Sales-Record until no more records.
3. Perform 220-Finish-Up.
4. Stop the run.

200-Start-Up.

1. Open the files.
2. Perform 300-Initialize-Items.
3. Perform 310-Read-Sales-Record.
4. Perform 510-Write-Page-Heading.

210-Process-Sales-Record.

1. Perform 320-Check-For-New-Store.
2. Add input current-sales to department-accumulator.
3. Perform 330-Prepare-Sales-Line.
4. Perform 310-Read-Sales-Record.

■ **Figure 8.24** continued

220-Finish-Up.

1. Perform 340-Prepare-Company-Footing.
2. Move End-Line to the output area Printline.
3. After advancing 4 lines, write the output record Printline.
4. Close the files.

300-Initialize-Items.

1. Obtain the date from the system.
2. Move the date to Top-Line date.
3. Set page-number to zero.
4. Set the end-of-file flag WS-MORE-RECORDS to "YES".
5. Set the company sales-accumulator to zero.
6. Clear the record area Sales-Line.

310-Read-Sales-Record.

1. Read an input Sales-Record.
2. Test for end-of-file record;
   if EOF record reached, set the flag WS-MORE-RECORDS to "NO ".

320-Check-For-New-Store.

1. If input store-number is not equal to store-control value,
   then, perform 410-Prepare-Store-Footing,
   else, perform 400-Check-For-New-Dept.

330-Prepare-Sales-Line.

1. Move input social-security-number to Sales-Line social-security-number.
2. Move input salesperson to Sales-Line salesperson.
3. Move input current-sales to Sales-Line current-sales.
4. Move Sales-Line to the output area Printline.
5. After advancing proper-spacing, write the output record Printline.
6. Set proper-spacing to 1.

340-Prepare-Company-Footing.

1. Perform 410-Prepare-Store-Footing.
2. Move company-accumulator to Company-Footing company-sales.
3. Move Company-Footing to the output area Printline.
4. After advancing 3 lines, write the output record Printline.

400-Check-For-New-Dept.

1. If input department-number is not equal to department-control,
   then, perform 500-Prepare-Dept-Footing and then
   perform 700-Write-Dept-Heading.

410-Prepare-Store-Footing.

1. Perform 500-Prepare-Dept-Footing.
2. Move store-control to Store-Footing store-number.
3. Move store-accumulator to Store-Footing store-sales.
4. Add store-accumulator to company-accumulator.
5. Move Store-Footing to the output area Printline.
6. After advancing 2 lines, write the output record Printline.
7. If the flag WS-MORE-RECORDS is equal to "YES",
   perform 510-Write-Page-Heading.

500-Prepare-Dept-Footing.

1. Move department-control to Dept-Footing department-number.
2. Move department-accumulator to Dept-Footing department-sales.
3. Add department-accumulator to store-accumulator.
4. Move Dept-Footing to the output area Printline.
5. After advancing 2 lines, write the output record Printline.

510-Write-Page-Heading.

1. Add 1 to page-number.
2. Move page-number to Top-Line page-number.
3. Move Top-Line to the output area Printline.
4. After advancing to the top of a new page,
   write the output record Printline.
5. Move Company-Name to the output area Printline.
6. After advancing 1 line, write the output record Printline.
7. Move Report-Name to the output area Printline.
8. After advancing 3 lines, write the output record Printline.
9. Perform 600-Write-Store-Heading.

600-Write-Store-Heading.

1. Move input store-number to store-control.
2. Test input store-number:
   if "10", then move "10 - NEW YORK" to Store-Heading store-id;
   if "20", then move "20 - BOSTON" to Store-Heading store-id;
   if "30", then move "30 - CHICAGO" to Store-Heading store-id;
   if "40", then move "40 - SEATTLE" to Store-Heading store-id;
   if any other, then display "Error in Store Number for " input salesperson.
3. Move Store-Heading to the output area Printline.
4. After advancing 2 lines, write the output record Printline.
5. Reset the store-accumulator to zero.
6. Perform 700-Write-Dept-Heading.

700-Write-Dept-Heading.

1. Move input department-number to department-control.
2. Test input department-number:
   if "02", then move "02 - FOOTWEAR" to Dept-Heading-1 department-id;
   if "04", then move "04 - APPAREL" to Dept-Heading-1 department-id;
   if "06", then move "06 - EQUIPMENT" to Dept-Heading-1 department-id;
   if "08", then move "08 - LETTERING" to Dept-Heading-1 department-id;
   if other, then display "Error in Department number for " input salesperson.
3. Move Dept-Heading-1 to the output area Printline.
4. After advancing 2 lines, write the output record Printline.
5. Move Dept-Heading-2 to the output area Printline.
6. After advancing 2 lines, write the output record Printline.
7. Set proper-spacing to 2.
8. Reset department-accumulator to zero.

■ **Figure 8.25** Program flowchart for the revised program

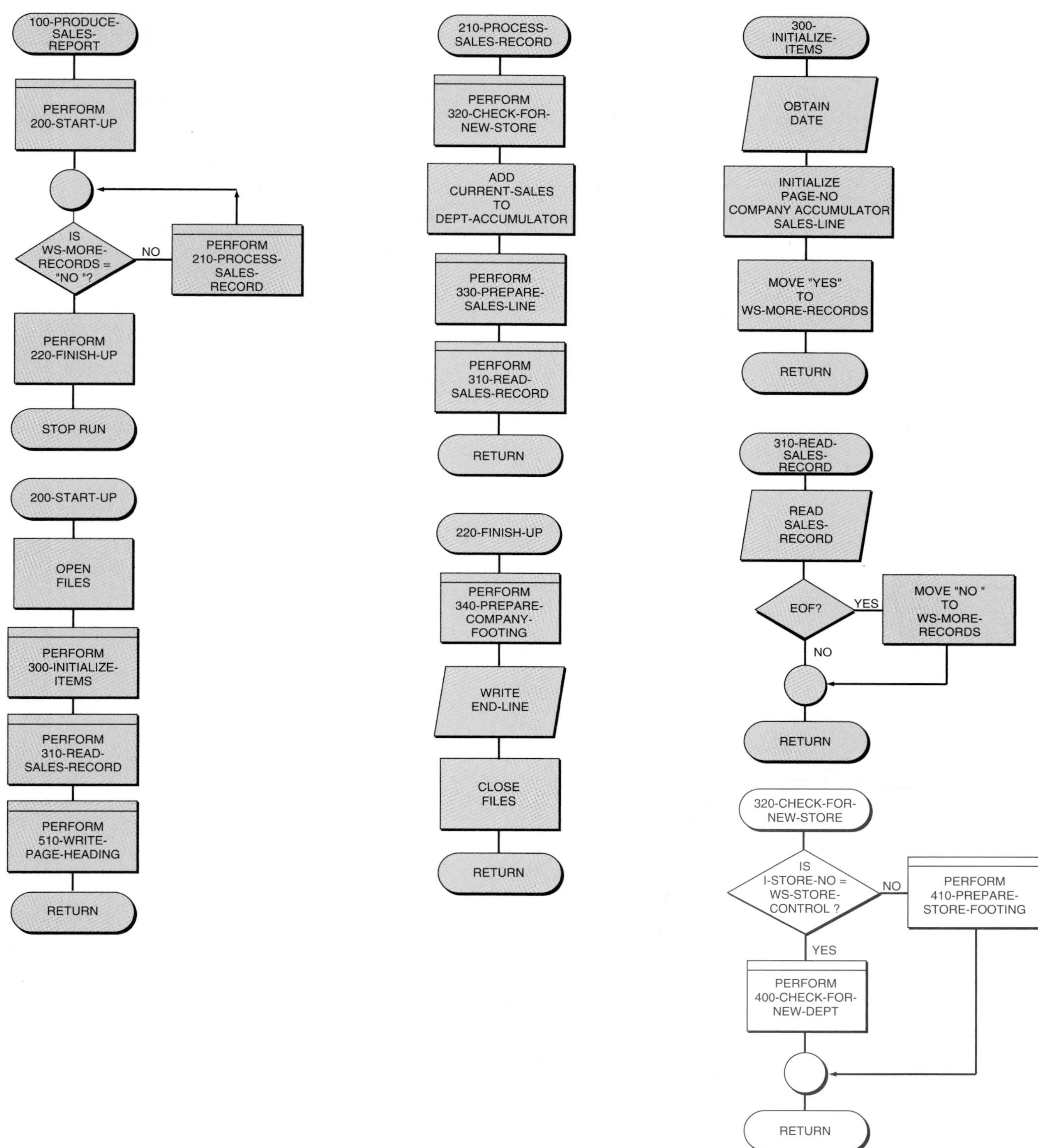

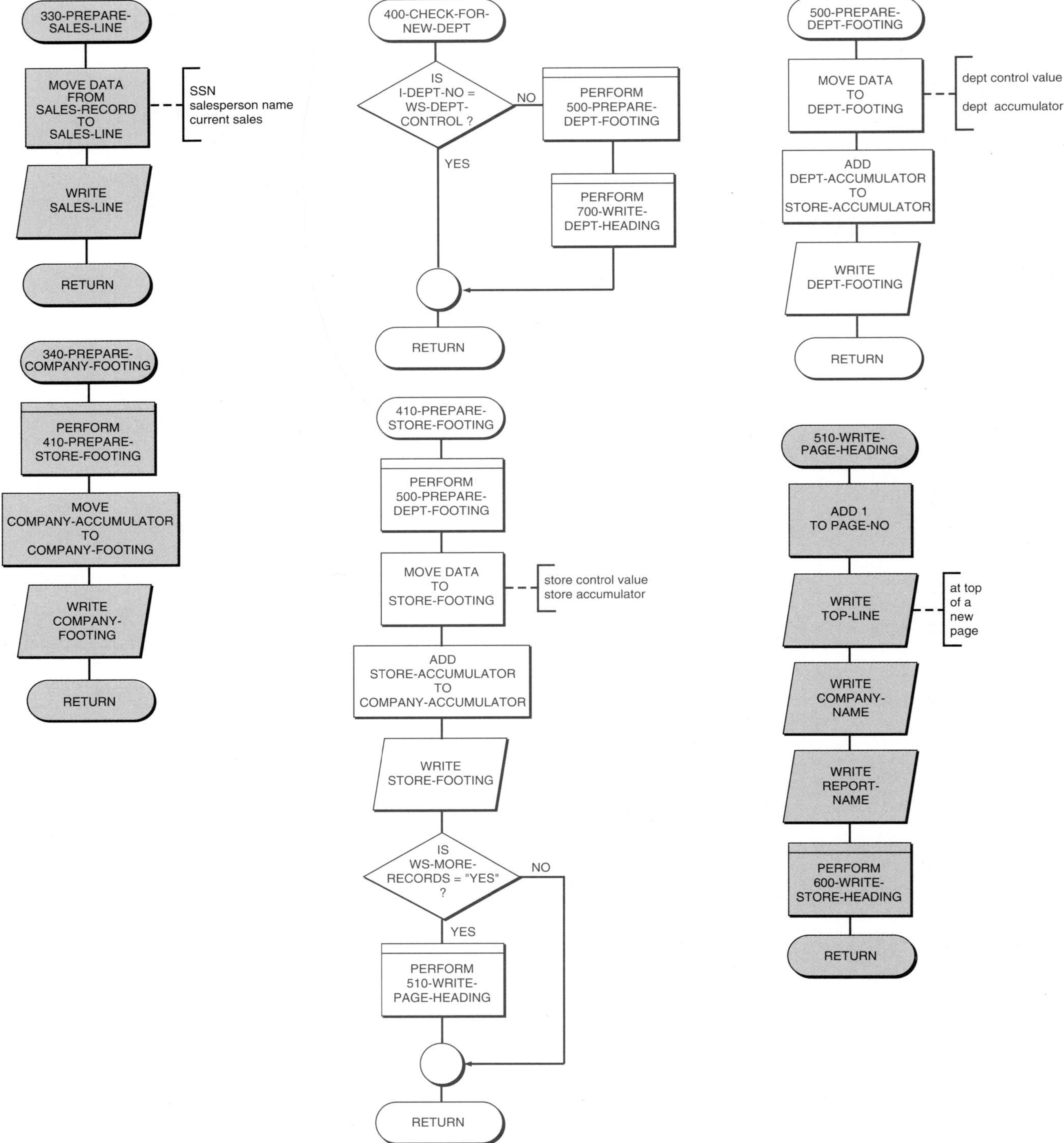
330-PREPARE-SALES-LINE
MOVE DATA FROM SALES-RECORD TO SALES-LINE
SSN
salesperson name
current sales
WRITE SALES-LINE
RETURN
340-PREPARE-COMPANY-FOOTING
PERFORM 410-PREPARE-STORE-FOOTING
MOVE COMPANY-ACCUMULATOR TO COMPANY-FOOTING
WRITE COMPANY-FOOTING
RETURN
400-CHECK-FOR-NEW-DEPT
IS I-DEPT-NO = WS-DEPT-CONTROL ?
NO
PERFORM 500-PREPARE-DEPT-FOOTING
PERFORM 700-WRITE-DEPT-HEADING
YES
RETURN
410-PREPARE-STORE-FOOTING
PERFORM 500-PREPARE-DEPT-FOOTING
MOVE DATA TO STORE-FOOTING
store control value
store accumulator
ADD STORE-ACCUMULATOR TO COMPANY-ACCUMULATOR
WRITE STORE-FOOTING
IS WS-MORE-RECORDS = "YES" ?
NO
YES
PERFORM 510-WRITE-PAGE-HEADING
RETURN
500-PREPARE-DEPT-FOOTING
MOVE DATA TO DEPT-FOOTING
dept control value
dept accumulator
ADD DEPT-ACCUMULATOR TO STORE-ACCUMULATOR
WRITE DEPT-FOOTING
RETURN
510-WRITE-PAGE-HEADING
ADD 1 TO PAGE-NO
WRITE TOP-LINE
at top of a new page
WRITE COMPANY-NAME
WRITE REPORT-NAME
PERFORM 600-WRITE-STORE-HEADING
RETURN

Figure 8.25 continued

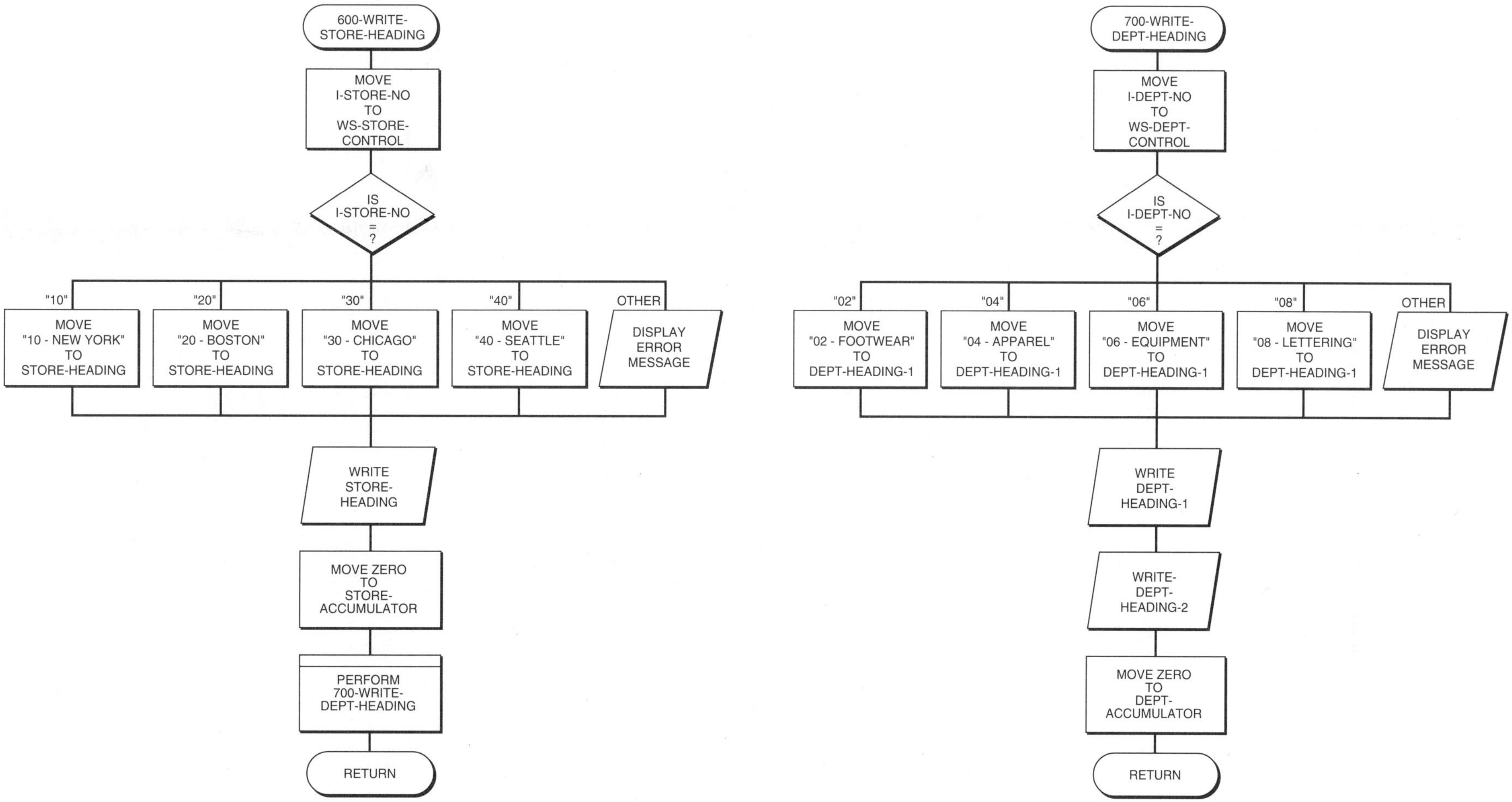

600-WRITE-STORE-HEADING

MOVE I-STORE-NO TO WS-STORE-CONTROL

IS I-STORE-NO = ?

"10": MOVE "10 - NEW YORK" TO STORE-HEADING

"20": MOVE "20 - BOSTON" TO STORE-HEADING

"30": MOVE "30 - CHICAGO" TO STORE-HEADING

"40": MOVE "40 - SEATTLE" TO STORE-HEADING

OTHER: DISPLAY ERROR MESSAGE

WRITE STORE-HEADING

MOVE ZERO TO STORE-ACCUMULATOR

PERFORM 700-WRITE-DEPT-HEADING

RETURN

700-WRITE-DEPT-HEADING

MOVE I-DEPT-NO TO WS-DEPT-CONTROL

IS I-DEPT-NO = ?

"02": MOVE "02 - FOOTWEAR" TO DEPT-HEADING-1

"04": MOVE "04 - APPAREL" TO DEPT-HEADING-1

"06": MOVE "06 - EQUIPMENT" TO DEPT-HEADING-1

"08": MOVE "08 - LETTERING" TO DEPT-HEADING-1

OTHER: DISPLAY ERROR MESSAGE

WRITE DEPT-HEADING-1

WRITE DEPT-HEADING-2

MOVE ZERO TO DEPT-ACCUMULATOR

RETURN

Figure 8.26 contains a listing of the records in the sample input file SALES-FILE. The symbol "-->" points to each record that triggers a department control break (the minor control break), and the department number that causes the break is underscored. The symbol "====>>" points to each record that triggers a store control break (the major control break), and the store number that causes the break is underscored.

It should be clear that the record preceding the one that triggers a store control break is the last record of the previous store, and it is also the last record of the last department of the previous store. Thus, a store control break must generate a department footing line as well as a store footing line.

■ **Figure 8.26** Records of SALES-FILE that trigger control breaks

Store number / Dept. number / Social Security number / Salesperson name / Current sales

```
        1002214365025ALLEN, ROBERT             150000
        1002218546010BROWN, RAYMOND            302255
        1002641275050BRANNIGAN, NICOLE         087525
        1002315463030FOGARTY, JANICE           105050
        1002642754040MAIN, CHARLES             128000
    --> 1004685264065CARLSON, HOPE             090000
        1004556234035CRANE, JOHN               105050
        1004696996055DANIELS, JULIA            287050
        1004251342020FARMER, SUSAN             162000
        1004263452070FEINGOLD, HAROLD          125050
        1004667451060HARRISON, LILY            142580
    --> 1006521244005DWYER, TERRENCE           142580
        1006564451045EDWARDS, PETER            108050
        1006644353075MANNING, ELIZABETH        135000
    --> 1008377568080HOWARD, RALPH             056050
        1008482131015JANKOWSKI, STANLEY        135000
        1008551164090KELLY, PATRICK            162500
        1008599231085LANGFORD, SARAH           115050
        1008521166100PRINGLY, ANNE             109805
 ====>> 2002408936050CORDEIRO, ANTONE          010050
        2002509862005CORTON, ALEXANDRA         100000
        2002509185045PINEAULT, NORMAN          098050
        2002480755030TALBOT, JILLIAN           127580
    --> 2004479210065BARRESI, JOHN             065000
        2004427560010COCHRANE, RUSSELL         146050
        2004360902035PENTA, ROBERT             165025
        2004472847080PROULX, PAULINE           115000
        2004375701060QUINN, SUZANNE            132050
    --> 2006683309020COSTELLO, JAMES           167050
        2006418090015CRAWFORD, SHIRLEY         139050
        2006566127070FELDMAN, WALTER           147080
        2006433406075FERNANDEZ, LOUISE         200000
        2006571904025LEMERISE, DONALD          185050
        2006572495090WORTHEN, MICHAEL          157000
    --> 2008762355100GOYETTE, FRANCES          095000
        2008812133085KOSINSKI, KATHERINE       112500
        2008804233040VERMETTE, GLORIA          156050
 ====>> 3002576400892KING, CHRISTOPHER         189070
        3002416892014BERNARD, ISIDORE          203569
        3002823144098MAHFUZ, IRENE             185025
    --> 3004566731251ROBINSON, GILBERT         210590
        3004788230154DONOHUE, PHIL             087500
        3004607044132CORRIGAN, ALENE           187550
        3004745645270FURTADO, MAUREEN          201540
    --> 3006820788914ABALLO, NORMA             235075
        3006785023157DOLLARHIDE, CHRIS         201570
        3006745635164LINCOURT, LORETTA         149500
    --> 3008466587165BRAZ, JOAN                231560
        3008557318974PRATT, ROBIN              215500
        3008487251099MELANSON, GARY            190550
 ====>> 4002452677143BEAUDOIN, ROCKY           221500
        4002787855623MARKLAND, MARY            198750
        4002674451231BISBANO, HENRY            219055
    --> 4004720954670VELOZO, MARIO             242390
        4004624166876PARISEAU, WILLIAM         178500
        4004712133463PERRY, MARTA              194550
    --> 4006452892153CARDIN, FRANCIS           204590
        4006551502546FORTIN, EMIL              225450
        4006574930461GALLAGHER, MICHAEL        197675
        4006683215467NOTTE, LORENZO            200500
    --> 4008721435472JOBIN, ANTONIO            214050
        4008490234571MILLER, RENEE             190570
        4008351566178TRAMONTE, ESTELLE         213500
```

A final reminder: For a control break program to work properly, it is necessary to have the records of the input file presorted by minor control groups within each major control group.

The Revised Program

The revised program and the report that it generated from the input file in Figure 8.26 are shown in Figure 8.27a and Figure 8.27b, respectively. (The program entries related to the control breaks are highlighted.)

■ **Figure 8.27a** The revised program

```
 IDENTIFICATION DIVISION.

 PROGRAM-ID.  SPORTSMAN-SALES-2.

****************************************************************
*                                                              *
*  AUTHOR.        PAQUETTE.                                    *
*  DATE WRITTEN.  AUGUST 1993.                                 *
*                                                              *
*      THIS PROGRAM ALSO PRODUCES A MULTILEVEL SALES ANALYSIS  *
*  REPORT FOR THE SPORTSMAN COMPANY.  HOWEVER, IT PRODUCES     *
*  INTERMEDIATE TOTALS AT THE DEPARTMENT LEVEL AS WELL AS AT   *
*  THE STORE LEVEL, IN ADDITION TO PRODUCING TOTALS FOR THE    *
*  COMPANY AS A WHOLE.                                         *
*                                                              *
****************************************************************

 ENVIRONMENT DIVISION.

 CONFIGURATION SECTION.

 SOURCE-COMPUTER.  VAX-VMS-8650.
 OBJECT-COMPUTER.  VAX-VMS-8650.

 INPUT-OUTPUT SECTION.

 FILE-CONTROL.
     SELECT SALES-FILE    ASSIGN TO COB$INPUT.
     SELECT SALES-REPORT  ASSIGN TO COB$OUTPUT.

 DATA DIVISION.

 FILE SECTION.

 FD  SALES-FILE
     RECORD CONTAINS 39 CHARACTERS.

 01  SALES-RECORD.
     05 I-STORE-NO          PIC XX.
        88 NEW-YORK         VALUE "10".
        88 BOSTON           VALUE "20".
        88 CHICAGO          VALUE "30".
        88 SEATTLE          VALUE "40".
        88 VALID-STORE-NO VALUES "10", "20", "30", "40".
     05 I-DEPT-NO           PIC XX.
        88 FOOTWEAR         VALUE "02".
        88 APPAREL          VALUE "04".
        88 EQUIPMENT        VALUE "06".
        88 LETTERING        VALUE "08".
        88 VALID-DEPT-NO    VALUES "02", "04", "06", "08".
     05 I-SSN               PIC X(9).
     05 I-SALESPERSON       PIC X(20).
     05 I-CURRENT-SALES     PIC 9(4)V99.

 FD  SALES-REPORT
     RECORD CONTAINS 133 CHARACTERS.

 01  PRINTLINE     PIC X(133).

 WORKING-STORAGE SECTION.

 01  PROGRAM-CONTROLS.
     05 WS-MORE-RECORDS           PIC XXX.
        88 THERE-IS-A-RECORD      VALUE "YES".
        88 NO-MORE-RECORDS        VALUE "NO ".
     05 WS-DEPT-CONTROL           PIC XX.
     05 WS-STORE-CONTROL          PIC XX.
     05 WS-PROPER-SPACING         PIC 99.
     05 WS-REPORT-DATE            PIC X(6).
     05 WS-PAGE-NO                PIC 99.
```

Figure 8.27a continued

```
01  PROGRAM-ACCUMULATORS       COMP.
    05 WS-DEPT-ACCUMULATOR     PIC S9(6)V99.
    05 WS-STORE-ACCUMULATOR    PIC S9(6)V99.
    05 WS-COMPANY-ACCUMULATOR  PIC S9(7)V99.

01  PAGE-HEADING.

    05 TOP-LINE.
        10                    PIC X(6)   VALUE SPACES.
        10                    PIC X(14)  VALUE "REPORT DATE:  ".
        10 O-REPORT-DATE      PIC XX/XX/XX.
        10                    PIC X(92)  VALUE SPACES.
        10                    PIC X(5)   VALUE "PAGE ".
        10 O-PAGE-NO          PIC Z9.
        10                    PIC X(6)   VALUE SPACES.

    05 COMPANY-NAME.
        10 PIC X(60)  VALUE SPACES.
        10 PIC X(13)  VALUE "THE SPORTSMAN".
        10 PIC X(60)  VALUE SPACES.

    05 REPORT-NAME.
        10 PIC X(56)  VALUE SPACES.
        10 PIC X(21)  VALUE "SALES ANALYSIS REPORT".
        10 PIC X(56)  VALUE SPACES.

01  STORE-HEADING.
    05              PIC X(15)  VALUE SPACES.
    05              PIC X(8)   VALUE "STORE:  ".
    05 O-STORE-ID   PIC X(15).
    05              PIC X(95)  VALUE SPACES.

01  DEPT-HEADING.

    05 DEPT-HEADING-1.
        10                PIC X(25)  VALUE SPACES.
        10                PIC X(11)  VALUE " DEPT NO:  ".
        10 O-DEPT-ID      PIC X(18).
        10                PIC X(80)  VALUE SPACES.

    05 DEPT-HEADING-2.
        10 PIC X(42)  VALUE SPACES.
        10 PIC X(15)  VALUE "SALESPERSON SSN".
        10 PIC X(11)  VALUE SPACES.
        10 PIC X(16)  VALUE "SALESPERSON NAME".
        10 PIC X(11)  VALUE SPACES.
        10 PIC X(13)  VALUE "CURRENT SALES".
        10 PIC X(25)  VALUE SPACES.

01  SALES-LINE.
    05                      PIC X(44).
    05 O-SSN                PIC XXXBXXBXXXX.
    05                      PIC X(11).
    05 O-SALESPERSON        PIC X(20).
    05                      PIC X(11).
    05 O-CURRENT-SALES      PIC $Z,ZZ9.99.
    05                      PIC X(27).

01  DEPT-FOOTING.
    05                    PIC X(84) VALUE SPACES.
    05                    PIC X(21) VALUE "TOTAL SALES FOR DEPT ".
    05 O-DEPT-NO          PIC XX.
    05                    PIC X(3)  VALUE " : ".
    05 O-DEPT-SALES       PIC $ZZZ,ZZ9.99-.
    05                    PIC XX    VALUE " *".
    05                    PIC X(9)  VALUE SPACES.

01  STORE-FOOTING.
    05                    PIC X(83) VALUE SPACES.
    05                    PIC X(22) VALUE "TOTAL SALES FOR STORE ".
    05 O-STORE-NO         PIC XX.
    05                    PIC X(3)  VALUE " : ".
    05 O-STORE-SALES      PIC $ZZZ,ZZ9.99-.
    05                    PIC X(3)  VALUE " **".
    05                    PIC X(8)  VALUE SPACES.

01  COMPANY-FOOTING.
    05                      PIC X(86) VALUE SPACES.
    05                      PIC X(22) VALUE "TOTAL COMPANY SALES : ".
    05 O-COMPANY-SALES      PIC $Z,ZZZ,ZZ9.99-.
    05                      PIC X(4)  VALUE " ***".
    05                      PIC X(7)  VALUE SPACES.

01  END-LINE.
    05 PIC X(55)  VALUE SPACES.
    05 PIC X(23)  VALUE "***  END OF REPORT  ***".
    05 PIC X(55)  VALUE SPACES.
```

■ **Figure 8.27a** continued

```
PROCEDURE DIVISION.

100-PRODUCE-SALES-REPORT.
    PERFORM 200-START-UP.
    PERFORM 210-PROCESS-SALES-RECORD
        UNTIL NO-MORE-RECORDS.
    PERFORM 220-FINISH-UP.
    STOP RUN.

200-START-UP.
    OPEN INPUT SALES-FILE
         OUTPUT SALES-REPORT.
    PERFORM 300-INITIALIZE-ITEMS.
    PERFORM 310-READ-SALES-RECORD.
    PERFORM 510-WRITE-PAGE-HEADING.

210-PROCESS-SALES-RECORD.
    PERFORM 320-CHECK-FOR-NEW-STORE.
    ADD I-CURRENT-SALES TO WS-DEPT-ACCUMULATOR.
    PERFORM 330-PREPARE-SALES-LINE.
    PERFORM 310-READ-SALES-RECORD.

220-FINISH-UP.
    PERFORM 340-PREPARE-COMPANY-FOOTING.
    WRITE PRINTLINE FROM END-LINE
        AFTER ADVANCING 4 LINES.
    CLOSE SALES-FILE
          SALES-REPORT.

300-INITIALIZE-ITEMS.
    ACCEPT WS-REPORT-DATE FROM DATE.
    MOVE WS-REPORT-DATE TO O-REPORT-DATE.
    SET THERE-IS-A-RECORD TO TRUE.
    INITIALIZE WS-COMPANY-ACCUMULATOR
               WS-PAGE-NO.
    MOVE SPACES TO SALES-LINE.

310-READ-SALES-RECORD.
    READ SALES-FILE RECORD
        AT END
            SET NO-MORE-RECORDS TO TRUE.

320-CHECK-FOR-NEW-STORE.
    IF I-STORE-NO = WS-STORE-CONTROL
        PERFORM 400-CHECK-FOR-NEW-DEPT
    ELSE
        PERFORM 410-PREPARE-STORE-FOOTING.

330-PREPARE-SALES-LINE.
    MOVE I-SSN TO O-SSN.
    MOVE I-SALESPERSON TO O-SALESPERSON.
    MOVE I-CURRENT-SALES TO O-CURRENT-SALES.
    WRITE PRINTLINE FROM SALES-LINE
        AFTER ADVANCING WS-PROPER-SPACING.
    MOVE 1 TO WS-PROPER-SPACING.

340-PREPARE-COMPANY-FOOTING.
    PERFORM 410-PREPARE-STORE-FOOTING.
    MOVE WS-COMPANY-ACCUMULATOR TO O-COMPANY-SALES.
    WRITE PRINTLINE FROM COMPANY FOOTING
        AFTER ADVANCING 3 LINES.

400-CHECK-FOR-NEW-DEPT.
    IF I-DEPT-NO = WS-DEPT-CONTROL
        NEXT SENTENCE
    ELSE
        PERFORM 500-PREPARE-DEPT-FOOTING
        PERFORM 700-WRITE-DEPT-HEADING.

410-PREPARE-STORE-FOOTING.
    PERFORM 500-PREPARE-DEPT-FOOTING.
    MOVE WS-STORE-CONTROL TO O-STORE-NO.
    MOVE WS-STORE-ACCUMULATOR TO O-STORE-SALES.
    ADD WS-STORE-ACCUMULATOR TO WS-COMPANY-ACCUMULATOR.
    WRITE PRINTLINE FROM STORE-FOOTING
        AFTER ADVANCING 2 LINES.
    IF THERE-IS-A-RECORD
        PERFORM 510-WRITE-PAGE-HEADING
    END-IF.

500-PREPARE-DEPT-FOOTING.
    MOVE WS-DEPT-CONTROL TO O-DEPT-NO.
    MOVE WS-DEPT-ACCUMULATOR TO O-DEPT-SALES.
    ADD WS-DEPT-ACCUMULATOR TO WS-STORE-ACCUMULATOR.
    WRITE PRINTLINE FROM DEPT-FOOTING
        AFTER ADVANCING 2 LINES.
```

■ **Figure 8.27a** continued

```
 510-WRITE-PAGE-HEADING.
     ADD 1 TO WS-PAGE-NO.
     MOVE WS-PAGE-NO TO O-PAGE-NO.
     WRITE PRINTLINE FROM TOP-LINE
         AFTER ADVANCING PAGE.
     WRITE PRINTLINE FROM COMPANY-NAME
         AFTER ADVANCING 1 LINE.
     WRITE PRINTLINE FROM REPORT-NAME
         AFTER ADVANCING 3 LINES.
     PERFORM 600-WRITE-STORE-HEADING.

 600-WRITE-STORE-HEADING.
     MOVE I-STORE-NO TO WS-STORE-CONTROL.
     EVALUATE I-STORE-NO
         WHEN "10"  MOVE "10 - NEW YORK" TO O-STORE-ID
         WHEN "20"  MOVE "20 - BOSTON" TO O-STORE-ID
         WHEN "30"  MOVE "30 - CHICAGO" TO O-STORE-ID
         WHEN "40"  MOVE "40 - SEATTLE" TO O-STORE-ID
         WHEN OTHER
             DISPLAY " ERROR IN STORE NO. FOR " I-SALESPERSON.
     WRITE PRINTLINE FROM STORE-HEADING
         AFTER ADVANCING 2 LINES.
     INITIALIZE WS-STORE-ACCUMULATOR.
     PERFORM 700-WRITE-DEPT-HEADING.

 700-WRITE-DEPT-HEADING.
     MOVE I-DEPT-NO TO WS-DEPT-CONTROL.
     EVALUATE I-DEPT-NO
         WHEN "02"  MOVE "02 - FOOTWEAR" TO O-DEPT-ID
         WHEN "04"  MOVE "04 - APPAREL" TO O-DEPT-ID
         WHEN "06"  MOVE "06 - EQUIPMENT" TO O-DEPT-ID
         WHEN "08"  MOVE "08 - LETTERING" TO O-DEPT-ID
         WHEN OTHER
             DISPLAY " ERROR IN DEPT NO FOR " I-SALESPERSON
     END-EVALUATE.
     WRITE PRINTLINE FROM DEPT-HEADING-1
         AFTER ADVANCING 2 LINES.
     WRITE PRINTLINE FROM DEPT-HEADING-2
         AFTER ADVANCING 2 LINES.
     MOVE 2 TO WS-PROPER-SPACING.
     INITIALIZE WS-DEPT-ACCUMULATOR.
```

■ **Figure 8.27b** The two-level control-break report

```
REPORT DATE:  93/08/25                                                          PAGE 1
                                        THE SPORTSMAN

                                     SALES ANALYSIS REPORT

       STORE:  10 - NEW YORK

              DEPT NO.:  02 - FOOTWEAR

                         SALESPERSON SSN        SALESPERSON NAME        CURRENT SALES

                           214 36 5025        ALLEN, ROBERT              $1,500.00
                           218 54 6010        BROWN, RAYMOND             $3,022.55
                           641 27 5050        BRANNIGAN, NICOLE          $  875.25
                           315 46 3030        FOGARTY, JANICE            $1,050.50
                           642 75 4040        MAIN, CHARLES              $1,280.00

                                                   TOTAL SALES FOR DEPT 02 : $ 7,728.30 *
              DEPT NO.:  04 - APPAREL

                         SALESPERSON SSN        SALESPERSON NAME        CURRENT SALES

                           685 26 4065        CARLSON, HOPE              $  900.00
                           556 23 4035        CRANE, JOHN                $1,050.50
                           696 99 6055        DANIELS, JULIA             $2,870.50
                           251 34 2020        FARMER, SUSAN              $1,620.00
                           263 45 2070        FEINGOLD, HAROLD           $1,250.50
                           667 45 1060        HARRISON, LILY             $1,425.80

                                                   TOTAL SALES FOR DEPT 04 : $ 9,117.30 *
              DEPT NO.:  06 - EQUIPMENT

                         SALESPERSON SSN        SALESPERSON NAME        CURRENT SALES

                           521 24 4005        DWYER, TERRENCE            $1,425.80
                           564 45 1045        EDWARDS, PETER             $1,080.50
                           644 35 3075        MANNING, ELIZABETH         $1,350.00

                                                   TOTAL SALES FOR DEPT 06 : $  3,856.30 *
```

Figure 8.27b continued

```
                    DEPT NO.:  08 - LETTERING

                               SALESPERSON SSN            SALESPERSON NAME        CURRENT SALES

                                 377 56 8080            HOWARD, RALPH               $  560.50
                                 482 13 1015            JANKOWSKI, STANLEY          $1,350.00
                                 551 16 4090            KELLY, PATRICK              $1,625.00
                                 599 23 1085            LANGFORD, SARAH             $1,150.50
                                 521 16 6100            PRINGLY, ANNE               $1,098.05

                                                             TOTAL SALES FOR DEPT 08 : $  5,784.05 *

                                                            TOTAL SALES FOR STORE 10 : $ 26,485.95 **

REPORT DATE:  93/08/25                                                                        PAGE 2
                                             THE SPORTSMAN

                                          SALES ANALYSIS REPORT

         STORE:  20 - BOSTON

                    DEPT NO.:  02 - FOOTWEAR

                               SALESPERSON SSN            SALESPERSON NAME        CURRENT SALES

                                 408 93 6050            CORDEIRO, ANTONE            $  100.50
                                 509 86 2005            CORTON, ALEXANDRA           $1,000.00
                                 509 18 5045            PINEAULT, NORMAN            $  980.50
                                 480 75 5030            TALBOT, JILLIAN             $1,275.80

                                                             TOTAL SALES FOR DEPT 02 : $  3,356.80 *

                    DEPT NO.:  04 - APPAREL

                               SALESPERSON SSN            SALESPERSON NAME        CURRENT SALES

                                 479 21 0065            BARRESI, JOHN               $  650.00
                                 427 56 0010            COCHRANE, RUSSELL           $1,460.50
                                 360 90 2035            PENTA, ROBERT               $1,650.25
                                 472 84 7080            PROULX, PAULINE             $1,150.00
                                 375 70 1060            QUINN, SUZANNE              $1,320.50

                                                             TOTAL SALES FOR DEPT 04 : $  6,231.25 *

                    DEPT NO.:  06 - EQUIPMENT

                               SALESPERSON SSN            SALESPERSON NAME        CURRENT SALES

                                 683 30 9020            COSTELLO, JAMES             $1,670.50
                                 418 09 0015            CRAWFORD, SHIRLEY           $1,390.50
                                 566 12 7070            FELDMAN, WALTER             $1,470.80
                                 433 40 6075            FERNANDEZ, LOUISE           $2,000.00
                                 571 90 4025            LEMERISE, DONALD            $1,850.50
                                 572 49 5090            WORTHEN, MICHAEL            $1,570.00

                                                             TOTAL SALES FOR DEPT 06 : $  9,952.30 *

                    DEPT NO.:  08 - LETTERING

                               SALESPERSON SSN            SALESPERSON NAME        CURRENT SALES

                                 762 35 5100            GOYETTE, FRANCES            $  950.00
                                 812 13 3085            KOSINSKI, KATHERINE         $1,125.00
                                 804 23 3040            VERMETTE, GLORIA            $1,560.50

                                                             TOTAL SALES FOR DEPT 08 : $  3,635.50 *

                                                            TOTAL SALES FOR STORE 20 : $ 23,175.85 **

REPORT DATE:  93/08/25                                                                        PAGE 3

                                             THE SPORTSMAN

                                          SALES ANALYSIS REPORT

         STORE:  30 - CHICAGO

                    DEPT NO.:  02 - FOOTWEAR

                               SALESPERSON SSN            SALESPERSON NAME        CURRENT SALES

                                 576 40 0892            KING, CHRISTOPHER           $1,890.70
                                 416 89 2014            BERNARD, ISIDORE            $2,035.69
                                 823 14 4098            MAHFUZ, IRENE               $1,850.25

                                                             TOTAL SALES FOR DEPT 02 : $  5,776.64 *
```

```
           DEPT NO.:  04 - APPAREL

                      SALESPERSON SSN            SALESPERSON NAME        CURRENT SALES

                        566 73 1251            ROBINSON, GILBERT          $2,105.90
                        788 23 0154            DONOHUE, PHIL              $  875.00
                        607 04 4132            CORRIGAN, ALENE            $1,875.50
                        745 64 5270            FURTADO, MAUREEN           $2,015.40

                                                       TOTAL SALES FOR DEPT 04 : $  6,871.80 *
           DEPT NO.:  06 - EQUIPMENT

                      SALESPERSON SSN            SALESPERSON NAME        CURRENT SALES

                        820 78 8914            ABALLO, NORMA              $2,350.75
                        785 02 3157            DOLLARHIDE, CHRIS          $2,015.70
                        745 63 5164            LINCOURT, LORETTA          $1,495.00

                                                       TOTAL SALES FOR DEPT 06 : $  5,861.45 *
           DEPT NO.:  08 - LETTERING

                      SALESPERSON SSN            SALESPERSON NAME        CURRENT SALES

                        466 58 7165            BRAZ, JOAN                 $2,315.60
                        557 31 8974            PRATT, ROBIN               $2,155.00
                        487 25 1099            MELANSON, GARY             $1,905.50

                                                       TOTAL SALES FOR DEPT 08 : $  6,376.10 *

                                                      TOTAL SALES FOR STORE 30 : $ 24,885.99 **

REPORT DATE:  93/08/25                                                                     PAGE 4

                                             THE SPORTSMAN

                                         SALES ANALYSIS REPORT

      STORE:  40 - SEATTLE

           DEPT NO.:  02 - FOOTWEAR

                      SALESPERSON SSN            SALESPERSON NAME        CURRENT SALES

                        452 67 7143            BEAUDOIN, ROCKY            $2,215.00
                        787 85 5623            MARKLAND, MARY             $1,987.50
                        674 45 1231            BISBANO, HENRY             $2,190.55

                                                       TOTAL SALES FOR DEPT 02 : $  6,393.05 *
           DEPT NO.:  04 - APPAREL

                      SALESPERSON SSN            SALESPERSON NAME        CURRENT SALES

                        720 95 4670            VELOZO, MARIO              $2,423.90
                        624 16 6876            PARISEAU, WILLIAM          $1,785.00
                        712 13 3463            PERRY, MARTA               $1,945.50

                                                       TOTAL SALES FOR DEPT 04 : $  6,154.40 *
           DEPT NO.:  06 - EQUIPMENT

                      SALESPERSON SSN            SALESPERSON NAME        CURRENT SALES

                        452 89 2153            CARDIN, FRANCIS            $2,045.90
                        551 50 2546            FORTIN, EMIL               $2,254.50
                        574 93 0461            GALLAGHER, MICHAEL         $1,976.75
                        683 21 5467            NOTTE, LORENZO             $2,005.00

                                                       TOTAL SALES FOR DEPT 06 : $  8,282.15 *
           DEPT NO.:  08 - LETTERING

                      SALESPERSON SSN            SALESPERSON NAME        CURRENT SALES

                        721 43 5472            JOBIN, ANTONIO             $2,140.50
                        490 23 4571            MILLER, RENEE              $1,905.70
                        351 56 6178            TRAMONTE, ESTELLE          $2,135.00

                                                       TOTAL SALES FOR DEPT 08 : $  6,181.20 *

                                                      TOTAL SALES FOR STORE 40 : $ 27,010.80 **

                                                         TOTAL COMPANY SALES : $  101,558.59 ***

                                        ***  END OF REPORT  ***
```

Data Validation

Before processing the records of a data file, it is most important to verify that they contain the data they are designed to contain. If this verification process is not performed, then the old adage "garbage in, garbage out" may very well apply again. If the file contains few records, it may be possible to validate the data visually at a terminal. However, data validation is usually carried out by special applications programs designed to test each data field of a record. The tests determine if a field value is missing, if the value is of the right class, if it falls within an acceptable range, and so on. The main objective of a data validation program is to identify the records that contain data entry errors so that the errors can be corrected.

The program that we develop in this part of the chapter serves to illustrate some data validation procedures. A variety of tests are used, such as the class test, the sign test, and the relational test; and a new statement, the INSPECT statement, is introduced.

The Problem

The Sportsman Company wants a data validation program to test the records of its sales file. The program must produce a *data validation* report (formatted as shown in Figure 8.28) and a new file containing only the validated records, that is, those records that successfully passed all the tests.

Each record of the sales file must be printed in the DATA RECORD area of the printer spacing chart, and for each error found on the record, if any, an appropriate message must be printed in the ERROR MESSAGES area. The specifics are listed in the following table.

Data Field	Tests to Be Performed	Error Messages to Be Printed
Store number	No entry	STORE NO. IS MISSING
	Not a numeric value	STORE NO. IS NOT NUMERIC
	Invalid code	INVALID STORE NO.
Department number	No entry	DEPT NO. IS MISSING
	Not a numeric value	DEPT NO. IS NOT NUMERIC
	Invalid code	INVALID DEPT NO.
Social Security number	No entry	SSN IS MISSING
	Not a numeric value	SSN IS NOT NUMERIC
Name	No entry	NAME IS MISSING
	Name is not left-justified	NAME IS NOT LEFT JUSTIFIED
	Not an alphabetic value	NAME IS NOT ALPHABETIC
	Not all uppercase letters	NAME LETTERS ARE NOT ALL CAPS
Current sales	No entry	SALES AMOUNT IS MISSING
	Not a numeric value	SALES AMOUNT IS NOT NUMERIC

Figure 8.28 Printer spacing chart for the data validation report

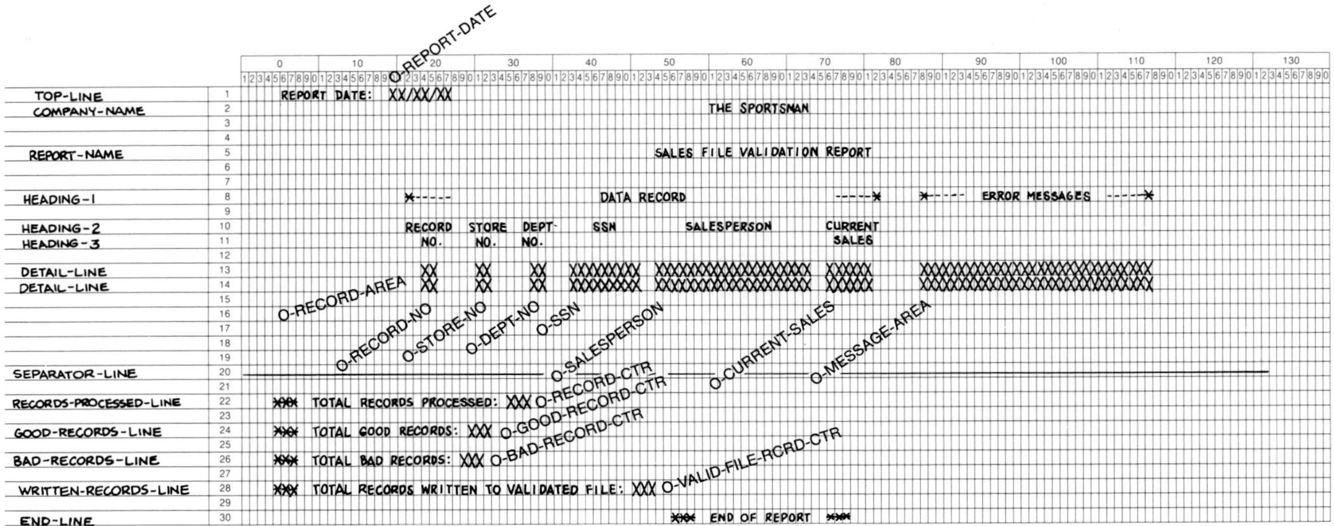

A record is printed in the record area only once, regardless of how many error messages must be printed for that record. At the end of the report, totals must show the number of records processed, the number of "good" records, the number of "bad" records, and the number of records written to the validated data file. (These totals provide an easy way of checking the accuracy of some program functions: The sum of the good records and the bad records must equal the number of records processed, and the number of records written to the validated file must be the same as the number of good records.)

The report is formatted as one continuous report without page breaks. The totals are printed between separator lines at the end of the report.

Program Design Phase

The layout of the input record SALES-RECORD is the one used in the first part of the chapter. The printer spacing chart of Figure 8.28 shows thirteen record layouts: TOP-LINE, COMPANY-NAME, REPORT-NAME, HEADING-1, HEADING-2, HEADING-3, DETAIL-LINE, SEPARATOR-LINE, RECORDS-PROCESSED-LINE, GOOD-RECORDS-LINE, BAD-RECORDS-LINE, WRITTEN-RECORDS-LINE, and END-LINE. The DETAIL-LINE contains at the first level the two data fields O-RECORD-AREA and O-MESSAGE-AREA; and at the second level, O-RECORD-AREA contains the elementary items O-RECORD-NO, O-STORE-NO, O-DEPT-NO, O-SSN, O-SALESPERSON, and O-CURRENT-SALES. The data fields that contain the totals are named in sequence: O-RECORD-CTR, O-GOOD-RECORD-CTR, O-BAD-RECORD-CTR, and O-VALID-FILE-RCRD-CTR.

Note that this program must produce two output files: the print file, VALIDATION-REPORT, and the storage file, VALIDATED-FILE. This requirement is shown in the system flowchart of Figure 8.29.

Structure Chart

The primary task of the program is to produce the data validation report. The initial breakdown of the overall task consists of the three standard subordinate tasks: doing the necessary start-up activities, setting up the main record processing routine, and ending with the finish-up activities.

The start-up activities include the normal "housekeeping" chores, such as opening the files, getting the date, initializing the EOF flag and the counters, and obtaining the first record of the input file to prime the main record processing loop. And, since the report must contain details for every record of the input file, the top-of-report documentation lines must be printed on the report **before** processing the first input record.

Within the main processing module, the input record currently in input memory must be copied to the record area of the output record, and then additional processes must be set up to test all the data fields of the input record. An error message will have to be produced on the report for each failed test. If the input record passes all the tests successfully, then it must be written to the new file VALIDATED-FILE. The next record of the input file is then accessed so that it can be processed in turn.

Figure 8.29 System flowchart for the data validation program

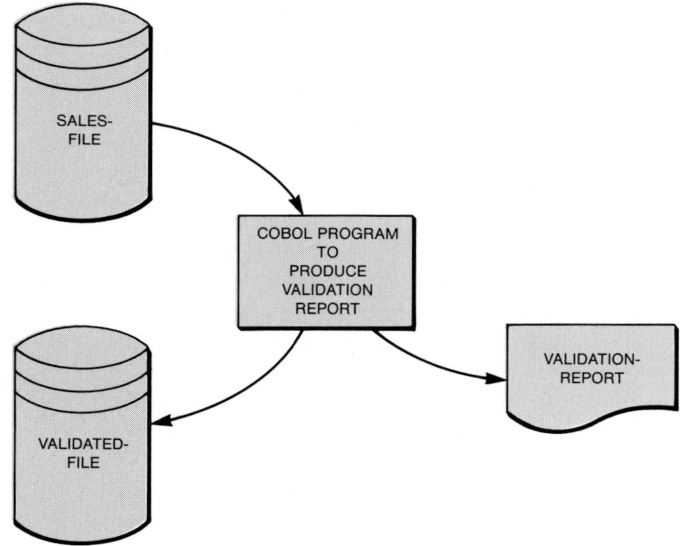

Figure 8.30 First three levels of the structure chart

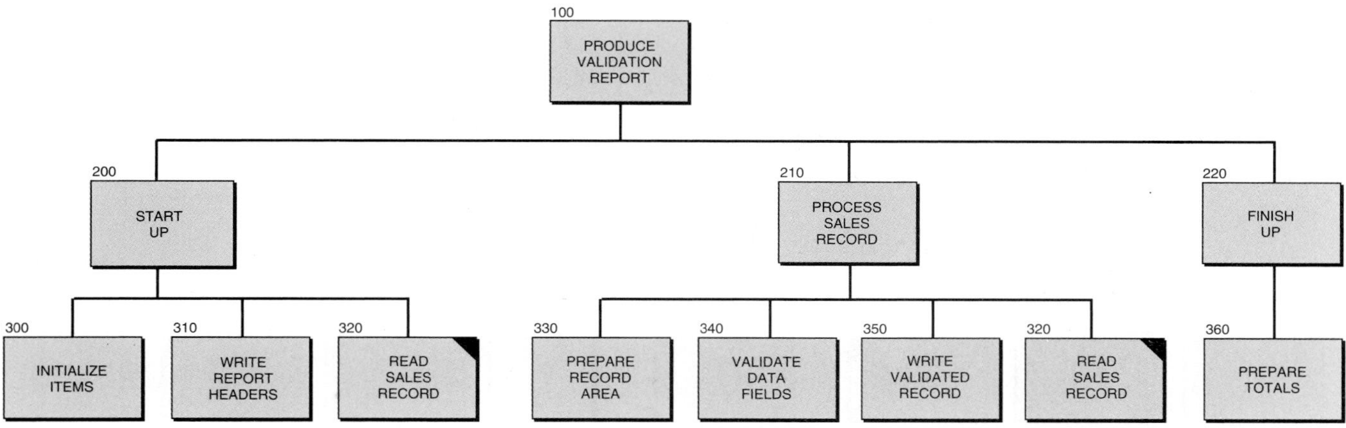

The finish-up activities must include the printing of the totals that were accumulated within the main record processing loop before printing the End-of-Report message and closing the files.

This brief analysis yields the first three levels of the structure chart shown in Figure 8.30.

We return to the main processing module 210 PROCESS SALES RECORD to further analyze its subtasks. It was briefly mentioned earlier that at the beginning of this process, the sales record currently in input memory is copied to the record area of the output record DETAIL-LINE. However, the line must not yet be written, since an error message may have to be assigned to the message area of the line. To determine if error messages are needed, the data fields of the record must be tested. When the first error is found, the appropriate message must be moved to the message area, and the DETAIL-LINE is printed. If more errors are found, then, according to the report requirements, only the error messages must be printed and consequently, the record area of DETAIL-LINE must be erased. If no error is found, DETAIL-LINE will be printed only after the last field test has been performed. And in that case, the record is validated and must be written to the file VALIDATED-FILE. This further analysis leads to the hierarchy of the subordinate tasks of module 210, as shown in Figure 8.31.

Figure 8.31 Subtasks of module 210-PROCESS-SALES-RECORD

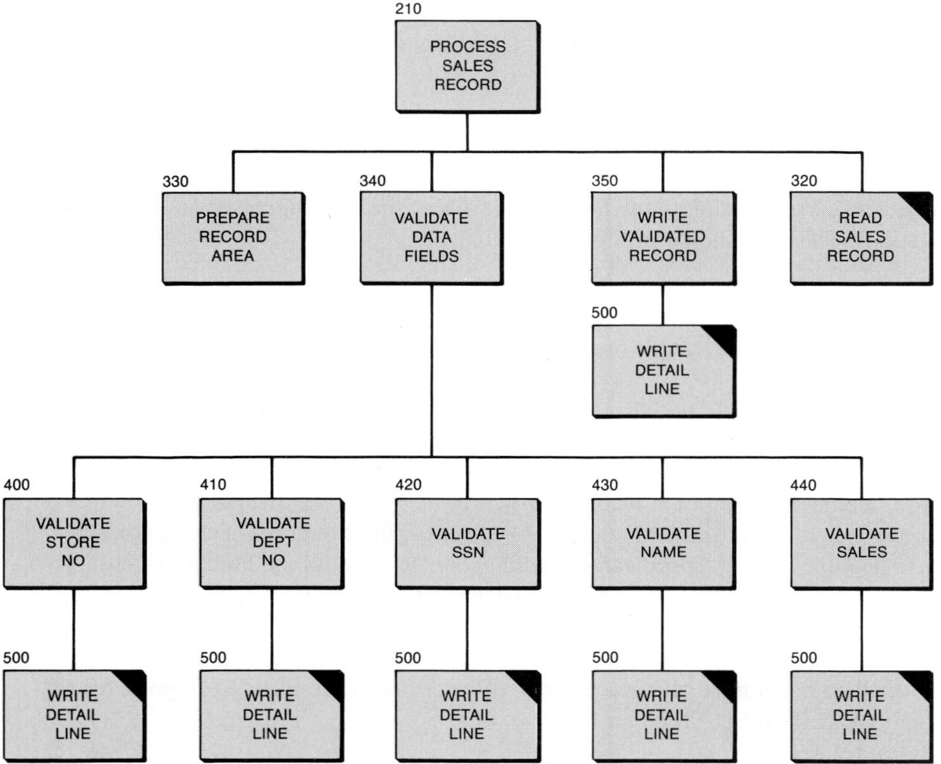

■ **Figure 8.32** Structure chart for the data validation program

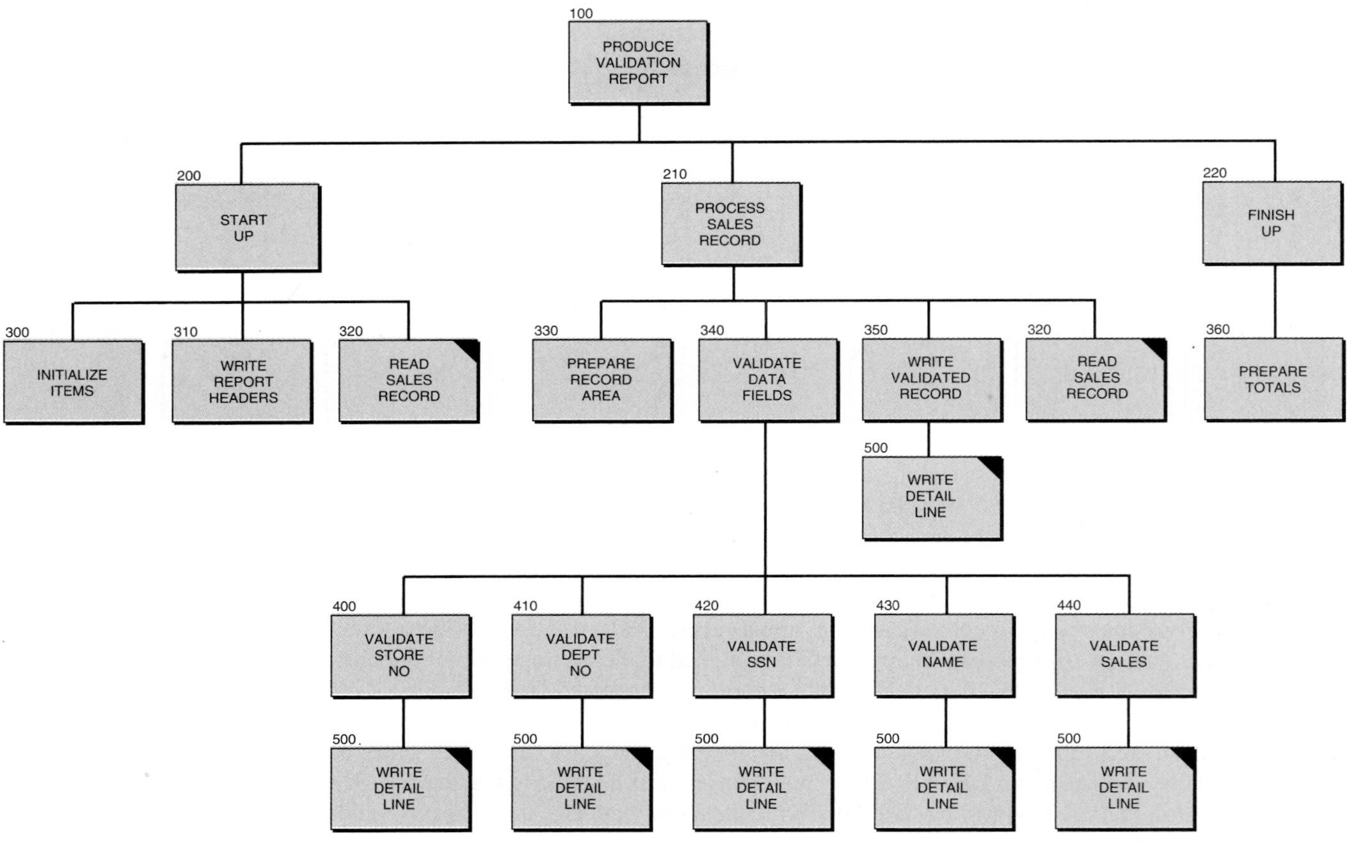

It is important to emphasize that after the tasks of module 340 VALIDATE DATA FIELDS have been completed, DETAIL-LINE will have been printed on the data validation report only if errors were found while testing the data fields. If no error was found, DETAIL-LINE must now be printed on the report without any error message, and the record SALES-RECORD must be written to the file VALIDATED-FILE. These functions will be performed within module 350 WRITE VALIDATED RECORD.

The complete structure chart is shown in Figure 8.32.

Program Pseudocode

The pseudocode paragraphs corresponding to the first three levels of the structure chart are straightforward and need few explanations. They are shown in Figure 8.33.

Brief comments:

1. In paragraph 200-Start-Up, step 1 is to "open the files." Remember that three files are needed, one input file (SALES-FILE) and two output files (the print file VALIDATION-REPORT and the storage file VALIDATED-FILE).

   Note the number of counters initialized in subordinate paragraph 300-Initialize-Items: A record counter to count the records read from the input file SALES-FILE, a "good record" counter to count the records with no errors, a "bad record" counter to count the records with errors, a "valid-file record" counter to count the records written to the file VALIDATED-FILE.

   In addition to the counters that accumulate the totals for the final part of the report, the program will use another counter, specifically, a space counter to count the number of spaces within a data field. The space counter is explained later in the discussion of the INSPECT statement.
2. In paragraph 210-Process-Sales-Record, note that the record counter is incremented in step 1. Also note that when the data fields have all been examined for errors, if the record is a good record, then it is written to VALIDATED-FILE.

Figure 8.33 Pseudocode corresponding to the first three levels of the structure chart

100-Produce-Validation-Report.

1. Perform 200-Start-Up.
2. Perform 210-Process-Sales-Record until no more records.
3. Perform 220-Finish-Up.
4. Stop the run.

200-Start-Up.

1. Open the files.
2. Perform 300-Initialize-Items.
3. Perform 310-Write-Report-Headers.
4. Perform 320-Read-Sales-Record.

210-Process-Sales-Record.

1. Add 1 to record-counter.
2. Perform 330-Prepare-Record-Area.
3. Perform 340-Validate-Data-Fields.
4. Test error-flag:
   if it is "OFF",
   perform 350-Write-Validated-Record.
5. Perform 320-Read-Sales-Record.

220-Finish-Up.

1. Perform 360-Prepare-Totals.
2. Move End-Line to the output area Printline.
3. After advancing 5 lines, write the output record printline.
4. Close the files.

300-Initialize-Items.

1. Obtain the date from the system.
2. Move the date to Top-Line date.
3. Set the end-of-file flag WS-MORE-RECORDS to "YES".
4. Set the counters to zero: record-counter, good-record-counter, bad-record-counter, valid-file-record-counter.
5. Clear the record area Detail-Line.

310-Write-Report-Headers.

1. Move Top-Line to the output area Printline.
2. After advancing to the top of a new page, write the output record Printline.
3. Move Company-Name to the output area Printline.
4. After advancing 1 line, write the output record Printline.
5. Move Report-Name to the output area Printline.
6. After advancing 3 lines, write the output record Printline.
7. Move Heading-1 to the output area Printline.
8. After advancing 3 lines, write the output record Printline.
9. Move Heading-2 to the output area Printline.
10. After advancing 2 lines, write the output record Printline.
11. Move Heading-3 to the output area Printline.
12. After advancing 1 line, write the output record Printline.
13. Set proper-spacing to 2.

320-Read-Sales-Record.

1. Read an input Sales-Record.
2. Test for end-of-file record;
   if EOF record reached, move "NO " to the end-of-file flag WS-MORE-RECORDS.

330-Prepare-Record-Area.

1. Move record-counter to Detail-Line record-number.
2. Move input store-number to Detail-Line store-number.
3. Move input department-number to Detail-Line department-number.
4. Move input social-security-number to Detail-Line social-security-number.
5. Move input salesperson to Detail-Line salesperson.
6. Move input current-sales to Detail-Line current-sales.

■ **Figure 8.33** continued

340-Validate-Data-Fields.

1. Set error-flag to "OFF".
2. Perform 400-Validate-Store-No.
3. Perform 410-Validate-Dept-No.
4. Perform 420-Validate-SSN.
5. Perform 430-Validate-Name.
6. Perform 440-Validate-Sales.
7. If error-flag is "OFF", add 1 to good-record-counter,
   else, add 1 to bad-record-counter.

350-Write-Validated-Record.

1. Perform 500-Write-Detail-Line.
2. Move Sales-Record to Validated-Record.
3. Write Validated-Record.
4. Add 1 to valid-file-record-counter.

360-Prepare-Totals.

1. Move Separator-line to the output area Printline.
2. After advancing 4 lines, write the output record Printline.
3. Move record-counter to Records-Processed-Line record-counter.
4. Move Records-Processed-Line to the output area Printline.
5. After advancing 3 lines, write the output record Printline.
6. Move good-record-counter to Good-Records-Line good-record-counter.
7. Move Good-Records-Line to the output area Printline.
8. After advancing 2 lines, write the output record Printline.
9. Move bad-record-counter to Bad-Records-Line bad-record-counter.
10. Move Bad-Records-Line to the output area Printline.
11. After advancing 2 lines, write the output record Printline.
12. Move valid-file-record-counter to Written-Records-Line valid-file-record-counter.
13. Move Written-Records-Line to the output area Printline.
14. After advancing 2 lines, write the output record Printline.
15. Move Separator-Line to the output area Printline.
16. After advancing 3 lines, write the output record Printline.

3. In paragraph 220-Finish-Up, the statement "Close the files" means **all** the files—three in this program.
4. In paragraph 330-Prepare-Record-Area, note the ordinal number assigned to the record in step 2. Also note that the data fields in the record area of DETAIL-LINE receive values, but, since it is not known at this point if error messages must be produced, the record DETAIL-LINE cannot be written on the report at this point.
5. In paragraph 340-Validate-Data-Fields, an error flag is set to "OFF" initially. Then all the data fields are tested. When a test detects an error, the error flag is set to "ON ". Following the tests, if the error flag is still set to "OFF", the record is a good record, and the good record counter is incremented by 1; otherwise, the record is a bad record, and the bad record counter is incremented by 1.
6. In paragraph 350-Write-Validated-Record, the good record previously copied into the record area of DETAIL-LINE is written on the data validation report without any error message. The original record SALES-RECORD is now written to the file VALIDATED-FILE, and the valid-file record counter is incremented by 1. (Note that the record is written to VALIDATED-FILE without using the "advancing" clause, since this file is a storage file, **not a print file.**)

In preparing pseudocode paragraph 400-Validate-Store-No, the program must implement all the tests specified for the data field I-STORE-NO. The tests are listed in the table contained in the statement of the problem: Test for the possibility of no entry in the field, test for the possibility of a nonnumeric code, and test for an invalid numeric entry. If any one of these errors occurs, the error flag (initially set to "OFF" in paragraph 340-Validate-Data-Fields) must be set to "ON ", the appropriate message must be moved to the message area of the record DETAIL-LINE, and the line must be printed on the report. If there is no error in this field, DETAIL-LINE is not printed at this point, since other data fields remain to be tested for errors. Paragraph 400-Validate-Store-No is shown below. Note that the tests should be **nested,** since, if the field is empty, the remaining tests do not apply; if there is an entry, but it is not numeric, the third test does not apply.

400-Validate-Store-No.

1. Test input store-number:
   - **a.** if empty field, set error-flag to "ON ",
     move "Store number is missing" to Detail-Line message-area, and
     perform 500-Write-Detail-Line;
   - **b.** if not numeric, set error-flag to "ON ",
     move "Store number is not numeric" to Detail-Line message-area, and
     perform 500-Write-Detail-Line;
   - **c.** if not "10" or "20" or "30" or "40",
     set error-flag to "ON",
     move "Invalid store number" to Detail-Line message-area, and
     perform 500-Write-Detail-Line.

The next paragraph is 410-Validate-Dept-No. As control enters this paragraph, realize that a detail line will have been printed for the current record only if an error was found in the store number field. If a line has already been printed, the record area of DETAIL-LINE must not be repeated on any other line that contains an error message. This requirement can be met by erasing the record area Detail-Line subsequent to printing the line on the report. This is the last step of paragraph 500-Write-Detail-Line. Upon returning from paragraph 500, the two major subdivisions of the record Detail-Line, namely O-Record-Area and O-Message-Area, are clear. If errors are found in any other data field of the input record, only the appropriate message is moved to Detail-Line and hence only the error message will be printed on the report, as required.

The pseudocode paragraphs that correspond to the remaining field validation modules are shown below.

410-Validate-Dept-No.

1. Test input department-number:
   - **a.** if empty field, set error-flag to "ON ",
     move "Dept number is missing" to Detail-Line message-area, and
     perform 500-Write-Detail-Line;
   - **b.** if not numeric, set error-flag to "ON ",
     move "Dept number is not numeric" to Detail-Line message-area, and
     perform 500-Write-Detail-Line;
   - **c.** if not "02" or "04" or "06" or "08",
     set error-flag to "ON ",
     move "Invalid dept number" to Detail-Line message-area, and
     perform 500-Write-Detail-Line:

420-Validate-SSN.

1. Test input social-security-number:
   - **a.** if empty field, set error-flag to "ON ",
     move "SSN is missing" to Detail-Line message-area, and
     perform 500-Write-Detail-Line;
   - **b.** if not numeric, set error-flag to "ON ",
     move "SSN is not numeric" to Detail-Line message-area, and
     perform 500-Write-Detail-Line.

430-Validate-Name.

1. Test input salesperson:
   - **a.** if empty field, set error-flag to "ON ",
     move "Name is missing" to Detail-Line message-area, and
     perform 500-Write-Detail-Line;
   - **b.** if not left-justified, set error-flag to "ON ",
     move "Name is not left-justified" to Detail-Line message-area, and
     perform 500-Write-Detail-Line;
   - **c.** if not alphabetic, set error-flag to "ON ",
     move "Name is not alphabetic" to Detail-Line message-area, and
     perform 500-Write-Detail-Line;
   - **d.** if not upper-case letters,
     set error-flag to "ON ",
     move "Name letters are not all caps" to Detail-Line message-area, and
     perform 500-Write-Detail-Line.

440-Validate-Sales.

1. Test input current-sales:
   a. if empty field, set error-flag to "ON ",
      move "Sales amount is missing" to Detail-Line message-area, and
      perform 500-Write-Detail-Line;
   b. if not numeric, set error-flag to "ON ",
      move "Sales amount is not numeric" to Detail-Line message-area, and
      perform 500-Write-Detail-Line.

500-Write-Detail-Line.

1. Move Detail-Line to the output area Printline.
2. After advancing proper-spacing, write the output record Printline.
3. Set proper-spacing to 1.
4. Clear the record area Detail-Line.

Program Flowchart

The program flowchart of Figure 8.34 may serve as an alternative to the program pseudocode. The brief comments above apply to the corresponding modules of the flowchart. In addition, note that the validation tests in modules 400 through 440 are nested. The nesting is due to the nature of these specific tests. Other data validation procedures may require sequential tests.

Figure 8.34 Program flowchart

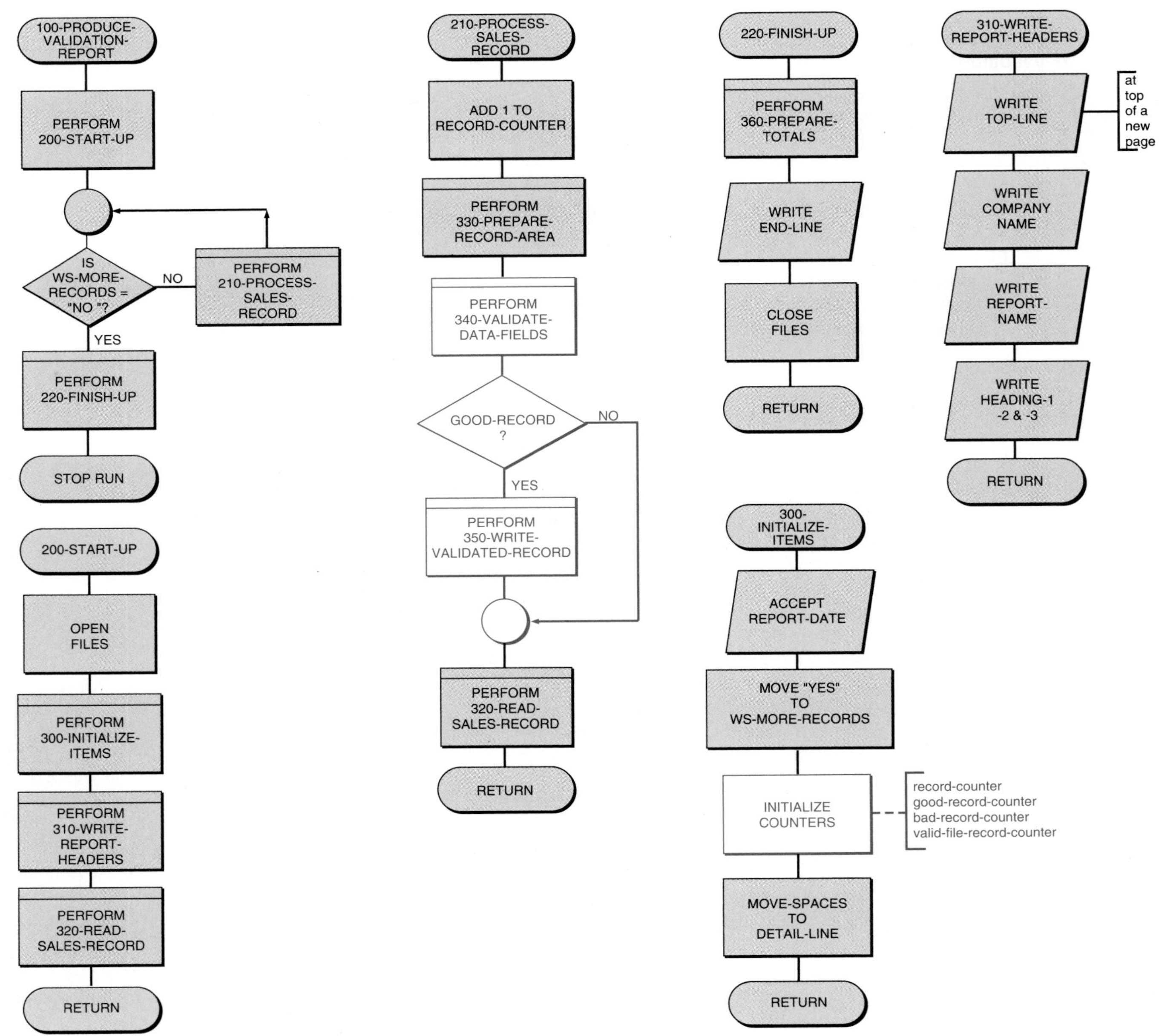

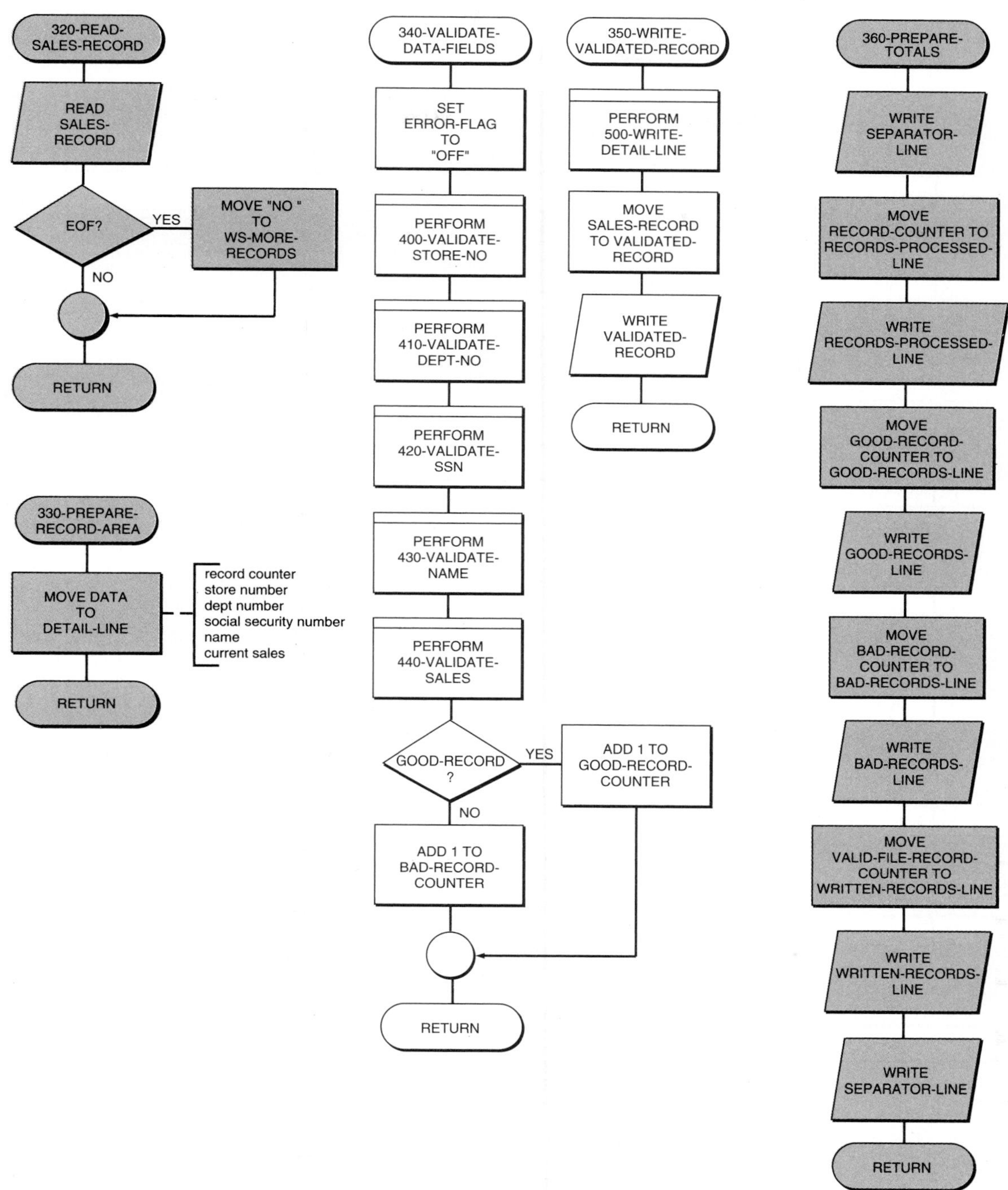
320-READ-SALES-RECORD
READ SALES-RECORD
EOF?
YES
MOVE "NO " TO WS-MORE-RECORDS
NO
RETURN
330-PREPARE-RECORD-AREA
MOVE DATA TO DETAIL-LINE
record counter
store number
dept number
social security number
name
current sales
RETURN
340-VALIDATE-DATA-FIELDS
SET ERROR-FLAG TO "OFF"
PERFORM 400-VALIDATE-STORE-NO
PERFORM 410-VALIDATE-DEPT-NO
PERFORM 420-VALIDATE-SSN
PERFORM 430-VALIDATE-NAME
PERFORM 440-VALIDATE-SALES
GOOD-RECORD ?
YES
ADD 1 TO GOOD-RECORD-COUNTER
NO
ADD 1 TO BAD-RECORD-COUNTER
RETURN
350-WRITE-VALIDATED-RECORD
PERFORM 500-WRITE-DETAIL-LINE
MOVE SALES-RECORD TO VALIDATED-RECORD
WRITE VALIDATED-RECORD
RETURN
360-PREPARE-TOTALS
WRITE SEPARATOR-LINE
MOVE RECORD-COUNTER TO RECORDS-PROCESSED-LINE
WRITE RECORDS-PROCESSED-LINE
MOVE GOOD-RECORD-COUNTER TO GOOD-RECORDS-LINE
WRITE GOOD-RECORDS-LINE
MOVE BAD-RECORD-COUNTER TO BAD-RECORDS-LINE
WRITE BAD-RECORDS-LINE
MOVE VALID-FILE-RECORD-COUNTER TO WRITTEN-RECORDS-LINE
WRITE WRITTEN-RECORDS-LINE
WRITE SEPARATOR-LINE
RETURN

■ **Figure 8.34** continued

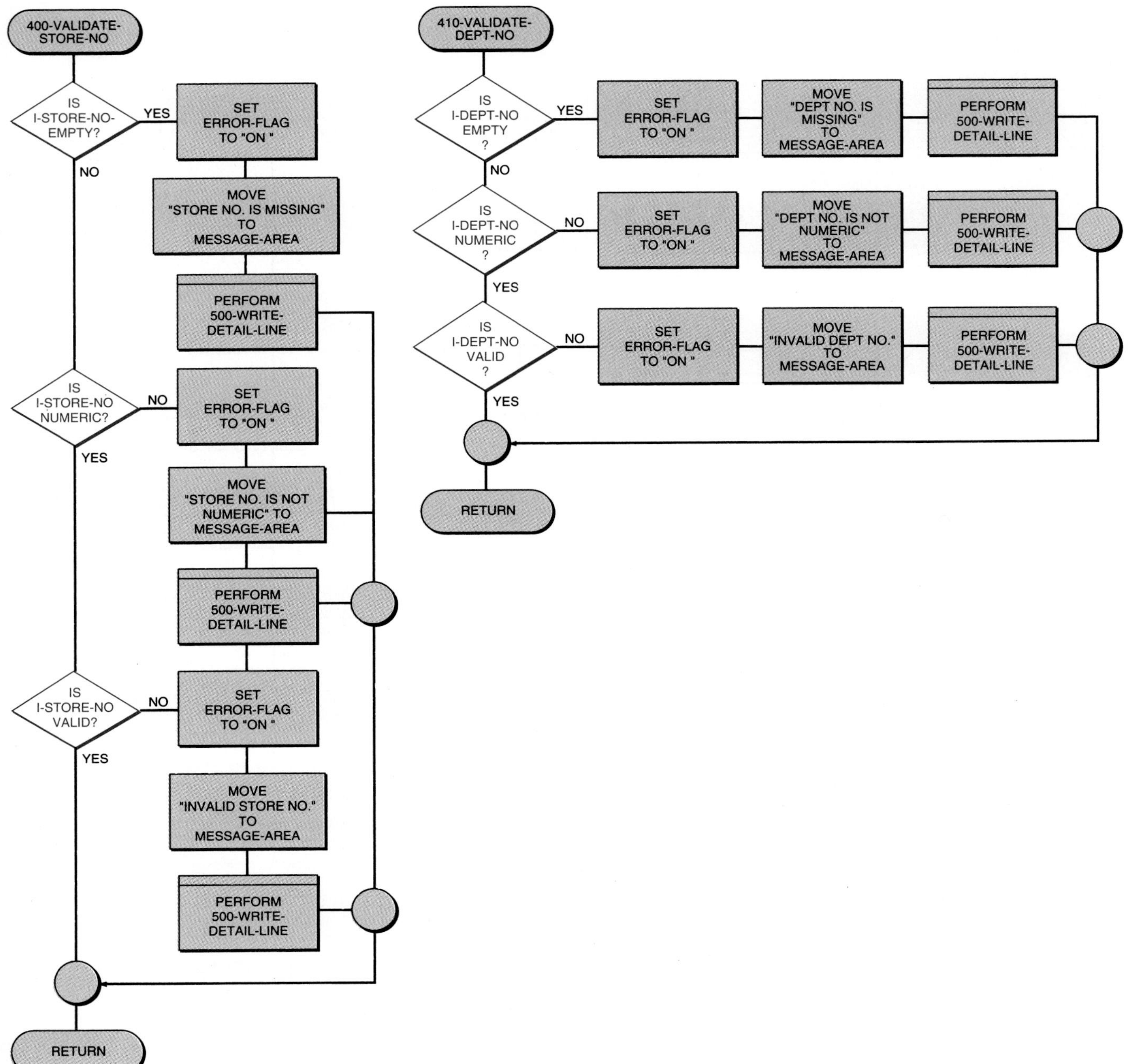

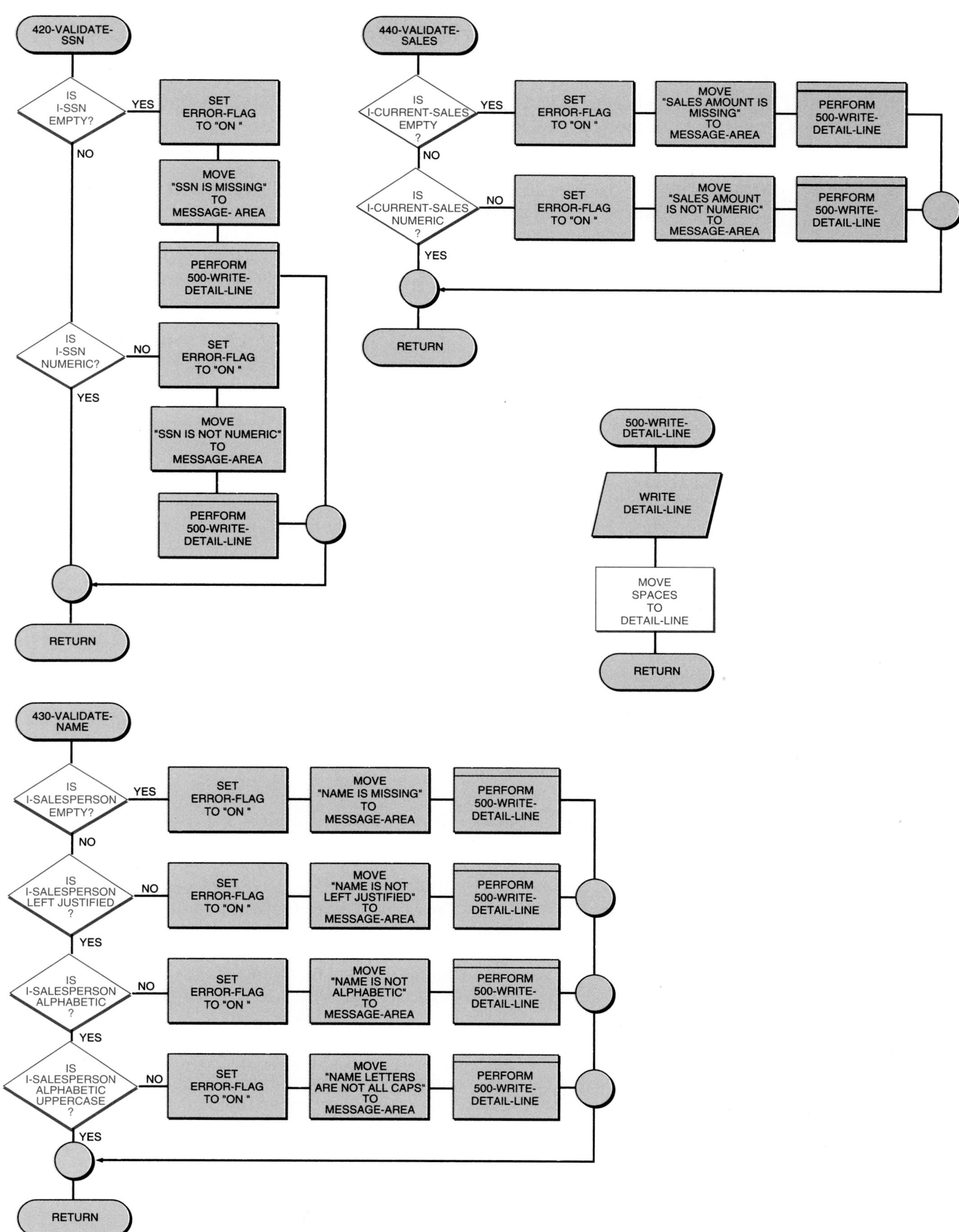
420-VALIDATE-SSN
IS I-SSN EMPTY?
YES
SET ERROR-FLAG TO "ON "
MOVE "SSN IS MISSING" TO MESSAGE- AREA
PERFORM 500-WRITE-DETAIL-LINE
NO
IS I-SSN NUMERIC?
NO
SET ERROR-FLAG TO "ON "
MOVE "SSN IS NOT NUMERIC" TO MESSAGE-AREA
PERFORM 500-WRITE-DETAIL-LINE
YES
RETURN
440-VALIDATE-SALES
IS I-CURRENT-SALES EMPTY ?
YES
SET ERROR-FLAG TO "ON "
MOVE "SALES AMOUNT IS MISSING" TO MESSAGE-AREA
PERFORM 500-WRITE-DETAIL-LINE
NO
IS I-CURRENT-SALES NUMERIC ?
NO
SET ERROR-FLAG TO "ON "
MOVE "SALES AMOUNT IS NOT NUMERIC" TO MESSAGE-AREA
PERFORM 500-WRITE-DETAIL-LINE
YES
RETURN
500-WRITE-DETAIL-LINE
WRITE DETAIL-LINE
MOVE SPACES TO DETAIL-LINE
RETURN
430-VALIDATE-NAME
IS I-SALESPERSON EMPTY?
YES
SET ERROR-FLAG TO "ON "
MOVE "NAME IS MISSING" TO MESSAGE-AREA
PERFORM 500-WRITE-DETAIL-LINE
NO
IS I-SALESPERSON LEFT JUSTIFIED ?
NO
SET ERROR-FLAG TO "ON "
MOVE "NAME IS NOT LEFT JUSTIFIED" TO MESSAGE-AREA
PERFORM 500-WRITE-DETAIL-LINE
YES
IS I-SALESPERSON ALPHABETIC ?
NO
SET ERROR-FLAG TO "ON "
MOVE "NAME IS NOT ALPHABETIC" TO MESSAGE-AREA
PERFORM 500-WRITE-DETAIL-LINE
YES
IS I-SALESPERSON ALPHABETIC UPPERCASE ?
NO
SET ERROR-FLAG TO "ON "
MOVE "NAME LETTERS ARE NOT ALL CAPS" TO MESSAGE-AREA
PERFORM 500-WRITE-DETAIL-LINE
YES
RETURN

Coding the Program

The coding of the first three divisions of the program requires no new entries; however, the following observations may be helpful:

1. Since this is the first program that requires the use of three files, we remind you that the FILE-CONTROL paragraph of the ENVIRONMENT DIVISION must contain three SELECT statements, and the FILE SECTION of the DATA DIVISION must contain three FD paragraphs, one for each of the three files. Recall that SALES-FILE will be the input file, whereas VALIDATION-REPORT is an output "print file," and VALIDATED-FILE is an output "storage file." Thus, there are two output files. On the VAX, only one file can be assigned to COB$OUTPUT. As in previous sample programs, the print file, named VALIDATION-REPORT in this program, will be assigned to the VAX logical name COB$OUTPUT. The programmer has the option of specifying a user-defined logical name or a specific file in the user's directory for the storage file. (See FILE-CONTROL subsection in Chapter 3.) To maintain the file independence of the program, the storage file VALIDATED-FILE is assigned to the user-defined logical name SPORTSDATA, as in

   ```
   SELECT VALIDATED-FILE ASSIGN TO SPORTSDATA.
   ```

   On the VAX, a DCL (Digital Control Language) command must be entered before executing the program to define the logical name SPORTSDATA. A sample sequence of DCL statements may be the following:

   ```
   $ COBOL/ANSI/LIS  C8SAM2.COB
   $ LINK C8SAM2.OBJ
   $ ASSIGN C8SAM2.DAT COB$INPUT
   $ ASSIGN C8SAM2.OT1 COB$OUTPUT
   $ DEFINE SPORTSDATA C8SAM2.OT2
   $ RUN C8SAM2.EXE
   $ PRINT/QUE=OS315 C8SAM2.LIS, C8SAM2.DAT, C8SAM2.OT1, C8SAM2.OT2
   ```

   [Ask your instructor for the procedures that are specific to your computer system.]

   Note that in the user's directory, the file C8SAM2.OT1 contains the validation report (Figure 8.39) and the file C8SAM2.OT2 contains all the validated records, that is, the records from the input file that are free of errors (Figure 8.40).
2. As the input record SALES-RECORD is being coded, condition-names can be attached to its data fields, where appropriate, to facilitate some of the tests that will be performed within the PROCEDURE DIVISION. For instance, the field I-STORE-NO must be tested for a missing value. By defining the condition-name STORE-NOT-ENTERED to correspond to "spaces" in the field, then the statement

   ```
   IF STORE-NOT-ENTERED
       SET BAD-RECORD TO TRUE ...
   ```

   can be used to perform the needed test. The complete description of SALES-RECORD is shown in Figure 8.35. Can you determine why it would be incorrect to attach the entry " 88 SALES-NOT-ENTERED VALUE SPACES." to the data item I-CURRENT-SALES?
3. The description of the error flag WS-ERROR-FLAG contains the condition-names GOOD-RECORD and BAD-RECORD. The condition-name GOOD-RECORD will be used to perform the test in step 4 of paragraph 210-Process-Sales-Record, and the condition-name BAD-RECORD will be used to set the error flag WS-ERROR-FLAG to "ON ", within modules 400 through 440, whenever an error is detected in a data field of the record.
4. The group item PROGRAM-COUNTERS contains the elementary item WS-SPACE-CTR. The use of this counter will become clear when the INSPECT statement is explained.
5. Note that the record DETAIL-LINE contains two data fields at the first level: O-RECORD-AREA and O-MESSAGE-AREA. The group item O-RECORD-AREA is subdivided so as to insert spaces between the field values of the input record SALES-RECORD. It is then easier for the user of the report to see the field values as separate items. Note, however, that no editing has been performed on the field values. The user sees the data as it is stored on the input record, except for the inserted spacing.

   The first three divisions of the program are contained in Figure 8.35.

■ **Figure 8.35** First three divisions of the data validation program

```
IDENTIFICATION DIVISION.

PROGRAM-ID.   DATA-VAL-PROGRAM.

****************************************************************
*                                                              *
*  AUTHOR.        PAQUETTE.                                    *
*  DATE WRITTEN.  SEPTEMBER, 1993.                             *
*                                                              *
****************************************************************

ENVIRONMENT DIVISION.

CONFIGURATION SECTION.

SOURCE-COMPUTER.  VAX-VMS-8650.
OBJECT-COMPUTER.  VAX-VMS-8650.

INPUT-OUTPUT SECTION.

FILE-CONTROL.
    SELECT SALES-FILE          ASSIGN TO COB$INPUT.
    SELECT VALIDATION-REPORT   ASSIGN TO COB$OUTPUT.
    SELECT VALIDATED-FILE      ASSIGN TO SPORTSDATA.

DATA DIVISION.

FILE SECTION.

FD  SALES-FILE
    RECORD CONTAINS 39 CHARACTERS.

01  SALES-RECORD.
    05 I-STORE-NO         PIC XX.
       88 STORE-NOT-ENTERED     VALUE SPACES.
       88 VALID-STORE-NO        VALUES "10", "20", "30", "40".
    05 I-DEPT-NO          PIC XX.
       88 DEPT-NOT-ENTERED      VALUE SPACES.
       88 VALID-DEPT-NO         VALUES "02", "04", "06", "08".
    05 I-SSN              PIC X(9).
       88 SSN-NOT-ENTERED       VALUE SPACES.
    05 I-SALESPERSON      PIC X(20).
       88 NAME-NOT-ENTERED      VALUE SPACES.
    05 I-CURRENT-SALES    PIC 9(4)V99.

FD  VALIDATION-REPORT
    RECORD CONTAINS 132 CHARACTERS.

01  PRINTLINE             PIC X(132).

FD  VALIDATED-FILE
    RECORD CONTAINS 39 CHARACTERS.

01  VALIDATED-RECORD      PIC X(39).

WORKING-STORAGE SECTION.

01  PROGRAM-CONTROLS.
    05 WS-MORE-RECORDS          PIC XXX.
       88 THERE-IS-A-RECORD              VALUE "YES".
       88 NO-MORE-RECORDS                VALUE "NO ".
    05 WS-ERROR-FLAG            PIC X(3).
       88 GOOD-RECORD                    VALUE "OFF".
       88 BAD-RECORD                     VALUE "ON ".
    05 WS-REPORT-DATE           PIC X(6).
    05 WS-PROPER-SPACING        PIC 9.

01  PROGRAM-COUNTERS.
    05 WS-RECORD-CTR            PIC S99.
    05 WS-GOOD-RECORD-CTR       PIC S99.
    05 WS-BAD-RECORD-CTR        PIC S99.
    05 WS-VALID-FILE-RCRD-CTR PIC S99.
    05 WS-SPACE-CTR             PIC S99.

01  PROGRAM-WORK-AREAS.
    05 WS-SALESPERSON           PIC X(20).
```

```
01  REPORT-HEADERS.

    05 TOP-LINE.
       10                   PIC X(5)    VALUE SPACES.
       10                   PIC X(14)   VALUE "REPORT DATE:  ".
       10 O-REPORT-DATE     PIC XX/XX/XX.
       10                   PIC X(120) VALUE SPACES.

    05 COMPANY-NAME.
       10 PIC X(60)    VALUE SPACES.
       10 PIC X(13)    VALUE "THE SPORTSMAN".
       10 PIC X(60)    VALUE SPACES.

    05 REPORT-NAME.
       10 PIC X(53)    VALUE SPACES.
       10 PIC X(28)    VALUE "SALES FILE VALIDATION REPORT".
       10 PIC X(52)    VALUE SPACES.

    05 HEADING-1.
       10 PIC X(21)    VALUE SPACES.
       10 PIC X(6)     VALUE "*-----".
       10 PIC X(19)    VALUE SPACES.
       10 PIC X(11)    VALUE "DATA RECORD".
       10 PIC X(19)    VALUE SPACES.
       10 PIC X(6)     VALUE "-----*".
       10 PIC X(6)     VALUE SPACES.
       10 PIC X(6)     VALUE "*-----".
       10 PIC XX       VALUE SPACES.
       10 PIC X(14)    VALUE "ERROR MESSAGES".
       10 PIC XX       VALUE SPACES.
       10 PIC X(6)     VALUE "-----*".
       10 PIC X(15)    VALUE SPACES.

    05 HEADING-2.
       10 PIC X(21)    VALUE SPACES.
       10 PIC X(6)     VALUE "RECORD".
       10 PIC XX       VALUE SPACES.
       10 PIC X(5)     VALUE "STORE".
       10 PIC XX       VALUE SPACES.
       10 PIC X(4)     VALUE "DEPT".
       10 PIC X(5)     VALUE SPACES.
       10 PIC XXX      VALUE "SSN".
       10 PIC X(9)     VALUE SPACES.
       10 PIC X(11)    VALUE "SALESPERSON".
       10 PIC X(7)     VALUE SPACES.
       10 PIC X(7)     VALUE "CURRENT".
       10 PIC X(51)    VALUE SPACES.

    05 HEADING-3.
       10 PIC X(23)    VALUE SPACES.
       10 PIC XXX      VALUE "NO.".
       10 PIC X(4)     VALUE SPACES.
       10 PIC XXX      VALUE "NO.".
       10 PIC XXX      VALUE SPACES.
       10 PIC XXX      VALUE "NO.".
       10 PIC X(37)    VALUE SPACES.
       10 PIC X(5)     VALUE "SALES".
       10 PIC X(51)    VALUE SPACES.

01  DETAIL-LINE.
    05                        PIC X(21).
    05 O-RECORD-AREA.
       10                     PIC XX.
       10 O-RECORD-NO         PIC Z9.
       10                     PIC X(5).
       10 O-STORE-NO          PIC XX.
       10                     PIC X(5).
       10 O-DEPT-NO           PIC XX.
       10                     PIC XXX.
       10 O-SSN               PIC X(9).
       10                     PIC XX.
       10 O-SALESPERSON       PIC X(20).
       10                     PIC XX.
       10 O-CURRENT-SALES     PIC 9999V99.
       10                     PIC X(7).
    05 O-MESSAGE-AREA         PIC X(30).
    05                        PIC X(15).

01  SUMMARY-LINES.
```

```
    05 RECORDS-PROCESSED-LINE.
       10 PIC X(4)        VALUE SPACES.
       10 PIC X(5)        VALUE "***  ".
       10 PIC X(25)       VALUE "TOTAL RECORDS PROCESSED: ".
       10 O-RECORD-CTR    PIC ZZ9.

    05 GOOD-RECORDS-LINE.
       10 PIC X(4)             VALUE SPACES.
       10 PIC X(5)             VALUE "***  ".
       10 PIC X(20)            VALUE "TOTAL GOOD RECORDS: ".
       10 O-GOOD-RECORD-CTR    PIC ZZ9.

    05 BAD-RECORDS-LINE.
       10 PIC X(4)             VALUE SPACES.
       10 PIC X(5)             VALUE "***  ".
       10 PIC X(19)            VALUE "TOTAL BAD RECORDS: ".
       10 O-BAD-RECORD-CTR     PIC ZZ9.

    05 WRITTEN-RECORDS-LINE.
       10 PIC X(4)               VALUE SPACES.
       10 PIC X(5)               VALUE "***  ".
       10 PIC X(41)              VALUE
              "TOTAL RECORDS WRITTEN TO VALIDATED FILE: ".
       10 O-VALID-FILE-RCRD-CTR    PIC ZZ9.

01  SEPARATOR-LINE   PIC X(132)    VALUE ALL "-".

01  END-LINE.
    05 PIC X(55)   VALUE SPACES.
    05 PIC X(23)   VALUE "***  END OF REPORT  ***".
    05 PIC X(55)   VALUE SPACES.
```

By using the program pseudocode or the program flowchart, you can code the PROCEDURE DIVISION with very few problems. However, as we learn more of the COBOL language, additional choices become available. For instance, in coding step 4 of paragraph 210-Process-Sales-Record, any one of the following statements is permitted:

1. `IF WS-ERROR-FLAG = "OFF"` (Relational Test)
   `PERFORM 350-WRITE-VALIDATED-RECORD.`
2. `IF GOOD-RECORD` (Condition-name Test)
   `PERFORM 350-WRITE-VALIDATED-RECORD.`
3. `IF NOT BAD-RECORD` (Negated Test)
   `PERFORM 350-WRITE-VALIDATED-RECORD.`
4. `EVALUATE WS-ERROR-CTR`
   `WHEN ZERO   PERFORM 350-WRITE-VALIDATED-RECORD.`
5. `EVALUATE  TRUE`
   `WHEN GOOD-RECORD PERFORM 350-WRITE-VALIDATED-RECORD.`

Of particular interest in this program are the procedures that can be used in paragraphs 400 through 440. As an example, consider paragraph 400-Validate-Store-No. Figure 8.36 shows the pseudocode paragraph and the corresponding COBOL paragraph.

Figure 8.36 Corresponding paragraphs 400-VALIDATE-STORE-NO

400-Validate-Store-No.

1. Test input store-number:
   a. if empty field, set error-flag to "ON ",
      move "Store number is missing" to Detail-Line message-area, and
      perform 500-Write-Detail-Line;
   b. if not numeric, set error-flag to "ON ",
      move "Store number is not numeric" to Detail-Line message-area, and
      perform 500-Write-Detail-Line;
   c. if not "10" or "20" or "30" or "40",
      set error-flag to "ON ",
      move "Invalid store number to Detail-Line message-area, and
      perform 500-Write-Detail-Line.

```
400-VALIDATE-STORE-NO.
    IF STORE-NOT-ENTERED
*   AN ALTERNATIVE TO THE USE OF THE CONDITION-NAME TEST IS THE
*   USE OF THE INSPECT STATEMENT. IT WOULD REQUIRE THE NEXT
*   THREE LINES.
*     INITIALIZE WS-SPACE-CTR.
*     INSPECT I-STORE-NO TALLYING WS-SPACE-CTR FOR ALL SPACES.
*     IF WS-SPACE-CTR = 2
        SET BAD-RECORD TO TRUE
        MOVE "STORE NO. IS MISSING" TO O-MESSAGE-AREA
        PERFORM 500-WRITE-DETAIL-LINE
    ELSE
        IF I-STORE-NO IS NOT NUMERIC
            SET BAD-RECORD TO TRUE
            MOVE "STORE NO. IS NOT NUMERIC" TO O-MESSAGE-AREA
            PERFORM 500-WRITE-DETAIL-LINE
        ELSE
            IF NOT VALID-STORE-NO
                SET BAD-RECORD TO TRUE
                MOVE "INVALID STORE NO." TO O-MESSAGE-AREA
                PERFORM 500-WRITE-DETAIL-LINE
            END-IF
        END-IF
    END-IF.
```

A second alternative is to code the following:

```
IF I-STORE-NO = SPACES
    MOVE "ON " TO WS-ERROR-FLAG
    MOVE "STORE NO. IS MISSING" TO O-MESSAGE-AREA
    PERFORM 500-WRITE-DETAIL-LINE
ELSE
    IF I-STORE-NO IS NOT NUMERIC
        MOVE "ON " TO WS-ERROR-FLAG
        MOVE "STORE NO. IS NOT NUMERIC" TO O-MESSAGE-AREA
        PERFORM 500-WRITE-DETAIL-LINE
    ELSE
        IF I-STORE-NO NOT = "10" OR "20" OR "30" OR "40"
            MOVE "ON " TO WS-ERROR-FLAG
            MOVE "INVALID STORE NO." TO O-MESSAGE-AREA
            PERFORM 500-WRITE-DETAIL-LINE
        END-IF
    END-IF
END-IF.
```

The INSPECT Statement

In the example of Figure 8.36 and the alternative that follows, the field I-STORE-NO is first tested to determine if it contains an entry. COBOL allows the use of the *INSPECT* statement to count spaces or other characters in a data item. Obviously, if the INSPECT statement counts two spaces in a two-byte field, the field is empty. The statement can be coded as follows:

```
INSPECT I-STORE-NO TALLYING WS-SPACE-CTR FOR ALL SPACES.
```

The clause TALLYING WS-SPACE-CTR keeps a tally in the counter WS-SPACE-CTR of the number of spaces found in the field I-STORE-NO. Naturally, the data item WS-SPACE-CTR should be initialized to zero before executing the INSPECT statement.

If the INSPECT statement is used in paragraph 400-Validate-Store-No, then the coding is as follows:

```
400-VALIDATE-STORE-NO.
    INITIALIZE WS-SPACE-CTR.
    INSPECT I-STORE-NO TALLYING WS-SPACE-CTR FOR ALL SPACES.
    IF WS-SPACE-CTR = 2
        SET BAD-RECORD TO TRUE
        MOVE "STORE NO. IS MISSING" TO O-MESSAGE-AREA
        PERFORM 500-WRITE-DETAIL-LINE
    ELSE
        etc.
```

It is obvious that the use of the condition-name STORE-NOT-ENTERED in Figure 8.36 allows for a simpler procedure to test for an empty store number field than the INSPECT statement, but the example is presented as a simple application of the INSPECT statement.

A more important application of the INSPECT statement occurs in the test of the field I-SALES-PERSON. How can a test be performed to determine if the name has been entered left-justified in the field? One of the options available in the INSPECT statement allows a test for "leading" characters (i.e., characters occurring to the left of a given character). If leading characters in the field I-SALES PERSON are spaces, then the name entry is not left-justified; and if there are 20 leading spaces, then the field entry is missing. The INSPECT statement can be coded as follows:

```
INSPECT I-SALESPERSON TALLYING WS-SPACE-CTR FOR LEADING SPACES.
IF WS-SPACE-CTR = 20
    SET BAD-RECORD TO TRUE
    MOVE "NAME IS MISSING" TO O-MESSAGE-AREA
    PERFORM 500-WRITE-DETAIL-LINE
ELSE
    IF WS-SPACE-CTR IS POSITIVE
        SET BAD-RECORD TO TRUE
        MOVE "NAME IS NOT LEFT JUSTIFIED" TO O-MESSAGE-AREA
        PERFORM 500-WRITE-DETAIL-LINE
    and so on.
```

These two tests can be paraphrased as follows: If there are 20 leading spaces, the name entry is missing; if there are some leading spaces but fewer than 20, the entry is not left-justified.

In addition to the above tests, the field I-SALESPERSON must also be tested to determine if all the characters are alphabetic. The initial reaction to this requirement is to say, "Use the class test IS ALPHABETIC." But consider that the name has been entered in the field as follows: last name, comma, space, and then first name. In general, names can also contain an apostrophe, a hyphen, and/or a period after a middle initial. These characters properly belong in the name field, but they are not alphabetic characters, and therefore the class test IS ALPHABETIC would fail.

The INSPECT statement contains a REPLACING option that allows the programmer to replace a specific character with another. If these special characters (',.–) are replaced by spaces, this would allow the use of the class test. Then, if the test fails, it is because of some other unacceptable character in the field. Now, to avoid changing characters in the original field I-SALESPERSON, a copy of the field should be made, and the tests should then be performed on the copy. Consider the following coding:

```
MOVE I-SALESPERSON TO WS-SALESPERSON.
INITIALIZE WS-SPACE-CTR.
INSPECT WS-SALESPERSON TALLYING WS-SPACE-CTR FOR LEADING SPACES
    REPLACING ALL "." BY SPACE
                  "," BY SPACE
                  "-" BY SPACE
                  "'" BY SPACE
IF WS-SALESPERSON IS NOT ALPHABETIC
    SET BAD-RECORD TO TRUE
    MOVE "NAME IS NOT ALPHABETIC" TO O-MESSAGE-AREA
    PERFORM 500-WRITE-DETAIL-LINE
ELSE
    IF WS-SALESPERSON IS NOT ALPHABETIC-UPPER
        SET BAD-RECORD TO TRUE
        MOVE "NAME LETTERS ARE NOT ALL CAPS" TO O-MESSAGE-AREA
        PERFORM 500-WRITE-DETAIL-LINE.
```

All of the above features can be used in paragraph 430-VALIDATE-NAME as follows:

```
430-VALIDATE-NAME.
    MOVE I-SALESPERSON TO WS-SALESPERSON.
    INITIALIZE WS-SPACE-CTR.
```

```
INSPECT WS-SALESPERSON TALLYING WS-SPACE-CTR FOR LEADING SPACES
    REPLACING ALL "." BY SPACE
                  "," BY SPACE
                  "-" BY SPACE
                  "'" BY SPACE.
IF WS-SPACE-CTR = 20
    SET BAD-RECORD TO TRUE
    MOVE "NAME IS MISSING" TO O-MESSAGE-AREA
    PERFORM 500-WRITE-DETAIL-LINE
ELSE
    IF WS-SPACE-CTR IS POSITIVE
        SET BAD-RECORD TO TRUE
        MOVE "NAME IS NOT LEFT JUSTIFIED" TO O-MESSAGE-AREA
        PERFORM 500-WRITE-DETAIL-LINE
    ELSE
        IF WS-SALESPERSON IS NOT ALPHABETIC
            SET BAD-RECORD TO TRUE
            MOVE "NAME IS NOT ALPHABETIC" TO O-MESSAGE-AREA
            PERFORM 500-WRITE-DETAIL-LINE
    ELSE
        IF WS-SALESPERSON IS NOT ALPHABETIC-UPPER
            SET BAD-RECORD TO TRUE
            MOVE "NAME LETTERS ARE NOT ALL CAPS" TO O-MESSAGE-AREA
            PERFORM 500-WRITE-DETAIL-LINE.
```

The PROCEDURE DIVISION of the data validation program is shown in Figure 8.37. Note that some coding alternatives are entered as comments within certain paragraphs.

The sample data file that was used as input to the program is shown in Figure 8.38. Figure 8.39 contains the data validation report, and Figure 8.40 contains a listing of the records written to the file VALIDATED-FILE.

■ **Figure 8.37** PROCEDURE DIVISION for the data validation program

```
PROCEDURE DIVISION.

100-PRODUCE-VALIDATION-REPORT.
    PERFORM 200-START-UP.
    PERFORM 210-PROCESS-SALES-RECORD
        UNTIL NO-MORE-RECORDS.
    PERFORM 220-FINISH-UP.
    STOP RUN.

200-START-UP.
    OPEN INPUT SALES-FILE
         OUTPUT VALIDATION-REPORT
         OUTPUT VALIDATED-FILE.
    PERFORM 300-INITIALIZE-ITEMS.
    PERFORM 310-WRITE-REPORT-HEADERS.
    PERFORM 320-READ-SALES-RECORD.

210-PROCESS-SALES-RECORD.
    ADD 1 TO WS-RECORD-CTR.
    PERFORM 330-PREPARE-RECORD-AREA.
    PERFORM 340-VALIDATE-DATA-FIELDS.
    IF GOOD-RECORD
        PERFORM 350-WRITE-VALIDATED-RECORD
    END-IF.
    PERFORM 320-READ-SALES-RECORD.

220-FINISH-UP.
    PERFORM 360-PREPARE-TOTALS.
    WRITE PRINTLINE FROM END-LINE
        AFTER ADVANCING 5 LINES.
    CLOSE SALES-FILE
          VALIDATION-REPORT
          VALIDATED-FILE.

300-INITIALIZE-ITEMS.
    ACCEPT WS-REPORT-DATE FROM DATE.
    MOVE WS-REPORT-DATE TO O-REPORT-DATE.
    SET THERE-IS-A-RECORD TO TRUE.
    INITIALIZE PROGRAM-COUNTERS.
    MOVE SPACES TO DETAIL-LINE.
```

```
 310-WRITE-REPORT-HEADERS.
     WRITE PRINTLINE FROM TOP-LINE
         AFTER ADVANCING PAGE.
     WRITE PRINTLINE FROM COMPANY-NAME
         AFTER ADVANCING 1 LINE.
     WRITE PRINTLINE FROM REPORT-NAME
         AFTER ADVANCING 3 LINES.
     WRITE PRINTLINE FROM HEADING-1
         AFTER ADVANCING 3 LINES.
     WRITE PRINTLINE FROM HEADING-2
         AFTER ADVANCING 2 LINES.
     WRITE PRINTLINE FROM HEADING-3
         AFTER ADVANCING 1 LINE.
     MOVE 2 TO WS-PROPER-SPACING.

 320-READ-SALES-RECORD.
     READ SALES-FILE RECORD
         AT END
             SET NO-MORE-RECORDS TO TRUE.

 330-PREPARE-RECORD-AREA.
     MOVE WS-RECORD-CTR TO O-RECORD-NO.
     MOVE I-STORE-NO TO O-STORE-NO.
     MOVE I-DEPT-NO TO O-DEPT-NO.
     MOVE I-SSN TO O-SSN.
     MOVE I-SALESPERSON TO O-SALESPERSON.
     MOVE I-CURRENT-SALES TO O-CURRENT-SALES.

 340-VALIDATE-DATA-FIELDS.
     SET GOOD-RECORD TO TRUE.
     PERFORM 400-VALIDATE-STORE-NO.
     PERFORM 410-VALIDATE-DEPT-NO.
     PERFORM 420-VALIDATE-SSN.
     PERFORM 430-VALIDATE-NAME.
     PERFORM 440-VALIDATE-SALES.
     IF GOOD-RECORD
         ADD 1 TO WS-GOOD-RECORD-CTR
     ELSE
         ADD 1 TO WS-BAD-RECORD-CTR.

 350-WRITE-VALIDATED-RECORD.
     PERFORM 500-WRITE-DETAIL-LINE.
     WRITE VALIDATED-RECORD FROM SALES-RECORD.
     ADD 1 TO WS-VALID-FILE-RCRD-CTR.

 360-PREPARE-TOTALS.
     WRITE PRINTLINE FROM SEPARATOR-LINE
         AFTER ADVANCING 4 LINES.
     MOVE WS-RECORD-CTR TO O-RECORD-CTR.
     WRITE PRINTLINE FROM RECORDS-PROCESSED-LINE
         AFTER ADVANCING 3 LINES.
     MOVE WS-GOOD-RECORD-CTR TO O-GOOD-RECORD-CTR.
     WRITE PRINTLINE FROM GOOD-RECORDS-LINE
         AFTER ADVANCING 2 LINES.
     MOVE WS-BAD-RECORD-CTR TO O-BAD-RECORD-CTR.
     WRITE PRINTLINE FROM BAD-RECORDS-LINE
         AFTER ADVANCING 2 LINES.
     MOVE WS-VALID-FILE-RCRD-CTR TO O-VALID-FILE-RCRD-CTR.
     WRITE PRINTLINE FROM WRITTEN-RECORDS-LINE
         AFTER ADVANCING 2 LINES.
     WRITE PRINTLINE FROM SEPARATOR-LINE
         AFTER ADVANCING 3 LINES.

 400-VALIDATE-STORE-NO.
     IF STORE-NOT-ENTERED

*   AN ALTERNATIVE TO THE USE OF THE CONDITION-NAME TEST IS THE
*   USE OF THE INSPECT STATEMENT.  IT WOULD REQUIRE THE NEXT
*   THREE LINES.
```

```
*     INITIALIZE WS-SPACE-CTR.
*     INSPECT I-STORE-NO TALLYING WS-SPACE-CTR FOR ALL SPACES.
*     IF WS-SPACE-CTR = 2

          SET BAD-RECORD TO TRUE
          MOVE "STORE NO. IS MISSING" TO O-MESSAGE-AREA
          PERFORM 500-WRITE-DETAIL-LINE
      ELSE
          IF I-STORE-NO IS NOT NUMERIC
              SET BAD-RECORD TO TRUE
              MOVE "STORE NO. IS NOT NUMERIC" TO O-MESSAGE-AREA
              PERFORM 500-WRITE-DETAIL-LINE
          ELSE
              IF NOT VALID-STORE-NO
                  SET BAD-RECORD TO TRUE
                  MOVE "INVALID STORE NO." TO O-MESSAGE-AREA
                  PERFORM 500-WRITE-DETAIL-LINE
              END-IF
          END-IF
      END-IF.

      410-VALIDATE-DEPT-NO.
          IF DEPT-NOT-ENTERED

*   AN ALTERNATIVE TO THE USE OF THE CONDITION-NAME TEST IS THE
*   USE OF THE INSPECT STATEMENT.  IT WOULD REQUIRE THE NEXT
*   THREE LINES.

*     INITIALIZE WS-SPACE-CTR.
*     INSPECT I-DEPT-NO TALLYING WS-SPACE-CTR FOR ALL SPACES.
*     IF WS-SPACE-CTR = 2

          SET BAD-RECORD TO TRUE
          MOVE "DEPT NO. IS MISSING" TO O-MESSAGE-AREA
          PERFORM 500-WRITE-DETAIL-LINE
      ELSE
          IF I-DEPT-NO IS NOT NUMERIC
              SET BAD-RECORD TO TRUE
              MOVE "DEPT NO. IS NOT NUMERIC" TO O-MESSAGE-AREA
              PERFORM 500-WRITE-DETAIL-LINE
          ELSE
              IF NOT VALID-DEPT-NO
                  SET BAD-RECORD TO TRUE
                  MOVE "INVALID DEPT NO." TO O-MESSAGE-AREA
                  PERFORM 500-WRITE-DETAIL-LINE
              END-IF
          END-IF
      END-IF.

  420-VALIDATE-SSN.
      IF SSN-NOT-ENTERED

*   AN ALTERNATIVE TO THE USE OF THE CONDITION-NAME TEST IS THE
*   USE OF THE INSPECT STATEMENT.  IT WOULD REQUIRE THE NEXT
*   THREE LINES.

*     INITIALIZE WS-SPACE-CTR.
*     INSPECT I-SSN TALLYING WS-SPACE-CTR FOR ALL SPACES.
*     IF WS-SPACE-CTR = 9

          SET BAD-RECORD TO TRUE
          MOVE "SSN IS MISSING" TO O-MESSAGE-AREA
          PERFORM 500-WRITE-DETAIL-LINE
      ELSE
          IF I-SSN IS NOT NUMERIC
              SET BAD-RECORD TO TRUE
              MOVE "SSN IS NOT NUMERIC" TO O-MESSAGE-AREA
              PERFORM 500-WRITE-DETAIL-LINE
          END-IF
      END-IF.
```

```
 430-VALIDATE-NAME.

*   A CONDITION-NAME TEST COULD BE USED TO DETECT A MISSING NAME.
*   HOWEVER, INSPECT IS USED HERE BECAUSE IT FACILITATES
*   THE ALPHABETIC TESTS THAT FOLLOW.

       MOVE I-SALESPERSON TO WS-SALESPERSON.
       INITIALIZE WS-SPACE-CTR.
       INSPECT WS-SALESPERSON
           TALLYING WS-SPACE-CTR FOR LEADING SPACES
           REPLACING ALL "." BY SPACE
                         "," BY SPACE
                         "'" BY SPACE
                         "-" BY SPACE.
       IF WS-SPACE-CTR = 20
           SET BAD-RECORD TO TRUE
           MOVE "NAME IS MISSING" TO O-MESSAGE-AREA
           PERFORM 500-WRITE-DETAIL-LINE
       ELSE
           IF WS-SPACE-CTR IS POSITIVE
               SET BAD-RECORD TO TRUE
               MOVE "NAME IS NOT LEFT JUSTIFIED" TO O-MESSAGE-AREA
               PERFORM 500-WRITE-DETAIL-LINE
           ELSE
               IF WS-SALESPERSON IS NOT ALPHABETIC
                   SET BAD-RECORD TO TRUE
                   MOVE "NAME IS NOT ALPHABETIC" TO O-MESSAGE-AREA
                   PERFORM 500-WRITE-DETAIL-LINE
           ELSE
               IF WS-SALESPERSON IS NOT ALPHABETIC-UPPER
                   SET BAD-RECORD TO TRUE
                   MOVE "NAME LETTERS ARE NOT ALL CAPS" TO
                        O-MESSAGE-AREA
                   PERFORM 500-WRITE-DETAIL-LINE
               END-IF
           END-IF
       END-IF
   END-IF.

 440-VALIDATE-SALES.
       INITIALIZE WS-SPACE-CTR.
       INSPECT I-CURRENT-SALES
           TALLYING WS-SPACE-CTR FOR LEADING SPACES.
       IF WS-SPACE-CTR = 6
           SET BAD-RECORD TO TRUE
           MOVE "SALES AMOUNT IS MISSING" TO O-MESSAGE-AREA
           PERFORM 500-WRITE-DETAIL-LINE
       ELSE
           IF I-CURRENT-SALES IS NOT NUMERIC
               SET BAD-RECORD TO TRUE
               MOVE "SALES AMOUNT IS NOT NUMERIC" TO O-MESSAGE-AREA
               PERFORM 500-WRITE-DETAIL-LINE
           END-IF
        END-IF.

 500-WRITE-DETAIL-LINE.
       WRITE PRINTLINE FROM DETAIL-LINE
           AFTER ADVANCING WS-PROPER-SPACING.
       MOVE 1 TO WS-PROPER-SPACING.
       MOVE SPACES TO DETAIL-LINE.
```

■ **Figure 8.38** Sample input file

Store number | Dept number | Social Security number | Salesperson name | Current sales

```
1002214365025ALLEN, ROBERT       150000
1002218546010BROWN, RAYMOND      302255
1002641275050BRANNIGAN, NICOLE   087525
10  315-63030FOGARTY, JANICE     105050
1002642754040MAIN, CHARLES       128000
1004685264065CARLSON, HOPE       090000
  40556-34-35CRANE, JOHN         105050
0104696996055Daniels, Julia      287050
1004251342020FARMER, SUSAN       162000
1004263452070FEINGOLD, HAROLD    125050
1004667451060HARRISON, LILY
1006521244005DWYER, TERRENCE     142580
1006564451045EDWARDS, PETER      108050
1006644353075MANNING, ELIZABETH  135000
1008           HOWARD, RALPH       0560
1008482131015JANKOWSKI, STANLEY  135000
1008551164090                    162500
1008599231085LANGFORD, SARAH     115050
1008521166100PRINGLY, ANNE       109805
2002408936050CORDEIRO, ANTONE    010050
2002509862005CORTON, ALEXANDRA   100000
0220509185045Pineault, Norman    098050
2002480755030TALBOT, JILLIAN     127580
2004479210065BARRESI, JOHN       065000
2004427560010COCHRANE, RUSSELL   146050
             PENTA, ROBERT       165025
2004472847080PROULX, PAULINE     115000
2004375701060QUINN, SUZANNE      132050
2006683309020COSTELLO, JAMES     167050
2006418090015Crawford, Shirley   139050
2006566127070FELDMAN, WALTER     147080
2006433406075FERNANDEZ, LOUISE   200000
2006571904025LEMERISE, DONALD    185050
2006572495090WORTHEN, MICHAEL    157000
2200762355100GOYETTE, FRANCES    095000
2008812133085KOSINSKI, KATHERINE 112500
2008804233040   VERMETTE, GLORIA    156
3002576400892KING, CHRISTOPHER   189070
3002416892014BERNARD, ISIDORE    203569
3002823144098MAHFUZ, IRENE       185025
3004566731251ROBINSON, GILBERT   210590
3004788230154DONOHUE, PHIL       087500
3004607044132CORRIGAN, ALENE     187550
3004745645270FURTADO, MAUREEN    201540
3006820788914ABALLO< NORMA       235075
3006785023157DOLLARHIDE, CHRIS   201570
3006745635164LINCOURT, LORETTA   149500
3008466587165BRAZ, JOAN          231560
3008557318974PRATT, ROBIN        215500
3008487251099MELANSON, GARY      190550
4002452677143BEAUDOIN, ROCKY     221500
4002787855623MARKLAND, MARY      198750
4002674451231BISBANO, HENRY      219055
4004720954670VELOZO, MARIO       242390
4004624166876PARISEAU, WILLIAM   178500
4004712133463PERRY, MARTA        194550
4006452892153CARDIN, FRANCIS     204590
4006551502546FORTIN, EMIL        225450
4006574930461GALLAGHER, MICHAEL  197675
4006683215467NOTTE, LORENZO      200500
4008721435472JOBIN, ANTONIO      214050
4008490234571MILLER, RENEE       190570
4008351566178TRAMONTE, ESTELLE   213500
```

Figure 8.39 The data validation report

```
REPORT DATE: 93/09/11
                                        THE SPORTSMAN

                                   SALES FILE VALIDATION REPORT

      *-----                    DATA RECORD                  -----*     *----- ERROR MESSAGES -----*

      RECORD  STORE  DEPT     SSN        SALESPERSON         CURRENT
        NO.    NO.   NO.                                      SALES

         1     10     02   214365025  ALLEN, ROBERT          150000
         2     10     02   218546010  BROWN, RAYMOND         302255     STORE NO. IS NOT NUMERIC
                                                                        SALES AMOUNT IS NOT NUMERIC
         3     10     02   641275050  BRANNIGAN, NICOLE      087525
         4     10          315-63030  FOGARTY, JANICE        105050     DEPT NO. IS MISSING
                                                                        SSN IS NOT NUMERIC
         5     10     02   642754040  MAIN, CHARLES          128000
         6     10     04   685264065  CARLSON, HOPE          090000
         7            40   556-34-35  CRANE, JOHN            105050     STORE NO. IS MISSING
                                                                        INVALID DEPT NO.
                                                                        SSN IS NOT NUMERIC
                                                                        SALES AMOUNT IS NOT NUMERIC
         8     01     04   696996055  Daniels, Julia         287050     INVALID STORE NO.
                                                                        NAME LETTERS ARE NOT ALL CAPS
         9     10     04   251342020  FARMER, SUSAN          162000
        10     10     04   263452070  FEINGOLD, HAROLD       125050
        11     10     04   667451060  HARRISON, LILY                    SALES AMOUNT IS MISSING
        12     10     06   521244005  DWYER, TERRENCE        142580
        13     10     06   564451045  EDWARDS, PETER         108050
        14     10     06   644353075  MANNING, ELIZABETH     135000
        15     10     08              HOWARD, RALPH            0560     SSN IS MISSING
                                                                        NAME IS NOT LEFT JUSTIFIED
                                                                        SALES AMOUNT IS NOT NUMERIC
        16     10     08   482131015  JANKOWSKI, STANLEY     135000
        17     10     08   551164090                         162500     NAME IS MISSING
        19     10     08   599231085  LANGFORD, SARAH        115050
        19     10     08   521166100  PRINGLY, ANNE          109805
        20     20     02   408936050  CORDEIRO, ANTONE       010050     NAME IS NOT ALPHABETIC
        21     20     02   509862005  CORTON, ALEXANDRA      100000
        22     02     20   509185045  Pineault, Norman       098050     INVALID STORE NO.
                                                                        INVALID DEPT NO.
                                                                        SSN IS NOT NUMERIC
                                                                        NAME LETTERS ARE NOT ALL CAPS
                                                                        SALES AMOUNT IS NOT NUMERIC
        23     20     02   480755030  TALBOT, JILLIAN        127580
        24     20     04   479210065  BARRESI, JOHN          065000
        25     20     04   427560010  COCHRANE, RUSSELL      146050
        26                            PENTA, ROBERT          165025     STORE NO. IS MISSING
                                                                        DEPT NO. IS MISSING
                                                                        SSN IS MISSING
        27     20     04   472847080  PROULX, PAULINE        115000
        28     20     04   375701060  QUINN, SUZANNE         132050
        29     20     06   683309020  COSTELLO, JAMES        167050
        30     20     06   418090015  Crawford, Shirley      139050     NAME LETTERS ARE NOT ALL CAPS
        31     20     06   566127070  FELDMAN, WALTER        147080
        32     20     06   433406075  FERNANDEZ, LOUISE      200000     STORE NOT IS NOT NUMERIC
                                                                        DEPT NO. IS NOT NUMERIC
                                                                        SSN IS NOT NUMERIC
                                                                        SALES AMOUNT IS NOT NUMERIC
        33     20     06   571904025  LEMERISE, DONALD       185050
        34     20     06   572495090  WORTHEN, MICHAEL       157000
        35     22     00   762355100  GOYETTE, FRANCES       095000     INVALID STORE NO.
                                                                        INVALID DEPT NO.
        36     20     08   812133085  KOSINSKI, KATHERINE    112500
        37     20     08   804233040  VERMETTE, GLORIA          156     NAME IS NOT LEFT JUSTIFIED
                                                                        SALES AMOUNT IS NOT NUMERIC
        38     30     02   576400892  KING, CHRISTOPHER      189070
        39     30     02   416892014  BERNARD, ISIDORE       203569
        40     30     02   823144098  MAHFUZ, IRENE          185025
        41     30     04   566731251  ROBINSON, GILBERT      210590
        42     30     04   788230154  DONOHUE, PHIL          087500
        43     30     04   607044132  CORRIGAN, ALENE        187550     NAME IS NOT ALPHABETIC
        44     30     04   745645270  FURTADO, MAUREEN       201540
        45     30     06   820788914  ABALLO< NORMA          235075     NAME IS NOT ALPHABETIC
        46     30     06   785023157  DOLLARHIDE, CHRIS      201570
        47     30     06   745635164  LINCOURT, LORETTA      149500
        48     30     08   466587165  BRAZ, JOAN             231560
        49     30     08   557318974  PRATT, ROBIN           215500
        50     30     08   487251099  MELANSON, GARY         190550
        51     40     02   452677143  BEAUDOIN, ROCKY        221500
        52     40     02   787855623  MARKLAND, MARY         198750
        53     40     02   674451231  BISBANO, HENRY         219055
        54     40     04   720954670  VELOZO, MARIO          242390
        55     40     04   624166876  PARISEAU, WILLIAM      178500
        56     40     04   712133463  PERRY, MARTA           194550
        57     40     06   452892153  CARDIN, FRANCIS        204590
        58     40     06   551502546  FORTIN, EMIL           225450
        59     40     06   574930461  GALLAGHER, MICHAEL     197675
```

■ Figure 8.39 continued

```
60      40      06     683215467  NOTTE, LORENZO         200500
61      40      08     721435472  JOBIN, ANTONIO         214050
62      40      08     490234571  MILLER, RENEE          190570
63      40      08     351566178  TRAMONTE, ESTELLE      213500


-----------------------------------------------------------------------------------------------

***   TOTAL RECORDS PROCESSED:  63

***   TOTAL GOOD RECORDS:  47

***   TOTAL BAD RECORDS:  16

***   TOTAL RECORDS WRITTEN TO VALIDATED FILE:  47

-----------------------------------------------------------------------------------------------


                              ***  END OF REPORT  ***
```

■ Figure 8.40 Listing of the records in VALIDATED-FILE

```
1002214365025ALLEN, ROBERT        150000
1002641275050BRANNIGAN, NICOLE    087525
1002642754040MAIN, CHARLES        128000
1004685264065CARLSON, HOPE        090000
1004251342020FARMER, SUSAN        162000
1004263452070FEINGOLD, HAROLD     125050
1006521244005DWYER, TERRENCE      142580
1006564451045EDWARDS, PETER       108050
1006644353075MANNING, ELIZABETH   135000
1008482131015JANKOWSKI, STANLEY   135000
1008599231085LANGFORD, SARAH      115050
1008521166100PRINGLY, ANNE        109805
2002509862005CORTON, ALEXANDRA    100000
2002480755030TALBOT, JILLIAN      127580
2004479210065BARRESI, JOHN        065000
2004427560010COCHRANE, RUSSELL    146050
2004472847080PROULX, PAULINE      115000
2004375701060QUINN, SUZANNE       132050
2006683309020COSTELLO, JAMES      167050
2006566127070FELDMAN, WALTER      147080
2006571904025LEMERISE, DONALD     185050
2006572495090WORTHEN, MICHAEL     157000
2008812133085KOSINSKI, KATHERINE  112500
3002576400892KING, CHRISTOPHER    189070
3002416892014BERNARD, ISIDORE     203569
3002823144098MAHFUZ, IRENE        185025
3004566731251ROBINSON, GILBERT    210590
3004788230154DONOHUE, PHIL        087500
3004745645270FURTADO, MAUREEN     201540
3006785023157DOLLARHIDE, CHRIS    201570
3006745635164LINCOURT, LORETTA    149500
3008466587165BRAZ, JOAN           231560
3008557318974PRATT, ROBIN         215500
3008487251099MELANSON, GARY       190550
4002452677143BEAUDOIN, ROCKY      221500
4002787855623MARKLAND, MARY       198750
4002674451231BISBANO, HENRY       219055
4004720954670VELOZO, MARIO        242390
4004624166876PARISEAU, WILLIAM    178500
4004712133463PERRY, MARTA         194550
4006452892153CARDIN, FRANCIS      204590
4006551502546FORTIN, EMIL         225450
4006574930461GALLAGHER, MICHAEL   197675
4006683215467NOTTE, LORENZO       200500
4008721435472JOBIN, ANTONIO       214050
4008490234571MILLER, RENEE        190570
4008351566178TRAMONTE, ESTELLE    213500
```

Figure 8.41 INSPECT statement formats

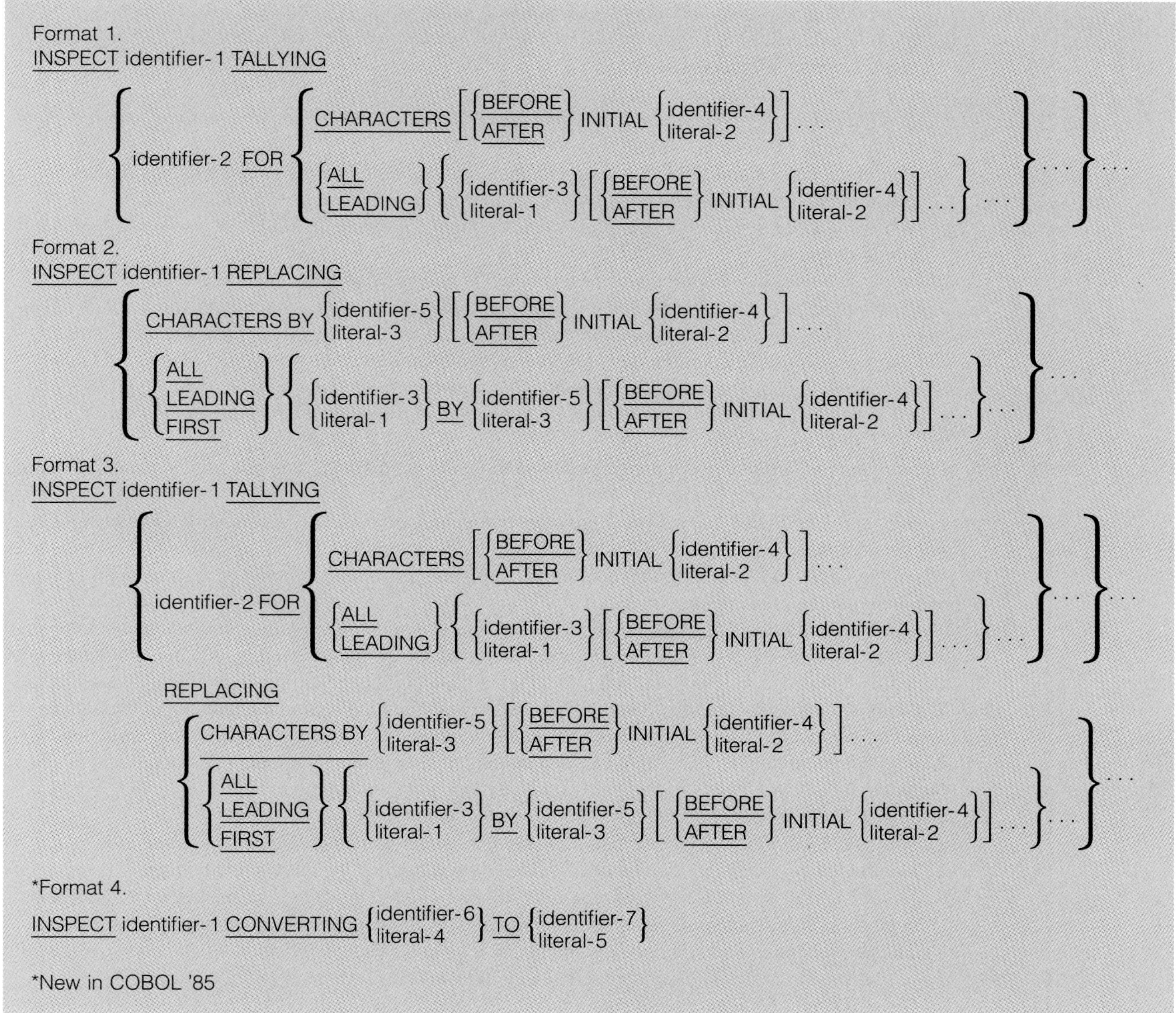

More on the INSPECT Statement

The INSPECT statement has four different formats. The various options allowed in these formats provide a wide range of applications for counting and replacing characters in data items. The formats are listed in Figure 8.41.

Rules Governing the Use of the INSPECT Statement

1. The INSPECT statement counts or replaces occurrences of single characters or groups of characters in a data item.
2. In the formats shown in Figure 8.41, the following definitions apply:
   a. Identifier-1 is the source item that the INSPECT operates on. It must be an elementary or group data item with DISPLAY usage.
   b. Identifier-2 is the tally-counter. It must be an elementary numeric data item. The INSPECT statement does not initialize the tally-counter.
   c. Identifier-3 or literal-1 specifies the character string that INSPECT uses for comparison.
   d. Identifier-4 or literal-2 specifies the character string that delimits the INSPECT operation.

   - **e.** Identifier-5 or literal-3 specifies the one character that replaces all characters.
   - **f.** Identifier-6 or literal-4 specifies the string that contains all the specific characters to be converted to the ones specified by identifier-7 or literal-5.
   - **g.** Identifier-7 or literal-5 specifies the string that contains all the characters that the characters in identifier-6 or literal-4 will convert to.

3. In all formats, a phrase that contains ALL, LEADING, CHARACTERS, FIRST, or CONVERTING can have no more than one BEFORE and one AFTER phrase following it.

4. In format 2, the following rules apply:
   - **a.** The items before and after the word BY must have the same size; if literal-3 is a figurative constant, its size is made equal to that of identifier-3 or literal-1.
   - **b.** When the CHARACTERS phrase is used, the item following INITIAL (if used) must be a single character.

5. In format 4, the items before and after the word TO must be of the same size.

6. The inspection performed by INSPECT includes comparison, setting delimiters for the BEFORE and AFTER phrases, and tallying and/or replacing characters. Inspection begins at the leftmost character position of the source item (or its substring) and proceeds to the rightmost.

7. During inspection of the source item, every matched occurrence of identifier-3 or literal-1 is tallied if the TALLYING format is used and/or replaced by identifier-5 or literal-3 if the REPLACING format is used.

8. The contents of any identifier are treated by INSPECT as character strings. Signed numeric items are treated as unsigned items.

9. If identifier-3 or literal-1 contains more than one character, a match occurs with a substring of the source item only if the strings are equal, character by character.

10. When the CHARACTERS phrase is used, no comparison occurs; rather, a straightforward tallying and/or replacing takes place.

11. Identifier-4 or literal-2 used in the BEFORE phrase specifies the rightmost character in the source item that delimits the substring of the source item subject to the inspection. All the characters to the left of identifier-4 or literal-2 are part of the substring, but identifier-4 or literal-2 is excluded.

12. Identifier-4 or literal-2 used in the AFTER phrase specifies the leftmost character in the source item that delimits the substring of the source item subject to the inspection. All the characters to the right of identifier-4 or literal-2 are part of the substring, but identifier-4 or literal-2 is excluded.

13. In format 1, the following rules apply:
   - **a.** If the ALL phrase is used, the tally-counter (identifier-2) is incremented by 1 for each occurrence of identifier-3 or literal-1 in the source item or its specified substring.
   - **b.** If the LEADING phrase is used, the tally-counter (identifier-2) is incremented by 1 for each contiguous occurrence of identifier-3 or literal-1 in the source item or its specified substring. The first of these occurrences must be at the leftmost character position. If the comparison fails at that position, the tally-counter remains at zero and no further inspection occurs.
   - **c.** If the CHARACTERS phrase is used, the tally-counter (identifier-2) is incremented by 1 for each character in the source item or its specified substring.

14. In format 2, the following rules apply:
   - **a.** The adjectives ALL, LEADING, and FIRST apply to all successive BY phrases until the next adjective (ALL, LEADING, or FIRST) appears.
   - **b.** If ALL is used, each occurrence of identifier-3 or literal-1 in the source item or its specified substring is replaced by identifier-5 or literal-3.
   - **c.** If LEADING is used, then each contiguous occurrence of identifier-3 or literal-1 is replaced by identifier-5 or literal-3, provided the first occurrence is at the leftmost character position in the source item or its specified substring.
   - **d.** If FIRST is used, the leftmost occurrence of identifier-3 or literal-1 in the source item or its specified substring is replaced by identifier-5 or literal-3.
   - **e.** If the CHARACTERS phrase is used, each character in the source item or its specified substring is replaced by identifier-5 or literal-3.

15. In format 3, the INSPECT statement is equivalent to a format 1 statement followed by a format 2 statement. All the format 1 and format 2 specifications apply.

16. Format 4 is equivalent to a format 2 statement using the ALL phrase for each character of identifier-6 or literal-4. For each character in identifier-6 or literal-4, the corresponding replacement character is the one in the same ordinal position in identifier-7 or literal-5.

More INSPECT Statement Examples

Example 1:

Suppose that the field I-SALESPERSON is validated to be alphabetic, but the letters are not all uppercase letters. The following statements change all lowercase letters to uppercase letters.

Option a.

```
INSPECT I-SALESPERSON REPLACING ALL "a" BY "A"
                                    "b" BY "B"
                                    "c" BY "C"
                                     .
                                     .
                                     .
                                    "z" BY "Z".
```

Option b.

```
INSPECT I-SALESPERSON
    CONVERTING "abcdefghijklmnopqrstuvwxyz" TO

               "ABCDEFGHIJKLMNOPQRSTUVWXYZ".
```

Example 2:

Suppose a data entry operator is permitted to enter a numeric value into the field I-CURRENT-SALES with leading spaces. For instance, $54.50 can be entered as (space)(space)5450. The following statement changes the spaces to leading zeros:

```
INSPECT I-CURRENT-SALES REPLACING LEADING SPACES BY ZEROS.
```

Example 3:

Given: `05 O-CURRENT-SALES  PIC $$$$9.99.`

The following statement substitutes an asterisk (*) for each dollar sign ($) beyond the first:

```
INSPECT O-CURRENT-SALES
    REPLACING ALL "$" BY "*" AFTER INITIAL "$".
```

Example 4:

The following statement counts the number of characters in the last name of a salesperson, where the data entry format is last name, comma, first name:

```
INSPECT I-SALESPERSON TALLYING WS-CHAR-COUNT
    FOR CHARACTERS BEFORE INITIAL ",".
```

Example 5:

The following statement tallies the occurrences of the letter *A* in a salesperson's name:

```
INSPECT I-SALESPERSON TALLYING A-CTR FOR ALL "A".
```

Example 6:

The following statement tallies the occurrences of the letter *A* in a salesperson's first name (recall the entry format):

```
INSPECT I-SALESPERSON TALLYING A-CTR FOR ALL "A" AFTER ",".
```

Example 7:

Given:
```
05 O-REPORT-DATE    PIC XX/XX/XX.
  MOVE WS-REPORT-DATE TO O-REPORT-DATE.
```

The following statement changes the format of the date:

```
INSPECT O-REPORT-DATE REPLACING ALL "/" BY "-".
```

For instance, the date 09/06/93 becomes 09-06-93.

Example 8:

Given:
```
05 O-SSN    PIC XXXBXXBXXXX.
  MOVE I-SSN TO O-SSN.
```

The spaces inserted by the B editing character are replaced by hyphens in the following statement:

```
INSPECT O-SSN REPLACING ALL SPACES BY "-".
```

For instance, 324 56 1459 becomes 324-56-1459.

Example 9:

Given:
```
05 WS-PERCENT-CHANGE        PIC S999.
05 O-PERCENT-CHANGE         PIC ZZ9+.
MOVE WS-PERCENT-CHANGE TO O-PERCENT-CHANGE.
```

The following statement changes the format specified by the PICTURE of O-PERCENT-CHANGE:

```
INSPECT O-PERCENT-CHANGE REPLACING LEADING SPACES BY "*"
                                   "+" BY SPACE.
```

If the value moved to the field is +045, the INSPECT statement changes it from (space)45+ to *45(space). If the value moved to the field is −045, the INSPECT statement changes it from (space)45− to *45−.

Reference Modification

Reference modification is a new feature in COBOL '85 that allows the programmer to reference a subgroup of characters that are stored in a data item. The reference is made by specifying first the position of the first character of the subgroup, and then the number of characters to be included in the subgroup. The general format is shown below.

data-name-1 (leftmost-character-position : [length])

For instance, if a Social Security number field is defined by

```
05 I-SSN   PIC X(9),
```

and the value stored in the field is "049523143", then the reference modification I-SSN (1:3) refers to the subgroup "049", I-SSN (4:2) refers to the subgroup "52", and I-SSN (6:4) refers to the subgroup "3143". Statements such as

a. `MOVE I-SSN (1:3) TO FIRST-PART`
b. `MOVE I-SSN (4:2) TO SECOND-PART`
c. `MOVE I-SSN (6:4) TO THIRD-PART`

are valid, provided that the receiving fields have appropriate definitions.

As a second example, suppose the current date is received from the operating system in the format YYMMDD, but for printout purposes, it must be stored in an edited field with format MM/DD/YY. The following data item descriptions and the statements using reference modification would accomplish the required date transfer:

```
05 WS-DATE   PIC X(6).
05 O-DATE    PIC XX/XX/XX.
.
.
ACCEPT WS-DATE FROM DATE.
MOVE WS-DATE (1:2) TO O-DATE (7:2).
MOVE WS-DATE (3:2) TO O-DATE (1:2).
MOVE WS-DATE (5:2) TO O-DATE (4:2).
```

As a third example, in the data validation program of this chapter, reference modification could be used to test the left-justification requirement for the field I-SALESPERSON as follows:

```
IF I-SALESPERSON (1:1) = SPACE
    SET BAD-RECORD TO TRUE
    MOVE "NAME IS NOT LEFT JUSTIFIED" TO O-MESSAGE-AREA
    .
    .
```

Note that I-SALESPERSON (1:1) references the first byte of the data item I-SALESPERSON. If the first byte contains a space, the name is not left-justified in the field.

As a final example, suppose the data item WS-MONTH is defined by PIC X(9), and it is used to store the name of the month. Suppose that the month name abbreviation is needed in the field O-MONTH. The statement MOVE WS-MOVE (1:3) TO O-MONTH moves the first three characters of the month name to the receiving field.

Rules Governing the Use of Reference Modification

In the format of the reference modification on page 502,

1. Data-name-1 can be of any class, but its usage must be DISPLAY. The usage can be specified explicitly or implicitly.
2. The two arguments within parentheses must be separated by a colon.
3. The first argument is required. It specifies the position within data-name-1 of the first character that must be included in the subgroup.
4. The second argument is optional. It specifies the number of characters within data-name-1 that are to be included in the subgroup. If the length argument is omitted, then the default is "the number of characters beginning with the character in leftmost-character-position up to and including the last character in data-name-1".
5. The values of the arguments must be positive integers, and the sum of the two arguments minus 1 must not be greater than the size of data-name-1.
6. The arguments can be literals, data-names, or arithmetic expressions.
7. Data-name-1 can be a subscripted or indexed item. If it is, then the reference modification specifications follow the subscript or index.

   Example: `MOVE WS-MONTH (MONTH-INDEX) (1:3) TO O-MONTH-ABBREV.`

The REDEFINES Clause

The description of a data item in the DATA DIVISION of a program causes the compiler to set aside a storage area whose size and function are specified in one or more PIC clauses. In some programs, it may be desirable to provide alternate descriptions of the same storage area so that the same area can be used in more than one way. For instance, in one case we may want an area to contain a numeric value, whereas in another case we may want the area to contain a brief message. In another situation, a group item may be defined with a particular set of subordinate items, and it may be redefined as another group of subordinate items. COBOL makes this possible by means of the *REDEFINES* clause. This clause provides an alternate description for a storage area that has previously been defined.

The format of the REDEFINES clause is shown in Figure 8.42.

Example 1:

Suppose an item file contains two different kinds of records, a regular-item record and a promotion-item record. On these two types of records, some data fields are identical and others are not. Consider the following descriptions:

```
01 REGULAR-ITEM-RECORD.
   05 REG-ITEM-CODE          PIC X(5)
   05 REG-ITEM-DESCR         PIC X(15).
   05 REG-ITEM-TYPE          PIC X.
      88 REG-ITEM                  VALUE "1".
   05                        PIC X(9).
   05 REG-ITEM-UNIT-PRICE    PIC 9(5)V99.
   05 REG-ITEM-TAX-CODE      PIC X(2).
   05 REG-ITEM-WEIGHT        PIC 9(4)V9.
   05                        PIC X(6).
```

```
01 PROMOTION-ITEM-RECORD.
   05 PROM-ITEM-CODE         PIC X(5).
   05 PROM-ITEM-DESCR        PIC X(15).
   05 PROM-ITEM-TYPE         PIC X.
      88 PROM-ITEM                  VALUE "2".
  05                         PIC X(9).
  05 PROM-ITEM-MAX-QTY       PIC 9(3).
  05 PROM-ITEM-SOURCE        PIC X(10).
  05                         PIC X(7).
```

Note that the first four data fields in both records have identical PIC clauses, whereas the remaining fields of the two records have little in common. In other words, the first thirty bytes of storage contain similar values in both records, but that is not the case for the remaining twenty bytes. The two record descriptions

Figure 8.42 REDEFINES format

level-number $\left\{\begin{array}{l}\text{data-name-1}\\ \text{FILLER}\end{array}\right\}$ <u>REDEFINES</u> data-name-2 can be combined into one provided the last twenty bytes of storage are defined in two different ways. Examine the following record description.

```
01   ITEM-RECORD.
     05 ITEM-CODE            PIC X(5).
     05 ITEM-DESCR           PIC X(15).
     05 ITEM-TYPE            PIC X.
        88 REG-ITEM                  VALUE "1".
        88 PROM-ITEM                 VALUE "2".
     05                      PIC X(9).
     05 REG-ITEM-DATA.
        10 ITEM-UNIT-PRICE   PIC 9(5)V99.
        10 ITEM-TAX-CODE     PIC X(2).
        10 ITEM-WEIGHT       PIC 9(4)V9.
        10                   PIC X(6).
     05 PROM-ITEM-DATA REDEFINES REG-ITEM-DATA.
        10 ITEM-MAX-QTY      PIC 9(3).
        10 ITEM-SOURCE       PIC X(10).
        10                   PIC X(7).
```

It is important for you to realize that the group item REG-ITEM-DATA and the group item PROM-ITEM-DATA both reference the same twenty bytes of storage (PROM-ITEM-DATA is a **redefinition** of REG-ITEM-DATA), but the usage of those twenty bytes is not the same. It should be clear that to properly reference a subordinate item in either of these two groups, the program will need to determine if the record is a regular item record or a promotion item record, and that is easily done by testing the condition name REG-ITEM or PROM-ITEM.

The use of the REDEFINES clause provides the flexibility needed to allow data items of different types within the record and additionally simplifies coding by requiring only one record description, ITEM-RECORD, instead of the two records REGULAR-ITEM-RECORD and PROMOTION-ITEM-RECORD, and by eliminating the need for duplicate data item names, such as REG-ITEM-CODE and PROM-ITEM-CODE.

Example 2:

Assume that a detail line must be printed for each ITEM-RECORD in example 1. One of the printed fields of the detail line must contain the edited value of the unit price if the record is a regular item record, but if the item is a promotion item, the same field of the detail line must contain the message "NO CHARGE". The description of that field might be as follows:

```
05 O-ITEM-UNIT-PRICE                                PIC $ZZ,ZZ9.99.
05 O-PROM-ITEM-PRICE   REDEFINES   O-ITEM-UNIT-PRICE   PIC X(10).
```

When the detail line is being prepared, the data field can be assigned its appropriate value by using a conditional statement, such as

```
IF REG-ITEM
    MOVE ITEM-UNIT-PRICE TO O-ITEM-UNIT-PRICE
ELSE
    MOVE "NO CHARGE" TO O-PROM-ITEM-PRICE
END-IF.
```

Note that the MOVE in the IF clause transfers a numeric value to a numeric-edited field, whereas the MOVE statement in the ELSE clause transfers an alphabetic value to an alphanumeric field. It would be incorrect to code `MOVE "NO CHARGE" TO O-ITEM-UNIT-PRICE` since such a data transfer is invalid; that is, an alphabetic value cannot be moved to a numeric-edited field.

The rules that apply to the use of the REDEFINES clause are listed below.

Rules Governing the Use of the REDEFINES Clause

1. The REDEFINES clause allows different data description entries to describe the same storage area.
2. Data-name-2 is the name that first defines the storage area.
3. The level-number of data-name-1 must be the same as the level-number of data-name-2.
4. The level-number can be any number in the range 01–49. However, it must not be a 01 in the FILE SECTION. (Recall that multiple record descriptions in an input file or an output file share the same storage area.)
5. Data-name-1 and FILLER are optional entries.
6. The description of the redefinition must immediately follow the description of data-name-2.
7. Data-name-2 can be redefined more than once, but, in each case, REDEFINES must be followed by the name that first defines the storage area.

8. The description of data-name-2 must not contain an OCCURS clause, though data-name-2 can be subordinate to one that contains an OCCURS clause. In that case, data-name-2 in the REDEFINES clause must not be subsripted.
9. If the REDEFINES clause is used at a level-number other than 01, the size of data-name-1 must not be greater than the size of data-name-2.
10. The description of data-name-1 must not contain the VALUE clause (unless it is used for a condition-name entry).

Important Terms in Chapter 8

AFTER
BEFORE
CHARACTERS
control break
control field
control group
control group footing
control group heading
CONVERTING
data validation
detail report
FIRST
forcing final totals
INITIAL
input record key field
INSPECT
intermediate totals
LEADING
major control break
minor control break
multilevel report
one-level control break
page heading
REDEFINES
reference modification
REPLACING
rolling forward
subtotaling
summary report
tally-counter
TALLYING
two-level control break

Exercises

1. Explain the general function of a control break.
2. Figure 8.43 shows elements needed in a control break.
   a. What is the first value that will be assigned to the store control field in working storage, WS-STORE-CONTROL?
   b. Code the statement that will be used to test for a control break.
   c. How many records will be read while the first store control value is in the field WS-STORE-CONTROL? Which ones?
   d. How many records will be processed while the first store control value is in the field WS-STORE-CONTROL? Which ones?
   e. At which point will the first value in the store control field WS-STORE-CONTROL be replaced by the second? What will be the second store control value?
   f. Explain what will signal the printing of the store summary for the first store, the second store, and the last store.

Figure 8.43

```
WORKING-STORAGE SECTION.
.
.
.
       05 WS-STORE-CONTROL   PIC XXX.
```

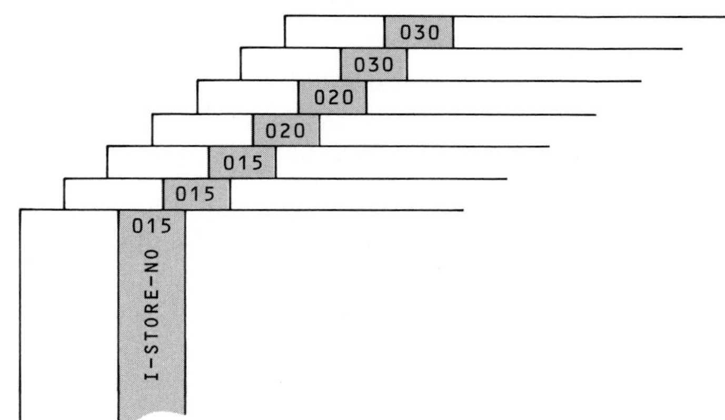

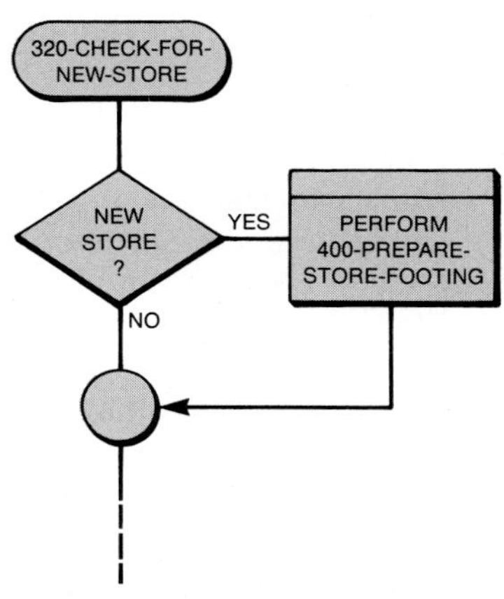

3. Answer the following questions about printed output:
   a. If a printed report contains a line for each input record that was processed, how is it classified?
   b. If in the preparation of a printed report, all the input records are processed before printing a line on the report, how is the report classified?
   c. If a report contains a line for each input record and a line corresponding to a group of records, how is the report classified?
4. In the preparation of a multilevel report, what scheme is often used to highlight summary information at the different levels?
5. A multilevel report must be prepared for the Jocelyn Originals Company. Figure 8.44 shows the format of the report, the input file record layout, and the input file.
   a. Specify the sequence in which the records must be arranged so that names on the report are listed alphabetically within each region, and regions are reported in ascending order.
   b. Name the key field of the input record that is used in the test for a control break.
   c. Which record will trigger the printing of the Region 1 summary? the Region 2 summary? the Region 3 summary? the Region 4 summary?
   d. Identify the lines on the printer spacing chart that belong to the region heading.
   e. Identify the lines on the printer spacing chart that belong to the region footing.
   f. Identify the lines on the printer spacing chart that belong to the company footing.
   g. Which procedure must be executed first, printing the first region heading or reading the first record of the input file? Explain.
   h. Assume that WS-REGION-TOTAL-SALES and WS-COMPANY-TOTAL-SALES name the region and company sales accumulators respectively, and I-YR-SALES contains the yearly sales for a salesperson.
      i. Code statements that will accumulate the region and company sales if subtotaling is used.
      ii. Code statements that will accumulate the region and company sales if rolling forward is used.
      iii. Specify the number of times each statement in part i would be executed and the number of times each statement in part ii would be executed.
6. Refer to Figure 8.44b.
   a. Code an INSPECT statement that will replace the region codes 1, 2, 3, and 4 by the letters A, B, C, and D, respectively.
   b. Code an INSPECT statement that will count the spaces in the name field.
   c. Code an INSPECT statement that will count the zeros in a record.
   d. Code an INSPECT statement that will change all uppercase letters to lowercase letters.
   e. Code an INSPECT statement that will replace a period (.) and a comma (,) in the name field by spaces.
   f. Code an INSPECT statement that will count the characters in a person's last name (characters before the first comma).
7. Given the following item:

```
O-REPORT-DATE    PIC XX/XX/XX.
```

   Code an INSPECT statement that will replace each "/" with a "–".
8. Given the following item:

```
O-NET-SALARY    PIC $$$,$$9.99.
```

   Code an INSPECT statement that will replace every dollar sign ($) except the first with an asterisk (*).
9. Given the following item:

```
O-NET-SALARY PIC $ZZ,ZZ9.99.
```

   Code an INSPECT statement that will replace every space with an asterisk (*).
10. Suppose that an employee identification code is constructed as follows: The first two characters identify the state, the next two identify the store, the next two identify the department in which the employee works, and the next nine are the employee's Social Security number. The code is stored in the field EMPLOYEE-CODE, and the code components are to be moved to WS-STATE, WS-STORE, WS-DEPT, and WS-SSN, respectively. Use reference modification in MOVE statements to effect the transfers.
11. Given the following data item descriptions:

```
05 FIELD-A PIC X(20)    VALUE "ABCDEFGHIJKLMNOPQRST".
05 FIELD-B PIC 9        VALUE 5.
05 FIELD-C PIC 99       VALUE 12.
```

■ Figure 8.44

a.

Printer Spacing Chart

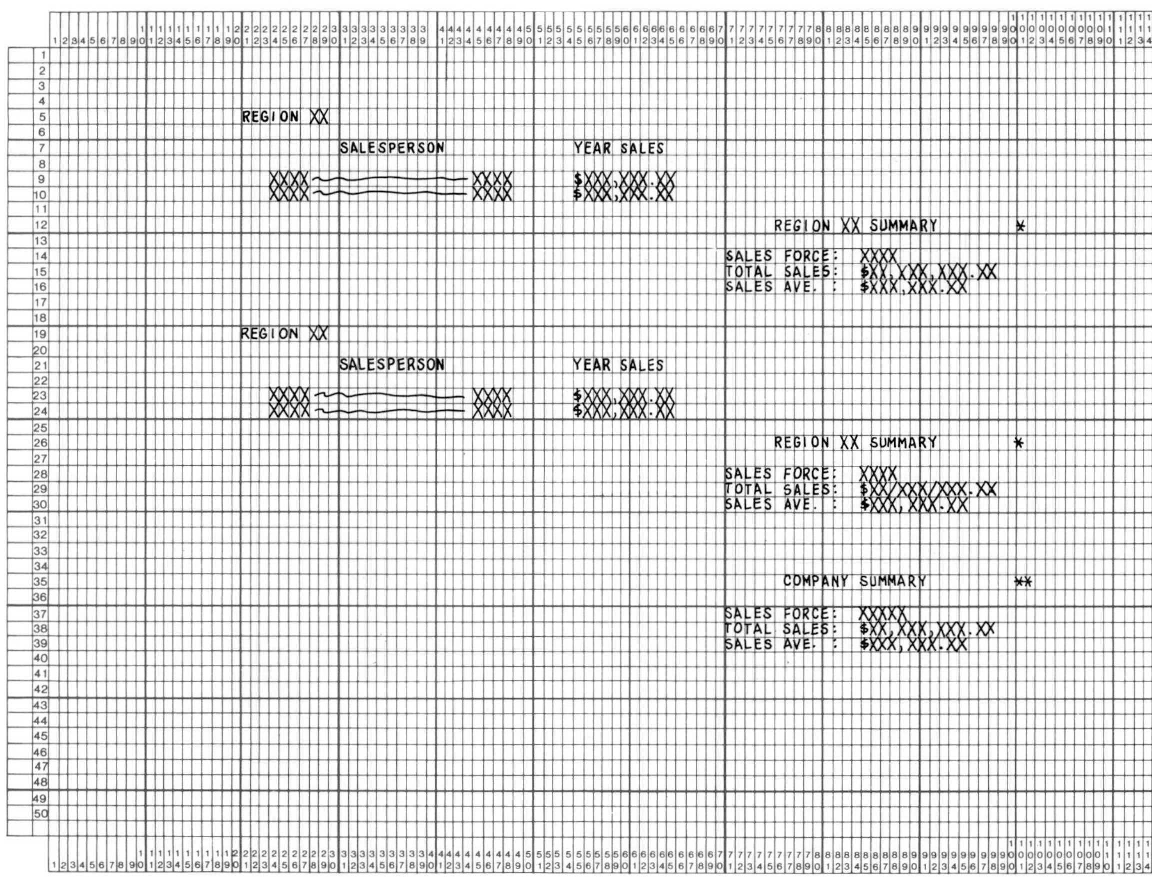

b.

Record Layout Form

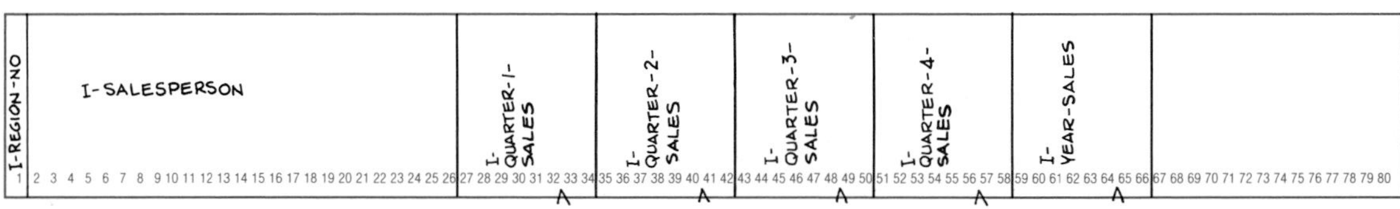

Record Name: SALESPERSON-RECORD

Identify the subgroup specified by each of the following reference modifications:

a. `FIELD-A (3:2)`
b. `FIELD-C (2:1)`
c. `FIELD-C (1:)`
d. `FIELD-A (1: FIELD-B)`
e. `FIELD-A (FIELD-C/2: FIELD-C - 2 * FIELD-B)`
f. `FIELD-A (FIELD-B * 3 + 1:)`

c.

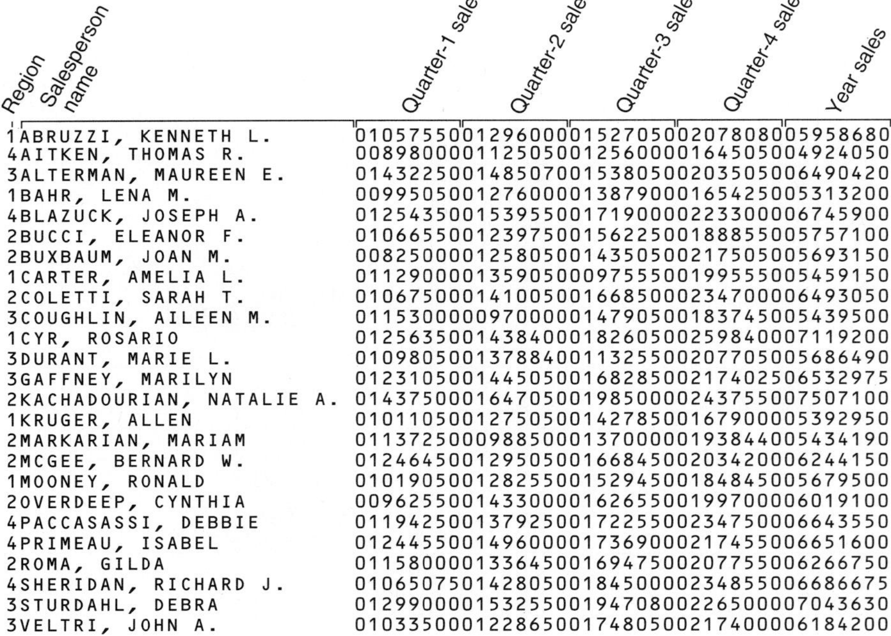


```
1ABRUZZI, KENNETH L.         0105755001296000015270500207808005958680
4AITKEN, THOMAS R.           00898000011250500125600001645050004924050
3ALTERMAN, MAUREEN E.        01432250014850700153805002035050006490420
1BAHR, LENA M.               00995050012760000138790001654250005313200
4BLAZUCK, JOSEPH A.          01254350015395500171900002233000006745900
2BUCCI, ELEANOR F.           01066550012397500156225001888550005757100
2BUXBAUM, JOAN M.            00825000012580500143505002175050005693150
1CARTER, AMELIA L.           01129000013590500097555001995550005459150
2COLETTI, SARAH T.           01067500014100500166850002347000006493050
3COUGHLIN, AILEEN M.         01153000009700000147905001837450005439500
1CYR, ROSARIO                01256350014384000182605002598400007119200
3DURANT, MARIE L.            01098050013788400113255002077050005686490
3GAFFNEY, MARILYN            01231050014450500168285002174025006532975
2KACHADOURIAN, NATALIE A.    01437500016470500198500002437550007507100
1KRUGER, ALLEN               01011050012750500142785001679000005392950
2MARKARIAN, MARIAM           01137250009885000137000001938440005434190
2MCGEE, BERNARD W.           01246450012950500166845002034200006244150
1MOONEY, RONALD              01019050012825500152945001848450005679500
2OVERDEEP, CYNTHIA           00962550014330000162655001997000006019100
4PACCASASSI, DEBBIE          01194250013792500172255002347500006643550
4PRIMEAU, ISABEL             01244550014960000173690002174550006651600
2ROMA, GILDA                 01158000013364500169475002077550006266750
4SHERIDAN, RICHARD J.        01065075014280500184500002348550006686675
3STURDAHL, DEBRA             01299000015325500194708002265000007043630
3VELTRI, JOHN A.             01033500012286500174805002174000006184200
```

12. Refer to example 1 in the REDEFINES section in the text (page 503).

a. What is the size of the record REGULAR-ITEM-RECORD?

b. What is the size of the record PROMOTION-ITEM-RECORD?

c. What is the size of the record ITEM-RECORD?

d. IF ITEM-CODE has value "1" and bytes 31–37 contain the value 01342-95, what is the value displayed by each of the following?

1. DISPLAY ITEM-UNIT-PRICE.
2. DISPLAY ITEM-MAX-QTY.
3. DISPLAY ITEM-SOURCE(1:2).

13. Given the following coding:

```
05 WS-DATE        PIC X(6).
05 WS-SYS-DATE   REDEFINES   WS-DATE.
   10 WS-YR       PIC 9(2).
   10 WS-MO       PIC 9(2).
   10 WS-DAY      PIC 9(2).

ACCEPT WS-DATE FROM DATE.
```

The statement is executed on October 5, 1993.

a. What is the value stored in WS-DATE?

b. What is the value stored in WS-DAY?

c. What is the value stored in WS-MO?

d. What is the value stored in WS-YR?

e. What is the value stored in WS-SYS-DATE?

f. What is the value stored in WS-DATE (3:2)?

Debugging Activities

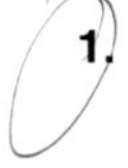

1. The report below contains errors as noted. Find the source of each error in the partial program that follows. (The data file that was used to produce this report is contained in Debugging Activity Data File Set 15 [DD/CD:VIC8DBG1.DAT].)

```
REPORT DATE:  93/09/15                                                                        PAGE  1
                                                 THE SPORTSMAN

                                             SALES ANALYSIS REPORT
                                  missing
                                  entry
           STORE:

                   DEPT NO.        SALESPERSON SSN        SALESPERSON NAME        CURRENT SALES   footing
                                                                                                   without
                                                                                                    detail
                                                             TOTAL SALES FOR STORE    : $    0.00  *  lines

           STORE:  10 - NEW YORK

                   DEPT NO.        SALESPERSON SSN        SALESPERSON NAME        CURRENT SALES

                     02             214 36 5025          ALLEN, ROBERT             $1,500.00
                     02             218 54 6010          BROWN, RAYMOND            $3,022.55
                     02             641 27 5050          BRANNIGAN, NICOLE         $  875.25
                     02             315 46 3030          FOGARTY, JANICE           $1,050.50
                     02             642 75 4040          MAIN, CHARLES             $1,280.00
                     04             685 26 4065          CARLSON, HOPE             $  900.00
                     04             556 23 4035          CRANE, JOHN               $1,050.50
                     04             696 99 6055          DANIELS, JULIA            $2,870.50
                     04             251 34 2020          FARMER, SUSAN             $1,620.00
                     04             263 45 2070          FEINGOLD, HAROLD          $1,250.50
                     04             667 45 1060          HARRISON, LILY            $1,425.80
                     06             521 24 4005          DWYER, TERRENCE           $1,425.80
                     06             564 45 1045          EDWARDS, PETER            $1,080.50
                     06             644 35 3075          MANNING, ELIZABETH        $1,350.00
                     08             377 56 8080          HOWARD, RALPH             $  560.50
                     08             482 13 1015          JANKOWSKI, STANLEY        $1,350.00
                     08             551 16 4090          KELLY, PATRICK            $1,625.00
                     08             599 23 1085          LANGFORD, SARAH           $1,150.50
                     08             521 16 6100          PRINGLY, ANNE             $1,098.05

                                                             TOTAL SALES FOR STORE 10 : $ 26,485.95  *


REPORT DATE:  93/09/15                                                                        PAGE  2
                                                 THE SPORTSMAN

                                             SALES ANALYSIS REPORT

           STORE:  20 - BOSTON

                   DEPT NO.        SALESPERSON SSN        SALESPERSON NAME        CURRENT SALES

                     02             408 93 6050          CORDEIRO, ANTONE          $  100.50
                     02             509 86 2005          CORTON, ALEXANDRA         $1,000.00
                     02             509 18 5045          PINEAULT, NORMAN          $  980.50
                     02             480 75 5030          TALBOT, JILLIAN           $1,275.80
                     04             479 21 0065          BARRESI, JOHN             $  650.00
                     04             427 56 0010          COCHRANE, RUSSELL         $1,460.50
                     04             360 90 2035          PENTA, ROBERT             $1,650.25
                     04             472 84 7080          PROULX, PAULINE           $1,150.00
                     04             375 70 1060          QUINN, SUZANNE            $1,320.50
                     06             683 30 9020          COSTELLO, JAMES           $1,670.50
                     06             418 09 0015          CRAWFORD, SHIRLEY         $1,390.50
                     06             566 12 7070          FELDMAN, WALTER           $1,470.80
                     06             433 40 6075          FERNANDEZ, LOUISE         $2,000.00
                     06             571 90 4025          LEMERISE, DONALD          $1,850.50
                     06             572 49 5090          WORTHEN, MICHAEL          $1,570.00
                     08             762 35 5100          GOYETTE, FRANCES          $  950.00
                     08             812 13 3085          KOSINSKI, KATHERINE       $1,125.00
                     08             804 23 3040          VERMETTE, GLORIA          $1,560.50

                                                             TOTAL SALES FOR STORE 20 : $ 23,175.85  *
```

```
STORE:  30 - CHICAGO

        DEPT NO.        SALESPERSON SSN         SALESPERSON NAME          CURRENT SALES

          02              576 40 0892          KING, CHRISTOPHER            $1,890.70
          02              416 89 2014          BERNARD, ISIDORE             $2,035.69
          02              823 14 4098          MAHFUZ, IRENE                $1,850.25
          04              566 73 1251          ROBINSON, GILBERT            $2,105.90
          04              788 23 0154          DONOHUE, PHIL                $  875.00
          04              607 04 4132          CORRIGAN, ALENE              $1,875.50
          04              745 64 5270          FURTADO, MAUREEN             $2,015.40
          06              820 78 8914          ABALLO, NORMA                $2,350.75
          06              785 02 3157          DOLLARHIDE, CHRIS            $2,015.70
          06              745 63 5164          LINCOURT, LORETTA            $1,495.00
          08              466 58 7165          BRAZ, JOAN                   $2,315.60
          08              557 31 8974          PRATT, ROBIN                 $2,155.00
          08              487 25 1099          MELANSON, GARY               $1,905.50

                                              TOTAL SALES FOR STORE 30 : $ 24,885.99  *

REPORT DATE:  93/09/15                  THE SPORTSMAN                              PAGE  3

                                    SALES ANALYSIS REPORT

STORE:  40 - SEATTLE

        DEPT NO.        SALESPERSON SSN         SALESPERSON NAME          CURRENT SALES

          02              452 67 7143          BEAUDOIN, ROCKY              $2,215.00
          02              787 85 5623          MARKLAND, MARY               $1,987.50
          02              674 45 1231          BISBANO, HENRY               $2,190.55
          04              720 95 4670          VELOZO, MARIO                $2,423.90
          04              624 16 6876          PARISEAU, WILLIAM            $1,785.00
          04              712 13 3463          PERRY, MARTA                 $1,945.50
          06              452 89 2153          CARDIN, FRANCIS              $2,045.90
          06              551 50 2546          FORTIN, EMIL                 $2,254.50
          06              574 93 0461          GALLAGHER, MICHAEL           $1,976.75
          06              683 21 5467          NOTTE, LORENZO               $2,005.00
          08              721 43 5472          JOBIN, ANTONIO               $2,140.50
          08              490 23 4571          MILLER, RENEE                $1,905.70
          08              351 56 6178          TRAMONTE, ESTELLE            $2,135.00

                                              TOTAL SALES FOR STORE 40 : $ 27,010.80  *

STORE:  40 - SEATTLE

        DEPT NO.        SALESPERSON SSN         SALESPERSON NAME          CURRENT SALES

                                                 TOTAL COMPANY SALES : $ 203,117.18  **

                                   ***  END OF REPORT  ***
```

Heading printed but all records processed!

Wrong total

```
PROCEDURE DIVISION.

100-PRODUCE-SALES-REPORT.
    PERFORM 200-START-UP.
    PERFORM 210-PROCESS-SALES-RECORD
        UNTIL NO-MORE-RECORDS.
    PERFORM 220-FINISH-UP.
    STOP RUN.

200-START-UP.
    OPEN INPUT SALES-FILE
         OUTPUT SALES-REPORT.
    PERFORM 300-INITIALIZE-ITEMS.
    PERFORM 600-WRITE-PAGE-HEADING.
    PERFORM 310-READ-SALES-RECORD.

210-PROCESS-SALES-RECORD.
    PERFORM 320-CHECK-FOR-NEW-STORE.
    PERFORM 330-UPDATE-ACCUMULATORS.
    PERFORM 340-PREPARE-SALES-LINE.
    PERFORM 310-READ-SALES-RECORD.
```

```
220-FINISH-UP.
    PERFORM 350-PREPARE-COMPANY-FOOTING.
    WRITE PRINTLINE FROM END-LINE
        AFTER ADVANCING 5 LINES.
    CLOSE SALES-FILE
          SALES-REPORT.

300-INITIALIZE-ITEMS.
    ACCEPT WS-REPORT-DATE FROM DATE.
    MOVE WS-REPORT-DATE TO O-REPORT-DATE.
    SET THERE-IS-A-RECORD TO TRUE.
    INITIALIZE PROGRAM-ACCUMULATORS
               WS-PAGE-NO.
    MOVE SPACES TO SALES-LINE.

310-READ-SALES-RECORD.
    READ SALES-FILE RECORD
        AT END
            SET NO-MORE-RECORDS TO TRUE.

320-CHECK-FOR-NEW-STORE.
    IF I-STORE-NO = WS-STORE-CONTROL
        NEXT SENTENCE
    ELSE
        PERFORM 400-PREPARE-STORE-FOOTING.

330-UPDATE-ACCUMULATORS.
    ADD I-CURRENT-SALES TO WS-STORE-ACCUMULATOR
                           WS-COMPANY-ACCUMULATOR.

340-PREPARE-SALES-LINE.
    MOVE I-DEPT-NO TO O-DEPT-NO.
    MOVE I-SSN TO O-SSN.
    MOVE I-SALESPERSON TO O-SALESPERSON.
    MOVE I-CURRENT-SALES TO O-CURRENT-SALES.
    WRITE PRINTLINE FROM SALES-LINE
        AFTER ADVANCING WS-PROPER-SPACING.
    MOVE 1 TO WS-PROPER-SPACING.

350-PREPARE-COMPANY-FOOTING.
    PERFORM 400-PREPARE-STORE-FOOTING.
    MOVE WS-COMPANY-ACCUMULATOR TO O-COMPANY-SALES.
    WRITE PRINTLINE FROM COMPANY-FOOTING
        AFTER ADVANCING 3 LINES.

400-PREPARE-STORE-FOOTING.
    MOVE WS-STORE-CONTROL TO O-STORE-NO.
    MOVE WS-STORE-ACCUMULATOR TO O-STORE-SALES.
    WRITE PRINTLINE FROM STORE-FOOTING
        AFTER ADVANCING 3 LINES.
    ADD WS-STORE-ACCUMULATOR TO WS-COMPANY-ACCUMULATOR.
    PERFORM 500-CHECK-STORE-CTR.

500-CHECK-STORE-CTR.
    ADD 1 TO WS-STORES-PER-PAGE-CTR.
    IF WS-STORES-PER-PAGE-CTR = 2
        PERFORM 600-WRITE-PAGE-HEADING
    ELSE
        PERFORM 700-WRITE-STORE-HEADING.

600-WRITE-PAGE-HEADING.
    ADD 1 TO WS-PAGE-NO.
    MOVE WS-PAGE-NO TO O-PAGE-NO.
    WRITE PRINTLINE FROM TOP-LINE
        AFTER ADVANCING PAGE.
    WRITE PRINTLINE FROM COMPANY-NAME
        AFTER ADVANCING 1 LINE.
    WRITE PRINTLINE FROM REPORT-NAME
        AFTER ADVANCING 3 LINES.
    INITIALIZE WS-STORES-PER-PAGE-CTR.
    PERFORM 700-WRITE-STORE-HEADING.

700-WRITE-STORE-HEADING.
    MOVE I-STORE-NO TO WS-STORE-CONTROL.
    EVALUATE I-STORE-NO
        WHEN "10"  MOVE "10 - NEW YORK" TO O-STORE-ID
        WHEN "20"  MOVE "20 - BOSTON" TO O-STORE-ID
        WHEN "30"  MOVE "30 - CHICAGO" TO O-STORE-ID
        WHEN "40"  MOVE "40 - SEATTLE" TO O-STORE-ID
        WHEN OTHER
            DISPLAY " ERROR IN STORE NO. FOR " I-SALESPERSON.
    WRITE PRINTLINE FROM STORE-HEADING-1
        AFTER ADVANCING 2 LINES.
    WRITE PRINTLINE FROM STORE-HEADING-2
        AFTER ADVANCING 2 LINES.
    MOVE 2 TO WS-PROPER-SPACING.
    INITIALIZE WS-STORE-ACCUMULATOR.
```

2. The report below contains errors as noted. Find the source of each error in the partial program that follows. (The data file that was used to produce this report is contained in Debugging Activity Data File Set 15 [DD/CD:VIC8DBG1.DAT].)

```
REPORT DATE:  93/09/15                        THE SPORTSMAN                                   PAGE   1


                                           SALES ANALYSIS REPORT
         STORE:   10 - NEW YORK

                   DEPT NO.          SALESPERSON SSN           SALESPERSON NAME           CURRENT SALES

                      02               214 36 5025            ALLEN, ROBERT                 $1,500.00
                      02               218 54 6010            BROWN, RAYMOND                $3,022.55
                      02               641 27 5050            BRANNIGAN, NICOLE             $  875.25
                      02               315 46 3030            FOGARTY, JANICE               $1,050.50
                      02               642 75 4040            MAIN, CHARLES                 $1,280.00
                      04               685 26 4065            CARLSON, HOPE                 $  900.00
                      04               556 23 4035            CRANE, JOHN                   $1,050.50
                      04               696 99 6055            DANIELS, JULIA                $2,870.50
                      04               251 34 2020            FARMER, SUSAN                 $1,620.00
                      04               263 45 2070            FEINGOLD, HAROLD              $1,250.50
                      04               667 45 1060            HARRISON, LILY                $1,425.80
                      06               521 24 4005            DWYER, TERRENCE               $1,425.80
                      06               564 45 1045            EDWARDS, PETER                $1,080.50
                      06               644 35 3075            MANNING, ELIZABETH            $1,350.00
                      08               377 56 8080            HOWARD, RALPH                 $  560.50
                      08               482 13 1015            JANKOWSKI, STANLEY            $1,350.00
                      08               551 16 4090            KELLY, PATRICK                $1,625.00
                      08               599 23 1085            LANGFORD, SARAH               $1,150.50
                      08               521 16 6100            PRINGLY, ANNE                 $1,098.05

                                                             TOTAL SALES FOR STORE 10 : $ 26,485.95 *

        STORE:   20 - BOSTON

                   DEPT NO.          SALESPERSON SSN           SALESPERSON NAME           CURRENT SALES

                      02               408 93 6050            CORDEIRO, ANTONE              $  100.50
                      02               509 86 2005            CORTON, ALEXANDRA             $1,000.00
                      02               509 18 5045            PINEAULT, NORMAN              $  980.50
                      02               480 75 5030            TALBOT, JILLIAN               $1,275.80
                      04               479 21 0065            BARRESI, JOHN                 $  650.00
                      04               427 56 0010            COCHRANE, RUSSELL             $1,460.50
                      04               360 90 2035            PENTA, ROBERT                 $1,650.25
                      04               472 84 7080            PROULX, PAULINE               $1,150.00
                      04               375 70 1060            QUINN, SUZANNE                $1,320.50
                      06               683 30 9020            COSTELLO, JAMES               $1,670.50
                      06               418 09 0015            CRAWFORD, SHIRLEY             $1,390.50
                      06               566 12 7070            FELDMAN, WALTER               $1,470.80
                      06               433 40 6075            FERNANDEZ, LOUISE             $2,000.00
                      06               571 90 4025            LEMERISE, DONALD              $1,850.50
                      06               572 49 5090            WORTHEN, MICHAEL              $1,570.00
                      08               762 35 5100            GOYETTE, FRANCES              $  950.00     Wrong total
                      08               812 13 3085            KOSINSKI, KATHERINE           $1,125.00
                      08               804 23 3040            VERMETTE, GLORIA              $1,560.50

                                                             TOTAL SALES FOR STORE 20 : $ 49,661.80 *

REPORT DATE:  93/09/15                        THE SPORTSMAN                                   PAGE   2

                                           SALES ANALYSIS REPORT

         STORE:   30 - CHICAGO

                   DEPT NO.          SALESPERSON SSN           SALESPERSON NAME           CURRENT SALES

                      02               576 40 0892            KING, CHRISTOPHER             $1,890.70
                      02               416 89 2014            BERNARD, ISIDORE              $2,035.69
                      02               823 14 4098            MAHFUZ, IRENE                 $1,850.25
                      04               566 73 1251            ROBINSON, GILBERT             $2,105.90
                      04               788 23 0154            DONOHUE, PHIL                 $  875.00
                      04               607 04 4132            CORRIGAN, ALENE               $1,875.50
                      04               745 64 5270            FURTADO, MAUREEN              $2,015.40
                      06               820 78 8914            ABALLO, NORMA                 $2,350.75
                      06               785 02 3157            DOLLARHIDE, CHRIS             $2,015.70
                      06               745 63 5164            LINCOURT, LORETTA             $1,495.00
                      08               466 58 7165            BRAZ, JOAN                    $2,315.60
                      08               557 31 8974            PRATT, ROBIN                  $2,155.00     Wrong total
                      08               487 25 1099            MELANSON, GARY                $1,905.50

                                                             TOTAL SALES FOR STORE 30 : $ 74,547.79   *
```

```
STORE:  40 - SEATTLE

        DEPT NO.        SALESPERSON SSN            SALESPERSON NAME          CURRENT SALES

           02             452 67 7143            BEAUDOIN, ROCKY              $2,215.00
           02             787 85 5623            MARKLAND, MARY               $1,987.50
           02             674 45 1231            BISBANO, HENRY               $2,190.55
           04             720 95 4670            VELOZO, MARIO                $2,423.90
           04             624 16 6876            PARISEAU, WILLIAM            $1,785.00
           04             712 13 3463            PERRY, MARTA                 $1,945.50
           06             452 89 2153            CARDIN, FRANCIS              $2,045.90
           06             551 50 2546            FORTIN, EMIL                 $2,254.50
           06             574 93 0461            GALLAGHER, MICHAEL           $1,976.75
           06             683 21 5467            NOTTE, LORENZO               $2,005.00
           08             721 43 5472            JOBIN, ANTONIO               $2,140.50
           08             490 23 4571            MILLER, RENEE                $1,905.70
           08             351 56 6178            TRAMONTE, ESTELLE            $2,135.00

                                                          TOTAL COMPANY SALES : $ 101,558.58  **

                                 ***  END OF REPORT  ***
```

Footing missing for last store

```
PROCEDURE DIVISION.

100-PRODUCE-SALES-REPORT.
    PERFORM 200-START-UP.
    PERFORM 210-PROCESS-SALES-RECORD
        UNTIL NO-MORE-RECORDS.
    PERFORM 220-FINISH-UP.
    STOP RUN.

200-START-UP.
    OPEN INPUT SALES-FILE
         OUTPUT SALES-REPORT.
    PERFORM 300-INITIALIZE-ITEMS.
    PERFORM 310-READ-SALES-RECORD.
    PERFORM 600-WRITE-PAGE-HEADING.

210-PROCESS-SALES-RECORD.
    PERFORM 320-CHECK-FOR-NEW-STORE.
    PERFORM 330-UPDATE-ACCUMULATORS.
    PERFORM 340-PREPARE-SALES-LINE.
    PERFORM 310-READ-SALES-RECORD.

220-FINISH-UP.
    PERFORM 350-PREPARE-COMPANY-FOOTING.
    WRITE PRINTLINE FROM END-LINE
        AFTER ADVANCING 5 LINES.
    CLOSE SALES-FILE
          SALES-REPORT.

300-INITIALIZE-ITEMS.
    ACCEPT WS-REPORT-DATE FROM DATE.
    MOVE WS-REPORT-DATE TO O-REPORT-DATE.
    SET THERE-IS-A-RECORD TO TRUE.
    INITIALIZE PROGRAM-ACCUMULATORS
               WS-PAGE-NO.
    MOVE SPACES TO SALES-LINE.

310-READ-SALES-RECORD.
    READ SALES-FILE RECORD
        AT END
            SET NO-MORE-RECORDS TO TRUE.

320-CHECK-FOR-NEW-STORE.
    IF I-STORE-NO = WS-STORE-CONTROL
        NEXT SENTENCE
    ELSE
        PERFORM 400-PREPARE-STORE-FOOTING.

330-UPDATE-ACCUMULATORS.
    ADD I-CURRENT-SALES TO WS-STORE-ACCUMULATOR
                           WS-COMPANY-ACCUMULATOR.

340-PREPARE-SALES-LINE.
    MOVE I-DEPT-NO TO O-DEPT-NO.
    MOVE I-SSN TO O-SSN.
    MOVE I-SALESPERSON TO O-SALESPERSON.
    MOVE I-CURRENT-SALES TO O-CURRENT-SALES.
    WRITE PRINTLINE FROM SALES-LINE
        AFTER ADVANCING WS-PROPER-SPACING.
    MOVE 1 TO WS-PROPER-SPACING.
```

```
350-PREPARE-COMPANY-FOOTING.
    MOVE WS-COMPANY-ACCUMULATOR TO O-COMPANY-SALES.
    WRITE PRINTLINE FROM COMPANY-FOOTING
        AFTER ADVANCING 3 LINES.

400-PREPARE-STORE-FOOTING.
    MOVE WS-STORE-CONTROL TO O-STORE-NO.
    MOVE WS-STORE-ACCUMULATOR TO O-STORE-SALES.
    WRITE PRINTLINE FROM STORE-FOOTING
        AFTER ADVANCING 2 LINES.
    PERFORM 500-CHECK-STORE-CTR.

500-CHECK-STORE-CTR.
    ADD 1 TO WS-STORES-PER-PAGE-CTR.
    IF WS-STORES-PER-PAGE-CTR = 2
        PERFORM 600-WRITE-PAGE-HEADING
    ELSE
        PERFORM 700-WRITE-STORE-HEADING.

600-WRITE-PAGE-HEADING.
    ADD 1 TO WS-PAGE-NO.
    MOVE WS-PAGE-NO TO O-PAGE-NO.
    WRITE PRINTLINE FROM TOP-LINE
        AFTER ADVANCING PAGE.
    WRITE PRINTLINE FROM COMPANY-NAME
        AFTER ADVANCING 1 LINE.
    WRITE PRINTLINE FROM REPORT-NAME
        AFTER ADVANCING 3 LINES.
    INITIALIZE WS-STORES-PER-PAGE-CTR.
    PERFORM 700-WRITE-STORE-HEADING.

700-WRITE-STORE-HEADING.
    MOVE I-STORE-NO TO WS-STORE-CONTROL.
    EVALUATE I-STORE-NO
        WHEN "10"  MOVE "10 - NEW YORK" TO O-STORE-ID
        WHEN "20"  MOVE "20 - BOSTON" TO O-STORE-ID
        WHEN "30"  MOVE "30 - CHICAGO" TO O-STORE-ID
        WHEN "40"  MOVE "40 - SEATTLE" TO O-STORE-ID
        WHEN OTHER
            DISPLAY " ERROR IN STORE NO. FOR " I-SALESPERSON.
    WRITE PRINTLINE FROM STORE-HEADING-1
        AFTER ADVANCING 2 LINES.
    WRITE PRINTLINE FROM STORE-HEADING-2
        AFTER ADVANCING 2 LINES.
    MOVE 2 TO WS-PROPER-SPACING.
```

3. The report below contains errors as noted. Find the source of each error in the partial program that follows. (The data file that was used to produce this output is contained in Debugging Activity, Data File Set 11.)

```
REPORT DATE:  93/09/15                     THE SPORTSMAN                              PAGE  1


                                       SALES ANALYSIS REPORT

        STORE:  10 - NEW YORK

             DEPT NO.        SALESPERSON SSN          SALESPERSON NAME          CURRENT SALES

               02              214 36 5025           ALLEN, ROBERT               $1,500.00
               02              218 54 6010           BROWN, RAYMOND              $3,022.55
               02              641 27 5050           BRANNIGAN, NICOLE           $  875.25
               02              315 46 3030           FOGARTY, JANICE             $1,050.50
               02              642 75 4040           MAIN, CHARLES               $1,280.00
               04              685 26 4065           CARLSON, HOPE               $  900.00
               04              556 23 4035           CRANE, JOHN                 $1,050.50
               04              696 99 6055           DANIELS, JULIA              $2,870.50
               04              251 34 2020           FARMER, SUSAN               $1,620.00
               04              263 45 2070           FEINGOLD, HAROLD            $1,250.50
               04              667 45 1060           HARRISON, LILY              $1,425.80
               06              521 24 4005           DWYER, TERRENCE             $1,425.80
               06              564 45 1045           EDWARDS, PETER              $1,080.50
               06              644 35 3075           MANNING, ELIZABETH          $1,350.00
               08              377 56 8080           HOWARD, RALPH               $  560.50
               08              482 13 1015           JANKOWSKI, STANLEY          $1,350.00
               08              551 16 4090           KELLY, PATRICK              $1,625.00
               08              599 23 1085           LANGFORD, SARAH             $1,150.50
               08              521 16 6100           PRINGLY, ANNE               $1,098.05
               02              408 93 6050           CORDEIRO, ANTONE            $  100.50   <-- Store 10 footing missing
               02              509 86 2005           CORTON, ALEXANDRA           $1,000.00
               02              509 18 5045           PINEAULT, NORMAN            $  980.50
               02              480 75 5030           TALBOT, JILLIAN             $1,275.80
               04              479 21 0065           BARRESI, JOHN               $  650.00
               04              427 56 0010           COCHRANE, RUSSELL           $1,460.50
               04              360 90 2035           PENTA, ROBERT               $1,650.25
               04              472 84 7080           PROULX, PAULINE             $1,150.00
```

```
           04          375 70 1060          QUINN, SUZANNE                $1,320.50
           06          683 30 9020          COSTELLO, JAMES               $1,670.50
           06          418 09 0015          CRAWFORD, SHIRLEY             $1,390.50
           06          566 12 7070          FELDMAN, WALTER               $1,470.80
           06          433 40 6075          FERNANDEZ, LOUISE             $2,000.00
           06          571 90 4025          LEMERISE, DONALD              $1,850.50
           06          572 49 5090          WORTHEN, MICHAEL              $1,570.00
           08          762 35 5100          GOYETTE, FRANCES              $  950.00
           08          812 13 3085          KOSINSKI, KATHERINE           $1,125.00
           08          804 23 3040          VERMETTE, GLORIA              $1,560.50
           02          576 40 0892          KING, CHRISTOPHER             $1,890.70
           02          416 89 2014          BERNARD, ISIDORE              $2,035.69
           02          823 14 4098          MAHFUZ, IRENE                 $1,850.25
           04          566 73 1251          ROBINSON, GILBERT             $2,105.90
           04          788 23 0154          DONOHUE, PHIL                 $  875.00
           04          607 04 4132          CORRIGAN, ALENE               $1,875.50
           04          745 64 5270          FURTADO, MAUREEN              $2,015.40
           06          820 78 8914          ABALLO, NORMA                 $2,350.75
           06          785 02 3157          DOLLARHIDE, CHRIS             $2,015.70
           06          745 63 5164          LINCOURT, LORETTA             $1,495.00
           08          466 58 7165          BRAZ, JOAN                    $2,315.60
           08          557 31 8974          PRATT, ROBIN                  $2,155.00
           08          487 25 1099          MELANSON, GARY                $1,905.50
           02          452 67 7143          BEAUDOIN, ROCKY               $2,215.00
           02          787 85 5623          MARKLAND, MARY                $1,987.50
           02          674 45 1231          BISBANO, HENRY                $2,190.55
           04          720 95 4670          VELOZO, MARIO                 $2,423.90
           04          624 16 6876          PARISEAU, WILLIAM             $1,785.00
           04          712 13 3463          PERRY, MARTA                  $1,945.50
           06          452 89 2153          CARDIN, FRANCIS               $2,045.90
           06          551 50 2546          FORTIN, EMIL                  $2,254.50
           06          574 93 0461          GALLAGHER, MICHAEL            $1,976.75
           06          683 21 5467          NOTTE, LORENZO                $2,005.00
           08          721 43 5472          JOBIN, ANTONIO                $2,140.50
           08          490 23 4571          MILLER, RENEE                 $1,905.70
           08          351 56 6178          TRAMONTE, ESTELLE             $2,135.00

                                        TOTAL SALES FOR STORE 40 :  $101,558.59*

    STORE:  40 - SEATTLE

            DEPT NO.       SALESPERSON SSN          SALESPERSON NAME          CURRENT SALES

                                                  TOTAL COMPANY SALES :
$ 101,558.59  **


                          ***  END OF REPORT  ***
```

Store 20 footing missing

Store 30 footing missing

Heading printed after all records have been processed

Wrong total for store 40

```
PROCEDURE DIVISION.

100-PRODUCE-SALES-REPORT.
    PERFORM 200-START-UP.
    PERFORM 210-PROCESS-SALES-RECORD
        UNTIL NO-MORE-RECORDS.
    PERFORM 220-FINISH-UP.
    STOP RUN.

200-START-UP.
    OPEN INPUT SALES-FILE
         OUTPUT SALES-REPORT.
    PERFORM 300-INITIALIZE-ITEMS.
    PERFORM 310-READ-SALES-RECORD.
    PERFORM 600-WRITE-PAGE-HEADING.

210-PROCESS-SALES-RECORD.
    MOVE I-STORE-NO TO WS-STORE-CONTROL.
    PERFORM 320-CHECK-FOR-NEW-STORE.
    PERFORM 330-UPDATE-ACCUMULATORS.
    PERFORM 340-PREPARE-SALES-LINE.
    PERFORM 310-READ-SALES-RECORD.

220-FINISH-UP.
    PERFORM 350-PREPARE-COMPANY-FOOTING.
    WRITE PRINTLINE FROM END-LINE
        AFTER ADVANCING 5 LINES.
    CLOSE SALES-FILE
          SALES-REPORT.
```

```
300-INITIALIZE-ITEMS.
    ACCEPT WS-REPORT-DATE FROM DATE.
    MOVE WS-REPORT-DATE TO O-REPORT-DATE.
    SET THERE-IS-A-RECORD TO TRUE.
    INITIALIZE PROGRAM-ACCUMULATORS
               WS-PAGE-NO.
    MOVE SPACES TO SALES-LINE.

310-READ-SALES-RECORD.
    READ SALES-FILE RECORD
        AT END
            SET NO-MORE-RECORDS TO TRUE.

320-CHECK-FOR-NEW-STORE.
    IF I-STORE-NO = WS-STORE-CONTROL
        NEXT SENTENCE
    ELSE
        PERFORM 400-PREPARE-STORE-FOOTING.

330-UPDATE-ACCUMULATORS.
    ADD I-CURRENT-SALES TO WS-STORE-ACCUMULATOR
                           WS-COMPANY-ACCUMULATOR.

340-PREPARE-SALES-LINE.
    MOVE I-DEPT-NO TO O-DEPT-NO.
    MOVE I-SSN TO O-SSN.
    MOVE I-SALESPERSON TO O-SALESPERSON.
    MOVE I-CURRENT-SALES TO O-CURRENT-SALES.
    WRITE PRINTLINE FROM SALES-LINE
        AFTER ADVANCING WS-PROPER-SPACING.
    MOVE 1 TO WS-PROPER-SPACING.

350-PREPARE-COMPANY-FOOTING.
    PERFORM 400-PREPARE-STORE-FOOTING.
    MOVE WS-COMPANY-ACCUMULATOR TO O-COMPANY-SALES.
    WRITE PRINTLINE FROM COMPANY-FOOTING
        AFTER ADVANCING 3 LINES.

400-PREPARE-STORE-FOOTING.
    MOVE WS-STORE-CONTROL TO O-STORE-NO.
    MOVE WS-STORE-ACCUMULATOR TO O-STORE-SALES.
    WRITE PRINTLINE FROM STORE-FOOTING
        AFTER ADVANCING 2 LINES.
    PERFORM 500-CHECK-STORE-CTR.

500-CHECK-STORE-CTR.
    ADD 1 TO WS-STORES-PER-PAGE-CTR.
    IF WS-STORES-PER-PAGE-CTR = 2
        PERFORM 600-WRITE-PAGE-HEADING
    ELSE
        PERFORM 700-WRITE-STORE-HEADING.

600-WRITE-PAGE-HEADING.
    ADD 1 TO WS-PAGE-NO.
    MOVE WS-PAGE-NO TO O-PAGE-NO.
    WRITE PRINTLINE FROM TOP-LINE
        AFTER ADVANCING PAGE.
    WRITE PRINTLINE FROM COMPANY-NAME
        AFTER ADVANCING 1 LINE.
    WRITE PRINTLINE FROM REPORT-NAME
        AFTER ADVANCING 3 LINES.
    INITIALIZE WS-STORES-PER-PAGE-CTR.
    PERFORM 700-WRITE-STORE-HEADING.

700-WRITE-STORE-HEADING.
    EVALUATE I-STORE-NO
        WHEN "10"  MOVE "10 - NEW YORK" TO O-STORE-ID
        WHEN "20"  MOVE "20 - BOSTON" TO O-STORE-ID
        WHEN "30"  MOVE "30 - CHICAGO" TO O-STORE-ID
        WHEN "40"  MOVE "40 - SEATTLE" TO O-STORE-ID
        WHEN OTHER
            DISPLAY " ERROR IN STORE NO. FOR " I-SALESPERSON.
    WRITE PRINTLINE FROM STORE-HEADING-1
        AFTER ADVANCING 2 LINES.
    WRITE PRINTLINE FROM STORE-HEADING-2
        AFTER ADVANCING 2 LINES.
    MOVE 2 TO WS-PROPER-SPACING.
    INITIALIZE WS-STORE-ACCUMULATOR.
```

Programming Exercises

Programming Exercise I

The management of International Haberdashery wants a sales analysis report that will list all of its salespersons by store. The report is to be multilevel; that is, it must provide sales information for individual salespersons, sales information for each store, and sales information for the company as a whole.

For each salesperson, the report must specify the current sales, interpret the current sales as a percent of the salesperson's quota, and provide a rating of the salesperson's performance: print a double star if sales are 20 percent or more above quota, and print one star if sales are 10 percent or more (but less than 20 percent) above quota.

For each store, the report must print a store heading and a store footing. The store footing must show the store's total sales, the average sales per salesperson, and the top salesperson for the store.

For the company, the report must print a company footing that shows the total sales and the top salesperson.

The input file consists of salespersons' records, arranged alphabetically by store, with store numbers in ascending order. Each record contains the following data:

cc 1–2	Store number
cc 3–22	Salesperson name
cc 48–55	Current sales (format: xxxxxx.xx)
cc 56–63	Sales quota (format: xxxxxx.xx)

The report should be formatted as shown in the printer spacing chart of Figure 8.45. There should be no more than two stores reported per page, and the company footing should be printed immediately following the store footing for the last store.

The layout of the input record, the printer spacing chart, the system flowchart, the structure chart, the program pseudocode, and the program flowchart are provided in Figure 8.45.

Your assignment is to implement the program design; that is, code, compile, debug, and run the program successfully. Use the data in Data File Set 5 (see Appendix C [DD/CD:VIC8EX1.DAT]) as a sample input file, and use the current date as the report date.

Figure 8.45

Record Layout Form

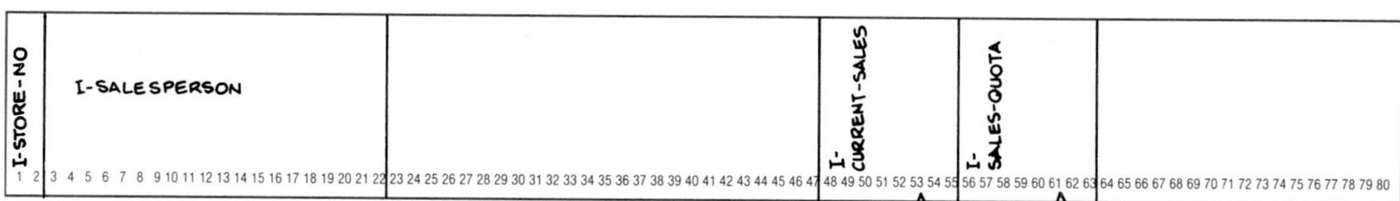

Record Name: SALES-RECORD

■ **Figure 8.45** continued

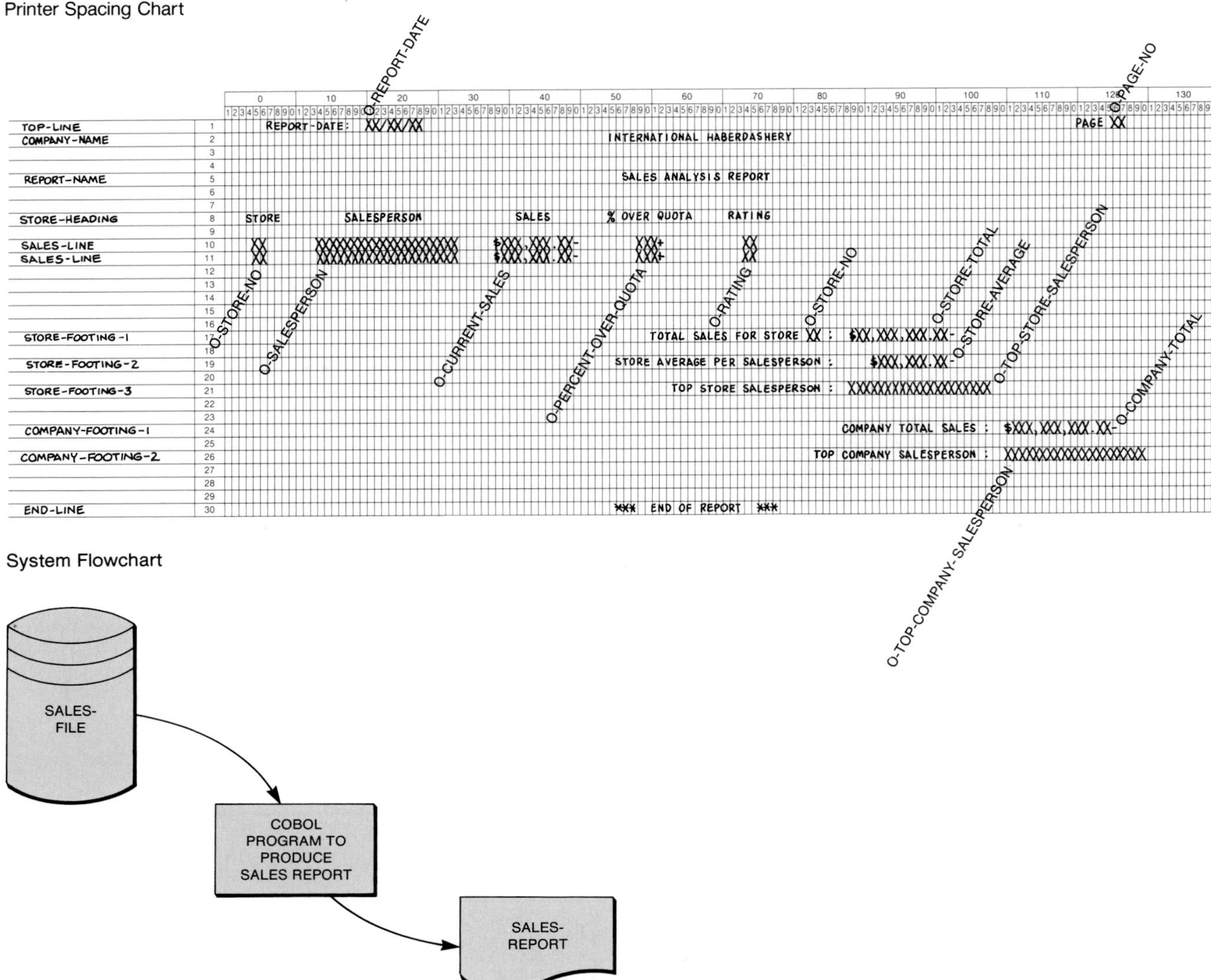

■ **Figure 8.45** continued

Structure Chart

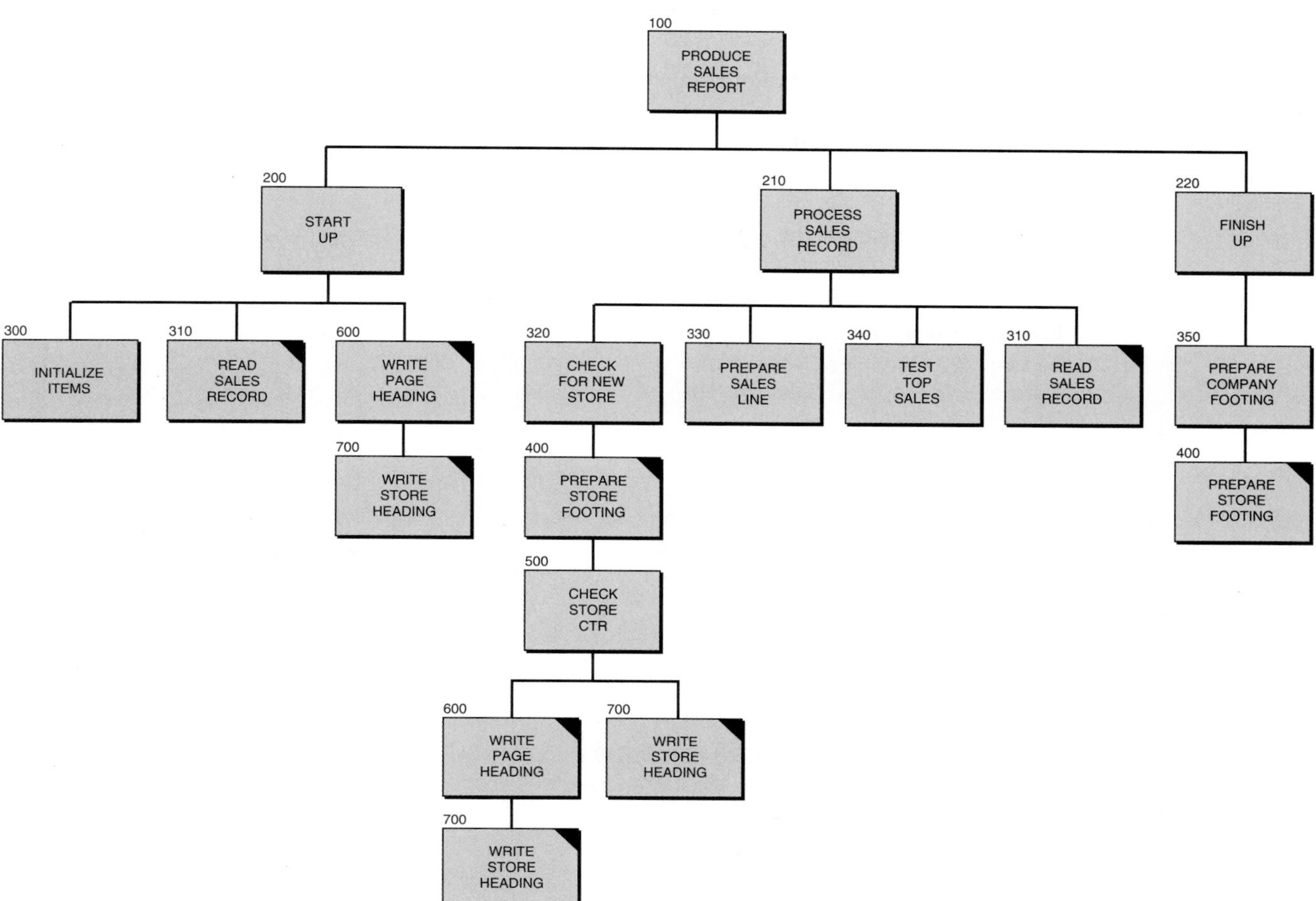

■ **Figure 8.45** continued

Program Pseudocode

100-Produce-Sales-Report.

1. Perform 200-Start-Up.
2. Perform 210-Process-Sales-Record until no more records.
3. Perform 220-Finish-Up.
4. Stop the run.

200-Start-Up.

1. Open the files.
2. Perform 300-Initialize-Items.
3. Perform 310-Read-Sales-Record.
4. Perform 600-Write-Page-Heading.

210-Process-Sales-Record.

1. Perform 320-Check-For-New-Store.
2. Perform 330-Prepare-Sales-Line.
3. Perform 340-Test-Top-Sales.
4. Perform 310-Read-Sales-Record.

220-Finish-Up.

1. Perform 350-Prepare-Company-Footing.
2. Move End-Line to the output area Printline.
3. After advancing 5 lines, write the output record Printline.
4. Close the files.

300-Initialize-Items.

1. Obtain the date from the system.
2. Move the date to Top-Line date.
3. Set page-number to zero.
4. Set the end-of-file flag WS-MORE-RECORDS to "YES".
5. Set the top-company-sales and the company-total-sales to zero.
6. Clear the record area Sales-Line.

310-Read-Sales-Record.

1. Read an input Sales-Record.
2. Test for end-of-file record;
   if EOF record reached, set the flag WS-MORE-RECORDS to "NO ".

320-Check-For-New-Store.

1. If input store-number is not equal to store-control value,
   perform 400-Prepare-Store-Footing.

330-Prepare-Sales-Line.

1. Move input store-number to Sales-Line store-number.
2. Move input salesperson to Sales-Line salesperson.
3. Move input current-sales to Sales-Line current-sales.
4. Subtract input sales-quota from input current-sales;
   then, divide the difference by input sales-quota,
   and multiply the quotient by 100 to equal percent-over-quota.
5. Move percent-over-quota to Sales-Line percent-over-quota.
6. Test input current-sales:
   a. if > or = 120% of input sales-quota, move "**" to Sales-Line rating;
   b. if < 120% but > or = 110% of input sales-quota, move "*" to Sales-Line rating;
   c. if < 110% of input sales-quota, move spaces to Sales-Line rating.
7. Move Sales-Line to the output area Printline.
8. After advancing proper-spacing, write the output record Printline.
9. Add 1 to salesperson-counter.
10. Add input current-sales to store-total-sales.
11. Set proper-spacing to 1.

340-Test-Top-Sales.

1. If input current-sales is greater than top-store-sales,
   then, move input current-sales to top-store-sales, and
   move input salesperson to top-store-salesperson.
2. If input current-sales is greater than top-company-sales,
   then, move input current-sales to top-company-sales, and
   move input salesperson to top-company-salesperson.

350-Prepare-Company-Footing.

1. Perform 400-Prepare-Store-Footing.
2. Move company-total-sales to Company-Footing-1 company-total.
3. Move Company-Footing-1 to the output area Printline.
4. After advancing 3 lines, write the output record Printline.
5. Move top-company-salesperson to Company-Footing-2 top-company-salesperson.
6. Move Company-Footing-2 to the output area Printline.
7. After advancing 2 lines, write the output record Printline.

400-Prepare-Store-Footing.

1. Move store-control to Store-Footing-1 store-number.
2. Move store-total-sales to Store-Footing-1 store-total.
3. Move Store-Footing-1 to the output area Printline.
4. After advancing 2 lines, write the output record Printline.
5. Divide store-total-sales by salesperson-counter to equal Store-Footing-2 store-average.
6. Move Store-Footing-2 to the output area Printline.
7. After advancing 2 lines, write the output record Printline.
8. Move top-store-salesperson to Store-Footing-3 top-store-salesperson.
9. Move Store-Footing-3 to the output area Printline.
10. After advancing 2 lines, write the output record Printline.
11. Add store-total-sales to company-total-sales.
12. If the flag WS-MORE-RECORDS is equal to "YES",
    then, perform 500-Check-Store-Ctr.

500-Check-Store-Ctr.

1. Add 1 to stores-per-page-ctr.
2. If stores-per-page-ctr is equal to 2,
   then, perform 600-Write-Page-Heading;
   else, perform 700-Write-Store-Heading.

600-Write-Page-Heading.

1. Add 1 to page-number.
2. Move page-number to Top-Line page-number.
3. Move Top-Line to the output area Printline.
4. After advancing to the top of a new page,
   write the output record Printline.
5. Move Company-Name to the output area Printline.
6. After advancing 1 line, write the output record Printline.
7. Move Report-Name to the output area Printline.
8. After advancing 3 lines, write the output record Printline.
9. Initialize the stores-per-page-counter.
10. Perform 700-Write-Store-Heading.

700-Write-Store-Heading.

1. Move input store-number to store-control.
2. Move Store-Heading to the output area Printline.
3. After advancing 3 lines, write the output record Printline.
4. Set salesperson-counter, top-store-sales, and store-total-sales to zero.
5. Move 2 to proper-spacing.

■ **Figure 8.45** continued

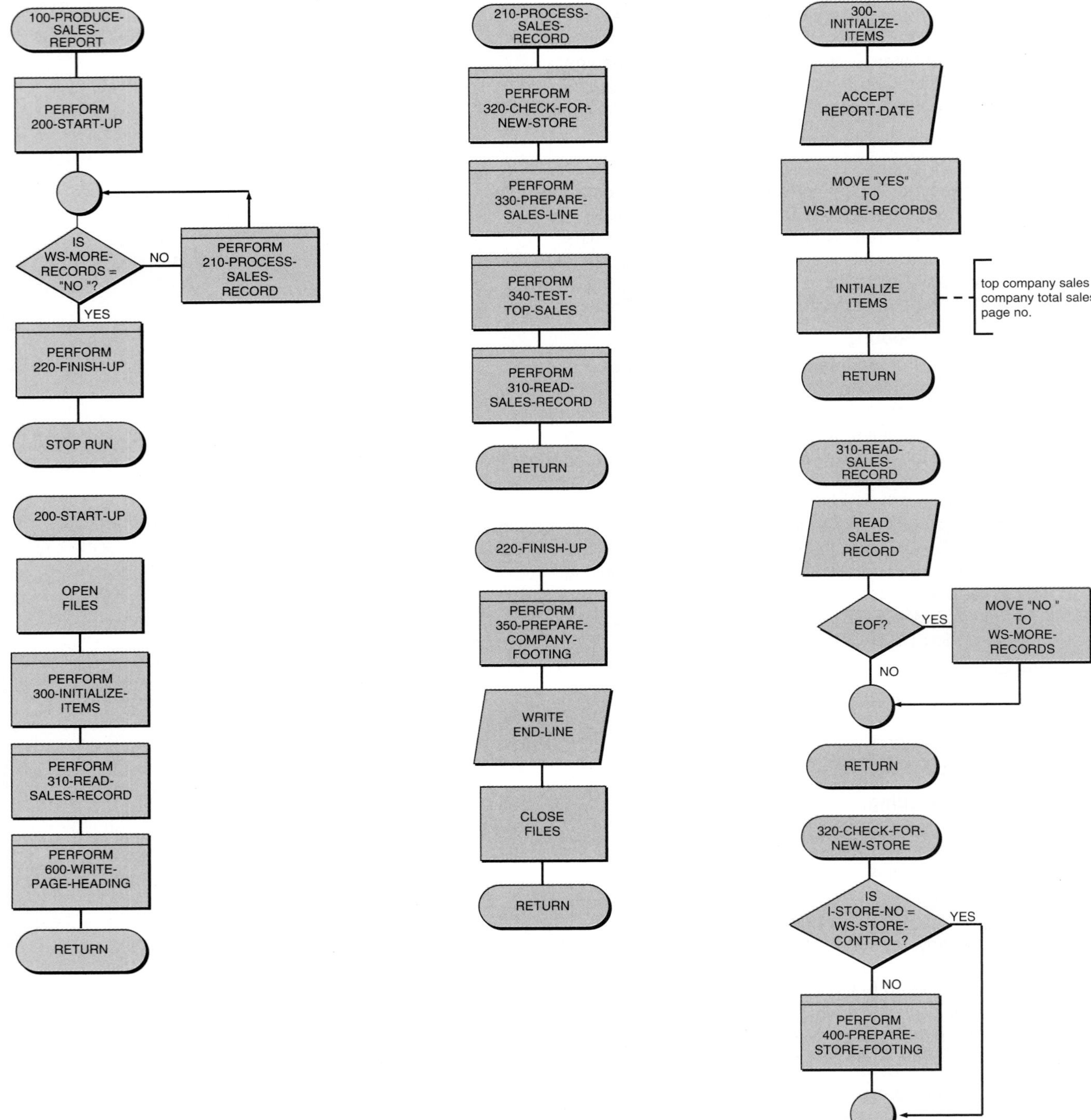

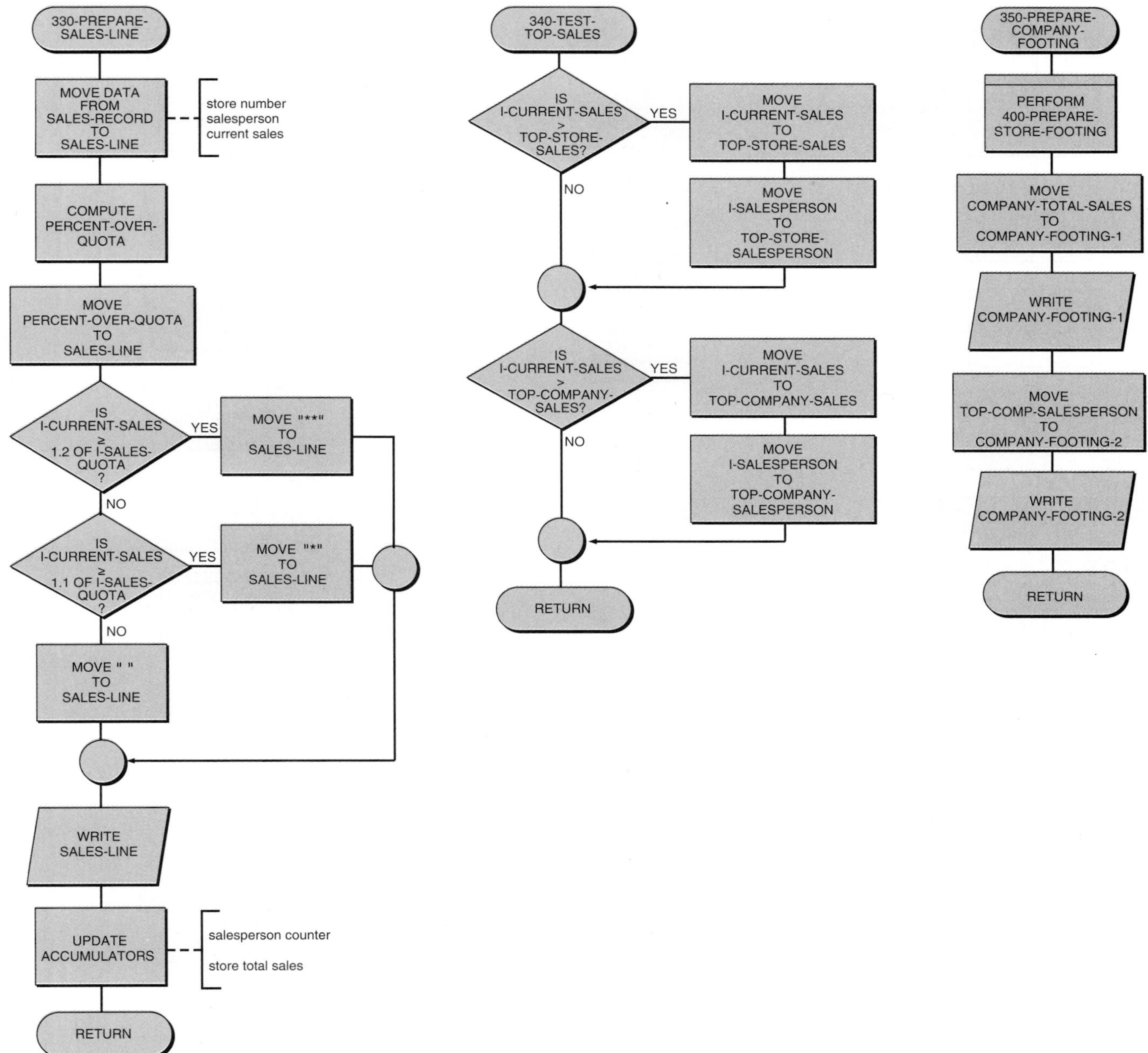
330-PREPARE-SALES-LINE
MOVE DATA FROM SALES-RECORD TO SALES-LINE
store number
salesperson
current sales
COMPUTE PERCENT-OVER-QUOTA
MOVE PERCENT-OVER-QUOTA TO SALES-LINE
IS I-CURRENT-SALES ≥ 1.2 OF I-SALES-QUOTA ?
YES
MOVE "***" TO SALES-LINE
NO
IS I-CURRENT-SALES ≥ 1.1 OF I-SALES-QUOTA ?
YES
MOVE "*" TO SALES-LINE
NO
MOVE " " TO SALES-LINE
WRITE SALES-LINE
UPDATE ACCUMULATORS
salesperson counter
store total sales
RETURN
340-TEST-TOP-SALES
IS I-CURRENT-SALES > TOP-STORE-SALES?
YES
MOVE I-CURRENT-SALES TO TOP-STORE-SALES
MOVE I-SALESPERSON TO TOP-STORE-SALESPERSON
NO
IS I-CURRENT-SALES > TOP-COMPANY-SALES?
YES
MOVE I-CURRENT-SALES TO TOP-COMPANY-SALES
MOVE I-SALESPERSON TO TOP-COMPANY-SALESPERSON
NO
RETURN
350-PREPARE-COMPANY-FOOTING
PERFORM 400-PREPARE-STORE-FOOTING
MOVE COMPANY-TOTAL-SALES TO COMPANY-FOOTING-1
WRITE COMPANY-FOOTING-1
MOVE TOP-COMP-SALESPERSON TO COMPANY-FOOTING-2
WRITE COMPANY-FOOTING-2
RETURN

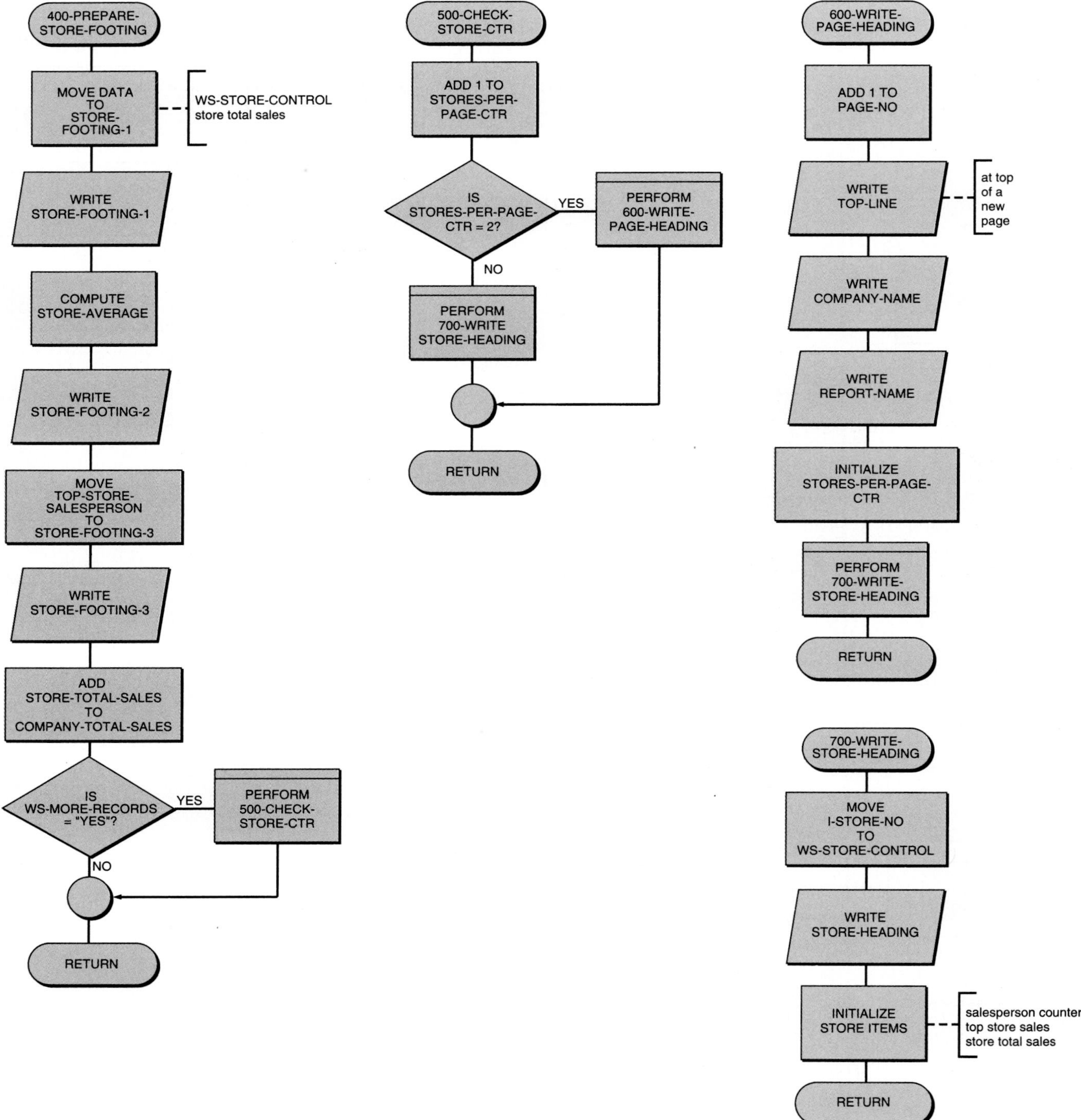
400-PREPARE-STORE-FOOTING
MOVE DATA TO STORE-FOOTING-1
WS-STORE-CONTROL
store total sales
WRITE STORE-FOOTING-1
COMPUTE STORE-AVERAGE
WRITE STORE-FOOTING-2
MOVE TOP-STORE-SALESPERSON TO STORE-FOOTING-3
WRITE STORE-FOOTING-3
ADD STORE-TOTAL-SALES TO COMPANY-TOTAL-SALES
IS WS-MORE-RECORDS = "YES"?
YES
PERFORM 500-CHECK-STORE-CTR
NO
RETURN
500-CHECK-STORE-CTR
ADD 1 TO STORES-PER-PAGE-CTR
IS STORES-PER-PAGE-CTR = 2?
YES
PERFORM 600-WRITE-PAGE-HEADING
NO
PERFORM 700-WRITE STORE-HEADING
RETURN
600-WRITE-PAGE-HEADING
ADD 1 TO PAGE-NO
WRITE TOP-LINE
at top of a new page
WRITE COMPANY-NAME
WRITE REPORT-NAME
INITIALIZE STORES-PER-PAGE-CTR
PERFORM 700-WRITE-STORE-HEADING
RETURN
700-WRITE-STORE-HEADING
MOVE I-STORE-NO TO WS-STORE-CONTROL
WRITE STORE-HEADING
INITIALIZE STORE ITEMS
salesperson counter
top store sales
store total sales
RETURN

Programming Exercise II

The management of the Modern Plastics Company wants its data processing department to prepare a multilevel payroll report, formatted as shown in Figure 8.46. It must show payroll information for each employee, for each department of each plant, for each plant of the company, and for the company as a whole.

For each employee, the detail line must show the employee's Social Security number, name, and the gross salary for the period.

For each department, the department heading must identify the department by number and description. The heading must be followed by a detail line for each department employee, and the department footing must show the total gross salaries and the average gross salary.

For each plant, the plant heading must identify the plant by number and location. The plant heading is followed by a department report for each of its departments. The plant footing must show the total gross salaries and the average gross salary. There must be no more than one plant report per page.

For the company, the company footing must show the total gross salaries and the average gross salary. This footing is to be printed two lines below the footing for the last plant.

Each page of the report begins with the page heading. It consists of the report-date line (TOP-LINE), the company name, and the report name. The pages are numbered consecutively.

For each employee, there is a record in the payroll file containing the following data:

cc 3–4	Plant number
cc 5–6	Department number
cc 7–15	Social Security number
cc 16–35	Employee name
cc 39–42	Pay rate (format: xx.xx)
cc 43–44	Hours worked at regular pay
cc 45–46	Hours worked at overtime pay (time and a half)
cc 77–80	Date hired

The records of the input file are arranged in seniority sequence by department within each plant. The department numbers and the plant numbers are in ascending order.

The plant numbers and locations are as follows:

10 – Boston
20 – Providence
30 – New Haven
40 – Stamford
50 – New York

The department numbers and identifiers are as follows:

10 – Administration
20 – Personnel
30 – Finance
40 – Research & Development
50 – Production
60 – Shipping & Receiving
70 – Maintenance
80 – Data Processing

Figure 8.46 contains the layout of the input record, the printer spacing chart, the system flowchart, and the structure chart. Your assignment is to complete the design phase. Next, you are to code, compile, debug, and run the program successfully. Use the data in Data File Set 4 (see Appendix C [DD/CD:VIC8EX2.DAT]) as a sample input file.

■ Figure 8.46

Record Layout Form

Columns	Field
1–2	
3–4	I-PLANT-NO
5–6	I-DEPT-NO
7–15	I-SSN
16–35	I-EMPLOYEE-NAME
36–38	
39–42	I-PAY-RATE
43–44	I-REG-HRS
45–46	I-OT-HRS
47–76	
77–80	I-DATE-HIRED

Record Name: EMPLOYEE-RECORD

Printer Spacing Chart

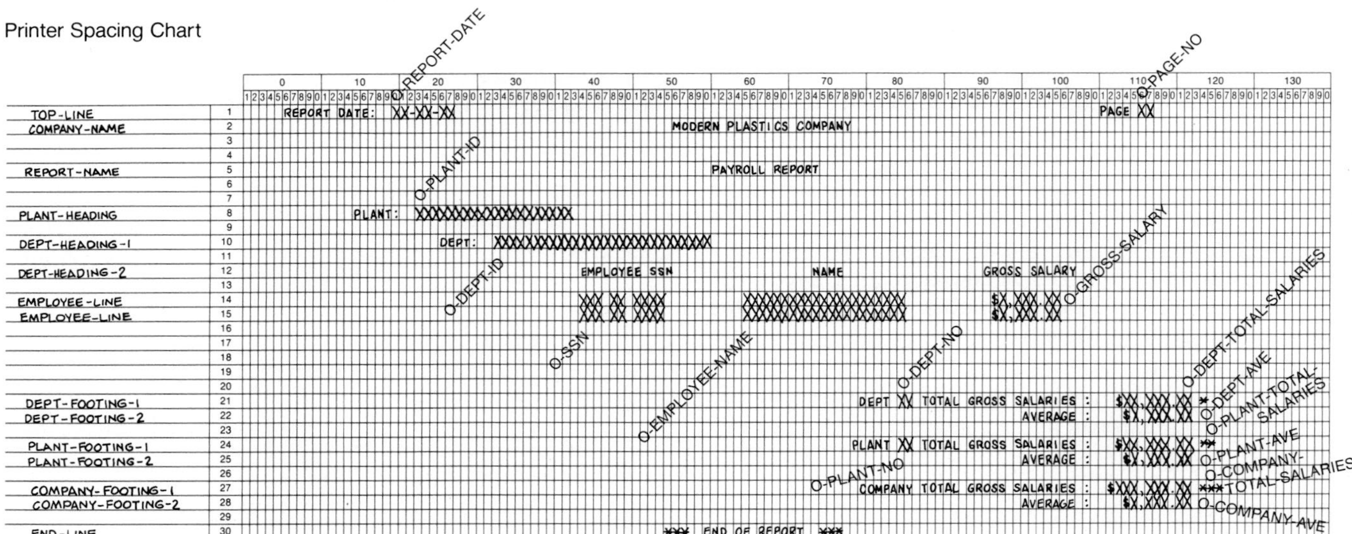

System Flowchart

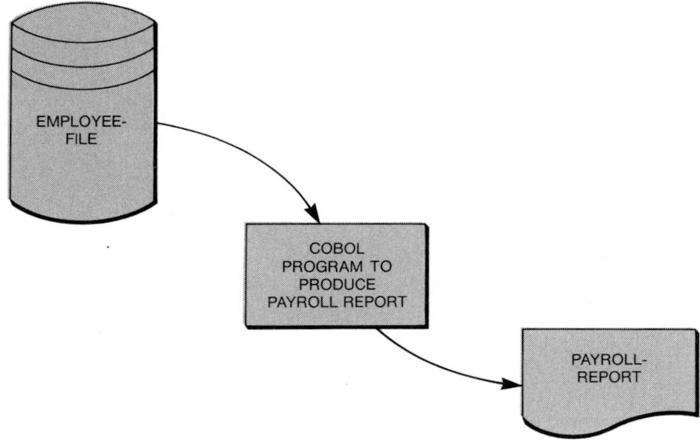

■ **Figure 8.46** continued

Structure Chart

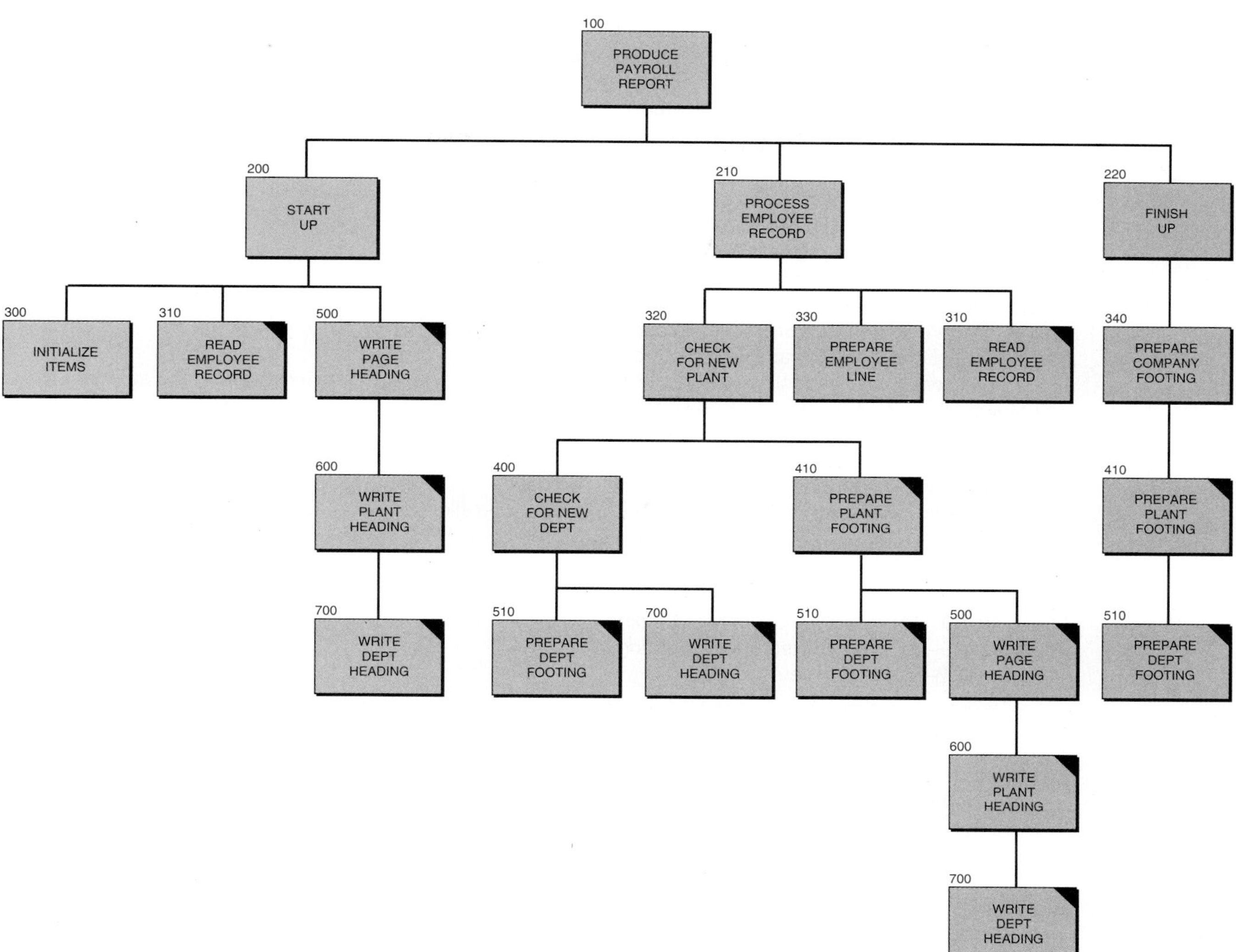

Programming Exercise III

The management of the Ponagansett Electric Company wants a multilevel usage report formatted as shown in Figure 8.47. It must show usage information for each customer of each area, usage information for each area of the company, and usage information for the company as a whole.

Only one area is reported per page. An area report begins with the area heading; the body of the report contains a detail line for each customer in the area; and the report ends with an area footing that contains summary information for the area.

Areas are identified by code and by location. They are as follows:

RI1 – Bristol
RI2 – Essex
RI3 – South

The area heading specifies the area identifier.

A detail line contains the following information for a customer: the classification of the customer as residential or commercial, the rate schedule that applies to the customer, the customer number and name, the previous and current meter readings, the KWH used by the customer for the current period, and the total charge to be assessed to the customer.

The area footing specifies the total KWH sold and the income to be derived from the sale of electricity to each of its customer classifications.

The company footing specifies the total KWH sold and the income to be derived from the sale of electricity to each of its customer classifications as a whole. In addition, it identifies the highest user in each classification and the actual number of KWH used.

For each customer, there is a record in the customer file that contains the following data:

cc 1–3	Area code (RI1, RI2, RI3)
cc 4–9	Customer number
cc 10–29	Customer name
cc 30–34	Previous meter reading
cc 35–39	Current meter reading
cc 74–76	Rate schedule

The records in this file are arranged sequentially by customer number within each area code.

The rate schedules are as follows:

1. Residential: A10
   Customer Charge: $1.61 per month
   Energy Charge: 7.974 cents per KWH
2. Residential: A11 (Electric Water Heater)
   Customer Charge:

$2.75	for first	20 KWH or less
10.435 cents per KWH	next	30 KWH
8.381 cents per KWH	next	150 KWH
5.529 cents per KWH	next	350 KWH
6.831 cents per KWH	next	1450 KWH
6.554 cents per KWH	excess of	2000 KWH

3. Residential: A12 (All Electric)
   Same as A11
4. Commercial: C-2 (General Service, Small Business)
   Customer Charge: $4.75 per month
   Energy Charge:
   8.913 cents per KWH for the first 2000 KWH
   8.313 cents per KWH in excess of 2000 KWH

For all rate schedules, the following additional charges apply: .006 cents per KWH for the Uniform Conservation Cost Adjustment, .042 cents per KWH for the Oil Conservation Adjustment, and .01413 cents Fuel Factor per KWH.

Your assignment is to design the program and then to implement it. Use the data in Data File Set 2 (see Appendix C [DD/CD:VIC8EX3.DAT]), and use the current date as the report date.

■ Figure 8.47

Printer Spacing Chart

Record	Line	Content
TOP-LINE	1	REPORT DATE: XX/XX/XX PAGE XX
COMPANY-NAME	2	PONAGANSETT ELECTRIC COMPANY
	3	
	4	
REPORT-NAME	5	CUSTOMER USAGE REPORT
	6	
AREA-HEADING-1	7	AREA: XXXXXXXXXXXX
	8	
AREA-HEADING-2	9	CUSTOMER RATE CUSTOMER CUSTOMER PREVIOUS CURRENT USAGE TOTAL
AREA-HEADING-3	10	CLASS SCHEDULE NUMBER NAME READING READING CHARGE
	11	
CUSTOMER-LINE	12	XXXXXXXXXX XXX XXXXX XXXXXXXXXXXXXXXXXX XXXXX XXXXX XXXXX- $XX,XXX.XX
CUSTOMER-LINE	13	XXXXXXXXXX XXX XXXXX XXXXXXXXXXXXXXXXXX XXXXX XXXXX XXXXX- $XX,XXX.XX
	14	
	15	
AREA-FOOTING-1	16	TOTALS FOR AREA XXX KWHS INCOME
	17	
AREA-FOOTING-2	18	COMMERCIAL XXX,XXX,XXX- $XXX,XXX,XXX.XX
	19	
AREA-FOOTING-3	20	RESIDENTIAL XXX,XXX,XXX- $XXX,XXX,XXX.XX
	21	
COMPANY-FOOTING-1	22	SUMMARY
	23	
COMPANY-FOOTING-2	24	1. TOTAL KWHS SOLD TO COMMERCIAL CUSTOMERS XXX,XXX,XXX-
COMPANY-FOOTING-3	25	TOTAL INCOME FROM COMMERCIAL CUSTOMERS $XXX,XXX,XXX.XX-
COMPANY-FOOTING-4	26	HIGHEST COMMERCIAL USER XXXXXXXXXXXXXXXXXX USAGE XXXXX-
	27	
COMPANY-FOOTING-5	28	2. TOTAL KWHS SOLD TO RESIDENTIAL CUSTOMERS XXX,XXX,XXX-
COMPANY-FOOTING-6	29	TOTAL INCOME FROM RESIDENTIAL CUSTOMERS $XXX,XXX,XXX.XX-
COMPANY-FOOTING-7	30	HIGHEST RESIDENTIAL USER XXXXXXXXXXXXXXXXXX USAGE XXXXX-
	31	
END-LINE	32	** END OF REPORT **

Programming Exercise IV

The data processing department of the Modern Plastics Company must prepare a data validation report on the payroll file. The file contains a record for each employee on the current payroll. Each record is supposed to contain the following data:

cc 3–4	Plant number
cc 5–6	Department number
cc 7–15	Social Security number
cc 16–35	Employee name
cc 39–42	Pay rate (format: xx.xx)
cc 43–44	Hours worked at regular pay
cc 45–46	Hours worked at overtime pay (time and a half)

The data validation program must perform all the tests indicated in the table on page 528. Each record must be printed on the report and if an error exists in any field, the appropriate message must also be printed. (A record is printed only once, even if it contains more than one error.) Any record found to be free of errors must be written to a validated payroll file.

The report must also show the following totals:

Number of records read from the payroll file
Number of "good" records (records free of any error)
Number of "bad" records (records with at least one error)
Number of records written to the validated payroll file

■ Figure 8.48

Printer Spacing Chart

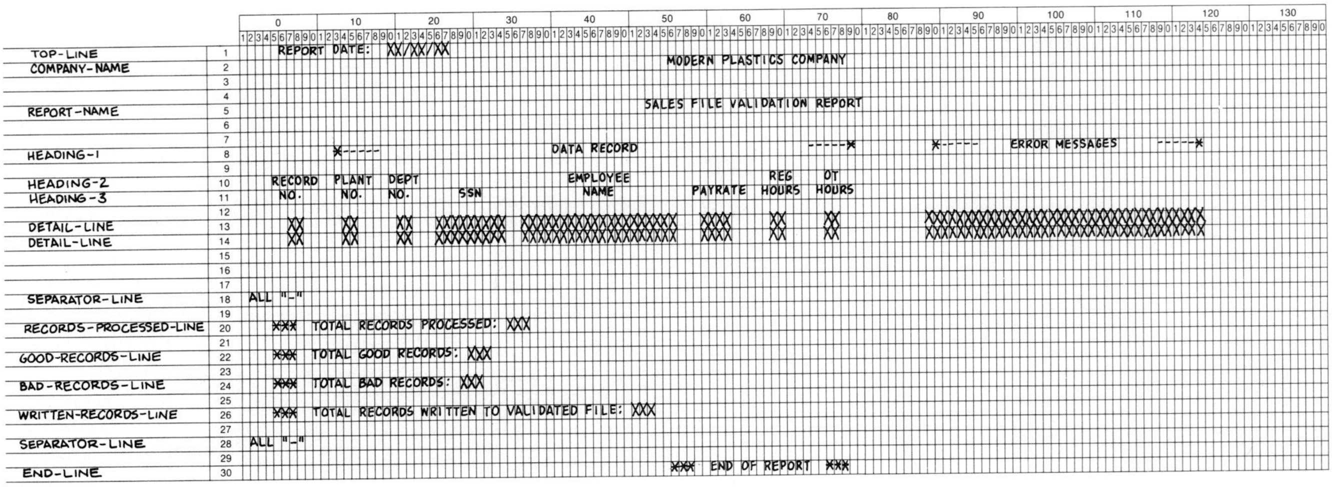

Line Name	Line	Content
TOP-LINE	1	REPORT DATE: XX/XX/XX
COMPANY-NAME	2	MODERN PLASTICS COMPANY
	3	
	4	
REPORT-NAME	5	SALES FILE VALIDATION REPORT
	6	
	7	
HEADING-1	8	X----- DATA RECORD -----X X----- ERROR MESSAGES -----X
	9	
HEADING-2	10	RECORD PLANT DEPT EMPLOYEE REG OT
HEADING-3	11	NO. NO. NO. SSN NAME PAYRATE HOURS HOURS
	12	
DETAIL-LINE	13	XX XX XX XXXXXXXXX XXXXXXXXXXXXXXXXXXXX XXXX XX XX XXXXXXXXXXXXXXXXXXXXXXXXXXXXXXXXXXX
DETAIL-LINE	14	XX XX XX XXXXXXXXX XXXXXXXXXXXXXXXXXXXX XXXX XX XX XXXXXXXXXXXXXXXXXXXXXXXXXXXXXXXXXXX
	15	
	16	
	17	
SEPARATOR-LINE	18	ALL "-"
	19	
RECORDS-PROCESSED-LINE	20	XXX TOTAL RECORDS PROCESSED: XXX
	21	
GOOD-RECORDS-LINE	22	XXX TOTAL GOOD RECORDS: XXX
	23	
BAD-RECORDS-LINE	24	XXX TOTAL BAD RECORDS: XXX
	25	
WRITTEN-RECORDS-LINE	26	XXX TOTAL RECORDS WRITTEN TO VALIDATED FILE: XXX
	27	
SEPARATOR-LINE	28	ALL "-"
	29	
END-LINE	30	XXX END OF REPORT XXX

Fields to Be Tested	Tests to Be Performed	Error Messages to Be Printed
Plant number	Missing entry	PLANT NUMBER IS MISSING
	Nonnumeric value	PLANT NUMBER IS NOT NUMERIC
	Not a valid plant number	INVALID PLANT NUMBER
Department number	Missing entry	DEPARTMENT NUMBER IS MISSING
	Nonnumeric value	DEPARTMENT NUMBER IS NOT NUMERIC
	Not a valid department number	INVALID DEPARTMENT NUMBER
Social Security number	Missing entry	SSN IS MISSING
	Nonnumeric value	SSN IS NOT NUMERIC
Employee name	Missing entry	NAME IS MISSING
	Name is not left justified	NAME IS NOT LEFT JUSTIFIED
	Name is not alphabetic	NAME IS NOT ALPHABETIC
	Not all uppercase letters	NAME LETTERS ARE NOT ALL UPPERCASE
Pay rate	Missing entry	PAY RATE IS MISSING
	Nonnumeric value	PAY RATE IS NOT NUMERIC
	Not between 0 and 30	PAY RATE IS OUT OF RANGE
Regular hours	Missing entry	REGULAR HOURS IS MISSING
	Nonnumeric value	REGULAR HOURS IS NOT NUMERIC
	Not between 1 and 40	REGULAR HOURS IS OUT OF RANGE
Overtime hours	Missing entry	OVERTIME HOURS IS MISSING
	Nonnumeric value	OVERTIME HOURS IS NOT NUMERIC
	Not between 0 and 20	OVERTIME HOURS IS OUT OF RANGE

The report is a continuous report. It begins with a report header on the first page, and detail lines are printed consecutively on continuous-form paper until the last record has been processed. The report then ends with the required totals followed by the "End of Report" message.

Your assignment is to design the program and then to implement it. The format of the report is shown in Figure 8.48. Use the data in Data File Set 6 (see Appendix C [DD/CD:VIC8EX4.DAT]) as a sample input file, and use the current date as the report date.

9 Table Handling Using Subscripts

In common everyday use, such as in newspapers and on television, tables are used to graphically display related data in a concise and visually meaningful way. In COBOL, as in any other programming language, tables are used, not for visual clarity, but for invisible, concise, and effective internal data storage.

In this chapter, you will learn how to define a table, how to initialize it with values, and how to access data stored in a table. Tables can be separated into two classes: those that contain static or permanent data, that is, data that never changes, such as the names of the months of the year; and those that contain volatile or nonpermanent data, that is, data that changes over time, such as the points scored by each player on a basketball team from one game to another. Most tables contain volatile data. Volatile data is generally stored in a separate file and is loaded into the table defined within the COBOL program during the execution phase of the program. On the other hand, permanent data is usually stored in the program by means of VALUE clauses and is therefore stored in the table when the program is compiled. For these reasons, "volatile" tables are often referred to as **input-loaded tables,** whereas "static" tables are referred to as **hard-coded tables.**

The sample program that is developed in this chapter illustrates both input-loaded and hard-coded tables. ■

Objectives You Should Achieve

After studying this chapter, you should:

1. Be able to correctly code the definition of a one-level table containing a single repeating elementary item.
2. Be able to correctly code the definition of a one-level table containing a repeating group item.
3. Be able to correctly reference each value in a one-level table by using a subscripted data name.
4. Given a table with sequential organization and records containing the data to be loaded into the table, be able to
   a. Organize the records in the sequence specified by the key or keys.
   b. Design the logic needed to load the table.
5. Given the data to be stored in a table with positional organization, be able to
   a. Correctly sequence the data.
   b. Design the logic needed to load the table.
6. Given a data file whose values must be stored in a table and the corresponding DATA DIVISION entries, be able to correctly code the PROCEDURE DIVISION statements needed to load the table.
7. Given a set of values that must be stored in a hard-coded table (one-level or two-level), be able to correctly code the entries that define the permanent table and redefine it in such a way that the individual values can be referenced.
8. Given a visual representation of a two-level table, be able to code the DATA DIVISION entries that define the table in a program.
9. Given DATA DIVISION entries that define a two-level table, be able to correctly draw a visual representation of the two-level table.
10. Given the DATA DIVISION entries that define a two-level table and the file that contains the data to be loaded into the table, be able to design and to code the table-loading procedure.
11. Given a two-level table containing numeric values and DATA DIVISION entries that define the table, be able to correctly code PROCEDURE DIVISION statements to find the average of the values in each row of the table.
12. Given a one-level table with random organization, be able to correctly code a table look-up procedure to retrieve a table element corresponding to a given input value.
13. Given a two-level table, be able to correctly code a table look-up procedure to retrieve a table element corresponding to given input values.

14. Given a programming assignment whose purpose is to prepare a report containing values that must be retrieved from tables with positional organization, and for which the design tools are provided, be able to successfully complete the task of coding and running the program. The table elements must be retrieved by direct referencing using subscripts.
15. Given a programming assignment whose purpose is to prepare a report containing values that must be retrieved from tables, and for which the design tools are provided, be able to successfully complete the task of coding and running the program. The table elements must be retrieved by using a table look-up procedure.
16. Given a programming assignment whose purpose is to prepare a report containing values that must be retrieved from tables, and for which the input record layouts, the printer spacing chart, and the system flowchart are provided, be able to successfully complete the task of designing, coding, and running the program.
17. Given a programming assignment whose purpose is to prepare a report containing values that must be retrieved from tables, be able to successfully complete the assignment, that is, develop the program design and then implement the design.

The Problem

The management of the Monster Burger Stores wants a weekly payroll report formatted as shown in Figure 9.1.

For each employee, the report must show the employee's store number, Social Security number, name, classification, pay rate, the pay base (/HR or /WK), hours worked, gross earnings, deductions for federal and state taxes and insurance premiums, and net earnings.

The report must contain a maximum of 30 payroll lines per page, and each page must begin with the documentation shown on the printer spacing chart of Figure 9.1.

The report ends with company totals that must show the total number of employees, the total gross earnings for all the employees, the total amounts withheld for federal taxes, state taxes, and insurance premiums, and, finally, the total net earnings for all the employees.

To prepare this report, the data processing department must use two data files. One file, Payroll File, contains a payroll record for each employee on the current payroll. Each payroll record contains the following data:

cc 1–2	Employee classification code
cc 3–11	Employee Social Security number
cc 12–31	Employee name
cc 32–33	Employee store code
cc 34–35	Employee pay code

Figure 9.1 Printer spacing chart for the sample program

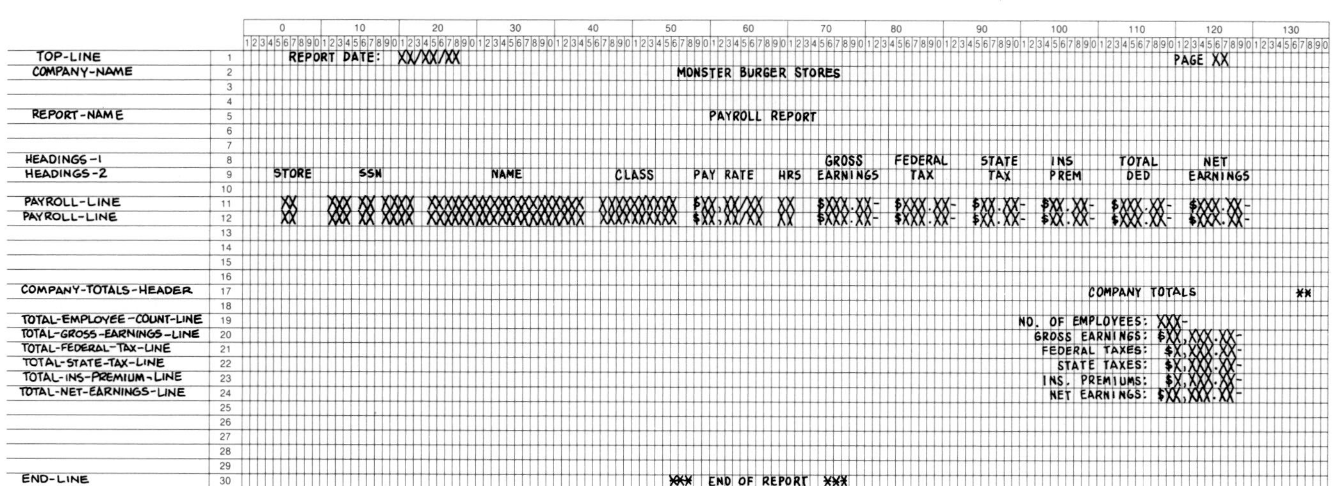

cc 36–37 Employee hours worked
cc 38–39 Number of store openings or closings (for assistant managers only)
cc 40–41 Employee insurance plan code
cc 42–43 Employee allowances claimed (for tax purposes)

Payroll File has been presorted in ascending order by store number. Within each store, the records are sorted alphabetically on employee names.

The other data file, called Tables File, contains records that are needed to do the following:

1. Load federal tax rates into a federal tax rate table.
2. Load the company's pay rates into a pay rate table.
3. Load the current insurance rates, for the various insurance plans the company offers, into an insurance rate table.

Each record of Tables File contains an identification code in the first byte. An "I" denotes an insurance rate record, a "P" denotes a pay rate record, and a "T" denotes a tax rate record. The rest of the record is the data that must be stored in one row of the corresponding table.

For purposes of this program, the rates are as shown in the tables below. The state tax is a "piggyback" tax of 19 percent applied to the federal tax.

In addition, the employee classifications are as follows:

Code	**Classification**
01	Apprentice
02	Beginner
03	Yearling
04	Standard
05	Assistant Manager
06	Store Manager

For this company, employee classifications are static, and thus the table can be hard-coded into the program.

■ Insurance Rates

		Plan Code	Premium per Week
Individual Coverage	Basic Plan "A"	IA	$ 6.73
	Major Medical Plan "B"	IB	$ 9.14
Family Coverage	Basic Plan "A"	FA	$ 8.65
	Major Medical Plan "B"	FB	$11.54

■ Federal Income Tax Withholding Table—Married (Simplified)

Weekly Income (Less Than)	Number of Withholding Allowances 1	2	3	4	5
100	.070	.030	.000	.000	.000
200	.100	.075	.045	.020	.000
300	.117	.100	.080	.063	.043
400	.125	.113	.098	.085	.070
500	.130	.120	.108	.098	.086
600	.135	.125	.115	.107	.097
700	.156	.141	.127	.113	.104
800	.171	.159	.146	.134	.121
900	.183	.172	.161	.150	.139
1000	.199	.187	.174	.163	.153

■ Company's Pay Schedule

Code	Pay Rate
01	$3.65/hr
02	$3.90/hr
03	$4.25/hr
04	$4.60/hr
05	$5.10/hr
06	$5.75/hr
07	$6.50/hr
08	$7.30/hr
09	$8.30/hr
10	$9.50/hr
11	$300.00/wk
12	$375.00/wk
13	$450.00/wk
14	$525.00/wk
15	$600.00/wk

All employees are paid hourly wages except store managers, who are paid weekly salaries. Only managers and assistant managers are responsible for opening and/or closing stores. Assistant managers receive a weekly bonus of $10 plus an additional $5 for each time they have to open or close a store, in addition to their hourly wages.

Note 1: To allow you to concentrate on table definitions, initialization, and access, the two input files have been validated. The program does not require tests related to data validation.

Note 2: The Federal Income Tax Withholding Table shown here is obviously incomplete. Such tables normally contain entries for 0 allowances as well as for more than 5. There are tables for single individuals and for heads of households. There are tables for weekly, biweekly, and monthly payrolls.

A Brief Analysis of the Problem

This is the first program in the text that requires two input files. Normally this is a very common occurrence, and you will experience it for yourself as you proceed into more advanced COBOL topics. Whenever two or more input files must be processed by a program, a very pertinent question must be asked: Must they be processed concurrently or sequentially? Some applications require that they be processed concurrently, and other applications require that they be processed in a specific sequence.

In the current program, the processing of a payroll record requires access to federal tax rate data, insurance premium data, and so on. It should be clear that the tables containing this data must be loaded **before** processing the payroll records. Thus, the program logic must be set up to process Tables File completely before beginning to process the Payroll File records.

The processing of a Tables File record must include the following steps:

1. Read a record of the file.
2. Determine the record identification code:
   a. If it is an "I," move the record contents to the appropriate row of the insurance rate table.
   b. If it is a "P," move the record contents to the appropriate row of the pay rate table.
   c. If it is a "T," move the record contents to the appropriate row of the tax rate table.

After the tables have received all their entries, the records of Payroll File must be processed. To process a payroll record, the following must occur:

1. Read the record from Payroll File.
2. Compute the employee's gross earnings.

   Note that the store managers are salaried, whereas all other employees are paid wages on an hourly basis. Consequently, the employee classification field must be tested first so the program can apply the appropriate formula to compute the week's gross earnings. In either case, the pay rate (hourly or weekly) must be retrieved from the pay rate table. The pay code on the employee record will be used to select the correct pay rate.

   For a store manager, the retrieved pay rate is the gross earnings for the week, whereas, for all other employees, the retrieved pay rate must be multiplied by the number of hours the employee worked during the week. In addition, an assistant manager receives a $10 bonus and an extra $5 for each time he or she had to open or close the store.
3. Compute the federal tax to be withheld from the gross earnings.

   The applicable federal tax rate is a function of the gross earnings and of the number of allowances claimed by the employee. For instance, the federal income tax withholding table on page 534 shows that if gross earnings are between 300 and 400 a week, the applicable tax rate is 12.5 percent if the employee claims no allowances, but it is 8.5 percent if the employee claims three allowances. The table clearly shows that the higher the income level, the higher the tax rate, and within any one income level, the higher the number of allowances claimed, the lower the tax rate.

   You can see that the gross earnings must be used to identify the appropriate row in the table, and the number of allowances claimed must be used to select the applicable tax rate in that row. The gross earnings are then simply multiplied by the tax rate to determine the amount to be withheld for the federal tax.
4. Compute the state tax.

   Since the state tax is tied to the federal tax, the amount to be withheld for the state tax is computed directly as 19 percent of the federal tax.

5. Determine the amount to be withheld for the employee's share of the insurance premium.

   Obviously, the amount to be withheld from gross earnings depends on the insurance plan the employee participates in. The payroll record contains an insurance plan code in bytes 40 and 41. This code must be matched against the codes in the insurance table. Matching codes will then indicate the amount to be withheld.

6. Compute the total deductions.

   Since the only payroll deductions in this program are the federal and state taxes and the insurance premium, they are added to determine the total deductions.

7. Compute the net earnings.

   Subtracting the total deductions from the gross earnings yields the net earnings for the week.

8. Subtotal the relevant amounts into the company accumulators.

   The company totals portion of the report format in Figure 9.1 indicates that the required accumulators are an employee counter, a gross earnings accumulator, a federal tax accumulator, a state tax accumulator, an insurance premium accumulator, and a net earnings accumulator.

9. Prepare the payroll line that must be printed on the report.

   The printer spacing chart of Figure 9.1 shows that all the values computed earlier (steps 2 through 7) must be copied into selected fields of the record PAYROLL-LINE. Of the remaining seven fields, four receive values from the input record (store number, Social Security number, name, and hours worked, except that a manager has no posted hours). The pay rate field receives a copy of the pay rate that was selected earlier, but a test is needed to determine if the suffix /HR or the suffix /WK is to be attached to the pay rate. Finally, the entry in the employee classification field must be retrieved from the employee classification table. The employee classification code in bytes 1 and 2 of the payroll record is tested against the codes in the table. A match then specifies the entry that must be moved to the class field of the payroll line. When all the data fields of the record PAYROLL-LINE have received their values, the line is then written on the report.

10. Test the line counter to determine if a new page is needed.

    No more than 30 lines are to be printed per page.

After processing the last record of Payroll File, the totals that have been accumulated for the company are printed on the report. As a last step, the End-of-Report message is printed, and this completes the payroll report.

The Design Phase

Step 1 of the problem-solving procedure calls for preparing the layouts of the input records. Payroll File contains only one kind of record, as specified in the statement of the problem. Its layout is shown in Figure 9.2a.

The second input file, Tables File, contains three different kinds of records: one that contains insurance rates, another that contains pay rates, and a third that contains tax rates. Though there are many ways of preparing the data that must be loaded into the tables (to be defined within the program), the most natural way is to prepare one record for each row of data in each of the tables. The first byte of each record contains a code used to identify the table that the record is associated with. Other data is stored as follows:

1. A federal tax rate record contains all the entries that must be stored in one row of the federal tax table, that is, the upper income limit for that row, and five tax rates. Its layout is shown in Figure 9.2b. Note that the row entries are grouped under a group name.
2. A pay rate record contains the pay rate to be stored in a row of the pay rate table. The record could be designed to contain the code as well. The code is purposely excluded because we intend to use this table to illustrate a special kind of table, referred to as a *positional* table. That is, the pay rate is to be stored in the row occurrence that corresponds to the pay rate code: 3.65 is to be stored in row 1 because its code is 1; 4.60 is to be stored in row 4 because its code is 4, and so on. The layout of this record is shown in Figure 9.2c.
3. An insurance premium record contains a plan code and the corresponding premium amount, since this data is to be stored in one row of the insurance table. Its layout is shown in Figure 9.2d. Note that the plan code and insurance premium are grouped under a group name.

■ Figure 9.2 Layouts of all input records

Record Layout Forms

a.

Positions	Field
1–2	I-EMPL-CLASS-CODE
3–11	I-EMPL-SSN
12–31	I-EMPL-NAME
32–33	I-EMPL-STORE
34–35	I-EMPL-PAY-CODE
36–37	I-EMPL-HRS
38–39	I-EMPL-OPEN-CLOSE
40–41	I-EMPL-INS-CODE
42–43	I-EMPL-ALLOWANCES
44–80	

Record Name: PAYROLL-RECORD

b.

Positions	Field	Group
1	I-RECORD-CODE	
2–5	I-UPPER-LIMIT	I-TAX-TABLE-ROW-VALUES
6–8	I-TAX-RATE (1)	I-TAX-TABLE-ROW-VALUES
9–11	I-TAX-RATE (2)	I-TAX-TABLE-ROW-VALUES
12–14	I-TAX-RATE (3)	I-TAX-TABLE-ROW-VALUES
15–17	I-TAX-RATE (4)	I-TAX-TABLE-ROW-VALUES
18–20	I-TAX-RATE (5)	I-TAX-TABLE-ROW-VALUES
21–80		

Record Name: FEDERAL-TAX-RATES-RECORD

c.

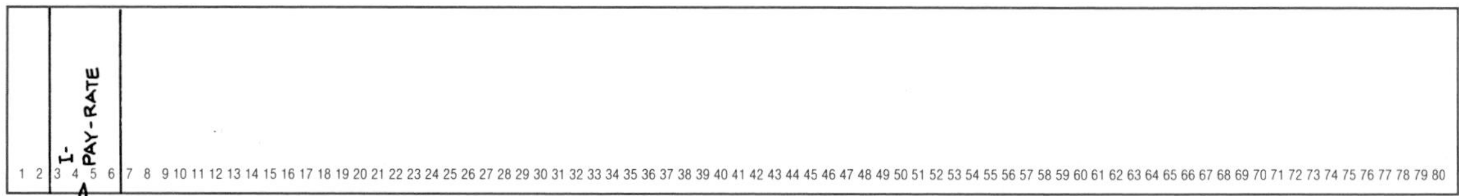

Record Name: PAY-RATE-RECORD

d.

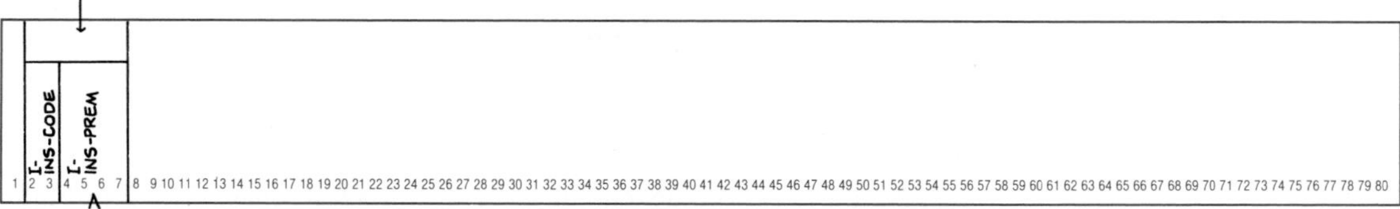

Record Name: INSURANCE-PREMIUM-RECORD

The records in Tables File are sequenced as follows: the ten federal tax rate records, in increasing order of upper income limits; the fifteen pay rate records, in increasing order of their pay rate codes; and the four insurance premium records in any order. (The sample Tables File used in this program is shown on page 541.)

The printer spacing chart of Figure 9.1 can be completed easily by attaching appropriate names to its data fields. It is shown in Figure 9.3.

System Flowchart

The system flowchart must show that the program must obtain data from **two** input files, Tables File and Payroll File, and it must produce one output file, Payroll Report. The system flowchart is shown in Figure 9.4.

■ **Figure 9.3** Printer spacing chart for the payroll report

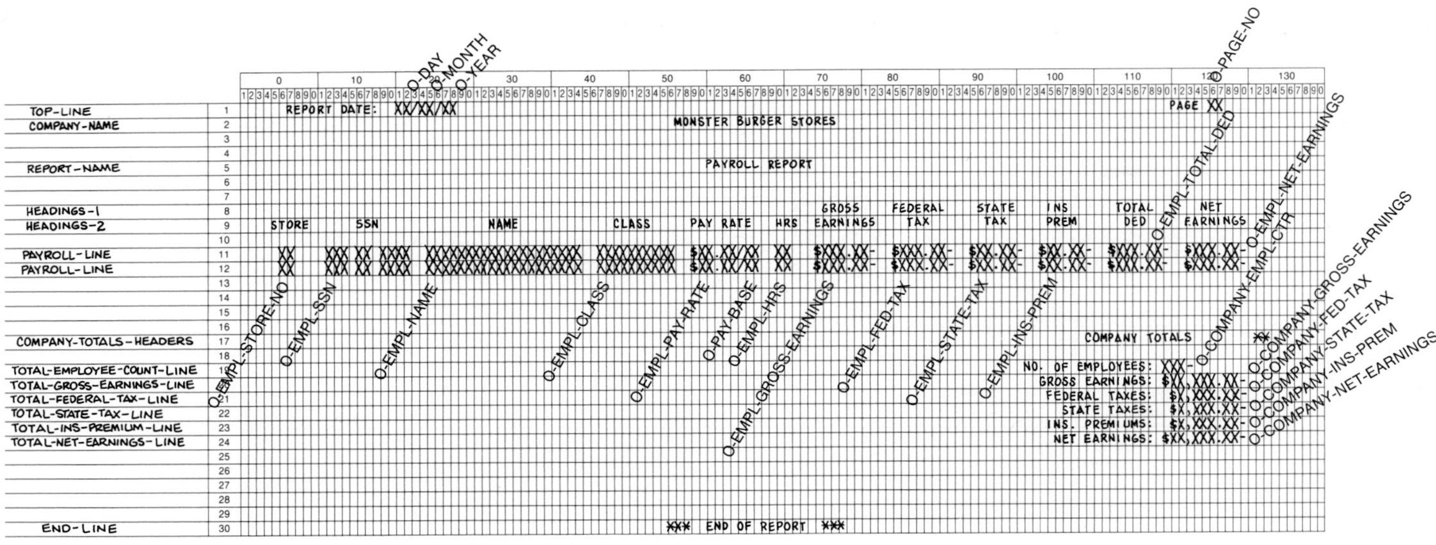

■ **Figure 9.4** System flowchart

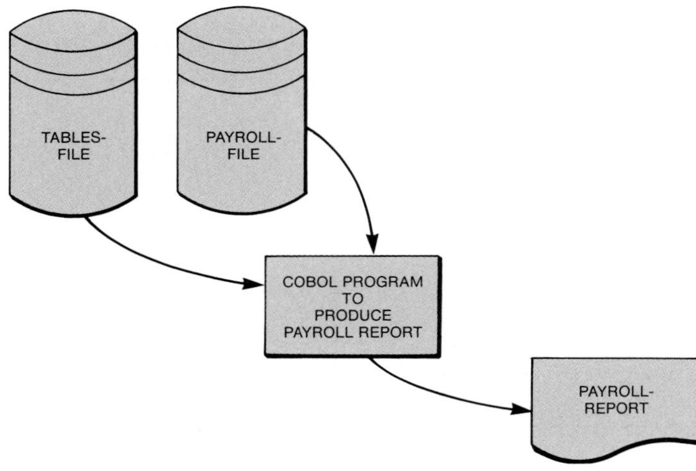

Structure Chart

The brief analysis of the problem is the basis for the development of the structure chart shown in Figure 9.5. Note that the table-loading functions have been placed under the control of module 300 INITIALIZE ITEMS. This is because all the program tables must be loaded at the very beginning of the program, before processing any of the payroll records. Also note that while processing a payroll record, module 320 COMPUTE EMPLOYEE ITEMS must carry out two table look-up procedures: one to retrieve the appropriate federal tax rate, and the other to retrieve the insurance premium amount to be withheld from the employee's gross earnings. In addition, while preparing the payroll line in module 340, another table look-up procedure must be executed to retrieve the appropriate employee classification.

Program Pseudocode

Paragraph 300-Initialize-Items

The pseudocode corresponding to the first two levels of the structure chart is straightforward and needs few explanations. Of greater interest is paragraph 300-Initialize-Items. The first five pseudocode paragraphs are shown in Figure 9.6.

■ **Figure 9.5** Structure chart

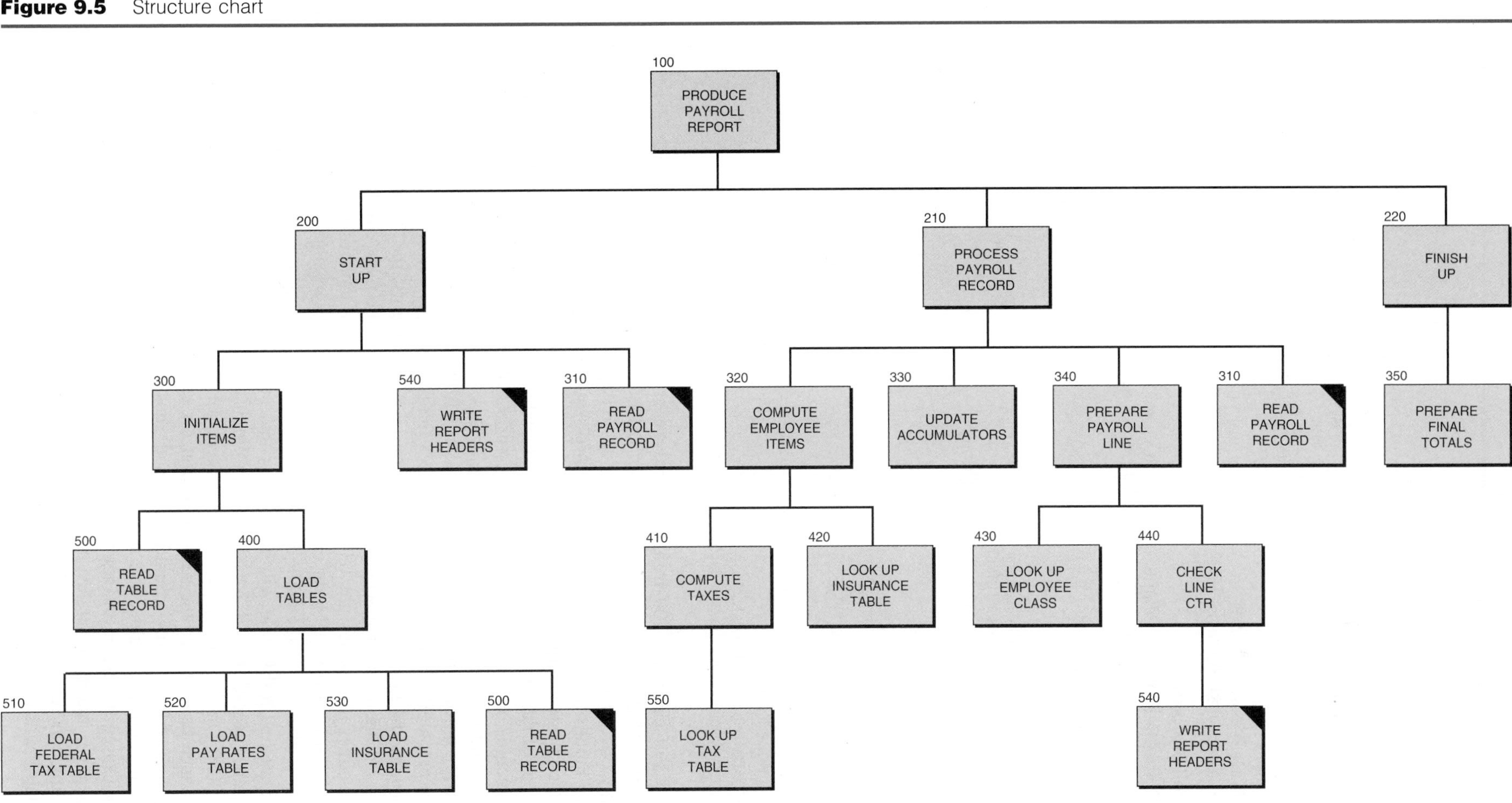

■ **Figure 9.6** The first five pseudocode paragraphs

100-Produce-Payroll-Report.

1. Perform 200-Start-Up.
2. Perform 210-Process-Payroll-Record until no more records.
3. Perform 220-Finish-Up.
4. Stop the run.

200-Start-Up.

1. Open the three files.
2. Perform 300-Initialize-Items.
3. Perform 540-Write-Report-Headers.
4. Perform 310-Read-Payroll-Record.

210-Process-Payroll-Record.

1. Perform 320-Compute-Employee-Items.
2. Perform 330-Update-Accumulators.
3. Perform 340-Prepare-Payroll-Line.
4. Perform 310-Read-Payroll-Record.

220-Finish-Up.

1. Perform 350-Prepare-Final-Totals.
2. Move End-Line to the output area Printline.
3. After advancing 5 lines, write the output record Printline.
4. Close the three files.

300-Initialize-Items.

1. Obtain the date from the system.
2. Move the date to Top-Line date.
3. Set the end-of-file flags WS-TABLE-RECORDS-FLAG and WS-PAYROLL-RECORDS-FLAG to "YES".
4. Set the company accumulators, the table row counters, and page-number to zero.
5. Perform 500-Read-Table-Record.
6. Perform 400-Load-Tables until no-more-table-records.

1. Note that step 3 of paragraph 300-Initialize-Items assigns initial values to two flags: WS-TABLE-RECORDS-FLAG and WS-PAYROLL-RECORDS-FLAG. In all prior programs, there was only one input file, and the flag that was consistently used was WS-MORE-RECORDS. Since the two input files in the current program are sequential files—that is, their records will be accessed in the physical sequence in which they reside on the file—a flag is associated with each file to help control the logic of the program. Specifically, when the Tables File flag indicates that all the table records have been processed, then control can proceed with the task of producing the payroll report. And when the Payroll File flag indicates that all the payroll records have been processed, then control is passed to the module that will print the company totals.
2. Step 4 of paragraph 300-Initialize-Items initializes the five company accumulators, specifically, the employee counter, the gross earnings and net earnings accumulators, the federal and state tax accumulators, and the insurance accumulator. It also initializes the table row counters. Recall that the program defines four tables: the table of federal tax rates, the table of pay rates, the table of insurance premiums, and the table of employee classifications. As a value is moved from an input record to a table, the row of the table that is to receive the value must be specified. The row counter associated with the table will be used for that purpose. For instance, in Figure 9.7, when the first insurance record is read, by adding 1 to the insurance table row counter, the program assigns the value 1 to the counter. Thus, the contents of the insurance record will be moved to row 1 of the insurance table. When the second insurance record is read, the program increments the value of the insurance table row counter by 1, and, thus, the contents of this record will be stored into row 2 of the insurance table, and so on.

   The procedure illustrated in Figure 9.7 will be used to load data into the federal tax table, the pay rates table, and the insurance table. Recall that the employee classification table is a hard-coded table, and consequently it is not loaded from input records. The procedure to set up a hard-coded table will be explained later.

■ **Figure 9.7** Loading the insurance table

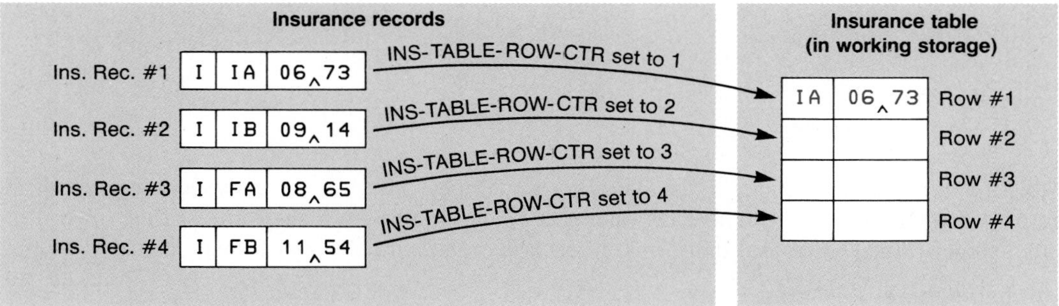

3. Step 5 of paragraph 300-Initialize-Items will result in reading the first record of the file Tables File. Control then enters step 6. This step contains a loop that is executed repeatedly until there are no more records in the file, or, equivalently, until the flag WS-TABLE-RECORDS-FLAG contains the value "NO ".

   As the procedure 400-Load-Tables is executed repeatedly, the data on the records of Tables File is loaded into the appropriate tables.

   When control leaves step 6 and returns to paragraph 200-Start-Up, step 3 will print the report headers on the first page of the report, and step 4 will read the first payroll record into input memory.

   Paragraphs 210 and 220 present no new concepts.

Loading the Tables

The function of structure chart module 500 READ TABLE RECORD is simply to access a record from the Tables File. Module 400 LOAD TABLES must then identify the table in working storage that must receive the data on the record. The selection is based on the code stored in the first byte of the record. If the code is a "T," the record data must be loaded into the federal tax table. If it is a "P," the data must be loaded into the pay rate table. And if it is an "I," the data must be loaded into the insurance table.

500-Read-Table-Record.

1. Read an input Table-File record.
2. Test for end-of-file record:
   if EOF record reached, set the flag WS-TABLE-RECORDS-FLAG to "NO ".

400-Load-Tables.

1. Test input record-code:
   a. if "T", then perform 510-Load-Federal-Tax-Table;
   b. if "P", then perform 520-Load-Pay-Rate-Table;
   c. if "I", then perform 530-Load-Insurance-Table.
2. Perform 500-Read-Table-Record.

Paragraphs 500 and 400 of the pseudocode are shown above. Note that paragraph 400 references paragraphs 510-Load-Federal-Tax-Table, 520-Load-Pay-Rate-Table, and 530-Load-Insurance-Table. They are shown below. These are the paragraphs that must transfer the data stored in Tables File to the tables established within the program. The records of Tables File are listed below in the sequence described earlier.

```
T0100070030000000000
T0200100075045020000
T0300117100080063043
T0400125113098085070
T0500130120108098086
T0600135125115107097
T0700156141127113104
T0800171159146134121
T0900183172161150139
T1000199187174163153
P00365
P00390
P00425
P00460
P00510
P00575
P00650
P00730
```

```
P00830
P00950
P30000
P37500
P45000
P52500
P60000
IIA0673
IIB0914
IFA0865
IFB1154
```

In this file, a record with code "T" contains the wage upper limit for the corresponding row of the table (see page 534), followed by the five tax rates that belong to that row. The format of the upper limit value is the integer format xxxx, and the format of each tax rate is the decimal format .xxx.

510-Load-Federal-Tax-Table.

1. Add 1 to tax-table-row-counter.
2. Move input tax-table-row-values
   to federal-tax-table wage-level-info (tax-table-row-counter).

520-Load-Pay-Rate-Table.

1. Add 1 to pay-rate-table-row-counter.
2. Move input pay-rate to pay-rate-table pay-rate (pay-rate-table-row-counter).

530-Load-Insurance-Table.

1. Add 1 to insurance-table-row-counter.
2. Move input insurance-table-row-values
   to insurance-table insurance-info (insurance-table-row-counter).

Now, examine paragraph 510-Load-Federal-Tax-Table. (Recall that all the table row counters were set to zero in paragraph 300-Initialize-Items.) The data on the first record, referred to by the group name *tax-table-row-values,* will be moved to row 1 of the federal tax table. Since each row of the tax table contains data related to a specific level of income, it is given the name *wage-level-info.* The first row is wage-level-info (1) [read "wage-level-info *sub* one"], the second row is wage-level-info (2) [wage-level-info *sub* two], and so on, so that the tenth row is referred to as wage-level-info (10). (The number within parentheses is called a *subscript.* It specifies a particular occurrence of the repeating table item wage-level-info.) When the second record of the file is read, the code "T" will cause paragraph 400-Load-Tables to send control to paragraph 510-Load-Federal-Tax-Table again. The tax table row counter is incremented by 1, and thus the data on the record is moved to wage-level-info (2). The pattern continues until the table is loaded. See Figure 9.8.

Figure 9.8 Loading the federal tax rate table

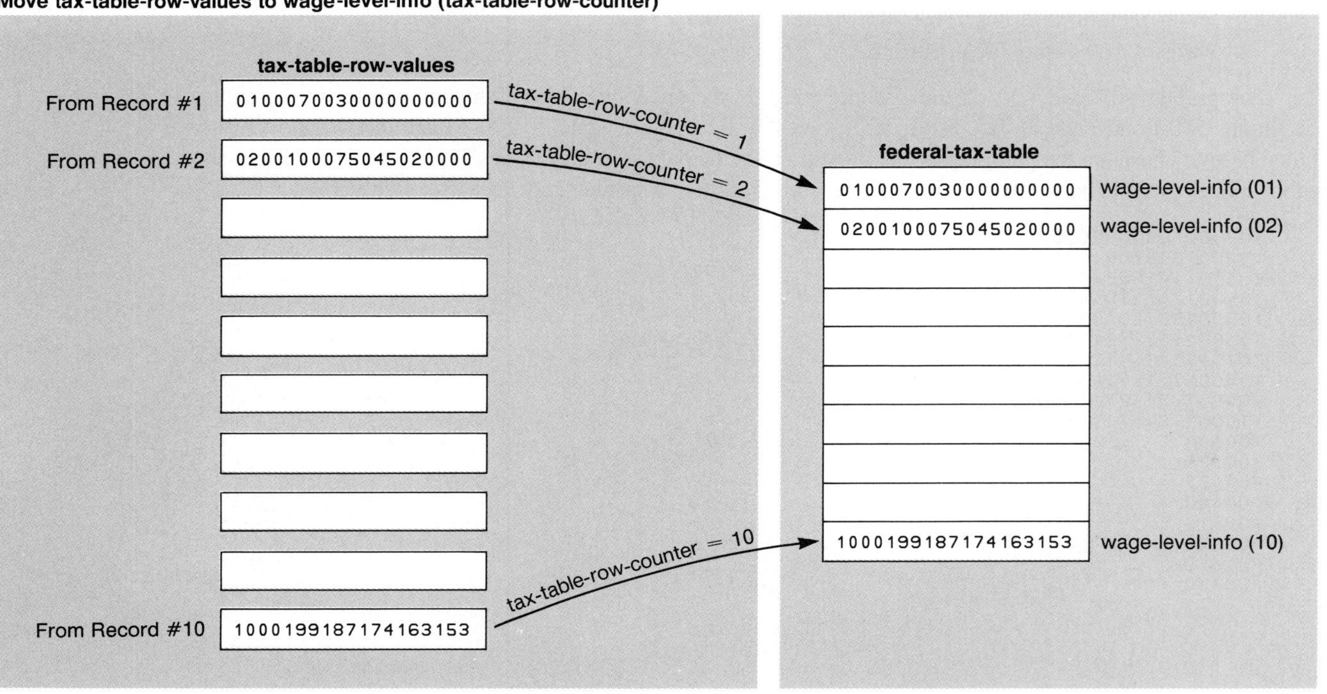

Whenever the code in byte 1 of the record is a "P", paragraph 400-Load-Tables sends control to paragraph 520-Load-Pay-Rate-Table, and similar steps are used to load the data into the pay-rate table. Whenever the code in byte 1 is an "I", control is sent to paragraph 530-Load-Insurance-Table, and the data on the record is then loaded into the next row of the insurance table.

Processing a Payroll Record

Paragraph 210-Process-Payroll-Record controls the execution of the procedures needed to process a payroll record. The first procedure is paragraph 320-Compute-Employee-Items.

320-Compute-Employee-Items

A look at the printer spacing chart clearly shows that the items that must be computed are the gross earnings, the federal and state taxes to be withheld, the insurance premium, the total payroll deductions, and, finally, the net earnings.

To compute the gross earnings, the applicable pay rate must be found. The pay rate is indicated by a code on the employee's payroll record. For instance, if the code is 06, the pay rate stored in row 6 of the pay rate table must be retrieved. Hence, the statement "move pay-rate-table pay-rate (06) to employee-pay-rate" accomplishes the retrieval. This move statement can be generalized as follows: If the pay rate code is stored in the input record field employee-pay-code, the statement becomes "move pay-rate-table pay-rate (input employee-pay-code) to employee-pay-rate." The procedure is illustrated in Figure 9.9.

Once the employee pay rate has been retrieved, then the gross earnings can be computed. You must recall that a manager's pay rate is a weekly rate, and thus the pay rate is the gross earnings. For all other employees, the pay rate is an hourly rate, and thus the gross earnings is the product of the pay rate and the number of hours worked. Assistant managers receive extra amounts as specified in the problem.

Figure 9.9 Retrieving a value from the pay-rate table

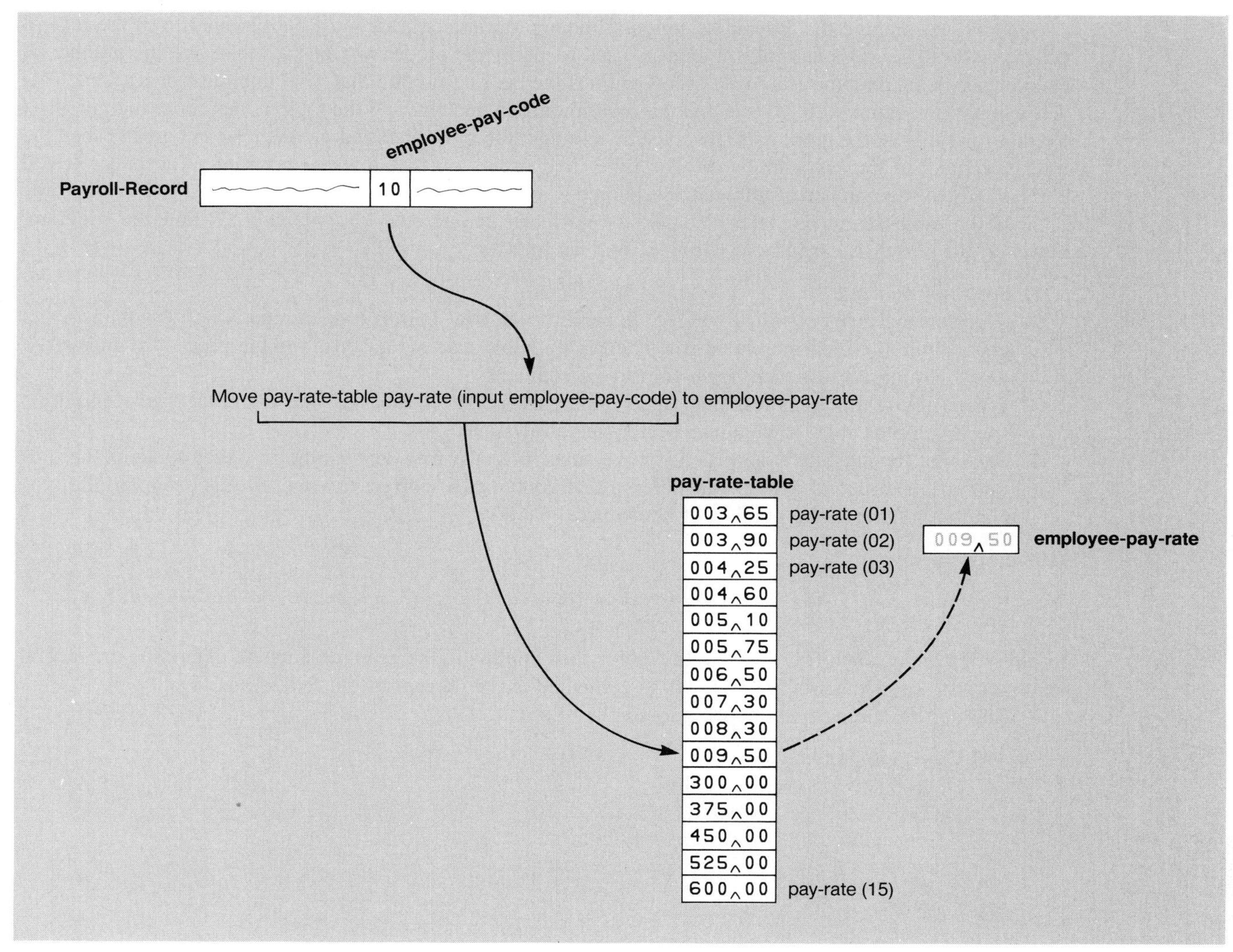

Figure 9.10 Retrieving the tax rate

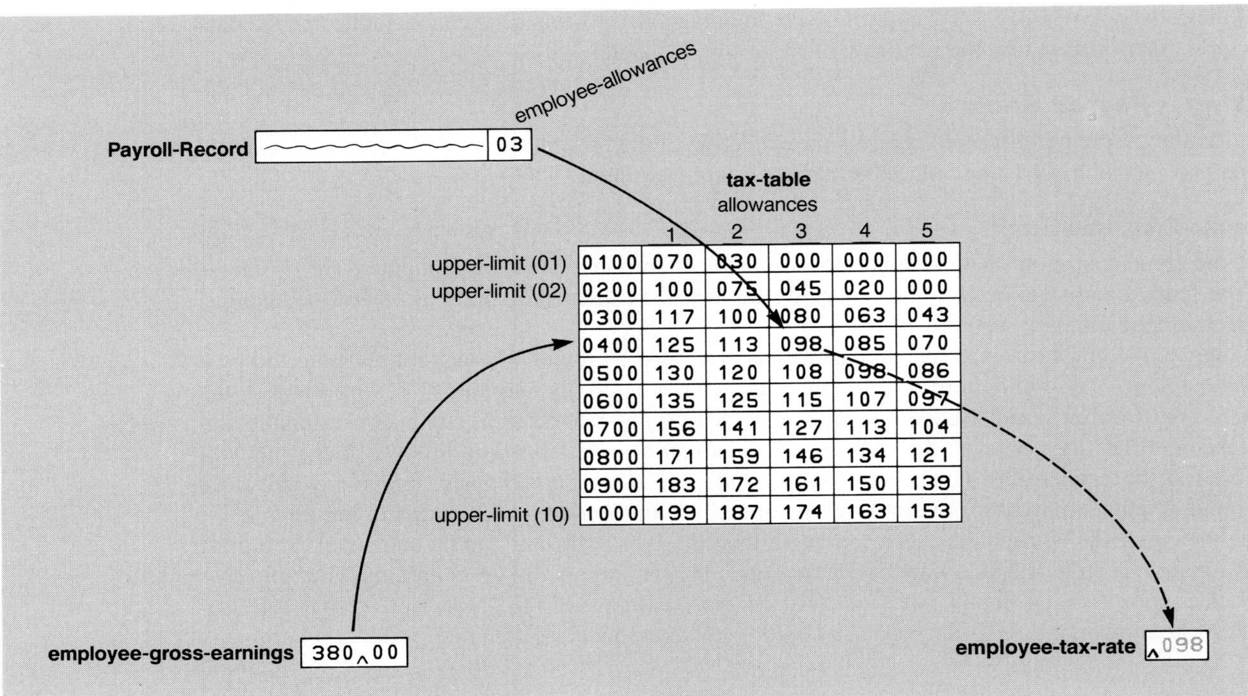

Next, to compute the federal tax amount, the appropriate tax rate must be retrieved from the federal tax rate table. The gross earnings amount is used to select the proper *row* of the table, and the number of allowances claimed by the employee then identifies the tax rate (within that row) that must be applied. This is illustrated in Figure 9.10. Recall that the first amount in each row of the table is the upper income limit for that row; that is, the gross earnings must be less than the limit specified on that row, but greater than the limit specified on the preceding row. The other five values on that row are tax rates. The one selected corresponds to the number of allowances claimed.

If the table search is done visually, the row can be selected very quickly. Within the program, however, the search is carried out within a loop, as follows:

1. Set row-counter to 1.
2. Compare the gross earnings with the upper limit on row 1. If gross-earnings is not less than upper-limit (1), then increment row-counter by 1 and test again, repeating the procedure until gross-earnings is less than upper-limit (row-counter).
3. When gross-earnings is less than upper-limit (row-counter), then tax-rate is in that row; it is specifically tax-rate (row-counter, employee-allowances).
4. Note that the tax rate is specified by **two** subscripts: the first denotes the row that contains the rate, and the second denotes the column that contains the correct tax-rate. In this program, the column number is the number of allowances claimed.

Hence, the statement

```
Move tax-table tax-rate (tax-table-row-counter, input employee-allowances) to
employee-tax-rate
```

retrieves the appropriate tax rate. The tax rate is then applied to the gross earnings to determine the federal tax amount to be withheld. The state tax is computed as 19 percent of the federal tax.

The corresponding pseudocode paragraphs follow.

410-Compute-Taxes.

1. Move "NO " to tax-table-flag.
2. Perform 550-Look-Up-Tax-Table
   varying tax-table-row-counter from initial value 1,
   incrementing it by 1, until tax-table-flag is equal to "YES".

3. Multiply employee-gross-earnings by employee-tax-rate
   to equal employee-federal-tax.
4. Multiply employee-federal-tax by .19 to equal employee-state-tax.

.

.

.

550-Look-Up-Tax-Table.

1. Test employee-gross-earnings
   against tax-table upper-limit (tax-table-row-counter);
2. When employee-gross-earnings is less than tax-table upper-limit (tax-table-row-counter),
   a. move tax-table tax-rate (tax-table-row-counter, input employee-allowances)
      to employee-tax-rate;
   b. move "YES" to tax-table-flag.

In paragraph 410, note that the loop that looks up the tax table is controlled by the flag tax-table-flag. Its function is to provide an exit from the loop as soon as the tax rate is found.

The next payroll deduction that must be found is the insurance premium. Recall that the premiums are stored in a table in working storage, whereas the payroll record contains a code that identifies the insurance plan the employee participates in. Here again, a table look-up procedure is needed as follows:

1. Set row-counter to 1.
2. Compare the code on the payroll record with the one in row 1 of the table:
   a. If the code on the payroll record matches the code in row 1 of the table, retrieve the premium in that row.
   b. If the codes do not match, increment row-counter by 1, and test again.
3. Repeat the process until the premium is found.
4. Exit from the table look-up procedure.

Figure 9.11 illustrates the table look-up procedure, and Figure 9.12 contains the related pseudocode entries.

Figure 9.11 Insurance table look-up

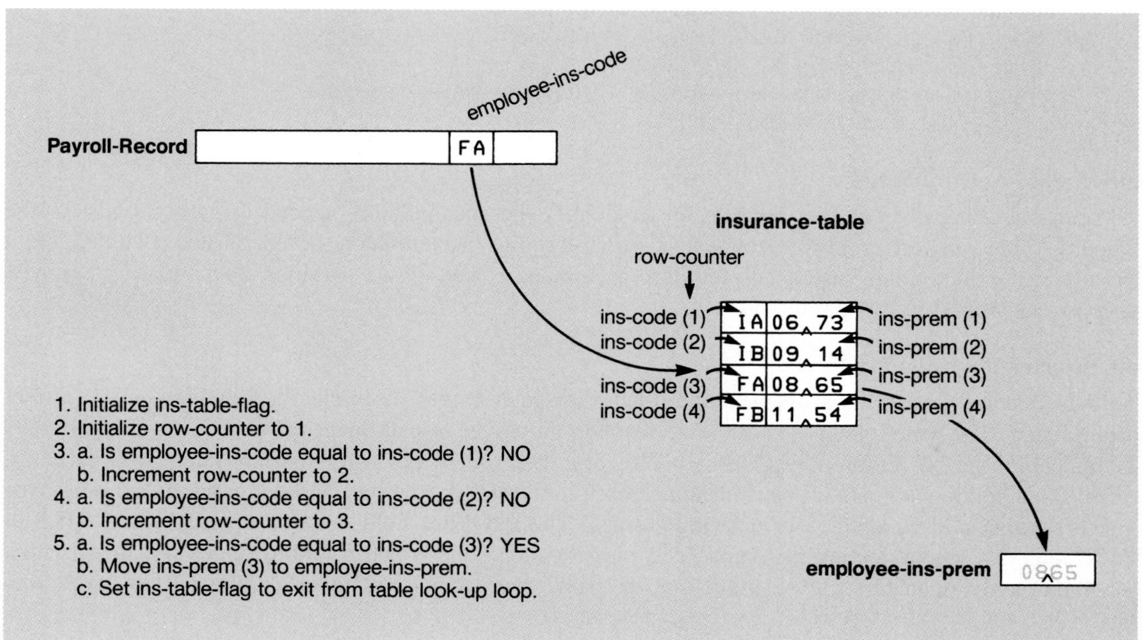

Figure 9.12 Pseudocode to retrieve the insurance premium

320-Compute-Employee-Items.

.
.
.

4. Set the insurance-table-flag to "NO ".
5. Perform 420-Look-Up-Insurance-Table
   varying insurance-table-row-counter from initial value 1,
   and incrementing it by 1, until insurance-table-flag is equal to "YES".

.
.
.

420-Look-Up-Insurance-Table.

1. Test input employee-insurance-code
   against insurance-table insurance-code (insurance-table-row-counter);
2. When they match,
   a. move insurance-table insurance-premium (insurance-table-row-counter)
      to employee-insurance-premium;
   b. move "YES" to insurance-table-flag.

At this point, all payroll deductions can be totaled, and the net earnings can be computed. The complete pseudocode paragraph 320-Compute-Employee-Items is shown below.

320-Compute-Employee-Items.

1. Move pay-rate (input employee-pay-code) from the pay-rate-table to employee-pay-rate.
2. Test input employee-class-code:
   a. if "06", move employee-pay-rate to employee-gross-earnings;
   b. if "05", multiply employee-pay-rate by input employee-hours,
      multiply input employee-open-close by 5,
      and add the two products and 10 to equal employee-gross-earnings;
   c. if any other, multiply employee-pay-rate by input employee-hours
      to equal employee-gross-earnings.
3. Perform 410-Compute-Taxes.
4. Set the insurance-table-flag to "NO ".
5. Perform 420-Look-Up-Insurance-Table
   varying insurance-table-row-counter from initial value 1,
   and incrementing it by 1, until insurance-table-flag is equal to "YES".
6. Add employee-federal-tax, employee-state-tax, employee-insurance-premium
   to equal employee-total-deductions.
7. Subtract employee-total-deductions from employee-gross-earnings
   to equal employee-net-earnings.

330-Update-Accumulators

The printer spacing chart is used here again to identify the accumulators needed to gather totals for the company. They are an employee-counter, a gross-earnings accumulator, a federal-tax accumulator, a state-tax accumulator, an insurance-premium accumulator, and a net-earnings accumulator. No new concepts are needed in this paragraph.

340-Prepare-Payroll-Line

The data that must be printed on the Payroll-Line for each employee is clearly identified in the printer spacing chart. The source fields for the store number, employee Social Security number, name, and hours (if applicable) are on the employee's Payroll-Record. The source fields for the pay rate, gross earnings, federal tax amount, state tax amount, insurance premium, total deductions, and net earnings are employee work areas that will be defined in working storage. The Pay-Base field must contain either a "/HR" or "/WK" entry. A simple test on the employee's classification code is performed to select the correct entry. Recall that only managers are salaried, that is, paid "per week"; all other employees are paid "per hour."

■ **Figure 9.13** Employee-class-table look-up procedure

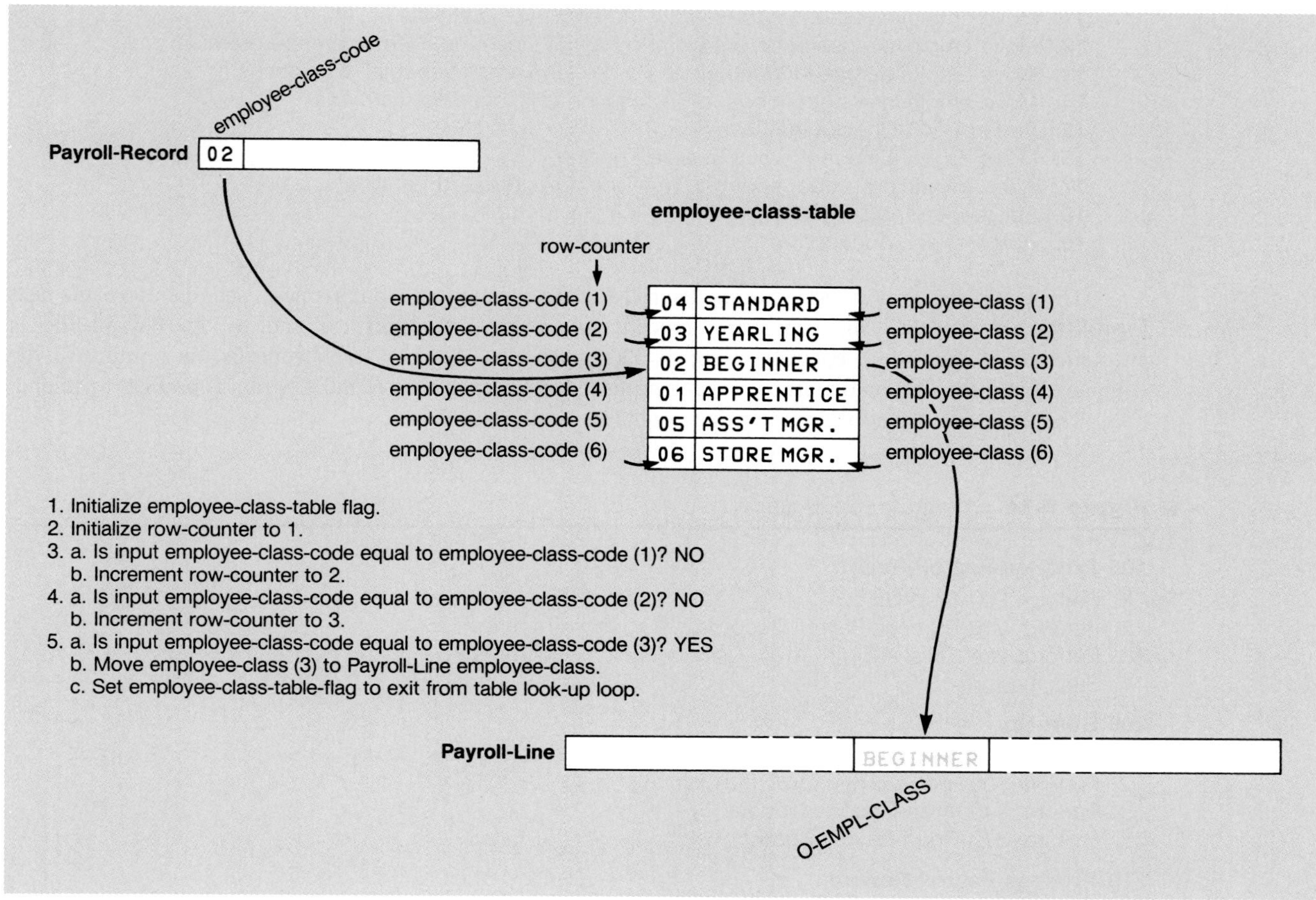

The one remaining field that must receive a value is the employee-class field. Since the input record contains only a class code, the hard-coded Employee-Class-Table in working storage has to be searched to find the corresponding classification entry. The table look-up procedure is similar to the one used to search the insurance table. It is illustrated in Figure 9.13.

When the input employee-class-code matches the class-code in a row of the table, the employee-class in that row is moved to the employee-class field of the output record Payroll-Line.

By now, the record Payroll-Line is completely prepared. Before the line is written onto the report, the procedure 440-Check-Line-Ctr is executed to determine if enough detail lines have been printed on the current page (30 lines max). Then, Payroll-Line is written to the Payroll-Report, and the line counter is incremented by 1. The pseudocode for paragraph 340-Prepare-Payroll-Line is shown below.

340-Prepare-Payroll-Line.

1. Clear the record area Payroll-line.
2. Move input employee-store-number to Payroll-Line employee-store-number.
3. Move input employee-SSN to Payroll-Line employee-SSN.
4. Move input employee-name to Payroll-Line employee-name.
5. Move "NO " to the employee-class-table-flag.
6. Perform 430-Look-Up-Employee-Class
   varying the employee-class-row-counter from initial value 1,
   and incrementing it by 1, until employee-class-table-flag is equal to "YES".
7. Move employee-pay-rate to Payroll-Line employee-pay-rate.
8. Test input employee-class-code:
   if "06", move "/WK" to Payroll-Line pay-base,
   else, move "/HR" to Payroll-Line pay-base, and
   move input employee-hours to Payroll-Line employee-hours.

9. Move employee-gross-earnings to Payroll-Line employee-gross-earnings.
10. Move employee-federal-tax to Payroll-Line employee-federal-tax.
11. Move employee-state-tax to Payroll-Line employee-state-tax.
12. Move employee-insurance-premium to Payroll-Line employee-insurance-premium.
13. Move employee-total-deductions to Payroll-Line employee-total-deductions.
14. Move employee-net-earnings to Payroll-Line employee-net-earnings.
15. Perform 440-Check-Line-Ctr.
16. Move Payroll-Line to the output area Printline.
17. After advancing proper-spacing, write the output record Printline.
18. Set proper-spacing to 1.
19. Add 1 to line-counter.

This completes the processing of the Payroll-Record currently in input memory, and, therefore, the next Payroll-Record is read. The processing procedures are repeated until the end of the Payroll-File is encountered. At that point, control is sent to 220-Finish-Up. This paragraph controls the printing of the company totals, the End-of-Report message is printed, and the execution of the program is brought to an end.

The complete program pseudocode is contained in Figure 9.14.

Figure 9.14 Program pseudocode

100-Produce-Payroll-Report.

1. Perform 200-Start Up.
2. Perform 210-Process-Payroll-Record until no more records.
3. Perform 220-Finish-Up.
4. Stop the run.

200-Start-Up.

1. Open the three files.
2. Perform 300-Initialize-Items.
3. Perform 540-Write-Report-Headers.
4. Perform 310-Read-Payroll-Record.

210-Process-Payroll-Record.

1. Perform 320-Compute-Employee-Items.
2. Perform 330-Update-Accumulators.
3. Perform 340-Prepare-Payroll-Line.
4. Perform 310-Read-Payroll-Record.

220-Finish-Up.

1. Perform 350-Prepare-Final-Totals.
2. Move End-Line to the output area Printline.
3. After advancing 5 lines, write the output record Printline.
4. Close the three files.

300-Initialize-Items.

1. Obtain the date from the system.
2. Move the date to Top-Line date.
3. Set the end-of-file flags WS-TABLE-RECORDS-FLAG and WS-PAYROLL-RECORDS-FLAG to "YES".
4. Set the company accumulators, the table row counters, and page-number to zero.
5. Perform 500-Read-Table-Record.
6. Perform 400-Load-Tables until no-more-table-records.

310-Read-Payroll-Record.

1. Read an input Payroll-Record.
2. Test for end-of-file record;
   if EOF record reached, set the flag WS-PAYROLL-RECORDS-FLAG to "NO ".

Figure 9.14 continued

320-Compute-Employee-Items.

1. Move payrate (input employee-paycode) from the payrate-table to employee-payrate.
2. Test input employee-class-code:
   a. if "06", move employee-payrate to employee-gross-earnings;
   b. if "05", multiply employee-payrate by input employee-hours,
      multiply input employee-open-close by 5,
      and add the two products and 10 to equal employee-gross-earnings;
   c. if any other, multiply employee-payrate by input employee-hours
      to equal employee-gross-earnings.
3. Perform 410-Compute-Taxes.
4. Set the insurance-table-flag to "NO ".
5. Perform 420-Look-Up-Insurance-Table
   varying insurance-table-row-counter from initial value 1,
   and incrementing it by 1, until insurance-table-flag is equal to "YES".
6. Add employee-federal-tax, employee-state-tax, employee-insurance-premium
   to equal employee-total-deductions.
7. Subtract employee-total-deductions from employee-gross-earnings
   to equal employee-net-earnings.

350-Update-Accumulators.

1. Add 1 to company-employee-counter.
2. Add employee-gross-earnings to company-gross-earnings.
3. Add employee-federal-tax to company-federal-tax.
4. Add employee-state-tax to company-state-tax.
5. Add employee-insurance-premium to company-insurance-premium.
6. Add employee-net-earnings to company-net-earnings.

340-Prepare-Payroll-Line.

1. Clear the record area Payroll-line.
2. Move input employee-store-number to Payroll-Line employee-store-number.
3. Move input employee-SSN to Payroll-Line employee-SSN.
4. Move input employee-name to Payroll-Line employee-name.
5. Move "NO " to the employee-class-table-flag.
6. Perform 430-Look-Up-Employee-Class
   varying the employee-class-row-counter from initial value 1,
   and incrementing it by 1, until employee-class-table-flag is equal to "YES".
7. Move employee-payrate to Payroll-Line employee-payrate.
8. Test input employee-class-code:
   if "06", move "/WK" to Payroll-Line pay-base,
   else, move "/HR" to Payroll-Line pay-base, and
   move input employee-hours to Payroll-Line employee-hours.
9. Move employee-gross-earnings to Payroll-Line employee-gross-earnings.
10. Move employee-federal-tax to Payroll-Line employee-federal-tax.
11. Move employee-state-tax to Payroll-Line employee-state-tax.
12. Move employee-insurance-premium to Payroll-Line employee-insurance-premium.
13. Move employee-total-deductions to Payroll-Line employee-total-deductions.
14. Move employee-net-earnings to Payroll-Line employee-net-earnings.
15. Perform 440-Check-Line-Ctr.
16. Move Payroll-Line to the output area Printline.
17. After advancing proper-spacing, write the output record Printline.
18. Set proper-spacing to 1.
19. Add 1 to line-counter.

350-Prepare-Final-Totals.

1. Move Company-Totals-Header to the output area Printline.
2. After advancing 5 lines, write the output record Printline.
3. Move company-employee-counter to Total-Employee-Count-Line company-employee-counter.
4. Move Total-Employee-Count-Line to the output area Printline.
5. After advancing 2 lines, write the output record Printline.
6. Move company-gross-earnings to Total-Gross-Earnings-Line company-gross-earnings.
7. Move Total-Gross-Earnings-Line to the output area Printline.
8. After advancing 1 line, write the output record Printline.
9. Move company-federal-tax to Total-Federal-Tax-Line company-federal-tax.
10. Move Total-Federal-Tax-Line to the output area Printline.
11. After advancing 1 line, write the output record Printline.
12. Move company-state-tax to Total-State-Tax-Line company-state-tax.
13. Move Total-State-Tax-Line to the output area Printline.
14. After advancing 1 line, write the output record Printline.
15. Move company-insurance-premiums to Total-Ins-Premium-Line company-insurance-premiums.
16. Move Total-Ins-Premium-Line to the output area Printline.
17. After advancing 1 line, write the output record Printline.
18. Move company-net-earnings to Total-Net-Earnings-Line company-net-earnings.
19. Move Total-Net-Earnings-Line to the output area Printline.
20. After advancing 1 line, write the output record Printline.

400-Load-Tables.

1. Test input record-code:
   a. if "T", then perform 510-Load-Federal-Tax-Table;
   b. if "P", then perform 520-Load-Payrate-Table;
   c. if "I", then perform 530-Load-Insurance-Table.
2. Perform 500-Read-Table-Record.

410-Compute-Taxes.

1. Move "NO " to tax-table-flag.
2. Perform 550-Look-Up-Tax-Table
   varying tax-table-row-counter from initial value 1,
   incrementing it by 1, until tax-table-flag is equal to "YES".
3. Multiply employee-gross-earnings by employee-tax-rate
   to equal employee-federal-tax.
4. Multiply employee-federal-tax by .19 to equal employee-state-tax.

420-Look-Up-Insurance-Table.

1. Test input employee-insurance-code
   against insurance-table insurance-code (insurance-table-row-counter);
2. When they match,
   a. move insurance-table insurance-premium (insurance-table-row-counter)
      to employee-insurance-premium;
   b. move "YES" to insurance-table-flag.

430-Look-Up-Employee-Class.

1. Test input employee-class-code
   against employee-class-table employee-class-code (employee-class-row-counter);
2. When they match,
   a. move employee-class-table employee-class (employee-class-row-counter)
      to Payroll-Line employee-class;
   b. move "YES" to employee-class-table-flag.

440-Check-Line-Ctr.

1. If line-counter is greater than or equal to line-limit,
   then, perform 540-Write-Report-Headers.

500-Read-Table-Record.

1. Read an input Table-File record.
2. Test for end-of-file record:
   if EOF record reached, set the flag WS-TABLE-RECORDS-FLAG to "NO ".

510-Load-Federal-Tax-Table.

1. Add 1 to tax-table-row-counter
2. Move input tax-table-row-values
   to federal-tax-table wage-level-info (tax-table-row-counter).

520-Load-Payrate-Table.

1. Add 1 to payrate-table-row-counter.
2. Move input payrate to payrate-table payrate (payrate-table-row-counter).

530-Load-Insurance-Table.

1. Add 1 to insurance-table-row-counter.
2. Move input insurance-table-row-values
   to insurance-table insurance-info (insurance-table-row-counter).

540-Write-Report-Headers.

1. Add 1 to page-number.
2. Move page-number to Top-Line page-number.
3. Move Top-Line to the output area Printline.
4. After advancing to the top of a new page,
   write the output record Printline.
5. Move Company-Name to the output area Printline.
6. After advancing 1 line, write the output record Printline.
7. Move Report-Name to the output area Printline.
8. After advancing 3 lines, write the output record Printline.
9. Move Headings-1 to the output area Printline.
10. After advancing 3 lines, write the output record Printline.
11. Move Headings-2 to the output area Printline.
12. After advancing 1 line, write the output record Printline.
13. Set line-counter to zero.
14. Set proper-spacing to 2.

550-Look-Up-Tax-Table.

1. Test employee-gross-earnings
   against tax-table upper-limit (tax-table-row-counter);
2. When employee-gross-earnings is less than tax-table upper-limit (tax-table-row-counter),
   a. move tax-table taxrate (tax-table-row-counter, input employee-allowances)
      to employee-taxrate;
   b. move "YES" to tax-table-flag.

■ **Figure 9.15** Flowchart structure for a PERFORM-VARYING statement

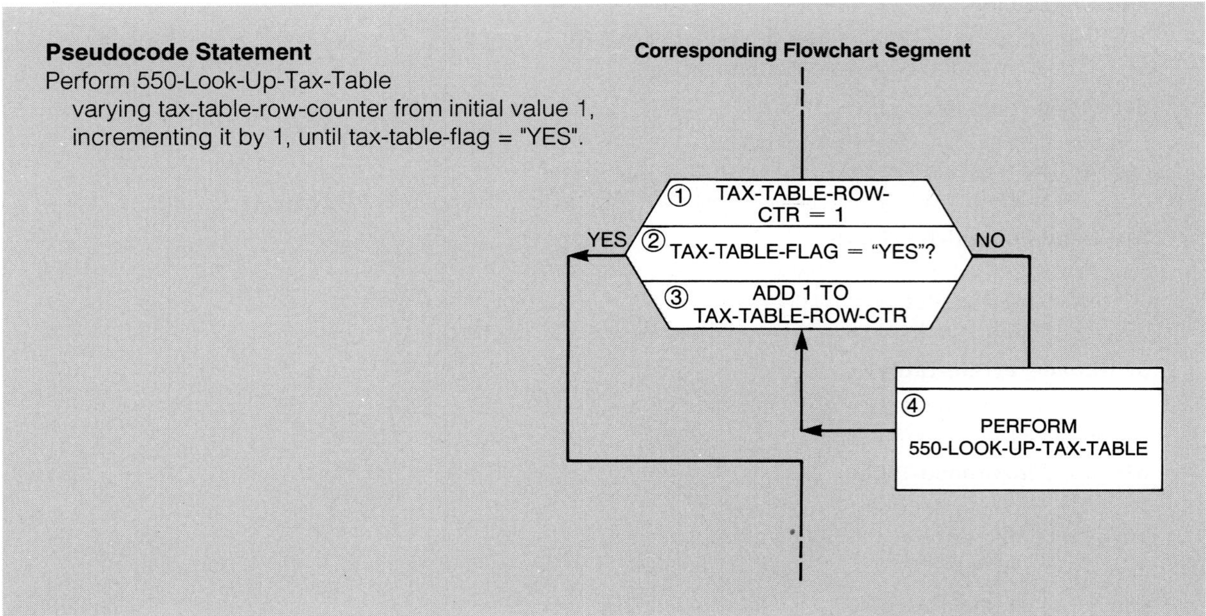

The Program Flowchart

The preceding discussion of the pseudocode paragraphs applies as well to the corresponding modules of the flowchart and therefore will not be repeated. However, there is a convenient flowchart structure that is often used in relation to tables. It is illustrated in Figure 9.15.

In the new flowchart segment of Figure 9.15, control enters the structure from above in the section labeled **1.** Here, the row counter is initialized to 1. Then control passes to the section labeled **2.** Here, the specified test is performed. If the tested condition is **not** satisfied, control follows the "NO" branch to the perform box. Control is then sent to the procedure 550-LOOK-UP-TAX-TABLE. When it returns, control enters the section labeled **3** from below. The row counter is incremented by 1. Control then enters section **2** again to perform the test. As long as the tested condition is not satisfied, the loop just described is executed repeatedly. Finally, when the tested condition is satisfied, control leaves section **3** along the "YES" branch and proceeds to the next function. This structure is used in modules 320-COMPUTE-EMPLOYEE-ITEMS, 340-PREPARE-PAYROLL-LINE, and 410-COMPUTE-TAXES to control the table look-up procedures. The complete program flowchart is shown in Figure 9.16.

This completes the design phase. Now, the programmer should review the design very carefully. In particular, he or she should "play computer" with the program pseudocode or the program flowchart and be on the lookout for existing logic errors and errors of omission. Does the design process the Tables File records correctly? Does it process the Payroll File records correctly? Are the correct values retrieved from the tables? Does the report satisfy the problem requirements? If corrections are needed, they should be made here, before beginning the coding of the program.

■ **Figure 9.16** Program flowchart

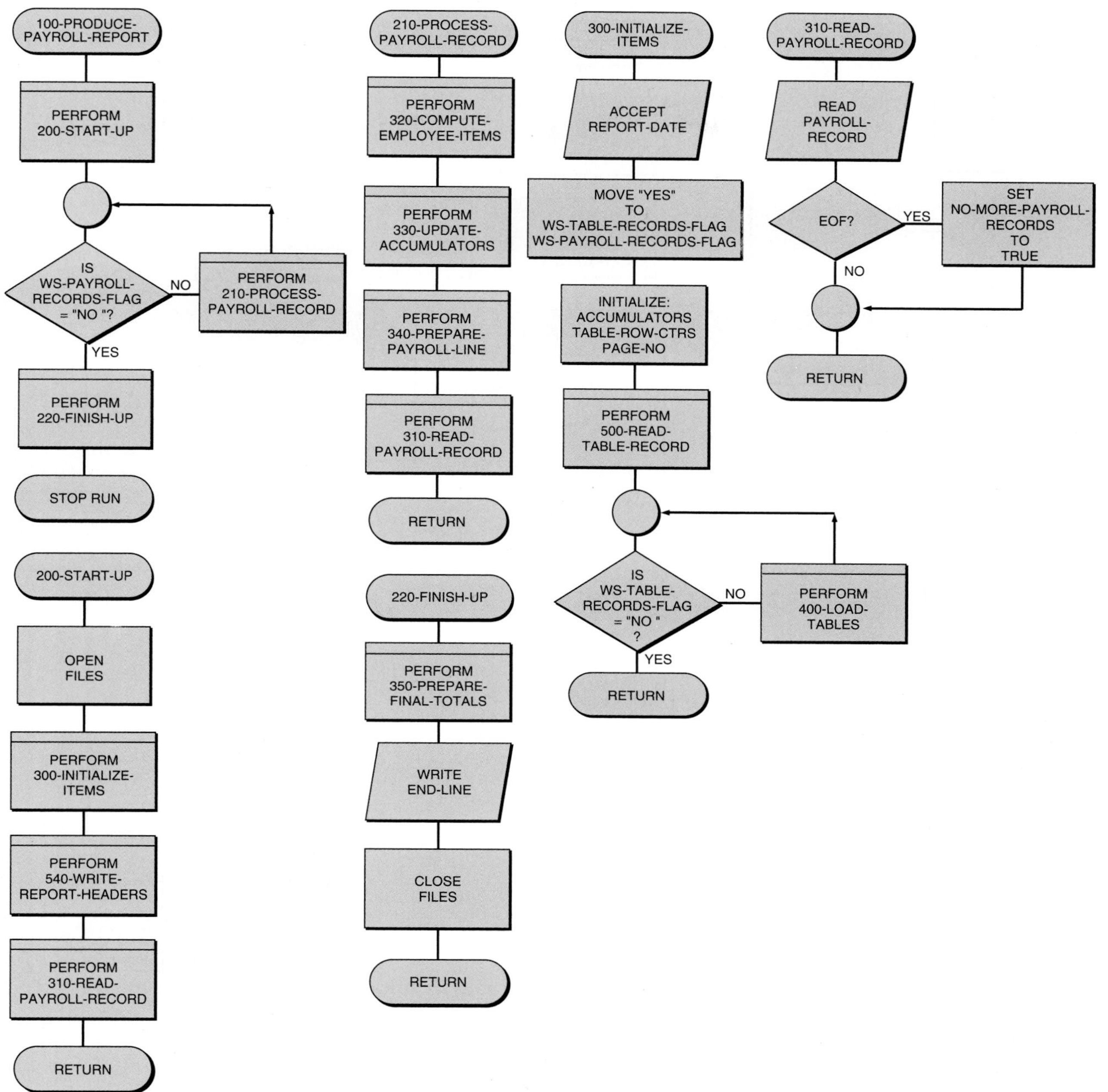

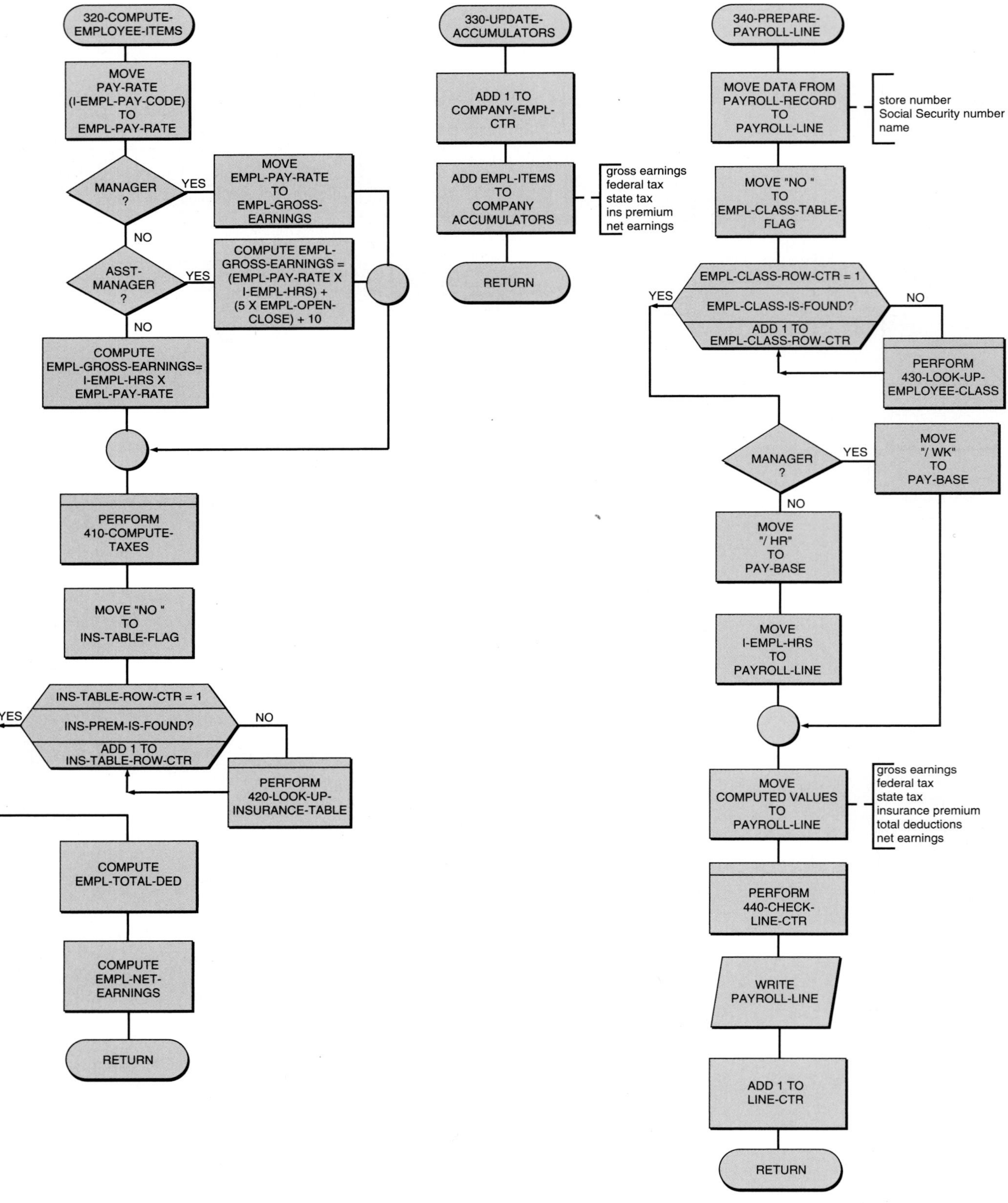
320-COMPUTE-EMPLOYEE-ITEMS
MOVE PAY-RATE (I-EMPL-PAY-CODE) TO EMPL-PAY-RATE
MANAGER ?
YES
MOVE EMPL-PAY-RATE TO EMPL-GROSS-EARNINGS
NO
ASST-MANAGER ?
YES
COMPUTE EMPL-GROSS-EARNINGS = (EMPL-PAY-RATE X I-EMPL-HRS) + (5 X EMPL-OPEN-CLOSE) + 10
NO
COMPUTE EMPL-GROSS-EARNINGS= I-EMPL-HRS X EMPL-PAY-RATE
PERFORM 410-COMPUTE-TAXES
MOVE "NO " TO INS-TABLE-FLAG
INS-TABLE-ROW-CTR = 1
INS-PREM-IS-FOUND?
ADD 1 TO INS-TABLE-ROW-CTR
YES
NO
PERFORM 420-LOOK-UP-INSURANCE-TABLE
COMPUTE EMPL-TOTAL-DED
COMPUTE EMPL-NET-EARNINGS
RETURN
330-UPDATE-ACCUMULATORS
ADD 1 TO COMPANY-EMPL-CTR
ADD EMPL-ITEMS TO COMPANY ACCUMULATORS
gross earnings
federal tax
state tax
ins premium
net earnings
RETURN
340-PREPARE-PAYROLL-LINE
MOVE DATA FROM PAYROLL-RECORD TO PAYROLL-LINE
store number
Social Security number
name
MOVE "NO " TO EMPL-CLASS-TABLE-FLAG
EMPL-CLASS-ROW-CTR = 1
EMPL-CLASS-IS-FOUND?
ADD 1 TO EMPL-CLASS-ROW-CTR
YES
NO
PERFORM 430-LOOK-UP-EMPLOYEE-CLASS
MANAGER ?
YES
MOVE "/ WK" TO PAY-BASE
NO
MOVE "/ HR" TO PAY-BASE
MOVE I-EMPL-HRS TO PAYROLL-LINE
MOVE COMPUTED VALUES TO PAYROLL-LINE
gross earnings
federal tax
state tax
insurance premium
total deductions
net earnings
PERFORM 440-CHECK-LINE-CTR
WRITE PAYROLL-LINE
ADD 1 TO LINE-CTR
RETURN

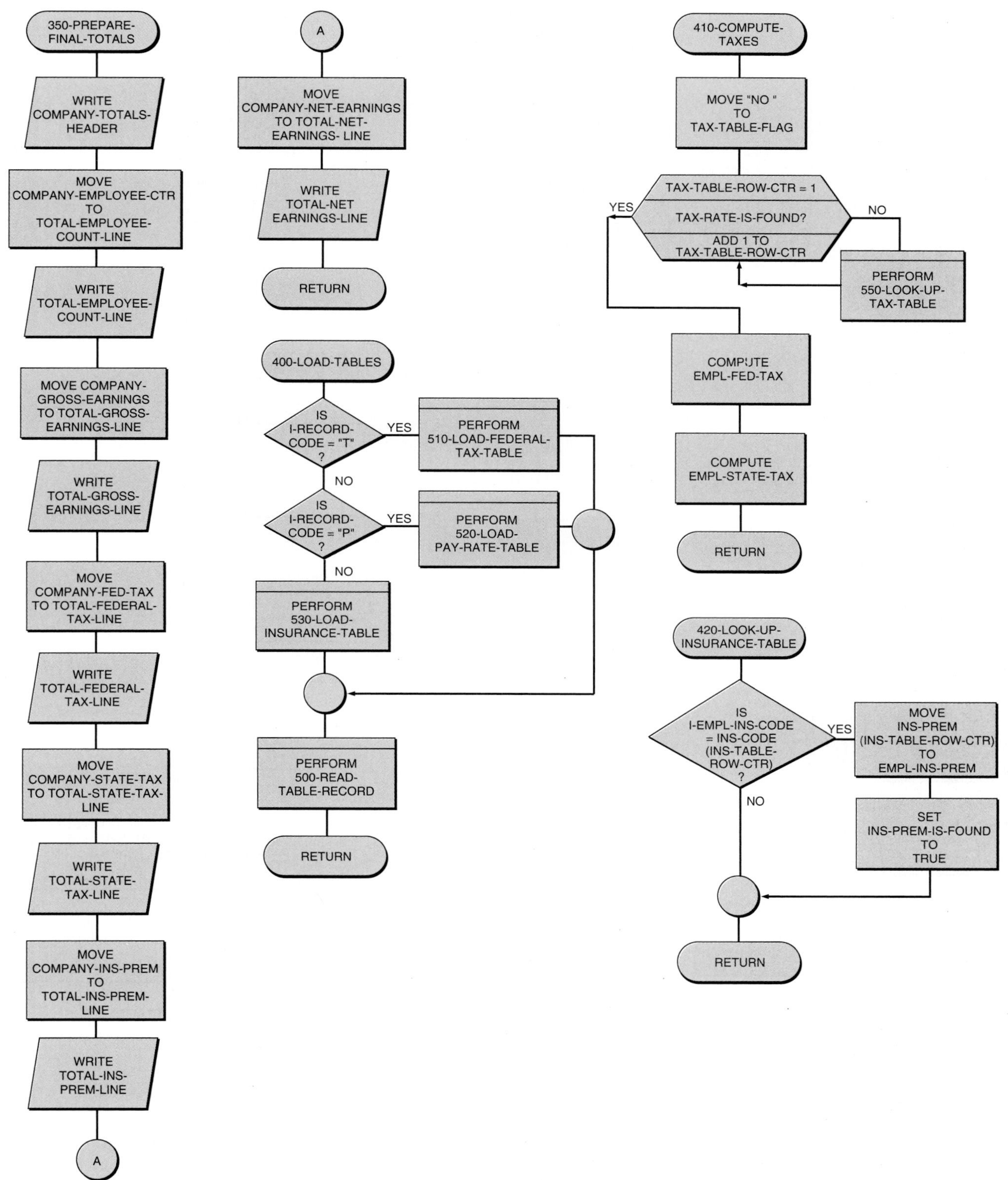
350-PREPARE-FINAL-TOTALS
WRITE COMPANY-TOTALS-HEADER
MOVE COMPANY-EMPLOYEE-CTR TO TOTAL-EMPLOYEE-COUNT-LINE
WRITE TOTAL-EMPLOYEE-COUNT-LINE
MOVE COMPANY-GROSS-EARNINGS TO TOTAL-GROSS-EARNINGS-LINE
WRITE TOTAL-GROSS-EARNINGS-LINE
MOVE COMPANY-FED-TAX TO TOTAL-FEDERAL-TAX-LINE
WRITE TOTAL-FEDERAL-TAX-LINE
MOVE COMPANY-STATE-TAX TO TOTAL-STATE-TAX-LINE
WRITE TOTAL-STATE-TAX-LINE
MOVE COMPANY-INS-PREM TO TOTAL-INS-PREM-LINE
WRITE TOTAL-INS-PREM-LINE
A
A
MOVE COMPANY-NET-EARNINGS TO TOTAL-NET-EARNINGS- LINE
WRITE TOTAL-NET EARNINGS-LINE
RETURN
400-LOAD-TABLES
IS I-RECORD-CODE = "T" ?
YES
PERFORM 510-LOAD-FEDERAL-TAX-TABLE
NO
IS I-RECORD-CODE = "P" ?
YES
PERFORM 520-LOAD-PAY-RATE-TABLE
NO
PERFORM 530-LOAD-INSURANCE-TABLE
PERFORM 500-READ-TABLE-RECORD
RETURN
410-COMPUTE-TAXES
MOVE "NO " TO TAX-TABLE-FLAG
TAX-TABLE-ROW-CTR = 1
YES
TAX-RATE-IS-FOUND?
NO
ADD 1 TO TAX-TABLE-ROW-CTR
PERFORM 550-LOOK-UP-TAX-TABLE
COMPUTE EMPL-FED-TAX
COMPUTE EMPL-STATE-TAX
RETURN
420-LOOK-UP-INSURANCE-TABLE
IS I-EMPL-INS-CODE = INS-CODE (INS-TABLE-ROW-CTR) ?
YES
MOVE INS-PREM (INS-TABLE-ROW-CTR) TO EMPL-INS-PREM
SET INS-PREM-IS-FOUND TO TRUE
NO
RETURN

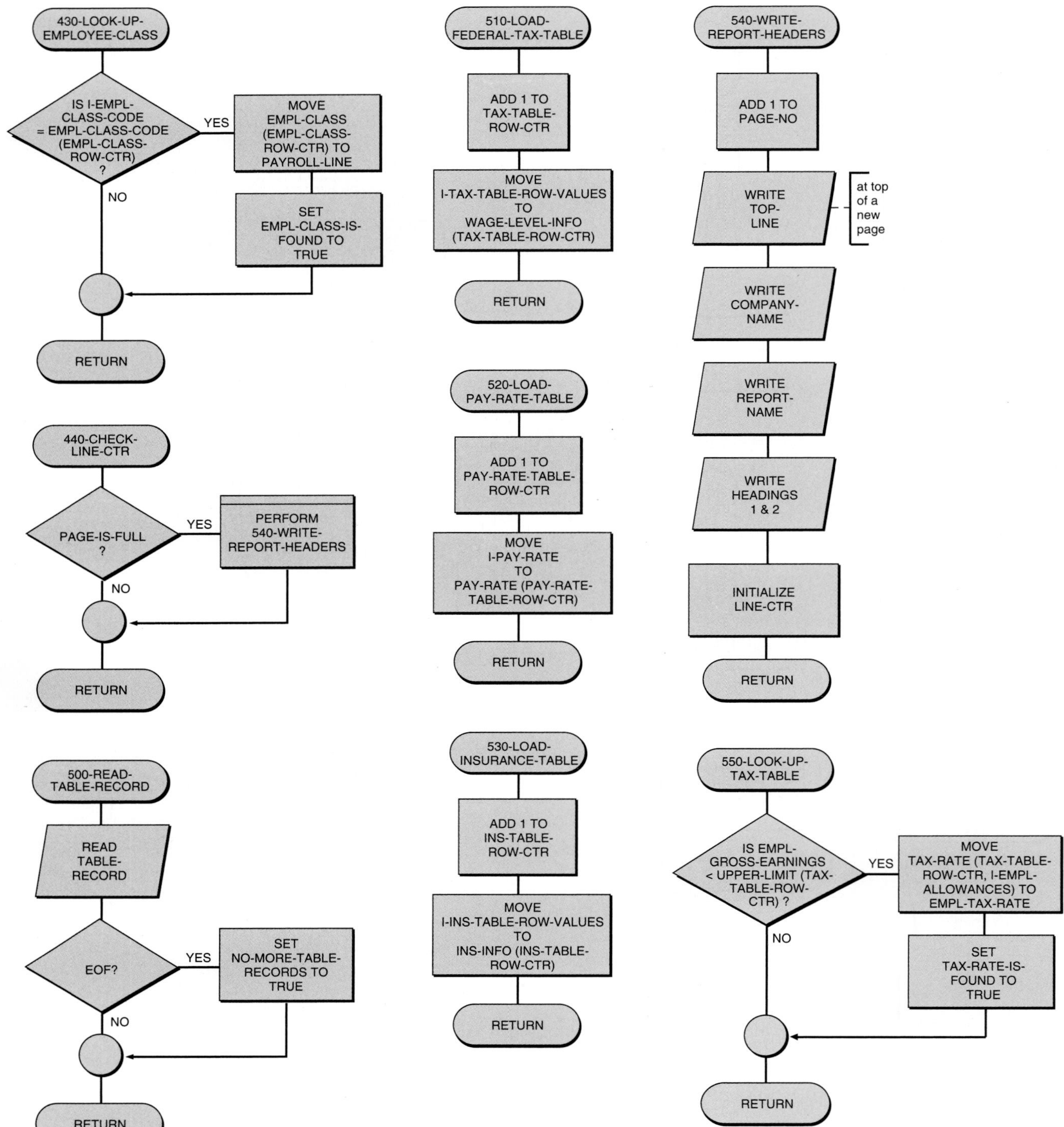
430-LOOK-UP-EMPLOYEE-CLASS
IS I-EMPL-CLASS-CODE = EMPL-CLASS-CODE (EMPL-CLASS-ROW-CTR) ?
YES
NO
MOVE EMPL-CLASS (EMPL-CLASS-ROW-CTR) TO PAYROLL-LINE
SET EMPL-CLASS-IS-FOUND TO TRUE
RETURN
440-CHECK-LINE-CTR
PAGE-IS-FULL ?
YES
NO
PERFORM 540-WRITE-REPORT-HEADERS
RETURN
500-READ-TABLE-RECORD
READ TABLE-RECORD
EOF?
YES
NO
SET NO-MORE-TABLE-RECORDS TO TRUE
RETURN
510-LOAD-FEDERAL-TAX-TABLE
ADD 1 TO TAX-TABLE-ROW-CTR
MOVE I-TAX-TABLE-ROW-VALUES TO WAGE-LEVEL-INFO (TAX-TABLE-ROW-CTR)
RETURN
520-LOAD-PAY-RATE-TABLE
ADD 1 TO PAY-RATE-TABLE-ROW-CTR
MOVE I-PAY-RATE TO PAY-RATE (PAY-RATE-TABLE-ROW-CTR)
RETURN
530-LOAD-INSURANCE-TABLE
ADD 1 TO INS-TABLE-ROW-CTR
MOVE I-INS-TABLE-ROW-VALUES TO INS-INFO (INS-TABLE-ROW-CTR)
RETURN
540-WRITE-REPORT-HEADERS
ADD 1 TO PAGE-NO
WRITE TOP-LINE
at top of a new page
WRITE COMPANY-NAME
WRITE REPORT-NAME
WRITE HEADINGS 1 & 2
INITIALIZE LINE-CTR
RETURN
550-LOOK-UP-TAX-TABLE
IS EMPL-GROSS-EARNINGS < UPPER-LIMIT (TAX-TABLE-ROW-CTR) ?
YES
NO
MOVE TAX-RATE (TAX-TABLE-ROW-CTR, I-EMPL-ALLOWANCES) TO EMPL-TAX-RATE
SET TAX-RATE-IS-FOUND TO TRUE
RETURN

Tables in COBOL

At this point, we interrupt the application of the problem-solving procedure to study the COBOL language requirements as they pertain to the table concepts discussed during the design phase.

There are three essential considerations:

1. Defining a table
2. Storing values in a table
3. Accessing data in a table

Defining a Table

A table is defined by coding the OCCURS clause in a data description entry. For instance, in the entry

```
01   TEST-TABLE.
     05 WS-TEST   OCCURS 10 TIMES   PIC 999.
```

the OCCURS clause specifies that WS-TEST is a repeating data item within the record TEST-TABLE. The literal 10 in the clause indicates the number of repetitions or occurrences of the data item WS-TEST, thereby creating the table. All occurrences share the PIC clause. A reference to any of the ten occurrences must use the data name WS-TEST, and it must be accompanied by a subscript entered within parentheses. The subscript indicates the occurrence within the table. For instance, WS-TEST (3) [read WS-TEST sub 3] is the name of the third occurrence, and WS-TEST (10) is the name of the tenth occurrence. The subscript must not have a value greater than the literal specified in the OCCURS clause. For instance, WS-TEST (12) is undefined, since there are only 10 occurrences of the item in the table. Since a subscript (or an index, as you will learn later) is needed to refer to a table item, the item is classified as a subscripted (or indexed) data item. The size of each item in the above table is 3; the size of the table itself is 30.

To aid in the conceptualization of a table, a visual representation is often used. A *one-level table,* like the one above, can be represented vertically or horizontally. See Figure 9.17.

In the above example, the data item that repeats within the table is an elementary item. The OCCURS clause can also be used at the group level. For instance, in the entry

```
01   STATES-TABLE.
     05 STATE-INFO OCCURS 51 TIMES.
        10 ST-ABBREV    PIC XX.
        10 ST-NAME      PIC X(20).
        10 ST-CAPITAL   PIC X(15).
```

Figure 9.17 Vertical and horizontal representations of a one-level table

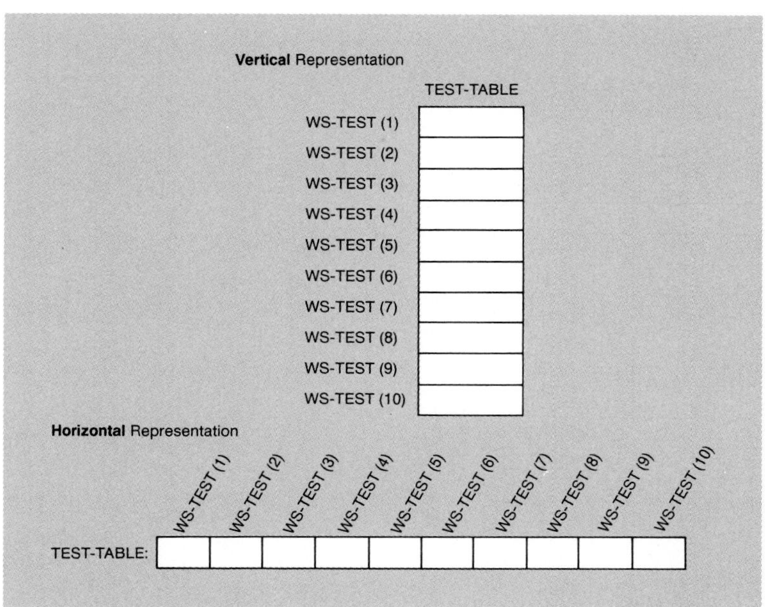

the data item defined using the OCCURS clause is STATE-INFO, a group item. The group item contains the three elementary items ST-ABBREV, ST-NAME, and ST-CAPITAL. It should be obvious that **every** occurrence of STATE-INFO also contains the three elementary items. In other words, there are as many occurrences of each of the three elementary items as there are occurrences of the group item. So, clearly, subscripting a group item (by using the OCCURS clause) automatically subscripts its subordinate elementary items. Thus, in the STATES-TABLE, four data items are subscripted: the group item STATE-INFO and the three elementary items ST-ABBREV, ST-NAME, and ST-CAPITAL. Assuming the table is loaded alphabetically by name, the 46th occurrence in the table contains the following data:

```
VTVERMONT_____________ MONTPELIER_____
```

The data name STATE-INFO (46) references the group of 37 characters in row 46; the data name ST-ABBREV (46) references the characters in the first two bytes of row 46, namely "VT"; the data name ST-NAME (46) references the characters in the next 20 bytes of row 46, namely, "VERMONT _____________"; and the data name ST-CAPITAL (46) references the characters in the last 15 bytes of row 46, namely, "MONTPELIER _____".

Note that the size of one occurrence of the group item STATE-INFO is 37, the sum of the sizes of its elementary items. The size of the table (STATES-TABLE) is therefore 51 × 37, or 1887. (The table is defined to contain 51 occurrences in order to allow the District of Columbia to be included.)

An illustration of STATES-TABLE and its subscripted data items is contained in Figure 9.18.

The sample program of this chapter needs tables of the two types illustrated above. Since the pay rate table contains only pay rates, it is of the type shown in Figure 9.17, but since the insurance table and the employee class table require more than one data item in each row of the table, they are of the type illustrated in Figure 9.18. These program tables can be defined as follows:

1.
```
01   PAYRATE-TABLE.
     05 WS-PAY-RATE OCCURS 15 TIMES PIC S999V99.
```
In this table, there are 15 occurrences of the data item WS-PAY-RATE, specifically, WS-PAY-RATE (1), WS-PAY-RATE (2), . . . , WS-PAY-RATE (15). The size of each item is 5, and the size of the table is 75.

2.
```
01   INSURANCE-TABLE.
     05 WS-INS-INFO OCCURS 4 TIMES.
        10 WS-INS-CODE      PIC XX.
        10 WS-INS-PREM      PIC S99V99.
```
In this table, there are four occurrences of the group item WS-INS-INFO. Each occurrence of WS-INS-INFO contains one occurrence of WS-INS-CODE, and one occurrence of

Figure 9.18 Subscripted data names in table—example

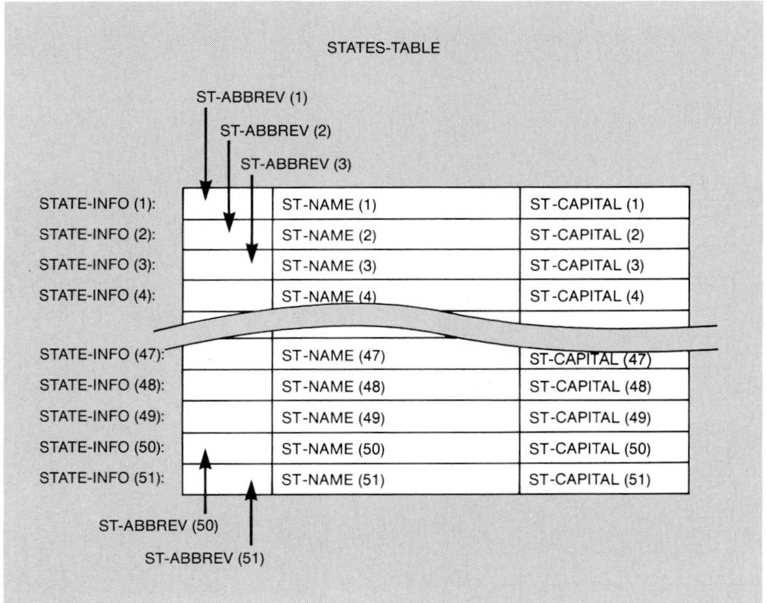

WS-INS-PREM. The size of one occurrence of the group item WS-INS-INFO is 6, and the size of the table is 24.

3.
```
01  EMPLOYEE-CLASS-TABLE.
    05 WS-EMPL-CLASS-INFO OCCURS 6 TIMES.
       10 WS-EMPL-CLASS-CODE  PIC 99.
       10 WS-EMPL-CLASS       PIC X(10).
```

In this table, there are six occurrences of the group item WS-EMPL-CLASS-INFO. Each occurrence of this group contains one occurrence of WS-EMPL-CLASS-CODE and one occurrence of WS-EMPL-CLASS. The size of one occurrence of the group item WS-EMPL-CLASS-INFO is 12, and the size of the table is 72.

Storing Values in a Table

Defining a table simply allocates storage areas. Additional coding is required to actually store values in the table. There are two distinct ways of storing values in a table: one is referred to as *hard-coding* a table, the other is *loading* a table. In hard-coding a table, the data is specified in VALUE clauses, whereas in loading a table, the data must be transferred into the table by executing instructions within the program. The data can be produced within the program and moved to the table, or it can be initially stored in a file external to the program. In that case, instructions must access the records of the file and MOVE the data into the table. Explanations and examples of both methods follow.

Hard-Coding a Table—Part I

Traditionally, a table has been hard-coded as follows:

1. A data item is defined using one or more VALUE clauses to specify its contents.
2. A successor data item REDEFINES the preceding item (see REDEFINES in Chapter 8). This redefinition uses the OCCURS clause, thereby storing the values of the preceding data description entry into the newly defined table.

Example 1:

```
01  MONTH-VALUES.
    05 PIC X(9)   VALUE "JANUARY  ".
    05 PIC X(9)   VALUE "FEBRUARY ".
    05 PIC X(9)   VALUE "MARCH    ".
    05 PIC X(9)   VALUE "APRIL    ".
    05 PIC X(9)   VALUE "MAY      ".
    05 PIC X(9)   VALUE "JUNE     ".
    05 PIC X(9)   VALUE "JULY     ".
    05 PIC X(9)   VALUE "AUGUST   ".
    05 PIC X(9)   VALUE "SEPTEMBER".
    05 PIC X(9)   VALUE "OCTOBER  ".
    05 PIC X(9)   VALUE "NOVEMBER ".
    05 PIC X(9)   VALUE "DECEMBER ".

01  MONTH-TABLE REDEFINES MONTH-VALUES.
    05 WS-MONTH   OCCURS 12 TIMES  PIC X(9).
```

The data item MONTH-VALUES contains 12 nameless elementary items, each with specific contents, as seen in Figure 9.19a. The data item MONTH-TABLE contains 12 occurrences of the elementary item WS-MONTH, as shown in Figure 9.19b. But, because MONTH-TABLE is a redefinition (REDEFINES) of MONTH-VALUES, it essentially allows the layout of Figure 9.19b to be superimposed upon Figure 9.19a. The net result is Figure 9.19c, in which the actual month names can be referenced as WS-MONTH (1), WS-MONTH (2), and so on.

Example 2:

```
01  MONTH-VALUES.
    05 PIC X(13)   VALUE "01JANUARY   31".
    05 PIC X(13)   VALUE "02FEBRUARY  28".
    05 PIC X(13)   VALUE "03MARCH     31".
    05 PIC X(13)   VALUE "04APRIL     30".
    05 PIC X(13)   VALUE "05MAY       31".
    05 PIC X(13)   VALUE "06JUNE      30".
    05 PIC X(13)   VALUE "07JULY      31".
    05 PIC X(13)   VALUE "08AUGUST    31".
    05 PIC X(13)   VALUE "09SEPTEMBER30".
    05 PIC X(13)   VALUE "10OCTOBER  31".
    05 PIC X(13)   VALUE "11NOVEMBER 30".
    05 PIC X(13)   VALUE "12DECEMBER 31".
```

```
01  MONTH-TABLE REDEFINES MONTH-VALUES.
    05 MONTH-INFO OCCURS 12 TIMES.
       10 WS-MONTH-NO         PIC 99.
       10 WS-MONTH            PIC X(9).
       10 WS-DAYS-IN-MONTH    PIC 99.
```

In this example, the redefinition of MONTH-VALUES, the storage area originally assigned values, allows references to any of the three components in each occurrence of the group item MONTH-INFO. Thus, MONTH-INFO (5) is "05MAY   31", but WS-MONTH-NO (5) is "05", WS-MONTH (5) is "MAY   ", and WS-DAYS-IN-MONTH (5) is "31".

Example 3:

```
01  MONTH-ABBREV-VALUES.
    05 PIC X(36)
       VALUE ''JANFEBMARAPRMAYJUNJULAUGSEPOCTNOVDEC".

01  MONTH-ABBREV-TABLE REDEFINES MONTH-ABBREV-VALUES.
    05 WS-MONTH-ABBREV   OCCURS 12 TIMES   PIC XXX.
```

In this example, the redefinition of MONTH-ABBREV-VALUES is a table consisting of 12 occurrences of the elementary item WS-MONTH-ABBREV. The size of each occurrence is 3. The characters in the literal of the VALUE clause are therefore separated into 12 items of 3 characters each, and, as a result, WS-MONTH-ABBREV (1) refers to "JAN", WS-MONTH-ABBREV (5) to "MAY" (the fifth grouping of 3 characters), and WS-MONTH-ABBREV (12) to "DEC" (the twelfth grouping of 3 characters).

Note: If month abbreviations are needed, and the table in example 2 is available, a separate table containing month abbreviations is not required, since the abbreviations can be obtained directly from the table in example 2 by using reference modification (see Chapter 8). For instance, in example 2, WS-MONTH (1) is "JANUARY   ", but WS-MONTH (1) (1:3) is "JAN"; WS-MONTH (12) is "DECEMBER ", but WS-MONTH (12) (1:3) is "DEC".

In the sample program, the table containing the employee classifications must be hard-coded. The coding might be as follows:

```
01  EMPLOYEE-CLASS-VALUES.
    05 PIC X(12)   VALUE "04STANDARD  ".
    05 PIC X(12)   VALUE "03YEARLING  ".
    05 PIC X(12)   VALUE "02BEGINNER  ".
    05 PIC X(12)   VALUE "01APPRENTICE".
    05 PIC X(12)   VALUE "05ASS'T MGR.".
    05 PIC X(12)   VALUE "06STORE MGR.".

01  EMPLOYEE-CLASS-TABLE REDEFINES EMPLOYEE-CLASS-VALUES.
    05 WS-EMPL-CLASS-INFO   OCCURS 6 TIMES.
       10 WS-EMPL-CLASS-CODE     PIC 99.
       10 WS-EMPL-CLASS          PIC X(10).
```

Figure 9.19 Illustration of the hard-coded table in Example 1

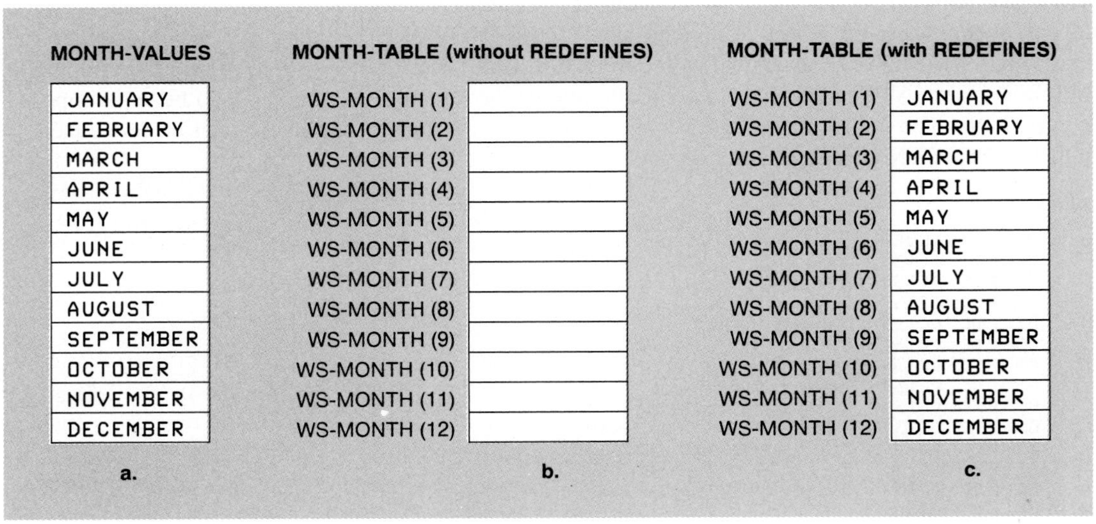

MONTH-VALUES	MONTH-TABLE (without REDEFINES)		MONTH-TABLE (with REDEFINES)	
JANUARY	WS-MONTH (1)		WS-MONTH (1)	JANUARY
FEBRUARY	WS-MONTH (2)		WS-MONTH (2)	FEBRUARY
MARCH	WS-MONTH (3)		WS-MONTH (3)	MARCH
APRIL	WS-MONTH (4)		WS-MONTH (4)	APRIL
MAY	WS-MONTH (5)		WS-MONTH (5)	MAY
JUNE	WS-MONTH (6)		WS-MONTH (6)	JUNE
JULY	WS-MONTH (7)		WS-MONTH (7)	JULY
AUGUST	WS-MONTH (8)		WS-MONTH (8)	AUGUST
SEPTEMBER	WS-MONTH (9)		WS-MONTH (9)	SEPTEMBER
OCTOBER	WS-MONTH (10)		WS-MONTH (10)	OCTOBER
NOVEMBER	WS-MONTH (11)		WS-MONTH (11)	NOVEMBER
DECEMBER	WS-MONTH (12)		WS-MONTH (12)	DECEMBER
a.		b.		c.

In this coding, the data item WS-EMPL-CLASS-CODE (1) contains "04", the data item WS-EMPL-CLASS (1) contains "STANDARD ", the data item WS-EMPL-CLASS-CODE (3) contains "02", the data item WS-EMPL-CLASS (3) contains "BEGINNER ", and so on. (The VALUE clauses have been entered in order of usage-frequency to make the table look-up procedure execute more efficiently. More comments about this later.)

Hard-Coding a Table—Part II

COBOL '85 makes it possible to initialize a hard-coded table without using the REDEFINES clause, by combining the use of the VALUE clause and the OCCURS clause in the same data description entry.

Example 4:

```
01  TEST-TOTALS-TABLE.
    05 WS-TEST-TOTAL   OCCURS 50 TIMES   PIC 999
                                         VALUE ZERO.
```

The net effect of the VALUE clause is to initialize each of the 50 occurrences of WS-TEST-TOTAL with zeros. Obviously, instructions within the PROCEDURE DIVISION can later change those values. This use of the VALUE clause produces the same results as the statement INITIALIZE TEST-TOTALS-TABLE. (You may want to consider the advantages of the greater self-documentation provided by the INITIALIZE statement.)

Example 5:

```
01  VALUE "JANFEBMARAPRMAYJUNJULAUGSEPOCTNOVDEC".
    05 WS-MONTH-ABBREV   OCCURS 12 TIMES   PIC XXX.
```

The result is similar to example 3, except that no name has been given to the table.

Example 6:

If the insurance table of the sample program were to be hard-coded, its description could be as follows:

```
01  INSURANCE-TABLE   VALUE "IA0673IB0914FA0865FB1154".
    05 WS-INS-INFO   OCCURS 4 TIMES.
       10 WS-INS-CODE    PIC XX.
       10 WS-INS-PREM    PIC 99V99.
```

Note that each occurrence of WS-INS-INFO consists of six bytes. In each of these groupings, the first two characters are in the field WS-INS-CODE (*x*), and the next four characters are in the field WS-INS-PREM (*x*). Thus, the data item WS-INS-CODE (3) contains "FA", and the data item WS-INS-PREM (3) contains "0865" with an assumed decimal point between the 8 and the 6.

Loading a Table

As noted earlier, the process of loading values into a table requires the execution of instructions in the PROCEDURE DIVISION. If the data to be loaded into a table is stored in a file, then a READ instruction must access a record of the file, and one or more MOVE statements must be executed to copy the data into the table.

Example 1:

Given the following table:

```
01  TEST-TABLE.
    05 WS-TEST   OCCURS 10 TIMES   PIC 999.
```

Suppose that the tests are available in a TEST-FILE, one test per record, and the record description is simply as follows:

```
01  TEST-RECORD.
    05 I-TEST   PIC 999.
```

It should be clear that a total of 10 records will have to be read to fully load the table. As a record is read into input memory, a MOVE statement will transfer the value to one occurrence of the repeating data item WS-TEST in the table. It is necessary to specify the occurrence. Since the READ and MOVE statements must be executed 10 times, a loop is in order. It can be set up as follows:

```
MOVE ZERO TO TEST-TABLE-CTR.
PERFORM 300-READ-N-MOVE
    UNTIL TEST-TABLE-CTR = 10.
```

```
        .
        .
        .
    300-READ-N-MOVE.
        PERFORM 400-READ-TEST-RECORD.
        ADD 1 TO TEST-TABLE-CTR.
        MOVE I-TEST TO WS-TEST (TEST-TABLE-CTR).
```

Since TEST-TABLE-CTR is being used as a subscript, it must be defined as a numeric integer data item. Do you see that the test value on the first record is moved into WS-TEST (1) because the value of the subscript TEST-TABLE-CTR is 1? Similarly, the test value on the second record is moved into WS-TEST (2) because the second time procedure 300-READ-N-MOVE is executed, the counter is incremented by 1, and therefore the subscript of WS-TEST is 2. Executing the procedure 10 times will load the test values from the 10 records into the 10 occurrences of the item WS-TEST in TEST-TABLE.

Note that the loop is controlled by the condition in the UNTIL clause: TEST-TABLE-CTR = 10.

An alternate way of coding the above instructions makes use of another form of the PERFORM statement. Examine the following coding:

```
        PERFORM 300-READ-N-MOVE
            VARYING TEST-TABLE-CTR FROM 1 BY 1
                UNTIL TEST-TABLE-CTR > 10.
        .
        .
        .
    300-READ-N-MOVE.
        PERFORM 400-READ-TEST-RECORD.
        MOVE I-TEST TO WS-TEST (TEST-TABLE-CTR).
```

Do you see that the VARYING clause of the PERFORM statement eliminates the need to initialize and to increment the counter TEST-TABLE-CTR in separate statements?

The logic of the PERFORM-VARYING statement is illustrated in Figure 9.20, and its execution proceeds as follows:

1. As control first enters the PERFORM-VARYING statement, TEST-TABLE-CTR is set to the initial value specified in the FROM phrase, namely 1.
2. The condition in the UNTIL clause is tested.
   a. If the condition is false, the procedure under the control of the PERFORM is executed; that is, control is sent to paragraph 300-READ-N-MOVE.
      When control returns from the procedure 300-READ-N-MOVE, it enters the VARYING clause, where TEST-TABLE-CTR is incremented by the value specified in the BY phrase, namely 1. The condition in the UNTIL clause is tested again, and then step 2a is repeated.
   b. If the condition is true, control leaves the PERFORM statement to execute the first statement beyond the scope of the PERFORM.

■ **Figure 9.20** Logic of the PERFORM-VARYING statement

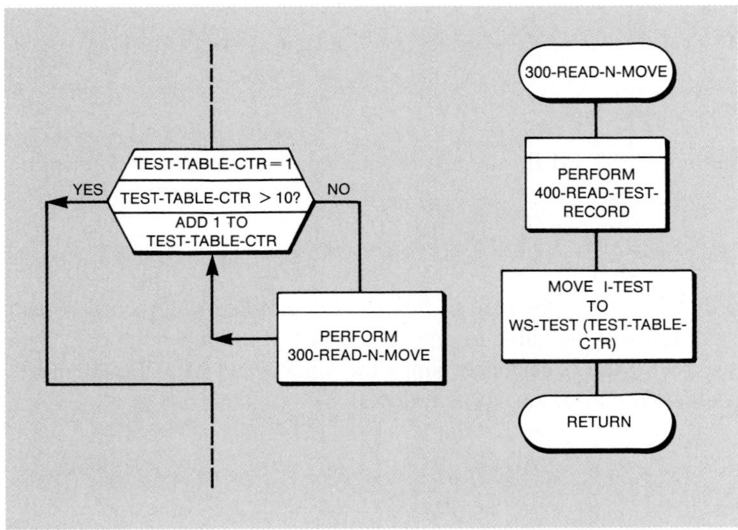

Figure 9.21 PERFORM-VARYING statement format

```
PERFORM [ procedure-name-1 [ {THROUGH} procedure-name-2 ] ]
                             {THRU   }
        [ WITH TEST {BEFORE} ]
                    {AFTER }
        VARYING {identifier-2 } FROM {identifier-3 } BY {identifier-4} UNTIL condition-1
                {index-name-1 }      {index-name-2 }    {literal-2   }
                                     {literal-1    }
        [imperative-statement END-PERFORM]
```

The format for this PERFORM statement is shown in Figure 9.21.

In this format, the only new entries are the ones contained in the VARYING clause. The following rules apply:

Rules Governing Use of the PERFORM-VARYING Statement

1. Identifier-2 must be the name of an elementary numeric data item. (Index-names will be explained later.)
2. Identifier-3 or literal-1 specifies the value of identifier-2 before any statement in the range of the PERFORM is executed. It must be an elementary numeric item.
3. Identifier-4 or literal-2 systematically changes the value of identifier-2 every time control returns from executing the statements in the range of the PERFORM. It must be a nonzero numeric item.
4. Condition-1 can be any condition, simple or compound.
5. If condition-1 is false, the PERFORM is executed once; then, identifier-2 is automatically incremented by the value of identifier-4 or literal-2, and condition-1 is tested again.
6. If condition-1 is true, control transfers to the first statement beyond the scope of the PERFORM statement.

In the preceding example of the PERFORM-VARYING statement, since paragraph 300-READ-N-MOVE consists of only two imperative statements, an in-line PERFORM can also be coded, as follows:

```
PERFORM VARYING TEST-TABLE-CTR FROM 1 BY 1
            UNTIL TEST-TABLE-CTR > 10
    PERFORM 400-READ-TEST-RECORD
    MOVE I-TEST TO WS-TEST (TEST-TABLE-CTR)
END-PERFORM.
```

Example 2:

Suppose that we change the layout of TEST-RECORD in example 1, so that the 10 test values are stored on **one** record. The record description then becomes the following:

```
01  TEST-RECORD.
    05 I-TEST   OCCURS 10 TIMES   PIC 999.
```

The OCCURS clause specifies 10 occurrences of the item I-TEST on the record. This allows the test values to be referenced individually, such as I-TEST (1), I-TEST (2), and so on, or as a group by using the record name TEST-RECORD.

Consider the following alternatives.

Alternative 1:

```
    PERFORM 400-READ-TEST-RECORD.
    PERFORM VARYING TEST-TABLE-CTR FROM 1 BY 1
                UNTIL TEST-TABLE-CTR > 10
        MOVE I-TEST (TEST-TABLE-CTR) TO WS-TEST (TEST-TABLE-CTR)
    END-PERFORM.
```

Alternative 2:

```
    PERFORM 400-READ-TEST-RECORD.
    PERFORM 300-MOVE-TEST
        VARYING TEST-TABLE-CTR FROM 1 BY 1
            UNTIL TEST-TABLE-CTR > 10.
300-MOVE-TEST.
    MOVE I-TEST (TEST-TABLE-CTR) TO WS-TEST (TEST-TABLE-CTR).
```

Alternative 3:

```
PERFORM 400-READ-TEST-RECORD.
MOVE TEST-RECORD TO TEST-TABLE.
```

Both alternatives 1 and 2 transfer the test values one at a time: I-TEST (1) is moved to WS-TEST (1), I-TEST (2) is moved to WS-TEST (2), and so on. The only difference between the two is that alternative 1 uses an in-line PERFORM.

In alternative 3, however, the test values are moved as a **group**. Do you see that TEST-RECORD contains 10 test values, and TEST-TABLE is a storage area that contains 10 occurrences of the item WS-TEST? The size of the source field and the size of the receiving field are the same. A group data transfer is always an alphanumeric data transfer. This means that the 30 incoming characters are stored left-justified in the receiving item TEST-TABLE. The three leftmost characters "fall" into the field WS-TEST (1), the next three into the field WS-TEST (2), and so on, so that each occurrence of WS-TEST receives the appropriate test value.

Example 3:

Suppose that the STATES-TABLE of Figure 9.18 is to be loaded. Assume that the needed data is available in the STATE-INFO-FILE, one record per state, and the records are sequenced in alphabetic order by state name. The record is defined as follows:

```
01  STATE-RECORD.
    05 I-STATE-INFO.
       10 I-ST-ABBREV    PIC XX.
       10 I-ST-NAME      PIC X(20).
       10 I-ST-CAPITAL   PIC X(15).
```

The task is to set up instructions that will read a STATE-RECORD and move the data to the STATES-TABLE. Since the file is presorted alphabetically, then the data on the first record must be stored in the first row of the table, the data on the second record must be stored in the second row of the table, and so on.

Consider the following alternatives.

Alternative 1:

```
    PERFORM 300-READ-STATE-RECORD.
    PERFORM 310-LOAD-TABLE
        VARYING ST-TABLE-ROW-CTR FROM 1 BY 1
            UNTIL ST-TABLE-ROW-CTR > 51.
310-LOAD-TABLE.
    MOVE I-ST-ABBREV TO ST-ABBREV (ST-TABLE-ROW-CTR).
    MOVE I-ST-NAME TO ST-NAME (ST-TABLE-ROW-CTR).
    MOVE I-ST-CAPITAL TO ST-CAPITAL (ST-TABLE-ROW-CTR).
    PERFORM 300-READ-STATE-RECORD.
```

In this coding, the three elementary items of a STATE-RECORD are moved **individually** to the corresponding elementary items of the appropriate row of the table STATES-TABLE. That is, the contents of record 1 are stored in row 1 of the table, one elementary item at a time; the contents of record 2 are stored in row 2 of the table, one elementary item at a time; and so on.

Alternative 2:

```
    PERFORM 300-READ-STATE-RECORD.
    PERFORM 310-LOAD-TABLE
        VARYING ST-TABLE-ROW-CTR FROM 1 BY 1
            UNTIL ST-TABLE-ROW-CTR > 51.
310-LOAD-TABLE.
    MOVE I-STATE-INFO TO STATE-INFO (ST-TABLE-ROW-CTR).
    PERFORM 300-READ-STATE-RECORD.
```

In this case, the data on a record is moved **as a group** to the appropriate row of the table. The source field I-STATE-INFO contains 37 characters. These characters are moved as an alphanumeric value, and they are stored left-justified in the receiving field STATE-INFO (ST-TABLE-ROW-CTR). The two leftmost characters are stored in ST-ABBREV (ST-TABLE-ROW-CTR), the next 20 are stored in ST-NAME (ST-TABLE-ROW-CTR), and the next 15 in ST-CAPITAL (ST-TABLE-ROW-CTR).

Figure 9.22 illustrates both procedures for the first record in the STATE-INFO-FILE.

■ **Figure 9.22** Loading a table—example

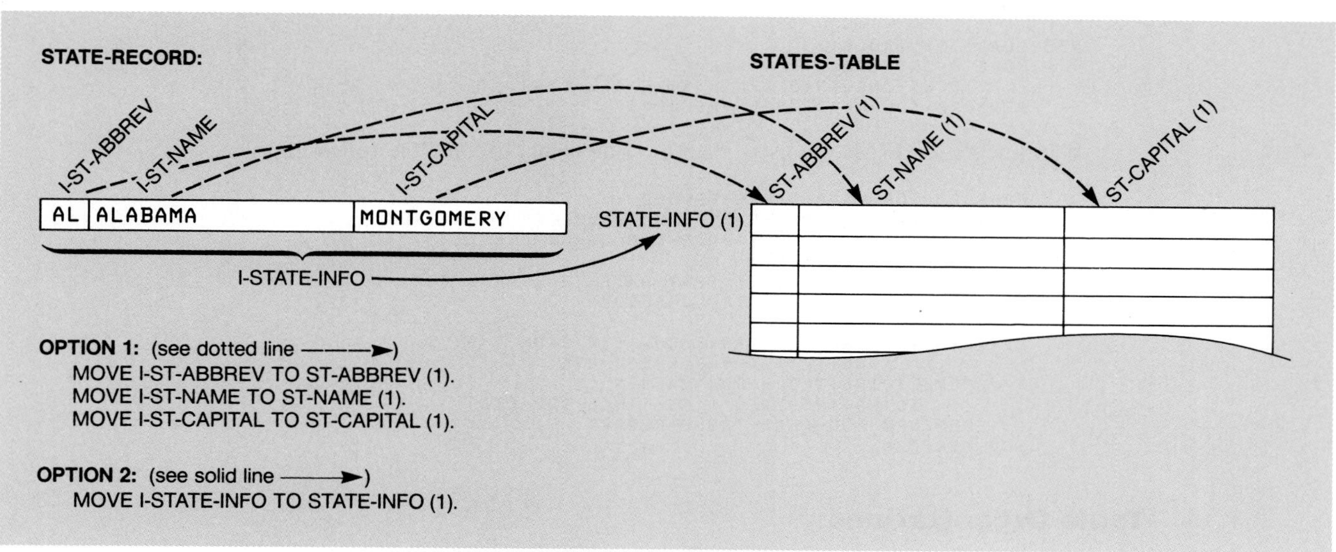

In the sample program, the following coding can be used to define and to load the pay rate table and the insurance table.

```
FILE SECTION.
.
.
.
01   PAY-RATE-RECORD.
     05                  PIC X.
     05 I-PAY-RATE       PIC 999V99.

01   INSURANCE-PREMIUM-RECORD.
     05                  PIC X.
     05 I-INS-TABLE-ROW-VALUES.
        10 I-INS-CODE    PIC XX.
        10 I-INS-PREM    PIC 99V99.
.
.
.
WORKING-STORAGE SECTION.
.
.
.
01   PAY-RATE-TABLE.
     05 WS-PAY-RATE   OCCURS 15 TIMES   PIC 999V99.

01   INSURANCE-TABLE.
     05 WS-INS-INFO   OCCURS 4 TIMES.
        10 WS-INS-CODE           PIC XX.
        10 WS-INS-PREM           PIC 99V99.

01   TABLE-CTRS.
     05 PAY-RATE-TABLE-ROW-CTR   PIC 99.
     05 INS-TABLE-ROW-CTR        PIC 99.
.
.
.
PROCEDURE DIVISION.
.
.
.
     PERFORM 500-READ-TABLE-RECORD.
     PERFORM 520-LOAD-PAY-RATE-TABLE
         VARYING PAY-RATE-TABLE-ROW-CTR FROM 1 BY 1
             UNTIL PAY-RATE-TABLE-ROW-CTR > 15.
     PERFORM 530-LOAD-INS-TABLE
         VARYING INS-TABLE-ROW-CTR FROM 1 BY 1
             UNTIL INS-TABLE-ROW-CTR > 4.
.
.
.
```

```
520-LOAD-PAY-RATE-TABLE.
    MOVE I-PAY-RATE TO WS-PAY-RATE (PAY-RATE-TABLE-ROW-CTR).
    PERFORM 500-READ-TABLE-RECORD.

530-LOAD-INS-TABLE.
    MOVE I-INS-TABLE-ROW-VALUES
        TO WS-INS-INFO (INS-TABLE-ROW-CTR).
    PERFORM 500-READ-TABLE-RECORD.
```

If in-line PERFORMs are used, then the statements become the following:

```
    PERFORM 500-READ-TABLE-RECORD.
    PERFORM VARYING PAY-RATE-TABLE-ROW-CTR FROM 1 BY 1
                UNTIL PAY-RATE-TABLE-ROW-CTR > 15
        MOVE I-PAY-RATE
            TO WS-PAY-RATE (PAY-RATE-TABLE-ROW-CTR)
        PERFORM 500-READ-TABLE-RECORD
    END-PERFORM.
    PERFORM VARYING INS-TABLE-ROW-CTR FROM 1 BY 1
                UNTIL INS-TABLE-ROW-CTR > 4
        MOVE I-INS-TABLE-ROW-VALUES
            TO WS-INS-INFO (INS-TABLE-ROW-CTR)
        PERFORM 500-READ-TABLE-RECORD
    END-PERFORM.
```

Table Organizations

The preceding discussions on table definitions and data initialization of tables have covered a variety of table organizations:

1. **Sequential.** In a table with sequential organization, the data is sequenced on the basis of some key field(s), either in ascending or descending order. The STATES-TABLE discussed earlier is an example of sequential organization. The data is stored in the table in alphabetic order, that is, in ascending order by state name.

   In the sample program, the federal tax table, although not discussed in detail yet, will have sequential organization, since the data will be stored in the table in ascending order by upper income limits, as seen on page 534.

   As another example, consider a company with many stores in one or more regions. Stores are usually given some kind of identification code. If a table is needed that contains the store IDs and locations, then the data could be stored in ascending order of the store IDs, as seen in Figure 9.23. To document the fact that the table has sequential organization, the table definition may contain an entry that specifies the key field, such as ASCENDING KEY IS STORE-ID, in this example. The KEY clause is not required here, but it will be required later in other special applications.
2. **Random.** In a table with random organization, the data is not ordered in any particular sequence. For instance, in the table of Figure 9.23, if the store numbers were stored from first to last occurrence in the order 200, 150, 100, 250, 350, and 300, the resulting table would have random organization.

Figure 9.23 Table with sequential organization—example

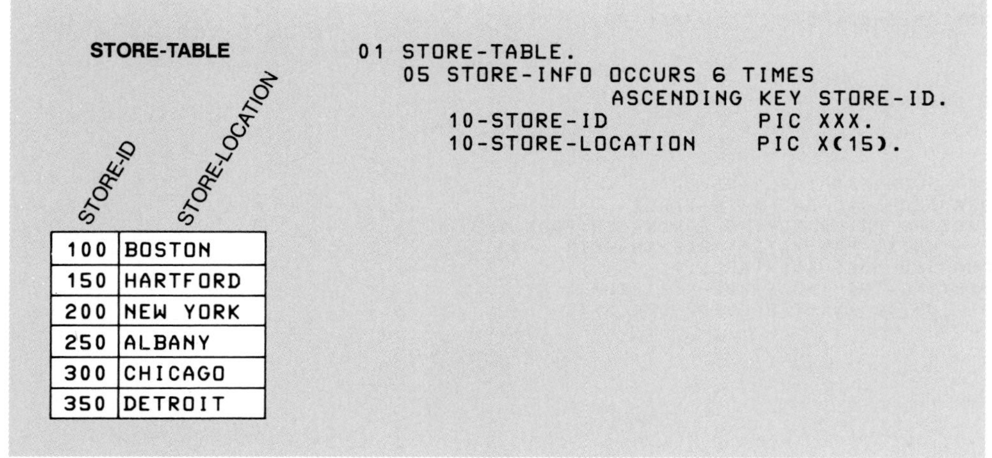

In the chapter program, the insurance table is an example of a table with random organization. See page 534.

3. **Positional.** In a table with positional organization, data is stored in a way that takes into account the relative position within the table where it is stored. There is a meaningful relation between the data and the occurrence number of the field in which it is stored. For example, in the TEST-TABLE example presented earlier, the test values are stored in the sequence in which the tests were taken. That is, WS-TEST (1) contains the result obtained on test 1; WS-TEST (2) contains the result obtained on test 2, and so on. So, since WS-TEST (5) occupies position 5 within the table, the value it contains is the result of test 5.

    In the sample program, the pay rates table is an example of a table with positional organization. WS-PAY-RATE (1) contains the pay rate whose code is 1; WS-PAY-RATE (2) contains the pay rate whose code is 2; and so on. If one needs the pay rate with code 8, it can be obtained by simply referencing WS-PAY-RATE (8). The relation is very clear: The subscript that specifies a particular occurrence of a pay rate is identical to the pay rate code.
4. **Usage-Frequency.** In a table with usage-frequency organization, the data is stored from first to last occurrence on the basis of most-frequent use to least-frequent use.

    In the sample program, the employee classification table has usage-frequency organization. The largest number of employees are STANDARD employees, so this class is stored in the first occurrence. The next largest number of employees are in the YEARLING class, so this entry is stored in the second occurrence. The remaining entries in decreasing order of frequency are BEGINNER, APPRENTICE, ASS'T MGR., and STORE MGR. The table is shown in Figure 9.24.

    It should be clear that in most cases where the table is searched, an early exit will occur, because the needed entry will be found near the beginning of the table. The efficiency of the table look-up procedure is therefore maximized. This organization is particularly beneficial for fairly large tables.

Figure 9.25 contains another example of tables with sequential, random, and usage-frequency organizations. Note the following:

1. In the table with sequential organization that uses the account number as the key, the numeric account numbers are in ascending order.
2. In the table with sequential organization that uses the name as the key, the names are in alphabetic order.
3. In the table with random organization, neither the account numbers nor the names are in any specific sequence.
4. In the table with usage-frequency, it is assumed that Grant, Smith, and Green write many more checks than the others. Since they are "looked up" more often, their names are placed at the beginning of the usage-frequency table to save look-up time.

Figure 9.24 Table with usage-frequency organization—example

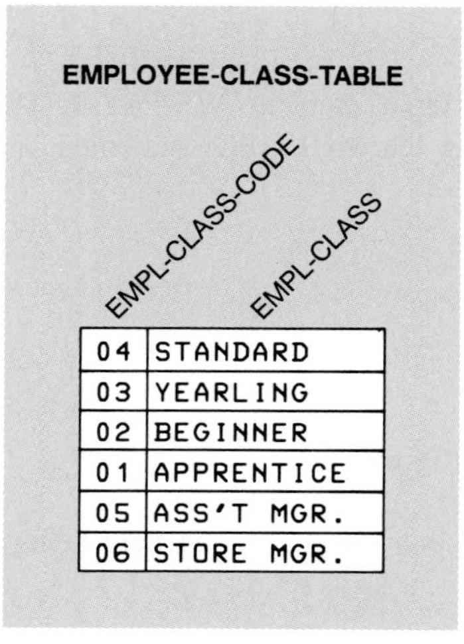
EMPLOYEE-CLASS-TABLE

EMPL-CLASS-CODE	EMPL-CLASS
04	STANDARD
03	YEARLING
02	BEGINNER
01	APPRENTICE
05	ASS'T MGR.
06	STORE MGR.

■ **Figure 9.25** Example of tables with various organizations

Sequential (by account #)		Sequential (by name)		Random		Usage-Frequency	
Acc't #	*Name*	*Acc't #*	*Name*	*Acc't #*	*Name*	*Acc't #*	*Name*
1001	Smith	1020	Grant	1011	Green	1020	Grant
1003	Thomas	1011	Green	1012	Riley	1001	Smith
1011	Green	1012	Riley	1001	Smith	1011	Green
1012	Riley	1001	Smith	1020	Grant	1003	Thomas
1020	Grant	1003	Thomas	1003	Thomas	1012	Riley

Accessing Data in a Table

The method that is used to retrieve data from a table is often a function of the table organization. If a table has positional organization, then the appropriate method is *direct referencing;* for tables with other organizations, a *table look-up* procedure must be used.

Using Direct Referencing

Suppose the task is to total the test results in the table TEST-TABLE. Since this table has positional organization, a simple ADD statement can be used, as follows:

```
ADD WS-TEST (1) WS-TEST (2) WS-TEST (3) WS-TEST (4) WS-TEST (5)
    WS-TEST (6) WS-TEST (7) WS-TEST (8) WS-TEST (9) WS-TEST (10)
        TO WS-TEST-TOTAL.
```

This statement is not particularly elegant, and it would be most impractical if the table contained 1000 entries. A much preferable procedure is to use a PERFORM-VARYING statement, as in the following coding (assume TEST-CTR and WS-TEST-TOTAL are properly defined):

```
MOVE ZERO TO WS-TEST-TOTAL.
PERFORM VARYING TEST-CTR FROM 1 BY 1
            UNTIL TEST-CTR > 10
    ADD WS-TEST (TEST-CTR) TO WS-TEST-TOTAL
END-PERFORM.
```

If the number of tests is 1000, the coding remains the same except that the literal 10 is replaced by 1000.

As another example, consider the pay rate table in the chapter program. Suppose that a payroll record is being processed, that the employee is on hourly wages, and that the pertinent fields of the record are the ones shown in Figure 9.26, along with the pay rate table description and representation. When the MOVE statement is executed, the subscript of WS-PAY-RATE, namely I-EMPL-PAY-CODE, takes on the value stored in the field I-EMPL-PAY-CODE of the Payroll-Record. Consequently, the MOVE statement is interpreted as

```
MOVE WS-PAY-RATE (05) TO WS-EMPL-PAY-RATE
```

and the value in that position of the table (005.10) is moved to the employee work area WS-EMPL-PAY-RATE. Do you see that the pay rate value is obtained by directly referencing the position in which it is stored?

The gross earnings can then be computed as follows:

```
MULTIPLY WS-EMPL-PAY-RATE BY I-EMPL-HRS
    GIVING WS-EMPL-GROSS-EARNINGS.
```

Now, since the value of WS-EMPL-PAY-RATE is the same as the table element WS-PAY-RATE (I-EMPL-PAYCODE), the MOVE statement can be eliminated by coding the MULTIPLY statement as follows:

```
MULTIPLY WS-PAY-RATE (I-EMPL-PAYCODE) BY I-EMPL-HRS
    GIVING WS-EMPL-GROSS-EARNINGS.
```

Using Table Look-Up

A table look-up procedure requires the following components:

1. A **search value,** either supplied as input or determined within the program
2. A **search field** that occurs repeatedly in the table
3. A **condition** that must be satisfied between the search value and the entry in the search field being looked at

■ **Figure 9.26** Using direct referencing—example

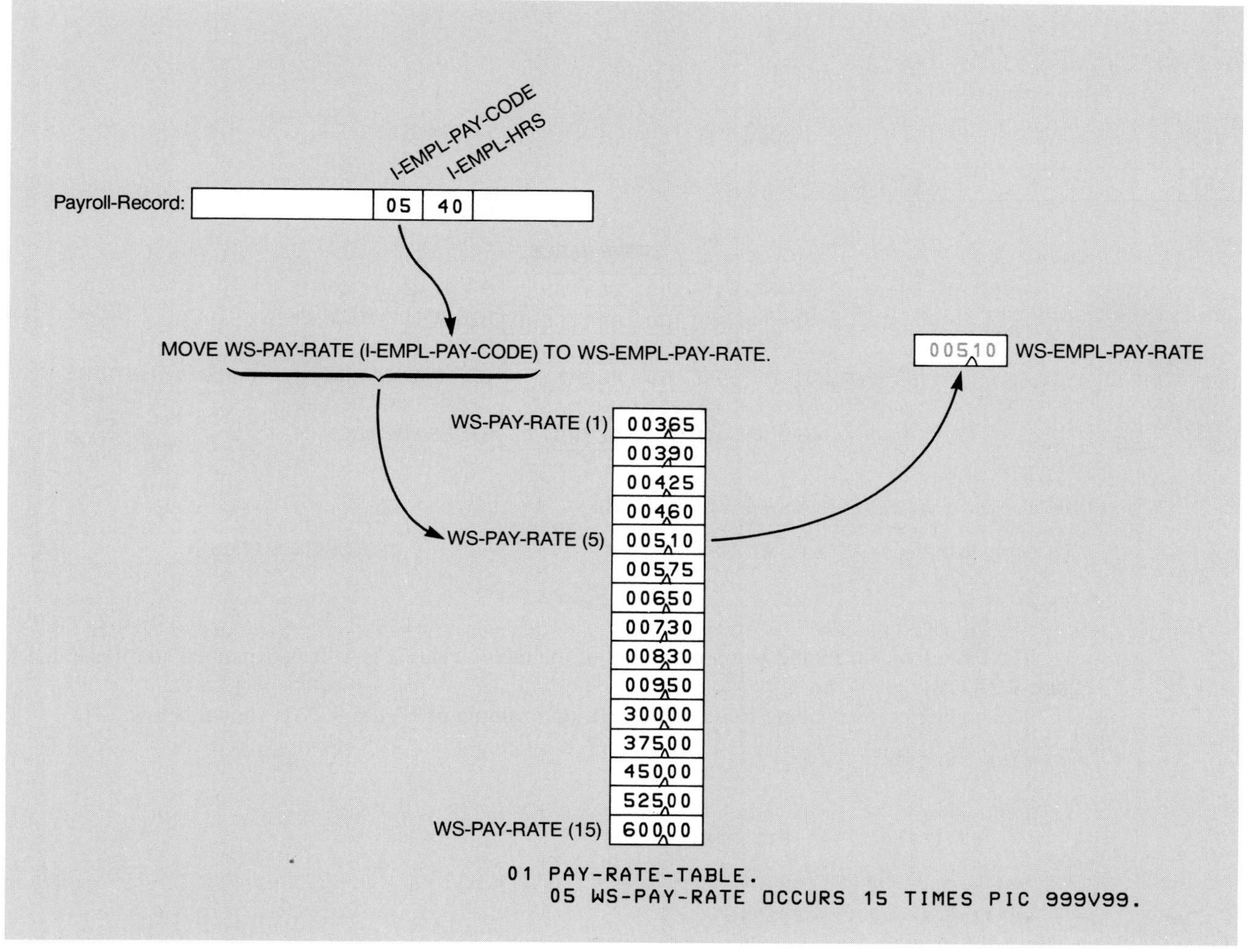

The procedure normally begins at the first occurrence of the search field in the table; that is, the table is searched sequentially (or serially). The required condition is tested. If it is not satisfied, the occurrence number is incremented by 1, and the condition is tested again. If the condition is not satisfied, the occurrence number is incremented by 1 again, and the condition is tested again. The pattern repeats until the condition is satisfied for a particular occurrence of the search field. The object of the table look-up will be found at that occurrence number.

At that point, the execution of the loop should be terminated to avoid searching the remaining entries in the table needlessly. A search flag is used for this purpose, as follows:

1. The search flag is initialized to some particular value before the loop begins.
2. When the condition is satisfied, a new value is assigned to the search flag.
3. Before returning to the look-up procedure, the search flag is tested to determine if it contains the new value. If it does, an exit from the loop is effected; otherwise, control remains within the loop.

Example 1:

Consider the STORE-TABLE of Figure 9.23. Suppose the task is to retrieve from the table the store location for a given store number. The given store number is in field I-STORE-ID.

In this case, the search value is I-STORE-ID, the search field in the table is STORE-ID, and the condition is that I-STORE-ID be the same as the value in STORE-ID (*x*), where *x* is a particular occurrence number.

Figure 9.27 Table look-up procedure—example 1

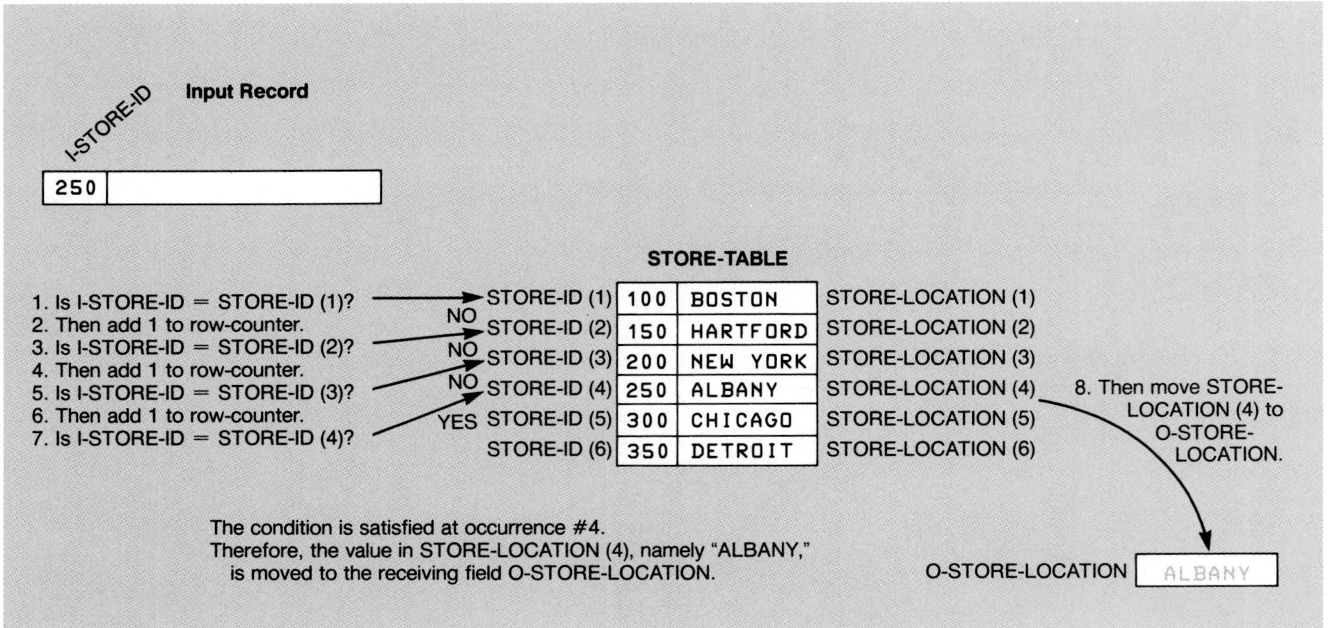

The table look-up should begin at the top of the table, where *x* is 1. It is explained and illustrated in Figure 9.27.

The coding corresponding to the table look-up example of Figure 9.27 is shown below.

```
FILE SECTION.
.
.
.
    05 I-STORE-ID  PIC XXX.
.
.
.
WORKING-STORAGE SECTION.
.
.
.
01  STORE-TABLE.
    05 STORE-INFO  OCCURS 6 TIMES.
       10 STORE-ID              PIC XXX.
       10 STORE-LOCATION        PIC X(15).
    05 STORE-TABLE-CONTROL.
       10 STORE-TABLE-FLAG      PIC XXX.
          88 STORE-IS-FOUND             VALUE "YES".
       10 STORE-TABLE-ROW-CTR   PIC 9.
.
.
.
PROCEDURE DIVISION.
.
.
.
    MOVE "NO " TO STORE-TABLE-FLAG.
    PERFORM 300-LOOK-UP-STORE-TABLE
        VARYING STORE-TABLE-ROW-CTR FROM 1 BY 1
            UNTIL STORE-IS-FOUND.
    .
    .
    .
300-LOOK-UP-STORE-TABLE.
    IF I-STORE-ID = STORE-ID (STORE-TABLE-ROW-CTR)
        MOVE STORE-LOCATION (STORE-TABLE-ROW-CTR)
            TO O-STORE-LOCATION
        SET STORE-IS-FOUND TO TRUE
    END-IF.
```

In this example, the search flag is STORE-TABLE-FLAG. It is initialized to "NO " prior to the PERFORM statement. It is tested in the UNTIL clause before control is sent to the procedure 300-LOOK-UP-STORE-TABLE, and its value is changed to "YES" in the SET statement when the condition is satisfied.

Figure 9.28 Table look-up procedure—example 2

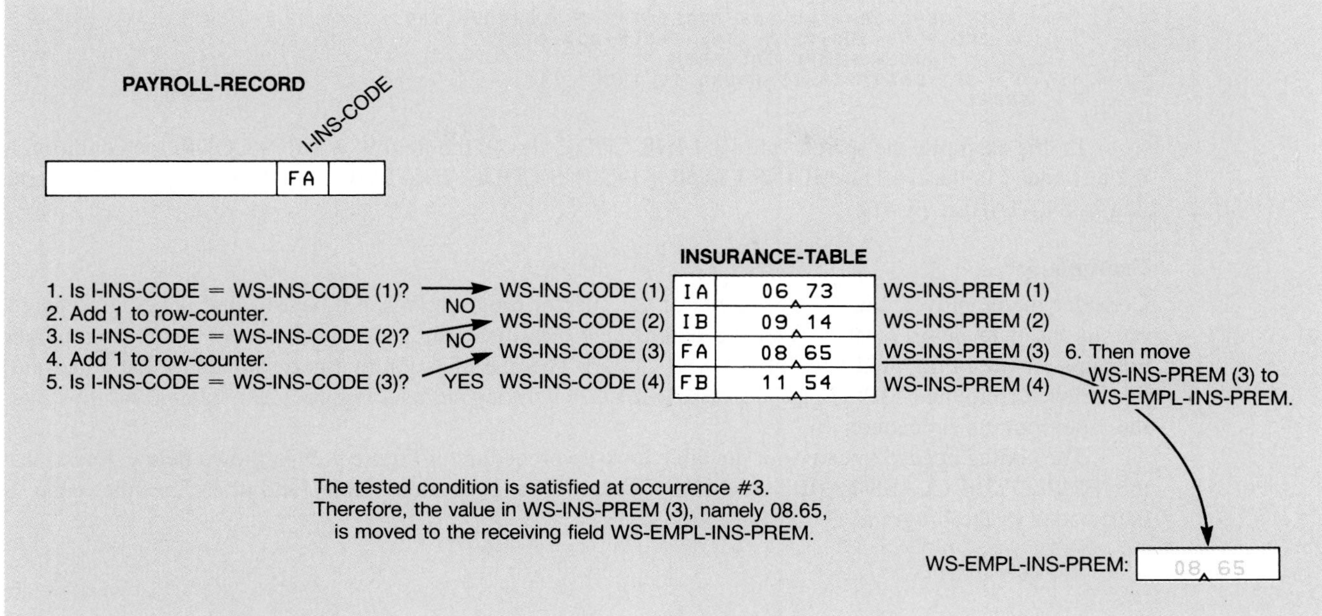

Example 2:

Consider the insurance table in the chapter program. Assume that a payroll record is being processed, and it is necessary to find the amount to be withheld from gross earnings for the employee's share of the insurance premium. The record contains an insurance plan code in the field I-INS-CODE. The situation is explained and illustrated in Figure 9.28.

The coding needed to carry out the table look-up procedure of Figure 9.28 is shown below.

```
.
.
.
FILE SECTION.
.
.
.
01   PAYROLL-RECORD.
     .
     .
     .
     05 I-INS-CODE    PIC XX.
.
.
.
WORKING-STORAGE SECTION.
.
.
.
01   INSURANCE-TABLE.
     05 WS-INS-INFO   OCCURS 4 TIMES.
        10 WS-INS-CODE        PIC XX.
        10 WS-INS-PREM        PIC 99V99.
     05 INSURANCE-TABLE-CONTROLS.
        10 INS-TABLE-FLAG     PIC XXX.
           88 INS-PREM-IS-FOUND       VALUE "YES".
        10 INS-TABLE-ROW-CTR  PIC 9.
.
.
.
PROCEDURE DIVISION.
.
.
.
     MOVE "NO " TO INS-TABLE-FLAG.
     PERFORM 420-LOOK-UP-INSURANCE-TABLE
         VARYING INS-TABLE-ROW-CTR FROM 1 BY 1
             UNTIL INS-PREM-IS-FOUND.
```

```
.
.
.
420-LOOK-UP-INSURANCE-TABLE.
    IF I-INS-CODE = WS-INS-CODE (INS-TABLE-ROW-CTR)
        MOVE WS-INS-PREM (INS-TABLE-ROW-CTR)
            TO WS-EMPL-INS-PREM
        SET INS-PREM-IS-FOUND TO TRUE
    END-IF.
```

In this example, the search value is I-INS-CODE, the search field is WS-INS-CODE, the condition is the test coded in the IF clause [I-INS-CODE = WS-INS-CODE (INS-TABLE-ROW-CTR)], and the search flag is INS-TABLE-FLAG.

Example 3:

Consider the employee classification table of the chapter program. When a payroll line is being prepared, one of the data fields must contain the employee's classification. The payroll record for that employee contains a code in the field I-EMPL-CLASS-CODE. The classification that corresponds to that code must be retrieved from the EMPLOYEE-CLASS-TABLE in working storage. Figure 9.29 explains and illustrates the table look-up procedure.

The coding needed to carry out the table look-up procedure of Figure 9.29 is shown below. Recall that the EMPLOYEE-CLASS-TABLE is being treated as a permanent table, and therefore the table is hard-coded in the program.

```
FILE SECTION.
.
.
.
01  PAYROLL-RECORD.
    .
    .
    .
    05 I-EMPL-CLASS-CODE  PIC 99.
.
.
.
WORKING-STORAGE SECTION.
.
.
.
01  EMPLOYEE-CLASS-VALUES.
    05 PIC X(12)  VALUE "04STANDARD  ".
    05 PIC X(12)  VALUE "03YEARLING  ".
    05 PIC X(12)  VALUE "02BEGINNER  ".
    05 PIC X(12)  VALUE "01APPRENTICE".
    05 PIC X(12)  VALUE "05ASS'T MGR.".
    05 PIC X(12)  VALUE "06STORE MGR.".

01  EMPLOYEE-CLASS-TABLE REDEFINES EMPLOYEE-CLASS-VALUES.
    05 WS-EMPL-CLASS-INFO  OCCURS 6 TIMES.
       10 WS-EMPL-CLASS-CODE      PIC 99.
       10 WS-EMPL-CLASS           PIC X(10).
01  EMPLOYEE-CLASS-CONTROLS.
    05 EMPL-CLASS-TABLE-FLAG      PIC XXX.
       88 EMPL-CLASS-IS-FOUND             VALUE "YES".
    05 EMPL-CLASS-ROW-CTR         PIC 9.
.
.
.
PROCEDURE DIVISION.
.
.
.
    MOVE "NO " TO EMPL-CLASS-TABLE-FLAG.
    PERFORM 430-LOOK-UP-EMPLOYEE-CLASS
        VARYING EMPL-CLASS-ROW-CTR FROM 1 BY 1
            UNTIL EMPL-CLASS-IS-FOUND.
.
.
.
430-LOOK-UP-EMPLOYEE-CLASS.
    IF I-EMPL-CLASS-CODE =
                   WS-EMPL-CLASS-CODE (EMPL-CLASS-ROW-CTR)
        MOVE WS-EMPL-CLASS (EMPL-CLASS-ROW-CTR)
            TO O-EMPL-CLASS
        SET EMPL-CLASS-IS-FOUND TO TRUE
    END-IF.
```

Figure 9.29 Table look-up procedure—example 3

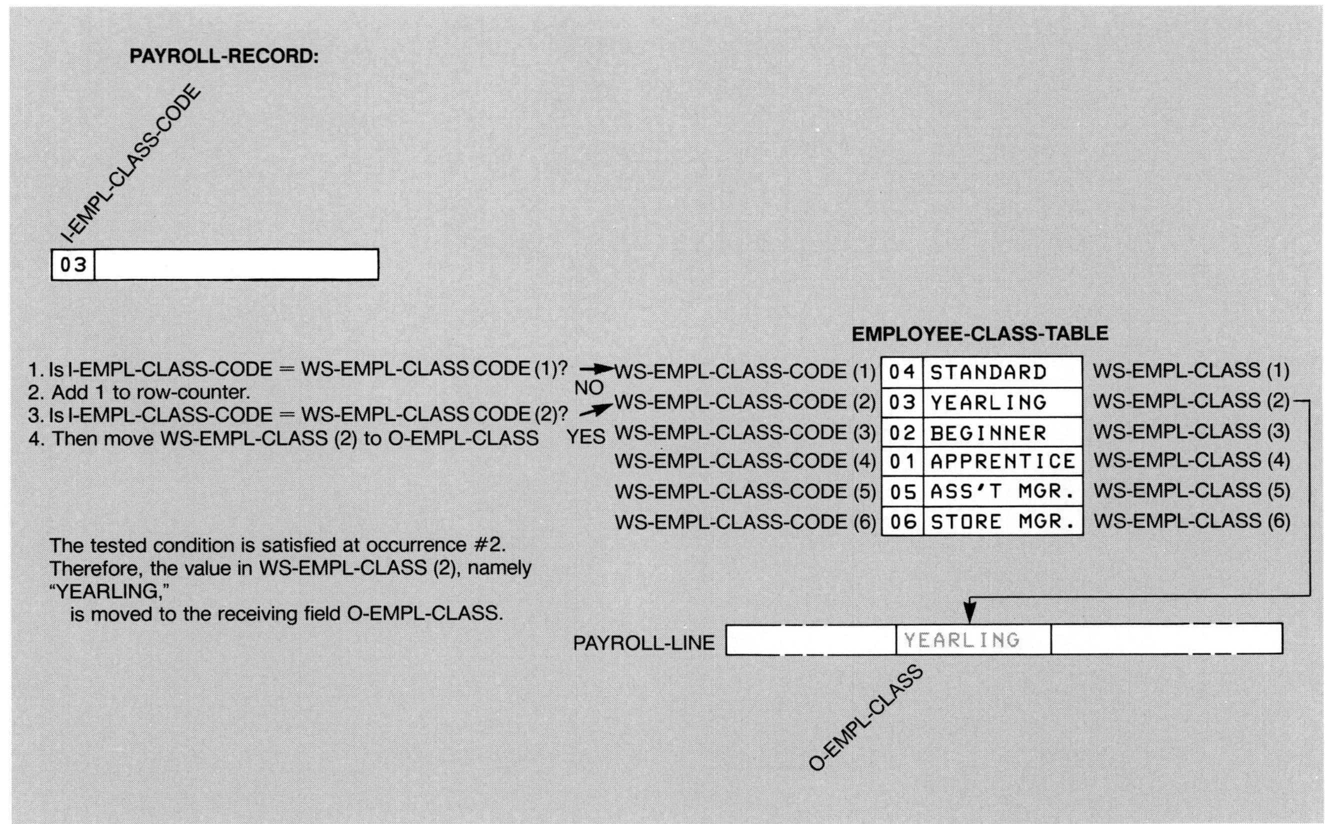

Two-Level Tables

The preceding discussions on the definitions of tables, the initialization of tables, and retrieving data from tables were limited to one-level tables. In addition to one-level tables, the chapter program also requires the use of a *two-level table,* namely, the federal tax rate table.

Just as a one-level table is defined using the OCCURS clause once, a two-level table is defined using the OCCURS clause twice within the data description entry, one OCCURS being nested within the other, essentially creating a table within a table. The most common visual representation of a two-level table is a rectangular array consisting of a number of rows and a number of columns. In each row, one or more data items occur in a repeating pattern.

Example 1:

A simple example of a non-COBOL two-level table is shown in Figure 9.30a.

In this table there are five rows, one for each of five players, and seven columns, one for each of seven games. An entry in the table is simply the points scored by a particular player in a particular game. For instance, ENTRY (3,4) references player 3 and game 4, and its value is 10, that is, player 3 scored 10 points in game 4. ENTRY (4,3) references player 4 and game 3, and its value is 02, that is, player 4 scored 2 points in game 3. Note that **two** subscripts are needed to reference a specific "cell" within the array: The first subscript denotes the number of the row that contains the cell, and the second subscript denotes the number of the column that contains the cell.

The data description entries for the definition of such a table must specify that the rows (the data items at the first level of the table) occur five times, and the columns (the data items that repeat within each row, the second level of the table) occur seven times, as illustrated in the following coding:

```
01  SCORE-TABLE.
    05 PLAYER   OCCURS 5 TIMES.
       10 GAME-PTS   OCCURS 7 TIMES   PIC 99.
```

■ **Figure 9.30a** Two-level table containing points scored per game for each player

	Game-1	Game-2	Game-3	Game-4	Game-5	Game-6	Game-7
Player-1	10	05	04	08	06	15	09
Player-2	06	02	05	07	10	04	03
Player-3	01	00	05	10	08	05	07
Player-4	06	03	02	07	09	04	06
Player-5	02	05	03	09	06	10	05

■ **Figure 9.30b** Data names attached to the two-level table followed by the table definition

SCORE-TABLE

PLAYER (1):	GAME-PTS (1,1)	GAME-PTS (1,2)	GAME-PTS (1,3)	GAME-PTS (1,4)	GAME-PTS (1,5)	GAME-PTS (1,6)	GAME-PTS (1,7)
PLAYER (2):	GAME-PTS (2,1)	GAME-PTS (2,2)	GAME-PTS (2,3)	GAME-PTS (2,4)	GAME-PTS (2,5)	GAME-PTS (2,6)	GAME-PTS (2,7)
PLAYER (3):	GAME-PTS (3,1)	GAME-PTS (3,2)	GAME-PTS (3,3)	GAME-PTS (3,4)	GAME-PTS (3,5)	GAME-PTS (3,6)	GAME-PTS (3,7)
PLAYER (4):	GAME-PTS (4,1)	GAME-PTS (4,2)	GAME-PTS (4,3)	GAME-PTS (4,4)	GAME-PTS (4,5)	GAME-PTS (4,6)	GAME-PTS (4,7)
PLAYER (5):	GAME-PTS (5,1)	GAME-PTS (5,2)	GAME-PTS (5,3)	GAME-PTS (5,4)	GAME-PTS (5,5)	GAME-PTS (5,6)	GAME-PTS (5,7)

```
01  SCORE-TABLE.
    05 PLAYER OCCURS 5 TIMES.
       10 GAME-PTS OCCURS 7 TIMES PIC 99.
```

Note the following in this description:

1. PLAYER is defined using a single OCCURS clause; hence, it is a *single-subscripted data item.*
2. GAME-PTS is defined using an OCCURS clause, but it is an elementary item of a group item defined using the OCCURS clause; hence, it is a *double-subscripted data item.*

Correspondingly, the single-subscripted item PLAYER (3) references all the characters stored in row 3 of the table in Figure 9.30a, specifically "01000510080507". No spacing is present between the successive numeric values, since each occurrence of PLAYER consists of seven elementary items, and each is defined by PIC 99. But the double-subscripted item GAME-PTS (3,5) references the fifth entry in that row, and its value is "08".

Note that GAME-PTS is the data name that must be accompanied by two subscripts, the first specifying the row (that is, the specific occurrence of PLAYER), and the second specifying the column to which the entry belongs (that is, the occurrence of GAME-PTS within that row).

In Figure 9.30b, the data names in the description of SCORE-TABLE are attached to the table illustrated in Figure 9.30a. Note again that the data name SCORE-TABLE names the whole table, data name PLAYER (*x*) names row *x* in the table, and data name GAME-PTS (*x,y*) names the data cell in row *x* and column *y*.

Figure 9.30a shows data in the table, but, of course, the definition of SCORE-TABLE above does **not** load the table. Let us consider some schemes that can be used to load the table.

Loading a Two-Level Table—Scheme A

Suppose the values are to be prepared in a data file so that only one value is stored on each record. The data file must then contain 35 records, and obviously the records must be carefully ordered. Suppose that the first seven records contain the game points for player 1 in games 1 through 7, respectively; the next group of seven records contain the game points for player 2 in games 1 through 7; and so on.

■ **Figure 9.31** Sample input record layout—only one value per record

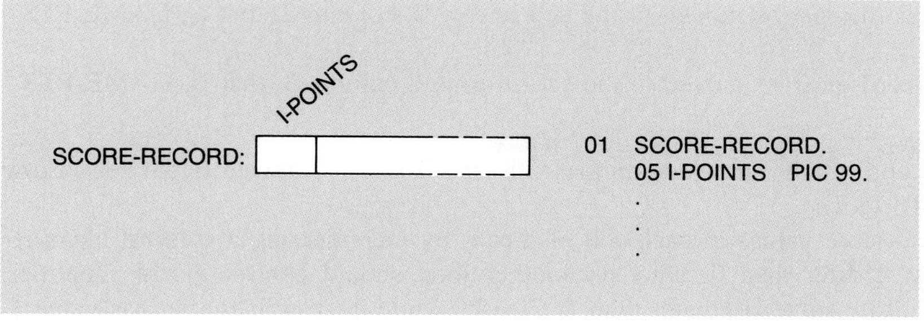

■ **Figure 9.32** Illustration showing the cell in which the value from each input record must be stored in the two-level table

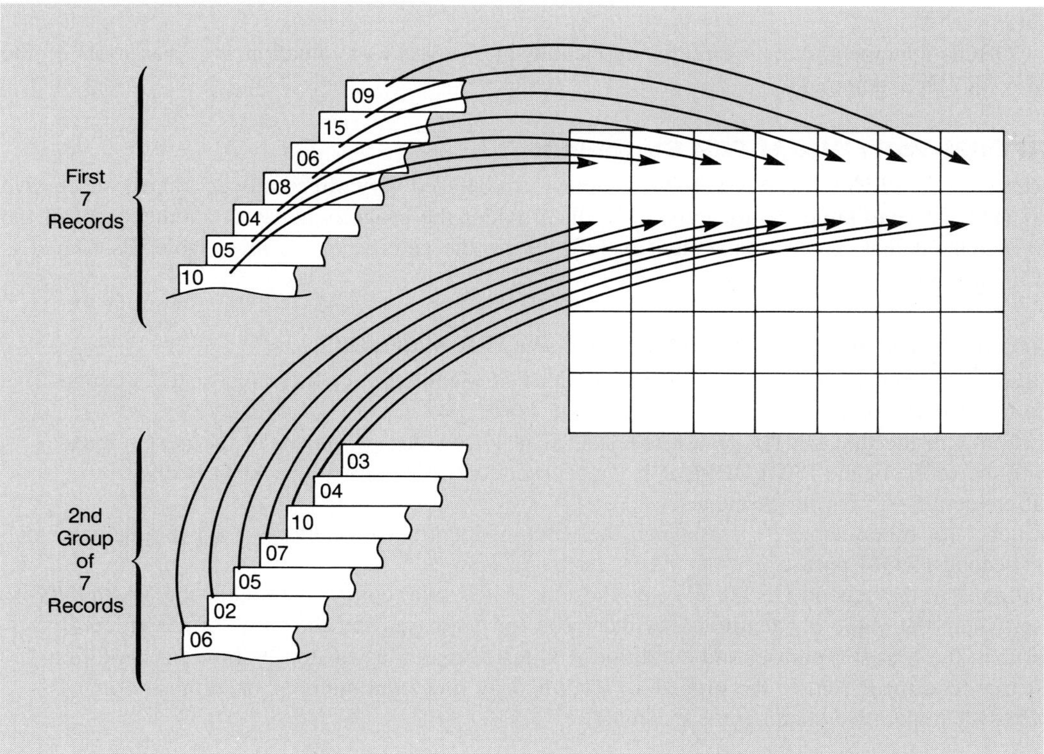

The input record layout and corresponding record description are shown in Figure 9.31. The task to be accomplished is illustrated in Figure 9.32, and is as follows:

1. The value on the first record must be moved to the cell in row 1, column 1, that is, GAME-PTS (1,1).
2. The value on the second record must be moved to the cell in row 1, column 2, that is, GAME-PTS (1,2).
3. The value on the third record must be moved to the cell in row 1, column 3, that is, GAME-PTS (1,3).
4. The value on the fourth record must be moved to the cell in row 1, column 4, that is, GAME-PTS (1,4).
5. The value on the fifth record must be moved to the cell in row 1, column 5, that is, GAME-PTS (1,5).
6. The value on the sixth record must be moved to the cell in row 1, column 6, that is, GAME-PTS (1,6).
7. The value on the seventh record must be moved to the cell in row 1, column 7, that is, GAME-PTS (1,7).

8. The value on the eighth record must be moved to the cell in row 2, column 1, that is, GAME-PTS (2,1).
9. The value on the ninth record must be moved to the cell in row 2, column 2, that is, GAME-PTS (2,2).
10. The value on the tenth record must be moved to the cell in row 2, column 3, that is, GAME-PTS (2,3).

This procedure continues until finally the value on the 35th record must be moved to the cell in row 5, column 7, that is, GAME-PTS (5,7).

A loop should be set up to store values in each cell of a row, by incrementing a **column** identifier from 1 by 1, until its value is greater than 7, whereas another loop should control a **row** identifier, incrementing it from 1 by 1, until its value is greater than 5. Clearly, while the row identifier has value 1, the column identifier must be allowed to assume values 1 through 7 successively to reference the seven cells in row 1. Then the row identifier is incremented to 2, and while that value is maintained, the column identifier will assume values 1 through 7 again to reference the seven cells in row 2, and so on.

Note: The loop that increments the column identifier must be nested within the loop that increments the row identifier.

The COBOL statement that is directly applicable in this kind of situation is a variation of the PERFORM-VARYING statement.

The PERFORM-VARYING-AFTER Statement

We have seen how the PERFORM-VARYING statement can be used very effectively to address successive occurrences in a one-level table. Fortunately, COBOL provides the programmer with another form of the PERFORM statement that is very convenient in referencing the cells in a two-level table. Its format is shown in Figure 9.33.

Rules Governing Use of the PERFORM-VARYING-AFTER Statement

1. Identifier-2 (or index-name-1) is assigned the value of identifier-3 or literal-1 (or index-name-2) in the first FROM phrase.
2. Condition-1 in the first UNTIL clause is tested; if it is true, control passes to the next sentence beyond the scope of the PERFORM; if it is not true, control passes to the AFTER clause to initialize identifier-5 (or index-name-3).
3. Identifier-5 (or index-name-3) is assigned the value of identifier-6 or literal-3 (or index-name-4) in the second FROM phrase.
4. Condition-2 in the second UNTIL clause is tested; if it is true, control returns to the VARYING clause, where the value of identifier-2 is increased (or decreased) by the value of identifier-4 or literal-2 in the first BY phrase, and condition-1 is tested again, as in step 2 above; if condition-2 is not true, control is sent to the procedure identified by procedure-name-1 or, in an in-line PERFORM, imperative-statement is executed.

Figure 9.33 PERFORM-VARYING-AFTER statement format

```
PERFORM [procedure-name-1 [{THROUGH | THRU} procedure-name-2]]

    [WITH TEST {BEFORE | AFTER}]

    VARYING {identifier-2 | index-name-1} FROM {identifier-3 | index-name-2 | literal-1} BY {identifier-4 | literal-2} UNTIL condition-1

    [AFTER {identifier-5 | index-name-3} FROM {identifier-6 | index-name-4 | literal-3} BY {identifier-7 | literal-4} until condition-2] . . .

    [imperative-statement END-PERFORM]
```

5. After executing the last statement in the procedure, or the last instruction in imperative-statement, control returns to the AFTER clause, where the value of identifier-5 is increased (or decreased) by the value of identifier-7 or literal-4 in the second BY phrase.
6. Condition-2 in the second UNTIL clause is tested again as in step 4.
7. The pattern repeats until an exit occurs by satisfying condition-1.
8. A PERFORM-VARYING-AFTER statement can contain up to six AFTER clauses. (This allows access to all the cells in seven-level tables, the new maximum in COBOL '85.)

The logic of the PERFORM-VARYING-AFTER format is shown in the flowchart segment of Figure 9.34.

From the above rules, note the following:

1. For **each** value of identifier-2 (or index-name-1), the procedure named in the PERFORM statement, or the imperative-statement, is executed **repeatedly** within the inner loop, incrementing the value of identifier-5 during each repetition, until condition-2 is satisfied.
2. When condition-1 is satisfied, control exits from the PERFORM statement.

By applying the logic of the PERFORM-VARYING-AFTER statement to the task of loading the SCORE-TABLE, the result is the flowchart segment in Figure 9.35, and the corresponding coding is shown below.

Assume that PLAYER-NO and GAME-NO are properly defined.

```
    PERFORM 300-READ-SCORE-RECORD.
    PERFORM 400-STORE-N-READ-SCORE
        VARYING PLAYER-NO FROM 1 BY 1
            UNTIL PLAYER-NO > 5
        AFTER GAME-NO FROM 1 BY 1
            UNTIL GAME-NO > 7.

400-STORE-N-READ-SCORE.
    MOVE I-POINTS TO GAME-PTS (PLAYER-NO, GAME-NO).
    PERFORM 300-READ-SCORE-RECORD.
```

In Figure 9.35, the specific sequence is as follows:

1. Read the first record: `PERFORM 300-READ-SCORE-RECORD.`
2. Enter the outer loop.
   a. Set PLAYER-NO equal to 1.
   b. Test: Is PLAYER-NO > 5?
   c. No, it's 1.
3. Enter the inner loop.
   a. Set GAME-NO equal to 1.
   b. Test: Is GAME-NO > 7?

Figure 9.34 General logic of the PERFORM-VARYING-AFTER statement

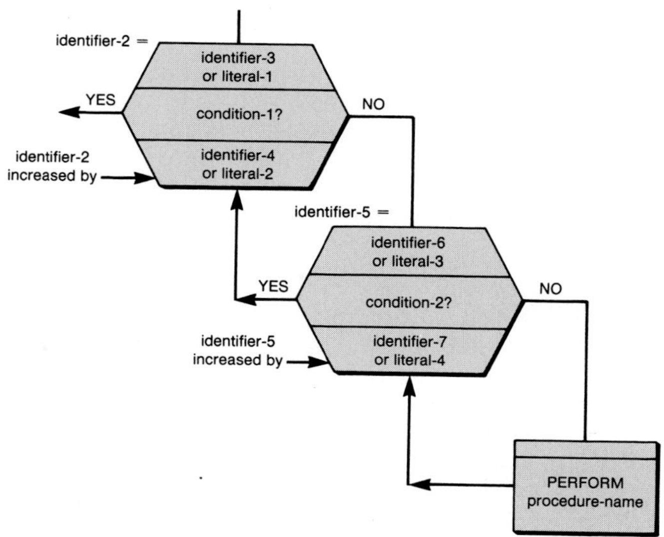

■ **Figure 9.35** Logic of the PERFORM-VARYING-AFTER statement—example

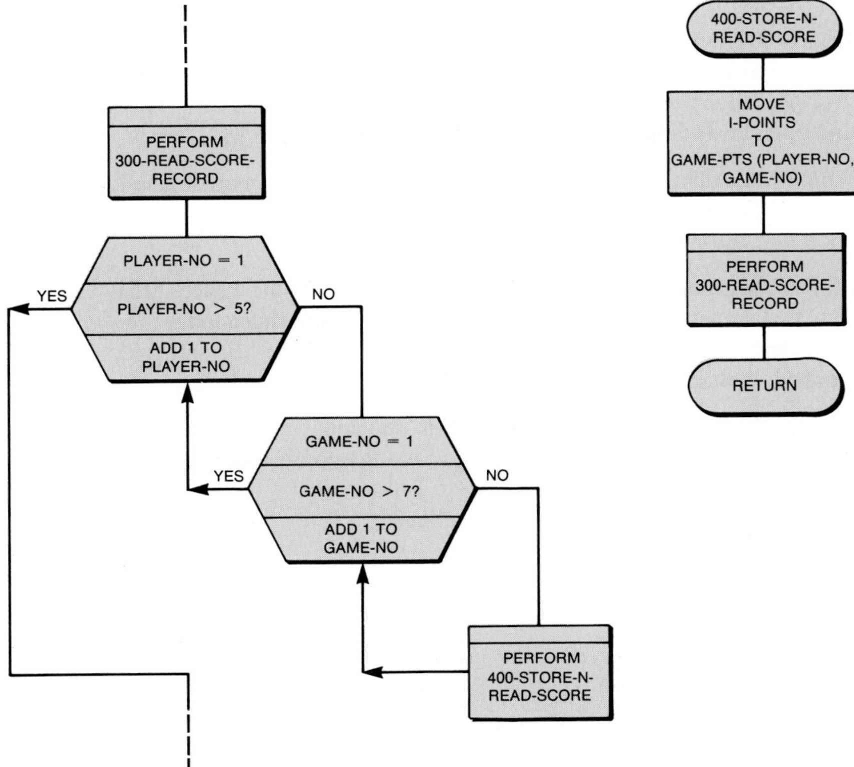

   c. No, it's 1.
   d. Execute the procedure 400-STORE-N-READ-SCORE:

```
MOVE I-POINTS TO GAME-PTS (1,1).
PERFORM 300-READ-SCORE-RECORD.
```

   e. Increment GAME-NO: ADD 1 TO GAME-NO.
   f. Test again: Is GAME-NO > 7?
   g. No, it's 2.
   h. Execute procedure 400 again:

```
MOVE I-POINTS TO GAME-PTS (1,2).
PERFORM 300-READ-SCORE-RECORD.
```

   i. Increment GAME-NO: ADD 1 TO GAME-NO.
   j. Test again: Is GAME-NO > 7?
   k. No, it's 3.
   And so on, until
   x. Test again: Is GAME-NO > 7?
   y. Yes, it's 8.
   z. **Exit** inner loop.

   At this point, the game points for the first player have been stored in the seven cells of the first row.

4. Return to outer loop to increment PLAYER-NO.
   a. Increment PLAYER-NO: ADD 1 TO PLAYER-NO.
   b. Test: Is PLAYER-NO > 5?
   c. No, it's 2.

5. Reenter the inner loop.
   a. Set GAME-NO equal to 1.
   b. Test: Is GAME-NO > 7?
   c. No, it's 1.
   d. Execute procedure 400-STORE-N-READ-SCORE:

```
MOVE I-POINTS TO GAME-PTS (2,1).
PERFORM 300-READ-SCORE-RECORD.
```

e. Increment GAME-NO: ADD 1 TO GAME-NO.
f. Test again: Is GAME-NO > 7?
g. No, it's 2.
And so on, until
x. Test again: Is GAME-NO > 7?
y. Yes, it's 8.
z. **Exit** inner loop.

At this point, the game points for the second player have been stored in the seven cells of the second row.

6. Return to outer loop to increment PLAYER-NO.
a. Increment PLAYER-NO: ADD 1 TO PLAYER-NO.
b. Test: Is PLAYER-NO > 5?
c. No, it's 3.
And so on, until
x. Test again: Is PLAYER-NO > 5?
y. Yes, it's 6.

7. **Exit** outer loop.

At this point, the execution of the nested loops controlled by the PERFORM-VARYING-AFTER statement terminates, and the table SCORE-TABLE has been loaded.

As you can see, the procedure 400-STORE-N-READ-SCORE will be executed seven times for each value of PLAYER-NO (and there are five of these), for a total of 35 times. During each execution of the procedure 400-STORE-N-READ-SCORE, the subscripts of the double-subscripted item GAME-PTS have a new pair of values that reference a different cell in the table. Note again that in this scheme, a row number is kept fixed while a value is assigned to each of its seven cells in that row. The row number is then increased by one, a value is assigned to each of the seven cells in that row, and so on until the table is completely loaded.

Loading a Two-Level Table—Scheme B

Suppose the table values are to be prepared in a data file so that each record contains all the game points for an individual player. This is a more natural way of preparing the data records than the one used in scheme A. With this scheme, the data file contains only five records rather than 35. The game points on the first record must be moved to the first row of the table; the game points on the second record must be moved to the second row of the table; and so on, as illustrated in Figure 9.36.

We can use either of two alternative approaches in this situation. In one approach, the SCORE-RECORD for one player is read, the game points are moved from the record to the table one game at a time for that player, then the next record is read, and the game points for that player are moved to the next row of the table, one game at a time, and so on until the table is loaded. In the other approach, an input record is read, and the whole group of game points for player 1 is moved to the first row of the table in a single MOVE statement, then the next record is read, and the whole group of game points for player 2 is moved to the second row of the table, and so on until the table is loaded.

Figure 9.36 Values on one input record to be transferred to one row of SCORE-TABLE

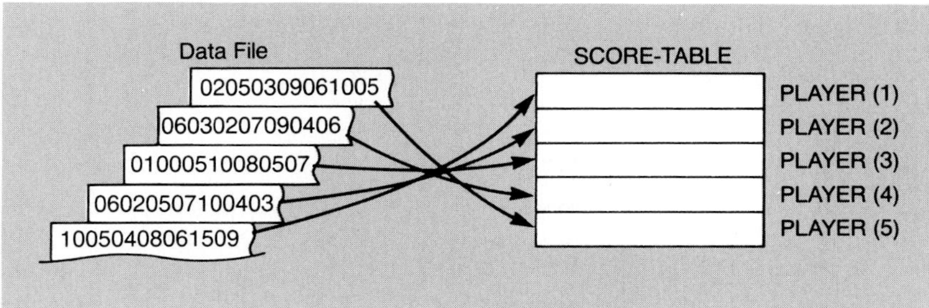

Approach 1

The record layout and record description for SCORE-RECORD are shown in Figure 9.37.

Examine the logic in the flowchart of Figure 9.38. Note that the outer loop is controlled by the data item PLAYER-NO. It will be executed a total of five times, once for each of five players. Prior to the first time, a SCORE-RECORD is read. Then, each time the outer loop is executed, the inner loop controlled by GAME-NO executes seven times, each time storing the points for one game in the appropriate cell. When control exits from the inner loop, the next SCORE-RECORD is read. Note the subscript of I-POINTS in the MOVE box. It references the appropriate occurrence on the input record as well as the cell in a particular row of the table.

The coding corresponding to Figure 9.38 is as follows:

```
    PERFORM 300-READ-SCORE-RECORD.
    PERFORM 400-PROCESS-SCORE-RECORD
        VARYING PLAYER-NO FROM 1 BY 1
            UNTIL PLAYER-NO > 5.

400-PROCESS-SCORE-RECORD.
    PERFORM VARYING GAME-NO FROM 1 BY 1
                UNTIL GAME-NO > 7
        MOVE I-POINTS (GAME-NO) TO GAME-PTS (PLAYER-NO, GAME-NO)
    END-PERFORM.
    PERFORM 300-READ-SCORE-RECORD.
```

It should be clear that for a given player, the game points are stored in the table one game at a time.

Figure 9.37 Sample input record layout and related coding showing seven elementary items

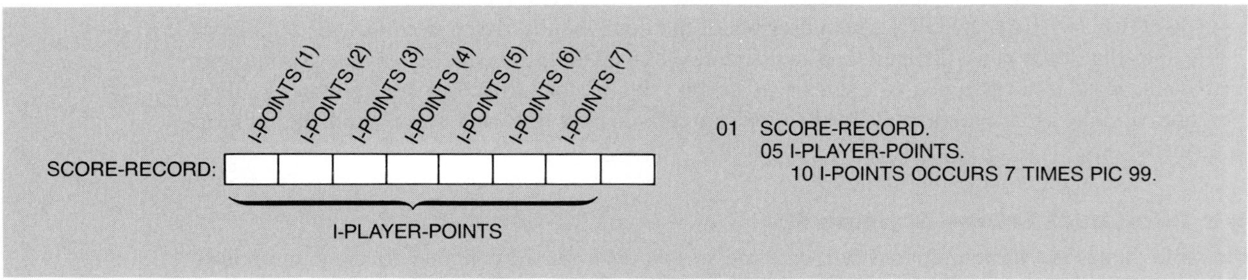

Figure 9.38 Logic used to transfer values one at a time to the table

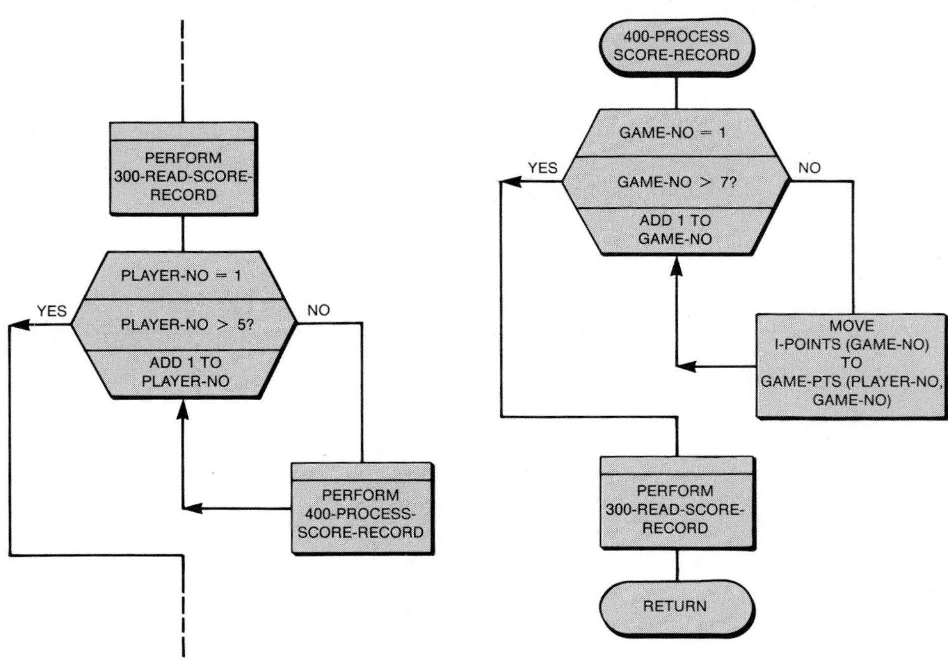

Approach 2

In the second approach, the table-loading procedure is more efficient. Only one loop is needed. Within the loop, the group of game points on the input record, namely, I-PLAYER-POINTS (see Figure 9.37), is moved in a single MOVE statement to a row occurrence in the table, that is, to PLAYER (*x*), where *x* is the occurrence number. Figure 9.39 shows the logic for this approach.

The coding corresponding to Figure 9.39 is shown below.

```
PERFORM 300-READ-SCORE-RECORD.
PERFORM VARYING PLAYER-NO FROM 1 BY 1
           UNTIL PLAYER-NO > 5
    MOVE I-PLAYER-POINTS TO PLAYER (PLAYER-NO)
    PERFORM 300-READ-SCORE-RECORD
END-PERFORM.
```

In this approach, it is most important to understand the correspondence between the data item I-PLAYER-POINTS (Figure 9.37) and the single-subscripted data item PLAYER (Figure 9.30b). I-PLAYER-POINTS is a parent or group item on the input record SCORE-RECORD. It is a group consisting of the seven elementary items I-POINTS (1), I-POINTS (2), . . . , I-POINTS (7), and each of these is a two-digit item. The size of the group is 14.

Similarly, PLAYER is a single-subscripted group item belonging to SCORE-TABLE. Each occurrence of PLAYER, say PLAYER (*x*), consists of the seven elementary items GAME-PTS (*x*,1), GAME-PTS (*x*,2), . . . , GAME-PTS (*x*,7), and each of these is a two-digit item. Consequently, the size of PLAYER (*x*) is also 14.

The statement MOVE I-PLAYER-POINTS TO PLAYER (*x*) moves a 14-character value from one group item to another. Since the characters will be stored left-justified in the receiving field, the game points fall into their proper cells.

Example 2:

The table of Figure 9.30 can be improved by adding a field at the beginning of each row to store the names of the players along with the points they scored in the seven games. Such a table is shown in Figure 9.40. The coding that defines the table is shown below. (The data items in SCORE-TABLE-CONTROLS will be used shortly.)

Figure 9.39 Logic used to transfer all values for one player as a group to a row of the table

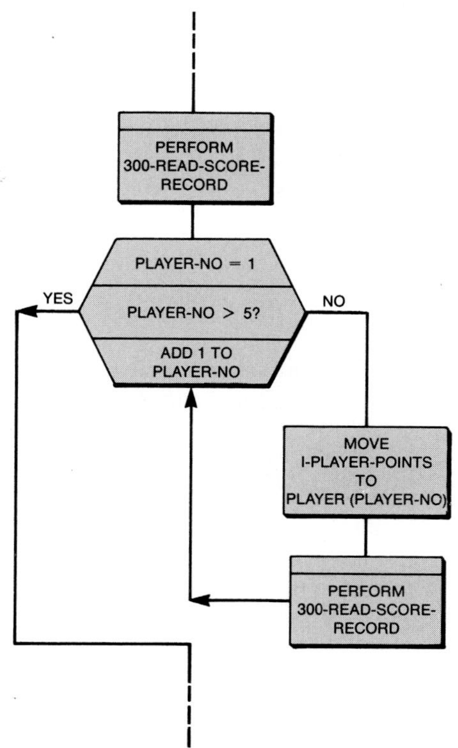

Figure 9.40 A two-level table—example

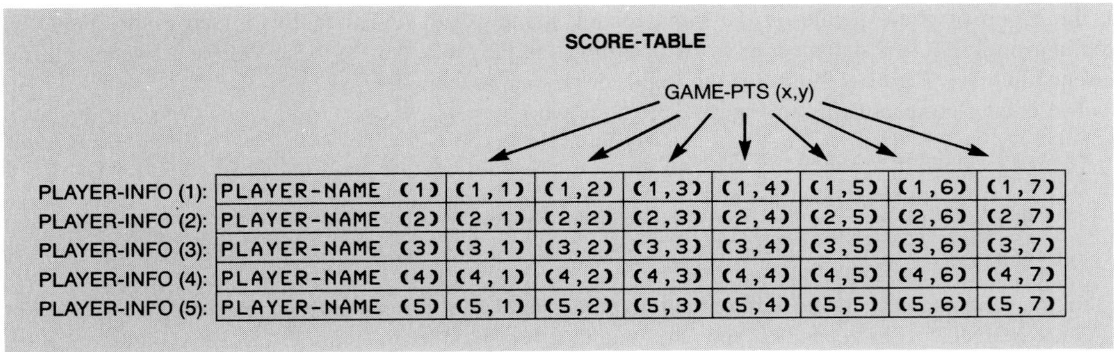


```
01  SCORE-TABLE.
    05 PLAYER-INFO   OCCURS 5 TIMES.
       10 PLAYER-NAME                  PIC X(20).
       10 GAME-PTS   OCCURS 7 TIMES    PIC 99.

01  SCORE-TABLE-CONTROLS.
    05 SCORE-TABLE-ROW-CTR             PIC 9.
    05 SCORE-TABLE-FLAG                PIC XXX.
       88 VALUE-IS-FOUND               VALUE "YES".
```

Note that PLAYER-INFO is a group item. Each of its five occurrences consists of a field PLAYER-NAME and seven repeating items, namely, GAME-PTS. In this definition, the single-subscripted data items are PLAYER-INFO and PLAYER-NAME. GAME-PTS is a double-subscripted data item.

Now, let's examine a procedure to load the revised table with data. The most natural way of proceeding is to prepare an input record for each player in such a way that it contains the player name and the points scored by that player in each of the seven games. The record description can be the following:

```
01  PLAYER-RECORD.
    05 I-PLAYER-INFO.
       10 I-PLAYER-NAME              PIC X(20).
       10 I-POINTS OCCURS 7 TIMES    PIC 99.
```

The record layout and the logic that will be used to load the table are shown in Figure 9.41.

Note that the MOVE box in Figure 9.41 specifies I-PLAYER-INFO as the source field and PLAYER-INFO (SCORE-TABLE-ROW-CTR) as the receiving field. Determine the sizes of the source and receiving fields. Do you see that they are equal?

The coding corresponding to the logic of Figure 9.41 is as follows:

```
    PERFORM 300-READ-PLAYER-RECORD.
    PERFORM VARYING SCORE-TABLE-ROW-CTR FROM 1 BY 1
              UNTIL SCORE-TABLE-ROW-CTR > 5
        MOVE I-PLAYER-INFO TO PLAYER-INFO (SCORE-TABLE-ROW-CTR)
        PERFORM 300-READ-PLAYER-RECORD
    END-PERFORM.
```

With this scheme, the table is loaded quickly.

Searching a Two-Level Table

Suppose that the same table must be searched for the points scored by a given player during a specific game. How can the value be found? If I-PLAYER and I-GAME-NO are supplied as input data, a table look-up might proceed as follows:

```
    MOVE "NO " TO SCORE-TABLE-FLAG.
    PERFORM 400-LOOK-UP-TABLE
        VARYING SCORE-TABLE-ROW-CTR FROM 1 BY 1
            UNTIL VALUE-IS-FOUND.
    .
    .
    .
400-LOOK-UP-TABLE.
    IF I-PLAYER = PLAYER-NAME (SCORE-TABLE-ROW-CTR)
        MOVE GAME-PTS (SCORE-TABLE-ROW-CTR, I-GAME-NO)
            TO O-GAME-PTS
        SET VALUE-IS-FOUND TO TRUE
    END-IF.
```

Figure 9.41 Loading a two-level table—example

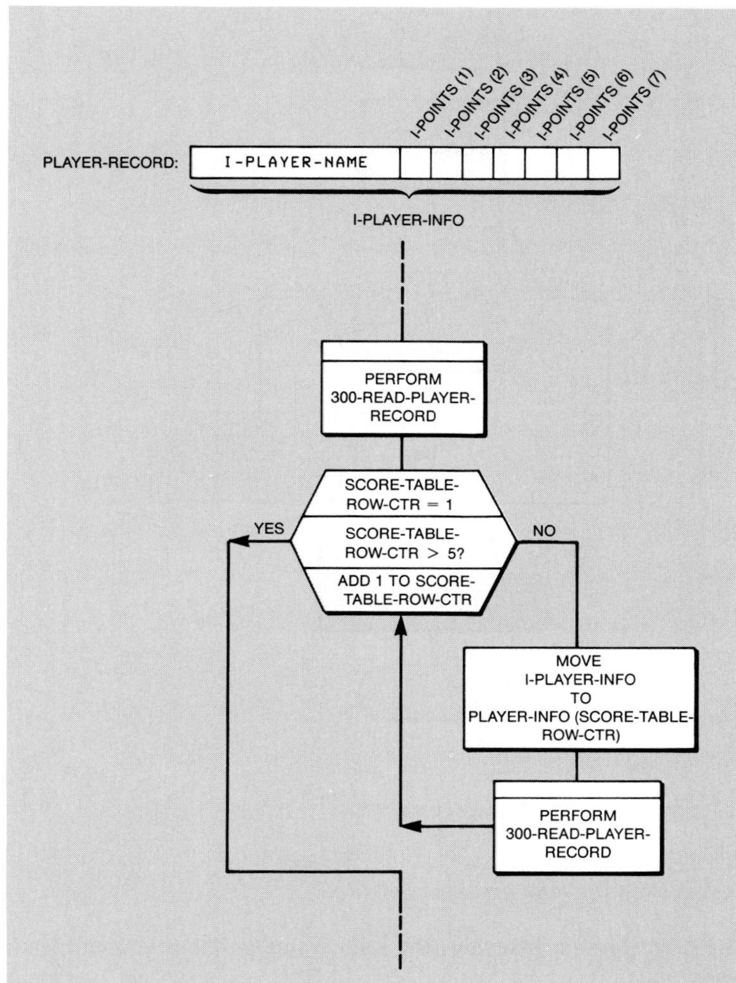

For instance, if the test is satisfied for SCORE-TABLE-ROW-CTR = 3, that is, if the player name on the input record matches the player name in row 3 of the table, and if I-GAME-NO = 5, the MOVE statement is interpreted as

```
MOVE GAME-PTS (3,5) TO O-GAME-PTS.
```

The required value is then stored in O-GAME-PTS, and the execution of the SET statement will cause an exit from the loop by satisfying the condition VALUE-IS-FOUND in the UNTIL clause.

Accessing Data from a Two-Level Table

Now, suppose that the average must be computed for each player, and the averages must be stored in a one-level table, defined as follows:

```
01  PLAYER-AVERAGE-TABLE.
    05 PLAYER-AVE  OCCURS 5 TIMES  PIC 99V9.
```

The logic is shown in Figure 9.42.

The coding corresponding to the logic of Figure 9.42 is as follows (assume all data names are properly defined):

```
    PERFORM 400-COMPUTE-AVE
        VARYING SCORE-TABLE-ROW-CTR FROM 1 BY 1
            UNTIL SCORE-TABLE-ROW-CTR > 5.

400-COMPUTE-AVE.
    INITIALIZE POINT-TOTAL.
    PERFORM VARYING GAME-CTR FROM 1 BY 1
```

■ **Figure 9.42** Accessing data in a two-level table—example

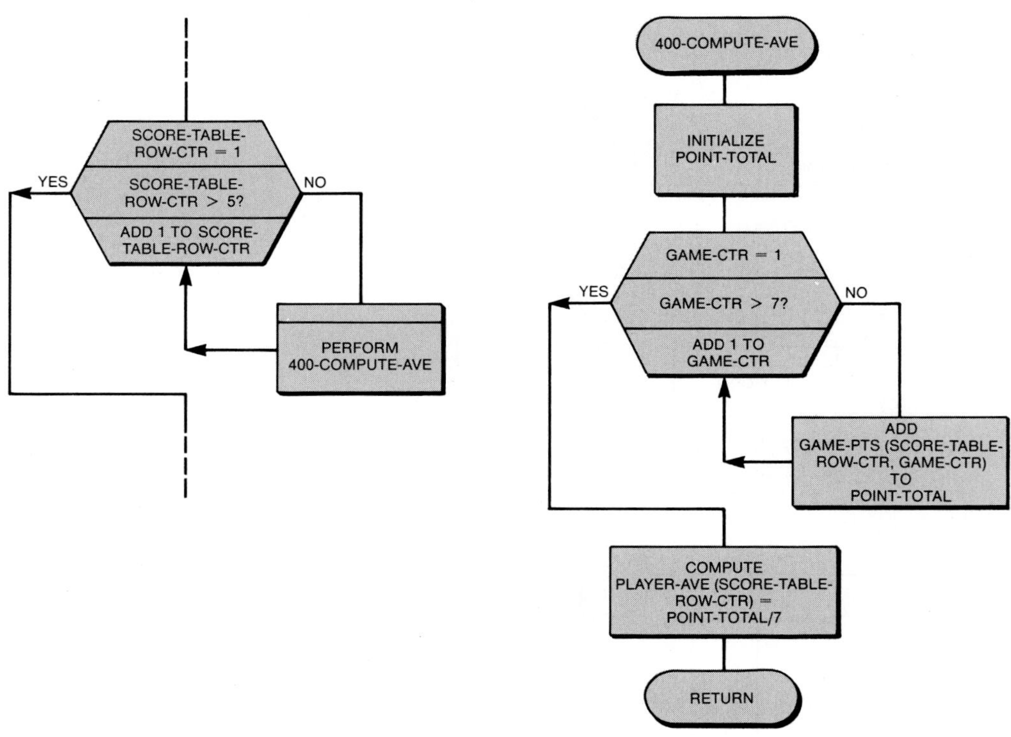


```
                UNTIL GAME-CTR > 7
        ADD GAME-PTS (SCORE-TABLE-ROW-CTR, GAME-CTR)
             TO POINT-TOTAL
    END-PERFORM.
    DIVIDE POINT-TOTAL BY 7
        GIVING PLAYER-AVE (SCORE-TABLE-ROW-CTR) ROUNDED.
```

Do you see that the subscript of PLAYER-AVE is always the same value as the row identifier in SCORE-TABLE? That is, the player whose name is in row 1 of SCORE-TABLE has her or his average in row 1 of PLAYER-AVERAGE-TABLE, and, in general, the player whose name is in row *x* of SCORE-TABLE has his or her average in row *x* of PLAYER-AVERAGE-TABLE. Do you see that the PLAYER-AVERAGE-TABLE is neither an input-loaded table nor a hard-coded table? It is loaded with values produced during the execution of the program.

The Federal Tax Table

We return to the chapter program to define the two-level federal tax table. Once it is defined, we will set up procedures to load it.

Page 534 shows the kind of data that the table must contain, and Figure 9.2b shows that each FEDERAL-TAX-RATES-RECORD contains the data that must be stored in one row of the table (Note that the group name given to the data on the input record is I-TAX-TABLE-ROW-VALUES). An appropriate table definition is the following:

```
01  FEDERAL-TAX-TABLE.
    05 WAGE-LEVEL-INFO   OCCURS 10 TIMES.
       10 UPPER-LIMIT                 PIC 9(4).
       10 WS-TAX-RATE OCCURS 5 TIMES  PIC V999.
    05 FEDERAL-TAX-TABLE-CONTROLS.
       10 TAX-TABLE-FLAG              PIC XXX.
          88 TAX-RATE-IS-FOUND                  VALUE "YES".
       10 TAX-TABLE-ROW-CTR           PIC 99.
```

Now, the task is to set up instructions that will read a FEDERAL-TAX-RATES-RECORD and transfer the data it contains to the appropriate row of the table. Consider the following alternatives:

```
1.      PERFORM 500-READ-TABLE-RECORD.
        PERFORM 510-LOAD-FEDERAL-TAX-TABLE
            VARYING TAX-TABLE-ROW-CTR FROM 1 BY 1
                UNTIL TAX-TABLE-ROW-CTR > 10.

    510-LOAD-FEDERAL-TAX-TABLE.
        MOVE I-TAX-TABLE-ROW-VALUES
            TO WAGE-LEVEL (TAX-TABLE-ROW-CTR).
        PERFORM 500-READ-TABLE-RECORD.

2.      PERFORM 500-READ-TABLE-RECORD.
        PERFORM VARYING TAX-TABLE-ROW-CTR FROM 1 BY 1
                    UNTIL TAX-TABLE-ROW-CTR > 10
            MOVE I-TAX-TABLE-ROW-VALUES
                TO WAGE-LEVEL (TAX-TABLE-ROW-CTR)
            PERFORM 500-READ-TABLE-RECORD
        END-PERFORM.
```

Both alternatives will successfully load the table. The table is shown in Figure 9.43.

As a payroll record is processed, it is necessary to search the federal tax table to retrieve the tax rate appropriate for this employee. Recall that the tax rate is a function of the wage level and of the allowances claimed by the employee. From work done earlier, we know that the computed gross earnings are in the field WS-EMPL-GROSS-EARNINGS. The tax table look-up procedure can be coded as follows:

```
        MOVE "NO " TO TAX-TABLE-FLAG.
        PERFORM 550-LOOK-UP-TAX-TABLE
            VARYING TAX-TABLE-ROW-CTR FROM 1 BY 1
                UNTIL TAX-RATE-IS-FOUND.
        MULTIPLY WS-EMPL-GROSS-EARNINGS BY WS-EMPL-TAX-RATE
            GIVING WS-EMPL-FED-TAX ROUNDED.
        .
        .
        .
    550-LOOK-UP-TAX-TABLE.
        IF WS-EMPL-GROSS-EARNINGS <
                                UPPER-LIMIT (TAX-TABLE-ROW-CTR)
            MOVE WS-TAX-RATE (TAX-TABLE-ROW-CTR, I-EMPL-ALLOWANCES)
                TO WS-EMPL-TAX-RATE
            SET TAX-RATE-IS-FOUND TO TRUE
        END-IF.
```

■ **Figure 9.43** Input-loaded federal tax table

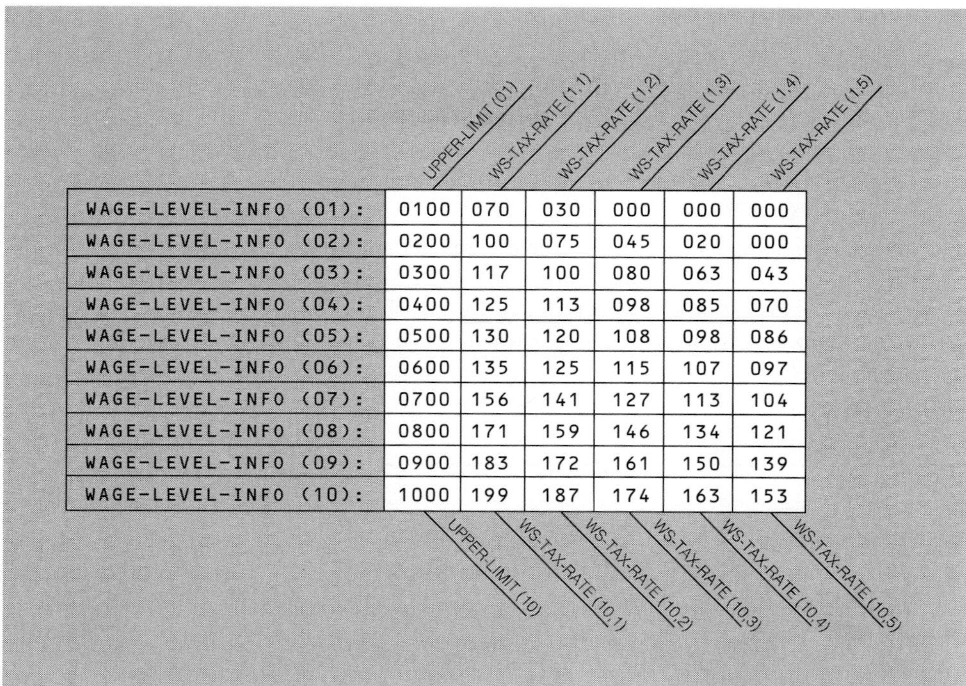

	UPPER-LIMIT	WS-TAX-RATE (n,1)	WS-TAX-RATE (n,2)	WS-TAX-RATE (n,3)	WS-TAX-RATE (n,4)	WS-TAX-RATE (n,5)
WAGE-LEVEL-INFO (01):	0100	070	030	000	000	000
WAGE-LEVEL-INFO (02):	0200	100	075	045	020	000
WAGE-LEVEL-INFO (03):	0300	117	100	080	063	043
WAGE-LEVEL-INFO (04):	0400	125	113	098	085	070
WAGE-LEVEL-INFO (05):	0500	130	120	108	098	086
WAGE-LEVEL-INFO (06):	0600	135	125	115	107	097
WAGE-LEVEL-INFO (07):	0700	156	141	127	113	104
WAGE-LEVEL-INFO (08):	0800	171	159	146	134	121
WAGE-LEVEL-INFO (09):	0900	183	172	161	150	139
WAGE-LEVEL-INFO (10):	1000	199	187	174	163	153

Note the key MOVE statement in paragraph 550-LOOK-UP-TAX-TABLE. WS-TAX-RATE requires two subscripts: The first specifies the row for which the condition in the IF statement is satisfied—that is, it specifies the appropriate UPPER-LIMIT row—whereas the second subscript specifies the number of allowances claimed on the employee's payroll record.

Once the tax rate is found, it is used to multiply the employee's gross earnings, thereby determining the amount to be withheld for the federal tax.

Hard-Coding a Two-Level Table

The federal tax table in the chapter program is an example of an input-loaded table. It is the appropriate way to handle such a table, since the tax rates are volatile, changing periodically, as we all know too well. Yet, in the next example, the federal tax table is hard-coded to provide an example of a two-level hard-coded table.

```
01  FEDERAL-TAX-VALUES.
    05 PIC X(19)   VALUE "0100070030000000000".
    05 PIC X(19)   VALUE "0200100075045020000".
    05 PIC X(19)   VALUE "0300117100080063043".
    05 PIC X(19)   VALUE "0400125113098085070".
    05 PIC X(19)   VALUE "0500130120108098086".
    05 PIC X(19)   VALUE "0600135125115107097".
    05 PIC X(19)   VALUE "0700156141127113104".
    05 PIC X(19)   VALUE "0800171159146134121".
    05 PIC X(19)   VALUE "0900183172161150139".
    05 PIC X(19)   VALUE "1000199187174163153".

01  FEDERAL-TAX-TABLE REDEFINES FEDERAL-TAX-VALUES.
    05 WAGE-LEVEL-INFO   OCCURS 10 TIMES.
       10 UPPER-LIMIT                      PIC 9(4).
       10 WS-TAX-RATE     OCCURS 5 TIMES   PIC V999.
```

The redefinition of FEDERAL-TAX-VALUES assigns the name WAGE-LEVEL-INFO to each row of the table. And, each occurrence of WAGE-LEVEL-INFO contains an UPPER-LIMIT value and five occurrences of the item WS-TAX-RATE. UPPER-LIMIT (x) references the first four characters in row x, and the successive items WS-TAX-RATE (x,y) reference successive groupings of three characters on that row, where $y = 1$ means the first grouping, $y = 2$ means the second grouping, and $y = 5$ the fifth grouping, thus accounting for a total of 19 characters on that row.

Table look-up procedures are the same whether a table is input-loaded or hard-coded.

Some Technical Considerations

All of the preceding examples have used the OCCURS clause in the table definitions, and they have used subscripts in referencing items within a table. The next two paragraphs summarize the rules for using OCCURS and subscripts. The format of the OCCURS clause is shown in Figure 9.44. The general format for subscripting is shown in Figure 9.45.

Rules Governing Use of the OCCURS Clause

1. The OCCURS clause is used to define a table. Table elements are subscripted (or indexed) data items.
2. The integer specifies the exact number of occurrences in the table.
3. In the format, if data-item is a group item, its subordinate data items are also subscripted (or indexed).

Figure 9.44 OCCURS clause format

```
data-item OCCURS integer TIMES

  [ {ASCENDING }  KEY IS {data-name} . . . ] . . .
    {DESCENDING}

  [INDEXED BY {index-name} . . .]
```

■ **Figure 9.45** General subscripting format

$$\left\{\begin{array}{l}\text{data-name}\\ \text{condition-name}\end{array}\right\}\left(\left\{\begin{array}{l}\text{subscript-name [\{\pm\} integer-1]}\\ \text{integer-2}\end{array}\right\}\ldots\right)$$

4. If the KEY clause is used, the values of data-name are the basis for the ascending or descending arrangement of the table elements. More than one data-name can be specified as a key. The position of the data-name in the list of data names indicates its level of significance: The first one is the most significant, the last is the least significant.
5. Any PROCEDURE DIVISION statement that references a data-item or any of its subordinate items must specify a subscript (or an index) for any such item.
6. If a PROCEDURE DIVISION statement contains a subscripted data item, the data item must be defined by an OCCURS clause or be subordinate to an item that is defined by an OCCURS clause.
7. The OCCURS clause can be used only in the definition of data items at levels 02 through 49.
8. The VALUE clause and the OCCURS clause can both be used in the same data-item description. (This is new in COBOL '85 and allows for the definition of hard-coded tables without using the REDEFINES clause.)
9. OCCURS clauses can be nested seven deep; that is, tables can contain up to seven levels. (This is new in COBOL '85. Prior versions allowed a maximum of three levels.)

Rules Governing the Use of Subscripts

1. A subscript-name must be the identifier of an elementary numeric item whose value is an integer. Subscript-name can itself be subscripted.
2. The lowest value of subscript-name or integer-2 is 1. This value points to the first occurrence within the table.
3. The highest value of subscript-name or integer-2 is the integer specified in the OCCURS clause. This value points to the last occurrence within the table.
4. The subscript, or set of subscripts, is always written within a pair of parentheses. The subscripts within a set are separated by a space, or a comma, or both. They are listed in descending order of inclusiveness from the left. A maximum of seven subscripts is allowed.
5. A data name followed by its subscripts is called a subscripted data name. A data name must have a subscript for each OCCURS clause defining the table elements to which it belongs.
6. In COBOL '85, a subscript can be a "relative subscript"; that is, subscript-name can be incremented or decremented by integer-1. For instance, ROW-CTR + 1 references the next occurrence in the table, and ROW-CTR – 1 references the prior occurrence in the table, relative to the current occurrence.

■ The Design Implementation Phase

Now that table-handling requirements of the COBOL language have been developed and illustrated, we turn our attention to completing the chapter program.

Coding the ENVIRONMENT DIVISION

No new entries are needed in the IDENTIFICATION DIVISION. However, the FILE-CONTROL paragraph of the ENVIRONMENT DIVISION must contain three SELECT statements, one for each of the three files required by the program. They are input file TABLES-FILE, input file PAYROLL-FILE, and output file PAYROLL-REPORT. Recall that implementor names specified in the ASSIGN clauses are system-dependent entries, and that you must obtain the appropriate information from your instructor. (Since all the programs in this text have been run on a VAX 8650, the system-related entries in the programs may not be appropriate for your operating system.) The coding of the first two divisions is contained in the printout below.

```
IDENTIFICATION DIVISION.

PROGRAM-ID.   MONSTER-BURGER-PAYROLL.
```

```
******************************************************************
*                                                                *
*   AUTHOR.         PAQUETTE.                                    *
*   DATE WRITTEN.   OCTOBER, 1993.                               *
*                                                                *
******************************************************************

 ENVIRONMENT DIVISION.

 CONFIGURATION SECTION.

 SOURCE-COMPUTER.  VAX-VMS-8650.
 OBJECT-COMPUTER.  VAX-VMS-8650.

 INPUT-OUTPUT SECTION.

 FILE-CONTROL.
     SELECT  TABLES-FILE     ASSIGN TO TABLESDATA.
     SELECT  PAYROLL-FILE    ASSIGN TO COB$INPUT.
     SELECT  PAYROLL-REPORT  ASSIGN TO COB$OUTPUT.
```

(In the first SELECT statement, TABLESDATA is a user-supplied logical name. Before the program is run on the VAX, it will be defined by a DCL statement, such as

$ DEFINE TABLESDATA C9SAM.DT2

where C9SAM.DT2 is the name of the file in the user's directory that contains the data to be stored in the tables within the program. Ask your instructor for corresponding procedures for the computer you are using.)

Coding the FILE SECTION of the DATA DIVISION

The FILE SECTION must contain a file description (FD) for each file referenced in the SELECT statements above. One of the files to be described is TABLES-FILE. Recall that this file contains three kinds of records. Each record description begins with level number 01. Consequently, the FD paragraph for TABLES-FILE is followed by three 01-level entries. Use the layouts of Figure 9.2b, c, and d as guides in checking the accuracy of the coding for these records. Note that the first field of each of these records is reserved for a code that identifies the record. Since these three records will use the same input buffer reserved for the file TABLES-FILE, it is sufficient to name the field for only one of the record layouts. Condition-names attached to this field can be used in the PROCEDURE DIVISION to conveniently test the field to determine which of the three types of records is currently in input memory.

Input file PAYROLL-FILE contains only one kind of record, PAYROLL-RECORD. Its layout is shown in Figure 9.2a. Condition-names are specified for I-EMPL-CLASS-CODE to simplify some of the record processing steps needed in the PROCEDURE DIVISION.

The resulting coding of the file section is shown below.

```
DATA DIVISION.

FILE SECTION.

FD  TABLES-FILE
    RECORD CONTAINS 6 TO 20 CHARACTERS.

01  FEDERAL-TAX-RATES-RECORD.
    05 I-RECORD-CODE                PIC X.
       88 TAX-RATE-RECORD                     VALUE "T".
       88 PAY-RATE-RECORD                     VALUE "P".
       88 INS-PREM-RECORD                     VALUE "I".
    05 I-TAX-TABLE-ROW-VALUES.
       10 I-UPPER-LIMIT             PIC 9(4).
       10 I-TAX-RATE  OCCURS 5 TIMES PIC V999.

01  PAY-RATE-RECORD.
    05                     PIC X.
    05 I-PAY-RATE          PIC 999V99.

01  INSURANCE-PREMIUM-RECORD.
    05                     PIC X.
    05 I-INS-TABLE-ROW-VALUES.
       10 I-INS-CODE       PIC XX.
       10 I-INS-PREM       PIC 99V99.

FD  PAYROLL-FILE
    RECORD CONTAINS 43 CHARACTERS.

01  PAYROLL-RECORD.
    05 I-EMPL-CLASS-CODE    PIC 99.
```

```
            88 MANAGER                     VALUE 06.
            88 ASST-MANAGER                VALUE 05.
            88 REG-EMPLOYEE                VALUES 01 THRU 04.
        05 I-EMPL-SSN            PIC X(9).
        05 I-EMPL-NAME           PIC X(20).
        05 I-EMPL-STORE-NO       PIC XX.
        05 I-EMPL-PAY-CODE       PIC 99.
        05 I-EMPL-HRS            PIC 99.
        05 I-EMPL-OPEN-CLOSE     PIC 99.
        05 I-EMPL-INS-CODE       PIC XX.
        05 I-EMPL-ALLOWANCES     PIC 99.

    FD  PAYROLL-REPORT
        RECORD CONTAINS 133 CHARACTERS.

    01  PRINTLINE                PIC X(133).
```

Coding the WORKING-STORAGE SECTION

In this section, we need the perennial control items, the various employee-related work areas, the company accumulators, the tables, the report headers, and so on. Of particular importance in this program are the tables that must be defined. Earlier discussions of these tables have presented them individually. Within the program, they are listed under the descriptive group name PROGRAM-TABLES. Each table is accompanied by its associated control items, specifically, a flag to expedite the table look-up procedures and a row-counter to be used as a subscript. (The pay rate table does not need a flag because of its positional organization.) The coding of the group PROGRAM-TABLES is shown below. (The remaining entries will be shown in the fully coded program later.)

```
     01  PROGRAM-TABLES.

    *   FEDERAL-TAX-TABLE IS A TWO-LEVEL INPUT-LOADED TABLE.  NOTE THE
    *   USE OF TWO 'OCCURS' CLAUSES.  IT HAS SEQUENTIAL ORGANIZATION.
    *   THE ASCENDING KEY (NOT CODED) IS UPPER-LIMIT.

         05 FEDERAL-TAX-TABLE.
            10 WAGE-LEVEL-INFO  OCCURS 10 TIMES.
               15 UPPER-LIMIT                     PIC S9(4).
               15 WS-TAX-RATE   OCCURS 5 TIMES PIC SV999.
         05 FEDERAL-TAX-TABLE-CONTROL.
            10 WS-TAX-TABLE-FLAG                  PIC XXX.
               88 TAX-RATE-IS-FOUND                        VALUE "YES".
            10 WS-TAX-TABLE-ROW-CTR               PIC S99.

    *   PAY-RATE-TABLE IS A ONE-LEVEL INPUT-LOADED TABLE WITH POSITIONAL
    *   ORGANIZATION.  THE CODE FOR EACH PAY RATE IS THE POSITION IT
    *   OCCUPIES IN THE TABLE.

         05 PAY-RATE-TABLE.
            10 WS-PAY-RATE  OCCURS 15 TIMES  PIC S999V99.
         05 PAY-RATE-TABLE-CONTROL.
            10 WS-PAY-RATE-TABLE-ROW-CTR     PIC 99.

    *   INSURANCE-TABLE IS A ONE-LEVEL INPUT-LOADED TABLE WITH RANDOM
    *   ORGANIZATION.

         05 INSURANCE-TABLE.
            10 WS-INS-INFO  OCCURS 4 TIMES.
               15 WS-INS-CODE          PIC XX.
               15 WS-INS-PREM          PIC 99V99.
         05 INSURANCE-TABLE-CONTROL.
            10 WS-INS-TABLE-FLAG       PIC XXX.
               88 INS-PREM-IS-FOUND             VALUE "YES".
            10 WS-INS-TABLE-ROW-CTR    PIC S9.

    *   EMPLOYEE-CLASS-TABLE IS A ONE-LEVEL HARD-CODED TABLE WITH
    *   USAGE-FREQUENCY ORGANIZATION.

         05 EMPLOYEE-CLASS-VALUES.
            10 PIC X(12)  VALUE "04STANDARD  ".
            10 PIC X(12)  VALUE "03YEARLING  ".
            10 PIC X(12)  VALUE "02BEGINNER  ".
            10 PIC X(12)  VALUE "01APPRENTICE".
            10 PIC X(12)  VALUE "05ASS'T MGR.".
            10 PIC X(12)  VALUE "06STORE MGR.".
         05 EMPLOYEE-CLASS-TABLE REDEFINES EMPLOYEE-CLASS-VALUES.
            10 WS-EMPL-CLASS-INFO  OCCURS 6 TIMES.
               15 WS-EMPL-CLASS-CODE     PIC 99.
               15 WS-EMPL-CLASS          PIC X(10).
         05 EMPLOYEE-CLASS-TABLE-CONTROL.
            10 WS-EMPL-CLASS-TABLE-FLAG  PIC XXX.
               88 EMPL-CLASS-IS-FOUND           VALUE "YES".
            10 WS-EMPL-CLASS-ROW-CTR     PIC S9.
```

Coding the PROCEDURE DIVISION

Coding the PROCEDURE DIVISION follows directly from the program pseudocode of Figure 9.14 or the program flowchart of Figure 9.16. Since the specific coding instructions needed to load the tables and to retrieve data from the tables have been explained and illustrated in detail earlier, no further explanations are provided here. However, comments have been inserted within the program to draw your attention to certain entries related to table-handling concepts.

The complete COBOL program for the chapter is contained in Figure 9.46.

Figure 9.46 COBOL program

```
 IDENTIFICATION DIVISION.

 PROGRAM-ID.  MONSTER-BURGER-PAYROLL.

*****************************************************************
*                                                               *
*  AUTHOR.         PAQUETTE.                                    *
*  DATE WRITTEN.   OCTOBER, 1993.                               *
*                                                               *
*****************************************************************

 ENVIRONMENT DIVISION.

 CONFIGURATION SECTION.

 SOURCE-COMPUTER.  VAX-VMS-8650.
 OBJECT-COMPUTER.  VAX-VMS-8650.

 INPUT-OUTPUT SECTION.

 FILE-CONTROL.
     SELECT  TABLES-FILE    ASSIGN TO TABLESDATA.
     SELECT  PAYROLL-FILE   ASSIGN TO COB$INPUT.
     SELECT  PAYROLL-REPORT ASSIGN TO COB$OUTPUT.

 DATA DIVISION.

 FILE SECTION.

 FD  TABLES-FILE
     RECORD CONTAINS 6 TO 20 CHARACTERS.

 01  FEDERAL-TAXRATES-RECORD.
     05 I-RECORD-CODE                PIC X.
        88 TAXRATE-REC                   VALUE "T".
        88 PAYRATE-REC                   VALUE "P".
        88 INS-PREM-REC                  VALUE "I".
     05 I-TAX-TABLE-ROW-VALUES.
        10 I-UPPER-LIMIT             PIC 9(4).
        10 I-TAXRATE OCCURS 5 TIMES PIC V999.

 01  PAYRATE-RECORD.
     05                      PIC X.
     05 I-PAYRATE            PIC 999V99.

 01  INSURANCE-PREMIUM-RECORD.
     05                      PIC X.
     05 I-INS-TABLE-ROW-VALUES.
        10 I-INS-CODE        PIC XX.
        10 I-INS-PREM        PIC 99V99.

 FD  PAYROLL-FILE
     RECORD CONTAINS 43 CHARACTERS.

 01  PAYROLL-RECORD.
     05 I-EMPL-CLASS-CODE    PIC 99.
        88 MANAGER                    VALUE 06.
        88 ASST-MANAGER               VALUE 05.
        88 REG-EMPLOYEE               VALUES 01 THRU 04.
     05 I-EMPL-SSN           PIC X(9).
     05 I-EMPL-NAME          PIC X(20).
     05 I-EMPL-STORE-NO      PIC XX.
     05 I-EMPL-PAYCODE       PIC 99.
     05 I-EMPL-HRS           PIC 99.
     05 I-EMPL-OPEN-CLOSE    PIC 99.
     05 I-EMPL-INS-CODE      PIC XX.
     05 I-EMPL-ALLOWANCES    PIC 99.
```

```
 FD   PAYROLL-REPORT
      RECORD CONTAINS 133 CHARACTERS.

 01   PRINTLINE              PIC X(133).

 WORKING-STORAGE SECTION.

 01   PROGRAM-CONTROLS.
      05 WS-PARYOLL-RECORDS-FLAG    PIC XXX.
         88 MORE-PAYROLL-RECORDS            VALUE "YES".
         88 NO-MORE-PAYROLL-RECORDS         VALUE "NO ".
      05 WS-TABLE-RECORDS-FLAG      PIC XXX.
         88 MORE-TABLE-RECORDS              VALUE "YES".
         88 NO-MORE-TABLE-RECORDS           VALUE "NO ".
      05 WS-LINE-CTR                PIC S99.
         88 PAGE-IS-FULL                    VALUE +30.
      05 WS-LINE-LIMIT              PIC S99 VALUE +30.
      05 WS-REPORT-DATE             PIC X(6).
      05 WS-PAGE-NO                 PIC S99.
      05 WS-PROPER-SPACING          PIC 9.

 01   EMPLOYEE-WORK-AREAS           COMP.
      05 WS-EMPL-PAYRATE            PIC S9(3)V99.
      05 WS-EMPL-GROSS-EARNINGS     PIC S9(3)V99.
      05 WS-EMPL-TAXRATE            PIC V999.
      05 WS-EMPL-FED-TAX            PIC S9(3)V99.
      05 WS-EMPL-STATE-TAX          PIC S9(2)V99.
      05 WS-EMPL-INS-PREM           PIC S9(2)V99.
      05 WS-EMPL-TOTAL-DED          PIC S9(3)V99.
      05 WS-EMPL-NET-EARNINGS       PIC S9(3)V99.

 01   COMPANY-ACCUMULATORS          COMP.
      05 WS-COMPANY-EMPL-CTR        PIC S9(3).
      05 WS-COMPANY-GROSS-EARNINGS  PIC S9(5)V99.
      05 WS-COMPANY-FED-TAX         PIC S9(5)V99.
      05 WS-COMPANY-STATE-TAX       PIC S9(5)V99.
      05 WS-COMPANY-INS-PREM        PIC S9(5)V99.
      05 WS-COMPANY-NET-EARNINGS    PIC S9(5)V99.

 01   PROGRAM-TABLES.

*   FEDERAL-TAX-TABLE IS A TWO-LEVEL INPUT-LOADED TABLE.  NOTE THE
*   USE OF TWO 'OCCURS' CLAUSES.  IT HAS SEQUENTIAL ORGANIZATION.
*   THE ASCENDING KEY (NOT CODED) IS UPPER-LIMIT.

      05 FEDERAL-TAX-TABLE.
         10 WAGE-LEVEL-INFO  OCCURS 10 TIMES.
            15 UPPER-LIMIT                  PIC S9(4).
            15 WS-TAXRATE    OCCURS 5 TIMES PIC SV999.
      05 FEDERAL-TAX-TABLE-CONTROL.
         10 WS-TAX-TABLE-FLAG               PIC XXX.
            88 TAXRATE-IS-FOUND                     VALUE "YES".
         10 WS-TAX-TABLE-ROW-CTR            PIC S99.

*   PAYRATE-TABLE IS A ONE-LEVEL INPUT-LOADED TABLE WITH POSITIONAL
*   ORGANIZATION.  THE CODE FOR EACH PAYRATE IS THE POSITION IT
*   OCCUPIES IN THE TABLE.

      05 PAYRATE-TABLE.
         10 WS-PAYRATE  OCCURS 15 TIMES  PIC S999V99.
      05 PAYRATE-TABLE-CONTROL.
         10 WS-PAYRATE-TABLE-ROW-CTR     PIC 99.

*   INSURANCE-TABLE IS A ONE-LEVEL INPUT-LOADED TABLE WITH RANDOM
*   ORGANIZATION.

      05 INSURANCE-TABLE.
         10 WS-INS-INFO  OCCURS 4 TIMES.
            15 WS-INS-CODE          PIC XX.
            15 WS-INS-PREM          PIC 99V99.
      05 INSURANCE-TABLE-CONTROL.
         10 WS-INS-TABLE-FLAG       PIC XXX.
            88 INS-PREM-IS-FOUND            VALUE "YES".
         10 WS-INS-TABLE-ROW-CTR    PIC S9.

*   EMPLOYEE-CLASS-TABLE IS A ONE-LEVEL HARD-CODED TABLE WITH
*   USAGE-FREQUENCY ORGANIZATION.
```

```
       05 EMPLOYEE-CLASS-VALUES.
          10 PIC X(12)  VALUE "04STANDARD  ".
          10 PIC X(12)  VALUE "03YEARLING  ".
          10 PIC X(12)  VALUE "02BEGINNER  ".
          10 PIC X(12)  VALUE "01APPRENTICE".
          10 PIC X(12)  VALUE "05ASS'T MGR.".
          10 PIC X(12)  VALUE "06STORE MGR.".
       05-EMPLOYEE-CLASS-TABLE REDEFINES EMPLOYEE-CLASS-VALUES.
          10 WS-EMPL-CLASS-INFO  OCCURS 6 TIMES.
             15 WS-EMPL-CLASS-CODE      PIC 99.
             15 WS-EMPL-CLASS           PIC X(10).
       05 EMPLOYEE-CLASS-TABLE-CONTROL.
          10 WS-EMPL-CLASS-TABLE-FLAG  PIC XXX.
             88 EMPL-CLASS-IS-FOUND            VALUE "YES".
          10 WS-EMPL-CLASS-ROW-CTR     PIC S9.

   01  REPORT-HEADERS.

       05 TOP-LINE.
          10                 PIC X(6)  VALUE SPACES.
          10                 PIC X(14) VALUE "REPORT DATE:  ".
          10 O-REPORT-DATE   PIC XX/XX/XX.
          10                 PIC X(92) VALUE SPACES.
          10                 PIC X(5)  VALUE "PAGE ".
          10 O-PAGE-NO       PIC Z9.
          10                 PIC X(6)  VALUE SPACES.

       05 COMPANY-NAME.
          10 PIC X(56)  VALUE SPACES.
          10 PIC X(21)  VALUE "MONSTER BURGER STORES".
          10 PIC X(56)  VALUE SPACES.

       05 REPORT-NAME.
          10 PIC X(60)  VALUE SPACES.
          10 PIC X(14)  VALUE "PAYROLL REPORT".
          10 PIC X(59)  VALUE SPACES.

       05 HEADINGS-1.
          10 PIC X(75)  VALUE SPACES.
          10 PIC X(5)   VALUE "GROSS".
          10 PIC X(4)   VALUE SPACES.
          10 PIC X(7)   VALUE "FEDERAL".
          10 PIC X(4)   VALUE SPACES.
          10 PIC X(5)   VALUE "STATE".
          10 PIC X(4)   VALUE SPACES.
          10 PIC X(3)   VALUE "INS".
          10 PIC X(6)   VALUE SPACES.
          10 PIC X(5)   VALUE "TOTAL".
          10 PIC X(6)   VALUE SPACES.
          10 PIC X(3)   VALUE "NET".
          10 PIC X(6)   VALUE SPACES.

       05 HEADINGS-2.
          10 PIC X(4)   VALUE SPACES.
          10 PIC X(5)   VALUE "STORE".
          10 PIC X(6)   VALUE SPACES.
          10 PIC X(3)   VALUE "SSN".
          10 PIC X(14)  VALUE SPACES.
          10 PIC X(4)   VALUE "NAME".
          10 PIC X(12)  VALUE SPACES.
          10 PIC X(5)   VALUE "CLASS".
          10 PIC X(5)   VALUE SPACES.
          10 PIC X(8)   VALUE "PAY RATE".
          10 PIC X(3)   VALUE SPACES.
          10 PIC X(3)   VALUE "HRS".
          10 PIC X(2)   VALUE SPACES.
          10 PIC X(8)   VALUE "EARNINGS".
          10 PIC X(4)   VALUE SPACES.
          10 PIC X(3)   VALUE "TAX".
          10 PIC X(7)   VALUE SPACES.
          10 PIC X(3)   VALUE "TAX".
          10 PIC X(5)   VALUE SPACES.
          10 PIC X(4)   VALUE "PREM".
          10 PIC X(6)   VALUE SPACES.
          10 PIC X(3)   VALUE "DED".
          10 PIC X(5)   VALUE SPACES.
          10 PIC X(8)   VALUE "EARNINGS".
          10 PIC X(3)   VALUE SPACES.
```

```
01  PAYROLL-LINE.
    05                        PIC X(5).
    05 O-EMPL-STORE-NO        PIC XX.
    05                        PIC X(4).
    05 O-EMPL-SSN             PIC XXXBXXBXXXX.
    05                        PIC XX.
    05 O-EMPL-NAME            PIC X(20).
    05                        PIC XX.
    05 O-EMPL-CLASS           PIC X(10).
    05                        PIC XX.
    05 O-EMPL-PAYRATE         PIC $Z9.99.
    05 O-PAY-BASE             PIC X(3).
    05                        PIC XX.
    05 O-EMPL-HRS             PIC Z9.
    05                        PIC X(3).
    05 O-EMPL-GROSS-EARNINGS  PIC $ZZ9.99-.
    05                        PIC XX.
    05 O-EMPL-FED-TAX         PIC $ZZ9.99-.
    05                        PIC XX.
    05 O-EMPL-STATE-TAX       PIC $Z9.99-.
    05                        PIC XX.
    05 O-EMPL-INS-PREM        PIC $Z9.99-.
    05                        PIC XX.
    05 O-EMPL-TOTAL-DED       PIC $ZZ9.99-.
    05                        PIC XX.
    05 O-EMPL-NET-EARNINGS    PIC $ZZ9.99-.
    05                        PIC X(3).

01  COMPANY-TOTALS.

    05 COMPANY-TOTALS-HEADER.
       10 PIC X(109)               VALUE SPACES.
       10 PIC X(14)                VALUE "COMPANY TOTALS ".
       10 PIC X(8)                 VALUE SPACES.
       10 PIC XX                   VALUE "**".

    05 TOTAL-EMPLOYEE-COUNT-LINE.
       10 PIC X(101)               VALUE SPACES.
       10 PIC X(18)                VALUE "NO. OF EMPLOYEES: ".
       10 O-COMPANY-EMPL-CTR       PIC ZZ9-.
       10 PIC X(10)                VALUE SPACES.

    05 TOTAL-GROSS-EARNINGS-LINE.
       10 PIC X(103)               VALUE SPACES.
       10 PIC X(16)                VALUE "GROSS EARNINGS: ".
       10 O-COMPANY-GROSS-EARNINGS PIC $ZZ,ZZ9.99-.
       10 PIC X(3)                 VALUE SPACES.

    05 TOTAL-FEDERAL-TAX-LINE.
       10 PIC X(104)               VALUE SPACES.
       10 PIC X(16)                VALUE "FEDERAL TAXES:   ".
       10 O-COMPANY-FED-TAX        PIC $Z,ZZ9.99-.
       10 PIC X(3)                 VALUE SPACES.

    05 TOTAL-STATE-TAX-LINE.
       10 PIC X(106)               VALUE SPACES.
       10 PIC X(14)                VALUE "STATE TAXES:   ".
       10 O-COMPANY-STATE-TAX      PIC $Z,ZZ9.99-.
       10 PIC X(3)                 VALUE SPACES.

    05 TOTAL-INS-PREMIUM-LINE.
       10 PIC X(104)               VALUE SPACES.
       10 PIC X(16)                VALUE "INS. PREMIUMS:   ".
       10 O-COMPANY-INS-PREM       PIC $Z,ZZ9.99-.
       10 PIC X(3)                 VALUE SPACES.

    05 TOTAL-NET-EARNINGS-LINE.
       10 PIC X(105)               VALUE SPACES.
       10 PIC X(14)                VALUE "NET EARNINGS: ".
       10 O-COMPANY-NET-EARNINGS   PIC $ZZ,ZZ9.99-.
       10 PIC X(3)                 VALUE SPACES.

    05 END-LINE.
       10 PIC X(55)                VALUE SPACES.
       10 PIC X(23)                VALUE "*** END OF REPORT ***".
       10 PIC X(55)                VALUE SPACES.

PROCEDURE DIVISION.

100-PRODUCE-PAYROLL-REPORT.
    PERFORM 200-START-UP.
    PERFORM 210-PROCESS-PAYROLL-RECORD
        UNTIL NO-MORE-PAYROLL-RECORDS.
    PERFORM 200-FINISH-UP.
    STOP RUN.
```

■ **Figure 9.46** continued

```
 200-START-UP.
     OPEN INPUT TABLES-FILE
          INPUT PAYROLL-FILE
          OUTPUT PAYROLL-REPORT.
     PERFORM 300-INITIALIZE-ITEMS.
     PERFORM 540-WRITE-REPORT-HEADERS.
     PERFORM 310-READ-PAYROLL-RECORD.

 210-PROCESS-PAYROLL-RECORD.
     PERFORM 320-COMPUTE-EMPLOYEE-ITEMS.
     PERFORM 330-UPDATE-ACCUMULATORS.
     PERFORM 340-PREPARE-PAYROLL-LINE.
     PERFORM 310-READ-PAYROLL-RECORD.

 220-FINISH-UP.
     PERFORM 350-PREPARE-FINAL-TOTALS.
     WRITE PRINTLINE FROM END-LINE
         AFTER ADVANCING 5 LINES.
     CLOSE TABLES-FILE
           PAYROLL-FILE
           PAYROLL-REPORT.

 300-INITIALIZE-ITEMS.
     ACCEPT WS-REPORT-DATE FROM DATE.
     MOVE WS-REPORT-DATE TO O-REPORT-DATE.
     MOVE "YES" TO WS-TABLE-RECORDS-FLAG
                   WS-PAYROLL-RECORDS-FLAG.
     INITIALIZE COMPANY-ACCUMULATORS
                WS-PAGE-NO
                WS-INS-TABLE-ROW-CTR
                WS-PAYRATE-TABLE-ROW-CTR
                WS-TAX-TABLE-ROW-CTR.
     PERFORM 500-READ-TABLE-RECORD.
     PERFORM 400-LOAD-TABLES
         UNTIL NO-MORE-TABLE-RECORDS.

 310-READ-PAYROLL-RECORD.
     READ PAYROLL-FILE RECORD
         AT END
             SET NO-MORE-PAYROLL-RECORDS TO TRUE.

*  THE FIRST MOVE STATEMENT IN THE NEXT PARAGRAPH USES DIRECT
*  REFERENCING TO RETRIEVE A PAYRATE FROM THE PAYRATE TABLE.

 320-COMPUTE-EMPLOYEE-ITEMS.
     MOVE WS-PAYRATE (I-EMPL-PAYCODE) TO WS-EMPL-PAYRATE.
     IF MANAGER
         MOVE WS-EMPL-PAYRATE TO WS-EMPL-GROSS-EARNINGS
     ELSE
         IF ASST-MANAGER
             COMPUTE WS-EMPL-GROSS-EARNINGS ROUNDED =
                 I-EMPL-HRS * WS-EMPL-PAYRATE +
                 5 * I-EMPL-OPEN-CLOSE + 10
         ELSE
             MULTIPLY I-EMPL-HRS BY WS-EMPL-PAYRATE
                 GIVING WS-EMPL-GROSS-EARNINGS ROUNDED
         END-IF
     END-IF.
     PERFORM 410-COMPUTE-TAXES.
     MOVE "NO " TO WS-INS-TABLE-FLAG.
     PERFORM 420-LOOK-UP-INSURANCE-TABLE
         VARYING WS-INS-TABLE-ROW-CTR FROM 1 BY 1
             UNTIL INS-PREM-IS-FOUND.
     ADD WS-EMPL-FED-TAX WS-EMPL-STATE-TAX WS-EMPL-INS-PREM
         GIVING WS-EMPL-TOTAL-DED.
     SUBTRACT WS-EMPL-TOTAL-DED FROM WS-EMPL-GROSS-EARNINGS
         GIVING WS-EMPL-NET-EARNINGS.

 330-UPDATE-ACCUMULATORS.
     ADD 1 TO WS-COMPANY-EMPL-CTR.
     ADD WS-EMPL-GROSS-EARNINGS TO WS-COMPANY-GROSS-EARNINGS.
     ADD WS-EMPL-FED-TAX TO WS-COMPANY-FED-TAX.
     ADD WS-EMPL-STATE-TAX TO WS-COMPANY-STATE-TAX.
     ADD WS-EMPL-INS-PREM TO WS-COMPANY-INS-PREM.
     ADD WS-EMPL-NET-EARNINGS TO WS-COMPANY-NET-EARNINGS.

 340-PREPARE-PAYROLL-LINE.
     MOVE SPACES TO PAYROLL-LINE.
     MOVE I-EMPL-STORE-NO TO O-EMPL-STORE-NO.
     MOVE I-EMPL-SSN TO O-EMPL-SSN.
     MOVE I-EMPL-NAME TO O-EMPL-NAME.
     MOVE "NO " TO WS-EMPL-CLASS-TABLE-FLAG.
```

```
       PERFORM 450-LOOK-UP-EMPLOYEE-CLASS
           VARYING WS-EMPL-CLASS-ROW-CTR FROM 1 BY 1
               UNTIL EMPL-CLASS-IS-FOUND.
       MOVE WS-EMPL-PAYRATE TO O-EMPL-PAYRATE.
       IF MANAGER
           MOVE "/WK" TO O-PAY-BASE
       ELSE
           MOVE "/HR" TO O-PAY-BASE
           MOVE I-EMPL-HRS TO O-EMPL-HRS.
       MOVE WS-EMPL-GROSS-EARNINGS TO O-EMPL-GROSS-EARNINGS.
       MOVE WS-EMPL-FED-TAX TO O-EMPL-FED-TAX.
       MOVE WS-EMPL-STATE-TAX TO O-EMPL-STATE-TAX.
       MOVE WS-EMPL-INS-PREM TO O-EMPL-INS-PREM.
       MOVE WS-EMPL-TOTAL-DED TO O-EMPL-TOTAL-DED.
       MOVE WS-EMPL-NET-EARNINGS TO O-EMPL-NET-EARNINGS.
       PERFORM 440-CHECK-LINE-CTR.
       WRITE PRINTLINE FROM PAYROLL-LINE
           AFTER ADVANCING WS-PROPER-SPACING.
       MOVE 1 TO WS-PROPER-SPACING.
       ADD 1 TO WS-LINE-CTR.

   350-PREPARE-FINAL-TOTALS.
       WRITE PRINTLINE FROM COMPANY-TOTALS-HEADER
           AFTER ADVANCING 5 LINES.
       MOVE WS-COMPANY-EMPL-CTR TO O-COMPANY-EMPL-CTR.
       WRITE PRINTLINE FROM TOTAL-EMPLOYEE-COUNT-LINE
           AFTER ADVANCING 2 LINES.
       MOVE WS-COMPANY-GROSS-EARNINGS TO O-COMPANY-GROSS-EARNINGS.
       WRITE PRINTLINE FROM TOTAL-GROSS-EARNINGS-LINE
           AFTER ADVANCING 1 LINE.
       MOVE WS-COMPANY-FED-TAX TO O-COMPANY-FED-TAX.
       WRITE PRINTLINE FROM TOTAL-FEDERAL-TAX-LINE
           AFTER ADVANCING 1 LINE.
       MOVE WS-COMPANY-STATE-TAX TO O-COMPANY-STATE-TAX.
       WRITE PRINTLINE FROM TOTAL-STATE-TAX-LINE
           AFTER ADVANCING 1 LINE.
       MOVE WS-COMPANY-INS-PREM TO O-COMPANY-INS-PREM.
       WRITE PRINTLINE FROM TOTAL-INS-PREMIUM-LINE
           AFTER ADVANCING 1 LINE.
       MOVE WS-COMPANY-NET-EARNINGS TO O-COMPANY-NET-EARNINGS.
       WRITE PRINTLINE FROM TOTAL-NET-EARNINGS-LINE
           AFTER ADVANCING 1 LINE.

   400-LOAD-TABLES.
       EVALUATE I-RECORD-CODE
           WHEN "T"  PERFORM 510-LOAD-FEDERAL-TAX-TABLE
           WHEN "P"  PERFORM 520-LOAD-PAYRATE-TABLE
           WHEN "I"  PERFORM 530-LOAD-INSURANCE-TABLE.
       PERFORM 500-READ-TABLE-RECORD.

   410-COMPUTE-TAXES.
       MOVE "NO " TO WS-TAX-TABLE-FLAG.
       PERFORM 550-LOOK-UP-TAX-TABLE
           VARYING WS-TAX-TABLE-ROW-CTR FROM 1 BY 1
               UNTIL TAXRATE-IS-FOUND.
       MULTIPLY WS-EMPL-GROSS-EARNINGS BY WS-EMPL-TAXRATE
           GIVING WS-EMPL-FED-TAX ROUNDED.
       MULTIPLY WS-EMPL-FED-TAX BY .19
           GIVING WS-EMPL-STATE-TAX ROUNDED.

  *  THE NEXT MOVE STATEMENT MOVES THE INSURANCE PREMIUM ON THE
  *  ROW FOR WHICH THE CONDITION IN THE "IF" CLAUSE IS SATISFIED
  *  TO A WORK AREA.

   420-LOOK-UP-INSURANCE-TABLE.
       IF I-EMPL-INS-CODE = WS-INS-CODE (WS-INS-TABLE-ROW-CTR)
           MOVE WS-INS-PREM (WS-INS-TABLE-ROW-CTR)
               TO WS-EMPL-INS-PREM
           SET INS-PREM-IS-FOUND TO TRUE
       END-IF.

  *  THE NEXT MOVE STATEMENT MOVES THE EMPLOYEE CLASS ON THE ROW
  *  FOR WHICH THE CONDITION IN THE "IF" CLAUSE IS SATISFIED TO A
  *  FIELD OF THE OUTPUT RECORD "PAYROLL-LINE".

   430-LOOK-UP-EMPLOYEE-CLASS.
       IF I-EMPL-CLASS-CODE =
                        WS-EMPL-CLASS-CODE (WS-EMPL-CLASS-ROW-CTR)
           MOVE WS-EMPL-CLASS (WS-EMPL-CLASS-ROW-CTR)
               TO O-EMPL-CLASS
           SET EMPL-CLASS-IS-FOUND TO TRUE
           END-IF.
```

```
 440-CHECK-LINE-CTR.
     IF WS-LINE-CTR >= WS-LINE-LIMIT
         PERFORM 540-WRITE-REPORT-HEADERS
     END-IF.

 500-READ-TABLE-RECORD.
     READ TABLE-FILE RECORD
         AT END
             SET NO-MORE-TABLE-RECORDS TO TRUE.

*   THE NEXT MOVE STATEMENT MOVES A GROUP OF 19 CHARACTERS FROM THE
*   INPUT RECORD TO THE ROW OF THE TWO-LEVEL TAX TABLE SPECIFIED BY
*   THE VALUE OF THE SUBSCRIPT.

 510-LOAD-FEDERAL-TAX-TABLE.
     ADD 1 TO WS-TAX-TABLE-ROW-CTR.
     MOVE I-TAX-TABLE-ROW-VALUES
         TO WAGE-LEVEL-INFO (WS-TAX-TABLE-ROW-CTR).

*   THE NEXT MOVE STATEMENT MOVES AN ELEMENTARY ITEM FROM THE INPUT
*   RECORD TO THE ROW OF THE ONE-LEVEL PAYRATE TABLE SPECIFIED BY
*   THE VALUE OF THE SUBSCRIPT.

 520-LOAD-PAYRATE-TABLE.
     ADD 1 TO WS-PAYRATE-TABLE-ROW-CTR.
     MOVE I-PAYRATE TO WS-PAYRATE (WS-PAYRATE-TABLE-ROW-CTR).

*   THE NEXT MOVE STATEMENT MOVES A GROUP OF 6 CHARACTERS FROM THE
*   INPUT RECORD TO THE ROW OF THE ONE-LEVEL INSURANCE TABLE
*   SPECIFIED BY THE VALUE OF THE SUBSCRIPT.

 530-LOAD-INSURANCE-TABLE.
     ADD 1 TO WS-INS-TABLE-ROW-CTR.
     MOVE I-INS-TABLE-ROW-VALUES
         TO WS-INS-INFO (WS-INS-TABLE-ROW-CTR).

 540-WRITE-REPORT-HEADERS.
     ADD 1 TO WS-PAGE-NO.
     MOVE WS-PAGE-NO TO O-PAGE-NO.
     WRITE PRINTLINE FROM TOP-LINE
         AFTER ADVANCING PAGE.
     WRITE PRINTLINE FROM COMPANY-NAME
         AFTER ADVANCING 1 LINE.
     WRITE PRINTLINE FROM REPORT-NAME
         AFTER ADVANCING 3 LINES.
     WRITE PRINTLINE FROM HEADINGS-1
         AFTER ADVANCING 3 LINES.
     WRITE PRINTLINE FROM HEADINGS-2
         AFTER ADVANCING 1 LINE.
     INITIALIZE WS-LINE-CTR.
     MOVE 2 TO WS-PROPER-SPACING.

*   THE NEXT MOVE STATEMENT MOVES A TAXRATE FROM THE ROW FOR WHICH
*   THE CONDITION IN THE "IF" CLAUSE IS SATISFIED TO A WORK AREA.
*   SINCE THERE ARE 5 TAXRATES IN EACH ROW, A SECOND SUBSCRIPT
*   "I-EMPL-ALLOWANCES" IS NEEDED TO SPECIFY WHICH OF THE 5 IN THAT
*   ROW IS TO BE RETRIEVED.

 550-LOOK-UP-TAX-TABLE.
     IF WS-EMPL-GROSS-EARNINGS <
                            UPPER-LIMIT (WS-TAX-TABLE-ROW-CTR)
         MOVE WS-TAXRATE (WS-TAX-TABLE-ROW-CTR, I-EMPL-ALLOWANCES)
             TO WS-EMPL-TAXRATE
         SET TAXRATE-IS-FOUND TO TRUE
     END-IF.
```

The input file TABLES-FILE is shown in Figure 9.47a [DD/CD:VIC9SP.DT1], and the input file PAYROLL-FILE is shown in Figure 9.47b [DD/CD:VIC9SP.DT2]. The report produced by the program is contained in Figure 9.48.

■ **Figure 9.47a** Input file TABLES-FILE

```
T0100070030000000000
T0200100075045020000
T0300117100080063043
T0400125113098085070
T0500130120108098086
T0600135125115107097
T0700156141127113104
T0800171159146134121
T0900183172161150139
T1000199187174163153
P00365
P00390
P00425
P00460
P00510
P00575
P00650
P00730
P00830
P00950
P30000
P37500
P45000
P52500
P60000
IIA0673
IIB0914
IFA0865
IFB1154
```

■ **Figure 9.47b** Input file PAYROLL-FILE

Class code | Social Security number | Employee name | Store | Pay code | Hours | Open-close | Insurance code | Allowances

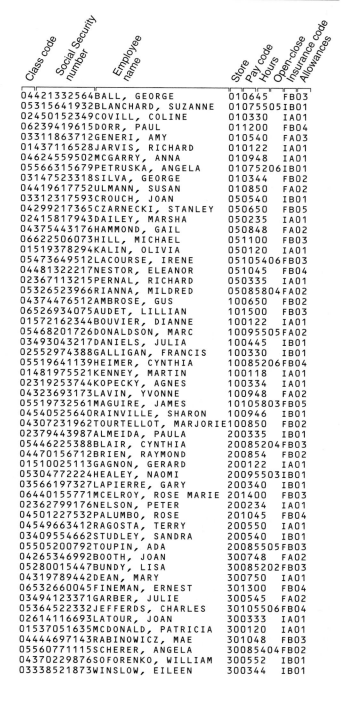

```
04421332564BALL, GEORGE        010645  FB03
05315641932BLANCHARD, SUZANNE  01075505IB01
02450152349COVILL, COLINE      010330  IA01
06239419615DORR, PAUL          011200  FB04
03311863712GENERI, AMY         010540  FA03
01437116528JARVIS, RICHARD     010122  IA01
04624559502MCGARRY, ANNA       010948  IA01
05566315679PETRUSKA, ANGELA    01075206IB01
03147523318SILVA, GEORGE       010344  FB02
04419617752ULMANN, SUSAN       010850  FA02
03312317593CROUCH, JOAN        050540  IB01
04299217365CZARNECKI, STANLEY  050650  FB05
02415817943DAILEY, MARSHA      050235  IA01
04375443176HAMMOND, GAIL       050848  FA02
06622506073HILL, MICHAEL       051100  FB03
01519378294KALIN, OLIVIA       050120  IA01
05473649512LACOURSE, IRENE     05105406FB03
04481322217NESTOR, ELEANOR     051045  FB04
02367113215PERNAL, RICHARD     050335  IA01
05326523966RIANNA, MILDRED     05085804FA02
04374476512AMBROSE, GUS        100650  FB02
06526934075AUDET, LILLIAN      101500  FB03
01572162344BOUVIER, DIANNE     100122  IA01
05468201726DONALDSON, MARC     10095505FA02
03493043217DANIELS, JULIA      100445  IB01
02552974388GALLIGAN, FRANCIS   100330  IB01
05519641139HEIMER, CYNTHIA     10085206FB04
01481975521KENNEY, MARTIN      100118  IA01
02319253744KOPECKY, AGNES      100334  IA01
04323693173LAVIN, YVONNE       100948  FA02
05519732561MAGUIRE, JAMES      10105803FB05
04540525640RAINVILLE, SHARON   100946  IB01
04307231962TOURTELLOT, MARJORIE100850  FB02
02379443987ALMEIDA, PAULA      200335  IB01
05446225388BLAIR, CYNTHIA      20085204FB03
04470156712BRIEN, RAYMOND      200854  FB02
01510025113GAGNON, GERARD      200122  IA01
05304772224HEALEY, NAOMI       20095503IB01
03566197327LAPIERRE, GARY      200340  IB01
06440155771MCELROY, ROSE MARIE 201400  FB03
02362799176NELSON, PETER       200234  IA01
04501227532PALUMBO, ROSE       201045  FB04
04549663412RAGOSTA, TERRY      200550  IA01
03409554662STUDLEY, SANDRA     200540  IB01
05505200792TOUPIN, ADA         20085505FB03
04265346992BOOTH, JOAN         300748  FA02
05280015447BUNDY, LISA         30085202FB03
04319789442DEAN, MARY          300750  IA01
06532660045FINEMAN, ERNEST     301300  FB04
03494123371GARBER, JULIE       300545  FA02
05364522332JEFFERDS, CHARLES   30105506FB04
02614116693LATOUR, JOAN        300333  IA01
01537051635MCDONALD, PATRICIA  300120  IA01
04444697143RABINOWICZ, MAE     301048  FB03
05560771115SCHERER, ANGELA     30085404FB02
04370229876SOFORENKO, WILLIAM  300552  IB01
03338521873WINSLOW, EILEEN     300344  IB01
```

Figure 9.48 Report produced by the program

REPORT DATE: 93/10/23 PAGE 1

MONSTER BURGER STORES

PAYROLL REPORT

STORE	SSN	NAME	CLASS	PAY RATE	HRS	GROSS EARNINGS	FEDERAL TAX	STATE TAX	INS PREM	TOTAL DED	NET EARNINGS
01	421 33 2564	BALL, GEORGE	STANDARD	$ 5.75/HR	45	$258.75	$ 20.70	$ 3.93	$11.54	$ 36.17	$222.58
01	315 64 1932	BLANCHARD, SUZANNE	ASS'T MGR.	$ 6.50/HR	55	$392.50	$ 49.06	$ 9.32	$ 9.14	$ 67.52	$324.98
01	450 15 2349	COVILL, COLINE	BEGINNER	$ 4.25/HR	30	$127.50	$ 12.75	$ 2.42	$ 6.73	$ 21.90	$105.60
01	239 41 9615	DORR, PAUL	STORE MGR.	$75.00/WK		$375.00	$ 31.88	$ 6.06	$11.54	$ 49.48	$325.52
01	311 86 3712	GENERI, AMY	YEARLING	$ 5.10/HR	40	$204.00	$ 16.32	$ 3.10	$ 8.65	$ 28.07	$175.93
01	437 11 6528	JARVIS, RICHARD	APPRENTICE	$ 3.65/HR	22	$ 80.30	$ 5.62	$ 1.07	$ 6.73	$ 13.42	$ 66.88
01	624 55 9502	MCGARRY, ANNA	STANDARD	$ 8.30/HR	48	$398.40	$ 49.80	$ 9.46	$ 6.73	$ 65.99	$332.41
01	566 31 5679	PETRUSKA, ANGELA	ASS'T MGR.	$ 6.50/HR	52	$378.00	$ 47.25	$ 8.98	$ 9.14	$ 65.37	$312.63
01	147 52 3318	SILVA, GEORGE	YEARLING	$ 4.25/HR	44	$187.00	$ 14.03	$ 2.67	$11.54	$ 28.24	$158.76
01	419 61 7752	ULMANN, SUSAN	STANDARD	$ 7.30/HR	50	$365.00	$ 41.25	$ 7.84	$ 8.65	$ 57.74	$307.26
05	312 31 7593	CROUCH, JOAN	YEARLING	$ 5.10/HR	40	$204.00	$ 23.87	$ 4.54	$ 9.14	$ 37.55	$166.45
05	299 21 7365	CZARNECKI, STANLEY	STANDARD	$ 5.75/HR	50	$287.50	$ 12.36	$ 2.35	$11.54	$ 26.25	$261.25
05	415 81 7943	DAILEY, MARSHA	BEGINNER	$ 3.90/HR	35	$136.50	$ 13.65	$ 2.59	$ 6.73	$ 22.97	$113.53
05	375 44 3176	HAMMOND, GAIL	STANDARD	$ 7.30/HR	48	$350.40	$ 39.60	$ 7.52	$ 8.65	$ 55.77	$294.63
05	622 50 6073	HILL, MICHAEL	STORE MGR.	$ 0.00/WK		$300.00	$ 29.40	$ 5.59	$11.54	$ 46.53	$253.47
05	519 37 8294	KALIN, OLIVIA	APPRENTICE	$ 3.65/HR	20	$ 73.00	$ 5.11	$ 0.97	$ 6.73	$ 12.81	$ 60.19
05	473 64 9512	LACOURSE, IRENE	ASS'T MGR.	$ 9.50/HR	54	$553.00	$ 63.60	$12.08	$11.54	$ 87.22	$465.78
05	481 32 2217	NESTOR, ELEANOR	STANDARD	$ 9.50/HR	45	$427.50	$ 41.90	$ 7.96	$11.54	$ 61.40	$366.10
05	367 11 3215	PERNAL, RICHARD	BEGINNER	$ 4.25/HR	35	$148.75	$ 14.88	$ 2.83	$ 6.73	$ 24.44	$124.31
05	326 52 3966	RIANNA, MILDRED	ASS'T MGR.	$ 7.30/HR	58	$453.40	$ 54.41	$10.34	$ 8.65	$ 73.40	$380.00
10	374 47 6512	AMBROSE, GUS	STANDARD	$ 5.75/HR	50	$287.50	$ 28.75	$ 5.46	$11.54	$ 45.75	$241.75
10	526 93 4075	AUDET, LILLIAN	STORE MGR.	$ 0.00/WK		$600.00	$ 76.20	$14.48	$11.54	$102.22	$497.78
10	572 16 2344	BOUVIER, DIANNE	APPRENTICE	$ 3.65/HR	22	$ 80.30	$ 5.62	$ 1.07	$ 6.73	$ 13.42	$ 66.88
10	468 20 1726	DONALDSON, MARC	ASS'T MGR.	$ 8.30/HR	55	$491.50	$ 58.98	$11.21	$ 8.65	$ 78.84	$412.66
10	493 04 3217	DANIELS, JULIA	YEARLING	$ 4.60/HR	45	$207.00	$ 24.22	$ 4.60	$ 9.14	$ 37.96	$169.04
10	552 97 4388	GALLIGAN, FRANCIS	BEGINNER	$ 4.25/HR	30	$127.50	$ 12.75	$ 2.42	$ 9.14	$ 24.31	$103.19
10	519 64 1139	HEIMER, CYNTHIA	ASS'T MGR.	$ 7.30/HR	52	$419.60	$ 41.12	$ 7.81	$11.54	$ 60.47	$359.13
10	481 97 5521	KENNEY, MARTIN	APPRENTICE	$ 3.65/HR	18	$ 65.70	$ 4.60	$ 0.87	$ 6.73	$ 12.20	$ 53.50
10	319 25 3744	KOPECKY, AGNES	BEGINNER	$ 4.25/HR	34	$144.50	$ 14.45	$ 2.75	$ 6.73	$ 23.93	$120.57
10	323 69 3173	LAVIN, YVONNE	STANDARD	$ 8.30/HR	48	$398.40	$ 45.02	$ 8.55	$ 8.65	$ 62.22	$336.18

REPORT DATE: 93/10/23 PAGE 2

MONSTER BURGER STORES

PAYROLL REPORT

STORE	SSN	NAME	CLASS	PAY RATE	HRS	GROSS EARNINGS	FEDERAL TAX	STATE TAX	INS PREM	TOTAL DED	NET EARNINGS
10	519 73 2561	MAGUIRE, JAMES	ASS'T MGR.	$ 9.50/HR	58	$576.00	$ 55.87	$10.62	$11.54	$ 78.03	$497.97
10	540 52 5640	RAINVILLE, SHARON	STANDARD	$ 8.30/HR	46	$381.80	$ 47.73	$ 9.07	$ 9.14	$ 65.94	$315.86
10	307 23 1962	TOURTELLOT, MARJORIE	STANDARD	$ 7.30/HR	50	$365.00	$ 41.25	$ 7.84	$11.54	$ 60.63	$304.37
20	379 44 3987	ALMEIDA, PAULA	BEGINNER	$ 4.25/HR	35	$148.75	$ 14.88	$ 2.83	$ 9.14	$ 26.85	$121.90
20	446 22 5388	BLAIR, CYNTHIA	ASS'T MGR.	$ 7.30/HR	52	$409.60	$ 44.24	$ 8.41	$11.54	$ 64.19	$345.41
20	470 15 6712	BRIEN, RAYMOND	STANDARD	$ 7.30/HR	54	$394.20	$ 44.54	$ 8.46	$11.54	$ 64.54	$329.66
20	510 02 5113	GAGNON, GERARD	APPRENTICE	$ 3.65/HR	22	$ 80.30	$ 5.62	$ 1.07	$ 6.73	$ 13.42	$ 66.88
20	304 77 2224	HEALEY, NAOMI	ASS'T MGR.	$ 8.30/HR	55	$481.50	$ 62.60	$11.89	$ 9.14	$ 83.63	$397.87
20	566 19 7327	LAPIERRE, GARY	YEARLING	$ 4.25/HR	40	$170.00	$ 17.00	$ 3.23	$ 9.14	$ 29.37	$140.63
20	440 15 5771	MCELROY, ROSE MARIE	STORE MGR.	$25.00/WK		$525.00	$ 60.38	$11.47	$11.54	$ 83.39	$441.61
20	362 79 9176	NELSON, PETER	BEGINNER	$ 3.90/HR	34	$132.60	$ 13.26	$ 2.52	$ 6.73	$ 22.51	$110.09
20	501 22 7532	PALUMBO, ROSE	STANDARD	$ 9.50/HR	45	$427.50	$ 41.90	$ 7.96	$11.54	$ 61.40	$366.10
20	549 66 3412	RAGOSTA, TERRY	STANDARD	$ 5.10/HR	50	$255.00	$ 29.84	$ 5.67	$ 6.73	$ 42.24	$212.76
20	409 55 4662	STUDLEY, SANDRA	YEARLING	$ 5.10/HR	40	$204.00	$ 23.87	$ 4.54	$ 9.14	$ 37.55	$166.45
20	505 20 0792	TOUPIN, ADA	ASS'T MGR.	$ 7.30/HR	55	$436.50	$ 47.14	$ 8.96	$11.54	$ 67.64	$368.86
30	265 34 6992	BOOTH, JOAN	STANDARD	$ 6.50/HR	48	$312.00	$ 35.26	$ 6.70	$ 8.65	$ 50.61	$261.39
30	280 01 5447	BUNDY, LISA	ASS'T MGR.	$ 7.30/HR	52	$399.60	$ 39.16	$ 7.44	$11.54	$ 58.14	$341.46
30	319 78 9442	DEAN, MARY	STANDARD	$ 6.50/HR	50	$325.00	$ 40.63	$ 7.72	$ 6.73	$ 55.08	$269.92
30	532 66 0045	FINEMAN, ERNEST	STORE MGR.	$50.00/WK		$450.00	$ 44.10	$ 8.38	$11.54	$ 64.02	$385.98
30	494 12 3371	GARBER, JULIE	YEARLING	$ 5.10/HR	45	$229.50	$ 22.95	$ 4.36	$ 8.65	$ 35.96	$193.54
30	364 52 2332	JEFFERDS, CHARLES	ASS'T MGR.	$ 9.50/HR	55	$562.50	$ 60.19	$11.44	$11.54	$ 83.17	$479.33
30	614 11 6693	LATOUR, JOAN	BEGINNER	$ 4.25/HR	33	$140.25	$ 14.03	$ 2.67	$ 6.73	$ 23.43	$116.82
30	537 05 1635	MCDONALD, PATRICIA	APPRENTICE	$ 3.65/HR	20	$ 73.00	$ 5.11	$ 0.97	$ 6.73	$ 12.81	$ 60.19
30	444 69 7143	RABINOWICZ, MAE	STANDARD	$ 9.50/HR	48	$456.00	$ 49.25	$ 9.36	$11.54	$ 70.15	$385.85
30	560 77 1115	SCHERER, ANGELA	ASS'T MGR.	$ 7.30/HR	54	$424.20	$ 50.90	$ 9.67	$11.54	$ 72.11	$352.09
30	370 22 9876	SOFORENKO, WILLIAM	STANDARD	$ 5.10/HR	52	$265.20	$ 31.03	$ 5.90	$ 9.14	$ 46.07	$219.13
30	338 52 1873	WINSLOW, EILEEN	YEARLING	$ 4.25/HR	44	$187.00	$ 18.70	$ 3.55	$ 9.14	$ 31.39	$155.61

COMPANY TOTALS

NO. OF EMPLOYEES:	57
GROSS EARNINGS:	$17,334.50
FEDERAL TAXES:	$1,860.58
STATE TAXES:	$ 353.54
INS. PREMIUMS:	$ 533.71
NET EARNINGS:	$14,586.67

*** END OF REPORT ***

More to Come

The COBOL language provides the programmer with two other very powerful tools to find and retrieve data from tables. They are the SEARCH and SEARCH ALL statements. Though a complete development of these facilities is beyond the intended scope of this material, an introduction is provided below. (These topics are treated fully in *Volume II.*)

To use the SEARCH statement, the table to be searched must be defined as an "indexed" table. This is accomplished by coding the INDEXED BY clause in the entry that contains the OCCURS clause. The clause INDEXED BY specifies an index, similar to a subscript, that can be associated with occurrences of a data item in that table only. In other words, an index is table-specific, as opposed to a subscript name, which is table-independent. The SEARCH statement uses the table index to refer to occurrences within the table.

1. Defining the table.

```
01   STORE-TABLE.
     05 STORE-INFO OCCURS 10 TIMES
                   INDEXED BY STORE-INDEX.
        10 STORE-ID          PIC XXX.
        10 STORE-LOCATION    PIC X(15).
```

2. Loading the table. Assume I-STORE-INFO of STORE-RECORD contains data for one occurrence of STORE-INFO in STORE-TABLE.

```
PERFORM 300-READ-STORE-RECORD.
PERFORM VARYING STORE-INDEX FROM 1 BY 1
            UNTIL STORE-INDEX > 10
    MOVE I-STORE-INFO TO STORE-INFO (STORE-INDEX)
    PERFORM 300-READ-STORE-RECORD
END-PERFORM.
```

3. Searching the table for the store location corresponding to I-STORE-ID and moving it to the field O-STORE-LOCATION. The SET statement specifies where the search begins in the table.

```
SET STORE-INDEX TO 1.
SEARCH STORE-INFO
    WHEN I-STORE-ID = STORE-ID (STORE-INDEX)
        MOVE STORE-LOCATION (STORE-INDEX)
            TO O-STORE-LOCATION.
```

The formats for the SET and SEARCH statements are shown in Figure 9.49. The logic of the SEARCH statement is shown in Figure 9.50.

Figure 9.49 SET and SEARCH statement formats

```
                                    ┌index-name-2┐
Format 1:   SET ┌index-name-1┐ . . . TO │identifier-2│
                └identifier-1┘          └integer-1  ┘

                                   ┌UP BY  ┐ ┌identifier-2┐
Format 2:   SET {index-name-3} . . . └DOWN BY┘ └integer-2  ┘

SEARCH identifier-1 [VARYING {identifier-2 / index-name-1}]

    [AT END imperative-statement-1]
                        ┌imperative-statement-2┐
    WHEN condition-1    └NEXT SENTENCE         ┘ . . .
[END-SEARCH]
```

Figure 9.50 Logic of the SEARCH statement

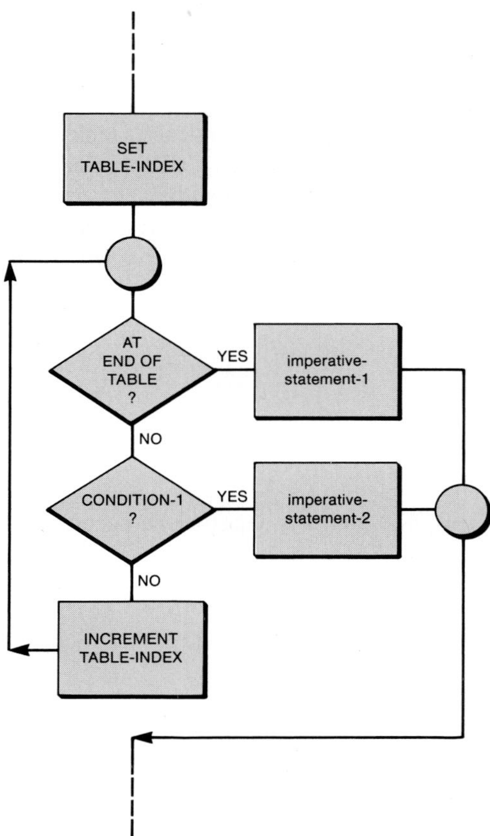

Rules Governing Use of the SEARCH Statement

1. The DATA DIVISION description of identifier-1 must contain an OCCURS clause and an INDEXED BY clause. Identifier-1 must not be a 01-level entry.
2. The VARYING entry is optional. It is used to increment the index of a related table in the same manner as the index of the table being searched is incremented. If identifier-2 is used, it must be an index-data item or a numeric integer item.
3. The AT END entry is optional. If it is used, the imperative statement it contains will be executed if the whole table is searched without satisfying the condition in the WHEN clause, and then control passes to the next statement after the SEARCH. That is, the AT END condition is satisfied when the index is incremented to a value higher than the highest occurrence number in the table.
4. At least one WHEN clause is required. If more than one is used, the search ends when any one of the tested conditions is satisfied. When a condition is satisfied, the imperative statement that follows will be executed, and control passes to the next statement beyond the scope of the SEARCH statement.
5. A condition can take the form of any test: relational, condition-name, class, or sign. It normally references the search value.
6. The SEARCH statement causes a serial search of the elements in the table. The search begins at the position in the table corresponding to the value of the index. The index is assigned its initial value in a SET statement that precedes the SEARCH statement.
7. The table being searched can have any organization.

SEARCH ALL

The SEARCH ALL statement causes the execution of a binary search of a table. Because of the nature of a binary search, it is necessary that the values in the table be arranged either in ascending or descending order, numeric or alphabetic, of one or more of the related items stored in the table. The selected items are called the *search keys.* The search keys must be specified in the ASCENDING or DESCENDING KEY clause, and they must be listed from most significant to least significant.

A table that will be the subject of a binary search must be both indexed and ordered; that is, it must have sequential organization. In the example using store locations and store numbers, if the store number is selected as the key, then the data must be entered in the table either in ascending or descending order by store number as specified in the KEY clause. The presence of the KEY clause **does not** internally order the data. The coding that defines the ordered table and an illustration of the table are shown in Figure 9.51. In this case, the table elements must be in ascending order of the key STORE-ID.

Suppose that the store location corresponding to a given I-STORE-ID must be moved to the field O-STORE-LOCATION. The statement calling for a binary search of the entries in the STORE-TABLE is coded as follows:

```
SEARCH ALL STORE-INFO
    AT END MOVE "UNKNOWN" TO O-STORE-LOCATION
    WHEN STORE-ID (STORE-INDEX) = I-STORE-ID
        MOVE STORE-LOCATION (STORE-INDEX)
            TO O-STORE-LOCATION.
```

The search procedure is executed as follows:

1. STORE-INDEX is set to the middle occurrence in the table (5 in the above table).
2. The value of I-STORE-ID is compared with the value of STORE-ID (5).
   a. If I-STORE-ID = STORE-ID (5), a match occurs, the MOVE is executed, and control passes out of the search.
   b. If I-STORE-ID < STORE-ID (5), then the second half of the table is disregarded.
   c. If I-STORE-ID > STORE-ID (5), then the first half of the table is disregarded.
3. If 2b or 2c occurred, the index STORE-INDEX is now set to the middle occurrence of the remaining half, either 3 or 8.
4. Steps 2 and 3 are repeated (with the appropriate occurrence numbers) until a match occurs.
5. If no match occurs, the AT END condition is satisfied. After MOVE "UNKNOWN" TO O-STORE-LOCATION is executed, control passes to the first statement beyond the scope of the SEARCH statement.

The general format of the SEARCH ALL statement is shown in Figure 9.52.

■ **Figure 9.51** Sample ordered table: Ascending key is STORE-ID

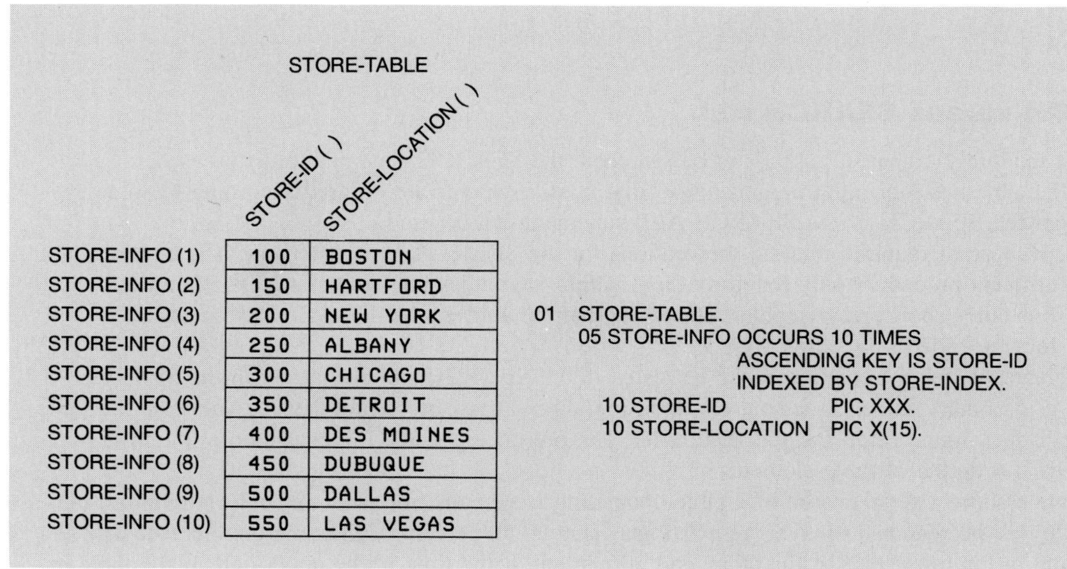

■ **Figure 9.52** SEARCH ALL statement format

```
SEARCH ALL identifier-1
    [AT END imperative-statement-1]

         { data-name-1  { IS EQUAL TO }   { identifier-3              } }
    WHEN {              { IS =        }   { literal-1                 } }
         {                                { arithmetic-expression-1   } }
         { condition-name-1                                             }

    [     { data-name-2  { IS EQUAL TO }   { identifier-4              } } ]
    [ AND {              { IS =        }   { literal-2                 } } ] ...
    [     {                                { arithmetic-expression-2   } } ]
    [     { condition-name-2                                             } ]

         { imperative-statement-2 }
         { NEXT SENTENCE          }

    [END-SEARCH]
```

Rules Governing Use of the SEARCH ALL Statement

1. The SET statement is not used to initialize the index. The index will automatically be set to the middle occurrence of the table entries.
2. Identifier-1 must be defined in the DATA DIVISION by an OCCURS clause; its description must contain the ASCENDING KEY or DESCENDING KEY clause and the INDEXED BY clause.
3. The AT END clause is optional. If used, and the condition is never satisfied, imperative-statement-1 is executed, and control passes to the next statement after SEARCH ALL.
4. The condition in the WHEN clause must contain either a relational test of equality or a condition-name test.
   a. If a relational test, the item specified in the KEY entry must be one of the operands.
   b. If a condition-name test, the data item to which the condition-name is attached must be specified in the KEY entry.
5. The condition in the WHEN clause can be a conjunctive compound condition, that is, two or more tests connected by AND.
6. When the condition in the WHEN clause is satisfied, then imperative-statement-2 or NEXT SENTENCE will be executed.
7. If the condition in the WHEN clause is never satisfied and the AT END clause is not used, control simply passes out of the SEARCH ALL procedure to the next statement in line.

SEARCH versus SEARCH ALL

1. If a randomly organized table is to be searched, the SEARCH statement must be used.
2. If the table has sequential organization—that is, its elements are ordered according to some key—either the SEARCH or the SEARCH ALL statement can be used.
   a. Because of required internal preparations for the SEARCH ALL statement, it is a more efficient procedure only for fairly large tables, say tables containing at least 50 entries.
   b. For fairly short ordered tables, say fewer than 50 entries, the SEARCH statement is recommended.
3. A greater variety of conditions can be tested in the SEARCH statement than in the SEARCH ALL.
4. To use a binary search in a program, the programmer must be certain that the values in the table are in fact organized in the specified order. The presence of the KEY clause does not ensure internal ordering of table elements.
5. If we assume a serial search of a table containing n elements for randomly selected values, the table will be searched on average $n/2$ times. That is, 50 percent of the time the element will be found in the lower half of the table, and 50 percent of the time in the upper half. If the table has 1000 elements, on average it will be searched 500 times before the correct entry is found.

6. If we assume a binary search of a table containing n elements for randomly selected values, the table will be searched at most x times, where 2^x is the smallest power of 2 greater than n. That is, the table size is reduced by a factor of 2 every time the test is not satisfied. If the table has 1000 elements, it will be searched no more than 10 times, since $2^{10} = 1024$.

Both searches are carried out exceedingly fast, so using the binary search is more worthwhile only when used on very large tables.

The concepts of indexed and ordered tables of various levels are developed fully in *Volume II, Advanced Structured COBOL,* the sequel to this text.

Important Terms in Chapter 9

array
ASCENDING KEY
DESCENDING KEY
direct referencing
double-subscripted data item
hard-coded table
initializing a table
input-loaded table
loading a table
nonpermanent table (volatile)
OCCURS
one-level table
PERFORM-VARYING-AFTER
PERFORM-VARYING-UNTIL
permanent table (static)
positional organization
random organization
retrieving a table element
SEARCH
SEARCH ALL
search keys
sequential organization
single-subscripted data item
subscript
table look-up with subscripts
table redefinition
two-level table
two-level table search
usage-frequency organization

Exercises

1. Write record description entries for the record layout shown in Figure 9.53.
2. The input data file QUARTER-SALES-FILE consists of records as shown in exercise 1. One of these records is shown below.

   MA-32503054300076050067550087000115025. . . . .

   a. What is the salesperson's number?
   b. The sales amounts are for which quarter?
   c. What are the salesperson's sales for the second week of the quarter? the fifth week?
3. Write record description entries for the table representation shown in Figure 9.54. Assume size 20 for each table element.
4. Write record description entries for the table representation shown in Figure 9.55. Assume size 6 for student number and size 20 for student name.
5. Given the two tables in Figure 9.56, and the record descriptions of exercise 3 and exercise 4, answer the following questions:
   a. What is the value associated with WS-STUDENT (5) of WS-CLASS-LIST-1?
   b. What is the value associated with WS-STUDENT (5) of WS-CLASS-LIST-2?
   c. What is the correct reference for the value RUCKSTER, JAMIE of WS-CLASS-LIST-1? of WS-CLASS-LIST-2?
   d. Is it correct to say that WS-CLASS-LIST-1 has sequential organization? If so, what is the basis or key for the sequencing? Is it ascending or descending?
   e. Repeat part d for WS-CLASS-LIST-2.

Figure 9.53

Record Layout Form

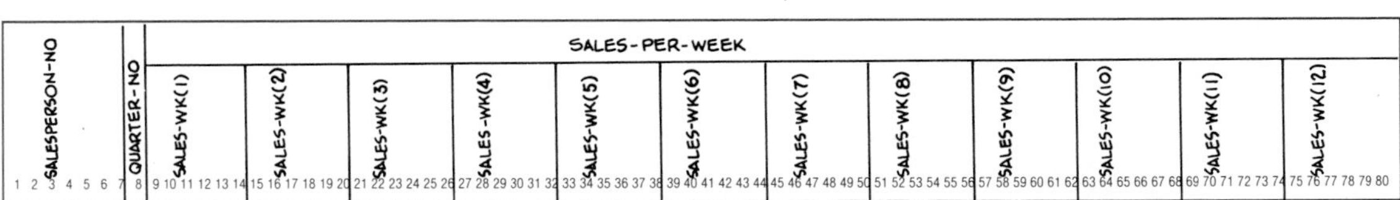

Record Name: QUARTER-SALES-RECORD

■ **Figure 9.54**

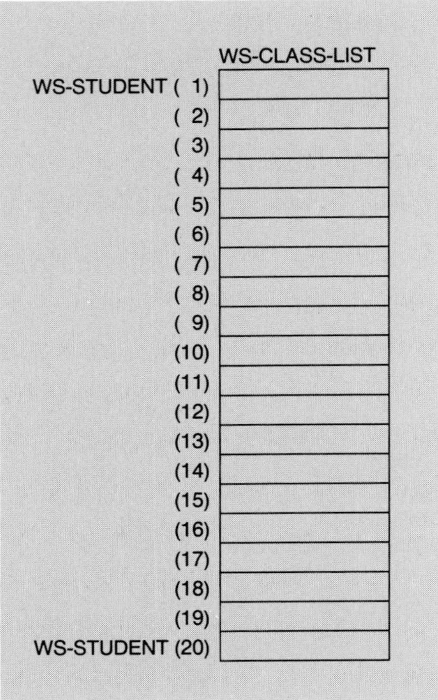

■ **Figure 9.55**

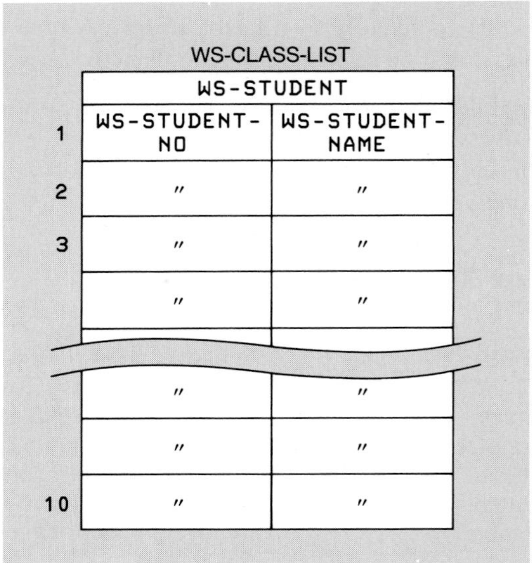

■ **Figure 9.56**

WS-CLASS-LIST-1

BENOIT, ALBERT
CLARK, ANNE
EARLEN, WOLF
HANSON, BARRY
KELLOGG, ROBERTA
PINCHON, LIZZY
PRENDA, ROBERT
QUINLON, ARNOLD
RUCKSTER, JAMIE
SILVIA, JOHN

WS-CLASS-LIST-2

672435	BENOIT, ALBERT
683277	CLARK, ANNE
653214	EARLEN, WOLF
667433	HANSON, BARRY
655342	KELLOGG, ROBERTA
688755	PINCHON, LIZZY
637566	PRENDA, ROBERT
654782	QUINLON, ARNOLD
685322	RUCKSTER, JAMIE
674451	SILVIA, JOHN

f. Rearrange the values of WS-CLASS-LIST-2 if ASCENDING KEY IS WS-STUDENT-NO.
  i. What is the value of WS-STUDENT-NAME (1)? WS-STUDENT-NAME (5)?
  ii. Write the new record description entries for WS-CLASS-LIST-2, and use the KEY entry.

g. Write the values that will be printed as a result of the following entries:

```
PERFORM VARYING ROW-CTR FROM 1 BY 2
        UNTIL ROW-CTR > 10
    DISPLAY WS-STUDENT OF WS-CLASS-LIST-1 (ROW-CTR)
END-PERFORM.
```

h. Write the values that will be printed as a result of the following entries:

```
PERFORM VARYING ROW-CTR FROM 10 BY -2
        UNTIL ROW-CTR < 5
    DISPLAY WS-STUDENT OF WS-CLASS-LIST-2 (ROW-CTR)
END-PERFORM.
```

6. Assume that the wholesale prices for 50 catalog items are kept in a data file (CATALOG-FILE), but they must be stored in a table in working storage. Wholesale prices have the format xxx.xxx.

a. Assume that the catalog numbers are in the range from 1 to 50, and the data file is sorted in ascending order on them.
   i. Write DATA DIVISION entries for the records of the data file and the required working storage table of wholesale prices. (The table should also include the catalog numbers.)
   ii. Write the pseudocode or design the flowchart segment(s) required to read the data file and store the wholesale price information in the table.
   iii. Write the COBOL statements corresponding to the pseudocode or flowchart of part ii above.
b. Assume that the catalog numbers are in the range 1 to 50, but the data file is **not** sorted. Repeat items i, ii, and iii of part a so that the table entries are stored in ascending order of catalog numbers.
c. Assume that the catalog numbers are seven-character identifiers: two letters, one hyphen, and four digits. Repeat items i, ii, and iii of part a.

7. A permanent table of day names is to be coded into a program. Write the WORKING-STORAGE SECTION entries required to define the table and to allow individual day-name references as WS-DAY (*x*).

8. Write the statement corresponding to the flowchart segment shown in Figure 9.57.

9. a. Draw a representation of the table defined by the following record description:

```
01  STUDENT-TESTS-TABLE.
    05 WS-STUDENT  OCCURS 20 TIMES.
    10 WS-TEST  OCCURS  4 TIMES  PIC 999.
```

   b. Write PROCEDURE DIVISION statements that will compute the average test grade for each student and store it in a table of averages, so that the first element of the table is the average for the first student, the second element of the table is the average for the second student, and so on. Use the following table description:

```
01  AVERAGES-TABLE.
    05 STUDENT-TEST-AVE OCCURS 20 TIMES PIC S999.
```

10. Given the table layout shown in Figure 9.58, complete the exercises below.
   a. Write the entries that are needed to define the table.
   b. Identify the single-subscripted data items and the double-subscripted data items.
   c. Assume that for each student, there is a record in a data file defined by the following entries:

```
FD  STUDENT-FILE
    RECORD CONTAINS 38 CHARACTERS.

01  STUDENT-RECORD.
    05 I-STUDENT-ID            PIC X(6).
    05 I-STUDENT-NAME          PIC X(20).
    05 I-TEST OCCURS 4 TIMES   PIC 999.
```

   Use the flowchart segment of Figure 9.59 to write the PROCEDURE DIVISION statements needed to store the student information in the table. Pay particular attention to the subscripts.

Figure 9.57

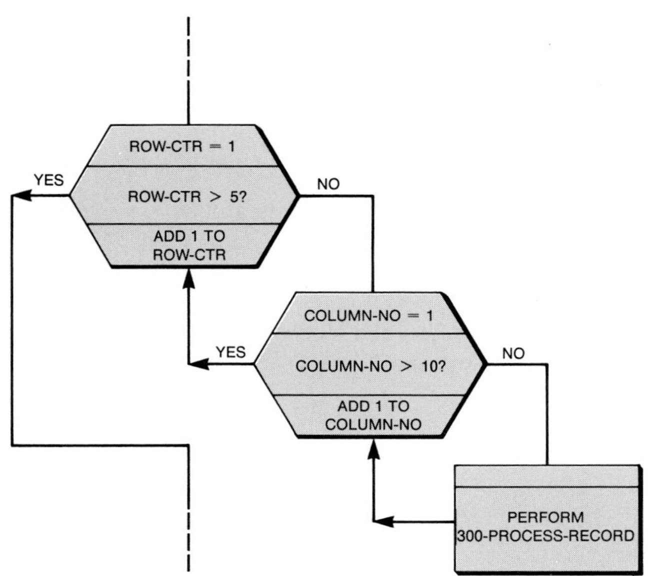

■ Figure 9.58

	WS-STUDENT-TABLE							
WS-STU-INFO (1):	WS-STU-ID (1)	WS-STU-NAME (1)	WS-TEST (1,1)	WS-TEST (1,2)	WS-TEST (1,3)	WS-TEST (1,4)	WS-TOTAL (1)	WS-AVE (1)
WS-STU-INFO (2):	WS-STU-ID (2)	WS-STU-NAME (2)	WS-TEST (2,1)	WS-TEST (2,2)	WS-TEST (2,3)	WS-TEST (2,4)	WS-TOTAL (2)	WS-AVE (2)
WS-STU-INFO (3):	WS-STU-ID (3)	WS-STU-NAME (3)	WS-TEST (3,1)	WS-TEST (3,2)	WS-TEST (3,3)	WS-TEST (3,4)	WS-TOTAL (3)	WS-AVE (3)
WS-STU-INFO (4):	WS-STU-ID (4)	WS-STU-NAME (4)	WS-TEST (4,1)	WS-TEST (4,2)	WS-TEST (4,3)	WS-TEST (4,4)	WS-TOTAL (4)	WS-AVE (4)
WS-STU-INFO (5):	WS-STU-ID (5)	WS-STU-NAME (5)	WS-TEST (5,1)	WS-TEST (5,2)	WS-TEST (5,3)	WS-TEST (5,4)	WS-TOTAL (5)	WS-AVE (5)
	[illegible] ID (6)	WS-STU-NAME (6)	WS-TEST (6,1)	WS-TEST [illegible]	[illegible]	[illegible]	[illegible]	[illegible] (6)
WS-STU-INFO (15):	WS-STU-[illegible]	[illegible]	[illegible]	[illegible] (15,2)	WS-TEST (15,3)	WS-TEST (15,4)	WS-TOTAL (15)	WS-AVE (15)
WS-STU-INFO (16):	WS-STU-ID (16)	WS-STU-NAME (16)	WS-TEST (16,1)	WS-TEST (16,2)	WS-TEST (16,3)	WS-TEST (16,4)	WS-TOTAL (16)	WS-AVE (16)
WS-STU-INFO (17):	WS-STU-ID (17)	WS-STU-NAME (17)	WS-TEST (17,1)	WS-TEST (17,2)	WS-TEST (17,3)	WS-TEST (17,4)	WS-TOTAL (17)	WS-AVE (17)
WS-STU-INFO (18):	WS-STU-ID (18)	WS-STU-NAME (18)	WS-TEST (18,1)	WS-TEST (18,2)	WS-TEST (18,3)	WS-TEST (18,4)	WS-TOTAL (18)	WS-AVE (18)
WS-STU-INFO (19):	WS-STU-ID (19)	WS-STU-NAME (19)	WS-TEST (19,1)	WS-TEST (19,2)	WS-TEST (19,3)	WS-TEST (19,4)	WS-TOTAL (19)	WS-AVE (19)
WS-STU-INFO (20):	WS-STU-ID (20)	WS-STU-NAME (20)	WS-TEST (20,1)	WS-TEST (20,2)	WS-TEST (20,3)	WS-TEST (20,4)	WS-TOTAL (20)	WS-AVE (20)

■ Figure 9.59

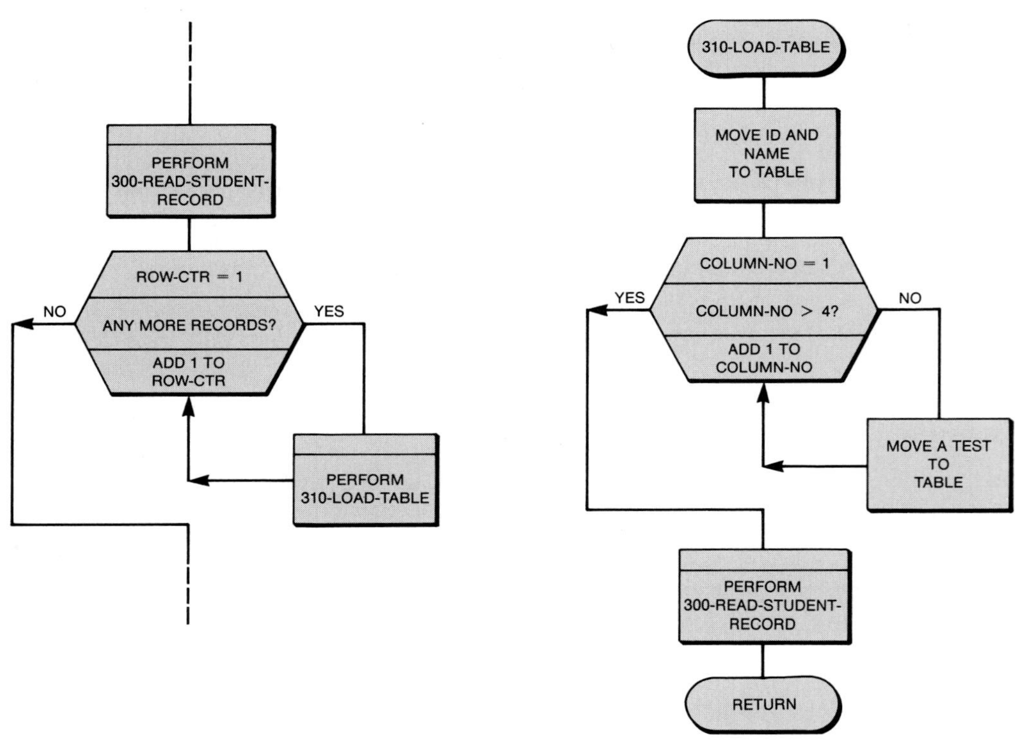

d. Write the pseudocode or design the flowchart segment needed to compute and store the total and the average for each student.

e. Write the PROCEDURE DIVISION statements corresponding to the pseudocode or the flowchart segment of part d.

11. Use WS-CLASS-LIST-2 of exercise 5, the following table definition and record description, and the flowchart segment in Figure 9.60 to complete the following exercises:

```
01  WS-CLASS-LIST-2.
    05 WS-STUDENT OCCURS 10 TIMES.
       10 WS-STUDENT-NO      PIC 9(6).
       10 WS-STUDENT-NAME    PIC X(20).
    05 CLASS-LIST-FLAG       PIC XXX.
       88 STUDENT-IS-FOUND           VALUE "YES".
    05 ROW-CTR               PIC 99.
```

■ Figure 9.60

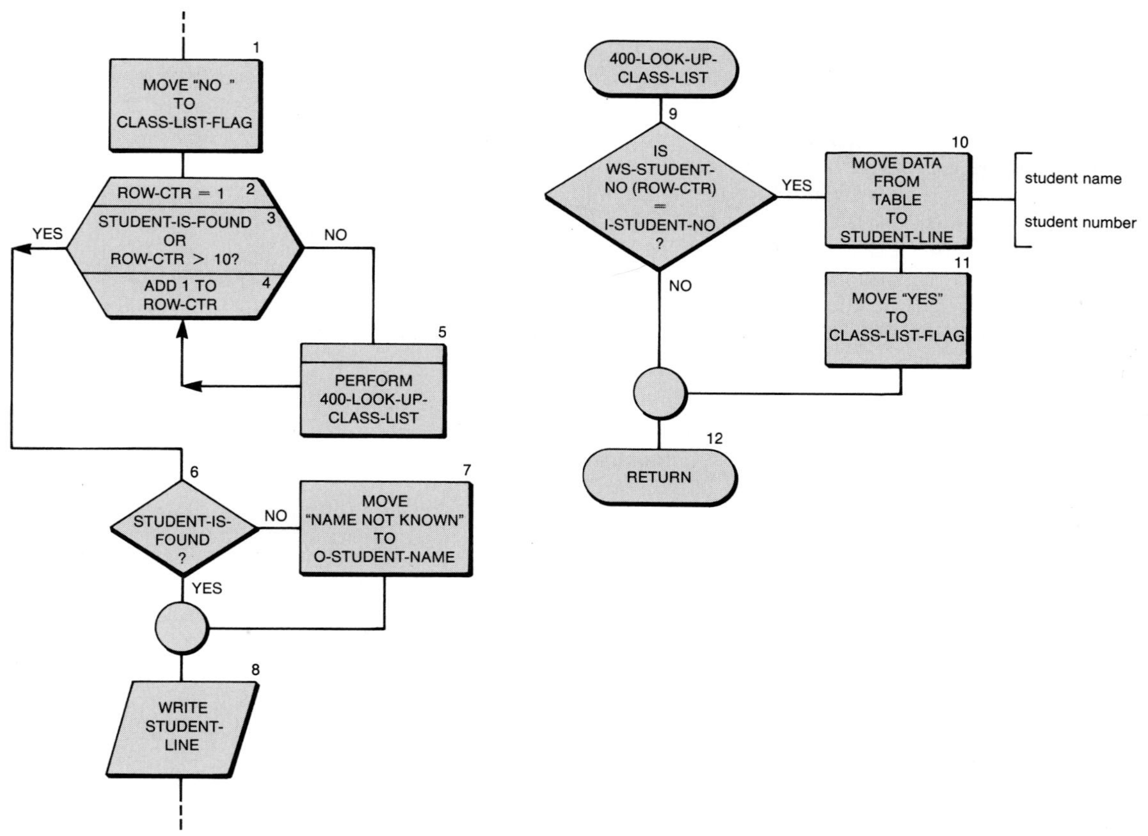


```
01  STUDENT-LINE.
    05                        PIC X(10).
    05 O-STUDENT-NO           PIC X(6).
    05                        PIC X(5).
    05 O-STUDENT-NAME         PIC X(20).
    05                        PIC X(10).
```

a. Write the PROCEDURE DIVISION statements corresponding to the flowchart segment.

b. If I-STUDENT-NO has value 667433, use the box numbers attached to the symbols in the flowchart segment to trace the control sequence.

c. If I-STUDENT-NO has value 767433, use the box numbers to trace the control sequence.

12. In exercise 11, assume the objective of the table look-up is to find the student number corresponding to an input student name. Revise the flowchart segment, and show the corresponding coding.

13. Suppose an inventory table is defined as follows:

```
01  INVENTORY-TABLE.
    05 WS-INVENTORY-ITEM   OCCURS 2000 TIMES
                           ASCENDING KEY IS WS-ITEM-NO.
       10 WS-ITEM-NO          PIC 9(4).
       10 WS-ITEM-DESCR       PIC X(15).
       10 WS-ITEM-UNIT-PR     PIC S9(4)V99.
       10 WS-ITEM-SELL-PR     PIC S9(4)V99.
    05 INVENTORY-TABLE-FLAG   PIC XXX.
       88 ITEM-IS-FOUND                 VALUE "YES".
    05 ROW-CTR                PIC 9(4).
```

a. A table look-up is needed to retrieve the description and unit price for an input item number I-ITEM-NO. The description and unit price are to be stored in the output record fields O-ITEM-DESCR and O-ITEM-UNIT-PR respectively. When the values are found, the output record ITEM-LINE is to be written.

   i. Design the logic for the table look-up procedure.

   ii. Write the COBOL statements needed to implement the table look-up procedure.

b. For a given input item number I-ITEM-NO, its markup (selling price – unit price) is to be stored in a separate table MARKUPS.

i. Define the table.

ii. Write the statements needed to get the job done.

14. The students in a course are given an objective-type test. Each student prepares a test record containing her or his answers, and the instructor prepares an answers record containing all the correct answers. The record layouts are shown in Figure 9.61.

a. Code the record description entries for each type of record.

b. The data on the answers record must be loaded into an answers table in working storage.

i. Show the coding needed to define the answers table.

ii. Write PROCEDURE DIVISION entries that can be used to load the table.

c. Plan the logic needed to read a student test record and grade the student responses. Be sure to test the course number and the test number before grading the student record.

d. Write the PROCEDURE DIVISION entries corresponding to part c.

15. Given the simplified tax table below, complete the exercises.

Tax Table

Gross Weekly Income		**Number of Dependents**			
At Least	*But Less Than*	*1*	*2*	*3*	*4*
000	100	.05	.02	.00	.00
100	200	.10	.09	.07	.05
200	250	.12	.11	.10	.08
250	300	.14	.12	.11	.10
300	350	.15	.14	.12	.11
350	400	.16	.15	.14	.13
400	450	.18	.16	.15	.14
450	500	.19	.18	.16	.15

a. Write the WORKING-STORAGE SECTION entries needed to hard-code the table into a program.

b. Write the WORKING-STORAGE SECTION entries for the tax table if the table is to be loaded from input records.

i. Show the layout and coding of the needed input records.

ii. Write the PROCEDURE DIVISION entries needed to load the table.

Figure 9.61

Record Layout Forms

a.

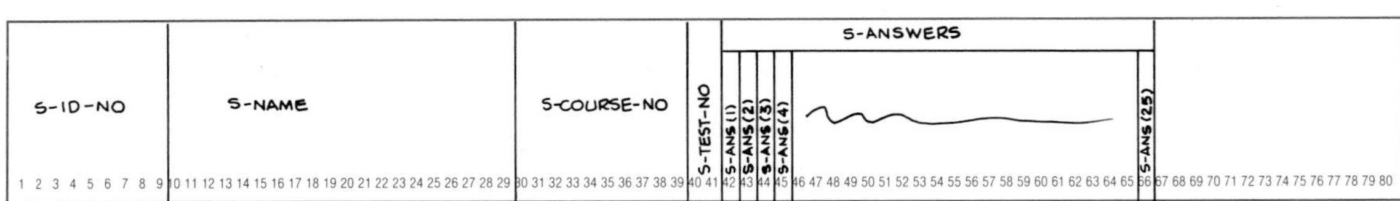

Record Name: TEST-RECORD

b.

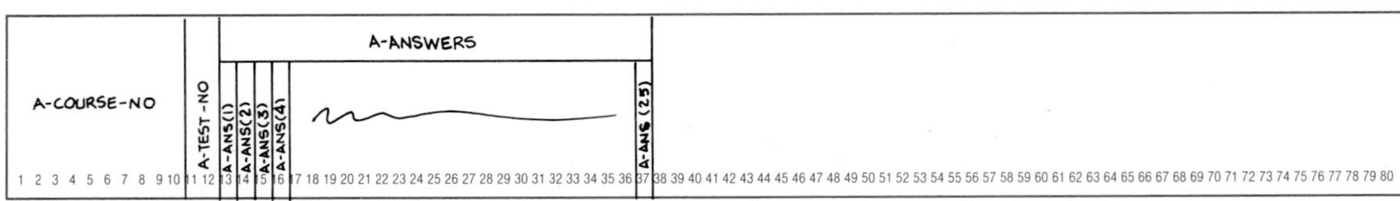

Record Name: ANSWERS-RECORD

Debugging Activities

1. The two-level table below shows tax amounts owed based on annual income and number of exemptions claimed. The table must be hard-coded into a program. It will be used within the program in a table look-up procedure in which the tax must be retrieved to compute net income.

Tax Table

Yearly Income		Number of Exemptions			
Over	*But Not Over*	*1*	*2*	*3*	*4*
0	2400	0	0	0	0
2400	7650	88	0	0	0
7650	10900	835	683	543	403
10900	15400	1505	1305	1135	975
15400	23250	2811	2561	2311	2080
23250	28900	4683	4373	4074	3824
28900	34200	6430	6090	5761	5451
34200	40000	8374	8004	7637	7297
40000	50000	11297	10927	10557	10187

Identify problems that might result from the following coding:

```
01  TAX-VALUES.
    05 PIC X(30) VALUE "    0 2400    0    0    0    0".
    05 PIC X(30) VALUE " 2400 7650   88    0    0    0".
    05 PIC X(30) VALUE " 765010900  835  683  543  403".
    05 PIC X(30) VALUE "1090015400 1505 1305 1135  975".
    05 PIC X(30) VALUE "1540023250 2811 2561 2311 2080".
    05 PIC X(30) VALUE "2325028900 4683 4373 4074 3824".
    05 PIC X(30) VALUE "2890034200 6430 6090 5761 5451".
    05 PIC X(30) VALUE "3420040000 8374 8004 7637 7297".
    05 PIC X(30) VALUE "400005000011297109271055710187".

01  TAX-TABLE.
    05 INCOME-LEVEL OCCURS 10 TIMES  PIC X(30).
    05 LOW-LIMIT                PIC X(5).
    05 UPPER-LIMIT              PIC X(5).
    05 WS-TAX   OCCURS 4 TIMES  PIC X(5).
```

2. Refer to the following partial program:

Part a.

```
FILE SECTION.

FD  CATALOG-FILE
    RECORD CONTAINS 35 CHARACTERS.

01  CATALOG-RECORD.
    05 I-PART-NO          PIC X(5).
    05 I-PART-DESCR       PIC X(20).
    05 I-PURCH-PRICE      PIC 999V99.
    05 I-SELL-PRICE       PIC 999V99.

FD  DETAIL-FILE
    RECORD CONTAINS 5 CHARACTERS.

01  DETAIL-RECORD.
    05 I-DETAIL-PART-NO PIC X(5).

FD  MARKUP-REPORT
    RECORD CONTAINS 80 CHARACTERS.

01  PRINTLINE             PIC X(80).

WORKING-STORAGE SECTION.

01  PROGRAM-CONTROLS.
    05 WS-MORE-DETAIL-RECORDS       PIC XXX.
       88 THERE-IS-A-DETAIL-RECORD          VALUE "YES".
       88 NO-MORE-DETAIL-RECORDS            VALUE "NO ".
    05 WS-MORE-CATALOG-RECORDS      PIC XXX.
       88 NO-MORE-CAT-RECORDS               VALUE "NO ".
    05 WS-PROPER-SPACING            PIC 9.

01  ITEM-WORK-AREAS.
    05 WS-PURCH-PRICE-WORK          PIC S999V99.
```

```
    05 WS-SELL-PRICE-WORK          PIC S999V99.
    05 WS-MARKUP-WORK              PIC S999V99.

01  PROGRAM-TABLES.
    05 CATALOG-TABLE.
       10 CAT-ITEM-INFO OCCURS 10 TIMES.
          15 WS-PART-NO            PIC X(5).
          15 WS-PART-DESCR         PIC X(20).
          15 WS-PURCH-PRICE        PIC S999V99.
    05 CATALOG-TABLE-CONTROLS.
       10 CAT-TABLE-FLAG           PIC XXX.
          88 ITEM-IS-FOUND                 VALUE "YES".
       10 CAT-TABLE-ROW-CTR        PIC S99.

PROCEDURE DIVISION.

100-PRODUCE-MARKUP-REPORT.
    PERFORM 200-START-UP.
    PERFORM 210-PROCESS-DETAIL-RECORD
        UNTIL NO-MORE-DETAIL-RECORDS.
    PERFORM 220-FINISH-UP.
    STOP RUN.

200-START-UP.
    OPEN INPUT CATALOG-FILE
         INPUT DETAIL-FILE
         OUTPUT MARK-UP-REPORT.
    PERFORM 300-INITIALIZE-ITEMS.
    PERFORM 310-WRITE-REPORT-HEADERS.
    PERFORM 320-READ-DETAIL-RECORD.

210-PROCESS-DETAIL-RECORD.
    PERFORM 330-COMPUTE-MARK-UP.
    PERFORM 340-PREPARE-MARK-UP-LINE.
    PERFORM 320-READ-DETAIL-RECORD.

220-FINISH-UP.
    WRITE PRINTLINE FROM END-LINE
        AFTER ADVANCING 5 LINES.
    CLOSE CATALOG-FILE
          DETAIL-FILE
          MARK-UP-REPORT.

300-INITIALIZE-ITEMS.
    MOVE "YES" TO WS-MORE-DETAIL-RECORDS
                  WS-MORE-CATALOG-RECORDS.
    MOVE SPACES TO MARK-UP-LINE.
    PERFORM 500-READ-CATALOG-RECORD.
    PERFORM VARYING CAT-TABLE-ROW-CTR FROM 1 BY 1
                UNTIL NO-MORE-CAT-RECORDS
        MOVE CATALOG-RECORD TO CAT-ITEM-INFO (CAT-TABLE-ROW-CTR)
        PERFORM 500-READ-CATALOG-RECORD
    END-PERFORM.

310-WRITE-REPORT-HEADERS.
    WRITE PRINTLINE FROM COMPANY-NAME
        AFTER ADVANCING PAGE.
    WRITE PRINTLINE FROM REPORT-NAME
        AFTER ADVANCING 3 LINES.
    WRITE PRINTLINE FROM HEADINGS
        AFTER ADVANCING 3 LINES.
    MOVE 2 TO WS-PROPER-SPACING.

320-READ-DETAIL-RECORD.
    READ DETAIL-FILE RECORD
        AT END
            SET NO-MORE-DETAIL-RECORDS TO TRUE.

330-COMPUTE-MARK-UP.
    MOVE "NO " TO CAT-TABLE-FLAG.
    PERFORM 410-LOOK-UP-CATALOG-TABLE
        VARYING CAT-TABLE-ROW-CTR FROM 1 BY 1
            UNTIL ITEM-IS-FOUND.
    MOVE WS-PURCH-PRICE (CAT-TABLE-ROW-CTR)
        TO WS-PURCH-PRICE-WORK.
    SUBTRACT WS-PURCH-PRICE-WORK FROM WS-SELL-PRICE-WORK
        GIVING WS-MARK-UP-WORK.

340-PREPARE-MARK-UP-LINE.
    MOVE I-DETAIL-PART-NO TO O-PART-NO.
    MOVE "NO " TO CAT-TABLE-FLAG.
    PERFORM 410-LOOK-UP-CATALOG-TABLE
        VARYING CAT-TABLE-ROW-CTR FROM 1 BY 1
            UNTIL CAT-PART-IS-FOUND.
    MOVE WS-PART-DESCR (CAT-TABLE-ROW-CTR) TO O-PART-DESCR.
    MOVE WS-PURCH-PRICE-WORK TO O-PURCH-PRICE.
```

```
       MOVE WS-SELL-PRICE-WORK TO O-SELL-PRICE.
       MOVE WS-MARK-UP-WORK TO O-MARK-UP.
       WRITE PRINTLINE FROM MARK-UP-LINE
           AFTER ADVANCING WS-PROPER-SPACING.
       MOVE 1 TO WS-PROPER-SPACING.

   410-LOOK-UP-CATALOG-TABLE.
       IF I-DETAIL-PART-NO = WS-PART-NO (CAT-TABLE-ROW-CTR)
           SET ITEM-IS-FOUND TO TRUE
       END-IF.

   500-READ-CATALOG-RECORD.
       READ CATALOG-FILE RECORD
           AT END
               SET NO-MORE-CAT-RECORDS TO TRUE.
```

Part b.

```
                      EXPRESS AUTO PARTS WAREHOUSE

                             MARK-UPS REPORT

ITEM NO.     ITEM DESCRIPTION      PURCH. PRICE    SELL. PRICE    MARKUP

 5507R     DISC BRAKE PADS            $ 12.46        $   0.00     $ 12.46-
 0359B     FLEXSOCKET WRENCH          $  1.91        $   0.00     $  1.91-
 1242W     TUNE-UP TESTER             $ 33.29        $   0.00     $ 33.29-
```

Part c.

```
0346RCB ANTENNA          0332903995
0359BCB CONVERTER        0207902495
0462UFLEXSOCKET WRENCH   0019100229
1242WRV ALARM SYSTEM     0166301995
1352VTUNE-UP TESTER      0332903995
1616WAIR DIESEL HARN     0141501698
2181XEXHAUST HEADERS     0566306795
5507RBONDED BRAKE SHOE   0066500798
5524YDISC BRAKE PADS     0124601495
7519YSOLID STATE TACH    0332903995
```

Part d.

```
5507R
0359B
1242W
7519Y
1352V
```

Part a shows relevant portions of the program that produced the report in part b. The catalog file (Debugging Activity Data File Set 16 [DD/CD:VIC9DBG2.DT1]) used to load CATALOG-TABLE is in part c. Each record in the detail file (Debugging Activity Data File Set 17 [DD/CD:VIC9DBG2.DT2]) in part d contains a catalog part number. The program must retrieve the appropriate table data, compute the markup for the item, and print the information on the report. Unfortunately, the report contains a number of errors, specifically:

a. The selling price prints as zero.
b. The markup is negative.
c. Only three items printed on the report; there should be five detail lines, followed by an End-of-Report message.
d. The item numbers and item descriptions (and associated prices) are mismatched.

Debug the program and run it so it produces the following report:

```
                      EXPRESS AUTO PARTS WAREHOUSE


                             MARK-UPS REPORT


ITEM NO.     ITEM DESCRIPTION      PURCH. PRICE    SELL. PRICE    MARKUP

 5507R     BONDED BRAKE SHOE          $  6.65        $  7.98      $   1.33
 0359B     CB CONVERTER               $ 20.79        $ 24.95      $   4.16
 1242W     RV ALARM SYSTEM            $ 16.63        $ 19.95      $   3.32
 7519Y     SOLID STATE TACH           $ 33.29        $ 39.95      $   6.66
 1352V     TUNE-UP TESTER             $ 33.29        $ 39.95      $   6.66



                          ***  END OF REPORT  ***
```

Programming Exercises

Programming Exercise I

The management of Modern Plastics Company wants its data processing department to prepare a two-level report listing all of its employees by plant. At the first level, it must print a detail line for each employee of a plant. At the second level, a plant summary must show the number of employees in each of its departments. The format of the report is shown in the printer spacing chart of Figure 9.62.

■ Figure 9.62

Record Layout Form

I-PLANT-NO	I-DEPT-NO	I-SSN	I-EMPL-NAME		I-DATE-HIRED
3 4	5 6	7–15	16–35	36–76	77–80

Record Name: EMPLOYEE-RECORD

Printer Spacing Chart

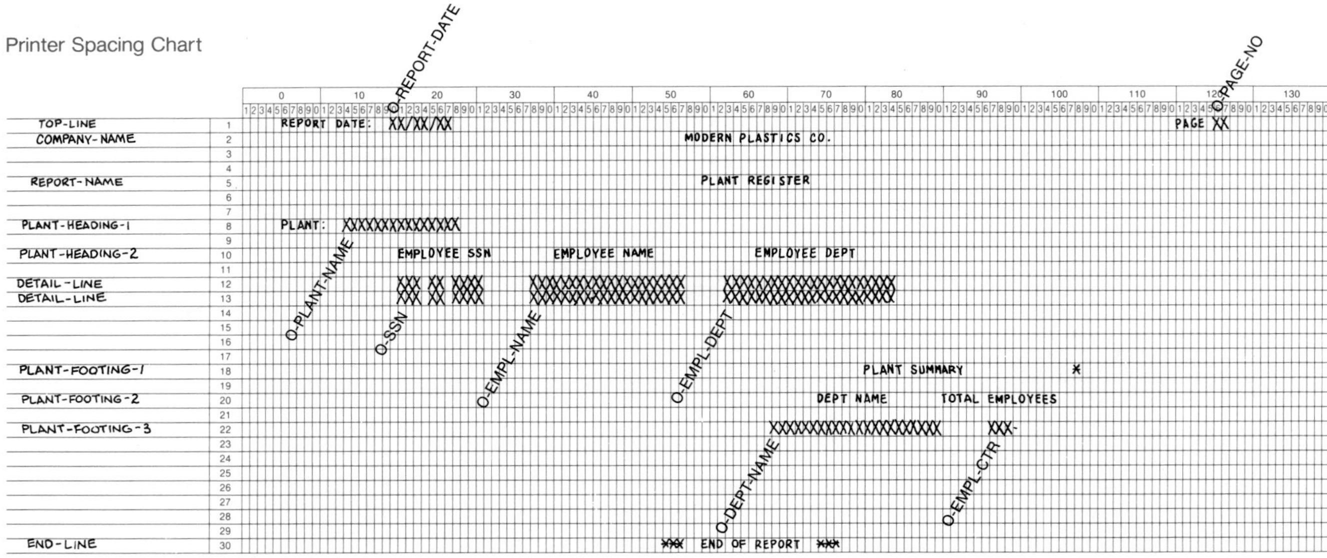

System Flowchart

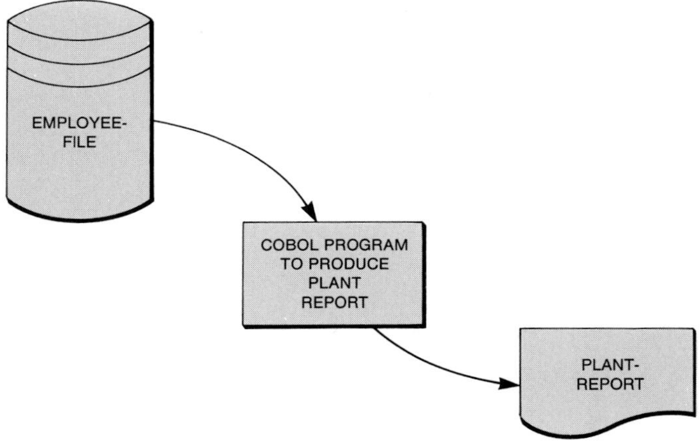

For each employee, there is a record in the employee register file containing the following data:

cc 3–4	Plant number
cc 5–6	Department number
cc 7–15	Social Security number
cc 16–35	Employee name
cc 77–80	Date hired

The records are ordered in seniority sequence within each department.

Figure 9.62 continued

Structure Chart

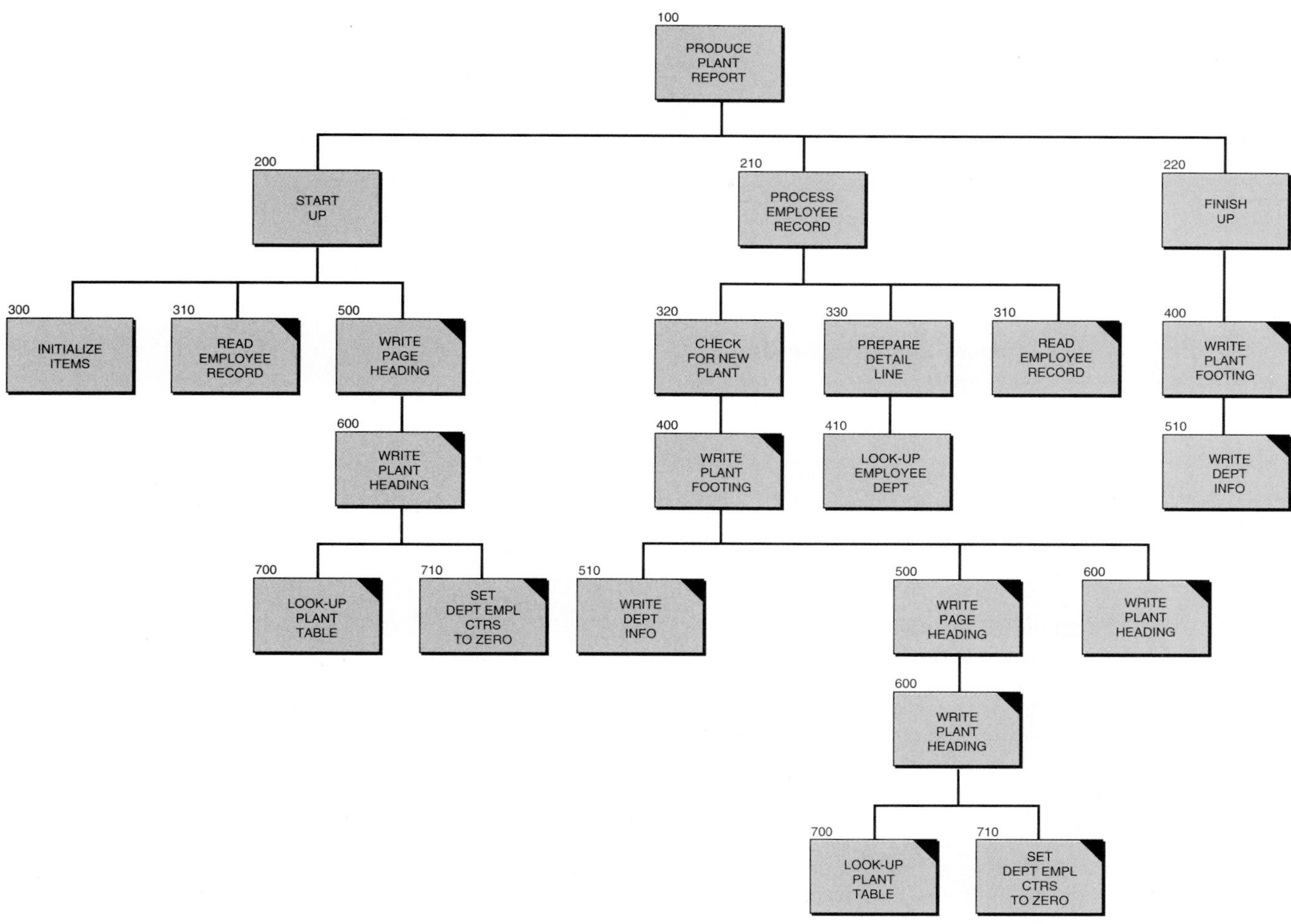

The program must convert plant numbers and department numbers into names. Hard-coded tables are to be used for that purpose. Since the report must produce intermediate totals for each plant, the program must use a plant control break.

The report must be properly documented on each page, and at most two plants are to be reported per page. The lists of plants and departments are shown below.

Plants		**Departments**	
Plant No.	Plant Name	Dept. No.	Dept. Name
10	Boston	10	Administration
20	Providence	20	Personnel
30	New Haven	30	Finance
40	Stamford	40	Research & Development
50	New York	50	Production
		60	Shipping & Receiving
		70	Maintenance
		80	Data Processing

The design tools are all supplied in Figure 9.62. Your task is to code, debug, compile, and run the program successfully. Use Data File Set 4 (see Appendix C) as the input file.

Program Pseudocode

100-Produce-Plant-Report.

1. Perform 200-Start-Up.
2. Perform 210-Process-Employee-Record until no more records.
3. Perform 220-Finish-Up.
4. Stop the run.

200-Start-Up.

1. Open the files.
2. Perform 300-Initialize-Items.
3. Perform 310-Read-Employee-Record.
4. Perform 500-Write-Page-Heading.

210-Process-Employee-Record.

1. Perform 320-Check-For-New-Plant.
2. Perform 330-Prepare-Detail-Line.
3. Perform 310-Read-Employee-Record.

220-Finish-Up.

1. Perform 400-Write-Plant-Footing.
2. Move End-Line to the output area Printline.
3. After advancing 5 lines, write the output record Printline.
4. Close the files.

300-Initialize-Items.

1. Obtain the date from the system.
2. Move the date to Top-Line date.
3. Set the end-of-file flag WS-MORE-RECORDS to "YES".
4. Set the page-number to zero.
5. Clear the record area Detail-Line.

310-Read-Employee-Record.

1. Read an input Employee-Record.
2. Test for end-of-file record;
   if EOF record reached, set the flag WS-MORE-RECORDS to "NO ".

320-Check-For-New-Plant.

1. If input plant-number is not equal to plant-control,
   then, perform 400-Write-Plant-Footing.

330-Prepare-Detail-Line.

1. Move input employee-SSN to Payroll-Line employee-SSN.
2. Move input employee-name to Payroll-Line employee-name.
3. Move "NO " to the department-table-flag.
4. Perform 410-Look-Up-Employee-Department
   varying the department-table-row-counter from initial value 1,
   and incrementing it by 1, until department-table-flag is equal to "YES".
5. Add 1 to department-employee-counter (department-table-row-counter - 1).
6. Move Detail-Line to the output area Printline.
7. After advancing proper-spacing, write the output record Printline.
8. Set proper-spacing to 1.

400-Write-Plant-Footing.

1. Move Plant-Footing-1 to the output area Printline.
2. After advancing 3 lines, write the output record Printline.
3. Move Plant-Footing-2 to the output area Printline.
4. After advancing 2 lines, write the output record Printline.
5. Set proper-spacing to 2.

6. Perform 510-Write-Dept-Info
    varying the department-table-row-counter from initial value 1,
    and incrementing it by 1, until its value is greater than 8.
7. Add 1 to the plants-per-page-counter.
8. If the flag WS-MORE-RECORDS is equal to "YES",
    then, if the plants-per-page-counter is equal to 2,
        perform 500-Write-Page-Heading, but otherwise, perform 600-Write-Plant-Heading.

410-Look-Up-Employee-Dept.

1. Test input department-number
    against department-table department-number (department-table-row-counter);
2. When they match,
    a. move department-table department-name (department-table-row-counter)
        to Detail-Line employee-department.
    b. move "YES" to department-table-flag.

500-Write-Page-Heading.

1. Add 1 to page-number.
2. Move page-number to Top-Line page-number.
3. Move Top-Line to the output area Printline.
4. After advancing to the top of a new page,
    write the output record Printline.
5. Move Company-Name to the output area Printline.
6. After advancing 1 line, write the output record Printline.
7. Move Report-Name to the output area Printline.
8. After advancing 3 lines, write the output record Printline.
9. Set the plants-per-page-counter to zero.
10. Perform 600-Write-Plant-Heading.

510-Write-Dept-Info.

1. Move department-table department-name (department-table-row-counter)
    to Detail-Line department-name.
2. Move department-employee-counter (department-table-row-counter)
    to Detail-Line employee-counter.
3. Move Plant-Footing-3 to the output area Printline.
4. After advancing proper-spacing, write the output record Printline.
5. Set proper-spacing to 1.

600-Write-Plant-Heading.

1. Move input plant-number to plant-control.
2. Move "NO " to the plant-table-flag.
3. Perform 700-Look-Up-Plant-Table
    varying the plant-table-row-counter from initial value 1,
    and incrementing it by 1, until plant-table-flag is equal to "YES".
4. Move Plant-Heading-1 to the output area Printline.
5. After advancing 2 lines, write the output record Printline.
6. Move Plant-Heading-2 to the output area Printline.
7. After advancing 2 lines, write the output record Printline.
8. Set proper-spacing to 2.
9. Perform varying department-table-row-counter from initial value 1,
    and incrementing it by 1, until department-table-row-counter is greater than 8
    "move zero to department-employee-counter (department-table-row-counter)."

700-Look-Up-Plant-Table.

1. Test input plant-number
    against plant-table plant-number (plant-table-row-counter);
2. When they match,
    a. move plant-table plant-name (plant-table-row-counter)
        to Detail-Line plant-name;
    b. move "YES" to plant-table-flag.

Note: Paragraph 710-Initialize-Dept-Empl-Ctrs is included in the in-line Perform in paragraph 600-Write-Plant-Heading.

Program Flowchart

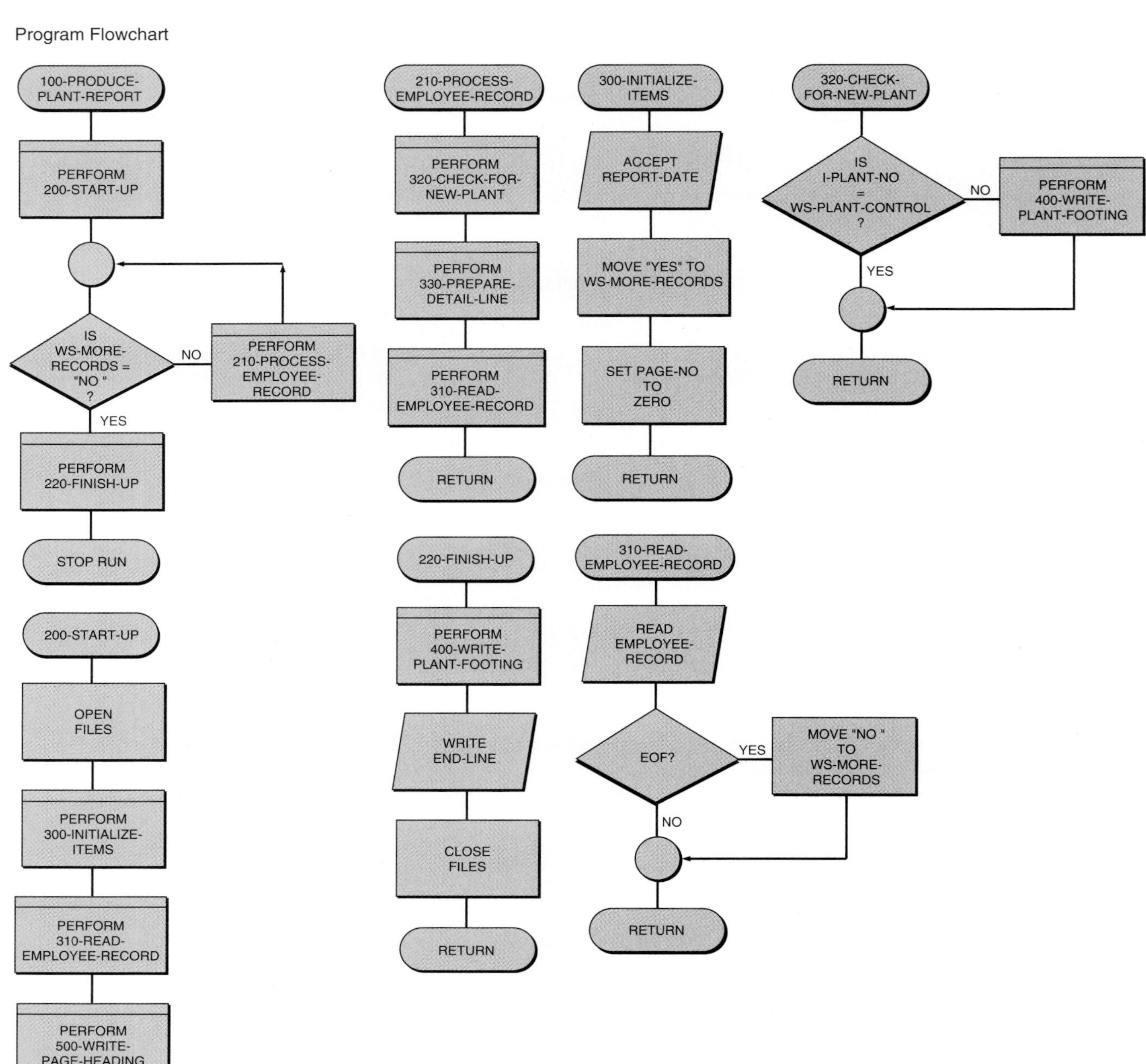

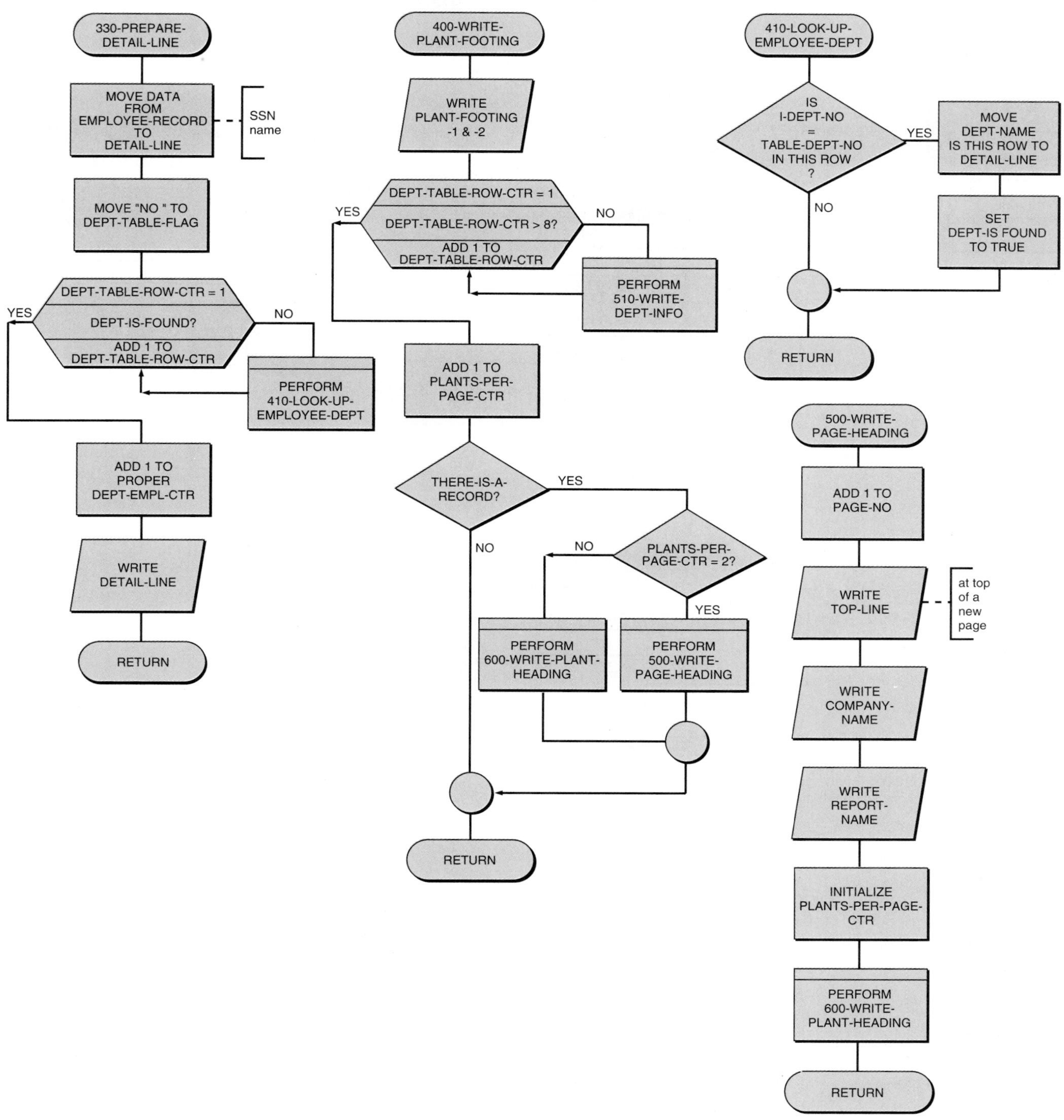

330-PREPARE-DETAIL-LINE
MOVE DATA FROM EMPLOYEE-RECORD TO DETAIL-LINE
SSN
name
MOVE "NO " TO DEPT-TABLE-FLAG
DEPT-TABLE-ROW-CTR = 1
DEPT-IS-FOUND?
ADD 1 TO DEPT-TABLE-ROW-CTR
YES
NO
PERFORM 410-LOOK-UP-EMPLOYEE-DEPT
ADD 1 TO PROPER DEPT-EMPL-CTR
WRITE DETAIL-LINE
RETURN
400-WRITE-PLANT-FOOTING
WRITE PLANT-FOOTING -1 & -2
DEPT-TABLE-ROW-CTR = 1
DEPT-TABLE-ROW-CTR > 8?
ADD 1 TO DEPT-TABLE-ROW-CTR
YES
NO
PERFORM 510-WRITE-DEPT-INFO
ADD 1 TO PLANTS-PER-PAGE-CTR
THERE-IS-A-RECORD?
YES
NO
PLANTS-PER-PAGE-CTR = 2?
NO
YES
PERFORM 600-WRITE-PLANT-HEADING
PERFORM 500-WRITE-PAGE-HEADING
RETURN
410-LOOK-UP-EMPLOYEE-DEPT
IS I-DEPT-NO = TABLE-DEPT-NO IN THIS ROW ?
YES
NO
MOVE DEPT-NAME IS THIS ROW TO DETAIL-LINE
SET DEPT-IS FOUND TO TRUE
RETURN
500-WRITE-PAGE-HEADING
ADD 1 TO PAGE-NO
WRITE TOP-LINE
at top of a new page
WRITE COMPANY-NAME
WRITE REPORT-NAME
INITIALIZE PLANTS-PER-PAGE-CTR
PERFORM 600-WRITE-PLANT-HEADING
RETURN

■ **Figure 9.62** continued

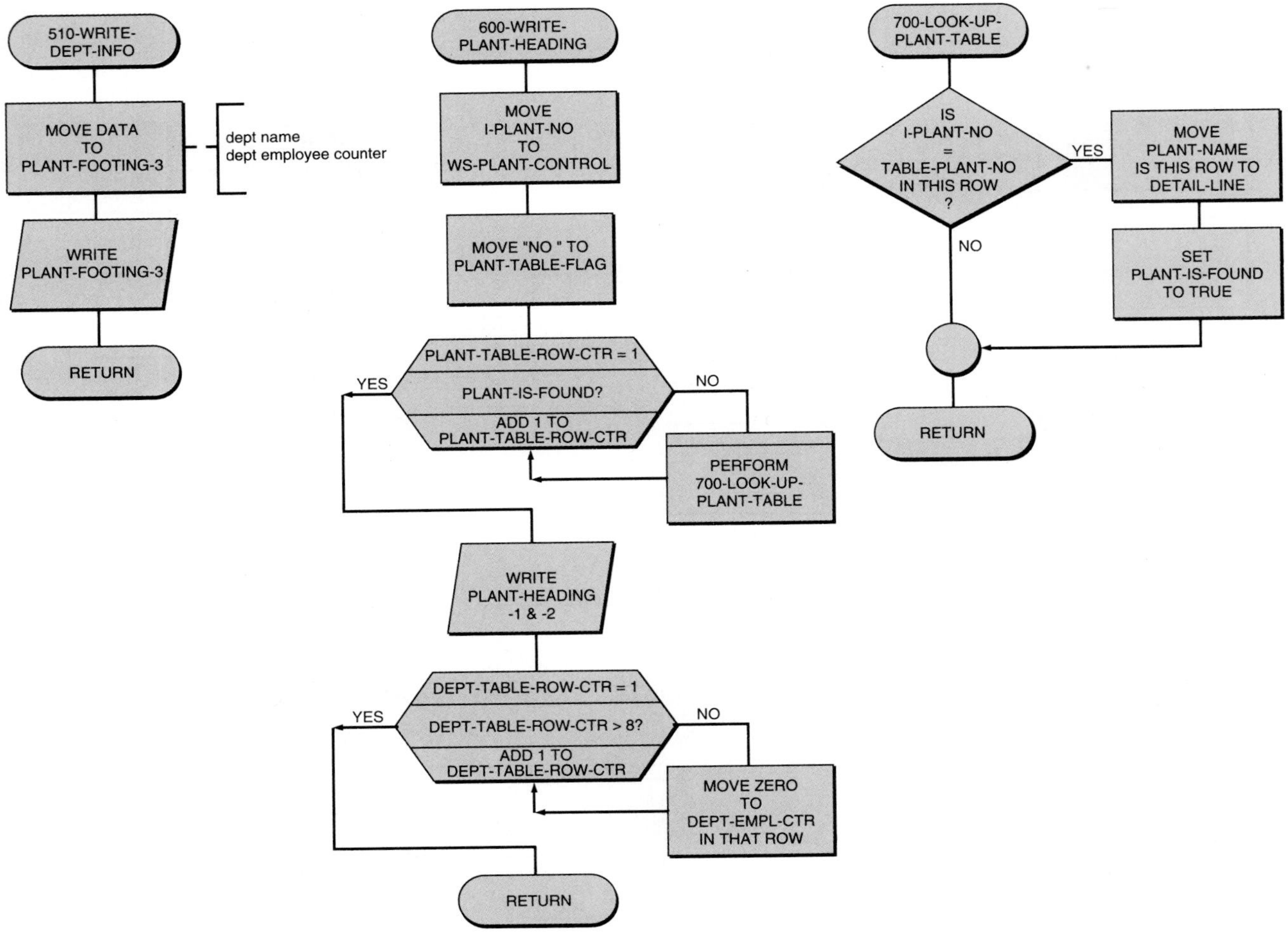

Note: Module 710-INITIALIZE-DEPT-EMPL-CTRS is included in the in-line PERFORM in module 600-WRITE-PLANT-HEADING.

Programming Exercise II

The management of Express Auto Parts Warehouse wants its data processing department to prepare a two-level activity listing for the week. For each item involved in a transaction during the week, a transaction record is prepared and contains the following data:

cc 1–5	Part number
cc 6–9	Quantity transacted
cc 10–11	Transaction code

The records in this transaction file are ordered by part number.

The program must contain a hard-coded table of transaction codes and types as shown below.

Code	Type
01	Cash & Carry
02	Charge & Carry
03	Charge & Deliver
04	Deliver COD
05	Layaway
06	Return for Cash
07	Return for Credit
08	Return/Exchange
09	Damaged

The program must load a catalog table before processing the transaction records. The catalog table must contain the part number, the part description, and the part unit price for each item in the catalog. This data is stored in a catalog file sorted on the part number. The layout of the record is as follows:

cc 1–5	Part number
cc 6–25	Part description
cc 26–30	Part unit price (format: xxx.xx)

At the first level, the printed report, entitled Activity Listing, must contain a detail line corresponding to each transaction. The detail line must identify the part number, the part description, the quantity involved in the transaction, and the type of transaction (not the transaction code).

At the second level, the report must print the total number of transactions for each type of transaction.

The input record layout, the printer spacing chart, the system flowchart, and the structure chart are provided in Figure 9.63.

Your task is to complete the design, and then implement the design for a successful run of the program.

Use Data File Set 7B [DD/CD:VIC9EX2.DT2] as the transaction file and Data File Set 7A [DD/CD:VIC9EX2.DT1] as the catalog file (see Appendix C).

Figure 9.63

Record Layout Forms

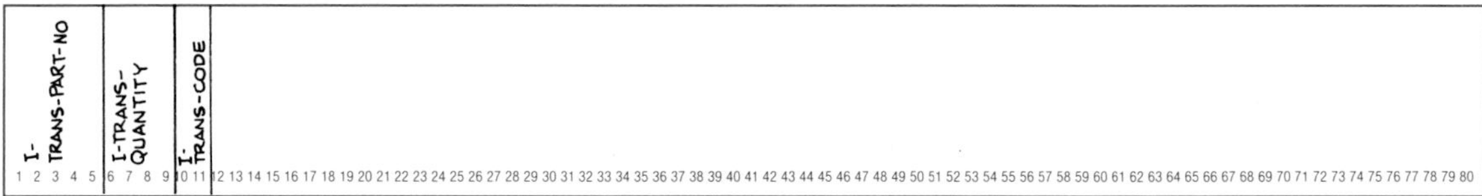

Record Name: TRANSACTION-RECORD

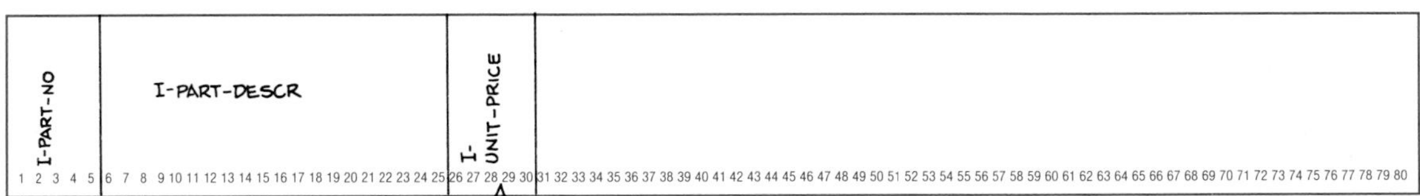

Record Name: CATALOG-RECORD

Printer Spacing Chart

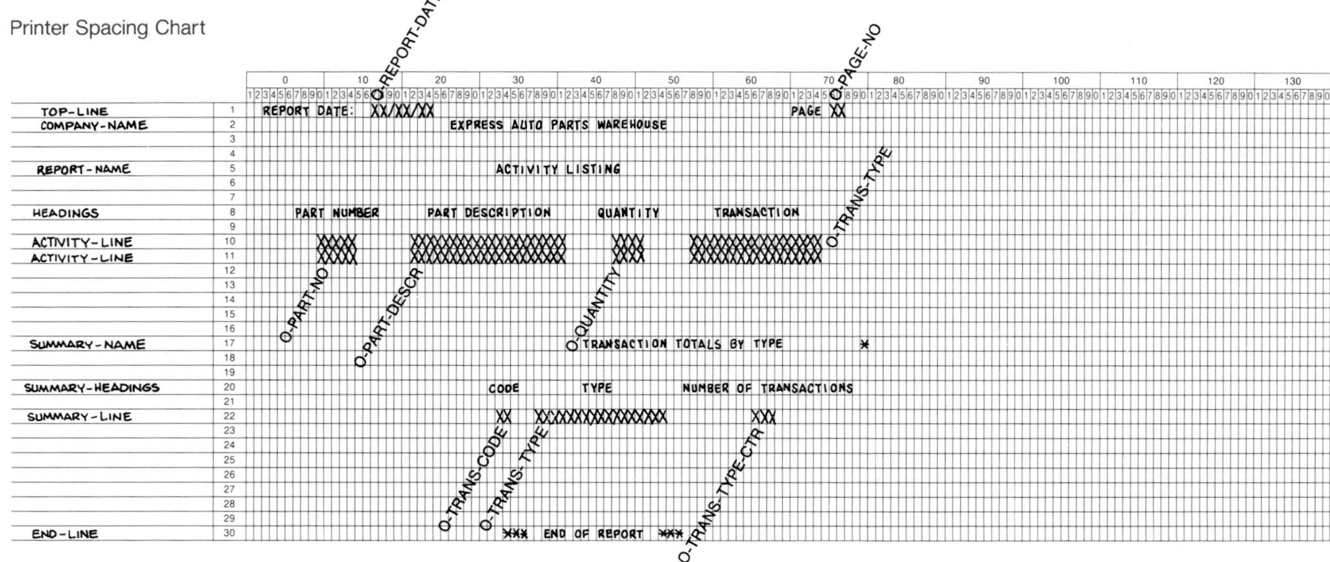

■ Figure 9.63

System Flowchart

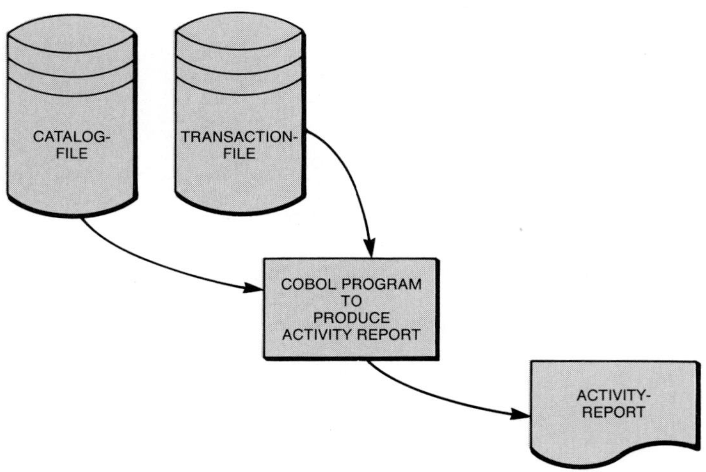

Structure Chart

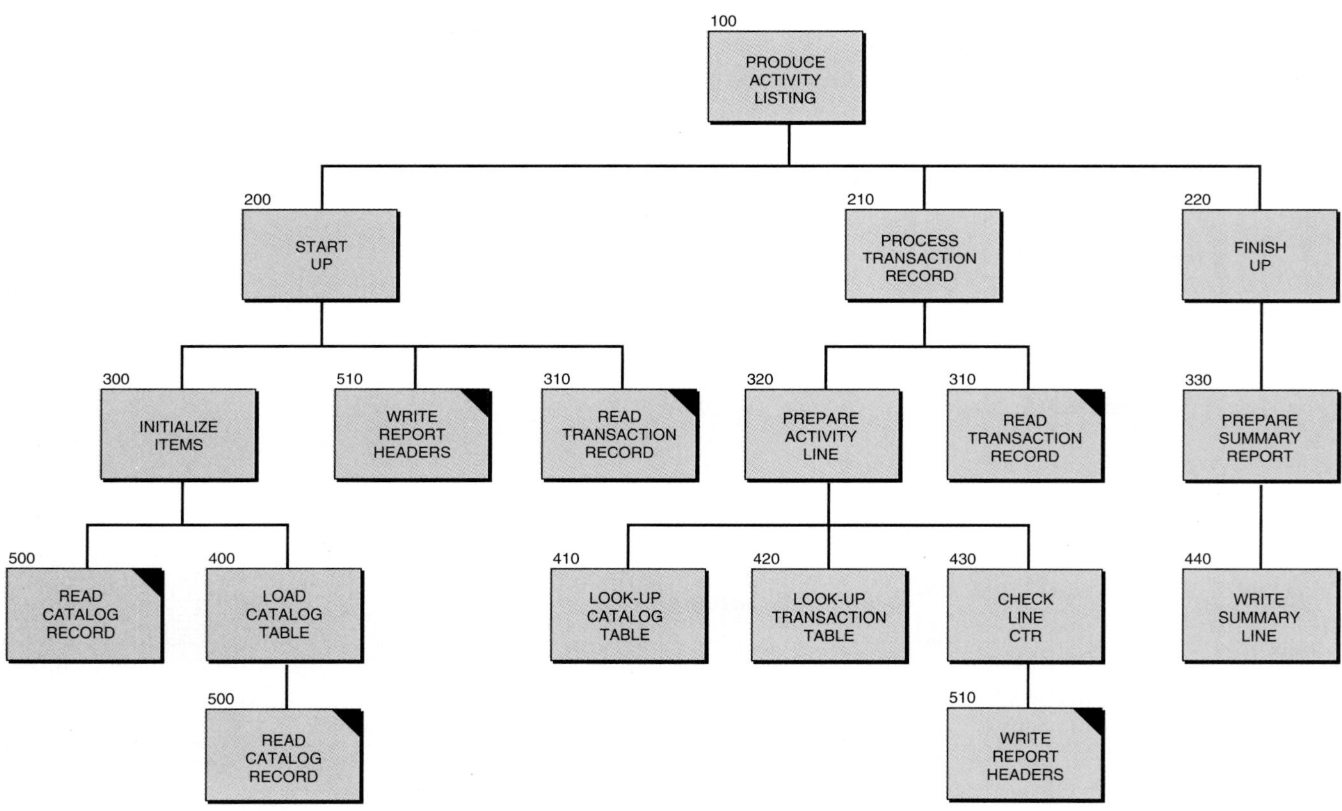

Programming Exercise III

The management of International Haberdashery wants its data processing department to prepare a two-level sales and quota report for the current period, formatted as shown in Figure 9.64.

At the first level, the report must list, for each salesperson, the Social Security number, name, current sales, sales quota, amount of current sales above or below quota, and percent of current sales above or below quota. There should be a maximum of 40 detail lines per page.

At the second level, the report must show, for each store, the number of salespersons in each of five percent ranges related to their sales quotas. The ranges are 20 percent or more above quota, 10 percent to 19.9 percent above quota, from exact quota to 9.9 percent above quota, between 9.9 percent and .1 percent below quota, and 10 percent or more below quota.

The program must contain a quota table that contains the Social Security number, name, store number, and sales quota for each salesperson. This table must be input-loaded using the records in a quota file. Each record in this file contains the following data:

cc 1–2	Store number
cc 3–22	Salesperson name
cc 23–31	Salesperson Social Security number
cc 32–39	Salesperson's sales quota (format: xxxxxx.xx)

The program must also define a hard-coded store table that contains the following data:

Store No.	Store Name
10	HELENA
20	GREAT FALLS
30	OMAHA
40	LINCOLN
50	TOPEKA

This table will be used to transform store numbers into store names as needed on the report.

The input sales file contains a current sales record for each salesperson. The Social Security number is used to identify the salesperson. The data is stored on each record as follows:

cc 1–9	Social Security number
cc 10–17	Current sales (format: xxxxxx.xx)

To prepare the summary report, the program must contain a two-level table of counters. There must be five counters for each store, one for each of the five percent ranges specified earlier.

Your task is to develop the program. It is recommended that you follow the steps of the problem-solving procedure.

Use Data File Set 8A [DD/CD:VIC9EX3.DT1] as the quota file and Data File Set 8B [DD/CD:VIC9EX3.DT2] as the sales file (see Appendix C).

Figure 9.64

Printer Spacing Chart

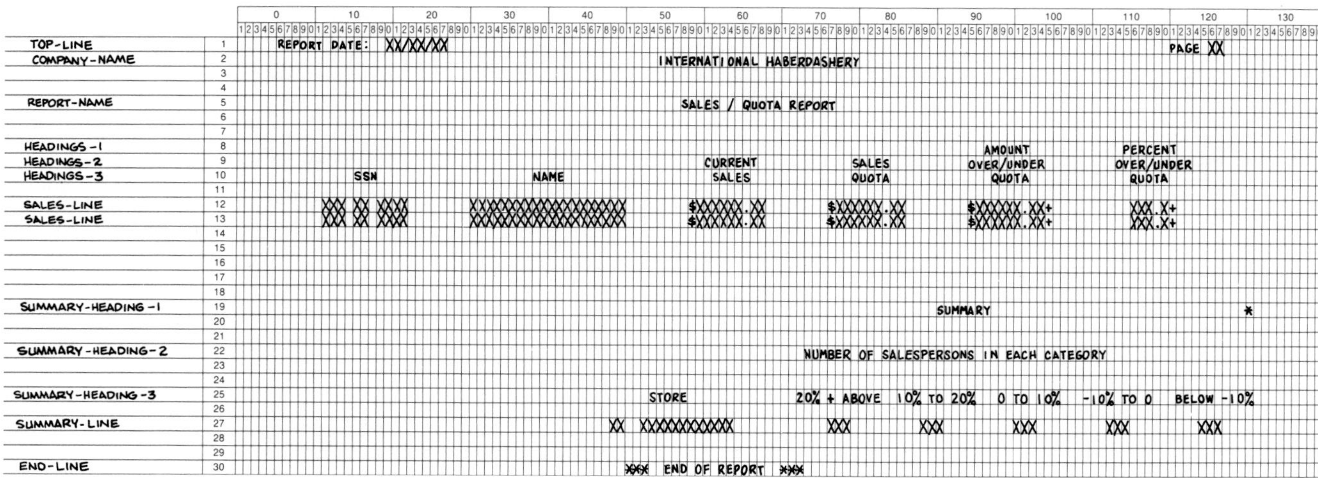

Programming Exercise IV

The management of the Modern Plastics Company wants its data processing department to prepare a weekly payroll tax report. For each employee, the report must list the Social Security number, name, number of allowances claimed, gross income for the week, the amount of federal tax to be withheld, and the resulting net income for the week. The format of the report is shown in Figure 9.65. There should be a maximum of 30 detail lines per page.

A time records file contains a time record for each employee with the following data:

cc 1–9	Social Security number
cc 10–11	Hours worked at regular pay
cc 12–13	Hours worked at overtime pay (time and a half)

To prepare the required report, the program must first load two tables in working storage: an employee information table and a federal withholding tax table.

An employee data file is to be used to load the information table. The records in the file contain the following data:

cc 1–9	Social Security number
cc 10–29	Employee name
cc 30–33	Pay rate (format: xx.xx)
cc 34	Number of allowances claimed

The data shown in the table on the next page is to be loaded into the tax table. You must enter this data into a tax rate file.

Note: To keep the assignment manageable, assume this excerpt from the "Wage Bracket Percentage Method Table" applies to all company employees.)

Your assignment, in addition to preparing the above file, is to develop the program. It is recommended that you follow the steps of the problem-solving procedure.

Use Data File Set 9B [DD/CD:VIC9EX4.DT2] as the employee data file and Data File Set 9C [DD/CD:VIC9EX4.DT3] as the time records file (see Appendix C).

Figure 9.65

Printer Spacing Chart

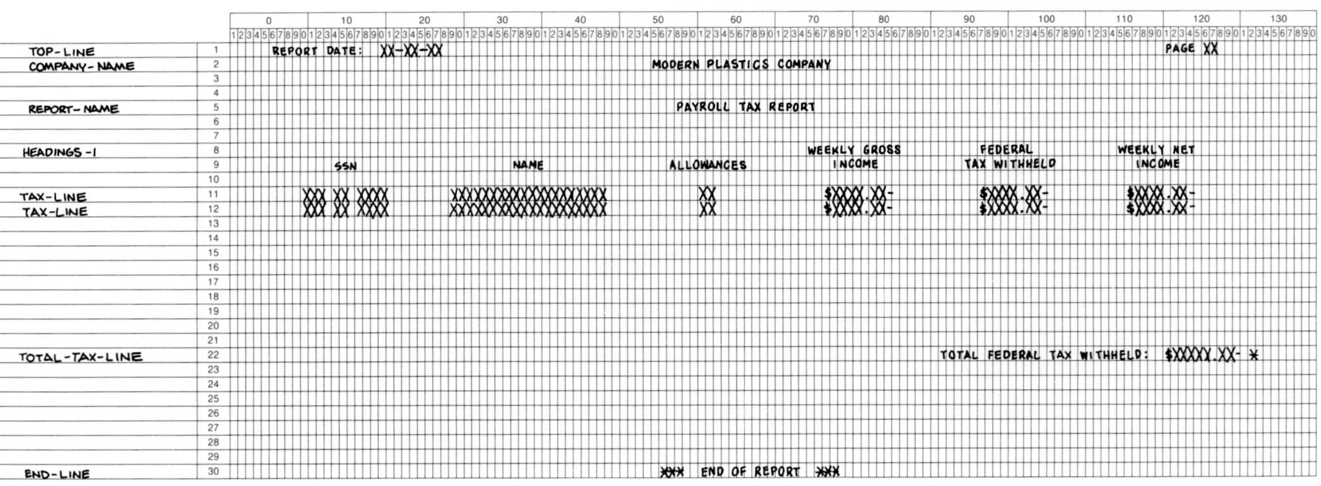

(For Wages Paid After December 1986)

Wage Bracket Percentage Method Table for Computing Income Tax Withholding from Wages Exceeding Allowance Amount

Weekly Payroll Period

Married Persons

If the number of allowances is—	*And gross wages are—*		*Subtract from excess wages*	*Multiply remainder by—*
	Over	*But not over*		
	$0	$93.00	$36.00	11.0%
	93.00	574.00	51.20	15.0%
0	547.00	901.00	293.93	28.0%
	901.00	1,767.00	415.34	35.0%
	1,767.00	....	538.22	38.5%
	$0	$129.54	$36.00	11.0%
	129.54	610.54	51.20	15.0%
1	610.54	937.54	293.93	28.0%
	937.54	1,803.54	415.34	35.0%
	1,803.54	....	538.22	38.5%
	$0	$166.08	$36.00	11.0%
	166.08	647.08	51.20	15.0%
2	647.08	974.08	293.93	28.0%
	974.08	1,840.08	415.34	35.0%
	1,840.08	....	538.22	38.5%
	$0	$202.62	$36.00	11.0%
	202.62	683.62	51.20	15.0%
3	683.62	1,010.62	293.93	28.0%
	1,010.62	1,876.62	415.34	35.0%
	1,876.62	....	538.22	38.5%
	$0	$239.16	$36.00	11.0%
	239.16	720.16	51.20	15.0%
4	720.16	1,047.16	293.93	28.0%
	1,047.16	1,913.16	415.34	35.0%
	1,913.16	....	538.22	38.5%

Instructions

A. For each employee, use the appropriate payroll period table and marital status section and select the subsection showing the number of allowances claimed.

B. Read across the selected subsection and locate the wage bracket range applicable to the employee's gross wage.

C. From the employee's "excess" wages (gross wages less amount for allowances claimed), subtract the amount shown on the next column of the appropriate row. [Amount for each allowance is $38.46. Excess wages = gross wages – (38.46 × number of allowances claimed).]

D. Multiply the remaining amount of wages by the withholding percentage rate shown in the last column. The result of this computation is the amount of tax to be withheld.

10 The SORT and MERGE Statements

Records in a file are usually arranged sequentially on the basis of a particular field of the records. An employee file may be set up alphabetically by employee last name or by employee number. An inventory file may be set up in ascending order by catalog number. An accounts receivable file may be arranged in customer number sequence, and so on. However, many files are needed in a variety of applications, and the record sequence that makes file processing efficient in one application may not be the sequence needed in another application.

The COBOL language makes available to the programmer very powerful sort-merge routines that allow files to be sorted internally in any desired sequence on the basis of one or more keys and that allow two or more files sorted on the same keys to be merged into a single file.

In addition to the essential function of sorting records in a file, the SORT statement provides options to process records before being sorted and after being sorted. These options are often referred to as presort processing (or simply preprocessing) and postsort processing (or simply postprocessing). In addition to the essential function of merging records from two or more files into a single file, the MERGE statement provides an option that allows the processing of the merged records after they are merged. In this chapter, we examine all of these options. ■

Objectives You Should Achieve

After studying this chapter, you should:

1. Given an example of a SORT statement, be able to correctly identify
   - **a.** the sorting keys on which the file will be sorted
   - **b.** the input file component option specified within the statement
   - **c.** the output file component option specified within the statement
   - **d.** the files that will be processed automatically by the computer without programmer control
2. Given an adequate statement of a programming problem in which a file must be sorted, be able to correctly
   - **a.** specify the sort keys
   - **b.** specify the input component option required by the program
   - **c.** specify the output component option required by the program
   - **d.** code the SORT statement
3. Given a SORT statement and sample records that will be released to the file, be able to rearrange the records in the same sequence produced by the SORT statement.
4. Given the program pseudocode or flowchart of the primary section that indicates a need for the sort routine, be able to correctly code the corresponding PROCEDURE DIVISION entries.
5. Given a complete program pseudocode or flowchart containing a sort structure with either one or both procedure options and needed data item names, be able to correctly code the corresponding PROCEDURE DIVISION.
6. Given the program pseudocode or flowchart containing a merge structure, with or without the OUTPUT PROCEDURE option and the needed data item names, be able to correctly code the corresponding PROCEDURE DIVISION entries.
7. Given a programming assignment whose purpose is to produce a report containing sorted records, for which the completed design tools are provided, be able to successfully complete the task of implementing the design.
8. Given a programming assignment whose purpose is to produce a report containing sorted records, for which the design tools through the structure chart are provided, be able to successfully complete the design of the program and code, compile, debug, and run the program.
9. Given a programming assignment whose purpose is to produce a report containing sorted records, for which the format of the report is specified, be able to successfully complete the assignment; that is, design the program and implement the design.

Problem 1—Sorting Only

The Chicago store has received a request from the national office of the Sportsman Company to submit a file of its salespersons' sales for the current period. The records in this file must be in alphabetic sequence by salesperson name. If two or more persons have the same name, they should be placed in ascending order by their Social Security numbers.

In addition to the name and Social Security number, each record must contain three other fields: store number, department number, and total sales of that salesperson for the current period.

Brief Analysis of the Problem

Since the record layout requested by the national office is the one in use in Chicago, the task of the data processing department is simply to sort the records in their current sales file. The layout of these records is shown in Figure 10.1. The records will be sorted on the basis of two key fields, the name field and the Social Security number field. In the SORT statement, the name field is the **primary** or **major** key, and the Social Security number field is the **minor** key.

The input to the program is the original sales file, and the output is simply a second file that contains the records sorted in the appropriate sequence. No printed report is required. The system flowchart is shown in Figure 10.2. Note that it shows a third file that has been named SORT-FILE. This file is a requirement of the SORT statement, and it will be explained shortly.

Figure 10.1 Layout of the input record SALESPERSON-RECORD

Record Layout Form

I-STORE-NO	I-DEPT-NO	I-SSN	I-SALESPERSON	I-CURRENT-SALES	
1 2	3 4	5 6 7 8 9 10 11 12 13	14 15 16 17 18 19 20 21 22 23 24 25 26 27 28 29 30 31 32 33	34 35 36 37 ^ 38 39	40 41 42 43 44 45 46 47 48 49 50 51 52 53 54 55 56 57 58 59 60 61 62 63 64 65 66 67 68 69 70 71 72 73 74 75 76 77 78 79 80

Record Name: SALESPERSON-RECORD

Figure 10.2 System flowchart for problem 1

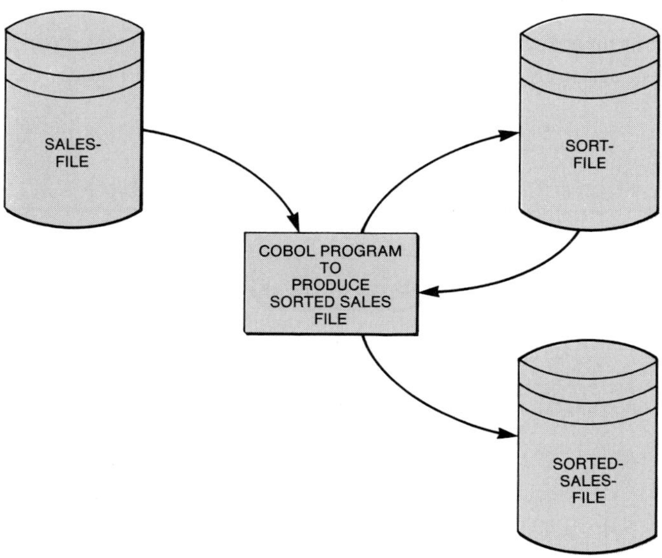

The Structure Chart for Problem 1

The task specified in the system flowchart as the function of the COBOL program is normally separated into a number of distinct subtasks, and the hierarchy of these tasks is shown in the structure chart. In the current problem, the major task is to sort the input file. All the sorting occurs in what is referred to as work files that are under the direct control of the sorting routine. The programmer does not code statements in the program to specify the functions of the work files; that is, the sorting itself takes place "behind the scenes." It is sufficient for the programmer to make sure that the records to be sorted are passed to the sort file. The COBOL sort function itself controls the sorting procedures. Once the sorting has taken place, the programmer must make sure that the sorted records are passed on to the output file.

It appears then that three steps are required to complete this task:

1. Read the records of the input file into the sort file.
2. Sort the records as specified.
3. Write the sorted records to the output file.

The structure chart is shown in Figure 10.3. Note that the second-level modules have not been assigned numbers. The reason will become clear shortly.

The Program Pseudocode for Problem 1

From the three steps identified above, you can see that the pseudocode is very brief:

100-Produce-Sorted-Sales-File.

1. Read all input Salesperson-Records into the Sort-File.
2. Sort the records of the Sort-File using the following keys:
   a. major key: names in ascending order
   b. minor key: Social-Security-numbers in ascending order
3. Write all the sorted records to the output file Sorted-Sales-File.
4. Stop the run.

The Program Flowchart for Problem 1

The flowchart is the visual representation of the above pseudocode. It is shown in Figure 10.4. Note that the symbol for the SORT statement is a perform box. This is because the SORT statement executes a predefined routine, and, once it has been accomplished, control automatically returns from the routine. The annotation to the right of the box specifies the options of the SORT statement that are being used, whereas the annotation to the left of the box specifies the keys used during the sorting process.

The SORT Statement in Problem 1

Now that we have reached the coding phase, it is time to examine the SORT statement format and consider the coding requirements it imposes in the different divisions of a program. The format is shown in Figure 10.5.

Figure 10.3 The structure chart for problem 1

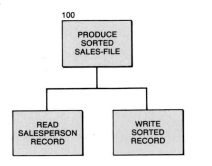

100
PRODUCE SORTED SALES-FILE

READ SALESPERSON RECORD

WRITE SORTED RECORD

Figure 10.4 The program flowchart for problem 1

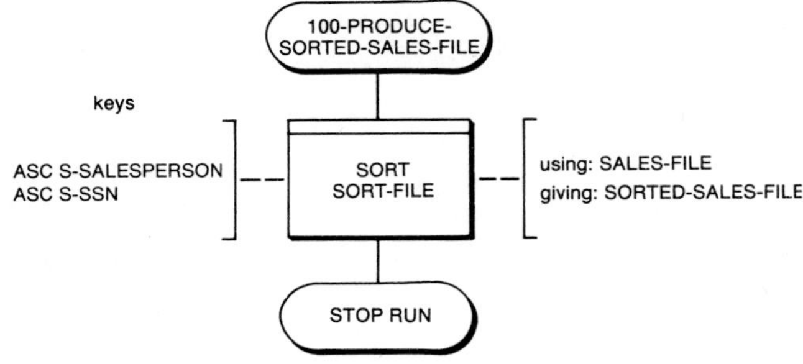

■ **Figure 10.5** The SORT statement format for problem 1

```
SORT file-name-1

    { ON {ASCENDING } KEY {data-name-1} . . . } . . .
         {DESCENDING}

    [WITH DUPLICATES IN ORDER]
    [COLLATING SEQUENCE IS alphabet-name-1]

    {USING {file-name-2} . . .                                                     }
    {INPUT PROCEDURE IS procedure-name-1 [ {THROUGH} procedure-name-2 ]            }
                                           {THRU   }

    {GIVING {file-name-3} . . .                                                    }
    {OUTPUT PROCEDURE IS procedure-name-3 [ {THROUGH} procedure-name-4 ]           }
                                            {THRU   }
```

■ **Figure 10.6** Schematic showing operation of the SORT statement for problem 1

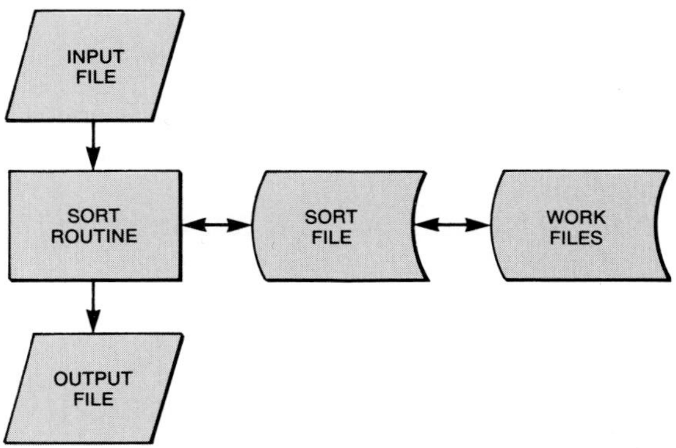

It is obvious from the numerous options in the SORT statement format that there are many possible variations in coding a SORT statement. Fortunately, the current program needs only the simplest application of all. But, before actually coding it, a few comments must be made regarding features of the COBOL sort function.

1. First, it is necessary to understand the overall operation of the sort function: It must obtain the records to be sorted from an input file; it must then sort them according to the specified key or keys; and it must then return them to an output file in the appropriate sequence, as shown in the schematic of Figure 10.6. (The schematic is similar to the system flowchart in Figure 10.2, except that the work files were not shown.)

Note that a sorting procedure requires at least three files: the sort file, an input file, and an output file. The work files shown in Figure 10.6 are internal to the sorting process; they are not controlled by the programmer, and they are not even referenced by the programmer.

In the SORT statement format,

a. File-name-1 is the name of the sort file.

b. File-name-2 is the name of the input file. Note that the format allows more than one input file.

c. File-name-3 is the name of the output file. Note that the format allows more than one output file.

The records of the input file must be accessed and then copied into the sort file. The sort routine rearranges the records of the sort file according to the specified sequence. Once the sorting is complete, the records of the sort file must then be written to the output file.

In the current program, the file that originally contains the records to be sorted is SALES-FILE; that is, SALES-FILE is the input file. The file that must receive all the sorted records is SORTED-SALES-FILE; that is, SORTED-SALES-FILE is the output file. The name of the sort file must be supplied by the programmer, and as seen in the system flowchart of Figure 10.2, it is simply named SORT-FILE.

2. Second, note that the SORT statement requires the following four components:

   a. SORT file-name-1

   This component specifies the name of the file that must receive all the records of the input file that are to be sorted. This file is the sort file.

   b. ON {ASCENDING | DESCENDING} KEY {data-name-1} . . . } . . .

   This component specifies the names of the fields of the sort records that will be used to arrange the records in the required sequence. Each of these fields is a sort key. The first one is the primary key. The sequence of the records may be based on a combination of sort keys, and, for each key, the ASCENDING or DESCENDING entry determines the specific order.

   In the current program, the primary key is the field that contains the salesperson's name, and the required order is ASCENDING, since the names must be in alphabetic order. Thus, if the field name is S-SALESPERSON, the first key phrase is ON ASCENDING KEY S-SALESPERSON.

   The statement of the problem specifies that in the case of identical names, the records must be arranged in ascending order by Social Security number. Thus, if the field name is S-SSN, then the second key phrase is ON ASCENDING KEY S-SSN.

   c. {USING file-name-2 . . . | INPUT PROCEDURE IS procedure-name-1 [{THROUGH | THRU} procedure-name-2]}

   This component deals with the input file. It either simply names it, if the USING option is used, or it names the procedure that processes the input records before they are released to the sort file, if the INPUT PROCEDURE option is used.

   In the current program, the option is USING SALES-FILE, since SALES-FILE is the input file, and there is no need to process these records individually before sorting them.

   d. {GIVING file-name-3 . . . | OUTPUT PROCEDURE IS procedure-name-3 [{THROUGH | THRU} procedure-name-4]}

   This component deals with the output file. It either simply names it, if the GIVING option is used, or it names the procedure that processes the sorted records before they are written to the output file, if the OUTPUT PROCEDURE option is used.

   In the current program, the option is GIVING SORTED-SALES-FILE, since SORTED-SALES-FILE is the output file, and there is no need to process these records individually after they have been sorted.

3. The sort file receives the records from the input file. During the sorting routine, the sort file will be used in conjunction with other internal files, called work files, to sort all the records according to the specified keys. Ultimately, the sort file will contain all the sorted records. The work files are internal files completely controlled by the sort routine. The programmer produces no code whatsoever in relation to these work files.

   Like any other file, the sort file must be specified in a SELECT statement of the FILE-CONTROL paragraph of the INPUT-OUTPUT SECTION of the ENVIRONMENT DIVISION. The ASSIGN clause must identify a mass storage device that provides sort capabilities, namely, magnetic disk or tape, as in SELECT SORT-FILE ASSIGN TO DA-3330-S-SORTF (disk: IBM system), or SELECT SORT-FILE ASSIGN TO UT-2400-S-SORTF (tape: IBM system), or SELECT SORT-FILE ASSIGN TO DISK10 (disk: VAX system). The most common storage medium for a sort file is a magnetic disk.

   The name of the sort file is user-defined and consequently does not have to be SORT-FILE. However, since it serves no other purpose than to name the sort file, the name SORT-FILE provides all the self-documentation that is needed, and, therefore, it will be used consistently in all the examples in this text.

   In the FILE SECTION of the DATA DIVISION, the sort file, like any other file, must be described in a file description entry. However, the entry SD is used instead of FD, as in

```
SD  SORT-FILE
    RECORD CONTAINS 80 CHARACTERS.
```

The SD paragraph then continues with the sort file record description. It is most important to note here that the sort keys are data fields of the sort file records, not of the input records.

In the current program, the following record description is appropriate:

```
01   SORT-RECORD.
     05 S-STORE-NO          PIC XX.
     05 S-DEPT-NO           PIC XX.
     05 S-SSN               PIC X(9).
     05 S-SALESPERSON       PIC X(20).
     05 S-CURRENT-SALES     PIC 9(4)V99.
```

Note that only the fields S-SALESPERSON and S-SSN are needed by the SORT statement to execute the required sorting. It is not necessary to name the other fields of the sort record (although it may be advisable to name them for documentation purposes), since they are not referenced in any statement. Hence, the above record description could be simplified to the following:

```
01   SORT-RECORD.
     05                     PIC X(4).
     05 S-SSN               PIC X(9).
     05 S-SALESPERSON       PIC X(20).
     05                     PIC X(6).
```

4. In the PROCEDURE DIVISION, the programmer is usually responsible for opening and closing files. The sort file is an exception. It is **never** opened or closed by the programmer. The sort routine initiated by the SORT statement will automatically assume the sort file handling requirements.

In the current program, the pseudocode and/or flowchart in Figure 10.4 make it clear that the PROCEDURE DIVISION contains only one paragraph, as follows:

```
100-PRODUCE-SORTED-SALES-FILE.
     SORT SORT-FILE
          ON ASCENDING KEY S-SALESPERSON
          ON ASCENDING KEY S-SSN
          USING SALES-FILE
          GIVING SORTED-SALES-FILE.
     STOP RUN.
```

In this case, not only does the programmer exercise no control over opening and closing the sort file, but he or she has no control over opening and closing the input and output files either. This occurs whenever the USING and GIVING options of the SORT statement are used.

The SORT statement is a very powerful statement. When the current program is executed, the following events occur:

a. Control is passed by the system to the SORT statement. The sort routine opens the input file SALES-FILE and the sort file SORT-FILE; it reads the first input record into input memory, moves it to the sort record area, and releases it to the sort file; then it reads the next input record, moves it to the sort record area, and releases it to the sort file. The pattern continues until the AT END condition for the input file is satisfied.

b. When all input records have been copied into the sort file, the sort routine closes the input file.

c. The sort routine sorts the records on the sort key S-SALESPERSON, that is, it rearranges them in alphabetic sequence, since this field is the primary key. If two or more salespersons have the same name, the sort routine will rearrange those records in ascending order of the Social Security numbers, since the field S-SSN is the secondary or minor key.

d. The sort routine then opens the output file SORTED-SALES-FILE.

e. The sort records are then returned one at a time to the output file. That is, the first sort record is read (that is, returned) from the sort file into the sort record area, it is moved to the output record area, and the output record is then written to the output file. The second sort record is returned from the sort file, it is moved to the output record area, and the output record is written to the output file. This pattern continues until the AT END condition occurs for the sort file.

f. After all the records have been written to the output file SORTED-SALES-FILE, the sort routine then closes the output file and the sort file.

g. Control passes from the SORT statement to the next statement, STOP RUN, and program execution is terminated.

Note again that with the USING option and with the GIVING option, there is no coding by the programmer to open or close the files. This is the reason for not numbering the READ and WRITE modules in the structure chart of Figure 10.3. Each module in a structure chart generally corresponds to a paragraph within the PROCEDURE DIVISION. But, in this case, since the read and write functions are completely under the control of the SORT statement, those two modules need not be shown at all.

Coding the Program for Problem 1

We are now ready to code the program. The program entries related to the comments made above are highlighted for your convenience. The complete program is shown in Figure 10.7. It is very short indeed. Note that the elementary data fields of the input record SALESPERSON-RECORD and the elementary data fields of the output record SORTED-SALESPERSON-RECORD have not been coded. There is no need to

Figure 10.7 The COBOL program for problem 1

```
 IDENTIFICATION DIVISION.

 PROGRAM-ID.      SORT-PROG-1.

*****************************************************************
*                                                               *
*   AUTHOR.          PAQUETTE.                                  *
*   DATE WRITTEN.    OCTOBER 1993.                              *
*                                                               *
*   THIS PROGRAM IS A SIMPLE APPLICATION OF THE SORT STATEMENT. *
*   THE SORT STATEMENT SPECIFIES TWO ASCENDING KEYS, AND IT     *
*   CONTAINS THE USING AND GIVING PHRASES.                      *
*                                                               *
*   THE FUNCTION OF THE PROGRAM IS TO SORT THE RECORDS OF AN    *
*   INPUT FILE IN ALPHABETIC ORDER BY SALESPERSON NAME AND,     *
*   IN THE CASE OF IDENTICAL NAMES, IN ASCENDING ORDER OF THE   *
*   SOCIAL SECURITY NUMBERS.                                    *
*                                                               *
*****************************************************************

 ENVIRONMENT DIVISION.

 CONFIGURATION SECTION.

 SOURCE-COMPUTER.   VAX-VMS-8650.
 OBJECT-COMPUTER.   VAX-VMS-8650.

 INPUT-OUTPUT SECTION.

 FILE-CONTROL.
    SELECT SALES-FILE          ASSIGN TO COB$INPUT.
    SELECT SORT-FILE           ASSIGN TO DISK10.
    SELECT SORTED-SALES-FILE   ASSIGN TO COB$OUTPUT.

 DATA DIVISION.

 FILE SECTION.

 FD   SALES-FILE
      RECORD CONTAINS 39 CHARACTERS.

 01   SALESPERSON-RECORD         PIC X(39).

 SD   SORT-FILE
      RECORD CONTAINS 39 CHARACTERS.

 01   SORT-RECORD.
      05                         PIC X(4).
      05 S-SSN                   PIC X(9).
      05 S-SALESPERSON           PIC X(20).
      05                         PIC X(6).

 FD   SORTED-SALES-FILE
      RECORD CONTAINS 39 CHARACTERS.

 01   SORTED-SALESPERSON-RECORD PIC X(39).

 PROCEDURE DIVISION.

 100-PRODUCE-SORTED-SALES-FILE.
      SORT SORT-FILE
          ON ASCENDING KEY S-SALESPERSON
          ON ASCENDING KEY S-SSN
          USING SALES-FILE
          GIVING SORTED-SALES-FILE.
      STOP RUN.
```

Figure 10.8a SALES-FILE for problem 1

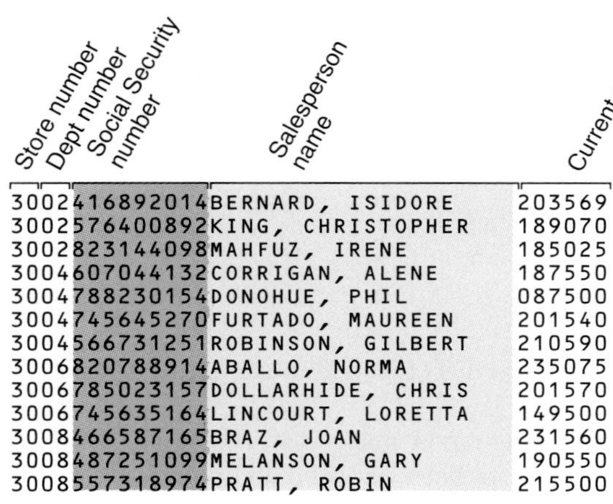


```
3002416892014BERNARD, ISIDORE      203569
3002576400892KING, CHRISTOPHER     189070
3002823144098MAHFUZ, IRENE         185025
3004607044132CORRIGAN, ALENE       187550
3004788230154DONOHUE, PHIL         087500
3004745645270FURTADO, MAUREEN      201540
3004566731251ROBINSON, GILBERT     210590
3006820788914ABALLO, NORMA         235075
3006785023157DOLLARHIDE, CHRIS     201570
3006745635164LINCOURT, LORETTA     149500
3008466587165BRAZ, JOAN            231560
3008487251099MELANSON, GARY        190550
3008557318974PRATT, ROBIN          215500
```

Figure 10.8b SORTED-SALES-FILE for problem 1

```
3006820788914ABALLO, NORMA         235075
3002416892014BERNARD, ISIDORE      203569
3008466587165BRAZ, JOAN            231560
3004607044132CORRIGAN, ALENE       187550
3006785023157DOLLARHIDE, CHRIS     201570
3004788230154DONOHUE, PHIL         087500
3004745645270FURTADO, MAUREEN      201540
3002576400892KING, CHRISTOPHER     189070
3006745635164LINCOURT, LORETTA     149500
3002823144098MAHFUZ, IRENE         185025
3008487251099MELANSON, GARY        190550
3008557318974PRATT, ROBIN          215500
3004566731251ROBINSON, GILBERT     210590
```

Figure 10.9 Printer spacing chart for problem 2

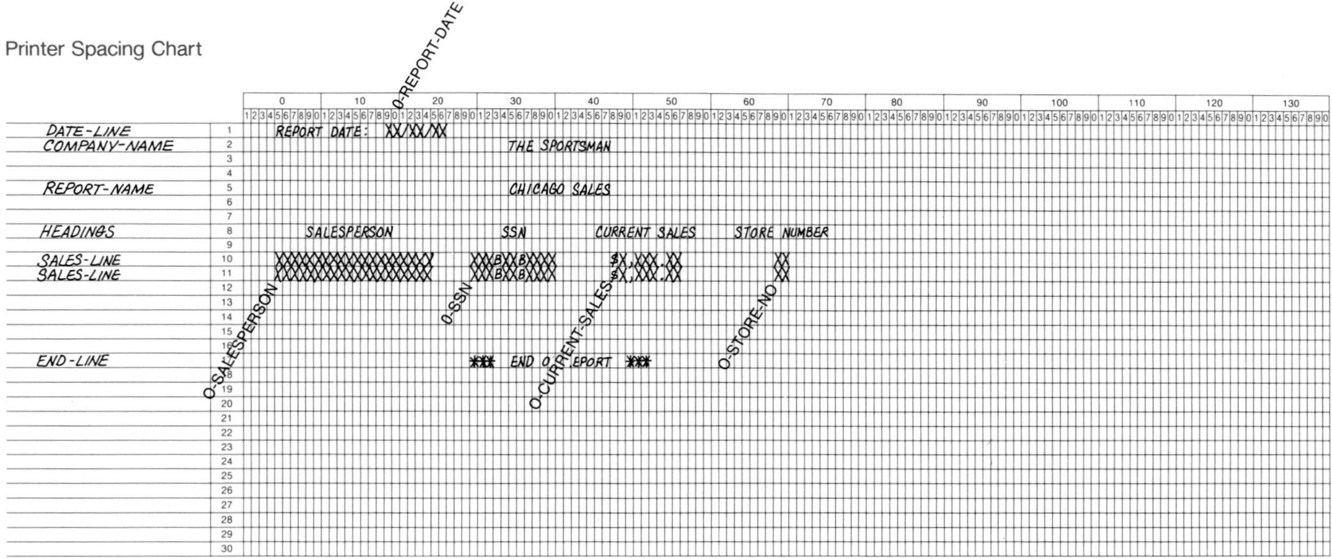

code them, since there are no statements in the PROCEDURE DIVISION that reference them. (As noted earlier, you may still want to code them to provide additional documentation). Also note that the WORKING-STORAGE SECTION header has not been coded either. It is not needed.

Figure 10.8a [DD/CD:VICIOSPI.DAT] shows the records of the input file SALES-FILE. These are the records that the program must sort in alphabetic order. The salesperson name fields have been highlighted to more clearly show the major sort key, and the Social Security number fields have been more deeply highlighted to draw your attention to the minor sort key. Figure 10.8b shows the records in the sequence produced by the sorting routine. These records belong to the output file SORTED-SALES-FILE.

Problem 2—Sorting and Postsort Processing

The Chicago store has received a request from the national office of the Sportsman Company for a sales report listing the sales of all its salespersons for the current period. The listing must be in alphabetic order by salesperson name, with the exception that if two or more salespersons have the same name, they should be listed in ascending order of their Social Security numbers. The format of the report is specified in the printer spacing chart of Figure 10.9. (The report does not require page breaks.)

The essential difference between these two problems is that in problem 1, a sorted file had to be sent to the national office, whereas in problem 2, a sorted report must be sent.

Brief Analysis of the Problem

The records in the sales file are currently ordered alphabetically by salesperson name within each department. (The record layout is the one shown in Figure 10.1.) It is clear that the file has to be sorted in order to satisfy the needs of the national office. Furthermore, since a report must be prepared, the data fields that contain the name, the Social Security number, the current sales, and the store number of the salesperson have to be referenced during the preparation of the output record SALES-LINE.

The data processing department decides to proceed as follows:

1. Begin by sorting the sales file as specified.
2. Prepare the report.
   a. Write the documentation at the top of the report.
   b. Retrieve the first record from the sort file.
   c. Move the appropriate values to the data fields of the record SALES-LINE and write the line on the report.
   d. Retrieve the next record from the sort file and prepare its report line.
   e. Repeat the pattern until all the records of the sort file have been retrieved and processed.

The system flowchart to accomplish the task is shown in Figure 10.10. The above list of processing activities indicates that the input file will be sent directly to the sort file, but once the sorting has occurred, the records must be processed individually. The implications for the SORT statement are twofold:

1. Of the two options available in the input file component of the SORT statement, the one that is needed is the USING option. That is, opening the input file SALES-FILE, reading its records, copying them into the sort file, and closing the input file are functions that are to be completely controlled by the SORT statement.
2. Of the two options available in the output file component of the SORT statement, the one that is needed is the OUTPUT PROCEDURE option. In this procedure, the programmer must code all the statements needed to retrieve a record from the sort file and to process it in the preparation of a detail line on the report. This means that the programmer is also responsible for opening and closing the output file SORTED-SALES-REPORT.

   Furthermore, the *procedure-name* referenced in the OUTPUT PROCEDURE clause must be the name of a *section* in the PROCEDURE DIVISION. Until now, all procedures in the PROCEDURE DIVISION have been paragraphs. A section is a collection of contiguous paragraphs, and a section header must contain the reserved word SECTION. COBOL syntax requires that if at least one paragraph is contained in a section within the PROCEDURE DIVISION, then all paragraphs must be contained within sections. Thus, in the current program, there is a need for two sections: the one that contains the "OUTPUT PROCEDURE" specified in the SORT statement, and the one that contains the paragraph in which the SORT statement is coded.

Figure 10.10 The system flowchart for problem 2

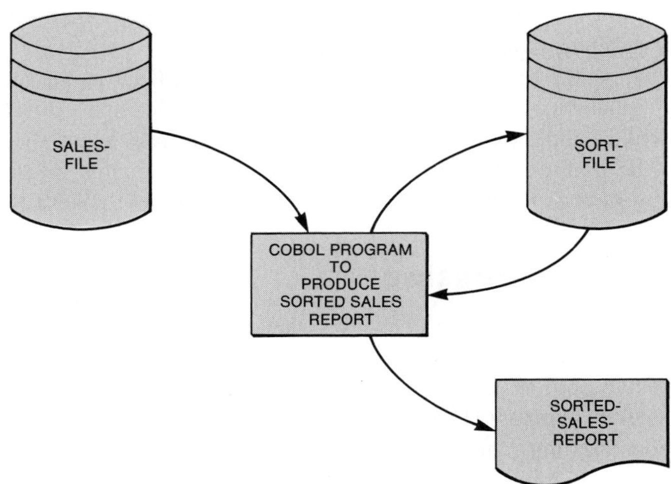

■ **Figure 10.11** The structure chart for problem 2

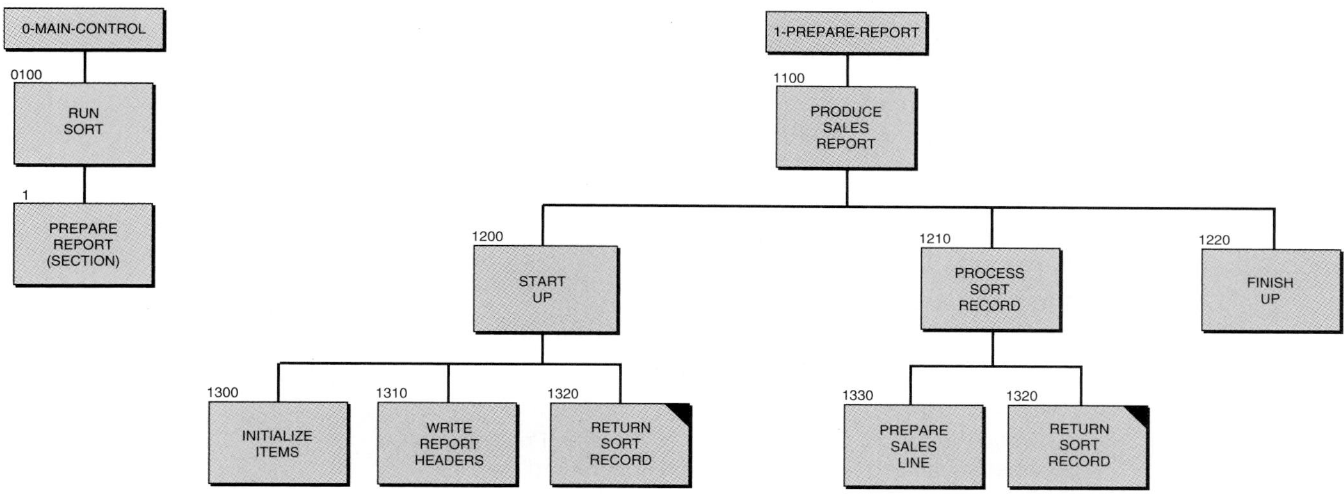

Now, since a PROCEDURE DIVISION can contain any number of sections, we will enhance the structure of the division by using a numeric prefix in each section name. The primary section is given the numeric prefix 0-, as in 0-MAIN-CONTROL SECTION. The next section is given the numeric prefix 1-, as in 1-PRODUCE-REPORT SECTION, and so on, where the numeric prefix indicates the relative position of the section within the PROCEDURE DIVISION.

To maintain the self-documentation provided by the numeric prefixes that have been used in paragraph names, the numeric prefix of the section name will now be attached as the first digit to the numeric prefix of a paragraph name. For instance, 1200-START-UP is the name of the start-up paragraph in the section with numeric prefix 1-, whereas 2200-START-UP is the name of the start-up paragraph in the section with numeric prefix 2-.

This adaptation of our paragraph-naming convention also carries over into the structure chart. The structure chart should show the need for sections within the program.

The Structure Chart for Problem 2

Figure 10.11 contains the structure chart for the current problem. Note that there are two sections in the chart: 0-MAIN-CONTROL and 1-PREPARE-REPORT. A section name is inserted in a long and narrow rectangle at the very top of the structure chart section.

In the structure chart for the section 0-MAIN-CONTROL, there is one paragraph, namely 0100-RUN-SORT, and this paragraph controls the execution of the section 1-PREPARE-REPORT. In the structure chart for the section 1-PREPARE-REPORT, there are seven paragraphs. Note how the first digit of a module number indicates the section that it belongs to.

The Program Pseudocode and Program Flowchart for Problem 2

The pseudocode related to the structure chart follows, and the corresponding program flowchart is shown in Figure 10.12.

0-Main-Control Section.

0100-Run-Sort.

1. Read all input Salesperson-Records into the Sort-file.
2. Sort the records of Sort-File using the following keys:
   a. major key: names in ascending order
   b. minor key: Social Security numbers in ascending order
3. Perform the output procedure 1-Prepare-Report.
4. Stop the run.

1-Prepare-Report Section.

1100-Produce-Sales-Report.

1. Perform 1200-Start-Up.
2. Perform 1210-Process-Sort-Record until no more sort records.
3. Perform 1220-Finish-Up.
4. Exit from the output procedure.

1200-Start-Up.

1. Open the output file Sorted-Sales-Report.
2. Perform 1300-Initialize-Items.
3. Perform 1310-Write-Report-Headers.
4. Perform 1320-Return-Sort-Record.

1210-Process-Sort-Record.

1. Perform 1330-Prepare-Sales-Line.
2. Perform 1320-Return-Sort-Record.

1220-Finish-Up.

1. Move the record End-Line to the output area Printline.
2. After advancing 5 lines, write the output record Printline.
3. Close the output file Sorted-Sales-Report.

1300-Initialize-Items.

1. Obtain the date from the system.
2. Move the date to Date-Line date.
3. Set the end-of-file flag WS-MORE-SORT-RECORDS to "YES".
4. Clear the record area Sales-Line.

1310-Write-Report-Headers.

1. Move the record Date-Line to the output area Printline.
2. After advancing to a new page, write the output record Printline.
3. Move the record Company-Name to the output area Printline.
4. After advancing 1 line, write the output record Printline.
5. Move the record Report-Name to the output area Printline.
6. After advancing 3 lines, write the output record Printline.
7. Move the record Headings to the output area Printline.
8. After advancing 3 lines, write the output record Printline.
9. Set proper-spacing to 2.

1320-Return-Sort-Record.

1. Return (read) a Sort-File record.
2. Test for end-of-file record;
   if EOF record reached, set WS-MORE-SORT-RECORDS to "NO ".

1330-Prepare-Sales-Line.

1. Move Sort-Record name to Sales-Line name.
2. Move Sort-Record SSN to Sales-Line SSN.
3. Move Sort-Record sales to Sales-Line sales.
4. Move Sort-Record store number to Sales-Line store number.
5. Move the record Sales-Line to the output area Printline.
6. After advancing proper-spacing, write the output record Printline.
7. Set proper-spacing to 1.

Note in the flowchart that program execution is terminated by executing the last statement in the primary module of the first section, 0-MAIN-CONTROL. When the procedure contained in section 1-PREPARE-REPORT is completely executed, control must be returned to the SORT statement in the primary module 0100-RUN-SORT. At that point, the SORT statement closes the sort file before passing control to the next statement, namely, STOP RUN.

To indicate that control must be returned from the procedure 1-PREPARE-REPORT, the flowchart terminal symbol of its primary module 1100-PRODUCE-SALES-REPORT contains the descriptive entry EXIT. Similarly, step 4 of the paragraph 1100-Produce-Sales-Report in the pseudocode contains the descriptive entry "Exit from the output procedure."

■ **Figure 10.12** The program flowchart for problem 2

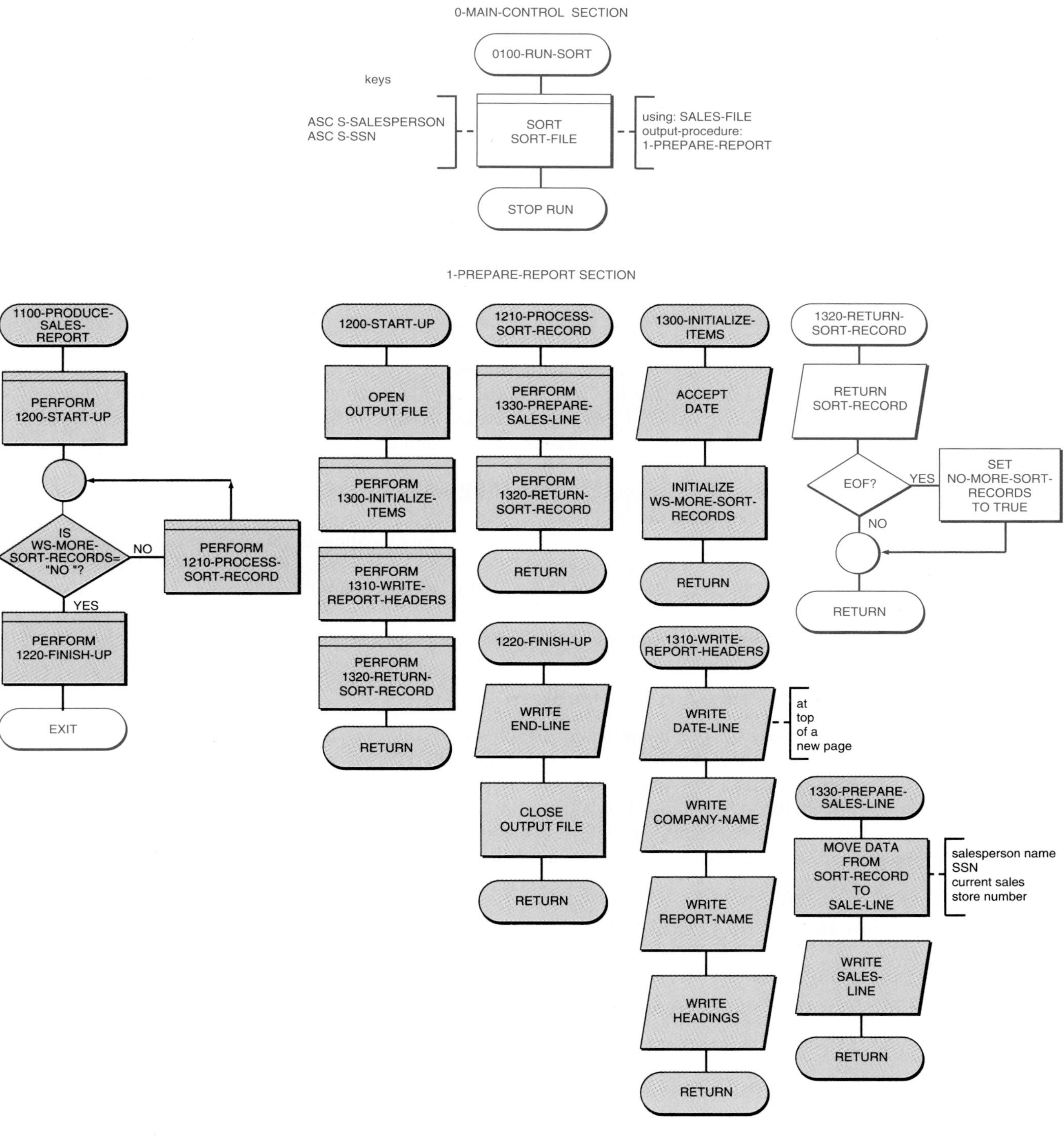

The SORT Statement in Problem 2

The analysis of the problem leads us to code the SORT statement as follows:

```
SORT SORT-FILE
    ON ASCENDING KEY S-SALESPERSON
    ON ASCENDING KEY S-SSN
    USING SALES-FILE
    OUTPUT PROCEDURE IS 1-PREPARE-REPORT.
```

When this statement is executed, the following sequence of events occurs:

1. As program execution begins, control passes to the SORT statement. The sort routine opens the sort file SORT-FILE and the input file SALES-FILE; it reads all the input records and copies them into the sort file, one at a time; it then closes the input file.
2. The sort routine then sequences all the sort records according to the specified keys, that is, in alphabetic order by salesperson name and in ascending order of the Social Security numbers in the case of identical names.
3. The sort routine then releases control to the output procedure (section) 1-PREPARE-REPORT.
4. While control is in the output procedure, the statements coded by the programmer are executed. That is, the output file SORTED-SALES-REPORT is opened; some items are initialized, the report headers are generated; the first record of the sort file is retrieved, using the RETURN statement; the output record SALES-LINE is prepared and printed on the report; the next record of the sort file is retrieved and processed; and the pattern continues until the end-of-file record in the sort file is encountered.
5. Control passes to paragraph 1220-FINISH-UP, where the end-of-report message is printed on the report, and the output file is closed.
6. Control must then return to the SORT statement by executing an EXIT statement at the end of the output procedure 1-PREPARE-REPORT.
7. The sort routine then closes the sort file, and it releases control to the next statement, namely, STOP RUN.
8. The STOP RUN statement is executed, and control returns to the operating system.

Coding the Program for Problem 2

We are now ready to code the program. The first three divisions are similar to those in the program for problem 1, except that the WORKING-STORAGE SECTION is needed in this one. It must contain the description of the flag WS-MORE-SORT-RECORDS as well as the descriptions of all the records related to the printed report. Also note that the fields of the sort record that contain the sales amount and the store number must be given names, in addition to the fields that are used as sort keys, since these values must be moved individually to corresponding fields of the output record SALES-LINE.

The program is contained in Figure 10.13.

Figure 10.13 The COBOL program for problem 2

```
 IDENTIFICATION DIVISION.

 PROGRAM-ID.      SORT-PROG-2.

******************************************************************
*                                                                *
*   AUTHOR.          PAQUETTE.                                   *
*   DATE WRITTEN.    OCTOBER 1993.                               *
*                                                                *
*   IN THIS PROGRAM, THE SORT STATEMENT SPECIFIES TWO ASCENDING  *
*   KEYS, AND IT USES THE USING PHRASE TO LOAD THE INPUT RECORDS *
*   INTO THE SORT FILE AND THE OUTPUT PROCEDURE CLAUSE TO        *
*   SPECIFY THE SECTION THAT CONTAINS THE STATEMENTS THAT WILL   *
*   BE EXECUTED TO PRODUCE THE REPORT.                           *
*                                                                *
*   THERE ARE TWO FUNCTIONS TO THIS PROGRAM:  FIRST, IT MUST     *
*   SORT THE RECORDS OF THE INPUT FILE IN ALPHABETIC ORDER BY    *
*   SALESPERSON NAME, AND IN THE CASE OF IDENTICAL NAMES, IN     *
*   ASCENDING ORDER OF THE SOCIAL SECURITY NUMBERS; SECOND, IT   *
*   MUST PRINT THE SORTED RECORDS ON A FORMATTED REPORT.         *
*                                                                *
******************************************************************
```

Figure 10.13 The COBOL program for problem 2

```
ENVIRONMENT DIVISION.

CONFIGURATION SECTION.

SOURCE-COMPUTER.   VAX-VMS-8650.
OBJECT-COMPUTER.   VAX-VMS-8650.

INPUT-OUTPUT SECTION.

FILE-CONTROL.
    SELECT SALES-FILE            ASSIGN TO COB$INPUT.
    SELECT SORT-FILE             ASSIGN TO DISK10.
    SELECT SORTED-SALES-REPORT   ASSIGN TO COB$OUTPUT.

DATA DIVISION.

FILE SECTION.

FD  SALES-FILE
    RECORD CONTAINS 39 CHARACTERS.

01  SALESPERSON-RECORD PIC X(39).

SD  SORT-FILE
    RECORD CONTAINS 39 CHARACTERS.

01  SORT-RECORD.
    05 S-STORE-NO       PIC X(2).
    05                  PIC X(2).
    05 S-SSN            PIC X(9).
    05 S-SALESPERSON    PIC X(20).
    05 S-CURRENT-SALES  PIC 9999V99.

FD  SORTED-SALES-REPORT
    RECORD CONTAINS 80 CHARACTERS.

01  PRINTLINE           PIC X(80).

WORKING-STORAGE SECTION.

01  PROGRAM-CONTROLS.

    05 WS-MORE-SORT-RECORDS     PIC XXX.
       88 NO-MORE-SORT-RECORDS  VALUE "NO ".
    05 WS-DATE                  PIC X(6).
    05 WS-PROPER-SPACING        PIC 9.

01  REPORT-HEADERS.

    05 DATE-LINE.
       10                PIC X(4)  VALUE SPACES.
       10                PIC X(14) VALUE "REPORT DATE:  ".
       10 O-REPORT-DATE  PIC XX/XX/XX.
       10                PIC X(54) VALUE SPACES.

    05 COMPANY-NAME.
       10 PIC X(34) VALUE SPACES.
       10 PIC X(13) VALUE "THE SPORTSMAN".
       10 PIC X(33) VALUE SPACES.

    05 REPORT-NAME.
       10 PIC X(34) VALUE SPACES.
       10 PIC X(13) VALUE "CHICAGO SALES".
       10 PIC X(33) VALUE SPACES.

    05 HEADINGS.
       10 PIC X(8)  VALUE SPACES.
       10 PIC X(11) VALUE "SALESPERSON".
       10 PIC X(14) VALUE SPACES.
       10 PIC X(3)  VALUE "SSN".
       10 PIC X(9)  VALUE SPACES.
       10 PIC X(13) VALUE "CURRENT SALES".
       10 PIC X(5)  VALUE SPACES.
       10 PIC X(12) VALUE "STORE NUMBER".
       10 PIC X(5)  VALUE SPACES.
```

```
01  SALES-LINE.
    05                   PIC X(4).
    05 O-SALESPERSON     PIC X(20).
    05                   PIC X(5).
    05 O-SSN             PIC XXXBXXBXXXX.
    05                   PIC X(7).
    05 O-CURRENT-SALES   PIC $Z,ZZ9.99.
    05                   PIC X(12).
    05 O-STORE-NO        PIC XX.
    05                   PIC X(10).

01  END-LINE.
    05 PIC X(29) VALUE SPACES.
    05 PIC X(23) VALUE "*** END OF REPORT ***".
    05 PIC X(28) VALUE SPACES.

PROCEDURE DIVISION.

O-MAIN-CONTROL SECTION.

0100-RUN-SORT.
    SORT SORT-FILE
        ON ASCENDING KEY S-SALESPERSON
        ON ASCENDING KEY S-SSN
        USING SALES-FILE
        OUTPUT PROCEDURE IS 1-PREPARE-REPORT.
    STOP RUN.
*********************************************************
*                                                       *
*                                                       *
*  THE OUTPUT PROCEDURE BEGINS HERE.                    *
*********************************************************

1-PREPARE-REPORT SECTION.

1100-PRODUCE-SALES-REPORT.
    PERFORM 1200-START-UP.
    PERFORM 1210-PROCESS-SORT-RECORD
        UNTIL NO-MORE-SORT-RECORDS.
    PERFORM 1220-FINISH-UP.
    GO TO 1999-EXIT-OUTPUT-SECTION.

1200-START-UP.
    OPEN OUTPUT SORTED-SALES-REPORT.
    PERFORM 1300-INITIALIZE-ITEMS.
    PERFORM 1310-WRITE-REPORT-HEADERS.
    PERFORM 1320-RETURN-SORT-RECORD.

1210-PROCESS-SORT-RECORD.
    PERFORM 1330-PREPARE-SALES-LINE.
    PERFORM 1320-RETURN-SORT-RECORD.

1220-FINISH-UP.
    WRITE PRINTLINE FROM END-LINE
        AFTER ADVANCING 5 LINES.
    CLOSE SORTED-SALES-REPORT.

1300-INITIALIZE-ITEMS.
    ACCEPT WS-DATE FROM DATE.
    MOVE WS-DATE TO O-REPORT-DATE.
    MOVE "YES" TO WS-MORE-SORT-RECORDS.
    MOVE SPACES TO SALES-LINE.

1310-WRITE-REPORT-HEADERS.
    WRITE PRINTLINE FROM DATE-LINE
        AFTER ADVANCING PAGE.
    WRITE PRINTLINE FROM COMPANY-NAME
        AFTER ADVANCING 1 LINE.
    WRITE PRINTLINE FROM REPORT-NAME
        AFTER ADVANCING 3 LINES.
    WRITE PRINTLINE FROM HEADINGS
        AFTER ADVANCING 3 LINES.
    MOVE 2 TO WS-PROPER-SPACING.

1320-RETURN-SORT-RECORD.
    RETURN SORT-FILE RECORD
        AT END
            SET NO-MORE-SORT-RECORDS TO TRUE.
```

■ **Figure 10.13** continued

```
1330-PREPARE-SALES-LINE.
    MOVE S-SALESPERSON TO O-SALESPERSON.
    MOVE S-SSN TO O-SSN.
    MOVE S-CURRENT-SALES TO O-CURRENT-SALES.
    MOVE S-STORE-NO TO O-STORE-NO.
    WRITE PRINTLINE FROM SALES-LINE
        AFTER ADVANCING WS-PROPER-SPACING.
    MOVE 1 TO WS-PROPER-SPACING.

1999-EXIT-OUTPUT-SECTION.
    EXIT.
```

■ **Figure 10.14** RETURN statement format

```
RETURN file-name RECORD [INTO identifier]
    AT END imperative-statement-1
    [NOT AT END imperative-statement-2]
    [END-RETURN]
```

We direct your attention to the coding of the output procedure 1-PREPARE-REPORT SECTION. There are two features of particular interest:

1. Due to the program pseudocode or flowchart prepared earlier, you probably expect to code the EXIT statement as the last statement in paragraph 1100-PRODUCE-SALES-REPORT. However, that is syntactically incorrect. The EXIT statement must be the sole statement in a paragraph of its own, and, furthermore, it must be coded as the very last statement of the section. To meet these requirements, it is necessary to use a GO TO statement to send control to the last paragraph of the section. And, since it must be the last paragraph, it is assigned the highest possible numeric prefix in the section, namely, 1999-, and the rest of the paragraph name documents its function. The paragraph name is 1999-EXIT-OUTPUT-SECTION, and the GO TO statement at the end of the primary paragraph is GO TO 1999-EXIT-OUTPUT-SECTION. Note that a PERFORM statement is not an appropriate substitute for GO TO. That is because a PERFORM contains an implied return, and there must not be a return in this situation. (There are very few situations in structured COBOL where a GO TO statement is allowed by structured programming purists. In the present case, however, it is not only allowed, it is mandatory.)

   In Figure 10.13, note the arrow lines that show

   i. How control flows from the SORT statement to the output procedure 1-PREPARE-REPORT SECTION (the solid arrow line).
   ii. Within the output procedure, the transfer of control from the statement GO TO 1999-EXIT-OUTPUT-SECTION to the Exit-paragraph (the dashed arrow line).
   iii. How control leaves the output procedure, from within paragraph 1999-EXIT-OUTPUT-SECTION, by executing the EXIT statement, to return to the SORT statement (the dot-dash arrow line).
2. The problem analysis performed earlier has made it clear that once the records have been sorted in the sort file, they must be retrieved from the sort file, one at a time. To retrieve a record from a sort file, the COBOL RETURN statement must be used. Its format is shown in Figure 10.14. Note that it is very similar to the sequential READ statement format.

Rules Govering Use of the RETURN statement

a. The verb RETURN must be followed by the name of the sort file.
b. The word RECORD is optional; its use is recommended to document that only one record is returned each time the statement is executed.
c. The returned record is stored in the buffer area in main memory associated with the sort file.
d. If the INTO phrase is used, the returned record is also copied into identifier.
e. The AT END clause is required. When the condition is satisfied, imperative-statement-1 is executed.
f. The NOT AT END clause provides an alternate path to the AT END path. If it is used, imperative-statement-2 is executed every time a record is returned from the sort file.
g. END-RETURN is the explicit scope terminator for the RETURN statement.

■ **Figure 10.15** The SORTED SALES REPORT for problem 2

```
REPORT DATE: 93/10/20
                              THE SPORTSMAN

                              CHICAGO SALES


    SALESPERSON               SSN          CURRENT SALES     STORE NUMBER

ABALLO, NORMA             820 78 8914       $2,350.75            30
BERNARD, ISIDORE          416 89 2014       $2,035.69            30
BRAZ, JOAN                466 58 7165       $2,315.60            30
CORRIGAN, ALENE           607 04 4132       $1,875.50            30
DOLLARHIDE, CHRIS         785 02 3157       $2,015.70            30
DONOHUE, PHIL             788 23 0154       $  875.00            30
FURTADO, MAUREEN          745 64 5270       $2,015.40            30
KING, CHRISTOPHER         576 40 0892       $1,890.70            30
LINCOURT, LORETTA         745 63 5164       $1,495.00            30
MAHFUZ, IRENE             823 14 4098       $1,850.25            30
MELANSON, GARY            487 25 1099       $1,905.50            30
PRATT, ROBIN              557 31 8974       $2,155.00            30
ROBINSON, GILBERT         566 73 1251       $2,105.90            30



                         ***  END OF REPORT  ***
```

Running the Program for Problem 2

Using the input file listed in Figure 10.8a [DD/CD:VICIOSPI.DAT], the program produced the report shown in Figure 10.15.

■ Problem 3—Sorting and Presort Processing

The Chicago store has received a request from the national office of the Sportsman Company for a file that contains the records of all the salespersons with sales of over $1200 for the period. The records are to be arranged from highest sales to lowest sales. If two or more salespersons have the same sales amount, those records are to be in alphabetic order by the salespersons' names. If two or more names are identical, those records are to be arranged in ascending order of their Social Security numbers.

Brief Analysis of the Problem

The records in the original sales file are arranged alphabetically by salesperson name within each department. (The record layout is the one shown in Figure 10.1.) You can see that only those records with current sales amounts that exceed $1200 need to be copied into the file that must be sent to the national office.

The data processing department sets down the following general guidelines:

1. Read the first record of the input file.
2. Determine if the sales amount for that salesperson exceeds $1200; if it does, then copy that record into the sort file; if it does not, then do nothing with it.
3. Read the next record of the input file, and repeat step 2.
4. Continue the pattern in step 3 until there are no more records in the input file.
5. Sort the records in the sort file using the criteria specified in the problem.
6. After the sorting is complete, write all the records into an output file.

The system flowchart for this job is shown in Figure 10.16. The list of guidelines clearly indicates that not all the input records are to be sent to the sort file. Consequently, each input record has to be processed carefully: It must be read from the input file, it must be tested to determine if it meets the selection criteria, and if it does, then it must be sent to the sort file. The implication this processing has on the SORT statement should be obvious: Of the two options available in the input file component, USING and INPUT PROCEDURE, the only one that allows the programmer to control the processing of the input records is the INPUT PROCEDURE.

Figure 10.16 The system flowchart for problem 3

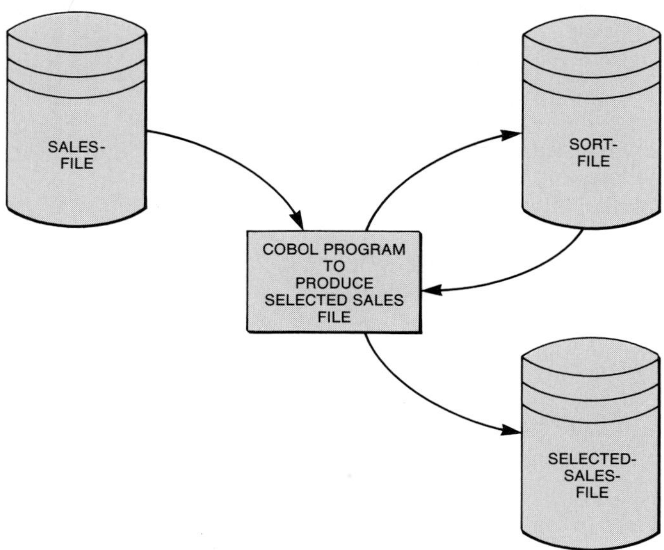

Figure 10.17 The structure chart for problem 3

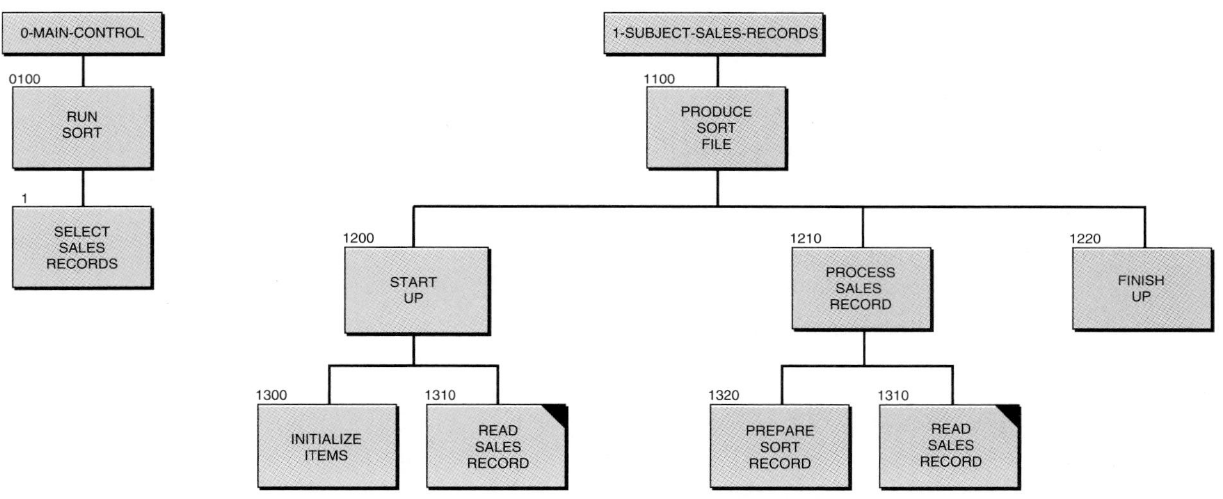

On the other hand, once the selected records have been sorted, they are copied directly to the output file. Of the two options available in the output file component of the SORT statement, the one that is needed is the GIVING option.

In other words, there is a need for an INPUT PROCEDURE section, but there is no need for an OUTPUT PROCEDURE section.

The Structure Chart for Problem 3

Figure 10.17 contains the structure chart. It shows two sections: 0-MAIN-CONTROL, which contains the SORT statement, and 1-SELECT-RECORDS, which contains all the functions required to select the records of the input file that must be sent (released) to the sort file.

The Program Pseudocode and Program Flowchart for Problem 3

The structure chart in Figure 10.17 leads to the pseudocode that follows and to the corresponding flowchart in Figure 10.18.

0-Main-Control Section.

0100-Run-Sort.

1. Perform the input procedure 1-Select-Sales-Records.
2. Sort the records of Sort-File using the following keys:
   a. major key: current sales in descending order
   b. intermediate key: names in alphabetic order
   c. minor key: Social Security numbers in ascending order
3. Write all the sorted records into the output file Selected-Sales-File.
4. Stop the run.

1-Select-Sales-Records Section.

1100-Produce-Sort-File.

1. Perform 1200-Start-Up.
2. Perform 1210-Process-Sales-Record until no more sales records.
3. Perform 1220-Finish-Up.
4. Exit from the input procedure.

1200-Start-Up.

1. Open the input file Sales-File.
2. Perform 1300-Initialize-Items.
3. Perform 1310-Read-Sales-Record.

1210-Process-Sales-Record.

1. Perform 1320-Prepare-Sort-Record.
2. Perform 1310-Read-Sales-Record.

1220-Finish-Up.

1. Close the input file Sales-File.

1300-Initialize-Items.

1. Set the end-of-file flag WS-MORE-SALES-RECORDS to "YES".

1310-Read-Sales-Record.

1. Read an input Sales-Record.
2. Test for end-of-file record;
   if EOF record reached, set WS-MORE-SALES-RECORDS to "NO ".

1320-Prepare-Sort-Record.

1. If input current-sales > 1200,
   a. Move input Sales-Record to Sort-Record.
   b. Release (write) Sort-Record to Sort-File.

The SORT Statement in Problem 3

The preceding analysis indicates that the specific version of the SORT statement needed in this problem is the following:

```
SORT SORT-FILE
    ON DESCENDING KEY S-CURRENT-SALES
    ON ASCENDING KEY S-SALESPERSON
    ON ASCENDING KEY S-SSN
    INPUT PROCEDURE IS 1-SELECT-SALES-RECORDS
    GIVING SELECTED-SALES-FILE.
```

When this statement is executed, the following events occur:

1. As program execution begins, control is passed from the operating system to the SORT statement. The sort routine opens the sort file and immediately sends control to the input procedure (section) 1-SELECT-SALES-RECORDS.
2. Within the input procedure section, the statements coded by the programmer are executed. Specifically, the input file SALES-FILE is opened; some items are initialized; the first input record is read; a test is performed to determine if this record should be selected (it is if the amount in the

■ **Figure 10.18** The program flowchart for problem 3

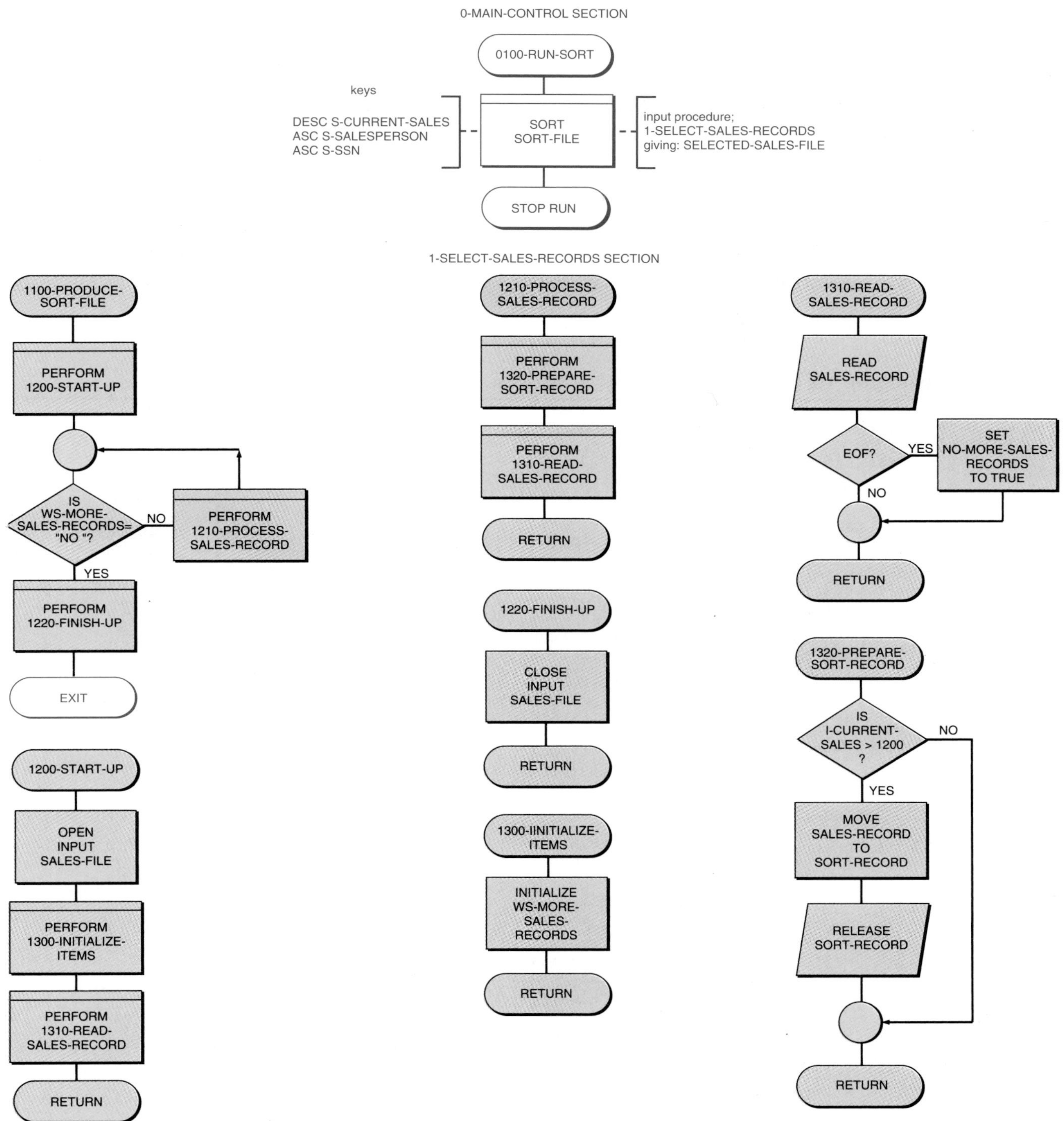

field I-CURRENT-SALES is greater than 1200); if it is selected, then it is copied into the sort record area, and the sort record is written (released) to the sort file; if it is not selected, no further processing occurs for this record. The next record is read and processed as just described. The pattern continues until all the records of the input file have been processed. The input file is then closed, and control is returned to the SORT statement by the execution of the EXIT statement at the end of the input procedure.

3. When control is returned to the SORT statement, the sort routine sorts all the records in the sort file, first from highest sales to lowest sales, then in alphabetic order in the case of matching sales,

and finally in ascending numeric order by Social Security number in the case of matching names. In other words, there are 3 sort keys: The major key is the current sales field, the intermediate key is the salesperson's name field, and the minor key is the Social Security number field.

4. The sort routine then automatically opens the output file and copies all the sort records to it; then it closes the output file.
5. The sort routine then closes the sort file and releases control to the first statement beyond the scope of the SORT statement, namely, STOP RUN.
6. When STOP RUN is executed, control returns to the operating system.

Coding the Program for Problem 3

We are ready to code the program. The first two divisions are similar to those in the problem 2 program. However, in the WORKING-STORAGE SECTION, the only data item needed is the flag WS-MORE-SALES-RECORDS, which is used in relation to the input file. The complete program is shown in Figure 10.19.

Figure 10.19 The COBOL program for problem 3

```
 IDENTIFICATION DIVISION.

 PROGRAM-ID.      SORT-PROG-3.

*****************************************************************
*                                                               *
*    AUTHOR.          PAQUETTE.                                 *
*    DATE WRITTEN.    OCTOBER 1993.                             *
*                                                               *
*    IN THIS PROGRAM, THE SORT STATEMENT SPECIFIES AN INPUT PRO-  *
*    CEDURE TO SELECT RECORDS FROM THE INPUT FILE AND WRITE THEM  *
*    TO THE SORT FILE.  THE SORT ROUTINE SORTS THE RECORDS IN     *
*    DESCENDING ORDER OF CURRENT SALES AMOUNTS, FURTHER SORTING   *
*    ALPHABETICALLY IF THE SALES AMOUNTS ARE THE SAME, AND IN     *
*    ASCENDING ORDER OF THE SOCIAL SECURITY NUMBERS IF THE NAMES  *
*    ARE IDENTICAL.                                             *
*                                                               *
*    THE SORT STATEMENT THEN USES THE GIVING OPTION TO SPECIFY  *
*    THE OUTPUT FILE THAT WILL RECEIVE THE SORTED RECORDS.      *
*                                                               *
*****************************************************************

 ENVIRONMENT DIVISION.

 CONFIGURATION SECTION.

 SOURCE-COMPUTER.   VAX-VMS-8650.
 OBJECT-COMPUTER.   VAX-VMS-8650.

 INPUT-OUTPUT SECTION.

 FILE-CONTROL.
     SELECT SALES-FILE            ASSIGN TO COB$INPUT.
     SELECT SORT-FILE             ASSIGN TO DISK10.
     SELECT SELECTED-SALES-FILE   ASSIGN TO COB$OUTPUT.

 DATA DIVISION.

 FILE SECTION.

 FD  SALES-FILE
     RECORD CONTAINS 39 CHARACTERS.

 01  SALESPERSON-RECORD.
     05                  PIC X(33).
     05 I-CURRENT-SALES  PIC 9999V99.

 SD  SORT-FILE
     RECORD CONTAINS 39 CHARACTERS.

 01  SORT-RECORD.
     05 S-STORE-NO        PIC X(2).
     05                   PIC X(2).
     05 S-SSN             PIC X(9).
     05 S-SALESPERSON     PIC X(20).
     05 S-CURRENT-SALES   PIC 9999V99.
```

■ **Figure 10.19** The COBOL program for problem 3

```
FD   SELECTED-SALES-FILE
     RECORD CONTAINS 39 CHARACTERS.

01   SORTED-SALES-RECORD PIC X(39).

WORKING-STORAGE SECTION.

01   PROGRAM-CONTROLS.
     05 WS-MORE-SALES-RECORDS      PIC XXX.
        88 NO-MORE-SALES-RECORDS   VALUE "NO ".

PROCEDURE DIVISION.

0-MAIN-CONTROL SECTION.

0100-RUN-SORT.
     SORT SORT-FILE
          ON DESCENDING S-CURRENT-SALES
          ON ASCENDING KEY S-SALESPERSON
          ON ASCENDING KEY S-SSN
          INPUT PROCEDURE IS 1-SELECT-SALES-RECORDS
          GIVING SELECTED-SALES-FILE.
     STOP RUN.
*******************************************************
*                                                     *
*                                                     *
*    THE INPUT PROCEDURE BEGINS HERE.                 *
*******************************************************

1-SELECT-SALES-RECORDS SECTION.

1100-PRODUCE-SORT-FILE.
     PERFORM 1200-START-UP.
     PERFORM 1210-PROCESS-SALES-RECORD
          UNTIL NO-MORE-SALES-RECORDS.
     PERFORM 1220-FINISH-UP.
     GO TO 1999-EXIT-INPUT-SECTION.

1200-START-UP.
     OPEN INPUT SALES-FILE.
     PERFORM 1300-INITIALIZE-ITEMS.
     PERFORM 1310-READ-SALES-RECORD.

1210-PROCESS-SALES-RECORD.
     PERFORM 1320-PREPARE-SORT-RECORD.
     PERFORM 1310-READ-SALES-RECORD.

1220-FINISH-UP.
     CLOSE SALES-FILE.

1300-INITIALIZE-ITEMS.
     MOVE "YES" TO WS-MORE-SALES-RECORDS.

1310-READ-SALES-RECORD.
     READ SALES-FILE RECORD
          AT END
               SET NO-MORE-SALES-RECORDS TO TRUE.

1320-PREPARE-SORT-RECORD.
     IF I-CURRENT-SALES > 1200
          MOVE SALESPERSON-RECORD TO SORT-RECORD
          RELEASE SORT-RECORD
     END-IF.

1999-EXIT-INPUT-SECTION.
     EXIT.
```

In this program, notice that again there are two sections, the primary section, 0-MAIN-CONTROL, and the section 1-SELECT-SALES-RECORDS, which is under the control of the SORT statement. The same scheme that was used to exit from the output procedure in problem 2 is used again here to exit from the input procedure. Specifically, the last statement in the primary paragraph of the input procedure section is GO TO 1999-EXIT-INPUT-SECTION, and this paragraph, which must be the last paragraph of the section, contains only one statement, namely, EXIT. Arrow lines have been inserted in Figure 10.19 to draw your attention to control transfers.

Of particular importance in this program is the statement that must be used to write records into a sort file. It is the RELEASE statement, and its format is shown in Figure 10.20.

Figure 10.20 RELEASE statement format

```
RELEASE record-name [FROM identifier]
```

Figure 10.21 The output file SELECTED-SALES-FILE

```
3006820788914ABALLO, NORMA        235075
3008466587165BRAZ, JOAN           231560
3008557318974PRATT, ROBIN         215500
3004566731251ROBINSON, GILBERT    210590
3002416892014BERNARD, ISIDORE     203569
3006785023157DOLLARHIDE, CHRIS    201570
3004745645270FURTADO, MAUREEN     201540
3008487251099MELANSON, GARY       190550
3002576400892KING, CHRISTOPHER    189070
3004607044132CORRIGAN, ALENE      187550
3002823144098MAHFUZ, IRENE        185025
3006745635164LINCOURT, LORETTA    149500
```

Rules Governing Use of the RELEASE Statement

1. Record-name is the name of the record area associated with the sort file.
2. Execution of the RELEASE record-name statement copies the record into the sort file.
3. The FROM phrase is optional. If it is used, identifier is the name of the source field whose contents are copied into the sort record area prior to execution of the RELEASE. It is equivalent to the explicit transfer caused by the statement "MOVE identifier TO record-name."
4. The RELEASE statement is valid only when writing a record to a sort file while control is within an input procedure.

Running the Program for Problem 3

The input file used for this run of the program is the one shown in Figure 10.8a, and the sorted file SELECTED-SALES-FILE generated by the program is shown in Figure 10.21. Note that the records are in descending order of the sales amounts. This column has been highlighted in the figure.

Problem 4—Sorting with Presort and Postsort Processing

The Chicago store has received a request from the national office of the Sportsman Company for a file that contains the records of all the salespersons with sales of over $1200 for the period. The records are to be arranged from highest sales to lowest sales. If two or more salespersons have the same sales amount, those records are to be in alphabetic order by salesperson name. If two or more names are identical, those records are to be arranged in ascending order of their Social Security numbers.

In addition to the file, the company wants a report formatted as shown in the printer spacing chart of Figure 10.22. The detail lines SALES-LINE are printed in the same sequence as the records in the output file SELECTED-SALES-FILE. (The report does not require page breaks.)

Brief Analysis of the Problem

This problem is an extension of problem 3. The only new feature is the need to prepare a report. The report is in addition to creating the output file SELECTED-SALES-FILE. The system flowchart is shown in Figure 10.23.

There are two different ways of proceeding.

Option 1

Maintain the SORT statement exactly as it is coded in problem 3. Then, create another procedure (section) under the control of a PERFORM statement whose sole function is the preparation of the report. In this procedure, the file created as an output file by the SORT statement is opened as an input file; its records are read and processed one at a time in generating the required report.

Figure 10.22 The printer spacing chart for problem 4

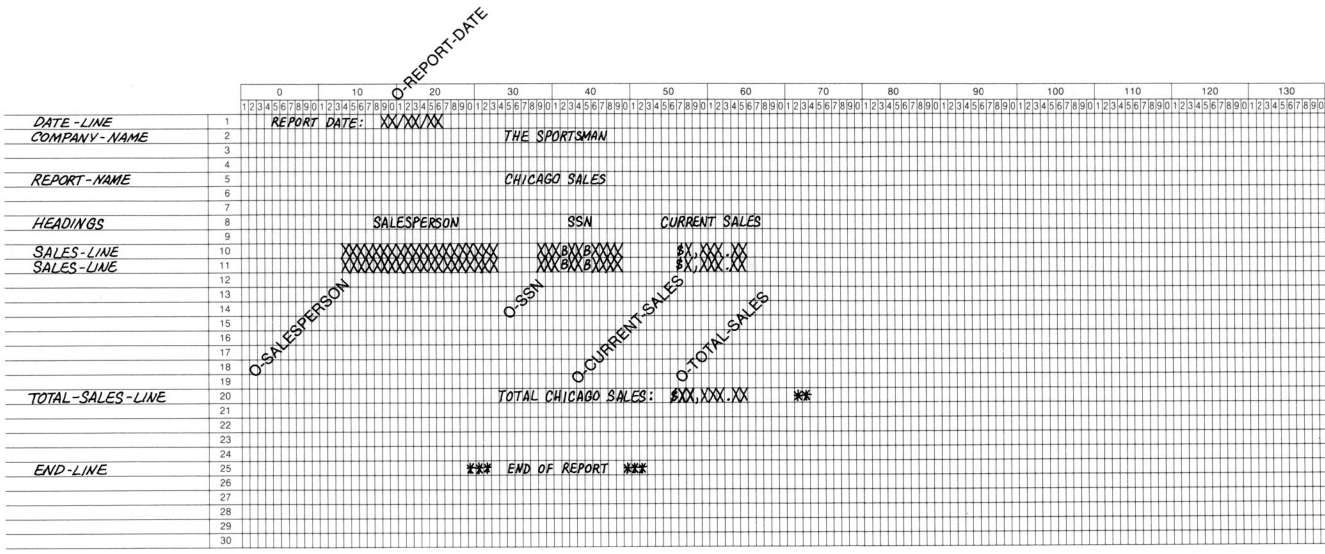

Figure 10.23 The system flowchart for problem 4

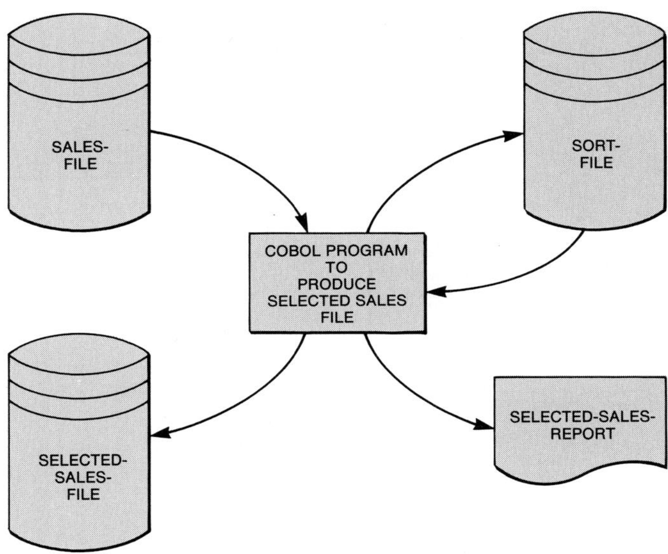

The structure chart for this approach is shown in Figure 10.24, and the three statements in the primary paragraph of 0-MAIN-CONTROL SECTION are as follows:

```
SORT SORT-FILE
    ON DESCENDING KEY S-CURRENT-SALES
    ON ASCENDING KEY S-SALESPERSON
    ON ASCENDING KEY S-SSN
    INPUT PROCEDURE IS 1-SELECT-SALES-RECORDS
    GIVING SELECTED-SALES-FILE.
PERFORM 2-PRODUCE-REPORT.
STOP RUN.
```

■ **Figure 10.24** Option 1 structure chart for problem 4

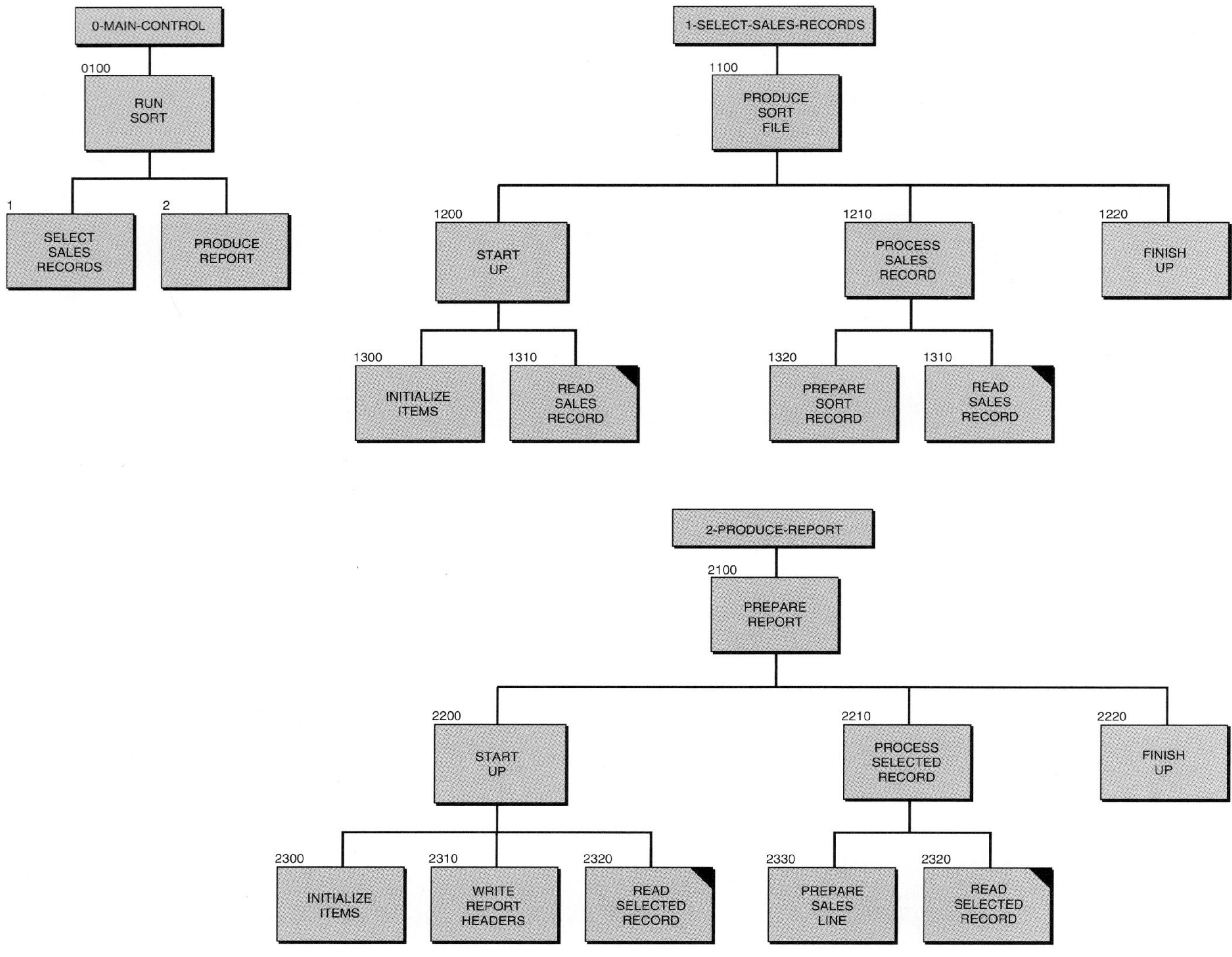

Option 2

Use the OUTPUT PROCEDURE option of the SORT statement to retrieve the records from the sort file, one at a time. As each record is retrieved from the sort file, write it to the output file SELECTED-SALES-FILE, and also prepare the corresponding detail line SALES-LINE on the report.

Since the main purpose of this chapter is to learn the SORT statement, we shall follow this development. The structure chart for this option is shown in Figure 10.25.

The Program Pseudocode and Program Flowchart for Problem 4

The structure chart serves as a guide in writing the program pseudocode. Note that the pseudocode for the section 1-SELECT-SALES-RECORDS is identical to the one for problem 3 and, for that reason, it is not repeated here. The other sections of the pseudocode are shown below, and the program flowchart is shown in Figure 10.26.

■ **Figure 10.25** Option 2 structure chart for problem 4

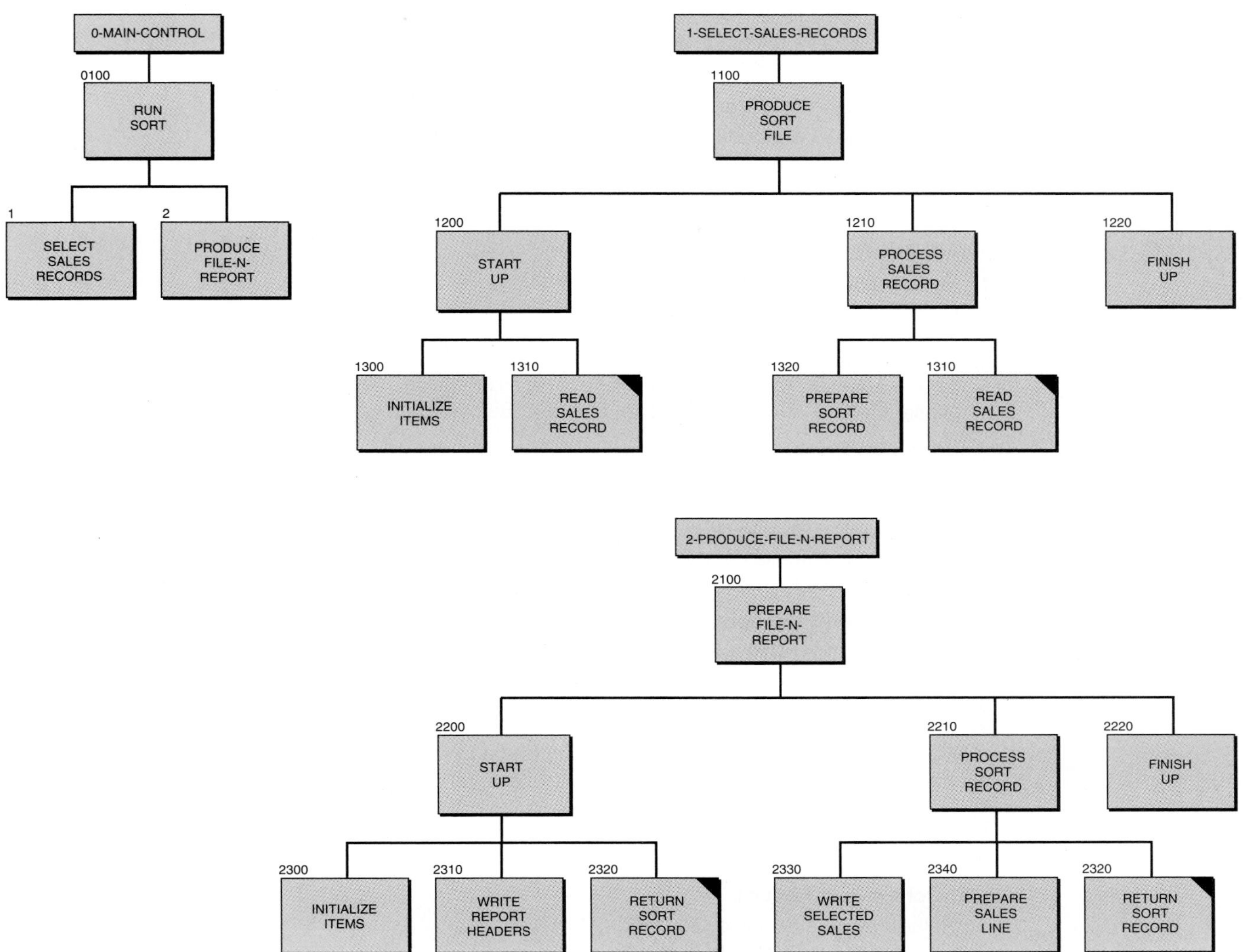

0-Main-Control Section.

0100-Run-Sort.

1. Perform the input procedure 1-Select-Sales-Records.
2. Sort the records of Sort-File using the following keys:
   a. major key: current sales in descending order
   b. intermediate key: names in alphabetic order
   c. minor key: Social Security numbers in ascending order
3. Perform the output procedure 2-Produce-File-N-Report.
4. Stop the run.

1-Select-Sales-Records Section.

(as in problem 3)

2-Produce-File-N-Report Section.

2100-Prepare-File-N-Report.

1. Perform 2200-Start-Up.
2. Perform 2210-Process-Sort-Record until no more sort records.
3. Perform 2220-Finish-Up.
4. Exit from the output procedure.

2200-Start-Up.

1. Open two output files, Selected-Sales-File, Selected-Sales-Report.
2. Perform 2300-Initialize-Items.
3. Perform 2310-Write-Report-Headers.
4. Perform 2320-Return-Sort-Record.

2210-Process-Sort-Record.

1. Add Sort-Record current-sales to current-sales accumulator.
2. Perform 2330-Write-Selected-Sales.
3. Perform 2340-Prepare-Sales-Line.
4. Perform 2320-Return-Sort-Record.

2220-Finish-Up.

1. Move current-sales accumulator to Total-Sales-Line total-sales.
2. Move the record Total-Sales-Line to the output area Printline.
3. After advancing 4 lines, write the output record Printline.
4. Move the record End-Line to the output area Printline.
5. After advancing 5 lines, write the output record Printline.
6. Close the files Selected-Sales-File, Selected-Sales-Report.

2300-Initialize-Items.

1. Obtain the date from the system.
2. Move the date to Date-Line.
3. Set the end-of-file flag WS-MORE-SORT-RECORDS to "YES".
4. Initialize current-sales accumulator.
5. Clear the record area Sales-Line.

2310-Write-Report-Headers.

1. Move the record Date-Line to the output area Printline.
2. After advancing to a new page, write the output record Printline.
3. Move the record Company-Name to the output area Printline.
4. After advancing 1 line, write the output record Printline.
5. Move the record Report-Name to the output area Printline.
6. After advancing 3 lines, write the output record Printline.
7. Move the record Headings to the output area Printline.
8. After advancing 3 lines, write the output record Printline.
9. Set proper-spacing to 2.

2320-Return-Sort-Record.

1. Return (read) a Sort-File record.
2. Test for end-of-file record;
   if EOF record reached, set WS-MORE-SORT-RECORDS to "NO ".

2330-Write-Selected-Sales.

1. Move Sort-Record to Selected-Sales-Record.
2. Write Selected-Sales-Record.

2340-Prepare-Sales-Line.

1. Move Sort-Record salesperson to Sales-Line salesperson.
2. Move Sort-Record SSN to Sales-Line SSN.
3. Move Sort-Record current-sales to Sales-Line current-sales.
4. Move the record Sales-Line to the output area Printline.
5. After advancing proper-spacing, write the output record Printline.
6. Set proper-spacing to 1.

■ **Figure 10.26** The program flowchart for problem 4

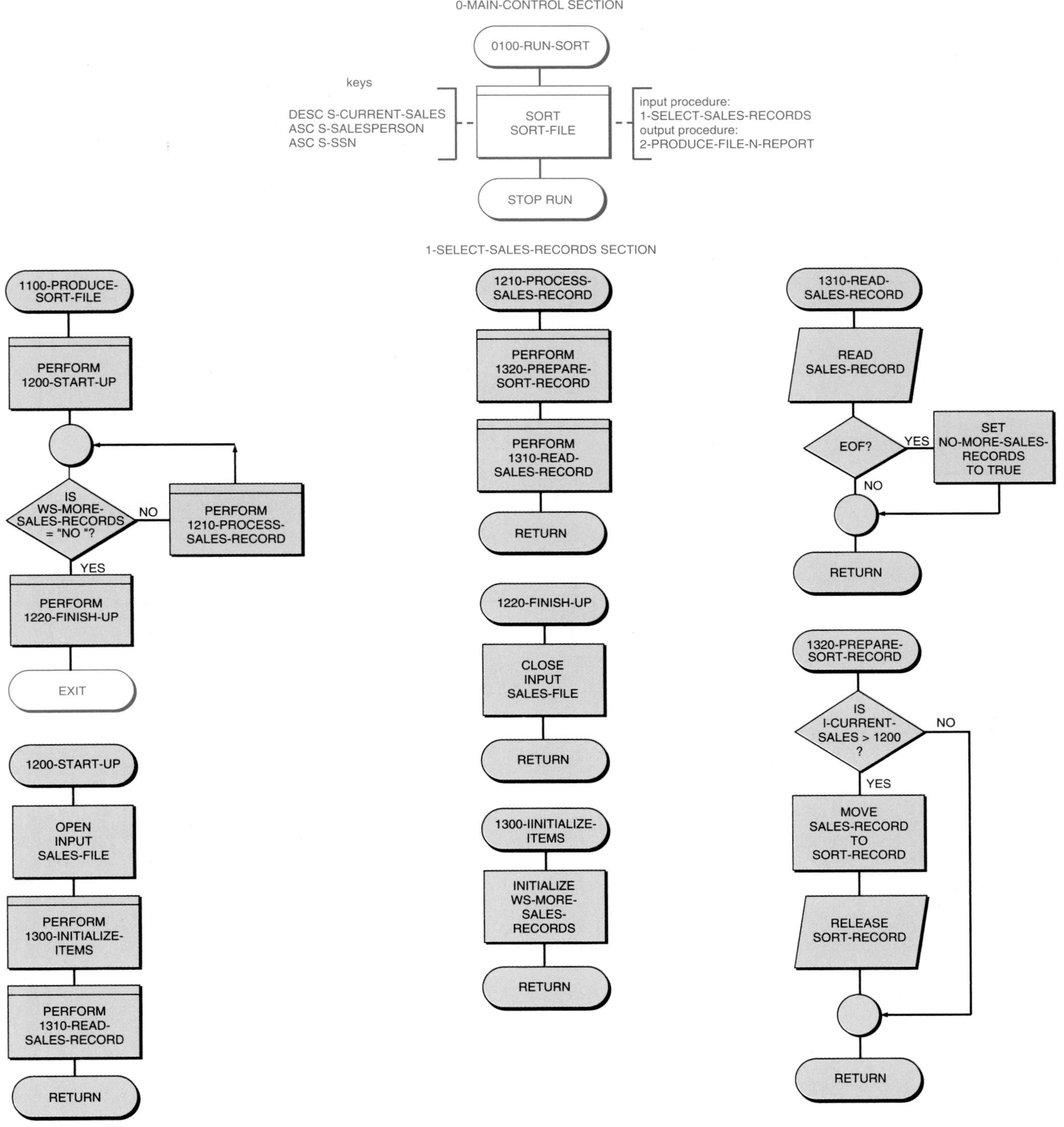

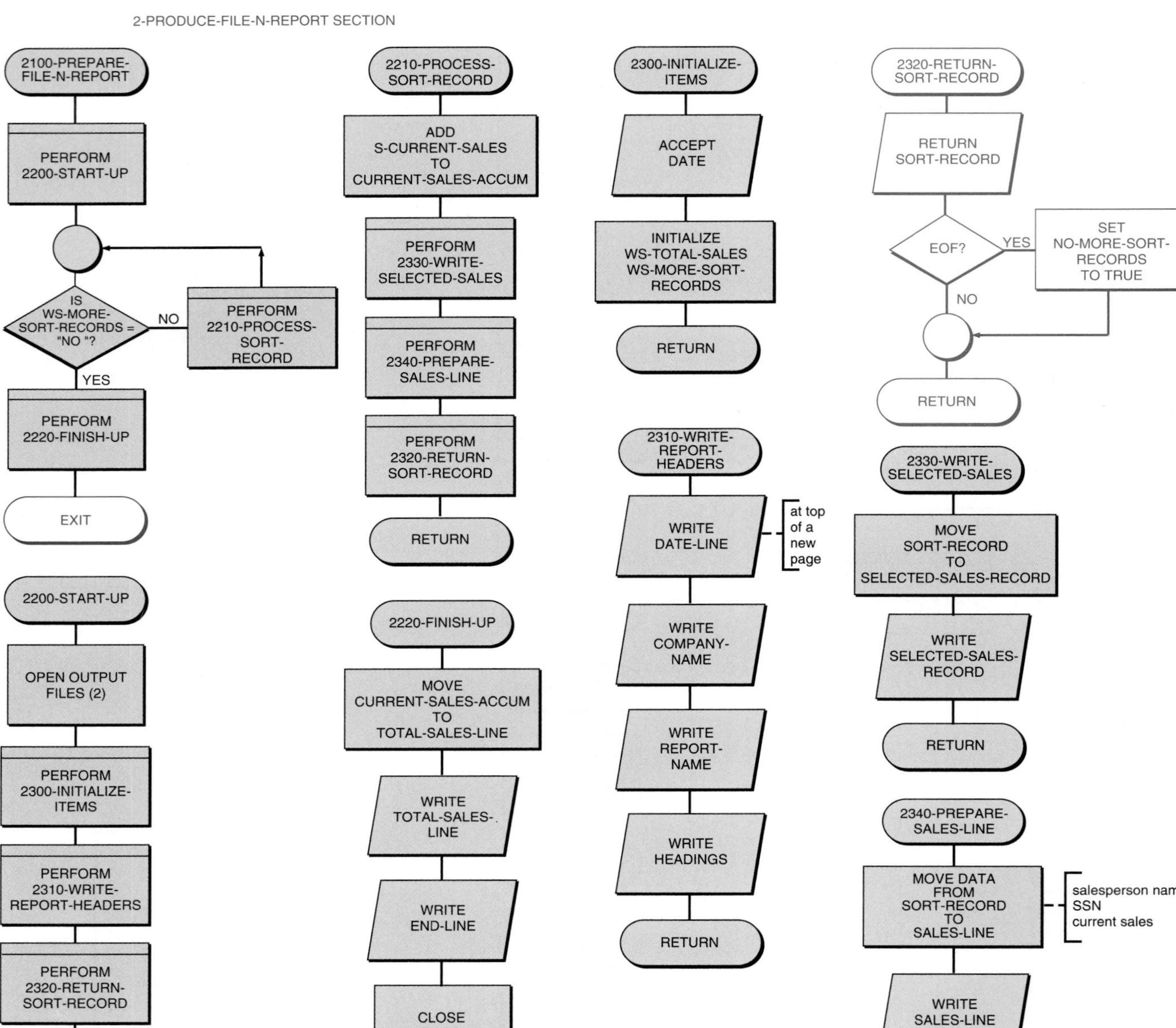
2-PRODUCE-FILE-N-REPORT SECTION
2100-PREPARE-FILE-N-REPORT
PERFORM 2200-START-UP
IS WS-MORE-SORT-RECORDS = "NO "?
NO
PERFORM 2210-PROCESS-SORT-RECORD
YES
PERFORM 2220-FINISH-UP
EXIT
2200-START-UP
OPEN OUTPUT FILES (2)
PERFORM 2300-INITIALIZE-ITEMS
PERFORM 2310-WRITE-REPORT-HEADERS
PERFORM 2320-RETURN-SORT-RECORD
RETURN
2210-PROCESS-SORT-RECORD
ADD S-CURRENT-SALES TO CURRENT-SALES-ACCUM
PERFORM 2330-WRITE-SELECTED-SALES
PERFORM 2340-PREPARE-SALES-LINE
PERFORM 2320-RETURN-SORT-RECORD
RETURN
2220-FINISH-UP
MOVE CURRENT-SALES-ACCUM TO TOTAL-SALES-LINE
WRITE TOTAL-SALES-LINE
WRITE END-LINE
CLOSE FILES
RETURN
2300-INITIALIZE-ITEMS
ACCEPT DATE
INITIALIZE WS-TOTAL-SALES WS-MORE-SORT-RECORDS
RETURN
2310-WRITE-REPORT-HEADERS
WRITE DATE-LINE
at top of a new page
WRITE COMPANY-NAME
WRITE REPORT-NAME
WRITE HEADINGS
RETURN
2320-RETURN-SORT-RECORD
RETURN SORT-RECORD
EOF?
YES
SET NO-MORE-SORT-RECORDS TO TRUE
NO
RETURN
2330-WRITE-SELECTED-SALES
MOVE SORT-RECORD TO SELECTED-SALES-RECORD
WRITE SELECTED-SALES-RECORD
RETURN
2340-PREPARE-SALES-LINE
MOVE DATA FROM SORT-RECORD TO SALES-LINE
salesperson name
SSN
current sales
WRITE SALES-LINE
RETURN

The SORT Statement in Problem 4

The flowchart in Figure 10.26 shows that the version of the SORT statement needed in this program is the following:

```
SORT SORT-FILE
    ON DESCENDING KEY S-CURRENT-SALES
    ON ASCENDING KEY S-SALESPERSON
    ON ASCENDING KEY S-SSN
    INPUT PROCEDURE IS 1-SELECT-SALES-RECORDS
    OUTPUT PROCEDURE IS 2-PRODUCE-FILE-N-REPORT.
```

When this statement is executed, the following events occur:

1. As program execution begins, control is passed from the operating system to the SORT statement. The sort routine opens the sort file and immediately sends control to the input procedure (section) 1-SELECT-SALES-RECORDS.
2. Within the input procedure section, the statements coded by the programmer are executed. Specifically, the input file SALES-FILE is opened; some items are initialized; the first input record is read; a test is performed to determine if this record should be selected (it is if the amount in the field I-CURRENT-SALES is greater than 1200); if it is selected, then it is copied into the sort record area, and the sort record is written (released) to the sort file; if it is not selected, no further processing occurs for this record. The next record is read and processed as just described. The pattern continues until all the records of the input file have been processed. The input file is then closed, and control is returned to the SORT statement by the execution of the EXIT statement at the end of the input procedure.
3. When control is returned to the SORT statement, the sort routine sorts all the records in the sort file, first from highest sales to lowest sales, then in alphabetic order in the case of matching sales, and finally in ascending numeric order of Social Security numbers in the case of matching names.
4. The sort routine then sends control to the output procedure (section) 2-PRODUCE-FILE-N-REPORT.
5. Within the output procedure section, the statements coded by the programmer are executed. Specifically, two output files are opened, the date is obtained from the system, the current sales accumulator is set to zero, the top-of-report documentation is printed on the report, and the first record is retrieved (returned) from the sort file. The current sales amount on that record is added into the current sales accumulator. The sort record is then copied into the output file SELECTED-SALES-FILE, and it is also used to print the corresponding detail line SALES-LINE on the report. The next sort record is returned from the sort file and processed as just described. The pattern repeats until there are no more records in the sort file. At that point, the TOTAL-SALES-LINE is prepared and printed on the report, and the End-of-Report message is printed. The two files opened earlier by the programmer are closed, and control returns to the SORT statement when the EXIT statement at the end of the output procedure section is executed.
6. At this point, the sort routine closes the sort file and releases control to the first statement beyond the scope of the SORT, namely, STOP RUN.
7. The execution of STOP RUN returns control to the operating system.

Coding the Program for Problem 4

In this program, the FILE-CONTROL paragraph must contain four SELECT statements, since there are four files: one input, two output, and the sort file. Consequently, there are three FD paragraphs and one SD paragraph in the FILE SECTION. The WORKING-STORAGE SECTION must describe the two flags WS-MORE-SALES-RECORDS and WS-MORE-SORT-RECORDS, it must describe the accumulator for the current sales, and it must describe all the records that must be printed on the report. The PROCEDURE DIVISION consists of three sections, namely, the primary section, the input procedure section, and the output procedure section. There are no new statement formats in this program. The program is shown in Figure 10.27.

■ **Figure 10.27** The COBOL program for problem 4

```
 IDENTIFICATION DIVISION.

 PROGRAM-ID.      SORT-PROG-4.

*****************************************************************
*                                                               *
*   AUTHOR.          PAQUETTE.                                  *
*   DATE WRITTEN.    OCTOBER 1993.                              *
*                                                               *
*   IN THIS PROGRAM, THE SORT STATEMENT SPECIFIES AN INPUT PRO- *
*   CEDURE TO SELECT RECORDS FROM THE INPUT FILE AND WRITE THEM *
*   TO THE SORT FILE.  THE SORT ROUTINE SORTS THE RECORDS IN    *
*   DESCENDING ORDER OF CURRENT SALES AMOUNTS, FURTHER SORTING  *
*   ALPHABETICALLY IF THE SALES AMOUNTS ARE THE SAME, AND IN    *
*   ASCENDING ORDER OF THE SOCIAL SECURITY NUMBERS IF THE NAMES *
*   ARE IDENTICAL.                                              *
*                                                               *
*   THE SORT STATEMENT THEN SPECIFIES AN OUTPUT PROCEDURE.  IT  *
*   MUST PREPARE A FILE THAT CONTAINS THE SORTED RECORDS, AND IT *
*   MUST ALSO PRINT A FORMATTED REPORT.  THE REPORT LISTS THE   *
*   RECORDS IN THE SEQUENCE IN WHICH THEY HAVE BEEN SORTED.     *
*                                                               *
*****************************************************************

 ENVIRONMENT DIVISION.

 CONFIGURATION SECTION.

 SOURCE-COMPUTER.   VAX-VMS-8650.
 OBJECT-COMPUTER.   VAX-VMS-8650.

 INPUT-OUTPUT SECTION.

 FILE-CONTROL.
     SELECT SALES-FILE              ASSIGN TO COB$INPUT.
     SELECT SORT-FILE               ASSIGN TO DISK10.
     SELECT SELECTED-SALES-FILE     ASSIGN TO COB$OUTPUT.
     SELECT SELECTED-SALES-REPORT ASSIGN TO REPORTFILE.

 DATA DIVISION.

 FILE SECTION.

 FD  SALES-FILE
     RECORD CONTAINS 39 CHARACTERS.

 01  SALESPERSON-RECORD.
     05                     PIC X(33).
     05 I-CURRENT-SALES     PIC 9999V99.

 SD  SORT-FILE
     RECORD CONTAINS 39 CHARACTERS.

 01  SORT-RECORD.
     05 S-STORE-NO          PIC X(2).
     05                     PIC X(2).
     05 S-SSN               PIC X(9).
     05 S-SALESPERSON       PIC X(20).
     05 S-CURRENT-SALES     PIC 9999V99.

 FD  SELECTED-SALES-FILE
     RECORD CONTAINS 39 CHARACTERS.

 01  SELECTED-SALES-RECORD PIC X(39).

 FD  SELECTED-SALES-REPORT
     RECORD CONTAINS 80 CHARACTERS.

 01  PRINTLINE              PIC X(80).

 WORKING-STORAGE SECTION.

 01  PROGRAM-CONTROLS.
     05 WS-MORE-SALES-RECORDS     PIC XXX.
        88 NO-MORE-SALES-RECORDS  VALUE "NO ".
     05 WS-MORE-SORT-RECORDS      PIC XXX.
        88 NO-MORE-SORT-RECORDS   VALUE "NO ".
     05 WS-DATE                   PIC X(6).
     05 WS-PROPER-SPACING         PIC 9.

 01  WORK-AREAS.
     05 WS-TOTAL-SALES            PIC S9(5)V99.
```

■ **Figure 10.27** continued

```
01  REPORT-HEADERS.

    05 DATE-LINE
       10                PIC X(4)  VALUE SPACES.
       10                PIC X(14) VALUE "REPORT DATE:  ".
       10 O-REPORT-DATE  PIC XX/XX/XX.
       10                PIC X(54) VALUE SPACES.

    05 COMPANY-NAME.
       10 PIC X(34) VALUE SPACES.
       10 PIC X(13) VALUE "THE SPORTSMAN".
       10 PIC X(33) VALUE SPACES.

    05 REPORT-NAME.
       10 PIC X(34) VALUE SPACES.
       10 PIC X(13) VALUE "CHICAGO SALES"
       10 PIC X(33) VALUE SPACES.

    05 HEADINGS.
       10 PIC X(17) VALUE SPACES.
       10 PIC X(11) VALUE "SALESPERSON".
       10 PIC X(14) VALUE SPACES.
       10 PIC X(3)  VALUE "SSN".
       10 PIC X(9)  VALUE SPACES.
       10 PIC X(13) VALUE "CURRENT SALES".
       10 PIC X(13) VALUE SPACES.

01  SALES-LINE.
    05                  PIC X(13).
    05 O-SALESPERSON    PIC X(20).
    05                  PIC X(5).
    05 O-SSN            PIC XXXBXXBXXXX.
    05                  PIC X(7).
    05 O-CURRENT-SALES  PIC $Z,ZZ9.99.
    05                  PIC X(15).

01  TOTAL-SALES-LINE.
    05                  PIC X(33) VALUE SPACES.
    05                  PIC X(22) VALUE "TOTAL CHICAGO SALES:  ".
    05 O-TOTAL-SALES    PIC $ZZ,ZZ9.99.
    05                  PIC X(8)  VALUE "      **".

01  END-LINE.
    05 PIC X(29) VALUE SPACES.
    05 PIC X(23) VALUE "***  END OF REPORT  ***".
    05 PIC X(28) VALUE SPACES.

PROCEDURE DIVISION.

O-MAIN-CONTROL SECTION.

0100-RUN-SORT.
    SORT SORT-FILE
        ON DESCENDING S-CURRENT-SALES
        ON ASCENDING KEY S-SALESPERSON
        ON ASCENDING KEY S-SSN
        INPUT PROCEDURE IS 1-SELECT-SALES-RECORDS
        OUTPUT PROCEDURE IS 2-PRODUCE-FILE-N-REPORT.
    STOP RUN.

*****************************************************************
*                                                               *
*   THE INPUT PROCEDURE BEGINS HERE.                            *
*                                                               *
*****************************************************************

1-SELECT-SALES-RECORDS SECTION.

1100-PRODUCE-SORT-FILE.
    PERFORM 1200-START-UP.
    PERFORM 1210-PROCESS-SALES-RECORD
        UNTIL NO-MORE-SALES-RECORDS.
    PERFORM 1220-FINISH-UP.
    GO TO 1999-EXIT-INPUT-SECTION.

1200-START-UP.
    OPEN INPUT SALES-FILE.
    PERFORM 1300-INITIALIZE-ITEMS.
    PERFORM 1310-READ-SALES-RECORD.

1210-PROCESS-SALES-RECORD.
    PERFORM 1320-PREPARE-SORT-RECORD.
    PERFORM 1310-READ-SALES-RECORD.
```

```
 1220-FINISH-UP.
     CLOSE SALES-FILE.

 1300-INITIALIZE-ITEMS.
     MOVE "YES" TO WS-MORE-SALES-RECORDS.

 1310-READ-SALES-RECORD.
     READ SALES-FILE RECORD
         AT END
             SET NO-MORE-SALES-RECORDS TO TRUE.

 1320-PREPARE-SORT-RECORD.
     IF I-CURRENT-SALES > 1200
         MOVE SALESPERSON-RECORD TO SORT-RECORD
         RELEASE SORT-RECORD
     END-IF.

 1999-EXIT-INPUT-SECTION.
     EXIT.

*****************************************************************
*                                                               *
*   THE OUTPUT PROCEDURE BEGINS HERE.                           *
*                                                               *
*****************************************************************

 2-PRODUCE-FILE-N-REPORT SECTION.

 2100-PREPARE-FILE-N-REPORT.
     PERFORM 2200-START-UP.
     PERFORM 2210-PROCESS-SORT-RECORD
         UNTIL NO-MORE-SORT-RECORDS.
     PERFORM 2220-FINISH-UP.
     GO TO 2999-EXIT-OUTPUT-SECTION.

 2200-START-UP.
     OPEN OUTPUT SELECTED-SALES-FILE
                 SELECTED-SALES-REPORT.
     PERFORM 2300-INITIALIZE-ITEMS.
     PERFORM 2310-WRITE-REPORT-HEADERS.
     PERFORM 2320-RETURN-SORT-RECORD.

 2210-PROCESS-SORT-RECORD.
     ADD S-CURRENT-SALES TO WS-TOTAL-SALES.
     PERFORM 2330-WRITE-SELECTED-SALES.
     PERFORM 2340-PREPARE-SALES-LINE.
     PERFORM 2320-RETURN-SORT-RECORD.

 2220-FINISH-UP.
     MOVE WS-TOTAL-SALES TO O-TOTAL-SALES.
     WRITE PRINTLINE FROM TOTAL-SALES-LINE
         AFTER ADVANCING 4 LINES.
     WRITE PRINTLINE FROM END-LINE
         AFTER ADVANCING 5 LINES.
     CLOSE SELECTED-SALES-FILE
           SELECTED-SALES-REPORT.

 2300-INITIALIZE-ITEMS.
     ACCEPT WS-DATE FROM DATE.
     MOVE WS-DATE TO O-REPORT-DATE.
     MOVE "YES" TO WS-MORE-SORT-RECORDS.
     INITIALIZE WS-TOTAL-SALES.
     MOVE SPACES TO SALES-LINE.

 2310-WRITE-REPORT-HEADERS.
     WRITE PRINTLINE FROM DATE-LINE
         AFTER ADVANCING PAGE.
     WRITE PRINTLINE FROM COMPANY-NAME
         AFTER ADVANCING 1 LINE.
     WRITE PRINTLINE FROM REPORT-NAME
         AFTER ADVANCING 3 LINES.
     WRITE PRINTLINE FROM HEADINGS
         AFTER ADVANCING 3 LINES.
     MOVE 2 TO WS-PROPER-SPACING.

 2320-RETURN-SORT-RECORD.
     RETURN SORT-FILE RECORD
         AT END
             SET NO-MORE-SORT-RECORDS TO TRUE.
```

■ **Figure 10.27** continued

```
2330-WRITE-SELECTED-SALES.
    WRITE SELECTED-SALES-RECORD FROM SORT-RECORD.

2340-PREPARE-SALES-LINE.
    MOVE S-SALESPERSON TO O-SALESPERSON.
    MOVE S-SSN TO O-SSN.
    MOVE S-CURRENT-SALES TO O-CURRENT-SALES.
    WRITE PRINTLINE FROM SALES-LINE
        AFTER ADVANCING WS-PROPER-SPACING.
    MOVE 1 TO WS-PROPER-SPACING.

2999-EXIT-OUTPUT-SECTION.
    EXIT.
```

■ **Figure 10.28** The report produced by the program in Figure 10.27

```
REPORT DATE:  93/10/20
                              THE SPORTSMAN

                              CHICAGO SALES

         SALESPERSON                 SSN          CURRENT SALES

      ABALLO, NORMA              820 78 8914        $2,350.75
      BRAZ, JOAN                 466 58 7165        $2,315.60
      PRATT, ROBIN               557 31 8974        $2,155.00
      ROBINSON, GILBERT          566 73 1251        $2,105.90
      BERNARD, ISIDORE           416 89 2014        $2,035.69
      DOLLARHIDE, CHRIS          785 02 3157        $2,015.70
      FURTADO, MAUREEN           745 64 5270        $2,015.40
      MELANSON, GARY             487 25 1099        $1,905.50
      KING, CHRISTOPHER          576 40 0892        $1,890.70
      CORRIGAN, ALENE            607 04 4132        $1,875.50
      MAHFUZ, IRENE              823 14 4098        $1,850.25
      LINCOURT, LORETTA          745 63 5164        $1,495.00

                             TOTAL CHICAGO SALES:  $24,010.99       **


                          ***  END OF REPORT  ***
```

Running the Program for Problem 4

This program has been run using the input file shown in Figure 10.8a [DD/CD:VICIOSPI.DAT]. The output file (SELECTED-SALES-FILE) containing the selected records, sorted in the specified sequence, is the one shown earlier in Figure 10.21. The report produced by the program is shown in Figure 10.28.

Problem 5—Sorting with Multiple Input Files and Postsort Processing

The national office of the Sportsman Company has requested and received a sales file for the current period from each of its major stores, namely, New York, Boston, Chicago, and Seattle. The files are shown in Figure 10.29. The management wants a sales analysis report that will list the sales force in descending order of sales amounts within each store and show the total sales for each store and for the company as a whole. The report is to be formatted as shown in Figure 10.30, and it must contain at most two stores per page.

Brief Analysis of the Problem

In this problem, there is a control break at the store level. There are four input files. The SORT statement should be used to load all of these files into the sort file, sort them in ascending order by store number, and, within each store, sort them in descending order of the current sales amounts. The records should further be sorted alphabetically if sales amounts within a store are equal and in ascending order of the Social Security numbers if the names are identical. The records must then be retrieved from the sort file and processed as they normally are in a control break program.

■ **Figure 10.29** The four sales files for problem 5

1. BOSTON File

```
2002408936050CORDEIRO, ANTONE      010050
2002509862005CORTON, LOUIS         100000
2002509185045PINEAULT, NORMAN      098050
2002480755030TALBOT, WILFRED       127580
2004479210065BARRESI, JOHN         065000
2004427560010COCHRANE, RUSSELL     146050
2004360902035PENTA, ROBERT         165025
2004472847080PROULX, PAULINE       115000
2004375701060QUINN, SUZANNE        132050
2006683309020COSTELLO, JAMES       167050
2006418090015CRAWFORD, SHIRLEY     139050
2006566127070FELDMAN, WALTER       147080
2006433406075FERNANDEZ, LOUISE     200000
2006571904025LEMERISE, DONALD      185050
2006572495090WORTHEN, MICHAEL      157000
2008762355100GOYETTE, FRANCES      095000
2008812133085KOSINSKI, KATHERINE 112500
2008804233040VERMETTE, GLORIA      156050
```

2. NEW YORK File

```
1002214365025ALLEN, ROBERT         150000
1002218546010BROWN, RAYMOND        302255
1002641275050BRANNIGAN, NICOLE     087525
1002315463030FOGARTY, JANICE       105050
1002642754040MAIN, CHARLES         128000
1004685264065CARLSON, HOPE         090000
1004556234035CRANE, JOHN           287050
1004696996055DANIELS, JULIA        162000
1004251342020FARMER, SUSAN         162000
1004263452070FEINGOLD, HAROLD      125050
1004667451060HARRISON, LILY        142580
1006521244005DWYER, TERRENCE       142580
1006564451045EDWARDS, PETER        108050
1006644353075MANNING, ELIZABETH    135000
1008377568080HOWARD, RALPH         056050
1008482131015JANKOWSKI, STANLEY    135000
1008551164090KELLY, PATRICK        162500
1008599231085LANGFORD, WAYNE       115050
1008521166100PRINGLY, ANNE         109805
```

3. CHICAGO File

```
3002576400892KING, CHRISTOPHER     189070
3002416892014BERNARD, ISIDORE      203569
3002823144098MAHFUZ, IRENE         185025
3004566731251ROBINSON, GILBERT     210590
3004788230154DONOHUE, PHIL         087500
3004607044132CORRIGAN, ALENE       187550
3004745645270FURTADO, MAUREEN      201540
3006820788914ABALLO, NORMA         235075
3006785023157DOLLARHIDE, CHRIS     201570
3006745635164LINCOURT, LORETTA     149500
3008466587165BRAZ, JOAN            231560
3008557318974PRATT, ROBIN          215500
3008487251099MELANSON, GARY        190550
```

4. SEATTLE File

```
4002452677143BEAUDOIN, ROCKY       221500
4002787855623MARKLAND, MARY        198750
4002674451231BISBANO, HENRY        219055
4004720954670OVELOZO, MARIO        242390
4004624166876PARISEAU, WILLIAM     178500
4004712133463PERRY, JOSEPH         194550
4006452892153CARDIN, FRANCIS       204590
4006551502546FORTIN, EMIL          225450
4006574930461GALLAGHER, MICHAEL    197675
4006683215467NOTTE, LORENZO        200500
4008721435472JOBIN, ANTONIO        214050
4008490234571MILLER, RENEE         190570
4008351566178TRAMONTE, ESTELLE     213500
```

■ **Figure 10.30** The printer spacing chart for problem 5

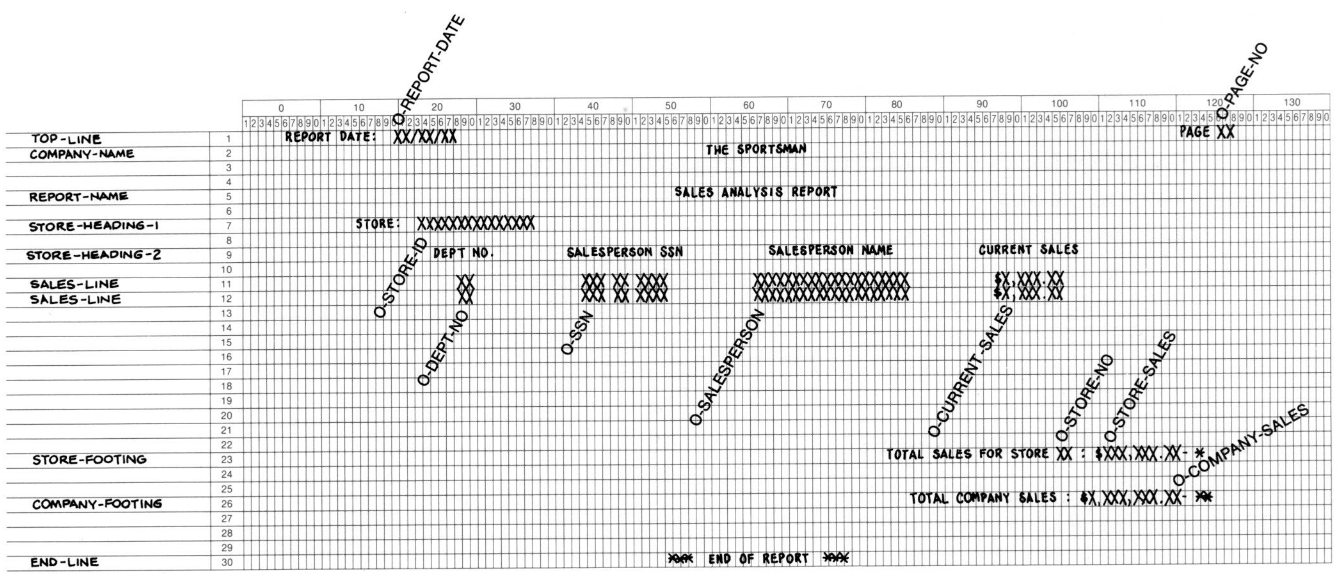

■ **Figure 10.31** The system flowchart for problem 5

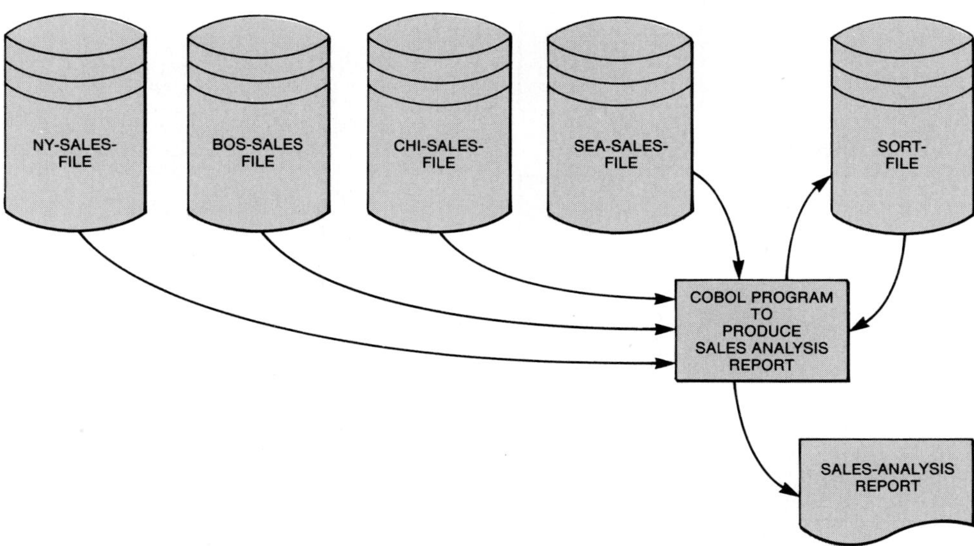

It should be clear that the SORT statement needed in this program should specify the USING phrase, with four input files, and it must specify the OUTPUT PROCEDURE clause to control the preparation of the multilevel report.

The system flowchart for this program is shown in Figure 10.31, and the structure chart is shown in Figure 10.32.

As you examine the structure chart, note that the section 1-PREPARE-REPORT contains the standard structure for a one-level control break program: The first subordinate module in 1210-PROCESS-SORT-RECORD is 1320-CHECK-FOR-NEW-STORE, the module that tests for a control break at the store level. Also note that the report on each store begins with a store heading and ends with a store footing. There is also a global footing for the company.

The pseudocode is listed in Figure 10.33, and the flowchart is shown in Figure 10.34.

Coding the Program for Problem 5

Since there are no new statement formats in this program, it is presented in its entirety in Figure 10.35. In particular, note the version of the SORT statement in the primary paragraph. It specifies S-STORE-NO as the major key, S-CURRENT-SALES as the first intermediate key, S-SALESPERSON as the second intermediate key, and S-SSN as the minor key. Also note that the USING phrase names all the input files and the OUTPUT PROCEDURE option identifies the section that contains the control break logic. The report produced by this program is shown in Figure 10.36.

Figure 10.32 The structure chart for problem 5

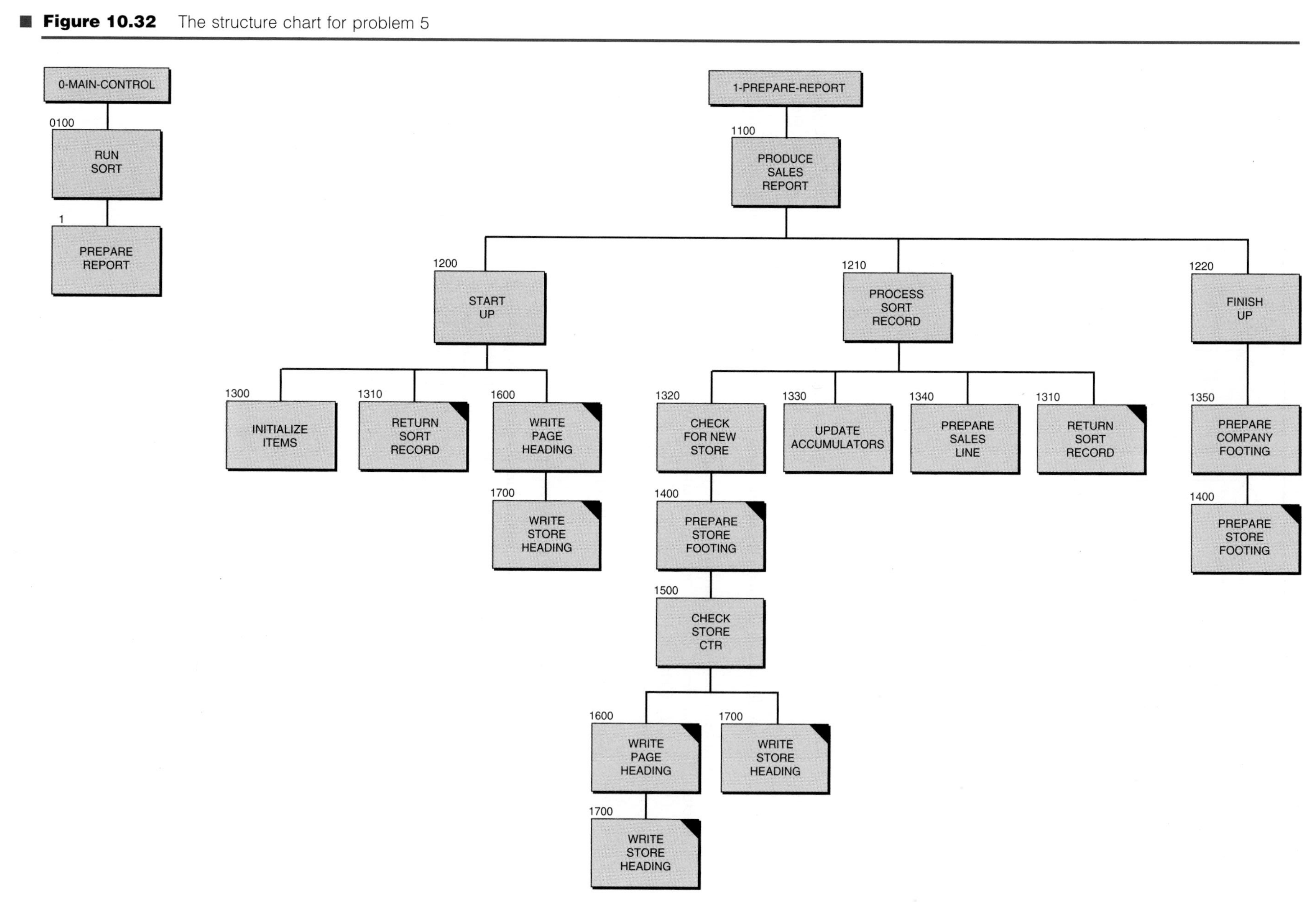

■ **Figure 10.33** The program pseudocode for problem 5

0-Main-Control Section.
0100-Run-Sort.

1. Read all records of the four input files into the Sort-file.
2. Sort the records of Sort-File using:
   major key: store numbers in ascending order
   intermediate key 1: current sales in descending order
   intermediate key 2: names in alphabetic order
   minor key: Social Security numbers in ascending order.
3. Perform the procedure 1-Prepare-Report.
4. Stop the run.

1-Prepare-Report Section.
1100-Produce-Sales-Report.

1. Perform 1200-Start-Up.
2. Perform 1210-Process-Sales-Record until no more sort records.
3. Perform 1220-Finish-Up.
4. Exit from the output procedure.

1200-Start-Up.

1. Open the output file Sales-Report.
2. Perform 1300-Initialize-Items.
3. Perform 1310-Return-Sort-Record.
4. Perform 1600-Write-Page-Heading.

1210-Process-Sort-Record.

1. Perform 1320-Check-For-New-Store.
2. Perform 1330-Update-Store-Accumulator.
3. Perform 1340-Prepare-Sales-Line.
4. Perform 1310-Return-Sort-Record.

1220-Finish-Up.

1. Perform 1350-Prepare-Company-Footing.
2. Move the record End-Line to the output area Printline.
3. After advancing 5 lines, write the output record Printline.
4. Close the file Sales-Report.

1300-Initialize-Items.

1. Obtain the date from the system.
2. Move the date to Date-Line.
3. Set the end-of-file flag WS-MORE-SORT-RECORDS to "YES".
4. Initialize company-sales accumulator and page-number.
5. Clear the record area Sales-Line.

1310-Return-Sort-Record.

1. Return (read) a Sort-File record.
2. Test for end-of-file record;
   if EOF record reached, set WS-MORE-SORT-RECORDS to "NO ".

1320-Check-For-New-Store.

1. If Sort-Record store-number is not equal to store-control,
   then, perform 1400-Prepare-Store-Footing.

1330-Update-Store-Accumulator.

1. Add Sort-Record current-sales to store-accumulator.

1340-Prepare-Sales-Line.

1. Move Sort-Record department-number to Sales-Line department-number.
2. Move Sort-Record SSN to Sales-Line SSN.
3. Move Sort-Record salesperson to Sales-Line salesperson.
4. Move Sort-Record current-sales to Sales-Line current-sales.
5. Move the record Sales-Line to the output area Printline.
6. After advancing proper-spacing, write the output record Printline.
7. Set proper-spacing to 1.

1350-Prepare-Company-Footing.

1. Perform 1400-Prepare-Store-Footing.
2. Move company-accumulator to Company-Footing company-sales.
3. Move the record Company-Footing to the output area Printline.
4. After advancing 3 lines, write the output record Printline.

1400-Prepare-Store-Footing.

1. Move store-control to Store-Footing store-number.
2. Add store-accumulator to company-accumulator.
3. Move store-accumulator to Store-Footing store-sales.
4. Move the record Store-Footing to the output area Printline.
5. After advancing 3 lines, write the output record Printline.
6. Add 1 to stores-per-page-counter.
7. If the flag WS-MORE-SORT-RECORDS is equal to "YES",
   then, perform 1500-Check-Store-Ctr.

1500-Check-Store-Ctr.

1. If stores-per-page-counter is greater than or equal to stores-per-page-limit,
   then, perform 1600-Write-Page-Heading;
   else, perform 1700-Write-Store-Heading.

1600-Write-Page-Heading.

1. Add 1 to page-number.
2. Move page-number to Top-Line page-number.
3. Move the record Top-Line to the output area Printline.
4. After advancing to a new page, write the output record Printline.
5. Move the record Company-Name to the output area Printline.
6. After advancing 1 line, write the output record Printline.
7. Move the record Report-Name to the output area Printline.
8. After advancing 3 lines, write the output record Printline.
9. Set stores-per-page-ctr to zero.
10. Perform 1700-Write-Store-Heading.

1700-Write-Store-Heading.

1. Move Sort-Record store-number to store-control.
2. Test Sort-Record store-number:
   a. if "10", then move "10 - New York" to Store-Heading-1 store-ID.
   b. if "20", then move "20 - Boston" to Store-Heading-1 store-ID.
   c. if "30", then move "30 - Chicago" to Store-Heading-1 store-ID.
   d. if "40", then move "40 - Seattle" to Store-Heading-1 store-ID.
   e. if any other, display message: "Error in Store No. for " Sort-Record salesperson.
3. Move the record Store-Heading-1 to the output area Printline.
4. After advancing 3 lines, write the output record Printline.
5. Move the record Store-Heading-2 to the output area Printline.
6. After advancing 3 lines, write the output record Printline.
7. Set proper-spacing to 2.
8. Set store-accumulator to zero.

Figure 10.34 The program flowchart for problem 5

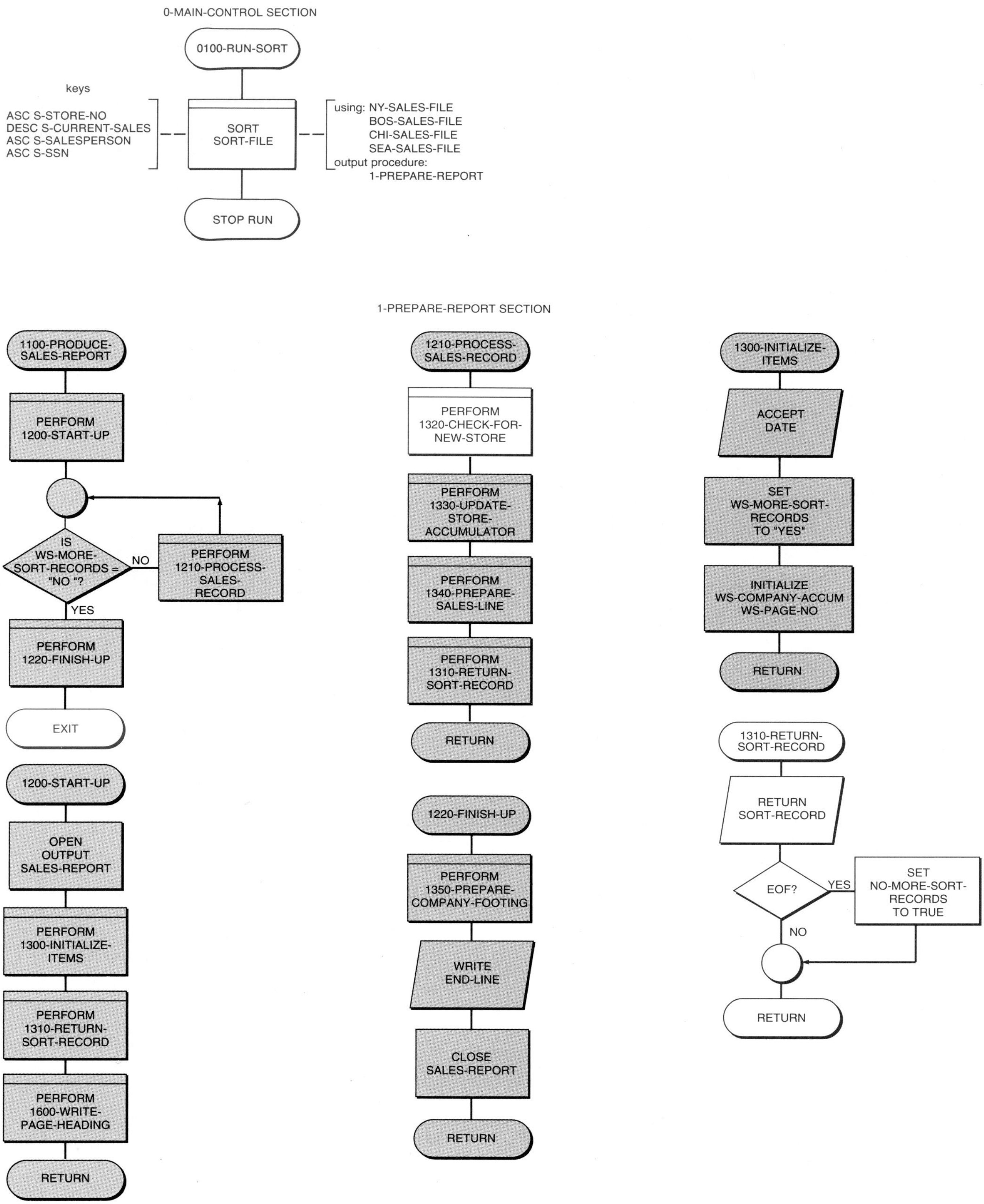

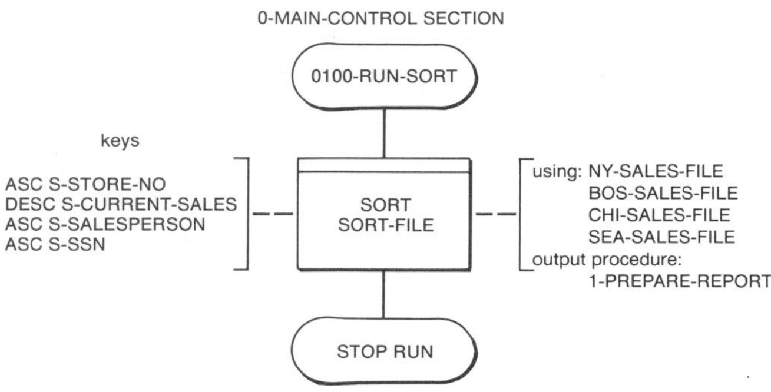

0-MAIN-CONTROL SECTION
0100-RUN-SORT
keys
ASC S-STORE-NO
DESC S-CURRENT-SALES
ASC S-SALESPERSON
ASC S-SSN
SORT SORT-FILE
using: NY-SALES-FILE
BOS-SALES-FILE
CHI-SALES-FILE
SEA-SALES-FILE
output procedure:
1-PREPARE-REPORT
STOP RUN
1-PREPARE-REPORT SECTION
1100-PRODUCE-SALES-REPORT
PERFORM 1200-START-UP
IS WS-MORE-SORT-RECORDS = "NO "?
NO
YES
PERFORM 1210-PROCESS-SALES-RECORD
PERFORM 1220-FINISH-UP
EXIT
1200-START-UP
OPEN OUTPUT SALES-REPORT
PERFORM 1300-INITIALIZE-ITEMS
PERFORM 1310-RETURN-SORT-RECORD
PERFORM 1600-WRITE-PAGE-HEADING
RETURN
1210-PROCESS-SALES-RECORD
PERFORM 1320-CHECK-FOR-NEW-STORE
PERFORM 1330-UPDATE-STORE-ACCUMULATOR
PERFORM 1340-PREPARE-SALES-LINE
PERFORM 1310-RETURN-SORT-RECORD
RETURN
1220-FINISH-UP
PERFORM 1350-PREPARE-COMPANY-FOOTING
WRITE END-LINE
CLOSE SALES-REPORT
RETURN
1300-INITIALIZE-ITEMS
ACCEPT DATE
SET WS-MORE-SORT-RECORDS TO "YES"
INITIALIZE WS-COMPANY-ACCUM WS-PAGE-NO
RETURN
1310-RETURN-SORT-RECORD
RETURN SORT-RECORD
EOF?
YES
SET NO-MORE-SORT-RECORDS TO TRUE
NO
RETURN

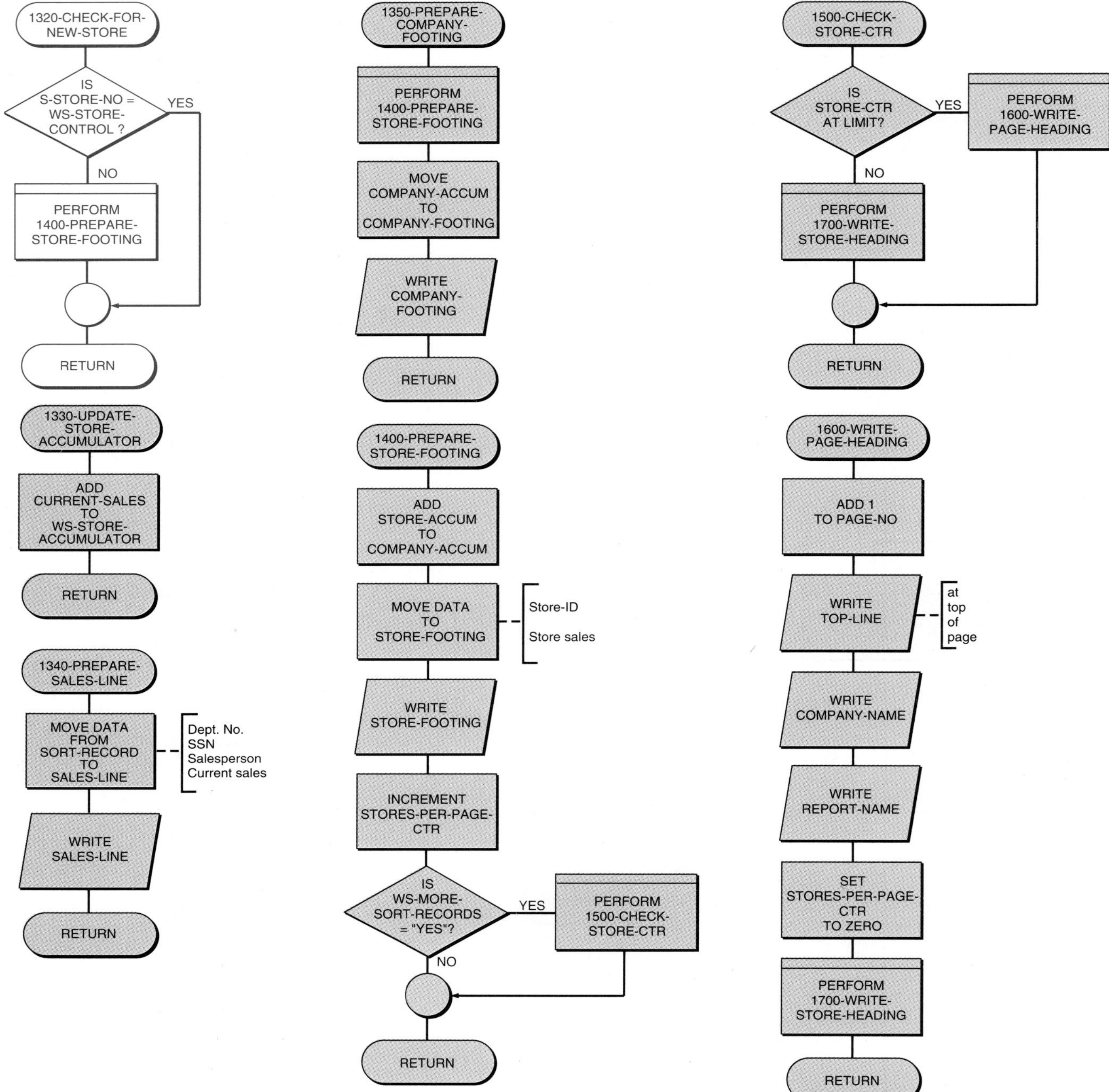
1320-CHECK-FOR-NEW-STORE
IS S-STORE-NO = WS-STORE-CONTROL ?
YES
NO
PERFORM 1400-PREPARE-STORE-FOOTING
RETURN
1330-UPDATE-STORE-ACCUMULATOR
ADD CURRENT-SALES TO WS-STORE-ACCUMULATOR
RETURN
1340-PREPARE-SALES-LINE
MOVE DATA FROM SORT-RECORD TO SALES-LINE
Dept. No.
SSN
Salesperson
Current sales
WRITE SALES-LINE
RETURN
1350-PREPARE-COMPANY-FOOTING
PERFORM 1400-PREPARE-STORE-FOOTING
MOVE COMPANY-ACCUM TO COMPANY-FOOTING
WRITE COMPANY-FOOTING
RETURN
1400-PREPARE-STORE-FOOTING
ADD STORE-ACCUM TO COMPANY-ACCUM
MOVE DATA TO STORE-FOOTING
Store-ID
Store sales
WRITE STORE-FOOTING
INCREMENT STORES-PER-PAGE-CTR
IS WS-MORE-SORT-RECORDS = "YES"?
YES
PERFORM 1500-CHECK-STORE-CTR
NO
RETURN
1500-CHECK-STORE-CTR
IS STORE-CTR AT LIMIT?
YES
PERFORM 1600-WRITE-PAGE-HEADING
NO
PERFORM 1700-WRITE-STORE-HEADING
RETURN
1600-WRITE-PAGE-HEADING
ADD 1 TO PAGE-NO
WRITE TOP-LINE
at top of page
WRITE COMPANY-NAME
WRITE REPORT-NAME
SET STORES-PER-PAGE-CTR TO ZERO
PERFORM 1700-WRITE-STORE-HEADING
RETURN

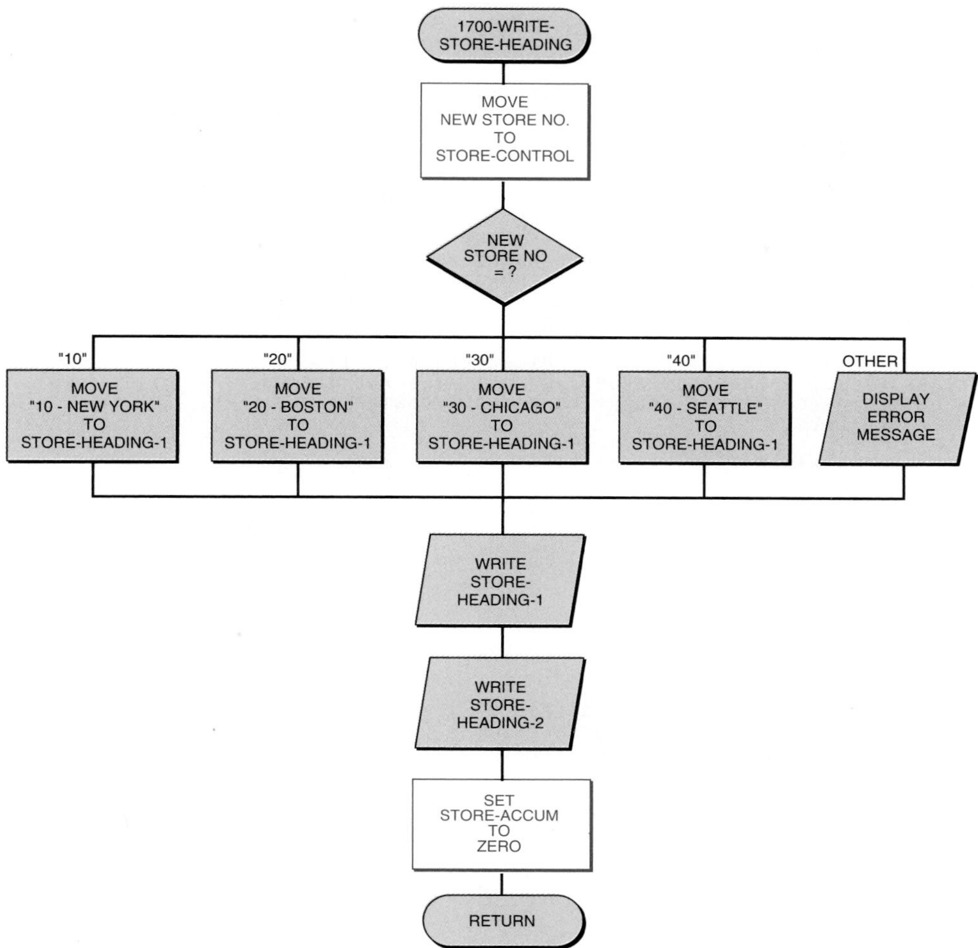
1700-WRITE-
STORE-HEADING
MOVE
NEW STORE NO.
TO
STORE-CONTROL
NEW
STORE NO
= ?
"10"
"20"
"30"
"40"
OTHER
MOVE
"10 - NEW YORK"
TO
STORE-HEADING-1
MOVE
"20 - BOSTON"
TO
STORE-HEADING-1
MOVE
"30 - CHICAGO"
TO
STORE-HEADING-1
MOVE
"40 - SEATTLE"
TO
STORE-HEADING-1
DISPLAY
ERROR
MESSAGE
WRITE
STORE-
HEADING-1
WRITE
STORE-
HEADING-2
SET
STORE-ACCUM
TO
ZERO
RETURN

Figure 10.35 The COBOL program for problem 5

```
 IDENTIFICATION DIVISION.

 PROGRAM-ID.      SORT-PROG-5.

*****************************************************************
*                                                               *
*   AUTHOR.           PAQUETTE.                                 *
*   DATE WRITTEN.     OCTOBER 1993.                             *
*                                                               *
*   IN THIS PROGRAM, THE SORT STATEMENT SPECIFIES THE USING     *
*   PHRASE TO LOAD FOUR FILES INTO THE SORT FILE.  THE SORT     *
*   ROUTINE THEN SEQUENCES THE RECORDS FROM ALL FOUR FILES INTO *
*   ASCENDING ORDER OF STORE NUMBERS, IN DESCENDING ORDER OF    *
*   CURRENT SALES AMOUNTS WITHIN EACH STORE, ALPHABETICALLY IF  *
*   THE SALES AMOUNTS ARE EQUAL, AND IN ASCENDING ORDER OF THE  *
*   SOCIAL SECURITY NUMBERS IF THE NAMES ARE IDENTICAL.         *
*                                                               *
*   THE SORT STATEMENT THEN SPECIFIES AN OUTPUT PROCEDURE.  IT  *
*   CONTROLS THE RETRIEVAL OF RECORDS FROM THE SORT FILE AND THE *
*   PREPARATION OF THE REPORT.  THE REPORT CONTAINS A CONTROL   *
*   BREAK AT THE STORE LEVEL.                                   *
*                                                               *
*****************************************************************

 ENVIRONMENT DIVISION.

 CONFIGURATION SECTION.

 SOURCE-COMPUTER.   VAX-VMS-8650.
 OBJECT-COMPUTER.   VAX-VMS-8650.

 INPUT-OUTPUT SECTION.

 FILE-CONTROL.
     SELECT NY-SALES-FILE       ASSIGN TO NYSALES.
     SELECT BOS-SALES-FILE      ASSIGN TO BOSSALES.
     SELECT CHI-SALES-FILE      ASSIGN TO CHISALES.
     SELECT SEA-SALES-FILE      ASSIGN TO SEASALES.
     SELECT SORT-FILE           ASSIGN TO DISK10.
     SELECT SALES-REPORT        ASSIGN TO REPORTFILE.

 DATA DIVISION.

 FILE SECTION.

 FD  NY-SALES-FILE
     RECORD CONTAINS 39 CHARACTERS.

 01  NY-SALES-RECORD        PIC X(39).

 FD  BOS-SALES-FILE
     RECORD CONTAINS 39 CHARACTERS.

 01  BOS-SALES-RECORD       PIC X(39).

 FD  CHI-SALES-FILE
     RECORD CONTAINS 39 CHARACTERS.

 01  CHI-SALES-RECORD       PIC X(39).

 FD  SEA-SALES-FILE
     RECORD CONTAINS 39 CHARACTERS.

 01  SEA-SALES-RECORD       PIC X(39).

 SD  SORT-FILE
     RECORD CONTAINS 39 CHARACTERS.

 01  SORT-RECORD.
     05 S-STORE-NO          PIC X(2).
     05 S-DEPT-NO           PIC X(2).
     05 S-SSN               PIC X(9).
     05 S-SALESPERSON       PIC X(20).
     05 S-CURRENT-SALES     PIC 9999V99.

 FD  SALES-REPORT
     RECORD CONTAINS 133 CHARACTERS.

 01  PRINTLINE              PIC X(133).
```

```
WORKING-STORAGE SECTION.

01  PROGRAM-CONTROLS.
    05 WS-MORE-SORT-RECORDS       PIC XXX.
       88 THERE-IS-A-SORT-RECORD VALUE "YES".
       88 NO-MORE-SORT-RECORDS   VALUE "NO ".
    05 WS-STORE-CONTROL           PIC XX.
    05 WS-STORES-PER-PAGE-CTR     PIC S9.
    05 WS-STORES-PER-PAGE-LIMIT   PIC 9     VALUE 2.
    05 WS-REPORT-DATE             PIC X(6).
    05 WS-PAGE-NO                 PIC 99.
    05 WS-PROPER-SPACING          PIC 9.

01  PROGRAM-ACCUMULATORS          COMP.
    05 WS-STORE-ACCUMULATOR       PIC S9(6)V99.
    05 WS-COMPANY-ACCUMULATOR     PIC S9(7)V99.

01  PAGE-HEADING.

    05 TOP-LINE.
        10                  PIC X(6)    VALUE SPACES.
        10                  PIC X(14)   VALUE "REPORT DATE:  ".
        10 O-REPORT-DATE    PIC XX/XX/XX.
        10                  PIC X(92)   VALUE SPACES.
        10                  PIC X(5)    VALUE "PAGE ".
        10 O-PAGE-NO        PIC Z9.
        10                  PIC X(6)    VALUE SPACES.

    05 COMPANY-NAME.
        10 PIC X(60)   VALUE SPACES.
        10 PIC X(13)   VALUE "THE SPORTSMAN".
        10 PIC X(60)   VALUE SPACES.

    05 REPORT-NAME.
        10 PIC X(56)   VALUE SPACES.
        10 PIC X(21)   VALUE "SALES ANALYSIS REPORT".
        10 PIC X(56)   VALUE SPACES.

01  STORE-HEADING.

    05 STORE-HEADING-1.
        10                PIC X(15)   VALUE SPACES.
        10                PIC X(8)    VALUE "STORE:  ".
        10 O-STORE-ID     PIC X(15).
        10                PIC X(95)   VALUE SPACES.

    05 STORE-HEADING-2.
        10 PIC X(25)   VALUE SPACES.
        10 PIC X(8)    VALUE "DEPT NO.".
        10 PIC X(9)    VALUE SPACES.
        10 PIC X(15)   VALUE "SALESPERSON SSN".
        10 PIC X(11)   VALUE SPACES.
        10 PIC X(16)   VALUE "SALESPERSON NAME".
        10 PIC X(11)   VALUE SPACES.
        10 PIC X(13)   VALUE "CURRENT SALES".
        10 PIC X(25)   VALUE SPACES.

01  SALES-LINE.
    05                    PIC X(28).
    05 O-DEPT-NO          PIC XX.
    05                    PIC X(14).
    05 O-SSN              PIC XXXBXXBXXXX.
    05                    PIC X(11).
    05 O-SALESPERSON      PIC X(20).
    05                    PIC X(11).
    05 O-CURRENT-SALES    PIC $Z,ZZ9.99.
    05                    PIC X(27).

01  STORE-FOOTING.
    05                  PIC X(83)   VALUE SPACES.
    05                  PIC X(22)   VALUE "TOTAL SALES FOR STORE ".
    05 O-STORE-NO       PIC XX.
    05                  PIC X(3)    VALUE " : ".
    05 O-STORE-SALES    PIC $ZZZ,ZZ9.99-.
    05                  PIC XX      VALUE " *".
    05                  PIC X(9)    VALUE SPACES.

01  COMPANY-FOOTING.
    05                    PIC X(86) VALUE SPACES.
    05                    PIC X(22) VALUE "TOTAL COMPANY SALES : ".
    05 O-COMPANY-SALES    PIC $Z,ZZZ,ZZ9.99-.
    05                    PIC X(3)  VALUE " **".
    05                    PIC X(8)  VALUE SPACES.
```

```
 01  END-LINE.
     05 PIC X(55)  VALUE SPACES.
     05 PIC X(23)  VALUE "***  END OF REPORT  ***".
     05 PIC X(55)  VALUE SPACES.

 PROCEDURE DIVISION.

 0-MAIN-CONTROL SECTION.

 0100-RUN-SORT.
     SORT SORT-FILE
         ON ASCENDING S-STORE-NO
         ON DESCENDING S-CURRENT-SALES
         ON ASCENDING KEY S-SALESPERSON
         ON ASCENDING KEY S-SSN
         USING NY-SALES-FILE
               BOS-SALES-FILE
               CHI-SALES-FILE
               SEA-SALES-FILE
         OUTPUT PROCEDURE IS 1-PREPARE-REPORT.
     STOP RUN.

******************************************************************
*                                                                *
*   THE OUTPUT PROCEDURE BEGINS HERE.                            *
*                                                                *
******************************************************************

 1-PREPARE-REPORT SECTION.

 1100-PRODUCE-SALES-REPORT.
     PERFORM 1200-START-UP.
     PERFORM 1210-PROCESS-SALES-RECORD
         UNTIL NO-MORE-SORT-RECORDS.
     PERFORM 1220-FINISH-UP.
     GO TO 1999-EXIT-OUTPUT-SECTION.

 1200-START-UP.
     OPEN OUTPUT SALES-REPORT.
     PERFORM 1300-INITIALIZE-ITEMS.
     PERFORM 1310-RETURN-SORT-RECORD.
     PERFORM 1600-WRITE-PAGE-HEADING.

 1210-PROCESS-SALES-RECORD.
     PERFORM 1320-CHECK-FOR-NEW-STORE.
     PERFORM 1330-UPDATE-STORE ACCUMULATOR.
     PERFORM 1340-PREPARE-SALES-LINE.
     PERFORM 1310-RETURN-SORT-RECORD.

 1220-FINISH-UP.
     PERFORM 1350-PREPARE-COMPANY-FOOTING.
     WRITE PRINTLINE FROM END-LINE
         AFTER ADVANCING 5 LINES.
     CLOSE SALES-REPORT.

 1300-INITIALIZE-ITEMS.
     ACCEPT WS-REPORT-DATE FROM DATE.
     MOVE WS-REPORT-DATE TO O-REPORT-DATE.
     SET THERE-IS-A-SORT-RECORD TO TRUE.
     INITIALIZE WS-COMPANY-ACCUMULATOR
                WS-PAGE-NO.
     MOVE SPACES TO SALES-LINE.

 1310-RETURN-SORT-RECORD.
     RETURN SORT-FILE RECORD
         AT END
             SET NO-MORE-SORT-RECORDS TO TRUE.

 1320-CHECK-FOR-NEW-STORE.
     IF S-STORE-NO = WS-STORE-CONTROL
         NEXT SENTENCE
     ELSE
         PERFORM 1400-PREPARE-STORE-FOOTING.

 1330-UPDATE-STORE-ACCUMULATOR.
     ADD S-CURRENT-SALES TO WS-STORE-ACCUMULATOR.

 1340-PREPARE-SALES-LINE.
     MOVE S-DEPT-NO TO O-DEPT-NO.
     MOVE S-SSN TO O-SSN.
     MOVE S-SALESPERSON TO O-SALESPERSON.
     MOVE S-CURRENT-SALES TO O-CURRENT-SALES.
     WRITE PRINTLINE FROM SALES-LINE
         AFTER ADVANCING WS-PROPER-SPACING.
     MOVE 1 TO WS-PROPER-SPACING.
```

■ **Figure 10.35** continued

```
1350-PREPARE-COMPANY-FOOTING.
    PERFORM 1400-PREPARE-STORE-FOOTING.
    MOVE WS-COMPANY-ACCUMULATOR TO O-COMPANY-SALES.
    WRITE PRINTLINE FROM COMPANY-FOOTING
        AFTER ADVANCING 3 LINES.

1400-PREPARE-STORE-FOOTING.
    MOVE WS-STORE-CONTROL TO O-STORE-NO.
    ADD WS-STORE-ACCUMULATOR TO
    WS-COMPANY-ACCUMULATOR.
    MOVE WS-STORE-ACCUMULATOR TO O-STORE-SALES.
    WRITE PRINTLINE FROM STORE-FOOTING
        AFTER ADVANCING 3 LINES.
    ADD 1 TO WS-STORES-PER-PAGE-CTR.
    IF THERE-IS-A-SORT-RECORD
        PERFORM 1500-CHECK-STORE-CTR
    END-IF.

1500-CHECK-STORE-CTR.
    IF WS-STORES-PER-PAGE-CTR >= WS-STORES-PER-PAGE-LIMIT
        PERFORM 1600-WRITE-PAGE-HEADING
    ELSE
        PERFORM 1700-WRITE-STORE-HEADING.

1600-WRITE-PAGE-HEADING.
    ADD 1 TO WS-PAGE-NO.
    MOVE WS-PAGE-NO TO O-PAGE-NO.
    WRITE PRINTLINE FROM TOP-LINE
        AFTER ADVANCING PAGE.
    WRITE PRINTLINE FROM COMPANY-NAME
        AFTER ADVANCING 1 LINE.
    WRITE PRINTLINE FROM REPORT-NAME
        AFTER ADVANCING 3 LINES.
    INITIALIZE WS-STORES-PER-PAGE-CTR.
    PERFORM 1700-WRITE-STORE-HEADING.

1700-WRITE-STORE-HEADING.
    MOVE S-STORE-NO TO WS-STORE-CONTROL.
    EVALUATE S-STORE-NO
        WHEN "10"  MOVE "10 - NEW YORK" TO O-STORE-ID
        WHEN "20"  MOVE "20 - BOSTON" TO O-STORE-ID
        WHEN "30"  MOVE "30 - CHICAGO" TO O-STORE-ID
        WHEN "40"  MOVE "40 - SEATTLE" TO O-STORE-ID
        WHEN OTHER
            DISPLAY " ERROR IN STORE NO. FOR " S-SALESPERSON.
    WRITE PRINTLINE FROM STORE-HEADING-1
        AFTER ADVANCING 3 LINES.
    WRITE PRINTLINE FROM STORE-HEADING-2
        AFTER ADVANCING 3 LINES.
    MOVE 2 TO WS-PROPER-SPACING.
    INITIALIZE WS-STORE-ACCUMULATOR.

1999-EXIT-OUTPUT-SECTION.
    EXIT.
```

The SORT Statement Rules

The complete format for the SORT statement is contained in Figure 10.5. The rules that apply to this statement are listed below.

Rules Governing Use of the SORT Statement

1. In this format,
   - **a.** File-name-1 is the name given to the sort file. This file must be described in a sort file description entry in the FILE SECTION of the DATA DIVISION. The sort file description entry begins with SD coded in Area A.
   - **b.** Data-name-1 is the name of a data item in a record of the sort file. It is referred to as a sort key.
   - **c.** Alphabet-name-1 is an alphabet-name defined in the SPECIAL-NAMES paragraph of the CONFIGURATION SECTION of the ENVIRONMENT DIVISION.
   - **d.** File-name-2 is the name of an input file. It must be described in a file description (FD) entry in the FILE SECTION of the DATA DIVISION.
   - **e.** Procedure-name-1 is the name of the first (or only) section specified in the INPUT PROCEDURE clause.
   - **f.** Procedure-name-2 is the name of the last section in the range of the INPUT PROCEDURE.

Figure 10.36 The report produced by the program in Figure 10.35

```
REPORT DATE:  93/10/22                                                                    PAGE  1
                                        THE SPORTSMAN

                                    SALES ANALYSIS REPORT

         STORE:   10 - NEW YORK

                   DEPT NO.         SALESPERSON SSN          SALESPERSON NAME          CURRENT SALES

                      02              218 54 6010          BROWN, RAYMOND                 $3,022.55
                      04              556 23 4035          CRANE, JOHN                    $2,870.50
                      08              551 16 4090          KELLY, PATRICK                 $1,625.00
                      04              696 99 6055          DANIELS, JULIA                 $1,620.00
                      04              251 34 2020          FARMER, SUSAN                  $1,620.00
                      02              214 36 5025          ALLEN, ROBERT                  $1,500.00
                      06              521 24 4005          DWYER, TERRENCE                $1,425.80
                      04              667 45 1060          HARRISON, LILY                 $1,425.80
                      08              482 13 1015          JANKOWSKI, STANLEY             $1,350.00
                      06              644 35 3075          MANNING, ELIZABETH             $1,350.00
                      02              642 75 4040          MAIN, CHARLES                  $1,280.00
                      04              263 45 2070          FEINGOLD, HAROLD               $1,250.50
                      08              599 23 1085          LANGFORD, WAYNE                $1,150.50
                      08              521 16 6100          PRINGLY, ANNE                  $1,098.05
                      06              564 45 1045          EDWARDS, PETER                 $1,080.50
                      02              315 46 3030          FOGARTY, JANICE                $1,050.50
                      04              685 26 4065          CARLSON, HOPE                  $   900.00
                      02              641 27 5050          BRANNIGAN, NICOLE              $   875.25
                      08              377 56 8080          HOWARD, RALPH                  $   560.50


                                                     TOTAL SALES FOR STORE 10 : $ 27,055.45   *


         STORE:   20 - BOSTON

                   DEPT NO.         SALESPERSON SSN          SALESPERSON NAME        CURRENT SALES

                      06              433 40 6075          FERNANDEZ, LOUISE              $2,000.00
                      06              571 90 4025          LEMERISE, DONALD               $1,850.50
                      06              683 30 9020          COSTELLO, JAMES                $1,670.50
                      04              360 90 2035          PENTA, ROBERT                  $1,650.25
                      06              572 49 5090          WORTHEN, MICHAEL               $1,570.00
                      08              804 23 3040          VERMETTE, GLORIA               $1,560.50
                      06              566 12 7070          FELDMAN, WALTER                $1,470.80
                      04              427 56 0010          COCHRANE, RUSSELL              $1,460.50
                      06              418 09 0015          CRAWFORD, SHIRLEY              $1,390.50
                      04              375 70 1060          QUINN, SUZANNE                 $1,320.50
                      02              480 75 5030          TALBOT, WILFRED                $1,275.80
                      04              472 84 7080          PROULX PAULINE                 $1,150.00
                      08              812 13 3085          KOSINSKI, KATHERINE            $1,125.00
                      02              509 86 2005          CORTON, LOUIS                  $1,000.00
                      02              509 18 5045          PINEAULT, NORMAN               $   980.50
                      08              762 35 5100          GOYETTE, FRANCES               $   950.00
                      04              479 21 0065          BARRESI, JOHN                  $   650.00
                      02              408 93 6050          CORDEIRO, ANTONE               $   100.50


                                                     TOTAL SALES FOR STORE 20 : $ 23,175.85   *
```

  g. File-name-3 is the name of an output file. It must be described in a file description (FD) entry in the FILE SECTION of the DATA DIVISION.
  h. Procedure-name-3 is the name of the first (or only) section specified in the OUTPUT PROCEDURE clause.
  i. Procedure-name-4 is the name of the last section in the range of the OUTPUT PROCEDURE.

2. The SORT statement may be coded anywhere in the PROCEDURE DIVISION except within an INPUT or OUTPUT PROCEDURE. That is, SORT statements must not be nested.
3. The size of the records in the sort file must accommodate the sizes of the records in both file-name-2 and file-name-3.
4. More than one sort key can be specified. Their level of significance is related strictly to the order in which they are named: The first sort key is the most significant, the last sort key is the least significant.
5. Sort keys can be qualified, but they must not be subscripted.

■ **Figure 10.36** continued

```
REPORT DATE:  93/10/22                                                                              PAGE  2
                                                  THE SPORTSMAN

                                              SALES ANALYSIS REPORT

         STORE:   30 - CHICAGO

                  DEPT NO.          SALESPERSON SSN             SALESPERSON NAME              CURRENT SALES

                     06              820 78 8914             ABALLO, NORMA                     $2,350.75
                     08              466 58 7165             BRAZ, JOAN                        $2,315.60
                     08              557 31 8974             PRATT, ROBIN                      $2,155.00
                     04              566 73 1251             ROBINSON, GILBERT                 $2,105.90
                     02              416 89 2014             BERNARD, ISIDORE                  $2,035.69
                     06              785 02 3157             DOLLARHIDE, CHRIS                 $2,015.70
                     04              745 64 5270             FURTADO, MAUREEN                  $2,015.40
                     08              487 25 1099             MELANSON, GARY                    $1,905.50
                     02              576 40 0892             KING, CHRISTOPHER                 $1,890.70
                     04              607 04 4132             CORRIGAN, ALENE                   $1,875.50
                     02              823 14 4098             MAHFUZ, IRENE                     $1,850.25
                     06              745 63 5164             LINCOURT, LORETTA                 $1,495.00
                     04              788 23 0154             DONOHUE, PHIL                     $  875.00

                                                               TOTAL SALES FOR STORE 30 : $ 24,885.99  *

         STORE:   40 - SEATTLE

                  DEPT NO.          SALESPERSON SSN             SALESPERSON NAME              CURRENT SALES

                     04              720 95 4670             VELOZO, MARIO                     $2,423.90
                     06              551 50 2546             FORTIN, EMIL                      $2,254.50
                     02              452 67 7143             BEAUDOIN, ROCKY                   $2,215.00
                     02              674 45 1231             BISBANO, HENRY                    $2,190.55
                     08              721 43 5472             JOBIN, ANTONIO                    $2,140.50
                     08              351 56 6178             TRAMONTE, ESTELLE                 $2,135.00
                     06              452 89 2153             CARDIN, FRANCIS                   $2,045.90
                     06              683 21 5467             NOTTE, LORENZO                    $2,005.00
                     02              787 85 5623             MARKLAND, MARY                    $1,987.50
                     06              574 93 0461             GALLAGHER, MICHAEL                $1,976.75
                     04              712 13 3463             PERRY, JOSEPH                     $1,945.50
                     08              490 23 4571             MILLER, RENEE                     $1,905.70
                     04              624 16 6876             PARISEAU, WILLIAM                 $1,785.00

                                                               TOTAL SALES FOR STORE 40 : $ 27,010.80 *

                                                                  TOTAL COMPANY SALES : $  102,128.09 **

                                              *** END OF REPORT ***
```

6. In determining the sequence (ASCENDING or DESCENDING) of values in the sort key fields, the system's default collating sequence is used unless the COLLATING SEQUENCE clause specifies another collating sequence.
7. The ASCENDING option causes the records to be sorted from the lowest to the highest value of the sort key.
8. The DESCENDING option causes the records to be sorted from the highest to the lowest value of the sort key.
9. If the DUPLICATES phrase is coded, it controls the order in which records with identical values for the sort keys are returned: the order corresponds to the order of file names in the USING option and/or to the order in which records were released to the sort file in the INPUT PROCEDURE. If the DUPLICATES phrase is not coded, the order in which records with identical values for the sort keys are returned is unpredictable.
10. If the INPUT PROCEDURE or OUTPUT PROCEDURE clause contains the THRU phrase, the sections belonging to the specified range must be coded contiguously. The range of an INPUT PROCEDURE must not overlap the range of an OUTPUT PROCEDURE.

11. An INPUT PROCEDURE must contain at least one RELEASE statement to send records to the sort file.
12. An OUTPUT PROCEDURE must contain at least one RETURN statement to retrieve records from the sort file.
13. During execution of a SORT statement, while control is within an INPUT PROCEDURE or an OUTPUT PROCEDURE, control may temporarily leave the procedure to perform paragraphs in another section, provided the section is not under the control of the SORT statement. However, the programmer must assure that control properly exits the INPUT PROCEDURE or OUTPUT PROCEDURE to return to the SORT statement. (This is a new feature in COBOL '85.)
14. Control can be transferred into the INPUT PROCEDURE or OUTPUT PROCEDURE by executing PERFORM statements in other paragraphs, provided these paragraphs are not under the control of the SORT statement. (This is a new feature in COBOL '85.)
15. If a SORT statement contains an INPUT PROCEDURE, all the statements in the range of the procedure are executed before the records of the sort file are sorted.
16. If a SORT statement contains an OUTPUT PROCEDURE, the records in the sort file are sorted before control is passed to the first statement in the range of the procedure. When the last statement in the range is executed, control leaves the SORT statement and passes on to the next statement.
17. If the USING phrase is used, all the records of the input file(s) are released to the sort file. The SORT statement implicitly opens an input file, reads all of its records sequentially into the sort file until the AT END condition occurs, and then it implicitly closes the input file.
18. If the GIVING phrase is used, all the records in the sort file are returned in the prescribed sequence to each output file. The SORT statement implicitly opens each output file, writes the records of the sort file sequentially, and implicitly closes each output file when the AT END condition occurs for the sort file.
19. The GIVING phrase can specify more than one output file. (This is a new feature in COBOL '85.)
20. The sort file is not opened or closed by the programmer.

The MERGE Statement

The MERGE statement is provided by the COBOL language for the purpose of merging records from two or more files into a single merge file. It is necessary that the records in the input files be identically sequenced, that is, sorted on the basis of the same keys before being made available as input files to the merge routine. The keys that are used to presort the records of each file are the ones specified as merge keys in the MERGE statement itself.

Once the records from all the input files have been merged on the basis of the merge keys, then they can be written directly by the merge routine to one or more output files by naming the files in the GIVING phrase, or the programmer can code specific processing steps in the OUTPUT PROCEDURE section. A record of the merge file is retrieved by the execution of a RETURN statement.

The format of the MERGE statement is shown in Figure 10.37.

Figure 10.37 The MERGE statement format

```
MERGE file-name-1
    {ON {ASCENDING } KEY {date-name-1} . . . } . . .
        {DESCENDING}
    [COLLATING SEQUENCE IS alphabet-name-1]
    USING file-name-2 {file-name-3} . . .
    {GIVING {file-name-4} . . .                                                   }
    {OUTPUT PROCEDURE IS procedure-name-1 [{THRU   } procedure-name-2]}
                                           {THROUGH}
```

Note that the MERGE statement is very similar to the SORT statement except for the absence of an INPUT PROCEDURE and the DUPLICATES phrase. Since there is no INPUT PROCEDURE option, the records of the input files cannot be processed individually under the control of the programmer before they are merged into a single file. This is a rather severe restriction, and it tends to minimize the usefulness of the statement. This is particularly true since if two or more files are used as input files in a SORT statement, the sort routine sorts the records and also merges them into a single file. Furthermore, recall that if preprocessing of the input files is needed, the INPUT PROCEDURE of the SORT statement allows that as well. In other words, whatever has to be accomplished by a MERGE statement can also be accomplished with a greater degree of flexibility with a SORT statement.

Nonetheless, the MERGE statement is presented here because it is usually associated with the SORT statement. Furthermore, all the rules that have been listed for the SORT statement also apply to the MERGE statement, except for the ones related to an INPUT PROCEDURE and the DUPLICATES option.

A Merge Problem

The national office of the Sportsman Company has requested and received sales files for the current period from its major stores. (The files are shown in Figure 10.38 [DD/CD:VICIOSP6.DTI-DT4].) The individual files are sorted from highest to lowest sales, and in the case of equal sales, in alphabetic order by salesperson name, and in the case of identical names, in ascending order of their Social Security numbers. The data processing department must merge all the files and produce a simple report listing all the salespersons' records in descending order of sales amounts. The format of the report is shown in Figure 10.39. At most 30 lines are to be printed on any one page. Note that the program must print the total of the sales displayed on each page of the report, and on the last page, the program must also print the total sales for the company.

A Brief Analysis of the Problem

Note that in each input file of Figure 10.38, the records are arranged in descending order of sales. When sales are equal, those records are sequenced in alphabetic order of salesperson names. The three sorting keys are

1. Major key: sales, in descending order
2. Intermediate key: names, in alphabetic order
3. Minor key: Social Security number, in ascending order

The minor key is used only if two or more people have the same sales and the same name. A careful examination of the files reveals that the minor key is not used in this program.

The merge routine will assemble the four files into a single file. Then, control must be sent to the OUTPUT PROCEDURE where the required report will be generated. After printing the report headers, the program must retrieve the merged records one at a time for processing. The sales must be accumulated into two accumulators: one to accumulate the sales listed on a page, and the other to accumulate the sales for the company as a whole. The subtotaling process could be used for both accumulators, but in this program, it will be used to accumulate the page total only, and the rolling-forward process will be used to accumulate the company total. Hence, as a record is processed, its sales are added to the page accumulator, and whenever a page break occurs, the page total is rolled forward into the company accumulator.

Because the system flowchart is very similar to the one in Figure 10.31, it is not repeated here. The structure chart is shown in Figure 10.40, the program pseudocode is in Figure 10.41, and the program flowchart is in Figure 10.42.

■ **Figure 10.38** The four sales files for the merge problem

1. BOSTON File

```
2006433406075FERNANDEZ, LOUISE      200000
2006571904025LEMERISE, DONALD       185050
2006683309020COSTELLO, JAMES        167050
2004360902035PENTA, ROBERT          165025
2006572495090WORTHEN, MICHAEL       157000
2008804233040VERMETTE, GLORIA       156050
2006566127070FELDMAN, WALTER        147080
2004427560010COCHRANE, RUSSELL      146050
2006418090015CRAWFORD, SHIRLEY      139050
2004375701060QUINN, SUZANNE         132050
2002480755030TALBOT, WILFRED        127580
2004472847080PROULX, PAULINE        115000
2008812133085KOSINSKI, KATHERINE    112500
2002509862005CORTON, LOUIS          100000
2002509185045PINEAULT, NORMAN       098050
2008762355100GOYETTE, FRANCES       095000
2004479210065BARRESI, JOHN          065000
2002408936050CORDEIRO, ANTONE       010050
```

2. NEW YORK File

```
1002218546010BROWN, RAYMOND         302255
1004556234035CRANE, JOHN            287050
1008551164090KELLY, PATRICK         162500
1004696996055DANIELS, JULIA         162000
1004251342020FARMER, SUSAN          162000
1002214365025ALLEN, ROBERT          150000
1006521244005DWYER, TERRENCE        142580
1004667451060HARRISON, LILY         142580
1008482131015JANKOWSKI, STANLEY     135000
1006644353075MANNING, ELIZABETH     135000
1002642754040MAIN, CHARLES          128000
1004263452070FEINGOLD, HAROLD       125050
1008599231085LANGFORD, WAYNE        115050
1008521166100PRINGLY, ANNE          109805
1006564451045EDWARDS, PETER         108050
1002315463060FOGARTY, JANICE        105050
1004685264065CARLSON, HOPE          090000
1002641275050BRANNIGAN, NICOLE      087525
1008377568080HOWARD, RALPH          056050
```

3. CHICAGO File

```
3006820788914ABALLO, NORMA          235075
3008466587165BRAZ, JOAN             231560
3008557318974PRATT, ROBIN           215500
3004566731251ROBINSON, GILBERT      210590
3002416892014BERNARD, ISIDORE       203569
3006785023157DOLLARHIDE, CHRIS      201570
3004745645270FURTADO, MAUREEN       201540
3008487251099MELANSON, GARY         190550
3002576400892KING, CHRISTOPHER      189070
3004607044132CORRIGAN, ALENE        187550
3002823144098MAHFUZ, IRENE          185025
3006745635164LINCOURT, LORETTA      149500
3004788230154DONOHUE, PHIL          087500
```

4. SEATTLE File

```
4004720954670VELOZO, MARIO          242390
4006551502546FORTIN, EMIL           225450
1002452677143BEAUDOIN, ROCKY        221500
4002674451231BISBANO, HENRY         219055
4008721435472JOBIN, ANTONIO         214050
4008351566178TRAMONTE, ESTELLE      213500
4006452892153CARDIN, FRANCIS        204590
4006683215467NOTTE, LORENZO         200500
4002787855623MARKLAND, MARY         198750
4006574930461GALLAGHER, MICHAEL     197675
4004712133463PERRY, JOSEPH          194550
4008490234571MILLER, RENEE          190570
4004624166876PARISEAU, WILLIAM      178500
```

■ **Figure 10.39** The printer spacing chart for the merge problem

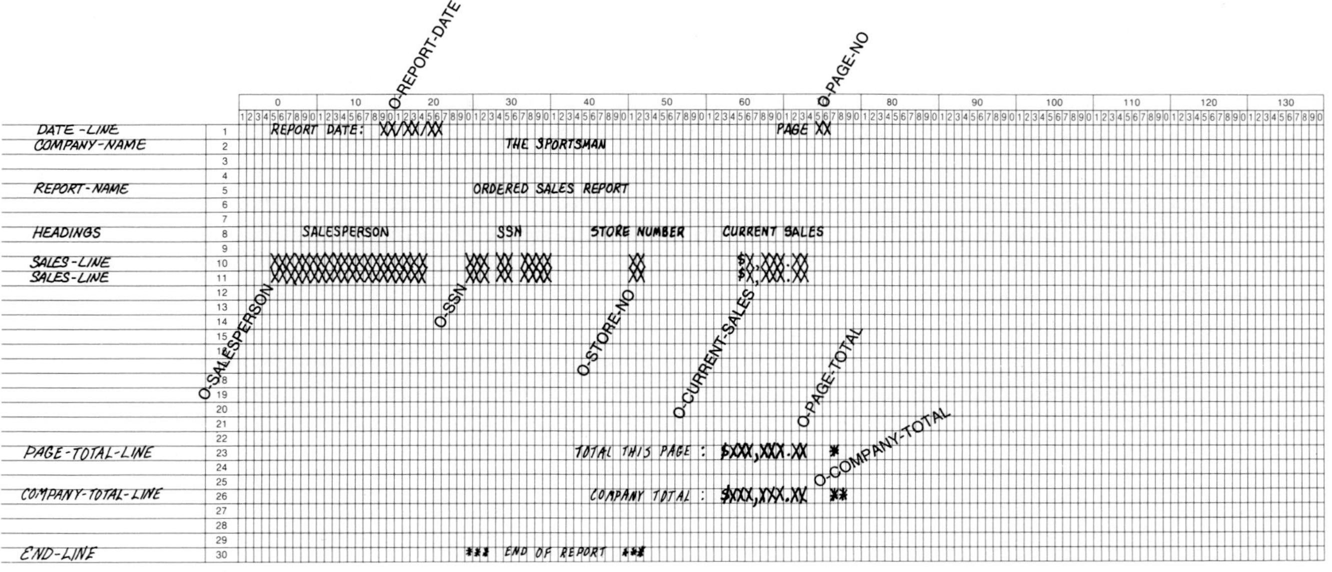

Figure 10.40 Structure chart for the merge problem

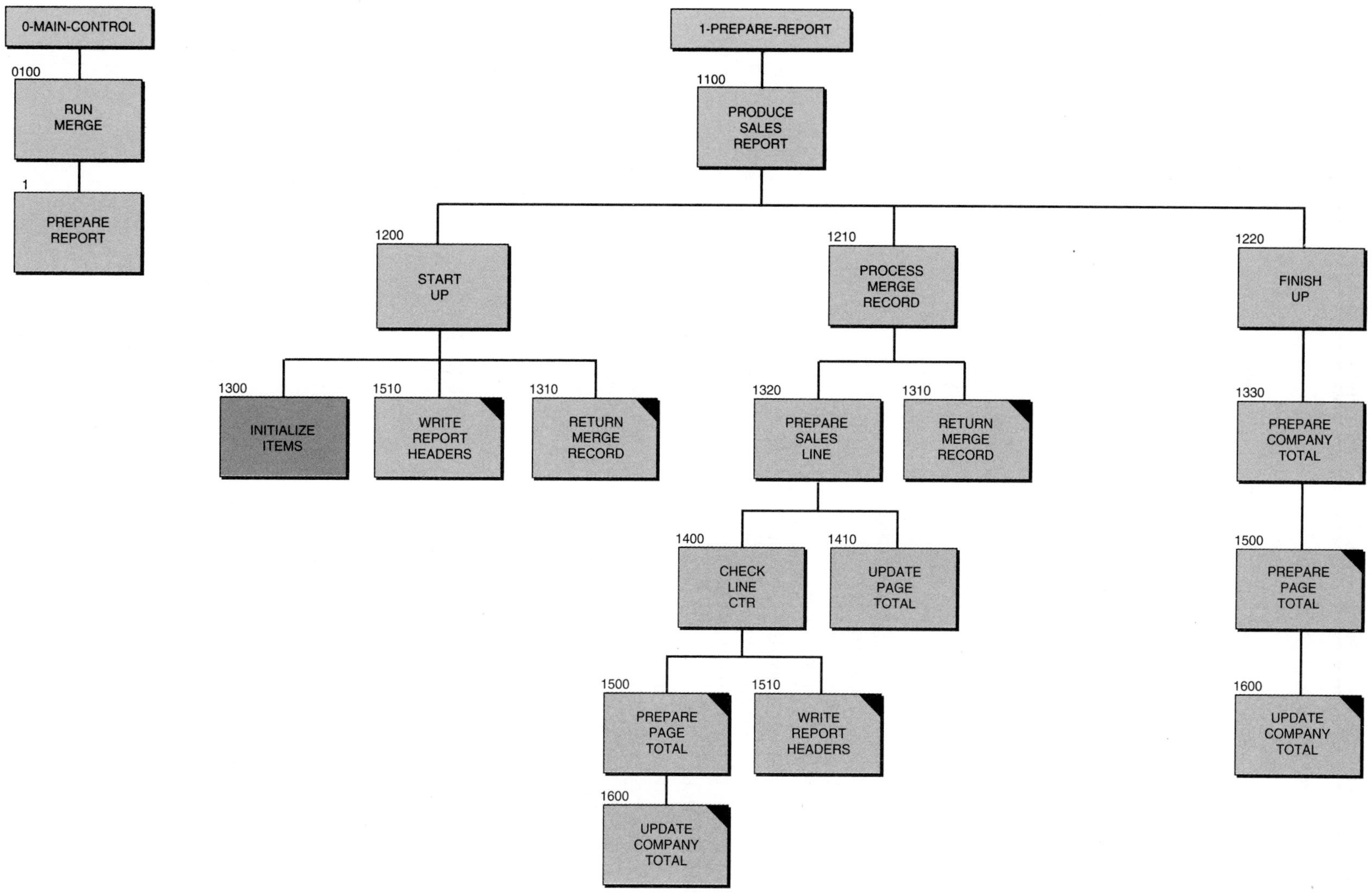

Figure 10.41 Program pseudocode for the merge problem

0-Main-Control Section.

0100-Run-Merge.

1. Read all records of the four input files into the Merge-file.
2. Merge the records of Merge-File using:
   major key: current sales in descending order
   intermediate key: names in alphabetic order
   minor key: Social Security numbers in ascending order.
3. Perform the procedure 1-Prepare-Report.
4. Stop the run.

1-Prepare-Report Section.

1100-Produce-Sales-Report.

1. Perform 1200-Start-Up.
2. Perform 1210-Process-Merge-Record until no more merge records.
3. Perform 1220-Finish-Up.
4. Exit from the output procedure.

1200-Start-Up.

1. Open the output file Ordered-Sales-Report.
2. Perform 1300-Initialize-Items.
3. Perform 1510-Write-Report-Headers.
4. Perform 1310-Return-Merge-Record.

1210-Process-Merge-Record.

1. Perform 1320-Prepare-Sales-Line.
2. Perform 1310-Return-Merge-Record.

1220-Finish-Up.

1. Perform 1330-Prepare-Company-Total.
2. Move the record End-Line to the output area Printline.
3. After advancing 4 lines, write the output record Printline.
4. Close the file Ordered-Sales-Report.

1300-Initialize-Items.

1. Obtain the date from the system.
2. Move the date to Date-Line.
3. Inspect Date-Line date and replace "/" by "-".
4. Set the end-of-file flag WS-MORE-MERGE-RECORDS to "YES".
5. Initialize company-total and page-number.
6. Clear the record area Sales-Line.

1310-Return-Merge-Record.

1. Return (read) a Merge-File record.
2. Test for end-of-file record;
   if EOF record reached, set WS-MORE-MERGE-RECORDS to "NO ".

1320-Prepare-Sales-Line.

1. Move Merge-Record salesperson to Sales-Line salesperson.
2. Move Merge-Record SSN to Sales-Line SSN.
3. Move Merge-Record current-sales to Sales-Line current-sales.
4. Perform 1400-Check-Line-Ctr.
5. Perform 1410-Update-Page-Total.
6. Move the record Sales-Line to the output area Printline.
7. After advancing proper-spacing, write the output record Printline.
8. Set proper-spacing to 1.
9. Add 1 to line-counter.

1330-Prepare-Company-Total.

1. Perform 1500-Prepare-Page-Total.
2. Move company-total to Company-Total-Line company-total.
3. Move the record Company-Total-Line to the output area Printline.
4. After advancing 3 lines, write the output record Printline.

1400-Check-Line-Ctr.

1. If line-counter is greater than or equal to line-limit,
   then, perform 1500-Prepare-Page-Total and
   perform 1510-Write-Report-Headers.

1410-Update-Page-Total.

1. Add current-sales to page-total.

1500-Prepare-Page-Total.

1. Perform 1600-Update-Company-Total.
2. Move page-total to Page-Total-Line page-total.
3. Move the record Page-Total-Line to the output area Printline.
4. After advancing 3 lines, write the output record Printline.

1510-Write-Report-Headers.

1. Add 1 to page-number.
2. Move page-number to Date-Line page-number.
3. Move the record Date-Line to the output area Printline.
4. After advancing to a new page, write the output record Printline.
5. Move the record Company-Name to the output area Printline.
6. After advancing 1 line, write the output record Printline.
7. Move the record Report-Name to the output area Printline.
8. After advancing 3 lines, write the output record Printline.
9. Move the record Headings to the output area Printline.
10. After advancing 3 lines, write the output record Printline.
11. Move 2 to proper-spacing.
12. Initialize page-total and line-counter.

1600-Update-Company-Total.

1. Add page-total to Company-Total-Line company-total.

Figure 10.42 Program flowchart for the merge problem

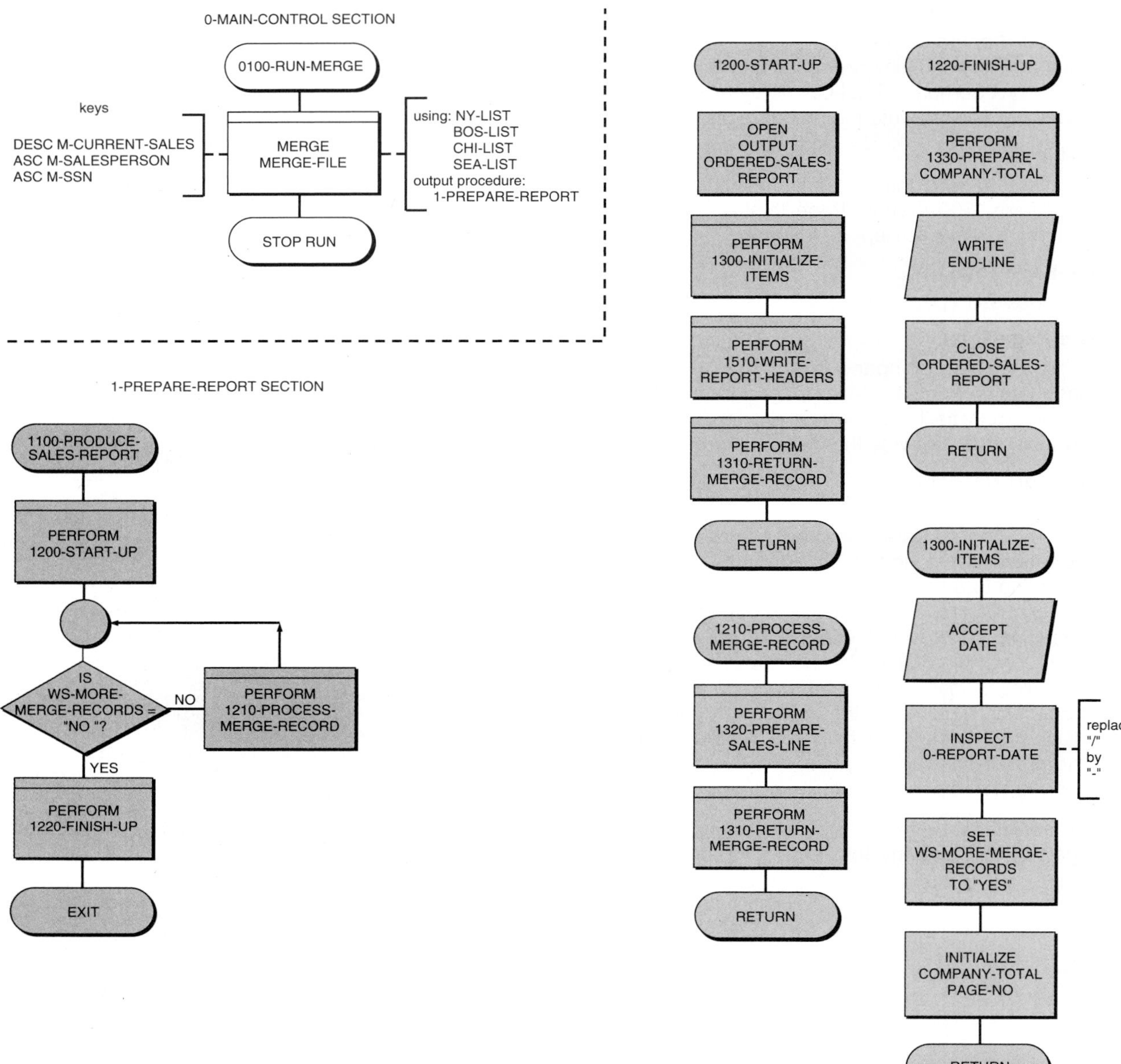

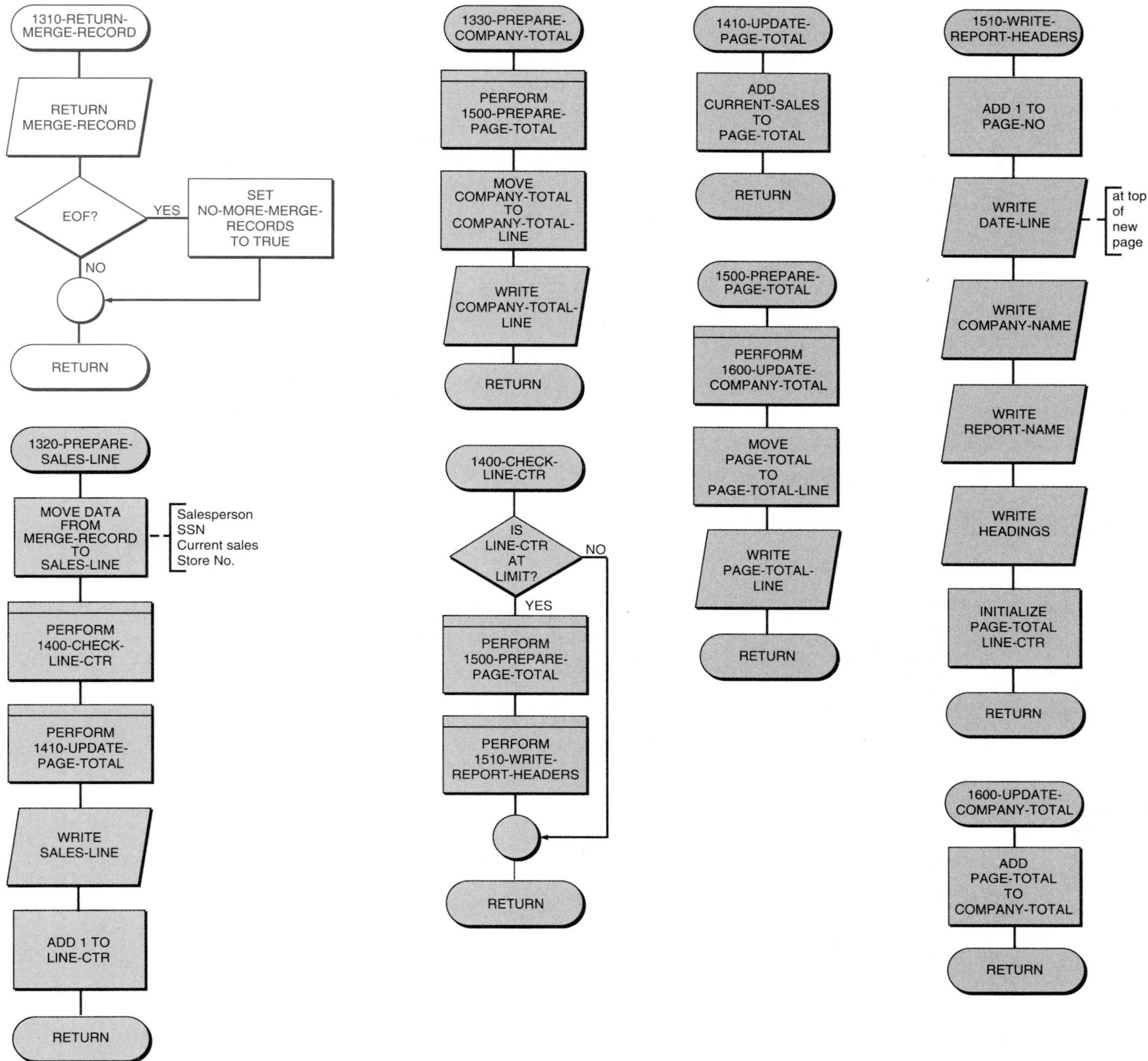

The Merge Program

The program in Figure 10.43 produces the report shown in Figure 10.44. Examine the MERGE statement coded in the primary paragraph of the section 0-MAIN-CONTROL. Note the four input files specified in the USING phrase and the corresponding SELECT statements in the FILE-CONTROL paragraph. The FD paragraph for each input file defines each record as an elementary item, since individual fields of the input records are not referenced anywhere in the program. However, the internal organization of the data fields within the records of each input file must be identical to the one specified for the records of the MERGE-FILE. Obviously, the data fields of MERGE-RECORD must be given names, since they are specified as the merge keys and are also referenced as the source fields during the preparation of the detail lines that must be printed on the report.

■ **Figure 10.43** The COBOL program for the merge problem

```
 IDENTIFICATION DIVISION.

 PROGRAM-ID.      MERGE-PROG-6.

*****************************************************************
*                                                               *
*   AUTHOR.           PAQUETTE.                                 *
*   DATE WRITTEN.     OCTOBER 1993.                             *
*                                                               *
*   THIS PROGRAM ILLUSTRATES THE USE OF THE MERGE STATEMENT.    *
*   IT MERGES FOUR FILES THAT HAVE BEEN PRESORTED IN DESCENDING *
*   ORDER OF CURRENT SALES AMOUNTS, ALPHABETICALLY IF SALES ARE *
*   EQUAL AND IN ASCENDING ORDER OF SOCIAL SECURITY NUMBERS IF  *
*   NAMES ARE IDENTICAL.                                        *
*                                                               *
*   ITS PURPOSE IS TO PRODUCE AN ORDERED SALES REPORT.  THE     *
*   MERGE STATEMENT USES THE OUTPUT PROCEDURE CLAUSE TO NAME THE *
*   SECTION THAT CONTROLS THE PRINTING OF THE REPORT.           *
*                                                               *
*   THE REPORT DISPLAYS THE TOTAL SALES PRINTED ON EACH PAGE AS *
*   WELL AS THE COMPANY TOTAL AT THE END OF THE REPORT.         *
*                                                               *
*****************************************************************

 ENVIRONMENT DIVISION.

 CONFIGURATION SECTION.

 SOURCE-COMPUTER.   VAX-VMS-8650.
 OBJECT-COMPUTER.   VAX-VMS-8650.

 INPUT-OUTPUT SECTION.

 FILE-CONTROL.
     SELECT NY-LIST               ASSIGN TO NYFILE.
     SELECT BOS-LIST              ASSIGN TO BOSFILE.
     SELECT CHI-LIST              ASSIGN TO CHIFILE.
     SELECT SEA-LIST              ASSIGN TO SEAFILE.
     SELECT MERGE-FILE            ASSIGN TO DISK10.
     SELECT ORDERED-SALES-REPORT  ASSIGN TO COB$OUTPUT.

 DATA DIVISION.

 FILE SECTION.

 FD  NY-LIST
     RECORD CONTAINS 39 CHARACTERS.

 01  NY-RECORD    PIC X(39).

 FD  BOS-LIST
     RECORD CONTAINS 39 CHARACTERS.

 01  BOS-RECORD   PIC X(39).

 FD  CHI-LIST
     RECORD CONTAINS 39 CHARACTERS.

 01  CHI-RECORD   PIC X(39).

 FD  SEA-LIST
     RECORD CONTAINS 39 CHARACTERS.

 01  SEA-RECORD   PIC X(39).

 SD  MERGE-FILE
     RECORD CONTAINS 39 CHARACTERS.

 01  MERGE-RECORD.
     05 M-STORE-NO         PIC X(2).
     05                    PIC X(2).
     05 M-SSN              PIC X(9).
     05 M-SALESPERSON      PIC X(20).
     05 M-CURRENT-SALES    PIC 9999V99.

 FD  ORDERED-SALES-REPORT
     RECORD CONTAINS 80 CHARACTERS.

 01  PRINTLINE             PIC X(80).

 WORKING-STORAGE SECTION.
```

```
01  PROGRAM-CONTROLS.
    05 WS-MORE-MERGE-RECORDS      PIC XXX.
       88 THERE-IS-A-MERGE-RECORD            VALUE "YES".
       88 NO-MORE-MERGE-RECORDS              VALUE "NO ".
    05 WS-REPORT-DATE             PIC X(6).
    05 WS-PROPER-SPACING          PIC 9.
    05 WS-LINE-CTR                PIC S99.
       88 PAGE-IS-FULL                       VALUE +30.
    05 WS-LINE-LIMIT              PIC 99.    VALUE 30.
    05 WS-PAGE-NO                 PIC 99.

01  PROGRAM-ACCUMULATORS.
    05 WS-PAGE-TOTAL              PIC S9(6)V99.
    05 WS-COMPANY-TOTAL           PIC S9(6)V99.

01  REPORT-HEADERS.

    05 DATE-LINE.
       10                PIC X(4)  VALUE SPACES.
       10                PIC X(14) VALUE "REPORT DATE:  ".
       10 O-REPORT-DATE  PIC XX/XX/XX.
       10                PIC X(43) VALUE SPACES.
       10                PIC X(5)  VALUE "PAGE ".
       10 O-PAGE-NO      PIC Z9.
       10                PIC X(4)  VALUE SPACES.

    05 COMPANY-NAME.
       10 PIC X(34) VALUE SPACES.
       10 PIC X(13) VALUE "THE SPORTSMAN".
       10 PIC X(33) VALUE SPACES.

    05 REPORT-NAME.
       10 PIC X(30) VALUE SPACES.
       10 PIC X(20) VALUE "ORDERED SALES REPORT".
       10 PIC X(30) VALUE SPACES.

    05 HEADINGS.
       10 PIC X(8)  VALUE SPACES.
       10 PIC X(11) VALUE "SALESPERSON".
       10 PIC X(14) VALUE SPACES.
       10 PIC X(3)  VALUE "SSN".
       10 PIC X(9)  VALUE SPACES.
       10 PIC X(12) VALUE "STORE NUMBER".
       10 PIC X(5)  VALUE SPACES.
       10 PIC X(13) VALUE "CURRENT SALES".
       10 PIC X(5)  VALUE SPACES.

01  SALES-LINE.
    05                  PIC X(4).
    05 O-SALESPERSON    PIC X(20).
    05                  PIC X(5).
    05 O-SSN            PIC XXXBXXBXXXX.
    05                  PIC X(10).
    05 O-STORE-NO       PIC XX.
    05                  PIC X(12).
    05 O-CURRENT-SALES  PIC $Z,ZZ9.99-.
    05                  PIC X(6).

01  PAGE-TOTAL-LINE.
    05                  PIC X(43)   VALUE SPACES.
    05                  PIC X(19)   VALUE "TOTAL THIS PAGE : ".
    05 O-PAGE-TOTAL     PIC $ZZZ,ZZ9.99-.
    05                  PIC X(3)    VALUE "  *".
    05                  PIC X(3)    VALUE SPACES.

01  COMPANY-TOTAL-LINE.
    05                  PIC X(45)   VALUE SPACES.
    05                  PIC X(17)   VALUE "COMPANY TOTAL :  ".
    05 O-COMPANY-TOTAL  PIC $ZZZ,ZZ9.99-.
    05                  PIC X(4)    VALUE "  **".
    05                  PIC X(2)    VALUE SPACES.

01  END-LINE.
    05 PIC X(29) VALUE SPACES.
    05 PIC X(23) VALUE "***  END OF REPORT  ***".
    05 PIC X(28) VALUE SPACES.

PROCEDURE DIVISION.

O-MAIN-CONTROL SECTION.
```

```
 0100-RUN-MERGE.
     MERGE MERGE-FILE
         ON DESCENDING KEY M-CURRENT-SALES
         ON ASCENDING KEY M-SALESPERSON
         ON ASCENDING KEY M-SSN
         USING NY-LIST
               BOS-LIST
               CHI-LIST
               SEA-LIST
         OUTPUT PROCEDURE IS 1-PREPARE-REPORT.
     STOP RUN.

*****************************************************************
*                                                               *
*   THE OUTPUT PROCEDURE BEGINS HERE.                           *
*                                                               *
*****************************************************************

 1-PREPARE-REPORT SECTION.

 1100-PRODUCE-SALES-REPORT.
     PERFORM 1200-START-UP.
     PERFORM 1210-PROCESS-MERGE-RECORD
         UNTIL NO-MORE-MERGE-RECORDS.
     PERFORM 1220-FINISH-UP.
     GO TO 1999-EXIT-OUTPUT-SECTION.

 1200-START-UP.
     OPEN OUTPUT ORDERED-SALES-REPORT.
     PERFORM 1300-INITIALIZE-ITEMS.
     PERFORM 1510-WRITE-REPORT-HEADERS.
     PERFORM 1310-RETURN-MERGE-RECORD.

 1210-PROCESS-MERGE-RECORD.
     PERFORM 1320-PREPARE-SALES-LINE.
     PERFORM 1310-RETURN-MERGE-RECORD.

 1220-FINISH-UP.
     PERFORM 1330-PREPARE-COMPANY-TOTAL.
     WRITE PRINTLINE FROM END-LINE
         AFTER ADVANCING 4 LINES.
     CLOSE ORDERED-SALES-REPORT.

 1300-INITIALIZE-ITEMS.
     ACCEPT WS-REPORT-DATE FROM DATE.
     MOVE WS-REPORT-DATE TO O-REPORT-DATE.
     INSPECT O-REPORT-DATE REPLACING ALL "/" BY "-".
     MOVE "YES" TO WS-MORE-MERGE-RECORDS.
     INITIALIZE WS-COMPANY-TOTAL
                WS-PAGE-NO.
     MOVE SPACES TO SALES-LINE.

 1310-RETURN-MERGE-RECORD.
     RETURN MERGE-FILE RECORD
         AT END
             SET NO-MORE-MERGE-RECORDS TO TRUE.

 1320-PREPARE-SALES-LINE.
     MOVE M-SALESPERSON TO O-SALESPERSON.
     MOVE M-SSN TO O-SSN.
     MOVE M-CURRENT-SALES TO O-CURRENT-SALES.
     MOVE M-STORE-NO TO O-STORE-NO.
     PERFORM 1400-CHECK-LINE-CTR.
     PERFORM 1410-UPDATE-PAGE-TOTAL.
     WRITE PRINTLINE FROM SALES-LINE
         AFTER ADVANCING WS-PROPER-SPACING.
     MOVE 1 TO WS-PROPER-SPACING.
     ADD 1 TO WS-LINE-CTR.

 1330-PREPARE-COMPANY-TOTAL.
     PERFORM 1500-PREPARE-PAGE-TOTAL.
     MOVE WS-COMPANY-TOTAL TO O-COMPANY-TOTAL.
     WRITE PRINTLINE FROM COMPANY-TOTAL-LINE
         AFTER ADVANCING 3 LINES.

 1400-CHECK-LINE-CTR.
     IF WS-LINE-CTR >= WS-LINE-LIMIT
         PERFORM 1500-PREPARE-PAGE-TOTAL
         PERFORM 1510-WRITE-REPORT-HEADERS
     END-IF.

 1410-UPDATE-PAGE-TOTAL.
     ADD M-CURRENT-SALES TO WS-PAGE-TOTAL.
```

Figure 10.43 continued

```
1500-PREPARE-PAGE-TOTAL.
    PERFORM 1600-UPDATE-COMPANY-TOTAL.
    MOVE WS-PAGE-TOTAL TO O-PAGE-TOTAL.
    WRITE PRINTLINE FROM PAGE-TOTAL-LINE
        AFTER ADVANCING 3 LINES.

1510-WRITE-REPORT-HEADERS.
    ADD 1 TO WS-PAGE-NO.
    MOVE WS-PAGE-NO TO O-PAGE-NO.
    WRITE PRINTLINE FROM DATE-LINE
        AFTER ADVANCING PAGE.
    WRITE PRINTLINE FROM COMPANY-NAME
        AFTER ADVANCING 1 LINE.
    WRITE PRINTLINE FROM REPORT-NAME
        AFTER ADVANCING 3 LINES.
    WRITE PRINTLINE FROM HEADINGS
        AFTER ADVANCING 3 LINES
    MOVE 2 TO WS-PROPER-SPACING.
    INITIALIZE WS-PAGE-TOTAL
               WS-LINE-CTR.
1600-UPDATE-COMPANY-TOTAL.
    ADD WS-PAGE-TOTAL TO WS-COMPANY-TOTAL.

1999-EXIT-OUTPUT-SECTION.
    EXIT.
```

Figure 10.44 The report produced by the program in Figure 10.43

```
REPORT DATE: 93-11-18                                                PAGE 1
                             THE SPORTSMAN

                         ORDERED SALES REPORT

    SALESPERSON                SSN           STORE NUMBER     CURRENT SALES

BROWN, RAYMOND          218 54 6010              10            $3,022.55
CRANE, JOHN             556 23 4035              10            $2,870.50
VELOZO, MARIO           720 95 4670              40            $2,423.90
ABALLO, NORMA           820 78 8914              30            $2,350.75
BRAZ, JOAN              466 58 7165              30            $2,315.60
FORTIN, EMIL            551 50 2546              40            $2,254.50
BEAUDOIN, ROCKY         452 67 7143              40            $2,215.00
BISBANO, HENRY          674 45 1231              40            $2,190.55
PRATT, ROBIN            557 31 8974              30            $2,155.00
JOBIN, ANTONIO          721 43 5472              40            $2,140.50
TRAMONTE, ESTELLE       351 56 6178              40            $2,135.00
ROBINSON, GILBERT       566 73 1251              30            $2,105.90
CARDIN, FRANCIS         452 89 2153              40            $2,045.90
BERNARD, ISIDORE        416 89 2014              30            $2,035.69
DOLLARHIDE, CHRIS       785 02 3157              30            $2,015.70
FURTADO, MAUREEN        745 64 5270              30            $2,015.40
NOTTE, LORENZO          683 21 5467              40            $2,005.00
FERNANDEZ, LOUISE       433 40 6075              20            $2,000.00
MARKLAND, MARY          787 85 5623              40            $1,987.50
GALLAGHER, MICHAEL      574 93 0461              40            $1,976.75
PERRY, JOSEPH           712 13 3463              40            $1,945.50
MILLER, RENEE           490 23 4571              40            $1,905.70
MELANSON, GARY          487 25 1099              30            $1,905.50
KING, CHRISTOPHER       576 40 0892              30            $1,890.70
CORRIGAN, ALENE         607 04 4132              30            $1,875.50
LEMERISE, DONALD        571 90 4025              20            $1,850.50
MAHFUZ, IRENE           823 14 4098              30            $1,850.25
PARISEAU, WILLIAM       624 16 6876              40            $1,785.00
COSTELLO, JAMES         683 30 9020              20            $1,670.50
PENTA, ROBERT           360 90 2035              20            $1,650.25

                                      TOTAL THIS PAGE : $ 62,591.09   *
```

■ **Figure 10.44** continued

```
REPORT DATE: 93-11-18                                              PAGE 2
                              THE SPORTSMAN

                          ORDERED SALES REPORT

    SALESPERSON               SSN          STORE NUMBER     CURRENT SALES

KELLY, PATRICK           551 16 4090           10             $1,625.00
DANIELS, JULIA           696 99 6055           10             $1,620.00
FARMER, SUSAN            251 34 2020           10             $1,620.00
WORTHEN, MICHAEL         572 49 5090           20             $1,570.00
VERMETTE, GLORIA         804 23 3040           20             $1,560.50
ALLEN, ROBERT            214 36 5025           10             $1,500.00
LINCOURT, LORETTA        745 63 5164           30             $1,495.00
FELDMAN, WALTER          566 12 7070           20             $1,470.80
COCHRANE, RUSSELL        427 56 0010           20             $1,460.50
DWYER, TERRENCE          521 24 4005           10             $1,425.80
HARRISON, LILY           667 45 1060           10             $1,425.80
CRAWFORD, SHIRLEY        418 09 0015           20             $1,390.50
JANKOWKSI, STANLEY       482 13 1015           10             $1,350.00
MANNING, ELIZABETH       644 35 3075           10             $1,350.00
QUINN, SUZANNE           375 70 1060           20             $1,320.50
MAIN, CHARLES            642 75 4040           10             $1,280.00
TALBOT, WILFRED          480 75 5030           20             $1,275.80
FEINGOLD, HAROLD         263 45 2070           10             $1,250.50
LANGFORD, WAYNE          599 23 1085           10             $1,150.50
PROULX, PAULINE          472 84 7080           20             $1,150.00
KOSINSKI, KATHERINE      812 13 3085           20             $1,125.00
PRINGLY, ANNE            521 16 6100           10             $1,098.05
EDWARDS, PETER           564 45 1045           10             $1,080.50
FOGARTY, JANICE          315 46 3030           10             $1,050.50
CORTON, LOUIS            509 86 2005           20             $1,000.00
PINEAULT, NORMAN         509 18 5045           20             $   980.50
GOYETTE, FRANCES         762 35 5100           20             $   950.00
CARLSON, HOPE            685 26 4065           10             $   900.00
BRANNIGAN, NICOLE        641 27 5050           10             $   875.25
DONOHUE, PHIL            788 23 0154           30             $   875.00

                                     TOTAL THIS PAGE : $ 38,226.00   *


REPORT DATE: 93-11-18                                              PAGE 3
                              THE SPORTSMAN

                          ORDERED SALES REPORT

    SALESPERSON               SSN          STORE NUMBER     CURRENT SALES

BARRESI, JOHN            479 21 0065           20             $   650.00
HOWARD, RALPH            377 56 8080           10             $   560.50
CORDEIRO, ANTONE         408 93 6050           20             $   100.50
                                     TOTAL THIS PAGE : $  1,311.00   *

                                       COMPANY TOTAL : $102,128.09   **

                     ***  END OF REPORT  ***
```

Internal Sort/Merge versus External Sort/Merge

In broad terms, sorting or merging programs can generally be classified either as *internal* or *external* sorts. An internal sort is a sorting routine that is incorporated within a COBOL program, whereas an external sort is a stand-alone program whose sole function is to sort files.

There are two kinds of internal sorts: programmer-generated sorting routines for which the programmer produces the logic and related coding, and the COBOL SORT statement, which makes available to the programmer a powerful sorting routine by simply coding the SORT statement. Programmer-generated sorting routines are similar in concept to sorting procedures you may have coded in other languages such as BASIC, Pascal, or C. However, because the COBOL SORT statement is generally available in most computer installations, very few programmer-generated sorting routines are being written today.

There is a substantial difference of opinion between advocates of the COBOL SORT and advocates of external sorts. External sorts are efficient, prepackaged programs generally available from the computer library by using appropriate system-related job-control statements. Those who favor external sorts point to their speed, to the little amount of coding they require (four or five lines of parameter specifications in system-related commands, i.e., DCL for the VAX or JCL for IBM), to the ease with which key fields can be changed, and to the fact that their use poses no problems whatsoever to structured programming features of COBOL programs.

Those who favor the COBOL SORT point to its portability from computer to computer, whereas DCL/JCL usually depend on the particular operating system. They also point to the fact that the INPUT/OUTPUT PROCEDUREs allow for direct processing of records pre- and postsort.

Obviously, it is important for the programmer to adhere to the standards of his or her particular computer installation.

Important Terms in Chapter 10

alphabet-name
COLLATING SEQUENCE
DUPLICATES
EXIT
exit paragraph
external sort
GIVING
GO TO
INPUT PROCEDURE
internal sort
MERGE
merge file
ON ASCENDING KEY
ON DESCENDING KEY
OUTPUT PROCEDURE
prefixing paragraph names in sections
PROCEDURE DIVISION sections
RELEASE
RETURN
SD
section name
SORT
sort file
sort keys
USING

Exercises

1. Use the following statement to answer the questions below:

```
SORT SORT-FILE
    ON ASCENDING KEY S-SSN
    USING IN-FILE
    GIVING OUT-FILE.
```

   a. What is the name of the input file?
   b. What is the name of the output file?
   c. How will the records of the output file be ordered?
   d. For which of the files, SORT-FILE, IN-FILE, OUT-FILE, will the programmer write OPEN and CLOSE statements?
   e. In which sequence will the files be opened and closed?

2. Answer the following questions about sort and merge files:
   a. In the SELECT statement, what kind of device must a sort file or a merge file be assigned to?
   b. In the FILE SECTION, what entry is used to begin a sort file or a merge file description?
   c. Must the records of a sort file always have the same description as that of the input file records? of the output file records?
   d. Must the records of a merge file always have the same description as that of the input file records? of the output file records?

3. Answer the following questions about the components of the SORT statement:
   a. If the records of the input file are to be processed individually while under control of the SORT statement before sorting, which input file component option must be used?
   b. If processing of the sorted records is required while under control of the SORT statement before being written to the output file, which output file component option must be used?
   c. If preprocessing of the input records is not required, which input file component option of the SORT statement can be used?
   d. If postprocessing of the sorted records is not required, which output file component option of the SORT statement can be used?
4. Refer to the following statement when answering the questions below:

```
SORT SORT-FILE
    ON DESCENDING KEY S-PRICE-PER-UNIT
    ON ASCENDING KEY S-ITEM-NO
    INPUT PROCEDURE IS 1-SELECT-SALE-ITEMS
    GIVING PRICE-LISTING.
```

   a. Explain the role of each of the following words: S-PRICE-PER-UNIT, S-ITEM-NO, 1-SELECT-SALE-ITEMS, PRICE-LISTING.
   b. What kind of statement will be used in the INPUT PROCEDURE to pass the records of the input file to the sort file?
   c. Identify at least three statements that must be contained in the INPUT PROCEDURE and that refer to files.
   d. Rearrange the following data in one vertical list according to the keys specified in the SORT statement above:

Item No.	Unit Price	Item No.	Unit Price
9794	10.99	6227	5.99
9796	18.99	6228	9.99
9740	10.99	6248	5.99
9741	18.99	6249	5.99
6226	5.99	6250	9.99

5. Write the PROCEDURE DIVISION corresponding to the following pseudocode:

   0-Main-Control Section.

   0100-Produce-Sorted-File.

   1. Load all the records of input file In-File into Sort-File.
   2. Sort the records of Sort-File using the following keys:
      a. major key: sales in descending order
      b. minor key: name in ascending order
   3. Write all the sorted records to output file Sorted-File.
   4. Stop the run.
6. Write the PROCEDURE DIVISION corresponding to the flowchart in Figure 10.45. Use S- as a prefix for sort file record fields and O- as a prefix for print file record fields. The output file record is PRINTLINE. Other records are prepared in the WORKING-STORAGE SECTION.
7. Explain the differences in the formats of the SORT and the MERGE statements.

Figure 10.45

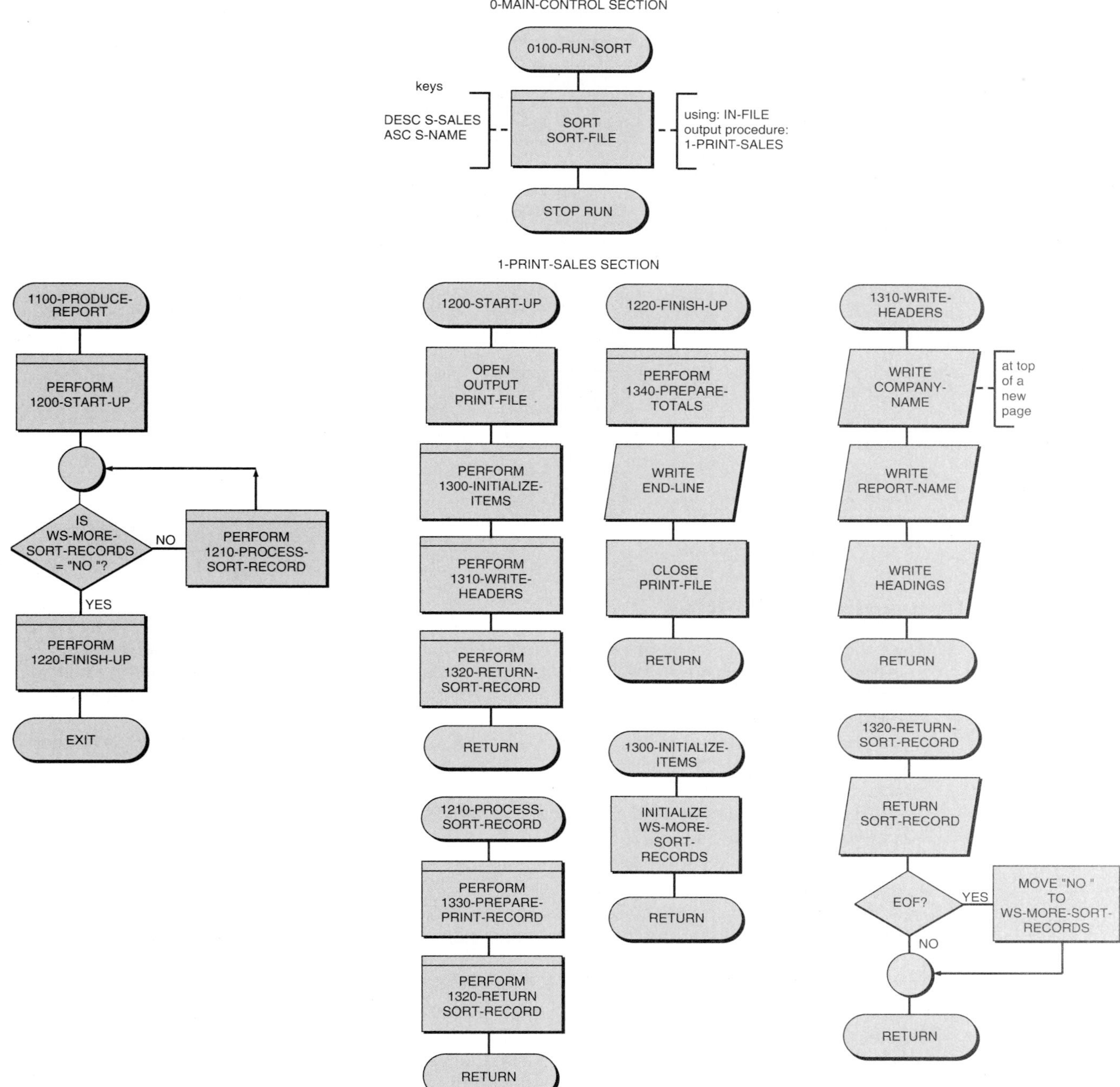
0-MAIN-CONTROL SECTION
0100-RUN-SORT
keys
DESC S-SALES
ASC S-NAME
SORT
SORT-FILE
using: IN-FILE
output procedure:
1-PRINT-SALES
STOP RUN
1-PRINT-SALES SECTION
1100-PRODUCE-REPORT
PERFORM 1200-START-UP
IS WS-MORE-SORT-RECORDS = "NO "?
NO
PERFORM 1210-PROCESS-SORT-RECORD
YES
PERFORM 1220-FINISH-UP
EXIT
1200-START-UP
OPEN OUTPUT PRINT-FILE
PERFORM 1300-INITIALIZE-ITEMS
PERFORM 1310-WRITE-HEADERS
PERFORM 1320-RETURN-SORT-RECORD
RETURN
1210-PROCESS-SORT-RECORD
PERFORM 1330-PREPARE-PRINT-RECORD
PERFORM 1320-RETURN SORT-RECORD
RETURN
1220-FINISH-UP
PERFORM 1340-PREPARE-TOTALS
WRITE END-LINE
CLOSE PRINT-FILE
RETURN
1300-INITIALIZE-ITEMS
INITIALIZE WS-MORE-SORT-RECORDS
RETURN
1310-WRITE-HEADERS
WRITE COMPANY-NAME
at top of a new page
WRITE REPORT-NAME
WRITE HEADINGS
RETURN
1320-RETURN-SORT-RECORD
RETURN SORT-RECORD
EOF?
YES
MOVE "NO " TO WS-MORE-SORT-RECORDS
NO
RETURN

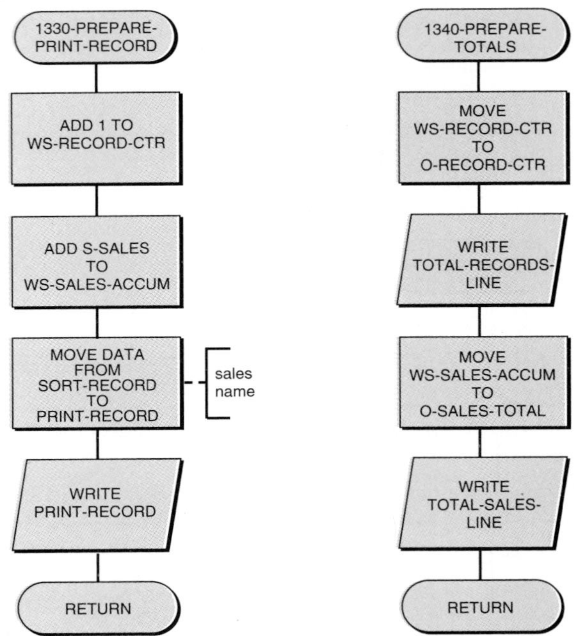

Debugging Activities

1. The program in Figure 10.46 was developed for the purpose of producing a report that lists the salespersons in each store of the International Haberdashery Company whose sales for the current period have fallen below quota. They are listed alphabetically within each store, and the store numbers are in ascending order.

   The report produced by the program is shown in Figure 10.47. However, it should have been the one in Figure 10.48. There are two errors in the program that contributed to the outcome. Find and correct them.

   The data file that was used as the input file for this run of the program is Data File Set 5 in Appendix C [DD/CD:VICIODBI.DAT].

2. Refer to the program in Figure 10.46. The detail lines that must be printed on the report correspond to "selected" salespersons' records.
   - **a.** Locate the statement that makes the selection of the records.
   - **b.** Study the major function of the program and then explain where the record selection statement should be placed to make the program run more efficiently.
   - **c.** Based on your answer in part b, make the necessary changes in the program.

3. Suppose the report specifications are changed so that salespersons must be listed from "most below" quota to "least below" quota within each store. If two or more salespersons are at the same amount below quota, they should be listed alphabetically.

   Explain the changes that must be made to the program, assuming that a detail line must still print the salesperson's name, Social Security number, store number, and amount below quota.

■ **Figure 10.46**

```
 IDENTIFICATION DIVISION.

 PROGRAM-ID.     DBG1-SORT.

*****************************************************************
*                                                               *
*  AUTHOR.          PAQUETTE.                                   *
*  DATE WRITTEN.    OCTOBER 1993.                               *
*                                                               *
*  THIS PROGRAM PRODUCES A REPORT FOR THE INTERNATIONAL HABER-  *
*  DASHERY COMPANY.  THE REPORT LISTS THE SALESPERSONS WHOSE    *
*  SALES FOR THE PERIOD ARE BELOW QUOTA.  FOR EACH PERSON, THE  *
*  REPORT PRINTS THE NAME, SOCIAL SECURITY NUMBER, STORE NUMBER, *
*  AND THE AMOUNT BELOW QUOTA.                                  *
*                                                               *
*  THE RECORDS ARE SORTED ALPHABETICALLY WITHIN EACH STORE.     *
*                                                               *
*****************************************************************

 ENVIRONMENT DIVISION.

 CONFIGURATION SECTION.

 SOURCE-COMPUTER.  VAX-VMS-8650.
 OBJECT-COMPUTER.  VAX-VMS-8650.

 INPUT-OUTPUT SECTION.

 FILE-CONTROL.
     SELECT SALES-FILE   ASSIGN TO COB$INPUT.
     SELECT SORT-FILE    ASSIGN TO DISK01.
     SELECT SALES-REPORT ASSIGN TO COB$OUTPUT.

 DATA DIVISION.

 FILE SECTION.

 FD  SALES-FILE
     RECORD CONTAINS 80 CHARACTERS.

 01  SALES-RECORD
     05 I-STORE-NO       PIC XX.
     05 I-SALESPERSON    PIC X(20).
     05 I-SSN            PIC X(9).
     05                  PIC X(16).
     05 I-CURRENT-SALES  PIC 9(6)V99.
     05 I-QUOTA          PIC 9(6)V99.
     05                  PIC X(17).

 SD  SORT-FILE
     RECORD CONTAINS 80 CHARACTERS.

 01  SORT-RECORD.
     05 S-STORE-NO       PIC XX.
     05 S-SALESPERSON    PIC X(20).
     05 S-SSN            PIC X(9).
     05                  PIC X(16).
     05 S-CURRENT-SALES  PIC 9(4)V9999.
     05 S-QUOTA          PIC 9(6)V99.
     05                  PIC X(17).

 FD  SALES-REPORT
     RECORD CONTAINS 80 CHARACTERS.

 01  PRINTLINE           PIC X(80).

 WORKING-STORAGE SECTION.

 01  PROGRAM-CONTROLS.
     05 WS-MORE-SALES-RECORDS  PIC XXX.
         88 NO-MORE-SALES-RECORDS       VALUE "NO ".
     05 WS-MORE-SORT-RECORDS   PIC XXX.
         88 NO-MORE-SORT-RECORDS        VALUE "NO ".
     05 PROPER-SPACING   PIC 9.

 01  COMPANY-NAME.
     05 PIC X(27)    VALUE SPACES.
     05 PIC X(26)    VALUE "INTERNATIONAL HABERDASHERY".
     05 PIC X(27)    VALUE SPACES.

 01  REPORT-NAME.
     05 PIC X(31)    VALUE SPACES.
     05 PIC X(18)    VALUE "BELOW QUOTA REPORT".
     05 PIC X(31)    VALUE SPACES.
```

```
01   HEADINGS.
     05 PIC X(8)      VALUE SPACES.
     05 PIC X(11)     VALUE "SALESPERSON".
     05 PIC X(11)     VALUE SPACES.
     05 PIC XXX       VALUE "SSN".
     05 PIC X(8)      VALUE SPACES.
     05 PIC X(5)      VALUE "STORE".
     05 PIC X(4)      VALUE SPACES.
     05 PIC X(18)     VALUE "AMOUNT BELOW QUOTA".
     05 PIC XX        VALUE SPACES.

01   SALES-LINE.
     05 CARRIAGE-CONTROL PIC X.
     05                  PIC X.
     05 O-SALESPERSON    PIC X(20).
     05                  PIC X(4).
     05 O-SSN            PIC XXXBXXBXXXX.
     05                  PIC X(6).
     05 O-STORE-NO       PIC XX.
     05                  PIC X(9).
     05 O-AMOUNT-BELOW   PIC $ZZZ,ZZ9.99.
     05                  PIC X(5).

PROCEDURE DIVISION.

O-MAIN-CONTROL SECTION.

0100-RUN-SORT.
    SORT SORT-FILE
        ON ASCENDING KEY S-STORE-NO
        ON ASCENDING KEY S-SALESPERSON
            INPUT PROCEDURE IS 1-PREPARE-SORT-FILE
            OUTPUT PROCEDURE IS 2-PREPARE-REPORT.
    STOP RUN.

1-PREPARE-SORT-FILE SECTION.

1100-PRODUCE-SORT-FILE.
    PERFORM 1200-START-UP.
    PERFORM 1210-PROCESS-SALES-RECORD
        UNTIL NO-MORE-SALES-RECORDS.
    PERFORM 1220-FINISH-UP.
    GO TO 1999-EXIT-INPUT-SECTION.

1200-START-UP.
    OPEN INPUT SALES-FILE.
    PERFORM 1300-INITIALIZE-ITEMS.
    PERFORM 1310-READ-SALES-RECORD.

1210-PROCESS-SALES-RECORD.
    PERFORM 1320-PREPARE-SORT-RECORD.
    PERFORM 1310-READ-SALES-RECORD.

1220-FINISH-UP.
    CLOSE SALES-FILE.

1300-INITIALIZE-ITEMS.
    MOVE "YES" TO WS-MORE-SALES-RECORDS.

1310-READ-SALES-RECORD.
    READ SALES-FILE RECORD
        AT END
            SET NO-MORE-SALES-RECORDS TO TRUE.

1320-PREPARE-SORT-RECORD.
    RELEASE SORT-RECORD FROM SALES-RECORD.

1999-EXIT-INPUT-SECTION.
    EXIT.

2-PREPARE-REPORT SECTION.

2100-PRODUCE-SALES-REPORT.
    PERFORM 2200-START-UP.
    PERFORM 2210-PROCESS-SORT-RECORD
        UNTIL NO-MORE-SORT-RECORDS.
    PERFORM 2220-FINISH-UP.
    GO TO 2999-EXIT-OUTPUT-SECTION.

2200-START-UP.
    OPEN OUTPUT SALES-REPORT.
    PERFORM 2300-INITIALIZE-ITEMS.
    PERFORM 2310-WRITE-REPORT-HEADERS.
    PERFORM 2320-RETURN-A-RECORD.
```

■ Figure 10.46 continued

```
 2210-PROCESS-SORT-RECORD.
     IF S-CURRENT-SALES < S-QUOTA
         PERFORM 2330-PREPARE-SALES-LINE
     END-IF.
     PERFORM 2320-RETURN-A-RECORD.

 2220-FINISH-UP.
     CLOSE SALES-REPORT.

 2300-INITIALIZE-ITEMS.
     MOVE "YES" TO WS-MORE-SORT-RECORDS.

 2310-WRITE-REPORT-HEADERS.
     WRITE PRINTLINE FROM COMPANY-NAME
         AFTER ADVANCING PAGE.
     WRITE PRINTLINE FROM REPORT-NAME
         AFTER ADVANCING 3 LINES.
     WRITE PRINTLINE FROM HEADINGS
         AFTER ADVANCING 2 LINES.
     MOVE SPACES TO SALES-LINE.
     MOVE 2 TO PROPER-SPACING.

 2320-RETURN-A-RECORD.
     RETURN SORT-FILE RECORD
         AT END
             SET NO-MORE-SORT-RECORDS TO TRUE.

 2330-PREPARE-SALES-LINE.
     SUBTRACT S-QUOTA FROM S-CURRENT-SALES
         GIVING O-AMOUNT-BELOW.
     MOVE S-STORE-NO TO O-STORE-NO.
     MOVE S-SALESPERSON TO O-SALESPERSON.
     MOVE S-SSN TO O-SSN.
     WRITE PRINTLINE FROM SALES-LINE
         AFTER ADVANCING PROPER-SPACING.
     MOVE 1 TO PROPER-SPACING.
     PERFORM 2320-RETURN-A-RECORD.

 2999-EXIT-OUTPUT-SECTION.
     EXIT.
```

■ Figure 10.47

```
                         INTERNATIONAL HABERDASHERY


                             BELOW QUOTA REPORT

     SALESPERSON             SSN          STORE     AMOUNT BELOW QUOTA

CAHILL, PAULA R.        623 45 5100        10          $    790.13
GAMELIN, JOSEPH         315 78 1243        10          $  1,184.75
LAUZON, MARIE L.        315 32 5123        10          $    495.34
REZENDES, PHILIP        788 40 7265        10          $    788.74
ROSS, ROBERT J.         571 34 9231        10          $  1,184.39
WOOD, RICHARD W.        028 12 5226        10          $    790.64
DAWICKI, WALTER         472 69 2314        20          $    792.29
LEONARDO, BARBARA       472 58 7311        20          $    495.64
PAQUIN, BRIDGET         186 73 7565        20          $  1,183.68
SHEEHAN, WILLIAM J.     218 39 4740        20          $    791.29
FOX, EVA M.             517 24 6302        30          $  1,973.75
PANKIEWICZ, ALLEN       410 42 5545        30          $    691.89
RAYMOND, VICTOR         518 17 7032        30          $    692.75
RENAUD, ANNE            269 31 3905        30          $  1,188.25
ROBILLARD, STEPHEN      121 31 5631        30          $  1,971.90
SEQUEIRA, PAUL M.       356 31 2251        30          $  1,181.74
DAWSON, THOMAS A.       678 33 1952        40          $    789.49
HELGER, ARTHUR          268 32 2166        40          $    789.49
PECKHAM, PHYLLIS        696 54 4213        40          $    790.14
SABRA, STEVEN S.        628 73 9394        40          $    493.90
VACHON, JULIA           477 71 3390        40          $  1,183.60
GAMACHE, NORMAN T.      414 67 4337        50          $    496.09
MALTAIS, VICTORIA       353 22 8728        50          $  1,182.49
REGO, FIRMINO           235 72 2152        50          $    493.34
SANTOS, JOSEPHINE       407 39 9168        50          $    791.84
```

■ **Figure 10.48**

```
                         INTERNATIONAL HABERDASHERY

                              BELOW QUOTA REPORT

      SALESPERSON                 SSN         STORE     AMOUNT BELOW QUOTA

CUSTER, GEORGE P.           611 72 3510        10            $      89.75
LAUZON, MARIE L.            315 32 5123        10            $      34.75
WHITMAN, ELEANOR            599 35 3423        10            $     134.80
DAWICKI, WALTER             472 69 2314        20            $      29.50
HARRINGTON, KATHY           232 46 3239        20            $     154.30
LEONARDO, BARBARA           472 58 7311        20            $      64.25
LARSON, ANTHONY             634 22 7460        30            $      25.50
RENAUD, ANNE                269 31 3905        30            $      25.50
RIENDEAU, NORMAN            461 21 7415        30            $     169.50
SHEEHAN, CHARLES A.         346 58 5714        40            $      19.50
CROWLEY, JOHN H.            449 83 4615        50            $      74.75
GAMACHE, NORMAN T.          414 67 4337        50            $     109.50
MELLO, ANTONIO              569 46 1603        50            $      74.75
```

Programming Exercises

Programming Exercise I

The management of International Haberdashery wants a sales analysis report that will list all of its salespersons by store in descending order of current sales. If two or more salespersons have the same current sales amounts, they are to be listed alphabetically. The store numbers are in ascending order. Each record in the input file contains the following data:

cc 1–2	Store number
cc 3–22	Salesperson name
cc 48–55	Current sales (format: xxxxxx.xx)

The size of each record is 80 characters. The report must be properly documented with the company name, the report name, and column headings.

The design phase of program development has been completed for you in Figure 10.49. Your assignment is to implement the design. That is, code, compile, debug, and run the program with a sample input file. Use the data in Data File Set 5 in Appendix C [DD/CD:VICIOEX1.DAT].

■ **Figure 10.49**

Record Layout Form

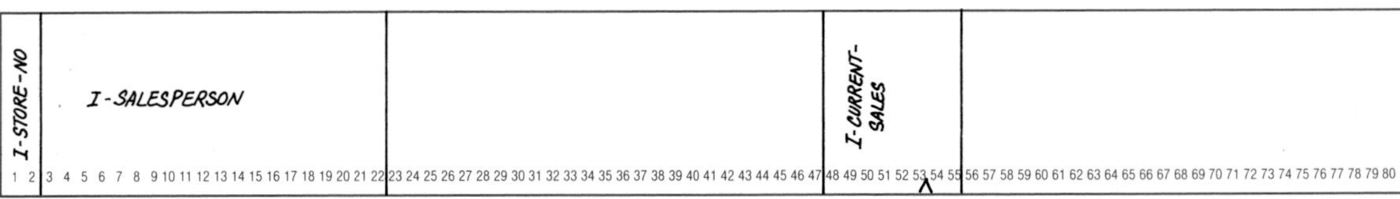

Record Name: SALES-RECORD

■ Figure 10.49 continued

Printer Spacing Chart

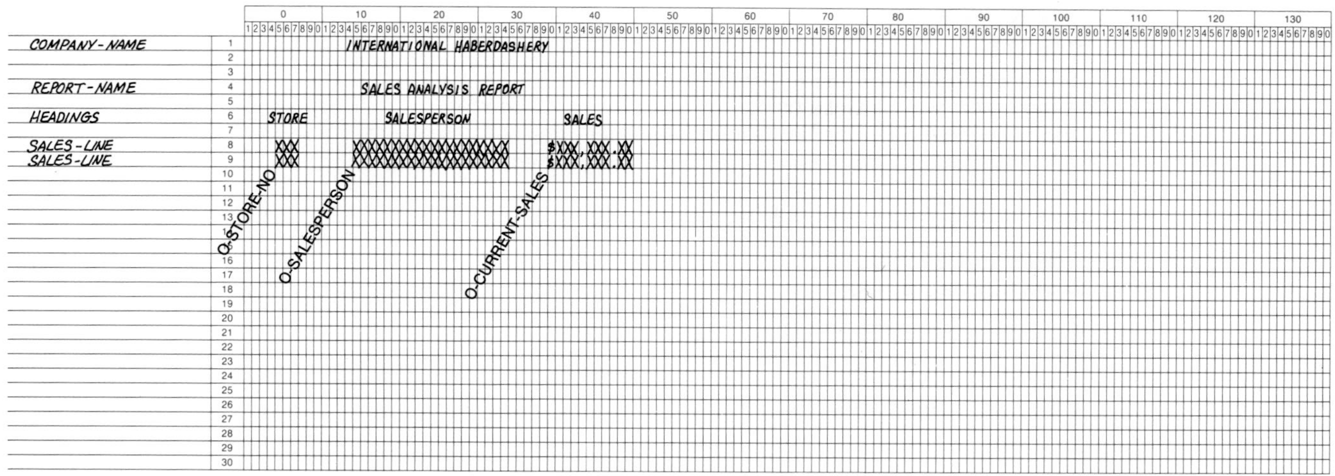

System Flowchart

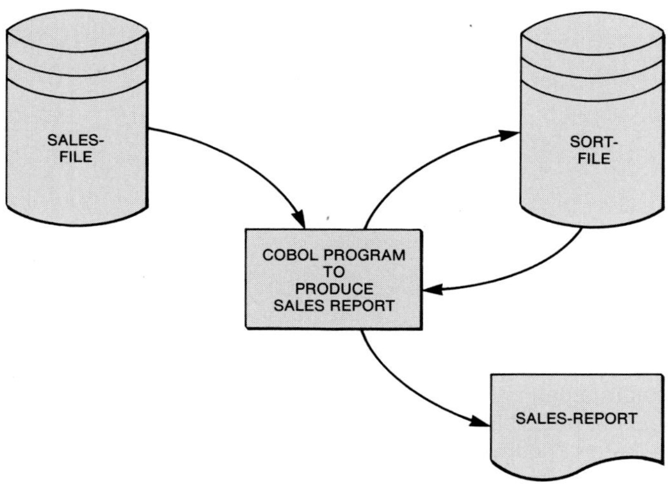

Structure Chart

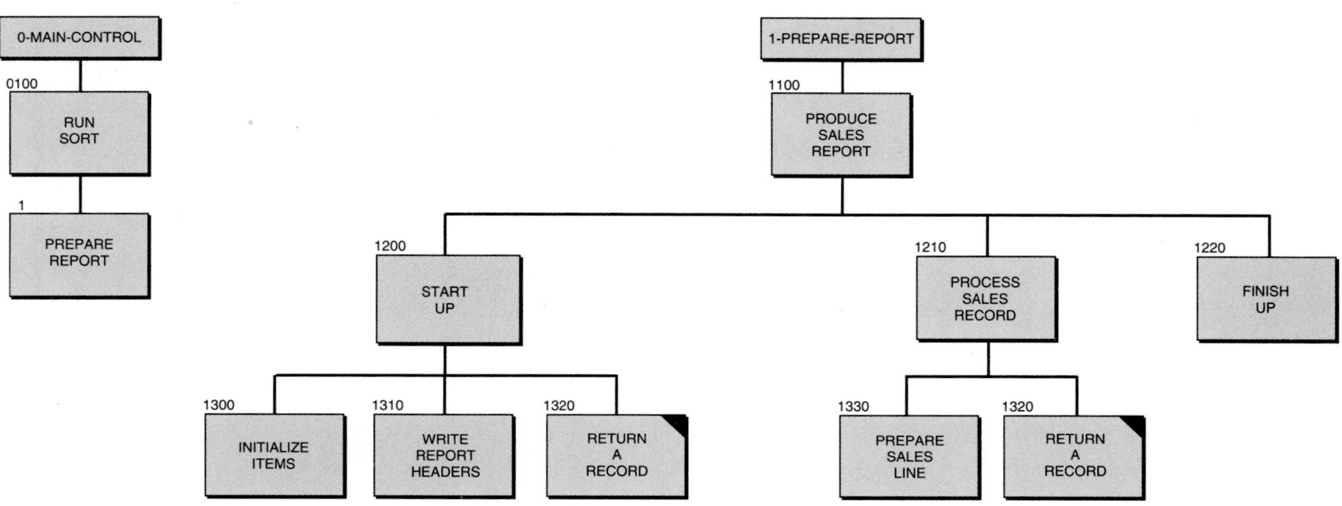

Program Pseudocode

0-Main-Control Section.

0100-Run-Sort.

1. Read all input Sales-Records into the Sort-file.
2. Sort the records of Sort-File using:
   major key: store-numbers in ascending order
   intermediate key: current-sales in descending order
   minor key: names in ascending order
3. Perform the output procedure 1-Prepare-Report.

1-Prepare-Report Section.

1100-Produce-Sales-Report.

1. Perform 1200-Start-Up.
2. Perform 1210-Process-Sort-Record until no more records.
3. Perform 1220-Finish-Up.
4. Exit from the output procedure.

1200-Start-Up.

1. Open the output file Sales-Report.
2. Perform 1300-Initialize-Items.
3. Perform 1310-Write-Report-Headers.
4. Perform 1320-Return-Sort-Record.

1210-Process-Sort-Record.

1. Perform 1330-Prepare-Sales-Line.
2. Perform 1320-Return-Sort-Record.

1220-Finish-Up.

1. Close the output file Sales-Report.

1300-Initialize-Items.

1. Set the end-of-file flag WS-MORE-RECORDS to "YES".
2. Clear the output record Sales-Line.

1310-Write-Report-Headers.

1. Move the record Company-Name to the output area Printline.
2. After advancing to a new page, write the output record Printline.
3. Move the record Report-Name to the output area Printline.
4. After advancing 3 lines, write the output record Printline.
5. Move the record Headings to the output area Printline.
6. After advancing 2 lines, write the output record Printline.
7. Set proper-spacing to 2.

1320-Return-Sort-Record.

1. Return (read) a Sort-File record.
2. Test for end-of-file record;
   if EOF record reached, set WS-MORE-RECORDS to "NO ".

1330-Prepare-Sales-Line.

1. Move Sort-Record store-number to Sales-Line store-number.
2. Move Sort-Record salesperson to Sales-Line salesperson.
3. Move Sort-Record current-sales to Sales-Line current-sales.
4. Move the record Sales-Line to the output area Printline.
5. After advancing proper-spacing, write the output record Printline.
6. Set proper-spacing to 1.

Program Flowchart

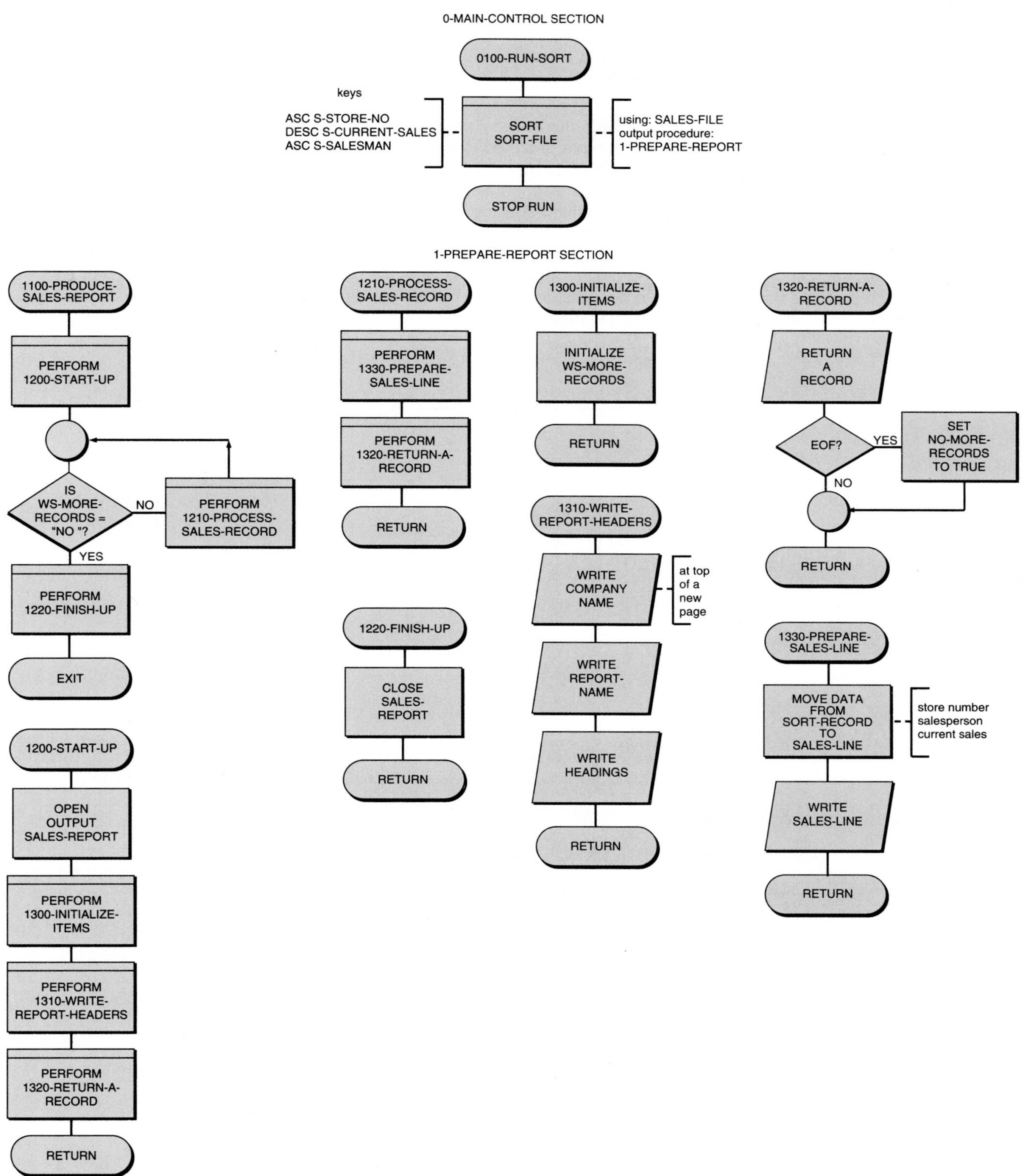

Programming Exercise II

The management of Express Auto Parts wants a reorder list prepared for all inventory items for which the quantity on hand is less than the reorder point. The inventory file records contain the following data:

cc 1–5	Catalog number
cc 6–25	Item description
cc 26–30	Unit purchase price (format: xxx.xx)
cc 36–39	Quantity on hand
cc 44–47	Reorder point

The size of each record is 80 characters. The items on the reorder list must be in ascending order of quantity on hand, that is, from most depleted stock to least depleted. If the quantity on hand is the same for two or more items, these items must be listed in descending order of the unit purchase price, and if any of these prices are the same, in catalog number sequence.

The input record layout, the printer spacing chart, the system flowchart, and the structure chart are contained in Figure 10.50. On the printer spacing chart, the reorder value is based on the requirement that the quantity in stock for each item should be replenished to 25 percent above the reorder point. Your assignment is to complete the design phase; that is, write the pseudocode or draw the flowchart and then implement the design to successful completion. Use the data in Data File Set 1 in Appendix C [DD/CD:VICIOEX2.DAT] as the sample input file.

Figure 10.50

Record Layout Form

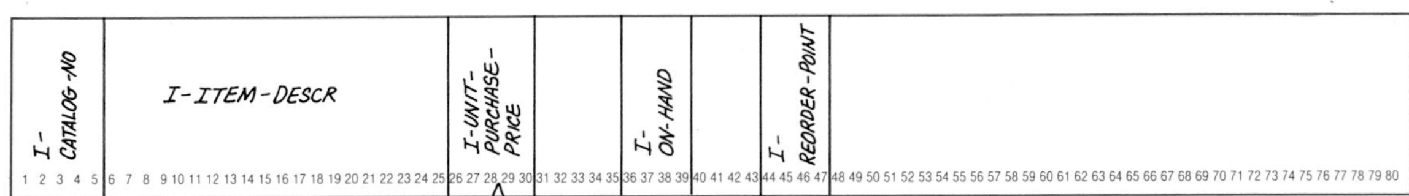

Record Name: ITEM-RECORD

Printer Spacing Chart

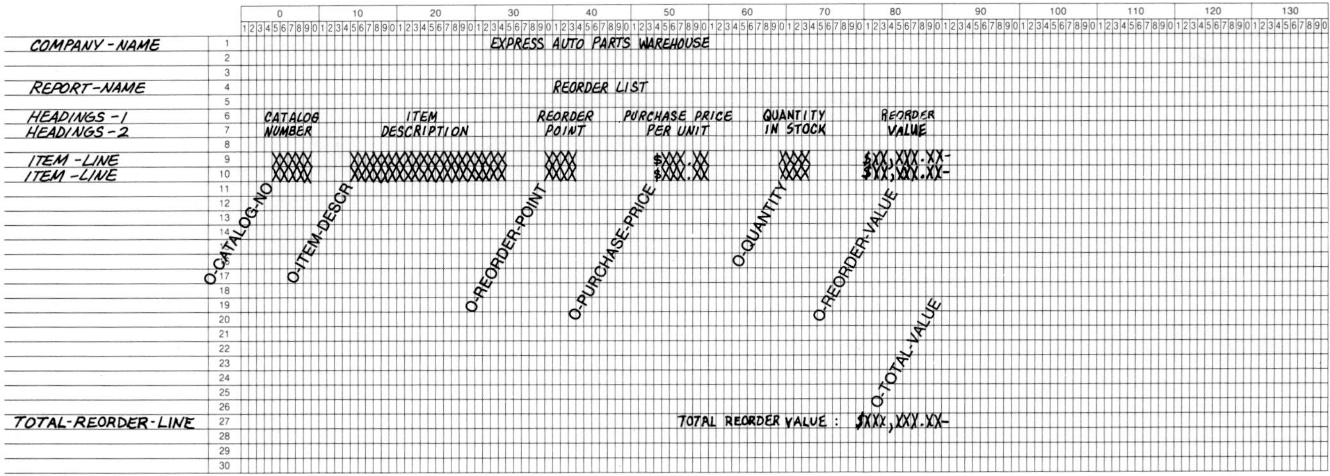

■ **Figure 10.50** continued

System Flowchart

INVENTORY-FILE
SORT-FILE
COBOL PROGRAM TO PRODUCE REORDER LIST
REORDER-LIST

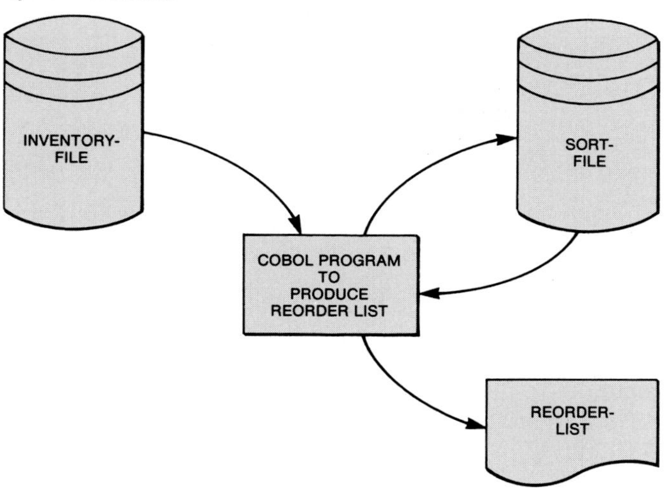

Structure Chart

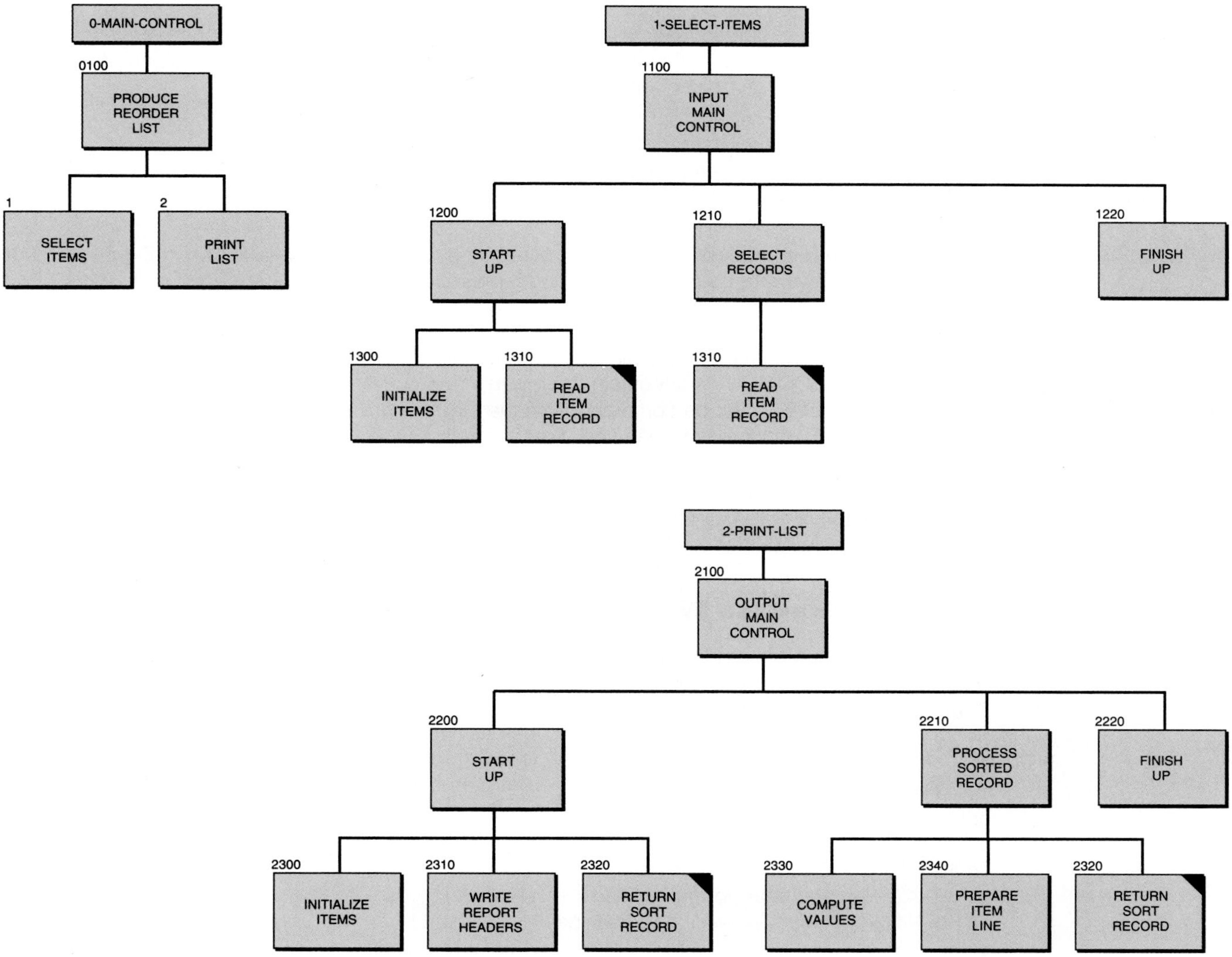

0-MAIN-CONTROL
0100
PRODUCE REORDER LIST
1
SELECT ITEMS
2
PRINT LIST
1-SELECT-ITEMS
1100
INPUT MAIN CONTROL
1200
START UP
1210
SELECT RECORDS
1220
FINISH UP
1300
INITIALIZE ITEMS
1310
READ ITEM RECORD
1310
READ ITEM RECORD
2-PRINT-LIST
2100
OUTPUT MAIN CONTROL
2200
START UP
2210
PROCESS SORTED RECORD
2220
FINISH UP
2300
INITIALIZE ITEMS
2310
WRITE REPORT HEADERS
2320
RETURN SORT RECORD
2330
COMPUTE VALUES
2340
PREPARE ITEM LINE
2320
RETURN SORT RECORD

■ **Figure 10.51**

Printer Spacing Chart

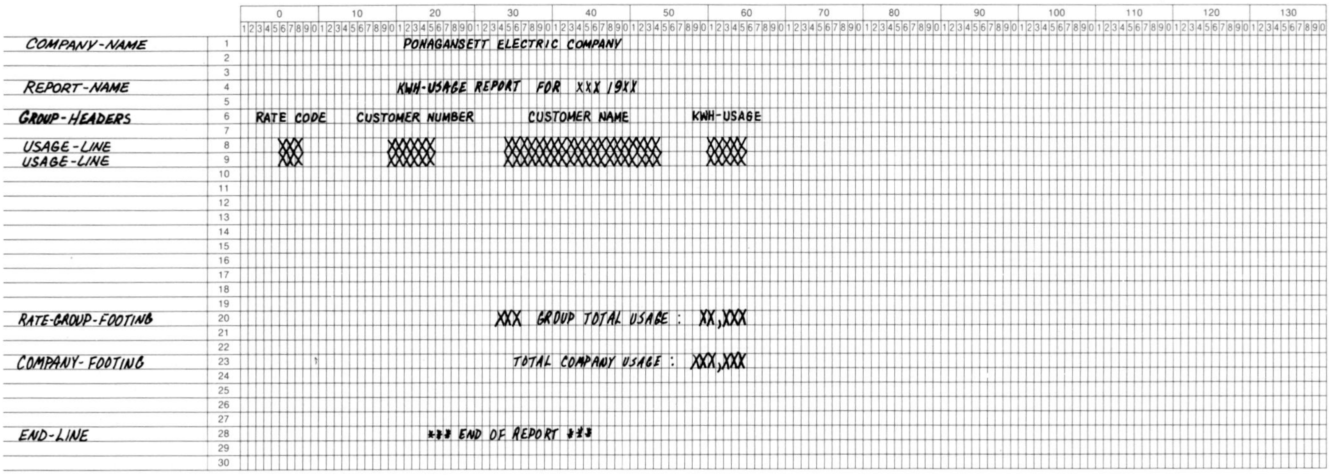

Line name	Line	Content
COMPANY-NAME	1	PONAGANSETT ELECTRIC COMPANY
REPORT-NAME	4	KWH-USAGE REPORT FOR XXX 19XX
GROUP-HEADERS	6	RATE CODE CUSTOMER NUMBER CUSTOMER NAME KWH-USAGE
USAGE-LINE	8	XXX XXXXXX XXXXXXXXXXXXXXXXXXXX XXXXX
USAGE-LINE	9	XXX XXXXXX XXXXXXXXXXXXXXXXXXXX XXXXX
RATE-GROUP-FOOTING	20	XXX GROUP TOTAL USAGE : XX,XXX
COMPANY-FOOTING	23	TOTAL COMPANY USAGE : XXX,XXX
END-LINE	28	*** END OF REPORT ***

Programming Exercise III

The management of the Ponagansett Electric Company wants a multilevel KWH-usage report on all of its customers, from heaviest to lightest user within each rate schedule. The schedule codes are: A10 for Residential, A11 for Residential with Electric Water Heater, A12 for All Electric Residential, and C-2 for Commercial. The input records contain the following data:

cc 4–9	Customer number
cc 10–29	Customer name
cc 30–34	Previous meter reading
cc 35–39	Current meter reading
cc 74–76	Rate schedule (format: xxx)

The size of each record is 80 characters. The report is to be formatted as shown in Figure 10.51. It must list no more than two rate codes per page and it must display the total KWH used by the customers within each rate code. At the end of the report, it must also display the total KWH used by all its customers. The report must list the codes in descending order: C-2 to A10. Within a rate schedule, if more than one customer has the same usage, the listing is to be by customer number. (The first field of the line RATE-GROUP-FOOTING must contain the group's rate code.)

Since the KWH-usage must be computed from the input record before entering the sorting routine, the INPUT PROCEDURE option has to be used. And, the description of the sort record must contain a KWH-usage field, since the usage is a key in the SORT statement.

Since the report must be formatted, the OUTPUT PROCEDURE option must also be used. Your task is to design the control-break program, and then implement the design to successful completion. Use the data in Data File Set 2 in Appendix C [DD/CD:VICIOEX3.DAT] as a sample input file.

Programming Exercise IV

The management of the Modern Plastics Company wants a multilevel payroll report formatted as shown in Figure 10.52. The report must list all employees within each department of each plant in descending order of gross wages earned. Plants and departments are to be reported in ascending sequence of their numeric codes. Within any one department, employees having the same gross wages must be listed in alphabetic order. The input file records contain the following data:

cc 3–4	Plant number
cc 5–6	Department number
cc 7–15	Social Security number
cc 16–35	Employee name
cc 39–42	Pay rate (format xx.xx)
cc 43–44	Hours worked at regular pay
cc 45–46	Hours worked at overtime pay (time and a half)

■ Figure 10.52

Printer Spacing Chart

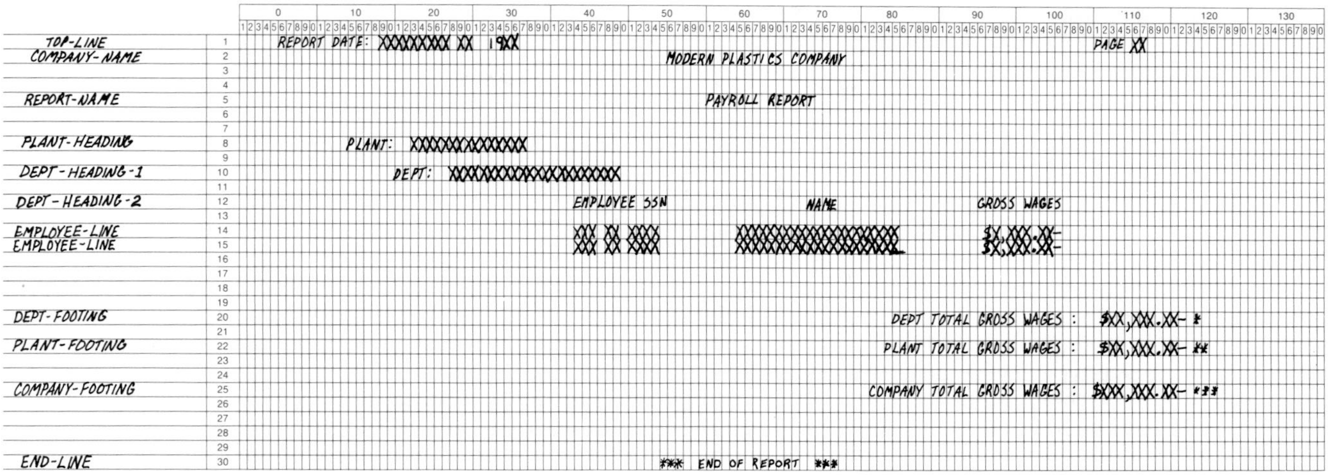

Record	Line	Content
TOP-LINE	1	REPORT DATE: XXXXXXXX XX 19XX PAGE XX
COMPANY-NAME	2	MODERN PLASTICS COMPANY
	3	
	4	
REPORT-NAME	5	PAYROLL REPORT
	6	
	7	
PLANT-HEADING	8	PLANT: XXXXXXXXXXXXX
	9	
DEPT-HEADING-1	10	DEPT: XXXXXXXXXXXXXXXXXXXX
	11	
DEPT-HEADING-2	12	EMPLOYEE SSN NAME GROSS WAGES
	13	
EMPLOYEE-LINE	14	XXX XX XXXX XXXXXXXXXXXXXXXXXXXX $X,XXX.XX-
EMPLOYEE-LINE	15	XXX XX XXXX XXXXXXXXXXXXXXXXXXXX $X,XXX.XX-
	16	
	17	
	18	
	19	
DEPT-FOOTING	20	DEPT TOTAL GROSS WAGES : $XX,XXX.XX- *
	21	
PLANT-FOOTING	22	PLANT TOTAL GROSS WAGES : $XX,XXX.XX- **
	23	
	24	
COMPANY-FOOTING	25	COMPANY TOTAL GROSS WAGES : $XXX,XXX.XX- ***
	26	
	27	
	28	
	29	
END-LINE	30	*** END OF REPORT ***

The size of each record is 80 characters. The format of the report shows a need for control breaks at two levels, the major being the plant level, and the minor being the department level. The plant control heading must display the location of the plant, and the department control heading must contain the name of the department. The control footings for each of these control items must show the total wages earned by the employees of the plant/department.

The program must contain a hard-coded table of plant codes and locations and a second hard-coded table of department codes and corresponding names. The plants are as follows:

Numeric Code	Location
10	Boston
20	Providence
30	New Haven
40	Stamford
50	New York

The departments are as follows:

Numeric Code	Dept. Name
10	Administration
20	Personnel
30	Finance
40	Research & Development
50	Production
60	Shipping & Receiving
70	Maintenance
80	Data Processing

Additionally, since the report date format requires the month name, the program must contain a hard-coded table of month names.

Preprocessing of the input records is required, since one of the sort keys is gross wages, which must be computed. Therefore, the INPUT PROCEDURE option is needed.

Postprocessing of the sort records is required, since the report must be formatted. Therefore, the OUTPUT PROCEDURE option is also required.

Your task is to design the control break program, and then implement the design to successful completion. Use the data in Data File Set 4 in Appendix C [DD/CD:VICIOEX4.DAT] as a sample input file and use the current date as the report date.

11 ■ File Handling

In some chapters of this text, you have been reminded that the data files supplied as input to the sample programs and to the programs in the exercises are sequential files. In this chapter, you will take a closer look at file organizations, in particular sequential organization, at the most common file storage mediums, and at some typical file maintenance activities.

There are three standard file organizations: *sequential, indexed,* and *relative.* A file is classified as **sequential,** that is, as having sequential organization, if the records are stored in it in some specified sequence and are then accessed and processed in that physical sequence. Generally, a key field of the record is selected, and the records of the file are then stored in the file in ascending or descending order of the values in the key field. Examples of such sequential files are an employee file in which the records are arranged alphabetically by employee name, an employee file in which the records are arranged in descending order by employee number, and an inventory file in which the records are arranged in ascending order by catalog number. It is not necessary that the records be sequenced on the basis of a key field. For instance, a transaction file created during a business day is a typical sequential file that is not key sequenced.

Sequential files can be stored on a variety of storage mediums, such as cards, printer paper, magnetic tapes, and magnetic disks. The storage mediums of particular interest to us are magnetic tapes and magnetic disks.

An **indexed file** is one whose logical structure allows records to be accessed either sequentially or randomly. When an indexed file is created, an index is generated for each record. The index contains a value that is unique to the record, called the **record key,** and it also contains a pointer indicating where the record is stored in the file. These indexes are stored in the file itself. The file's records can be retrieved sequentially—that is, in the same sequence in which they were written to the file—or they can be retrieved randomly simply by specifying a record's record key value. Indexed files must, however, be stored on direct-access storage devices such as magnetic disks.

Relative file organization also allows records to be accessed sequentially or randomly. Each record in a relative file has a relative number that indicates its ordinal position in the file. Records can be accessed sequentially from the first to the last, or a record can be accessed randomly simply by specifying its relative number.

There are programming considerations that are peculiar to each file organization. In this chapter, sequential organization will be examined in detail, and indexed and relative file organizations will be introduced. ■

■ Objectives You Should Achieve

After studying this chapter, you should:

1. Be able to explain the terms *sequential organization* and *sequential access.*
2. Be able to explain the meaning of *BPI, IBG, DASD,* and the term *block.*
3. Be able to name advantages and disadvantages of magnetic tapes and disks.
4. Given an adequate description of a master file, be able to select an appropriate data field of its records which could serve as a key for sequencing the records.
5. Be able to explain the function of an audit trail report.
6. Be able to explain the function of the EXTEND and I-O file open modes.
7. Be able to briefly explain the nature of an indexed file.
8. Be able to briefly explain the nature of a relative file.
9. Given a programming problem that requires deleting records from and adding new records to a master file with sequential organization, be able to correctly design the program and implement the design to successful completion.

10. Given a programming problem that requires changing selected field values in records of a master file with sequential organization, be able to correctly design the program and implement the design to successful completion. The master file may be a tape file or a disk file.
11. Given a programming problem that requires a complete update of a master file with sequential organization, be able to correctly design the program and implement the design to successful completion.

Uses of Sequential Files

One of the most common uses of sequential files is the maintenance of master files. A *master file* is the collection of all the records that pertain to a particular application within the business environment. Typical master files are master payroll files, master inventory files, master accounts payable files, master sales files, master employee information files, and so on.

A master file is created once and maintained periodically from then on. To maintain a master file means to keep it current. In a master payroll file, for instance, records must be deleted for those employees who leave, records must be added for new employees, and some record field values must be changed when employees are reclassified or receive pay raises, change addresses or phone numbers, and so on.

In this chapter, we develop programs to create sequential master files on magnetic tape and on magnetic disk, and programs to update such master files. As we study various file organizations, in this chapter and in later chapters, we will encounter programs whose essential function is to produce output directly on a tape or on a disk. Such files are classified as *storage files;* that is, files that are stored on magnetic medium for further processing or referencing later. As such, they cannot be "seen" as they are being produced, and program execution will terminate without giving any evidence that the programmed task has been accomplished. Although the programmer can display the contents of a storage file on the screen of a terminal to verify that the program ran successfully, procedures are normally included in the program itself for the explicit purpose of producing a hard-copy report that provides a trail of what took place internally. Examples of such reports are audit trail reports, error audit reports, and exception reports. The reports can be designed to be very complete or to contain minimal information, as desired by the data processing department. We will illustrate some of these procedures to ascertain the outcome of such programs.

Creating Sequential Files

There are various ways of creating sequential files. Some of them are the following:

1. Use a key-to-tape encoder or converter to enter data directly onto magnetic tape. The machine consists of a keyboard and a magnetic tape drive. Pressing a key of the keyboard causes the corresponding magnetic character to be stored on the tape. The data that must be stored on a record is keyed in at the keyboard, and then pressing the ENTER key delimits the record on the tape. After all the records are encoded, the result is a tape file. It is usually recommended that the records be arranged in some specific sequence, that is, in ascending or descending order of the values in one or more key fields of the records. A sample system flowchart for this method is shown in Figure 11.1. (Key-to-disk encoders transfer data directly onto a magnetic disk, thereby creating a disk file.)

Figure 11.1 Key-to-tape system flowchart

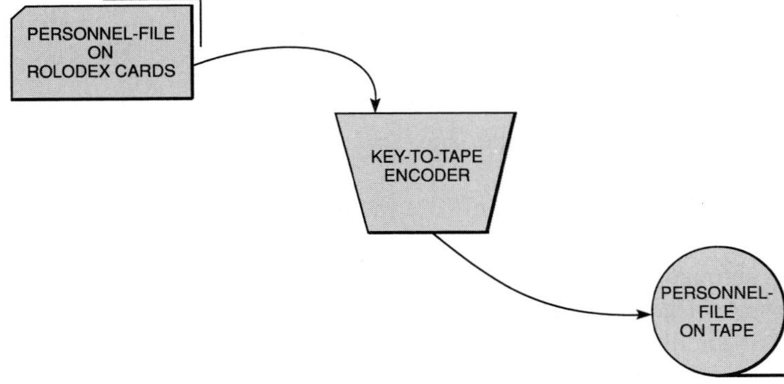

■ **Figure 11.2** Terminal-to-disk system flowchart

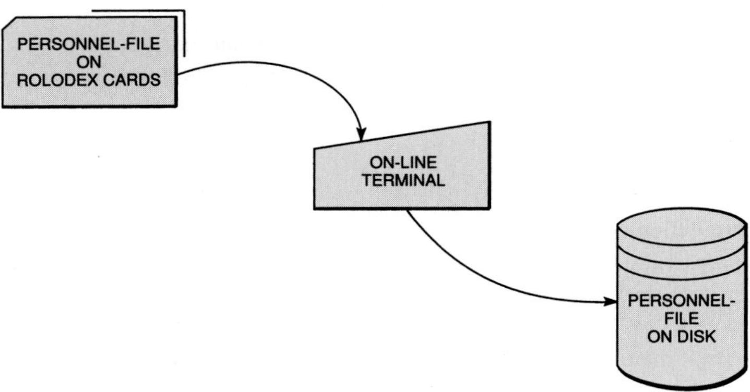

■ **Figure 11.3** Input-file-to-tape file system flowchart

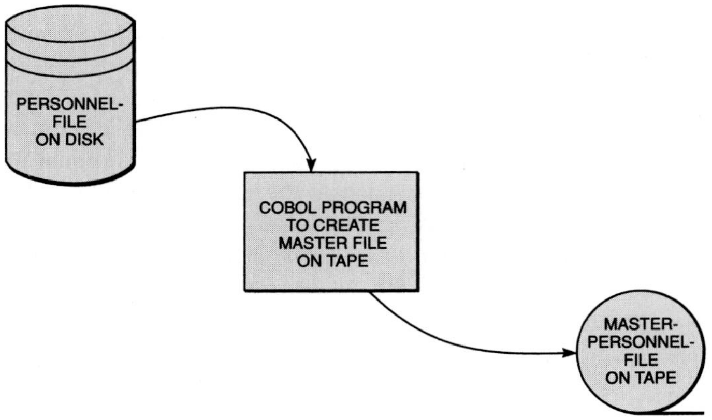

2. Use an on-line terminal. An on-line terminal is a keyboard, with a built-in printer and/or visual display terminal (VDT), connected directly to the computer. By using appropriate system commands and an editor, data can be entered at the terminal and stored directly on a storage medium, generally a magnetic disk, and the result is a disk file. Obviously, system commands and editors are system-specific. A sample system flowchart for this method is shown in Figure 11.2.
3. Code a COBOL program whose major functions are to access data from some input file, such as the editor-generated file referred to above, and to copy the input records onto magnetic tape or disk. The system flowchart for this method is shown in Figure 11.3.

Of these three methods, the one we want to study is the third. We want to write programs to create sequential files on tape, other programs to update tape master files, and then later in the chapter, programs to create sequential files on disk and to update sequential disk files. The symbols used in system flowcharts are shown in Figure 11.4.

Some Tape File Characteristics

We now examine some characteristics of files stored on magnetic tape. Later in the chapter, we examine characteristics of files stored on magnetic disks.

Tape files necessarily have a sequential organization. Not only are the records written onto the tape in physical sequence, but they are also read in the same physical sequence. To read the 1000th record on a tape, the preceding 999 records must pass through the read-write heads of the tape drive mechanism. The sequential nature of a tape file is an important consideration in selecting magnetic tape as a storage medium. When a file is selected for a program, if most or all of its records must be accessed during the program run, then magnetic tape is an efficient storage medium. If only a selected few records must be accessed during

Figure 11.4 System flowchart symbols

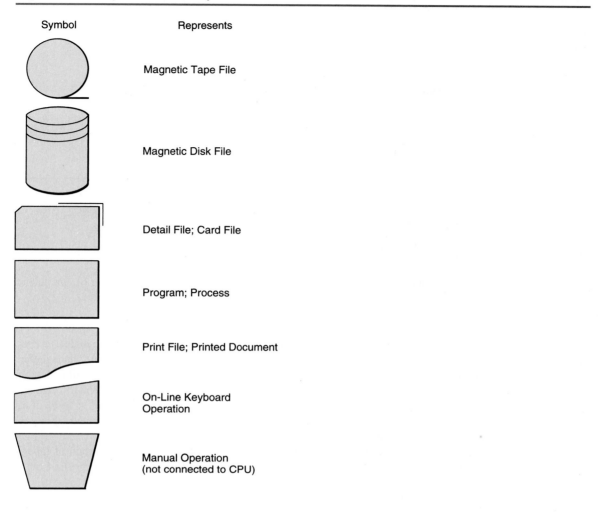

Symbol	Represents
	Magnetic Tape File
	Magnetic Disk File
	Detail File; Card File
	Program; Process
	Print File; Printed Document
	On-Line Keyboard Operation
	Manual Operation (not connected to CPU)

Figure 11.5 Relationship between BPIs and characters per inch

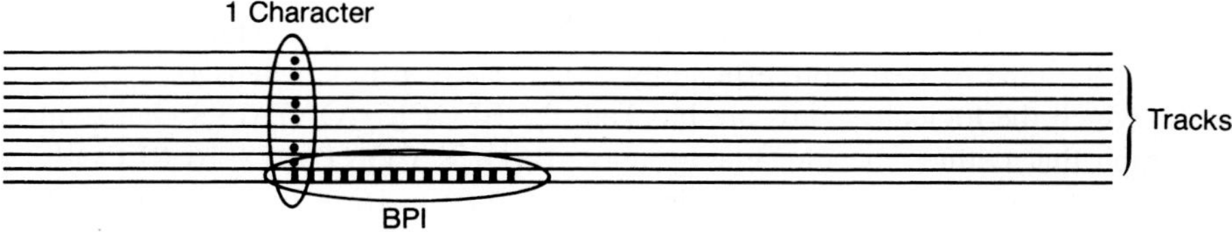

the program run, magnetic tape is not an efficient storage medium for the file, since much of the run time is wasted reading numerous records of the tape that are not needed in the program.

Some typical files for which magnetic tapes are very suitable are master files for payroll, inventory, accounts payable, and accounts receivable. As noted earlier, a master file is the main data file that contains all the current information for a company, a subdivision of the company, or a particular phase of management. A computer run of a master file usually accesses most, if not all, records of the file. A sample master file run is one that produces a current inventory list.

Magnetic tapes are generally 2400 to 3600 feet long and a half-inch wide, and they come in a range of densities. Density is expressed in BPIs (bits per inch). Standard densities are 556, 800, 1600, 3200, and 6250. Furthermore, tapes are seven-track or nine-track tapes. Thus, on a seven-track tape, a character is represented as a group of seven bits across the width of the tape (a 7-bit byte), whereas on a nine-track tape, a character is represented as a group of nine bits across the width of the tape. So, BPIs along one track correspond to bytes per inch or characters per inch across the width of the tape, as shown in Figure 11.5.

Figure 11.6 Blocked records on a tape

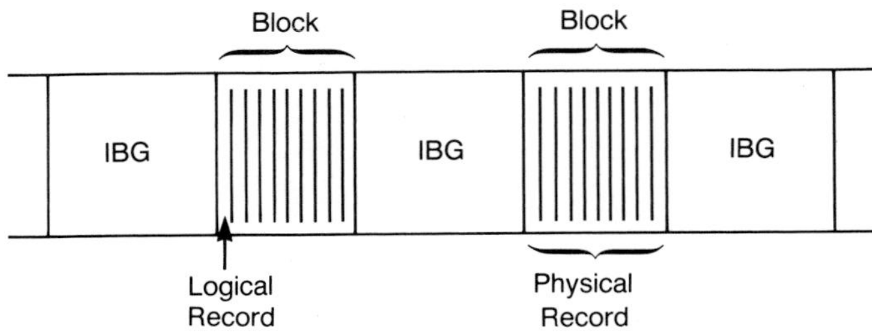

Figure 11.7 BLOCK CONTAINS clause format

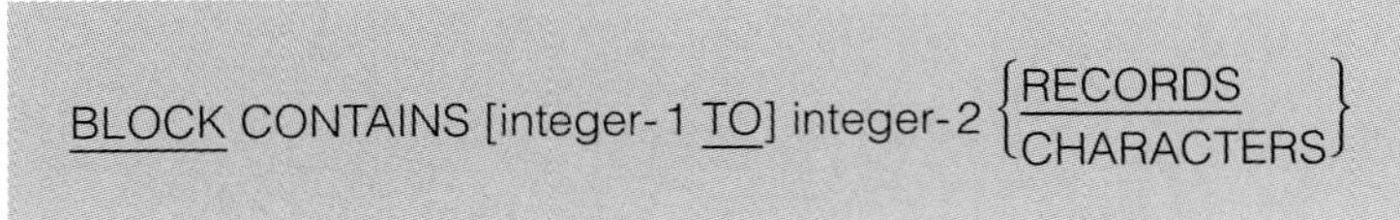

Theoretically, a 3600-foot tape with density 1600 BPI could store the following number of characters:

1600 BPI 12 inches/foot 3600 feet = 69,120,000 characters

In reality, this will never be the case. Characters are always grouped according to the layout specified for a record. A tape record can contain hundreds of characters or only a few. It is generally recommended to keep the length fairly small (for instance, one hundred character positions) to make the records more manageable.

Suppose the size of a tape record is fixed at 100 characters. On a 1600-BPI tape, the record uses only $1/16$ of an inch of tape. When the record is read (or written), $1/16$ of an inch of tape is pulled through the read-write head of the tape drive, but the inertia of the spinning reels causes anywhere from $3/5$ to $3/4$ of an inch of tape to slip through the head. Because of this fact, tape records are normally separated by a gap, called an *interblock gap* (IBG), of $3/5$ to $3/4$ of an inch.

In the situation just described, for each $1/16$ of an inch of usable tape, up to $12/16$ of an inch of tape is wasted. Therefore, most of the tape remains unused, and only about 53,000 records could be stored on it. Clearly, the tape is not being used efficiently.

To use the tape more efficiently, the logical records can be *blocked,* or grouped, to form a larger *physical record.* When blocking is used, the IBG is not inserted between the logical records, but rather between the physical records, that is, the blocks of logical records. The resulting pattern is shown in Figure 11.6.

In the above example, using 1600-BPI tape and 100-character records, 16 records could be blocked per inch, followed by a $3/4$-inch IBG. In this case, a 3600-foot tape could store approximately 395,000 records. Obviously in this case the tape is used more efficiently, since less of it is left unused.

To create a tape file in which the logical records are blocked, the BLOCK CONTAINS clause must be entered in the FD paragraph that defines the file. For instance, BLOCK CONTAINS 16 RECORDS specifies the blocking factor as 16 logical records per physical record, that is, 16 records per block. The general format of the BLOCK CONTAINS clause is shown in Figure 11.7.

Rules Governing Use of the BLOCK CONTAINS Clause

1. The BLOCK CONTAINS clause specifies the size of a physical record in a file. The file can be a storage file or a print file. The storage medium can be a magnetic tape or a magnetic disk.
2. The clause must be coded in the FD entry for the file to which it applies.
3. *Integer-1* is an integer that specifies the minimum size of a physical record.
4. *Integer-2* is an integer that specifies the exact size of a physical record if *integer-1* is not specified; otherwise, *integer-2* specifies the maximum size of a physical record.
5. If the RECORDS option is used, the clause specifies the size in logical records:
   a. Each block or physical record, except possibly the last, contains *integer-2* logical records.
   b. If the records in the file are variable-length records, the size of the physical record is *integer-2* times the size of the largest logical record.
6. If the CHARACTERS option is used, the clause specifies the size in characters. Each block, except possibly the last, contains *integer-2* characters, or the number of characters in the largest logical record, whichever is greater.

7. **a.** If the clause is not used in the creation of a file, there is only one logical record per physical record. The size of the block is the size of the largest logical record. An *interrecord gap (IRG)* separates successive records in the file.
   b. If the clause is used in the creation of a file, the physical records are separated by interblock gaps (IBGs).
8. The maximum physical record size in a sequential file is system-dependent. (For instance, on a VAX, the maximum is 65,535 characters for a tape file and 65,024 characters for a disk file.)
9. The ideal blocking factor depends on a number of factors, such as the file organization, the storage medium, the record size, and the size of the input and output buffers. It is usually determined by a systems analyst, not by the COBOL programmer.
10. Input and output operations occur on the basis of the specified physical record size.

Example

Suppose that an input file has a blocking factor of 5. The first READ statement accesses the first physical record (block) from the input file, stores it in the read buffer, and makes the first logical record of the block available for processing. The second READ statement makes the second logical record currently in the buffer available for processing. The third, fourth, and fifth READ statements have the same effect. At this point, all the logical records of the first block have been processed. Consequently, the sixth READ statement will access the second block or physical record, store it in the read buffer, and make the first logical record of this block available for processing, and the pattern continues.

Other than the BLOCK CONTAINS clause, no special COBOL statements are required to process files containing blocked records.

The format shown in Figure 11.7 also allows the programmer to specify the blocking factor by the number of characters in the block rather than the number of records. Assuming 100 characters per record and a record blocking factor of 5, the following entries are equivalent:

```
BLOCK CONTAINS 5 RECORDS
BLOCK CONTAINS 500 CHARACTERS.
```

Many programmers prefer to state the number of records per block, because it appears to simplify documentation. This is particularly true if the BLOCK CONTAINS clause is used in conjunction with the RECORD CONTAINS clause; for instance,

```
RECORD CONTAINS 100 CHARACTERS
BLOCK CONTAINS 5 RECORDS
```

seems to provide clearer documentation than

```
RECORD CONTAINS 100 CHARACTERS
BLOCK CONTAINS 500 CHARACTERS.
```

More Tape File Considerations

From the above discussion, it is obvious that tape files can store millions of characters. Data can be read from or written onto tape at rates of 100,000 to 300,000 characters per second, so large volumes of data can be processed very quickly.

One disadvantage of a tape file is that in a given computer run, it can be used only as an input file or as an output file, never as both at the same time. If a tape master file is to be updated, that is, some record field values are to be changed, or new records are to be added, or some records are to be deleted, this tape file is the input file and a *new* tape master file has to be created as the updated (output) file. The process of updating a tape master file then requires two tape drives, one through which the old master tape records will be read and the other through which the new updated master file will be written. Later in this chapter, we will present a tape master file update program.

In a computer installation, there may be hundreds or thousands of magnetic tapes. It is important that some efficient system be set up to properly identify, catalog, and store all the tape reels to facilitate the retrieval of a particular tape when it is needed. Naturally, this is not a responsibility of the COBOL programmer. It is mentioned here to point out the need for *external* labels on the tape reels.

An external label, like the one shown in Figure 11.8, must provide pertinent information about the file (or files) contained on the tape: name of the file, date written, retention, tape number, reel number, and the like.

In addition to external labels, tape files are generally required to have *internal* labels. These are labels that provide similar information to that contained on external labels. Of course, they are not visible to the

■ **Figure 11.8** Sample external label

SUBJECT		
TAPE NO.	OUTPUT FROM	DATE
REEL NO. OF	INPUT TO	RETENTION

■ **Figure 11.9** General tape file organization

TAKE-UP LEAD	HEADER LABELS	RECORD BLOCK	IBG	RECORD BLOCK	IBG	....	RECORD BLOCK	END-OF-FILE LABELS	TAKE-UP LEAD

naked eye, but they can be read by the operating system or other software to ascertain whether the file is the correct file and can be used as specified.

Each computer installation has standardized procedures that create the internal labels as label records on output files. When the file is used as an input file, the label records will be checked as noted above. These are the labels that were normally referenced in the FD paragraph clause LABEL RECORDS ARE STANDARD. This entry is no longer required, because monitoring of label records is better handled by the system manager than by the COBOL program.

The layout of a typical tape file is shown in Figure 11.9. The tape file characteristics examined above are taken into account in the sample problem that follows.

Problem 1

The Jocelyn Originals Company wants its data processing department to create a master personnel file, and the file is to be stored on tape. It has been decided that the file should have sequential organization, mainly because it is anticipated that when it is needed in a program run, all or most of its records will have to be accessed for processing.

Currently, the records reside on a file that was generated by an editor. They are supposed to be in alphabetic sequence by employee name. (The file is contained in Figure 11.16 [DD/CD:VICIISPI.DAT])

In addition to creating the master personnel file, the program must also produce an audit trail report and an error file. The report must list the records in the sequence in which they were written to the file, and it must flag records that were not written to the master file because they were out of sequence. The error file must capture the records that were out of sequence so that they can be added to the file later.

The records in the current employee file contain the following data:

cc 1–20	Employee name
cc 21–35	Street address
cc 36–53	City and state
cc 54–58	ZIP code
cc 59–67	Social Security number
cc 68–73	Date of birth (month, day, year)
cc 74–79	Date hired (month, day, year)

The records in the new master personnel file should be formatted with a size of 100 characters to allow for the addition of new data items later.

The records in the error file are simply copies of the records as they exist in the current employee file.

The audit trail report should be formatted as shown in the printer spacing chart of Figure 11.10.

Brief Analysis of the Problem

The statement of the problem makes it clear that the program requires one input file, namely, the current employee file, and three output files, namely, the master personnel file, the error file, and the audit report. The system flowchart is shown in Figure 11.11.

Though the problem requires multiple tasks, the logical analysis is simple. The main steps are as follows:

1. Read an employee record.
2. Test the employee name to determine if it is in the proper alphabetic order.

■ **Figure 11.10** Printer spacing chart for the audit trail report of problem 1

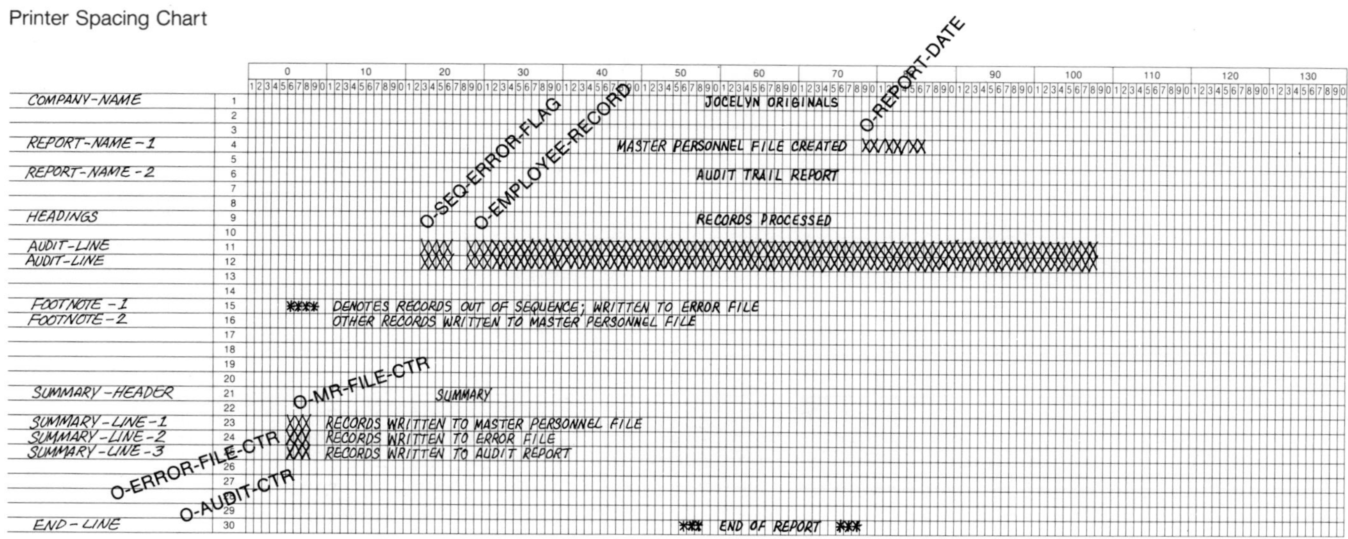

■ **Figure 11.11** System flowchart for problem 1

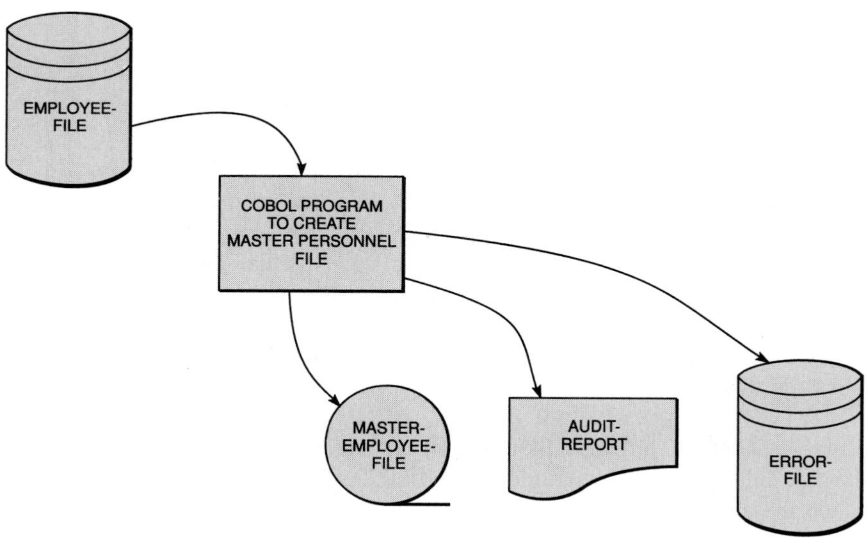

   a. If it is, write it to the master personnel file, write it on the audit report, increment the appropriate counters, and save this name so that the name on the next record can be compared with it.
   b. If it is not, write it to the error file, set the flag on the audit report, write the record on the audit report, and increment the appropriate counters.

3. Repeat steps 1 and 2 until all the employee records have been processed.
4. Write the summary information.

The structure chart is shown in Figure 11.12.

The Program Pseudocode

In preparing to write the pseudocode or to design the flowchart, a number of details must be taken into account, as follows:

1. The flag WS-MORE-RECORDS used to control the input record processing loop must be initialized.
2. Three record counters are needed: one to count the records written to the master file, one to count the records written to the error file, and one to count the records written to the audit report. All three should be initialized to zero. We'll name the counters WS-MR-FILE-CTR, WS-ERROR-FILE-CTR, and WS-AUDIT-CTR, respectively.

■ **Figure 11.12** Structure chart for problem 1

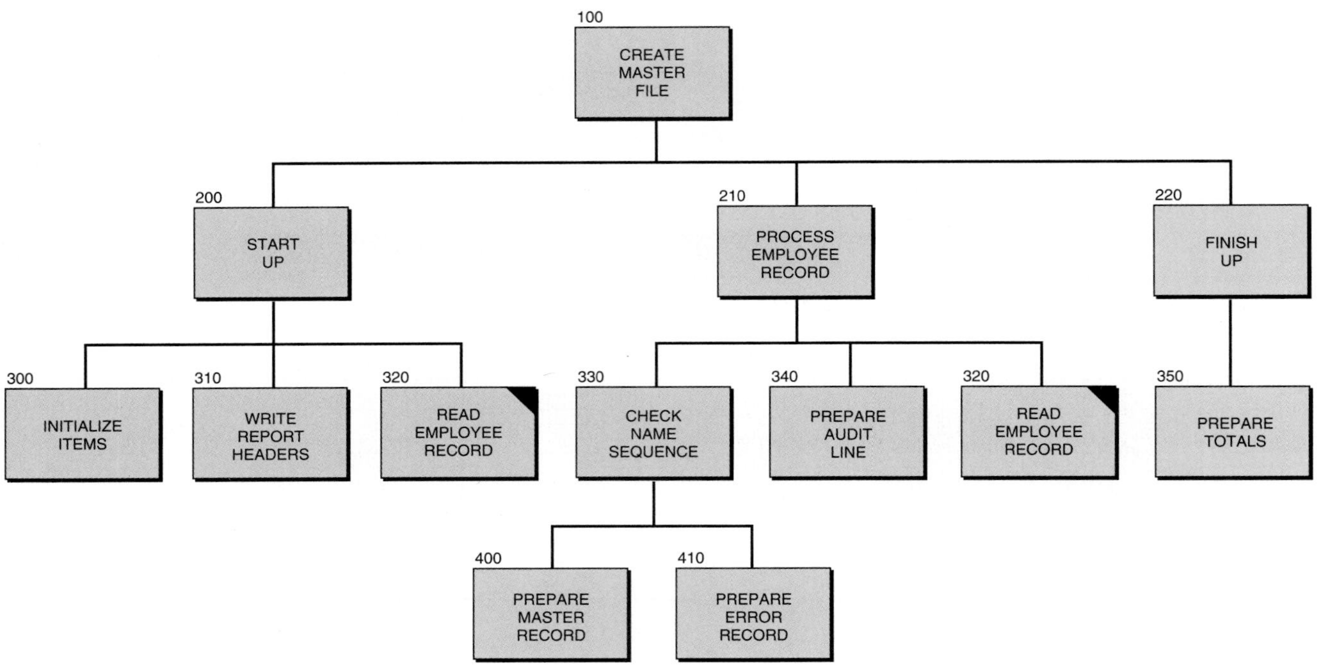

3. In relation to ensuring correct alphabetic sequence, a data item is needed to hold the employee name from the previous record written to the master file so that the name on the current record can be compared with it. We'll name this item WS-NAME-TEST-FLD and initialize it with spaces. Recall that in any collating sequence, a space has a smaller value than any letter of the alphabet. As a result, when the name on the first record is tested against WS-NAME-TEST-FLD, the condition I-EMPL-NAME > WS-NAME-TEST-FLD is satisfied and the first record is written to the master file. For any record written to the master file, the value in I-EMPL-NAME is moved to WS-NAME-TEST-FLD so that alphabetic sequence for the name on the next input record can be correctly tested.
4. In structure chart module 330 CHECK NAME SEQUENCE, the name on the input record is tested against the name-test field, that is, the condition I-EMPL-NAME > WS-NAME-TEST-FLD is tested. If it is true, then the employee record in input memory is in the correct alphabetic sequence and consequently, the value of I-EMPL-NAME must be moved to WS-NAME-TEST-FLD and module 400 PREPARE MASTER RECORD is executed to write the record to the new master file. On the other hand, if the tested condition is false, the employee record in input memory is out of sequence and consequently, the sequence-error flag on the audit line must be set, and module 410 PREPARE ERROR RECORD must be executed to write the record to the error file.

The program pseudocode follows below, and the corresponding flowchart is shown in Figure 11.13.

100-Create-Master-File.

1. Perform 200-Start-Up.
2. Perform 210-Process-Employee-Record until no more records.
3. Perform 220-Finish-Up.
4. Stop the run.

200-Start-Up.

1. Open Employee-File as input file and open Master-Employee-File, Error-File, and Audit-Report-File as output files.
2. Perform 300-Initialize-Items.
3. Perform 310-Write-Report-Headers.
4. Perform 320-Read-Employee-Record.

210-Process-Employee-Record.

1. Move spaces to the record Audit-Line.
2. Perform 330-Check-Name-Sequence.
3. Perform 340-Prepare-Audit-Line.
4. Perform 320-Read-Employee-Record.

220-Finish-Up.

1. Move the record Footnote-1 to the output area Printline.
2. After advancing 5 lines, write the output record Printline.
3. Move the record Footnote-2 to the output area Printline.
4. After advancing 1 line, write the output record Printline.
5. Perform 350-Prepare-Totals.
6. Move the record End-Line to the output area Printline.
7. After advancing 5 lines, write the output record Printline.
8. Close the four files.

300-Initialize-Items.

1. Obtain the date from the system.
2. Move the date to Report-Name-1 report-date.
3. Set the flag WS-MORE-RECORDS to "YES" and set
   the test item name-test-field to spaces.
4. Set the counters master-file-counter, error-file-counter, and audit-counter
   to zero.

310-Write-Report-Headers.

1. Move the record Company-Name to the output area Printline.
2. After advancing to a new page, write the output record Printline.
3. Move the record Report-Name-1 to the output area Printline.
4. After advancing 3 lines, write the output record Printline.
5. Move the record Report-Name-2 to the output area Printline.
6. After advancing 2 lines, write the output record Printline.
7. Move the record Headings to the output area Printline.
8. After advancing 2 lines, write the output record Printline.
9. Move 2 to proper-spacing.

320-Read-Employee-Record.

1. Read an input Employee-File record.
2. Test for end-of-file record;
   if EOF record reached, set the flag WS-MORE-RECORDS to "NO ".

330-Check-Name-Sequence.

1. Test if input name is greater than name-test-field value.
   - **a.** if it is, move input name to name-test-field and
     perform 400-Prepare-Master Record;
   - **b.** if it is not, perform 410-Prepare-Error-Record, and
     move "****" to Audit-Line sequence-error-flag.

340-Prepare-Audit-Line.

1. Move input employee-record to Audit-Line employee-record.
2. Move the record Audit-Line to the output area Printline.
3. After advancing proper-spacing, write the output record Printline.
4. Add 1 to audit counter.
5. Move 1 to proper-spacing.

350-Prepare-Totals.

1. Move the record Summary-Header to the output area Printline.
2. After advancing 5 lines, write the output record Printline.
3. Move the item master-file-counter to Summary-Line-1 master-file-record-counter.
4. Move the record Summary-Line-1 to the output area Printline.
5. After advancing 2 lines, write the output record Printline.
6. Move the item error-file-counter to Summary-Line-2 error-file-record-counter.
7. Move the record Summary-Line-2 to the output area Printline.
8. After advancing 1 line, write the output record Printline.
9. Move the item audit-counter to Summary-Line-3 audit-record-counter.
10. Move the record Summary-Line-3 to the output area Printline.
11. After advancing 1 line, write the output record Printline.

400-Prepare-Master-Record.

1. Move input employee-record to Employee-Master-File employee-record.
2. Write Employee-Master-File employee-record.
3. Add 1 to master-file-counter.

410-Prepare-Error-Record.

1. Move input employee-record to Error-File employee-record.
2. Write Error-File employee-record.
3. Add 1 to error-file-counter.

Figure 11.13 Program flowchart for problem 1

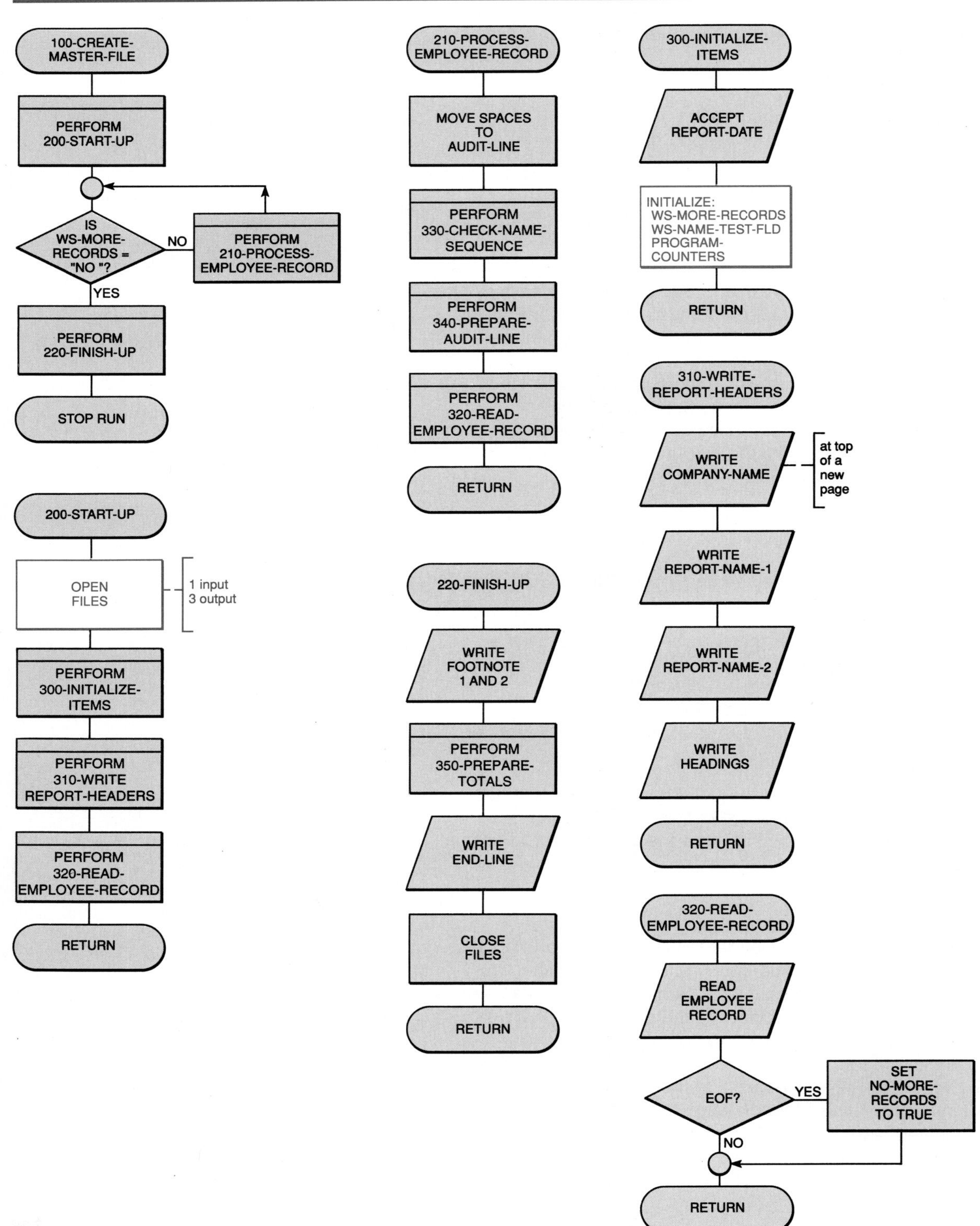

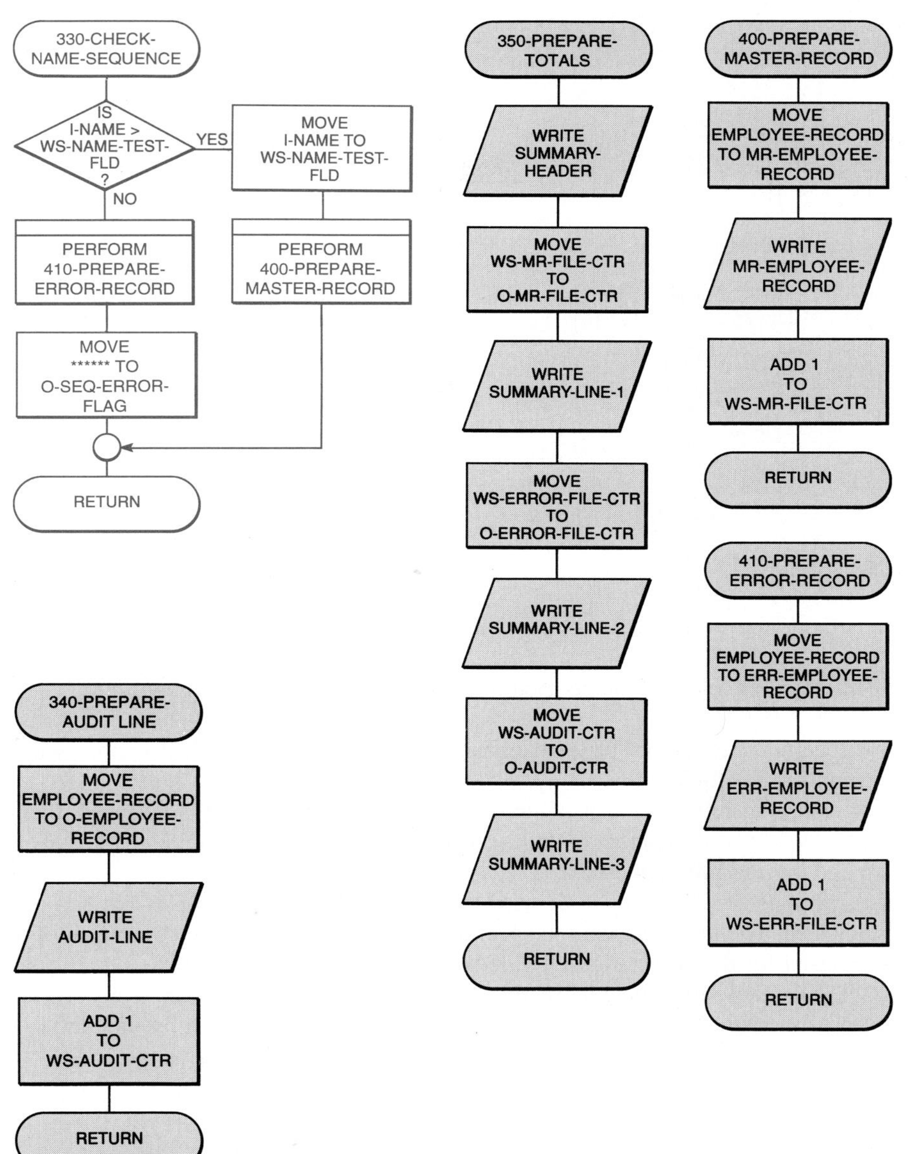

The next step in the problem-solving procedure is normally to code the program. However, some program entries that we wish to examine are specifically related to the nature of various file organizations. The first of these is in the FILE-CONTROL paragraph.

FILE-CONTROL Entries

Recall that the function of the FILE-CONTROL paragraph is to contain file-related specifications. Until now, the only entry that has been coded in a SELECT statement for a particular file has been the ASSIGN clause. Additional entries related to file organizations are now taken into account. The general format of the SELECT statement for sequential files is shown in Figure 11.14.

Rules Governing Use of the SELECT Statement-Sequential Files

1. *File-name-1* is the internal name of the file, and it must be defined in an FD entry.
2. The word OPTIONAL must be specified only for input files that need not be present when the program is run.

Figure 11.14 SELECT statement entries for sequential files

```
SELECT [OPTIONAL] file-name-1

    ASSIGN TO {implementor-name-1} ...
              {literal-1         }

   [RESERVE integer-1 [AREA ]]
                      [AREAS]

   [[ORGANIZATION IS] SEQUENTIAL]

   [PADDING CHARACTER IS {data-name-1}]
                         {literal-2  }

   [RECORD DELIMITER IS {STANDARD-1         }]
                        {implementor-name-2}

   [ACCESS MODE IS SEQUENTIAL]

   [FILE STATUS IS data-name-2]
```

3. *Implementor-name-1* is the name of the system-specific device that connects the internal file with an external file.
4. *Literal-1* is a file specification or a logical name used in connecting the internal file with an external file.
5. The RESERVE clause specifies the number of input or output buffers for the file. If it is not used, the operating system supplies a default value.
6. The ORGANIZATION clause specifies the logical structure of a file. If the clause is not used, the default is SEQUENTIAL. When a file is created with a specific organization, the organization of the file cannot be changed for the life of the file.
7. The PADDING clause specifies the character to be used to fill up the unused portion at the end of each block in sequential files. The character can be specified as a literal, or it can be the value of a data item. The clause is used for documentation only. [It will not be used in this text.]
8. The RECORD DELIMITER clause indicates the method used to determine the length of a variable-length record on an external storage medium. The method can be indicated by the ANSI specification STANDARD-1 or by a system-specific *implementor-name.* The clause is used for documentation only. [It will not be used in this text.]
9. The ACCESS clause specifies the order in which the records of the file must be accessed. For sequential files, the mode of access is necessarily sequential and the sequence is the one established by the execution of WRITE statements when the file was created. If the ACCESS clause is not coded, the access mode is sequential by default.
10. The FILE STATUS clause names the data item that contains the status code generated by an input or an output operation in relation to the file. The data item must be defined, usually in the WORKING-STORAGE SECTION, as a two-character alphanumeric item. The code is stored in *data-name-2* after the input/output operation has been executed.

Note that the ORGANIZATION clause and the ACCESS clause are clearly stated characteristics of sequential files, and, though they are optional clauses, their use is recommended because of the explicit documentation they provide. In the current program, the FILE-CONTROL paragraph can be coded as follows:

```
FILE-CONTROL.
    SELECT EMPLOYEE-FILE        ASSIGN TO COB$INPUT.
    SELECT MASTER-EMPLOYEE-FILE ASSIGN TO "JOCPERS.DAT"
                                ORGANIZATION IS SEQUENTIAL
                                ACCESS MODE IS SEQUENTIAL.
    SELECT ERROR-FILE           ASSIGN TO "JOCERR.DAT".
    SELECT AUDIT-REPORT-FILE    ASSIGN TO COB$OUTPUT.
```

Note that the organization and access mode for MASTER-EMPLOYEE-FILE are stated explicitly as SEQUENTIAL, whereas the organization and the access mode for each of the other three files are sequential by **default.**

The FILE STATUS clause is not needed in the current program. Since it is used in *Advanced Structured COBOL,* the sequel to this text, it is explained in that text.

Back to the Program

We can now complete the steps of the problem-solving procedure. Specifically, the program is coded, debugged, and compiled, and a test run of the program is made using a sample input file. The sample file contains some records out of sequence to verify that the program does in fact detect them and process them as originally planned.

The program is shown in Figure 11.15, the sample input file is shown in Figure 11.16, and the audit report is shown in Figure 11.17. The records in the new master personnel file are listed in Figure 11.18a, and the records that were written to the error file are listed in Figure 11.18b.

In the program listed in Figure 11.15, note that the FILE-CONTROL paragraph selects four files, as follows:

1. EMPLOYEE-FILE is the internal name of the input file. Through its ASSIGN clause and other operating system commands, it is connected to the sample data file in the user's directory. Since there is no ORGANIZATION clause and no ACCESS clause in the SELECT statement, the implied organization and the implied access mode are sequential. Its open mode within the program is specified in paragraph 200-START-UP as INPUT.
2. MASTER-EMPLOYEE-FILE is the internal name given to the master personnel file that the program will create on a magnetic tape. The ASSIGN clause contains a file specification (JOCPERS.DAT), and operating system commands will be used to store the file on a magnetic tape. An implementor-name could have been specified in the ASSIGN clause, but since such entries are system-specific, this choice was not selected.

   Note that the clauses ORGANIZATION IS SEQUENTIAL and ACCESS MODE IS SEQUENTIAL have been coded for this file. Though not required, since the default values would have been appropriate, they were coded to more clearly document the program.

   This file is opened as an output file in paragraph 200-START-UP. Note that it is a storage file and that the WRITE statement in paragraph 400-PREPARE-MASTER-RECORD that writes records to the file does not contain the ADVANCING clause.

   Note that the FD paragraph that defines this file contains the clause BLOCK CONTAINS 10 RECORDS. Consequently, the output buffer reserved for this file will accumulate 10 logical records (MR-EMPLOYEE-RECORD) before writing a physical record (the block) onto the magnetic tape.
3. ERROR-FILE is the internal name given to the file that will receive the records that are not in the correct alphabetic order. The ASSIGN clause connects this file to the file JOCERR.DAT in the user's directory. The system will store this file on a disk.

   Note that this file is also opened as an output file in paragraph 200-START-UP, and records are written to it in paragraph 410-PREPARE-ERROR-RECORD. Do you see that this file is also a storage file and that it has sequential organization?

   The records in this file will be added to the master personnel file later.
4. AUDIT-REPORT-FILE is the internal name given to the file that will contain the audit report. Through its ASSIGN clause and other operating system commands, it is connected to a specific file in the user's directory.

   Note that the open mode for this file is also OUTPUT (see paragraph 200-START-UP), and note that it is a print file, since the WRITE statements that write records to this file, in paragraphs 220-FINISH-UP, 310-WRITE-REPORT-HEADERS, 340-PREPARE-AUDIT-LINE, and 350-PREPARE-TOTALS, all contain the ADVANCING clause.

   A print file necessarily has sequential organization, and the access mode for the file is also necessarily sequential. Though the ORGANIZATION and ACCESS clauses could have been coded, they were not, since the default values are appropriate.

■ **Figure 11.15** COBOL program for problem 1

```
 IDENTIFICATION DIVISION.

 PROGRAM-ID.  MASTER-PERSONNEL-FILE.

*****************************************************************
*                                                               *
*  AUTHOR.        PAQUETTE.                                     *
*  DATE WRITTEN.  OCTOBER 1993.                                 *
*                                                               *
*****************************************************************

 ENVIRONMENT DIVISION.

 CONFIGURATION SECTION.

 SOURCE-COMPUTER.  VAX-VMS-8650.
 OBJECT-COMPUTER.  VAX-VMS-8650.

 INPUT-OUTPUT SECTION.

 FILE-CONTROL.
     SELECT EMPLOYEE-FILE          ASSIGN TO COB$INPUT.
     SELECT MASTER-EMPLOYEE-FILE   ASSIGN TO "JOCPERS.DAT"
                                   ORGANIZATION IS SEQUENTIAL
                                   ACCESS MODE IS SEQUENTIAL
     SELECT ERROR-FILE             ASSIGN TO "JOCERR.DAT".
     SELECT AUDIT-REPORT-FILE      ASSIGN TO COB$OUTPUT.

 DATA DIVISION.

 FILE SECTION.

 FD  EMPLOYEE-FILE
     RECORD CONTAINS 80 CHARACTERS.

 01  EMPLOYEE-RECORD.
     05 I-NAME        PIC X(20).
     05 I-ST-ADDRESS  PIC X(15).
     05 I-CITY-STATE  PIC X(17).
     05 I-ZIP         PIC X(5).
     05 I-SSN         PIC X(9).
     05 I-DATES.
        10 I-BIRTH    PIC X(6).
        10 I-HIRED    PIC X(6).
     05               PIC X(2).

 FD  MASTER-EMPLOYEE-FILE
     RECORD CONTAINS 100 CHARACTERS
     BLOCK CONTAINS 10 RECORDS.

 01  MR-EMPLOYEE-RECORD.
     05 MR-DATA        PIC X(80).
     05                PIC X(20).

 FD  ERROR-FILE
     RECORD CONTAINS 80 CHARACTERS.

 01  ERR-EMPLOYEE-RECORD PIC X(80).

 FD  AUDIT-REPORT-FILE
     RECORD CONTAINS 132 CHARACTERS.

 01  PRINTLINE         PIC X(132).

 WORKING-STORAGE SECTION.

 01  PROGRAM-CONTROLS.
     05 WS-MORE-RECORDS       PIC XXX.
        88 NO-MORE-RECORDS              VALUE "NO ".
     05 WS-NAME-TEST-FLD      PIC X(20).
     05 WS-REPORT-DATE        PIC X(6).
     05 WS-PROPER-SPACING     PIC 99.

 01  PROGRAM-COUNTERS         COMP.
     05 WS-MR-FILE-CTR        PIC S9(3).
     05 WS-ERROR-FILE-CTR     PIC S9(3).
     05 WS-AUDIT-CTR          PIC S9(3).

 01  REPORT-HEADERS.
     05 COMPANY-NAME.
        10 PIC X(58)    VALUE SPACES.
        10 PIC X(17)    VALUE "JOCELYN ORIGINALS".
        10 PIC X(57)    VALUE SPACES.
```

```
    05 REPORT-NAME-1.
       10                 PIC X(47) VALUE SPACES.
       10                 PIC X(31) VALUE
          "MASTER PERSONNEL FILE CREATED  ".
       10 O-REPORT-DATE   PIC XX/XX/XX.
       10                 PIC X(46) VALUE SPACES.

    05 REPORT-NAME-2.
       10 PIC X(57)  VALUE SPACES.
       10 PIC X(18)  VALUE "AUDIT TRAIL REPORT".
       10 PIC X(57)  VALUE SPACES.

    05 HEADINGS.
       10 PIC X(57)  VALUE SPACES.
       10 PIC X(17)  VALUE "RECORDS PROCESSED".
       10 PIC X(58)  VALUE SPACES.

01  AUDIT-LINE.
    05                     PIC X(22).
    05 O-SEQ-ERROR-FLAG    PIC X(4).
    05                     PIC X(2).
    05 O-EMPLOYEE-RECORD   PIC X(80).
    05                     PIC X(24).

01  REPORT-ENDERS.
    05 FOOTNOTE-1.
       10 PIC X(5)    VALUE SPACES.
       10 PIC X(6)    VALUE " **** ".
       10 PIC X(54)   VALUE
        "DENOTES RECORDS OUT OF SEQUENCE; WRITTEN TO ERROR FILE".

    05 FOOTNOTE-2.
       10 PIC X(11)   VALUE SPACES.
       10 PIC X(46)   VALUE
        "OTHER RECORDS WRITTEN TO MASTER PERSONNEL FILE".

    05 SUMMMARY-HEADER.
       10 PIC X(24)    VALUE SPACES.
       10 PIC X(7)     VALUE "SUMMARY".

    05 SUMMARY-LINE-1.
       10                    PIC X(5)  VALUE SPACES.
       10 O-MR-FILE-CTR      PIC ZZ9.
       10                    PIC X(42) VALUE
                "  RECORDS WRITTEN TO MASTER PERSONNEL FILE".

    05 SUMMARY-LINE-2.
       10                   PIC X(5)   VALUE SPACES.
       10 O-ERROR-FILE-CTR  PIC ZZ9.
       10                   PIC X(31)  VALUE
                "  RECORDS WRITTEN TO ERROR FILE".

    05 SUMMARY-LINE-3.
       10                   PIC X(5)  VALUE SPACES.
       10 O-AUDIT-CTR       PIC ZZ9.
       10                   PIC X(33) VALUE
                "  RECORDS WRITTEN TO AUDIT REPORT".

    05 END-LINE.
       10 PIC X(55)   VALUE SPACES.
       10 PIC X(23)   VALUE "***  END OF REPORT  ***".
       10 PIC X(54)   VALUE SPACES.

PROCEDURE DIVISION.

100-CREATE-MASTER-FILE.
    PERFORM 200-START-UP.
    PERFORM 210-PROCESS-EMPLOYEE-RECORD
       UNTIL NO-MORE-RECORDS.
    PERFORM 220-FINISH-UP.
    STOP RUN.

200-START-UP.
    OPEN INPUT EMPLOYEE-FILE
         OUTPUT MASTER-EMPLOYEE-FILE
                ERROR-FILE
                AUDIT-REPORT-FILE.
    PERFORM 300-INITIALIZE-ITEMS.
    PERFORM 310-WRITE-REPORT-HEADERS.
    PERFORM 320-READ-EMPLOYEE-RECORD.
```

```
210-PROCESS-EMPLOYEE-RECORD.
    MOVE SPACES TO AUDIT-LINE.
    PERFORM 330-CHECK-NAME-SEQUENCE.
    PERFORM 340-PREPARE-AUDIT-LINE.
    PERFORM 320-READ-EMPLOYEE-RECORD.

220-FINISH-UP.
    WRITE PRINTLINE FROM FOOTNOTE-1
        AFTER ADVANCING 5 LINES.
    WRITE PRINTLINE FROM FOOTNOTE-2
        AFTER ADVANCING 1 LINE.
    PERFORM 350-PREPARE-TOTALS.
    WRITE PRINTLINE FROM END-LINE.
        AFTER ADVANCING 5 LINES.
    CLOSE EMPLOYEE-FILE
          MASTER-EMPLOYEE-FILE
          ERROR-FILE
          AUDIT-REPORT-FILE.

300-INITIALIZE-ITEMS.
    ACCEPT WS-REPORT-DATE FROM DATE.
    MOVE WS-REPORT-DATE TO O-REPORT-DATE.
    MOVE "YES" TO WS-MORE-RECORDS.
    INITIALIZE WS-NAME-TEST-FLD
               PROGRAM-COUNTERS.

310-WRITE-REPORT-HEADERS.
    WRITE PRINTLINE FROM COMPANY-NAME
        AFTER ADVANCING PAGE.
    WRITE PRINTLINE FROM REPORT-NAME-1
        AFTER ADVANCING 3 LINES.
    WRITE PRINTLINE FROM REPORT-NAME-2
        AFTER ADVANCING 2 LINES.
    WRITE PRINTLINE FROM HEADINGS
        AFTER ADVANCING 2 LINES.
    MOVE 2 TO WS-PROPER-SPACING.

320-READ-EMPLOYEE-RECORD.
    READ EMPLOYEE-FILE RECORD
        AT END
            SET NO-MORE-RECORDS TO TRUE.

330-CHECK-NAME-SEQUENCE.
    IF I-NAME > WS-NAME-TEST-FLD
        MOVE I-NAME TO WS-NAME-TEST-FLD
        PERFORM 400-PREPARE-MASTER-RECORD
    ELSE
        PERFORM 410-PREPARE-ERROR-RECORD
        MOVE "****" TO O-SEQ-ERROR-FLAG
    END-IF.

340-PREPARE-AUDIT-LINE.
    MOVE EMPLOYEE-RECORD TO O-EMPLOYEE-RECORD.
    WRITE PRINTLINE FROM AUDIT-LINE
        AFTER ADVANCING WS-PROPER-SPACING.
    ADD 1 TO WS-AUDIT-CTR.
    MOVE 1 TO WS-PROPER-SPACING.

350-PREPARE-TOTALS.
    WRITE PRINTLINE FROM SUMMARY-HEADER
        AFTER ADVANCING 5 LINES.
    MOVE WS-MR-FILE-CTR TO O-MR-FILE-CTR.
    WRITE PRINTLINE FROM SUMMARY-LINE-1
        AFTER ADVANCING 2 LINES.
    MOVE WS-ERROR-FILE-CTR TO O-ERROR-FILE-CTR.
    WRITE PRINTLINE FROM SUMMARY-LINE-2
        AFTER ADVANCING 1 LINE.
    MOVE WS-AUDIT-CTR TO O-AUDIT-CTR.
    WRITE PRINTLINE FROM SUMMARY-LINE-3
        AFTER ADVANCING 1 LINE.

400-PREPARE-MASTER-RECORD.
    MOVE EMPLOYEE-RECORD TO MR-EMPLOYEE-RECORD.
    WRITE MR-EMPLOYEE-RECORD.
    ADD 1 TO WS-MR-FILE-CTR.

410-PREPARE-ERROR-RECORD.
    MOVE EMPLOYEE-RECORD TO ERR-EMPLOYEE-RECORD.
    WRITE ERR-EMPLOYEE-RECORD.
    ADD 1 TO WS-ERROR-FILE-CTR.
```

Figure 11.16 Sample input file for problem 1

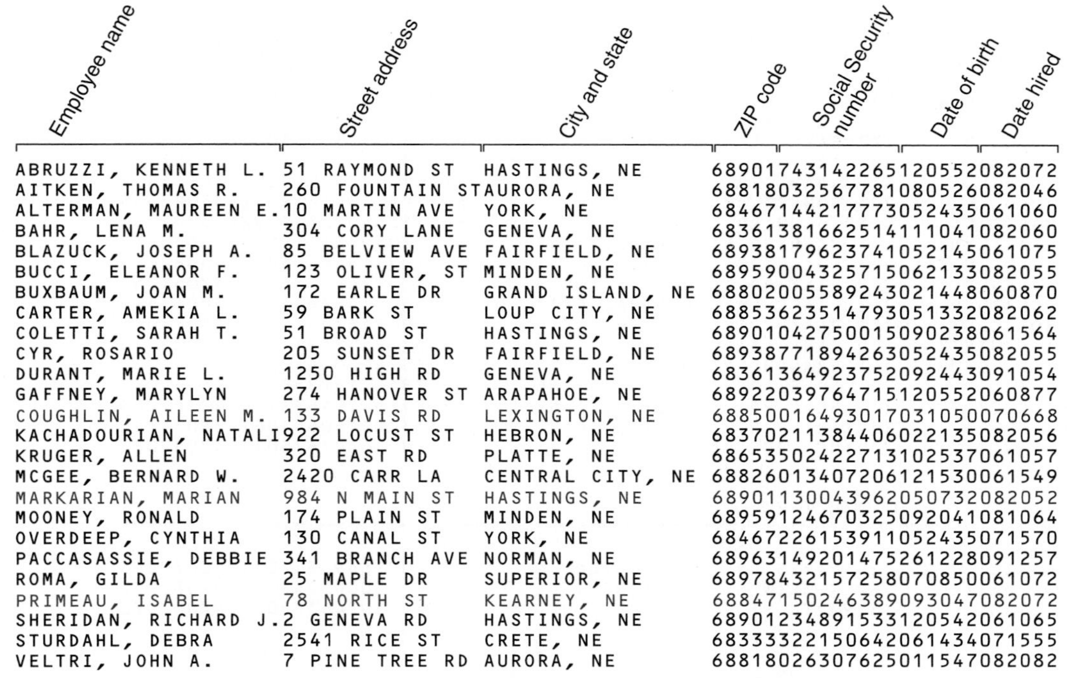


```
ABRUZZI, KENNETH L. 51 RAYMOND ST   HASTINGS, NE      6890174314226512055208207 2
AITKEN, THOMAS R.   260 FOUNTAIN STAURORA, NE         688180325677810805260820 46
ALTERMAN, MAUREEN E.10 MARTIN AVE   YORK, NE          684671442177730524350610 60
BAHR, LENA M.       304 CORY LANE   GENEVA, NE        683613816625141110410820 60
BLAZUCK, JOSEPH A.  85 BELVIEW AVE  FAIRFIELD, NE     689381796237410521450610 75
BUCCI, ELEANOR F.   123 OLIVER, ST  MINDEN, NE        689590043257150621330820 55
BUXBAUM, JOAN M.    172 EARLE DR    GRAND ISLAND, NE  688020055892430214480608 70
CARTER, AMEKIA L.   59 BARK ST      LOUP CITY, NE     688536235147930513320820 62
COLETTI, SARAH T.   51 BROAD ST     HASTINGS, NE      689010427500150902380615 64
CYR, ROSARIO        205 SUNSET DR   FAIRFIELD, NE     689387718942630524350820 55
DURANT, MARIE L.    1250 HIGH RD    GENEVA, NE        683613649237520924430910 54
GAFFNEY, MARYLYN    274 HANOVER ST  ARAPAHOE, NE      689220397647151205520608 77
COUGHLIN, AILEEN M. 133 DAVIS RD    LEXINGTON, NE     688500164930170310500706 68
KACHADOURIAN, NATALI922 LOCUST ST   HEBRON, NE        683702113844060221350820 56
KRUGER, ALLEN       320 EAST RD     PLATTE, NE        686535024227131025370610 57
MCGEE, BERNARD W.   2420 CARR LA    CENTRAL CITY, NE  688260134072061215300615 49
MARKARIAN, MARIAN   984 N MAIN ST   HASTINGS, NE      689011300439620507320820 52
MOONEY, RONALD      174 PLAIN ST    MINDEN, NE        689591246703250920410810 64
OVERDEEP, CYNTHIA   130 CANAL ST    YORK, NE          684672261539110524350715 70
PACCASASSIE, DEBBIE 341 BRANCH AVE  NORMAN, NE        689631492014752612280912 57
ROMA, GILDA         25 MAPLE DR     SUPERIOR, NE      689784321572580708500610 72
PRIMEAU, ISABEL     78 NORTH ST     KEARNEY, NE       688471502463890930470820 72
SHERIDAN, RICHARD J.2 GENEVA RD     HASTINGS, NE      689012348915331205420610 65
STURDAHL, DEBRA     2541 RICE ST    CRETE, NE         683333221506420614340715 55
VELTRI, JOHN A.     7 PINE TREE RD  AURORA, NE        688180263076250115470820 82
```

Figure 11.17 The audit report for problem 1

```
                                   JOCELYN ORIGINALS

                         MASTER PERSONNEL FILE CREATED 93/10/17

                                  AUDIT TRAIL REPORT

                                  RECORDS PROCESSED

          ABRUZZI, KENNETH L. 51 RAYMOND ST   HASTINGS, NE      68901743142265120552082072
          AITKEN, THOMAS R.   260 FOUNTAIN STAURORA, NE         68818032567781080526082046
          ALTERMAN, MAUREEN E.10 MARTIN AVE   YORK, NE          68467144217773052435061060
          BAHR, LENA M.       304 CORY LANE   GENEVA, NE        68361381662514111041082060
          BLAZUCK, JOSEPH A.  85 BELVIEW AVE  FAIRFIELD, NE     68938179623741052145061075
          BUCCI, ELEANOR F.   123 OLIVER, ST  MINDEN, NE        68959004325715062133082055
          BUXBAUM, JOAN M.    172 EARLE DR    GRAND ISLAND, NE  68802005589243021448060870
          CARTER, AMEKIA L.   59 BARK ST      LOUP CITY, NE     68853623514793051332082062
          COLETTI, SARAH T.   51 BROAD ST     HASTINGS, NE      68901042750015090238061564
          CYR, ROSARIO        205 SUNSET DR   FAIRFIELD, NE     68938771894263052435082055
          DURANT, MARIE L.    1250 HIGH RD    GENEVA, NE        68361364923752092443091054
          GAFFNEY, MARYLYN    274 HANOVER ST  ARAPAHOE, NE      68922039764715120552060877
     **** COUGHLIN, AILEEN M. 133 DAVIS RD    LEXINGTON, NE     68850016493017031050070668
          KACHADOURIAN, NATALI922 LOCUST ST   HEBRON, NE        68370211384406022135082056
          KRUGER, ALLEN       320 EAST RD     PLATTE, NE        68653502422713102537061057
          MCGEE, BERNARD W.   2420 CARR LA    CENTRAL CITY, NE  68826013407206121530061549
     **** MARKARIAN, MARIAN   984 N MAIN ST   HASTINGS, NE      68901130043962050732082052
          MOONEY, RONALD      174 PLAIN ST    MINDEN, NE        68959124670325092041081064
          OVERDEEP, CYNTHIA   130 CANAL ST    YORK, NE          68467226153911052435071570
          PACCASASSIE, DEBBIE 341 BRANCH AVE  NORMAN, NE        68963149201475261228091257
          ROMA, GILDA         25 MAPLE DR     SUPERIOR, NE      68978432157258070850061072
     **** PRIMEAU, ISABEL     78 NORTH ST     KEARNEY, NE       68847150246389093047082072
          SHERIDAN, RICHARD J.2 GENEVA RD     HASTINGS, NE      68901234891533120542061065
          STURDAHL, DEBRA     2541 RICE ST    CRETE, NE         68333322150642061434071555
          VELTRI, JOHN A.     7 PINE TREE RD  AURORA, NE        68818026307625011547082082


****  DENOTES RECORDS OUT OF SEQUENCE; WRITTEN TO ERROR FILE
      OTHER RECORDS WRITTEN TO MASTER PERSONNEL FILE


                SUMMARY

22  RECORDS WRITTEN TO MASTER PERSONNEL FILE
 3  RECORDS WRITTEN TO ERROR FILE
25  RECORDS WRITTEN TO AUDIT REPORT


                         ***  END OF REPORT  ***
```

Figure 11.18a The records in the master personnel file

```
ABRUZZI, KENNETH L. 51 RAYMOND ST  HASTINGS, NE     68901743142265120552082072
AITKEN, THOMAS R.   260 FOUNTAIN STAURORA, NE       68818032567781080526082046
ALTERMAN, MAUREEN E.10 MARTIN AVE  YORK, NE         68467144217773052435061060
BAHR, LENA M.       304 CORY LANE  GENEVA, NE       68361381662514111041082060
BLAZUCK, JOSEPH A.  85 BELVIEW AVE FAIRFIELD,NE     68938179623741052145061075
BUCCI, ELEANOR F.   123 OLIVER, ST MINDEN, NE       68959004325715062133082055
BUXBAUM, JOAN M.    172 EARLE DR   GRAND ISLAND, NE 68802005589243021448060870
CARTER, AMEKIA L.   59 BARK ST     LOUP CITY, NE    68853623514793051332082062
COLETTI, SARAH T.   51 BROAD ST    HASTINGS, NE     68901042750015090238061564
CYR, ROSARIO        205 SUNSET DR  FAIRFIELD, NE    68938771894263052435082055
DURANT, MARIE L.    1250 HIGH RD   GENEVA, NE       68361364923752092443091054
GAFFNEY, MARYLYN    274 HANOVER ST ARAPAHOE, NE     68922039764715120552060877
KACHADOURIAN, NATALI922 LOCUST ST  HEBRON, NE       68370211384406022135082056
KRUGER, ALLEN       320 EAST RD    PLATTE, NE       68653502422713102537061057
MCGEE, BERNARD W.   2420 CARR LA   CENTRAL CITY, NE 68826013407206121530061549
MOONEY, RONALD      174 PLAIN ST   MINDEN, NE       68969124670325092041081064
OVERDEEP, CYNTHIA   130 CANAL ST   YORK, NE         68467226153911052435071570
PACCASASSIE, DEBBIE 341 BRANCH AVE NORMAN, NE       68963149201475261228091257
ROMA, GILDA         25 MAPLE DR    SUPERIOR, NE     68978432157258070850061072
SHERIDAN, RICHARD J.2 GENEVA RD    HASTINGS, NE     68901234891533120542061065
STURDAHL, DEBRA     2541 RICE ST   CRETE, NE        68333322150642061434071555
VELTRI, JOHN A.     7 PINE TREE RD AURORA, NE       68818026307625011547082082
```

Figure 11.18b The records in the error file

```
COUGHLIN, AILEEN M. 133 DAVIS RD   LEXINGTON, NE    68850016493017031050070668
MARKARIAN, MARIAN   984 N MAIN ST  HASTINGS, NE     68901130043962050732082052
PRIMEAU, ISABEL     78 NORTH ST    KEARNEY, NE      68847150246389093047082072
```

Updating the Master Personnel Tape File

Suppose that many records were found to be out of sequence in the program of problem 1. How are they inserted in the master personnel file? Also, suppose that, over a period of time, new employees are hired, other employees leave, and still others change addresses. How is the master personnel file kept up-to-date? These are typical examples of conditions that require the master file to be updated. A brief examination of each case follows.

1. A record was found to be out of sequence.
   Action needed: Insert it in the master file where it belongs in order to maintain alphabetic sequence.
2. A new employee has been hired.
   Action needed: Prepare a record for the new employee, then insert it in the master file where it belongs. (Except for preparing a new record, the procedure is the same as the one needed in step 1.)
3. An employee leaves the company.
   Action needed: Delete the corresponding record from the master file.
4. An employee's address is changed.
   Action needed: Replace the old information with the new.

One way of updating the master tape file is to proceed as follows:

1. Prepare a file containing a record for each employee involved in the updating task. Decide on a code to be inserted in each record to indicate the action that must be taken with respect to that record. The codes, referred to as process codes, might be the following:

   a "1" means that the record must be added to the master file;

   a "2" means that the matching record in the master file must be deleted;

   a "3" means that the record contains a new address that must replace the address on the old master record.

   The process code should be stored in the first byte of the record.

   For a record with a process code of 1, the rest of the record must contain employee data as specified in problem 1, namely, the name, street address, city and state, ZIP code, Social Security number, date of birth, and date hired.

   For a record with a process code of 2, the only other data field that must have a value is the name field. It will be used to identify the matching record in the old master file.

Figure 11.19 Detail record layout

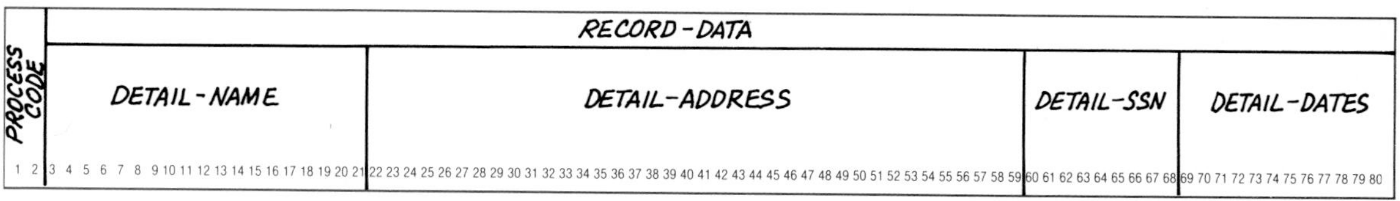
Record Layout Form

PROCESS CODE	RECORD-DATA			
	DETAIL-NAME	DETAIL-ADDRESS	DETAIL-SSN	DETAIL-DATES
1 2	3–21	22–59	60–68	69–80

Record Name: DETAIL-RECORD

Figure 11.20 System flowchart

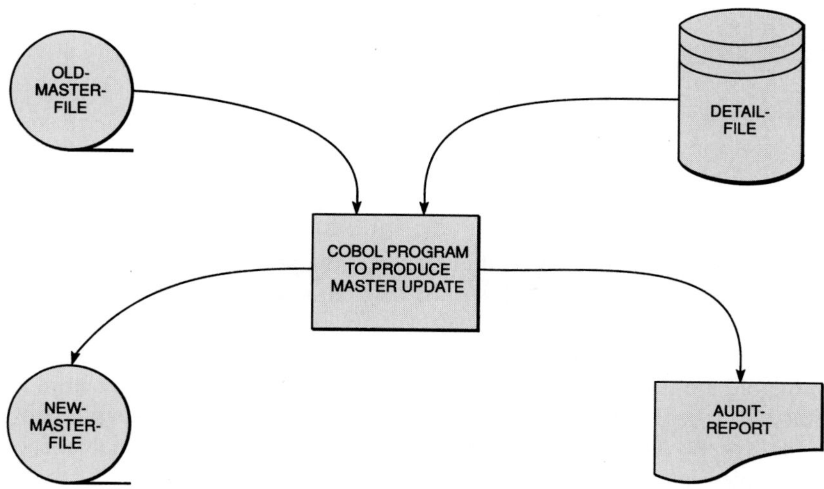

For a record with a process code of 3, both the name field and the address field must contain values. The name field will be used to identify the matching record in the old master file, and the address field contains the new address.

The layout of these records is shown in Figure 11.19. The file that contains these records is called a *detail file,* and its records should be sequenced alphabetically by employee name.

2. There must be at least three files: the old master file, the detail file, and the new master file. In addition, an audit report will be produced, and thus a total of four files are needed in this program. The system flowchart is shown in Figure 11.20.

   It should be clear that to update a master file stored on a magnetic tape, it is necessary to create a **new** master file on a second magnetic tape. Since the records on a tape have been written sequentially, it is impossible to write new records between existing ones. It is also impossible to update fields of records on tape, since this requires reading the record to be updated, inserting the new values, and then rewriting the revised record. The REWRITE statement cannot be executed for a tape file, hence the need to produce the updated master file on a new tape.

   Obviously, many records of the old master file will simply be written onto the updated master file. Those are the records not involved in the update. Other records of the old master file are to be deleted. When such a record is being processed, it is simply not copied into the new master file. When a record requiring an address change is being processed, the new address is copied into the field and the revised record is written into the new master file.

   All the records of the old master file must be accessed, and all the records of the detail file must also be accessed.

3. The program must be designed to accomplish the following:
   a. Read a record from the old master file and a record from the detail file.
   b. Test the employee name of the detail record against the employee name of the old master record. (Recall that both files are in alphabetic order by employee name.) If they match, then

■ **Figure 11.21** Processing the input records

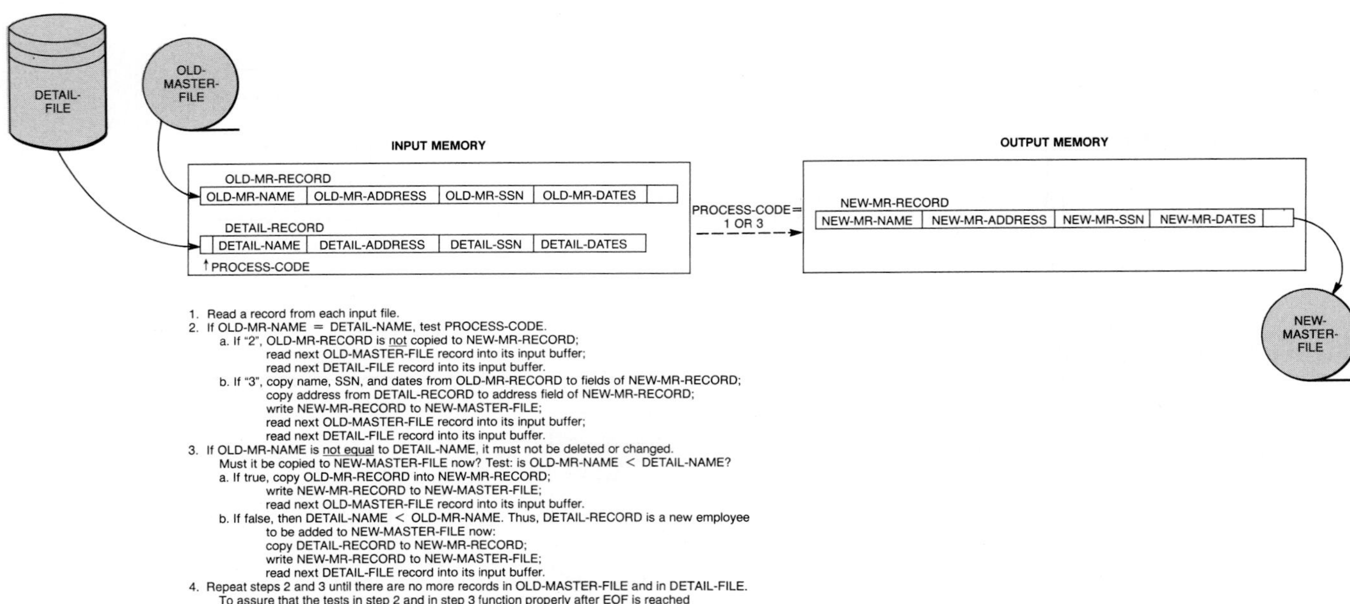

the old master record is involved in the update. In this case, test the process code on the detail record to determine whether the old master record is to be deleted or simply needs an address change. Then, proceed accordingly.

DETAIL-FILE
OLD-MASTER-FILE
INPUT MEMORY
OLD-MR-RECORD
OLD-MR-NAME
OLD-MR-ADDRESS
OLD-MR-SSN
OLD-MR-DATES
DETAIL-RECORD
DETAIL-NAME
DETAIL-ADDRESS
DETAIL-SSN
DETAIL-DATES
PROCESS-CODE
PROCESS-CODE= 1 OR 3
OUTPUT MEMORY
NEW-MR-RECORD
NEW-MR-NAME
NEW-MR-ADDRESS
NEW-MR-SSN
NEW-MR-DATES
NEW-MASTER-FILE
1. Read a record from each input file.
2. If OLD-MR-NAME = DETAIL-NAME, test PROCESS-CODE.
a. If "2", OLD-MR-RECORD is not copied to NEW-MR-RECORD;
read next OLD-MASTER-FILE record into its input buffer;
read next DETAIL-FILE record into its input buffer.
b. If "3", copy name, SSN, and dates from OLD-MR-RECORD to fields of NEW-MR-RECORD;
copy address from DETAIL-RECORD to address field of NEW-MR-RECORD;
write NEW-MR-RECORD to NEW-MASTER-FILE;
read next OLD-MASTER-FILE record into its input buffer;
read next DETAIL-FILE record into its input buffer.
3. If OLD-MR-NAME is not equal to DETAIL-NAME, it must not be deleted or changed.
Must it be copied to NEW-MASTER-FILE now? Test: is OLD-MR-NAME < DETAIL-NAME?
a. If true, copy OLD-MR-RECORD into NEW-MR-RECORD;
write NEW-MR-RECORD to NEW-MASTER-FILE;
read next OLD-MASTER-FILE record into its input buffer.
b. If false, then DETAIL-NAME < OLD-MR-NAME. Thus, DETAIL-RECORD is a new employee
to be added to NEW-MASTER-FILE now:
copy DETAIL-RECORD to NEW-MR-RECORD;
write NEW-MR-RECORD to NEW-MASTER-FILE;
read next DETAIL-FILE record into its input buffer.
4. Repeat steps 2 and 3 until there are no more records in OLD-MASTER-FILE and in DETAIL-FILE.
To assure that the tests in step 2 and in step 3 function properly after EOF is reached
in either input file, move HIGH-VALUES to the name field in the input buffer for that file.

If the names do not match, the old master record is not involved in the update. In that case, test the name on the old master record against the name on the detail record to determine which comes first alphabetically. If it's the old master record that comes first, then simply copy it into the new master file. On the other hand, if it's the detail record that comes first, this is a new record that must be copied into the new master file at this point.

See Figure 11.21, which illustrates input record processing.

c. In part b,

  i. If a record deletion occurred, then the next record of the old master file and the next record of the detail file must be read, since the previous detail record has accomplished its purpose, and the test pattern in part b is repeated.

  ii. If the old master record was copied into the new master file, then read the next record in the old master file, and repeat the test pattern in part b.

  iii. If a new record was added to the master file, then read the next record in the detail file, and repeat the test pattern in part b.

d. The procedures in parts b and c must be repeated until there are no more records in either input file.

e. The audit report should list each record processed along with an indication of the action taken with respect to it.

The printer spacing chart for the audit report is shown in Figure 11.22. The structure chart for the program analyzed in item 3 on page 719 is shown in Figure 11.23. The program flowchart is shown in Figure 11.24, and the pseudocode is listed below.

100-Produce-Master-Update.

1. Perform 200-Start-Up.
2. Perform 210-Process-Update until no more records in Old-Master-File and in Detail-File.
3. Perform 220-Finish-Up.
4. Stop the run.

200-Start-Up.

1. Open Old-Master-File and Detail-File as input files, and New-Master-File and Audit-Report as output files.
2. Perform 300-Initialize-Items.

■ **Figure 11.22** Printer spacing chart for audit report on the master file update

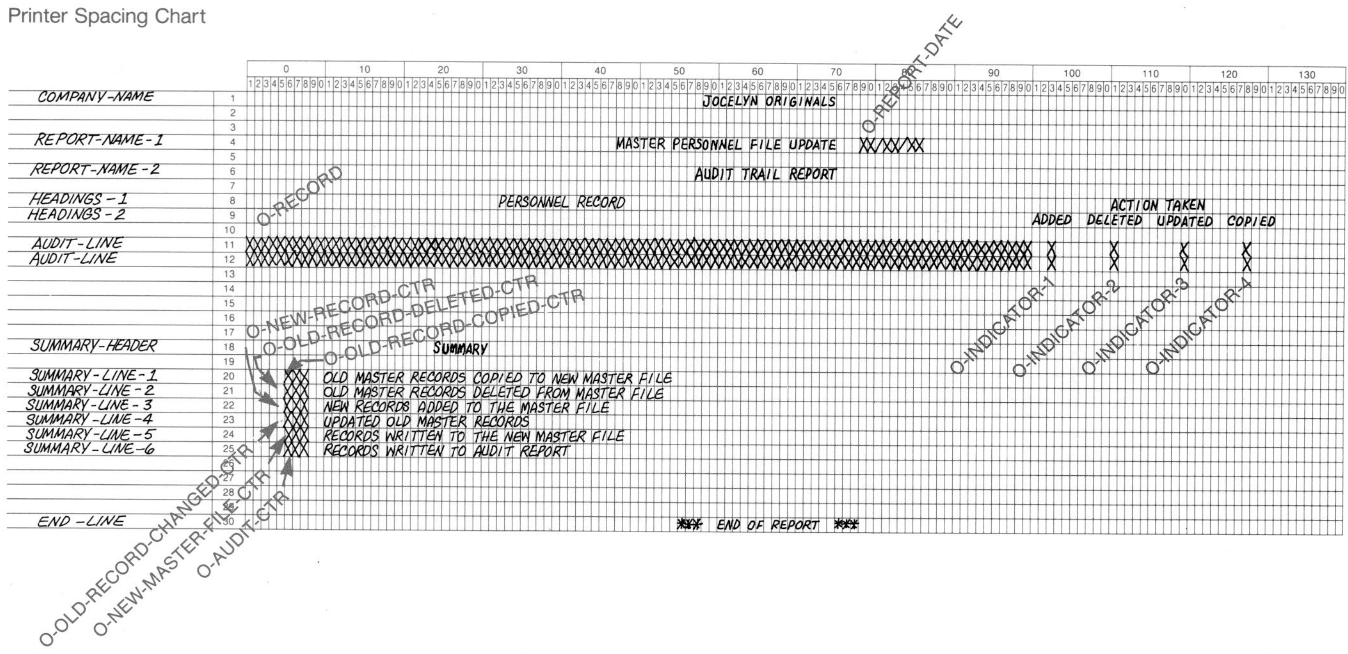

■ **Figure 11.23** Structure chart

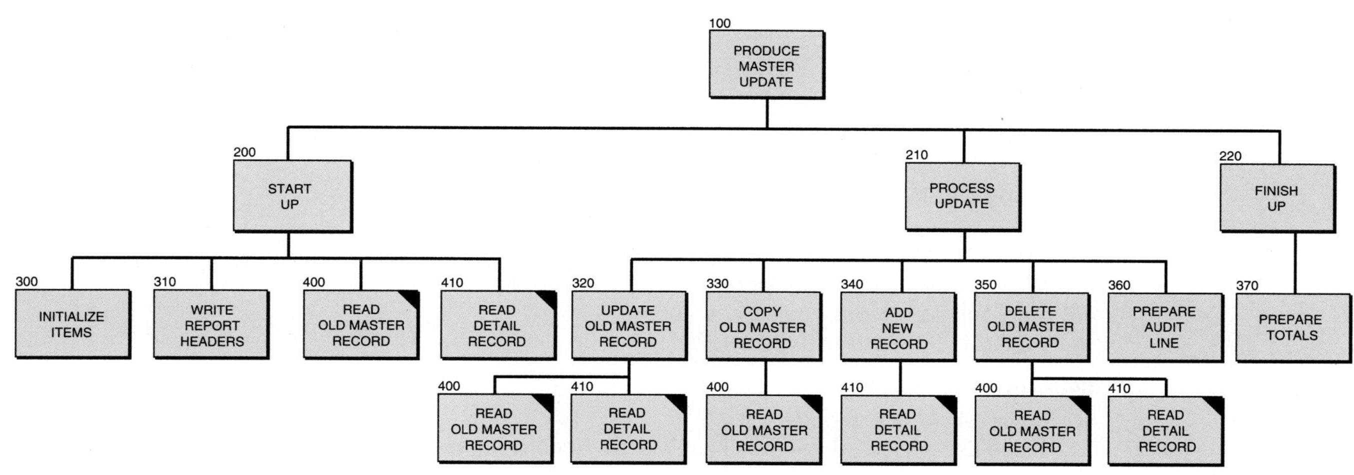

3. Perform 310-Write-Report-Headers.
4. Perform 400-Read-Old-Master-Record.
5. Perform 410-Read-Detail-Record.

210-Process-Update.

1. Test old-master-record name against detail-record name;
   a. if they match, test detail-record process-code:
      if process-code = 3, perform 320-Update-Old-Master-Record;
      otherwise, perform 350-Delete-Old-Master-Record.
   b. if they do not match, test if old-master-record name is less than detail-record name;
      if so, perform 330-Copy-Old-Master-Record;
      if not so, perform 340-Add-New-Record.
2. Perform 360-Prepare-Audit-Line.

220-Finish-Up.

1. Perform 370-Prepare-Totals.
2. Move the record End-Line to the output area Printline.
3. After advancing 5 lines, write the output record Printline.
4. Close the four files.

300-Initialize-Items.

1. Obtain the date from the system.
2. Move the date to Report-Name-1 date.
3. Set all the counters to zero: old-record-copied-counter, old-record-deleted-counter, new-record-counter, old-record-changed-counter, new-master-record-counter, and audit-counter.

310-Write-Report-Headers.

1. Move the record Company-Name to the output area Printline.
2. After advancing to a new page, write the output record Printline.
3. Move the record Report-Name-1 to the output area Printline.
4. After advancing 3 lines, write the output record Printline.
5. Move the record Report-Name-2 to the output area Printline.
6. After advancing 2 lines, write the output record Printline.
7. Move the record Headings-1 to the output area Printline.
8. After advancing 2 lines, write the output record Printline.
9. Move the record Headings-2 to the output area Printline.
10. After advancing 1 line, write the output record Printline.
11. Move 2 to proper-spacing.

320-Update-Old-Master-Record.

1. Move "U" to action-code.
2. Move Old-Master-Record name to New-Master-Record name.
3. Move Detail-Record address to New-Master-Record address.
4. Move Old-Master-Record Social-Security-number to New-Master-Record Social-Security-number.
5. Move Old-Master-Record dates to New-Master-Record dates.
6. Write the record New-Master-Record to the New-Master-File.
7. Add 1 to old-record-changed-counter.
8. Perform 400-Read-Old-Master-Record.
9. Perform 410-Read-Detail-Record.

330-Copy-Old-Master-Record.

1. Move "C" to action-code.
2. Move Old-Master-Record to New-Master-Record.
3. Write the record New-Master-Record to the New-Master-File.
4. Add 1 to old-record-copied-counter.
5. Perform 400-Read-Old-Master-Record.

340-Add-New-Record.

1. Move "A" to action-code.
2. Move Detail-Record name to New-Master-Record name.
3. Move Detail-Record address to New-Master-Record address.
4. Move Detail-Record Social-Security-number to New-Master-Record Social-Security-number.
5. Move Detail-Record dates to New-Master-Record dates.
6. Write the record New-Master-Record to the New-Master-File.
7. Add 1 to new-record-counter.
8. Perform 410-Read-Detail-Record.

350-Delete-Old-Master-Record.

1. Move "D" to action-code.
2. Move Old-Master-Record to working-area old-master-record.
3. Add 1 to old-record-deleted-counter.
4. Perform 400-Read-Old-Master-Record.
5. Perform 410-Read-Detail-Record.

360-Prepare-Audit-Line.

1. Test action-code:
   a. if "A", move New-Master-Record to Audit-Line record area,
      move "X" to Audit-Line indicator-1.
   b. if "D", move working-area old-master-record to Audit-Line record area,
      move "X" to Audit-Line indicator-2.
   c. if "U", move New-Master-Record to Audit-Line record area,
      move "X" to Audit-Line indicator-3.
   d. if "C", move New-Master-Record to Audit-Line record area,
      move "X" to Audit-Line indicator-4.
2. Move the record Audit-Line to the output area Printline.
3. After advancing proper-spacing, write the output record Printline.
4. Move 1 to proper-spacing.
5. Add 1 to audit-counter.

370-Prepare-Totals.

1. Move the record Summary-Header to the output area Printline.
2. After advancing 5 lines, write the output record Printline.
3. Move old-record-copied-counter to Summary-Line-1 old-record-copied-counter.
4. Move the record Summary-Line-1 to the output area Printline.
5. After advancing 2 lines, write the output record Printline.
6. Move old-record-deleted-counter to Summary-Line-2 old-record-deleted-counter.
7. Move the record Summary-Line-2 to the output area Printline.
8. After advancing 1 line, write the output record Printline.
9. Move new-record-counter to Summary-Line-3 new-record-counter.
10. Move the record Summary-Line-3 to the output area Printline.
11. After advancing 1 line, write the output record Printline.
12. Move old-record-changed-counter to Summary-Line-4 old-record-changed-counter.
13. Move the record Summary-Line-4 to the output area Printline.
14. After advancing 1 line, write the output record Printline.
15. Move new-master-record-counter to Summary-Line-5 new-master-record-counter.
16. Move the record Summary-Line-5 to the output area Printline.
17. After advancing 1 line, write the output record Printline.
18. Move audit-counter to Summary-Line-6 audit-counter.
19. Move the record Summary-Line-6 to the output area Printline.
20. After advancing 1 line, write the output record Printline.

400-Read-Old-Master-Record.

1. Read the next input Old-Master-File record.
2. Test for end-of-file record;
   if EOF record reached, move High-Values to Old-Master-Record name.

410-Read-Detail-Record.

1. Read the next input Detail-File record.
2. Test for end-of-file record;
   if EOF record reached, move High-Values to Detail-Record name.

Figure 11.24 Program flowchart for master file update

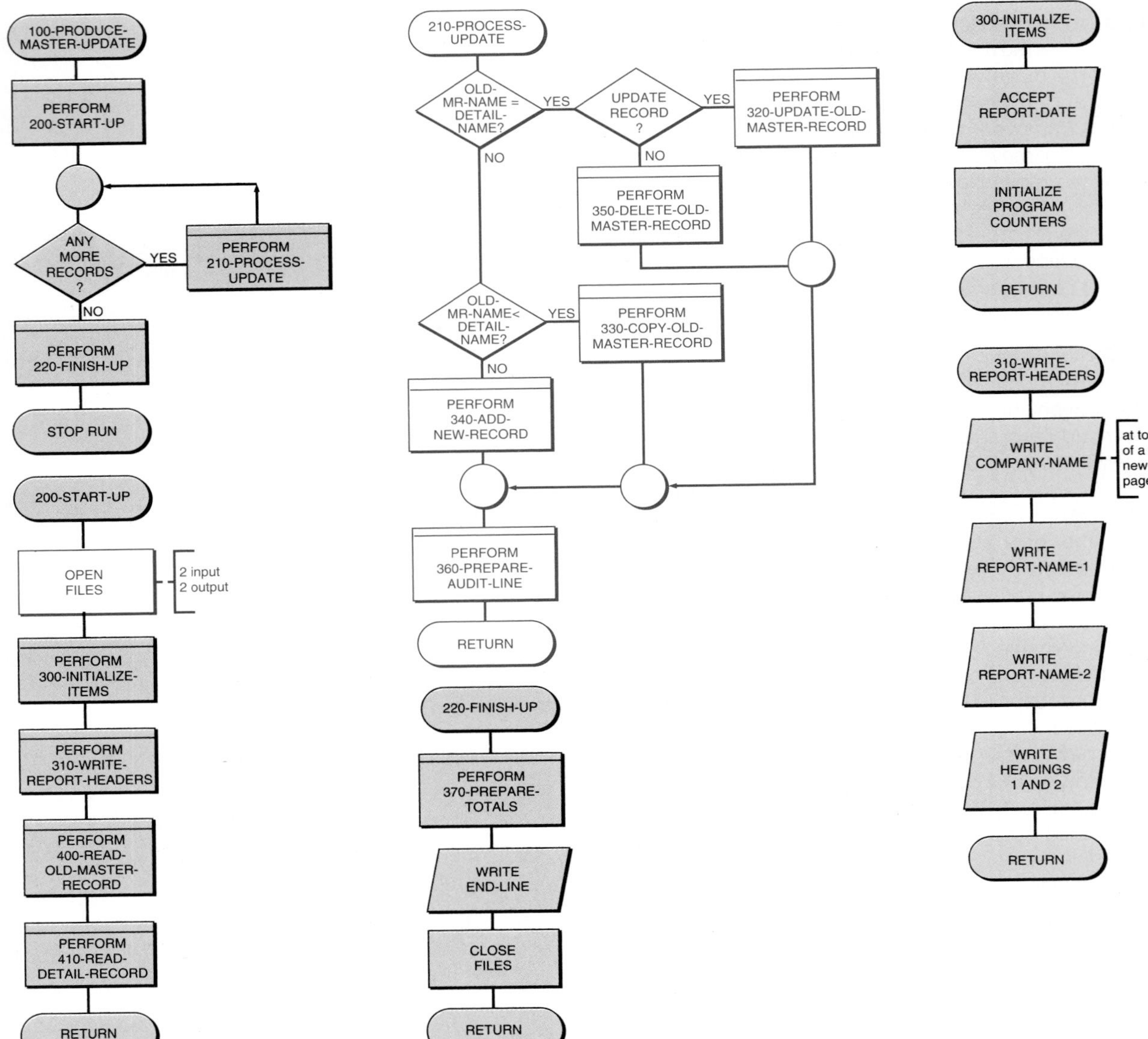

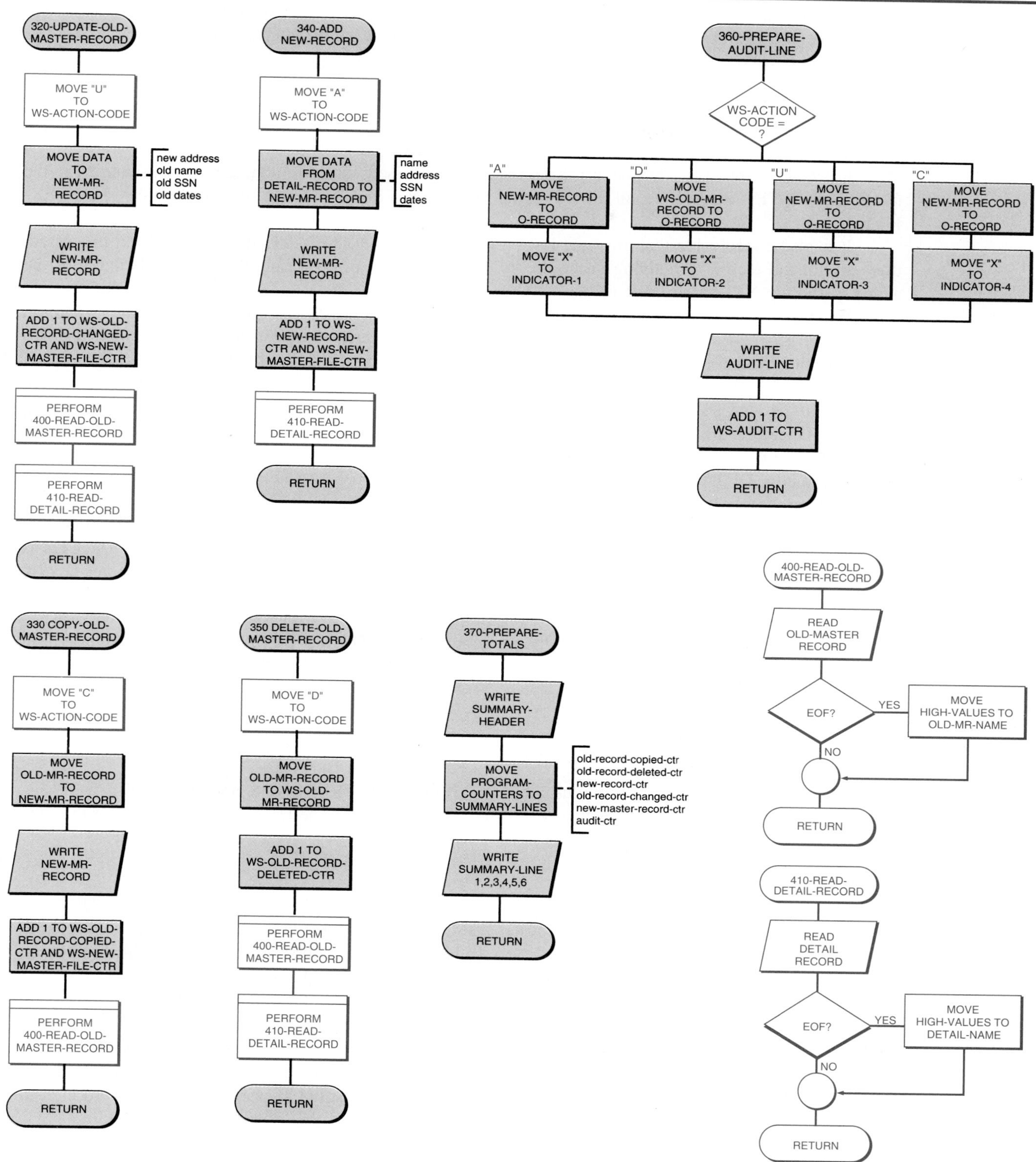

320-UPDATE-OLD-MASTER-RECORD
MOVE "U" TO WS-ACTION-CODE
MOVE DATA TO NEW-MR-RECORD
new address
old name
old SSN
old dates
WRITE NEW-MR-RECORD
ADD 1 TO WS-OLD-RECORD-CHANGED-CTR AND WS-NEW-MASTER-FILE-CTR
PERFORM 400-READ-OLD-MASTER-RECORD
PERFORM 410-READ-DETAIL-RECORD
RETURN
340-ADD NEW-RECORD
MOVE "A" TO WS-ACTION-CODE
MOVE DATA FROM DETAIL-RECORD TO NEW-MR-RECORD
name
address
SSN
dates
WRITE NEW-MR-RECORD
ADD 1 TO WS-NEW-RECORD-CTR AND WS-NEW-MASTER-FILE-CTR
PERFORM 410-READ-DETAIL-RECORD
RETURN
360-PREPARE-AUDIT-LINE
WS-ACTION CODE = ?
"A"
MOVE NEW-MR-RECORD TO O-RECORD
MOVE "X" TO INDICATOR-1
"D"
MOVE WS-OLD-MR-RECORD TO O-RECORD
MOVE "X" TO INDICATOR-2
"U"
MOVE NEW-MR-RECORD TO O-RECORD
MOVE "X" TO INDICATOR-3
"C"
MOVE NEW-MR-RECORD TO O-RECORD
MOVE "X" TO INDICATOR-4
WRITE AUDIT-LINE
ADD 1 TO WS-AUDIT-CTR
RETURN
330 COPY-OLD-MASTER-RECORD
MOVE "C" TO WS-ACTION-CODE
MOVE OLD-MR-RECORD TO NEW-MR-RECORD
WRITE NEW-MR-RECORD
ADD 1 TO WS-OLD-RECORD-COPIED-CTR AND WS-NEW-MASTER-FILE-CTR
PERFORM 400-READ-OLD-MASTER-RECORD
RETURN
350 DELETE-OLD-MASTER-RECORD
MOVE "D" TO WS-ACTION-CODE
MOVE OLD-MR-RECORD TO WS-OLD-MR-RECORD
ADD 1 TO WS-OLD-RECORD-DELETED-CTR
PERFORM 400-READ-OLD-MASTER-RECORD
PERFORM 410-READ-DETAIL-RECORD
RETURN
370-PREPARE-TOTALS
WRITE SUMMARY-HEADER
MOVE PROGRAM-COUNTERS TO SUMMARY-LINES
old-record-copied-ctr
old-record-deleted-ctr
new-record-ctr
old-record-changed-ctr
new-master-record-ctr
audit-ctr
WRITE SUMMARY-LINE 1,2,3,4,5,6
RETURN
400-READ-OLD-MASTER-RECORD
READ OLD-MASTER RECORD
EOF?
YES
MOVE HIGH-VALUES TO OLD-MR-NAME
NO
RETURN
410-READ-DETAIL-RECORD
READ DETAIL RECORD
EOF?
YES
MOVE HIGH-VALUES TO DETAIL-NAME
NO
RETURN

Comments on the Flowchart

The logic built into the program pseudocode and/or program flowchart is initially difficult to completely understand. You must work your way through the logic repeatedly until you feel comfortable with it. The comments that follow should help you achieve a deeper understanding.

Comment 1

The procedure 210-PROCESS-UPDATE must be executed until there are no more records. Since there are two input files, "there are no more records" means **in both files.**

It is conceivable that after the last detail record is processed, there are unread records remaining in the file OLD-MASTER-FILE. If so, all the remaining records must also be copied into the file NEW-MASTER-FILE.

It is also conceivable that after the last record in the file OLD-MASTER-FILE has been processed, there are unread records remaining in the file DETAIL-FILE. If so, these are all new records that must be added to the file NEW-MASTER-FILE.

When the end-of-file record is encountered for the file OLD-MASTER-FILE, program execution must not be stopped automatically, since there may be remaining records in the file DETAIL-FILE. To make sure that all these records do get processed, the COBOL reserved word HIGH-VALUES is assigned to the field OLD-MR-NAME so that the tests in the procedure 210-PROCESS-UPDATE will be executed properly. HIGH-VALUES corresponds to the highest value of any character in the computer's collating sequence. Therefore, when the test OLD-MR-NAME = DETAIL-NAME is executed, it is necessarily false. Then, the test OLD-MR-NAME < DETAIL-NAME is performed, and it also will always be false. As a result, the record DETAIL-RECORD will be added to the file NEW-MASTER-FILE.

Similarly, when the end-of-file record is encountered for the file DETAIL-FILE, the program must not be terminated automatically here either, since there may be records in the file OLD-MASTER-FILE that have not yet been processed. To make sure that these are copied into the new file, HIGH-VALUES is assigned to the field DETAIL-NAME, so that the test OLD-MR-NAME = DETAIL-NAME is necessarily false. Then, the test OLD-MR-NAME < DETAIL-NAME is always true, and this results in the remaining old master records being copied into the file NEW-MASTER-FILE.

These comments make it clear that the procedure 210-PROCESS-UPDATE must be executed until OLD-MR-NAME = HIGH-VALUES **and** DETAIL-NAME = HIGH-VALUES. The control statement could be written as follows:

```
PERFORM 210-PROCESS-UPDATE
     UNTIL OLD-MR-NAME = HIGH-VALUES AND
           DETAIL-NAME = HIGH-VALUES.
```

For our sample program, the condition-names NO-MORE-OLD-RECORDS and NO-MORE-DETAIL-RECORDS will be substituted, respectively, for the relational tests in the UNTIL clause above for the sake of improved documentation.

Comment 2

Regarding the first test in the procedure 210-PROCESS-UPDATE, if OLD-MR-NAME is equal to DETAIL-NAME, the presence of the detail record indicates that the corresponding old master record is to be deleted or updated. Consequently, a second test is needed to decide the specific course of action. To facilitate this test, the condition-name UPDATE-RECORD will be set up to correspond to the process code 3.

If the UPDATE-RECORD condition is satisfied, then the new address contained on the detail record and the unchanged employee data on the old master record will be copied to a record in the buffer associated with the file NEW-MASTER-FILE, and then the updated record is written to the file NEW-MASTER-FILE. If the UPDATE-RECORD condition is not satisfied, this indicates that the old master record is to be deleted. To delete the record, it is simply not copied into the file NEW-MASTER-FILE. In either case, the next record in each file is accessed, and control returns to the PERFORM-UNTIL loop of the primary module.

If OLD-MR-NAME is not equal to DETAIL-NAME, then it is important to determine the correct relationship between them. If OLD-MR-NAME is less than DETAIL-NAME, this indicates that the old master record must be written to the new file, because the name on the old master record occurs alphabetically before the name on the detail record. The next old master record is then accessed so that it can be compared with the detail record currently in input memory.

If OLD-MR-NAME is not less than or equal to DETAIL-NAME, it is therefore greater than DETAIL-NAME. This condition means that the detail record is a new record, and it must be written to the file NEW-MASTER-FILE at this point to conform to the alphabetic ordering. Then, the next detail record is accessed so that it can be compared with the old master record currently in input memory.

Comment 3

Since the purpose of the audit report is to show on a hard copy the action taken with respect to every record accessed from the old master file and from the detail file, an action code has been selected for each available type of action, namely, "U" to represent an **updated** old master record written to the new master file, "C" to represent an old master record simply **copied** to the new master file, "A" to represent a new record **added** to the master file, and "D" to represent an old master record **deleted** from the master file (by simply not writing it to the new master file). Note that the appropriate code is assigned to the data item WS-ACTION-CODE at the beginning of an "action" module. These modules are, respectively, 320-UPDATE-OLD-MASTER-RECORD, 330-COPY-OLD-MASTER-RECORD, 340-ADD-NEW-RECORD, and 350-DELETE-OLD-MASTER-RECORD.

In module 360-PREPARE-AUDIT-LINE, the value of WS-ACTION-CODE determines how the particular audit line should be prepared. If the record being processed is a new record, it is displayed on the report and an X is inserted under the header "ADDED". If the record being processed is a record from the file OLD-MASTER-FILE for which there is no corresponding record in the detail file, the record is displayed and an X is inserted under the header "COPIED". If the record being processed is a record from the file OLD-MASTER-FILE for which the corresponding record in the detail file indicates a deletion, the record is displayed and an X is inserted under the header "DELETED". And finally, if the record being processed is a record from the file OLD-MASTER-FILE for which the corresponding detail file record indicates a need to change the address, the record with the updated information is displayed and an X is inserted under the header "UPDATED".

Comment 4

The summary part of the audit report must print the number of records copied from the old master file to the new one, the number of records deleted from the master file, the number of records added to the master file, the number of old records that needed an address change, the total number of records written into the new master file, and the number of audit lines written on the report. These numbers obviously serve as a check on the accuracy of the program's procedures.

Six counters are needed to obtain these numbers. The counters are set to zero in module 300-INITIALIZE-ITEMS, and they are incremented by 1 in appropriate modules. The counter WS-OLD-RECORD-COPIED-CTR is incremented in module 330-COPY-OLD-MASTER-RECORD, the counter WS-OLD-RECORD-DELETED-CTR is incremented in module 350-DELETE-OLD-MASTER-RECORD, the counter WS-NEW-RECORD-CTR is incremented in module 340-ADD-NEW-RECORD, the counter WS-OLD-RECORD-CHANGED-CTR is incremented in module 320-UPDATE-OLD-MASTER-RECORD, the counter WS-NEW-MASTER-FILE-CTR is incremented in each module that writes a record to the new master file, and, finally, the counter WS-AUDIT-CTR is incremented in module 360-PREPARE-AUDIT-LINE.

Comment 5

Note that the output file NEW-MASTER-FILE is a pure storage file. Consequently, the WRITE statements that write records to the file must not contain the ADVANCING clause. On the other hand, the output file AUDIT-REPORT is a print file, and every WRITE statement that writes records to this file should contain the ADVANCING clause to control vertical spacing on the report.

The COBOL program that corresponds to the pseudocode beginning on page 720 and flowchart beginning on page 724 is shown in Figure 11.25.

Figure 11.25 COBOL program to update the master file

```
 IDENTIFICATION DIVISION.

 PROGRAM-ID.     JOCELYN-TAPE-UPDATE.

*****************************************************************
*                                                               *
*   AUTHOR.          PAQUETTE.                                  *
*   DATE WRITTEN.    OCTOBER 1993.                              *
*                                                               *
*   THIS PROGRAM UPDATES THE MASTER PERSONNEL TAPE FILE FOR THE *
*   JOCELYN ORIGINALS COMPANY, USING RECORDS FROM A DETAIL FILE. *
*   THE UPDATE INCLUDES:  ADDING A RECORD, DELETING A RECORD,   *
*   AND UPDATING FIELD VALUES ON A RECORD.  THE UPDATED FILE IS *
*   ANOTHER TAPE FILE.  THE PROGRAM ALSO PRODUCES AN AUDIT TRAIL *
*   REPORT.  THE REPORT SPECIFIES THE ACTION TAKEN FOR EACH     *
*   RECORD PROCESSED.                                           *
*                                                               *
*****************************************************************
```

■ **Figure 11.25** continued

```
ENVIRONMENT DIVISION.

CONFIGURATION SECTION.

SOURCE-COMPUTER.  VAX-VMS-8650.
OBJECT-COMPUTER.  VAX-VMS-8650.

INPUT-OUTPUT SECTION.

FILE-CONTROL.
    SELECT DETAIL-FILE          ASSIGN TO COB$INPUT.
    SELECT OLD-MASTER-FILE      ASSIGN TO OLDMASTER
                                ORGANIZATION IS SEQUENTIAL
                                ACCESS MODE IS SEQUENTIAL.
    SELECT NEW-MASTER-FILE      ASSIGN TO NEWMASTER
                                ORGANIZATION IS SEQUENTIAL
                                ACCESS MODE IS SEQUENTIAL.
    SELECT AUDIT-REPORT         ASSIGN TO COB$OUTPUT.

DATA DIVISION.

FILE SECTION.

FD  DETAIL-FILE
    RECORD CONTAINS 80 CHARACTERS.

01  DETAIL-RECORD.
    05 PROCESS-CODE       PIC 9.
       88 NEW-RECORD                VALUE 1.
       88 DELETE-RECORD             VALUE 2.
       88 UPDATE-RECORD             VALUE 3.
    05 DETAIL-NAME        PIC X(20).
       88 NO-MORE-DETAIL-RECORDS    VALUE HIGH-VALUES.
    05 DETAIL-ADDRESS     PIC X(37).
    05 DETAIL-SSN         PIC X(9).
    05 DETAIL-DATES       PIC X(12).
    05                    PIC X.

FD  OLD-MASTER-FILE
    RECORD CONTAINS 100 CHARACTERS
    BLOCK CONTAINS 10 RECORDS.

01  OLD-MR-RECORD.
    05 OLD-MR-NAME        PIC X(20).
        88 NO-MORE-OLD-RECORDS      VALUE HIGH-VALUES.
    05 OLD-MR-ADDRESS     PIC X(37).
    05 OLD-MR-SSN         PIC X(9).
    05 OLD-MR-DATES       PIC X(12).
    05                    PIC X(22).

FD  NEW-MASTER-FILE
    RECORD CONTAINS 100 CHARACTERS
    BLOCK CONTAINS 10 RECORDS.

01  NEW-MR-RECORD.
    05 NEW-MR-NAME        PIC X(20).
    05 NEW-MR-ADDRESS     PIC X(37).
    05 NEW-MR-SSN         PIC X(9).
    05 NEW-MR-DATES       PIC X(12).
    05                    PIC X(22).

FD  AUDIT-REPORT
    RECORD CONTAINS 132 CHARACTERS.

01  PRINTLINE             PIC X(132).

WORKING-STORAGE SECTION.

01  PROGRAM-CONTROLS.
    05 WS-DATE               PIC 9(6).
    05 WS-PROPER-SPACING     PIC 9.

01  WORK-AREAS.
    05 WS-ACTION-CODE        PIC X.
    05 WS-OLD-MR-RECORD      PIC X(100).

01  PROGRAM-COUNTERS              COMP.
    05 WS-OLD-RECORD-COPIED-CTR  PIC S999.
    05 WS-OLD-RECORD-DELETED-CTR PIC S999.
    05 WS-NEW-RECORD-CTR         PIC S999.
    05 WS-OLD-RECORD-CHANGED-CTR PIC S999.
    05 WS-NEW-MASTER-FILE-CTR    PIC S999.
    05 WS-AUDIT-CTR              PIC S999.
```

```
 01   REPORT-HEADERS.
      05 COMPANY-NAME.
         10 PIC X(58)    VALUE SPACES.
         10 PIC X(17)    VALUE "JOCELYN ORIGINALS".
         10 PIC X(57)    VALUE SPACES.

      05 REPORT-NAME-1.
         10 PIC X(47)    VALUE SPACES.
         10 PIC X(31)    VALUE "MASTER PERSONNEL FILE UPDATE
         10 O-DATE       PIC XX/XX/XX.
         10 PIC X(46)    VALUE SPACES.

      05 REPORT-NAME-2.
         10 PIC X(57)    VALUE SPACES.
         10 PIC X(18)    VALUE "AUDIT TRAIL REPORT".
         10 PIC X(57)    VALUE SPACES.

      05 HEADINGS-1.
         10 PIC X(32)    VALUE SPACES.
         10 PIC X(16)    VALUE "PERSONNEL RECORD".
         10 PIC X(62)    VALUE SPACES.
         10 PIC X(12)    VALUE "ACTION TAKEN".
         10 PIC X(10)    VALUE SPACES.

      05 HEADINGS-2.
         10 PIC X(100)   VALUE SPACES.
         10 PIC X(7)     VALUE "ADDED  ".
         10 PIC X(9)     VALUE "DELETED  ".
         10 PIC X(9)     VALUE "UPDATED  ".
         10 PIC X(7)     VALUE "COPIED ".

 01   AUDIT-LINE.
      05 CARRIAGE-CONTROL PIC X.
      05 O-RECORD          PIC X(100).
      05                   PIC X(2).
      05 INDICATOR-1       PIC X.
      05                   PIC X(7).
      05 INDICATOR-2       PIC X.
      05                   PIC X(8).
      05 INDICATOR-3       PIC X.
      05                   PIC X(7).
      05 INDICATOR-4       PIC X.
      05                   PIC X(4).

 01   REPORT-ENDERS.
      05 SUMMARY-HEADER.
         10 PIC X(24)   VALUE SPACES.
         10 PIC X(7)    VALUE "SUMMARY".

      05 SUMMARY-LINE-1.
         10                            PIC X(5)   VALUE SPACES.
         10 O-OLD-RECORD-COPIED-CTR    PIC ZZ9.
         10                            PIC X(46)  VALUE
            "  OLD MASTER RECORDS COPIED TO NEW MASTER FILE".

      05 SUMMARY-LINE-2.
         10                            PIC X(5)   VALUE SPACES.
         10 O-OLD-RECORD-DELETED-CTR PIC ZZ9.
         10                            PIC X(45)  VALUE
            "  OLD MASTER RECORDS DELETED FROM MASTER FILE".

      05 SUMMARY-LINE-3.
         10                            PIC X(5)   VALUE SPACES.
         10 O-NEW-RECORD-CTR           PIC ZZ9.
         10                            PIC X(38)  VALUE
            "  NEW RECORDS ADDED TO THE MASTER FILE".

      05 SUMMARY-LINE-4.
         10                            PIC X(5)   VALUE SPACES.
         10 O-OLD-RECORD-CHANGED-CTR PIC ZZ9.
         10                            PIC X(28)  VALUE
            "  UPDATED OLD MASTER RECORDS".

      05 SUMMARY-LINE-5.
         10                            PIC X(5)   VALUE SPACES.
         10 O-NEW-MASTER-FILE-CTR      PIC ZZ9.
         10                            PIC X(36)  VALUE
            "  RECORDS WRITTEN TO NEW MASTER FILE".

      05 SUMMARY-LINE-6.
         10                            PIC X(5)   VALUE SPACES.
         10 O-AUDIT-CTR                PIC ZZ9.
         10                            PIC X(33)  VALUE
            "  RECORDS WRITTEN TO AUDIT REPORT".
```

```
        05 END-LINE.
           10 PIC X(55)   VALUE SPACES.
           10 PIC X(23)   VALUE "***  END OF REPORT  ***."
           10 PIC X(54)   VALUE SPACES.

    PROCEDURE DIVISION.

    100-PRODUCE-MASTER-FILE-UPDATE.
        PERFROM 200-START-UP.
        PERFROM 210-PROCESS-UPDATE
             UNTIL NO-MORE-OLD-RECORDS AND NO-MORE-DETAIL-RECORDS.
        PERFORM 220-FINISH-UP.
        STOP RUN.

    200-START-UP.
        OPEN INPUT DETAIL-FILE
                   OLD-MASTER-FILE
             OUTPUT NEW-MASTER-FILE
                    AUDIT-REPORT.
        PERFORM 300-INITIALIZE-ITEMS.
        PERFORM 310-WRITE-REPORT-HEADERS.
        PERFORM 400-READ-OLD-MASTER-RECORD.
        PERFROM 410-READ-DETAIL-RECORD.

    210-PROCESS-UPDATE.
        MOVE SPACES TO AUDIT-LINE.
        IF OLD-MR-NAME = DETAIL-NAME
           THEN
               IF UPDATE-RECORD
                   PERFORM 320-UPDATE-OLD-MASTER-RECORD
               ELSE
                   PERFORM 350-DELETE-OLD-MASTER-RECORD
               END-IF
        ELSE
            IF OLD-MR-NAME < DETAIL-NAME
                PERFORM 330-COPY-OLD-MASTER-RECORD
            ELSE
                PERFORM 340-ADD-NEW-RECORD
            END-IF
        END-IF.
        PERFORM 360-PREPARE-AUDIT-LINE.

    220-FINISH-UP.
        PERFORM 370-PREPARE-TOTALS.
        WRITE PRINTLINE FROM END-LINE
            AFTER ADVANCING 5 LINES.
        CLOSE DETAIL-FILE
            OLD-MASTER-FILE
            NEW-MASTER-FILE
            AUDIT-REPORT.

    300-INITIALIZE-ITEMS.
        ACCEPT WS-DATE FROM DATE.
        MOVE WS-DATE TO O-DATE.
        INITIALIZE PROGRAM-COUNTERS.

    310-WRITE-REPORT-HEADERS.
        WRITE PRINTLINE FROM COMPANY-NAME
            AFTER ADVANCING PAGE.
        WRITE PRINTLINE FROM REPORT-NAME-1
            AFTER ADVANCING 3 LINES.
        WRITE PRINTLINE FROM REPORT-NAME-2
            AFTER ADVANCING 2 LINES.
        WRITE PRINTLINE FROM HEADINGS-1
            AFTER ADVANCING 2 LINES.
        WRITE PRINTLINE FROM HEADINGS-2
            AFTER ADVANCING 1 LINE.
        MOVE 2 TO WS-PROPER-SPACING.

    320-UPDATE-OLD-MASTER-RECORD.
        MOVE "U" TO WS-ACTION-CODE.
        MOVE OLD-MR-NAME TO NEW-MR-NAME.
        MOVE DETAIL-ADDRESS TO NEW-MR-ADDRESS.
        MOVE OLD-MR-SSN TO NEW-MR-SSN.
        MOVE OLD-MR-DATES TO NEW-MR-DATES.
        WRITE NEW-MR-RECORD.
        ADD 1 TO WS-OLD-RECORD-CHANGED-CTR
                 WS-NEW-MASTER-FILE-CTR.
        PERFORM 400-READ-OLD-MASTER-RECORD.
        PERFORM 410-READ-DETAIL-RECORD.
```

```
330-COPY-OLD-MASTER-RECORD.
    MOVE "C" TO WS-ACTION-CODE.
    MOVE OLD-MR-RECORD TO NEW-MR-RECORD.
    WRITE NEW-MR-RECORD.
    ADD 1 TO WS-OLD-RECORD-COPIED-CTR
             WS-NEW-MASTER-FILE-CTR.
    PERFORM 400-READ-OLD-MASTER-RECORD.

340-ADD-NEW-RECORD.
    MOVE "A" TO WS-ACTION-CODE.
    MOVE DETAIL-NAME TO NEW-MR-NAME.
    MOVE DETAIL-ADDRESS TO NEW-MR-ADDRESS.
    MOVE DETAIL-SSN TO NEW-MR-SSN.
    MOVE DETAIL-DATES TO NEW-MR-DATES.
    WRITE NEW-MR-RECORD.
    ADD 1 TO WS-NEW-RECORD-CTR
             WS-NEW-MASTER-FILE-CTR.
    PERFORM 410-READ-DETAIL-RECORD.

350-DELETE-OLD-MASTER-RECORD.
    MOVE "D" TO WS-ACTION-CODE.
    MOVE OLD-MR-RECORD TO WS-OLD-MR-RECORD.
    ADD 1 TO WS-OLD-RECORD-DELETED-CTR.
    PERFORM 400-READ-OLD-MASTER-RECORD.
    PERFORM 410-READ-DETAIL-RECORD.

360-PREPARE-AUDIT-LINE.
    EVALUATE WS-ACTION-CODE
        WHEN "A"
            MOVE NEW-MR-RECORD TO O-RECORD
            MOVE "X" TO INDICATOR-1
        WHEN "D"
            MOVE WS-OLD-MR-RECORD TO O-RECORD
            MOVE "X" TO INDICATOR-2
        WHEN "U"
            MOVE NEW-MR-RECORD TO O-RECORD
            MOVE "X" TO INDICATOR-3
        WHEN "C"
            MOVE NEW-MR-RECORD TO O-RECORD
            MOVE "X" TO INDICATOR-4.
    WRITE PRINTLINE FROM AUDIT-LINE
        AFTER ADVANCING WS-PROPER-SPACING.
    MOVE 1 TO WS-PROPER-SPACING.
    ADD 1 TO WS-AUDIT-CTR.

370-PREPARE-TOTALS.
    WRITE PRINTLINE FROM SUMMARY-HEADER
        AFTER ADVANCING 5 LINES.
    MOVE WS-OLD-RECORD-COPIED-CTR TO O-OLD-RECORD-COPIED-CTR.
    WRITE PRINTLINE FROM SUMMARY-LINE-1
        AFTER ADVANCING 2 LINES.
    MOVE WS-OLD-RECORD-DELETED-CTR TO O-OLD-RECORD-DELETED-CTR.
    WRITE PRINTLINE FROM SUMMARY-LINE-2
        AFTER ADVANCING 1 LINE.
    MOVE WS-NEW-RECORD-CTR TO O-NEW-RECORD-CTR.
    WRITE PRINTLINE FROM SUMMARY-LINE-3
        AFTER ADVANCING 1 LINE.
    MOVE WS-OLD-RECORD-CHANGED-CTR TO O-OLD-RECORD-CHANGED-CTR.
    WRITE PRINTLINE FROM SUMMARY-LINE 4
        AFTER ADVANCING 1 LINE.
    MOVE WS-NEW-MASTER-FILE-CTR TO O-NEW-MASTER-FILE-CTR.
    WRITE PRINTLINE FROM SUMMARY-LINE-5
        AFTER ADVANCING 1 LINE.
    MOVE WS-AUDIT-CTR TO O-AUDIT-CTR.
    WRITE PRINTLINE FROM SUMMARY-LINE-6
        AFTER ADVANCING 1 LINE.

400-READ-OLD-MASTER-RECORD.
    READ OLD-MASTER-FILE NEXT RECORD
        AT END
            MOVE HIGH-VALUES TO OLD-MR-NAME.

410-READ-DETAIL-RECORD.
    READ DETAIL-FILE RECORD
        AT END
            MOVE HIGH-VALUES TO DETAIL-NAME.
```

The file used as the OLD-MASTER-FILE is the master file created by the program in Figure 11.15 [DD/CD:VICIISP2.DT2]. The sample detail file is shown in Figure 11.26 [DD/CD:VICIISP2.DT1]. The records in the file NEW-MASTER-FILE are listed in Figure 11.27a, and the audit report is shown in Figure 11.27b.

Figure 11.26 Sample detail file for the master file update

```
2BUCCI, ELEANOR F.
1COUGHLIN, AILEEN M. 133 DAVIS RD   LEXINGTON, NE     68850016493017031050070668
2KRUGER, ALLEN
1MARKARIAN, MARIAN   984 N MAIN ST  HASTINGS, NE      68901130043962050732082052
3MOONEY, RONALD      220 N MAIN ST  HASTINGS, NE      68901
1PRIMEAU, ISABEL     78 NORTH ST    KEARNEY, NE       68847150246389093047082072
3VELTRI, JOHN A.     54 SOUTH ST    AURORA, NE        68818
```

Figure 11.27a Records of NEW-MASTER-FILE

```
ABRUZZI, KENNETH L. 51 RAYMOND ST  HASTINGS, NE      68901743142265120552082072
AITKEN, THOMAS R.   260 FOUNTAIN STAURORA, NE        68818032567781080526082046
ALTERMAN, MAUREEN E.10 MARTIN AVE  YORK, NE          68467144217773052435061060
BAHR, LENA M.       304 CORY LANE  GENEVA, NE        68361381662514111041082060
BLAZUCK, JOSEPH A.  85 BELVIEW AVE FAIRFIELD, NE     68938179623741052145061075
BUXBAUM, JOAN M.    172 EARLE DR   GRAND ISLAND, NE 68802005589243021448060870
CARTER, AMEKIA L.   59 BARK ST     LOUP CITY, NE     68853623514793051332082062
COLETTI, SARAH T.   51 BROAD ST    HASTINGS, NE      68901042750015090238061564
COUGHLIN, AILEEN M. 133 DAVIS RD   LEXINGTON, NE     68850016493017031050070668
CYR, ROSARIO        205 SUNSET DR  FAIRFIELD, NE     68938771894263052435082055
DURANT, MARIE L.    1250 HIGH RD   GENEVA, NE        68361364923752092443091054
GAFFNEY, MARYLYN    274 HANOVER ST ARAPAHOE, NE      68922039764715120552060877
KACHADOURIAN, NATALI922 LOCUST ST  HEBRON, NE        68370211384406022135082056
MARKARIAN, MARIAN   984 N MAIN ST  HASTINGS, NE      68901130043962050732082052
MCGEE, BERNARD W.   2420 CARR LA   CENTRAL CITY, NE 68901124670325092041081064
MOONEY, RONALD      220 N MAIN ST  HASTINGS, NE      68949124670325092041081064
OVERDEEP, CYNTHIA   130 CANAL ST   YORK, NE          68467226153911052435071570
PACCASASSIE, DEBBIE 341 BRANCH AVE NORMAN, NE        68963149201475261228091257
PRIMEAU, ISABEL     78 NORTH ST    KEARNEY, NE       68847150246389093047082072
ROMA, GILDA         25 MAPLE DR    SUPERIOR, NE      68978432157258070850061072
SHERIDAN, RICHARD J.2 GENEVA RD    HASTINGS, NE      68901234891533120542061065
STURDAHL, DEBRA     2541 RICE ST   CRETE, NE         68333322150642061434071555
VELTRI, JOHN A.     54 SOUTH ST    AURORA, NE        68818026307625011547082082
```

Figure 11.27b Audit report for the master file update

```
                                             JOCELYN ORIGINALS

                                  MASTER PERSONNEL FILE UPDATE    93/10/07

                                             AUDIT TRAIL REPORT

                         PERSONNEL RECORD                                                   ACTION TAKEN
                                                                                   ADDED   DELETED  UPDATED    COPIED

ABRUZZI, KENNETH L. 51 RAYMOND ST  HASTINGS, NE      68901743142265120552082072                                  X
AITKEN, THOMAS R.   260 FOUNTAIN STAURORA, NE        68818032567781080526082046                                  X
ALTERMAN, MAUREEN E.10 MARTIN AVE  YORK, NE          68467144217773052435061060                                  X
BAHR, LENA M.       304 CORY LANE  GENEVA, NE        68361381662514111041082060                                  X
BLAZUCK, JOSEPH A.  85 BELVIEW AVE FAIRFIELD, NE     68938179623741052145061075                                  X
BUCCI, ELEANOR F.   123 OLIVER, ST MINDEN, NE        68959004325715062133082055                 X
BUXBAUM, JOAN M.    172 EARLE DR   GRAND ISLAND, NE 68802005589243021448060870                                  X
CARTER, AMEKIA L.   59 BARK ST     LOUP CITY, NE     68853623514793051332082062                                  X
COLETTI, SARAH T.   51 BROAD ST    HASTINGS, NE      68901042750015090238061564                                  X
COUGHLIN, AILEEN M. 133 DAVIS RD   LEXINGTON, NE     68850016493017031050070668        X
CYR, ROSARIO        205 SUNSET DR  FAIRFIELD, NE     68938771894263052435082055                                  X
DURANT, MARIE L.    1250 HIGH RD   GENEVA, NE        68361364923752092443091054                                  X
GAFFNEY, MARYLYN    274 HANOVER ST ARAPAHOE, NE      68922039764715120552060877                                  X
KACHADOURIAN, NATALI922 LOCUST ST  HEBRON, NE        68370211384406022135082056                                  X
KRUGER, ALLEN       320 EAST RD    PLATTE, NE        68653502422713102537061057                 X
MARKARIAN, MARIAN   984 N MAIN ST  HASTINGS, NE      68901130043962050732082052        X
MCGEE, BERNARD W.   2420 CARR LA   CENTRAL CITY, NE 68826013407206121530061549                                  X
MOONEY, RONALD      220 N MAIN ST  HASTINGS, NE      68901124670325092041081064                          X
OVERDEEP, CYNTHIA   130 CANAL ST   YORK, NE          68467226153911052435071570                                  X
PACCASASSIE, DEBBIE 341 BRANCH AVE NORMAN, NE        68963149201475261228091257                                  X
PRIMEAU, ISABEL     78 NORTH ST    KEARNEY, NE       68847150246389093047082072        X
ROMA, GILDA         25 MAPLE DR    SUPERIOR, NE      68978432157258070850061072                                  X
SHERIDAN, RICHARD J.2 GENEVA RD    HASTINGS, NE      68901234891533120542061065                                  X
STURDAHL, DEBRA     2541 RICE ST   CRETE, NE         68333322150642061434071555                                  X
VELTRI, JOHN A.     54 SOUTH ST    AURORA, NE        68818026307625011547082082                          X


                    SUMMARY

   18  OLD MASTER RECORDS COPIED TO NEW MASTER FILE
    2  OLD MASTER RECORDS DELETED FROM MASTER FILE
    3  NEW RECORDS ADDED TO THE MASTER FILE
    2  UPDATED OLD MASTER RECORDS
   23  RECORDS WRITTEN TO NEW MASTER FILE
   25  RECORDS WRITTEN TO AUDIT REPORT


                                        ***  END OF REPORT  ***
```

Backing Up the Master File

Within a business environment, several versions of updated master files are usually retained for a period of time. These are backup copies that can be used to reconstruct a current master file that may be damaged or so full of errors that it is rendered useless. A minimum of three generations of master files is usually kept, but in some situations where updates are needed more frequently, a large number of generations is normal. A company sets its own criteria for determining its margin of safety and, consequently, the number of backup copies it should retain at any one time.

The illustration in Figure 11.28 assumes that a master file is updated weekly. It shows that the master file generated in Week 1 is the father master file for the Week 2 generation, the grandfather master file for Week 3, and so on. In other words, the current master file is the son, the previous one is the father, and the one before that is the grandfather. If the critical number of generations for this company is three, then during Week 4 the great-grandfather master file will be discarded; that is, the tape can be erased and used for some other application.

Figure 11.28 Master file generations

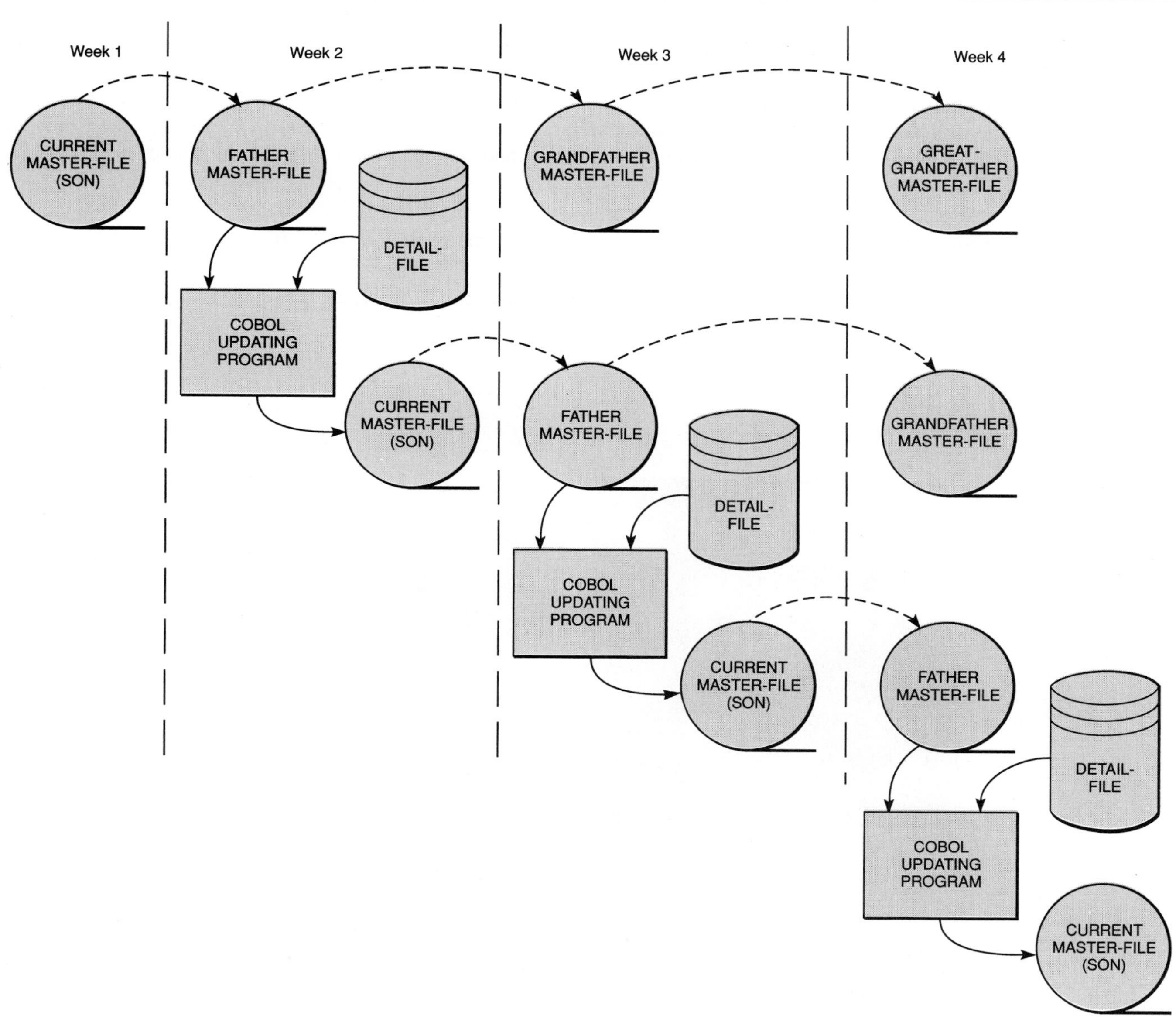

Disk Files

You have seen that a tape file is necessarily sequential. That is, to access a record on tape, it is necessary to "read" all the records physically preceding it on the tape. A disk file, on the other hand, can be set up either as a *sequential* file or a *direct-access* file. A sequential file on disk has many of the same properties as one on tape. For instance, to read the 1000th disk record, the read-write heads on the disk drive must scan the preceding 999 records. However, as a direct-access file, the records can be accessed directly, without having to read all the records that precede it in the file. Devices that support direct access to records of a file are classified as *direct-access storage devices* (DASD). Many different kinds of disks are available today. Some examples are shown in Figure 11.29.

A brief look at some physical characteristics of a disk will help to develop a better understanding of the process of accessing records sequentially or directly. The IBM 3330 Disk Drive will be used as a typical example.

Some Disk File Characteristics

A disk is similar in appearance to a phonograph record. Its surface consists of magnetized concentric circles rather than a spiral groove as is found on a record. It is generally mounted along with other disks (a total of 11 in the 3330) on a central spindle, to make what is known as a *disk pack.* (The IBM 3336 Disk Pack is used in the IBM 3330 Disk Drive.) The pack is then placed within a cabinet-type unit, called the *disk drive.* There is sufficient space between any two disks on the spindle to allow a read-write head, attached to a movable arm much like the pickup arm of a phonograph, to be positioned anywhere on the surface of the disk above the arm as well as on the surface of the disk below the arm. In an 11-disk pack, only 19 surfaces are available to store data, since the top and bottom surfaces are not used and one surface is

Figure 11.29 A sampling of magnetic media: **a,** $5\frac{1}{4}$-inch floppy diskette; **b,** $3\frac{1}{2}$-inch low-density floppy diskette; **c,** $3\frac{1}{2}$-inch high-density floppy diskette; **d,** 80 megabyte hard disk drive; **e,** 9-track tape in an IBM tape drive

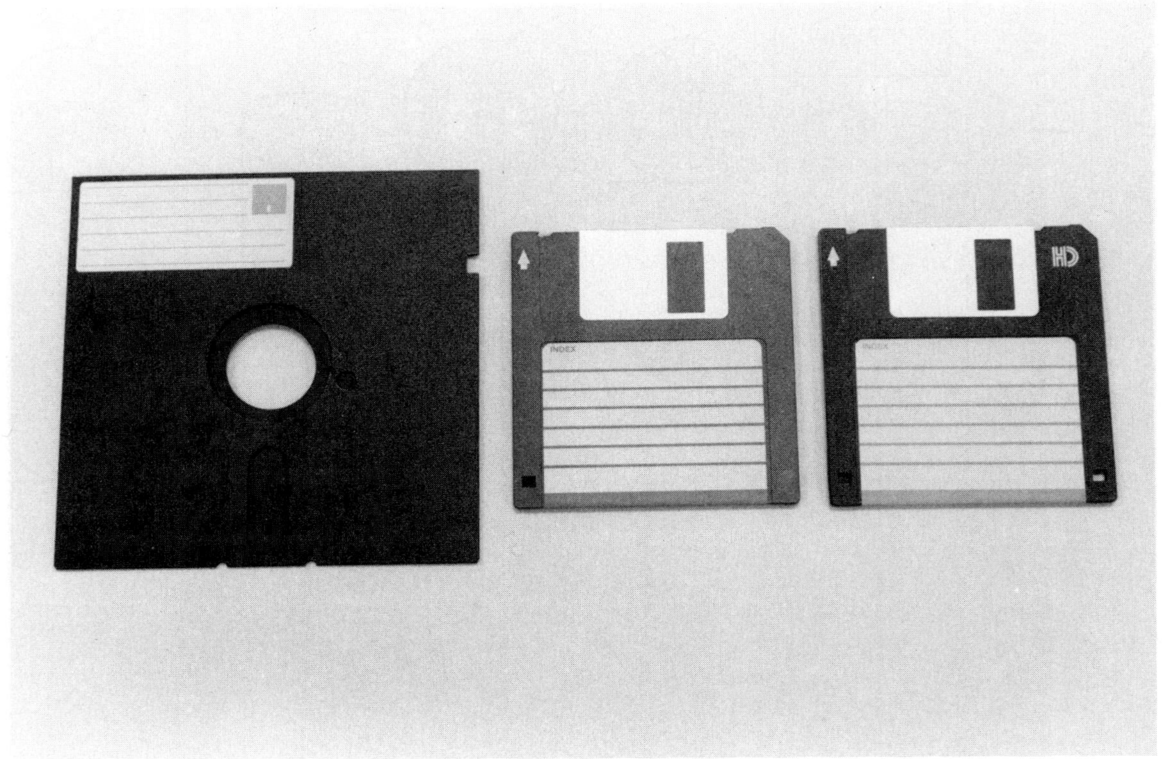

a. b. c.

WARRANTY VOID IF SEAL BROKEN
P/N : 79F4013
MLC : C81555
02/06/92 FRU : 56F8892
MODEL WD-380S
80MB
IBM
MADE BY IBM CORP ROCHESTER MN. USA
WARRANTY VOID IF THIS SEAL IS BROKEN
WARRANTY VOID IF SEAL BROKEN

d.

e.

Figure 11.30 Schematic of a disk access mechanism and disk tracks

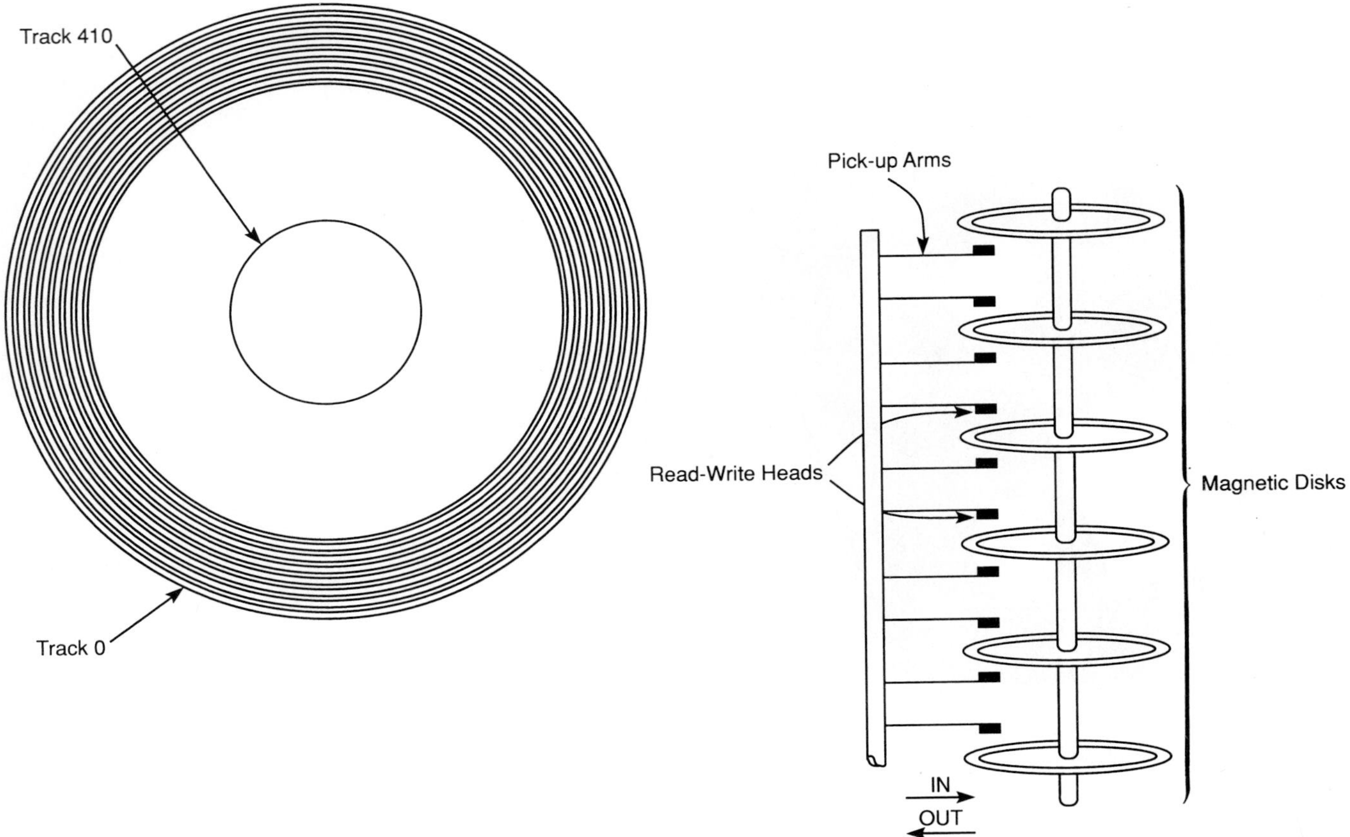

Source: Paquette, Gerard A., *Structured COBOL: A Problem-Solving Approach.* © 1984 by PWS-Kent Publishers, Boston, MA. Reprinted by permission of the author.

reserved for system use. Each disk surface consists of 411 concentric circles, called *tracks,* as shown in Figure 11.30. Of those, 404 can be used to store data.

The tracks on each surface are numbered, and the surfaces are numbered. Furthermore, by "looking down" at the disk pack, corresponding tracks on all the disk surfaces align into *cylinders.* There are as many cylinders as there are tracks on a given surface. The cylinders are also numbered, as shown in Figure 11.31.

By moving the arm access mechanism toward or away from the spindle, the read-write heads can be made to read or write data on any track of any surface. The disk pack rotates at a constant speed, and the head can access any position on a given track of any surface.

As with magnetic tape, a limited number of bytes, or characters, can be recorded per track. On the IBM 3330 there is a maximum of 13,030 bytes per track. (A density gradient assures that innermost tracks can store as many characters as outermost tracks.) Since there are 404 usable tracks out of the 411 tracks per surface, each surface can store 5,264,120 characters, or approximately 5 megabytes (a megabyte is one million bytes). An 11-disk pack can store approximately 100 million characters, or approximately 100 megabytes.

The records to be stored on a disk may vary in length, just like tape records. On a track, the records are separated by a gap, much like records on tape. Consequently, disk records are also often blocked, depending on the file organization, to increase the efficiency of the storage medium.

Suppose, for instance, that on a particular disk configuration, twenty 100-character records can be stored per track. Each record can easily be given an address by specifying (1) the cylinder, (2) the disk surface, and (3) the record position on that track. Example: Cylinder 200, Surface 5, Record 3. Can you visualize its approximate position in Figure 11.31?

As a result of the physical characteristics of disks, the records of a disk file can be accessed sequentially, that is, in the physical order in which they were written to the file, or a record can be accessed directly by referencing the position on the disk where the record is stored. If records are to be processed sequentially, no new considerations are required of the programmer, other than the ones specified earlier for

■ **Figure 11.31** Cylinders on a disk pack

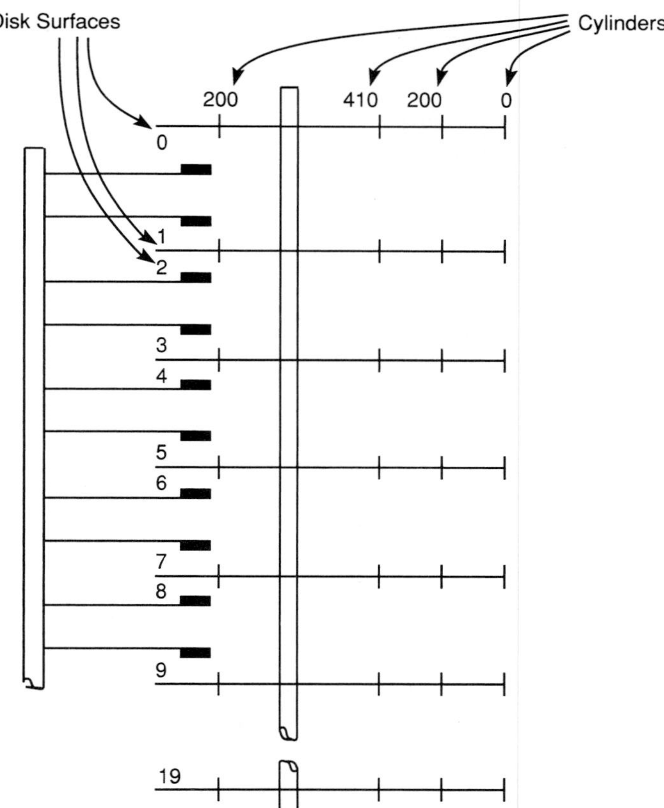

Source: Paquette, Gerard A., *Structured COBOL: A Problem-Solving Approach.* © 1984 by PWS-Kent Publishers, Boston, MA. Reprinted by permission of the author.

sequential files on tape. On the other hand, if a record is to be accessed directly, then additional considerations do apply. We shall examine these considerations later in this chapter.

Creating a Sequential File on Disk

We now consider the task of creating the master personnel file for the Jocelyn Originals Company on disk. Suppose that the master file is currently on tape, and suppose that a number of new records not yet on the master file must be added to the new file.

There are two approaches we could use. In one approach, the new records are added to the end of the current tape master file before creating the disk file. In the second approach, the old master file is copied to a disk file, and then the new records are added to the end of the disk file. In both cases, the disk master file must then be sorted in alphabetic order by employee name to maintain the required record sequence. As an example, we shall develop the program to accomplish the latter approach.

The system flowchart is shown in Figure 11.32. Note that the old tape master file is an input file, and the detail file containing the new records that must be added to the file is also an input file. The file labeled as DISK-FILE receives copies of the records from OLD-MASTER-FILE and DETAIL-FILE, and thus is an output file. The records of DISK-FILE must then be accessed so that they can be released to the sort file, and in that part of the program, DISK-FILE has to be opened in input mode. After the records are sorted, they are written to the new disk master file NEW-MASTER-FILE by the sorting routine. The audit report identifies the records copied from the old master file as well as the detail file records added to the new master file and, as expected, provides summary data. The printer spacing chart is shown in Figure 11.33.

In designing this program, three separate tasks are planned:

1. Copy the old master file records to a disk file.
2. Add the detail file records to the disk file created in step 1.
3. Sort the disk file produced in steps 1 and 2 to yield the required master file on disk.

■ **Figure 11.32** System flowchart to create and sort a master file on disk

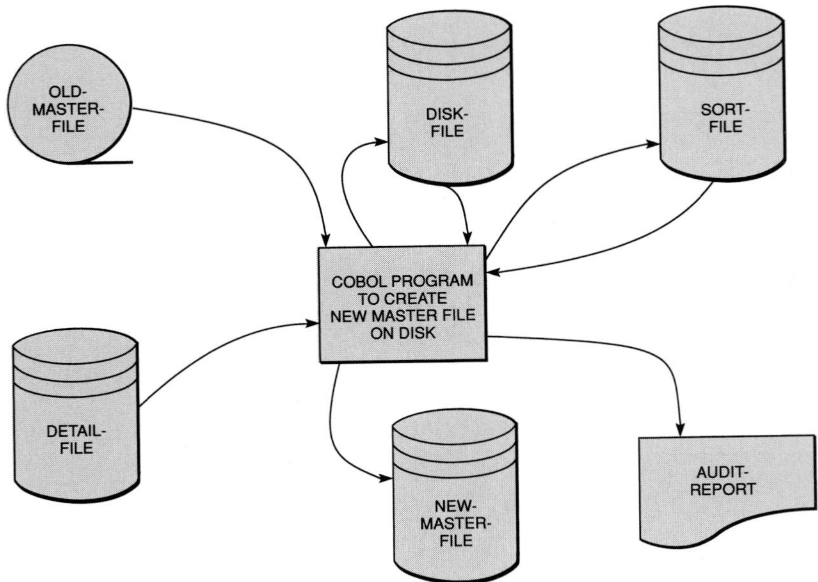

■ **Figure 11.33** Printer spacing chart for the audit report

Printer Spacing Chart

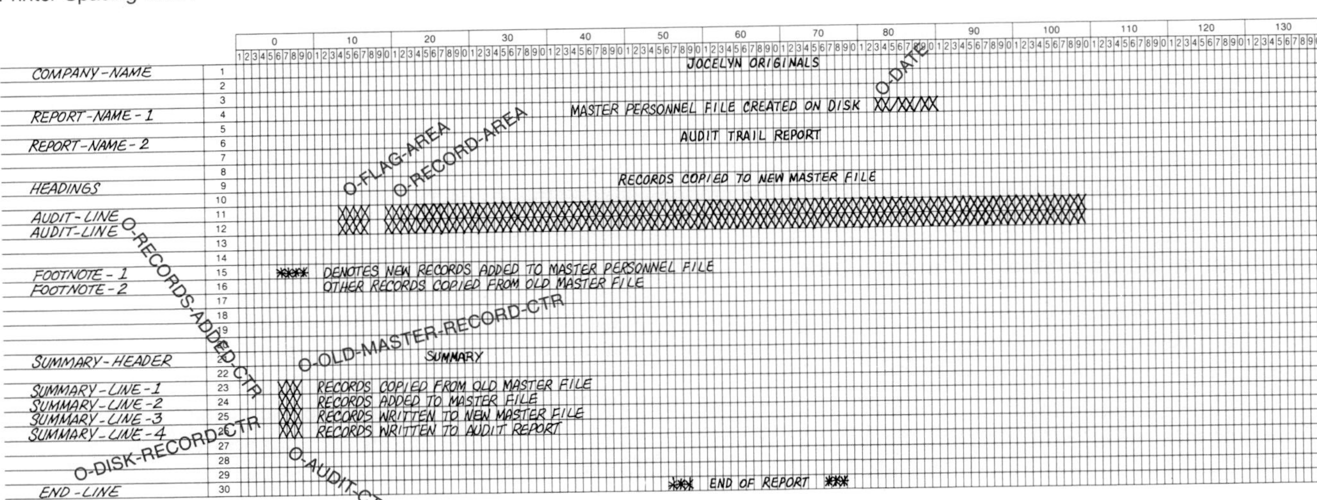

In task 1, OLD-MASTER-FILE is the input file, whereas DISK-FILE and AUDIT-REPORT are output files. Each record of OLD-MASTER-FILE must be copied to both output files. When this job is done, OLD-MASTER-FILE and DISK-FILE are closed, but AUDIT-REPORT is kept open. (Note that DISK-FILE could be kept open, since the new records in DETAIL-FILE remain to be copied into it. It is closed to provide an opportunity to use the EXTEND open mode for sequential files. This statement will be explained shortly.)

In task 2, DETAIL-FILE is the input file and DISK-FILE is again opened as an output file using the EXTEND mode. This mode allows records to be written beyond the EOF marker that indicated the end of the file when it was first created in task 1. Each record of DETAIL-FILE is copied to DISK-FILE and also to AUDIT-REPORT. When this job is done, the summary information is printed on the report, and the three files, DISK-FILE, DETAIL-FILE, and AUDIT-REPORT, are closed.

In task 3, DISK-FILE is supplied as input to the sort routine, and the sorted records are copied to the file NEW-MASTER-FILE.

The structure chart is shown in Figure 11.34. Note that each task is treated as a section, so the program then contains four sections: the main driver 0-MAIN-CONTROL, the task 1 section 1-COPY-OLD-MASTER-FILE, the task 2 section 2-ADD-DETAIL-FILE, and the task 3 section 3-SORT-DISK-FILE.

Figure 11.34 Structure chart to create NEW-MASTER-FILE on disk

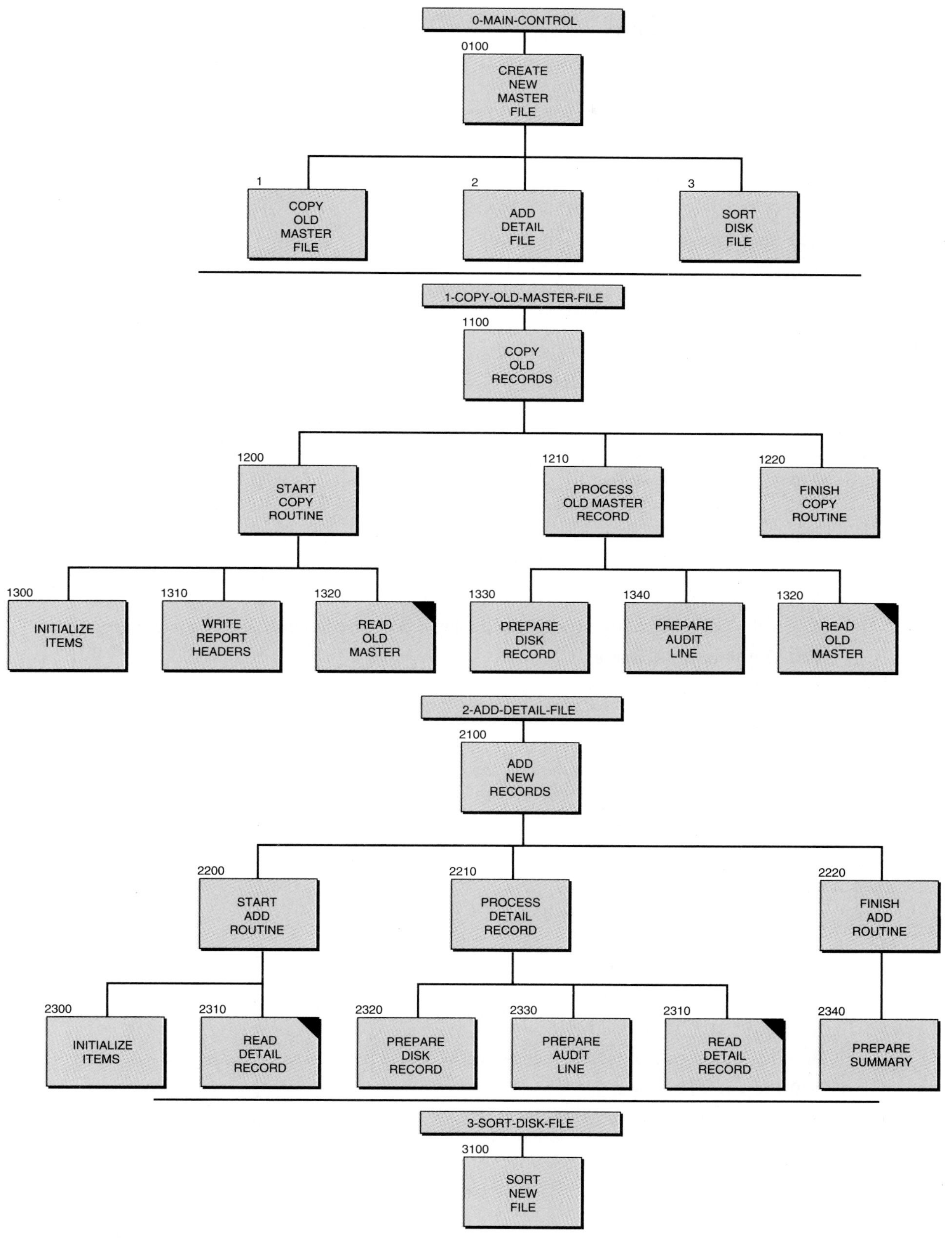

The pseudocode itemizing the processing steps required to complete the tasks identified in the structure chart follows.

0-Main-Control Section.

0100-Create-New-Master-File.

1. Perform 1-Copy-Old-Master-File section.
2. Perform 2-Add-Detail-File section.
3. Perform 3-Sort-Disk-File section.
4. Stop the run.

1-Copy-Old-Master-File Section.

1100-Copy-Old-Records.

1. Perform 1200-Start-Copy-Routine.
2. Perform 1210-Process-Old-Master-Record until no more old master records.
3. Perform 1220-Finish-Copy-Routine.
4. Exit from the section 1-Copy-Old-Master-File.

1200-Start-Copy-Routine.

1. Open the file Old-Master-File as input, and the files
   Disk-File and Audit-Report as output files.
2. Perform 1300-Initialize-Items.
3. Perform 1310-Write-Report-Headers.
4. Perform 1320-Read-Old-Master-Record.

1210-Process-Old-Master-Record.

1. Perform 1330-Prepare-Disk-Record.
2. Perform 1340-Prepare-Audit-Line.
3. Perform 1320-Read-Old-Master-Record.

1220-Finish-Copy-Routine.

1. Close the files Old-Master-File and Disk-File.

1300-Initialize-Items.

1. Obtain the date from the operating system.
2. Move date to Report-Name-1 date.
3. Set the flag WS-MORE-OLD-RECORDS to "YES".
4. Set the counters old-master-record-counter, disk-record-counter, audit-counter to zero.

1310-Write-Report-Headers.

1. Move the record Company-Name to the output area Printline.
2. After advancing to a new page, write the output record Printline.
3. Move the record Report-Name-1 to the output area Printline.
4. After advancing 3 lines, write the output record Printline.
5. Move the record Report-Name-2 to the output area Printline.
6. After advancing 2 lines, write the output record Printline.
7. Move the record Headings to the output area Printline.
8. After advancing 3 lines, write the output record Printline.
9. Move 2 to proper-spacing.

1320-Read-Old-Master-Record.

1. Read an input Old-Master-Record.
2. Test for end-of-file record;
   if EOF record reached, set the flag WS-MORE-OLD-RECORDS to "NO ".

1330-Prepare-Disk-Record.

1. Move input Old-Master-Record to Disk-Record.
2. Write Disk-Record.
3. Add 1 to old-master-record-counter and to disk-record-counter.

1340-Prepare-Audit-Line.

1. Move input Old-Master-Record to Audit-Line record-area.
2. Move the record Audit-Line to the output area Printline.
3. After advancing proper-spacing, write the output record Printline.
4. Add 1 to audit-counter.
5. Move 1 to proper-spacing.

2-Add-Detail-File Section.

2100-Add-New-Records.

1. Perform 2200-Start-Add-Routine.
2. Perform 2210-Process-Detail-Record until no more detail records.
3. Perform 2220-Finish-Add-Routine.
4. Exit from the section 2-Add-Detail-File.

2200-Start-Add-Routine.

1. Open the file Detail-File as input and the file Disk-File as
   an output file in EXTEND mode.
2. Perform 2300-Initialize-Items.
3. Perform 2310-Read-Detail-Record.

2210-Process-Detail-Record.

1. Perform 2320-Prepare-Disk-Record.
2. Perform 2330-Prepare-Audit-Line.
3. Perform 2310-Read-Detail-Record.

2220-Finish-Add-Routine.

1. Move the record Footnote-1 to the output area Printline.
2. After advancing 5 lines, write the output record Printline.
3. Move the record Footnote-2 to the output area Printline.
4. After advancing 1 line, write the output record Printline.
5. Perform 2340-Prepare-Summary.
6. Move the record End-Line to the output area Printline.
7. After advancing 5 lines, write the output record Printline.
8. Close the files Detail-File, Disk-File and Audit-Report.

2300-Initialize-Items.

1. Set the flag WS-MORE-DETAIL-RECORDS to "YES".
2. Set the counter records-added-counter to zero.

2310-Read-Detail-Record.

1. Read an input Detail-Record.
2. Test for end-of-file record;
   if EOF record reached, set the flag WS-MORE-DETAIL-RECORDS to "NO ".

2320-Prepare-Disk-Record.

1. Move Detail-Record to Disk-Record.
2. Write Disk-Record.
3. Add 1 to records-added-counter and to disk-record-counter.

2330-Prepare-Audit-Line.

1. Move Detail-Record to Audit-Line record-area.
2. Move "****" to Audit-Line flag-area.
3. Move the record Audit-Line to the output area Printline.
4. After advancing proper-spacing, write the output record Printline.
5. Add 1 to audit-counter.
6. Move 1 to proper-spacing.

2340-Prepare-Summary.

1. Move the record Summary-Header to the output area Printline.
2. After advancing 5 lines, write the output record Printline.
3. Move old-master-record-counter to Summary-Line-1 old-master-record-counter.
4. Move the record Summary-Line-1 to the output area Printline.
5. After advancing 2 lines, write the output record Printline.
6. Move records-added-counter to Summary-Line-2 records-added-counter.
7. Move the record Summary-Line-2 to the output area Printline.
8. After advancing 1 line, write the output record Printline.
9. Move disk-record-counter to Summary-Line-3 disk-record-counter.
10. Move the record Summary-Line-3 to the output area Printline.
11. After advancing 1 line, write the output record Printline.
12. Move audit-counter to Summary-Line-4 audit-counter.
13. Move the record Summary-Line-4 to the output area Printline.
14. After advancing 1 line, write the output record Printline.

3-Sort-Disk-File Section.

3100-Sort-New-File.

1. Read all Disk-File records into the Sort-File.
2. Sort the records of Sort-File using the following key:
   a. major key: names in ascending order.
3. Write all the sorted records to the output file New-Master-File.
4. Exit from the section 3-Sort-Disk-File.

The program flowchart that corresponds to the preceding pseudocode is shown in Figure 11.35.

Coding the Program

The task of coding the program is greatly facilitated by using the design tools that have been developed. No new COBOL statements are required other than the EXTEND mode of the OPEN statement. It is used to reopen the file DISK-FILE so that the new records, currently in DETAIL-FILE, can be added to the end of DISK-FILE. The format of the EXTEND option is as follows:

```
OPEN EXTEND file-name
```

Rules Governing Use of the EXTEND Mode of the OPEN Statement

1. The access mode specified for *file-name* must be SEQUENTIAL.
2. *File-name* may have any organization, namely, sequential, indexed, or relative.
   a. For a file with sequential organization, the execution of an OPEN EXTEND statement positions the file's pointer after the last logical record previously written to the file.
   b. For a file with indexed organization, the execution of the OPEN EXTEND statement positions the file's pointer after the record with the highest record key value.
   c. For a file with relative organization, the execution of the OPEN EXTEND statement positions the file's pointer after the record with the highest relative record number.
3. If *file-name* is a Report Writer file, the execution of the OPEN EXTEND statement positions the file's pointer after the last logical record written to the file.
4. The execution of the statement makes *file-name* available to the program.
   a. If *file-name* already exists, a normal open occurs as specified in step 2. The description of the file must be the same as when it was first created.
   b. If *file-name* does not exist, the statement creates it, but the file does not contain any record.
5. Within a program, the statement can be the initial open statement with respect to the file. If it is not, its execution must be preceded by a CLOSE statement for *file-name*.

The program to create the master personnel file on disk, to add new records to the master file, and to sort the file in the required sequence is shown in Figure 11.36. Some lines have been numbered to facilitate references in the comments that follow.

1. The FILE-CONTROL paragraph contains six SELECT statements, one for each file (see line 1). OLD-MASTER-FILE is the master personnel file on tape as updated by the program in Figure 11.25 [DD/CD:VICIISP3.DT1]. All of its records must be copied to the new master file created on disk, namely, DISK-FILE. This occurs in the section 1-COPY-OLD-MASTER-FILE (see line 5). Note that OLD-MASTER-FILE is opened in INPUT mode and DISK-FILE is opened in OUTPUT mode (see lines 7 and 8). Also note that both files are closed before leaving the section (see lines 10 and 11).

   DETAIL-FILE [DD/CD:VICIISP3.DT2] contains the new records to be added to the disk master file DISK-FILE. This occurs in section 2-ADD-DETAIL-FILE (see line 13). The file DETAIL-FILE is opened in INPUT mode, and DISK-FILE, which was closed at the end of section 1-COPY-OLD-MASTER, is reopened in EXTEND mode to make possible the addition of new master records to the end of the master file (see lines 14 and 15). Both files are then closed before leaving the section (see lines 16 and 17).

   The file AUDIT-REPORT is opened in OUTPUT mode in section 1-COPY-OLD-MASTER-FILE (see line 9) and is closed in section 2-ADD-DETAIL-FILE subsequent to the processing of the records in DETAIL-FILE (see line 18).

   The file SORT-FILE is activated in section 3-SORT-DISK-FILE (see line 19). It is never opened or closed by the programmer. It uses DISK-FILE as the input file (see line 21). DISK-FILE must be closed prior to the execution of the SORT statement. It is closed at the end of section 2-ADD-DETAIL-FILE (see line 17). The SORT statement creates the file NEW-MASTER-FILE as output (see line 22).

■ **Figure 11.35** Program flowchart to create NEW-MASTER-FILE

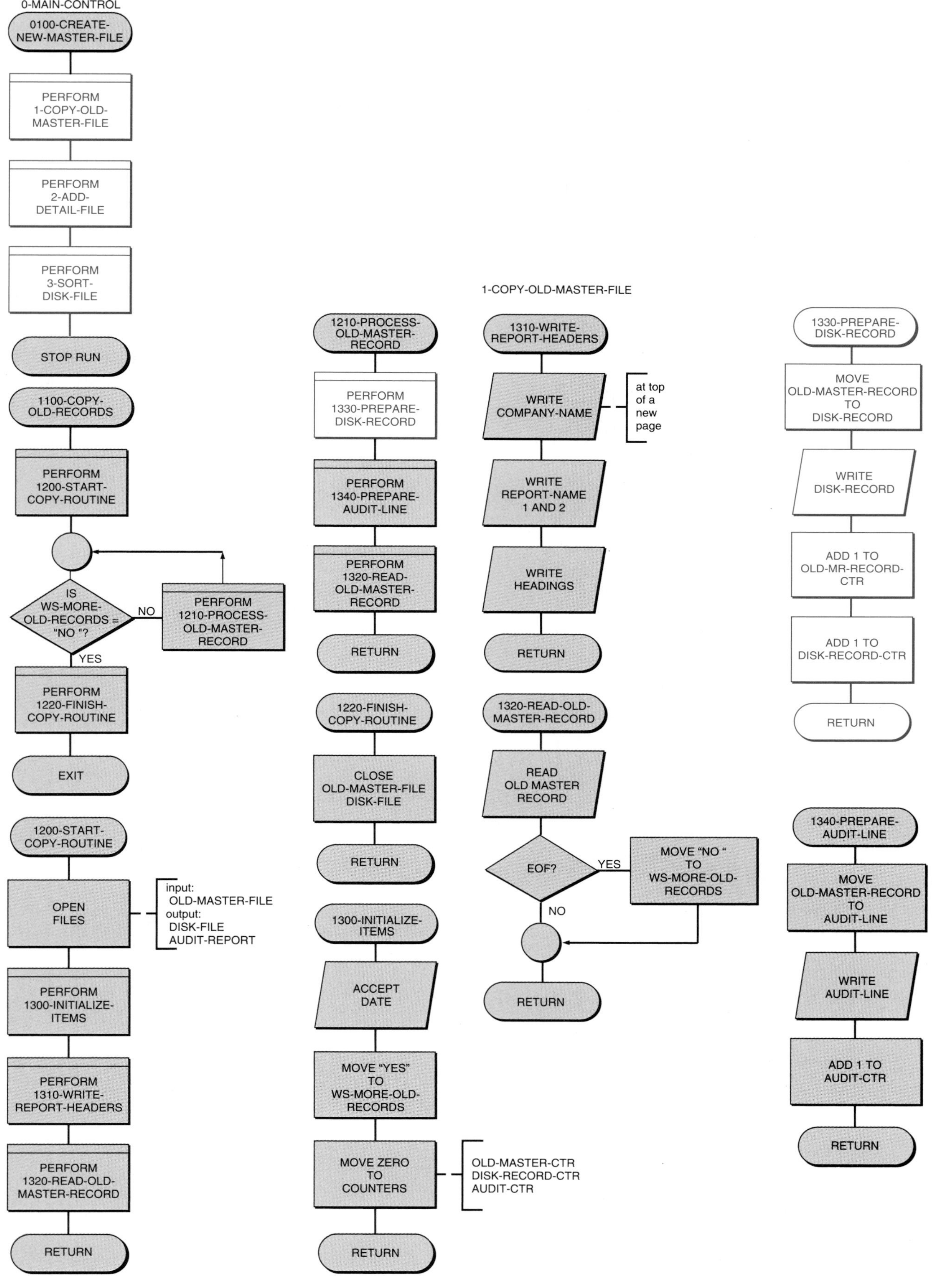

Figure 11.35 continued

2-ADD-DETAIL-FILE

2100-ADD-NEW-RECORDS
PERFORM 2200-START-ADD-ROUTINE
IS WS-MORE-DETAIL-RECORDS = "NO "?
NO
PERFORM 2210-PROCESS-DETAIL-RECORD
YES
PERFORM 2220-FINISH-ADD-ROUTINE
EXIT
2200-START-ADD-ROUTINE
OPEN INPUT DETAIL-FILE EXTEND DISK-FILE
PERFORM 2300-INITIALIZE-ITEMS
PERFORM 2310-READ-DETAIL-RECORD
RETURN
2210-PROCESS-DETAIL-RECORDS
PERFORM 2320-PREPARE-DISK-RECORD
PERFORM 2330-PREPARE-AUDIT-LINE
PERFORM 2310-READ-DETAIL-RECORD
RETURN
2220-FINISH-ADD-ROUTINE
WRITE FOOTNOTE 1 AND 2
PERFORM 2340-PREPARE-SUMMARY
WRITE END-LINE
CLOSE DETAIL-FILE DISK-FILE AUDIT-REPORT
RETURN
2300-INITIALIZE-ITEMS
MOVE "YES" TO WS-MORE-DETAIL-RECORDS
MOVE ZERO TO RECORDS-ADDED-CTR
RETURN
2310-READ-DETAIL-RECORD
READ DETAIL RECORD
EOF?
YES
MOVE "NO " TO WS-MORE-DETAIL-RECORDS
NO
RETURN
2320-PREPARE-DISK-RECORD
MOVE DETAIL-RECORD TO DISK-RECORD
WRITE DISK-RECORD
ADD 1 TO RECORDS-ADDED-CTR
ADD 1 TO DISK-RECORD-CTR
RETURN
2330-PREPARE-AUDIT-LINE
MOVE DETAIL-RECORD TO AUDIT-LINE
MOVE ****** TO FLAG-AREA
WRITE AUDIT-LINE
ADD 1 TO AUDIT-CTR
RETURN
2340-PREPARE-SUMMARY
MOVE COUNTERS TO SUMMARY-LINES
WRITE SUMMARY-HEADER
WRITE SUMMARY-LINE 1,2,3, and 4
RETURN

3-SORT-DISK-FILE

3100-SORT-NEW-FILE
KEY
ASC S-NAME
SORT SORT-FILE
Using: DISK FILE
Giving: NEW-MASTER-FILE
EXIT

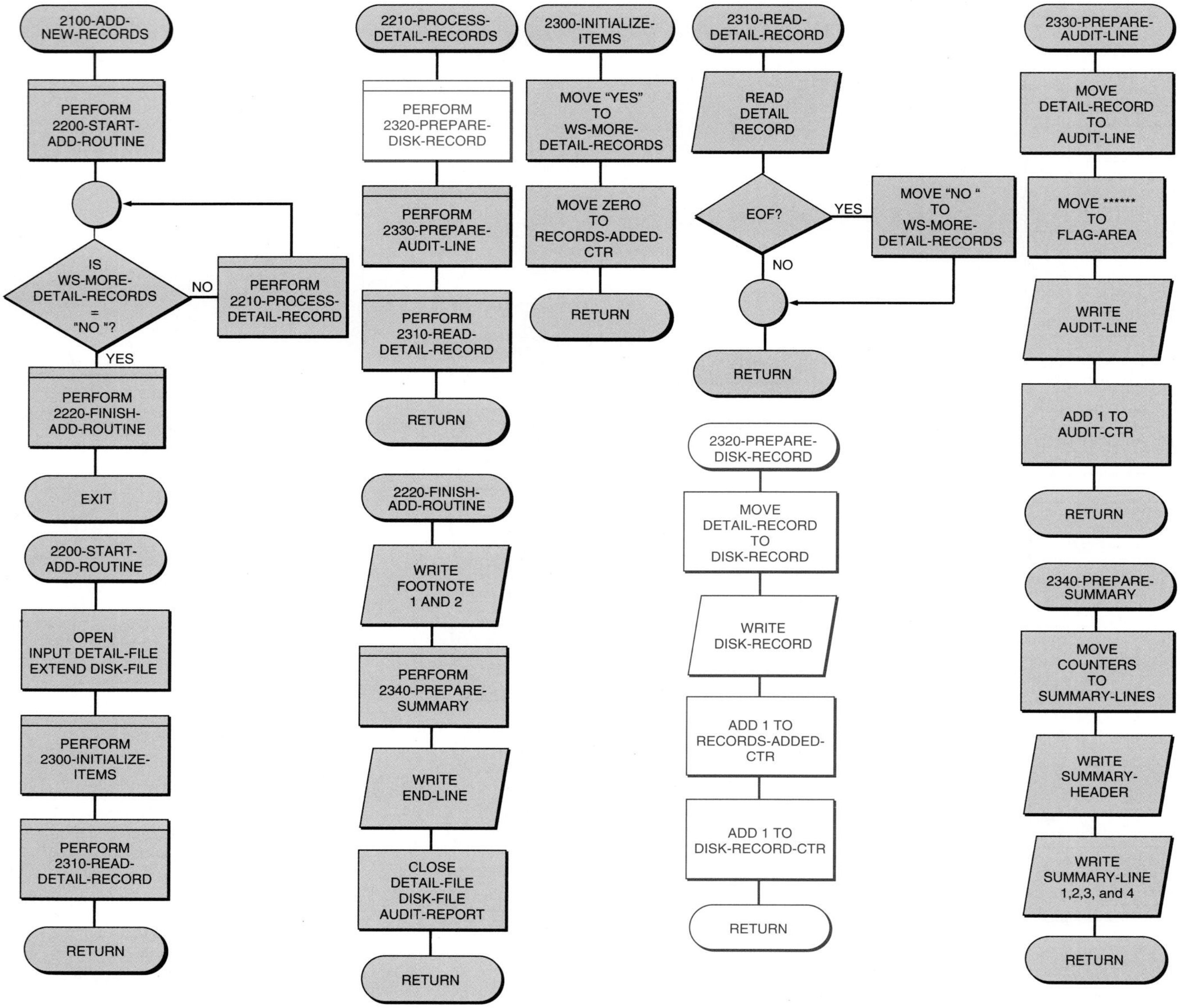

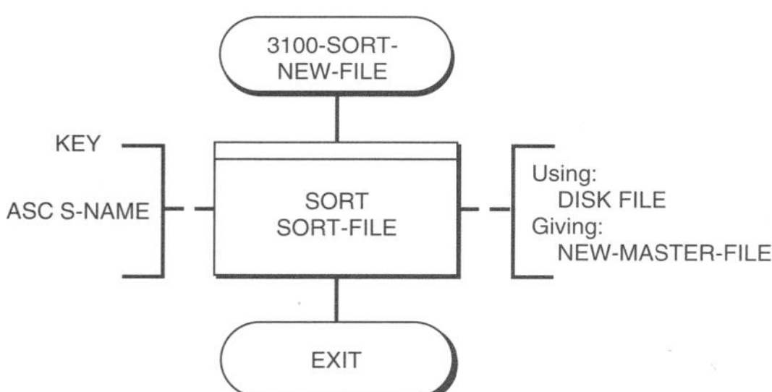

■ **Figure 11.36** COBOL program to create the master personnel file on disk

```
       IDENTIFICATION DIVISION.

       PROGRAM-ID.     JOCELYN-DISK-MASTER.

      ******************************************************************
      *                                                                *
      *    AUTHOR.          PAQUETTE.                                  *
      *    DATE WRITTEN.    OCTOBER 1993.                              *
      *                                                                *
      ******************************************************************

       ENVIRONMENT DIVISION.

       CONFIGURATION SECTION.

       SOURCE-COMPUTER.  VAX-VMS-8650.
       OBJECT-COMPUTER.  VAX-VMS-8650.

       INPUT-OUTPUT SECTION.

1      FILE-CONTROL.
           SELECT OLD-MASTER-FILE      ASSIGN TO OLDMASTER
                                       ORGANIZATION IS SEQUENTIAL
                                       ACCESS MODE IS SEQUENTIAL.
           SELECT DISK-FILE            ASSIGN TO NEWDISK
                                       ORGANIZATION IS SEQUENTIAL
                                       ACCESS MODE IS SEQUENTIAL.
           SELECT DETAIL-FILE          ASSIGN TO COB$INPUT.
           SELECT AUDIT-REPORT         ASSIGN TO COB$OUTPUT.
           SELECT SORT-FILE            ASSIGN TO SORTDISK.
           SELECT NEW-MASTER-FILE      ASSIGN TO DISKMASTER
                                       ORGANIZATION IS SEQUENTIAL
                                       ACCESS MODE IS SEQUENTIAL.

       DATA DIVISION.

       FILE SECTION.

       FD  OLD-MASTER-FILE
           RECORD CONTAINS 100 CHARACTERS
           BLOCK CONTAINS 10 RECORDS.

       01  OLD-MASTER-RECORD.
           05 OLD-MR-NAME          PIC X(20).
           05 OLD-MR-ADDRESS       PIC X(37).
           05 OLD-MR-SSN           PIC X(9).
           05 OLD-MR-DATES         PIC X(12).
           05                      PIC X(22).

       FD  DISK-FILE
           RECORD CONTAINS 100 CHARACTERS
           BLOCK CONTAINS 10 RECORDS.

       01  DISK-MASTER-RECORD.
           05 DISK-MR-NAME          PIC X(20).
           05 DISK-MR-ADDRESS       PIC X(37).
           05 DISK-MR-SSN           PIC X(9).
           05 DISK-MR-DATES         PIC X(12).
           05                       PIC X(22).

       FD  DETAIL-FILE
           RECORD CONTAINS 80 CHARACTERS.

       01  DETAIL-RECORD.
           05 DETAIL-NAME          PIC X(20).
           05 DETAIL-ADDRESS       PIC X(37).
           05 DETAIL-SSN           PIC X(9).
           05 DETAIL-DATES         PIC X(12).
           05                      PIC X(2).

       FD  AUDIT-FILE
           RECORD CONTAINS 132 CHARACTERS.

       01  PRINTLINE               PIC X(132).

       SD  SORT-FILE
           RECORD CONTAINS 100 CHARACTERS.

       01  SORT-RECORD.
2          05 S-NAME               PIC X(20).
           05                      PIC X(80).
```

```
FD  NEW-MASTER-FILE
    RECORD CONTAINS 100 CHARACTERS
    BLOCK CONTAINS 10 RECORDS.

01  NEW-MASTER-RECORD.
    05 NEW-MR-NAME        PIC X(20).
    05 NEW-MR-ADDRESS     PIC X(37).
    05 NEW-MR-SSN         PIC X(9).
    05 NEW-MR-DATES       PIC X(12).
    05                    PIC X(22).

WORKING-STORAGE SECTION.

01  PROGRAM-CONTROLS.
    05 WS-MORE-OLD-RECORDS         PIC XXX.
       88 NO-MORE-OLD-RECORDS              VALUE "NO ".
    05 WS-MORE-DETAIL-RECORDS      PIC XXX.
       88 NO-MORE-DETAIL-RECORDS           VALUE "NO ".
    05 WS-DATE                     PIC 9(6).
    05 WS-PROPER-SPACING           PIC 9.

01  PROGRAM-COUNTERS               COMP.
    05 WS-OLD-MASTER-RECORD-CTR    PIC S999.
    05 WS-DISK-RECORD-CTR          PIC S999.
    05 WS-RECORDS-ADDED-CTR        PIC S999.
    05 WS-AUDIT-CTR                PIC S999.

01  REPORT-HEADERS.
    05 COMPANY-NAME.
       10 PIC X(58)    VALUE SPACES.
       10 PIC X(17)    VALUE "JOCELYN ORIGINALS".
       10 PIC X(57)    VALUE SPACES.

    05 REPORT-NAME-1.
       10 PIC X(43)    VALUE SPACES.
       10 PIC X(39)    VALUE
          "MASTER PERSONNEL FILE CREATED ON DISK  ".
       10 O-DATE       PIC XX/XX/XX.
       10 PIC X(42)    VALUE SPACES.

    05 REPORT-NAME-2.
       10 PIC X(57)    VALUE SPACES.
       10 PIC X(18)    VALUE "AUDIT TRAIL REPORT".
       10 PIC X(57)    VALUE SPACES.

    05 HEADINGS.
       10 PIC X(49)    VALUE SPACES.
       10 PIC X(33)    VALUE "RECORDS COPIED TO NEW MASTER FILE".
       10 PIC X(50)    VALUE SPACES.

01  AUDIT-LINE.
    05                    PIC X(13)  VALUE SPACES.
    05 O-FLAG-AREA        PIC X(6).
    05 O-RECORD-AREA      PIC X(100).
    05                    PIC X(23)  VALUE SPACES.

01  FOOTNOTE-1.
    05 PIC X(5)    VALUE SPACES.
    05 PIC X(6)    VALUE "****  ".
    05 PIC X(50)   VALUE
       "DENOTES NEW RECORDS ADDED TO MASTER PERSONNEL FILE".

01  FOOTNOTE-2.
    05 PIC X(11)   VALUE SPACES.
    05 PIC X(41)   VALUE
       "OTHER RECORDS COPIED FROM OLD MASTER FILE".

01  REPORT-ENDERS.
    05 SUMMARY-HEADER.
       10 PIC X(24)  VALUE SPACES.
       10 PIC X(7)   VALUE "SUMMARY".

    05 SUMMARY-LINE-1.
       10                             PIC X(5)  VALUE SPACES.
       10 O-OLD-MASTER-RECORD-CTR     PIC ZZ9.
       10                             PIC X(37) VALUE
          "  RECORDS COPIED FROM OLD MASTER FILE".

    05 SUMMARY-LINE-2.
       10                             PIC X(5)  VALUE SPACES.
       10 O-RECORDS-ADDED-CTR         PIC ZZ9.
       10                             PIC X(30) VALUE
          "  RECORDS ADDED TO MASTER FILE".
```

Figure 11.36 continued

```
           05 SUMMARY-LINE-3.
              10                        PIC X(5)   VALUE SPACES.
              10 O-DISK-RECORD-CTR      PIC ZZ9.
              10                        PIC X(36) VALUE
                 "  RECORDS WRITTEN TO NEW MASTER FILE".

           05 SUMMARY-LINE-4.
              10                            PIC X(5)   VALUE SPACES.
              10 O-AUDIT-CTR                PIC ZZ9.
              10                            PIC X(33) VALUE
                 "  RECORDS WRITTEN TO AUDIT REPORT".

           05 END-LINE.
              10 PIC X(55)  VALUE SPACES.
              10 PIC X(23)  VALUE "***  END OF REPORT  ***".
              10 PIC X(54)  VALUE SPACES.
       PROCEDURE DIVISION.

      ******************************
3      O-MAIN-CONTROL SECTION.
      ******************************

4      0100-CREATE-NEW-MASTER-FILE.
           PERFORM 1-COPY-OLD-MASTER-FILE.
           PERFORM 2-ADD-DETAIL-FILE.
           PERFORM 3-SORT-DISK-FILE.
           STOP RUN.

      ******************************
5      1-COPY-OLD-MASTER-FILE SECTION.
      ******************************

       1100-COPY-OLD-RECORDS.
           PERFORM 1200-START-COPY-ROUTINE.
           PERFORM 1210-PROCESS-OLD-MASTER-RECORD
               UNTIL NO-MORE-OLD-RECORDS.
           PERFORM 1220-FINISH-COPY-ROUTINE.
6          GO TO 1999-EXIT-SECTION.

       1200-START-COPY-ROUTINE.
7          OPEN INPUT OLD-MASTER-FILE
8               OUTPUT DISK-FILE
9                      AUDIT-REPORT.
           PERFORM 1300-INITIALIZE-ITEMS.
           PERFORM 1310-WRITE-REPORT-HEADERS.
           PERFORM 1320-READ-OLD-MASTER-RECORD.

       1210-PROCESS-OLD-MASTER-RECORD.
           PERFORM 1330-PREPARE-DISK-RECORD.
           PERFORM 1340-PREPARE-AUDIT-LINE.
           PERFORM 1320-READ-OLD-MASTER-RECORD.

       1220-FINISH-COPY-ROUTINE.
10         CLOSE OLD-MASTER-FILE
11               DISK-FILE.

       1300-INITIALIZE-ITEMS.
           ACCEPT WS-DATE FROM DATE.
           MOVE WS-DATE TO O-DATE.
           INITIALIZE PROGRAM-COUNTERS.

       1310-WRITE-REPORT-HEADERS.
           WRITE PRINTLINE FROM COMPANY-NAME
               AFTER ADVANCING PAGE.
           WRITE PRINTLINE FROM REPORT-NAME-1
               AFTER ADVANCING 3 LINES.
           WRITE PRINTLINE FROM REPORT-NAME-2
               AFTER ADVANCING 2 LINES.
           WRITE PRINTLINE FROM HEADINGS
               AFTER ADVANCING 3 LINES.
           MOVE 2 TO WS-PROPER-SPACING.

       1320-READ-OLD-MASTER-RECORD.
           READ OLD-MASTER-FILE NEXT RECORD
               AT END
                   SET NO-MORE-OLD-RECORDS TO TRUE.

       1330-PREPARE-DISK-RECORD.
           WRITE DISK-MASTER-RECORD FROM OLD-MASTER-RECORD.
           ADD 1 TO WS-OLD-MASTER-RECORD-CTR
                    WS-DISK-RECORD-CTR.
```

```
       1340-PREPARE-AUDIT-LINE.
           MOVE OLD-MASTER-RECORD TO O-RECORD-AREA.
           WRITE PRINTLINE FROM AUDIT-LINE
               AFTER ADVANCING WS-PROPER-SPACING.
           MOVE 1 TO WS-PROPER-SPACING.
           ADD 1 TO WS-AUDIT-CTR.

       1999-EXIT-SECTION.
12         EXIT.

      ******************************
13     2-ADD-DETAIL-FILE-SECTION.
      ******************************

       2100-ADD-NEW-RECORDS.
           PERFORM 2200-START-ADD-ROUTINE.
           PERFORM 2210-PROCESS-DETAIL-RECORD
               UNTIL NO-MORE-DETAIL-RECORDS.
           PERFORM 2220-FINISH-ADD-ROUTINE.

       2200-START-ADD-ROUTINE.
14         OPEN INPUT DETAIL-FILE
15              EXTEND DISK-FILE.
           PERFORM 2300-INITIALIZE-ITEMS.
           PERFORM 2310-READ-DETAIL-RECORD.

       2210-PROCESS-DETAIL-RECORD.
           PERFORM 2320-PREPARE-DISK-RECORD.
           PERFORM 2330-PREPARE-AUDIT-LINE.
           PERFORM 2310-READ-DETAIL-RECORD.

       2220-FINISH-ADD-ROUTINE.
           WRITE PRINTLINE FROM FOOTNOTE-1
               AFTER ADVANCING 5 LINES.
           WRITE PRINTLINE FROM FOOTNOTE-2
               AFTER ADVANCING 1 LINE.
           PERFORM 2340-PREPARE-SUMMARY.
               WRITE PRINTLINE FROM END-LINE
               AFTER ADVANCING 5 LINES.
16         CLOSE DETAIL-FILE
17               DISK-FILE
18               AUDIT-REPORT.

       2300-INITIALIZE-ITEMS.
            MOVE "YES" TO WS-MORE-DETAIL-RECORDS.
            INITIALIZE WS-RECORDS-ADDED-CTR.

       2310-READ-DETAIL-RECORD.
           READ DETAIL-FILE RECORD
               AT END
                   SET NO-MORE-DETAIL-RECORDS TO TRUE.

       2320-PREPARE-DISK-RECORD.
           WRITE DISK-MASTER-RECORD FROM DETAIL-RECORD.
           ADD 1 TO WS-RECORDS-ADDED-CTR
                    WS-DISK-RECORD-CTR.

       2330-PREPARE-AUDIT-LINE.
           MOVE DETAIL-RECORD TO O-RECORD-AREA.
           MOVE "****" TO O-FLAG-AREA.
           WRITE PRINTLINE FROM AUDIT-LINE
               AFTER ADVANCING WS-PROPER-SPACING.
           MOVE 1 TO WS-PROPER-SPACING.
           ADD 1 TO WS-AUDIT-CTR.

       2340-PREPARE-SUMMARY.
           WRITE PRINTLINE FROM SUMMARY-HEADER
               AFTER ADVANCING 5 LINES.
           MOVE WS-OLD-MASTER-RECORD-CTR TO O-OLD-MASTER-RECORD-CTR.
           WRITE PRINTLINE FROM SUMMARY-LINE-1
               AFTER ADVANCING 2 LINES.
           MOVE WS-RECORDS-ADDED-CTR TO O-RECORDS-ADDED-CTR.
           WRITE PRINTLINE FROM SUMMARY-LINE-2
               AFTER ADVANCING 1 LINE.
           MOVE WS-DISK-RECORD-CTR TO O-DISK-RECORD-CTR.
           WRITE PRINTLINE FROM SUMMARY-LINE-3
               AFTER ADVANCING 1 LINE.
           MOVE WS-AUDIT-CTR TO O-AUDIT-CTR.
           WRITE PRINTLINE FROM SUMMARY-LINE-4
               AFTER ADVANCING 1 LINE.

       2999-EXIT-SECTION.
           EXIT.
```

Figure 11.36 continued

```
         *******************************
19        3-SORT-DISK-FILE SECTION.
         *******************************

          3100-SORT-NEW-FILE.
              SORT SORT-FILE
20                ON ASCENDING S-NAME
21                USING DISK-FILE
22                GIVING NEW-MASTER-FILE.

          3999-EXIT-SECTION.
              EXIT.
```

2. The FILE SECTION contains a file description (FD or SD) for each file named in SELECT statements of the FILE-CONTROL paragraph. Recall that a sort file description must begin with SD, not FD.

   Note that the record descriptions provided for OLD-MASTER-RECORD, DETAIL-RECORD, DISK-RECORD, and NEW-MASTER-RECORD need not be detailed, since references to elementary items in those records are not required in the program. The descriptions could have been as follows:

```
01   OLD-MASTER-RECORD   PIC X(100).
01   DETAIL-RECORD       PIC X(80).
01   DISK-RECORD         PIC X (100).
01   NEW-MASTER-RECORD   PIC X(100).
```

   The detailed descriptions simply provide more documentation.

   The record description of SORT-RECORD, however, **must** identify the elementary item S-NAME, since it is a sort key within the SORT statement (see lines 2 and 20).
3. The sections within the PROCEDURE DIVISION have been highlighted by asterisks to provide convenient visual points of reference. Note the four sections: 0-MAIN-CONTROL SECTION at line 3, 1-COPY-OLD-MASTER-FILE SECTION at line 5, 2-ADD-DETAIL-FILE SECTION at line 13, and 3-SORT-DISK-FILE SECTION at line 19.
4. The paragraph 0100-CREATE-NEW-MASTER-FILE at line 4 is the main driver for the program. When control is passed from the operating system to the program, it enters at the beginning of this paragraph, and when the last statement in this paragraph is executed, control returns to the operating system—the PERFORM statements in this paragraph control the execution of **sections,** not paragraphs.
5. Recall that when a paragraph is under the control of a PERFORM statement, control returns to the PERFORM statement when the last statement in the paragraph is executed. Similarly, when a **section** is under the control of a PERFORM statement, control returns to the PERFORM statement when the last statement in the **section** is executed. To accomplish this while maintaining the integrity of the structure of the section, the last paragraph of the section is designed as an exit-section paragraph. It contains only the key statement EXIT. Control is explicitly sent to this paragraph by a GO TO statement at the end of the primary paragraph of the section. For instance, see lines 6 and 12 in section 1-COPY-OLD-MASTER-FILE.
6. Since the audit report keeps track of the activity in sections 1-COPY-OLD-MASTER-FILE and 2-ADD-DETAIL-FILE, the file AUDIT-REPORT is opened at the beginning of section 1-COPY-OLD-MASTER-FILE, and it is closed at the end of section 2-ADD-DETAIL-FILE. See lines 9 and 18.
7. The role of DISK-FILE is to receive copies of the old records in the tape file OLD-MASTER-FILE and the new records in the file DETAIL-FILE. It is opened in OUTPUT mode at the beginning of section 1-COPY-OLD-MASTER-FILE (see line 8) and closed at the end of that section (see line 11). Within section 2-ADD-DETAIL-FILE, it must be reopened to receive copies of the new records in DETAIL-FILE, but its open mode must be specified as EXTEND in order to add the new records to the end of the file (see line 15). Before leaving section 2-ADD-DETAIL-FILE, the file DISK-FILE is closed (see line 17). Then, in section 3-SORT-DISK-FILE, DISK-FILE is named as the input file in the USING phrase of the SORT statement (see line 21). Here it is reopened in INPUT mode by the sort routine, and it is closed by the sort routine when all of its records have been copied to SORT-FILE.

8. In section 3-SORT-DISK-FILE, note that a GO TO statement is not needed, since the EXIT statement in paragraph 3999-EXIT-SECTION is automatically executed following the SORT statement simply because it is the next statement in line.

The records in OLD-MASTER-FILE are shown in Figure 11.37a [DD/CD:VICIISP3.DT1], the records in DETAIL-FILE are shown in Figure 11.37b [DD/CD:VICIISP3.DT2], and the records in NEW-MASTER-FILE are shown in Figure 11.37c. The records in NEW-MASTER-FILE that come from DETAIL-FILE have been highlighted for your convenience. The audit report produced by the program is shown in Figure 11.38.

Figure 11.37a OLD-MASTER-FILE records

```
ABRUZZI, KENNETH L. 51 RAYMOND ST  HASTINGS, NE     68901743142265120552082072
AITKEN, THOMAS R.   260 FOUNTAIN STAURORA, NE       68818032567781080526082046
ALTERMAN, MAUREEN E.10 MARTIN AVE  YORK, NE         68467144217773052435061060
BAHR, LENA M.       304 CORY LANE  GENEVA, NE       68361381662514111041082060
BLAZUCK, JOSEPH A.  85 BELVIEW AVE FAIRFIELD, NE    68938179623741052145061075
BUXBAUM, JOAN M.    172 EARLE DR   GRAND ISLAND, NE 68802005589243021448060870
CARTER, AMEKIA L.   59 BARK ST     LOUP CITY, NE    68853623514793051332082062
COLETTI, SARAH T.   51 BROAD ST    HASTINGS, NE     68901042750015090238061564
COUGHLIN, AILEEN M. 133 DAVIS RD   LEXINGTON, NE    68850016493017031050070668
CYR, ROSARIO        205 SUNSET DR  FAIRFIELD, NE    68938771894263052435082055
DURANT, MARIE L.    1250 HIGH RD   GENEVA, NE       68361364923752092443091054
GAFFNEY, MARYLYN    274 HANOVER ST ARAPAHOE, NE     68922039764715120552060877
KACHADOURIAN, NATALI922 LOCUST ST  HEBRON, NE       68370211384406022135082056
MARKARIAN, MARIAN   984 N MAIN ST  HASTINGS, NE     68901130043962050732082052
MCGEE, BERNARD W.   2420 CARR LA   CENTRAL CITY, NE 68826013407206121530061549
MOONEY, RONALD      220 N MAIN ST  HASTINGS, NE     68901124670325092041081064
OVERDEEP, CYNTHIA   130 CANAL ST   YORK, NE         68467226153911052435071570
PACCASASSIE, DEBBIE 341 BRANCH AVE NORMAN, NE       68963149201475261228091257
PRIMEAU, ISABEL     78 NORTH ST    KEARNEY, NE      68847150246389093047082072
ROMA, GILDA         25 MAPLE DR    SUPERIOR, NE     68978432157258070850061072
SHERIDAN, RICHARD J.2 GENEVA RD    HASTINGS, NE     68901234891533120542061065
STURDAHL, DEBRA     2541 RICE ST   CRETE, NE        68333221506420614340715555
VELTRI, JOHN A.     54 SOUTH ST    AURORA, NE       68818026307625011547082082
```

Figure 11.37b DETAIL-FILE records

```
ARMSTRONG, GEORGE   105 STATE ST   PLATTE, NE    68653014766691032048081683
CUMMINGS, DOROTHEA  97 POWER AVE   NORMAN, NE    68963215137814040753082283
DESROSIERS, RICHARD 92 REGAN RD    LOUP CITY, NE 68853314764532122158081583
LAKE, SUE           252 EAST RD    CRETE, NE     68333253749144070741081583
MAYO, EVANGELINA    895 POTTERS AVEGENEVA, NE    68361032561579080562080783
PEARSON, ARTHUR     1020 GOLDEN RD HASTINGS, NE  68901033281512112550080283
```

Figure 11.37c NEW-MASTER-FILE records

```
ABRUZZI, KENNETH L. 51 RAYMOND ST  HASTINGS, NE     68901743142265120552082072
AITKEN, THOMAS R.   260 FOUNTAIN STAURORA, NE       68818032567781080526082046
ALTERMAN, MAUREEN E.10 MARTIN AVE  YORK, NE         68467144217773052435061060
ARMSTRONG, GEORGE   105 STATE ST   PLATTE, NE       68653014766691032048081683
BAHR, LENA M.       304 CORY LANE  GENEVA, NE       68361381662514111041082060
BLAZUCK, JOSEPH A.  85 BELVIEW AVE FAIRFIELD, NE    68938179623741052145061075
BUXBAUM, JOAN M.    172 EARLE DR   GRAND ISLAND, NE 68802005589243021448060870
CARTER, AMEKIA L.   59 BARK ST     LOUP CITY, NE    68853623514793051332082062
COLETTI, SARAH T.   51 BROAD ST    HASTINGS, NE     68901042750015090238061564
COUGHLIN, AILEEN M. 133 DAVIS RD   LEXINGTON, NE    68850016493017031050070668
CUMMINGS, DOROTHEA  97 POWER AVE   NORMAN, NE       68963215137814040753082283
CYR, ROSARIO        205 SUNSET DR  FAIRFIELD, NE    68938771894263052435082055
DESROSIERS, RICHARD 92 REGAN RD    LOUP CITY, NE    68853314764532122158081583
DURANT, MARIE L.    1250 HIGH RD   GENEVA, NE       68361364923752092443091054
GAFFNEY, MARYLYN    274 HANOVER ST ARAPAHOE, NE     68922039764715120552060877
KACHADOURIAN, NATALI922 LOCUST ST  HEBRON, NE       68370211384406022135082056
LAKE, SUE           252 EAST RD    CRETE, NE        68333253749144070741081583
MARKARIAN, MARIAN   984 N MAIN ST  HASTINGS, NE     68901130043962050732082052
MAYO, EVANGELINA    895 POTTERS AVEGENEVA, NE       68361032561579080562080783
MCGEE, BERNARD W.   2420 CARR LA   CENTRAL CITY, NE 68826013407206121530061549
MOONEY, RONALD      220 N MAIN ST  HASTINGS, NE     68901124670325092041081064
OVERDEEP, CYNTHIA   130 CANAL ST   YORK, NE         68467226153911052435071570
PACCASASSIE, DEBBIE 341 BRANCH AVE NORMAN, NE       68963149201475261228091257
PEARSON, ARTHUR     1020 GOLDEN RD HASTINGS, NE     68901033281512112550080283
PRIMEAU, ISABEL     78 NORTH ST    KEARNEY, NE      68847150246389093047082072
ROMA, GILDA         25 MAPLE DR    SUPERIOR, NE     68978432157258070850061072
SHERIDAN, RICHARD J.2 GENEVA RD    HASTINGS, NE     68901234891533120542061065
STURDAHL, DEBRA     2541 RICE ST   CRETE, NE        68333221506420614340715555
VELTRI, JOHN A.     54 SOUTH ST    AURORA, NE       68818026307625011547082082
```

Figure 11.38 The audit report produced by the program

```
                                                  JOCELYN ORIGINALS

                                     MASTER PERSONNEL FILE CREATED ON DISK  93/10/28
                                                  AUDIT TRAIL REPORT

                                            RECORDS COPIED TO NEW MASTER FILE

           ABRUZZI, KENNETH L. 51 RAYMOND ST  HASTINGS, NE      68901743142265120552082072
           AITKEN, THOMAS R.   260 FOUNTAIN STAURORA, NE        68818032567781080526082046
           ALTERMAN, MAUREEN E.10 MARTIN AVE  YORK, NE          68467144217773052435061060
           BAHR, LENA M.       304 CORY LANE  GENEVA, NE        68361381552514111041082060
           BLAZUCK, JOSEPH A.  85 BELVIEW AVE FAIRFIELD, NE     68938179623741052145061075
           BUXBAUM, JOAN M.    172 EARLE DR   GRAND ISLAND, NE  68802005589243021448060870
           CARTER, AMEKIA L.   59 BARK ST     LOUP CITY, NE     68853623514793051332082062
           COLETTI, SARAH T.   51 BROAD ST    HASTINGS, NE      68901042750015090238061564
           COUGHLIN, AILEEN M. 133 DAVIS RD   LEXINGTON, NE     68850016493017031050070668
           CYR, ROSARIO        205 SUNSET DR  FAIRFIELD, NE     68938771894263052435082055
           DURANT, MARIE L.    1250 HIGH RD   GENEVA, NE        68361364923752092443091054
           GAFFNEY, MARYLYN    274 HANOVER ST ARAPAHOE, NE      68922039764715120552060877
           KACHADOURIAN, NATALI922 LOCUST ST  HEBRON, NE        68370211384406022135082056
           MARKARIAN, MARIAN   984 N MAIN ST  HASTINGS, NE      68901130043962050732082052
           MCGEE, BERNARD W.   2420 CARR LA   CENTRAL CITY, NE  68826013407206121530061549
           MOONEY, RONALD      220 N MAIN ST  HASTINGS, NE      68901124670325092041081064
           OVERDEEP, CYNTHIA   130 CANAL ST   YORK, NE          68467226153911052435071570
           PACCASASSIE, DEBBIE 341 BRANCH AVE NORMAN, NE        68963149201475261228091257
           PRIMEAU, ISABEL     78 NORTH ST    KEARNEY, NE       68847150246389093047082072
           ROMA, GILDA         25 MAPLE DR    SUPERIOR, NE      68978432157258070850061072
           SHERIDAN, RICHARD J.2 GENEVA RD    HASTINGS, NE      68901234891533120542061065
           STURDAHL, DEBRA     2541 RICE ST   CRETE, NE         68333221506420614340715555
           VELTRI, JOHN A.     54 SOUTH ST    AURORA, NE        68818026307625011547082082
      **** ARMSTRONG, GEORGE   105 STATE ST   PLATTE, NE        68653014766691032048081683
      **** CUMMINGS, DOROTHEA  97 POWER AVE   NORMAN,NE         68963215137814040753082283
      **** DESROSIERS, RICHARD 92 REGAN RD    LOUP CITY, NE     68853314764532122158081583
      **** LAKE, SUE           252 EAST RD    CRETE, NE         68333253749144070741081583
      **** MAYO, EVANGELINA    895 POTTERS AVEGENEVA, NE        68361032561579080562080783
      **** PEARSON, ARTHUR     1020 GOLDEN RD HASTINGS, NE      68901033281512112550080283


****  DENOTES NEW RECORDS ADDED TO MASTER PERSONNEL FILE
      OTHER RECORDS COPIED FROM OLD MASTER FILE


                      SUMMARY

 23  RECORDS COPIED FROM OLD MASTER FILE
  6  RECORDS ADDED TO MASTER FILE
 29  RECORDS WRITTEN TO NEW MASTER FILE
 29  RECORDS WRITTEN TO AUDIT REPORT


                                                ***  END OF REPORT   ***
```

Updating Records in a Disk Sequential File

If a file with sequential organization is a tape file and some of its records contain values that must be changed and updated, a new tape file must be produced, as seen in the program of Figure 11.25. However, if the file is a disk file, existing records that must be brought up to date can be rewritten to the same file. The process consists essentially of the following three steps:

1. Read the record that must be updated into the buffer associated with the file.
2. Copy the new values into the appropriate fields of the record.
3. Rewrite the record to the file.

Suppose that some records in the new master file created by the program in Figure 11.36 must be brought up to date because some employees have changed address. A simple analysis of the task is as follows:

1. Prepare a detail file containing a record for each employee who has a new address. Each record must contain the employee name and the new address. The records should be presorted in alphabetic order by employee name to match the sequencing of the records in the master file.

Figure 11.39 System flowchart to update records in a disk sequential file

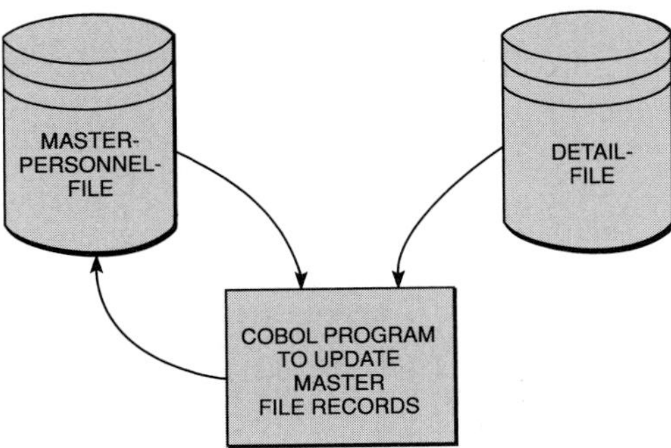

2. Design the program to do the following:
   a. Read a detail file record.
   b. Read a master file record.
   c. Compare the names on the two records. If the names do not match, read the next record of the master file and test the names again. If they do not match, continue reading successive records of the master file until a match occurs.

      When the names match, move the new address to the address field of the master record and then rewrite the record to the master file.
   d. Repeat steps a, b, and c until there are no more detail records or no more master records.
   e. If an exit occurs from the loop established in steps a, b, and c because there are no more master records while there are more detail records, display an appropriate error message. The message should indicate that there is no record in the master file corresponding to the name on the detail record currently in input memory.

Since you are already familiar with procedures to prepare an audit report, such procedures are omitted from this program for the sake of simplicity. The system flowchart is shown in Figure 11.39.

Note that only two files are needed: DETAIL-FILE, whose records contain the new addresses for particular employees, and MASTER-PERSONNEL-FILE, whose corresponding records contain addresses that must be changed. Since the master file must be read and also written to, it must be opened in a dual mode, that is, in input and in output modes. This will be accomplished by specifying I-O in the OPEN statement for the file.

Based on the brief analysis above, the structure chart is simple, as shown in Figure 11.40.

Figure 11.40 Structure chart to update records in a disk sequential file

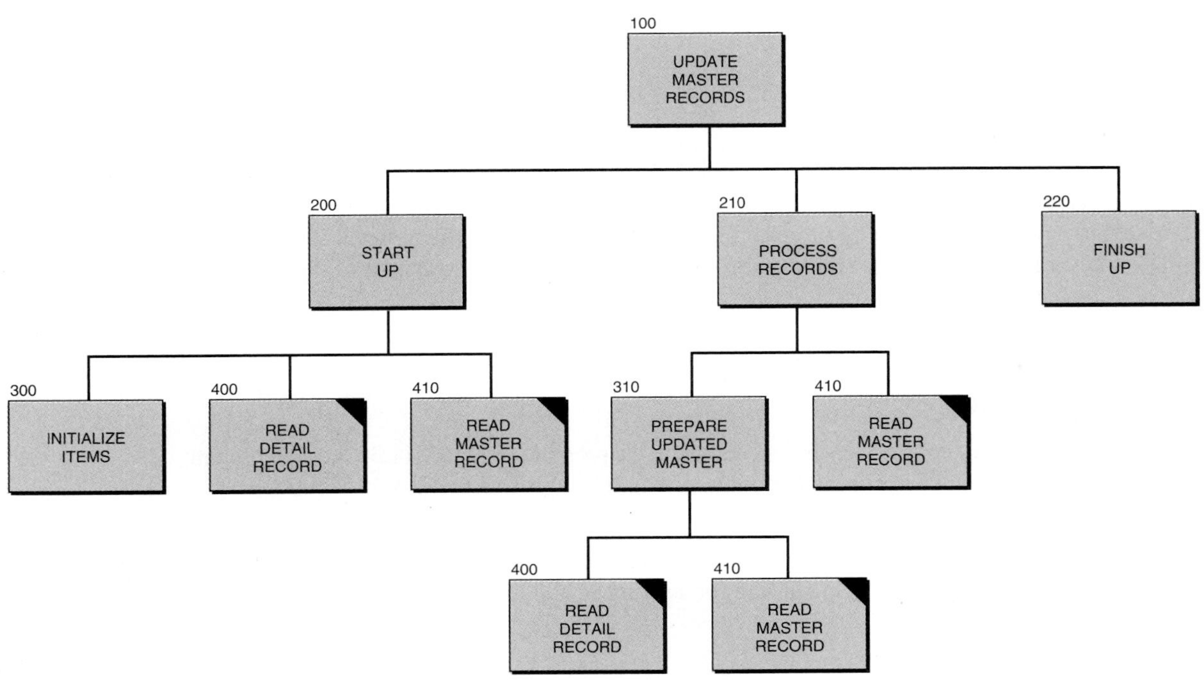

The pseudocode is as follows:

100-Update-Master-Records.

1. Perform 200-Start-Up.
2. Perform 210-Process-Records until no more detail records or no more master records.
3. Perform 220-Finish-Up.
4. Stop the run.

200-Start-Up.

1. Open Detail-File as an input file and Master-Personnel-File as an input-output file.
2. Perform 300-Initialize-Items.
3. Perform 400-Read-Detail-Record.
4. Perform 410-Read-Master-Record.

210-Process-Records.

1. Test input master-record name against input detail-record name.
   a. If they match, perform 310-Prepare-Updated-Master.
   b. If they do not match, perform 410-Read-Master-Record.

220-Finish-Up.

1. If there are no more master records and there are more detail records,
   display "No master record for " input detail-name, and
   display "Remaining records in detail file not processed".
2. Close the files.

300-Initialize-Items.

1. Set the flags WS-MORE-DETAIL-RECORDS and WS-MORE-MASTER-RECORDS to "YES".

310-Prepare-Updated-Master.

1. Move input detail-record address to input master-record address.
2. Rewrite master-record to Master-Personnel-File.
3. Perform 400-Read-Detail-Record.
4. Perform 410-Read-Master-Record.

400-Read-Detail-Record.

1. Read input detail-record.
2. Test for end-of-file record;
   if EOF record reached, move "NO " to the flag WS-MORE-DETAIL-RECORDS.

410-Read-Master-Record.

1. Read input master-record.
2. Test for end-of-file record;
   if EOF record reached, move "NO " to the flag WS-MORE-MASTER-RECORDS.

The program flowchart corresponding to the pseudocode is shown in Figure 11.41.

Coding the Program

Before coding the program, we must examine the two new statements required by the program. These statements are related to the functions specified in step 1 of pseudocode paragraph 200-Start-Up and step 2 of paragraph 310-Prepare-Updated-Master, namely, opening the master file in an input *and* output mode, and rewriting to the master file a record that was previously accessed from the master file by a READ statement.

I-O Open Mode

One of the options specified in the format for the OPEN statement is

<u>OPEN I-O</u> {file-name-3} . . .

In this format,

1. *File-name-3* is made available to the program in the dual mode INPUT and OUTPUT.
2. The I-O option can be used only for files on mass storage devices, such as disks.
3. If *file-name-3* is in a sequential access mode,
   a. The input statement that can reference the file is READ-AT END, and the only output statement that can reference the file is REWRITE.
   b. The OPEN statement is successful only if the file already exists. Otherwise, the OPEN statement fails. That is, *file-name-3* is not created by the OPEN I-O statement.

Figure 11.41 Program flowchart to update records in a disk sequential file

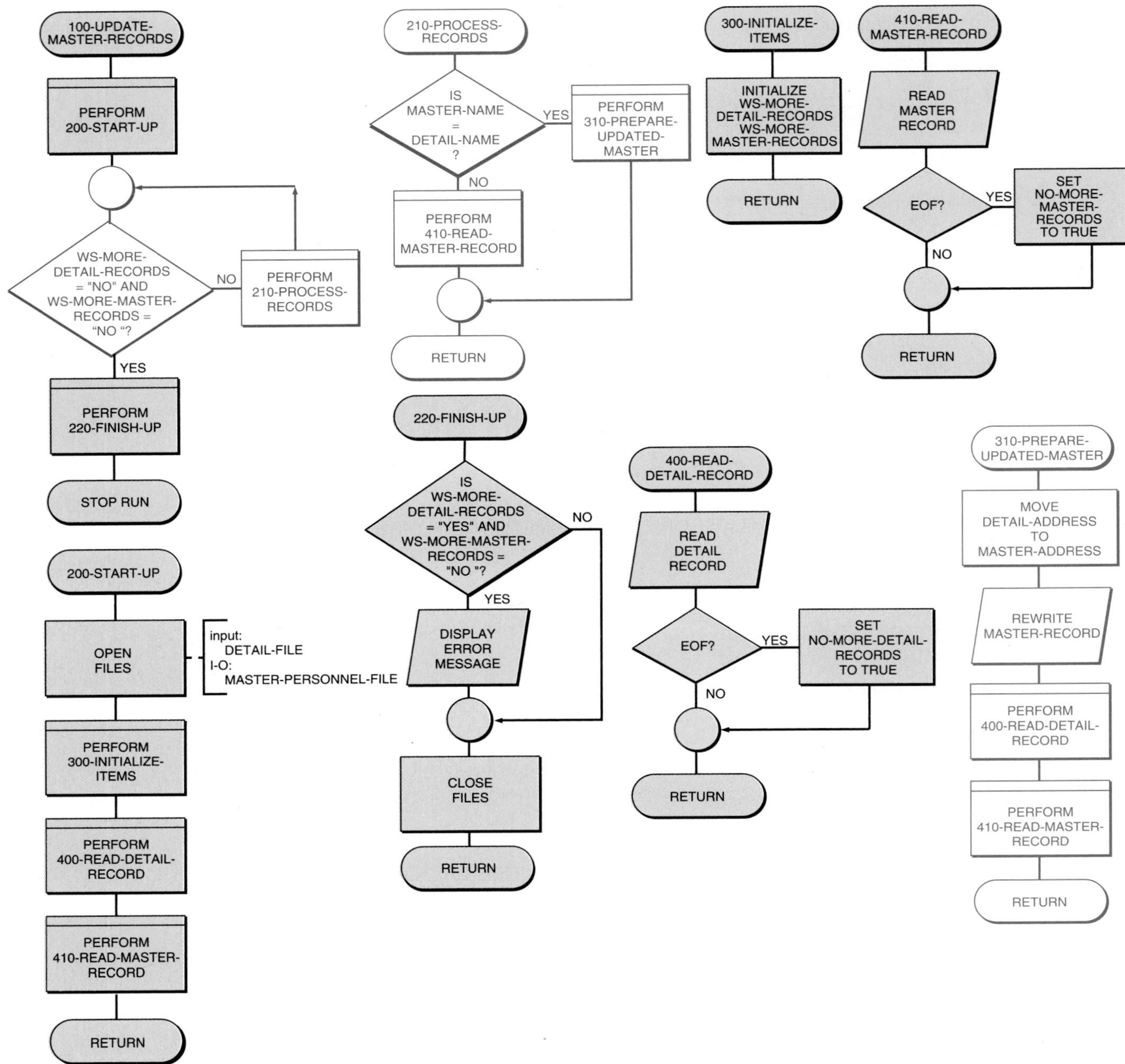

Figure 11.42 REWRITE statement format

<u>REWRITE</u> record-name-1 [<u>FROM</u> identifier-1]

In the current program, MASTER-PERSONNEL-FILE, which has sequential organization, must be opened in I-O mode, since its records must be read and the records that receive a new address must be rewritten to the file.

REWRITE Statement

The format of the REWRITE statement for sequential files is shown in Figure 11.42.

Rules Governing Use of the REWRITE Statement

1. The function of the REWRITE statement is to logically replace a record belonging to a file on a mass storage device.
2. *Record-name-1* is the name of a record defined in the FILE SECTION.
3. *Identifier-1* is a source data item. The FROM phrase copies its contents into *record-name-1* prior to the execution of the REWRITE operation.
4. The record named by *record-name-1* must be the same size as the record it replaces.
5. The file being written to must be on a mass storage device, and at the time of the REWRITE operation, it must be opened in I-O mode.
6. Prior to the execution of the REWRITE statement, a successful READ operation must have occurred, and the record being logically replaced is the one that was accessed by the READ operation.
7. Following the REWRITE operation, the record is no longer available in the buffer associated with the file.

Figure 11.43 illustrates the steps required to complete a successful REWRITE operation. In step 1, a master record is read from MASTER-PERSONNEL-FILE into the MASTER-RECORD area in main memory, and a detail record is read from DETAIL-FILE into the DETAIL-RECORD area in main memory. The figure illustrates a case where the names match. In step 2, the address in the DETAIL-RECORD is copied into the address field of MASTER-RECORD. In step 3, the updated MASTER-RECORD is rewritten to MASTER-PERSONNEL-FILE in the same record area that was accessed by the READ in step 1.

The COBOL program corresponding to the pseudocode or to the flowchart in Figure 11.41 is shown in Figure 11.44. Some key entries have been highlighted for your convenience. Figure 11.45a [DD/CD:VICIISP4.DT1] shows the master file records before the program run, and Figure 11.45b shows the master file records after the program run. The master records with new addresses are highlighted. Figure 11.45c [DD/CD:VICIISP4.DT2] shows the records in the sample DETAIL-FILE.

Figure 11.43 A READ and REWRITE operation illustration

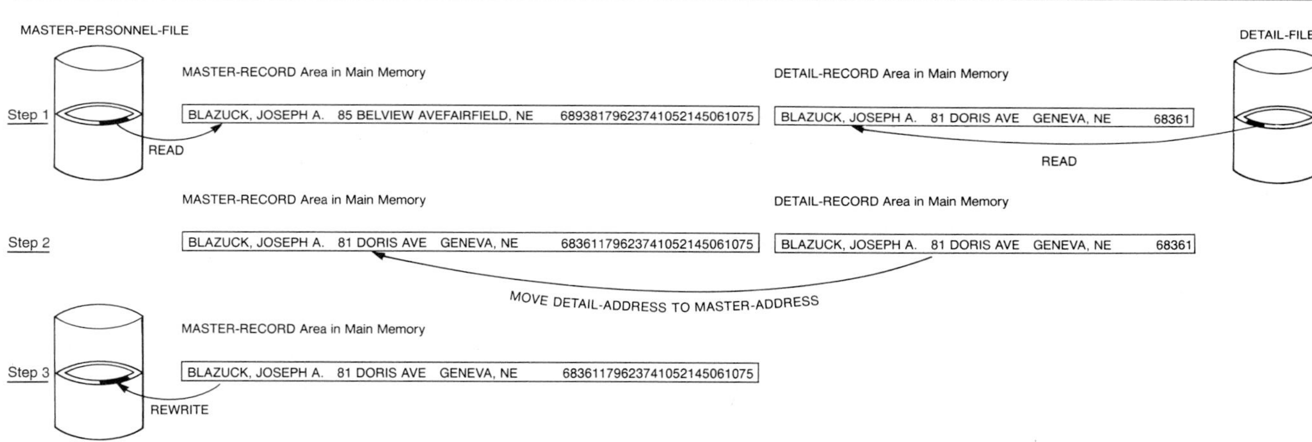

Figure 11.44 COBOL program to update records in a disk sequential file

```
 IDENTIFICATION DIVISION.

 PROGRAM-ID.     JOCELYN-DISK-UPDATE.

*****************************************************************
*                                                               *
*    AUTHOR.          PAQUETTE.                                 *
*    DATE WRITTEN.    OCTOBER 1993.                             *
*                                                               *
*    THIS PROGRAM UPDATES RECORDS IN THE MASTER PERSONNEL DISK  *
*    FILE FOR THE JOCELYN ORIGINALS COMPANY.  RECORDS IN A DETAIL *
*    FILE CONTAIN NEW ADDRESSES FOR SOME EMPLOYEES.             *
*    UPDATED RECORDS ARE REWRITTEN TO THE MASTER FILE.          *
*                                                               *
*****************************************************************

 ENVIRONMENT DIVISION.

 CONFIGURATION SECTION.
```

```
SOURCE-COMPUTER.  VAX-VMS-8650.
OBJECT-COMPUTER.  VAX-VMS-8650.

INPUT-OUTPUT SECTION.

FILE-CONTROL.
    SELECT DETAIL-FILE             ASSIGN TO COB$INPUT.
    SELECT MASTER-PERSONNEL-FILE   ASSIGN TO MASTERFILE
                                   ORGANIZATION IS SEQUENTIAL
                                   ACCESS MODE IS SEQUENTIAL.

DATA DIVISION.

FILE SECTION.

FD  DETAIL-FILE
    RECORD CONTAINS 57 CHARACTERS.

01  DETAIL-RECORD.
    05 DETAIL-NAME       PIC X(20).
    05 DETAIL-ADDRESS    PIC X(37).

FD  MASTER-PERSONNEL-FILE
    RECORD CONTAINS 100 CHARACTERS
    BLOCK CONTAINS 10 RECORDS.

01  MASTER-RECORD.
    05 MASTER-NAME       PIC X(20).
    05 MASTER-ADDRESS    PIC X(37).
    05 MASTER-SSN        PIC X(9).
    05 MASTER-DATES      PIC X(12).
    05                   PIC X(22).

WORKING-STORAGE SECTION.

01  PROGRAM-CONTROLS.
    05 WS-MORE-DETAIL-RECORDS    PIC X(3).
       88 MORE-DETAIL-RECORDS              VALUE "YES".
       88 NO-MORE-DETAIL-RECORDS           VALUE "NO ".
    05 WS-MORE-MASTER-RECORDS    PIC X(3).
       88 MORE-MASTER-RECORDS              VALUE "YES".
       88 NO-MORE-MASTER-RECORDS           VALUE "NO ".

PROCEDURE DIVISION.

100-UPDATE-MASTER-RECORDS.
    PERFORM 200-START-UP.
    PERFORM 210-PROCESS-RECORDS
        UNTIL NO-MORE-DETAIL-RECORDS OR NO-MORE-MASTER-RECORDS.
    PERFORM 220-FINISH-UP.
    STOP RUN.

200-START-UP.
    OPEN INPUT DETAIL-FILE
         I-O   MASTER-PERSONNEL-FILE.
    PERFORM 300-INITIALIZE-ITEMS.
    PERFORM 400-READ-DETAIL-RECORD.
    PERFORM 410-READ-MASTER-RECORD.

210-PROCESS-RECORDS.
    IF MASTER-NAME = DETAIL-NAME
       THEN
           PERFORM 310-PREPARE-UPDATED-MASTER
       ELSE
           PERFORM 410-READ-MASTER-RECORD
    END-IF.

220-FINISH-UP.
    IF NO-MORE-MASTER-RECORDS AND MORE-DETAIL-RECORDS
        DISPLAY "NO MASTER RECORD FOR " DETAIL-NAME
        DISPLAY "REMAINING RECORDS IN DETAIL FILE NOT PROCESSED"
    END-IF.
    CLOSE DETAIL-FILE
          MASTER-PERSONNEL-FILE.

300-INITIALIZE-ITEMS.
    SET MORE-DETAIL-RECORDS
        MORE-MASTER-RECORDS TO TRUE.

310-PREPARE-UPDATED-MASTER.
    MOVE DETAIL-ADDRESS TO MASTER-ADDRESS.
    REWRITE MASTER-RECORD.
    PERFORM 400-READ-DETAIL-RECORD.
    PERFORM 410-READ-MASTER-RECORD.

400-READ-DETAIL-RECORD.
    READ DETAIL-FILE RECORD
        AT END
            SET NO-MORE-DETAIL-RECORDS TO TRUE.

410-READ-MASTER-RECORD.
    READ MASTER-PERSONNEL-FILE NEXT RECORD
        AT END
            SET NO-MORE-MASTER-RECORDS TO TRUE.
```

Figure 11.45a MASTER-PERSONNEL-FILE before the program run

```
ABRUZZI, KENNETH L. 51 RAYMOND ST  HASTINGS, NE     68901743142265120552082072
AITKEN, THOMAS R.   260 FOUNTAIN STAURORA, NE       68818032567781080526082046
ALTERMAN, MAUREEN E.10 MARTIN AVE  YORK, NE         68467144217773052435061060
ARMSTRONG, GEORGE   105 STATE ST   PLATTE, NE       68653014766691032048081683
BAHR, LENA M.       304 CORY LANE  GENEVA, NE       68361381662514111041082060
BLAZUCK, JOSEPH A.  85 BELVIEW AVE FAIRFIELD, NE    68938179623741052145061075
BUXBAUM, JOAN M.    172 EARLE DR   GRAND ISLAND, NE 68802005589243021448060870
CARTER, AMEKIA L.   59 BARK ST     LOUP CITY, NE    68853623514793051332082062
COLETTI, SARAH T.   51 BROAD ST    HASTINGS, NE     68901042750015090238061564
COUGHLIN, AILEEN M. 133 DAVIS RD   LEXINGTON, NE    68850016493017031050070668
CUMMINGS, DOROTHEA  97 POWER AVE   NORMAN,NE        68963215137814040753082283
CYR, ROSARIO        205 SUNSET DR  FAIRFIELD, NE    68938771894263052435082055
DESROSIERS, RICHARD 92 REGAN RD    LOUP CITY, NE    68853314764532122158081583
DURANT, MARIE L.    1250 HIGH RD   GENEVA, NE       68361364923752092443091054
GAFFNEY, MARYLYN    274 HANOVER ST ARAPAHOE, NE     68922039764715120552060877
KACHADOURIAN, NATALI922 LOCUST ST  HEBRON, NE       68370211384406022135082056
LAKE, SUE           252 EAST RD    CRETE, NE        68333253749144070741081583
MARKARIAN, MARIAN   984 N MAIN ST  HASTINGS, NE     68901130043962050732082052
MAYO, EVANGELINA    895 POTTERS AVEGENEVA, NE       68361032561579080562080783
MCGEE, BERNARD W.   2420 CARR LA   CENTRAL CITY, NE 68826013407206121530061549
MOONEY, RONALD      220 N MAIN ST  HASTINGS, NE     68901124670325092041081064
OVERDEEP, CYNTHIA   130 CANAL ST   YORK, NE         68467226153911052435071570
PACCASASSIE, DEBBIE 341 BRANCH AVE NORMAN, NE       68963149201475261228091257
PEARSON, ARTHUR     1020 GOLDEN RD HASTINGS, NE     68901033281512112550080283
PRIMEAU, ISABEL     78 NORTH ST    KEARNEY, NE      68847150246389093047082072
ROMA, GILDA         25 MAPLE DR    SUPERIOR, NE     68978432157258070850061072
SHERIDAN, RICHARD J.2 GENEVA RD    HASTINGS, NE     68901234891533120542061065
STURDAHL, DEBRA     2541 RICE ST   CRETE, NE        68333322150642061434071555
VELTRI, JOHN A.     54 SOUTH ST    AURORA, NE       68818026307625011547082082
```

Figure 11.45b MASTER-PERSONNEL-FILE after the program run

```
ABRUZZI, KENNETH L. 51 RAYMOND ST  HASTINGS, NE     68901743142265120552082072
AITKEN, THOMAS R.   260 FOUNTAIN STAURORA, NE       68818032567781080526082046
ALTERMAN, MAUREEN E.10 MARTIN AVE  YORK, NE         68467144217773052435061060
ARMSTRONG, GEORGE   105 STATE ST   PLATTE, NE       68653014766691032048081683
BAHR, LENA M.       304 CORY LANE  GENEVA, NE       68361381662514111041082060
BLAZUCK, JOSEPH A.  81 DORIS AVE   GENEVA, NE       68361179623741052145061075
BUXBAUM, JOAN M.    172 EARLE DR   GRAND ISLAND, NE 68802005589243021448060870
CARTER, AMEKIA L.   59 BARK ST     LOUP CITY, NE    68853623514793051332082062
COLETTI, SARAH T.   51 BROAD ST    HASTINGS, NE     68901042750015090238061564
COUGHLIN, AILEEN M. 133 DAVIS RD   LEXINGTON, NE    68850016493017031050070668
CUMMINGS, DOROTHEA  97 POWER AVE   NORMAN,NE        68963215137814040753082283
CYR, ROSARIO        205 SUNSET DR  FAIRFIELD, NE    68938771894263052435082055
DESROSIERS, RICHARD 92 REGAN RD    LOUP CITY, NE    68853314764532122158081583
DURANT, MARIE L.    1250 HIGH RD   GENEVA, NE       68361364923752092443091054
GAFFNEY, MARYLYN    76 MAIN ST     PLATTE, NE       68653039764715120552060877
KACHADOURIAN, NATALI922 LOCUST ST  HEBRON, NE       68370211384406022135082056
LAKE, SUE           252 EAST RD    CRETE, NE        68333253749144070741081583
MARKARIAN, MARIAN   984 N MAIN ST  HASTINGS, NE     68901130043962050732082052
MAYO, EVANGELINA    895 POTTERS AVEGENEVA, NE       68361032561579080562080783
MCGEE, BERNARD W.   2420 CARR LA   CENTRAL CITY, NE 68826013407206121530061549
MOONEY, RONALD      220 N MAIN ST  HASTINGS, NE     68901124670325092041081064
OVERDEEP, CYNTHIA   130 CANAL ST   YORK, NE         68467226153911052435071570
PACCASASSIE, DEBBIE 341 BRANCH AVE NORMAN, NE       68963149201475261228091257
PEARSON, ARTHUR     1020 GOLDEN RD HASTINGS, NE     68901033281512112550080283
PRIMEAU, ISABEL     78 NORTH ST    KEARNEY, NE      68847150246389093047082072
ROMA, GILDA         25 MAPLE DR    SUPERIOR, NE     68978432157258070850061072
SHERIDAN, RICHARD J.850 SUN CIRCLE AURORA, NE       68818234891533120542061065
STURDAHL, DEBRA     2541 RICE ST   CRETE, NE        68333322150642061434071555
VELTRI, JOHN A.     312 PERCH DR.  HASTINGS, NE     68901026307625011547082082
```

Figure 11.45c Sample DETAIL-FILE

```
BLAZUCK, JOSEPH A.  81 DORIS AVE   GENEVA, NE       68361
GAFFNEY, MARYLYN    76 MAIN ST     PLATTE, NE       68653
SHERIDAN, RICHARD J.850 SUN CIRCLE AURORA, NE       68818
VELTRI, JOHN A.     312 PERCH DR.  HASTINGS, NE     68901
```

Updating a Disk Sequential File

We have examined procedures that can be used to add records to a disk sequential file and to change record field values. In a full-scale disk master file update, procedures must be included to delete records from the file as well as to add records and to change field values in existing records. However, records cannot be directly deleted from a file with sequential organization. It is necessary to create a new master file and copy all the records of the old master file except those that must be deleted. As a result, a full-scale update of a master sequential file on disk is done following the logic used to update a master sequential file on tape (see the program in Figure 11.25). For that reason, the procedures are not repeated here.

Sequential Files in Brief

The essential features of sequential files that a programmer must know are listed below.

1. A file's organization is specified in the SELECT statement for the file. The clause ORGANIZATION IS SEQUENTIAL specifies a sequential file. If the ORGANIZATION clause is omitted, the file's organization is sequential by default.
2. The only valid access mode for a sequential file is sequential. The access mode is specified in the SELECT statement by the clause ACCESS MODE IS SEQUENTIAL. If the ACCESS MODE clause is omitted, access is sequential by default.
3. To **create** a sequential file,
   a. The organization must be sequential.
   b. The access mode must be sequential.
   c. The file must be opened either in OUTPUT mode or in EXTEND mode.
   d. The statement used to write records to the file is WRITE.
4. To **read** a sequential file,
   a. The file must be opened in INPUT mode or in I-O mode.
   b. The READ-AT END statement is used.
5. To **update** records in a sequential file on a mass storage device,
   a. The file must be opened in I-O mode.
   b. The record to be updated must be accessed by a READ statement.
   c. The new values are copied to fields of the record by MOVE statements.
   d. The updated record is rewritten to the file by the REWRITE statement.
6. To **add** records to a sequential file,
   a. The file must be opened in EXTEND mode.
   b. The new records are written to the file by WRITE statements.
7. If the open mode for a sequential file is
   a. INPUT, the only valid input statement that can reference the file is READ-AT END.
   b. OUTPUT, the only valid output statement that can reference the file is WRITE.
   c. I-O, the valid input-output statements that can reference the file are READ-AT END and REWRITE.
   d. EXTEND, the only valid output statement that can reference the file is WRITE.
8. A sequential file may be a storage file or a print file. Print files are created by the ADVANCING clause of the WRITE statement, by the Report Writer, and by the LINAGE clause of the file description entry.

Indexed Files

Indexed organization can be selected for a file if

1. Some intended uses of the file will require access to all the records of the file.
2. Some other uses of the file will require access to relatively few records.
3. Each record of the file has a key field whose value is unique to that record.
4. The computer hardware contains at least one direct-access storage device.

Examples of files that can be given indexed organization are the following:

1. A master employee file in which employee Social Security numbers are used to identify employee records.
2. A master inventory file in which item or part numbers are used to identify item records.
3. A master accounts receivable file in which customer numbers are used to identify customer records.

Figure 11.46 Index file with index records and data records

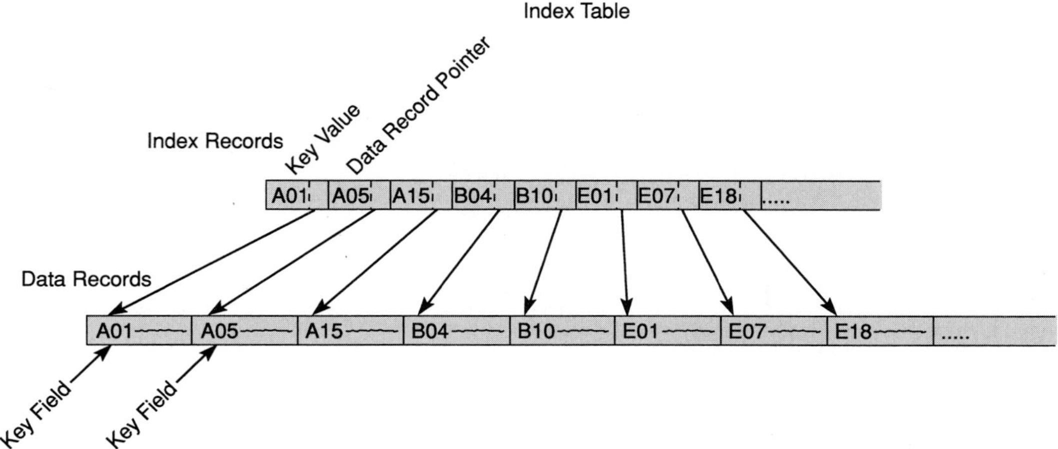

The key field of the record whose value is used to identify the record is called the file's *prime record key,* or simply its record key. When an indexed file is to be created, the records are first presorted in ascending order of the prime record key field values. As each record is written to the indexed file, an index record consisting of the record's record key field value and a pointer indicating where the record is stored in the file are stored in an index block at the beginning of the file. The index records are stored in ascending order of key values, that is, in the same order as the data records themselves, as shown in Figure 11.46.

The program that creates an indexed file typically contains entries similar to the ones that follow. In this example, the indexed file being created is MASTER-EMPLOYEE-FILE, and the prime record key is MR-SSN, a data field of the record MASTER-EMPLOYEE-RECORD. The following lines of code are sample program entries:

```
SELECT MASTER-EMPLOYEE-FILE ASSIGN TO . . .
                            ORGANIZATION IS INDEXED
                            ACCESS MODE IS SEQUENTIAL
                            RECORD KEY IS MR-SSN

.
.
.
FD MASTER-EMPLOYEE FILE . . .

01 MASTER-EMPLOYEE-RECORD.
   05 MR-SSN         PIC X(9).
   05 MR-NAME        PIC X(20).
   .
   .
   .
   OPEN OUTPUT MASTER-EMPLOYEE-FILE.
   .
   .
   .
   MOVE I-SSN TO MR-SSN.
   MOVE I-NAME TO MR-NAME.
   .
   .
   .
   WRITE MASTER-EMPLOYEE-RECORD
       INVALID KEY
           DISPLAY "RECORD KEY VALUE OUT OF SEQUENCE FOR "
                   I-SSN

   END-WRITE.
```

In the SELECT statement, the clauses ORGANIZATION IS INDEXED and RECORD KEY IS . . . are required. The clause ACCESS MODE IS SEQUENTIAL is optional, since access is sequential by default. However, its presence adds to the self-documentation of the program. The prime record key is MR-SSN, and it must be coded explicitly within the record description. The location of the record key within the record must not change during the life of the file.

Because the file is being written to, it must be opened in output mode. Note that the WRITE statement contains the INVALID KEY clause. Since the records must be written to the file in ascending order of

■ **Figure 11.47** WRITE-INVALID KEY statement format

```
WRITE record-name-1 [FROM identifier-1]
      [INVALID KEY imperative-statement-1]
      [NOT INVALID KEY imperative-statement-2]
      [END-WRITE]
```

■ **Figure 11.48** READ-INVALID KEY statement format

```
READ file-name-1 RECORD [INTO identifier-1]
      [KEY IS data-name-1]
      [INVALID KEY imperative-statement-3]
      [NOT INVALID KEY imperative-statement-4]
      [END-READ]
```

record key field values, an invalid key condition occurs whenever the key value for the record being written is not greater than the key value for the previous record written to the file. When an invalid key condition occurs, the record is not stored in the file.

If the WRITE statement executes successfully, the data record is stored in the file, and its index record is stored in the file's index block.

The format of the WRITE statement is shown in Figure 11.47.

Accessing Records of an Indexed File

The records of an indexed file can be accessed sequentially—that is, in ascending order of record key field values (the same order in which they were written to the file)—and they can be accessed randomly.

Accessing Records Sequentially

When the records of an indexed file must be retrieved sequentially, the file's SELECT statement must contain the clause ACCESS MODE IS SEQUENTIAL (either explicitly or by default), in addition to the clauses ORGANIZATION IS INDEXED and RECORD KEY IS. . . . The file must be open in input mode (INPUT or I-O), and the READ statement must contain the AT END clause.

Accessing Records Randomly

When selected records of an indexed file must be retrieved randomly, the file's SELECT statement must contain the clause ACCESS MODE IS RANDOM, in addition to the clauses ORGANIZATION IS INDEXED and RECORD KEY IS . . . . The file must be open in input mode (INPUT or I-O), and the READ statement must contain the INVALID KEY clause. The READ statement format is shown in Figure 11.48.

Before executing the READ statement, the program must assign the record key value of the record to be accessed to the file's record key. When the READ statement executes, the index records in the file's index block are searched serially for the matching key value, and the index record's pointer then allows direct access to the corresponding data record. For instance, look at the following statements:

```
MOVE I-SSN TO MR-SSN.
READ MASTER-EMPLOYEE-FILE RECORD
    INVALID KEY
        DISPLAY "NO RECORD IN MASTER EMPLOYEE FILE WITH SSN= "
                MR-SSN
END-READ.
```

If I-SSN = 345231412, the master record for the employee whose Social Security number is 345231412 is accessed directly. If no employee has this Social Security number, an invalid key condition occurs.

Figure 11.49 DELETE statement format

```
DELETE file-name-1 RECORD
    [INVALID KEY imperative-statement-1]
    [NOT INVALID KEY imperative-statement-2]
    [END-DELETE]
```

Maintaining an Indexed File

An indexed file can be updated either sequentially or randomly.

1. In a sequential update,
   a. Specify the access mode as SEQUENTIAL.
   b. Open the file in I-O mode.
   c. Access the target record using READ-AT END.
   d. If field values are to be changed, do so, and then rewrite the record using the REWRITE statement.
   e. If the record is to be deleted, verify that it is the correct one, and then use the DELETE statement to effectively delete it from the file. The DELETE statement format is shown in Figure 11.49. The INVALID KEY clause is not coded when the access mode is sequential.
2. In a random update,
   a. Specify the access mode as RANDOM.
   b. Open the file in I-O mode.
   c. Assign to the prime record key the key value of the target record:
      i. If field values are to be changed, access the record with the READ-INVALID KEY statement. Update the field values, and use the REWRITE-INVALID KEY statement to rewrite the record to the file.
      ii. If the record is to be deleted, use the DELETE-INVALID KEY statement to logically delete it from the file.
      iii. If a new record is to be added to the file, use the WRITE-INVALID KEY statement to write it to the file.

More to Come on Indexed Files

The material presented here on indexed files serves merely as an introduction. A complete development of indexed files is contained in this author's textbook *Advanced Structured COBOL*. You may wish to refer to it for a variety of sample programs illustrating the creation and maintenance of indexed files, the production of audit reports in relation to file maintenance, and various uses of indexed files. Sample programs also illustrate the use of alternate record keys as well as the use of the dynamic access mode.

Relative Files

Relative organization also provides for sequential access and random access to a relative file's records. Theoretically, it can make more efficient use of the disk space allotted to the file than is the case for indexed organization, since none of the storage capacity is reserved for index records. That is, the storage area can be used exclusively to store data records, since index records do not exist in a relative file. The location of a record is determined within the PROCEDURE DIVISION, and the relative record is then accessed directly.

In considering the possibility of using relative organization for a new file, the following factors are usually examined:

1. Are there file maintenance activities expected at times to have to access all the records of the file and, at other times, to have to access relatively few records? Relative organization supports both modes of access.
2. Are the records of this new file fixed-length records? If not, is the maximum record size known? All record areas in a relative file must be the same length. If the records are fixed-length, that length determines the size of the record areas. Otherwise, the maximum record length is used to create record areas of the same size.

3. How many records will be stored in the file? Will the number of records remain the same for the life of the file, or is it expected to grow? If the latter, can a reasonable estimate be made as to the growth during the life of the file? Is the capacity of the disk pack sufficient to meet the needs of the file? The size of a relative file cannot be changed once it has been created.
4. Does each record contain a key field whose value can be used, directly or indirectly, to specify the record's location in the file? Each record must be assigned a relative number that specifies its location in the file relative to the beginning of the file. For instance, if a record's relative number is 5, it will occupy the fifth record area from the beginning of the file.

If these considerations do not reveal insurmountable problems and a strong case can be made to give the file relative organization, the decision can be made to proceed.

Creating a Relative File

The first step in creating a file with relative organization is to format the file. Formatting a file means to separate the file's storage area into the required number of record areas. This can be done by simply writing blank fixed-length records to the file, or by writing "dummy" records whose key fields contain a dummy value (such as all zeros in a Social Security number field). When the file has been formatted, each record area then has an ordinal number that denotes its location when counting from the beginning of the file. The result is illustrated in Figure 11.50.

When an actual record is stored in a record area, the area's ordinal number is the record's relative number.

A relative file can be formatted sequentially or randomly. Suppose that MASTER-CUSTOMER-FILE has to be formatted sequentially by writing dummy records to it. A simple program to do the formatting contains the following typical entries:

```
SELECT MASTER-CUSTOMER-FILE   ASSIGN TO . . .
                              ORGANIZATION IS RELATIVE
                              ACCESS MODE IS SEQUENTIAL
                              RELATIVE KEY IS WS-LOCATION-NO.

.
.
.
FD   MASTER-CUSTOMER-FILE . . .

01   MASTER-CUSTOMER-RECORD.
     05 MR-CUSTOMER-NO    PIC 9(4).
     05                   PIC X (96).
.
.
.
WORKING-STORAGE SECTION.
.
.
.
01   WS-LOCATION-NO       PIC 9(4).
.
.
.
     OPEN OUTPUT MASTER-CUSTOMER-FILE.
     .
     .
     .
     MOVE SPACES TO MR-CUSTOMER-RECORD.
     MOVE ZEROS TO MR-CUSTOMER-NO.
     WRITE MASTER-CUSTOMER-RECORD
         INVALID KEY
             DISPLAY "ERROR WRITING TO RECORD AREA " WS-LOCATION-NO
     END-WRITE.
```

The SELECT statement must contain the clause ORGANIZATION IS RELATIVE. Since formatting is sequential, the clauses ACCESS MODE IS SEQUENTIAL and RELATIVE KEY IS . . . are

Figure 11.50 A formatted relative file

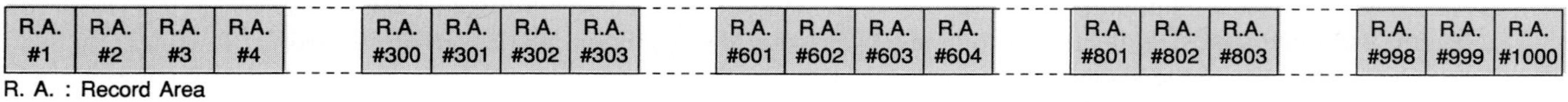

R.A. #1	R.A. #2	R.A. #3	R.A. #4		R.A. #300	R.A. #301	R.A. #302	R.A. #303		R.A. #601	R.A. #602	R.A. #603	R.A. #604		R.A. #801	R.A. #802	R.A. #803		R.A. #998	R.A. #999	R.A. #1000

R. A. : Record Area

coded for documentation only. If formatting had been on a random basis, the clause ACCESS MODE IS RANDOM and the RELATIVE KEY clause would have been required. The data item in the RELATIVE KEY clause (WS-LOCATION-NO in this case) is defined in working storage. It is not a data field of the record. During the formatting process, it receives the record's relative number when the WRITE statement is executed.

Since the file is being written to, it must be open in output mode. The master record is assigned spaces, and the record's key field (in this case MR-CUSTOMER-NO) is assigned zeros to create a dummy master record. It is then written to the file as many times as necessary to fill the file's storage space by means of the WRITE-INVALID KEY statement. (An invalid key condition occurs if an attempt is made to write a record beyond the externally defined boundaries for the file.)

Loading a Relative File

After the file has been formatted, the actual records can be loaded into it. They can be loaded sequentially or randomly. In either case, since the relative file already contains records, albeit "dummy" records, it must be open in I-O mode.

In sequential mode, the file's dummy records are read from the beginning of the file until the dummy record's relative number matches the relative number of the actual record that must be written in that area. (During sequential READ operations, the relative record's relative number is stored in the relative key data item.) The actual record's data items are then moved to the data fields of the dummy record, and the newly constructed relative record is rewritten to the file.

In random mode, the actual record's relative number is first determined and assigned to the relative key data item. The execution of a random READ statement accesses the corresponding relative record (a dummy record). The actual record's data items are moved to the dummy relative record, and the newly constructed record is rewritten to the file.

As an example, suppose that the customer numbers for the actual records that must be stored in the MASTER-CUSTOMER-FILE formatted on page 762 can be used directly to specify the record areas in which the customer records must be stored.

If the records are to be loaded sequentially, the loading program would contain entries similar to the following:

```
SELECT MASTER-CUSTOMER-FILE  ASSIGN TO. . .
                             ORGANIZATION IS RELATIVE
                             ACCESS MODE IS SEQUENTIAL
                             RELATIVE KEY IS WS-LOCATION-NO.
SELECT DETAIL-CUSTOMER-FILE  ASSIGN TO. . .
.
.
.
FD   MASTER-CUSTOMER-FILE. . .

01   MASTER-CUSTOMER-RECORD.
     05 MR-CUSTOMER-NO      PIC 9(4).
     05 MR-CUSTOMER-NAME    PIC X(20).
.
.
.
FD   DETAIL-CUSTOMER-FILE. . .

01   DETAIL-CUSTOMER-RECORD.
     05 DETAIL-CUSTOMER-NO   PIC 9(4).
     05 DETAIL-CUSTOMER-NAME PIC X(20).
.
.
.
WORKING-STORAGE SECTION.

01   PROGRAM-CONTROLS.
     05 WS-MORE-DETAIL-RECORDS     PIC X(3).
        88 NO-MORE-DETAIL-RECORDS            VALUE "NO ".
     05 WS-MORE-MASTER-RECORDS     PIC X(3).
        88 END-OF-MASTER-FILE                VALUE "NO ".
     05 WS-LOCATION-NO             PIC 9(4).

.
.
.
100-LOAD-MASTER-FILE.
     PERFORM 200-START-UP.
```

```
     PERFORM 210-PROCESS-DETAIL-RECORD
         UNTIL NO-MORE-DETAIL-RECORDS OR END-OF-MASTER-FILE.

 .
 .
 .
 200-START-UP.
     OPEN I-O MASTER-CUSTOMER-FILE
          INPUT DETAIL-CUSTOMER-FILE.
     PERFORM 300-READ-DETAIL-RECORD.

 .
 .
 .
 210-PROCESS-DETAIL-RECORD.
     PERFORM 310-READ-MASTER-RECORD
         UNTIL WS-LOCATION-NO = DETAIL-CUSTOMER-NO.
     PERFORM 320-LOAD-NEW-RECORD.
     PERFORM 300-READ-DETAIL-RECORD.

 .
 .
 .
 300-READ-DETAIL-RECORD.
     READ DETAIL-CUSTOMER-FILE RECORD
         AT END
              SET NO-MORE-DETAIL-RECORDS TO TRUE.
 310-READ-MASTER-RECORD.
     READ MASTER-CUSTOMER-FILE RECORD
         AT END
              SET END-OF-MASTER-FILE TO TRUE.
 320-LOAD-NEW-RECORD.
     MOVE DETAIL-CUSTOMER-NO TO MR-CUSTOMER-NO.
     MOVE DETAIL-CUSTOMER-NAME TO MR-CUSTOMER-NAME.
     .
     .
     .
     REWRITE MASTER-CUSTOMER-RECORD
         INVALID KEY
              DISPLAY "CANNOT REWRITE MASTER RECORD FOR CUSTOMER NO. "
                      DETAIL-CUSTOMER-NO
     END-REWRITE.
```

The sequential READ statement in paragraph 310 accesses records in ascending order by relative key values, namely 1, 2, 3, and so on. The relative key value is stored in WS-LOCATION-NO, the data item named in the RELATIVE KEY clause. When the condition WS-LOCATION-NO = DETAIL-CUSTOMER-NO is true, the target dummy record has been found. It is assigned the values of the detail record and is then rewritten to the master file.

If the records are to be loaded randomly, the loading program would contain entries similar to the following:

```
 SELECT MASTER-CUSTOMER-FILE  ASSIGN TO. . .
                              ORGANIZATION IS RELATIVE
                              ACCESS MODE IS RANDOM
                              RELATIVE KEY IS WS-LOCATION-NO.
 SELECT DETAIL-CUSTOMER-FILE  ASSIGN TO. . .
 .
 .
 .
 FD  MASTER-CUSTOMER-FILE. . .

 01  MASTER-CUSTOMER-RECORD.
     05 MR-CUSTOMER-NO      PIC 9(4).
     05 MR-CUSTOMER-NAME    PIC X(20).
     .
     .
     .
 FD  DETAIL-CUSTOMER-FILE. . .

 01  DETAIL-CUSTOMER-RECORD.
     05 DETAIL-CUSTOMER-NO   PIC 9(4).
     05 DETAIL-CUSTOMER-NAME PIC X(20).

 .
 .
 .
 WORKING-STORAGE SECTION.

 01  PROGRAM-CONTROLS.
     05 WS-MORE-DETAIL-RECORDS     PIC X(3).
        88 NO-MORE-DETAIL-RECORDS            VALUE "NO ".
```

```
    05 WS-MORE-MASTER-RECORDS     PIC X(3).
       88 END-OF-MASTER-FILE               VALUE "NO ".
    05 WS-LOCATION-NO             PIC 9(4).

.
.
.
100-LOAD-MASTER-FILE.
    PERFORM 200-START-UP.
    PERFORM 210-PROCESS-DETAIL-RECORD
        UNTIL NO-MORE-DETAIL-RECORDS.

.
.
.
200-START-UP.
    OPEN I-O MASTER-CUSTOMER-FILE
         INPUT DETAIL-CUSTOMER-FILE.
    PERFORM 300-READ-DETAIL-RECORD.

.
.
.
210-PROCESS-DETAIL-RECORD.
    MOVE DETAIL-CUSTOMER-NO TO WS-LOCATION-NO.
    PERFORM 310-READ-MASTER-RECORD.
    PERFORM 320-LOAD-NEW-RECORD.
    PERFORM 300-READ-DETAIL-RECORD.

.
.
.
300-READ-DETAIL-RECORD.
    READ DETAIL-CUSTOMER-FILE RECORD
        AT END
            SET NO-MORE-DETAIL-RECORDS TO TRUE.
310-READ-MASTER-RECORD.
    READ MASTER-CUSTOMER-FILE RECORD
        INVALID KEY
            DISPLAY "NO RECORD IN MASTER FILE WITH RELATIVE NO = "
                    WS-LOCATION-NO
    END-READ.
320-LOAD-NEW-RECORD.
    MOVE DETAIL-CUSTOMER-NO TO MR-CUSTOMER-NO.
    MOVE DETAIL-CUSTOMER-NAME TO MR-CUSTOMER-NAME.
    .
    .
    .
    REWRITE MASTER-CUSTOMER-RECORD
        INVALID KEY
            DISPLAY "CANNOT REWRITE MASTER RECORD FOR CUSTOMER NO. "
                    DETAIL-CUSTOMER-NO
    END-REWRITE.
```

Note that the access mode for the file is specified as RANDOM. The MOVE statement in paragraph 210 identifies the dummy record to be read by assigning DETAIL-CUSTOMER-NO to the relative key WS-LOCATION-NO. When the random READ statement in paragraph 310 is executed, it reads the dummy record whose relative number is the value in WS-LOCATION-NO. This dummy record is assigned the values of the detail record, and then it is rewritten to the master file.

Randomization Procedure

More often than not, records to be stored in a relative file do not contain a data field whose value can be used directly to specify the location of the record in the file. Usually, when a key field of the relative record has been selected to be the one whose value will be used to generate a relative number, the value must be transformed by some *randomization procedure* into the record's relative number. There are many such procedures. A popular one is the *division algorithm method.* In this method, the numeric value in the record's key field is divided by the number of record areas in the file, that is, the file size, or it is divided by the largest prime number that does not exceed the file size. The remainder, in the range from 0 to (file-size minus 1), or in the range from 0 to (largest prime number minus 1), is increased by 1 to yield the record's relative number.

For instance, if a record's key field value is 743142265 and the file size is 250, the division algorithm yields the following:

743142265 / 250 = 2972569, remainder 15

By adding 1 to the remainder, the record's relative number is 16.

Since it is possible for more than one record to initially receive the same relative number by applying a randomization procedure, the program must include other steps to prevent such record "collisions." An examination of these steps is beyond the scope of this chapter.

Updating a Relative File

A relative file can be updated sequentially or randomly.

1. In a sequential update,
   a. The access mode is specified as SEQUENTIAL.
   b. The file is open in I-O mode.
   c. The target record is accessed by using the READ-AT END statement (or by using the START statement before a READ-AT END statement).
   d. If field values are to be changed, new values are copied to the relative record and then the record is rewritten to the file using the REWRITE statement.
   e. If the record is to be deleted, it is first verified as the correct one, and then the DELETE statement is used to delete it from the file.
2. In a random update,
   a. The access mode is specified as RANDOM.
   b. The file is open in I-O mode.
   c. The relative key data item is assigned the relative key value of the record to be accessed.
      i. If field values are to be changed, the target record is accessed by using the READ-INVALID KEY statement. The field values are updated, and the REWRITE-INVALID KEY statement is used to rewrite the record to the file.
      ii. If the record is to be deleted, the DELETE-INVALID KEY statement is used to logically delete it from the file.

More to Come on Relative Files

A complete development of relative files is contained in this author's textbook *Advanced Structured COBOL*. Sample programs are included. A number of randomization techniques are examined in detail. Complete lists of rules accompany the input/output statement formats that apply to relative files.

Important Terms in Chapter 11

ACCESS MODE IS RANDOM
ACCESS MODE IS SEQUENTIAL
audit report
bits per inch (BPI)
block
BLOCK CONTAINS
bytes-per-inch
creating an indexed file
creating a relative file
cylinders
DELETE
detail file
direct-access file
direct-access storage device (DASD)
disk drive
disk pack
disk surface
division algorithm method
dummy record
EXTEND
external tape label
file backup
file record pointer
format a relative file
HIGH-VALUES
I-O
indexed file
indexed organization
index record
interblock gap (IBG)
internal tape label
interrecord gap (IRG)
loading a relative file
logical record
master file
megabyte
ORGANIZATION IS INDEXED
ORGANIZATION IS RELATIVE
ORGANIZATION IS SEQUENTIAL
physical record
prime record key
print file
random access
randomization procedure
READ-INVALID KEY
RECORD KEY IS
relative file
relative key data item
RELATIVE KEY IS
relative organization
REWRITE
sequential access
sequential file
sequential organization
sequential update
storage file
tape file
tracks
updating an indexed file
updating a relative file
WRITE-INVALID KEY

Exercises

1. What is a file with sequential organization?
2. What is the meaning of sequential access?
3. Suppose that the length of a magnetic tape is 2400 feet, its density is 3200 BPI, and the tape drive leaves a 3/4-inch IBG. How many 100-character records can be written to the tape
   a. If there is no blocking factor?
   b. If the blocking factor is 5?
   c. If the blocking factor is 10?
4. What is the main reason for using a blocking factor?
5. What does a blocking factor of 10 mean? Explain in terms of logical and physical records.
6. Explain the effect of a blocking factor on input/output operations.
7. Suppose that a master file contains the records shown in Figure 11.51a and it must be updated with the records of the detail file in Figure 11.51b. In both files, the records are in alphabetic order by employee name.

   The first character in a detail record is the process code. A code of 1 means a record to be added to the master file; a code of 2 means a record to be deleted from the master file; a code of 3 means that a current master record must have its address field value changed.

   The records in the updated master file must remain in alphabetic order by employee name.

   The system flowchart is shown in Figure 11.51c. When the EOF marker is reached in either input file, HIGH-VALUES is moved to the name field of the corresponding record.

   Answer the following questions in sequence:

   a. Read the first record of each file into its own buffer. (Write the employee names on the spaces provided.)
   Master record: ______________________________
   Detail record: ______________________________

   b. Since records in the updated master file must remain in alphabetic order, check the name on each record in part a.
   i. Are they the same?
   ii. If not, which one comes first alphabetically?
   iii. What must be done with it?

   c. Read the next master file record.
   Master record: ______________________________
   i. What is the current detail record?
   Detail record: ______________________________
   ii. Check the names on the two records. Are they the same?
   iii. If not, which one comes first alphabetically?
   iv. What must be done with it?
   When done, go to part d.

   d. Read the next master file record.
   Master record: ______________________________
   i. What is the current detail record?
   Detail record: ______________________________
   ii. Check the names on the two records. Are they the same?
   iii. If so, check the process code on the detail record. What is it?
   iv. What process must be carried out?
   v. How is the process indicated by the code carried out?
   At this point, the detail record in the buffer has served its purpose. Go on to part e.

   e. Read the next master record and the next detail record.
   Master record: ______________________________
   Detail record: ______________________________
   i. Check the names on the two records. Are they the same?

Figure 11.51a Old master file

```
GAFFNEY, MARYLYN    274 HANOVER ST ARAPAHOE, NE     6892203976471512055206087 7
KACHADOURIAN, NATALI922 LOCUST ST  HEBRON, NE       68370211384406022135082056
KRUGER, ALLEN       320 EAST RD    PLATTE, NE       68653502422713102537061057
MCGEE, BERNARD W.   2420 CARR LA   CENTRAL CITY, NE 68826013407206121530061549
MOONEY, RONALD      174 PLAIN ST   MINDEN, NE       68959124670325092041081064
OVERDEEP, CYNTHIA   130 CANAL ST   YORK, NE         68467226153911052435071570
PACCASASSIE, DEBBIE 341 BRANCH AVE NORMAN, NE       68963149201475261228091257
ROMA, GILDA         25 MAPLE DR    SUPERIOR, NE     68978432157258070850061072
```

■ **Figure 11.51b** Detail file

```
2KRUGER, ALLEN
1MARKARIAN, MARIAN    984 N MAIN ST   HASTINGS, NE      68901130043962050732082052
3MOONEY, RONALD       220 N MAIN ST   HASTINGS, NE      68901
1PRIMEAU, ISABEL      78 NORTH ST     KEARNEY, NE       68847150246389093047082072
```

■ **Figure 11.51c** System flowchart

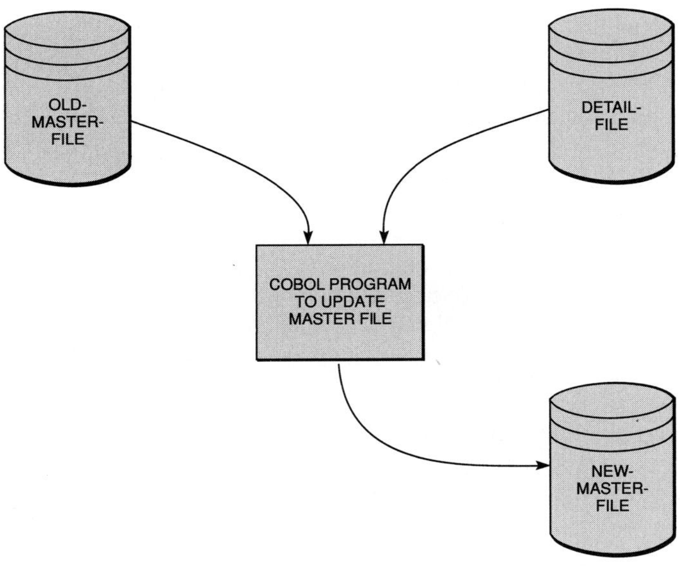

- **ii.** If not, which one comes first alphabetically?
- **iii.** What must be done with it?

When done, go to part f.

f. Read the next detail file record.
Detail record: ______________________________

- **i.** What is the current master record?
  Master record: ______________________________
- **ii.** Check the names on the two records. Are they the same?
- **iii.** If not, which one comes first alphabetically?
- **iv.** What must be done with it?

When done, go to part g.

g. Read the next master file record.
Master record: ______________________________

- **i.** What is the current detail record?
  Detail record: ______________________________
- **ii.** Check the names on the two records. Are they the same?
- **iii.** If so, check the process code on the detail record. What is it?
- **iv.** What process must be carried out?
- **v.** How is the process indicated by the code carried out?

When done, the detail record in the buffer has served its purpose. Go on to part h.

h. Read the next master record and the next detail record.
Master record: ______________________________
Detail record: ______________________________

- **i.** Check the names on the two records. Are they the same?
- **ii.** If not, which one comes first alphabetically?
- **iii.** What must be done with it?

When done, go to part i.

i. Read the next master file record.
Master record: ______________________________

- **i.** What is the current detail record?
  Detail record: ______________________________
- **ii.** Check the names on the two records. Are they the same?
- **iii.** If not, which one comes first alphabetically?

iv. What must be done with it?
When done, go to part j.

j. Read the next master file record.
Master record: ______________________________

i. What is the current detail record?
Detail record: ______________________________

ii. Check the names on the two records. Are they the same?

iii. If not, which one comes first alphabetically?

iv. What must be done with it?
When done, go on to part k.

k. Read the next detail file record.
Detail record: ______________________________
Recall that when the EOF record is reached (for either file), HIGH-VALUES is moved to the record area's name field.

i. What is the current master record?
Master record: ______________________________

ii. Check the name fields of the two records. Do they have the same value?

iii. If not, which one comes first alphabetically?

iv. What must be done with it?
When done, go on to part l.

l. Read the next master file record.
Master record: ______________________________

i. What is the current detail record?
Detail record: ______________________________

ii. What do the contents of the two buffers indicate?

8. Given the following record descriptions in a program designed to update a master personnel file,

```
01  OLD-MR-RECORD.
    05 OLD-MR-NAME        PIC X(20).
       88 NO-MORE-OLD-RECORDS
                          VALUE HIGH-VALUES.
    05 OLD-MR-ADDRESS     PIC X(37).
    05 OLD-MR-SSN         PIC X(9).
    05 OLD-MR-DATES       PIC X(12).
    05                    PIC X(22).

01  NEW-MR-RECORD.
    05 NEW-MR-NAME        PIC X(20).
    05 NEW-MR-ADDRESS     PIC X(37).
    05 NEW-MR-SSN         PIC X(9).
    05 NEW-MR-DATES       PIC X(12).
    05                    PIC X(22).

01  DETAIL-RECORD.
    05 PROCESS-CODE       PIC 9.
       88 NEW-RECORD          VALUE 1.
       88 DELETE-RECORD       VALUE 2.
       88 CHANGE-RECORD       VALUE 3.
    05 DETAIL-NAME        PIC X(20).
       88 NO-MORE-DETAIL-RECORDS
                          VALUE HIGH-VALUES.
    05 DETAIL-ADDRESS     PIC X(37).
    05 DETAIL-SSN         PIC X(9).
    05 DETAILS-DATES      PIC X(12).
    05                    PIC X(22).
```

a. Code the statements needed if the process code on a detail record is 1.
b. Code the statements needed if the process code on a detail record is 2.
c. Code the statements needed if the process code on a detail record is 3.

9. a. If the blocking factor for OLD-MASTER-FILE, shown in the system flowchart of Figure 11.51c, is 5, and the update procedure of exercise 7 is executed, what is the maximum number of I/O accesses to the disk that contains the file?

b. If the blocking factor for NEW-MASTER-FILE, shown in the system flowchart Figure 11.51c, is 5, and the update procedure of exercise 7 is executed, what is the maximum number of I/O accesses to the disk that contains the file?

c. If no blocking factor is specified for DETAIL-FILE, shown in the system flowchart of Figure 11.51c, what is the maximum number of I/O accesses to the disk that contains the file?

10. What is a file with indexed organization?

11. What main advantage does an indexed file provide over a sequential file?

12. What is the RECORD KEY clause used for?

13. What is a file with relative organization?
14. What access modes can be used to access records of a relative file?
15. What is the RELATIVE KEY clause used for?
16. What is meant by the relative number of a record in a relative file?

Debugging Activities

1. A student was given the task of planning a program that is supposed to update the master personnel file for the Monster Burger Company. This file has sequential organization and is stored on disk.
   During the compilation phase, the compiler produced the listing that follows. Your task is to correct all the syntax errors that have been flagged.
2. When the syntax errors in the listing that begins below are corrected, the program produces the audit report shown in Figure 11.52c and the updated master file shown in Figure 11.52d. The old master personnel file is shown in Figure 11.52a (Debugging Activity Data File, Set 18 [DD/CD:VICIIDB2.DT1]), and the detail file is shown in Figure 11.52b (Debugging Activity Data File, Set 19 [DD/CD:VICIIDB2.DT2]). However, the new master file should be the one shown in Figure 11.53a, and the audit report should be the one shown in Figure 11.53b. Find and correct the remaining logic errors in the program.

```
                                             18-Nov-1993 16:06:14     VAX COBOL V5.1-10                   Page   1
Source Listing                               18-Nov-1993 13:06:01     FACULTY$DISK:[PAQUETTEG.WCBTXT]C11DB1.CB1;1


           IDENTIFICATION DIVISION.

           PROGRAMID.      MONSTER-BURGER-DBG1.
           1
%COBOL-F-ERROR  222, (1) "PROGRAM-ID" required at this point

          ******************************************************************
          *                                                                *
          *   AUTHOR.           PAQUETTE.                                  *
          *   DATE WRITTEN.     OCTOBER 1993.                              *
          *                                                                *
          *   THIS PROGRAM UPDATES THE MASTER PAYROLL FILE FOR THE MONSTER *
          *   BURGER COMPANY, USING RECORDS FROM A DETAIL FILE.            *
          *   THE UPDATE INCLUDES:  ADDING A RECORD, DELETING A RECORD,    *
          *   AND UPDATING FIELD VALUES ON A RECORD.                       *
          *   THE PROGRAM ALSO PRODUCES AN  AUDIT TRAIL REPORT.  THE       *
          *   REPORT SPECIFIES THE ACTION TAKEN FOR EACH RECORD PROCESSED. *
          *                                                                *
          ******************************************************************


           ENVIRONMENT DIVISION.
           1
%COBOL-W-ERROR  297, (1) Processing of source program resumes at this point
%COBOL-E-ERROR   65, (1) Missing period is assumed
%COBOL-F-ERROR  226, (1) Missing required word

           CONFIGURATION SECTION.

           SOURCE-COMPUTER.  VAX-VMS-8650.
           OBJECT-COMPUTER.  VAX-VMS-8650.

           INPUT-OUTPUT SECTION.

           FILE-CONTROL.
               SELECT DETAIL-FILE          ASSIGN TO COB$INPUT.
                      1
%COBOL-F-ERROR   52, (1) File has no definition in File Section - definition assumed
               SELECT OLD-MASTER-FILE      ASSIGN TO OLDMASTER
                      1
%COBOL-W-ERROR   16, (1) RECORD CONTAINS value is greater than length of longest record
                                           ORGANIZATION IS SEQUENTAL
                                                           1
%COBOL-F-ERROR  111, (1) Invalid organization
                                           ACCESS MODE IS SEQUENTIAL.
               SELECT NEW-MASTER-FILE      ASSIGN TO NEWMASTER
                      1
%COBOL-W-ERROR   16, (1) RECORD CONTAINS value is greater than length of longest record
                                           ORGANIZATION IS SEQUENTIAL
                                           ACCESS NODE IS SEQUENTIAL.
                                                  1       2
%COBOL-F-ERROR  112, (1) Invalid access mode
%COBOL-W-ERROR  297, (2) Processing of source program resumes at this point
%COBOL-E-ERROR   47, (2) Duplicate clause - this clause supersedes previous
               SELECT AUDIT-REPORT         ASSIGN TO COB$OUTPUT.
                      1
%COBOL-E-ERROR   17, (1) Longest record is longer than RECORD CONTAINS value - Longest record size used

           DATA DIVISION.

           FILE SECTION.

           FD  DETAL-FILE
               1
```

```
                                        18-Nov-1993 16:06:14    VAX COBOL V5.1-10                   Page   2
Source Listing                          18-Nov-1993 13:06:01    FACULTY$DISK:[PAQUETTEG.WCBTXT]C11DB1.CB1;1

%COBOL-E-ERROR   51, (1) File has no definition in FILE-CONTROL paragraph - definition assumed
                RECORD CONTAINS 39 CHARACTERS.

            01  DETAIL-RECORD.
                05 PROCESS-CODE      PIC X.
                   88 NEW-RECORD              VALUE 1.
                      1
%COBOL-E-ERROR   83, (1) Condition VALUE conflicts with description of conditional variable
                   88 DELETE-RECORD           VALUE 2.
                      1
%COBOL-E-ERROR   83, (1) Condition VALUE conflicts with description of conditional variable
                   88 UPDATE-RECORD           VALUE 3.
                      1
%COBOL-E-ERROR   83, (1) Condition VALUE conflicts with description of conditional variable
                05 DETAIL-SSN        PIC 9(9).
                    88 NO-MORE-DETAIL-RECORDS VALUE HIGH-VALUES.
                      1
%COBOL-E-ERROR   83, (1) Condition VALUE conflicts with description of conditional variable
                05 DETAIL-NAME       PIC X(20).
                05 DETAIL-STORE-NO   PIC X(2).
                05 DETAIL-PAY-CODE   PIC 9(2).
                05 DETAIL-INS-CODE   PIC X(2).
                05 DETAIL-EXEMPT     PIC 9(1).
                05 DETAIL-CLASS-CODE PIC X(2).

            FD  OLD-MASTER-FILE
                RECORD CONTAINS 100 CHARACTERS
                BLOCK CONTAINS 10 RECORDS.

            01  OLD-MR-RECORD.
                05 OLD-MR-RECORD-CODE PIC X(2).
                05 OLD-MR-SSN         PIC X(9).
                   88 NO-MORE-OLD-RECORDS     VALUE HIGH-VALUES.
                05 OLD-MR-NAME        PIC X(20).
                05 OLD-MR-STORE-NO    PIC X(2).
                05 OLD-MR-PAY-CODE    PIC 9(2).
                05 OLD-MR-INS-CODE    PIC X(2).
                05 OLD-MR-EXEMPT      PIC 9(1).
                05 OLD-MR-CLASS-CODE  PIC X(2).

            FD  NEW-MASTER-FILE
                RECORD CONTAINS 100 CHARACTERS
                BLOCK CONTAINS 10 RECORDS.

            01  NEW-MR-RECORD.
                05 NEW-MR-RECRD-CODE  PIC X(2).
                05 NEW-MR-SSN         PIC X(9).
                05 NEW-MR-NAME        PIC X(20).
                05 NEW-MR-STORE-NO    PIC X(2).
                05 NEW-MR-PAY-CODE    PIC 9(2).
                05 NEW-MR-INS-CODE    PIC X(2).
                05 NEW-MR-EXEMPT      PIC 9(1).
                05 NEW-MR-CLASS-CODE  PIC X(2).

            FD  AUDIT-REPORT
                RECORD CONTAINS 80 CHARACTERS.

            01  PRINTLINE             PIC X(132).

            WORKING-STORAGE SECTION.

            01  PROGRAM-CONTROLS.
                05 WS-DATE             PIC 9(6).
                05 WS-PROPER-SAPCING   PIC 9.

            01  WORK-AREAS.
                05 WS-ACTION-CODE      PIC X.
                05 WS-OLD-MR-RECORD    PIC X(100).

            01  PROGRAM-COUNTERS.
                05 WS-OLD-RECORD-COPIED-CTR  PIC 999.
                05 WS-OLD-RECORD-DELETED-CTR PIC 999.
                05 WS-NEW-RECORD-CTR         PIC 999.
                05 WS-OLD-RECORD-CHANGED-CTR PIC 999.
                05 WS-NEW-MASTER-FILE-CTR    PIC 999.
                05 WS-AUDIT-LINE-CTR         PIC 999.

            01  REPORT-HEADERS.
                05 COMPANY-NAME.
                   10 PIC X(49)   VALUE SPACES.
                   10 PIC X(20)   VALUE "MONSTER BURGER COMPANY".
                       1
%COBOL-E-ERROR   84, (1) Literal in VALUE clause conflicts with description - clause ignored
                   10 PIC X(29)   VALUE SPACES.

                05 REPORT-NAME-1.
                   10 PIC X(22)   VALUE SPACES.
                   10 PIC X(29)   VALUE "MASTER PAYROLL FILE UPDATE   ".
                   10 O-DATE      PIC XX/XX/XX.
                   10 PIC X(21)   VALUE SPACES.

                05 REPORT-NAME-2.
                   10 PIC X(13)   VALUE SPACES.
                   10 PIC X(20)   VALUE "AUDIT TRAIL REPORT".
                   10 PIC X(31)   VALUE SPACES.

```

```
                                                  18-Nov-1993 16:06:14    VAX COBOL V5.1-10                Page   3
Source Listing                                    18-Nov-1993 13:06:01    FACULTY$DISK:[PAQUETTEG.WCBTXT]C11DB1.CB1;1
               05 HEADINGS-1.
                  10 PIC X(14)   VALUE SPACES.
                  10 PIC X(14)   VALUE "PAYROLL RECORD ".
                     1
%COBOL-E-ERROR   84, (1) Literal in VALUE clause conflicts with description - clause ignored
                  10 PIC X(30)   VALUE SPACES.
                  10 PIC X(12)   VALUE "ACTION TAKEN".
                  10 PIC X(10)   VALUE SPACES.

               05 HEADINGS-2.
                  10 PIC X(48)   VALUE SPACES.
                  10 PIC X(7)    VALUE "ADDED  ".
                  10 PIC X(9)    VALUE "DELETED  ".
                  10 PIC X(9)    VALUE "UPDATED  ".
                  10 PIC X(7)    VALUE "COPIED ".

           01  AUDIT-LINE.
               05 O-RECORD          PIC X(48).
               05                   PIC X(2).
               05 O-ACTION-FLD-1    PIC 9.
               05                   PIC X(7).
               05 O-ACTION-FLD-2    PIC 9.
               05                   PIC X(8).
               05 O-ACTION-FLD-3    PIC 9.
               05                   PIC X(7).
               05 O-ACTION-FLD-4    PIC 9.
               05                   PIC X(4).

           01  REPORT-ENDERS.
               05 SUMMARY-HEADER.
                  10 PIC X(24)  VALUE SPACES.
                  10 PIC X(7)   VALUE "SUMMARY".

               05 SUMMARY-LINE-1.
                  10                           PIC X(5)  VALUE SPACES.
                  10 O-OLD-RECORD-COPIED-CTR   PIC ZZ9.
                  10                           PIC X(46) VALUE
                     "  OLD MASTER RECORDS COPIED TO NEW MASTER FILE".

               05 SUMMARY-LINE-2.
                  10                           PIC X(5)  VALUE SPACES.
                  10 O-OLD-RECORD-DELETED-CTR  PIC ZZ9.
                  10                           PIC X(45) VALUE
                     "  OLD MASTER RECORDS DELETED FROM MASTER FILE".

               05 SUMMARY-LINE-3.
                  10                           PIC X(5)  VALUE SPACES.
                  10 O-NEW-RECORD-CTR          PIC ZZ9.
                  10                           PIC X(38) VALUE
                     "  NEW RECORDS ADDED TO THE MASTER FILE".

               05 SUMMARY-LINE-3.
                  10                           PIC X(5)  VALUE SPACES.
                  10 O-OLD-RECORD-CHANGED-CTR  PIC ZZ9.
                  10                           PIC X(28) VALUE
                     "  UPDATED OLD MASTER RECORDS".

               05 SUMMARY-LINE-5.
                  10                           PIC X(5)  VALUE SPACES.
                  10 O-NEW-MASTER-FILE-CTR     PIC ZZ9.
                  10                           PIC X(36) VALUE
                     "  RECORDS WRITTEN TO NEW MASTER FILE".

               05 SUMMARY-LINE-6.
                  10                           PIC X(5)  VALUE SPACES.
                  10 O-AUDIT-CTR               PIC ZZ9.
                  10                           PIC X(33) VALUE
                     "  RECORDS WRITTEN TO AUDIT REPORT".

               05 END-LINE.
                  10 PIC X(28)  VALUE SPACES.
                  10 PIC X(23)  VALUE "***  END OF REPORT  ***".
                  10 PIC X(29)  VALUE SPACES.

           PROCEDURE DIVISION.

           100-PRODUCE-MASTER-FILE-UPDATE.
               PERFORM 200-START-UP.
               PERFORM 210-PROCESS-UPDATE
                   UNTIL NO-MORE-OLD-RECORDS.
               PERFORM 220-FINISH-UP.
               STOP RUN.

           200-START-UP.
               OPEN INPUT DETAIL-FILE
                          OLD-MASTER-FILE
                    OUTPUT NEW-MASTER-FILE
                           AUDIT-REPORT.
               PERFORM 300-INITIALIZE-ITEMS.
               PERFORM 310-WRITE-REPORT-HEADERS.
               PERFORM 320-READ-OLD-MASTER-RECORD.

           210-PROCESS-UPDATE.
               IF OLD-MR-SSN = DETAIL-SSN
                  THEN
                      IF PROCES-CODE = 2
                         1
```

```
                                          18-Nov-1993 16:06:14    VAX COBOL V5.1-10                  Page    4
Source Listing                            18-Nov-1993 13:06:01    FACULTY$DISK:[PAQUETTEG.WCBTXT]C11DB1.CB1;1

%COBOL-F-ERROR  349, (1) Undefined name
                         PERFORM 340-UPDATE-OLD-MASTER-RECORD
                         1
%COBOL-W-ERROR  297, (1) Processing of source program resumes at this point
                     ELSE
                     1
%COBOL-F-ERROR  222, (1) "." required at this point
                         PERFORM 370-DELETE-OLD-MASTER-RECORD
                     END-IF
                     1
%COBOL-F-ERROR  222, (1) "." required at this point
              ELSE
                  IF OLD-MR-SSN > DETAIL-SSN
                  1
%COBOL-W-ERROR  297, (1) Processing of source program resumes at this point
                      PERFORM 350-COPY-OLD-MASTER-RECORD
                  ELSE
                      PERFORM 360-ADD-NEW-RECORD
                  END-IF
              END-IF.
              1
%COBOL-F-ERROR  222, (1) "." required at this point
              PERFORM 380-PREPARE-AUDIT-LINE.
              1
%COBOL-W-ERROR  297, (1) Processing of source program resumes at this point

          220-FINISH-UP.
              PERFORM 390-PREPARE-TOTALS.
              WRITE PRINTLINE FROM END-LINE
                  AFTER ADVANCING.
                                 1
%COBOL-F-ERROR  321, (1) Invalid statement syntax
              CLOSE DETAIL-FILE
                    OLD-MASTER-FILE
                    NEW-MASTER-FILE
                    AUDIT-REPORT.

          300-INITIALIZE-ITEMS.
              ACCEPT WS-REPORT-DATE FROM DATE.
l;2                     1
%COBOL-F-ERROR  349, (1) Undefined name
              INITALIZE PROGRAM-COUNTERS.
              1
%COBOL-F-ERROR  349, (1) Undefined name

          310-WRITE-REPORT-HEADERS.
          1
%COBOL-W-ERROR  297, (1) Processing of source program resumes at this point
              WRITE PRINTLINE FROM COMPANY-NAME
                  AFTER ADVANCING WS-PAGE.
                                  1
%COBOL-F-ERROR  349, (1) Undefined name
              WRITE PRINTLINE FROM REPORT-NAME-1
                  AFTER ADVANCING 3 LINES.
              WRITE PRINTLINE FROM REPORT-NAME-2
                  AFTER ADVANCING 2 LINES.
              WRITE PRINTLINE FROM HEADINGS-1
                  AFTER ADVANCING 2 LINES.
              WRITE PRINTLINE FROM HEADINGS-2
                  AFTER ADVANCING 1 LINES.
              MOVE 2 TO WS-PROPER-SPACING.
                        1
%COBOL-F-ERROR  349, (1) Undefined name

          320-READ-OLD-MASTER-RECORD.
              READ OLD-MASTER-FILE RECORD
                  AT END
                      SET NO-MORE-OLD-RECORDS TO TRUE.

          330-READ-DETAIL-RECORD.
              READ DETAIL-FILE RECORD
                  AT END
                      SET NO-MORE-DETAL-RECORDS TO TRUE.
                          1
%COBOL-F-ERROR  349, (1) Undefined name

          340-UPDATE-OLD-MASTER-RECORD.
              MOVE "U" TO WS-ACTION-CODE.
              MOVE OLD-MR-RECORD-CODE TO NEW-MR-RECORD-CODE.
                                         1
%COBOL-F-ERROR  349, (1) Undefined name
              MOVE OLD-MR-SSN TO NEW-MR-SSN
              MOVE OLD-MR-NAME TO NEW-MR-NAME.
              MOVE OLD-MR-STORE-NO TO NEW-MR-STORE-NO.
              MOVE OLD-MR-INS-CODE TO NEW-MR-INS-CODE.
              MOVE OLD-MR-EXEMPT TO NEW-MR-EXEMPT.
              WRITE NEW-RECORD.
                    1
%COBOL-F-ERROR  202, (1) Operand must be a level 01 record-name subordinate to a file defined by FD
              ADD 1 TO WS-OLD-RECORD-CHANGED-CTR
                       WS-NEW-MASTER-FILE-CTR.
              PERFORM 320-READ-OLD-MASTER-RECORD.
              PERFORM 330-READ-DETAIL-RECORD.
```

```
              350-COPY-OLD-MASTER-RECORD.
                  MOVE "C" TO WS-ACTION-CODE.
                  MOVE OLD-MR-RECORD TO NEW-MR-RECORD.
                  WRITE NEW-MR-RECORD.
                  ADD 1 TO WS-OLD-RECORD-COPIED-CTR
                           WS-NEW-MASTER-FILE-CTR.
                  PERFORM 320-READ-OLD-MR-RECORD.
                          1
%COBOL-F-ERROR  349, (1) Undefined name

              360-ADD-NEW-RECORD.
              1
%COBOL-W-ERROR  297, (1) Processing of source program resumes at this point
                  MOVE "A" TO WS-ACTION-CODE.
                  MOVE "PM" TO NEW-MR-RECORD-CODE.
                               1
%COBOL-F-ERROR  349, (1) Undefined name
                  MOVE DETAIL-SSN TO NEW-MR-SSN.
                  MOVE DETAIL-NAME TO NEW-MR-NAME.
                  MOVE DETAIL-STORE-NO TO NEW-MR-STORE-NO.
                  MOVE DETAIL-PAY-CODE TO NEW-MR-PAY-CODE.
                  MOVE DETAIL-INS-CODE TO NEW-MR-INS-CODE.
                  MOVE DETAIL-EXEMPT TO NEW-MR-EXEMPT.
                  MOVE DETAIL-CLASS-CODE TO NEW-MR-CLASS-CODE.
                  WRITE NEW-MR-RECORD.
                  ADD 1 TO WS-NEW-RECORD-CTR
                           WS-NEW-MASTER-FILE-CTR.
                  PERFORM 330-READ-DETAIL-RECORD.

              370-DELETE-OLD-MASTER-RECORD.
                  MOVE "D" TO WS-ACTION-CODE.
                  MOVE OLD-MR-RECORD TO WS-OLD-MR-RECORD.
                  ADD 1 TO WS-OLD-RECORD-DELETED-CTR.
                  PERFORM 320-READ-OLD-MASTER-RECORD.
                  PERFORM 330-READ-DETAIL-RECORD.

              380-PREPARE-AUDIT-LINE.
                  MOVE SPACES TO AUDT-LINE.
                                 1
%COBOL-F-ERROR  349, (1) Undefined name
                  EVALUATE WS-ACTION-CODE
                      WHEN "A"
                          MOVE NEW-MR-RECORD TO O-RECORD
                          MOVE "X" TO O-ACTION-FLD-1
                      WHEN "D"
                          MOVE WS-OLD-MR-RECORD TO O-RECORD
                          MOVE "X" TO O-ACTION-FLD-2
                      WHEN "U"
                          MOVE NEW-MR-RECORD TO O-RECORD
                          MOVE "X" TO O-ACTION-FLD-3
                      WHEN "C"
                          MOVE NEW-MR-RECORD TO O-RECORD
                          MOVE "X" TO O-ACTION-FLD-4.
                  WRITE PRINTLINE FROM AUDIT-LINE
                      AFTER ADVANCING WS-PROPER-SPACING.
                                      1
%COBOL-F-ERROR  349, (1) Undefined name
                  MOVE 1 TO WS-PROPER-SPACING.
                            1
%COBOL-F-ERROR  349, (1) Undefined name
                  ADD 1 TO WS-AUDIT-LINE-CTR.

              390-PREPARE-TOTALS.
                  WRITE PRINTLINE FROM SUMARY-HEADER
                                       1
%COBOL-F-ERROR  349, (1) Undefined name
                      AFTER ADVANCING 5 LINES.
                                             1
%COBOL-W-ERROR  297, (1) Processing of source program resumes at this point
                  MOVE WS-OLD-RECORD-COPIED-CTR TO O-OLD-RECORD-COPIED-CTR.
                  WRITE PRINTLINE FROM SUMMARY-LINE-1
                     AFTER ADVANCING 2 LINES.
                  MOVE WS-OLD-RECORD-DELETED-CTR TO O-OLD-RECORD-DELETED-CTR.
                  WRITE PRINTLINE FROM SUMMARY-LINE-2
                      AFTER ADVANCING 1 LINE.
                  MOVE WS-NEW-RECORD-CTR TO O-NEW-RECORD-CTR.
                  WRITE PRINTLINE FROM SUMMARY-LINE-3
                                       1
%COBOL-F-ERROR  337, (1) Ambiguous reference - check name qualification
                      AFTER ADVANCING 1 LINE.
                  MOVE WS-OLD-RECORD-CHANGED-CTR TO O-OLD-RECORD-CHANGED-CTR.
                  WRITE PRINTLINE FROM SUMMARY-LINE-4
                                       1
%COBOL-F-ERROR  349, (1) Undefined name
                      AFTER ADVANCING 1 LINE.
                                            1
%COBOL-W-ERROR  297, (1) Processing of source program resumes at this point
                  MOVE WS-NEW-MASTER-FILE-CTR TO O-NEW-MASTER-FILE-CTR.
                  WRITE PRINTLINE FROM SUMMARY-LINE-5
                      AFTER ADVANCING 1 LINE.
                  MOVE WS-AUDIT-LINE-CTR TO O-AUDIT-CTR.
                  WRITE PRINTLINE FROM SUMMARY-LINE-6
                      AFTER ADVANCING 1 LINE.
```

Figure 11.52a Old master personnel file

Record code | Social Security number | Name | Store number | Pay code | Ins. code | Exemptions | Class code

```
PM147523318SILVA, GEORGE       0103FB205
PM147523318SILVA, GEORGE       0103FB205
PM239419615DORR, PAUL          0112FB406
PM323693173LAVIN, YVONNE       1009FA204
PM326523966RIANNA, MILDRED     0508FA205
PM338521873WINSLOW, EILEEN     3003IB103
PM362799176NELSON, PETER       2002IA102
PM364522332JEFFERDS, CHARLES   3010FB405
PM367113215PERNAL, RICHARD     0503IA102
PM379443987ALMEIDA, PAULA      2003IB102
PM409554662STUDLEY, SANDRA     2005IB103
PM415817943DAILEY, MARSHA      0502IA102
PM419617752ULMANN, SUSAN       0108FA204
PM421332564BALL, GEORGE        0106FB304
PM437116528JARVIS, RICHARD     0101IA101
PM450152349COVILL, COLINE      0103IA102
PM468201726DONALDSON, MARC     1009FA205
PM470156712BRIEN, RAYMOND      2008FB204
PM481975521KENNEY, MARTIN      1001IA101
PM493043217DANIELS, JULIA      1004IB103
PM494123371GARBER, JULIE       3005FA203
PM505200792TOUPIN, ADA         2008FB305
PM510025113GAGNON, GERARD      2001IA101
PM519378294KALIN, OLIVIA       0501IA101
PM519641139HEIMER, CYNTHIA     1008FB405
PM540525640RAINVILLE, SHARON   1009IB104
PM549663412RAGOSTA, TERRY      2005IA104
PM552974388GALLIGAN, FRANCIS    1003IB102
PM560771115SCHERER, ANGELA     3008FB205
PM566197327LAPIERRE, GARY      2003IB103
PM566315679PETRUSKA, ANGELA    0107IB105
```

Figure 11.52b Detail file to update the master personnel file

Process code | Social Security number | Name | Store number | Pay code | Ins. code | Exemptions | Class code

```
1035287413PEEBLES, CARL W.     0503IA102
1035287413PEEBLES, CARL W.     0503IA102
3362799176                       04   03
2364522332
1415726750RYAN, FRANCIS X.     2008FB404
2415817943
3419617752                       10   05
3450152349                       05   03
3493043217                       07   04
1515031329COTTRELL, SARA       1004FB304
2549663412
1706314816GRAGNANI, CLORINDA   0502IA101
```

■ **Figure 11.52c** Audit report produced by program free of syntax errors

```
                                                          MONSTER BURGER COMPANY


                         MASTER PAYROLL FILE UPDATE

                AUDIT TRAIL REPORT

                 PAYROLL RECORD                                     ACTION TAKEN
                                                         ADDED  DELETED  UPDATED  COPIED

PM147523318SILVA, GEORGE       0103FB205                                            X
PM239419615DORR, PAUL          0112FB406                                            X
PM323693173LAVIN, YVONNE       1009FA204                                            X
PM326523966RIANNA, MILDRED     0508FA205                                            X
PM338521873WINSLOW, EILEEN     3003IB103                                            X
PM362799176NELSON, PETER       2002IA102                                            X
PM364522332JEFFERDS, CHARLES   3010FB405                                            X
PM367113215PERNAL, RICHARD     0503IA102                                            X
PM379443987ALMEIDA, PAULA      2003IB102                                            X
PM409554662STUDLEY, SANDRA     2005IB103                                            X
PM415817943DAILEY, MARSHA      0502IA102                                            X
PM419617752ULMANN, SUSAN       0108FA204                                            X
PM421332564BALL, GEORGE        0106FB304                                            X
PM437116528JARVIS, RICHARD     0101IA101                                            X
PM450152349COVILL, COLINE      0103IA102                                            X
PM468201726DONALDSON, MARC     1009FA205                                            X
PM470156712BRIEN, RAYMOND      2008FB204                                            X
PM481975521KENNEY, MARTIN      1001IA101                                            X
PM493043217DANIELS, JULIA      1004IB103                                            X
PM494123371GARBER, JULIE       3005FA203                                            X
PM505200792TOUPIN, ADA         2008FB305                                            X
PM510025113GAGNON, GERARD      2001IA101                                            X
PM519378294KALIN, OLIVIA       0501IA101                                            X
PM519641139HEIMER, CYNTHIA     1008FB405                                            X
PM540525640RAINVILLE, SHARON   1009IB104                                            X
PM549663412RAGOSTA, TERRY      2005IA104                                            X
PM552974388GALLIGAN, FRANCIS   1003IB102                                            X
PM560771115SCHERER, ANGELA     3008FB205                                            X
PM566197327LAPIERRE, GARY      2003IB103                                            X
PM566315679PETRUSKA, ANGELA    0107IB105                                            X



                          SUMMARY
     30   OLD MASTER RECORDS COPIED TO NEW MASTER FILE
      0   OLD MASTER RECORDS DELETED FROM MASTER FILE
      0   NEW RECORDS ADDED TO THE MASTER FILE
      0   UPDATED OLD MASTER RECORDS
     30   RECORDS WRITTEN TO NEW MASTER FILE
     30   RECORDS WRITTEN TO AUDIT REPORT


                              ***  END OF REPORT  ***
```

Figure 11.52d New master personnel file produced by program free of syntax errors

```
PM147523318SILVA, GEORGE       0103FB205
PM239419615DORR, PAUL          0112FB406
PM323693173LAVIN, YVONNE       1009FA204
PM326523966RIANNA, MILDRED     0508FA205
PM338521873WINSLOW, EILEEN     3003IB103
PM362799176NELSON, PETER       2002IA102
PM364522332JEFFERDS, CHARLES   3010FB405
PM367113215PERNAL, RICHARD     0503IA102
PM379443987ALMEIDA, PAULA      2003IB102
PM409554662STUDLEY, SANDRA     2005IB103
PM415817943DAILEY, MARSHA      0502IA102
PM419617752ULMANN, SUSAN       0108FA204
PM421332564BALL, GEORGE        0106FB304
PM437116528JARVIS, RICHARD     0101IA101
PM450152349COVILL, COLINE      0103IA102
PM468201726DONALDSON, MARC     1009FA205
PM470156712BRIEN, RAYMOND      2008FB204
PM481975521KENNEY, MARTIN      1001IA101
PM493043217DANIELS, JULIA      1004IB103
PM494123371GARBER, JULIE       3005FA203
PM505200792TOUPIN, ADA         2008FB305
PM510025113GAGNON, GERARD      2001IA101
PM519378294KALIN, OLIVIA       0501IA101
PM519641139HEIMER, CYNTHIA     1008FB405
PM540525640RAINVILLE, SHARON   1009IB104
PM549663412RAGOSTA, TERRY      2005IA104
PM552974388GALLIGAN, FRANCIS   1003IB102
PM560771115SCHERER, ANGELA     3008FB205
PM566197327LAPIERRE, GARY      2003IB103
PM566315679PETRUSKA, ANGELA    0107IB105
```

Figure 11.53a Correct new master personnel file

```
PM035287413PEEBLES, CARL W.    0503IA102
PM147523318SILVA, GEORGE       0103FB205
PM239419615DORR, PAUL          0112FB406
PM323693173LAVIN, YVONNE       1009FA204
PM326523966RIANNA, MILDRED     0508FA205
PM338521873WINSLOW, EILEEN     3003IB103
PM362799176NELSON, PETER       2002IA103
PM367113215PERNAL, RICHARD     0503IA102
PM379443987ALMEIDA, PAULA      2003IB102
PM409554662STUDLEY, SANDRA     2005IB103
PM415726750RYAN, FRANCIS X.    2008FB404
PM419617752ULMANN, SUSAN       0110FA205
PM421332564BALL, GEORGE        0106FB304
PM437116528JARVIS, RICHARD     0101IA101
PM450152349COVILL, COLINE      0105IA103
PM468201726DONALDSON, MARC     1009FA205
PM470156712BRIEN, RAYMOND      2008FB204
PM481975521KENNEY, MARTIN      1001IA101
PM493043217DANIELS, JULIA      1007IB104
PM494123371GARBER, JULIE       3005FA203
PM505200792TOUPIN, ADA         2008FB305
PM510025113GAGNON, GERARD      2001IA101
PM515031329COTTRELL, SARA      1004FB304
PM519378294KALIN, OLIVIA       0501IA101
PM519641139HEIMER, CYNTHIA     1008FB405
PM540525640RAINVILLE, SHARON   1009IB104
PM552974388GALLIGAN, FRANCIS   1003IB102
PM560771115SCHERER, ANGELA     3008FB205
PM566197327LAPIERRE, GARY      2003IB103
PM566315679PETRUSKA, ANGELA    0107IB105
PM706314816GRAGNANI, CLORINDA  0502IA101
```

Figure 11.53b Correct audit report

```
                              MONSTER BURGER COMPANY

                    MASTER PAYROLL FILE UPDATE    93/11/31

                                AUDIT TRAIL REPORT

             PAYROLL RECORD                                  ACTION TAKEN
                                                 ADDED   DELETED  UPDATED   COPIED

PM035287413PEEBLES, CARL W.     0503IA102          X
PM147523318SILVA, GEORGE        0103FB205                                     X
PM239419615DORR, PAUL           0112FB406                                     X
PM323693173LAVIN, YVONNE        1009FA204                                     X
PM326523966RIANNA, MILDRED      0508FA205                                     X
PM338521873WINSLOW, EILEEN      3003IB103                                     X
PM362799176NELSON, PETER        2004IA103                            X
PM364522332JEFFERDS, CHARLES    3010FB405                   X
PM367113215PERNAL, RICHARD      0503IA102                                     X
PM379443987ALMEIDA, PAULA       2003IB102                                     X
PM409554662STUDLEY, SANDRA      2005IB103                                     X
PM415726750RYAN, FRANCIS X.     2008FB404          X
PM415817943DAILEY, MARSHA       0502IA102                   X
PM419617752ULMANN, SUSAN        0110FA205                            X
PM421332564BALL, GEORGE         0106FB304                                     X
PM437116528JARVIS, RICHARD      0101IA101                                     X
PM450152349COVILL, COLINE       0105IA103                            X
PM468201726DONALDSON, MARC      1009FA205                                     X
PM470156712BRIEN, RAYMOND       2008FB204                                     X
PM481975521KENNEY, MARTIN       1001IA101                                     X
PM493043217DANIELS, JULIA       1007IB104                            X
PM494123371GARBER, JULIE        3005FA203                                     X
PM505200792TOUPIN, ADA          2008FB305                                     X
PM510025113GAGNON, GERARD       2001IA101                                     X
PM515031329COTTRELL, SARA       1004FB304          X
PM519378294KALIN, OLIVIA        0501IA101                                     X
PM519641139HEIMER, CYNTHIA      1008FB405                                     X
PM540525640RAINVILLE, SHARON    1009IB104                                     X
PM549663412RAGOSTA, TERRY       2005IA104                   X
PM552974388GALLIGAN, FRANCIS    1003IB102                                     X
PM560771115SCHERER, ANGELA      3008FB205                                     X
PM566197327LAPIERRE, GARY       2003IB103                                     X
PM566315679PETRUSKA, ANGELA     0107IB105                                     X
PM706314816GRAGNANI, CLORINDA   0502IA101          X


                          SUMMARY

     23   OLD MASTER RECORDS COPIED TO NEW MASTER FILE
      3   OLD MASTER RECORDS DELETED FROM MASTER FILE
      4   NEW RECORDS ADDED TO THE MASTER FILE
      4   UPDATED OLD MASTER RECORDS
     28   RECORDS WRITTEN TO NEW MASTER FILE
     34   RECORDS WRITTEN TO AUDIT REPORT


                    ***   END OF REPORT   ***
```

Programming Exercises

Programming Exercise I

The management of the Express Auto Parts Warehouse Company wants its data processing department to create a master inventory file, with sequential organization, that will contain a master record for each catalog item it maintains in inventory. The size of the master record is 100, and its layout is as follows:

cc 1–2	Record code (IM for Item Master)
cc 3–7	Item catalog number
cc 8–27	Item description
cc 28–32	Item unit purchase price (format: xxx.xx)
cc 33–37	Item unit selling price (format: xxx.xx)
cc 38–41	Item quantity on hand
cc 42–45	Item quantity on order
cc 46–49	Item reorder point
cc 50–100	Not used

The blocking factor for the master file is 10.

The item records are currently in a file called ITEM-FILE, and each record contains data as shown in Figure 11.54a.

The records in ITEM-FILE are supposed to be in ascending order by item catalog numbers, and the new master records must be written to the master file in that sequence. If a record is out of sequence, it must not be written to the master file.

The program must produce an audit report as formatted in Figure 11.54b. Not more than 30 detail lines must be written on each page. Counters are needed to produce the summary on the report.

The system flowchart and the structure chart have been developed for you and are shown in Figure 11.54c and 11.54d, respectively.

Figure 11.54a Input record layout

Record Layout Form

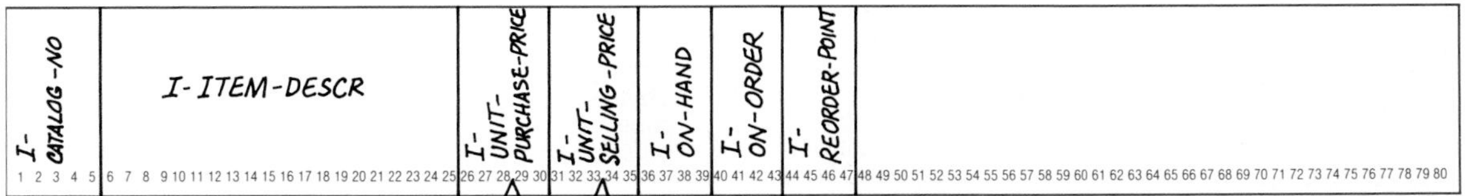

Record Name: ITEM-RECORD

Figure 11.54b Printer spacing chart for the audit report

Printer Spacing Chart

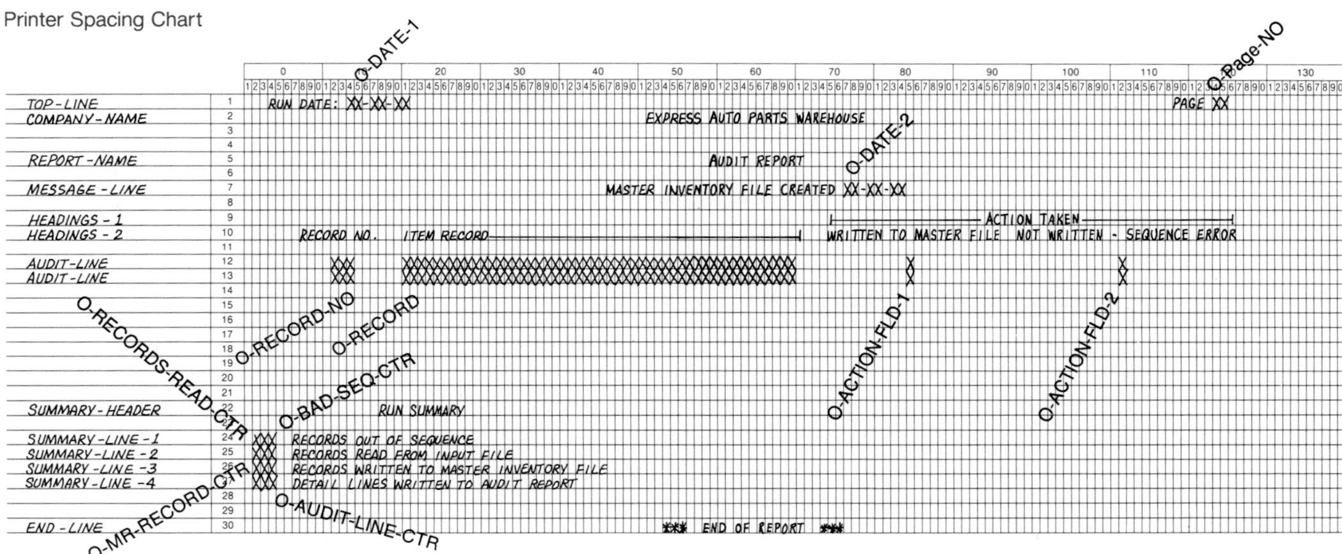

Figure 11.54c System flowchart

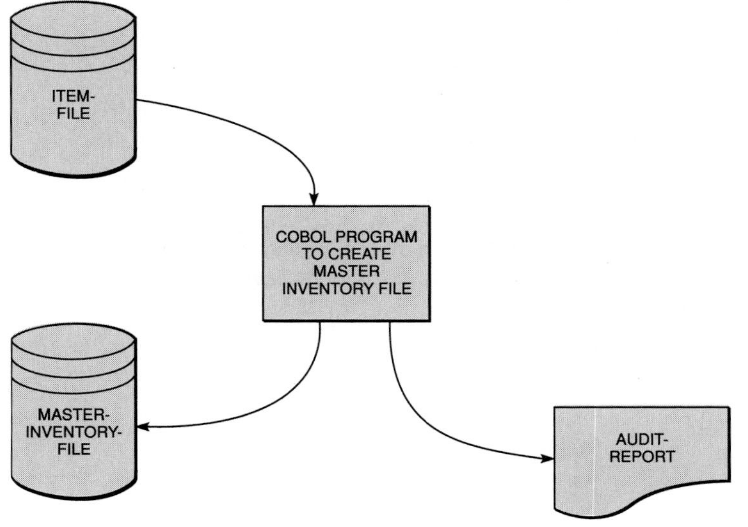

■ **Figure 11.54d** Structure chart

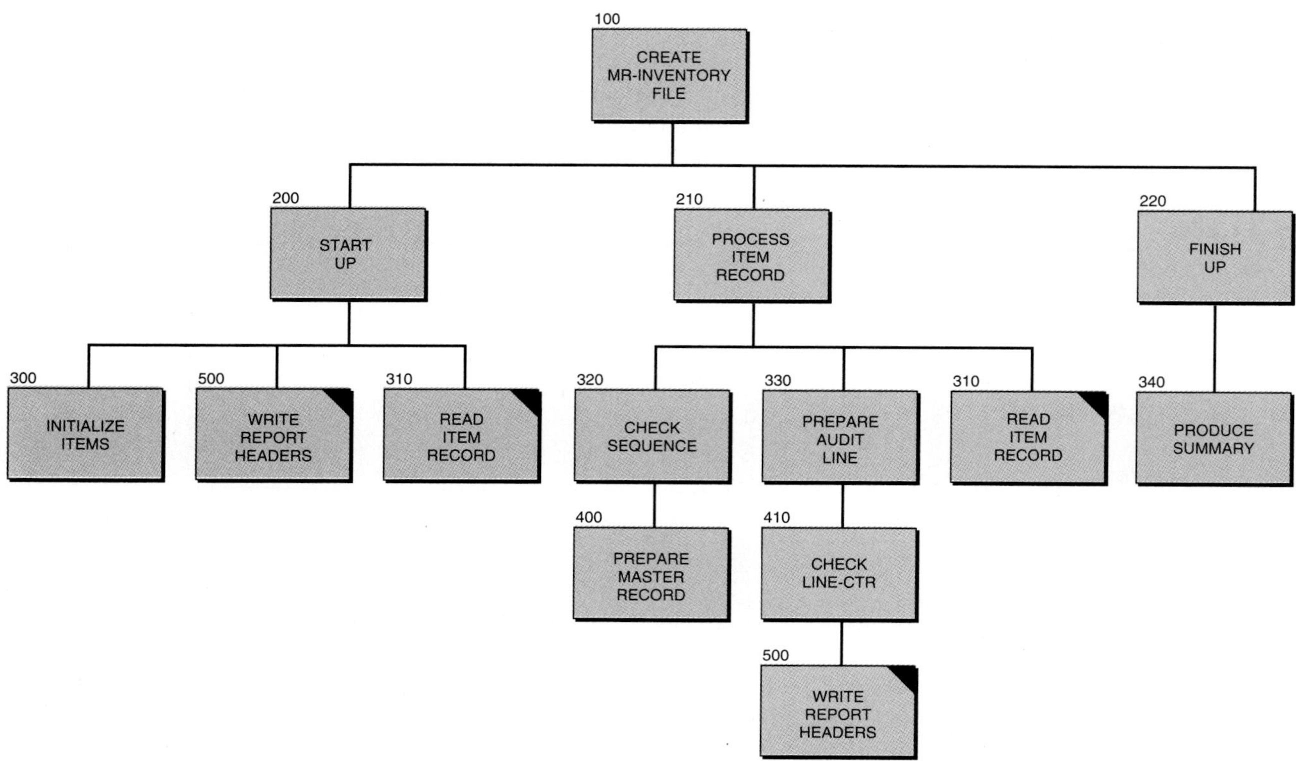

Your task is to complete the design and then implement the design to successful completion. Use the current date for the date fields on the report, and use Data File Set 1 (see Appendix C [DD/CD: VICIIEX1.DAT]) as the input file.

Programming Exercise II

The Allied Stock Company has accumulated a number of new customers during the past month. Management wants its data processing department to add these customers to its master customer file.

A record has been prepared for each new customer, and these records are currently in a detail file, in ascending order by customer number. The record layout is shown in Figure 11.55a.

Each record in the master customer file contains the following data:

cc 1–2	Record code (CM for Customer Master)
cc 3–6	Customer number
cc 7–26	Customer name
cc 27–51	Customer street address
cc 52–74	Customer city and state
cc 75–94	Not used
cc 95–100	Customer last activity date

These records are sequenced in ascending order by customer number. The master customer file has sequential organization, and it uses a blocking factor of 10.

The program must add the new customer records to the master file in a way that maintains the proper sequence. In addition, the current date must be entered as the last activity date for the new records. An audit report must also be produced, formatted as shown in Figure 11.55b. A report page must contain no more than 30 detail lines.

The system flowchart is provided for you in Figure 11.55c.

Your task is to complete the design phase and then to implement the design to successful completion. Assume both data files have been validated and no two customers have the same customer number.

Use Master Customer File Set 10A [DD/CD:VICIIEX2.DT1] and Detail File Set 10B [DD/CD: VICIIEX2.DT2] (see Appendix C). Use the current date as the report date.

Figure 11.55a Detail record layout

Record Layout Form

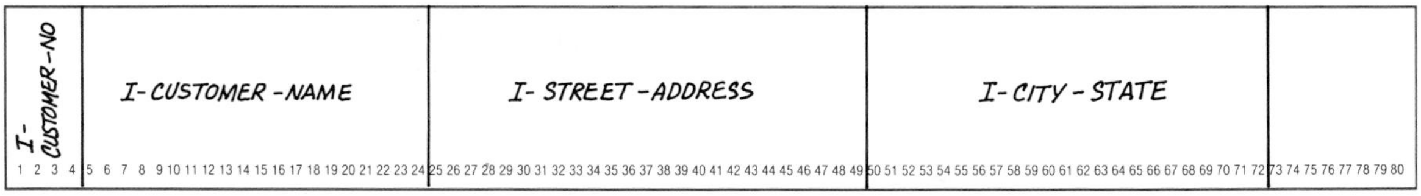

I-CUSTOMER-NO	I-CUSTOMER-NAME	I-STREET-ADDRESS	I-CITY-STATE	
1 2 3 4	5 6 7 8 9 10 11 12 13 14 15 16 17 18 19 20 21 22 23 24	25 26 27 28 29 30 31 32 33 34 35 36 37 38 39 40 41 42 43 44 45 46 47 48 49	50 51 52 53 54 55 56 57 58 59 60 61 62 63 64 65 66 67 68 69 70 71 72	73 74 75 76 77 78 79 80

Record Name: CUSTOMER-RECORD

Figure 11.55b Printer spacing chart for the audit report

Printer Spacing Chart

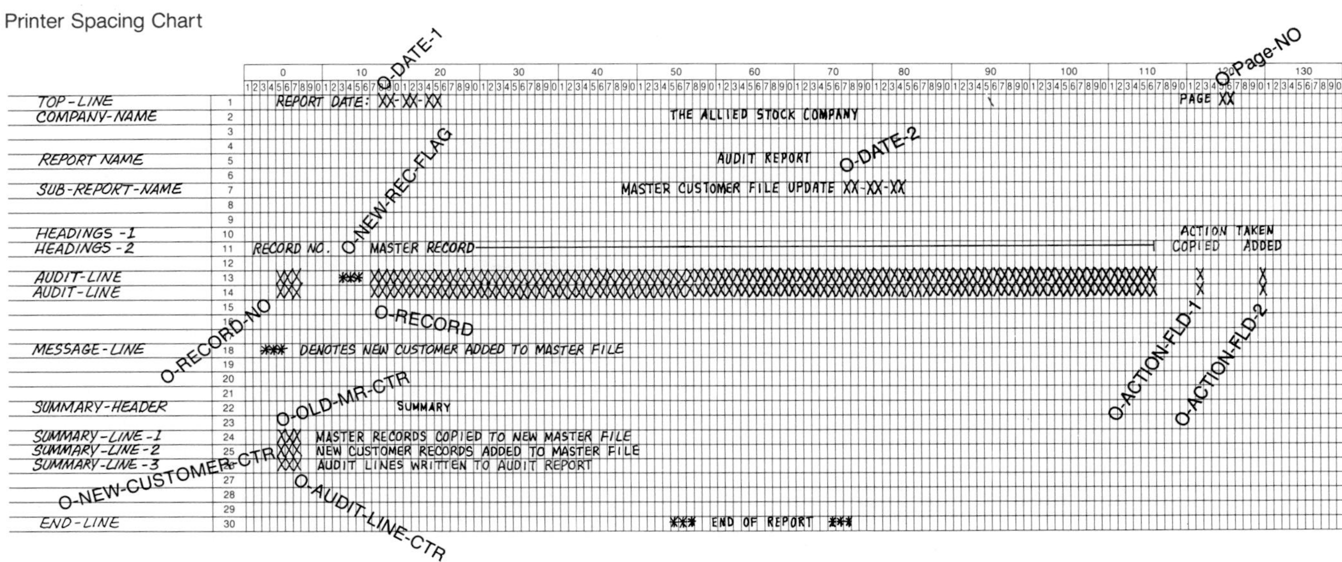

Figure 11.55c System flowchart

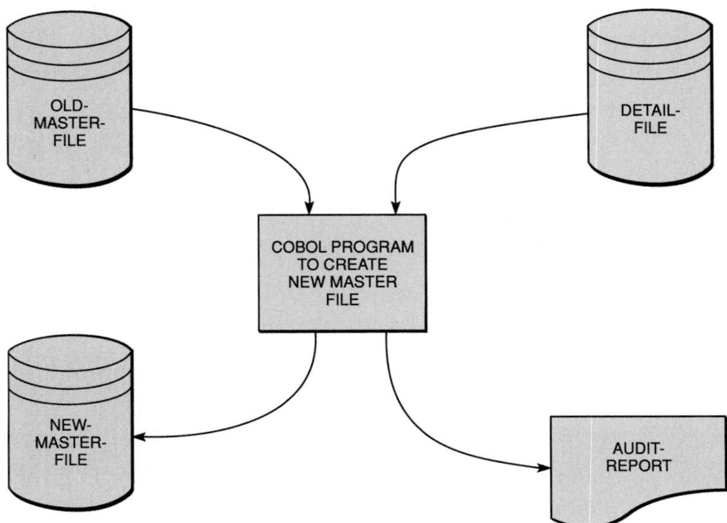

Programming Exercise III

The Express Auto Parts Warehouse Company has had some unexpected expenditures that are straining its cash flow. As a result, management has decided to add 2 percent to the selling price of each item in its inventory. At the same time, a few catalog items are no longer available and thus are to be removed from its master inventory file. The data processing department must produce a program that will accomplish both of these tasks.

A detail file is prepared that contains two kinds of records: One record contains the rate by which the selling price of each catalog item is to be increased; the other record contains the catalog number for an item to be removed from the master file. The rate record is the first one in the detail file. All the other records in the detail file identify catalog items to be deleted from the master file. The layouts of these records are as follows:

Rate Record:
cc 1–3 Rate of increase (format: .xxx)
Detail Record:
cc 1–5 Catalog number

The detail records have been validated and are in ascending order by catalog number.

The master inventory file records contain the following data:

cc 1–2	Record code (IM for Item Master)
cc 3–7	Item catalog number
cc 8–27	Item description
cc 28–32	Item unit purchase price (format: xxx.xx)
cc 33–37	Item unit selling price (format: xxx.xx)
cc 38–41	Item quantity on hand
cc 42–45	Item quantity on order
cc 46–49	Item reorder point
cc 50–100	Not used

The file has a blocking factor of 10, and its records are in ascending order by catalog number.

The program must produce an audit report formatted as shown in Figure 11.56. An audit line must be printed for each catalog item in the master file. If the item is being removed from the master file, the action taken field must indicate a deletion; otherwise, the action taken must indicate a price change, and the old and new selling prices must be shown. A maximum of 30 detail lines are to be printed on each page of the report.

A summary report must show how many items were deleted, how many catalog items remain in the master inventory file, and how many detail lines were written to the report.

Use Detail File Set 11A [DD/CD:VICIIEX3.DT1] and Master Inventory File Set 11B [DD/CD:VICIIEX3.DT2] (see Appendix C). Use the current date as the report date.

Figure 11.56 Printer spacing chart for the audit report

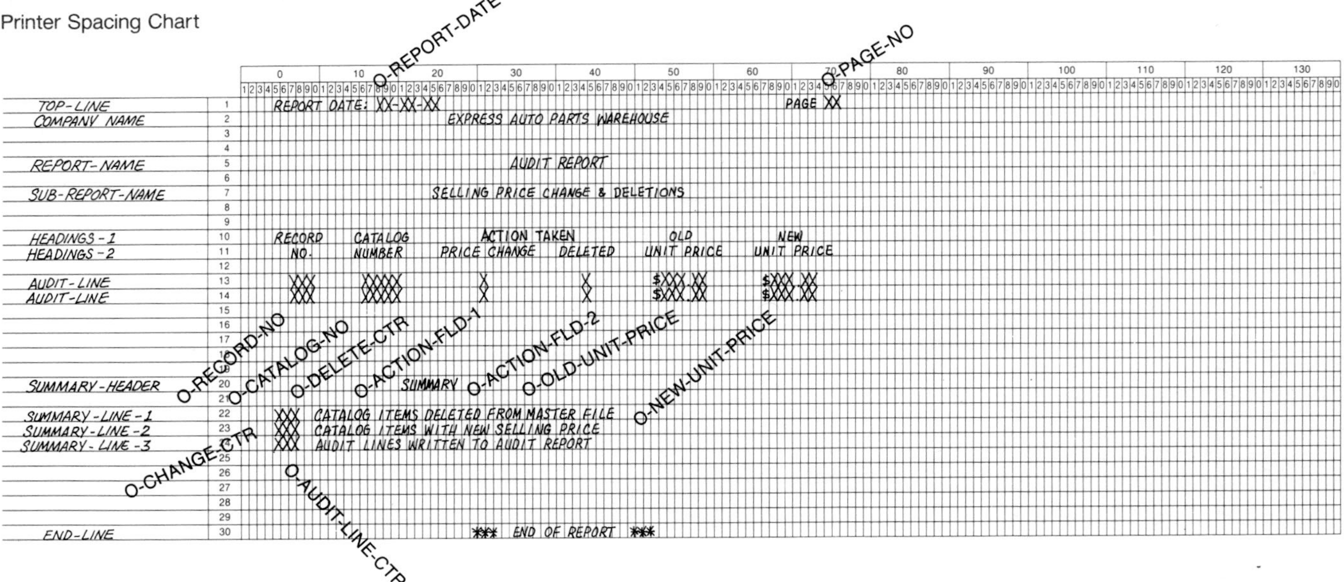

Programming Exercise IV

The management of Ponagansett Electric wants to update its master customer file. During the past month, the company signed up new customers, other customers closed their accounts as they left the area, and other customers changed from one rate schedule to another.

A detail file contains a record for each customer involved in the master file update. Each record contains a process code in byte 1. A 1 indicates a new customer to be added to the master file; a 2 indicates a customer to be deleted from the master file; a 3 indicates a customer record in which some field values must be changed. The detail record layout is as follows:

cc 1	Process code (value 1, 2, or 3)
cc 2–9	Meter number
cc 10–12	Electric rate code (A10, A11, A12, or C-2)
cc 13–18	Customer number
cc 19–38	Customer name
cc 39–63	Customer address
cc 64–86	Customer city, state, and ZIP code

If the process code is 1, the record contains a value in each data field. If the process code is 2, the record contains only the customer's meter number, since this value is sufficient to identify the record to be deleted. If the process code is 3, the record contains the customer's meter number and the new rate code that will be used for future billings. The records in the detail file are in ascending order by customer meter number.

The records in the master customer file contain the following data:

cc 1–2	Record code (CM for Customer Master)
cc 3–10	Customer meter number
cc 11–13	Customer rate code
cc 14–19	Customer number
cc 20–39	Customer name
cc 40–64	Customer address
cc 65–87	Customer city, state, and ZIP code
cc 88–100	Not used

The records in the master file are in ascending order by meter number. The file's organization is sequential, and its records are blocked with a factor of 10.

The program must produce an updated master customer file and an audit report formatted as shown in Figure 11.57. The report must contain no more than 30 detail lines per page.

Use Detail File Set 12A [DD/CD:VICIIEX4.DT1] and Master Customer File Set 12B [DD/CD: VICIIEX4.DT2] (see Appendix C). Use the current date as the report date.

Figure 11.57 Printer spacing chart for the audit report

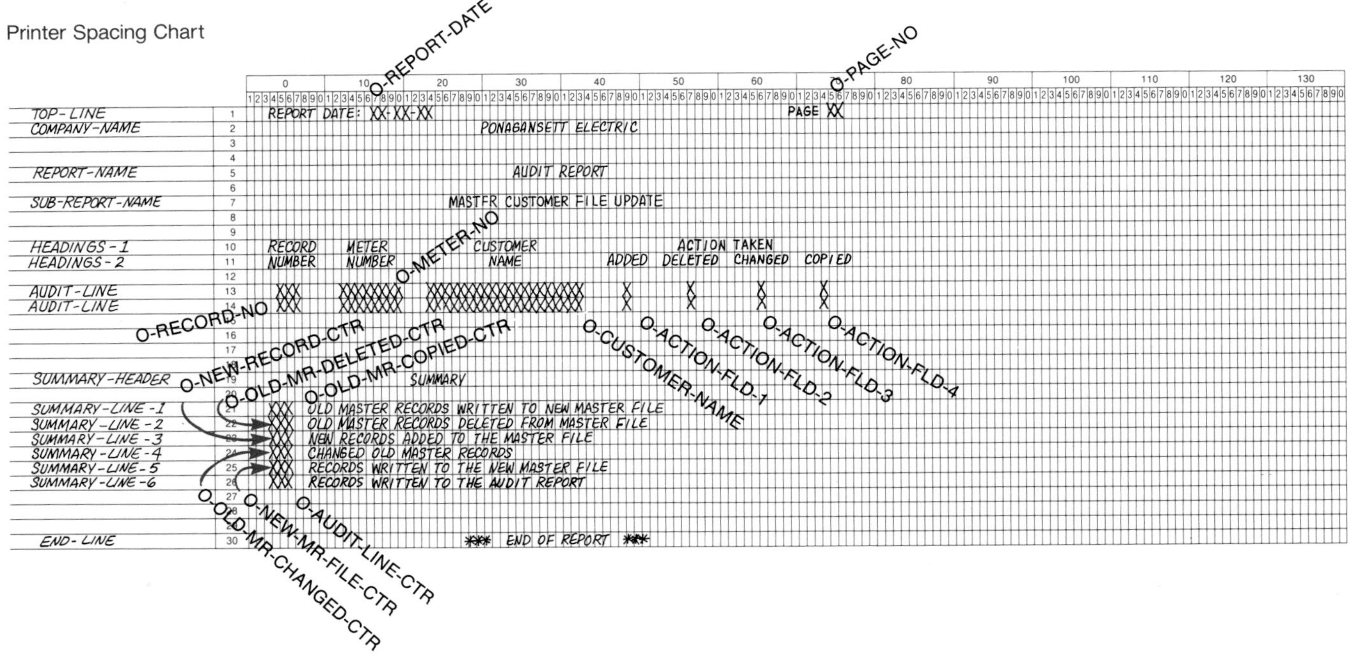

Appendix A
COBOL Reference Formats

The general COBOL Reference Formats listed in this appendix are contained in the American National Standard ANSI X3.23–1985. Highlighted formats are new to COBOL '85.

IDENTIFICATION DIVISION Formats

```
IDENTIFICATION DIVISION.

PROGRAM-ID. program-name [ { | COMMON  | } PROGRAM ] .
                         [ { | INITIAL | }         ]
[AUTHOR. [comment-entry] . . .]
[INSTALLATION. [comment-entry] . . .]
[DATE-WRITTEN. [comment-entry] . . .]
[DATE-COMPILED. [comment-entry] . . .]
[SECURITY. [comment-entry] . . .]
```

ENVIRONMENT DIVISION Formats

```
[ENVIRONMENT DIVISION.
[CONFIGURATION SECTION.
[SOURCE-COMPUTER. [computer-name [with DEBUGGING MODE].]]
[OBJECT-COMPUTER. [computer-name
                            { WORDS      }
    [MEMORY SIZE integer    { CHARACTERS } ]
                            { MODULES    }
    [PROGRAM COLLATING SEQUENCE IS alphabet-name]
    [SEGMENT-LIMIT IS segment-number].]]
[SPECIAL-NAMES. [[implementor-name-1
{ IS mnemonic-name-1 [ON STATUS IS condition-name-1 [OFF STATUS IS condition-name-2]] } ]
{ IS mnemonic-name-2 [OFF STATUS IS condition-name-2 [ON STATUS IS condition-name-1]] } ] . . .
{ ON STATUS IS condition-name-1 [OFF STATUS IS condition-name-2]                      } ]
{ OFF STATUS IS condition-name-2 [ON STATUS IS condition-name-1]                      } ]
                           { STANDARD-1                                            } ]
                           { STANDARD-2                                            } ]
                           { NATIVE                                                } ]
 ALPHABET alphabet-name-1 IS { implementor-name-2                                   } ] . . .
                           {          [ { THROUGH }             ]                   } ]
                           { { literal-1 [ { THRU    } literal-2 ] } . . .           } ]
                           {          [ {ALSO literal-3} . . .  ]                   } ]
[SYMBOLIC CHARACTERS { { {symbolic-character-1} . . . { IS  } {integer-1} . . . } . . . [IN alphabet-name-2] } ] . . .
                                                      { ARE }
[CLASS class-name IS { literal-4 [ { THROUGH } literal-5 ] } . . . ] . . .
                                 [ { THRU    }           ]
[CURRENCY SIGN IS literal-6]
[DECIMAL-POINT IS COMMA].]]]
[INPUT-OUTPUT SECTION.
FILE-CONTROL.
    {file-control-entry} . . .
[I-O-CONTROL.
```

```
[[RERUN [ON {file-name-1
            implementor-name}] EVERY {integer-1 RECORDS
                                      [END OF] {REEL
                                                UNIT} OF file-name-2
                                      integer-2 CLOCK-UNITS
                                      condition-name-1}]] . . .

[[SAME [RECORD
        SORT
        SORT-MERGE] AREA FOR file-name-3 {file-name-4} . . .] . . .

[MULTIPLE FILE TAPE CONTAINS {file-name-5 [POSITION integer-3]} . . .].]]]
```

FILE-CONTROL ENTRY Formats

Sequential File

```
SELECT [OPTIONAL] file-name-1 ASSIGN TO {implementor-name-1
                                         literal-1} . . .

[RESERVE integer-1 [AREA
                    AREAS]]
[[ORGANIZATION IS] SEQUENTIAL]
[PADDING CHARACTER IS {data-name-1
                       literal-2}]

[RECORD DELIMITER IS {STANDARD-1
                      implementor-name-2}]

[ACCESS MODE IS SEQUENTIAL]
[FILE STATUS IS data-name-2].
```

Relative File

```
SELECT [OPTIONAL] file-name-1 ASSIGN TO {implementor-name-1
                                         literal-1} . . .

[RESERVE integer-1 [AREA
                    AREAS]]
[ORGANIZATION IS] RELATIVE
[ACCESS MODE IS {SEQUENTIAL [RELATIVE KEY IS data-name-1]
                 {RANDOM
                  DYNAMIC} RELATIVE KEY IS data-name-1}]
[FILE STATUS IS data-name-2].
```

Indexed File

```
SELECT [OPTIONAL] file-name-1 ASSIGN TO {implementor-name-1
                                         literal-1} . . .

[RESERVE integer-1 [AREA
                    AREAS]]
[ORGANIZATION IS] INDEXED
[ACCESS MODE IS {SEQUENTIAL
                 RANDOM
                 DYNAMIC}]
RECORD KEY IS data-name-1
[ALTERNATE RECORD KEY IS data-name-2 [WITH DUPLICATES]] . . .
[FILE STATUS IS data-name-3].
```

Report File

```
SELECT [OPTIONAL] file-name-1 ASSIGN TO {implementor-name-1} . . .
                                        {literal-1         }
[RESERVE integer-1 [AREA ]]
                   [AREAS]
[[ORGANIZATION IS] SEQUENTIAL]
[PADDING CHARACTER IS {data-name-1}]
                      {literal-1  }
[RECORD DELIMITER IS {STANDARD-1         }]
                     {implementor-name-2 }
[ACCESS MODE IS SEQUENTIAL]
[FILE STATUS IS data-name-2].
```

Sort or Merge File

```
SELECT file-name-1 ASSIGN TO {implementor-name-1} . . .
                             {literal-1         }
```

DATA DIVISION Formats

```
[DATA DIVISION.
[FILE SECTION.
    [file-description-entry {record-description entry} . . .                      ]      ]
    [sort-merge-file-description-entry {record-description-entry} . . .           ] . . . ]
    [report-file-description-entry                                                 ]      ]
[WORKING-STORAGE SECTION.
    [77-level-description-entry]
    [record-description-entry  ] . . . ]
[LINKAGE SECTION.
    [77-level-description-entry]
    [record-description-entry  ] . . . ]
[COMMUNICATION SECTION.
    [communication-description-entry {record-description-entry} . . . ]
[REPORT SECTION.
    [report-description-entry
    {report-group-description-entry} . . . ] . . . ]]
```

FILE DESCRIPTION ENTRY Formats

Sequential File

```
FD file-name-1
  [IS EXTERNAL]
  [IS GLOBAL]
  [BLOCK CONTAINS [integer-1 TO] integer-2 {RECORDS   }]
                                           {CHARACTERS}
  [        {CONTAINS integer-3 CHARACTERS                                         }]
  [RECORD  {IS VARYING IN SIZE [[FROM integer-4] [TO integer-5] CHARACTERS]       }]
  [        {     [DEPENDING ON data-name-1]                                       }]
  [        {CONTAINS integer-6 TO integer-7 CHARACTERS                            }]
  [LABEL {RECORD IS   } {STANDARD}]
  [      {RECORDS ARE } {OMITTED }]
  [VALUE OF {implementor-name-1 IS {data-name-2}} . . . ]
  [                                {literal-1  }        ]
  [DATA {RECORD IS  } {data-name-3} . . . ]
  [     {RECORDS ARE}                     ]
```

[LINAGE IS {data-name-4 / integer-8} LINES [WITH FOOTING AT {data-name-5 / integer-9}]

[LINES AT TOP {data-name-6 / integer-10}] [LINES AT BOTTOM {data-name-7 / integer-11}]]

[CODE-SET IS alphabet-name-1].

Relative File

FD file-name-1

[IS EXTERNAL]

[IS GLOBAL]

[BLOCK CONTAINS [integer-1 TO] integer-2 {RECORDS / CHARACTERS}]

[RECORD {CONTAINS integer-3 CHARACTERS
IS VARYING IN SIZE [[FROM integer-4] [TO integer-5] CHARACTERS]
[DEPENDING ON data-name-1]
CONTAINS integer-6 TO integer-7 CHARACTERS}]

[LABEL {RECORD IS / RECORDS ARE} {STANDARD / OMITTED}]

[VALUE OF {implementor-name-1 IS {data-name-2 / literal-1}} . . .]

[DATA {RECORD IS / RECORDS ARE} {data-name-3} . . .].

Indexed File

FD file-name-1

[IS EXTERNAL]

[IS GLOBAL]

[BLOCK CONTAINS [integer-1 TO] integer-2 {RECORDS / CHARACTERS}]

[RECORD {CONTAINS integer-3 CHARACTERS
IS VARYING IN SIZE [[FROM integer-4] [TO integer-5] CHARACTERS]
[DEPENDING ON data-name-1]
CONTAINS integer-6 TO integer-7 CHARACTERS}]

[LABEL {RECORD IS / RECORDS ARE} {STANDARD / OMITTED}]

[VALUE OF {implementor-name-1 IS {data-name-2 / literal-1}} . . .]

[DATA {RECORD IS / RECORDS ARE} {data-name-3} . . .].

Report File

FD file-name-1

[IS EXTERNAL]

[IS GLOBAL]

[BLOCK CONTAINS [integer-1 TO] integer-2 {RECORDS / CHARACTERS}]

[RECORD {CONTAINS integer-3 CHARACTERS / CONTAINS integer-4 TO integer-5 CHARACTERS}]

[LABEL {RECORD IS / RECORDS ARE} {STANDARD / OMITTED}]

[VALUE OF {implementor-name-1 IS {data-name-2 / literal-1}} . . .]

[CODE-SET IS alphabet-name-1]

{REPORT IS / REPORTS ARE} {report-name-1} . . . .

Sort-Merge File

SD file-name-1

[RECORD {CONTAINS integer-1 CHARACTERS / IS VARYING IN SIZE [[FROM integer-2] [TO integer-3 CHARACTERS] [DEPENDING ON data-name-1] / CONTAINS integer-4 TO integer-5 CHARACTERS}]

[DATA {RECORD IS / RECORDS ARE} {data-name-2} . . .] .

■ DATA DESCRIPTION ENTRY Formats

Format 1

level-number [data-name-1 / FILLER]

[REDEFINES data-name-2]

[IS EXTERNAL]

[IS GLOBAL]

[{PICTURE / PIC} IS character-string]

[[USAGE IS] {INDEX / DISPLAY / COMPUTATIONAL / COMP / BINARY / PACKED-DECIMAL}]

[[SIGN IS] {LEADING / TRAILING} [SEPARATE CHARACTER]]

[OCCURS {integer-1 TO integer-2 TIMES DEPENDING ON data-name-4 / integer-2 TIMES}

[{ASCENDING / DESCENDING} KEY IS {data-name-3} . . .] . . .

[INDEXED BY {index-name-1} . . .]]

[{SYNCHRONIZED / SYNC} [LEFT / RIGHT]]

[{JUSTIFIED / JUST} RIGHT]

[BLANK WHEN ZERO]

[VALUE IS literal-1].

Format 2

66 data-name-1 RENAMES data-name-2 [{THROUGH / THRU} data-name-3].

Format 3

88 condition-name-1 {VALUE IS / VALUES ARE} {literal-1 [{THROUGH / THRU} literal-2]} . . . .

COMMUNICATION DESCRIPTION ENTRY Formats

Format 1

```
CD cd-name-1
                      ┌ [[SYMBOLIC QUEUE IS data-name-1]                                        ┐
                      │       [SYMBOLIC SUB-QUEUE-1 IS data-name-2]                             │
                      │       [SYMBOLIC SUB-QUEUE-2 IS data-name-3]                             │
                      │       [SYMBOLIC SUB-QUEUE-3 IS data-name-4]                             │
                      │       [MESSAGE DATE IS data-name-5]                                     │
                      │       [MESSAGE TIME IS data-name-6]                                     │
FOR [INITIAL] INPUT   │       [SYMBOLIC SOURCE IS data-name-7]                                  │
                      │       [TEXT LENGTH IS data-name-8]                                      │
                      │       [END KEY IS data-name-9]                                          │
                      │       [STATUS KEY IS data-name-10]                                      │
                      │       [MESSAGE COUNT IS data-name-11]]                                  │
                      │ [data-name-1, data-name-2, data-name-3, data-name-4, data-name-5, data-name-6, │
                      └       data-name-7, data-name-8, data-name-9, data-name-10, data-name-11] ┘
```

Format 2

```
CD cd-name-1 FOR OUTPUT
      [DESTINATION COUNT IS data-name-1]
      [TEXT LENGTH IS data-name-2]
      [STATUS KEY IS data-name-3]
      [DESTINATION TABLE OCCURS integer-1 TIMES [INDEXED BY {index-name-1} . . . ]]
      [ERROR KEY IS data-name-4]
      [SYMBOLIC DESTINATION IS data-name-5].
```

Format 3

```
CD cd-name-1
                      ┌ [[MESSAGE DATE IS data-name-1]                                          ┐
                      │       [MESSAGE TIME IS data-name-2]                                     │
                      │       [SYMBOLIC TERMINAL IS data-name-3]                                │
FOR [INITIAL] I-O     │       [TEXT LENGTH IS data-name-4]                                      │
                      │       [END KEY IS data-name-5]                                          │
                      │       [STATUS KEY IS data-name-6]]                                      │
                      └ [data-name-1, data-name-2, data-name-3, data-name-4, data-name-5, data-name-6] ┘
```

REPORT DESCRIPTION ENTRY Format

```
RD report-name-1
  [IS GLOBAL]
  [CODE literal-1]
  [{CONTROL IS   } {{data-name-1} . . .          }]
  [{CONTROLS ARE } {FINAL [data-name-1] . . .    }]
  [PAGE [LIMIT IS  ] integer-1 [LINE ] [HEADING integer-2]
  [     [LIMITS ARE]           [LINES]
        [FIRST DETAIL integer-3] [LAST DETAIL integer-4]
        [FOOTING integer-5]].
```

REPORT GROUP DESCRIPTION ENTRY Formats

Format 1

```
01  [data-name-1]
            ⎧ ⎧REPORT HEADING⎫                                  ⎫
            ⎪ ⎩RH            ⎭                                  ⎪
            ⎪ ⎧PAGE HEADING⎫                                    ⎪
            ⎪ ⎩PH          ⎭                                    ⎪
            ⎪ ⎧CONTROL HEADING⎫ ⎧data-name-2⎫                   ⎪
            ⎪ ⎩CH             ⎭ ⎩FINAL      ⎭                   ⎪
    TYPE IS ⎨ ⎧DETAIL⎫                                          ⎬
            ⎪ ⎩DE    ⎭                                          ⎪
            ⎪ ⎧CONTROL FOOTING⎫ ⎧data-name-3⎫                   ⎪
            ⎪ ⎩CF             ⎭ ⎩FINAL      ⎭                   ⎪
            ⎪ ⎧PAGE FOOTING⎫                                    ⎪
            ⎪ ⎩PF          ⎭                                    ⎪
            ⎪ ⎧REPORT FOOTING⎫                                  ⎪
            ⎩ ⎩RF            ⎭                                  ⎭
    [LINE NUMBER IS {integer-1 [ON NEXT PAGE]}]
                    {PLUS integer-2          }
    [                 ⎧integer-3     ⎫ ]
    [ NEXT GROUP IS   ⎨PLUS integer-4⎬ ]
    [                 ⎩NEXT PAGE     ⎭ ]
    [[USAGE IS] DISPLAY].
```

Format 2

```
level-number [data-name-1]
    [LINE NUMBER IS {integer-1 [ON NEXT PAGE]}]
                    {PLUS integer-2          }
    [[USAGE IS] DISPLAY].
```

Format 3

```
level-number [data-name-1]
  {PICTURE} IS character-string
  {PIC    }
  [[USAGE IS] DISPLAY]
  [[SIGN IS] {LEADING } SEPARATE CHARACTER]
             {TRAILING}
  [{JUSTIFIED} RIGHT]
  [{JUST     }      ]
  [BLANK WHEN ZERO]
  [LINE NUMBER IS {integer-1 [ON NEXT PAGE]}]
                  {PLUS integer-2          }
  [COLUMN NUMBER IS integer-3]
  ⎧ SOURCE IS identifier-1                                       ⎫
  ⎪ VALUE IS literal-1                                           ⎪
  ⎨ {SUM {identifier-2} . . . [UPON {data-name-2} . . . ]} . . . ⎬
  ⎪                                                              ⎪
  ⎩       [RESET ON {data-name-3}]                               ⎭
                    {FINAL      }
  [GROUP INDICATE].
```

PROCEDURE DIVISION Formats

Format 1

[PROCEDURE DIVISION [USING {data-name-1} . . .] .
[DECLARATIVES.
{section-name SECTION [segment-number].
USE statement.
[paragraph-name.
[sentence] . . .] . . . } . . .
END DECLARATIVES.]
{section-name SECTION [segment-number].
[paragraph-name.
[sentence] . . .] . . . } . . .]

Format 2

[PROCEDURE DIVISION [USING {data-name-1} . . .].
{paragraph-name.
[sentence] . . . } . . .]

Formats for COBOL Verbs

ACCEPT identifier-1 [FROM mnemonic-name-1]

ACCEPT identifier-2 FROM { DATE | DAY | DAY-OF-WEEK | TIME }

ACCEPT cd-name-1 MESSAGE COUNT

ADD { identifier-1 | literal-1 } . . . TO {identifier-2 [ROUNDED]} . . .
[ON SIZE ERROR imperative-statement-1]
[NOT ON SIZE ERROR imperative-statement-2]
[END-ADD]

ADD { identifier-1 | literal-1 } . . . TO { identifier-2 | literal-2 } GIVING {identifier-3 [ROUNDED]} . . .
[ON SIZE ERROR imperative-statement-1]
[NOT ON SIZE ERROR imperative-statement-2]
[END-ADD]

ADD { CORRESPONDING | CORR } identifier-1 TO identifier-2 [ROUNDED]
[ON SIZE ERROR imperative-statement-1]
[NOT ON SIZE ERROR imperative-statement-2]
[END-ADD]

ALTER {procedure-name-1 TO [PROCEED TO] procedure-name-2} . . .

CALL { identifier-1 | literal-1 } [USING { [BY REFERENCE] {identifier-2} . . . | BY CONTENT {identifier-2} . . . } . . .]
[ON OVERFLOW imperative-statement-1] [END-CALL]

CALL { identifier-1 | literal-1 } [USING { [BY REFERENCE] {identifier-2} . . . | BY CONTENT {identifier-2} . . . } . . .]
[ON EXCEPTION imperative-statement-1]
[NOT ON EXCEPTION imperative-statement-2]
[END-CALL]

CANCEL {identifier-1 | literal-1} . . .

CLOSE {file-name-1 [{REEL | UNIT} [FOR REMOVAL] | WITH {NO REWIND | LOCK}]} . . .

CLOSE {file-name-1 [WITH LOCK]} . . .

COMPUTE {identifier-1 [ROUNDED]} . . . = arithmetic-expression-1
[ON SIZE ERROR imperative-statement-1]
[NOT ON SIZE ERROR imperative-statement-2]
[END-COMPUTE]

CONTINUE

DELETE file-name-1 RECORD
[INVALID KEY imperative-statement-1]
[NOT INVALID KEY imperative-statement-2]
[END-DELETE]

DISABLE {INPUT [TERMINAL] | I-O TERMINAL | OUTPUT} cd-name-1 [WITH KEY {identifier-1 | literal-1}]

DISPLAY {identifier-1 | literal-1} . . . [UPON mnemonic-name-1] [WITH NO ADVANCING]

DIVIDE {identifier-1 | literal-1} INTO {identifier-2 [ROUNDED]} . . .
[ON SIZE ERROR imperative-statement-1]
[NOT ON SIZE ERROR imperative-statement-2]
[END-DIVIDE]

DIVIDE {identifier-1 | literal-1} {INTO | BY} {identifier-2 | literal-2} GIVING {identifier-3 [ROUNDED]} . . .
[ON SIZE ERROR imperative-statement-1]
[NOT ON SIZE ERROR imperative-statement-2]
[END-DIVIDE]

DIVIDE {identifier-1 | literal-1} {INTO | BY} {identifier-2 | literal-2} GIVING identifier-3 [ROUNDED]
REMAINDER identifier-4
[ON SIZE ERROR imperative-statement-1]
[NOT ON SIZE ERROR imperative-statement-2]
[END-DIVIDE]

ENABLE {INPUT [TERMINAL] | I-O TERMINAL | OUTPUT} cd-name-1 [WITH KEY {identifier-1 | literal-1}]

ENTER language-name-1 [routine-name-1]

EVALUATE {identifier-1 | literal-1 | expression-1 | TRUE | FALSE} [ALSO {identifier-2 | literal-2 | expression-2 | TRUE | FALSE}] . . .

```
{ { WHEN
      { ANY
        condition-1
        TRUE
        FALSE
        [NOT] { { identifier-3 | literal-3 | arithmetic-expression-1 } [ { THROUGH | THRU } { identifier-4 | literal-4 | arithmetic-expression-2 } ] } }
    [ ALSO
      { ANY
        condition-2
        TRUE
        FALSE
        [NOT] { { identifier-5 | literal-5 | arithmetic-expression-3 } [ { THROUGH | THRU } { identifier-6 | literal-6 | arithmetic-expression-4 } ] } } ] . . . } . . .
  imperative-statement-1} . . .
  [WHEN OTHER imperative-statement-2]
  [END-EVALUATE]

EXIT

EXIT PROGRAM

GENERATE { data-name-1 | report-name-1 }

GO TO [procedure-name-1]

GO TO {procedure-name-1} . . . DEPENDING ON identifier-1

IF condition-1 THEN { {statement-1} . . . | NEXT SENTENCE } [ { ELSE {statement-2} . . . [END-IF] | ELSE NEXT SENTENCE | END-IF } ]

INITIALIZE {identifier-1} . . .
[ REPLACING { { ALPHABETIC | ALPHANUMERIC | NUMERIC | ALPHANUMERIC-EDITED | NUMERIC-EDITED } DATA BY { identifier-2 | literal-1 } } . . . ]

INITIATE {report-name-1} . . .

INSPECT identifier-1 TALLYING
{ identifier-2 FOR { CHARACTERS [ { BEFORE | AFTER } INITIAL { identifier-4 | literal-2 } ] . . .
                     { ALL | LEADING } { { identifier-3 | literal-1 } [ { BEFORE | AFTER } INITIAL { identifier-4 | literal-2 } ] . . . } . . . } . . . } . . .

INSPECT identifier-1 REPLACING
{ CHARACTERS BY { identifier-5 | literal-3 } [ { BEFORE | AFTER } INITIAL { identifier-4 | literal-2 } ] . . .
  { ALL | LEADING | FIRST } { { identifier-3 | literal-1 } BY { identifier-5 | literal-3 } [ { BEFORE | AFTER } INITIAL { identifier-4 | literal-2 } ] . . . } . . . } . . .

INSPECT identifier-1 TALLYING
{ identifier-2 FOR { CHARACTERS [ { BEFORE | AFTER } INITIAL { identifier-4 | literal-2 } ] . . .
                     { ALL | LEADING } { { identifier-3 | literal-1 } [ { BEFORE | AFTER } INITIAL { identifier-4 | literal-2 } ] . . . } . . . } . . . } . . .
```

```
REPLACING
   { CHARACTERS BY {identifier-5} [ {BEFORE} INITIAL {identifier-4} ] . . .
                   {literal-3   }   {AFTER }         {literal-2   }
   { {ALL    } { {identifier-3} BY {identifier-5} [ {BEFORE} INITIAL {identifier-4} ] . . . } . . . } . . .
   { {LEADING} { {literal-1   }    {literal-3   }   {AFTER }         {literal-2   }           }       }
   { {FIRST  }

INSPECT identifier-1 CONVERTING {identifier-6} TO {identifier-7}
                                {literal-4   }    {literal-5   }
   [ {BEFORE} INITIAL {identifier-4} ] . . .
     {AFTER }         {literal-2   }

MERGE file-name-1 {ON {ASCENDING } KEY {data-name-1} . . . } . . .
                      {DESCENDING}
   [COLLATING SEQUENCE IS alphabet-name-1]
   USING file-name-2 {file-name-3} . . .
   { OUTPUT PROCEDURE IS procedure-name-1 [ {THROUGH} procedure-name-2 ] }
   {                                        {THRU   }                    }
   { GIVING {file-name-4} . . .                                          }

MOVE {identifier-1} TO {identifier-2} . . .
     {literal-1   }

MOVE {CORRESPONDING} identifier-1 TO identifier-2
     {CORR         }

MULTIPLY {identifier-1} BY {identifier-2 [ROUNDED]} . . .
         {literal-1   }
   [ON SIZE ERROR imperative-statement-1]
   [NOT ON SIZE ERROR imperative-statement-2]
   [END-MULTIPLY]

MULTIPLY {identifier-1} BY {identifier-2} GIVING {identifier-3 [ROUNDED]} . . .
         {literal-1   }    {literal-2   }
   [ON SIZE ERROR imperative-statement-1]
   [NOT ON SIZE ERROR imperative-statement-2]
   [END-MULTIPLY]

       { INPUT {file-name-1 [REVERSED         ]} . . . }
       {                    [WITH NO REWIND   ]         }
OPEN   { OUTPUT {file-name-2 [WITH NO REWIND]} . . .    } . . .
       { I-O {file-name-3} . . .                        }
       { EXTEND {file-name-4} . . .                     }

OPEN {OUTPUT {file-name-1 [WITH NO REWIND]} . . .} . . .
     {EXTEND {file-name-2} . . .                 }

PERFORM [ procedure-name-1 [ {THROUGH} procedure-name-2 ] ]
                             {THRU   }
   [imperative-statement-1 END-PERFORM]

PERFORM [ procedure-name-1 [ {THROUGH} procedure-name-2 ] ]
                             {THRU   }
   {identifier-1} TIMES [imperative-statement-1 END-PERFORM]
   {integer-1   }

PERFORM [ procedure-name-1 [ {THROUGH} procedure-name-2 ] ]
                             {THRU   }
   [ WITH TEST {BEFORE} ] UNTIL condition-1
               {AFTER }
   [imperative-statement-1 END-PERFORM]
```

```
PERFORM [procedure-name-1 [{THROUGH} procedure-name-2]]
                           {THRU   }
    [WITH TEST {BEFORE}]
               {AFTER }

    VARYING {identifier-2 } FROM {identifier-3 } BY {identifier-4} UNTIL condition-1
            {index-name-1 }      {index-name-2 }    {literal-2   }
                                 {literal-1    }

    [AFTER {identifier-5 } FROM {identifier-6 } BY {identifier-7} UNTIL condition-2] . . .
           {index-name-3 }      {index-name-4 }    {literal-4   }
                                {literal-3    }

    [imperative-statement-1 END-PERFORM]

PURGE cd-name-1

READ file-name-1 [NEXT] RECORD [INTO identifier-1]
    [AT END imperative-statement-1]
    [NOT AT END imperative-statement-2]
    [END-READ]

READ file-name-1 RECORD [INTO identifier-1]
    [INVALID KEY imperative-statement-3]
    [NOT INVALID KEY imperative-statement-4]
    [END-READ]

READ file-name-1 RECORD [INTO identifier-1]
    [KEY IS data-name-1]
    [INVALID KEY imperative-statement-3]
    [NOT INVALID KEY imperative-statement-4]
    [END-READ]

RECEIVE cd-name-1 {MESSAGE} INTO identifier-1
                  {SEGMENT}
    [NO DATA imperative-statement-1]
    [WITH DATA imperative-statement-2]
    [END-RECEIVE]

RELEASE record-name-1 [FROM identifier-1]

RETURN file-name-1 RECORD [INTO identifier-1]
    AT END imperative-statement-1
    [NOT AT END imperative-statement-2]
    [END-RETURN]

REWRITE record-name-1 [FROM identifier-1]

REWRITE record-name-1 [FROM identifier-1]
    [INVALID KEY imperative-statement-1]
    [NOT INVALID KEY imperative-statement-2]
    [END-REWRITE]

SEARCH identifier-1 [VARYING {identifier-2 }]
                             {index-name-1 }

    [AT END imperative-statement-1]
    {WHEN condition-1 {imperative-statement-2}} . . .
                      {NEXT SENTENCE         }
    [END-SEARCH]

SEARCH ALL identifier-1 [AT END imperative-statement-1]

    WHEN {data-name-1 {IS EQUAL TO} {identifier-3           }}
         {            {IS =       } {literal-1              }}
         {                          {arithmetic-expression-1}}
         {condition-name-1                                   }

    [AND {data-name-2 {IS EQUAL TO} {identifier-4           }}] . . .
    [    {            {IS =       } {literal-2              }}]
    [    {                          {arithmetic-expression-2}}]
    [    {condition-name-2                                   }]

    {imperative-statement-2}
    {NEXT SENTENCE         }
```

```
[END-SEARCH]
SEND cd-name-1 FROM identifier-1
                                    { WITH identifier-2 }
SEND cd-name-1 [FROM identifier-1]  { WITH ESI          }
                                    { WITH EMI          }
                                    { WITH EGI          }

    [                      { {identifier-3} [LINE ] } ]
    [ {BEFORE} ADVANCING   { {integer-1   } [LINES] } ]
    [ {AFTER }             { {mnemonic-name-1}      } ]
    [                      { {PAGE           }      } ]
    [REPLACING LINE]

                                  {index-name-2}
SET {index-name-1} . . . TO       {identifier-2}
    {identifier-1}                {integer-1   }

SET {index-name-3} . . . {UP BY  } {identifier-2}
                         {DOWN BY} {integer-2   }

SET { {mnemonic-name-1} . . . TO {ON } } . . .
                                 {OFF}

SET {condition-name-1} . . . TO TRUE

SORT file-name-1 { ON {ASCENDING } KEY {data-name-1} . . . } . . .
                      {DESCENDING}
    [WITH DUPLICATES IN ORDER]
    [COLLATING SEQUENCE IS alphabet-name-1]
    { INPUT PROCEDURE IS procedure-name-1 [ {THROUGH} procedure-name-2 ] }
    {                                       {THRU   }                    }
    { USING {file-name-2} . . .                                          }
    { OUTPUT PROCEDURE IS procedure-name-3 [ {THROUGH} procedure-name-4 ] }
    {                                        {THRU   }                    }
    { GIVING {file-name-3} . . .                                          }

                       [          { EQUAL TO                    }             ]
                       [          { =                           }             ]
                       [          { GREATER THAN                }             ]
START file-name-1      [ KEY IS   { >                           } data-name-1 ]
                       [          { NOT LESS THAN               }             ]
                       [          { NOT <                       }             ]
                       [          { GREATER THAN OR EQUAL TO    }             ]
                       [          { >=                          }             ]
    [INVALID KEY imperative-statement-1]
    [NOT INVALID KEY imperative-statement-2]
    [END-START]

STOP {RUN      }
     {literal-1}

                                                 {identifier-2}
STRING { {identifier-1} . . . DELIMITED BY       {literal-2   } } . . . INTO identifier-3
       { {literal-1   }                          {SIZE        } }
    [WITH POINTER identifier-4]
    [ON OVERFLOW imperative-statement-1]
    [NOT ON OVERFLOW imperative-statement-2]
    [END-STRING]

SUBTRACT {identifier-1} . . . FROM {identifier-3 [ROUNDED]} . . .
         {literal-1   }

    [ON SIZE ERROR imperative-statement-1]
    [NOT ON SIZE ERROR imperative-statement-2]
    [END-SUBTRACT]
```

```
SUBTRACT {identifier-1} . . . FROM {identifier-2} GIVING {identifier-3 [ROUNDED]} . . .
         {literal-1   }             {literal-2   }

    [ON SIZE ERROR imperative-statement-1]
    [NOT ON SIZE ERROR imperative-statement-2]
    [END-SUBTRACT]

SUBTRACT {CORRESPONDING} identifier-1 FROM identifier-2 [ROUNDED]
         {CORR         }

    [ON SIZE ERROR imperative-statement-1]
    [NOT ON SIZE ERROR imperative-statement-2]
    [END-SUBTRACT]

SUPPRESS PRINTING

TERMINATE {report-name-1} . . .

UNSTRING identifier-1 [DELIMITED BY [ALL] {identifier-2} [OR [ALL] {identifier-3}] . . . ]
                                          {literal-1   }           {literal-2   }

    INTO {identifier-4 [DELIMITER IN identifier-5] [COUNT IN identifier-6]} . . .
    [WITH POINTER identifier-7]
    [TALLYING IN identifier-8]
    [ON OVERFLOW imperative-statement-1]
    [NOT ON OVERFLOW imperative-statement-2]
    [END-UNSTRING]

                                                               {{file-name-1} . . .}
                                                               {INPUT              }
USE [GLOBAL] AFTER STANDARD {EXCEPTION} PROCEDURE ON {OUTPUT             }
                            {ERROR    }                        {I-O                }
                                                               {EXTEND             }

                                                    {{file-name-3} . . .}
USE AFTER STANDARD {EXCEPTION} PROCEDURE ON {OUTPUT             }
                   {ERROR    }                      {EXTEND             }

USE [GLOBAL] BEFORE REPORTING identifier-1

                      {cd-name-1                            }
                      {[ALL REFERENCES OF] identifier-1     }
USE FOR DEBUGGING ON  {file-name-1                          } . . .
                      {procedure-name-1                     }
                      {ALL PROCEDURES                       }

WRITE record-name-1 [FROM identifier-1]

    [                      {{identifier-2} [LINE ]}]
    [{BEFORE}              {{integer-1   } [LINES]}]
    [{AFTER } ADVANCING    {                      }]
    [                      {{mnemonic-name-1}     }]
    [                      {{PAGE           }     }]

    [AT {END-OF-PAGE} imperative-statement-1]
    [   {EOP        }                       ]

    [NOT AT {END-OF-PAGE} imperative-statement-2]
    [       {EOP        }                       ]

    [END-WRITE]

WRITE record-name-1 [FROM identifier-1]
    [INVALID KEY imperative-statement-1]
    [NOT INVALID KEY imperative-statement-2]
    [END-WRITE]
```

■ COPY and REPLACE Statement Formats

COPY text-name-1 [{ OF / IN } library-name-1]

[REPLACING { { ==pseudo-text-1== / identifier-1 / literal-1 / word-1 } BY { ==pseudo-text-2== / identifier-2 / literal-2 / word-2 } } . . .]

REPLACE {==pseudo-text-1== BY ==pseudo-text-2==} . . .

REPLACE OFF

■ Condition Formats

Relation Condition

{ identifier-1 / literal-1 / arithmetic-expression-1 / index-name-1 }

{
IS [NOT] GREATER THAN
IS [NOT] >
IS [NOT] LESS THAN
IS [NOT] <
IS [NOT] EQUAL TO
IS [NOT] =
IS GREATER THAN OR EQUAL TO
IS >=
IS LESS THAN OR EQUAL TO
IS <=
}

{ identifier-2 / literal-2 / arithmetic-expression-2 / index-name-2 }

Class Condition

identifier IS [NOT] { NUMERIC / ALPHABETIC / ALPHABETIC-LOWER / ALPHABETIC-UPPER / class-name }

Sign Condition

arithmetic-expression IS [NOT] { POSITIVE / NEGATIVE / ZERO }

Condition-name Condition

condition-name-1

Negated Condition

NOT condition-1

Switch-status Condition

condition-name-1

Combined Condition

condition-1 { { AND / OR } condition-2 } . . .

Abbreviated Combined Relation Condition

```
                     { {AND}                                   }
relation-condition   { {OR }  [NOT] [relational-operator] object } . . .
```

Qualification Formats

Format 1

```
                     ( { {IN} data-name-2 } . . . [ {IN} {file-name} ] )
{data-name-1    }    ( { {OF}             }       [ {OF} {cd-name  } ] )
{condition-name }    (                                                   )
                     (   {IN} {file-name}                                )
                     (   {OF} {cd-name  }                                )
```

Format 2

```
paragraph-name {IN} section-name
               {OF}
```

Format 3

```
text-name {IN} library-name
          {OF}
```

Format 4

```
LINAGE-COUNTER {IN} report-name
               {OF}
```

Format 5

```
{PAGE-COUNTER} {IN} report-name
{LINE-COUNTER} {OF}
```

Format 6

```
              ( {IN} data-name-4 [ {IN} report-name ] )
data-name-3   ( {OF}             [ {OF}             ] )
              (                                       )
              ( {IN} report-name                      )
              ( {OF}                                  )
```

Miscellaneous Formats

Subscripting

```
                     ( {integer-1                          }       )
{condition-name-1}   ( {data-name-2 [{±} integer-2]        } . . . )
{data-name-1     }   ( {index-name-1 [{±} integer-3]       }       )
```

Reference Modification

data-name-1 (leftmost-character-position: [length])

Identifier

data-name-1 [{IN / OF} data-name-2] . . . [{IN / OF} {cd-name / file-name / report-name}]

[({subscript} . . .)] [(leftmost-character-position: [length])]

General Format for Nested Source Programs

IDENTIFICATION DIVISION.
PROGRAM-ID. program-name-1 [IS INITIAL PROGRAM].
[ENVIRONMENT DIVISION. environment-division-content]
[DATA DIVISION. data-division-content]
[PROCEDURE DIVISION. procedure-division-content]
[[nested-source-program] . . .
END PROGRAM program-name-1.]

General Format for Nested-Source-Program

IDENTIFICATION DIVISION.

PROGRAM-ID. program-name-2 [IS {|COMMON / INITIAL|} PROGRAM].

[ENVIRONMENT DIVISION. environment-division-content]
[DATA DIVISION. data-division-content]
[PROCEDURE DIVISION. procedure-division-content]
[nested-source-program] . . .
END PROGRAM program-name-2.

General Format for Multiple Source Programs

{IDENTIFICATION DIVISION.
PROGRAM-ID. program-name-3 [IS INITIAL PROGRAM].
[ENVIRONMENT DIVISION. environment-division-content]
[DATA DIVISION. data-division-content]
[PROCEDURE DIVISION. procedure-division-content]
[nested-source-program] . . .
END PROGRAM program-name-3} . . .
IDENTIFICATION DIVISION.
PROGRAM-ID. program-name-4 [IS INITIAL PROGRAM].
[ENVIRONMENT DIVISION. environment-division-content]
[DATA DIVISION. data-division-content]
[PROCEDURE DIVISION. procedure-division-content]
[[nested-source-program] . . .
END PROGRAM program-name-4.]

Appendix B

Collating Sequences

ASCII (American Standard Code for Information Interchange)

7-bit Code	Decimal Code	Hexadecimal Code	Symbol	Meaning
0000000	000	00	NUL	Null
0000001	001	01	SOH	Start of Heading
0000010	002	02	STX	Start of Text
0000011	003	03	ETX	End of Text
0000100	004	04	EOT	End of Transmission
0000101	005	05	ENQ	Enquiry
0000110	006	06	ACK	Acknowledge
0000111	007	07	BEL	Bell
0001000	008	08	BS	Backspace
0001001	009	09	HT	Horizontal Tabulation
0001010	010	0A	LF	Line Feed
0001011	011	0B	VT	Vertical Tabulation
0001100	012	0C	FF	Form Feed
0001101	013	0D	CR	Carriage Return
0001110	014	0E	SO	Shift Out
0001111	015	0F	SI	Shift In
0010000	016	10	DLE	Data Link Escape
0010001	017	11	DC1	Device Control 1
0010010	018	12	DC2	Device Control 2
0010011	019	13	DC3	Device Control 3
0010100	020	14	DC4	Device Control 4
0010101	021	15	NAK	Negative Acknowledge
0010110	022	16	SYN	Synchronous Idle
0010111	023	17	ETB	End of Transmission Block
0011000	024	18	CAN	Cancel
0011001	025	19	EM	End of Medium
0011010	026	1A	SUB	Substitute
0011011	027	1B	ESC	Escape
0011100	028	1C	FS	File Separator
0011101	029	1D	GS	Group Separator
0011110	030	1E	RS	Record Separator
0011111	031	1F	US	Unit Separator
0100000	032	20	SP	Space (Nonprinting)
0100001	033	21	!	Exclamation Point
0100010	034	22	"	Quotation Mark
0100011	035	23	#	Number Sign
0100100	036	24	$	Dollar Sign
0100101	037	25	%	Percent Sign
0100110	038	26	&	Ampersand
0100111	039	27	'	Apostrophe (Closing Single Quotation Mark)
0101000	040	28	(	Opening Parenthesis
0101001	041	29	)	Closing Parenthesis
0101010	042	2A	*	Asterisk
0101011	043	2B	+	Plus Sign
0101100	044	2C	,	Comma

7-bit Code	Decimal Code	Hexadecimal Code	Symbol	Meaning
0101101	045	2D	-	Hyphen (Minus Sign)
0101110	046	2E	.	Period (Decimal Point)
0101111	047	2F	/	Slant (Forward Slash)
0110000	048	30	0	Digit 0
0110001	049	31	1	Digit 1
0110010	050	32	2	Digit 2
0110011	051	33	3	Digit 3
0110100	052	34	4	Digit 4
0110101	053	35	5	Digit 5
0110110	054	36	6	Digit 6
0110111	055	37	7	Digit 7
0111000	056	38	8	Digit 8
0111001	057	39	9	Digit 9
0111010	058	3A	:	Colon
0111011	059	3B	;	Semicolon
0111100	060	3C	<	Less Than
0111101	061	3D	=	Equals
0111110	062	3E	>	Greater Than
0111111	063	3F	?	Question Mark
1000000	064	40	@	Commercial At
1000001	065	41	A	Uppercase Latin Letter A
1000010	066	42	B	Uppercase Latin Letter B
1000011	067	43	C	Uppercase Latin Letter C
1000100	068	44	D	Uppercase Latin Letter D
1000101	069	45	E	Uppercase Latin Letter E
1000110	070	46	F	Uppercase Latin Letter F
1000111	071	47	G	Uppercase Latin Letter G
1001000	072	48	H	Uppercase Latin Letter H
1001001	073	49	I	Uppercase Latin Letter I
1001010	074	4A	J	Uppercase Latin Letter J
1001011	075	4B	K	Uppercase Latin Letter K
1001100	076	4C	L	Uppercase Latin Letter L
1001101	077	4D	M	Uppercase Latin Letter M
1001110	078	4E	N	Uppercase Latin Letter N
1001111	079	4F	O	Uppercase Latin Letter O
1010000	080	50	P	Uppercase Latin Letter P
1010001	081	51	Q	Uppercase Latin Letter Q
1010010	082	52	R	Uppercase Latin Letter R
1010011	083	53	S	Uppercase Latin Letter S
1010100	084	54	T	Uppercase Latin Letter T
1010101	085	55	U	Uppercase Latin Letter U
1010110	086	56	V	Uppercase Latin Letter V
1010111	087	57	W	Uppercase Latin Letter W
1011000	088	58	X	Uppercase Latin Letter X
1011001	089	59	Y	Uppercase Latin Letter Y
1011010	090	5A	Z	Uppercase Latin Letter Z
1011011	091	5B	[	Opening Bracket
1011100	092	5C	\	Reverse Slant (Back Slash)
1011101	093	5D	]	Closing Bracket
1011110	094	5E	^	Circumflex
1011111	095	5F	_	Underline
1100000	096	60	'	Opening Single Quotation Mark
1100001	097	61	a	Lowercase Latin Letter a
1100010	098	62	b	Lowercase Latin Letter b
1100011	099	63	c	Lowercase Latin Letter c
1100100	100	64	d	Lowercase Latin Letter d
1100101	101	65	e	Lowercase Latin Letter e
1100110	102	66	f	Lowercase Latin Letter f
1100111	103	67	g	Lowercase Latin Letter g
1101000	104	68	h	Lowercase Latin Letter h

7-bit Code	Decimal Code	Hexadecimal Code	Symbol	Meaning
1101001	105	69	i	Lowercase Latin Letter i
1101010	106	6A	j	Lowercase Latin Letter j
1101011	107	6B	k	Lowercase Latin Letter k
1101100	108	6C	l	Lowercase Latin Letter l
1101101	109	6D	m	Lowercase Latin Letter m
1101110	110	6E	n	Lowercase Latin Letter n
1101111	111	6F	o	Lowercase Latin Letter o
1110000	112	70	p	Lowercase Latin Letter p
1110001	113	71	q	Lowercase Latin Letter q
1110010	114	72	r	Lowercase Latin Letter r
1110011	115	73	s	Lowercase Latin Letter s
1110100	116	74	t	Lowercase Latin Letter t
1110101	117	75	u	Lowercase Latin Letter u
1110110	118	76	v	Lowercase Latin Letter v
1110111	119	77	w	Lowercase Latin Letter w
1111000	120	78	x	Lowercase Latin Letter x
1111001	121	79	y	Lowercase Latin Letter y
1111010	122	7A	z	Lowercase Latin Letter z
1111011	123	7B	{	Opening Brace
1111100	124	7C	|	Vertical Line
1111101	125	7D	}	Closing Brace
1111110	126	7E	~	Tilde
1111111	127	7F	DEL	Delete

EBCDIC (Extended Binary Coded Decimal Interchange Code)*

Left Digit(s)	Right Digit 0	1	2	3	4	5	6	7	8	9
6										
7					¢	.	<	(	+	|
8	&									
9	!	$	*	)	;		-	/		
10							¦	,	%	—
11	>	?								
12		`	:	#	@	'	=	"		a
13	b	c	d	e	f	g	h	i		
14						j	k	l	m	n
15	o	p	q	r						
16		~	s	t	u	v	w	x	y	z
17				[						]
18										
19			{	A	B	C	D	E	F	G
20	H	I							}	J
21	K	L	M	N	O	P	Q	R		
22							S	T	U	V
23	W	X	Y	Z	\					
24	0	1	2	3	4	5	6	7	8	9

Codes 00 to 63 and 250 to 255 represent nonprintable control characters. Code 64 is the blank.

*This table shows decimal codes only, and only printable characters are listed.

CDC Scientific, with 64 Characters*

Left Digit(s)	Right Digit 0	1	2	3	4	5	6	7	8	9
0	:	A	B	C	D	E	F	G	H	I
1	J	K	L	M	N	O	P	Q	R	S
2	T	U	V	W	X	Y	Z	0	1	2
3	3	4	5	6	7	8	9	+	−	*
4	/	(	)	$	=		,	.	≡	[
5	]	%	≠	→	∨	∧	↑	↓	<	>
6	≤	≥		;						

*This table shows decimal codes only.

Appendix C

Data Sets

Express Auto Parts Warehouse Data File, Set 1

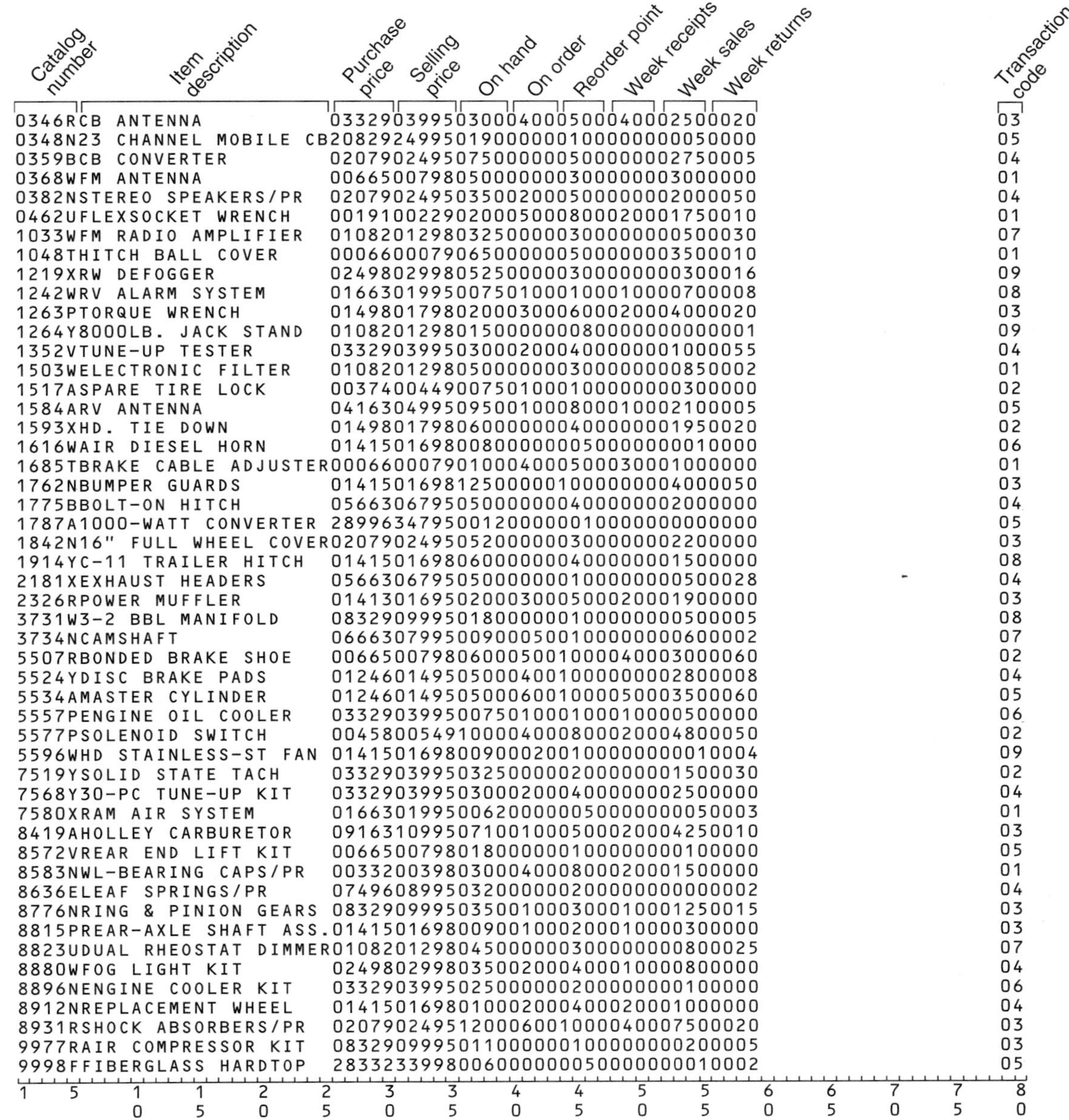

Catalog number | Item description | Purchase price | Selling price | On hand | On order | Reorder point | Week receipts | Week sales | Week returns | Transaction code

```
0346RCB ANTENNA         0332903995030004000500040002500020                    03
0348N23 CHANNEL MOBILE CB2082924995019000000100000000050000                    05
0359BCB CONVERTER       0207902495075000000500000002750005                    04
0368WFM ANTENNA         0066500798050000000300000003000000                    01
0382NSTEREO SPEAKERS/PR 0207902495035002000500000002000050                    04
0462UFLEXSOCKET WRENCH  0019100229020005000800020001750010                    01
1033WFM RADIO AMPLIFIER 0108201298032500000300000000500030                    07
1048THITCH BALL COVER   0006600079065000000500000003500010                    01
1219XRW DEFOGGER        0249802998052500000300000000300016                    09
1242WRV ALARM SYSTEM    0166301995007501000100010000700008                    08
1263PTORQUE WRENCH      0149801798020003000600020004000020                    03
1264Y8000LB. JACK STAND 0108201298015000000800000000000001                    09
1352VTUNE-UP TESTER     0332903995030002000400000001000055                    04
1503WELECTRONIC FILTER  0108201298050000000300000000850002                    01
1517ASPARE TIRE LOCK    0037400449007501000100000000300000                    02
1584ARV ANTENNA         0416304995095001000800010002100005                    05
1593XHD. TIE DOWN       0149801798060000000400000001950020                    02
1616WAIR DIESEL HORN    0141501698008000000500000000010000                    06
1685TBRAKE CABLE ADJUSTER0006600079010004000500030001000000                    01
1762NBUMPER GUARDS      0141501698125000001000000004000050                    03
1775BBOLT-ON HITCH      0566306795050000000400000002000000                    04
1787A1000-WATT CONVERTER 2899634795001200000010000000000000                    05
1842N16" FULL WHEEL COVER0207902495052000000300000002200000                    03
1914YC-11 TRAILER HITCH 0141501698060000000400000001500000                    08
2181XEXHAUST HEADERS    0566306795050000000100000000500028                    04
2326RPOWER MUFFLER      0141301695020003000500020001900000                    03
3731W3-2 BBL MANIFOLD   0832909995018000000100000000500005                    08
3734NCAMSHAFT           0666307995009000500100000000600002                    07
5507RBONDED BRAKE SHOE  0066500798060005001000040003000060                    02
5524YDISC BRAKE PADS    0124601495050004001000000002800008                    04
5534AMASTER CYLINDER    0124601495050006001000050003500060                    05
5557PENGINE OIL COOLER  0332903995007501000100010000500000                    06
5577PSOLENOID SWITCH    0045800549100004000800020004800050                    02
5596WHD STAINLESS-ST FAN 0141501698009000200100000000010004                    09
7519YSOLID STATE TACH   0332903995032500000200000001500030                    02
7568Y30-PC TUNE-UP KIT  0332903995030002000400000002500000                    04
7580XRAM AIR SYSTEM     0166301995006200000500000000050003                    01
8419AHOLLEY CARBURETOR  0916310995071001000500020004250010                    03
8572VREAR END LIFT KIT  0066500798018000000100000000100000                    05
8583NWL-BEARING CAPS/PR 0033200398030004000800020001500000                    01
8636ELEAF SPRINGS/PR    0749608995032000000200000000000002                    04
8776NRING & PINION GEARS 0832909995035001000300010001250015                    03
8815PREAR-AXLE SHAFT ASS.0141501698009001000200010000300000                    03
8823UDUAL RHEOSTAT DIMMER0108201298045000000300000000800025                    07
8880WFOG LIGHT KIT      0249802998035002000400010000800000                    04
8896NENGINE COOLER KIT  0332903995025000000200000000100000                    06
8912NREPLACEMENT WHEEL  0141501698010002000400020001000000                    04
8931RSHOCK ABSORBERS/PR 0207902495120006001000040007500020                    03
9977RAIR COMPRESSOR KIT 0832909995011000000100000000200005                    03
9998FFIBERGLASS HARDTOP 2833233998006000000050000000010002                    05
1   5    1    1    2    2    3    3    4    4    5    5    6    6    7    7    8
         0    5    0    5    0    5    0    5    0    5    0    5    0    5    0
```

Ponagansett Electric Company Data File, Set 2

Area code | Customer number | Customer name | Previous meter reading | Current meter reading | Rate schedule | Flat rate | Month number

```
RI1100140NARDONE, MARY E.    1402414997                                  A124208
RI1101235FLYNN, ROGER P.     4213142482                                  A106508
RI1103041BEST FURNITURE INC. 6656568711                                  C-28608
RI1106176KOLAKOWSKI, CASIMIR 0524005712                                  A106508
RI1110025ASSELIN, JANICE M.  2142122300                                  A124208
RI1115722GLORIA'S BEAUTY SHOP3485839208                                  C-28608
RI1120190WAREHAM, JOSEPH F.  1396214387                                  A106508
RI1131211KEATING, SUSAN A.   0707008110                                  A114208
RI1135400CONNELL, FRED C.    3523536157                                  A124208
RI1138625FRYE, LOUISE N.     0110601523                                  A106508
RI1150950TINY-TOT NURSERY    1272014355                                  C-28608
RI1153276BERGERON, FRANK S.  4103841756                                  A114208
RI1155900LOUGHERY, KATRINA   3048131624                                  A124208
RI1157133GOUDREAU, ELIZABETH 6565966235                                  A106508
RI1159005COPTER SERVICE      4330945292                                  C-28608
RI1160216GATTO, JANICE L.    1051811450                                  A114208
RI1161394JOZEFOWICZ, SANDRA  3769238007                                  A106508
RI1173731MCFADDEN, MICHAEL R.5808359347                                  A124208
RI1175571LETENDRE, THOMAS F. 4621247210                                  A124208
RI1177505MASSE, EUGENE       0517005703                                  A106508
RI1182162EVA'S FRUIT STORE   3257134713                                  C-28608
RI1190324MANDEL, ROLANDE J.  1076811240                                  A106508
RI1193005SCULLY, CLARA B.    0693407446                                  A106508
RI2201055NICOLETTA, JOHN J.  5193552917                                  A124208
RI2205182RAY TRUCKING CO.    3482137197                                  C-28608
RI2212433DION, GERARD M.     2347423995                                  A106508
RI2220020CHOW, SHUI          0978810714                                  A124208
RI2223944HODGE, KEVIN J.     7731977824                                  A106508
RI2232132PETE'S AUTO SUPPLIES6865270636                                  C-28608
RI2241694LAMOUNTAIN, LOUISE  4024141016                                  A114208
RI2245400PATALANO, SAMANTHA  0252703435                                  A124208
RI2248375CADY, RAYMOND F.    1517615533                                  A106508
RI2252100GASPAR, RAOUL       2357524027                                  A106508
RI2262025KLEIN, LAURALYNN    5708257811                                  A114208
RI2275364DORIS BAKERY SHOP   7499278134                                  C-28608
RI2275690HENNESSY, ROBERT J. 3901539517                                  A106508
RI2278170LUDOVICI, LUIGI     0286003224                                  A106508
RI2282985HUMMEL, STELLA      4010741153                                  A124208
RI2285374PARKS, EMERY R.     1074611158                                  A106508
RI3302010BENNETT, CLARENCE W.2374524228                                  A106508
RI3305327PETRUSKA, MARIE     0124002219                                  A124208
RI3320400MARK MARINE SERVICE 4937351447                                  C-28608
RI3331166DIGUILIO, EMILIO M. 5661356997                                  A106508
RI3342314CALLAHAN, JOHN J.   1040611459                                  A124208
RI3345943MCCARTHY, EUGENE F. 2753428646                                  A114208
RI3363770GERRY'S SEAFOODS    4519848660                                  C-28608
RI3367150BROWN, GEORGE W.    3206532589                                  A106508
RI3384000PRECOURT, JEAN M.   0862509562                                  A114208
RI3391450DEWEY, FRANCES D.   1121211624                                  A106508
RI3394765GARDNER, LEO F.     3543736562                                  A124208
1   5    1    1    2    2    3    3    4    4    5    5    6    6    7   7     8
         0    5    0    5    0    5    0    5    0    5    0    5    0   4     0
```

Allied Stock Company Data File, Set 3

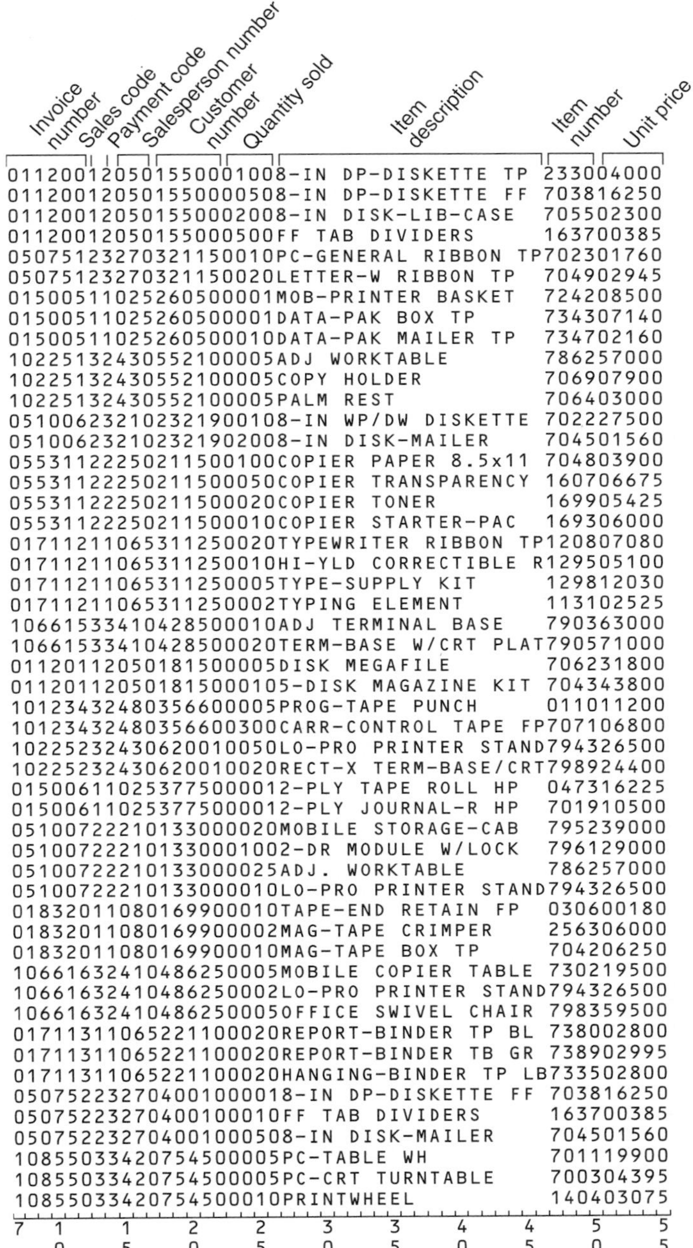

Invoice number | Sales code | Payment code | Salesperson number | Customer number | Quantity sold | Item description | Item number | Unit price

```
011200120501550001008-IN DP-DISKETTE TP 233004000
011200120501550000508-IN DP-DISKETTE FF 703816250
011200120501550002008-IN DISK-LIB-CASE  705502300
0112001205015500005OOFF TAB DIVIDERS    163700385
050751232703211500010PC-GENERAL RIBBON TP702301760
050751232703211500020LETTER-W RIBBON TP  704902945
015005110252605000001MOB-PRINTER BASKET  724208500
015005110252605000001DATA-PAK BOX TP     734307140
015005110252605000010DATA-PAK MAILER TP  734702160
102251324305521000005ADJ WORKTABLE       786257000
102251324305521000005COPY HOLDER         706907900
102251324305521000005PALM REST           706403000
051006232102321900108-IN WP/DW DISKETTE 702227500
051006232102321902008-IN DISK-MAILER    704501560
055311222502115001000COPIER PAPER 8.5x11 704803900
055311222502115000050COPIER TRANSPARENCY 160706675
055311222502115000020COPIER TONER        169905425
055311222502115000010COPIER STARTER-PAC  169306000
017112110653112500020TYPEWRITER RIBBON TP120807080
017112110653112500010HI-YLD CORRECTIBLE R129505100
017112110653112500005TYPE-SUPPLY KIT     129812030
017112110653112500002TYPING ELEMENT      113102525
106615334104285000010ADJ TERMINAL BASE   790363000
106615334104285000020TERM-BASE W/CRT PLAT790571000
011201120501815000005DISK MEGAFILE       706231800
011201120501815000105-DISK MAGAZINE KIT 704343800
101234324803566000005PROG-TAPE PUNCH     011011200
101234324803566003000CARR-CONTROL TAPE FP707106800
102252324306200100050LO-PRO PRINTER STAND794326500
102252324306200100020RECT-X TERM-BASE/CRT798924400
015006110253775000012-PLY TAPE ROLL HP  047316225
015006110253775000012-PLY JOURNAL-R HP  701910500
051007222101330000020MOBILE STORAGE-CAB  795239000
051007222101330001002-DR MODULE W/LOCK  796129000
051007222101330000025ADJ. WORKTABLE      786257000
051007222101330000010LO-PRO PRINTER STAND794326500
018320110801699000010TAPE-END RETAIN FP  030600180
018320110801699000002MAG-TAPE CRIMPER    256306000
018320110801699000010MAG-TAPE BOX TP     704206250
106616324104862500005MOBILE COPIER TABLE 730219500
106616324104862500002LO-PRO PRINTER STAND794326500
106616324104862500005OFFICE SWIVEL CHAIR 798359500
017113110652211000020REPORT-BINDER TP BL 738002800
017113110652211000020REPORT-BINDER TB GR 738902995
017113110652211000020HANGING-BINDER TP LB733502800
050752232704001000018-IN DP-DISKETTE FF 703816250
050752232704001000010FF TAB DIVIDERS     163700385
050752232704001000508-IN DISK-MAILER    704501560
108550334207545000005PC-TABLE WH         701119900
108550334207545000005PC-CRT TURNTABLE    700304395
108550334207545000010PRINTWHEEL          140403075
7 1    1    2    2    3    3    4    4    5    5
  0    5    0    5    0    5    0    5    0    5
```

Modern Plastics Company Data File, Set 4

Plant number | Department number | Social Security number | Employee name | Classification code | Pay rate | Reg-hours | OT-hours | Allowances | Date hired

```
1010456235100PALMER, WALTER R.   11020002005     2                          1960
5050419426056SORAFINE, JULIO     55010504006     2                          1970
5050228728353BELANGER, NORMAND   55010504000     2                          1970
5050461602956GREENE, WILMA       55009004000     3                          1974
5050722199235POTTER, RICHARD     55009004000     4                          1974
5050673372239LOBO, ALBERT P.     55008004000     1                          1978
5050399168704CELANO, LOUISE      55006004005     1                          1980
5060294933154WOLFE, LILETH       56008754005     2                          1976
5060325042172AIKEN, MARTINA      56007004000     4                          1980
5070426435893JUSTINO, KIRA       57006504000     3                          1979
1010723510611READY, MARIA ELENA  11018003008     1                          1975
1010781207315CAPARCO, DOMENIC A. 11015504000     3                          1982
1020861745201JACKVONY, WEBSTER P.12020003005     2                          1965
1020325123315GRAHAM, JUDITH L.   12012504000     1                          1978
1030017429976PESARE, KAROLYN S.  13018003500     2                          1975
1030407265788KRAUS, DONALD D.    13017504000     4                          1979
1080724844532CHARNIAK, NELSON T. 18020003005     3                          1970
1080349231175JACKSON, JESSICA    18016504005     1                          1974
1080125263028CANARIO, MARGARETTA 18012504005     2                          1982
2010288916795SILVIA, ROBERTA S.  21018003510     4                          1968
2020231769472LOISELLE, CYNTHIA   22016504005     1                          1970
2040463239232MACDONALD, PHILIP A.24018504000     3                          1964
2040587311472PAINE, JAMES H.     24015954000     4                          1972
2040387428531CALIFANO, CONCETTA  24016004000     1                          1975
2040737565186AFFLECK, SCOTT      24014504000     3                          1978
2040215311637CANTWELL, CLAUDIA   24012504000     1                          1982
2070394740218ALMEIDA, RICHARD    27007504005     4                          1972
3010170347173SHERMAN, MILTON L.  31020003005     2                          1970
3020246302715PAPADOPOULOS, JOE E.32018004005     1                          1968
3050227460634GOSSELIN, ANDREW P. 35012004000     3                          1963
3050425545014CHAN, SUKOM         35012004000     2                          1963
3050261197635SANTOS, MANUELA     35010004000     4                          1968
3050177032815JOUBERT, BERTHA M.  35009504000     1                          1970
3050466219366CHAPPELLE, BARBARA  35008004000     1                          1974
3050313905926ANDREWS, EARLE M.   35008004000     2                          1974
3050217415641PERRY, CHARLENE     35006254005     4                          1980
3050315631121SOSNICKI, STANLEY   35005504008     3                          1982
3060235596158KOSTEER, RICHARD G. 36008004010     3                          1975
3060312251653WINFIELD, LEWIS     36006504008     2                          1980
3070346795384LYNCH, WILLIAM S.   37006004000     2                          1976
4010331952867PELLETIER, VINCENT  41020002005     4                          1968
4020433405713POPKIN, ISABELLA M. 42014504005     1                          1974
4050322114268BARBER, MICHELLE K. 45008754005     3                          1972
4050392407915SAULNIER, ROBERT J. 45007504000     2                          1974
4050544287696ROCK, DONALD R.     45007504000     3                          1974
4050419712334ABRUZZI, GENE D.    45007003500     2                          1978
4050739394862PROULX, OSCAR R.    45006504000     4                          1980
4060585731346HIGGINS, DANIEL J.  46007504000     4                          1977
4070713390477CAMPBELL, ROBIN     47004504000     1                          1980
5010834615944CAPPUCCI, NAOMI     51020002505     1                          1966
5020674337414KLINGER, MICHAEL A. 52016004005     3                          1970
5050419426056SORAFINE, JULIO     55010504006     2                          1970
5050228728353BELANGER, NORMAND   55010504000     2                          1970
5050461602956GREENE, WILMA       55009004000     3                          1974
5050722199235POTTER, RICHARD     55009004000     4                          1974
5050673372239LOBO, ALBERT P.     55008004000     1                          1978
5050399168704CELANO, LOUISE      55006004005     1                          1980
5060294933154WOLFE, LILETH       56008754005     2                          1976
5060325042172AIKEN, MARTINA      56007004000     4                          1980
5070426435893JUSTINO, KIRA       57006504000     3                          1979
3 5  1    1    2    2    3    3    4    4    5    5    6    6    7    7    8
     0    5    0    5    0    5    0    5    0    5    0    5    0    5    0
```

International Haberdashery Data File, Set 5

Store number	Salesperson	Social Security number	Current sales	Sales quota
10	CAHILL, PAULA R.	623455100	0009865	0080000
10	CUSTER, GEORGE P.	611723510	0007102	5000800
10	GAMELIN, JOSEPH	315781243	0015250	0012000
10	JONES, EARLE B.	201861752	0005257	5000500
10	LAUZON, MARIE L.	315325123	0004652	5000500
10	MCMAHON, CHERYL	679017429	0009355	0008000
10	REZENDES, PHILIP	788407265	0011257	5000800
10	RICHARDS, ROBERT B.	325724844	0006352	5000500
10	ROSS, ROBERT J.	571349231	0015603	0012000
10	WHITMAN, ELEANOR	599353423	0010652	0012000
10	WOOD, RICHARD W.	028125226	0009355	0008000
20	BERARD, NORBERT V.	795288916	0008705	0008000
20	DAWICKI, WALTER	472692314	0007705	0008000
20	HARRINGTON, KATHY	232463239	0010457	0012000
20	LEONARDO, BARBARA	472587311	0004357	5000500
20	O'LEARY, KENNY	531387428	0010457	0008000
20	PAQUIN, BRIDGET	186737565	0016320	0012000
20	SANDERSON, JED	367215324	0008500	0005000
20	SHEEHAN, WILLIAM J.	218394740	0008705	0008000
30	ALBIN, EVELYN C.	173170347	0014355	0012000
30	FOX, EVA M.	517246302	0026250	0020000
30	LARSON, ANTHONY	634227460	0011745	0012000
30	PANKIEWICZ, ALLEN	410425545	0008102	0007000
30	PURCELL, HARRY C.	356261197	0028150	0020000
30	RAYMOND, VICTOR	518177032	0007242	0007000
30	REED, MARGARET	366466219	0014355	0012000
30	RENAUD, ANNE	269313905	0011745	0012000
30	RIENDEAU, NORMAN	461217415	0005305	0007000
30	ROBILLARD, STEPHEN	121315631	0028100	0020000
30	ROGERS, NANCY A.	581235596	0022405	0020000
30	SEQUEIRA, PAUL M.	356312251	0018258	0012000
30	THURSTON, SAMUEL	384346722	0007242	0007000
40	DAWSON, THOMAS A.	678331952	0010502	0008000
40	FULLER, ROSE E.	317433405	0007805	0005000
40	HELGER, ARTHUR	268322166	0010502	0008000
40	LEMAIRE, HERVE	519392407	0016450	0012000
40	PECKHAM, PHYLLIS	696544213	0009852	5000800
40	REAGAN, HELEN P.	334419701	0010050	0008000
40	SABRA, STEVEN S.	628739394	0006100	0005000
40	SHEEHAN, CHARLES A.	346585714	0007805	0008000
40	VACHON, JULIA	477713390	0016400	0012000
50	CROWLEY, JOHN H.	449834615	0007252	5000800
50	GAMACHE, NORMAN T.	414674337	0003905	0005000
50	IWANSKI, JENNIE	056419426	0013275	0012000
50	MALTAIS, VICTORIA	353228728	0017502	0012000
50	MELLO, ANTONIO	569461603	0007252	5000800
50	REGO, FIRMINO	235722152	0006652	5000500
50	REGO, JOSEPH C.	239673372	0010100	0008000
50	SANTOS, JOSEPHINE	407399168	0008155	0008000
50	TREMBLAY, ALPHONSE	451294933	0008695	0008000

Column positions: 1 5 10 15 20 25 30 35 40 45 50 55 60 63

■ Modern Plastics Company Data Validation File, Set 6

Plant number | Department number | Social Security number | Employee name | Classification code | Pay rate | Reg-hours | OT-hours | Allowances | Date hired

```
1010456235100PALMER, WALTER R.   11020002005   2                          1960
1010723510611READY, MARIA ELENA  11018003008   1                          1975
10  781207315CAPARCO, DOMENIC A. 11035504000   3                          1982
1020861745201JACKVONY, WEBSTER P.12020003055   2                          1965
1020325123315GRAHAM, JUDITH L.   1201250       1                          1978
1030017429976  PESARE, KAROLYN S.130    3500   2                          1975
  30407265788                    13017504000   4                          1979
1080724844532CHARNIAK, NELSON T. 18020003005   3                          1970
1080349231175JACKSON, JESSICA    18016504005   1                          1974
1080125263028CANARIO, MARGARETTA 18032505005   2                          1982
2010288916795SILVIA, ROBERTA S.  21018003510   4                          1968
    231769472loiselle, cynthia   22016504005   1                          1970
2040463239232MACDONALD, PHILIP A.24018504000   3                          1964
2040         PAINE, JAMES H.     24015954000   4                          1972
2040387428531CALIFANO, CONCETTA  24016000000   1                          1975
2040737565186AFFLECK, SCOTT      24014504000   3                          1978
2040215311637CANTWELL, CLAUDIA   24012504000   1                          1982
2070394740218ALMEIDA, RICHARD    27007504005   4                          1972
3010170347173SHERMAN, MILTON L.  31020003005   2                          1970
3020246302715PAPADOPOULOS, JOE E.32018004005   1                          1968
3050227460634GOSSELIN, ANDREW P. 35012004000   3                          1963
3050425545014CHAN, SUKOM         35012004000   2                          1963
3050261197635SANTOS, MANUELA     35010004000   4                          1968
3050177032815JOUBERT, BERTHA M.  35009504000   1                          1970
3050466219366CHAPPELLE, BARBARA  35008004000   1                          1974
3050313905926ANDREWS, EARLE M.   35008004000   2                          1974
3050217415641PERRY, CHARLENE     35006254005   4                          1980
3050315631121SOSNICKI, STANLEY   35005504008   3                          1982
3060235596158KOSTEER, RICHARD G. 36008004010   3                          1975
3060312251653WINFIELD, LEWIS     36006504008   2                          1980
3070346795384LYNCH, WILLIAM S.   37006004000   2                          1976
4010331952867PELLETIER, VINCENT  41020002005   4                          1968
4020433405713POPKIN, ISABELLA M. 42014504005   1                          1974
4050322114268BARBER, MICHELLE K. 45008754005   3                          1972
4050392407915SAULNIER, ROBERT J. 45007504000   2                          1974
4050544287696ROCK, DONALD R.     45007504000   3                          1974
4050419712334ABRUZZI, GENE D.    45007003500   2                          1978
4050739394862PROULX, OSCAR R.    45006504000   4                          1980
4060585731346HIGGINS, DANIEL J.  46007504000   4                          1977
4070713390477CAMPBELL, ROBIN     47004504000   1                          1980
5010834615944CAPPUCCI, NAOMI     51020002505   1                          1966
5020674337414KLINGER, MICHAEL A. 52016004005   3                          1970
5050419426056SORAFINE, JULIO     55010504006   2                          1970
5050228728353BELANGER, NORMAND   55010504000   2                          1970
5050461602956GREENE, WILMA       55009004000   3                          1974
5050722199235POTTER, RICHARD     55009004000   4                          1974
5050673372239LOBO, ALBERT P.     55008004000   1                          1978
5050399168704CELANO, LOUISE      55006004005   1                          1980
5060294933154WOLFE, LILETH       56008754005   2                          1976
5060325042172AIKEN, MARTINA      56007004000   4                          1980
5070426435893JUSTINO, KIRA       57006504000   3                          1979
3 5     1    1    2    2    3    3    4    4    5    5    6    6    7    7    8
        0    5    0    5    0    5    0    5    0    5    0    5    0    5    0
```

Express Auto Parts Warehouse Data File, Set 7A

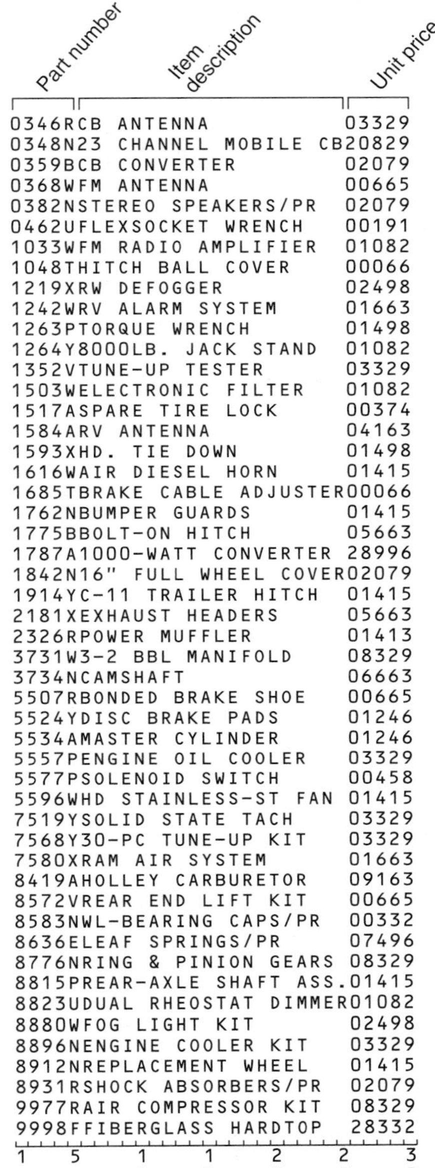


```
0346RCB ANTENNA          03329
0348N23 CHANNEL MOBILE CB20829
0359BCB CONVERTER        02079
0368WFM ANTENNA          00665
0382NSTEREO SPEAKERS/PR  02079
0462UFLEXSOCKET WRENCH   00191
1033WFM RADIO AMPLIFIER  01082
1048THITCH BALL COVER    00066
1219XRW DEFOGGER         02498
1242WRV ALARM SYSTEM     01663
1263PTORQUE WRENCH       01498
1264Y8000LB. JACK STAND  01082
1352VTUNE-UP TESTER      03329
1503WELECTRONIC FILTER   01082
1517ASPARE TIRE LOCK     00374
1584ARV ANTENNA          04163
1593XHD. TIE DOWN        01498
1616WAIR DIESEL HORN     01415
1685TBRAKE CABLE ADJUSTER00066
1762NBUMPER GUARDS       01415
1775BBOLT-ON HITCH       05663
1787A1000-WATT CONVERTER 28996
1842N16" FULL WHEEL COVER02079
1914YC-11 TRAILER HITCH  01415
2181XEXHAUST HEADERS     05663
2326RPOWER MUFFLER       01413
3731W3-2 BBL MANIFOLD    08329
3734NCAMSHAFT            06663
5507RBONDED BRAKE SHOE   00665
5524YDISC BRAKE PADS     01246
5534AMASTER CYLINDER     01246
5557PENGINE OIL COOLER   03329
5577PSOLENOID SWITCH     00458
5596WHD STAINLESS-ST FAN 01415
7519YSOLID STATE TACH    03329
7568Y30-PC TUNE-UP KIT   03329
7580XRAM AIR SYSTEM      01663
8419AHOLLEY CARBURETOR   09163
8572VREAR END LIFT KIT   00665
8583NWL-BEARING CAPS/PR  00332
8636ELEAF SPRINGS/PR     07496
8776NRING & PINION GEARS 08329
8815PREAR-AXLE SHAFT ASS.01415
8823UDUAL RHEOSTAT DIMMER01082
8880WFOG LIGHT KIT       02498
8896NENGINE COOLER KIT   03329
8912NREPLACEMENT WHEEL   01415
8931RSHOCK ABSORBERS/PR  02079
9977RAIR COMPRESSOR KIT  08329
9998FFIBERGLASS HARDTOP  28332
1   5    1    1    2    2    3
         0    5    0    5    0
```

Express Auto Parts Warehouse Data File, Set 7B

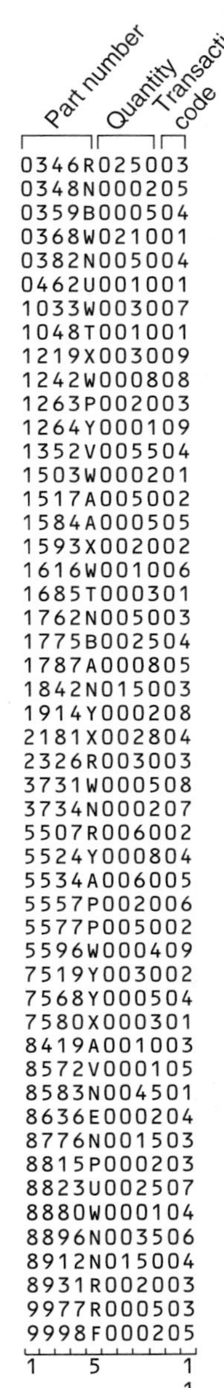


```
0346R025003
0348N000205
0359B000504
0368W021001
0382N005004
0462U001001
1033W003007
1048T001001
1219X003009
1242W000808
1263P002003
1264Y000109
1352V005504
1503W000201
1517A005002
1584A000505
1593X002002
1616W001006
1685T000301
1762N005003
1775B002504
1787A000805
1842N015003
1914Y000208
2181X002804
2326R003003
3731W000508
3734N000207
5507R006002
5524Y000804
5534A006005
5557P002006
5577P005002
5596W000409
7519Y003002
7568Y000504
7580X000301
8419A001003
8572V000105
8583N004501
8636E000204
8776N001503
8815P000203
8823U002507
8880W000104
8896N003506
8912N015004
8931R002003
9977R000503
9998F000205
1   5     1
          1
```

International Haberdashery Data File, Set 8A

Store number | Salesperson | Social Security number | Sales quota

```
10CAHILL, PAULA R.    62345510000080000
10CUSTER, GEORGE P.   61172351000080000
10GAMELIN, JOSEPH     31578124300120000
10JONES, EARLE B.     20186175200050000
10LAUZON, MARIE L.    31532512300050000
10MCMAHON, CHERYL     67901742900080000
10REZENDES, PHILIP    78840726500080000
10RICHARDS, ROBERT B. 32572484400050000
10ROSS, ROBERT J.     57134923100120000
10WHITMAN, ELEANOR    59935342300120000
10WOOD, RICHARD W.    02812522600080000
20BERARD, NORBERT V.  79528891600080000
20DAWICKI, WALTER     47269231400080000
20HARRINGTON, KATHY   23246323900120000
20LEONARDO, BARBARA   47258731100050000
20O'LEARY, KENNY      53138742800080000
20PAQUIN, BRIDGET     18673756500120000
20SANDERSON, JED      36721532400050000
20SHEEHAN, WILLIAM J. 21839474000080000
30ALBIN, EVELYN C.    17317034700120000
30FOX, EVA M.         51724630200200000
30LARSON, ANTHONY     63422746000120000
30PANKIEWICZ, ALLEN   41042554500070000
30PURCELL, HARRY C.   35626119700200000
30RAYMOND, VICTOR     51817703200070000
30REED, MARGARET      36646621900120000
30RENAUD, ANNE        26931390500120000
30RIENDEAU, NORMAN    46121741500070000
30ROBILLARD, STEPHEN  12131563100200000
30ROGERS, NANCY A.    58123559600200000
30SEQUEIRA, PAUL M.   35631225100120000
30THURSTON, SAMUEL    38434672200070000
40DAWSON, THOMAS A.   67833195200080000
40FULLER, ROSE E.     31743340500050000
40HELGER, ARTHUR      26832216600080000
40LEMAIRE, HERVE      51939240700120000
40PECKHAM, PHYLLIS    69654421300080000
40REAGAN, HELEN P.    33441970100080000
40SABRA, STEVEN S.    62873939400050000
40SHEEHAN, CHARLES A. 34658571400080000
40VACHON, JULIA       47771339000120000
50CROWLEY, JOHN H.    44983461500080000
50GAMACHE, NORMAN T.  41467433700050000
50IWANSKI, JENNIE     05641942600120000
50MALTAIS, VICTORIA   35322872800120000
50MELLO, ANTONIO      56946160300080000
50REGO, FIRMINO       23572215200050000
50REGO, JOSEPH C.     23967337200080000
50SANTOS, JOSEPHINE   40739916800080000
50TREMBLAY, ALPHONSE  45129493300080000
1   5    1    1    2    2    3    3   3
         0    5    0    5    0    5   9
```

International Haberdashery Data File, Set 8B

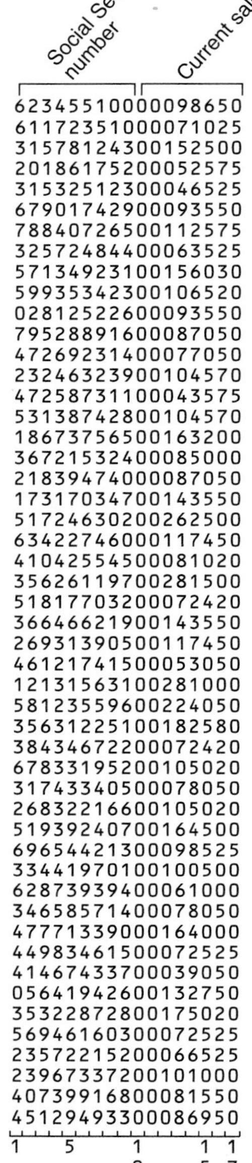

Social Security number | Current sales

```
62345510000098650
61172351000071025
31578124300152500
20186175200052575
31532512300046525
67901742900093550
78840726500112575
32572484400063525
57134923100156030
59935342300106520
02812522600093550
79528891600087050
47269231400077050
23246323900104570
47258731100043575
53138742800104570
18673756500163200
36721532400085000
21839474000087050
17317034700143550
51724630200262500
63422746000117450
41042554500081020
35626119700281500
51817703200072420
36646621900143550
26931390500117450
46121741500053050
12131563100281000
58123559600224050
35631225100182580
38434672200072420
67833195200105020
31743340500078050
26832216600105020
51939240700164500
69654421300098525
33441970100100500
62873939400061000
34658571400078050
47771339000164000
44983461500072525
41467433700039050
05641942600132750
35322872800175020
56946160300072525
23572215200066525
23967337200101000
40739916800081550
45129493300086950
1   5    1    11
         0    57
```

Modern Plastics Company Data File, Set 9A

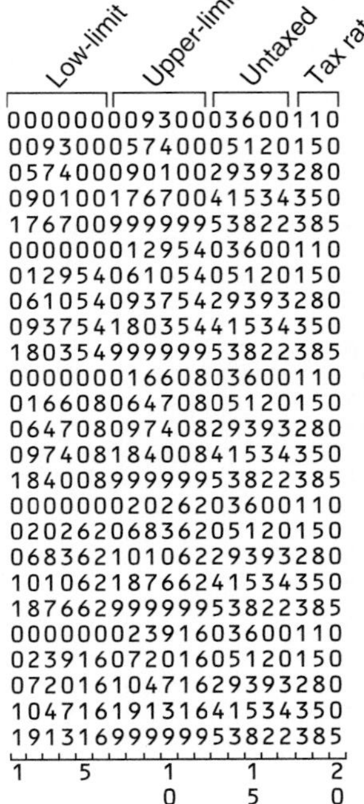

```
Low-limit Upper-limit Untaxed Tax rate
00000000930003600110
00930005740005120150
05740009010029393280
09010017670041534350
17670099999953822385
00000001295403600110
01295406105405120150
06105409375429393280
09375418035441534350
18035499999953822385
00000001660803600110
01660806470805120150
06470809740829393280
09740818400841534350
18400899999953822385
00000002026203600110
02026206836205120150
06836210106229393280
10106218766241534350
18766299999953822385
00000002391603600110
02391607201605120150
07201610471629393280
10471619131641534350
19131699999953822385
1   5    1    1    2
         0    5    0
```

Modern Plastics Company Data File, Set 9B

Social Security number | Employee name | Pay rate | Allowances

```
456235100PALMER, WALTER R.   20002
723510611READY, MARIA ELENA  18001
781207315CAPARCO, DOMENIC A. 15503
861745201JACKVONY, WEBSTER P.20002
325123315GRAHAM, JUDITH L.   12501
017429976PESARE, KAROLYN S.  18002
407265788KRAUS, DONALD D.    17504
724844532CHARNIAK, NELSON T. 20003
349231175JACKSON, JESSICA    16501
125263028CANARIO, MARGARETTA 12502
288916795SILVIA, ROBERTA S.  18004
231769472LOISELLE, CYNTHIA   16501
463239232MACDONALD, PHILIP A.18503
587311472PAINE, JAMES H.     15954
387428531CALIFANO, CONCETTA  16001
737565186AFFLECK, SCOTT      14503
215311637CANTWELL, CLAUDIA   12501
394740218ALMEIDA, RICHARD    07504
170347173SHERMAN, MILTON L.  20002
246302715PAPADOPOULOS, JOE E.18001
227460634GOSSELIN, ANDREW P. 12003
425545014CHAN, SUKOM         12002
261197635SANTOS, MANUELA     10004
177032815JOUBERT, BERTHA M.  09501
466219366CHAPPELLE, BARBARA  08001
313905926ANDREWS, EARLE M.   08002
217415641PERRY, CHARLENE     06254
315631121SOSNICKI, STANLEY   05503
235596158KOSTEER, RICHARD G. 08003
312251653WINFIELD, LEWIS     06502
346795384LYNCH, WILLIAM S.   06002
331952867PELLETIER, VINCENT  20004
433405713POPKIN, ISABELLA M. 14501
322114268BARBER, MICHELLE K. 08753
392407915SAULNIER, ROBERT J. 07502
544287696ROCK, DONALD R.     07503
419712334ABRUZZI, GENE D.    07002
739394862PROULX, OSCAR R.    06504
585731346HIGGINS, DANIEL J.  07504
713390477CAMPBELL, ROBIN     04501
834615944CAPPUCCI, NAOMI     20001
674337414KLINGER, MICHAEL A. 16003
419426056SORAFINE, JULIO     10502
228728353BELANGER, NORMAND   10502
461602956GREENE, WILMA       09003
722199235POTTER, RICHARD     09004
673372239LOBO, ALBERT P.     08001
399168704CELANO, LOUISE      06001
294933154WOLFE, LILETH       08752
325042172AIKEN, MARTINA      07004
426435893JUSTINO, KIRA       06503
1   5    1    1    2    2    3   3
         0    5    0    5    0   4
```

Modern Plastics Company Data File, Set 9C

Social Security number | Reg-hours | OT-hours

```
4562351002005
7235106113008
7812073154000
8617452013005
3251233154000
0174299763500
4072657884000
7248445323005
3492311754005
1252630284005
2889167953510
2317694724005
4632392324000
5873114724000
3874285314000
7375651864000
2153116374000
3947402184005
1703471733005
2463027154005
2274606344000
4255450144000
2611976354000
1770328154000
4662193664000
3139059264000
2174156414005
3156311214008
2355961584010
3122516534008
3467953844000
3319528672005
4334057134005
3221142684005
3924079154000
5442876964000
4197123343500
7393948624000
5857313464000
7133904774000
8346159442505
6743374144005
4194260564006
2287283534000
4616029564000
7221992354000
6733722394000
3991687044005
2949331544005
3250421724000
4264358934000
1   5    1  1
         0  3
```

■ Allied Stock Company Master Customer Data File, Set 10A

Record code | Customer number | Customer name | Street address | City/State/ZIP | Last activity date

```
CM0003HALEY, ETHEL          99 SUNSET DR.           PORT LAVACA, TX    77979                    890215
CM0008PANNONNI, NICHOLAS    3 COLT DRIVE            WHARTON, TX        77488                    890207
CM0015HARVEY, SIDNEY        814 REAGAN AVE.         GEORGETOWN, TX     78628                    890214
CM0037CORREIA, HERMAN       293 CRESCENT DR.        AUSTIN, TX         78722                    890124
CM0046WARD, BRUNO           289 ALMY RD.            AUSTIN, TX         78734                    890216
CM0061OLSON, HELENA         2050 EAST KING RD.      WHARTON, TX        77488                    890110
CM0105COUSIN, RAYMOND       698 WALNUT AVE.         MIDLAND, TX        79701                    890124
CM0210TYRELL, ROBERT T.     292 STOCKTON AVE.       FORT WORTH, TX     76106                    890223
CM0432ALVES, HERMANO        350 PILOT DR.           BROWNSVILLE, TX    78521                    890125
CM0530RAPOZA, JUDITH        609 DAVOL ST.           WACO, TX           76704                    890112
CM0700ROY, ALBERT F.        655 N. MAIN ST.         EL PASO, TX        79901                    890224
CM0701O'NEIL, EUGENE        151 RANCHERO DR.        PECOS, TX          79772                    890301
CM0702TAYLOR, MAXINE        64 ANAWAN AVE.          LAREDO, TX         78040                    890126
CM0703FARNHAM, NORMAN       1255 WILSON RD.         BROWNSVILLE, TX    78521                    890112
CM0704FAY, MARGO            815 BEDFORD ST.         CRYSTAL CITY, TX   78839                    890217
CM0705BORDEN REPAIR         1 TINMAN RD.            SWEETWATER, TX     79556                    890303
CM0706GOVERNO, MARY T.      170 WILLIAM ST.         WACO, TX           76705                    890221
CM0707LOU'S PLACE           190 NEWHALL AVE.        LUFKIN, TX         75901                    890118
CM0708POCASSET JEWELERS     201 SOUTH MAIN ST.      LAREDO, TX         78040                    890120
CM0709LOFTY BALLOONS        45 FREEDOM RD.          FORT WORTH, TX     76104                    890209
CM0711PIPEIRA, MARCIA       835 VALENTINE DR.       GEORGETOWN, TX     78626                    890206
CM0713PIELA, ELIZABETH      360 BUFFINGTON AVE.     PECOS, TX          79772                    890123
CM0715TYSON, URSULA         594 MAPLE AVE           ABILENE, TX        79602                    890203
CM0717TRIPLE-A AUTO PARTS 4095 COUNTY RD.           LAREDO, TX         78041                    890314
CM0819DUPRE, DIANE          345 DURFEE AVE.         DALLAS, TX         75223                    890206
CM1723CARPENTER, HAZEL      189 DENHAM DR.          MIDLAND, TX        79705                    890210
CM1765BURNS SERVICE CENTER480 RIDGE RD.             BIG SPRING, TX     79721                    890201
CM2150HAGUE, RUSSELL        126 PRESIDENT AVE.      SAN ANTONIO, TX    78219                    890303
CM2200WALLACE, EDWARD       64 WILLOW LANE          GEORGETOWN, TX     78628                    890207
CM2201BELMORE, ALICE        15 STEVEN AVE.          TEMPLE, TX         76503                    890119
CM2203BARRY, JEAN           177 MARKET DR.          KILLEEN, TX        76544                    890320
CM2205DOSTER, MARY          287 BROADWAY ST.        SAN ANGELO, TX     76902                    890209
CM2207PLUNKETT, GARY A.     750 RODEO BLVD.         ABILENE, TX        79608                    890301
CM2520PLUNKETT, LILLIAN     110 CAMPION AVE.        DALLAS, TX         75223                    890208
CM2875TURCOTTE, THEODORE    530 S. MAIN ST.         CRYSTAL CITY, TX   78839                    890302
CM3200UNDERWOOD, LLOYD      25 ISLAND VIEW RD.      PORT LAVACA, TX    77979                    890310
CM3201HAMILTON, RUTH        13 BAKER ST.            AUSTIN, TX         78721                    890111
CM3203HANCOCK, LENA         229 RIVERSIDE DR.       SWEETWATER, TX     79556                    890209
CM3205LECKY, PAUL M.        111 BORDEN ST.          MIDLAND, TX        79707                    890306
CM3207MCNERNEY, MARIE J.    144 MAPLE AVE           SAN ANTONIO, TX    78212                    890309
CM3209PERRY, MARY T.        75 HIGH HILL RD.        SAN ANGELO, TX     76904                    890126
CM4100PINTO, VICTOR         540 ALDEN ST.           ABILENE, TX        79601                    890213
CM4121AMIDON, PATRICIA      35 BANK ST.             MIDLAND, TX        79701                    890308
CM4203SAHADY, MARY L.       207 STAFFORD RD.        ODESSA, TX         79764                    890317
CM5213HAYES, EDNA           750 MAPLE AVE.          ABILENE, TX        79602                    890222
CM5645CABRAL, CAROL         1530 COUNTY RD.         TEMPLE, TX         76504                    890116
CM6001PRUITT, LARRY         603 ROCK ST.            ATHENS, TX         75751                    890310
CM7752ROY, VICTOR           135 WILCOX ST.          PORT LAVACA, TX    77979                    890215
CM8342LATANO, CATHERINE     2120 MAIN RD.           SEGUIN, TX         78156                    890125
CM8515OLSON, ROBERT M.      108 FRESNO LANE         LAREDO, TX         78040                    890316
CM8611SUTCLIFFE, LOUISE F.1384 PLEASANT ST.         WICHITA FALLS, TX 76304                     890207
CM8612BELANGER, AIME        1685 PLEASANT ST.       WICHITA FALLS, TX 76304                     890313
CM8614GOULART, GALE M.      740 WILLOW RANCH RD.    DALLAS, TX         75244                    890206
CM8617O'NEIL, FRANCIS L.    37 ADAMS RD.            FORT WORTH, TX     76106                    890323
CM8618BARTLETT, MICHELLE    96 BAYSIDE DR.          BIG SPRING, TX     79721                    890118
CM8619HOOKS, TRUDY          491 WARREN AVE.         ODESSA, TX         79763                    890220
CM8633HAYES, TOM            35 COMMONS RD.          BIG SPRING, TX     79721                    890320
CM9009PONTES, EDMUND        195 FROST ST.           HOUSTON, TX        77058                    890216
CM9551DELICIO, RAYMOND      52 KILBURN ST.          ALVIN, TX          77511                    890310
CM9999BENTSON, JAMES R.     254 WEST MAIN RD.       JACKSONVILLE, TX   75766                    890227
1   5    10   15   20   25   30   35   40   45   50   55   60   65   70   75   80   85   90   95   100
```

Allied Stock Company Detail Data File, Set 10B

Customer number | Customer name | Street address | City/State/ZIP

```
0075BEAUMONT CONTRACTORS96 SAMSON AVE.        SAN ANTONIO, TX    78219
0092KINGMAN, RUTH       46 SNELL ST.          ALVIN, TX          77511
0125CANTIN, LEONA       66 TURNER AVE.        SEGUIN, TX         78156
0167ROY, JEANNE         168 FULTON ST.        MIDLAND, TX        79701
1235TAYLOR, MANTON      146 STEWART ST.       HOUSTON, TX        77058
2280SYNNOTT, IDA        34 NEPTUNE DR.        SWEETWATER, TX     79556
2325DESMOND, P HENRY    90 SUFFOLK AVE.       CRYSTAL CITY, TX   78839
4315DEPIN, PHYLLIS      110 BLUFF AVE.        WICHITA FALLS, TX  76304
5744LEMAY, WALTER       309 PALMER ST.        BIG SPRING, TX     79721
6100COLONIAL BEAUTY SHOP161 LONSDALE AVE      DALLAS, TX         75223
1   5    1    1    2    2    3    3    4    4    5    5    6    6    7 7
         0    5    0    5    0    5    0    5    0    5    0    5    0 2
```

Express Auto Parts Warehouse Detail Data File, Set 11A

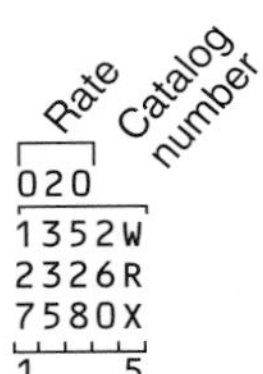


```
020
1352W
2326R
7580X
1   5
```

Express Auto Parts Warehouse Master Inventory Data File, Set 11B

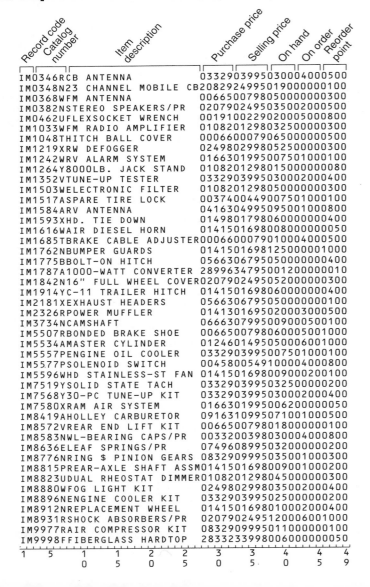

Record code | Catalog number | Item description | Purchase price | Selling price | On hand | On order | Reorder point

```
IM0346RCB ANTENNA                0332903995030004000500
IM0348N23 CHANNEL MOBILE CB2082924995019000000100
IM0368WFM ANTENNA                0066500798050000000300
IM0382NSTEREO SPEAKERS/PR        0207902495035002000500
IM0462UFLEXSOCKET WRENCH         0019100229020005000800
IM1033WFM RADIO AMPLIFIER        0108201298032500000300
IM1048THITCH BALL COVER          0006600079065000000500
IM1219XRW DEFOGGER               0249802998052500000300
IM1242WRV ALARM SYSTEM           0166301995007501000100
IM1264Y8000LB. JACK STAND        0108201298015000000080
IM1352VTUNE-UP TESTER            0332903995030002000400
IM1503WELECTRONIC FILTER         0108201298050000000300
IM1517ASPARE TIRE LOCK           0037400449007501000100
IM1584ARV ANTENNA                0416304995095001000800
IM1593XHD. TIE DOWN              0149801798060000000400
IM1616WAIR DIESEL HORN           0141501698008000000050
IM1685TBRAKE CABLE ADJUSTER0006600079010004000500
IM1762NBUMPER GUARDS             0141501698125000001000
IM1775BBOLT-ON HITCH             0566306795050000000400
IM1787A1000-WATT CONVERTER 2899634795001200000010
IM1842N16" FULL WHEEL COVER0207902495052000000300
IM1914YC-11 TRAILER HITCH        0141501698060000000400
IM2181XEXHAUST HEADERS           0566306795050000000100
IM2326RPOWER MUFFLER             0141301695020003000500
IM3734NCAMSHAFT                  0666307995009000500100
IM5507RBONDED BRAKE SHOE         0066500798060005001000
IM5534AMASTER CYLINDER           0124601495050006001000
IM5557PENGINE OIL COOLER         0332903995007501000100
IM5577PSOLENOID SWITCH           0045800549100004000800
IM5596WHD STAINLESS-ST FAN 0141501698009000200100
IM7519YSOLID STATE TACH          0332903995032500000200
IM7568Y30-PC TUNE-UP KIT         0332903995030002000400
IM7580XRAM AIR SYSTEM            0166301995006200000050
IM8419AHOLLEY CARBURETOR         0916310995071001000500
IM8572VREAR END LIFT KIT         0066500798018000000100
IM8583NWL-BEARING CAPS/PR        0033200398030004000800
IM8636ELEAF SPRINGS/PR           0749608995032000000200
IM8776NRING $ PINION GEARS 0832909995035001000300
IM8815PREAR-AXLE SHAFT ASSM0141501698009001000200
IM8823UDUAL RHEOSTAT DIMMER0108201298045000000300
IM8880WFOG LIGHT KIT             0249802998035002000400
IM8896NENGINE COOLER KIT         0332903995025000000200
IM8912NREPLACEMENT WHEEL         0141501698010002000400
IM8931RSHOCK ABSORBERS/PR        0207902495120006001000
IM9977RAIR COMPRESSOR KIT        0832909995011000000100
IM9998FFIBERGLASS HARDTOP        2833233998006000000050
1   5    1    1    2    2    3    3    4    4   4
         0    5    0    5    0    5    0    5   9
```

Ponagansett Electric Company Detail Data File, Set 12A

Process code | Meter number | Rate code | Customer number | Customer name | Street address | City/State/ZIP

```
300154397A11
100154430A12357118DUVAL, ROBERT J.    25 CENTER AVE.           FOREST PARK, GA 30050
100154560C-2173502NATIONWIDE TRAVEL   300 SOUTH MAIN ST.       MARIETTA, GA    30060
200154792
200155520
100155800A10136714SCARPETTI, JAMES A. 120 JEPSON LANE          FOREST PARK, GA 30050
301201413A10
101525200A11345113COFFEY, KENNETH W.  530 BEDFORD ST.          DECATUR, GA     30033
101700150C-2268375LUCIA MUSIC CO.     225 ESSEX ST.            ATLANTA, GA     30339
201702505
1   5    1    1    2    2    3    3    4    4    5    5    6    6    7    7    8    8
         0    5    0    5    0    5    0    5    0    5    0    5    0    5    0    5
```

Ponagansett Electric Company Master Customer Data File, Set 12B

Record code | Meter number | Rate code | Customer number | Customer name | Street address | City/State/ZIP

```
CM00154324A12100140NARDONE, MARY E.    152 JEFFERSON ST.        ATLANTA, GA     30315
CM00154352A10101235FLYNN, ROGER P.     21 NOTRE DAME ST.        N. ATLANTA, GA  30341
CM00154365C-2103041BEST FURNITURE INC. 550 SAKONNET POINT       EAST POINT, GA  30328
CM00154381A10106176KOLAKOWSKI, CASIMIR 386 CLARKSON ST.         DECATUR, GA     30035
CM00154388A12110025ASSELIN, JANICE M.  245 NO. MARION ST.       ATLANTA, GA     30312
CM00154395C-2115722GLORIA'S BEAUTY SHOP260 WM. SOUZA RD.        HAPEVILLE, GA   30354
CM00154397A10120190WAREHAM, JOSEPH F.  196 NEWHALL AVE.         MOUNTAIN VIEW, GA 30328
CM00154405A11131211KEATING, SUSAN A.   106 FAIRHAVEN AVE.       FOREST PARK, GA 30050
CM00154413A12135400CONNELL, FRED C.    645 CHERRY ST.           EAST POINT, GA  30315
CM00154417A10138625FRYE, LOUISE N.     43 STEWART ST.           EMORY, GA       30307
CM00154422C-2150950TINY-TOT NURSERY    142 SPRUCE ST.           ATLANTA, GA     30307
CM00154427A11153276BERGERON, FRANK S.  73 DOVER ST.             N. ATLANTA, GA  30331
CM00154438A12155900LOUGHERY, KATRINA   298 SOUTH MAIN ST.       MARIETTA, GA    30060
CM00154444A10157133GOUDREAU, ELIZABETH 24 DAVIS ST.             DECATUR, GA     30030
CM00154452C-2159005COPTER SERVICE      29 PERSHING AVE.         COLLEGE PARK, GA 30337
CM00154469A11160216GATTO, JANICE L.    55 CRESTWOOD AVE.        EAST POINT, GA  30316
CM00154473A10161394JOZEFOWICZ, SANDRA  45 DUKE AVE.             HAPEVILLE, GA   30354
CM00154485A12173731MCFADDEN, MICHAEL R.780 ATLANTIC BLVD.       FOREST PARK, GA 30050
CM00154499A12175571LETENDRE, THOMAS F. 205 MASON ST.            ATLANTA, GA     30349
CM00154550A10177505MASSE, EUGENE       131 CENTER AVE.          FOREST PARK, GA 30050
CM00154785C-2182162EVA'S FRUIT STORE   10 SPRING LANE           MARIETTA, GA    30060
CM00154792A10190324MANDEL, ROLANDE J.  2446 HIGHLAND AVE.       FOREST PARK, GA 30050
CM00154830A10193005SCULLY, CLARA B.    383 NICHOLS ST.          COLLEGE PARK, GA 30337
CM00154942A12201055NICOLETTA, JOHN J.  1012 MADISON AVE.        DECATUR, GA     30030
CM00155010C-2205182RAY TRUCKING CO.    81 STAFFORD RD.          DECATUR, GA     30032
CM00155100A10212433DION, GERARD M.     315 WASHINGTON ST.       EAST POINT, GA  30344
CM00155250A12220020CHOW, SHUI          140 ESSEX ST.            ATLANTA, GA     30339
CM00155520A10223944HODGE, KEVIN J.     560 EASTERN AVE.         EAST POINT, GA  30331
CM00155723C-2232132PETE'S AUTO SUPPLIES440 JEFFERSON BLVD.      N. ATLANTA, GA  30344
CM01201413A11241694LAMOUNTAIN, LOUISE  770 BEDFORD ST.          DECATUR, GA     30033
CM01201450A12245400PATALANO, SAMANTHA  50 AETNA ST.             COLLEGE PARK, GA 30337
CM01204300A10248375CADY, RAYMOND F.    70 NORTH COURT           N. ATLANTA, GA  30331
CM01204375A10252100GASPAR, RAOUL       86 COPLEY DR.            MARIETTA, GA    30060
CM01204423A11262025KLEIN, LAURALYNN    105 ALBION ST.           MABLETON, GA    30059
CM01204715C-2275364DORIS BAKERY SHOP   74 SIDNEY AVE.           SMYRNA, GA      30080
CM01523741A10275690HENNESSY, ROBERT J. 46 PALMER ST.            ATLANTA, GA     30305
CM01523742A10278170LUDOVICI, LUIGI     780 COTTAGE AVE.         FOREST PARK, GA 30050
CM01524001A12282985HUMMEL, STELLA      228 POWELL ST.           ATLANTA, GA     30316
CM01524023A10285374PARKS, EMERY R.     131 BARLOW ST.           MABLETON, GA    30059
CM01530437A10302010BENNETT, CLARENCE W.5021 KNIGHT ST.          SMYRNA, GA      30080
CM01680142A12305327PETRUSKA, MARIE     379 EAST MAIN RD.        EAST POINT, GA  30312
CM01702325C-2320400MARK MARINE SERVICE 270 COURTNEY ST.         ATLANTA, GA     30306
CM01702465A10331166DIGUILIO, EMILIO M. 52 WALNUT AVE.           MARIETTA, GA    30064
CM01702505A12342314CALLAHAN, JOHN J.   275 DUNCAN DR.           N. ATLANTA, GA  30341
CM01702580A11345943MCCARTHY, EUGENE F. 68 FARNUM ST.            DECATUR, GA     30032
CM01702640C-2363770GERRY'S SEAFOODS    86 WARREN AVE.           COLLEGE PARK, GA 30337
CM01705314A10367150BROWN, GEORGE W.    3964 NORTH MAIN ST.      N. ATLANTA, GA  30318
CM01705520A11384000PRECOURT, JEAN M.   140 JEPSON LANE          FOREST PARK, GA 30050
CM01721325A10391450DEWEY, FRANCES D.   532 BEAVER RD.           FOREST PARK, GA 30050
CM01734250A12394765GARDNER, LEO F.     25 GARDEN AVE.           COLLEGE PARK, GA 30337
1   5    1    1    2    2    3    3    4    4    5    5    6    6    7    7    8    8
         0    5    0    5    0    5    0    5    0    5    0    5    0    5    0    5
```

Debugging Activity Data File, Set 13

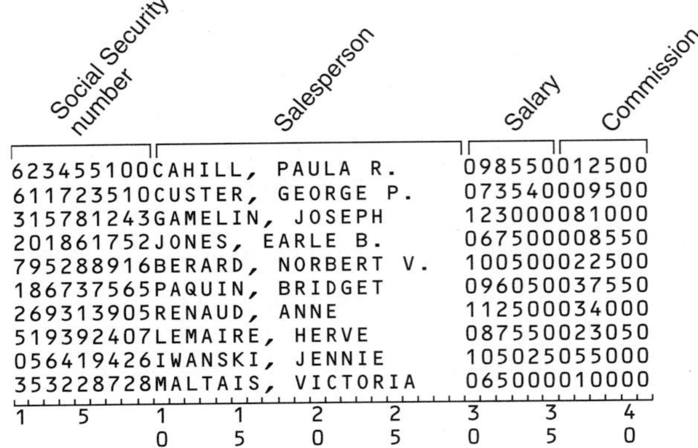


```
623455100CAHILL, PAULA R.      098550012500
611723510CUSTER, GEORGE P.     073540009500
315781243GAMELIN, JOSEPH       123000081000
201861752JONES, EARLE B.       067500008550
795288916BERARD, NORBERT V.    100500022500
186737565PAQUIN, BRIDGET       096050037550
269313905RENAUD, ANNE          112500034000
519392407LEMAIRE, HERVE        087550023050
056419426IWANSKI, JENNIE       105025055000
353228728MALTAIS, VICTORIA     065000010000
```

Debugging Activity Data File, Set 14

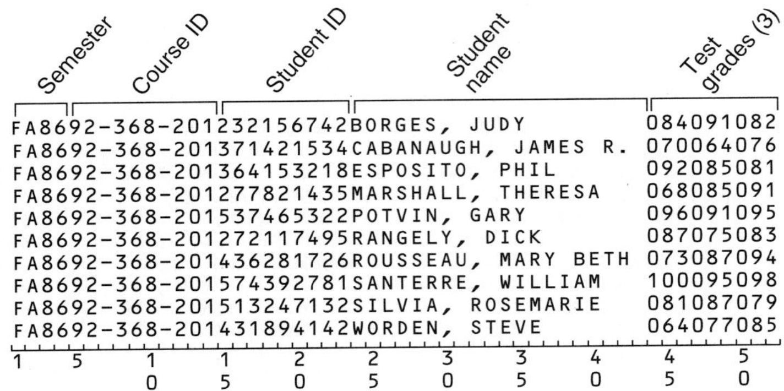


```
FA8692-368-201232156742BORGES, JUDY              084091082
FA8692-368-201371421534CABANAUGH, JAMES R.       070064076
FA8692-368-201364153218ESPOSITO, PHIL            092085081
FA8692-368-201277821435MARSHALL, THERESA         068085091
FA8692-368-201537465322POTVIN, GARY              096091095
FA8692-368-201272117495RANGELY, DICK             087075083
FA8692-368-201436281726ROUSSEAU, MARY BETH       073087094
FA8692-368-201574392781SANTERRE, WILLIAM         100095098
FA8692-368-201513247132SILVIA, ROSEMARIE         081087079
FA8692-368-201431894142WORDEN, STEVE             064077085
```

Debugging Activity Data File, Set 15

Store number | Department number | Social Security number | Salesperson | Sales

```
1002214365025ALLEN, ROBERT        150000
1002218546010BROWN, RAYMOND       302255
1002641275050BRANNIGAN, NICOLE    087525
1002315463030FOGARTY, JANICE      105050
1002642754040MAIN, CHARLES        128000
1004685264065CARLSON, HOPE        090000
1004556234035CRANE, JOHN          105050
1004696996055DANIELS, JULIA       287050
1004251342020FARMER, SUSAN        162000
1004263452070FEINGOLD, HAROLD     125050
1004667451060HARRISON, LILY       142580
1006521244005DWYER, TERRENCE      142580
1006564451045EDWARDS, PETER       108050
1006644353075MANNING, ELIZABETH   135000
1008377568080HOWARD, RALPH        056050
1008482131015JANKOWSKI, STANLEY   135000
1008551164090KELLY, PATRICK       162500
1008599231085LANGFORD, SARAH      115050
1008521166100PRINGLY, ANNE        109805
2002408936050CORDEIRO, ANTONE     010050
2002509862005CORTON, ALEXANDRA    100000
2002509185045PINEAULT, NORMAN     098050
2002480755030TALBOT, JILLIAN      127580
2004479210065BARRESI, JOHN        065000
2004427560010COCHRANE, RUSSELL    146050
2004360902035PENTA, ROBERT        165025
2004472847080PROULX, PAULINE      115000
2004375701060QUINN, SUZANNE       132050
2006683309020COSTELLO, JAMES      167050
2006418090015CRAWFORD, SHIRLEY    139050
2006566127070FELDMAN, WALTER      147080
2006433406075FERNANDEZ, LOUISE    200000
2006571904025LEMERISE, DONALD     185050
2006572495090WORTHEN, MICHAEL     157000
2008762355100GOYETTE, FRANCES     095000
2008812133085KOSINSKI, KATHERINE  112500
2008804233040VERMETTE, GLORIA     156050
3002576400892KING, CHRISTOPHER    189070
3002416892014BERNARD, ISIDORE     203569
3002823144098MAHFUZ, IRENE        185025
3004566731251ROBINSON, GILBERT    210590
3004788230154DONOHUE, PHIL        087500
3004607044132CORRIGAN, ALENE      187550
3004745645270FURTADO, MAUREEN     201540
3006820788914ABALLO, NORMA        235075
3006785023157DOLLARHIDE, CHRIS    201570
3006745635164LINCOURT, LORETTA    149500
3008466587165BRAZ, JOAN           231560
3008557318974PRATT, ROBIN         215500
3008487251099MELANSON, GARY       190550
4002452677143BEAUDOIN, ROCKY      221500
4002787855623MARKLAND, MARY       198750
4002674451231BISBANO, HENRY       219055
4004720954670VELOZO, MARIO        242390
4004624166876PARISEAU, WILLIAM    178500
4004712133463PERRY, MARTA         194550
4006452892153CARDIN, FRANCIS      204590
4006551502546FORTIN, EMIL         225450
4006574930461GALLAGHER, MICHAEL   197675
4006683215467NOTTE, LORENZO       200500
4008721435472JOBIN, ANTONIO       214050
4008490234571MILLER, RENEE        190570
4008351566178TRAMONTE, ESTELLE    213500
+---+----+----+----+----+----+----+---+
1   5    1    1    2    2    3    3   3
         0    5    0    5    0    5   9
```

Debugging Activity Data File, Set 16

Part number | Part description | Purchase price | Selling price

```
0346RCB ANTENNA         0332903995
0359BCB CONVERTER       0207902495
0462UFLEXSOCKET WRENCH  0019100229
1242WRV ALARM SYSTEM    0166301995
1352VTUNE-UP TESTER     0332903995
1616WAIR DIESEL HARN    0141501698
2181XEXHAUST HEADERS    0566306795
5507RBONDED BRAKE SHOE  0066500798
5524YDISC BRAKE PADS    0124601495
7519YSOLID STATE TACH   0332903995
```

Debugging Activity Data File, Set 17

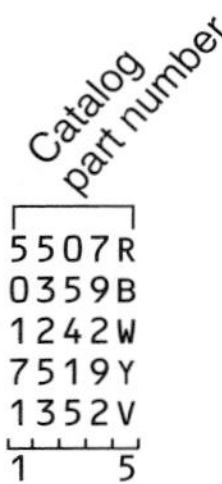

Catalog part number

```
5507R
0359B
1242W
7519Y
1352V
```

Debugging Activity Data File, Set 18

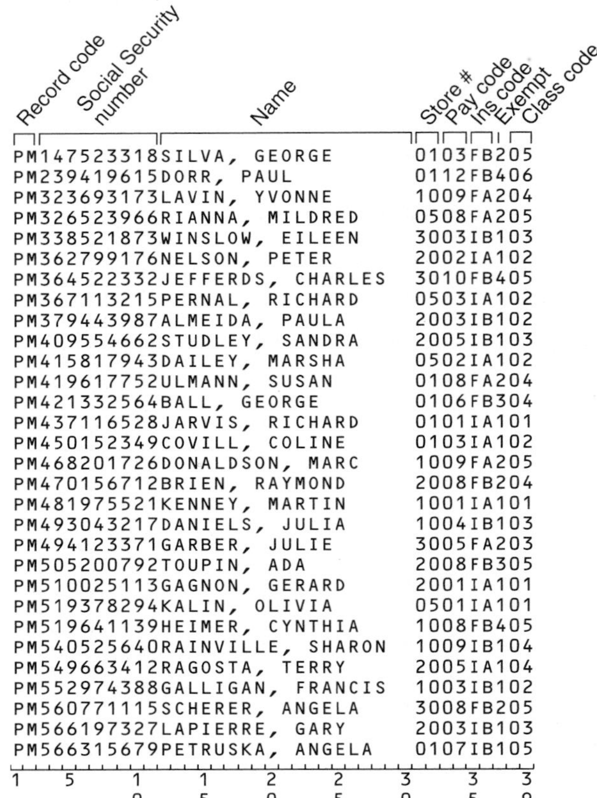

Record code | Social Security number | Name | Store # | Pay code | Ins code | Exempt | Class code

```
PM147523318SILVA, GEORGE      0103FB205
PM239419615DORR, PAUL         0112FB406
PM323693173LAVIN, YVONNE      1009FA204
PM326523966RIANNA, MILDRED    0508FA205
PM338521873WINSLOW, EILEEN    3003IB103
PM362799176NELSON, PETER      2002IA102
PM364522332JEFFERDS, CHARLES  3010FB405
PM367113215PERNAL, RICHARD    0503IA102
PM379443987ALMEIDA, PAULA     2003IB102
PM409554662STUDLEY, SANDRA    2005IB103
PM415817943DAILEY, MARSHA     0502IA102
PM419617752ULMANN, SUSAN      0108FA204
PM421332564BALL, GEORGE       0106FB304
PM437116528JARVIS, RICHARD    0101IA101
PM450152349COVILL, COLINE     0103IA102
PM468201726DONALDSON, MARC    1009FA205
PM470156712BRIEN, RAYMOND     2008FB204
PM481975521KENNEY, MARTIN     1001IA101
PM493043217DANIELS, JULIA     1004IB103
PM494123371GARBER, JULIE      3005FA203
PM505200792TOUPIN, ADA        2008FB305
PM510025113GAGNON, GERARD     2001IA101
PM519378294KALIN, OLIVIA      0501IA101
PM519641139HEIMER, CYNTHIA    1008FB405
PM540525640RAINVILLE, SHARON  1009IB104
PM549663412RAGOSTA, TERRY     2005IA104
PM552974388GALLIGAN, FRANCIS  1003IB102
PM560771115SCHERER, ANGELA    3008FB205
PM566197327LAPIERRE, GARY     2003IB103
PM566315679PETRUSKA, ANGELA   0107IB105
```

Debugging Activity Data File, Set 19

Process code | Social Security number | Name | Store # | Pay code | Ins code | Exempt | Class code

```
1035287413PEEBLES, CARL W.    0503IA102
3362799176                      04   03
2364522332
1415726750RYAN, FRANCIS X.    2008FB404
2415817943
3419617752                      10   05
3450152349                      05   03
3493043217                      07   04
1515031329COTTRELL, SARA      1004FB304
2549663412
1706314816GRAGNANI, CLORINDA  0502IA101
```

Appendix D
ANSI COBOL 1985 Reserved Words

The *new* words in ANSI COBOL '85 are highlighted.

ACCEPT
ACCESS
ADD
ADVANCING
AFTER
ALL
ALPHABET
ALPHABETIC
ALPHABETIC-LOWER
ALPHABETIC-UPPER
ALPHANUMERIC
ALPHANUMERIC-EDITED
ALSO
ALTER
ALTERNATE
AND
ANY
ARE
AREA
AREAS
ASCENDING
ASSIGN
AT
AUTHOR

BEFORE
BINARY
BLANK
BLOCK
BOTTOM
BY

CALL
CANCEL
CD
CF
CH
CHARACTER
CHARACTERS
CLASS
CLOCK-UNITS
CLOSE
COBOL
CODE
CODE-SET
COLLATING
COLUMN
COMMA
COMMON
COMMUNICATION
COMP
COMPUTATIONAL
COMPUTE
CONFIGURATION
CONTAINS
CONTENT
CONTINUE
CONTROL
CONTROLS
CONVERTING
COPY
CORR
CORRESPONDING
COUNT
CURRENCY

DATA
DATE
DATE-COMPILED
DATE-WRITTEN
DAY
DAY-OF-WEEK
DE
DEBUG-CONTENTS
DEBUG-ITEM
DEBUG-LINE
DEBUG-NAME
DEBUG-SUB-1
DEBUG-SUB-2
DEBUG-SUB-3
DEBUGGING
DECIMAL-POINT
DECLARATIVES
DELETE
DELIMITED
DELIMITER
DEPENDING
DESCENDING
DESTINATION
DETAIL
DISABLE
DISPLAY
DIVIDE
DIVISION
DOWN
DUPLICATES
DYNAMIC

EGI
ELSE
EMI
ENABLE
END
END-ADD
END-CALL
END-COMPUTE
END-DELETE
END-DIVIDE
END-EVALUATE
END-IF
END-MULTIPLY
END-OF-PAGE
END-PERFORM
END-READ
END-RECEIVE
END-RETURN
END-REWRITE
END-SEARCH
END-START
END-STRING
END-SUBTRACT
END-UNSTRING
END-WRITE
ENTER
ENVIRONMENT
EOP
EQUAL
ERROR
ESI
EVALUATE
EVERY
EXCEPTION
EXIT
EXTEND
EXTERNAL

FALSE
FD
FILE
FILE-CONTROL
FILLER
FINAL
FIRST
FOOTING
FOR
FROM

GENERATE
GIVING
GLOBAL
GO
GREATER
GROUP

HEADING
HIGH-VALUE
HIGH-VALUES

I-O
I-O-CONTROL
IDENTIFICATION
IF
IN
INDEX
INDEXED
INDICATE
INITIAL
INITIALIZE
INITIATE
INPUT
INPUT-OUTPUT
INSPECT
INSTALLATION
INTO
INVALID
IS

JUST
JUSTIFIED

KEY

LABEL
LAST
LEADING
LEFT
LENGTH
LESS
LIMIT
LIMITS
LINAGE
LINAGE-COUNTER
LINE
LINE-COUNTER
LINES

LINKAGE
LOCK
LOW-VALUE
LOW-VALUES

MEMORY
MERGE
MESSAGE
MODE
MODULES
MOVE
MULTIPLE
MULTIPLY

NATIVE
NEGATIVE
NEXT
NO
NOT
NUMBER
NUMERIC
NUMERIC-EDITED

OBJECT-COMPUTER
OCCURS
OF
OFF
OMITTED
ON
OPEN
OPTIONAL
OR
ORDER
ORGANIZATION
OTHER
OUTPUT
OVERFLOW

PACKED-DECIMAL
PADDING
PAGE
PAGE-COUNTER
PERFORM
PF
PH
PIC
PICTURE
PLUS
POINTER
POSITION
POSITIVE
PRINTING
PROCEDURE
PROCEDURES
PROCEED
PROGRAM
PROGRAM-ID
PURGE

QUEUE
QUOTE
QUOTES

RANDOM
RD
READ
RECEIVE
RECORD
RECORDS
REDEFINES
REEL
REFERENCE
REFERENCES
RELATIVE
RELEASE
REMAINDER
REMOVAL
RENAMES
REPLACE
REPLACING
REPORT
REPORTING
REPORTS
RERUN
RESERVE
RESET
RETURN
REVERSED
REWIND
REWRITE
RF
RH
RIGHT
ROUNDED
RUN

SAME
SD
SEARCH
SECTION
SECURITY
SEGMENT
SEGMENT-LIMIT
SELECT
SEND
SENTENCE
SEPARATE
SEQUENCE
SEQUENTIAL
SET
SIGN
SIZE
SORT
SORT-MERGE
SOURCE
SOURCE-COMPUTER
SPACE
SPACES
SPECIAL-NAMES
STANDARD
STANDARD-1
STANDARD-2
START
STATUS
STOP
STRING
SUB-QUEUE-1
SUB-QUEUE-2
SUB-QUEUE-3
SUBTRACT
SUM
SUPPRESS
SYMBOLIC
SYNC
SYNCHRONIZED

TABLE
TALLYING
TAPE
TERMINAL
TERMINATE
TEST
TEXT
THAN
THEN
THROUGH
THRU
TIME
TIMES
TO
TOP
TRAILING
TRUE
TYPE

UNIT
UNSTRING
UNTIL
UP
UPON
USAGE
USE
USING

VALUE
VALUES
VARYING

WHEN
WITH
WORDS
WORKING-STORAGE
WRITE

ZERO
ZEROES
ZEROS

————————

COBOL Symbols:
+
−
*
/
**
>
<
=
>=
<=

Note: Each COBOL compiler has its own set of reserved words. It generally contains most or all of the words in the ANSI set, but may also contain others.

Glossary

01 Entry
The first entry in a record description. The level number 01 is coded in Area A and the record name in Area B. The record may be either an elementary item or a group item.

02–49 Level Numbers
The level numbers assigned to data items of a record to show their hierarchical positions within the record.

77 Level Number
The level number traditionally assigned to an independent data item in working storage. It has been labeled as obsolete and is scheduled for deletion from the standards.

88 Level Entry
The entry used to define a condition-name.

Abbreviated Compound Conditionals
A compound test whose components are relational tests and in which one or more subjects and/or predicates are implied.

ACCEPT
A COBOL verb that executes an input function. It is used to make low-volume data available to the program. The data may be supplied by the user or by the system. It is stored in the data item named after the verb.

Accumulator
A numeric data item defined in working storage used to accumulate specific values during a predetermined processing cycle. The accumulator is normally initialized to zero at the beginning of each cycle.

ADD CORRESPONDING
A format of the ADD statement that adds values stored in numeric items of one group to identically named items (including qualifiers if necessary) of another group.

ADD-GIVING
One of two simple arithmetic statements in which the operation of addition is performed on two or more operands. The sum of all the operands before the word GIVING is stored in each identifier following the word GIVING.

ADD-TO
One of two simple arithmetic statements in which the operation of addition is performed on two or more operands. The sum is stored in each identifier following the word TO.

ADD-TO-GIVING
See ADD-GIVING.

ADVANCING Identifier
An option of the ADVANCING clause that allows the use of a variable data item to provide greater flexibility in controlling vertical line spacing on a print file.

AFTER ADVANCING
An optional clause of the WRITE statement. It is used to control vertical spacing of records being written to a print file.

Alphabetic Item
A data item defined in such a way that the only characters it may contain are letters of the alphabet and spaces. The PICTURE clause that defines the item must contain only the class code A.

Alphanumeric Item
A data item defined in such a way that it may contain any character of the available character set. The PICTURE clause that defines the item usually contains only the class code X, but it may contain combinations of As, Xs, and 9s. It must not contain all As or all 9s.

Alphanumeric-Edited Item
A data item defined by a PICTURE clause whose character string contains at least one class code A or X and at least one of the editing characters B, 0, or /.

ANSI
An acronym for *A*merican *N*ational *S*tandards *I*nstitute. ANSI is an organization that sets standards for American industry.

Application Program
A program whose function is a specific data processing requirement.

Area A
The third-leftmost area on a standard COBOL coding form or in a standard COBOL program, which consists of columns 8 through 11. Division headers, section headers, paragraph names, FD, and 01 entries are examples of entries that must be coded beginning in Area A.

Area B
The fourth-leftmost area on a standard COBOL coding form or in a standard COBOL program, which consists of columns 12 through 72. All program entries, except Area A entries, must be coded in this area. Area A entries may extend into Area B.

Array
A general term used to refer to a collection of contiguous data fields arranged in a one-dimensional row or column or in a two-dimensional table.

ASCENDING KEY
A clause that may be used in table definition entries. It specifies the data items that are the basis for the ordering of the table elements. ASCENDING means that the table elements are in ascending order of the values contained in the key fields. See DESCENDING KEY.

Assembly Language
An intermediate-level programming language. An assembler is required to translate assembly-language instructions into machine-language instructions.

ASSIGN
The clause of the SELECT statement that specifies the input/output device or logical name associated with the file named in the statement.

Assumed Decimal
The indication that a decimal point is logically needed, though it is not physically present. The indicator in a PICTURE clause is the special character V.

Asterisk (*)
The symbol used to denote the operation of multiplication. It may also be used to tag comment lines in a COBOL program, and when it is used for this purpose, it is entered in the Continuation Area (column 7) of each line that contains a comment.

AT END
The clause coded in a READ statement that accesses records of a file sequentially. Its function is to detect the end-of-file record. When the condition occurs, the statements contained in this clause are executed.

■ **Basic Logic Structure**
Any one of the three elementary logic constructs: simple sequence, selection, iteration. They are the building blocks used to develop more complex logic.

Batch
A batch is a collection of records; a batch program is one that is designed to process a batch of records collected into a file over a specific period of time.

Blank Field-name
See FILLER.

■ **Carriage Control**
A system-generated character that controls vertical spacing when records are written to a print file.

Case Structure
A logic construct that provides for more than two possible branches emanating from a single test. Typically, each branch or path corresponds to one or more specific values of the test item.

Character String
The sequence of characters used in the PICTURE clause that defines the class and size of the item being defined. In a more general sense, it may also mean the set of contiguous characters that form a literal or a COBOL word.

CLASS
An optional clause in the SPECIAL-NAMES paragraph that permits the user to assign a user-defined class-name to a specified set of characters. The class-name can then be used in a class test.

Class Codes: 9, A, X
The codes used in a PICTURE clause to specify a character as being numeric, alphabetic, or alphanumeric, respectively.

Class of a Data Item
The characteristic of a data item that specifies the kind of characters it consists of. A data item may be classified as alphabetic, numeric, alphanumeric, numeric-edited, or alphanumeric-edited.

Class Test
A test that determines if the characters in a data item are all numeric, all alphabetic (all uppercase, all lowercase, or mixed), or all of a specified set. The key words in the test are:
ALPHABETIC
ALPHABETIC-LOWER
ALPHABETIC-UPPER
class-name
NUMERIC

CLOSE
The COBOL verb that begins the statement that terminates the open mode of a file. Following the execution of this statement, the file that is closed is no longer accessible by the program.

COBOL
An acronym for *CO*mmon *B*usiness *O*riented *L*anguage. COBOL is the most popular high-level programming language for business applications.

COBOL Coding Form
A preprinted form designed to facilitate the coding of COBOL program entries. It identifies the Sequence Area, the Continuation Area, Area A, Area B, and the Identification Area. On some forms, the last of these areas is no longer shown, because it is seldom used today.

COBOL Reserved Word
A technical word of the COBOL language. It has a specific meaning to the compiler, and it must not be used as a user-defined name.

CODASYL
An acronym for *CO*nference on *DA*ta *SY*stems *L*anguages. CODASYL was the primary moving force behind the development of COBOL.

Collating Sequence
The sequence in which all the characters of a character set are assigned numeric codes for computer-related applications such as comparing, sorting, and merging.

Compiler
A translator program that translates a high-level-language program into a machine-language program. A COBOL compiler translates a COBOL source program into its corresponding object program. The compiler is also designed to generate diagnostics when it detects syntax errors in the program.

Compiling a Program
Calling the compiler so that it can generate the object program that corresponds to the source program. Equivalently, generating the machine-language instructions that correspond to the source code.

Compound Test
A test consisting of two or more tests connected by the logical operators AND and/or OR.

COMPUTE
A COBOL arithmetic statement whose format allows for the evaluation of an arithmetic expression containing one or more arithmetic operators. In particular, it is the only COBOL statement that permits the use of exponentiation.

Condition-Name
A user-defined name assigned to one or more values that the data item to which it is attached may assume. It must be defined in an 88-level entry.

Condition-Name Test
A test that uses a condition-name to determine if the data item to which it is attached contains a value specified in the definition of the condition-name.

Conditional Statement
A statement that contains a condition to be tested and for which the subsequent course of action depends on the results of the test.

CONFIGURATION SECTION
A section of the ENVIRONMENT DIVISION. It contains entries that identify the source and object computers.

Conjunction
A compound test whose components are connected by the logical operator AND.

Constant
A fixed value. In COBOL, the three classifications of constants are: numeric literal, nonnumeric literal, and figurative constant.

Continuation Area
It is the second-leftmost area on a standard COBOL coding form or in a standard COBOL program, and it consists of column 7. A hyphen is entered in this area to indicate the continuation of a literal. It may also contain other special-purpose characters, such as the asterisk.

Control Break
The temporary interruption of a processing routine caused by the presence of a new value in a control item. During the interruption, special processing requirements are executed, and then the interrupted processing routine is resumed.

Control Field
A data item for which a new value signals the need for a control break. See Input Record Key Field.

Control Item Footing
A footing, generally containing summary information, that is printed following a number of detail lines, as a result of a control break.

Control Item Heading
A heading printed on a report as a result of a control break.

Controlling Vertical Spacing
Procedures used within the program to position print lines on a report. Vertical spacing of lines is used to enhance the clarity of the printed report.

CPU
The Central Processing Unit. It is the component of a computer in which all processing occurs.

Creating a Data File
Producing the related data that must be stored on the records of a data file. The term also applies to keying data records into a file and to producing a data file as an output file to a program.

■ **Data Classification**
A scheme by which data is classified as numeric, alphabetic, alphanumeric, numeric-edited, or alphanumeric-edited.

DATA DIVISION
The third division of a COBOL program. This division contains entries that define all the data items needed by the program.

Data Field
A subdivision of a record. In order to reference data in the field, the field must be assigned a user-defined name.

Data Field Name
The name assigned to a data field.

Data File
A file whose records contain input data to be processed by a program or output data produced by the program. Output data files are also called storage files. In this text, most data files are input files.

Data Item
A unit of data defined within a COBOL program.

Data Item Description Entry
The collection of clauses that define a data item.

Data Item Name
The name given to a data item.

DATA RECORD IS Clause
An optional clause of the FD entry. It specifies the name(s) of the record(s) belonging to the file named in the FD entry.

Data Transfer
The act of transferring or "copying" a source value into a receiving field. COBOL statements such as MOVE, READ, WRITE, and COPY effect data transfers.

Data Validation
Processes used to verify that data stored in a field in fact possesses the attributes and characteristics it is supposed to possess.

Debugging
The process of searching a program to detect and to correct syntax and/or logic errors.

Decision Box
A flowcharting symbol used to denote a condition to be tested. It consists of a lozenge or diamond-shaped figure.

DESCENDING KEY
A clause that may be used in table definition entries. It specifies the data items that are the basis for the ordering of the table elements. DESCENDING means that the table elements are in descending order of the values contained in the key fields. See ASCENDING KEY.

Descriptive Name
A name constructed so as to provide self-documentation for the entity being named.

Design Implementation Phase
The second phase of the problem-solving procedure. In this phase, the program is coded; it is entered into a file; it is compiled by the compiler, debugged if necessary, and executed with sample data.

Design Phase
The first phase of the problem-solving procedure. In this phase, the layouts of input and output records are prepared, the system flowchart and the structure chart are developed, the program pseudocode is written, and/or the program flowchart is drawn.

Detail Report
A report classification. In this type of report, each input record processed usually results in an output record being written to the print file.

Diagnostics
Error messages produced by the translator program. They are inserted in the listing of the source program.

Direct Referencing
Referencing a table value solely by the occurrence number of the field in which it is stored. The table must have positional organization.

Disjunction
A compound test whose components are connected by the logical operator OR.

DISPLAY
A COBOL verb that executes an output function. All literals that follow the verb and the values of all data items that follow the verb are outputted by the program either on the screen of a terminal or onto an output file. Also see USAGE IS DISPLAY.

DIVIDE
A simple arithmetic statement in which the operation of division is performed.

Dividend
In a DIVIDE statement, the operand following the word INTO or the operand preceding the word BY.

Divisor
In a DIVIDE statement, the operand preceding the word INTO or the operand following the word BY.

Double-Subscripted Data Item
A table element whose reference requires the use of two subscripts.

■ **Edited Field**
The field associated with an edited data item. See Numeric-Edited and Alphanumeric-Edited Items.

Editing Characters
Special characters inserted in the character string of a PICTURE clause to make the corresponding printed value more meaningful to the user. They are: $. , * + – CR DB 0 / Z B.

Elementary Item
A data item that does not contain subordinate data items.

END-ADD
The explicit scope terminator for the ADD statement.

END-COMPUTE
The explicit scope terminator for the COMPUTE statement.

END-DIVIDE
The explicit scope terminator for the DIVIDE statement.

END-EVALUATE
The explicit scope terminator for the EVALUATE statement.

END-IF
The explicit scope terminator for the IF statement.

END-MULTIPLY
The explicit scope terminator for the MULTIPLY statement.

"End of Report" Message
A message printed on the last page of a report to show explicitly where a report ends. Without it, questions may arise as to whether the report is complete or not.

END-PERFORM
The explicit scope terminator for an in-line PERFORM statement.

END-READ
The explicit scope terminator for the READ statement.

END-SUBTRACT
The explicit scope terminator for the SUBTRACT statement.

ENVIRONMENT DIVISION
The second division of a COBOL program. This division contains entries that specify the hardware to be used by the program.

EOF Record
The end-of-file record.

EOF Test
A test for the end-of-file record or marker.

EVALUATE
A COBOL verb that begins a conditional statement in which any one of a number of program actions is selected on the basis of one or more conditions being satisfied. It is the statement used to implement the case structure.

Executive Program
The first program that is loaded into main memory when the computer is first turned on. It is the master program that controls all the major functions of the computer system. It is often referred to as the "operating system."

■ **FD Entry**
The entry in the FILE SECTION that begins a *F*ile *D*escription. It must be coded in Area A.

Figurative Constant
A COBOL reserved word that causes the compiler to generate a specific value. Each character in the following set is a figurative constant:
ALL "literal": represents the value of the literal; the literal is repeated until the field is "filled."
HIGH-VALUE: represents the highest character value in the collating sequence in use.
LOW-VALUE: represents the lowest character value in the collating sequence in use.
QUOTE: represents either the single quote (apostrophe) or double quote (quotation mark), depending on the specific implementor.
SPACE: represents the space character.
ZERO: represents the numeric value zero.

File
A collection of related records.

File Name
The user-defined name assigned to a file.

FILE SECTION
A section of the DATA DIVISION. It contains entries that define all of the program files.

FILE-CONTROL
A paragraph of the INPUT-OUTPUT SECTION of the ENVIRONMENT DIVISION. In this paragraph, the program files are assigned to the input/output devices or logical names through which they are made available to the program.

FILLER
A COBOL reserved word usually used to name a field that does not need a user-defined name. In COBOL '85, since a field is not required to have a name, the word FILLER is falling into disuse.

Floating Character
One of three insertion editing characters ($, +, −) that are allowed to be repeated in the character string of the PICTURE clause. The use of a floating character replaces all leading zeros with spaces except the rightmost. It is replaced by the floating character.

Forcing Final Totals
The term "forcing" is applied to the printing of final accumulated values because control breaks cannot cause them to be printed.

FROM DATE
An ACCEPT statement option that obtains the date from the system. The date is supplied as a six-digit value in the format YYMMDD. It is stored in the data item named after the ACCEPT verb.

FROM DAY
An ACCEPT statement option that obtains the day from the system. The day is supplied as a five-digit value in the format YYDDD. It is stored in the data item named after the ACCEPT verb.

FROM DAY-OF-WEEK
An ACCEPT statement option that obtains the day of the week from the system. The day of the week is supplied as a one-digit value in the range from 1 to 7, where 1 is Monday. It is stored in the data item named after the ACCEPT verb.

FROM TIME
An ACCEPT statement option that obtains the time of the day from the system. The time is supplied as elapsed time on a 24-hour clock in the format HHMMSShh. It is stored in the data item named after the ACCEPT verb.

Functional Module
A module in a program flowchart or an entry in a structure chart related to a specific function or subtask. The term may also be applied to the portion of the program that corresponds to the flowchart or structure chart module.

■ **Group (Parent) Item**
A data item that contains subordinate data items.

Grouping Report Headers
A coding technique in which each report header is coded as a subordinate item of a group. It enhances the self-documentation of the program and increases the efficiency of paging functions in VMS operating systems.

■ **Hard-Coded Table**
See Permanent Table.

High-Order Truncation
The truncation of leftmost characters.

■ **Identification Area**
The rightmost area on a standard COBOL coding form or in a standard COBOL program, which consists of columns 73 through 80. Traditionally, it contained a program identification entry. Because it is seldom used today, some preprinted coding forms do not include it.

IDENTIFICATION DIVISION
The first division of a COBOL program. This division contains an entry that names the program. Often, it also contains program documentation.

IF-ELSE
A COBOL conditional statement that allows alternate procedures to be executed depending on whether the tested condition is true or false.

Imperative Statement
A statement that must be executed unconditionally whenever control is passed to it.

Implementor Name
A system-dependent name that identifies a specific feature available on that computer system.

In-Line PERFORM
A form of the PERFORM statement in which a procedure is not named. Rather, the statements that make up the procedure are coded within the PERFORM statement itself. This type of PERFORM statement must end with the END-PERFORM scope terminator.

Independent Item
A "stand-alone" data item. It has no subordinate items, nor is it subordinate to a group data item. Traditionally assigned level number 77, it may now be assigned level number 01. Level number 77 is scheduled for deletion from the standards.

Initializing an Accumulator
Assigning to the accumulator the value it should contain at the beginning of the cycle during which it must perform its function. The initial value is normally zero.

Initializing a Table
Assigning initial values to a table.

Input Buffer
A storage area reserved in main memory for storing the contents of an input record as it is "read" from a file.

Input File
A file containing the data records that are supplied as input to a program.

INPUT PROCEDURE
An option of a SORT statement that specifies a section of the PROCEDURE DIVISION within which records are processed prior to being released to the sort file.

Input Record
A record belonging to an input file. The data contained on the record is entered into the input buffer by the execution of a READ statement, and it is then processed by the program.

Input Record Key Field
In this text, a field on an input record in which the presence of a new value causes a control break to occur. (The term also has important applications in file organizations.)

Input Record Layout
A form used to show the bytes reserved for and the names assigned to each data field of an input record. It also contains the name of the record itself.

Input Unit
One of the three major components of a computer system. It consists of the physical device that is used to supply data and/or instructions to the Central Processing Unit.

Input-Loaded Table
A table whose values are obtained from input records.

INPUT-OUTPUT SECTION
A section of the ENVIRONMENT DIVISION. It contains entries that associate program files with input/output devices or logical names.

Input/Output Symbol
A flowcharting symbol used to represent an input or an output function. It consists of a parallelogram that is not a rectangle.

Insertion Character
An editing character whose use increases the size of the item in which it is inserted. The insertion characters are: $. , + − CR DB 0 B /.

INSPECT
A COBOL verb that begins a statement that can be used to count and/or replace specified characters in a data item.

Integer Numeric Field
The field associated with a numeric data item whose PICTURE clause does not contain a V, implied or explicit.

Intermediate Totals
Values that are accumulated during the processing of some, but not all, records. The term is usually applied to values of accumulators that are printed during control breaks, with the accumulators reset to zero for the next control break cycle.

Invalid Data Transfer
An attempt at a data transfer that breaks one or more data transfer rules.

Iteration Structure
A logic structure in which one or more instructions must be executed repeatedly

until a specified condition is satisfied. Also called a repetition structure or a loop.

■ **JUSTIFIED RIGHT**
An optional phrase that may be coded in the data description entry of a nonnumeric item. It causes data transferred to this item to be stored right justified into the field.

■ **Keying a Program into a File**
The physical act of typing the program at a keyboard to enter it into a file on a disk (or tape).

■ **LABEL RECORDS Clause**
An optional clause of the FD entry. It specifies whether the label records are standard or omitted.

Left Justified
Storing characters in a field from the leftmost byte to the rightmost byte. If truncation occurs, then the rightmost characters are lost.

Linker
A utility program whose function is to adapt an object program to a particular operating system so that it can be executed by that system.

Literal Continuation
The procedure by which the coding of a literal on a line may be continued on the next line. This occurs if column 72 is encountered before the coding can be completed. In that case, a hyphen is entered in the Continuation Area of the next line, and the coding of the literal is completed in Area B.

Loader
A utility program whose function is to copy the object program into main memory so that it can be executed by the operating system.

Loading a Table
The process of assigning values to table elements in a nonpermanent table.

Low-Order Truncation
The truncation of rightmost characters.

Lower-level Paragraph
A paragraph of the PROCEDURE DIVISION other than the primary or main-control paragraph. In this text, the higher the numeric prefix in the paragraph name, the lower the level it belongs to. The primary paragraph has numeric prefix 100-.

■ **Machine Language**
A low-level language directly executable by the computer.

Main-Control Paragraph
The first paragraph of the PROCEDURE DIVISION. It is also called the primary paragraph.

MERGE
A COBOL verb that begins a statement, which activates a merge subroutine. It is followed by the name of the merge file. Its function is to merge the records of two or more files whose records have been presorted on the basis of identical keys into one file.

Mnemonic Name
A user-defined name associated with an implementor name in the SPECIAL-NAMES paragraph of the ENVIRONMENT DIVISION.

MOVE
The COBOL verb that begins a statement whose execution causes a data transfer.

MOVE CORRESPONDING
A format of the MOVE statement that transfers data from elementary items of one group to identically named items (including qualifiers if needed) of another group.

Multilevel Report
A report classification. In this type of report, a detail line is produced for each input record, and summary information is printed on the report for groups of input records.

Multiple Receiving Fields
The characteristic applied to any statement in which data, computed or transferred, is to be stored in more than one receiving field.

MULTIPLY-BY
One of two simple arithmetic statements in which the operation of multiplication is performed. The operand before the word BY multiplies each identifier after the word BY, and the product is stored in that identifier.

MULTIPLY-BY-GIVING
One of two simple arithmetic statements in which the operation of multiplication is performed. The operand before the word BY is multiplied by the operand after the word BY, and the product is stored in each identifier after the word GIVING.

Multipunch
Traditionally, it meant the keypunching of two or more characters in one column of a punchcard. Today, the term is sometimes applied to keying a character that corresponds to the combination of a digit and a "plus" or "minus" sign.

■ **Negated Compound Test**
A compound test (within parentheses) preceded by the logical operator NOT.

Negated Test
A test that is preceded by the word NOT.

Negative Test
A test whose predicate contains the word NOT.

Nested Conditional Statements
A set of conditional statements in which the first is executed unconditionally, but the remaining conditional statements are executed only if a prior condition is satisfied.

Nested Tests
A set of tests in which the first is performed unconditionally, but the remaining tests in the set are performed only if a prior condition is satisfied.

Noninteger Numeric Field
The field associated with a numeric data item whose PICTURE clause contains a V, implied or explicit.

Nonnumeric Data Item
A data item defined by its PICTURE clause as an alphabetic, alphanumeric, alphanumeric-edited, or numeric-edited item.

Nonnumeric Literal
A constant (or literal) enclosed within literal marks. In this text, literal marks are quotation marks.

Nonnumeric Relational Operands
Nonnumeric data items on which a relational test is performed.

Nonpermanent Table (Volatile)
A table whose values may change during one run of the program or from one run to another. Also see Input Loaded Table.

NOT
See Negative Test or Negated Test.

NOT AT END
An optional clause that may be coded in a READ statement to provide an alternative to the AT END path. If the record being read is not the EOF record, the statements in this clause are executed.

NOT ON SIZE ERROR
An optional clause that may be coded in an arithmetic statement to provide an alternative to the ON SIZE ERROR path. If there is no size error in the execution of the arithmetic statement, the statements contained in this clause are executed.

Numeric Data Item
A data item defined by a PICTURE clause whose character string contains only the class code 9.

Numeric Item
A data item defined in such a way that the only characters it may contain are the digits 0 through 9. It may also contain a + or a – sign if the PICTURE clause begins with S.

Numeric Item Characters: V, S, P
The special characters that may be coded in the PICTURE clause of a numeric data item in addition to the class code 9. The V indicates the position of an assumed decimal point; the S defines the item as a signed numeric item; the P represents an assumed zero.

Numeric Literal
A numeric constant.

Numeric Prefixes: 100-, 200-, 300-
The prefixes initially attached to the modules of the structure chart to

document the hierarchy level to which they belong. They are also attached to the corresponding paragraph names of the program pseudocode, to the corresponding module names of the program flowchart, and ultimately to the corresponding paragraph names within the PROCEDURE DIVISION of the COBOL program.

Numeric-Edited Item
A data item defined by a PICTURE clause whose character string contains editing characters in addition to the class code 9.

■ **Object Program**
The version of the program produced by the translator (compiler for COBOL programs). It consists of machine-language instructions, executable by the computer.

OBJECT-COMPUTER
An entry in the CONFIGURATION SECTION of the ENVIRONMENT DIVISION. It contains the name of the computer that executes the object program.

OCCURS
The key verb in the clause that defines a table. The integer that follows the verb indicates the number of occurrences of the data item that precedes the verb.

ON ASCENDING KEY
A phrase in a SORT statement that specifies that records of the sort file are to be sequenced from the lowest to the highest value of the sort key(s) named in the phrase.

ON DESCENDING KEY
A phrase in a SORT statement that specifies that records of the sort file are to be sequenced from the highest to the lowest value of the sort key(s) named in the phrase.

On-line Program
A program that requires communications with the user during the execution of the program.

ON SIZE ERROR
The optional clause that may be coded in an arithmetic statement to prevent a high-order truncation of the computed value. If a high-order truncation is indicated, the computed value is not stored, and the statements contained in this clause are executed.

One-level Control Break
A control break caused by a single control data item.

One-level Table
In COBOL, a one-dimensional collection of contiguous data fields defined by using the OCCURS clause once.

OPEN
The COBOL verb that begins the statement that specifies the open mode for a file. The open mode may be specified as INPUT, OUTPUT, I-O, or EXTEND. A file must be opened before it can be accessed by the program.

Operand
An entity (constant or variable) that is acted upon within a statement. For instance, in MOVE A TO B, the data items A and B are operands.

OUTPUT PROCEDURE
An option of a SORT statement that specifies a section of the PROCEDURE DIVISION within which records are processed individually subsequent to being returned from the sort file.

Output Record
A record belonging to an output file. It contains data that has been processed by the program. Output records generally belong either to print files or to storage files. In this text, most output records belong to print files.

Output Record Layout
A form used to show the bytes reserved for and the names assigned to each data field of an output record. It also contains the name of the record itself. In this text, most output records belong to print files, and their layouts are prepared on a printer spacing chart.

Output Unit
One of the three major components of a computer system. It consists of the physical device that is used to record the output produced by the program.

■ **PAGE**
An optional entry in the ADVANCING clause of the WRITE statement. It causes the printer to position the paper at the beginning of the next page.

Page Heading
A heading that is printed at the top of each page of a report.

Paragraph Name
A user-defined name that names and begins a paragraph of the PROCEDURE DIVISION.

PERFORM
The COBOL verb that transfers control to a procedure in such a way that control automatically returns after executing the last statement in the procedure. Also see In-line PERFORM.

Perform Box
A flowcharting symbol used to denote transfer of control to another flowchart module. It consists of a rectangle with a double bar at the top.

PERFORM WITH TEST
A form of the PERFORM-UNTIL statement which specifies explicitly whether the condition in the UNTIL clause is to be tested BEFORE or AFTER executing the procedure.

PERFORM-UNTIL
A form of the PERFORM statement in which the procedure is executed repeatedly until the condition specified in the UNTIL clause is satisfied.

PERFORM-VARYING-UNTIL
A form of the PERFORM-UNTIL statement in which the value of an identifier is incremented or decremented by a specified amount each time control returns from the procedure being performed.

Permanent Table (Static)
A table whose entries always remain the same. The table entries are specified by one or more VALUE clauses.

PICTURE Clause
The clause of a data item description entry that specifies the class and size and editing requirements (if any) of the elementary item being defined. The word PICTURE is usually abbreviated PIC.

Positional Organization
A table organization that requires that the values to be stored in the table have associated codes that are consecutive positive integers beginning with 1. The values are stored in increasing order of their codes. This allows for direct referencing of table elements.

Posttest Iteration
An iteration structure in which the test that controls the loop is performed after the instructions are executed.

Prefix I-
The prefix often attached to a data field name to document the fact that the data field belongs to an input record.

Prefix O-
The prefix often attached to a data field name to document the fact that the data field belongs to an output record.

Prefix WS-
The prefix often attached to a data field name to document the fact the data field resides in working storage.

Pretest Iteration
One of the basic logic structures in which the test that controls the looping is performed before executing the first statement of the set of statements that are to be repeated within the loop.

Primary Module
The highest-level functional module in a structure chart. It identifies the whole job to be accomplished by the program. The term is also applied to the corresponding module in the program flowchart, and, within the program, to the paragraph of the PROCEDURE DIVISION that corresponds to it (the primary paragraph).

Print Channel
A subdivision of a printer page consisting of a number of lines.

Printer Spacing Chart
A preprinted form used to prepare the layout of each type of line to be printed on a report.

Problem-Solving Procedure
A procedure whose systematic application facilitates the programmer's task of designing a program, coding it, debugging it, and running it.

PROCEDURE DIVISION
The last division of a COBOL program. It contains all the COBOL instructions to be executed by the program. The instructions are grouped within paragraphs and sections.

Procedure Name
A programmer-supplied name that labels and begins a procedure within the PROCEDURE DIVISION. A procedure is either a paragraph or a section.

Process Box
A flowchart symbol used to denote a process or operation. It consists of a rectangle.

Processor Unit
One of the three major components of a computer system. It consists of the Central Processing Unit and the main memory of the computer. The term is often used to refer to the computer itself.

Program
A set of instructions designed to accomplish a specific function. The program is a source program if it contains instructions coded by the programmer; it is an object program if it contains the instructions generated by the compiler or translator.

Program Documentation
Comments that are inserted in a program listing to provide useful information to the user.

Program Flowchart
A graphical representation of the functions to be executed or operations performed within a program, as well as the sequence in which they are to be executed or performed.

Program Name
A user-defined name assigned to a COBOL program. It is coded in the PROGRAM-ID paragraph of the IDENTIFICATION DIVISION.

Program Pseudocode
The set of instructions that must be executed in a program, written in a form that is English-like, which is not restricted by the COBOL language rules of syntax and yet maps out the complete logic of the program.

Program Walk-Through
A very careful reading of every entry in a COBOL program for the purpose of discovering errors in the program. They may be syntax errors, errors of omission, mathematical errors in formulas, and logic errors.

PROGRAM-ID
The only required paragraph in the IDENTIFICATION DIVISION. It contains the program name.

Programmer
A person who designs a program and writes the coded instructions that are needed to implement the design.

Proper Program
A program in which control enters the primary module, proceeds through all other modules by entering and exiting properly (that is, entering at the beginning and exiting at the end of the module), and ultimately leaves the program by executing the last statement of the primary module.

■ **Qualification**
A process used to reference a unique data item. The data item being referenced is followed by one or more phrases of the form "OF identifier" or "IN identifier," so that the data item is directly subordinate to the first identifier, and each identifier is subordinate to the next one.

Quotient
In a DIVIDE statement, the result produced by the operation. It is stored in the identifier following the word GIVING or in the identifier following the word INTO if the GIVING form is not used.

■ **Random Organization**
A table organization in which values are stored randomly.

READ
The COBOL verb that begins a statement that copies a record of the input file into the input buffer associated with that file.

READ-INTO
A form of the READ statement that causes an implicit transfer of the data stored in the input buffer to the field specified by the data name in the INTO phrase.

Receiving Field
The field that receives data as the result of a data transfer operation; also the field into which a value computed by the program is stored.

RECORD CONTAINS Clause
An optional clause of the FD entry. It specifies the number of characters contained in the records of the file name in the FD entry.

Record Counter
A numeric data item defined in working storage used to count the records that satisfy specified criteria.

Record Description
The collection of all the data item descriptions associated with a particular record.

Record Name
The user-defined name assigned to a record.

Reference Modification
A way of referencing a subgroup of contiguous characters within a data field. In a reference modification, the data name of the field is followed by two arguments, separated by a colon. The first argument identifies the position of the first character of the subgroup, and the second argument specifies the length of the subgroup.

Relational Operator
See Relational Test.

Relational Test
A test in which the relationship between the value of one arithmetic expression or data item and the value of a second arithmetic expression or data item is determined. The relational operators are:
EQUAL TO (=)
GREATER THAN (>)
GREATER THAN OR EQUAL TO (>=)
LESS THAN (<)
LESS THAN OR EQUAL TO (<=)

RELEASE
A COBOL verb used within an INPUT PROCEDURE under the control of a SORT statement. The verb is followed by the name of a sort record. Its effect is to copy the record into the sort file.

REMAINDER
An optional phrase that may be specified in a DIVIDE statement. The word REMAINDER is followed by the identifier that will contain the remainder after the division is performed.

Replacement Characters
The editing character *, which replaces leading zeros with asterisks, and the editing character Z, which replaces leading zeros with spaces.

Retrieving a Table Element
The process by which a table value is located and subsequently copied elsewhere or used as needed by the program.

RETURN
A COBOL verb used within an OUTPUT PROCEDURE under the control of a SORT statement. The verb is followed by the name of the sort file. Its effect is to copy the next available record of the sort file into the input buffer associated with the file.

Right Justified
Storing characters in a field from the rightmost byte to the leftmost byte. If truncation occurs, then the leftmost characters are lost.

Rolling-Forward
See Rolling-Over.

Rolling-Over
The process of updating an accumulator by adding to it the contents of another accumulator. This usually occurs during a control break and toward the end of a program when final totals are needed.

ROUNDED
The optional phrase that may be coded in an arithmetic statement to cause the computed value to be stored rounded in the receiving field. The rounding occurs in the rightmost byte specified in the PICTURE of the receiving field.

Running a Program
Executing the object program produced by the compiler or translator.

Running a Trace of a Flowchart
A step-by-step walk through a flowchart with carefully selected input records for the purpose of verifying that the program logic is in fact doing what it is designed to do.

■ **Scope Terminator**
An entry that terminates the scope of a statement. The scope may be terminated implicitly by a period or explicitly by a terminator of the form END-..., where ... is the statement verb, as in END-PERFORM.

Second-Level Module
A module whose execution is under the control of the primary module. In this text, second-level modules have numeric prefixes in the 200s.

SELECT
The statement of the FILE-CONTROL paragraph that identifies the file being assigned.

Selection Structure
One of the basic logic structures. Essentially, it provides alternate paths, the selection of which depends on the outcome of a preceding test.

Sending Field
The field that contains the value to be copied into a receiving field during a data transfer operation. Same as source field.

Sentence
A set of one or more statements terminated by a separator period.

SEPARATE CHARACTER
The phrase used in the description of a signed numeric data item to indicate that the sign occupies a byte by itself. If it is not used, the sign is stored along with a digit either in the rightmost byte or the leftmost byte depending on the SIGN clause.

Sequence Area
The leftmost area on a standard COBOL coding form or in a standard COBOL program, which consists of columns 1 through 6. It is separated into a three-digit page number area and a three-digit line number area. Entries are coded into the program in ascending order of sequence area numbers. These numbers may be coded into the program itself, but they are not required.

Sequential File
A file with sequential organization. A file in which the records are accessed in the physical sequence in which they reside on the file and in the same sequence in which they were written on the file. A file in which each record, except the first and the last, has a predecessor and a successor.

Sequential Organization
A table organization in which table elements are stored either in ascending order or descending order of the values in a key field at each occurrence. The key field values need not be consecutive.

Sequential Tests
A set of tests performed unconditionally in the sequence in which they are coded.

Sign Test
A test that determines if the algebraic value of a data item or arithmetic expression is greater than zero, less than zero, or equal to zero. The key words used in a sign test are:
POSITIVE
NEGATIVE
ZERO

SIGN IS LEADING
See SIGN IS TRAILING.

SIGN IS TRAILING
An optional clause that may be coded in the description of a signed numeric data item to specify explicitly the position of the sign. The alternate to TRAILING is LEADING. The option TRAILING means that the sign is in the rightmost byte; LEADING means the sign is in the leftmost byte.

Signed Data Field
The field associated with a signed numeric data item.

Signed Number
A number that is accompanied by a sign so that its algebraic value can be classified as greater than, less than, or equal to zero.

Simple Sequence Structure
A logic structure in which two or more instructions must be executed unconditionally in a specified sequence.

Single-Subscripted Data Item
A data item within a table that can be referenced by a single subscript.

Size of a Data Item
The characteristic of a data item that specifies the number of characters it consists of.

SORT
A COBOL verb that begins a statement that activates a sorting subroutine. It is followed by the name of the sort file. This file contains the records that are to be sorted on the basis of the sort keys specified within the statement.

Sort Keys
Fields of a record in a sort file whose values are used to resequence the records of the file.

Source Field
See Sending Field.

Source Program
The program in the form written by the programmer. The source program must be translated into machine language by a translator (compiler for COBOL source programs).

Source Value
The value that is to be stored in a receiving field.

SOURCE-COMPUTER
An entry in the CONFIGURATION SECTION of the ENVIRONMENT DIVISION. It contains the name of the computer that accepts the source program as input.

SPECIAL-NAMES
A paragraph of the ENVIRONMENT DIVISION in which implementor names are related to user-defined mnemonic names.

Statement
A syntactically valid combination of words and symbols that begins with a COBOL verb.

Static Table
See Permanent Table or Hard-Coded Table.

STOP
The COBOL verb in the STOP RUN statement. The execution of this statement returns control from the program to the operating system.

Structure Chart
A graphical representation of the hierarchy of the major task and its related subtasks that must be accomplished by a program.

Structure Chart Module
A functional module in a structure chart that identifies a particular task.

Subscript
An integer or a data item whose value is an occurrence number for an element within a table.

Subtotaling
The process by which an accumulator is updated every time a record is processed.

SUBTRACT CORRESPONDING
A format of the SUBTRACT statement that subtracts values stored in numeric elementary items of one group from identically named (including qualifiers if needed) items of another group.

SUBTRACT-FROM
One of the simple arithmetic statements in which the operation of subtraction is performed. The sum of the operands before the word FROM is subtracted from each identifier after the word FROM. The identifiers after the word FROM store the results.

SUBTRACT-FROM-GIVING
One of two simple arithmetic statements in which the operation of subtraction is performed. The sum of the operands before the word FROM is subtracted from the operand after the word FROM, and the result is stored in each identifier after the word GIVING.

Summary Report
A report classification. In this type of report, data is accumulated during the processing of all the input records, with summary information only printed on the report after the EOF record has been encountered.

System Flowchart
A flowchart that illustrates the data-flow requirements of a particular program. In this text, it shows the source of the data before it is supplied as input to the program, and it shows the type of file that contains the output produced by the program.

■ **Table Look-up With Subscripts**
Searching for data in a table by using subscripted identifiers. The subscripts

specify ordinal positions of fields within the table.

Table Redefinition
A procedure used in the definition of a hard-coded table. The original table definition uses the VALUE clause to specify the values in the table. The redefinition attaches subscripted data names to the table elements.

Tally Counter
A data item used within an INSPECT statement that keeps a tally (or count) of the number of occurrences of a specified string of characters.

Terminal Symbol
One of the standard flowcharting symbols used in a program flowchart to indicate the beginning and the end of a flowchart module.

Testing for an Empty Input File
A programming technique whose function is to intentionally terminate the execution of the program if the input file is empty.

Trailing Minus Sign
A minus sign that must be stored in the rightmost byte of a numeric field whenever the value assigned to the field is negative. The term is usually applied to the use of the minus sign (−) editing character in the trailing byte of a numeric-edited field. Its function is normally that of a flag to draw attention to values that should be examined more closely.

Translator
A program whose function is to convert a source program into a machine-language program.

Two-Level Control Break
In a two-level control break, the major control item is inclusive of the other, the minor. Control breaks usually occur a number of times for the minor without a break occurring for the major. A major control break is always accompanied by a minor control break.

Two-Level Table
In COBOL, a two-dimensional array of contiguous data items defined by using the OCCURS clause twice, where the second OCCURS applies to a data item subordinate to a data item qualified by the first OCCURS.

■ **USAGE IS BINARY**
An optional clause in a numeric data description entry. It specifies that the data item is stored in its binary form. The entry BINARY is the abbreviation for the entry USAGE IS BINARY.

USAGE IS COMP
Same as USAGE IS COMPUTATIONAL.

USAGE IS COMPUTATIONAL
An optional clause in a numeric data description entry. It specifies that the data item is in the appropriate computational form for the particular operating system. COMPUTATIONAL and COMP are abbreviations for the entry USAGE IS COMPUTATIONAL.

USAGE IS DISPLAY
An optional clause in a data description entry. It specifies that the data item is in the standard data format (or character format). DISPLAY is the abbreviation for the entry USAGE IS DISPLAY.

USAGE IS PACKED-DECIMAL
An optional entry in a numeric data description entry. It specifies that the data item is stored in a packed-decimal form. PACKED-DECIMAL is the abbreviation for the entry USAGE IS PACKED-DECIMAL.

Usage-Frequency Organization
A table organization in which data is stored in descending order of usage frequency, that is, the most frequently used data is stored at the top of the table, and the least frequently used data is stored at the bottom of the table.

User-Defined Name
A word supplied by the user to name such items as paragraphs, files, records, data fields, and so on. A COBOL reserved word must not be used as a user-defined word.

■ **Valid Data Transfer**
A data transfer that abides by the data transfer rules.

VALUE Clause
The clause used to define values associated with condition-names, or the initial value of a working storage data item.

Volatile Table
See Nonpermanent Table.

■ **Work Areas**
Independent or elementary data items defined in working storage that are needed to store values temporarily during the execution of the program.

Working Storage Record
A record that resides in working storage. Its data fields may contain constants or variable data.

WORKING-STORAGE SECTION
A section of the DATA DIVISION. It contains descriptions of records and their subordinate data items. These records do not belong explicitly to program files.

WRITE
The COBOL verb that begins a statement that copies an output record onto an output file.

WRITE-FROM
A form of the WRITE statement that includes an implicit data transfer from the source field specified in the FROM phrase to the output record area prior to the record being written onto the output file.

■ **Zero Suppressor**
The editing character Z. It suppresses leading zeros and replaces them with spaces. The term may also apply to the editing character *. It suppresses leading zeros and replaces them with asterisks. Also see Floating Character.

Index

Photograph credits: p. 3, *both,* p. 4, *top* and *middle,* p. 6, *bottom left* and *bottom right,* p. 12, *bottom,* and p. 13: courtesy of International Business Machines Corporation; p. 734, p. 735, *both:* by Mark VanOsdol.

Printer Spacing Chart

1 SSN NAME RATE CODE COMPENSATION

4 SSN RATE HRS CDM GROSS TAX NET

5 XXX-XX-XXXX

ʼlaster

Record Layout Forms

1 2 3 4 5 6 7 8 9 10 11 12 13 14 15 16 17 18 19 20 21 22 23 24 25 26 27 28 29 30 31 32 33 34 35 36 37 38 39 40 41 42 43 44 45 46 47 48 49 50 51 52 53 54 55 56 57 58 59 60 61 62 63 64 65 66 69 70 71 72 73 74 75 76 77 78 79 80

Record Name: ______________________________

1 2 3 4 5 6 7 8 9 10 11 12 13 14 15 16 17 18 19 20 21 22 23 24 25 26 27 28 29 30 31 32 33 34 35 36 37 38 39 40 41 42 43 44 45 46 47 48 49 50 51 52 53 54 55 56 57 58 59 60 61 62 63 64 65 66 67 68 69 72 73 74 75 76 77 78 79 80

Record Name: ______________________________

1 2 3 4 5 6 7 8 9 10 11 12 13 14 15 16 17 18 19 20 21 22 23 24 25 26 27 28 29 30 31 32 33 34 35 36 37 38 39 40 41 42 43 44 45 46 47 48 49 50 51 52 53 54 55 56 57 58 59 60 61 62 63 64 65 66 67 68 69 70 71 74 75 76 77 78 79 80

Record Name: ______________________________

1 2 3 4 5 6 7 8 9 10 11 12 13 14 15 16 17 18 19 20 21 22 23 24 25 26 27 28 29 30 31 32 33 34 35 36 37 38 39 40 41 42 43 44 45 46 47 48 49 50 51 52 53 54 55 56 57 58 59 60 61 62 63 64 65 66 67 68 69 70 71 72 73 74 76 77 78 79 80

Record Name: ______________________________

Photcopy Master

Photocopy